Can We Walk, Together?

Aerobics for the Heart

By
Richard D. Smith

Can We Walk, Together?

This edition published 2006

Cover design by Penny Hall
Cover Photo by Super Stock

Printed by Remnant Publications
Coldwater, MI

ISBN 0-9777445-0-7

Introduction

"I've got to get out of bed and go for a walk! I feel lousy!" Coping with personal health issues is a stress point for most of us. We don't feel good about ourselves because we are inactive, overweight, or feeling sluggish. Infomercials try to capitalize on this worry, by marketing all kinds of gadgets and solutions to improve our physical well-being. People spend good money. They resolve to time commitments for walking, jogging, or going to the fitness clubs which are popping up in every neighborhood.

Can We Walk, Together? takes this life-style changing concern for physical health, and brings forward from the back of our minds the questions, What about my spiritual health? Is it also sluggish? Am I inactive? My walk with God isn't as meaningful and fulfilling as it once was, so what's wrong? What can I do to improve my spiritual sense of well-being?

We need to exercise more, physically and spiritually. We need a daily commitment to improve our health. Enoch is written up as having an excellent exercise program. He walked with God. He valued his relationship with God so much, that God took him to heaven (Genesis 5:24). Isn't that the goal for all of us? To have a walk that prepares us for heavenly face-to-face communion and fellowship with God? How did Enoch walk with God? In the book LAST DAY EVENTS, in the chapter entitled "The Devotional Life of the Remnant," it is suggested that Enoch educated his mind and heart to ever feel that he was in the presence of God (page 71). That was Enoch's walk. And it can be ours!

Enoch treasured the experience of Psalm 16:11 – "Thou wilt shew me the path of life: in thy presence is fullness of joy; at thy right hand there are pleasures for evermore." Being in God's presence is our longing, our desire. So how do I train my mind and my heart to ever be in God's presence? Here is a suggestion for our walk: "It would be well for us to spend a thoughtful hour each day in contemplation of the life of Christ. We should take it point by point, and let the imagination grasp each scene, especially the closing ones." That suggestion comes from a book on the life of Christ, entitled DESIRE OF AGES by E. G. White. To walk like Enoch did, I want to read and meditate on the life of Jesus Christ. "The humble, self-denying life of our divine Lord we are to keep constantly in view." Amazing Grace, November 30.

Based on the four gospels, the book DESIRE OF AGES has brought my mind and heart to Christ, has aided and guided my walk with Him, and my experience with Him as a Friend. W. E. Bement of the Library of Congress, Washington, D.C., when asked to make his personal selection of the more than 10,000 volumes written on the life of Christ in the last 300 years had this to say, "My preference of choice would be guided by what I wish to get from the book or books to be read. Let me put it this way—I would put DESIRE OF AGES...first for spiritual discernment and practical application. I will say that the DESIRE OF AGES is well thought of in the Library of Congress." (1946).

Do you want spiritual health? Do you need an exercise program? Do you want to walk like Enoch did? Then Can We Walk, Together? is for you. Learn of the promise of His presence, and how your affections will go out after God. As you read the DESIRE OF AGES and walk with Him, respond to the thought questions and let your heart be drawn to God's heart.

For our spiritual health
Can We Walk, Together? Aerobics for the Heart
Suggested exercise program: read and meditate on one chapter per week.

Week 1: DA 1 – God with us.
Week 2: DA 2 – The Chosen People
Week 3: DA 3 – The Fullness of the Time
Week 4: DA 4 – Unto You a Savior
Week 5: DA 5 – The Dedication
Week 6: DA 6 – We Have Seen the Star
Week 7: DA 7 – As a Child
Week 8: DA 8 – The Passover Visit
Week 9: DA 9 – Days of Conflict
Week 10: DA 10 – The Voice in the Wilderness
Week 11: DA 11 – The Baptism
Week 12: STC 1 – God's Love for Man (STC represents *Steps to Christ*)
Week 13: STC 2 – The Sinner's Need of Christ
Week 14: DA 12 – The Temptation
Week 15: DA 13 – The Victory
Week 16: DA 14 – "We Have Found the Messias"
Week 17: DA 15 – At the Marriage Feast
Week 18: DA 16 – In His Temple
Week 19: DA 17 – Nicodemus
Week 20: DA 18 – "He Must Increase"
Week 21: DA 19 – At Jacob's Well
Week 22: DA 20 – "Except Ye See Signs and Wonders"
Week 23: DA 21 – Bethesda and the Sanhedrin
Week 24: DA 22 – Imprisonment and Death of John
Week 25: DA 23 – "The Kingdom of God Is at Hand"
Week 26: STC 3 – Repentance
Week 27: DA 24 – "Is Not This the Carpenter's Son?"
Week 28: DA 25 – The Call by the Sea
Week 29: DA 26 – At Capernaum
Week 30: DA 27 – "Thou Canst Make Me Clean"
Week 31: DA 28 – Levi-Matthew
Week 32: DA 29 – The Sabbath
Week 33: DA 30 – "He Ordained Twelve"
Week 34: DA 31 – The Sermon on the Mount
Week 35: DA 32 – The Centurion
Week 36: DA 33 – Who Are My Brethren?
Week 37: DA 34 – The Invitation
Week 38: STC 4 – Confession
Week 39: STC 5 – Consecration
Week 40: DA 35 – "Peace, Be Still"
Week 41: DA 36 – The Touch of Faith
Week 42: DA 37 – The First Evangelists
Week 43: DA 38 – Come Rest Awhile
Week 44: DA 39 – "Give Ye Them to Eat"
Week 45: DA 40 – A Night on the Lake
Week 46: DA 41 – The Crisis in Galilee
Week 47: DA 42 – Tradition
Week 48: DA 43 – Barriers Broken Down
Week 49: DA 44 – The True Sign
Week 50: DA 45 – The Foreshadowing of the Cross
Week 51: STC 6 – Faith and Acceptance
Week 52: STC 7 – The Test of Discipleship

Week 1: DA 46 – He was Transfigured
Week 2: DA 47 – Ministry
Week 3: DA 48 – Who Is the Greatest?
Week 4: DA 49 – At the Feast of Tabernacles
Week 5: DA 50 – Among Snares
Week 6: DA 51 – "The Light of Life"
Week 7: DA 52 – The Divine Shepherd
Week 8: DA 53 – The Last Journey From Galilee
Week 9: DA 54 – The Good Samaritan
Week 10: DA 55 – Not With Outward Show
Week 11: DA 56 – Blessing the Children
Week 12: DA 57 – "One Thing Thou Lackest"
Week 13: STC 8 – Growing Up Into Christ
Week 14: DA 58 – "Lazarus, Come Forth"
Week 15: DA 59 – Priestly Plottings
Week 16: DA 60 – The Law of the New Kingdom
Week 17: DA 61 – Zacchaeus
Week 18: DA 62 – The Feast at Simon's House
Week 19: DA 63 – "Thy King Cometh"
Week 20: DA 64 – A Doomed People
Week 21: DA 65 – The Temple Cleansed Again
Week 22: DA 66 – Controversy
Week 23: DA 67 – Woes on the Pharisees
Week 24: DA 68 – In the Outer Court
Week 25: DA 69 – On the Mount of Olives
Week 26: STC 9 – The Work and the Life
Week 27: DA 70 – "The Least of These My Brethren"
Week 28: DA 71 – A Servant of Servants
Week 29: DA 72 – "In Remembrance of Me"
Week 30: DA 73 – "Let Not Your Heart Be Troubled" part 1
Week 31: DA 73 – "Let Not Your Heart Be Troubled" part 2
Week 32: DA 74 – Gethsemane
Week 33: DA 75 – Before Annas and the Court of Caiaphas – part 1
Week 34: DA 75 – Before Annas and the Court of Caiaphas – part 2
Week 35: DA 76 – Judas
Week 36: DA 77 – In Pilate's Judgment Hall – part 1
Week 37: DA 77 – In Pilate's Judgment Hall – part 2
Week 38: STC 10 – A Knowledge of God
Week 39: STC 11 – The Privilege of Prayer
Week 40: DA 78 – Calvary – part 1
Week 41: DA 78 – Calvary – part 2
Week 42: DA 79 – "It Is Finished"
Week 43: DA 80 – In Joseph's Tomb
Week 44: DA 81 – "The Lord Is Risen"
Week 45: DA 82 – "Why Weepest Thou?"
Week 46: DA 83 – The Walk to Emmaus
Week 47: DA 84 – "Peace Be Unto You"
Week 48: DA 85 – By the Sea Once More
Week 49: DA 86 – Go Teach All Nations
Week 50: DA 87 – "To My Father, and Your Father"
Week 51: STC 12 – What to Do with Doubt
Week 52: STC 13 – Rejoicing in the Lord

Continue your walk with your Friend! Keep up your aerobics for your heart, and repeat this exercise!

Chapter 1

"God With Us"

"His name shall be called Immanuel, . . . God with us." "The light of the knowledge of the glory of God" is seen "in the face of Jesus Christ." From the days of eternity the Lord Jesus Christ was one with the Father; He was "the image of God," the image of His greatness and majesty, "the outshining of His glory." It was to manifest this glory that He came to our world. To this sin-darkened earth He came to reveal the light of God's love,--to be "God with us." Therefore it was prophesied of Him, "His name shall be called Immanuel."

By coming to dwell with us, Jesus was to reveal God both to men and to angels. He was the Word of God,-- God's thought made audible. In His prayer for His disciples He says, "I have declared unto them Thy name,"--"merciful and gracious, long-suffering, and abundant in goodness and truth,"--"that the love wherewith Thou hast loved Me may be in them, and I in them." But not alone for His earthborn children was this revelation given. Our little world is the lesson book of the universe. God's wonderful purpose of grace, the mystery of redeeming love, is the theme into which "angels desire to look," and it will be their study throughout endless ages. Both the redeemed [19-20] and the unfallen beings will find in the cross of Christ their science and their song. It will be seen that the glory shining in the face of Jesus is the glory of self-sacrificing love. In the light from Calvary it will be seen that the law of self-renouncing love is the law of life for earth and heaven; that the love which "seeketh not her own" has its source in the heart of God; and that in the meek and lowly One is manifested the character of Him who dwelleth in the light which no man can approach unto.

In the beginning, God was revealed in all the works of creation. It was Christ that spread the heavens, and laid the foundations of the earth. It was His hand that hung the worlds in space, and fashioned the flowers of the field. "His strength setteth fast the mountains." "The sea is His, and He made it." Ps. 65:6; 95:5. It was He that filled the earth with beauty, and the air with song.

1. What is the significance of the name "Immanuel?" God w_____ us. What does this say about God's intentions with me?_____

_____

The need of sin-darkened earth, and of my sin-darkened life, is the light of the knowledge of the glory of God, seen in the f_____ of Jesus Christ . Where is my focus, Lord? _____

_____

2. "Jesus was to r_____ God both to m_____ and to a_____." Is there something different from what the Son of God revealed on earth, and what He revealed in heaven? What were the respective inhabitants to learn?

_____

_____

_____

That God reveals, says something about the kind of response God wants from me: _____

_____

3. The heart of God, His character, is the source of "self-s_____ love" and "self-r_____ love", which is the glory shining in the face of Jesus. As I contemplate Your life, Lord, how does Your glory contrast with the world's definition of glory, or my definition of

glory? _____
_____
_____
_____
_____
_____
_____(20)

And upon all things in earth, and air, and sky, He wrote the message of the Father's love.

Now sin has marred God's perfect work, yet that handwriting remains. Even now all created things declare the glory of His excellence. There is nothing, save the selfish heart of man, that lives unto itself. No bird that cleaves the air, no animal that moves upon the ground, but ministers to some other life. There is no leaf of the forest, or lowly blade of grass, but has its ministry. Every tree and shrub and leaf pours forth that element of life without which neither man nor animal could live; and man and animal, in turn, minister to the life of tree and shrub and leaf. The flowers breathe fragrance and unfold their beauty in blessing [20-21] to the world. The sun sheds its light to gladden a thousand worlds. The ocean, itself the source of all our springs and fountains, receives the streams from every land, but takes to give. The mists ascending from its bosom fall in showers to water the earth, that it may bring forth and bud.

The angels of glory find their joy in giving,--giving love and tireless watchcare to souls that are fallen and unholy. Heavenly beings woo the hearts of men; they bring to this dark world light from the courts above; by gentle and patient ministry they move upon the human spirit, to bring the lost into a fellowship with Christ which is even closer than they themselves can know.

4. What words of Jesus "set forth the great principle which is the law of life for the universe?" Seek not my g_____ but the Father's. (21). How is the Holy Spirit impressing me to be more open to this life-fulfilling principle?

_____
_____
_____
_____

But turning from all lesser representations, we behold God in Jesus. Looking unto Jesus we see that it is the glory of our God to give. "I do nothing of Myself," said Christ; "the living Father hath sent Me, and I live by the Father." "I seek not Mine own glory," but the glory of Him that sent Me. John 8:28; 6:57; 8:50; 7:18. In these words is set forth the great principle which is the law of life for the universe. All things Christ received from God, but He took to give. So in the heavenly courts, in His ministry for all created beings: through the beloved Son, the Father's life flows out to all; through the Son it returns, in praise and joyous service, a tide of love, to the great Source of all. And thus through Christ the circuit of beneficence is complete, representing the character of the great Giver, the law of life.

5. How was this principle/ law broken in heaven? "Sin originated in self-s_____." How does this relate to my failures, my falling short of Your glory? _____

_____
_____
_____
_____

In heaven itself this law was broken. Sin originated in self-seeking. Lucifer, the covering cherub, desired to be first in heaven. He sought to gain control of heavenly beings, to draw them away from their Creator, and to win their homage to himself. Therefore he misrepresented God, [21-22] attributing to Him the desire for self-exaltation. With his own evil characteristics he sought to invest the loving Creator. Thus he deceived angels. Thus he deceived men. He led them to doubt the word of God, and to distrust His goodness. Because God is a God of justice and terrible majesty, Satan caused them to look upon Him as severe and unforgiving. Thus he drew men to join him in rebellion against God, and the night of woe settled down upon the world.

The earth was dark through misapprehension of God. That the gloomy shadows might be lightened, that the world might be brought back to God, Satan's deceptive power was to be broken. This could not be done by force. The exercise of force is contrary to the principles of God's government; He desires only the service of love; and love cannot be commanded; it cannot be won by force or authority. Only by love is love awakened. To know God is to love Him; His character must be manifested in contrast to the character of Satan. This work only one Being in all the universe could do. Only He who knew the height and depth of the love of God could make it known. Upon the world's dark night the Sun of Righteousness must rise, "with healing in His wings." Mal. 4:2.

The plan for our redemption was not an afterthought, a plan formulated after the fall of Adam. It was a revelation of "the mystery which hath been kept in silence through times eternal." Rom. 16:25, R. V. It was an unfolding of the principles that from eternal ages have been the foundation of God's throne. From the beginning, God and Christ knew of the apostasy of Satan, and of the fall of man through the deceptive power of the apostate. God did not ordain that sin should exist, but He foresaw its existence, and made provision to meet the terrible emergency. So great was His love for the world, that He covenanted to give His only-begotten Son, "that whosoever believeth in Him should not perish, but have everlasting life." John 3:16.

Lucifer had said, "I will exalt my throne above the stars of God; . . . I will be like the Most High." Isa. 14:13, 14. But Christ, "being in the form of God, counted it not a thing to be grasped to be on an equality with God, but emptied Himself, taking the form of a servant, being made in the likeness of men." Phil. 2:6, 7, R. V.,

6. Lucifer "misrepresented God, attributing to Him the desire for s_____ _____." (22). Does Satan cause me to look upon You, Lord, as severe and unforgiving? _____
_____
_____
_____

Is my life dark through mis-a_____ of You? _____

_____

"His character must be manifested in contrast to the character of Satan."

margin.

This was a voluntary sacrifice. Jesus might have remained at the Father's side. He might have retained the glory of heaven, and the homage of the angels. But He chose to give back the scepter into [22-23] the Father's hands, and to step down from the throne of the universe, that He might bring light to the benighted, and life to the perishing.

Nearly two thousand years ago, a voice of mysterious import was heard in heaven, from the throne of God, "Lo, I come." "Sacrifice and offering Thou wouldest not, but a body hast Thou prepared Me. . . . Lo, I come (in the volume of the Book it is written of Me,) to do Thy will, O God." Heb. 10:5-7. In these words is announced the fulfillment of the purpose that had been hidden from eternal ages. Christ was about to visit our world, and to become incarnate. He says, "A body hast Thou prepared Me." Had He appeared with the glory that was His with the Father before the world was, we could not have endured the light of His presence. That we might behold it and not be destroyed, the manifestation of His glory was shrouded. His divinity was veiled with humanity,--the invisible glory in the visible human form.

7. Christ's "manifestation" of the Father's glory was "s_____." In the burning bush, "the all merciful God shrouded His glory in a most humble type, that Moses could look upon it and l_____ ___." In Christ, "His glory was veiled, His greatness and majesty were hidden, that He might d_____ n_____ to sorrowful, tempted men." (23). How can I better lift You up and let myself be drawn to You?

_____
_____
_____
_____

This great purpose had been shadowed forth in types and symbols. The burning bush, in which Christ appeared to Moses, revealed God. The symbol chosen for the representation of the Deity was a lowly shrub, that seemingly had no attractions. This enshrined the Infinite. The all-merciful God shrouded His glory in a most humble type, that Moses could look upon it and live. So in the pillar of cloud by day and the pillar of fire by night, God communicated with Israel, revealing to men His will, and imparting to them His grace. God's glory was subdued, and His majesty veiled, that the weak vision of finite men might behold it. So Christ was to come in "the body of our humiliation" (Phil. 3:21, R. V.), "in the likeness of men." In the eyes of the world He possessed no beauty that they should desire Him; yet He was the incarnate God, the light of heaven and earth. His glory was veiled, His greatness and majesty were hidden, that He might draw near to sorrowful, tempted men.

God commanded Moses for Israel, "Let them make Me a sanctuary; that I may dwell among them" (Ex.

25:8), and He abode in the sanctuary, in the midst of His people. Through all their weary wandering in the desert, the symbol of His presence was with them. So Christ set up His tabernacle in the midst of our human encampment. He pitched His tent by the side of the tents of men, that He might dwell among us, and make us familiar with His divine character and life. "The Word became flesh, and tabernacled among us (and we beheld His glory, glory as of [23-24] the Only Begotten from the Father), full of grace and truth." John 1:14, R. V., margin.

Since Jesus came to dwell with us, we know that God is acquainted with our trials, and sympathizes with our griefs. Every son and daughter of Adam may understand that our Creator is the friend of sinners. For in every doctrine of grace, every promise of joy, every deed of love, every divine attraction presented in the Saviour's life on earth, we see "God with us."

Satan represents God's law of love as a law of selfishness. He declares that it is impossible for us to obey its precepts. The fall of our first parents, with all the woe that has resulted, he charges upon the Creator, leading men to look upon God as the author of sin, and suffering, and death. Jesus was to unveil this deception. As one of us He was to give an example of obedience. For this He took upon Himself our nature, and passed through our experiences. "In all things it behooved Him to be made like unto His brethren." Heb. 2:17. If we had to bear anything which Jesus did not endure, then upon this point Satan would represent the power of God as insufficient for us. Therefore Jesus was "in all points tempted like as we are." Heb. 4:15. He endured every trial to which we are subject. And He exercised in His own behalf no power that is not freely offered to us. As man, He met temptation, and overcame in the strength given Him from God. He says, "I delight to do Thy will, O My God: yea, Thy law is within My heart." Ps. 40:8. As He went about doing good, and healing all who were afflicted by Satan, He made plain to men the character of God's law and the nature of His service. His life testifies that it is possible for us also to obey the law of God.

By His humanity, Christ touched humanity; by His divinity, He lays hold upon the throne of God. As the Son of man, He gave us an example of obedience; as the

8. "Satan represents God's law of love as a law of s_____ ...that it is impossible for us to o_____...As the Son of Man, He gave us an example of o_____ _____, as the Son of God, He gives us p_____ to obey." (24). How? He "overcame in the strength given Him from God," and the same power is freely offered to me. _____

_____
_____
_____

Son of God, He gives us power to obey. It was Christ who from the bush on Mount Horeb spoke to Moses saying, "I Am That I Am. . . . Thus shalt thou say unto the children of Israel, I Am hath sent me unto you." Ex. 3:14. This was the pledge of Israel's deliverance. So when He came "in the likeness of men," He declared Himself the I Am. The Child of Bethlehem, the meek and lowly Saviour, is God "manifest in the flesh." 1 Tim. 3:16. And to us He says: "I Am the Good Shepherd." "I Am the living Bread." "I Am the Way, the Truth, and the Life." "All power is given [24-25] unto Me in heaven and in earth." John 10:11; 6:51; 14:6; Matt. 28:18. I Am the assurance of every promise. I Am; be not afraid. "God with us" is the surety of our deliverance from sin, the assurance of our power to obey the law of heaven.

In stooping to take upon Himself humanity, Christ revealed a character the opposite of the character of Satan. But He stepped still lower in the path of humiliation. "Being found in fashion as a man, He humbled Himself, and became obedient unto death, even the death of the cross." Phil. 2:8. As the high priest laid aside his gorgeous pontifical robes, and officiated in the white linen dress of the common priest, so Christ took the form of a servant, and offered sacrifice, Himself the priest, Himself the victim. "He was wounded for our transgressions, He was bruised for our iniquities: the chastisement of our peace was upon Him." Isa. 53:5.

Christ was treated as we deserve, that we might be treated as He deserves. He was condemned for our sins, in which He had no share, that we might be justified by His righteousness, in which we had no share. He suffered the death which was ours, that we might receive the life which was His. "With His stripes we are healed."

9. "It was Satan's purpose to bring about an eternal separation between God and man; but in Christ we become more c_____ united to God than if we had n_____ fallen... bonds of i_____ _____ union." (25, 26)

10. Am I experiencing this close union with Him, by beholding God's glory, in the face of Jesus Christ?

_____
_____
_____

By His life and His death, Christ has achieved even more than recovery from the ruin wrought through sin. It was Satan's purpose to bring about an eternal separation between God and man; but in Christ we become more closely united to God than if we had never fallen. In taking our nature, the Saviour has bound Himself to humanity by a tie that is never to be broken. Through the eternal ages He is linked with us. "God so loved the world, that He gave His only-begotten Son." John 3:16. He gave Him not only to bear our sins, and to die as our sacrifice; He gave Him to the fallen race. To assure us of

His immutable counsel of peace, God gave His only-begotten Son to become one of the human family, forever to retain His human nature. This is the pledge that God will fulfill His word. "Unto us a child is born, unto us a son is given: and the government shall be upon His shoulder." God has adopted human nature in the person of His Son, and has carried the same into the highest heaven. It is the "Son of man" who shares the throne of the universe. It is the "Son of man" whose name shall be called, "Wonderful, Counselor, The mighty God, The everlasting Father, The Prince of Peace." Isa. 9:6. The I Am is the Daysman between God and humanity, laying His hand upon both. He who is "holy, harmless, undefiled, separate from sinners," is not ashamed to call us brethren. Heb. 7:26; 2:11. In Christ the family of earth and the family of heaven are [25-26] bound together. Christ glorified is our brother. Heaven is enshrined in humanity, and humanity is enfolded in the bosom of Infinite Love.

Of His people God says, "They shall be as the stones of a crown, lifted up as an ensign upon His land. For how great is His goodness, and how great is His beauty!" Zech. 9:16, 17. The exaltation of the redeemed will be an eternal testimony to God's mercy. "In the ages to come," He will "show the exceeding riches of His grace in His kindness toward us through Christ Jesus." "To the intent that . . . unto the principalities and the powers in the heavenly places might be made known . . . the manifold wisdom of God, according to the eternal purpose which He purposed in Christ Jesus our Lord." Eph. 2:7; 3:10, 11, R. V.

Through Christ's redeeming work the government of God stands justified. The Omnipotent One is made known as the God of love. Satan's charges are refuted, and his character unveiled. Rebellion can never again arise. Sin can never again enter the universe. Through eternal ages all are secure from apostasy. By love's self-sacrifice, the inhabitants of earth and heaven are bound to their Creator in bonds of indissoluble union.

The work of redemption will be complete. In the place where sin abounded, God's grace much more abounds. The earth itself, the very field that Satan claims as his, is to be not only ransomed but exalted. Our little world, under the curse of sin the one dark blot in His glorious creation, will be honored above all other

Prayer Journal:

_____
_____
_____
_____
_____
_____
_____

worlds in the universe of God. Here, where the Son of God tabernacled in humanity; where the King of glory lived and suffered and died,--here, when He shall make all things new, the tabernacle of God shall be with men, "and He will dwell with them, and they shall be His people, and God Himself shall be with them, and be their God." And through endless ages as the redeemed walk in the light of the Lord, they will praise Him for His unspeakable Gift,--

Immanuel, "God with us."

Chapter 2

The Chosen People

For more than a thousand years the Jewish people had awaited the Saviour's coming. Upon this event they had rested their brightest hopes. In song and prophecy, in temple rite and household prayer, they had enshrined His name. And yet at His coming they knew Him not. The Beloved of heaven was to them "as a root out of a dry ground;" He had "no form nor comeliness;" and they saw in Him no beauty that they should desire Him. "He came unto His own, and His own received Him not." Isa. 53:2; John 1:11.

Yet God had chosen Israel. He had called them to preserve among men the knowledge of His law, and of the symbols and prophecies that pointed to the Saviour. He desired them to be as wells of salvation to the world. What Abraham was in the land of his sojourn, what Joseph was in Egypt, and Daniel in the courts of Babylon, the Hebrew people were to be among the nations. They were to reveal God to men.

In the call of Abraham the Lord had said, "I will bless thee; . . . and thou shalt be a blessing: . . . and in thee shall all families of the earth be blessed." Gen. 12:2, 3. The same teaching was repeated through the prophets. Even after Israel had been wasted by war and captivity, the promise was theirs, "The remnant of Jacob shall be in the midst of many people as a dew from the Lord, as the showers upon the grass, that tarrieth not for man, nor waiteth for the sons of men." Micah 5:7. Concerning the temple at Jerusalem, the Lord declared through Isaiah, "Mine house shall be called an house of prayer for all peoples." Isa. 56:7, R. V. [27-28]

But the Israelites fixed their hopes upon worldly greatness. From the time of their entrance to the land of Canaan, they departed from the commandments of God, and followed the ways of the heathen. It was in vain that God sent them warning by His prophets. In vain they suffered the chastisement of heathen oppression. Every reformation was followed by deeper apostasy.

Had Israel been true to God, He could have accomplished His purpose through their honor and exaltation.

1. God chose Israel; He called them, "to be as wells of s_____ _____ to the world," to "reveal G_____ to men." Lord, do You have the same aspirations for me? To be Your ambassador? To reveal You suggests knowing You; so how well am I revealing You? _____ _____ _____

If they had walked in the ways of obedience, He would have made them "high above all nations which He hath made, in praise, and in name, and in honor." "All people of the earth," said Moses, "shall see that thou art called by the name of the Lord; and they shall be afraid of thee." "The nations which shall hear all these statutes" shall say, "Surely this great nation is a wise and understanding people." Deut. 26:19; 28:10; 4:6. But because of their unfaithfulness, God's purpose could be wrought out only through continued adversity and humiliation.

They were brought into subjection to Babylon, and scattered through the lands of the heathen. In affliction many renewed their faithfulness to His covenant. While they hung their harps upon the willows, and mourned for the holy temple that was laid waste, the light of truth shone out through them, and a knowledge of God was spread among the nations. The heathen systems of sacrifice were a perversion of the system that God had appointed; and many a sincere observer of heathen rites learned from the Hebrews the meaning of the service divinely ordained, and in faith grasped the promise of a Redeemer.

Many of the exiles suffered persecution. Not a few lost their lives because of their refusal to disregard the Sabbath and to observe the heathen festivals. As idolaters were roused to crush out the truth, the Lord brought His servants face to face with kings and rulers, that they and their people might receive the light. Time after time the greatest monarchs were led to proclaim the supremacy of the God whom their Hebrew captives worshiped.

By the Babylonish captivity the Israelites were effectually cured of the worship of graven images. During the centuries that followed, they suffered from the oppression of heathen foes, until the conviction became fixed that their prosperity depended upon their obedience to the law of God. But with too many of the people obedience was not prompted by love. The motive was selfish. They rendered outward service to God [28-29] as the means of attaining to national greatness. They did not become the light of the world, but shut themselves away from the world in order to escape temptation to idolatry. In the instruction given through Moses, God had placed restrictions upon their association with idolaters; but this teaching had been misinterpreted. It

2. Israel experienced a cycle of reformation and apostasy, reformation and apostasy. In the affliction of heathen oppression though, "many renewed their f_____ to His covenant." (28) Lord, why shouldn't I complain when I experience affliction? What do I find to be the relationship between affliction and faithfulness? _____
_____
_____
_____
_____

was intended to prevent them from conforming to the practices of the heathen. But it was used to build up a wall of separation between Israel and all other nations. The Jews looked upon Jerusalem as their heaven, and they were actually jealous lest the Lord should show mercy to the Gentiles.

After the return from Babylon, much attention was given to religious instruction. All over the country, synagogues were erected, where the law was expounded by the priests and scribes. And schools were established, which, together with the arts and sciences, professed to teach the principles of righteousness. But these agencies became corrupted. During the captivity, many of the people had received heathen ideas and customs, and these were brought into their religious service. In many things they conformed to the practices of idolaters.

As they departed from God, the Jews in a great degree lost sight of the teaching of the ritual service. That service had been instituted by Christ Himself. In every part it was a symbol of Him; and it had been full of vitality and spiritual beauty. But the Jews lost the spiritual life from their ceremonies, and clung to the dead forms. They trusted to the sacrifices and ordinances themselves, instead of resting upon Him to whom they pointed. In order to supply the place of that which they had lost, the priests and rabbis multiplied requirements of their own; and the more rigid they grew, the less of the love of God was manifested. They measured their holiness by the multitude of their ceremonies, while their hearts were filled with pride and hypocrisy.

With all their minute and burdensome injunctions, it was an impossibility to keep the law. Those who desired to serve God, and who tried to observe the rabbinical precepts, toiled under a heavy burden. They could find no rest from the accusings of a troubled conscience. Thus Satan worked to discourage the people, to lower their conception of the character of God, and to bring the faith of Israel into contempt. He hoped to establish the claim put forth when he rebelled in heaven,--that the requirements of God were unjust, and could not be obeyed. Even Israel, he declared, did not keep the law.

While the Jews desired the advent of the Messiah, they had no true [29-30] conception of His mission. They did not seek redemption from sin, but deliverance from the Romans. They looked for the Messiah to come

3. How did the Israelites interpret God's restrictions upon association with idolaters? _____

_____

_____. Lord, why is it, that when I feel chosen, special, I believe myself to be better than others? ____

_____

_____

_____

_____(29)

4. As they departed from God, "the Jews lost the spiritual life from their ceremonies, and clung to the d_____ forms... They measured their holiness not by the manifestation of the love of God, but by the multitude of their c_____."
Lord, do I take any pride in my spiritual disciplines? Have any of them lost their spiritual life?

_____

_____ What do You suggest I do about it? ___

_____

_____

_____

_____

5. The way was prepared for God's chosen people to reject the Savior by their not having the true conception of His m_____.
(30). Could a misconception cause me to reject You, Lord? _____

_____
_____ Do I value
Your character of meek-
ness?_____
Do I reject You when
I fail to minister to the
"least of these?" _____
_____

6. Had God's people
studied the prophecies?
Yes, but without s_____
_____ insight. Lord,
how can I avoid interpret-
ing scriptures according
to my "selfish desires?"

_____
_____
(Pray a prayer of openness
to God, to be teachable).

Prayer Journal: _____
_____
_____
_____
_____
_____
_____
_____

as a conqueror, to break the oppressor's power, and exalt Israel to universal dominion. Thus the way was prepared for them to reject the Saviour.

At the time of the birth of Christ the nation was
chafing under the rule of her foreign masters, and
racked with internal strife. The Jews had been permitted to maintain the form of a separate government; but
nothing could disguise the fact that they were under
the Roman yoke, or reconcile them to the restriction
of their power. The Romans claimed the right of appointing and removing the high priest, and the office
was often secured by fraud, bribery, and even murder.
Thus the priesthood became more and more corrupt.
Yet the priests still possessed great power, and they employed it for selfish and mercenary ends. The people
were subjected to their merciless demands, and were
also heavily taxed by the Romans. This state of affairs
caused widespread discontent. Popular outbreaks were
frequent. Greed and violence, distrust and spiritual apa-
thy, were eating out the very heart of the nation.

Hatred of the Romans, and national and spiritual
pride, led the Jews still to adhere rigorously to their
forms of worship. The priests tried to maintain a reputation for sanctity by scrupulous attention to the ceremonies of religion. The people, in their darkness and oppression, and the rulers, thirsting for power, longed for
the coming of One who would vanquish their enemies
and restore the kingdom to Israel. They had studied
the prophecies, but without spiritual insight. Thus they
overlooked those scriptures that point to the humiliation
of Christ's first advent, and misapplied those that speak
of the glory of His second coming. Pride obscured their
vision. They interpreted prophecy in accordance with
their selfish desires.

Chapter 3

"The Fullness of the Time"

"When the fullness of the time was come, God sent forth His Son, . . . to redeem them that were under the law, that we might receive the adoption of sons." Gal. 4:4, 5.

The Saviour's coming was foretold in Eden. When Adam and Eve first heard the promise, they looked for its speedy fulfillment. They joyfully welcomed their first-born son, hoping that he might be the Deliverer. But the fulfillment of the promise tarried. Those who first received it died without the sight. From the days of Enoch the promise was repeated through patriarchs and prophets, keeping alive the hope of His appearing, and yet He came not. The prophecy of Daniel revealed the time of His advent, but not all rightly interpreted the message. Century after century passed away; the voices of the prophets ceased. The hand of the oppressor was heavy upon Israel, and many were ready to exclaim, "The days are prolonged, and every vision faileth." Ezek. 12:22. [31-32] But like the stars in the vast circuit of their appointed path, God's purposes know no haste and no delay. Through the symbols of the great darkness and the smoking furnace, God had revealed to Abraham the bondage of Israel in Egypt, and had declared that the time of their sojourning should be four hundred years. "Afterward," He said, "shall they come out with great substance." Gen. 15:14. Against that word, all the power of Pharaoh's proud empire battled in vain. On "the self-same day" appointed in the divine promise, "it came to pass, that all the hosts of the Lord went out from the land of Egypt." Ex. 12:41. So in heaven's council the hour for the coming of Christ had been determined. When the great clock of time pointed to that hour, Jesus was born in Bethlehem.

"When the fullness of the time was come, God sent forth His Son." Providence had directed the movements of nations, and the tide of human impulse and influence, until the world was ripe for the coming of the Deliverer. The nations were united under one government.

One language was widely spoken, and was everywhere recognized as the language of literature. From all lands the Jews of the dispersion gathered to Jerusalem to the annual feasts. As these returned to the places of their sojourn, they could spread throughout the world the tidings of the Messiah's coming.

At this time the systems of heathenism were losing their hold upon the people. Men were weary of pageant and fable. They longed for a religion that could satisfy the heart. While the light of truth seemed to have departed from among men, there were souls who were looking for light, and who were filled with perplexity and sorrow. They were thirsting for a knowledge of the living God, for some assurance of a life beyond the grave.

As the Jews had departed from God, faith had grown dim, and hope had well-nigh ceased to illuminate the future. The words of the prophets were uncomprehended. To the masses of the people, death was a dread mystery; beyond was uncertainty and gloom. It was not alone the wailing of the mothers of Bethlehem, but the cry from the great heart of humanity, that was borne to the prophet across the centuries,--the voice heard in Ramah, "lamentation, and weeping, and great mourning, Rachel weeping for her children, and would not be comforted, because they are not." Matt. 2:18. In "the region and shadow of death," men sat unsolaced. With longing eyes they looked for the [32-33] coming of the Deliverer, when the darkness should be dispelled, and the mystery of the future should be made plain.

Outside of the Jewish nation there were men who foretold the appearance of a divine instructor. These men were seeking for truth, and to them the Spirit of Inspiration was imparted. One after another, like stars in the darkened heavens, such teachers had arisen. Their words of prophecy had kindled hope in the hearts of thousands of the Gentile world.

For hundreds of years the Scriptures had been translated into the Greek language, then widely spoken throughout the Roman Empire. The Jews were scattered everywhere, and their expectation of the Messiah's coming was to some extent shared by the Gentiles. Among those whom the Jews styled heathen were men who had a better understanding of the Scripture prophecies concerning the Messiah than had the teachers in

---

1. What does it mean that Israel longed for a religion that could satisfy the heart? They were "weary of p____ _____ and f_____." (32) Lord, is my heart satisfied? Why? or why not?

Lord, will I be satisfied, blessed, if I hunger and thirst after righteousness? How can my walk with You be more than formality, and come from the heart?

2. "Among those whom the Jews styled h____ _____ were men who had a better understanding of the Scripture prophecies concerning the M_____ than had the teachers in Is-

Israel. There were some who hoped for His coming as a deliverer from sin. Philosophers endeavored to study into the mystery of the Hebrew economy. But the bigotry of the Jews hindered the spread of the light. Intent on maintaining the separation between themselves and other nations, they were unwilling to impart the knowledge they still possessed concerning the symbolic service. The true [33-34] Interpreter must come. The One whom all these types prefigured must explain their significance.

Through nature, through types and symbols, through patriarchs and prophets, God had spoken to the world. Lessons must be given to humanity in the language of humanity. The Messenger of the covenant must speak. His voice must be heard in His own temple. Christ must come to utter words which should be clearly and definitely understood. He, the author of truth, must separate truth from the chaff of man's utterance, which had made it of no effect. The principles of God's government and the plan of redemption must be clearly defined. The lessons of the Old Testament must be fully set before men.

Among the Jews there were yet steadfast souls, descendants of that holy line through whom a knowledge of God had been preserved. These still looked for the hope of the promise made unto the fathers. They strengthened their faith by dwelling upon the assurance given through Moses, "A Prophet shall the Lord your God raise up unto you of your brethren, like unto me; Him shall ye hear in all things whatsoever He shall say unto you." Acts 3:22. Again, they read how the Lord would anoint One "to preach good tidings unto the meek," "to bind up the brokenhearted, to proclaim liberty to the captives," and to declare the "acceptable year of the Lord." Isa. 61:1, 2. They read how He would "set judgment in the earth," how the isles should "wait for His law," how the Gentiles should come to His light, and kings to the brightness of His rising. Isa. 42:4; 60:3.

The dying words of Jacob filled them with hope: "The scepter shall not depart from Judah, nor a lawgiver from between his feet, until Shiloh come." Gen. 49:10. The waning power of Israel testified that the Messiah's coming was at hand. The prophecy of Daniel pictured the glory of His reign over an empire which should succeed all earthly kingdoms; and, said the prophet, "It

rael." (33). How do You feel Lord, about my lack of comprehension of spiritual truth? About my lack of intimacy with You? __

_____
_____
_____
_____
_____

3. Jesus came that He might speak in the language of humanity. "The principles of God's government and the plan of r_____ _____ must be c_____ defined." (34). Lord, what response from me are You hoping for, when You say in John 3:16 "whosoever believeth?"

_____
_____
_____

My believing must be important to You, for You sure went through a lot, to give me that opportunity! _____

_____
_____

4. "The fullness of the time had c_____…Satan had been working to make the gulf deep and impassable between earth and heaven… It was his purpose to wear out the f_____ of God, and to extinguish His l_____ for man." Was Satan successful? _____. Romans 8:35-39 says: _____

_____

_____. What about a fullness of the time in my life? What is happening to the gulf, the separation, that Satan has caused?

_____

_____

_____

5. Satan "won his great triumph in perverting the f_____ of Israel…The principle that man can save h_____ by his own works…had now become the principle of the Jewish religion. Satan had implanted this principle. Wherever it is held, men have no b_____ against sin." (35-6). Why? Why does self works eliminate the barrier? _____

_____

_____

Relying on my own "filthy rags" righteousness, is sin, which is to go my own way, straying away from You like sheep. Being away from You, there is no

shall stand forever." Dan. 2:44. While few understood the nature of Christ's mission, there was a widespread expectation of a mighty prince who should establish his kingdom in Israel, and who should come as a deliverer to the nations.

The fullness of the time had come. Humanity, becoming more degraded through ages of transgression, called for the coming of the Redeemer. Satan had been working to make the gulf deep and impassable between earth and heaven. By his falsehoods he had emboldened [34-35] men in sin. It was his purpose to wear out the forbearance of God, and to extinguish His love for man, so that He would abandon the world to satanic jurisdiction.

Satan was seeking to shut out from men a knowledge of God, to turn their attention from the temple of God, and to establish his own kingdom. His strife for supremacy had seemed to be almost wholly successful. It is true that in every generation God had His agencies. Even among the heathen there were men through whom Christ was working to uplift the people from their sin and degradation. But these men were despised and hated. Many of them suffered a violent death. The dark shadow that Satan had cast over the world grew deeper and deeper.

Through heathenism, Satan had for ages turned men away from God; but he won his great triumph in perverting the faith of Israel. By contemplating and worshiping their own conceptions, the heathen had lost a knowledge of God, and had become more and more corrupt. So it was with Israel. The principle that man can save himself by his own works lay at the foundation of every heathen religion; it had now [35-36] become the principle of the Jewish religion. Satan had implanted this principle. Wherever it is held, men have no barrier against sin.

The message of salvation is communicated to men through human agencies. But the Jews had sought to make a monopoly of the truth which is eternal life. They had hoarded the living manna, and it had turned to corruption. The religion which they tried to shut up to themselves became an offense. They robbed God of His glory, and defrauded the world by a counterfeit of the gospel. They had refused to surrender themselves to God for the salvation of the world, and they became agents of Satan for its destruction.

The people whom God had called to be the pillar and ground of the truth had become representatives of Satan. They were doing the work that he desired them to do, taking a course to misrepresent the character of God, and cause the world to look upon Him as a tyrant. The very priests who ministered in the temple had lost sight of the significance of the service they performed. They had ceased to look beyond the symbol to the thing signified. In presenting the sacrificial offerings they were as actors in a play. The ordinances which God Himself had appointed were made the means of blinding the mind and hardening the heart. God could do no more for man through these channels. The whole system must be swept away.

The deception of sin had reached its height. All the agencies for depraving the souls of men had been put in operation. The Son of God, looking upon the world, beheld suffering and misery. With pity He saw how men had become victims of satanic cruelty. He looked with compassion upon those who were being corrupted, murdered, and lost. They had chosen a ruler who chained them to his car as captives. Bewildered and deceived, they were moving on in gloomy procession toward eternal ruin,--to death in which is no hope of life, toward night to which comes no morning. Satanic agencies were incorporated with men. The bodies of human beings, made for the dwelling place of God, had become the habitation of demons. The senses, the nerves, the passions, the organs of men, were worked by supernatural agencies in the indulgence of the vilest lust. The very stamp of demons was impressed upon the countenances of men. Human faces reflected the expression of the legions of evil with which they were possessed. Such was the prospect upon which the world's Redeemer looked. What a spectacle for Infinite Purity to behold! [36-37]

Sin had become a science, and vice was consecrated as a part of religion. Rebellion had struck its roots deep into the heart, and the hostility of man was most violent against heaven. It was demonstrated before the universe that, apart from God, humanity could not be uplifted. A new element of life and power must be imparted by Him who made the world.

With intense interest the unfallen worlds had watched to see Jehovah arise, and sweep away the in-

barrier against sin. Lord, I choose to stay close to You. May I have confidence only in You, and not my self.

6. The fullness of the time for Christ's coming, also included a monopoly of the truth by the Jews. "They hoarded the living m_____...The religion which they tried to s_____ up to themselves became an offense." Instead of being a pillar of truth, they became representatives of S_____, misrepresenting the character of God. (36). What is the lesson, Lord?

_____
_____
_____

A religious experience that is focused on myself, that benefits myself, will be corrupted, will be an offense, even to myself? _____

_____
_____

habitants of the earth. And if God should do this, Satan was ready to carry out his plan for securing to himself the allegiance of heavenly beings. He had declared that the principles of God's government make forgiveness impossible. Had the world been destroyed, he would have claimed that his accusations were proved true. He was ready to cast blame upon God, and to spread his rebellion to the worlds above. But instead of destroying the world, God sent His Son to save it. Though corruption and defiance might be seen in every part of the alien province, a way for its recovery was provided. At the very crisis, when Satan seemed about to triumph, the Son of God came with the embassage of divine grace. Through every age, through every hour, the love of God had been exercised toward the fallen race. Notwithstanding the perversity of men, the signals of mercy had been continually exhibited. And when the fullness of the time had come, the Deity was glorified by pouring upon the world a flood of healing grace that was never to be obstructed or withdrawn till the plan of salvation should be fulfilled.

Satan was exulting that he had succeeded in debasing the image of God in humanity. Then Jesus came to restore in man the image of his [37-38] Maker. None but Christ can fashion anew the character that has been ruined by sin. He came to expel the demons that had controlled the will. He came to lift us up from the dust, to reshape the marred character after the pattern of His divine character, and to make it beautiful with His own glory.

7. "And when the fullness of the time had come, the Deity was glorified by pouring upon the world a flood [not of destruction, like Satan expected (why?), but a flood] of healing g_____ that was never to be obstructed or withdrawn till the plan of salvation should be fulfilled." (37). What a awesome God You are, Lord! I need Your healing grace! Help me to be open to the fulfilling of the plan of salvation in my life! ____

_____
_____
_____
_____

Prayer Journal: _____
_____
_____
_____
_____
_____

Chapter 4

Unto You a Saviour

[This chapter is based on Luke 2:1-20.]

The King of glory stooped low to take humanity. Rude and forbidding were His earthly surroundings. His glory was veiled, that the majesty of His outward form might not become an object of attraction. He shunned all outward display. Riches, worldly honor, and human greatness can never save a soul from death; Jesus purposed that no attraction of an earthly nature should call men to His side. Only the beauty of heavenly truth must draw those who would follow Him. The character of the Messiah had long been foretold in prophecy, and He desired men to accept Him upon the testimony of the word of God.

The angels had wondered at the glorious plan of redemption. They watched to see how the people of God would receive His Son, clothed in the garb of humanity. Angels came to the land of the chosen people. Other nations were dealing in fables and worshiping false gods. To the land where the glory of God had been revealed, and the light of prophecy had shone, the angels came. They came unseen to Jerusalem, to the appointed expositors of the Sacred Oracles, and the ministers of God's [43-44] house. Already to Zacharias the priest, as he ministered before the altar, the nearness of Christ's coming had been announced. Already the forerunner was born, his mission attested by miracle and prophecy. The tidings of his birth and the wonderful significance of his mission had been spread abroad. Yet Jerusalem was not preparing to welcome her Redeemer.

With amazement the heavenly messengers beheld the indifference of that people whom God had called to communicate to the world the light of sacred truth. The Jewish nation had been preserved as a witness that Christ was to be born of the seed of Abraham and of David's line; yet they knew not that His coming was now at hand. In the temple the morning and the evening sacrifice daily pointed to the Lamb of God; yet even here was no preparation to receive Him. The priests and teachers of the nation knew not that the greatest event of the ages was about to take place. They rehearsed their meaningless

1. When Jesus came to earth, "His glory was v_____." He wanted to be accepted not for the majesty of His outward form, but to let the beauty of heavenly truth "d_____ those that would follow Him," to be accepted for His character. (43). What am I more impressed with: majesty and miracles, or character and beauty of heavenly truth? _____ The latter requires more contemplation and openness to the leading of the Holy Spirit. Lord, is there a sufficient longing in my heart, for the time that is needed for contemplation, to be set aside and made a priority? ____

_____

_____

_____

2. "The angels had wondered at the glorious plan of redemption...With a__ _____ the heavenly messengers beheld the i_____ _____ of that people whom God had called to c_____ to the world the light of sacred truth." (43, 44). Lord, are my prayers / rites of worship meaningless and untouched by the joy and thrill at the nearness of the Your second coming? ____

_____

_____ What can I do about it? _____

_____

_____

prayers, and performed the rites of worship to be seen by men, but in their strife for riches and worldly honor they were not prepared for the revelation of the Messiah. The same indifference pervaded the land of Israel. Hearts selfish and world-engrossed were untouched by the joy that thrilled all heaven. Only a few were longing to behold the Unseen. To these heaven's embassy was sent.

Angels attend Joseph and Mary as they journey from their home in Nazareth to the city of David. The decree of imperial Rome for the enrollment of the peoples of her vast dominion has extended to the dwellers among the hills of Galilee. As in old time Cyrus was called to the throne of the world's empire that he might set free the captives of the Lord, so Caesar Augustus is made the agent for the fulfillment of God's purpose in bringing the mother of Jesus to Bethlehem. She is of the lineage of David, and the Son of David must be born in David's city. Out of Bethlehem, said the prophet, "shall He come forth . . . that is to be ruler in Israel; whose goings forth have been from of old, from the days of eternity." Micah 5:2, margin. But in the city of their royal line, Joseph and Mary are unrecognized and unhonored. Weary and homeless, they traverse the entire length of the narrow street, from the gate of the city to the eastern extremity of the town, vainly seeking a resting place for the night. There is no room for them at the crowded inn. In a rude building where the beasts are sheltered, they at last find refuge, and here the Redeemer of the world is born. [44-47]

Men know it not, but the tidings fill heaven with rejoicing. With a deeper and more tender interest the holy beings from the world of light are drawn to the earth. The whole world is brighter for His presence. Above the hills of Bethlehem are gathered an innumerable throng of angels. They wait the signal to declare the glad news to the world. Had the leaders in Israel been true to their trust, they might have shared the joy of heralding the birth of Jesus. But now they are passed by.

God declares, "I will pour water upon him that is thirsty, and floods upon the dry ground." "Unto the upright there ariseth light in the darkness." Isa. 44:3; Ps. 112:4. To those who are seeking for light, and who accept it with gladness, the bright rays from the throne of God will shine.

In the fields where the boy David had led his flock,

3. A weary Joseph and Mary traverse the entire length of the street, "v_____ seeking a resting place for the night. There is no r_____ for them at the crowded inn." (44). Lord, are You vainly seeking a resting place in my heart? What do I need to do make room for You? _____
_____
_____

4. What trust had the leaders of Israel been untrue to? _____
_____
What joy did they miss out on? _____
_____(47).
Do I have a trust? What is it? _____
_____
_____

5. "To those who are s_____ for light, and who a_____ it with gladness, the bright rays from the throne of God w_____ shine." Lord,

shepherds were still keeping watch by night. Through the silent hours they talked together of the promised Saviour, and prayed for the coming of the King to David's throne. "And, lo, the angel of the Lord came upon them, and the glory of the Lord shone round about them: and they were sore afraid. And the angel said unto them, Fear not: for, behold, I bring you good tidings of great joy, which shall be to all people. For unto you is born this day in the city of David a Saviour, which is Christ the Lord."

At these words, visions of glory fill the minds of the listening shepherds. The Deliverer has come to Israel! Power, exaltation, triumph, are associated with His coming. But the angel must prepare them to recognize their Saviour in poverty and humiliation. "This shall be a sign unto you," he says; "Ye shall find the babe wrapped in swaddling clothes, lying in a manger."

The heavenly messenger had quieted their fears. He had told them how to find Jesus. With tender regard for their human weakness, he had [47-48] given them time to become accustomed to the divine radiance. Then the joy and glory could no longer be hidden. The whole plain was lighted up with the bright shining of the hosts of God. Earth was hushed, and heaven stooped to listen to the song,--

"Glory to God in the highest,
And on earth peace, good will toward men."

Oh that today the human family could recognize that song! The declaration then made, the note then struck, will swell to the close of time, and resound to the ends of the earth. When the Sun of Righteousness shall arise, with healing in His wings, that song will be re-echoed by the voice of a great multitude, as the voice of many waters, saying, "Alleluia: for the Lord God omnipotent reigneth." Rev. 19:6.

As the angels disappeared, the light faded away, and the shadows of night once more fell on the hills of Bethlehem. But the brightest picture ever beheld by human eyes remained in the memory of the shepherds. "And it came to pass, as the angels were gone away from them into heaven, the shepherds said one to another, Let us now go even unto Bethlehem, and see this thing which is come to pass, which the Lord hath made known unto us. And they came with haste, and found Mary, and Joseph, and the babe lying in a manger."

---

if I see Your advice for me today as a bit uncomfortable, and I am less than enthusiastic about it, might I short-change myself of Your bright rays?

Would a prayer for an attitude shift help?

---

6. "'Glory to God in the highest, and on earth, peace, g_____ will toward men.' Oh that today the human family could r_____ that song!" (48). DO I recognize it? Does it resound in my heart? I should take time to hear the joy and the glory!

7. "Heaven and earth are n___ w_____ a_____ today than when the shepherds listened to the angels' song." Lord, let me hear Your heart's passion to be near! And to have the same longing! _____

_____

_____

8. Why does human pride and self-sufficiency stand rebuked in the story of Bethlehem? (49)_____

_____

_____

_____

(Jesus accepted humanity when the race had been w_____ by four thousand years of sin. See DA 311, 5 SDABC 1128).

9. What are two reasons that Jesus accepted the results of the working of the great law of heredity: 1) to share _____

_____

2) to give us the _____

_____

(See DA 24.2 - strength given Him from God). Lord, inspire me with the intimate reliance You had on the Father.

10. What risk did the Father and Jesus take? f__ _____ and e_____ loss. Lord, I should wonder and be astonished at

Departing with great joy, they made known the things they had seen and heard. "And all they that heard it wondered at those things which were told them by the shepherds. But Mary kept all these things, and pondered them in her heart. And the shepherds returned, glorifying and praising God."

Heaven and earth are no wider apart today than when shepherds listened to the angels' song. Humanity is still as much the object of heaven's solicitude as when common men of common occupations met angels at noonday, and talked with the heavenly messengers in the vineyards and the fields. To us in the common walks of life, heaven may be very near. Angels from the courts above will attend the steps of those who come and go at God's command.

The story of Bethlehem is an exhaustless theme. In it is hidden "the depth of the riches both of the wisdom and knowledge of God." Rom. 11:33. We marvel at the Saviour's sacrifice in exchanging the throne of heaven for the manger, and the companionship of adoring angels for the [48-49] beasts of the stall. Human pride and self-sufficiency stand rebuked in His presence. Yet this was but the beginning of His wonderful condescension. It would have been an almost infinite humiliation for the Son of God to take man's nature, even when Adam stood in his innocence in Eden. But Jesus accepted humanity when the race had been weakened by four thousand years of sin. Like every child of Adam He accepted the results of the working of the great law of heredity. What these results were is shown in the history of His earthly ancestors. He came with such a heredity to share our sorrows and temptations, and to give us the example of a sinless life.

Satan in heaven had hated Christ for His position in the courts of God. He hated Him the more when he himself was dethroned. He hated Him who pledged Himself to redeem a race of sinners. Yet into the world where Satan claimed dominion God permitted His Son to come, a helpless babe, subject to the weakness of humanity. He permitted Him to meet life's peril in common with every human soul, to fight the battle as every child of humanity must fight it, at the risk of failure and eternal loss.

The heart of the human father yearns over his son. He looks into the face of his little child, and trembles at the thought of life's peril. He longs to shield his dear one from Satan's power, to hold him back from temptation and conflict. To meet a bitterer conflict and a more fearful risk, God gave His only-begotten Son, that the path of life might be made sure for our little ones. "Herein is love." Wonder, O heavens! and be astonished, O earth!

this love! This was not a calculated risk, one that You could absorb and go on. Everything, everything was on the line! It is unbelievable that You would do it! Who am I that You would do this? _____

_____

_____

Prayer Journal: _____

_____

_____

_____

_____

_____

_____

_____

Chapter 5

The Dedication

[This chapter is based on Luke 2:21-38.]

About forty days after the birth of Christ, Joseph and Mary took Him to Jerusalem, to present Him to the Lord, and to offer sacrifice. This was according to the Jewish law, and as man's substitute Christ must conform to the law in every particular. He had already been subjected to the rite of circumcision, as a pledge of His obedience to the law.

As an offering for the mother, the law required a lamb of the first year for a burnt offering, and a young pigeon or a turtledove for a sin offering. But the law provided that if the parents were too poor to bring a lamb, a pair of turtledoves or two young pigeons, one for a burnt offering, the other for a sin offering, might be accepted.

The offerings presented to the Lord were to be without blemish. These offerings represented Christ, and from this it is evident that Jesus Himself was free from physical deformity. He was the "lamb without blemish and without spot." 1 Peter 1:19. His physical structure was not marred by any defect; His body was strong and healthy. And throughout His lifetime He lived in conformity to nature's laws. Physically [50-51] as well as spiritually, He was an example of what God designed all humanity to be through obedience to His laws.

The dedication of the first-born had its origin in the earliest times. God had promised to give the First-born of heaven to save the sinner. This gift was to be acknowledged in every household by the consecration of the first-born son. He was to be devoted to the priesthood, as a representative of Christ among men.

In the deliverance of Israel from Egypt, the dedication of the first-born was again commanded. While the children of Israel were in bondage to the Egyptians, the Lord directed Moses to go to Pharaoh, king of Egypt, and say, "Thus saith the Lord, Israel is My son, even My first-born: and I say unto thee, Let My son go, that he

---

1. The consecration of each family's first-born son, was an acknowledgment that "God had promised to give the First-born of h_____ _____ to save the sinner." (51). Lord, how can I acknowledge Your great gift? _____ _____ Does my mechanical practice of communion and footwashing make light of Your gift?

_____

_____

may serve Me: and if thou refuse to let him go, behold, I will slay thy son, even thy first-born." Ex. 4:22, 23.

Moses delivered his message; but the proud king's answer was, "Who is the Lord, that I should obey His voice to let Israel go? I know not the Lord, neither will I let Israel go." Ex. 5:2. The Lord worked for His people by signs and wonders, sending terrible judgments upon Pharaoh. At length the destroying angel was bidden to slay the first-born of man and beast among the Egyptians. That the Israelites might be spared, they were directed to place upon their doorposts the blood of a slain lamb. Every house was to be marked, that when the angel came on his mission of death, he might pass over the homes of the Israelites.

After sending this judgment upon Egypt, the Lord said to Moses, "Sanctify unto Me all the first-born, . . . both of man and of beast: it is Mine;" "for on the day that I smote all the first-born in the land of Egypt I hallowed unto Me all the first-born in Israel, both man and beast: Mine shall they be: I am the Lord." Ex. 13:2; Num. 3:13. After the tabernacle service was established, the Lord chose the tribe of Levi in the place of the first-born of all Israel to minister in the sanctuary. But the first-born were still to be regarded as the Lord's, and were to be bought back by a ransom.

Thus the law for the presentation of the first-born was made particularly significant. While it was a memorial of the Lord's wonderful deliverance of the children of Israel, it prefigured a greater deliverance, to be wrought out by the only-begotten Son of God. As the blood sprinkled on the doorposts had saved the first-born of Israel, so the blood of Christ has power to save the world. [51-52]

What meaning then was attached to Christ's presentation! But the priest did not see through the veil; he did not read the mystery beyond. The presentation of infants was a common scene. Day after day the priest received the redemption money as the babes were presented to the Lord. Day after day he went through the routine of his work, giving little heed to the parents or children, unless he saw some indication of the wealth or high rank of the parents. Joseph and Mary were poor; and when they came with their child, the priests saw only a man and woman dressed as Galileans, and in the humblest garments. There was nothing in their appear-

2. Presentation of the first-born was a memorial of God's deliverance: 1) for the children of Israel, 2) in the Son of God saving the w_____. Lord, may I better appreciate and value the cost of Your great deliverance. _____
_____
_____

ance to attract attention, and they presented only the offering made by the poorer classes.

The priest went through the ceremony of his official work. He took the child in his arms, and held it up before the altar. After handing it back to its mother, he inscribed the name "Jesus" on the roll of the first-born. Little did he think, as the babe lay in his arms, that it was the Majesty of heaven, the King of glory. The priest did not think that this babe was the One of whom Moses had written, "A Prophet shall the Lord your God raise up unto you of your brethren, like unto me; Him shall ye hear in all things whatsoever He shall say unto you." Acts 3:22. He did not think that this babe was He whose glory Moses had asked to see. But One greater than Moses lay in the priest's arms; and when he enrolled the child's name, he was enrolling the name of One who was the foundation of the whole Jewish economy. That name was to be its death warrant; for the system of sacrifices and offerings was waxing old; the type had almost reached its antitype, the shadow its substance.

The Shekinah had departed from the sanctuary, but in the Child of Bethlehem was veiled the glory before which angels bow. This unconscious babe was the promised seed, to whom the first altar at the gate of Eden pointed. This was Shiloh, the peace giver. It was He who declared Himself to Moses as the I am. It was He who in the pillar of cloud and of fire had been the guide of Israel. This was He whom seers had long foretold. He was the Desire of all nations, the Root and the Offspring of David, and the Bright and Morning Star. The name of that helpless little babe, inscribed in the roll of Israel, declaring Him our brother, was the hope of fallen humanity. The child for whom the redemption money had been paid was He who was to pay the ransom for the sins of the whole world. He was the true "high priest over the house of God," the head of "an unchangeable priesthood," the intercessor [52-55] at "the right hand of the Majesty on high." Heb. 10:21; 7:24; 1:3.

Spiritual things are spiritually discerned. In the temple the Son of God was dedicated to the work He had come to do. The priest looked upon Him as he would upon any other child. But though he neither saw nor felt anything unusual, God's act in giving His Son to the world was acknowledged. This occasion did not pass without some recognition of Christ. "There was a man

---

3. Little did the priest think, as the babe lay in his arms, that it was the "Majesty of heaven, the King of glory." (52). Why do I sometimes miss the special significance and privilege of Your presence, Lord? Could I be going through the motions, saying the right things with my lips, while my heart is far away? ___
_____
_____

4. What does the phrase 'type had almost reached its anti-type,' mean? ____
_____
_____
_____ (system of sacrifices vs THE Sacrifice / shadow vs substance). Have I at times confused the means with the end? For instance: paying tithe, without trust being nurtured; Sabbath observance rules being less than convincing (because it is so detached from a relationship-with-God motive); church attendance for guilt's sake:
_____
_____
_____
_____

in Jerusalem, whose name was Simeon; and the same man was just and devout, waiting for the Consolation of Israel: and the Holy Ghost was upon him. And it was revealed unto him by the Holy Ghost, that he should not see death, before he had seen the Lord's Christ."

As Simeon enters the temple, he sees a family presenting their first-born son before the priest. Their appearance bespeaks poverty; but Simeon understands the warnings of the Spirit, and he is deeply impressed that the infant being presented to the Lord is the Consolation of Israel, the One he has longed to see. To the astonished priest, Simeon appears like a man enraptured. The child has been returned to Mary, and he takes it in his arms and presents it to God, while a joy that he has never before felt enters his soul. As he lifts the infant Saviour toward heaven, he says, "Lord, now lettest Thou Thy servant depart in peace, according to Thy word: for mine eyes have seen Thy salvation, which Thou hast prepared before the face of all people; a light to lighten the Gentiles, and the glory of Thy people Israel."

The spirit of prophecy was upon this man of God, and while Joseph and Mary stood by, wondering at his words, he blessed them, and said unto Mary, "Behold, this child is set for the fall and rising again of many in Israel; and for a sign which shall be spoken against; (yea, a sword shall pierce through thy own soul also,) that the thoughts of many hearts may be revealed."

Anna also, a prophetess, came in and confirmed Simeon's testimony concerning Christ. As Simeon spoke, her face lighted up with the glory of God, and she poured out her heartfelt thanks that she had been permitted to behold Christ the Lord.

These humble worshipers had not studied the prophecies in vain. But those who held positions as rulers and priests in Israel, though they too had before them the precious utterances of prophecy, were not walking in the way of the Lord, and their eyes were not open to behold the Light of life. [55-56]

So it is still. Events upon which the attention of all heaven is centered are undiscerned, their very occurrence is unnoticed, by religious leaders, and worshipers in the house of God. Men acknowledge Christ in history, while they turn away from the living Christ. Christ in His word calling to self-sacrifice, in the poor and suffering who plead for relief, in the righteous cause

5. Simeon and Anna were enraptured. "But those who held positions as rulers and priests in Israel, though they too had before them the precious utterances of prophecy, were not w_____ in the way of the Lord, and their eyes were not open to behold the Light of life." (55). So, Lord, if I don't want to miss any closeness with You, any intimacy with You, I need to be walking in the way, and teachable as to where I am not walking in the way. Show me Lord: _

_____
_____
_____
_____

that involves poverty and toil and reproach, is no more readily received today than He was eighteen hundred years ago.

Mary pondered the broad and far-reaching prophecy of Simeon. As she looked upon the child in her arms, and recalled the words spoken by the shepherds of Bethlehem, she was full of grateful joy and bright hope. Simeon's words called to her mind the prophetic utterances of Isaiah: "There shall come forth a rod out of the stem of Jesse, and a Branch shall grow out of his roots: and the Spirit of the Lord shall rest upon Him, the spirit of wisdom and understanding, the spirit of counsel and might, the spirit of knowledge and of the fear of the Lord. . . . And righteousness shall be the girdle of His loins, and faithfulness the girdle of His reins." "The people that walked in darkness have seen a great light: they that dwell in the land of the shadow of death, upon them hath the light shined. . . . For unto us a child is born, unto us a son is given: and the government shall be upon His shoulder: and His name shall be called Wonderful, Counselor, The mighty God, The everlasting Father, The Prince of Peace." Isa. 11:1-5; 9:2-6.

6. What gets the attention of all heaven, yet is unnoticed and undiscerned by us, is Christ's call for self-s_____. "Mary [and most of Israel] did not understand Christ's mission." (56) "If we would know the glory of Christ's spiritual kingdom," self must be d_____, pride must be h_____. (57). Lord, help me notice and learn what a 'walk' with You involves: to "fall upon the Rock" means self and pride are dethroned. Dare I be hard on the leaders of Israel for rejecting You, when I struggle with the same issues? _____

_____

_____

Yet Mary did not understand Christ's mission. Simeon had prophesied of Him as a light to lighten the Gentiles, as well as a glory to Israel. Thus the angels had announced the Saviour's birth as tidings of joy to all peoples. God was seeking to correct the narrow, Jewish conception of the Messiah's work. He desired men to behold Him, not merely as the deliverer of Israel, but as the Redeemer of the world. But many years must pass before even the mother of Jesus would understand His mission.

Mary looked forward to the Messiah's reign on David's throne, but she saw not the baptism of suffering by which it must be won. Through Simeon it is revealed that the Messiah is to have no unobstructed passage through the world. In the words to Mary, "A sword shall pierce through thy own soul also," God in His tender mercy gives to the mother of Jesus an intimation of the anguish that already for His sake she had begun to bear.

"Behold," Simeon had said, "this child is set for the fall and rising again of many in Israel; and for a sign which shall be spoken against." [56-57] They must fall who would rise again. We must fall upon the Rock and be broken before we can be uplifted in Christ. Self must be dethroned, pride must be humbled, if we would know the glory of the spiritual kingdom. The Jews would not accept the honor that is reached through humiliation. Therefore they would not receive their Redeemer. He was a sign that was spoken against.

"That the thoughts of many hearts may be revealed." In the light of the Saviour's life, the hearts of all, even from the Creator to the prince of darkness, are revealed. Satan has represented God as selfish and oppressive, as claiming all, and giving nothing, as requiring the service of His creatures for His own glory, and making no sacrifice for their good. But the gift of Christ reveals the Father's heart. It testifies that the thoughts of God toward us are "thoughts of peace, and not of evil." Jer. 29:11. It declares that while God's hatred of sin is as strong as death, His love for the sinner is stronger than death. Having undertaken our redemption, He will spare nothing, however dear, which is necessary to the completion of His work. No truth essential to our salvation is withheld, no miracle of mercy is neglected, no divine agency is left unemployed. Favor is heaped upon favor, gift upon gift. The whole treasury of heaven is open to those He seeks to save. Having collected the riches of the universe, and laid open the resources of infinite power, He gives them all into the hands of Christ, and says, All these are for man. Use these gifts to convince him that there is no love greater than Mine in earth or heaven. His greatest happiness will be found in loving Me.

At the cross of Calvary, love and selfishness stood face to face. Here was their crowning manifestation. Christ had lived only to comfort and bless, and in putting Him to death, Satan manifested the malignity of his hatred against God. He made it evident that the real purpose of his rebellion was to dethrone God, and to destroy Him through whom the love of God was shown.

By the life and the death of Christ, the thoughts of men also are brought to view. From the manger to the cross, the life of Jesus was a call to self-surrender, and to fellowship in suffering. It unveiled the purposes of men. Jesus came with the truth of heaven, and all who were listening to the voice of the Holy Spirit were drawn to Him. The worshipers of self belonged to Satan's kingdom. In their attitude toward Christ, all would show on

7. "In the light of the Saviour's life, the hearts of all" are r_____.
(A) Satan has represented God as s_____ and oppressive. The gift of Christ reveals the Father's heart: the whole t_____ of heaven is open, nothing is spared.

(B) Satan's malignity of hatred, a crowning manifestation of selfishness.
(C) Each person shows on which side they stand, by "their attitude toward Christ" (self-surrender or worshipping self). "And

thus everyone passes j_____" on themselves. (57). Lord, may Your life, and this contemplation of Your life, reveal my heart; and may it be transformed to be like Yours. _____

_____

8. "When the thoughts of all hearts shall be revealed, both the loyal and the rebellious will unite in declaring, 'J_____ and true are Thy ways, Thou King of saints.'" (58). Lord, I don't want to discover that I am in the rebellious camp at that point. I need to be open today, to You revealing to me my heart, and letting You transform my heart. _____

_____
_____
_____

which side they stood. And thus everyone passes judgment on himself. [57-58]

In the day of final judgment, every lost soul will understand the nature of his own rejection of truth. The cross will be presented, and its real bearing will be seen by every mind that has been blinded by transgression. Before the vision of Calvary with its mysterious Victim, sinners will stand condemned. Every lying excuse will be swept away. Human apostasy will appear in its heinous character. Men will see what their choice has been. Every question of truth and error in the long-standing controversy will then have been made plain. In the judgment of the universe, God will stand clear of blame for the existence or continuance of evil. It will be demonstrated that the divine decrees are not accessory to sin. There was no defect in God's government, no cause for disaffection. When the thoughts of all hearts shall be revealed, both the loyal and the rebellious will unite in declaring, "Just and true are Thy ways, Thou King of saints. Who shall not fear Thee, O Lord, and glorify Thy name? . . . for Thy judgments are made manifest." Rev. 15:3, 4.

Prayer Journal: _____

_____
_____
_____
_____
_____

Chapter 6

"We Have Seen His Star"
[This chapter is based on Matthew 2.]

"Now when Jesus was born in Bethlehem of Judea in the days of Herod the king, behold, there came wise men from the East to Jerusalem, saying, Where is He that is born King of the Jews? for we have seen His star in the East, and are come to worship Him."

The wise men from the East were philosophers. They belonged to a large and influential class that included men of noble birth, and comprised much of the wealth and learning of their nation. Among these were many who imposed on the credulity of the people. Others were upright men who studied the indications of Providence in nature, and who were honored for their integrity and wisdom. Of this character were the wise men who came to Jesus.

The light of God is ever shining amid the darkness of heathenism. As these magi studied the starry heavens, and sought to fathom the mystery hidden in their bright paths, they beheld the glory of the Creator. Seeking clearer knowledge, they turned to the Hebrew Scriptures. In their own land were treasured prophetic writings that predicted the coming of a divine teacher. Balaam belonged to the magicians, though at one time a prophet of God; by the Holy Spirit he had foretold the prosperity of Israel and the appearing of the Messiah; and his prophecies [59-60] had been handed down by tradition from century to century. But in the Old Testament the Saviour's advent was more clearly revealed. The magi learned with joy that His coming was near, and that the whole world was to be filled with a knowledge of the glory of the Lord.

The wise men had seen a mysterious light in the heavens upon that night when the glory of God flooded the hills of Bethlehem. As the light faded, a luminous star appeared, and lingered in the sky. It was not a fixed star nor a planet, and the phenomenon excited the keenest interest. That star was a distant company of shining angels, but of this the wise men were ignorant. Yet they were impressed that the star was of special import to them. They consulted priests and philosophers, and

1. "Seeking clearer knowledge, they [the magi] turned to the Hebrew Scriptures...[and] learned with j_____ that His [the Savior's] coming was near...The magi had welcomed the light of heaven-sent truth; now it was shed upon them in b_____ ___ rays." (59, 60). Lord, do I restrict You from sharing greater light with me? Didn't You say in John 16:12 that there was more that You would have liked to share, but the disciples weren't ready yet? How responsive to current light am I? _____

_____

_____Why should I settle for less than ALL of Your bright rays? _____

_____

_____

searched the scrolls of the ancient records. The prophecy of Balaam had declared, "There shall come a Star out of Jacob, and a Scepter shall rise out of Israel." Num. 24:17. Could this strange star have been sent as a harbinger of the Promised One? The magi had welcomed the light of heaven-sent truth; now it was shed upon them in brighter rays. Through dreams they were instructed to go in search of the newborn Prince.

As by faith Abraham went forth at the call of God, "not knowing whither he went" (Heb. 11:8); as by faith Israel followed the pillar of cloud to the Promised Land, so did these Gentiles go forth to find the promised Saviour. The Eastern country abounded in precious things, and the magi did not set out empty-handed. It was the custom to offer presents as an act of homage to princes or other personages of rank, and the richest gifts the land afforded were borne as an offering to Him in whom all the families of the earth were to be blessed. It was necessary to journey by night in order to keep the star in view; but the travelers beguiled the hours by repeating traditional sayings and prophetic utterances concerning the One they sought. At every pause for rest they searched the prophecies; and the conviction deepened that they were divinely guided. While they had the star before them as an outward sign, they had also the inward evidence of the Holy Spirit, which was impressing their hearts, and inspiring them with hope. The journey, though long, was a happy one to them.

They have reached the land of Israel, and are descending the Mount of Olives, with Jerusalem in sight, when, lo, the star that has guided them all the weary way rests above the temple, and after a season fades from their view. With eager steps they press onward, confidently expecting the Messiah's birth to be the joyful burden of every tongue. But their [60-61] inquiries are in vain. Entering the holy city, they repair to the temple. To their amazement they find none who seem to have a knowledge of the newborn king. Their questions call forth no expressions of joy, but rather of surprise and fear, not unmingled with contempt.

The priests are rehearsing traditions. They extol their religion and their own piety, while they denounce the Greeks and Romans as heathen, and sinners above others. The wise men are not idolaters, and in the sight of God they stand far higher than do these, His professed worshipers; yet they are looked upon by the Jews

2. "At every pause for rest they [magi] searched the prophecies; and the conviction deepened that they were d_____ guided. While they had the star before them as an outward sign, they had also the i_____ evidence of the Holy Spirit, which was impressing their hearts, and inspiring them with hope." Isn't it a thrill to know that I am divinely guided, right in the middle of God's will? Lord, keep sending that inward evidence of the Holy Spirit, impressing and inspiring me. I seek the filling of Your Spirit. ____

3. "Entering the holy city… their [magi] questions call forth no expressions of joy, but rather of surprise and fear, not unmingled with c_____." (61)

as heathen. Even among the appointed guardians of the Holy Oracles their eager questionings touch no chord of sympathy.

The arrival of the magi was quickly noised throughout Jerusalem. Their strange errand created an excitement among the people, which penetrated to the palace of King Herod. The wily Edomite was aroused at the intimation of a possible rival. Countless murders had stained his pathway to the throne. Being of alien blood, he was hated by the people over whom he ruled. His only security was the favor of Rome. But this new Prince had a higher claim. He was born to the kingdom.

Herod suspected the priests of plotting with the strangers to excite a popular tumult and unseat him from the throne. He concealed his mistrust, however, determined to thwart their schemes by superior cunning. Summoning the chief priests and the scribes, he questioned [61-62] them as to the teaching of their sacred books in regard to the place of the Messiah's birth.

This inquiry from the usurper of the throne, and made at the request of strangers, stung the pride of the Jewish teachers. The indifference with which they turned to the rolls of prophecy enraged the jealous tyrant. He thought them trying to conceal their knowledge of the matter. With an authority they dared not disregard, he commanded them to make close search, and to declare the birthplace of their expected King. "And they said unto him, In Bethlehem of Judea: for thus it is written by the prophet,

"And thou Bethlehem, land of Judah,
Art in nowise least among the princes of Judah: For out of thee shall come forth a governor, Which shall be shepherd of My people Israel." R. V.

Herod now invited the magi to a private interview. A tempest of wrath and fear was raging in his heart, but he preserved a calm exterior, and received the strangers courteously. He inquired at what time the star had appeared, and professed to hail with joy the intimation of the birth of Christ. He bade his visitors, "Search diligently for the young child; and when ye have found Him, bring me word again, that I may come and worship Him also." So saying, he dismissed them to go on their way to Bethlehem.

The priests and elders of Jerusalem were not as ig-

Lord, do I not sometimes put down someone else's way of worshiping You, or their theology? Or see my own walk with You as more mature? How does this contempt impact a quest for spiritual growth? ____

4. "The priests and elders of Jerusalem were not as ignorant concerning the birth of Christ as they pretended...[But] now,

pride and e_____ closed the door against the light." (62) Lord, similar attitudes on my part, can't help. A significant portion of what You want to reveal to me, may be a bit pointed. As uncomfortable as it may be, I need to remember that You only want to help remove barriers to our relationship. _____

_____

_____

5. "They led the people to regard the interest in Jesus as a f_____ excitement. Here began the rejection of Christ by the priests and rabbis. From this point their pride and stubbornness grew into a settled h_____ of the Savior." (63). Is there such a thing as "just a little, white pride?" _____

_____. I should be very afraid of it. How? _____

_____

_____ (Be in awe of the humility of Christ?)

norant concerning the birth of Christ as they pretended. The report of the angels' visit to the shepherds had been brought to Jerusalem, but the rabbis had treated it as unworthy of their notice. They themselves might have found Jesus, and might have been ready to lead the magi to His birthplace; but instead of this, the wise men came to call their attention to the birth of the Messiah. "Where is He that is born King of the Jews?" they said; "for we have seen His star in the East, and are come to worship Him."

Now pride and envy closed the door against the light. If the reports brought by the shepherds and the wise men were credited, they would place the priests and rabbis in a most unenviable position, disproving their claim to be the exponents of the truth of God. These learned teachers would not stoop to be instructed by those whom they termed heathen. It could not be, they said, that God had passed them by, to communicate [62-63] with ignorant shepherds or uncircumcised Gentiles. They determined to show their contempt for the reports that were exciting King Herod and all Jerusalem. They would not even go to Bethlehem to see whether these things were so. And they led the people to regard the interest in Jesus as a fanatical excitement. Here began the rejection of Christ by the priests and rabbis. From this point their pride and stubbornness grew into a settled hatred of the Saviour. While God was opening the door to the Gentiles, the Jewish leaders were closing the door to themselves.

The wise men departed alone from Jerusalem. The shadows of night were falling as they left the gates, but to their great joy they again saw the star, and were directed to Bethlehem. They had received no such intimation of the lowly estate of Jesus as was given to the shepherds. After the long journey they had been disappointed by the indifference of the Jewish leaders, and had left Jerusalem less confident than when they entered the city. At Bethlehem they found no royal guard stationed to protect the newborn King. None of the world's honored men were in attendance. Jesus was cradled in a manger. His parents, uneducated peasants, were His only guardians. Could this be He of whom it was written, that He should "raise up the tribes of Jacob," and "restore the preserved of Israel;" that He should be "a light to the Gentiles," and for "salvation unto the end of the earth"? Isa. 49:6.

"When they were come into the house, they saw the young child with Mary His mother, and fell down, and worshiped Him." Beneath the lowly guise of Jesus, they recognized the presence of Divinity. They gave their hearts to Him as their Saviour, and then poured out their gifts,--"gold, and frankincense, and myrrh." What a faith was theirs! [63-64] It might have been said of the wise men from the East, as afterward of the Roman centurion, "I have not found so great faith, no, not in Israel." Matt. 8:10.

The wise men had not penetrated Herod's design toward Jesus. When the object of their journey was accomplished, they prepared to return to Jerusalem, intending to acquaint him with their success. But in a dream they received a divine message to hold no further communication with him. Avoiding Jerusalem, they set out for their own country by another route.

In like manner Joseph received warning to flee into Egypt with Mary and the child. And the angel said, "Be thou there until I bring thee word: for Herod will seek the young child to destroy Him." Joseph obeyed without delay, setting out on the journey by night for greater security.

Through the wise men, God had called the attention of the Jewish nation to the birth of His Son. Their inquiries in Jerusalem, the popular interest excited, and even the jealousy of Herod, which compelled the attention of the priests and rabbis, directed minds to the prophecies concerning the Messiah, and to the great event that had just taken place. [64-65]

Satan was bent on shutting out the divine light from the world, and he used his utmost cunning to destroy the Saviour. But He who never slumbers nor sleeps was watching over His beloved Son. He who had rained manna from heaven for Israel and had fed Elijah in the time of famine provided in a heathen land a refuge for Mary and the child Jesus. And through the gifts of the magi from a heathen country, the Lord supplied the means for the journey into Egypt and the sojourn in a land of strangers.

The magi had been among the first to welcome the Redeemer. Their gift was the first that was laid at His feet. And through that gift, what privilege of ministry was theirs! The offering from the heart that loves, God delights to honor, giving it highest efficiency in service for Him. If we have given our hearts to Jesus, we also

6. "They gave their h_____ to Him as their Savior, and then poured out their gifts (63)...

If we have given our h_____ to Jesus, we also shall bring our gifts to Him. Our gold and silver,

our most precious earthly possessions, our highest mental and spiritual endowments, will be freely d_____ to Him who loved us, and gave Himself for us." (65). Is giving my heart to Him, part of my daily prayer? Lord, help me to not forget; to be incomplete till I do: _____
_____
_____

7. "This calamity the Jews had brought upon themselves." They had (a) s_____ themselves from God by their sins, (b) r_____ the Holy Spirit, which was their only s_____, (c) not studied the Scriptures with a desire to c_____ to the will of God, (d) searched for prophecies which could be interpreted to e_____ themselves, and to show how God despised all other nations." (65). Lord, how open am I to the Holy Spirit, as I read the Scriptures? _____
_____
_____

8. "Through their [the Jews'] misrepresentation of Christ's mission, Satan had purposed to compass the d_____ of the Savior, but instead of this, it returned upon their own heads." (66). Does

shall bring our gifts to Him. Our gold and silver, our most precious earthly possessions, our highest mental and spiritual endowments, will be freely devoted to Him who loved us, and gave Himself for us.

Herod in Jerusalem impatiently awaited the return of the wise men. As time passed, and they did not appear, his suspicions were roused. The unwillingness of the rabbis to point out the Messiah's birthplace seemed to indicate that they had penetrated his design, and that the magi had purposely avoided him. He was maddened at the thought. Craft had failed, but there was left the resort to force. He would make an example of this child-king. Those haughty Jews should see what they might expect in their attempts to place a monarch on the throne.

Soldiers were at once sent to Bethlehem, with orders to put to death all the children of two years and under. The quiet homes of the city of David witnessed those scenes of horror that, six hundred years before, had been opened to the prophet. "In Ramah was there a voice heard, lamentation, and weeping, and great mourning, Rachel weeping for her children, and would not be comforted, because they are not."

This calamity the Jews had brought upon themselves. If they had been walking in faithfulness and humility before God, He would in a signal manner have made the wrath of the king harmless to them. But they had separated themselves from God by their sins, and had rejected the Holy Spirit, which was their only shield. They had not studied the Scriptures with a desire to conform to the will of God. They had searched for prophecies which could be interpreted to exalt themselves, and to show how God despised all other nations. It was their proud boast that the [65-66] Messiah was to come as a king, conquering His enemies, and treading down the heathen in His wrath. Thus they had excited the hatred of their rulers. Through their misrepresentation of Christ's mission, Satan had purposed to compass the destruction of the Saviour; but instead of this, it returned upon their own heads.

This act of cruelty was one of the last that darkened the reign of Herod. Soon after the slaughter of the innocents, he was himself compelled to yield to that doom which none can turn aside. He died a fearful death.

Joseph, who was still in Egypt, was now bidden by

an angel of God to return to the land of Israel. Regarding Jesus as the heir of David's throne, Joseph desired to make his home in Bethlehem; but learning that Archelaus reigned in Judea in his father's stead, he feared that the father's designs against Christ might be carried out by the son. Of all the sons of Herod, Archelaus most resembled him in character. Already his succession to the government had been marked by a tumult in Jerusalem, and the slaughter of thousands of Jews by the Roman guards.

Again Joseph was directed to a place of safety. He returned to Nazareth, his former home, and here for nearly thirty years Jesus dwelt, "that it might be fulfilled which was spoken by the prophets, He shall be called a Nazarene." Galilee was under the control of a son of Herod, but it had a much larger admixture of foreign inhabitants than Judea. [66-67] Thus there was less interest in matters relating especially to the Jews, and the claims of Jesus would be less likely to excite the jealousy of those in power.

Such was the Saviour's reception when He came to the earth. There seemed to be no place of rest or safety for the infant Redeemer. God could not trust His beloved Son with men, even while carrying forward His work for their salvation. He commissioned angels to attend Jesus and protect Him till He should accomplish His mission on earth, and die by the hands of those whom He came to save.

Satan misrepresent the nature of sin, with the purpose of my destruction, to devour me? Lord, how can I be more alert to Satan's designs? _____
_____
_____
_____
_____

9. What was the Savior's reception like, when He came to the earth?
_____
_____
_____
_____
_____

What kind of reception do I give Him? (at church time, beginning of Sabbath, or devotion time) _____
_____
_____
_____
_____

Prayer Journal: _____
_____
_____
_____
_____
_____

Chapter 7

As a Child

[This chapter is based on Luke 2:39,40.]

The childhood and youth of Jesus were spent in a little mountain village. There was no place on earth that would not have been honored by His presence. The palaces of kings would have been privileged in receiving Him as a guest. But He passed by the homes of wealth, the courts of royalty, and the renowned seats of learning, to make His home in obscure and despised Nazareth.

Wonderful in its significance is the brief record of His early life: "The child grew, and waxed strong in spirit, filled with wisdom: and the grace of God was upon Him." In the sunlight of His Father's countenance, Jesus "increased in wisdom and stature, and in favor with God and man." Luke 2:52. His mind was active and penetrating, with a thoughtfulness and wisdom beyond His years. Yet His character was beautiful in its symmetry. The powers of mind and body developed gradually, in keeping with the laws of childhood.

As a child, Jesus manifested a peculiar loveliness of disposition. His willing hands were ever ready to serve others. He manifested a patience [68-69] that nothing could disturb, and a truthfulness that would never sacrifice integrity. In principle firm as a rock, His life revealed the grace of unselfish courtesy.

With deep earnestness the mother of Jesus watched the unfolding of His powers, and beheld the impress of perfection upon His character. With delight she sought to encourage that bright, receptive mind. Through the Holy Spirit she received wisdom to co-operate with the heavenly agencies in the development of this child, who could claim only God as His Father.

From the earliest times the faithful in Israel had given much care to the education of the youth. The Lord had directed that even from babyhood the children should be taught of His goodness and His greatness, especially as revealed in His law, and shown in the history of Israel. Song and prayer and lessons from the Scriptures were to be adapted to the opening mind. Fathers and mothers were to instruct their children that the law of God is an expression of His character, and that as

1. "As a child Jesus manifested a peculiar loveliness of disposition. His willing hands were ever ready to s_____ others. He manifested a patience that nothing could d_____ _____, and a truthfulness that would never s_____ integrity." (68-9). Oh to have You as my own Child! Or to have You as my own Friend! Of course, that's what You want, and what I want. Lord, may I be like You, with a patience that can't be disturbed! By staying in Your friendship, throughout the day, may my mind be stayed on You, and inspired by Your character. _____ _____ _____

2. "The faithful of Israel gave much care to the education of the youth." They instructed "their children that the law of God is an e_____ of His c_____...the

they received the principles of the law into the heart, the image of God was traced on mind and soul. Much of the teaching was oral; but the youth also learned to read the Hebrew writings; and the parchment rolls of the Old Testament Scriptures were open to their study.

In the days of Christ the town or city that did not provide for the religious instruction of the young was regarded as under the curse of God. Yet the teaching had become formal. Tradition had in a great degree supplanted the Scriptures. True education would lead the youth to "seek the Lord, if haply they might feel after Him, and find Him." Acts 17:27. But the Jewish teachers gave their attention to matters of ceremony. The mind was crowded with material that was worthless to the learner, and that would not be recognized in the higher school of the courts above. The experience which is obtained through a personal acceptance of God's word had no place in the educational system. Absorbed in the round of externals, the students found no quiet hours to spend with God. They did not hear His voice speaking to the heart. In their search after knowledge, they turned away from the Source of wisdom. The great essentials of the service of God were neglected. The principles of the law were obscured. That which was regarded as superior education was the greatest hindrance to real development. Under the training of the rabbis the powers of the youth were repressed. Their minds became cramped and narrow. [69-70]

The child Jesus did not receive instruction in the synagogue schools. His mother was His first human teacher. From her lips and from the scrolls of the prophets, He learned of heavenly things. The very words which He Himself had spoken to Moses for Israel He was now taught at His mother's knee. As He advanced from childhood to youth, He did not seek the schools of the rabbis. He needed not the education to be obtained from such sources; for God was His instructor.

The question asked during the Saviour's ministry, "How knoweth this man letters, having never learned?" does not indicate that Jesus was unable to read, but merely that He had not received a rabbinical education. John 7:15. Since He gained knowledge as we may do, His intimate acquaintance with the Scriptures shows how diligently His early years were given to the study of God's word. And spread out before Him was the great library of God's created works. He who had

image of God was traced on m_____ and soul." (69). Lord, to know You intimately, is to know Your character. I need to re-evaluate the law, and see it not as a burdensome restriction, but as part of the meaningful friendship that You offer me. _____

_____

_____

3. "Jewish teachers gave their attention to matters of c_____...the students found no quiet hours to spend w_____ God. They did not hear His voice speaking to the h_____." (69). Instead of dwelling on the shortcomings of the educational system, I need to recognize the lack of a major component of the spiritual walk in my life: quiet hours with You, Lord. The attempted excuse of not enough time, doesn't make up for the lack. I need to make time, by understanding the true priorities. Lord, show what changes I need to make today:

_____

_____

_____

_____

4. "How knoweth this man letters, having never learned?" Jesus had not received a r_____ ____ education. But His m_____ was

His first human teacher; "G____ was His instructor." Jesus studied "the word and the w_____ of God." (70). Lord, can You be my instructor? What should I do to nurture that? _____

_____

_____May I be possessed with the one purpose You had, living to b_____ others: _____

_____

5. I "may gain knowledge as Jesus did. As we try to become a_____ _____ with our Heavenly Father through His word…our characters will be elevated and r_____. We shall become more like our Saviour… Our a_____ go out after God…Communion with God through p_____ develops the mental and m_____ faculties, and the spiritual powers strengthen as we c_____ thoughts upon spiritual things." (70, 71). That's what I want, Lord! Be acquainted with You, be like You. So it's spending time with You in Your Word, right? Keep drawing me, Lord! Tell me

made all things studied the lessons which His own hand had written in earth and sea and sky. Apart from the unholy ways of the world, He gathered stores of scientific knowledge from nature. He studied the life of plants and animals, and the life of man. From His earliest years He was possessed of one purpose; He lived to bless others. For this He found resources in nature; new ideas of ways and means flashed into His mind as He studied plant life and animal life. Continually He was seeking to draw from things seen illustrations by which to present the living oracles of God. The parables by which, during His ministry, He loved to teach His lessons of truth show how open His spirit was to the influences of nature, and how He had gathered the spiritual teaching from the surroundings of His daily life.

Thus to Jesus the significance of the word and the works of God was unfolded, as He was trying to understand the reason of things. Heavenly beings were His attendants, and the culture of holy thoughts and communings was His. From the first dawning of intelligence He was constantly growing in spiritual grace and knowledge of truth.

Every child may gain knowledge as Jesus did. As we try to become acquainted with our heavenly Father through His word, angels will draw near, our minds will be strengthened, our characters will be elevated and refined. We shall become more like our Saviour. And as we behold the beautiful and grand in nature, our affections go out after God. While the spirit is awed, the soul is invigorated by coming in contact with the Infinite through His works. Communion with God through [70-71] prayer develops the mental and moral faculties, and the spiritual powers strengthen as we cultivate thoughts upon spiritual things.

The life of Jesus was a life in harmony with God. While He was a child, He thought and spoke as a child; but no trace of sin marred the image of God within Him. Yet He was not exempt from temptation. The inhabitants of Nazareth were proverbial for their wickedness. The low estimate in which they were generally held is shown by Nathanael's question, "Can there any good thing come out of Nazareth?" John 1:46. Jesus was placed where His character would be tested. It was necessary for Him to be constantly on guard in order to preserve His purity. He was subject to all the conflicts which we have to meet, that He might be an example to us in childhood, youth, and manhood.

Satan was unwearied in his efforts to overcome the Child of Nazareth. From His earliest years Jesus was guarded by heavenly angels, yet His life was one long struggle against the powers of darkness. That there should be upon the earth one life free from the defilement of evil was an offense and a perplexity to the prince of darkness. He left no means untried to ensnare Jesus. No child of humanity will ever be called to live a holy life amid so fierce a conflict with temptation as was our Saviour. [71-72]

The parents of Jesus were poor, and dependent upon their daily toil. He was familiar with poverty, self-denial, and privation. This experience was a safeguard to Him. In His industrious life there were no idle moments to invite temptation. No aimless hours opened the way for corrupting associations. So far as possible, He closed the door to the tempter. Neither gain nor pleasure, applause nor censure, could induce Him to consent to a wrong act. He was wise to discern evil, and strong to resist it.

Christ was the only sinless one who ever dwelt on earth; yet for nearly thirty years He lived among the wicked inhabitants of Nazareth. This fact is a rebuke to those who think themselves dependent upon place, fortune, or prosperity, in order to live a blameless life. Temptation, poverty, adversity, is the very discipline needed to develop purity and firmness.

Jesus lived in a peasant's home, and faithfully and cheerfully acted His part in bearing the burdens of the household. He had been the Commander of heaven, and angels had delighted to fulfill His word; now He was a willing servant, a loving, obedient son. He learned a trade, and with His own hands worked in the carpenter's shop with Joseph. In the simple garb of a common laborer He walked the streets of the little town, going to and returning from His humble work. He did not employ His divine power to lessen His burdens or to lighten His toil.

As Jesus worked in childhood and youth, mind and body were developed. He did not use His physical powers recklessly, but in such a way as to keep them in health, that He might do the best work in every line. He was not willing to be defective, even in the handling of tools. He was perfect as a workman, as He was perfect in character. By His own example He taught that it is

how I can cultivate thoughts upon spiritual things?

_____

_____

(What did Enoch do? Educated his heart and mind to ever be in the presence of God).

6. "[Satan] left no means u_____ to ensnare Jesus. No child of humanity will ever be called to live a holy life amid so f_____ a conflict with temptation as was our Savior." (71).

7. Am I dependent upon "fortune or prosperity, in order to live a blameless life? Temptation, poverty, adversity, is the very d_____ needed to develop purity and firmness." (72). I normally thought I should completely avoid temptation, Lord. And You're saying, temptation is not an excuse for failure, but rather should be an opportunity to trust You for strength, to be pure. Remind me, Lord, how available You are at the moment of temptation. _____

_____

_____

our duty to be industrious, that our work should be performed with exactness and thoroughness, and that such labor is honorable. The exercise that teaches the hands to be useful and trains the young to bear their share of life's burdens gives physical strength, and develops every faculty. All should find something to do that will be beneficial to themselves and helpful to others. God appointed work as a blessing, and only the diligent worker finds the true glory and joy of life. The approval of God rests with loving assurance upon children and youth who cheerfully take their part in the duties of the household, sharing the burdens of father and mother. Such children will go out from the home to be useful members of society. [72-73]

Throughout His life on earth, Jesus was an earnest and constant worker. He expected much; therefore He attempted much. After He had entered on His ministry, He said, "I must work the works of Him that sent Me, while it is day: the night cometh, when no man can work." John 9:4. Jesus did not shirk care and responsibility, as do many who profess to be His followers. It is because they seek to evade this discipline that so many are weak and inefficient. They may possess precious and amiable traits, but they are nerveless and almost useless when difficulties are to be met or obstacles surmounted. The positiveness and energy, the solidity and strength of character, manifested in Christ are to be developed in us, through the same discipline that He endured. And the grace that He received is for us.

So long as He lived among men, our Saviour shared the lot of the poor. He knew by experience their cares and hardships, and He could comfort and encourage all humble workers. Those who have a true conception of the teaching of His life will never feel that a distinction must be made between classes, that the rich are to be honored above the worthy poor.

Jesus carried into His labor cheerfulness and tact. It requires much patience and spirituality to bring Bible religion into the home life and into the workshop, to bear the strain of worldly business, and yet keep the eye single to the glory of God. This is where Christ was a helper. He was never so full of worldly care as to have no time or thought for heavenly things. Often He expressed the gladness of His heart by singing psalms and heavenly songs. Often the dwellers in Nazareth heard His voice raised in praise and thanksgiving to God. He

8. Jesus "was never so full of worldly care as to have no time or t_____ for heavenly things." He sang

held communion with heaven in song; and as His companions complained of weariness from labor, they were cheered by the sweet melody from His lips. His praise seemed to banish the evil angels, and, like incense, fill the place with fragrance. The minds of His hearers were carried away from their earthly exile, to the heavenly home. [73-74]

Jesus was the fountain of healing mercy for the world; and through all those secluded years at Nazareth, His life flowed out in currents of sympathy and tenderness. The aged, the sorrowing, and the sin-burdened, the children at play in their innocent joy, the little creatures of the groves, the patient beasts of burden,--all were happier for His presence. He whose word of power upheld the worlds would stoop to relieve a wounded bird. There was nothing beneath His notice, nothing to which He disdained to minister.

Thus as He grew in wisdom and stature, Jesus increased in favor with God and man. He drew the sympathy of all hearts by showing Himself capable of sympathizing with all. The atmosphere of hope and courage that surrounded Him made Him a blessing in every home. And often in the synagogue on the Sabbath day He was called upon to read the lesson from the prophets, and the hearts of the hearers thrilled as a new light shone out from the familiar words of the sacred text.

Yet Jesus shunned display. During all the years of His stay in Nazareth, He made no exhibition of His miraculous power. He sought no high position and assumed no titles. His quiet and simple life, and even the silence of the Scriptures concerning His early years, teach an important lesson. The more quiet and simple the life of the child,--the more free from artificial excitement, and the more in harmony with nature,--the more favorable is it to physical and mental vigor and to spiritual strength.

Jesus is our example. There are many who dwell with interest upon the period of His public ministry, while they pass unnoticed the teaching of His early years. But it is in His home life that He is the pattern for all children and youth. The Saviour condescended to poverty, that He might teach how closely we in a humble lot may walk with God. He lived to please, honor, and glorify His Father in the common things of life. His work began in consecrating the lowly trade of the craftsmen who toil for their daily bread. He was doing

songs and "His praise seemed to b_____ the evil angels." (73).

"The Savior condescended to poverty, that He might teach how closely we in a humble lot may w_____ with God. He lived to please, h_____, and glorify His Father in the c_____ things of life." (74). Lord,

Enoch walked with You, and he did not have Your earthly life as an example. I want to also walk with You, in everyday life, to glorify You and the Father: _____

_____

_____

Prayer Journal: _____

_____

_____

_____

_____

_____

_____

God's service just as much when laboring at the carpenter's bench as when working miracles for the multitude. And every youth who follows Christ's example of faithfulness and obedience in His lowly home may claim those words spoken of Him by the Father through the Holy Spirit, "Behold My Servant, whom I uphold; Mine Elect, in whom My soul delighteth." Isa. 42:1.

Chapter 8

The Passover Visit
[This chapter is based on Luke 2:41-51.]

Among the Jews the twelfth year was the dividing line between childhood and youth. On completing this year a Hebrew boy was called a son of the law, and also a son of God. He was given special opportunities for religious instruction, and was expected to participate in the sacred feasts and observances. It was in accordance with this custom that Jesus in His boyhood made the Passover visit to Jerusalem. Like all devout Israelites, Joseph and Mary went up every year to attend the Passover; and when Jesus had reached the required age, they took Him with them.

There were three annual feasts, the Passover, the Pentecost, and the Feast of Tabernacles, at which all the men of Israel were commanded to appear before the Lord at Jerusalem. Of these feasts the Passover was the most largely attended. Many were present from all countries where the Jews were scattered. From every part of Palestine the worshipers came in great numbers. The journey from Galilee occupied several days, and the travelers united in large companies for companionship and protection. The women and aged men rode upon oxen or asses over the steep [75-76] and rocky roads. The stronger men and the youth journeyed on foot. The time of the Passover corresponded to the close of March or the beginning of April, and the whole land was bright with flowers, and glad with the song of birds. All along the way were spots memorable in the history of Israel, and fathers and mothers recounted to their children the wonders that God had wrought for His people in ages past. They beguiled their journey with song and music, and when at last the towers of Jerusalem came into view, every voice joined in the triumphant strain,--

"Our feet shall stand
Within thy gates, O Jerusalem. . . .
Peace be within thy walls,

52   Can We Walk, Together?

1. "When your children shall say unto you, What m_____ ye by this service? That ye shall say, It is the sacrifice of the Lord's passover, who passed over the houses of the children of Israel in Egypt." (77). God didn't want the annual service to be a meaningless ritual, so He instructed that the significance be passed on from generation to generation. The friendship that God offers is based on appreciation of Who God is and buying into His values, not based on God's superior power or mysterious ways. He wants me to believe in Him, to come and reason with Him. Jesus said, I no longer call you servants, but friends, because I have explained these things to you, John 15:15. Lord, help me to take the time to appreciate Your character, the rich meaning of Your friendship. _____

_____

_____

2. "The deliverance of Israel from Egypt was an object lesson of r_____, which the Passover was intended to keep in memory." (77). They sprinkled blood on the doorposts. Should I have an object lesson? Is redemption unimpressive to me?

And prosperity within thy palaces."
                    Ps. 122: 2-7.

The observance of the Passover began with the birth of the Hebrew nation. On the last night of their bondage in Egypt, when there appeared [76-77] no token of deliverance, God commanded them to prepare for an immediate release. He had warned Pharaoh of the final judgment on the Egyptians, and He directed the Hebrews to gather their families within their own dwellings. Having sprinkled the doorposts with the blood of the slain lamb, they were to eat the lamb, roasted, with unleavened bread and bitter herbs. "And thus shall ye eat it," He said, "with your loins girded, your shoes on your feet, and your staff in your hand; and ye shall eat it in haste: it is the Lord's passover." Ex. 12:11. At midnight all the first-born of the Egyptians were slain. Then the king sent to Israel the message, "Rise up, and get you forth from among my people; . . . and go, serve the Lord, as ye have said." Ex. 12:31. The Hebrews went out from Egypt an independent nation. The Lord had commanded that the Passover should be yearly kept. "It shall come to pass," He said, "when your children shall say unto you, What mean ye by this service? that ye shall say, It is the sacrifice of the Lord's passover, who passed over the houses of the children of Israel in Egypt, when He smote the Egyptians." Thus from generation to generation the story of this wonderful deliverance was to be repeated.

The Passover was followed by the seven days' feast of unleavened bread. On the second day of the feast, the first fruits of the year's harvest, a sheaf of barley, was presented before the Lord. All the ceremonies of the feast were types of the work of Christ. The deliverance of Israel from Egypt was an object lesson of redemption, which the Passover was intended to keep in memory. The slain lamb, the unleavened bread, the sheaf of first fruits, represented the Saviour.

With most of the people in the days of Christ, the observance of this feast had degenerated into formalism. But what was its significance to the Son of God! [77-78]

For the first time the child Jesus looked upon the temple. He saw the white-robed priests performing their solemn ministry. He beheld the bleeding victim upon the altar of sacrifice. With the worshipers He bowed in prayer, while the cloud of incense ascended before

God. He witnessed the impressive rites of the paschal service. Day by day He saw their meaning more clearly. Every act seemed to be bound up with His own life. New impulses were awakening within Him. Silent and absorbed, He seemed to be studying out a great problem. The mystery of His mission was opening to the Saviour.

Rapt in the contemplation of these scenes, He did not remain beside His parents. He sought to be alone. When the paschal services were ended, He still lingered in the temple courts; and when the worshipers departed from Jerusalem, He was left behind.

In this visit to Jerusalem, the parents of Jesus wished to bring Him in connection with the great teachers in Israel. While He was obedient in every particular to the word of God, He did not conform to the rabbinical rites and usages. Joseph and Mary hoped that He might be led to reverence the learned rabbis, and give more diligent heed to their requirements. But Jesus in the temple had been taught by God. That which He had received, He began at once to impart.

At that day an apartment connected with the temple was devoted to a sacred school, after the manner of the schools of the prophets. Here leading rabbis with their pupils assembled, and hither the child Jesus came. Seating Himself at the feet of these grave, learned men, He listened to their instruction. As one seeking for wisdom, He questioned these teachers in regard to the prophecies, and to events then taking place that pointed to the advent of the Messiah.

Jesus presented Himself as one thirsting for a knowledge of God. His questions were suggestive of deep truths which had long been obscured, yet which were vital to the salvation of souls. While showing how narrow and superficial was the wisdom of the wise men, every question put before them a divine lesson, and placed truth in a new aspect. The rabbis spoke of the wonderful elevation which the Messiah's coming would bring to the Jewish nation; but Jesus presented the prophecy of Isaiah, and asked them the meaning of those scriptures that point to the suffering and death of the Lamb of God.

The doctors turned upon Him with questions, and they were amazed at His answers. With the humility of a child He repeated the words of [78-79] Scripture, giving them a depth of meaning that the wise men had not

How can I help keep the Lord's Supper experience from becoming a ritual?

_____
_____
_____
_____

3. As the child Jesus witnessed the impressive rites of the paschal service, "day by day He saw their meaning more c_____ …The mystery of His mission was o_____ to the Savior." (78). What amazing openness and receptivity to spiritual understanding. Lord, teach me to be that responsive to You: _____
_____
_____

4. In the temple sacred school, Jesus asked questions; "every question put before them [rabbis] a divine lesson, and placed truth in a n_____ aspect...."

(78). If f_____,
the lines of truth He pointed out would have worked
a r_____ in
the religion of the day."
(79). "The words of Je-
sus had m_____
their hearts as they had
never before been moved
by words from human
lips." (80). How often do
I sense the stirrings of the
Spirit, only to have little
come from it, because of
a lack of follow-through?
Lord, help the insights of
Your Spirit be brought to
mind during the day, at
the opportunity of appli-
cation into my life. Move
me, stir my heart, Lord.

_____
_____
_____

conceived of. If followed, the lines of truth He pointed out would have worked a reformation in the religion of the day. A deep interest in spiritual things would have been awakened; and when Jesus began His ministry, many would have been prepared to receive Him. [79-80]

The rabbis knew that Jesus had not been instructed in their schools; yet His understanding of the prophecies far exceeded theirs. In this thoughtful Galilean boy they discerned great promise. They desired to gain Him as a student, that He might become a teacher in Israel. They wanted to have charge of His education, feeling that a mind so original must be brought under their molding.

The words of Jesus had moved their hearts as they had never before been moved by words from human lips. God was seeking to give light to those leaders in Israel, and He used the only means by which they could be reached. In their pride they would have scorned to admit that they could receive instruction from anyone. If Jesus had appeared to be trying to teach them, they would have disdained to listen. But they flattered themselves that they were teaching Him, or at least testing His knowledge of the Scriptures. The youthful modesty and grace of Jesus disarmed their prejudices. Unconsciously their minds were opened to the word of God, and the Holy Spirit spoke to their hearts.

They could not but see that their expectation in regard to the Messiah was not sustained by prophecy; but they would not renounce the theories that had flattered their ambition. They would not admit that they had misapprehended the Scriptures they claimed to teach. From one to another passed the inquiry, How hath this youth knowledge, having never learned? The light was shining in darkness; but "the darkness apprehended it not." John 1:5, R. V.

Meanwhile Joseph and Mary were in great perplexity and distress. In the departure from Jerusalem they had lost sight of Jesus, and they knew not that He had tarried behind. The country was then densely populated, and the caravans from Galilee were very large. There was much confusion as they left the city. On the way the pleasure of traveling with friends and acquaintances absorbed their attention, and they did not notice His absence till night came on. Then as they halted for rest, they missed the helpful hand of their child. Supposing Him to be with their company, they had felt no anxiety.

Young as He was, they had trusted Him implicitly, expecting that when needed, He would be ready to assist them, anticipating their wants as He had always done. But now their fears were roused. They searched for Him throughout their company, but in vain. Shuddering they remembered how Herod had tried to destroy Him in His infancy. Dark forebodings filled their hearts. They bitterly reproached themselves. [80-81]

Returning to Jerusalem, they pursued their search. The next day, as they mingled with the worshipers in the temple, a familiar voice arrested their attention. They could not mistake it; no other voice was like His, so serious and earnest, yet so full of melody.

In the school of the rabbis they found Jesus. Rejoiced as they were, they could not forget their grief and anxiety. When He was with them again, the mother said, in words that implied reproof, "Son, why hast Thou thus dealt with us? Behold, Thy father and I have sought Thee sorrowing."

"How is it that ye sought Me?" answered Jesus. "Wist ye not that I must be about My Father's business?" And as they seemed not to understand His words, He pointed upward. On His face was a light at which they wondered. Divinity was flashing through humanity. On finding Him in the temple, they had listened to what was passing between Him and the rabbis, and they were astonished at His questions and answers. His words started a train of thought that would never be forgotten.

And His question to them had a lesson. "Wist ye not," He said, "that I must be about My Father's business?" Jesus was engaged in the work that He had come into the world to do; but Joseph and Mary had neglected theirs. God had shown them high honor in committing to them His Son. Holy angels had directed the course of Joseph in order to preserve the life of Jesus. But for an entire day they had lost sight of Him whom they should not have forgotten for a moment. And when their anxiety was relieved, they had not censured themselves, but had cast the blame upon Him.

It was natural for the parents of Jesus to look upon Him as their own child. He was daily with them, His life in many respects was like that of other children, and it was difficult for them to realize that He was the Son of God. They were in danger of failing to appreciate the blessing granted them in the presence of the world's Redeemer. The grief of their separation from Him, and the gentle reproof which His words conveyed, were designed to impress them with the sacredness of their trust.

In the answer to His mother, Jesus showed for the first time that He understood His relation to God. Before His birth the angel had said to Mary, "He shall be great, and shall be called the Son of the Highest: and the Lord God shall give unto Him the throne of His [81-82] father David: and He shall reign over the house of Jacob forever." Luke 1:32, 33. These words Mary had pondered in her heart; yet while she believed that her child was to be Israel's Messiah, she did not comprehend His mission. Now she did not understand His words; but she knew that He had disclaimed kinship to Joseph, and had declared His Sonship to God.

Jesus did not ignore His relation to His earthly parents. From Jerusalem He returned home with them, and aided them in their life of toil. He hid in His own heart the mystery of His mission, waiting submissively for the appointed time for Him to enter upon His work. For eighteen years after He had recognized that He was the Son of God, He acknowledged the tie that bound Him to the home at Nazareth, and performed the duties of a son, a brother, a friend, and a citizen.

As His mission had opened to Jesus in the temple, He shrank from contact with the multitude. He wished to return from Jerusalem in quietness, with those who knew the secret of His life. By the paschal service, God was seeking to call His people away from their worldly cares, and to remind them of His wonderful work in their deliverance from Egypt. In this work He desired them to see a promise of deliverance from sin. As the blood of the slain lamb sheltered the homes of Israel, so the blood of Christ was to save their souls; but they could be saved through Christ only as by faith they should make His life their own. There was virtue in the symbolic service only as it directed the worshipers to Christ as their personal Saviour. God desired that they should be led to prayerful study and meditation in regard to Christ's mission. But as the multitudes left Jerusalem, the excitement of travel and social intercourse too often absorbed their attention, and the service they had witnessed was forgotten. The Saviour was not attracted to their company.

As Joseph and Mary should return from Jerusalem alone with Jesus, He hoped to direct their minds to the prophecies of the suffering Saviour. Upon Calvary He sought to lighten His mother's grief. He was thinking of her now. Mary was to witness His last agony, and Jesus desired her to understand His mission, that she might be strengthened to endure, when the sword should pierce through her soul. As Jesus had been separated from her, and she had sought Him sorrowing three days, so when He should be offered up for the sins of the world, He would again be lost to her for three days. And as He should come forth from the tomb, her sorrow would again be turned to joy. But how much better [82-83] she could have borne the anguish of His death if she had understood the Scriptures to which He was now trying to turn her thoughts!

If Joseph and Mary had stayed their minds upon God by meditation and prayer, they would have realized the sacredness of their trust, and would not have lost sight of Jesus. By one day's neglect they lost the Saviour; but it cost them three days of anxious search to find Him. So with us; by idle talk, evilspeaking, or neglect of prayer, we may in one day lose the Saviour's presence, and it may take many days of sorrowful search to find Him, and regain the peace that we have lost.

In our association with one another, we should take heed lest we forget Jesus, and pass along unmindful that He is not with us. When we become absorbed in worldly things so that we have no thought for Him in whom our hope of eternal life is centered, we separate ourselves from Jesus and from the heavenly angels. These holy beings cannot remain where the Saviour's presence is not desired, and His absence is not marked. This is why discouragement so often exists among the professed followers of Christ.

Many attend religious services, and are refreshed and comforted by the word of God; but through neglect of meditation, watchfulness, and prayer, they lose the blessing, and find themselves more destitute than before they received it. Often they feel that God has dealt hardly with them. They do not see that the fault is their own. By separating themselves from Jesus, they have shut away the light of His presence.

It would be well for us to spend a thoughtful hour each day in contemplation of the life of Christ. We should take it point by point, and let the imagination

5. "By one day's neglect Joseph and Mary lost the Savior; but it cost them three days of anxious search to find Him." (83) So it is with me; by i___ _____ talk, e_____ _____, or neglect of p_____, I may in one day lose the Savior's presence. Lord help me. What can I do? "If Joseph and Mary had s_____ their minds upon God by meditation and prayer, they would have realized the sacredness of their t_____, and not have lost sight of Jesus." Do I have a sacred trust? _____ _____ (to guard my relationship with Jesus?)

_____

_____

6. "When we become a_____ in worldly things so that we have no thought for him…we s_____ ourselves from Jesus and from the heavenly angels. These holy beings cannot remain where the Savior's presence is not d_____, and His absence is not m_____. This is why d_____ __ so often exists among the professed followers of Christ." Lord, do I notice a difference in Your absence, when I haven't invited You in? _____

_____

_____

7. "It would be well for us to spend a t_____ h_____ each day in contemplation of the life of Christ." (83). What three things will happen?

    a. c_____ in Him more constant,

    b. l_____ quickened,

    c. more deeply i_____ with His spirit. Lord, may this walk of contemplating Your life quicken my love and passion for You: _____

_____

_____

8. Beholding the beauty of His c_____, we shall be "changed into the same image from glory to glory." 2 Cor 3:18. Lord, the more I behold, the longer I want to behold! Thank You for this hungering, and for fulfilling it! _____

_____

Prayer Journal: _____

_____
_____
_____
_____
_____
_____

grasp each scene, especially the closing ones. As we thus dwell upon His great sacrifice for us, our confidence in Him will be more constant, our love will be quickened, and we shall be more deeply imbued with His spirit. If we would be saved at last, we must learn the lesson of penitence and humiliation at the foot of the cross.

As we associate together, we may be a blessing to one another. If we are Christ's, our sweetest thoughts will be of Him. We shall love to talk of Him; and as we speak to one another of His love, our hearts will be softened by divine influences. Beholding the beauty of His character, we shall be "changed into the same image from glory to glory." 2 Cor. 3:18.

Chapter 9

Days of Conflict

From its earliest years the Jewish child was surrounded with the requirements of the rabbis. Rigid rules were prescribed for every act, down to the smallest details of life. Under the synagogue teachers the youth were instructed in the countless regulations which as orthodox Israelites they were expected to observe. But Jesus did not interest Himself in these matters. From childhood He acted independently of the rabbinical laws. The Scriptures of the Old Testament were His constant study, and the words, "Thus saith the Lord," were ever upon His lips.

As the condition of the people began to open to His mind, He saw that the requirements of society and the requirements of God were in constant collision. Men were departing from the word of God, and exalting theories of their own invention. They were observing traditional rites that possessed no virtue. Their service was a mere round of ceremonies; the sacred truths it was designed to teach were hidden from the worshipers. He saw that in their faithless services they found no peace. They did not know the freedom of spirit that would come to them by serving God in truth. Jesus had come to teach the meaning of the worship of God, and He could not sanction the mingling of human requirements with the divine precepts. He did not attack the precepts or [84-85] practices of the learned teachers; but when reproved for His own simple habits, He presented the word of God in justification of His conduct.

In every gentle and submissive way, Jesus tried to please those with whom He came in contact. Because He was so gentle and unobtrusive, the scribes and elders supposed that He would be easily influenced by their teaching. They urged Him to receive the maxims and traditions that had been handed down from the ancient rabbis, but He asked for their authority in Holy Writ. He would hear every word that proceeds from the mouth of God; but He could not obey the inventions of men. Jesus seemed to know the Scriptures from beginning to end, and He presented them in their true import. The rabbis were ashamed to be instructed by a child. They

1. "The sacred truths it designed to teach were h_____ from the worshippers. He saw that in their f_____ services they found no peace...Jesus had come to teach the meaning of the w_____ of God." Lord, what do You think of my worship? Is it faithless? Is my heart disconnected from what my lips are doing? _____
_____
_____

claimed that it was their office to explain the Scriptures, and that it was His place to accept their interpretation. They were indignant that He should stand in opposition to their word.

They knew that no authority could be found in Scripture for their traditions. They realized that in spiritual understanding Jesus was far in advance of them. Yet they were angry because He did not obey their [85-86] dictates. Failing to convince Him, they sought Joseph and Mary, and set before them His course of noncompliance. Thus He suffered rebuke and censure.

At a very early age, Jesus had begun to act for Himself in the formation of His character, and not even respect and love for His parents could turn Him from obedience to God's word. "It is written" was His reason for every act that varied from the family customs. But the influence of the rabbis made His life a bitter one. Even in His youth He had to learn the hard lesson of silence and patient endurance.

His brothers, as the sons of Joseph were called, sided with the rabbis They insisted that the traditions must be heeded, as if they were the requirements of God. They even regarded the precepts of men more highly than the word of God, and they were greatly annoyed at the clear penetration of Jesus in distinguishing between the false and the true His strict obedience to the law of God they condemned as stubbornness. They were surprised at the knowledge and wisdom He showed in answering the rabbis. They knew that He had not received instruction from the wise men, yet they could not but see that He was an instructor to them. They recognized that His education was of a higher type than their own. But they did not discern that He had access to the tree of life, a source of knowledge of which they were ignorant.

Christ was not exclusive, and He had given special offense to the Pharisees by departing in this respect from their rigid rules. He found the domain of religion fenced in by high walls of seclusion, as too sacred a matter for everyday life. These walls of partition He overthrew. In His contact with men He did not ask, What is your creed? To what church do you belong? He exercised His helping power in behalf of all who needed help. Instead of secluding Himself in a hermit's cell in order to show His heavenly character, He labored earnestly for humanity. He inculcated the principle that Bible religion does not consist in the mortification of the body.

2. "At a very early age, Jesus had begun to act for Himself in the formation of His c_____." (86). What does this mean? _____

_____ "It is written" was His reason for every act that varied from family customs. The Scriptures were His "c_____ study, and the words, "Thus saith the Lord," were e_____ upon His lips." (84). The phrases "constant study" and "ever on His lips", point out an attitude that facilitates this walk with You, doesn't it? Lord, bring to mind an awareness of Your presence 24-7: _____

3. In Jesus' walk, did He seclude "Himself in a h_____ cell in order to show His heavenly character?" (86). No! "At a____ times and in all plac-

He taught that pure and undefiled religion is not meant only for set times and special occasions. At all times and in all places He manifested a loving interest in men, and shed about Him the light of a cheerful piety. All this was a rebuke to the Pharisees. It showed that religion does not consist in selfishness, and that their morbid devotion to personal interest was far from being true godliness. This had roused their enmity against Jesus, so that they tried to enforce His conformity to their regulations. [86-87]

Jesus worked to relieve every case of suffering that He saw. He had little money to give, but He often denied Himself of food in order to relieve those who appeared more needy than He. His brothers felt that His influence went far to counteract theirs. He possessed a tact which none of them had, or desired to have. When they spoke harshly to poor, degraded beings, Jesus sought out these very ones, and spoke to them words of encouragement. To those who were in need He would give a cup of cold water, and would quietly place His own meal in their hands. As He relieved their sufferings, the truths He taught were associated with His acts of mercy, and were thus riveted in the memory.

All this displeased His brothers. Being older than Jesus, they felt that He should be under their dictation. They charged Him with thinking Himself superior to them, and reproved Him for setting Himself above their teachers and the priests and rulers of the people. Often they threatened and tried to intimidate Him; but He passed on, making the Scriptures His guide.

Jesus loved His brothers, and treated them with unfailing kindness; but they were jealous of Him, and manifested the most decided unbelief and contempt. They could not understand His conduct. Great contradictions presented themselves in Jesus. He was the divine Son of God, [87-88] and yet a helpless child. The Creator of the worlds, the earth was His possession, and yet poverty marked His life experience at every step. He possessed a dignity and individuality wholly distinct from earthly pride and assumption; He did not strive for worldly greatness, and in even the lowliest position He was content. This angered His brothers. They could not account for His constant serenity under trial and deprivation. They did not know that for our sake He had become poor, that we "through His poverty might be rich." 2 Cor. 8:9. They could understand the mystery

es He manifested a loving i_____ in men, and shed about Him the light of a cheerful piety." Could this be part of what "constantly studying the Scriptures" mean, applying Biblical principles into my daily relationships? _____
_____

4. Is "light of cheerful piety" a contradiction in terms?
_____
Why or Why not? _____
_____
_____
_____

Lord, may my walk with You lend me a cheerful attitude.

5. How were the truths Jesus taught riveted in the memory? "As He relieved their sufferings, the truths He taught were a_____ with His acts of mercy. (87). My walk, then, is more than what I say, but how I treat others. Lord, may Your love flow throw me to others, this day. Tell me specifically what to do: __
_____
_____

6. Jesus "did not strive for worldly greatness, and in even the lowliest positions He was c_____ _____. This angered His brothers. They could not account for His constant s_____ under trial and deprivation...The ex-

of His mission no more than the friends of Job could understand his humiliation and suffering.

Jesus was misunderstood by His brothers because He was not like them. His standard was not their standard. In looking to men they had turned away from God, and they had not His power in their lives. The forms of religion which they observed could not transform the character. They paid "tithe of mint and anise and cummin," but omitted "the weightier matters of the law, judgment, mercy, and faith." Matt. 23:23. The example of Jesus was to them a continual irritation. He hated but one thing in the world, and that was sin. He could not witness a wrong act without pain which it was impossible to disguise. Between the formalists, whose sanctity of appearance concealed the love of sin, and a character in which zeal for God's glory was always paramount, the contrast was unmistakable. Because the life of Jesus condemned evil, He was opposed, both at home and abroad. His unselfishness and integrity were commented on with a sneer. His forbearance and kindness were termed cowardice.

Of the bitterness that falls to the lot of humanity, there was no part which Christ did not taste. There were those who tried to cast contempt upon Him because of His birth, and even in His childhood He had to meet their scornful looks and evil whisperings. If He had responded by an impatient word or look, if He had conceded to His brothers by even one wrong act, He would have failed of being a perfect example. Thus He would have failed of carrying out the plan for our redemption. Had He even admitted that there could be an excuse for sin, Satan would have triumphed, and the world would have been lost. This is why the tempter worked to make His life as trying as possible, that He might be led to sin.

But to every temptation He had one answer, "It is written." He rarely rebuked any wrongdoing of His brothers, but He had a word [88-89] from God to speak to them. Often He was accused of cowardice for refusing to unite with them in some forbidden act; but His answer was, It is written, "The fear of the Lord, that is wisdom; and to depart from evil is understanding." Job 28:28.

There were some who sought His society, feeling at peace in His presence; but many avoided Him, because they were rebuked by His stainless life. Young compan-

---

ample of Jesus was to them a continual i_____ _____." (88). If I am grounded firm and deep in Your love, wouldn't there be serenity under frustrations and stress? _____

How is it that I let these worries have priority over Your love? _____
_____
_____

ions urged Him to do as they did. He was bright and cheerful; they enjoyed His presence, and welcomed His ready suggestions; but they were impatient at His scruples, and pronounced Him narrow and strait-laced. Jesus answered, It is written, "Wherewithal shall a young man cleanse his way? by taking heed thereto according to Thy word." "Thy word have I hid in mine heart, that I might not sin against Thee." Ps. 119:9, 11.

Often He was asked, Why are you bent on being so singular, so different from us all? It is written, He said, "Blessed are the undefiled in the way, who walk in the law of the Lord. Blessed are they that keep His testimonies, and that seek Him with the whole heart. They also do no iniquity; they walk in His ways." Ps. 119:1-3.

When questioned why He did not join in the frolics of the youth of Nazareth, He said, It is written, "I have rejoiced in the way of Thy testimonies, as much as in all riches. I will meditate in Thy precepts, and have respect unto Thy ways. I will delight myself in Thy statutes; I will not forget Thy word." Ps. 119:14-16.

Jesus did not contend for His rights. Often His work was made unnecessarily severe because He was willing and uncomplaining. Yet He did not fail nor become discouraged. He lived above these difficulties, as if in the light of God's countenance. He did not retaliate when roughly used, but bore insult patiently.

Again and again He was asked, Why do You submit to such despiteful usage, even from Your brothers? It is written, He said, "My son, forget not My law; but let thine heart keep My commandments: for length of days, and long life, and peace, shall they add to thee. Let not mercy and truth forsake thee: bind them about thy neck; write them upon the table of thine heart: so shalt thou find favor and good understanding in the sight of God and man." Prov. 3:1-4.

From the time when the parents of Jesus found Him in the temple, His course of action was a mystery to them. He would not enter into controversy, yet His example was a constant lesson. He seemed as one [89-90] who was set apart. His hours of happiness were found when alone with nature and with God. Whenever it was His privilege, He turned aside from the scene of His labor, to go into the fields, to meditate in the green valleys, to hold communion with God on the mountainside or amid the trees of the forest. The early morning often found Him in some secluded place, meditating,

7. "Jesus did not c____ _____ for His rights. Often His work was made unnecessarily severe because He was willing and uncomplaining...He lived above these difficulties, as if in the light of God's c_____. He did not retaliate when roughly used, but bore insult patiently." (89). How can I be like You, Lord? Help me to live, to walk, in the light of Your countenance: ____

_____
_____
_____
_____

8. When were Jesus' hours of happiness found? (90). _____
_____
_____

(Though I have to remember that Jesus wasn't

a hermit. "From these quiet hours He would r_____ to His home to take up His duties again."). Lord, may I discover that my happiest hours are when I am with You: _____

_____

_____

searching the Scriptures, or in prayer. From these quiet hours He would return to His home to take up His duties again, and to give an example of patient toil.

The life of Christ was marked with respect and love for His mother. Mary believed in her heart that the holy child born of her was the long-promised Messiah, yet she dared not express her faith. Throughout His life on earth she was a partaker in His sufferings. She witnessed with sorrow the trials brought upon Him in His childhood and youth. By her vindication of what she knew to be right in His conduct, she herself was brought into trying positions. She looked upon the associations of the home, and the mother's tender watchcare over her children, as of vital importance in the formation of character. The sons and daughters of Joseph knew this, and by appealing to her anxiety, they tried to correct the practices of Jesus according to their standard.

Mary often remonstrated with Jesus, and urged Him to conform to the usages of the rabbis. But He could not be persuaded to change His habits of contemplating the works of God and seeking to alleviate the suffering of men or even of dumb animals. When the priests and teachers required Mary's aid in controlling Jesus, she was greatly troubled; but peace came to her heart as He presented the statements of Scripture upholding His practices.

At times she wavered between Jesus and His brothers, who did not believe that He was the Sent of God; but evidence was abundant that His was a divine character. She saw Him sacrificing Himself for the good of others. His presence brought a purer atmosphere into the home, and His life was as leaven working amid the elements of society. Harmless and undefiled, He walked among the thoughtless, the rude, the uncourteous; amid the unjust publicans, the reckless prodigals, the unrighteous Samaritans, the heathen soldiers, the rough peasants, and the mixed multitude. He spoke a word of sympathy here and a word there, as He saw men weary, yet compelled to bear heavy burdens. He shared their burdens, and repeated to them the lessons He had learned from nature, of the love, the kindness, the goodness of God. [90-91]

He taught all to look upon themselves as endowed with precious talents, which if rightly employed would secure for them eternal riches. He weeded all vanity from life, and by His own example taught that every

9. "By His own example, Jesus taught that every

moment of time is fraught with eternal results; that it is to be cherished as a treasure, and to be employed for holy purposes. He passed by no human being as worthless, but sought to apply the saving remedy to every soul. In whatever company He found Himself, He presented a lesson that was appropriate to the time and the circumstances. He sought to inspire with hope the most rough and unpromising, setting before them the assurance that they might become blameless and harmless, attaining such a character as would make them manifest as the children of God. Often He met those who had drifted under Satan's control, and who had no power to break from his snare. To such a one, discouraged, sick, tempted, and fallen, Jesus would speak words of tenderest pity, words that were needed and could be understood. Others [91-92] He met who were fighting a hand-to-hand battle with the adversary of souls. These He encouraged to persevere, assuring them that they would win; for angels of God were on their side, and would give them the victory. Those whom He thus helped were convinced that here was One in whom they could trust with perfect confidence. He would not betray the secrets they poured into His sympathizing ear.

Jesus was the healer of the body as well as of the soul. He was interested in every phase of suffering that came under His notice, and to every sufferer He brought relief, His kind words having a soothing balm. None could say that He had worked a miracle; but virtue--the healing power of love--went out from Him to the sick and distressed. Thus in an unobtrusive way He worked for the people from His very childhood. And this was why, after His public ministry began, so many heard Him gladly.

Yet through childhood, youth, and manhood, Jesus walked alone. In His purity and His faithfulness, He trod the wine press alone, and of the people there was none with Him. He carried the awful weight of responsibility for the salvation of men. He knew that unless there was a decided change in the principles and purposes of the human race, all would be lost. This was the burden of His soul, and none could appreciate the weight that rested upon Him. Filled with intense purpose, He carried out the design of His life that He Himself should be the light of men.

m_____ of time is fraught with eternal results; that it is to be cherished as a treasure, and to be employed for h_____ purposes." (91) Lord, that's a challenge! How can that principle be employed in my every day life? _____

_____

_____ "His presence brought a purer atmosphere into the home." (90).

10. "He sought to inspire with h_____ the most rough and uncompromising, setting before them the assurance that they might become b_____ and harmless, attaining such a character as would make them manifest as the c_____ of God." (91) What is more effective to me as a motivator, being inspired or scolded? _____

_____

_____

_____

Lord, how do I treat others?_____

_____

May my approach be Your approach: _____

_____

_____

Prayer Journal: _____

_____

_____

_____

_____

_____

Chapter 10

The Voice in the Wilderness
[This chapter is based on Luke 1:5-23, 57-80; 3:1-18; Matt.3:1-12; Mark 1:1-8.]

From among the faithful in Israel, who had long
waited for the coming of the Messiah, the forerunner
of Christ arose. The aged priest Zacharias and his wife
Elisabeth were "both righteous before God;" and in
their quiet and holy lives the light of faith shone out
like a star amid the darkness of those evil days. To this
godly pair was given the promise of a son, who should
"go before the face of the Lord to prepare His ways."

Zacharias dwelt in "the hill country of Judea," but
he had gone up to Jerusalem to minister for one week
in the temple, a service required twice a year from the
priests of each course. "And it came to pass, that while
he executed the priest's office before God in the order
of his course, according to the custom of the priest's office, his lot was to burn incense when he went into the
temple of the Lord."

He was standing before the golden altar in the holy
place of the sanctuary. The cloud of incense with the
prayers of Israel was ascending before God. Suddenly
he became conscious of a divine presence. An angel of
the Lord was "standing on the right side of the altar."
The position of the angel was an indication of favor, but
Zacharias took no [97-98] note of this. For many years
he had prayed for the coming of the Redeemer; now
heaven had sent its messenger to announce that these
prayers were about to be answered; but the mercy of
God seemed too great for him to credit. He was filled
with fear and self-condemnation.

But he was greeted with the joyful assurance: "Fear
not, Zacharias: for thy prayer is heard; and thy wife
Elisabeth shall bear thee a son, and thou shalt call his
name John. And thou shalt have joy and gladness; and
many shall rejoice at his birth. For he shall be great in
the sight of the Lord, and shall drink neither wine nor
strong drink; and he shall be filled with the Holy Ghost.
. . . And many of the children of Israel shall he turn to
the Lord their God. And he shall go before Him in the
spirit and power of Elias, to turn the hearts of the fathers

to the children, and the disobedient to the wisdom of the just; to make ready a people prepared for the Lord. And Zacharias said unto the angel, Whereby shall I know this? for I am an old man, and my wife well stricken in years."

Zacharias well knew how to Abraham in his old age a child was given because he believed Him faithful who had promised. But for a moment the aged priest turns his thought to the weakness of humanity. He forgets that what God has promised, He is able to perform. What a contrast between this unbelief and the sweet, childlike faith of Mary, the maiden of Nazareth, whose answer to the angel's wonderful announcement was, "Behold the handmaid of the Lord; be it unto me according to thy word"! Luke 1:38.

The birth of a son to Zacharias, like the birth of the child of Abraham, and that of Mary, was to teach a great spiritual truth, a truth that we are slow to learn and ready to forget. In ourselves we are incapable of doing any good thing; but that which we cannot do will be wrought by the power of God in every submissive and believing soul. It was through faith that the child of promise was given. It is through faith that spiritual life is begotten, and we are enabled to do the works of righteousness.

To the question of Zacharias, the angel said, "I am Gabriel, that stand in the presence of God; and am sent to speak unto thee, and to show thee these glad tidings." Five hundred years before, Gabriel had made known to Daniel the prophetic period which was to extend to the coming of Christ. The knowledge that the end of this period was near had moved Zacharias to pray for the Messiah's advent. Now the very messenger through whom the prophecy was given had come to announce its fulfillment. [98-99]

The words of the angel, "I am Gabriel, that stand in the presence of God," show that he holds a position of high honor in the heavenly courts. When he came with a message to Daniel, he said, "There is none that holdeth with me in these things, but Michael [Christ] your Prince." Dan. 10:21. Of Gabriel the Saviour speaks in the Revelation, saying that "He sent and signified it by His angel unto His servant John." Rev. 1:1. And to John the angel declared, "I am a fellow servant with thee and with thy brethren the prophets." Rev. 22:9, R. V. Wonderful thought--that the angel who stands next in honor

1. Aged Zacharias, being told of Elizabeth's pregnancy with John, for a moment "turns his thoughts to the weakness of humanity. He forgets that what God has promised, He is able to p_____." (98).

Lord, help me to view my walk not in terms of the weakness of humanity, but in terms of Your promise. "Come follow Me," You invite. "Abide in Me." It is Your vision, Your promise. You will perform, as I allow You too. What hinders me from allowing the fulfillment of Your promise?

_____
_____
_____

to the Son of God is the one chosen to open the purposes of God to sinful men.

Zacharias had expressed doubt of the angel's words. He was not to speak again until they were fulfilled. "Behold," said the angel, "thou shalt be dumb, . . . until the day that these things shall be performed, because thou believest not my words, which shall be fulfilled in their season." It was the duty of the priest in this service to pray for the pardon of public and national sins, and for the coming of the Messiah; but when Zacharias attempted to do this, he could not utter a word.

Coming forth to bless the people, "he beckoned unto them, and remained speechless." They had waited long, and had begun to fear, lest he had been cut down by the judgment of God. But as he came forth from the holy place, his face was shining with the glory of God, "and they perceived that he had seen a vision in the temple." Zacharias communicated to them what he had seen and heard; and "as soon as the days of his ministration were accomplished, he departed to his own house."

Soon after the birth of the promised child, the father's tongue was loosed, "and he spake, and praised God. And fear came on all that dwelt round about them: and all these sayings were noised abroad throughout all the hill country of Judea. And all they that heard them laid them up [99-100] in their hearts, saying, What manner of child shall this be!" All this tended to call attention to the Messiah's coming, for which John was to prepare the way.

The Holy Spirit rested upon Zacharias, and in these beautiful words he prophesied of the mission of his son:

> "Thou, child, shalt be called the prophet of the Highest;
> For thou shalt go before the face of the Lord to prepare His ways;
> To give knowledge of salvation unto His people
> By the remission of their sins,
> Through the tender mercy of our God,
> Whereby the Dayspring from on high hath visited us,
> To give light to them that sit in darkness and in the shadow of death,
> To guide our feet into the way of peace."

"And the child grew, and waxed strong in spirit, and

was in the deserts till the day of his showing unto Israel." Before the birth of John, the angel had said, "He shall be great in the sight of the Lord, and shall drink neither wine nor strong drink; and he shall be filled with the Holy Ghost." God had called the son of Zacharias to a great work, the greatest ever committed to men. In order to accomplish this work, he must have the Lord to work with him. And the Spirit of God would be with him if he heeded the instruction of the angel.

John was to go forth as Jehovah's messenger, to bring to men the light of God. He must give a new direction to their thoughts. He must impress them with the holiness of God's requirements, and their need of His perfect righteousness. Such a messenger must be holy. He must be a temple for the indwelling Spirit of God. In order to fulfill his mission, he must have a sound physical constitution, and mental and spiritual strength. Therefore it would be necessary for him to control the appetites and passions. He must be able so to control all his powers that he could stand among men as unmoved by surrounding circumstances as the rocks and mountains of the wilderness.

In the time of John the Baptist, greed for riches, and the love of luxury and display had become widespread. Sensuous pleasures, feasting and drinking, were causing physical disease and degeneracy, benumbing the spiritual perceptions, and lessening the sensibility to sin. John was to stand as a reformer. By his abstemious life and plain dress he was to [100-101] rebuke the excesses of his time. Hence the directions given to the parents of John,--a lesson of temperance by an angel from the throne of heaven.

In childhood and youth the character is most impressible. The power of self-control should then be acquired. By the fireside and at the family board influences are exerted whose results are as enduring as eternity. More than any natural endowment, the habits established in early years decide whether a man will be victorious or vanquished in the battle of life. Youth is the sowing time. It determines the character of the harvest, for this life and for the life to come.

As a prophet, John was "to turn the hearts of the fathers to the children, and the disobedient to the wisdom of the just; to make ready a people prepared for the Lord." In preparing the way for Christ's first advent, he was a representative of those who are to prepare

2. John was called to a great work: "bring to men the l_____ of God." As a reformer, John was to avoid anything "benumbing the spiritual perceptions, and l_____ the sensibility to sin." (100). In my walk with You, Lord, preparing for the second advent, temperance will enable me to "understand and to practice the sacred truths of God's Word." (101). Teach me, guide me, show me, Lord, the importance of temperance, and how to not be self-righteous about it: _____

_____

_____

a people for our Lord's second coming. The world is given to self-indulgence. Errors and fables abound. Satan's snares for destroying souls are multiplied. All who would perfect holiness in the fear of God must learn the lessons of temperance and self-control. The appetites and passions must be held in subjection to the higher powers of the mind. This self-discipline is essential to that mental strength and spiritual insight which will enable us to understand and to practice the sacred truths of God's word. For this reason temperance finds its place in the work of preparation for Christ's second coming.

In the natural order of things, the son of Zacharias would have been educated for the priesthood. But the training of the rabbinical schools would have unfitted him for his work. God did not send him to the teachers of theology to learn how to interpret the Scriptures. He called him to the desert, that he might learn of nature and nature's God.

It was a lonely region where he found his home, in the midst of barren hills, wild ravines, and rocky caves. But it was his choice to forgo the enjoyments and luxuries of life for the stern discipline of the wilderness. Here his surroundings were favorable to habits of simplicity and self-denial. Uninterrupted by the clamor of the world, he could here study the lessons of nature, of revelation, and of Providence. The words of the angel to Zacharias had been often repeated to John by his God-fearing parents. From childhood his mission had been kept before him, and he had accepted the holy trust. To him the solitude of the desert was a welcome escape from society in which suspicion, unbelief, and impurity had become well-nigh all-pervading. He distrusted his own [101-102] power to withstand temptation, and shrank from constant contact with sin, lest he should lose the sense of its exceeding sinfulness.

Dedicated to God as a Nazarite from his birth, he made the vow his own in a life-long consecration. His dress was that of the ancient prophets, a garment of camel's hair, confined by a leather girdle. He ate the "locusts and wild honey" found in the wilderness, and drank the pure water from the hills.

But the life of John was not spent in idleness, in ascetic gloom, or in selfish isolation. From time to time he went forth to mingle with men; and he was ever an interested observer of what was passing in the world. From his quiet retreat he watched the unfolding of events. With vision illuminated by the divine Spirit he studied the characters of men, that he might understand how to reach their hearts with the message of heaven. The burden of his mission was upon him. In solitude, by meditation and prayer, he sought to gird up his soul for the lifework before him.

Although in the wilderness, he was not exempt from temptation. So far as possible, he closed every avenue by which Satan could enter, yet he was still assailed by the tempter. But his spiritual perceptions were clear; he had developed strength and decision of character, and through the aid of the Holy Spirit he was able to detect Satan's approaches, and to resist his power.

John found in the wilderness his school and his sanctuary. Like Moses amid the mountains of Midian, he was shut in by God's presence, and surrounded by the evidences of His power. It was not his lot to dwell, as did Israel's great leader, amid the solemn majesty of the mountain solitudes; but before him were the heights of Moab, beyond Jordan, speaking of Him who had set fast the mountains, and girded them with strength. The gloomy and terrible aspect of nature in his wilderness home vividly pictured the condition of Israel. The fruitful vineyard of the Lord had become a desolate waste. But above the desert the heavens bent bright and beautiful. The clouds that gathered, dark with tempest, were arched by the rainbow of promise. So above Israel's degradation shone the promised glory of the Messiah's reign. The clouds of wrath were spanned by the rainbow of His covenant-mercy.

Alone in the silent night he read God's promise to Abraham of a seed numberless as the stars. The light of dawn, gilding the mountains of Moab, told of Him who should be as "the light of the morning, when the [102-103] sun riseth, even a morning without clouds." 2 Sam. 23:4. And in the brightness of noontide he saw the splendor of His manifestation, when "the glory of the Lord shall be revealed, and all flesh shall see it together." Isa. 40:5.

With awed yet exultant spirit he searched in the prophetic scrolls the revelations of the Messiah's coming,-- the promised seed that should bruise the serpent's head; Shiloh, "the peace giver," who was to appear before a king should cease to reign on David's throne. Now the time had come. A Roman ruler sat in the palace upon Mount Zion. By the sure word of the Lord, already the

3. Assailed by the tempter, John's "spiritual perceptions were c_____...and through the aid of the Holy Spirit he was able to detect Satan's approaches." (102). Lord, help my sensiblity to sin be sharpened. As I turn my eyes on You, may the desirability of that which lessens my sensibility to sin, grow dim: ___

Christ was born.

Isaiah's rapt portrayals of the Messiah's glory were his study by day and by night,--the Branch from the root of Jesse; a King to reign in righteousness, judging "with equity for the meek of the earth;" "a covert from the tempest; . . . the shadow of a great rock in a weary land;" Israel no longer to be termed "Forsaken," nor her land "Desolate," but to be called of the Lord, "My Delight," and her land "Beulah." Isa. 11:4; 32:2; 62:4, margin. The heart of the lonely exile was filled with the glorious vision.

He looked upon the King in His beauty, and self was forgotten. He beheld the majesty of holiness, and felt himself to be inefficient and unworthy. He was ready to go forth as Heaven's messenger, unawed by the human, because he had looked upon the Divine. He could stand erect and fearless in the presence of earthly monarchs, because he had bowed low before the King of kings.

John did not fully understand the nature of the Messiah's kingdom. He looked for Israel to be delivered from her national foes; but the coming of a King in righteousness, and the establishment of Israel as a holy nation, was the great object of his hope. Thus he believed would be accomplished the prophecy given at his birth,--

> "To remember His holy covenant; . . .
> That we being delivered out of the hand of our enemies
> Might serve Him without fear,
> In holiness and righteousness before Him, all the days of our life."

He saw his people deceived, self-satisfied, and asleep in their sins. He longed to rouse them to a holier life. The message that God had given him to bear was designed to startle them from their lethargy, and [103-104] cause them to tremble because of their great wickedness. Before the seed of the gospel could find lodgment, the soil of the heart must be broken up. Before they would seek healing from Jesus, they must be awakened to their danger from the wounds of sin.

4. "God does not send messengers to flatter the sinner...He lays heavy burdens upon the c_____ _____...and pierces the

God does not send messengers to flatter the sinner. He delivers no message of peace to lull the unsanctified into fatal security. He lays heavy burdens upon the conscience of the wrongdoer, and pierces the soul with arrows of conviction. The ministering angels present to him the fearful judgments of God to deepen the sense of need, and prompt the cry, "What must I do to be saved?" Then the hand that has humbled in the dust, lifts up the penitent. The voice that has rebuked sin, and put to shame pride and ambition, inquires with tenderest sympathy, "What wilt thou that I shall do unto thee?"

When the ministry of John began, the nation was in a state of excitement and discontent verging on revolution. At the removal of Archelaus, Judea had been brought directly under the control of Rome. The tyranny and extortion of the Roman governors, and their determined efforts to introduce the heathen symbols and customs, kindled revolt, which had been quenched in the blood of thousands of the bravest of Israel. All this intensified the national hatred against Rome, and increased the longing to be freed from her power.

Amid discord and strife, a voice was heard from the wilderness, a voice startling and stern, yet full of hope: "Repent ye; for the kingdom of heaven is at hand." With a new, strange power it moved the people. Prophets had foretold the coming of Christ as an event far in the future; but here was an announcement that it was at hand. John's singular appearance carried the minds of his hearers back to the ancient seers. In his manner and dress he resembled the prophet Elijah. With the spirit and power of Elijah he denounced the national corruption, and rebuked the prevailing sins. His words were plain, pointed, and convincing. Many believed him to be one of the prophets risen from the dead. The whole nation was stirred. Multitudes flocked to the wilderness.

John proclaimed the coming of the Messiah, and called the people to repentance. As a symbol of cleansing from sin, he baptized them in the waters of the Jordan. Thus by a significant object lesson he declared that those who claimed to be the chosen people of God were defiled by sin, and that without purification of heart and life they could have no part in the Messiah's kingdom.

Princes and rabbis, soldiers, publicans, and peasants came to hear the prophet. For a time the solemn warning from God alarmed them. Many were brought to repentance, and received baptism. Persons of all ranks submitted to the requirement of the Baptist, in order to participate in the kingdom he announced.

Many of the scribes and Pharisees came confess-

soul with arrows of c___ _____ ... to deepen the sense of n_____, to prompt the cry, 'What must I do to be saved?' [John's]... words were plain, p_____, and convincing." (104). Lord, may I not squirm at, avoid, or deny Your Spirit's convictions, but be receptive and open to them. Show me the areas of resistence, and how to be receptive:

_____
_____
_____
_____

ing their sins, and asking for baptism. They had exalted themselves as better than other men, and had led the people to entertain a high opinion of their piety; now the guilty secrets of their lives were unveiled. But John was impressed by the Holy Spirit that many of these men had no real conviction of sin. They were timeservers. As friends of the prophet, they hoped to find favor with the coming Prince. And by receiving baptism at the hands of this popular young teacher, they thought to strengthen their influence with the people.

John met them with the scathing inquiry, "O generation of vipers, who hath warned you to flee from the wrath to come? Bring forth therefore fruits meet for repentance; and think not to say within yourselves, [105-106] We have Abraham to our father: for I say unto you, that God is able of these stones to raise up children unto Abraham."

The Jews had misinterpreted God's promise of eternal favor to Israel: "Thus saith the Lord, which giveth the sun for a light by day, and the ordinances of the moon and of the stars for a light by night, which divideth the sea when the waves thereof roar; The Lord of hosts is His name: If those ordinances depart from before Me, saith the Lord, then the seed of Israel also shall cease from being a nation before Me forever. Thus saith the Lord; If heaven above can be measured, and the foundations of the earth searched out beneath, I will also cast off all the seed of Israel for all that they have done, saith the Lord." Jer. 31:35-37. The Jews regarded their natural descent from Abraham as giving them a claim to this promise. But they overlooked the conditions which God had specified. Before giving the promise, He had said, "I will put My law in their inward parts, and write it in their hearts; and will be their God, and they shall be My people. . . . For I will forgive their iniquity, and I will remember their sin no more." Jer. 31:33, 34.

To a people in whose hearts His law is written, the favor of God is assured. They are one with Him. But the Jews had separated themselves from God. Because of their sins they were suffering under His judgments. This was the cause of their bondage to a heathen nation. Their minds were darkened by transgression, and because in times past the Lord had shown them so great favor, they excused their sins. They flattered themselves that they were better than other men, and entitled to His blessings.

These things "are written for our admonition, upon whom the ends of the world are come." 1 Cor. 10:11. How often we misinterpret God's blessings, and flatter ourselves that we are favored on account of some goodness in us! God cannot do for us that which He longs to do. His gifts are used to increase our self-satisfaction, and to harden our hearts in unbelief and sin.

John declared to the teachers of Israel that their pride, selfishness, and cruelty showed them to be a generation of vipers, a deadly curse to the people, rather than the children of just and obedient Abraham. In view of the light they had received from God, they were even worse than the heathen, to whom they felt so much superior. They had forgotten the rock whence they were hewn, and the hole of the pit from which they had been digged. God was not dependent upon them for the fulfilling of [106-107] His purpose. As He had called Abraham out from a heathen people, so He could call others to His service. Their hearts might now appear as lifeless as the stones of the desert, but His Spirit could quicken them to do His will, and receive the fulfillment of His promise.

"And now also," said the prophet, "the ax is laid unto the root of the trees: therefore every tree which bringeth not forth good fruit is hewn down, and cast into the fire." Not by its name, but by its fruit, is the value of a tree determined. If the fruit is worthless, the name cannot save the tree from destruction. John declared to the Jews that their standing before God was to be decided by their character and life. Profession was worthless. If their life and character were not in harmony with God's law, they were not His people.

Under his heart-searching words, his hearers were convicted. They came to him with the inquiry, "What shall we do then?" He answered, "He that hath two coats, let him impart to him that hath none; and he that hath meat, let him do likewise." And he warned the publicans against injustice, and the soldiers against violence.

All who became the subjects of Christ's kingdom, he said, would give evidence of faith and repentance. Kindness, honesty, and fidelity would be seen in their lives. They would minister to the needy, and bring their offerings to God. They would shield the defenseless, and give an example of virtue and compassion. So the followers of Christ will give evidence of the transform-

5. "How often we misinterpret God's blessings, and flatter ourselves that we are f_____ on account of some goodness in us! God c_____ ____ do for us that which He longs to do. His gifts are used to increase our self-satisfaction, and to harden our hearts in unbelief and sin."(106). I need to hear John's cry of "Repent!" There are things in my life that are in the way of my relationship with You, Lord, things that slow me down spiritually. I need to let them go:

_____

_____

_____

6. "Not by its name, but by its f_____, is the value of a tree determined...John declared to the Jews that their standing before God was to be decided by their c_____ and life. Profession was worthless." (107). If my life and character is not in harmony with Your law, Lord, I am not Your people, I've wandered off, I'm not walking with You. Show me how to reverse this: _____

_____

_____

ing power of the Holy Spirit. In the daily life, justice, mercy, and the love of God will be seen. Otherwise they are like the chaff that is given to the fire.

"I indeed baptize you in water unto repentance," said John; "but He that cometh after me is mightier than I, whose shoes I am not worthy to bear: He shall baptize you with the Holy Ghost and with fire." Matt. 3:11, R. V., margin. The prophet Isaiah had declared that the Lord would cleanse His people from their iniquities "by the spirit of judgment, and by the spirit of burning." The word of the Lord to Israel was, "I will turn My hand upon thee, and purely purge away thy dross, and take away all thy tin." Isa. 4:4; 1:25. To sin, wherever found, "our God is a consuming fire." Heb. 12:29. In all who submit to His power the Spirit of God will consume sin. But if men cling to sin, they become identified with it. Then the glory of God, which destroys sin, must destroy them. Jacob, after his night of wrestling with the Angel, exclaimed, "I have seen God face to face, and my life is preserved." Gen. 32: 30. [107-108] Jacob had been guilty of a great sin in his conduct toward Esau; but he had repented. His transgression had been forgiven, and his sin purged; therefore he could endure the revelation of God's presence. But wherever men came before God while willfully cherishing evil, they were destroyed. At the second advent of Christ the wicked shall be consumed "with the Spirit of His mouth," and destroyed "with the brightness of His coming." 2 Thess. 2:8. The light of the glory of God, which imparts life to the righteous, will slay the wicked.

In the time of John the Baptist, Christ was about to appear as the revealer of the character of God. His very presence would make manifest to men their sin. Only as they were willing to be purged from sin could they enter into fellowship with Him. Only the pure in heart could abide in His presence.

Thus the Baptist declared God's message to Israel. Many gave heed to his instruction. Many sacrificed all in order to obey. Multitudes followed this new teacher from place to place, and not a few cherished the hope that he might be the Messiah. But as John saw the people turning to him, he sought every opportunity of directing their faith to Him who was to come.

7. "In all who s_____ to His power the Spirit of God will consume sin." (107). Just like at the second coming, "the light of the glory of God, which imparts life to the righteous, will slay the wicked…Only as they were willing to be purged from sin could they enter into f_____ _____ with Him." (108). Am I preparing the way of the Lord, for You? Am I willing to be purged of sin, to be transparent, be in harmony with Your holy character? I want that fellowship, Lord, so help me be willing! _____

Prayer Journal: _____

Chapter 11

The Baptism

[This chapter is based on Matt. 3:13-17;
Mark 1:9-11; Luke 3:21, 22.]

Tidings of the wilderness prophet and his wonderful announcement, spread throughout Galilee. The message reached the peasants in the remotest hill towns, and the fisher folk by the sea, and in these simple, earnest hearts found its truest response. In Nazareth it was told in the carpenter shop that had been Joseph's, and One recognized the call. His time had come. Turning from His daily toil, He bade farewell to His mother, and followed in the steps of His countrymen who were flocking to the Jordan.

Jesus and John the Baptist were cousins, and closely related by the circumstances of their birth; yet they had had no direct acquaintance with each other. The life of Jesus had been spent at Nazareth in Galilee; that of John, in the wilderness of Judea. Amid widely different surroundings they had lived in seclusion, and had had no communication with each other. Providence had ordered this. No occasion was to be given for the charge that they had conspired together to support each other's claims.

John was acquainted with the events that had marked the birth of Jesus. He had heard of the visit to Jerusalem in His boyhood, and of what had passed in the school of the rabbis. He knew of His sinless life, and believed Him to be the Messiah; but of this he had no positive assurance. The fact that Jesus had for so many years remained in obscurity, giving no special evidence of His mission, gave occasion for [109-110] doubt as to whether He could be the Promised One. The Baptist, however, waited in faith, believing that in God's own time all would be made plain. It had been revealed to him that the Messiah would seek baptism at his hands, and that a sign of His divine character should then be given. Thus he would be enabled to present Him to the people.

When Jesus came to be baptized, John recognized in Him a purity of character that he had never before

1. "The fact that Jesus had for so many years remained in obscurity, giving no special evidence of His mission, gave occasion for d_____ as to whether He could be the Promised One. [John] the Baptist, however, waited in f_____, believing that in God's own time all would be made plain." (109-110). Lord, I should remember from prior experience with You, that Your way is best, that though I don't see where You're going at this point, I can trust You, waiting in faith:

_____

_____

2. "When Jesus came to be baptized, John recognized in Him a p_____

of character that he had never before perceived in any man. The very a_____ of His presence was holy and awe-inspiring." (110). When Jesus abides in my heart, can the same atmosphere surround me? What is my atmosphere like now? Lord, I invite You to abide. May my influence be elevating: _____

_____

_____

3. "Jesus did not receive baptism as a c_____ of guilt on His own account." (111). So why was He baptized? "He identified Himself w_____ sinners." God will do what it takes, to be one with us: Word became flesh, Immanuel (God with us), was made sin (the worst of sinners); He even risked failure. Lord, I don't want to leave You waiting alone, any longer, waiting for me. Thank You for identifying with me, and being one with me:

_____

_____

4. Upon coming up out of the water, why, "though He was the Prince of Peace, His coming must be as the unsheathing of a s_____?" (111). His kingdom was the opposite of what was

perceived in any man. The very atmosphere of His presence was holy and awe-inspiring. Among the multitudes that had gathered about him at the Jordan, John had heard dark tales of crime, and had met souls bowed down with the burden of myriad sins; but never had he come in contact with a human being from whom there breathed an influence so divine. All this was in harmony with what had been revealed to John regarding the Messiah. Yet he shrank from granting the request of Jesus. How could he, a sinner, baptize the Sinless One? And why should He who needed no repentance submit to a rite that was a confession of guilt to be washed away? [110-111]

As Jesus asked for baptism, John drew back, exclaiming, "I have need to be baptized of Thee, and comest Thou to me?" With firm yet gentle authority, Jesus answered, "Suffer it to be so now: for thus it becometh us to fulfill all righteousness." And John, yielding, led the Saviour down into the Jordan, and buried Him beneath the water. "And straightway coming up out of the water," Jesus "saw the heavens opened, and the Spirit like a dove descending upon Him."

Jesus did not receive baptism as a confession of guilt on His own account. He identified Himself with sinners, taking the steps that we are to take, and doing the work that we must do. His life of suffering and patient endurance after His baptism was also an example to us.

Upon coming up out of the water, Jesus bowed in prayer on the river bank. A new and important era was opening before Him. He was now, upon a wider stage, entering on the conflict of His life. Though He was the Prince of Peace, His coming must be as the unsheathing of a sword. The kingdom He had come to establish was the opposite of that which the Jews desired. He who was the foundation of the ritual and economy of Israel would be looked upon as its enemy and destroyer. He who had proclaimed the law upon Sinai would be condemned as a transgressor. He who had come to break the power of Satan would be denounced as Beelzebub. No one upon earth had understood Him, and during His ministry He must still walk alone. Throughout His life His mother and His brothers did not comprehend His mission. Even His disciples did not understand Him. He had dwelt in eternal light, as one with God, but His life on earth must be spent in solitude.

As one with us, He must bear the burden of our guilt and woe. The Sinless One must feel the shame of sin. The peace lover must dwell with strife, the truth must abide with falsehood, purity with vileness. Every sin, every discord, every defiling lust that transgression had brought, was torture to His spirit.

Alone He must tread the path; alone He must bear the burden. Upon Him who had laid off His glory and accepted the weakness of humanity the redemption of the world must rest. He saw and felt it all, but His purpose remained steadfast. Upon His arm depended the salvation of the fallen race, and He reached out His hand to grasp the hand of Omnipotent Love.

The Saviour's glance seems to penetrate heaven as He pours out His soul in prayer. Well He knows how sin has hardened the hearts of men, [111-112] and how difficult it will be for them to discern His mission, and accept the gift of salvation. He pleads with the Father for power to overcome their unbelief, to break the fetters with which Satan has enthralled them, and in their behalf to conquer the destroyer. He asks for the witness that God accepts humanity in the person of His Son.

Never before have the angels listened to such a prayer. They are eager to bear to their loved Commander a message of assurance and comfort. But no; the Father Himself will answer the petition of His Son. Direct from the throne issue the beams of His glory. The heavens are opened, and upon the Saviour's head descends a dovelike form of purest light,--fit emblem of Him, the meek and lowly One.

Of the vast throng at the Jordan, few except John discerned the heavenly vision. Yet the solemnity of the divine Presence rested upon the assembly. The people stood silently gazing upon Christ. His form was bathed in the light that ever surrounds the throne of God. His upturned face was glorified as they had never before seen the face of man. From the open heavens a voice was heard saying, "This is My beloved Son, in whom I am well pleased."

These words of confirmation were given to inspire faith in those who witnessed the scene, and to strengthen the Saviour for His mission. Notwithstanding that the sins of a guilty world were laid upon Christ, notwithstanding the humiliation of taking upon Himself our fallen nature, the voice from heaven declared Him to be the Son of the Eternal.

expected; He would walk alone; and the burden of guilt (every sin, every discord) was t_____ to His spirit. Oh, Lord, help me not to trivialize what You went through, what sin does to You, and to me: _____

_____

_____

_____

5. "The Savior's glance seems to p_____ heaven as He pours out His soul in prayer." He pleads with the Father for power to

1) o_____ their unbelief,

2) break the fetters with which Satan has e_____ ____ them,

3) c_____ the destroyer. (111-112).

Lord, keep praying that prayer for me. Satan still has ways of enthralling me. You have the power to break Satan's power: _____

_____

6. "The F_____ Himself will answer the petition of His Son. Direct from the throne issue the beams of His g_____."
[Jesus] "was bathed in the light that e_____ surrounds throne of God... 'This is my beloved Son, in whom I am well p_____.'" (112).
Lord, You pray for my oneness with Yourself, just as You and the Father

are one (John 17). Since the Father is pleased with You, can I understand that He is also pleased with me? (see page 113)___

_____

7. Did John "discern the import of these words, "the Lamb of God?" (112). _____ Lord, do I understand? I want to dig into the science of salvation. Teach me more:

_____

_____

(their gift vs God's gift?)

_____

_____

8. "Many of them regarded the sacrificial offerings much as the heathen looked upon their sacrifices,-- as gifts by which they t_____ might propitiate the Deity. God desired to teach them that from His o_____ love comes the gift which reconciles them to Himself." (113). Jesus, You are the Lamb given by a loving Father (Jn 3:16). Help me to see the Lamb's blood as the cost, how far You were willing to go; to see Your blood as Your love (Rm 5:8). How do You want me to respond, to the announcement that You are the Lamb of God? _____

_____

John had been deeply moved as he saw Jesus bowed as a suppliant, pleading with tears for the approval of the Father. As the glory of God encircled Him, and the voice from heaven was heard, John recognized the token which God had promised. He knew that it was the world's Redeemer whom he had baptized. The Holy Spirit rested upon him, and with outstretched hand pointing to Jesus, he cried, "Behold the Lamb of God, which taketh away the sin of the world."

None among the hearers, and not even the speaker himself, discerned the import of these words, "the Lamb of God." Upon Mount Moriah, Abraham had heard the question of his son, "My father, . . . where is the lamb for a burnt offering?" The father answered, "My son, God will provide Himself a lamb for a burnt offering." Gen. 22:7, 8. And in the ram divinely provided in the place of Isaac, Abraham saw a symbol of Him who was to die for the sins of men. The Holy Spirit through Isaiah, taking up the illustration, prophesied of the Saviour, "He is [112-113] brought as a lamb to the slaughter," "and the Lord hath laid on Him the iniquity of us all" (Isa. 53:7, 6); but the people of Israel had not understood the lesson. Many of them regarded the sacrificial offerings much as the heathen looked upon their sacrifices,--as gifts by which they themselves might propitiate the Deity. God desired to teach them that from His own love comes the gift which reconciles them to Himself.

And the word that was spoken to Jesus at the Jordan, "This is My beloved Son, in whom I am well pleased," embraces humanity. God spoke to Jesus as our representative. With all our sins and weaknesses, we are not cast aside as worthless. "He hath made us accepted in the Beloved." Eph. 1:6. The glory that rested upon Christ is a pledge of the love of God for us. It tells us of the power of prayer,--how the human voice may reach the ear of God, and our petitions find acceptance in the courts of heaven. By sin, earth was cut off from heaven, and alienated from its communion; but Jesus has connected it again with the sphere of glory. His love has encircled man, and reached the highest heaven. The light which fell from the open portals upon the head of our Saviour will fall upon us as we pray for help to resist temptation. The voice which spoke to Jesus says to every believing soul, This is My beloved child, in whom I am well pleased.

"Beloved, now are we the sons of God, and it doth

not yet appear what we shall be: but we know that, when He shall appear, we shall be like Him; for we shall see Him as He is." 1 John 3:2. Our Redeemer has opened the way so that the most sinful, the most needy, the most oppressed and despised, may find access to the Father. All may have a home in the mansions which Jesus has gone to prepare. "These things saith He that is holy, He that is true, He that hath the key of David, He that openeth, and no man shutteth; and shutteth, and no man openeth; . . . behold, I have set before thee an open door, and no man can shut it." Rev. 3:7, 8.

9. "The light which fell from the open portals upon the head of our Savior will fall upon u__ as we p_____ for help to resist temptation." (113). That's money in the bank that I rarely use. Why not?

_____

_____

What a help, and blessing!

Prayer Journal:_____

_____

_____

_____

_____

_____

_____

_____

Chapter 12

The Temptation

[This chapter is based on Matt. 4:1-11;
Mark 1:12, 13; Luke 4:1-13.]

And Jesus being full of the Holy Ghost returned from Jordan, and was led by the Spirit into the wilderness." The words of Mark are still more significant. He says, "Immediately the Spirit driveth Him into the wilderness. And He was there in the wilderness forty days, tempted of Satan; and was with the wild beasts." "And in those days He did eat nothing."

When Jesus was led into the wilderness to be tempted, He was led by the Spirit of God. He did not invite temptation. He went to the wilderness to be alone, to contemplate His mission and work. By fasting and prayer He was to brace Himself for the bloodstained path He must travel. But Satan knew that the Saviour had gone into the wilderness, and he thought this the best time to approach Him.

Mighty issues for the world were at stake in the conflict between the Prince of light and the leader of the kingdom of darkness. After tempting man to sin, Satan claimed the earth as his, and styled himself the prince of this world. Having conformed to his own nature the father and mother of our race, he thought to establish here his empire. He declared that men had chosen him as their sovereign. Through his [114-115] control of men, he held dominion over the world. Christ had come to disprove Satan's claim. As the Son of man, Christ would stand loyal to God. Thus it would be shown that Satan had not gained complete control of the human race, and that his claim to the world was false. All who desired deliverance from his power would be set free. The dominion that Adam had lost through sin would be recovered.

Since the announcement to the serpent in Eden, "I will put enmity between thee and the woman, and between thy seed and her seed" (Gen. 3:15), Satan had known that he did not hold absolute sway over the world. There was seen in men the working of a power that withstood his dominion. With intense interest he

---

1. When Jesus went into the wilderness, why did He fast? (114). Along with prayer, it was to b_____ Himself for the bloodstained path He must travel. "M_____ issues for the world were at stake in the conflict between the Prince of light and the leader of the kingdom of darkness." Do I see the mighty issues? Or do I think this is kid's stuff? If Jesus fasted and prayed, what should my response be? _____

_____ How does fasting and prayer brace myself?

_____

_____

_____

_____

2. Satan intercepted the communion between earth and heaven by m_____ God and misinterpreting the sacrifices Adam and

watched the sacrifices offered by Adam and his sons. In these ceremonies he discerned a symbol of communion between earth and heaven. He set himself to intercept this communion. He misrepresented God, and misinterpreted the rites that pointed to the Saviour. Men were led to fear God as one who delighted in their destruction. The sacrifices that should have revealed His love were offered only to appease His wrath. Satan excited the evil passions of men, in order to fasten his rule upon them. When God's written word was given, Satan studied the prophecies of the Saviour's advent. From generation to generation he worked to blind the people to these prophecies, that they might reject Christ at His coming.

At the birth of Jesus, Satan knew that One had come with a divine commission to dispute his dominion. He trembled at the angel's message attesting the authority of the newborn King. Satan well knew the position that Christ had held in heaven as the Beloved of the Father. That the Son of God should come to this earth as a man filled him with amazement and with apprehension. He could not fathom the mystery of this great sacrifice. His selfish soul could not understand such love for the deceived race. The glory and peace of heaven, and the joy of communion with God, were but dimly comprehended by men; but they [115-116] were well known to Lucifer, the covering cherub. Since he had lost heaven, he was determined to find revenge by causing others to share his fall. This he would do by causing them to undervalue heavenly things, and to set the heart upon things of earth.

Not without hindrance was the Commander of heaven to win the souls of men to His kingdom. From the time when He was a babe in Bethlehem, He was continually assailed by the evil one. The image of God was manifest in Christ, and in the councils of Satan it was determined that He should be overcome. No human being had come into the world and escaped the power of the deceiver. The forces of the confederacy of evil were set upon His track to engage in warfare against Him, and if possible to prevail over Him.

At the Saviour's baptism, Satan was among the witnesses. He saw the Father's glory overshadowing His Son. He heard the voice of Jehovah testifying to the divinity of Jesus. Ever since Adam's sin, the human race had been cut off from direct communion with God; the

his sons made. "Men were led to f_____ God as one who delighted in their destruction. The sacrifices that should have revealed His l_____ were offered only to a_____ His wrath." (115). How cleverly Satan switches things: he lets me think that I am doing God's bidding, while the affect is opposite. He can appear as an angel of light, but he is a lion that devours. Lord, I need You to guide me, and guard me. Give me discernment to know I am truly in Your will: ____

_____

3. "The glory and peace of heaven, and the joy of c_____ with God, were but dimly comprehended by men... [Satan's goal is to cause me to] u_____ heavenly things, and set my heart upon the things of e_____." (115, 116). I don't want Satan to have his way. Lord, help me to differentiate between eternal and earthy things, to taste the joy of communion with You: _____

_____

_____

_____

4. "Satan had hoped that God's abhorrence of evil would bring an eternal s_____ be-tween heaven and earth. But now it was manifest that the connection between God and man had been r_____." (116). Lord, help me to hate anything that causes separation between us. May I see sin as You do:

_____

5. "Within the domain of every human h_____ this controversy [between Christ and Satan] is repeat-ed." Lord, impress upon me the daily decisions I make, the daily attitudes I have, that impact this con-troversy in my heart: _____

_____

_____

_____

6. "The enticements... were urged upon Him in as much g_____ degree as His c_____ _____ is superior to ours...Christ withstood the test upon a_____, upon the love of the w_____, and upon that love of d_____ that leads to presumption." Lord, show me how the enemy entices me in the same areas: _____

_____

_____

7. "Christ took upon Him

intercourse between heaven and earth had been through Christ; but now that Jesus had come "in the likeness of sinful flesh" (Rom. 8:3), the Father Himself spoke. He had before communicated with humanity through Christ; now He communicated with humanity in Christ. Satan had hoped that God's abhorrence of evil would bring an eternal separation between heaven and earth. But now it was manifest that the connection between God and man had been restored.

Satan saw that he must either conquer or be con-quered. The issues of the conflict involved too much to be entrusted to his confederate angels. He must person-ally conduct the warfare. All the energies of apostasy were rallied against the Son of God. Christ was made the mark of every weapon of hell.

Many look on this conflict between Christ and Sa-tan as having no special bearing on their own life; and for them it has little interest. But within the domain of every human heart this controversy is repeated. Never does one leave the ranks of evil for the service of God without encountering the assaults of Satan. The entice-ments which Christ resisted were those that we find it so difficult to withstand. They were urged upon Him in as much greater degree as His character is superior to ours. With the terrible weight of the sins of the world upon Him, Christ withstood the test upon appetite, upon the love of the world, and upon that love of display which leads to presumption. These were the [116-117] tempta-tions that overcame Adam and Eve, and that so readily overcome us.

Satan had pointed to Adam's sin as proof that God's law was unjust, and could not be obeyed. In our hu-manity, Christ was to redeem Adam's failure. But when Adam was assailed by the tempter, none of the effects of sin were upon him. He stood in the strength of perfect manhood, possessing the full vigor of mind and body. He was surrounded with the glories of Eden, and was in daily communion with heavenly beings. It was not thus with Jesus when He entered the wilderness to cope with Satan. For four thousand years the race had been decreasing in physical strength, in mental power, and in moral worth; and Christ took upon Him the infirmities of degenerate humanity. Only thus could He rescue man from the lowest depths of his degradation.

Many claim that it was impossible for Christ to be overcome by temptation. Then He could not have been placed in Adam's position; He could not have gained the victory that Adam failed to gain. If we have in any sense a more trying conflict than had Christ, then He would not be able to succor us. But our Saviour took humanity, with all its liabilities. He took the nature of man, with the possibility of yielding to temptation. We have nothing to bear which He has not endured.

With Christ, as with the holy pair in Eden, appetite was the ground of the first great temptation. Just where the ruin began, the work of our redemption must begin. As by the indulgence of appetite Adam fell, so by the denial of appetite Christ must overcome. "And when He had fasted forty days and forty nights, He was afterward an hungred. And when the tempter came to Him, he said, If Thou be the Son of God, command that these stones be made bread. But He answered and said, It is written, Man shall not live by bread alone, but by every word that proceedeth out of the mouth of God."

From the time of Adam to that of Christ, self-indulgence had increased the power of the appetites and passions, until they had almost unlimited control. Thus men had become debased and diseased, and of themselves it was impossible for them to overcome. In man's behalf, Christ conquered by enduring the severest test. For our sake He exercised a self-control stronger than hunger or death. And in this first victory were involved other issues that enter into all our conflicts with the powers of darkness. [117-118]

When Jesus entered the wilderness, He was shut in by the Father's glory. Absorbed in communion with God, He was lifted above human weakness. But the glory departed, and He was left to battle with temptation. It was pressing upon Him every moment. His human nature shrank from the conflict that awaited Him. For forty days He fasted and prayed. Weak and emaciated from hunger, worn and haggard with mental agony, "His visage was so marred more than any man, and His form more than the sons of men." Isa. 52:14. Now was Satan's opportunity. Now he supposed that he could overcome Christ.

There came to the Saviour, as if in answer to His prayers, one in the guise of an angel from heaven. He claimed to have a commission from God to declare that Christ's fast was at an end. As God had sent an angel to stay the hand of Abraham from offering Isaac, so, satisfied with Christ's willingness to enter the bloodstained

the infirmities of degenerate humanity," 4,000 years of decreasing physical strength, mental power, and m_____ worth. "Our Savior took humanity, with all its liabilities." (117). Lord, you then know my struggles, and how to uplift me. May I rely only on You and look to You for encouragement. Bring my thoughts to You, at the moment of temptation: _____

_____

_____

path, the Father had sent an angel to deliver Him; this was the message brought to Jesus. The Saviour was faint from hunger, He was craving for food, when Satan came suddenly upon Him. Pointing to the stones which strewed the desert, and which had the appearance of loaves, the tempter said, "If Thou be the Son of God, command that these stones be made bread."

Though he appears as an angel of light, these first words betray his character. "If Thou be the Son of God." Here is the insinuation of distrust. Should Jesus do what Satan suggests, it would be an acceptance of the doubt. The tempter plans to overthrow Christ by the same means that were so successful with the human race in the beginning. How artfully had Satan approached Eve in Eden! "Yea, hath God said, Ye shall not eat of every tree of the garden?" Gen 3:1. Thus far the tempter's words were truth; but in his manner of speaking them there was a disguised contempt for the words of God. There was a covert negative, a doubt of the divine truthfulness. Satan sought to instill into the mind of Eve the thought that God would not do as He had said; that the withholding of such beautiful fruit was a contradiction of His love and compassion for man. So now the tempter seeks to inspire Christ with his own sentiments. "If Thou be the Son of God." The words rankle with bitterness in his mind. In the tones of his voice is an expression of utter incredulity. Would God treat His own Son thus? Would He leave Him in the desert with wild beasts, without food, without companions, without comfort? He insinuates that God never meant His Son to be in such a state as this. "If Thou be the Son of God," show Thy power by [118-119] relieving Thyself of this pressing hunger. Command that this stone be made bread.

The words from heaven, "This is My beloved Son, in whom I am well pleased" (Matt. 3:17), were still sounding in the ears of Satan. But he was determined to make Christ disbelieve this testimony. The word of God was Christ's assurance of His divine mission. He had come to live as a man among men, and it was the word that declared His connection with heaven. It was Satan's purpose to cause Him to doubt that word. If Christ's confidence in God could be shaken, Satan knew that the victory in the whole controversy would be his. He could overcome Jesus. He hoped that under the force of despondency and extreme hunger, Christ

8. "'If thou be the Son of God.'" Here is the insinuation of d_____."
Satan approached Eve in the same artful way, with disguised c_____ for the words of God, and a d_____ of the divine truthfulness ("Yea, hath God said?"). He suggested that God's "withholding of such beautiful fruit was a c_____ of His love and compassion for man." (118). Satan approaches me with the same doubt about You, Lord, Your character and purposes. Lord, help me to see through it all. Help me to have confidence that Your will is best for me: _____

_____

_____

_____

9. "This is My beloved Son, in whom I am well pleased." Satan was "determined to make Christ d_____ this testimony... If Christ's

would lose faith in His Father, and work a miracle in His own behalf. Had He done this, the plan of salvation would have been broken.

When Satan and the Son of God first met in conflict, Christ was the commander of the heavenly hosts; and Satan, the leader of revolt in heaven, was cast out. Now their condition is apparently reversed, and Satan makes the most of his supposed advantage. One of the most powerful of the angels, he says, has been banished from heaven. The appearance of Jesus indicates that He is that fallen angel, forsaken by God, and deserted by man. A divine being would be able to sustain his claim by working a miracle; "if Thou be the Son of God, command this stone that it be made bread." Such an act of creative power, urges the tempter, would be conclusive evidence of divinity. It would bring the controversy to an end.

Not without a struggle could Jesus listen in silence to the arch-deceiver. But the Son of God was not to prove His divinity to Satan, or to explain the reason of His humiliation. By conceding to the demands of the rebel, nothing for the good of man or the glory of God would be gained. Had Christ complied with the suggestion of the enemy, Satan would still have said, Show me a sign that I may believe you to be the Son of God. Evidence would have been worthless to break the power of rebellion in his heart. And Christ was not to exercise divine power for His own benefit. He had come to bear trial as we must do, leaving us an example of faith and submission. Neither here nor at any subsequent time in His earthly life did He work a miracle in His own behalf. His wonderful works were all for the good of others. Though Jesus recognized Satan from the beginning, He was not provoked to enter into controversy with him. Strengthened with the memory of the voice [119-120] from heaven, He rested in His Father's love. He would not parley with temptation.

Jesus met Satan with the words of Scripture. "It is written," He said. In every temptation the weapon of His warfare was the word of God. Satan demanded of Christ a miracle as a sign of His divinity. But that which is greater than all miracles, a firm reliance upon a "Thus saith the Lord," was a sign that could not be controverted. So long as Christ held to this position, the tempter could gain no advantage.

It was in the time of greatest weakness that Christ

c_____ in God could be shaken, Satan knew that the victory in the whole controversy would be his." (119). He suggests that from the appearance, Jesus is the fallen angel, banished from heaven, forsaken by God, and deserted by man. How does Satan also try to shake my relationship with You, my confidence in You, Lord? _____
_____
_____
_____
_____

10. Using power to turn stones into bread would actually be a lack of confidence in God, to doubt God. No, Christ would leave us an "example of f_____ and submission." Lord, inspire me with Your example. May my confidence in You grow through practice: _____
_____
_____
_____

was assailed by the fiercest temptations. Thus Satan thought to prevail. By this policy he had gained the victory over men. When strength failed, and the will power weakened, and faith ceased to repose in God, then those who had stood long and valiantly for the right were overcome. Moses was wearied with the forty years' wandering of Israel, when for the moment his faith let go its hold upon infinite power. He failed just upon the borders of the Promised Land. So with Elijah, who had stood undaunted before King Ahab, who had faced the whole nation of Israel, with the four hundred and fifty prophets of Baal at their head. After that terrible day upon Carmel, when the false prophets had been slain, and the people had declared their allegiance to God, Elijah fled for his life before the threats of the idolatrous Jezebel. Thus Satan has taken advantage of the weakness of humanity. And he will still work in the same way. Whenever one is encompassed with clouds, perplexed by circumstances, or afflicted by poverty or distress, Satan is at hand to tempt and annoy. He attacks our weak points of character. He seeks to shake our confidence in God, who suffers such a condition of things to exist. We are tempted to distrust God, to question His love. Often the tempter comes to us as he came to Christ, arraying before us our [120-121] weakness and infirmities. He hopes to discourage the soul, and to break our hold on God. Then he is sure of his prey. If we would meet him as Jesus did, we should escape many a defeat. By parleying with the enemy, we give him an advantage.

When Christ said to the tempter, "Man shall not live by bread alone, but by every word that proceedeth out of the mouth of God," He repeated the words that, more than fourteen hundred years before, He had spoken to Israel: "The Lord thy God led thee these forty years in the wilderness. . . . And He humbled thee, and suffered thee to hunger, and fed thee with manna, which thou knewest not, neither did thy fathers know; that He might make thee know that man doth not live by bread only, but by every word that proceedeth out of the mouth of the Lord doth man live." Deut. 8:2, 3. In the wilderness, when all means of sustenance failed, God sent His people manna from heaven; and a sufficient and constant supply was given. This provision was to teach them that while they trusted in God and walked in His ways He would not forsake them. The Saviour now practiced the

11. Satan "attacks our w_____ points of character. He seeks to shake our confidence in God... We are tempted to distrust God, to question His l_____...[Satan] hopes to d_____ the soul, and to break our h_____ on God." (120, 121). Lord, I don't want Satan to have any success on me. I don't want to lose my hold on You. Keep me focused, not on him, but on You:

_____

_____

_____

_____

lesson He had taught to Israel. By the word of God succor had been given to the Hebrew host, and by the same word it would be given to Jesus. He awaited God's time to bring relief. He was in the wilderness in obedience to God, and He would not obtain food by following the suggestions of Satan. In the presence of the witnessing universe, He testified that it is a less calamity to suffer whatever may befall than to depart in any manner from the will of God.

"Man shall not live by bread alone, but by every word of God." Often the follower of Christ is brought where he cannot serve God and carry forward his worldly enterprises. Perhaps it appears that obedience to some plain requirement of God will cut off his means of support. Satan would make him believe that he must sacrifice his conscientious convictions. But the only thing in our world upon which we can rely is the word of God. "Seek ye first the kingdom of God, and His righteousness; and all these things shall be added unto you." Matt. 6:33. Even in this life it is not for our good to depart from the will of our Father in heaven. When we learn the power of His word, we shall not follow the suggestions of Satan in order to obtain food or to save our lives. Our only questions will be, What is God's command? and what His promise? Knowing these, we shall obey the one, and trust the other.

In the last great conflict of the controversy with Satan those who are loyal to God will see every earthly support cut off. Because they refuse [121-122] to break His law in obedience to earthly powers, they will be forbidden to buy or sell. It will finally be decreed that they shall be put to death. See Rev. 13:11-17. But to the obedient is given the promise, "He shall dwell on high: his place of defense shall be the munitions of rocks: bread shall be given him; his waters shall be sure." Isa. 33:16. By this promise the children of God will live. When the earth shall be wasted with famine, they shall be fed. "They shall not be ashamed in the evil time: and in the days of famine they shall be satisfied." Ps. 37:19. To that time of distress the prophet Habakkuk looked forward, and his words express the faith of the church: "Although the fig tree shall not blossom, neither shall fruit be in the vines; the labor of the olive shall fail, and the fields shall yield no meat; the flock shall be cut off from the fold, and there shall be no herd in the stalls: yet I will rejoice in the Lord, I will joy in the God of my salvation." Hab. 3:17,18.

Of all the lessons to be learned from our Lord's first great temptation none is more important than that bearing upon the control of the appetites and passions. In all ages, temptations appealing to the physical nature have been most effectual in corrupting and degrading mankind. Through intemperance, Satan works to destroy the mental and moral powers that God gave to man as a priceless endowment. Thus it becomes impossible for men to appreciate things of eternal worth. Through sensual indulgence, Satan seeks to blot from the soul every trace of likeness to God.

The uncontrolled indulgence and consequent disease and degradation that existed at Christ's first advent will again exist, with intensity of evil, before His second coming. Christ declares that the condition of the world will be as in the days before the Flood, and as in Sodom and Gomorrah. Every imagination of the thoughts of the heart will be evil continually. Upon the very verge of that fearful time we are now living, and to us should come home the lesson of the Saviour's fast. Only by the inexpressible anguish which Christ endured can we estimate the evil of unrestrained indulgence. His example declares that our only hope of eternal life is through bringing the appetites and passions into subjection to the will of God.

In our own strength it is impossible for us to deny the clamors of our fallen nature. Through this channel Satan will bring temptation upon us. Christ knew that the enemy would come to every human being, to take advantage of hereditary weakness, and by his false insinuations to ensnare all whose trust is not in God. And by passing over the ground which [122-123] man must travel, our Lord has prepared the way for us to overcome. It is not His will that we should be placed at a disadvantage in the conflict with Satan. He would not have us intimidated and discouraged by the assaults of the serpent. "Be of good cheer," He says; "I have overcome the world." John 16:33.

Let him who is struggling against the power of appetite look to the Saviour in the wilderness of temptation. See Him in His agony upon the cross, as He exclaimed, "I thirst." He has endured all that it is possible for us to bear. His victory is ours.

Jesus rested upon the wisdom and strength of His heavenly Father. He declares, "The Lord God will help

---

12. "Through intemperance, Satan works to destroy the mental and m_____ powers that God gave to man as a priceless endowment. Thus it becomes impossible for men to appreciate things of e_____ worth. Through sensual i_____, Satan seeks to blot from the soul every trace of l_____ to God." (122). Lord, guide me in not becoming self-righteous through diet and temperance, but to value how it enhances my walk with You, my awareness of our friendship: _____
_____
_____
_____
_____

13. "His victory is o_____ ...He came to make us partakers of the divine nature. So long as we are

Me; therefore shall I not be confounded: . . . and I know that I shall not be ashamed. . . . Behold, the Lord God will help Me." Pointing to His own example, He says to us, "Who is among you that feareth the Lord, . . . that walketh in darkness, and hath no light? let him trust in the name of the Lord, and stay upon his God." Isa. 50:7-10.

"The prince of this world cometh," said Jesus, "and hath nothing in Me." John 14:30. There was in Him nothing that responded to Satan's sophistry. He did not consent to sin. Not even by a thought did He yield to temptation. So it may be with us. Christ's humanity was united with divinity; He was fitted for the conflict by the indwelling of the Holy Spirit. And He came to make us partakers of the divine nature. So long as we are united to Him by faith, sin has no more dominion over us. God reaches for the hand of faith in us to direct it to lay fast hold upon the divinity of Christ, that we may attain to perfection of character.

And how this is accomplished, Christ has shown us. By what means did He overcome in the conflict with Satan? By the word of God. Only by the word could He resist temptation. "It is written," He said. And unto us are given "exceeding great and precious promises: that by these ye might be partakers of the divine nature, having escaped the corruption that is in the world through lust." 2 Peter 1:4. Every promise in God's word is ours. "By every word that proceedeth out of the mouth of God" are we to live. When assailed by temptation, look not to circumstances or to the weakness of self, but to the power of the word. All its strength is yours. "Thy word," says the psalmist, "have I hid in mine heart, that I might not sin against Thee." "By the word of Thy lips I have kept me from the paths of the destroyer." Ps. 119:11; 17:4.

u_____ to Him by f_____, sin has no more dominion over us. God reaches for the hand of faith in us to direct it to lay f_____ hold upon the divinity of Christ, that we may attain to perfection of character." (123). How? By the Word. "Every promise in God's Word is o_____." Oh Lord, to experience that union with You, that sin would have no more dominion over me, that is what I want! Help me today, to practice faith in Your Word, Your promises: _____

_____

_____

Prayer Journal: _____

_____

_____

_____

_____

_____

_____

_____

Chapter 13

The Victory

[This chapter is based on Matt. 4:5-11;
Mark 1:12, 13; Luke 4:5-13.]

Then the devil taketh Him up into the holy city, and setteth Him on a pinnacle of the temple, and saith unto Him, If Thou be the Son of God, cast Thyself down: for it is written,-- countenance his deception. He claims

> "He shall give His angels charge concerning Thee: And in their hands they shall bear Thee up, Lest at any time Thou dash Thy foot against a stone."

1. With the first temptation, Satan "claims that he has been only t_____ the fidelity of Jesus, and now he c_____ His steadfastness. As the Savior has manifested t_____ in God, Satan urges Him to give still another evidence of his faith." (124). I have to be careful with flattery, don't I, Lord? Satan will use any trick, including praising my religious disciplines. Am I susceptible to this? _____

_____

_____

Satan now supposes that he has met Jesus on His own ground. The wily foe himself presents words that proceeded from the mouth of God. He still appears as an angel of light, and he makes it evident that he is acquainted with the Scriptures, and understands the import of what is written. As Jesus before used the word of God to sustain His faith, the tempter now uses it to countence his deception. He claims that he has been only testing the fidelity of Jesus, and he now commends His steadfastness. As the Saviour has manifested trust in God, Satan urges Him to give still another evidence of His faith.

But again the temptation is prefaced with the insinuation of distrust, "If Thou be the Son of God." Christ was tempted to answer the "if;" but He refrained from the slightest acceptance of the doubt. He would not imperil His life in order to give evidence to Satan. [124-125]

2. "While Satan can solicit, he cannot c_____ to sin...The w_____ must consent, faith must let g____ its hold upon Christ,

The tempter thought to take advantage of Christ's humanity, and urge Him to presumption. But while Satan can solicit, he cannot compel to sin. He said to Jesus, "Cast Thyself down," knowing that he could not cast Him down; for God would interpose to deliver Him. Nor could Satan force Jesus to cast Himself down. Unless Christ should consent to temptation, He could not be overcome. Not all the power of earth or hell could force Him in the slightest degree to depart from the will of His Father.

The tempter can never compel us to do evil. He cannot control minds unless they are yielded to his control. The will must consent, faith must let go its hold upon Christ, before Satan can exercise his power upon us. But every sinful desire we cherish affords him a foothold. Every point in which we fail of meeting the divine standard is an open door by which he can enter to tempt and destroy us. And every failure or defeat on our part gives occasion for him to reproach Christ.

When Satan quoted the promise, "He shall give His angels charge over Thee," he omitted the words, "to keep Thee in all Thy ways;" that is, in all the ways of God's choosing. Jesus refused to go outside the path of obedience. While manifesting perfect trust in His Father, He would not place Himself, unbidden, in a position that would necessitate the interposition of His Father to save Him from death. He would not force Providence to come to His rescue, and thus fail of giving man an example of trust and submission.

Jesus declared to Satan, "It is written again, Thou shalt not tempt the Lord thy God." These words were spoken by Moses to the children of Israel when they thirsted in the desert, and demanded that Moses should give them water, exclaiming, "Is the Lord among [125-126] us, or not?" Exodus 17:7. God had wrought marcountence his deception. He claims that he has been only testing the fidelity of Jesus, and he now commends His steadfastness. As the Saviour has manifested trust in God, Satan urges Him to give still another evidence of His faith.

But again the temptation is prefaced with the insinuation of distrust, "If Thou be the Son of God." Christ was tempted to answer the "if;" but He refrained from the slightest acceptance of the doubt. He would not imperil His life in order to give evidence to Satan. [124-125]

The tempter thought to take advantage of Christ's humanity, and urge Him to presumption. But while Satan can solicit, he cannot compel to sin. He said to Jesus, "Cast Thyself down," knowing that he could not cast Him down; for God would interpose to deliver Him. Nor could Satan force Jesus to cast Himself down. Unless Christ should consent to temptation, He could not

before Satan can exercise his power upon us. But every sinful desire we cherish affords Satan a f_____ … Every failure or defeat on our part gives occasion for him to reproach Christ." (125). Satan is NOT that powerful! So why do I let him reproach Christ? _____

_____

_____

_____

be overcome. Not all the power of earth or hell could force Him in the slightest degree to depart from the will of His Father.

The tempter can never compel us to do evil. He cannot control minds unless they are yielded to his control. The will must consent, faith must let go its hold upon Christ, before Satan can exercise his power upon us. But every sinful desire we cherish affords him a foothold. Every point in which we fail of meeting the divine standard is an open door by which he can enter to tempt and destroy us. And every failure or defeat on our part gives occasion for him to reproach Christ.

When Satan quoted the promise, "He shall give His angels charge over Thee," he omitted the words, "to keep Thee in all Thy ways;" that is, in all the ways of God's choosing. Jesus refused to go outside the path of obedience. While manifesting perfect trust in His Father, He would not place Himself, unbidden, in a position that would necessitate the interposition of His Father to save Him from death. He would not force Providence to come to His rescue, and thus fail of giving man an example of trust and submission.

Jesus declared to Satan, "It is written again, Thou shalt not tempt the Lord thy God." These words were spoken by Moses to the children of Israel when they thirsted in the desert, and demanded that Moses should give them water, exclaiming, "Is the Lord among [125-126] us, or not?" Exodus 17:7. God had wrought marvelously for them; yet in trouble they doubted Him, and demanded evidence that He was with them. In their unbelief they sought to put Him to the test. And Satan was urging Christ to do the same thing. God had already testified that Jesus was His Son; and now to ask for proof that He was the Son of God would be putting God's word to the test,--tempting Him. And the same would be true of asking for that which God had not promised. It would manifest distrust, and be really proving, or tempting, Him. We should not present our petitions to God to prove whether He will fulfill His word, but because He will fulfill it; not to prove that He loves us, but because He loves us. "Without faith it is impossible to please Him: for he that cometh to God must believe that He is, and that He is a rewarder of them that diligently seek Him." Heb. 11:6.

But faith is in no sense allied to presumption. Only he who has true faith is secure against presumption. For presumption is Satan's counterfeit of faith. Faith claims God's promises, and brings forth fruit in obedience. Presumption also claims the promises, but uses them as Satan did, to excuse transgression. Faith would have led our first parents to trust the love of God, and to obey His commands. Presumption led them to transgress His law, believing that His great love would save them from the consequence of their sin. It is not faith that claims the favor of Heaven without complying with the conditions on which mercy is to be granted. Genuine faith has its foundation in the promises and provisions of the Scriptures.

Often when Satan has failed of exciting distrust, he succeeds in leading us to presumption. If he can cause us to place ourselves unnecessarily in the way of temptation, he knows that the victory is his. God will preserve all who walk in the path of obedience; but to depart from it is to venture on Satan's ground. There we are sure to fall. The Saviour has bidden us, "Watch ye and pray, lest ye enter into temptation." Mark 14:38. Meditation and prayer would keep us from rushing unbidden into the way of danger, and thus we should be saved from many a defeat.

Yet we should not lose courage when assailed by temptation. Often when placed in a trying situation we doubt that the Spirit of God has been leading us. But it was the Spirit's leading that brought Jesus into the wilderness to be tempted by Satan. When God brings us into trial, He has a purpose to accomplish for our good. Jesus did not presume on God's promises by going unbidden into temptation, neither did He give [126-129] up to despondency when temptation came upon Him. Nor should we. "God is faithful, who will not suffer you to be tempted above that ye are able; but will with the temptation also make a way to escape, that ye may be able to bear it." He says, "Offer unto God thanksgiving; and pay thy vows unto the Most High: and call upon Me in the day of trouble: I will deliver thee, and thou shalt glorify Me." 1 Cor. 10:13; Ps. 50:14, 15.

Jesus was victor in the second temptation, and now Satan manifests himself in his true character. But he does not appear as a hideous monster, with cloven feet and bat's wings. He is a mighty angel, though fallen. He avows himself the leader of rebellion and the god of this world.

Placing Jesus upon a high mountain, Satan caused

3. "P_____ is Satan's counterfeit of faith... Faith would have led our first parents to t_____ the love of God, and to o_____ His commands. Presumption led them to transgress His law, believing that His great l_____ would save them from the consequence of their sin." (126). Is it not presumption to think that the effects of a little sin have minimal consequence, that they won't hurt me? _____

_____

_____

Lord, what does it mean to trust Your love? _____

_____

_____

_____

_____

4. "Genuine faith has its foundation in the p_____ and p_____ of the Scriptures." Lord, You had that faith, in the face of temptation. My faith, and my walk, should also be grounded in Your Word, daily relying on its provisions. Lord, what can I do to make that happen, moment by moment?

_____

_____

_____

5. Since we should not "place ourselves u_____ _____ in the way of temptation," why does God sometimes bring us "into trial"? (126). _____ _____ _____ (He has a purpose to accomplish for our good?)

6. What is the promise of 1 Cor 10:13? _____ _____ God, You know me, how much I can endure with Your help. Remind me of this promise at the moment of temptation: _____ _____ _____ _____

7. The third temptation: Christ might deliver Himself from the dreadful future (life of sorrow, hardship, conflict, ignominious death, sins of the world, s_____ from the Father's love), and instead receive from Satan all the glory and power of the world, all that, for merely acknowledging the s_____ of Satan. Wasn't this an easier way to gain the world back? "But to do this was to yield the v_____ in the great controversy." (129). How do I at times acknowledge Satan's supremacy? _____ _____

the kingdoms of the world, in all their glory, to pass in panoramic view before Him. The sunlight lay on templed cities, marble palaces, fertile fields, and fruit-laden vineyards. The traces of evil were hidden. The eyes of Jesus, so lately greeted by gloom and desolation, now gazed upon a scene of unsurpassed loveliness and prosperity. Then the tempter's voice was heard: "All this power will I give Thee, and the glory of them: for that is delivered unto me; and to whomsoever I will I give it. If Thou therefore wilt worship me, all shall be Thine."

Christ's mission could be fulfilled only through suffering. Before Him was a life of sorrow, hardship, and conflict, and an ignominious death. He must bear the sins of the whole world. He must endure separation from His Father's love. Now the tempter offered to yield up the power he had usurped. Christ might deliver Himself from the dreadful future by acknowledging the supremacy of Satan. But to do this was to yield the victory in the great controversy. It was in seeking to exalt himself above the Son of God that Satan had sinned in heaven. Should he prevail now, it would be the triumph of rebellion.

When Satan declared to Christ, The kingdom and glory of the world are delivered unto me, and to whomsoever I will I give it, he stated what was true only in part, and he declared it to serve his own purpose of deception. Satan's dominion was that wrested from Adam, but Adam was the vicegerent of the Creator. His was not an independent rule. The earth is God's, and He has committed all things to His Son. Adam was to reign subject to Christ. When Adam betrayed his sovereignty into Satan's hands, Christ still remained the rightful King. Thus the Lord had said to King Nebuchadnezzar, "The Most High ruleth in the [129-130] kingdom of men, and giveth it to whomsoever He will." Dan. 4:17. Satan can exercise his usurped authority only as God permits.

When the tempter offered to Christ the kingdom and glory of the world, he was proposing that Christ should yield up the real kingship of the world, and hold dominion subject to Satan. This was the same dominion upon which the hopes of the Jews were set. They desired the kingdom of this world. If Christ had consented to offer them such a kingdom, they would gladly have received Him. But the curse of sin, with all its woe, rested upon it. Christ declared to the tempter, "Get thee behind Me,

Satan: for it is written, Thou shalt worship the Lord thy God, and Him only shalt thou serve."

By the one who had revolted in heaven the kingdoms of this world were offered Christ, to buy His homage to the principles of evil; but He would not be bought; He had come to establish a kingdom of righteousness, and He would not abandon His purpose. With the same temptation Satan approaches men, and here he has better success than with Christ. To men he offers the kingdom of this world on condition that they will acknowledge his supremacy. He requires that they sacrifice integrity, disregard conscience, indulge selfishness. Christ bids them seek first the kingdom of God, and His righteousness; but Satan walks by their side and says: Whatever may be true in regard to life eternal, in order to make a success in this world you must serve me. I hold your welfare in my hands. I can give you riches, pleasures, honor, and happiness. Hearken to my counsel. Do not allow yourselves to be carried away with whimsical notions of honesty or self-sacrifice. I will prepare the way before you. Thus multitudes are deceived. They consent to live for the service of self, and Satan is satisfied. While he allures them with the hope of worldly dominion, he gains dominion over the soul. But he offers that which is not his to bestow, and which is soon to be wrested from him. In return he beguiles them of their title to the inheritance of the sons of God.

Satan had questioned whether Jesus was the Son of God. In his summary dismissal he had proof that he could not gainsay. Divinity flashed through suffering humanity. Satan had no power to resist the command. Writhing with humiliation and rage, he was forced to withdraw from the presence of the world's Redeemer. Christ's victory was as complete as had been the failure of Adam.

So we may resist temptation, and force Satan to depart from us. Jesus gained the victory through submission and faith in God, and by [130-131] the apostle He says to us, "Submit yourselves therefore to God. Resist the devil, and he will flee from you. Draw nigh to God, and He will draw nigh to you." James 4:7, 8. We cannot save ourselves from the tempter's power; he has conquered humanity, and when we try to stand in our own strength, we shall become a prey to his devices; but "the name of the Lord is a strong tower: the righteous run-

Whenever I "sacrifice i_____, disregard c_____ indulges _____.(130).

8. "We may resist temptation, and force Satan to d_____ f_____ us." (130). How? In the same way that Jesus did. He "gained the victory through s_____ and f_____ in God."

9. What can I do in my life, to help resist the devil? s_____, d_____ nigh, call on the mighty name of 'Jesus.' (131).

10. "N_____ can the c_____ of our redemption be realized until the redeemed shall stand with the Redeemer before the throne of God." Then is when they realize that (1) Jesus left all these glories of heaven, so He could redeem, (2) Jesus took the risk of failure and eternal l____. What a Savior! I want to be there to thank You face to face, Lord! I want to show my appreciation now, by a life of devotion and love?_____
_____
_____

Prayer Journal: _____
_____
_____
_____
_____
_____
_____
_____

neth into it, and is safe." Prov. 18:10. Satan trembles and flees before the weakest soul who finds refuge in that mighty name.

After the foe had departed, Jesus fell exhausted to the earth, with the pallor of death upon His face. The angels of heaven had watched the conflict, beholding their loved Commander as He passed through inexpressible suffering to make a way of escape for us. He had endured the test, greater than we shall ever be called to endure. The angels now ministered to the Son of God as He lay like one dying. He was strengthened with food, comforted with the message of His Father's love and the assurance that all heaven triumphed in His victory. Warming to life again, His great heart goes out in sympathy for man, and He goes forth to complete the work He has begun; to rest not until the foe is vanquished, and our fallen race redeemed.

Never can the cost of our redemption be realized until the redeemed shall stand with the Redeemer before the throne of God. Then as the glories of the eternal home burst upon our enraptured senses we shall remember that Jesus left all this for us, that He not only became an exile from the heavenly courts, but for us took the risk of failure and eternal loss. Then we shall cast our crowns at His feet, and raise the song, "Worthy is the Lamb that was slain to receive power, and riches, and wisdom, and strength, and honor, and glory, and blessing." Rev. 5:12.

Chapter 14

"We Have Found the Messias"

[This chapter is based on John 1:19-51.]

John the Baptist was now preaching and baptizing at Bethabara, beyond Jordan. It was not far from this spot that God had stayed the river in its flow until Israel had passed over. A little distance from here the stronghold of Jericho had been overthrown by the armies of heaven. The memory of these events was at this time revived, and gave a thrilling interest to the Baptist's message. Would not He who had wrought so wonderfully in ages past again manifest His power for Israel's deliverance? Such was the thought stirring the hearts of the people who daily thronged the banks of the Jordan.

The preaching of John had taken so deep a hold on the nation as to demand the attention of the religious authorities. The danger of insurrection caused every popular gathering to be looked upon with suspicion by the Romans, and whatever pointed toward an uprising of the people excited the fears of the Jewish rulers. John had not recognized the authority of the Sanhedrin by seeking their sanction for his work; and [132-133] he had reproved rulers and people, Pharisees and Sadducees alike. Yet the people followed him eagerly. The interest in his work seemed to be continually increasing. Though he had not deferred to them, the Sanhedrin accounted that, as a public teacher, he was under their jurisdiction.

This body was made up of members chosen from the priesthood, and from the chief rulers and teachers of the nation. The high priest was usually the president. All its members were to be men advanced in years, though not aged; men of learning, not only versed in Jewish religion and history, but in general knowledge. They were to be without physical blemish, and must be married men, and fathers, as being more likely than others to be humane and considerate. Their place of meeting was an apartment connected with the temple at Jerusalem. In the days of Jewish independence the Sanhedrin was the supreme court of the nation, possessing secular as well as ecclesiastical authority. Though now subordinated by the Roman governors, it still exercised a strong influ-

1. "Though now subordinated by the Roman governors, it [the Sanhedrin] still exercised a strong

influence in c_____ as well as r_____ matters...[John the Baptist's] preaching was a direct a_____ of the Messiah...Such was the popular enthusiasm that the Sanhedrin would soon be forced either to sanction or r_____ John's work. Already their power over the people was waning. It was becoming a serious question how to maintain their p_____." (133). That kind of concern can only get in the way of a spiritual walk, the Spirit having a difficult time getting through. Lord, how is the same Sanhedrin's ambition manifested in me, at home, at work? _____

_____

_____

_____

_____

2. "It was long since Israel had had a prophet, long since such a r_____ _____ as was now in progress had been witnessed. The demand for confession of sin seemed new and s_____." How long has it been for me? Is confession novel? How long has it been, since I talked with You, Lord, from the heart? _____

_____

_____

ence in civil as well as religious matters.

The Sanhedrin could not well defer an investigation of John's work. There were some who recalled the revelation made to Zacharias in the temple, and the father's prophecy, that had pointed to his child as the Messiah's herald. In the tumults and changes of thirty years, these things had in a great measure been lost sight of. They were now called to mind by the excitement concerning the ministry of John.

It was long since Israel had had a prophet, long since such a reformation as was now in progress had been witnessed. The demand for confession of sin seemed new and startling. Many among the leaders would not go to hear John's appeals and denunciations, lest they should be led to disclose the secrets of their own lives. Yet his preaching was a direct announcement of the Messiah. It was well known that the seventy weeks of Daniel's prophecy, covering the Messiah's advent, were nearly ended; and all were eager to share in that era of national glory which was then expected. Such was the popular enthusiasm that the Sanhedrin would soon be forced either to sanction or to reject John's work. Already their power over the people was waning. It was becoming a serious question how to maintain their position. In the hope of arriving at some conclusion, they dispatched to the Jordan a deputation of priests and Levites to confer with the new teacher.

A multitude were gathered, listening to his words, when the delegates approached. With an air of authority designed to impress the people [133-134] and to command the deference of the prophet the haughty rabbis came. With a movement of respect, almost of fear, the crowd opened to let them pass. The great men, in their rich robes, in the pride of rank and power, stood before the prophet of the wilderness.

"Who art thou?" they demanded.

Knowing what was in their thoughts, John answered, "I am not the Christ."

"What then? Art thou Elias?"

"I am not."

"Art thou that prophet?"

"No."

"Who art thou? that we may give an answer to them that sent us. What sayest thou of thyself?"

"I am the voice of one crying in the wilderness, Make straight the way of the Lord, as said the prophet

Esaias."

The scripture to which John referred is that beautiful prophecy of Isaiah: "Comfort ye, comfort ye My people, saith your God. Speak [134-135] ye comfortably to Jerusalem, and cry unto her, that her appointed time is accomplished, that her iniquity is pardoned. . . . The voice of him that crieth in the wilderness, Prepare ye the way of the Lord, make straight in the desert a highway for our God. Every valley shall be exalted, and every mountain and hill shall be made low: and the crooked shall be made straight, and the rough places plain: and the glory of the Lord shall be revealed, and all flesh shall see it together." Isa. 40:1-5, margin.

Anciently, when a king journeyed through the less frequented parts of his dominion, a company of men was sent ahead of the royal chariot to level the steep places and to fill up the hollows, that the king might travel in safety and without hindrance. This custom is employed by the prophet to illustrate the work of the gospel. "Every valley shall be exalted, and every mountain and hill shall be made low." When the Spirit of God, with its marvelous awakening power, touches the soul, it abases human pride. Worldly pleasure and position and power are seen to be worthless. "Imaginations, and every high thing that exalteth itself against the knowledge of God" are cast down; every thought is brought into captivity "to the obedience of Christ." 2 Cor. 10:5. Then humility and self-sacrificing love, so little valued among men, are exalted as alone of worth. This is the work of the gospel, of which John's message was a part.

The rabbis continued their questioning: "Why baptizest thou then, if thou be not that Christ, nor Elias, neither that prophet?" The words "that prophet" had reference to Moses. The Jews had been inclined to the belief that Moses would be raised from the dead, and taken to heaven. They did not know that he had already been raised. When the Baptist began his ministry, many thought that he might be the prophet Moses risen from the dead, for he seemed to have a thorough knowledge of the prophecies and of the history of Israel.

It was believed also that before the Messiah's advent, Elijah would personally appear. This expectation John met in his denial; but his words had a deeper meaning. Jesus afterward said, referring to John, "If ye are willing to receive it, this is Elijah, which is to come." Matt. 11:14, R. V. John came in the spirit and power

3. 'Prepare the way of the Lord,' John quoted from Isaiah, is the work of the gospel. 'Hills shall be made low' refers to the Holy Spirit teaching us that human p_____, worldly pleasure, position, and power are w_____. "Humility and self-sacrificing l_____, so little valued among men, are exalted as alone of w_____." (135). Lord, may Your Spirit teach me. My heart is not humble like it should be. Let me die to self. Prepare the way of the Lord, of my walk with You; make my mountains low: _____

_____

_____

of Elijah, to do such a work as Elijah did. If the Jews had received him, it would have been accomplished for them. But they did not receive his message. To them he was not Elijah. He could not fulfill for them the mission he came to accomplish. [135-136]

Many of those gathered at the Jordan had been present at the baptism of Jesus; but the sign then given had been manifest to but few among them. During the preceding months of the Baptist's ministry, many had refused to heed the call to repentance. Thus they had hardened their hearts and darkened their understanding. When Heaven bore testimony to Jesus at His baptism, they perceived it not. Eyes that had never been turned in faith to Him that is invisible beheld not the revelation of the glory of God; ears that had never listened to His voice heard not the words of witness. So it is now. Often the presence of Christ and the ministering angels is manifest in the assemblies of the people, and yet there are many who know it not. They discern nothing unusual. But to some the Saviour's presence is revealed. Peace and joy animate their hearts. They are comforted, encouraged, and blessed.

The deputies from Jerusalem had demanded of John, "Why baptizest thou?" and they were awaiting his answer. Suddenly, as his glance swept over the throng, his eye kindled, his face was lighted up, his whole being was stirred with deep emotion. With outstretched hands he cried, "I baptize in water: in the midst of you standeth One whom ye know not, even He that cometh after me, the latchet of whose shoe I am not worthy to unloose." John 1:27, R. V., margin.

The message was distinct and unequivocal, to be carried back to the Sanhedrin. The words of John could apply to no other than the long-promised One. The Messiah was among them! In amazement priests and rulers gazed about them, hoping to discover Him of whom John had spoken. But He was not distinguishable among the throng.

When at the baptism of Jesus, John pointed to Him as the Lamb of God, a new light was shed upon the Messiah's work. The prophet's mind was directed to the words of Isaiah, "He is brought as a lamb to the slaughter." Isa. 53:7. During the weeks that followed, John with new interest studied the prophecies and the teaching of the sacrificial service. He did not distinguish clearly the two phases of Christ's work,--as a suffering

4. When Heaven bore testimony to Jesus at His baptism, why did most of those gathered at the Jordan not perceive it? _____

"So it is now. Often the presence of Christ and the ministering angels is manifest in the assemblies of the people, and yet there are many who k_____ it n_____." (136). That is disturbing to me, Lord. I could be at a prayer meeting, the Holy Spirit being poured out around me, and I not know it, missing out on the gift completely! Lord, help me to NEVER delay in response to Your Spirit: _____

sacrifice and a conquering king,--but he saw that His [136-137] coming had a deeper significance than priests or people had discerned. When he beheld Jesus among the throng on His return from the desert, he confidently looked for Him to give the people some sign of His true character. Almost impatiently he waited to hear the Saviour declare His mission; but no word was spoken, no sign given. Jesus did not respond to the Baptist's announcement of Him, but mingled with the disciples of John, giving no outward evidence of His special work, and taking no measures to bring Himself to notice.

The next day John sees Jesus coming. With the light of the glory of God resting upon him, the prophet stretches out his hands, declaring, "Behold the Lamb of God, which taketh away the sin of the world! This is He of whom I said, After me cometh a man which is become before me. . . . And I knew Him not; but that He should be made manifest to Israel, for this cause came I baptizing in water. . . . I have beheld the Spirit descending as a dove out of heaven; and it abode upon Him. And I knew Him not: but He that sent me to baptize in water, He said unto me, Upon whomsoever thou shalt see the Spirit descending, and abiding upon Him, the same is He that baptizeth with the Holy Spirit. And I have seen, and have borne witness that this is the Son of God." John 1:29-34, R. V., margin.

Was this the Christ? With awe and wonder the people looked upon the One just declared to be the Son of God. They had been deeply moved by the words of John. He had spoken to them in the name of God. They had listened to him day after day as he reproved their sins, and daily the conviction that he was sent of Heaven had strengthened. But who was this One greater than John the Baptist? In His dress and bearing there was nothing that betokened rank. He was apparently a simple personage, clad like themselves in the humble garments of the poor.

There were in the throng some who at Christ's baptism had beheld the divine glory, and had heard the voice of God. But since that time the Saviour's appearance had greatly changed. At His baptism they had seen His countenance transfigured in the light of heaven; now, pale, worn, and emaciated, He had been recognized only by the prophet John.

But as the people looked upon Him, they saw a face where divine compassion was blended with conscious

5. "They saw a face where divine compassion was blended with conscious

power. Every glance of the eye, every feature of the countenance, was marked with h_____, and expressive of unutterable l____." (137). Lord, I need Your Spirit to abide and change my spirit. May this daily walk provide the inspiration for humility. Help me to recognize when self pops up, and to let it go, let go of my rights, to die to self:

_____

_____

_____

6. "Many were disappointed and greatly p_____... [A king] who sought to establish in their hearts a kingdom of r_____ and peace, they would not a_____." (138). Am I also disappointed? _____

_____

Shouldn't I be more thrilled about a kingdom in my heart, of righteousness? _____

_____

power. Every glance of the eye, every feature of the countenance, was marked with humility, and expressive of unutterable love. He seemed to be surrounded by an [137-138] atmosphere of spiritual influence. While His manners were gentle and unassuming, He impressed men with a sense of power that was hidden, yet could not be wholly concealed. Was this the One for whom Israel had so long waited?

Jesus came in poverty and humiliation, that He might be our example as well as our Redeemer. If He had appeared with kingly pomp, how could He have taught humility? how could He have presented such cutting truths as in the Sermon on the Mount? Where would have been the hope of the lowly in life had Jesus come to dwell as a king among men?

To the multitude, however, it seemed impossible that the One designated by John should be associated with their lofty anticipations. Thus many were disappointed, and greatly perplexed.

The words which the priests and rabbis so much desired to hear, that Jesus would now restore the kingdom to Israel, had not been spoken. For such a king they had been waiting and watching; such a king they were ready to receive. But one who sought to establish in their hearts a kingdom of righteousness and peace, they would not accept.

On the following day, while two disciples were standing near, John again saw Jesus among the people. Again the face of the prophet was lighted up with glory from the Unseen, as he cried, "Behold the Lamb of God!" The words thrilled the hearts of the disciples. They did not fully understand them. What meant the name that John had given Him,--"the Lamb of God"? John himself had not explained it.

Leaving John, they went to seek Jesus. One of the two was Andrew, the brother of Simon; the other was John the evangelist. These were Christ's first disciples. Moved by an irresistible impulse, they followed Jesus,--anxious to speak with Him, yet awed and silent, lost in the overwhelming significance of the thought, "Is this the Messiah?"

Jesus knew that the disciples were following Him. They were the first fruits of His ministry, and there was joy in the heart of the divine Teacher as these souls responded to His grace. Yet turning, He asked only, "What seek ye?" He would leave them free to turn back or to speak of their desire.

Of one purpose only were they conscious. One presence filled their thought. They exclaimed, "Rabbi, . . . where dwellest Thou?" In a brief interview by the wayside they could not receive that for which they longed. They desired to be alone with Jesus, to sit at His feet, and hear His words. [138-139]

"He saith unto them, Come and see. They came and saw where He dwelt, and abode with Him that day."

If John and Andrew had possessed the unbelieving spirit of the priests and rulers, they would not have been found as learners at the feet of Jesus. They would have come to Him as critics, to judge His words. Many thus close the door to the most precious opportunities. But not so did these first disciples. They had responded to the Holy Spirit's call in the preaching of John the Baptist. Now they recognized the voice of the heavenly Teacher. To them the words of Jesus were full of freshness and truth and beauty. A divine illumination was shed upon the teaching of the Old Testament Scriptures. The many-sided themes of truth stood out in new light.

It is contrition and faith and love that enable the soul to receive wisdom from heaven. Faith working by love is the key of knowledge, and everyone that loveth "knoweth God." 1 John 4:7.

The disciple John was a man of earnest and deep affection, ardent, yet contemplative. He had begun to discern the glory of Christ,--not the worldly pomp and power for which he had been taught to hope, but "the glory as of the Only-begotten of the Father, full of grace and truth." John 1:14. He was absorbed in contemplation of the wondrous theme.

Andrew sought to impart the joy that filled his heart. Going in search of his brother Simon, he cried, "We have found the Messias." Simon waited for no second bidding. He also had heard the preaching of John the Baptist, and he hastened to the Saviour. The eye of Christ rested upon him, reading his character and his life history. His impulsive nature, his loving, sympathetic heart, his ambition and self-confidence, the history of his fall, his repentance, his labors, and his martyr death,--the Saviour read it all, and He said, "Thou art Simon the son of Jona: thou shalt be called Cephas, which is by interpretation, A stone."

"The day following Jesus would go forth into Galilee, and findeth Philip, and saith unto him, Follow Me."

7. Who were Christ's first disciples? A_____, J_____(138). "They desired to be alone w_____ Jesus, to sit at His feet, and hear His words." They did not possess an unbelieving spirit, a critical and judgmental attitude. Many who do, "c_____ the door to the most precious opportunities." (139. Lord, I do NOT want to close the door to sitting at your feet. Cleanse me of a critical attitude:

_____
_____
_____
_____

8. "Andrew sought to impart the j_____ that filled his heart. Going in search of his brother Simon, he cried, 'We have found the Messias.'" (139). Won't this be my joy also? _____
____ Lord, You are too good to keep to myself!

_____
_____

Philip obeyed the command, and straightway he also became a worker for Christ.

Philip called Nathanael. The latter had been among the throng when the Baptist pointed to Jesus as the Lamb of God. As Nathanael looked upon Jesus, he was disappointed. Could this man, who bore the marks of toil and poverty, be the Messiah? Yet Nathanael could not decide to reject Jesus, for the message of John had brought conviction to his heart. [139-140]

At the time when Philip called him, Nathanael had withdrawn to a quiet grove to meditate upon the announcement of John and the prophecies concerning the Messiah. He prayed that if the one announced by John was the deliverer, it might be made known to him, and the Holy Spirit rested upon him with assurance that God had visited His people and raised up a horn of salvation for them. Philip knew that his friend was searching the prophecies, and while Nathanael was praying under a fig tree, Philip discovered his retreat. They had often prayed together in this secluded spot hidden by the foliage.

The message, "We have found Him, of whom Moses in the law, and the prophets, did write," seemed to Nathanael a direct answer to his prayer. But Philip had yet a trembling faith. He added doubtfully, "Jesus of Nazareth, the son of Joseph." Again prejudice arose in Nathanael's heart. He exclaimed, "Can there any good thing come out of Nazareth?"

Philip entered into no controversy. He said, "Come and see. Jesus saw Nathanael coming to Him, and saith of him, Behold an Israelite indeed, in whom is no guile!" In surprise Nathanael exclaimed, "Whence knowest Thou me? Jesus answered and said unto him, Before that Philip called thee, when thou wast under the fig tree, I saw thee."

It was enough. The divine Spirit that had borne witness to Nathanael in his solitary prayer under the fig tree now spoke to him in the words of Jesus. Though in doubt, and yielding somewhat to prejudice, Nathanael had come to Christ with an honest desire for truth, and now his desire was met. His faith went beyond that of the one who had brought him to Jesus. He answered and said, "Rabbi, Thou art the Son of God; Thou art the King of Israel."

If Nathanael had trusted to the rabbis for guidance, he would never have found Jesus. It was by seeing and judging for himself that he [140-141] became a disciple. So in the case of many today whom prejudice withholds from good. How different would be the result if they would "come and see"!

While they trust to the guidance of human authority, none will come to a saving knowledge of the truth. Like Nathanael, we need to study God's word for ourselves, and pray for the enlightenment of the Holy Spirit. He who saw Nathanael under the fig tree will see us in the secret place of prayer. Angels from the world of light are near to those who in humility seek for divine guidance.

With the calling of John and Andrew and Simon, of Philip and Nathanael, began the foundation of the Christian church. John directed two of his disciples to Christ. Then one of these, Andrew, found his brother, and called him to the Saviour. Philip was then called, and he went in search of Nathanael. These examples should teach us the importance of personal effort, of making direct appeals to our kindred, friends, and neighbors. There are those who for a lifetime have professed to be acquainted with Christ, yet who have never made a personal effort to bring even one soul to the Saviour. They leave all the work for the minister. He may be well qualified for his calling, but he cannot do that which God has left for the members of the church.

There are many who need the ministration of loving Christian hearts. Many have gone down to ruin who might have been saved if their neighbors, common men and women, had put forth personal effort for them. Many are waiting to be personally addressed. In the very family, the neighborhood, the town, where we live, there is work for us to do as missionaries for Christ. If we are Christians, this work will be our delight. No sooner is one converted than there is born within him a desire to make known to others what a precious friend he has found in Jesus. The saving and sanctifying truth cannot be shut up in his heart.

All who are consecrated to God will be channels of light. God makes them His agents to communicate to others the riches of His grace. His promise is, "I will make them and the places round about My hill a blessing; and I will cause the shower to come down in his season; there shall be showers of blessing." Ezek. 34:26.

Philip said to Nathanael, "Come and see." He did

9. "There are those who for a lifetime have professed to be a_____ _____ with Christ, yet who have never made a personal effort to bring even one soul to the Savior...No sooner is one converted than there is born within him a desire to make known to others what a p_____ f_____ he has found in Jesus. The saving and sanctifying truth c_____ be shut up in his heart." (141). Am I 'acquainted' with You, Lord? How do I know? _____
_____
_____
_____

10. "One of the most effective ways of winning souls to Him is in e_____ His c_____ in our daily life. Our influence upon others depends not so much upon what we say as upon what we a_____." (141, 142). My verbal witness will be wasted if my life witness is not in harmony with it. Lord, to have found You is the best thing in life! May my life not discourage anyone from making the same joyful discovery: _____
_____
_____

not ask him to accept another's testimony, but to behold Christ for himself. Now that Jesus has ascended to heaven, His disciples are His representatives among men, and one of the most effective ways of winning souls to Him is in [141-142] exemplifying His character in our daily life. Our influence upon others depends not so much upon what we say as upon what we are. Men may combat and defy our logic, they may resist our appeals; but a life of disinterested love is an argument they cannot gainsay. A consistent life, characterized by the meekness of Christ, is a power in the world.

The teaching of Christ was the expression of an inwrought conviction and experience, and those who learn of Him become teachers after the divine order. The word of God, spoken by one who is himself sanctified through it, has a life-giving power that makes it attractive to the hearers, and convicts them that it is a living reality. When one has received the truth in the love of it, he will make this manifest in the persuasion of his manner and the tones of his voice. He makes known that which he himself has heard, seen, and handled of the word of life, that others may have fellowship with him through the knowledge of Christ. His testimony, from lips touched with a live coal from off the altar, is truth to the receptive heart, and works sanctification upon the character.

And he who seeks to give light to others will himself be blessed. "There shall be showers of blessing." "He that watereth shall be watered also himself." Prov. 11:25. God could have reached His object in saving sinners without our aid; but in order for us to develop a character like Christ's, we must share in His work. In order to enter into His joy,--the joy of seeing souls redeemed by His sacrifice,--we must participate in His labors for their redemption.

Nathanael's first expression of his faith, so full and earnest and sincere, fell like music on the ears of Jesus. And He "answered and said unto him, Because I said unto thee, I saw thee under the fig tree, believest thou? thou shalt see greater things than these." The Saviour looked forward with joy to His work in preaching good tidings to the meek, binding up the brokenhearted, and proclaiming liberty to the captives of Satan. At thought of the precious blessings He had brought to men, Jesus added, "Verily, verily, I say unto you, Hereafter ye shall see heaven open, and the angels of God ascending and descending upon the Son of man."

Here Christ virtually says, On the bank of the Jordan the heavens were opened, and the Spirit descended like a dove upon Me. That scene was but a token that I am the Son of God. If you believe on Me as such, your faith shall be quickened. You shall see that the heavens are opened, and are never to be closed. I have opened them to you. The [142-143] angels of God are ascending, bearing the prayers of the needy and distressed to the Father above, and descending, bringing blessing and hope, courage, help, and life, to the children of men.

The angels of God are ever passing from earth to heaven, and from heaven to earth. The miracles of Christ for the afflicted and suffering were wrought by the power of God through the ministration of the angels. And it is through Christ, by the ministration of His heavenly messengers, that every blessing comes from God to us. In taking upon Himself humanity, our Saviour unites His interests with those of the fallen sons and daughters of Adam, while through His divinity He grasps the throne of God. And thus Christ is the medium of communication of men with God, and of God with men.

Prayer Journal: _____

_____
_____
_____
_____
_____
_____
_____

Chapter 15

At the Marriage Feast

[This chapter is based on John 2:1-11.]

Jesus did not begin His ministry by some great work before the Sanhedrin at Jerusalem. At a household gathering in a little Galilean village His power was put forth to add to the joy of a wedding feast. Thus He showed His sympathy with men, and His desire to minister to their happiness. In the wilderness of temptation He Himself had drunk the cup of woe. He came forth to give to men the cup of blessing, by His benediction to hallow the relations of human life.

From the Jordan, Jesus had returned to Galilee. There was to be a marriage at Cana, a little town not far from Nazareth; the parties were relatives of Joseph and Mary; and Jesus, knowing of this family gathering, went to Cana, and with His disciples was invited to the feast.

Again He met His mother, from whom He had for some time been separated. Mary had heard of the manifestation at the Jordan, at His baptism. The tidings had been carried to Nazareth, and had brought to her mind afresh the scenes that for so many years had been hidden in her heart. In common with all Israel, Mary was deeply stirred by the mission of John the Baptist. Well she remembered the prophecy given at his birth. Now his connection with Jesus kindled her hopes [144-145] anew. But tidings had reached her also of the mysterious departure of Jesus to the wilderness, and she was oppressed with troubled forebodings.

From the day when she heard the angel's announcement in the home at Nazareth Mary had treasured every evidence that Jesus was the Messiah. His sweet, unselfish life assured her that He could be no other than the Sent of God. Yet there came to her also doubts and disappointments, and she had longed for the time when His glory should be revealed. Death had separated her from Joseph, who had shared her knowledge of the mystery of the birth of Jesus. Now there was no one to whom she could confide her hopes and fears. The past two months had been very sorrowful. She had been parted from Jesus, in whose sympathy she found comfort; she pondered upon the words of Simeon, "A sword

1. "Mary had treasured every e_____ that Jesus was the Messiah. His s_____, u_____ life assured her that He could be no other than the Sent of God." (145). What is the evidence that You, Lord, are my abiding Savior (in my heart)? ___
_____
_____
_____

shall pierce through thy own soul also" (Luke 2:35); she recalled the three days of agony when she thought Jesus lost to her forever; and with an anxious heart she awaited His return.

At the marriage feast she meets Him, the same tender, dutiful son. Yet He is not the same. His countenance is changed. It bears the traces of His conflict in the wilderness, and a new expression of dignity and power gives evidence of His heavenly mission. With Him is a group of young men, whose eyes follow Him with reverence, and who call Him Master. These companions recount to Mary what they have seen and heard at the baptism and elsewhere. They conclude by declaring, "We have found Him, of whom Moses in the law, and the prophets, did write." John 1:45.

As the guests assemble, many seem to be preoccupied with some topic of absorbing interest. A suppressed excitement pervades the company. Little groups converse together in eager but quiet tones, and wondering glances are turned upon the Son of Mary. As Mary had heard the disciples' testimony in regard to Jesus, she had been gladdened with the assurance that her long-cherished hopes were not in vain. Yet she would have been more than human if there had not mingled with this holy joy a trace of the fond mother's natural pride. As she saw the many glances bent upon Jesus, she longed to have Him prove to the company that He was really the Honored of God. She hoped there might be opportunity for Him to work a miracle before them.

It was the custom of the times for marriage festivities to continue several days. On this occasion, before the feast ended it was found that the supply of wine had failed. This discovery caused much perplexity and regret. It was unusual to dispense with wine on festive occasions, and [145-146] its absence would seem to indicate a want of hospitality. As a relative of the parties, Mary had assisted in the arrangements for the feast, and she now spoke to Jesus, saying, "They have no wine." These words were a suggestion that He might supply their need. But Jesus answered, "Woman, what have I to do with thee? Mine hour is not yet come."

This answer, abrupt as it seems to us, expressed no coldness or discourtesy. The Saviour's form of address to His mother was in accordance with Oriental custom. It was used toward persons to whom it was desired to show respect. Every act of Christ's earthly life was in

2. At the marriage feast, Jesus "bears the traces of His c_____ in the wilderness, and a new expression of d_____ and power gives evidence of His heavenly mission." How does my countenance reflect spiritual conflict?_____
_____
_____
_____

3. Jesus' response to His mother's statement "They have no wine" was not expressed in coldness or discourtesy. "The love

expressed in t_____ and l_____ and manner interpreted His words." (146). Communication involves more than just the words I choose, but how I speak. Lord, show me how Your love might affect my tone and my expression: _____

_____

_____

4. Jesus' response teaches us that "the claims of God are p_____ even to the ties of human relationship." (147). I want to honor both God and neighbor (parent, boss), but God comes first. How true is that Lord? Are You my first priority and passion? _____

_____

_____

harmony with the precept He Himself had given, "Honor thy father and thy mother." Ex. 20:12. On the cross, in His last act of tenderness toward His mother, Jesus again addressed her in the same way, as He committed her to the care of His best-loved disciple. Both at the marriage feast and upon the cross, the love expressed in tone and look and manner interpreted His words.

At His visit to the temple in His boyhood, as the mystery of His lifework opened before Him, Christ had said to Mary, "Wist ye not that I must be about My Father's business?" Luke 2:49. These words [146-147] struck the keynote of His whole life and ministry. Everything was held in abeyance to His work, the great work of redemption which He had come into the world to accomplish. Now He repeated the lesson. There was danger that Mary would regard her relationship to Jesus as giving her a special claim upon Him, and the right, in some degree, to direct Him in His mission. For thirty years He had been to her a loving and obedient son, and His love was unchanged; but He must now go about His Father's work. As Son of the Most High, and Saviour of the world, no earthly ties must hold Him from His mission, or influence His conduct. He must stand free to do the will of God. This lesson is also for us. The claims of God are paramount even to the ties of human relationship. No earthly attraction should turn our feet from the path in which He bids us walk.

The only hope of redemption for our fallen race is in Christ; Mary could find salvation only through the Lamb of God. In herself she possessed no merit. Her connection with Jesus placed her in no different spiritual relation to Him from that of any other human soul. This is indicated in the Saviour's words. He makes clear the distinction between His relation to her as the Son of man and as the Son of God. The tie of kinship between them in no way placed her on an equality with Him.

The words, "Mine hour is not yet come," point to the fact that every act of Christ's life on earth was in fulfillment of the plan that had existed from the days of eternity. Before He came to earth, the plan lay out before Him, perfect in all its details. But as He walked among men, He was guided, step by step, by the Father's will. He did not hesitate to act at the appointed time. With the same submission He waited until the time had come.

In saying to Mary that His hour had not yet come, Jesus was replying to her unspoken thought,--to the expectation she cherished in common with her people. She hoped that He would reveal Himself as the Messiah, and take the throne of Israel. But the time had not come. Not as a King, but as "a Man of Sorrows, and acquainted with grief," had Jesus accepted the lot of humanity.

But though Mary had not a right conception of Christ's mission, she trusted Him implicitly. To this faith Jesus responded. It was to honor Mary's trust, and to strengthen the faith of His disciples, that the first miracle was performed. The disciples were to encounter many and great temptations to unbelief. To them the prophecies had made it [147-148] clear beyond all controversy that Jesus was the Messiah. They looked for the religious leaders to receive Him with confidence even greater than their own. They declared among the people the wonderful works of Christ and their own confidence in His mission, but they were amazed and bitterly disappointed by the unbelief, the deep-seated prejudice, and the enmity to Jesus, displayed by the priests and rabbis. The Saviour's early miracles strengthened the disciples to stand against this opposition.

In nowise disconcerted by the words of Jesus, Mary said to those serving at table, "Whatsoever He saith unto you, do it." Thus she did what she could to prepare the way for the work of Christ.

Beside the doorway stood six large stone water jars, and Jesus bade the servants fill these with water. It was done. Then as the wine was wanted for immediate use, He said, "Draw out now, and bear unto the governor of the feast." Instead of the water with which the vessels had been filled, there flowed forth wine. Neither the ruler of the feast nor the guests generally were aware that the supply of wine had failed. Upon tasting that which the servants brought, the ruler found it superior to any he had ever before drunk, and very different from that served at the beginning of the feast. Turning to the bridegroom, he said, "Every man at the beginning doth set forth good wine; and when men have well drunk, then that which is worse: but thou hast kept the good wine until now."

As men set forth the best wine first, then afterward that which is worse, so does the world with its gifts. That which it offers may please the eye and fascinate the senses, but it proves to be unsatisfying. The wine turns to bitterness, the gaiety to gloom. That which was

5. The disciples "were amazed and bitterly disappointed by the u_____, the deep-seated prejudice, and the enmity to Jesus, displayed by the priests and rabbis. The Savior's early miracles s_____ the disciples to stand against this opposition." (148). Thank You, Lord, for reminding me of the evidences of Your presence, that strengthens me in the face of trials: I remember when

_____

_____

_____

6. Unlike the custom of offering inferior wine later,
"the gifts of Jesus are ever
fresh and n_____. The
feast that He provides for
the soul never fails to give
s_____ and
joy." (148). Nothing else
satisfies like Jesus. Do I believe that? Why do I try to
find satisfaction elsewhere?

_____
_____
_____
_____

begun with songs and mirth ends in weariness and dis-
gust. But the gifts of Jesus are ever fresh and new. The
feast that He provides for the soul never fails to give
satisfaction and joy. Each new gift increases the capacity of the receiver to appreciate and enjoy the blessings
of the Lord. He gives grace for grace. There can be no
failure of supply. If you abide in Him, the fact that you
receive a rich gift today insures the reception of a richer
gift tomorrow. The words of Jesus to Nathanael express
the law of God's dealing with the children of faith. With
every fresh revelation of His love, He declares to the
receptive heart, "Believest thou? thou shalt see greater
things than these." John 1:50.

The gift of Christ to the marriage feast was a symbol. The water represented baptism into His death; the
wine, the shedding of His blood [148-149] for the sins
of the world. The water to fill the jars was brought by
human hands, but the word of Christ alone could impart
to it life-giving virtue. So with the rites which point to
the Saviour's death. It is only by the power of Christ,
working through faith, that they have efficacy to nourish the soul.

The word of Christ supplied ample provision for
the feast. So abundant is the provision of His grace to
blot out the iniquities of men, and to renew and sustain
the soul.

At the first feast He attended with His disciples, Jesus gave them the cup that symbolized His work for
their salvation. At the last supper He gave it again, in
the institution of that sacred rite by which His death was
to be shown forth "till He come." 1 Cor. 11:26. And the
sorrow of the disciples at parting from their Lord was
comforted with the promise of reunion, as He said, "I
will not drink henceforth of this fruit of the vine, until
that day when I drink it new with you in My Father's
kingdom." Matt. 26:29.

The wine which Christ provided for the feast, and
that which He gave to the disciples as a symbol of His
own blood, was the pure juice of the grape. To this the
prophet Isaiah refers when he speaks of the new wine
"in the cluster," and says, "Destroy it not; for a blessing
is in it." Isa. 65:8.

It was Christ who in the Old Testament gave the
warning to Israel, "Wine is a mocker, strong drink is
raging: and whosoever is deceived thereby is not wise."
Prov. 20:1. And He Himself provided no such bever-

age. Satan tempts men to indulgence that will becloud reason and benumb the spiritual perceptions, but Christ teaches us to bring the lower nature into subjection. His whole life was an example of self-denial. In order to break the power of appetite, He suffered in our behalf the severest test that humanity could endure. It was Christ who directed that John the Baptist should drink neither wine nor strong drink. It was He who enjoined similar abstinence upon the wife of Manoah. And He pronounced a curse upon the man who should put the bottle to his neighbor's lips. Christ did not contradict His own teaching. The unfermented wine which He provided for the wedding guests was a wholesome and refreshing drink. Its effect was to bring the taste into harmony with a healthful appetite.

As the guests at the feast remarked upon the quality of the wine, inquiries were made that drew from the servants an account of the [149-150] miracle. The company were for a time too much amazed to think of Him who had performed the wonderful work. When at length they looked for Him, it was found that He had withdrawn so quietly as to be unnoticed even by His disciples.

The attention of the company was now turned to the disciples. For the first time they had the opportunity of acknowledging their faith in Jesus. They told what they had seen and heard at the Jordan, and there was kindled in many hearts the hope that God had raised up a deliverer for His people. The news of the miracle spread through all that region, and was carried to Jerusalem. With new interest the priests and elders searched the prophecies pointing to Christ's coming. There was eager desire to learn the mission of this new teacher, who appeared among the people in so unassuming a manner.

The ministry of Christ was in marked contrast to that of the Jewish elders. Their regard for tradition and formalism had destroyed all real freedom of thought or action. They lived in continual dread of defilement. To avoid contact with the "unclean," they kept aloof, not only from the Gentiles, but from the majority of their own people, seeking neither to benefit them nor to win their friendship. By dwelling constantly on these matters, they had dwarfed their minds and narrowed the orbit of their lives. Their example encouraged egotism and intolerance among all classes of the people.

7. "Satan tempts men to indulgence that will becloud reason and b_____ spiritual perceptions." (149). So the reason to abstain from wine is not that I will be more holy, but rather, to enhance my spiritual alertness. Lord, I don't want anything to benumb spiritual perceptions: overeating, lack of sleep, cherishing an attitude that clashes with the fruits of the Spirit. Please alert me to these: _____

_____

_____

_____

Jesus began the work of reformation by coming into close sympathy with humanity. While He showed the greatest reverence for the law of God, He rebuked the pretentious piety of the Pharisees, and tried to free the people from the senseless rules that bound them. He was seeking to break down the barriers which separated the different classes of society, that He might bring men together as children of one family. His attendance at the marriage feast was designed to be a step toward effecting this.

God had directed John the Baptist to dwell in the wilderness, that he might be shielded from the influence of the priests and rabbis, and be prepared for a special mission. But the austerity and isolation of his life were not an example for the people. John himself had not directed his hearers to forsake their former duties. He bade them give evidence of their repentance by faithfulness to God in the place where He had called them.

8. "Jesus reproved self-indulgence in all its forms, yet He was social in His nature." (150). Is there balance in that statement? What happens if I focus on just one side of that statement? How do I reproove self-indulgence in others, and yet be failing to follow Christ's nature of being social?

_____
_____
_____
_____

Jesus reproved self-indulgence in all its forms, yet He was social in His nature. He accepted the hospitality of all classes, visiting the homes [150-151] of the rich and the poor, the learned and the ignorant, and seeking to elevate their thoughts from questions of commonplace life to those things that are spiritual and eternal. He gave no license to dissipation, and no shadow of worldly levity marred His conduct; yet He found pleasure in scenes of innocent happiness, and by His presence sanctioned the social gathering. A Jewish marriage was an impressive occasion, and its joy was not displeasing to the Son of man. By attending this feast, Jesus honored marriage as a divine institution.

In both the Old and the New Testament, the marriage relation is employed to represent the tender and sacred union that exists between Christ and His people. To the mind of Jesus the gladness of the wedding festivities pointed forward to the rejoicing of that day when He shall bring home His bride to the Father's house, and the redeemed with the Redeemer shall sit down to the marriage supper of the Lamb. He says, "As the bridegroom rejoiceth over the bride, so shall thy God rejoice over thee." "Thou shalt no more be termed Forsaken; . . . but thou shalt be called My Delight; . . . for the Lord delighteth in thee." "He will rejoice over thee with joy; He will rest in His love, He will joy over thee with singing." Isa. 62:5, 4, margin; Zeph. 3:17. When the vision of heavenly things was granted to John the apostle, he wrote: "I heard as it were the voice of a great multitude, and as the voice of many waters, and as the voice of mighty thunderings, saying, Alleluia: for the Lord God omnipotent reigneth. Let us be glad and rejoice, and give honor to Him: for the marriage of the Lamb is come, and His wife hath made herself ready." "Blessed are they which are called unto the marriage supper of the Lamb." Rev. 19:6, 7, 9.

Jesus saw in every soul one to whom must be given the call to His kingdom. He reached the hearts of the people by going among them as one who desired their good. He sought them in the public streets, in private houses, on the boats, in the synagogue, by the shores of the lake, and at the marriage feast. He met them at their daily vocations, and manifested an interest in their secular affairs. He carried His instruction into the household, bringing families in their own homes under the influence of His divine presence. His strong personal sympathy helped to win hearts. He often repaired to the mountains for solitary prayer, but this was a preparation for His labor among men in active life. From these seasons He came forth to relieve the sick, to instruct the ignorant, and to break the chains from the captives of Satan. [151-152]

It was by personal contact and association that Jesus trained His disciples. Sometimes He taught them, sitting among them on the mountainside; sometimes beside the sea, or walking with them by the way, He revealed the mysteries of the kingdom of God. He did not sermonize as men do today. Wherever hearts were open to receive the divine message, He unfolded the truths of the way of salvation. He did not command His disciples to do this or that, but said, "Follow Me." On His journeys through country and cities He took them with Him, that they might see how He taught the people. He linked their interest with His, and they united with Him in the work.

The example of Christ in linking Himself with the interests of humanity should be followed by all who preach His word, and by all who have received the gospel of His grace. We are not to renounce social communion. We should not seclude ourselves from others. In order to reach all classes, we must meet them where they are. They will seldom seek us of their own accord. Not alone from the pulpit are the hearts of men touched by divine truth. There is another field of labor, hum-

9. Jesus "reached the hearts of the people by going among them as one who desired their good... He met them at their d_____ vocations, and manifested an interest in their s_____ affairs." (151). What does this tell me about my witness? _____ _____ _____Why do I hesitate? _____ _____ _____

10. "Not alone from the pulpit are the hearts of men touched by divine truth. There is another f_____ of labor." (152). Where is that? _____ _____ _____ (gatherings for innocent social enjoyment). Lord, let me be sensitive to Your Spirit; prompt me to be Your witness in any setting: _____ _____ _____ _____

11. "We should a_____ become witnesses for Jesus...Let the world see that we are not selfishly absorbed in our own i_____...Let them see that our religion does not make us unsympathetic or exacting...gloomy, u_____ people."

12. "If our eyes are f_____ on Jesus, we shall see a compassionate Redeemer, and shall c_____ light from His countenance. Wherever His Spirit reigns, there peace abides. And there will be j_____ also, for there is a calm, holy trust in God...The light that shines upon them [His followers] they are to reflect upon others, in works that are luminous with the l_____ of Christ." (153). Wow, there's a personal mission statement for me: catch the light of Your countenance and reflect it to others:

_____
_____
_____
_____
_____

Prayer Journal: _____
_____
_____
_____
_____
_____
_____

bler, it may be, but fully as promising. It is found in the home of the lowly, and in the mansion of the great; at the hospitable board, and in gatherings for innocent social enjoyment.

As disciples of Christ we shall not mingle with the world from a mere love of pleasure, to unite with them in folly. Such associations can result only in harm. We should never give sanction to sin by our words or our deeds, our silence or our presence. Wherever we go, we are to carry Jesus with us, and to reveal to others the preciousness of our Saviour. But those who try to preserve their religion by hiding it within stone walls lose precious opportunities of doing good. Through the social relations, Christianity comes in contact with the world. Everyone who has received the divine illumination is to brighten the pathway of those who know not the Light of life.

We should all become witnesses for Jesus. Social power, sanctified by the grace of Christ, must be improved in winning souls to the Saviour. Let the world see that we are not selfishly absorbed in our own interests, but that we desire others to share our blessings and privileges. Let them see that our religion does not make us unsympathetic or exacting. Let all who profess to have found Christ, minister as He did for the benefit of men.

We should never give to the world the false impression that Christians are a gloomy, unhappy people. If our eyes are fixed on Jesus, we shall [152-153] see a compassionate Redeemer, and shall catch light from His countenance. Wherever His Spirit reigns, there peace abides. And there will be joy also, for there is a calm, holy trust in God.

Christ is pleased with His followers when they show that, though human, they are partakers of the divine nature. They are not statues, but living men and women. Their hearts, refreshed by the dews of divine grace, open and expand to the Sun of Righteousness. The light that shines upon them they reflect upon others in works that are luminous with the love of Christ.

In His Temple

[This chapter is based on John 2:12-22.]

"After this He went down to Capernaum, He, and His mother, and His brethren, and His disciples: and they continued there not many days. And the Jews' Passover was at hand, and Jesus went up to Jerusalem."

In this journey, Jesus joined one of the large companies that were making their way to the capital. He had not yet publicly announced His mission, and He mingled unnoticed with the throng. Upon these occasions, the coming of the Messiah, to which such prominence had been given by the ministry of John, was often the theme of conversation. The hope of national greatness was dwelt upon with kindling enthusiasm. Jesus knew that this hope was to be disappointed, for it was founded on a misinterpretation of the Scriptures. With deep earnestness He explained the prophecies, and tried to arouse the people to a closer study of God's word.

The Jewish leaders had instructed the people that at Jerusalem they were to be taught to worship God. Here during the Passover week large numbers assembled, coming from all parts of Palestine, and even from distant lands. The temple courts were filled with a promiscuous throng. Many were unable to bring with them the sacrifices that were to be [154-155] offered up as typifying the one great Sacrifice. For the convenience of these, animals were bought and sold in the outer court of the temple. Here all classes of people assembled to purchase their offerings. Here all foreign money was exchanged for the coin of the sanctuary.

Every Jew was required to pay yearly a half shekel as "a ransom for his soul;" and the money thus collected was used for the support of the temple. Ex. 30:12-16. Besides this, large sums were brought as freewill offerings, to be deposited in the temple treasury. And it was required that all foreign coin should be changed for a coin called the temple shekel, which was accepted for the service of the sanctuary. The money changing gave opportunity for fraud and extortion, and it had grown into a disgraceful traffic, which was a source of revenue to the priests.

1. "The worshippers had been taught to believe that if they did not offer sacrifice, the b_____ of God would not rest upon their children or their lands...They were s_____ aware of how far they had wandered from the original purpose of the service instituted by God Himself." (155). Could this happen to me? Do I see tithing, Sabbath observance, the health message as a means of ensuring God's blessing? What is God's original purpose?

_____
_____
_____
_____ Lord, what is the difference between ensuring and enhancing my relationship with You?) _____
_____

2. The experience on Mt. Sinai "taught the lesson that wherever God manifests His presence, the place is h_____." (156). This includes the temple, the burning bush, my quiet corner. Lord, thanks for coming close, and making the moments so special:

_____

The dealers demanded exorbitant prices for the animals sold, and they shared their profits with the priests and rulers, who thus enriched themselves at the expense of the people. The worshipers had been taught to believe that if they did not offer sacrifice, the blessing of God would not rest on their children or their lands. Thus a high price for the animals could be secured; for after coming so far, the people would not return to their homes without performing the act of devotion for which they had come.

A great number of sacrifices were offered at the time of the Passover, and the sales at the temple were very large. The consequent confusion indicated a noisy cattle market rather than the sacred temple of God. There could be heard sharp bargaining, the lowing of cattle, the bleating of sheep, the cooing of doves, mingled with the chinking of coin and angry disputation. So great was the confusion that the worshipers were disturbed, and the words addressed to the Most High were drowned in the uproar that invaded the temple. The Jews were exceedingly proud of their piety. They rejoiced over their temple, and regarded a word spoken in its disfavor as blasphemy; they were very rigorous in the performance of ceremonies connected with it; but the love of money had overruled their scruples. They were scarcely aware how far they had wandered from the original purpose of the service instituted by God Himself.

When the Lord descended upon Mount Sinai, the place was consecrated by His presence. Moses was commanded to put bounds around the mount and sanctify it, and the word of the Lord was heard in [155-156] warning: "Take heed to yourselves, that ye go not up into the mount, or touch the border of it: whosoever toucheth the mount shall be surely put to death: there shall not an hand touch it, but he shall surely be stoned, or shot through; whether it be beast or man, it shall not live." Ex. 19:12, 13. Thus was taught the lesson that wherever God manifests His presence, the place is holy. The precincts of God's temple should have been regarded as sacred. But in the strife for gain, all this was lost sight of.

The priests and rulers were called to be the representatives of God to the nation; they should have corrected the abuses of the temple [156-157] court. They should have given to the people an example of integrity and compassion. Instead of studying their own profit, they should have considered the situation and needs of the worshipers, and should have been ready to assist those who were not able to buy the required sacrifices. But this they did not do. Avarice had hardened their hearts.

There came to this feast those who were suffering, those who were in want and distress. The blind, the lame, the deaf, were there. Some were brought on beds. Many came who were too poor to purchase the humblest offering for the Lord, too poor even to buy food with which to satisfy their own hunger. These were greatly distressed by the statements of the priests. The priests boasted of their piety; they claimed to be the guardians of the people; but they were without sympathy or compassion. The poor, the sick, the dying, made their vain plea for favor. Their suffering awakened no pity in the hearts of the priests.

As Jesus came into the temple, He took in the whole scene. He saw the unfair transactions. He saw the distress of the poor, who thought that without shedding of blood there would be no forgiveness for their sins. He saw the outer court of His temple converted into a place of unholy traffic. The sacred enclosure had become one vast exchange.

Christ saw that something must be done. Numerous ceremonies were enjoined upon the people without the proper instruction as to their import. The worshipers offered their sacrifices without understanding that they were typical of the only perfect Sacrifice. And among them, unrecognized and unhonored, stood the One symbolized by all their service. He had given directions in regard to the offerings. He understood their symbolical value, and He saw that they were now perverted and misunderstood. Spiritual worship was fast disappearing. No link bound the priests and rulers to their God. Christ's work was to establish an altogether different worship.

With searching glance, Christ takes in the scene before Him as He stands upon the steps of the temple court. With prophetic eye He looks into futurity, and sees not only years, but centuries and ages. He sees how priests and rulers will turn the needy from their right, and forbid that the gospel shall be preached to the poor. He sees how the love of God will be concealed from sinners, and men will make merchandise of His grace. As He beholds the scene, indignation, authority, and power

3. "Jesus saw the distress of the poor, who t_____ that without shedding of b_____ there would be no forgiveness for their sins." (157). How does this thought fit with Hebrews 9:22? _____

_____
_____
_____
_____

(a) Blood is essential, and there is an understanding that is responsive to all the evidence of Scripture. (b) Jesus saw people as "without the proper instruction as to their import." (c) The heathen view is appeasement; the Christian view is, God provides. (d) Lord, help me to take time, to understand Your ways, Your character: _____

_____
_____
_____

4. Do I, or does my church "conceal the love of God from sinners," and "make merchandise of His g_____?" _____

_____
_____

(Do I judge, withhold acceptance, withhold involvement?)

are expressed in His countenance. The attention of the people is attracted to Him. The eyes of those engaged in their unholy traffic [157-158] are riveted upon His face. They cannot withdraw their gaze. They feel that this Man reads their inmost thoughts, and discovers their hidden motives. Some attempt to conceal their faces, as if their evil deeds were written upon their countenances, to be scanned by those searching eyes.

The confusion is hushed. The sound of traffic and bargaining has ceased. The silence becomes painful. A sense of awe overpowers the assembly. It is as if they were arraigned before the tribunal of God to answer for their deeds. Looking upon Christ, they behold divinity flash through the garb of humanity. The Majesty of heaven stands as the Judge will stand at the last day,--not now encircled with the glory that will then attend Him, but with the same power to read the soul. His eye sweeps over the multitude, taking in every individual. His form seems to rise above them in commanding dignity, and a divine light illuminates His countenance. He speaks, and His clear, ringing voice--the same that upon Mount Sinai proclaimed the law that priests and rulers are transgressing--is heard echoing through the arches of the temple: "Take these things hence; make not My Father's house an house of merchandise."

Slowly descending the steps, and raising the scourge of cords gathered up on entering the enclosure, He bids the bargaining company depart from the precincts of the temple. With a zeal and severity He has never before manifested, He overthrows the tables of the money-changers. The coin falls, ringing sharply upon the marble pavement. None presume to question His authority. None dare stop to gather up their ill-gotten gain. Jesus does not smite them with the whip of cords, but in His hand that simple scourge seems terrible as a flaming sword. Officers of the temple, speculating priests, brokers and cattle traders, with their sheep and oxen, rush from the place, with the one thought of escaping from the condemnation of His presence.

A panic sweeps over the multitude, who feel the overshadowing of His divinity. Cries of terror escape from hundreds of blanched lips. Even the disciples tremble. They are awestruck by the words and manner of Jesus, so unlike His usual demeanor. They remember that it is written of Him, "The zeal of Thine house hath eaten Me up." Ps. 69:9. Soon the tumultuous throng

5. "Take these things h_____; make not My Father's house an house of merchandise." (158). Lord, what things, what attitudes need to be removed from the time of worship, from my time of devotion?

_____
_____
_____

6. There is one thought in the minds of those who flee: escape from the c_____ of His presence. "They are awestruck by the words and manner of Jesus, so u_____ His usual demeanor." Lord, help me to appreciate Your passion for purity of worship and devotion: _____

_____
_____

with their merchandise are far removed from the temple of the Lord. The courts are free from unholy traffic, and a deep silence and solemnity settles upon the scene of confusion. [158-161] The presence of the Lord, that of old sanctified the mount, has now made sacred the temple reared in His honor.

In the cleansing of the temple, Jesus was announcing His mission as the Messiah, and entering upon His work. That temple, erected for the abode of the divine Presence, was designed to be an object lesson for Israel and for the world. From eternal ages it was God's purpose that every created being, from the bright and holy seraph to man, should be a temple for the indwelling of the Creator. Because of sin, humanity ceased to be a temple for God. Darkened and defiled by evil, the heart of man no longer revealed the glory of the Divine One. But by the incarnation of the Son of God, the purpose of Heaven is fulfilled. God dwells in humanity, and through saving grace the heart of man becomes again His temple. God designed that the temple at Jerusalem should be a continual witness to the high destiny open to every soul. But the Jews had not understood the significance of the building they regarded with so much pride. They did not yield themselves as holy temples for the Divine Spirit. The courts of the temple at Jerusalem, filled with the tumult of unholy traffic, represented all too truly the temple of the heart, defiled by the presence of sensual passion and unholy thoughts. In cleansing the temple from the world's buyers and sellers, Jesus announced His mission to cleanse the heart from the defilement of sin,--from the earthly desires, the selfish lusts, the evil habits, that corrupt the soul. "The Lord, whom ye seek, shall suddenly come to His temple, even the Messenger of the covenant, whom ye delight in: behold, He shall come, saith the Lord of hosts. But who may abide the day of His coming? and who shall stand when He appeareth? for He is like a refiner's fire, and like fullers' soap: and He shall sit as a refiner and purifier of silver: and He shall purify the sons of Levi, and purge them as gold and silver." Mal. 3:1-3.

"Know ye not that ye are the temple of God, and that the Spirit of God dwelleth in you? If any man defile the temple of God, him shall God destroy; for the temple of God is holy, which temple ye are." 1 Cor. 3:16, 17. No man can of himself cast out the evil throng that have taken possession of the heart. Only Christ can cleanse

7. "In cleansing the temple, Jesus was announcing His   m_____ as the Messiah, and entering upon His work...to cleanse the heart from of the defilement of sin,-- from the earthly desires, the s_____ lusts, the evil habits, that corrupt the soul" (161). Lord, I want You to do Your work of cleansing in me; I give You permission. Show me what needs to be removed: _____
_____
_____
_____
_____

the soul temple. But He will not force an entrance. He comes not into the heart as to the temple of old; but He says, "Behold, I stand at the door, and knock: if any man hear My voice, and open the door, I will come in to him." Rev. 3:20. He will come, not for one day merely; for He says, "I will dwell in them, and walk in them; . . . and they shall [161-162] be My people." "He will subdue our iniquities; and Thou wilt cast all their sins into the depths of the sea." 2 Cor. 6:16; Micah 7:19. His presence will cleanse and sanctify the soul, so that it may be a holy temple unto the Lord, and "an habitation of God through the Spirit." Eph. 2:21, 22.

Overpowered with terror, the priests and rulers had fled from the temple court, and from the searching glance that read their hearts. In their flight they met others on their way to the temple, and bade them turn back, telling them what they had seen and heard. Christ looked upon the fleeing men with yearning pity for their fear, and their ignorance of what constituted true worship. In this scene He saw symbolized the dispersion of the whole Jewish nation for their wickedness and impenitence.

8. Did Jesus exalt at His success in getting rid of the offenders? "Christ looked upon the fleeing men with yearning p_____ for their fear, and their ignorance of what constituted true w_____." (162). Lord, what is my attitude when I talk to someone about their influence?

_____
_____
_____
_____
_____

And why did the priests flee from the temple? Why did they not stand their ground? He who commanded them to go was a carpenter's son, a poor Galilean, without earthly rank or power. Why did they not resist Him? Why did they leave the gain so ill acquired, and flee at the command of One whose outward appearance was so humble?

Christ spoke with the authority of a king, and in His appearance, and in the tones of His voice, there was that which they had no power to resist. At the word of command they realized, as they had never realized before, their true position as hypocrites and robbers. When divinity flashed through humanity, not only did they see indignation on Christ's countenance; they realized the import of His words. They felt as if before the throne of the eternal Judge, with their sentence passed on them for time and for eternity. For a time they were convinced that Christ was a prophet; and many believed Him to be the Messiah. The Holy Spirit flashed into their minds the utterances of the prophets concerning Christ. Would they yield to this conviction?

Repent they would not. They knew that Christ's sympathy for the poor had been aroused. They knew that they had been guilty of extortion in their dealings with the people. Because Christ discerned their thoughts they hated Him. His public rebuke was humiliating to their pride, and they were jealous of His growing influence with the people. They determined to challenge Him as to the power by which He had driven them forth, and who gave Him this power.

Slowly and thoughtfully, but with hate in their hearts, they returned to the temple. But what a change had taken place during their absence! [162-163] When they fled, the poor remained behind; and these were now looking to Jesus, whose countenance expressed His love and sympathy. With tears in His eyes, He said to the trembling ones around Him: Fear not; I will deliver thee, and thou shalt glorify Me. For this cause came I into the world.

The people pressed into Christ's presence with urgent, pitiful appeals: Master, bless me. His ear heard every cry. With pity exceeding that of a tender mother He bent over the suffering little ones. All received attention. Everyone was healed of whatever disease he had. The dumb opened their lips in praise; the blind beheld the face of their Restorer. The hearts of the sufferers were made glad.

As the priests and temple officials witnessed this great work, what a revelation to them were the sounds that fell on their ears! The people were relating the story of the pain they had suffered, of their disappointed hopes, of painful days and sleepless nights. When the last spark of hope seemed to be dead, Christ had healed them. The burden was so heavy, one said; but I have found a helper. He is the Christ of God, and I will devote my life to His service. Parents said to their children, He has saved your life; lift up your voice and praise Him. The voices of children and youth, fathers and mothers, friends and spectators, blended in thanksgiving and praise. Hope and gladness filled their hearts. Peace came to their minds. They were restored soul and body, and they returned home, proclaiming everywhere the matchless love of Jesus.

At the crucifixion of Christ, those who had thus been healed did not join with the rabble throng in crying, "Crucify Him, crucify Him." Their sympathies were with Jesus; for they had felt His great sympathy and wonderful power. They knew Him to be their Saviour; for He had given them health of body and soul. They listened to the preaching of the apostles, and the

9. "Because Christ discerned their thoughts they h_____ Him." (162). As You read my heart, Lord, I want to be like Judas, and thrill to confess, thrill to be so open and transparent with You (see page 645). But I do not want to be like Judas in how he closed the door. Search me Lord, know my thoughts:

_____

_____

_____

10. When the priests return to the temple to challenge Jesus, what a difference in the temple scene. Instead of merchandise traffic, there is thanksgiving and praise. The p_____ had stayed behind. With heavy burdens, they found hope and healing. Children, youth, fathers, mothers, friends blended in song. (163). So some people did not feel condemned in Jesus' presence, but rather felt drawn to Him. That's what I want, Lord: to experience a life that is close to You. May I

be responsive to Your drawing, and comfortable in Your presence:

_____

_____

_____

entrance of God's word into their hearts gave them understanding. They became agents of God's mercy, and instruments of His salvation.

The crowd that had fled from the temple court after a time slowly drifted back. They had partially recovered from the panic that had seized them, but their faces expressed irresolution and timidity. They looked with amazement on the works of Jesus, and were convicted that in Him the prophecies concerning the Messiah were fulfilled. The sin of the desecration of the temple rested, in a great degree, upon the priests. It [163-164] was by their arrangement that the court had been turned into a market place. The people were comparatively innocent. They were impressed by the divine authority of Jesus; but with them the influence of the priests and rulers was paramount. They regarded Christ's mission as an innovation, and questioned His right to interfere with what was permitted by the authorities of the temple. They were offended because the traffic had been interrupted, and they stifled the convictions of the Holy Spirit.

Above all others the priests and rulers should have seen in Jesus the anointed of the Lord; for in their hands were the sacred scrolls that described His mission, and they knew that the cleansing of the temple was a manifestation of more than human power. Much as they hated Jesus, they could not free themselves from the thought that He might be a prophet sent by God to restore the sanctity of the temple. With a deference born of this fear, they went to Him with the inquiry, "What sign showest Thou unto us, seeing that Thou doest these things?"

Jesus had shown them a sign. In flashing light into their hearts, and in doing before them the works which the Messiah was to do, He had given convincing evidence of His character. Now when they asked for a sign, He answered them by a parable, showing that He read their malice, and saw to what lengths it would lead them. "Destroy this temple," He said, "and in three days I will raise it up."

In these words His meaning was twofold. He referred not only to the destruction of the Jewish temple and worship, but to His own death,--the destruction of the temple of His body. This the Jews were already plotting. As the priests and rulers returned to the temple, they had proposed to kill Jesus, and thus rid themselves of the troubler. Yet when He set before them their purpose, they did not understand Him. They took His words as applying only to the temple at Jerusalem, and with indignation exclaimed, "Forty and six years was this temple in building, and wilt Thou rear it up in three days?" Now they felt that Jesus had justified their unbelief, and they were confirmed in their rejection of Him.

Christ did not design that His words should be understood by the unbelieving Jews, nor even by His disciples at this time. He knew that they would be misconstrued by His enemies, and would be turned against Him. At His trial they would be brought as an accusation, and on Calvary they would be flung at Him as a taunt. But to explain them now would give His disciples a knowledge of His sufferings, and bring [164-165] upon them sorrow which as yet they were not able to bear. And an explanation would prematurely disclose to the Jews the result of their prejudice and unbelief. Already they had entered upon a path which they would steadily pursue until He should be led as a lamb to the slaughter.

It was for the sake of those who should believe on Him that these words of Christ were spoken. He knew that they would be repeated. Being spoken at the Passover, they would come to the ears of thousands, and be carried to all parts of the world. After He had risen from the dead, their meaning would be made plain. To many they would be conclusive evidence of His divinity.

Because of their spiritual darkness, even the disciples of Jesus often failed of comprehending His lessons. But many of these lessons were made plain to them by subsequent events. When He walked no more with them, His words were a stay to their hearts.

As referring to the temple at Jerusalem, the Saviour's words, "Destroy this temple, and in three days I will raise it up," had a deeper meaning than the hearers perceived. Christ was the foundation and life of the temple. Its services were typical of the sacrifice of the Son of God. The priesthood was established to represent the mediatorial character and work of Christ. The entire plan of sacrificial worship was a foreshadowing of the Saviour's death to redeem the world. There would be no efficacy in these offerings when the great event toward which they had pointed for ages was consummated.

Since the whole ritual economy was symbolical of Christ, it had no value apart from Him. When the Jews sealed their rejection of Christ by delivering Him to death, they rejected all that gave significance to the temple and its services. Its sacredness had departed. It was doomed to destruction. From that day sacrificial offerings and the service connected with them were meaningless. Like the offering of Cain, they did not express faith in the Saviour. In putting Christ to death, the Jews virtually destroyed their temple. When Christ was crucified, the inner veil of the temple was rent in twain from top to bottom, signifying that the great final sacrifice had been made, and that the system of sacrificial offerings was forever at an end.

"In three days I will raise it up." In the Saviour's death the powers of darkness seemed to prevail, and they exulted in their victory. But from the rent sepulcher of Joseph, Jesus came forth a conqueror. "Having spoiled principalities and powers, He made a show of them openly, triumphing over them." Col.2:15. By virtue of His death and resurrection [165-166] He became the minister of the "true tabernacle, which the Lord pitched, and not man." Heb. 8:2. Men reared the Jewish tabernacle; men builded the Jewish temple; but the sanctuary above, of which the earthly was a type, was built by no human architect. "Behold the Man whose name is The Branch; . . . He shall build the temple of the Lord; and He shall bear the glory, and shall sit and rule upon His throne; and He shall be a priest upon His throne." Zech. 6:12, 13.

The sacrificial service that had pointed to Christ passed away; but the eyes of men were turned to the true sacrifice for the sins of the world. The earthly priesthood ceased; but we look to Jesus, the minister of the new covenant, and "to the blood of sprinkling, that speaketh better things than that of Abel." "The way into the holiest of all was not yet made manifest, while as the first tabernacle was yet standing: . . . but Christ being come an high priest of good things to come, by a greater and more perfect tabernacle, not made with hands, . . . by His own blood He entered in once into the holy place, having obtained eternal redemption for us." Heb. 12:24; 9:8-12.

"Wherefore He is able also to save them to the uttermost that come unto God by Him, seeing He ever liveth to make intercession for them." Heb. 7:25. Though the ministration was to be removed from the earthly to the heavenly temple; though the sanctuary and our great high priest would be invisible to human sight, yet the

11. "Though the ministration was to be removed from the earthly to the heavenly temple...the

disciples were to suffer no loss thereby. They would realize no break in their communion, and no diminution of power because of the Saviour's absence. While Jesus ministers in the sanctuary above, He is still by His Spirit the minister of the church on earth. He is withdrawn from the eye of sense, but His parting promise is fulfilled, "Lo, I am with you alway, even unto the end of the world." Matt. 28:20. While He delegates His power to inferior ministers, His energizing presence is still with His church.

"Seeing then that we have a great high priest, . . . Jesus, the Son of God, let us hold fast our profession. For we have not an high priest which cannot be touched with the feeling of our infirmities; but was in all points tempted like as we are, yet without sin. Let us therefore come boldly unto the throne of grace, that we may obtain mercy, and find grace to help in time of need." Heb 4:14-16.

disciples were to suffer no l_____ thereby. They would realize no break in their c_____, and no diminution of power because of the Savior's absence. While Jesus ministers in the sanctuary above, He is still by His Spirit the minister of the church on earth." (166). Lord, You are my God, my Friend, and You are always there for me, a constant Companion, as long as I invite You and make myself available to You:

_____
_____
_____

Prayer Journal: _____

_____
_____
_____
_____
_____
_____
_____

Chapter 17

Nicodemus

[This chapter is based on John 3:1-17.]

Nicodemus held a high position of trust in the Jewish nation. He was highly educated, and possessed talents of no ordinary character, and he was an honored member of the national council. With others, he had been stirred by the teaching of Jesus. Though rich, learned, and honored, he had been strangely attracted by the humble Nazarene. The lessons that had fallen from the Saviour's lips had greatly impressed him, and he desired to learn more of these wonderful truths.

Christ's exercise of authority in the cleansing of the temple had roused the determined hatred of the priests and rulers. They feared the power of this stranger. Such boldness on the part of an obscure Galilean was not to be tolerated. They were bent on putting an end to His work. But not all were agreed in this purpose. There were some that feared to oppose One who was so evidently moved upon by the Spirit of God. They remembered how prophets had been slain for rebuking the sins of the leaders in Israel. They knew that the bondage of the Jews to a heathen nation was the result of their stubbornness in rejecting reproofs from God. They feared that in plotting against Jesus the priests and rulers were following in the steps of their fathers, and would bring fresh calamities upon the nation. Nicodemus shared these feelings. In a [167-168] council of the Sanhedrin, when the course to be pursued toward Jesus was considered, Nicodemus advised caution and moderation. He urged that if Jesus was really invested with authority from God, it would be perilous to reject His warnings. The priests dared not disregard this counsel, and for the time they took no open measures against the Saviour.

Since hearing Jesus, Nicodemus had anxiously studied the prophecies relating to the Messiah; and the more he searched, the stronger was his conviction that this was the One who was to come. With many others in Israel he had been greatly distressed by the profana-

1. "In a council of the Sanhedrin, when a course to be pursued toward Jesus was considered [many wanted to put an end to this obscure Galilean's work], Nicodemus advised c_____ and moderation. He urged that if Jesus was really invested with authority from God, it would be p_____ to re-

tion of the temple He was a witness of the scene when Jesus drove out the buyers and the sellers; he beheld the wonderful manifestation of divine power; he saw the Saviour receiving the poor and healing the sick; he saw their looks of joy, and heard their words of praise; and he could not doubt that Jesus of Nazareth was the Sent of God.

He greatly desired an interview with Jesus, but shrank from seeking Him openly. It would be too humiliating for a ruler of the Jews to acknowledge himself in sympathy with a teacher as yet so little known. And should his visit come to the knowledge of the Sanhedrin, it would draw upon him their scorn and denunciation. He resolved upon a secret interview, excusing this on the ground that if he were to go openly, others might follow his example. Learning by special inquiry the Saviour's place of retirement in the Mount of Olives, he waited until the city was hushed in slumber, and then sought Him.

In the presence of Christ, Nicodemus felt a strange timidity, which he endeavored to conceal under an air of composure and dignity. "Rabbi," he said, "we know that Thou art a teacher come from God: for no man can do these miracles that Thou doest, except God be with him." By speaking of Christ's rare gifts as a teacher, and also of His wonderful power to perform miracles, he hoped to pave the way for his interview. His words were designed to express and to invite confidence; but they really expressed unbelief. He did not acknowledge Jesus to be the Messiah, but only a teacher sent from God.

Instead of recognizing this salutation, Jesus bent His eyes upon the speaker, as if reading his very soul. In His infinite wisdom He saw before Him a seeker after truth. He knew the object of this visit, and with a desire to deepen the conviction already resting upon His listener's mind, He came directly to the point, saying solemnly, yet kindly, "Verily, verily, I say unto thee, Except a man be born from above, he cannot see the kingdom of God." John 3:3, margin. [168-171]

Nicodemus had come to the Lord thinking to enter into a discussion with Him, but Jesus laid bare the foundation principles of truth. He said to Nicodemus, It is not theoretical knowledge you need so much as spiritual regeneration. You need not to have your curiosity satisfied, but to have a new heart. You must receive a

ject His warnings." (168). That's good counsel for me, too. And I already believe in You, Lord. Nicodemus was just open to You. So why do I discount so much of Your counsel? Do I not see, that to do so is perilous? _____

_____

2. "It would be too h_____ for a ruler of the Jews to acknowledge himself in sympathy with a teacher as yet so little known... it would draw their [Sanhedrin's] scorn and d_____." How could I be letting pride, or fear of what others might think of me, limit my walk with You, Lord?

_____
_____
_____
_____.
(I'll be seen as too fanatical? Too self-righteous? Too simple-minded?)_____

3. "Except a man be born from above, he cannot see the kingdom of God...It is not theoretical knowledge you need so much as spiritual r_____." (168,171). What is the difference? _____

_____
_____
(curiosity vs heart?) _____
_____
_____
_____

new life from above before you can appreciate heavenly things. Until this change takes place, making all things new, it will result in no saving good for you to discuss with Me My authority or My mission.

Nicodemus had heard the preaching of John the Baptist concerning repentance and baptism, and pointing the people to One who should baptize with the Holy Spirit. He himself had felt that there was a lack of spirituality among the Jews, that, to a great degree, they were controlled by bigotry and worldly ambition. He had hoped for a better state of things at the Messiah's coming. Yet the heart-searching message of the Baptist had failed to work in him conviction of sin. He was a strict Pharisee, and prided himself on his good works. He was widely esteemed for his benevolence and his liberality in sustaining the temple service, and he felt secure of the favor of God. He was startled at the thought of a kingdom too pure for him to see in his present state.

The figure of the new birth, which Jesus had used, was not wholly unfamiliar to Nicodemus. Converts from heathenism to the faith of Israel were often compared to children just born. Therefore he must have perceived that the words of Christ were not to be taken in a literal sense. But by virtue of his birth as an Israelite he regarded himself as sure of a place in the kingdom of God. He felt that he needed no change. Hence his surprise at the Saviour's words. He was irritated by their close application to himself. The pride of the Pharisee was struggling against the honest desire of the seeker after truth. He wondered that Christ should speak to him as He did, not respecting his position as ruler in Israel.

Surprised out of his self-possession, he answered Christ in words full of irony, "How can a man be born when he is old?" Like many others when cutting truth is brought home to the conscience, he revealed the fact that the natural man receiveth not the things of the Spirit of God. There is in him nothing that responds to spiritual things; for spiritual things are spiritually discerned.

But the Saviour did not meet argument with argument. Raising His hand with solemn, quiet dignity, He pressed the truth home with greater [171-172] assurance, "Verily, verily, I say unto thee, Except a man be born of water and of the Spirit, he cannot enter into the kingdom of God." Nicodemus knew that Christ here referred to water baptism and the renewing of the heart by the Spirit of God. He was convinced that he was in the

4. Nicodemus, a strict Pharisee, "felt secure of the favor of God," based on his good w_____, on his benevolence and liberality for the temple. But he had no conviction of s____. "He was s_____ at the thought of a kingdom too pure for him to see in his present state...The p_____ of a Pharisee was struggling against the honest desire of the seeker after truth." (171). It is easy to pat myself on the back, when I notice how evil the hearts of others' are. "I'm not like them!" Lord, is Your kingdom purer than where I am at? _____

presence of the One whom John the Baptist had fore-told.

Jesus continued: "That which is born of the flesh is flesh; and that which is born of the Spirit is spirit." By nature the heart is evil, and "who can bring a clean thing out of an unclean? not one." Job 14:4. No human invention can find a remedy for the sinning soul. "The carnal mind is enmity against God: for it is not subject to the law of God, neither indeed can be." "Out of the heart proceed evil thoughts, murders, adulteries, fornications, thefts, false witness, blasphemies." Rom. 8:7; Matt. 15:19. The fountain of the heart must be purified before the streams can become pure. He who is trying to reach heaven by his own works in keeping the law is attempting an impossibility. There is no safety for one who has merely a legal religion, a form of godliness. The Christian's life is not a modification or improvement of the old, but a transformation of nature. There is a death to self and sin, and a new life altogether. This change can be brought about only by the effectual working of the Holy Spirit.

Nicodemus was still perplexed, and Jesus used the wind to illustrate His meaning: "The wind bloweth where it listeth, and thou hearest the sound thereof, but canst not tell whence it cometh, and whither it goeth: so is everyone that is born of the Spirit."

The wind is heard among the branches of the trees, rustling the leaves and flowers; yet it is invisible, and no man knows whence it comes or whither it goes. So with the work of the Holy Spirit upon the heart. It can no more be explained than can the movements of the wind. A person may not be able to tell the exact time or place, or to trace all the circumstances in the process of conversion; but this does not prove him to be un-converted. By an agency as unseen as the wind, Christ is constantly working upon the heart. Little by little, perhaps unconsciously to the receiver, impressions are made that tend to draw the soul to Christ. These may be received through meditating upon Him, through reading the Scriptures, or through hearing the word from the living preacher. Suddenly, as the Spirit comes with more direct appeal, the soul gladly surrenders itself to Jesus. By many this is called sudden conversion; but it is the result of long wooing by the Spirit of God,--a patient, protracted process. [172-173]

While the wind is itself invisible, it produces effects

5. The kingdom of God is entered into through a birth with water and S_____. "The Christian's life is not a m_____ or improvement of the old, but a transformation of na-ture...This change can be brought about o_____ by the effectual working of the H_____ S_____." (172). Change for the sake of appearance is not of the Spirit. Nor is change attempted, to help others think better of me. Only change accomplished, by being available to the Holy Spirit, is what this birth is about:. What steps can I take to be available?

_____

_____

_____

6. "By an agency as un-seen as the wind, Christ is c_____ working upon the heart. Little by little, perhaps unconsciously to the receiver, impres-sions are made that tend to d_____ the soul to Christ." (172). How can I place myself where the Spirit is? _____

_____

_____

_____

(By m_____ upon Him, reading Scripture, hearing the word from preaching). Walking with God, then, as Enoch did, involves the Holy Spirit, daily drawing me.

7. "When the Spirit of God takes possession of the heart, it t_____ the life...Love, humility, and peace take the place of a_____, envy, and strife. Joy takes the place of sadness, and the countenance reflects the light of h_____." (173). If I don't see those transformations in my life, I should keep being available to the wind of the Spirit (through reading, meditating, preaching of the Word), and praying for the fruits of the Spirit: _____
_____
_____

that are seen and felt. So the work of the Spirit upon the soul will reveal itself in every act of him who has felt its saving power. When the Spirit of God takes possession of the heart, it transforms the life. Sinful thoughts are put away, evil deeds are renounced; love, humility, and peace take the place of anger, envy, and strife. Joy takes the place of sadness, and the countenance reflects the light of heaven. No one sees the hand that lifts the burden, or beholds the light descend from the courts above. The blessing comes when by faith the soul surrenders itself to God. Then that power which no human eye can see creates a new being in the image of God.

It is impossible for finite minds to comprehend the work of redemption. Its mystery exceeds human knowledge; yet he who passes from death to life realizes that it is a divine reality. The beginning of redemption we may know here through a personal experience. Its results reach through the eternal ages.

While Jesus was speaking, some gleams of truth penetrated the ruler's mind. The softening, subduing influence of the Holy Spirit impressed his heart. Yet he did not fully understand the Saviour's words. He was not so much impressed by the necessity of the new birth as by the manner of its accomplishment. He said wonderingly, "How can these things be?"

"Art thou a master of Israel, and knowest not these things?" Jesus asked. Surely one entrusted with the religious instruction of the people should not be ignorant of truths so important. His words conveyed the lesson that instead of feeling irritated over the plain words of truth, Nicodemus should have had a very humble opinion of himself, because of his spiritual ignorance. Yet Christ spoke with such solemn dignity, and both look and tone expressed such earnest love, that Nicodemus was not offended as he realized his humiliating condition.

But as Jesus explained that His mission on earth was to establish a spiritual instead of a temporal kingdom, His hearer was troubled. Seeing this, Jesus added, "If I have told you earthly things, and ye believe not, how shall ye believe, if I tell you of heavenly things?" If Nicodemus could not receive Christ's teaching, illustrating the work of grace upon the heart, how could he comprehend the nature of His glorious heavenly kingdom? Not discerning the nature of Christ's work on earth, he could not understand His work in heaven.

The Jews whom Jesus had driven from the temple

claimed to be children of Abraham, but they fled from the Saviour's presence because [173-174] they could not endure the glory of God which was manifested in Him. Thus they gave evidence that they were not fitted by the grace of God to participate in the sacred services of the temple. They were zealous to maintain an appearance of holiness, but they neglected holiness of heart. While they were sticklers for the letter of the law, they were constantly violating its spirit. Their great need was that very change which Christ had been explaining to Nicodemus,--a new moral birth, a cleansing from sin, and a renewing of knowledge and holiness.

There was no excuse for the blindness of Israel in regard to the work of regeneration. Under the inspiration of the Holy Spirit, Isaiah had written, "We are all as an unclean thing, and all our righteousnesses are as filthy rags." David had prayed, "Create in me a clean heart, O God; and renew a right spirit within me." And through Ezekiel the promise had been given, "A new heart also will I give you, and a new spirit will I put within you: and I will take away the stony heart out of your flesh, and I will give you an heart of flesh. And I will put My Spirit within you, and cause you to walk in My statutes." Isa. 64:6; Ps. 51:10; Ezek. 36:26, 27.

Nicodemus had read these scriptures with a clouded mind; but he now began to comprehend their meaning. He saw that the most rigid obedience to the mere letter of the law as applied to the outward life could entitle no man to enter the kingdom of heaven. In the estimation of men, his life had been just and honorable; but in the presence of Christ he felt that his heart was unclean, and his life unholy.

Nicodemus was being drawn to Christ. As the Saviour explained to him concerning the new birth, he longed to have this change wrought in himself. By what means could it be accomplished? Jesus answered the unspoken question: "As Moses lifted up the serpent in the wilderness, even so must the Son of man be lifted up: that whosoever believeth in Him should not perish, but have eternal life."

Here was ground with which Nicodemus was familiar. The symbol of the uplifted serpent made plain to him the Saviour's mission. When the people of Israel were dying from the sting of the fiery serpents, God directed Moses to make a serpent of brass, and place it on high in the midst of the congregation. Then the word

8. The Jews that fled from the temple, and the Savior's presence, "were zealous to maintain an appearance of h_____, but they neglected holiness of the h_____." They needed a change— "a new moral birth, a cleansing from sin, and a r_____ of knowledge and holiness." (174). Of the heart, Lord, my inner self. I want my heart to be drawn to You, not just my behavior: _____
_____
_____

9. "By what means could it [the change] be accomplished?" The Son of Man must be l_____ up." (174). How do I lift You up in my life, Lord?
_____
_____
_____
_____
_____

was sounded throughout the encampment that all who would look upon the serpent should live. The people well knew that in itself the serpent had no power to help them. It was a symbol of Christ. As the image made in the likeness of the [174-175] destroying serpents was lifted up for their healing, so One made "in the likeness of sinful flesh" was to be their Redeemer. Rom. 8:3. Many of the Israelites regarded the sacrificial service as having in itself virtue to set them free from sin. God desired to teach them that it had no more value than that serpent of brass. It was to lead their minds to the Saviour. Whether for the healing of their wounds or the pardon of their sins, they could do nothing for themselves but show their faith in the Gift of God. They were to look and live.

10. "Many of the Israelites regarded the sacrificial service as having in itself v_____ to set them free from sin. God desired to teach them that it had no more value than the serpent of b_____. It was to lead their minds to the Savior." (175). Lord, what should my attitude be towards tithing and temperance? _____

_____

_____

Those who had been bitten by the serpents might have delayed to look. They might have questioned how there could be efficacy in that brazen symbol. They might have demanded a scientific explanation. But no explanation was given. They must accept the word of God to them through Moses. To refuse to look was to perish.

Not through controversy and discussion is the soul enlightened. We must look and live. Nicodemus received the lesson, and carried it with him. He searched the Scriptures in a new way, not for the discussion of a theory, but in order to receive life for the soul. He began to see the kingdom of heaven as he submitted himself to the leading of the Holy Spirit.

There are thousands today who need to learn the same truth that was taught to Nicodemus by the uplifted serpent. They depend on their obedience to the law of God to commend them to His favor. When they are bidden to look to Jesus, and believe that He saves them solely through His grace, they exclaim, "How can these things be?"

11. "Faith is not our Savior." What does this mean? _____

_____

_____

_____

(the hand--lays hold on _____). Should I be impressed with someone's faith? _____

Like Nicodemus, we must be willing to enter into life in the same way as the chief of sinners. Than Christ, "there is none other name under heaven given among men, whereby we must be saved." Acts 4:12. Through faith we receive the grace of God; but faith is not our Saviour. It earns nothing. It is the hand by which we lay hold upon Christ, and appropriate His merits, the remedy for sin. And we cannot even repent without the aid of the Spirit of God. The Scripture says of Christ, "Him hath God exalted with His right hand to be a Prince and a Saviour, for to give repentance to Israel, and forgiveness of sins." Acts 5:31. Repentance comes from Christ as truly as does pardon.

How, then, are we to be saved? "As Moses lifted up the serpent in the wilderness," so the Son of man has been lifted up, and everyone who has been deceived and bitten by the serpent may look and live. "Behold the Lamb of God, which taketh away the sin of the [175-176] world." John 1:29. The light shining from the cross reveals the love of God. His love is drawing us to Himself. If we do not resist this drawing, we shall be led to the foot of the cross in repentance for the sins that have crucified the Saviour. Then the Spirit of God through faith produces a new life in the soul. The thoughts and desires are brought into obedience to the will of Christ. The heart, the mind, are created anew in the image of Him who works in us to subdue all things to Himself. Then the law of God is written in the mind and heart, and we can say with Christ, "I delight to do Thy will, O my God." Ps. 40:8.

In the interview with Nicodemus, Jesus unfolded the plan of salvation, and His mission to the world. In none of His subsequent discourses did He explain so fully, step by step, the work necessary to be done in the hearts of all who would inherit the kingdom of heaven. At the very beginning of His ministry He opened the truth to a member of the Sanhedrin, to the mind that was most receptive, and to an appointed teacher of the people. But the leaders of Israel did not welcome the light. Nicodemus hid the truth in his heart, and for three years there was little apparent fruit.

But Jesus was acquainted with the soil into which He cast the seed. The words spoken at night to one listener in the lonely mountain were not lost. For a time Nicodemus did not publicly acknowledge Christ, but he watched His life, and pondered His teachings. In the Sanhedrin council he repeatedly thwarted the schemes of the priests to destroy Him. When at last Jesus was lifted up on the cross, Nicodemus remembered the teaching upon Olivet: "As Moses lifted up the serpent in the wilderness, even so must the Son of man be lifted up: that whosoever believeth [176-177] in Him should not perish, but have eternal life." The light from that secret interview illumined the cross upon Calvary, and Nicodemus saw in Jesus the world's Redeemer.

After the Lord's ascension, when the disciples were

12. "We cannot even repent without the aid of the Spirit of God...Repentance comes from Christ as truly as does p_____ _____." Lord, what is the difference between a repentant heart and an unrepentant heart?

_____
_____

13. When we lift up the Son, "the cross reveals the love of God. His love is d_____ us to Himself. If we do not resist this drawing, we shall be l_____ to the foot of the cross in repentance for the sins that have crucified the Savior." (176). Resist the devil, but don't resist the drawing of God's love. It WILL happen! Lord, forgive me for my sin against Your heart, my sin that caused Your death: _____

_____
_____
_____

scattered by persecution, Nicodemus came boldly to the front. He employed his wealth in sustaining the infant church that the Jews had expected to be blotted out at the death of Christ. In the time of peril he who had been so cautious and questioning was firm as a rock, encouraging the faith of the disciples, and furnishing means to carry forward the work of the gospel. He was scorned and persecuted by those who had paid him reverence in other days. He became poor in this world's goods; yet he faltered not in the faith which had its beginning in that night conference with Jesus.

Nicodemus related to John the story of that interview, and by his pen it was recorded for the instruction of millions. The truths there taught are as important today as they were on that solemn night in the shadowy mountain, when the Jewish ruler came to learn the way of life from the lowly Teacher of Galilee.

Chapter 18

"He Must Increase"

[This chapter is based on John 3:22-36.]

For a time the Baptist's influence over the nation had been greater than that of its rulers, priests, or princes. If he had announced himself as the Messiah, and raised a revolt against Rome, priests and people would have flocked to his standard. Every consideration that appeals to the ambition of the world's conquerors Satan had stood ready to urge upon John the Baptist. But with the evidence before him of his power, he had steadfastly refused the splendid bribe. The attention which was fixed upon him he had directed to Another.

Now he saw the tide of popularity turning away from himself to the Saviour. Day by day the crowds about him lessened. When Jesus came from Jerusalem to the region about Jordan, the people flocked to hear Him. The number of His disciples increased daily. Many came for baptism, and while Christ Himself did not baptize, He sanctioned the administration of the ordinance by His disciples. Thus He set His seal upon the mission of His forerunner. But the disciples of John looked with jealousy upon the growing popularity of Jesus. They stood ready to criticize His work, and it was not long before they found occasion. A question arose between them and the Jews as to whether baptism availed to cleanse the soul from sin; they maintained that the baptism of Jesus differed essentially from that of John. Soon they were in dispute with Christ's disciples in regard to the form of words proper to use at baptism, and finally as to the right of the latter to baptize at all. [178-179]

The disciples of John came to him with their grievances, saying, "Rabbi, He that was with thee beyond Jordan, to whom thou bearest witness, behold, the same baptizeth, and all men come to Him." Through these words, Satan brought temptation upon John. Though John's mission seemed about to close, it was still possible for him to hinder the work of Christ. If he had sympathized with himself, and expressed grief or disappointment at being superseded, he would have sown the

1. "The disciples of John looked with jealousy upon the growing popularity of Jesus. They stood ready to c_____ His work." What occasions in my own life, do I recognize that criticism finds birth in jealousy? _____

2. "If he had s_____ _____ with himself, and expressed grief or disappointment at being superseded, he would have sown the seeds of d_____, would have encouraged envy and jealousy, and would seriously have impeded the progress of the g_____." (179). Lord, help me not to sow seeds of dissension. I don't need it in my life, and I don't want to hinder the gospel. Help me to be secure in who I am in Your love: _____

_____

_____

3. John manifested no sympathy with the d_____ _____ of his disciples. "He dwelt in an atmosphere uncontaminated with s_____ and a_____, and far above the miasma of jealousy." Where did that atmosphere come from?

_____

_____

And how can I have it?

_____

_____

4. How was John's joy fulfilled? _____

__ _____

_____

(direct people to Christ; witness success of Christ's work). "John had risen to the height of self-a_____." Isn't

seeds of dissension, would have encouraged envy and jealousy, and would seriously have impeded the progress of the gospel.

John had by nature the faults and weaknesses common to humanity, but the touch of divine love had transformed him. He dwelt in an atmosphere uncontaminated with selfishness and ambition, and far above the miasma of jealousy. He manifested no sympathy with the dissatisfaction of his disciples, but showed how clearly he understood his relation to the Messiah, and how gladly he welcomed the One for whom he had prepared the way.

He said, "A man can receive nothing, except it be given him from heaven. Ye yourselves bear me witness, that I said, I am not the Christ, but that I am sent before Him. He that hath the bride is the bridegroom: but the friend of the bridegroom, which standeth and heareth him, rejoiceth greatly because of the bridegroom's voice." John represented himself as the friend who acted as a messenger between the betrothed parties, preparing the way for the marriage. When the bridegroom had received his bride, the mission of the friend was fulfilled. He rejoiced in the happiness of those whose union he had promoted. So John had been called to direct the people to Jesus, and it was his joy to witness the success of the Saviour's work. He said, "This my joy therefore is fulfilled. He must increase, but I must decrease."

Looking in faith to the Redeemer, John had risen to the height of self-abnegation. He sought not to attract men to himself, but to lift their thoughts higher and still higher, until they should rest upon the Lamb of God. He himself had been only a voice, a cry in the wilderness. Now with joy he accepted silence and obscurity, that the eyes of all might be turned to the Light of life.

Those who are true to their calling as messengers for God will not seek honor for themselves. Love for self will be swallowed up in love for Christ. No rivalry will mar the precious cause of the gospel. They will recognize that it is their work to proclaim, as did John the Baptist, [179-180] "Behold the Lamb of God, which taketh away the sin of the world." John 1:29. They will lift up Jesus, and with Him humanity will be lifted up. "Thus saith the high and lofty One that inhabiteth eternity, whose name is Holy; I dwell in the high and holy place, with him also that is of a contrite and humble spirit, to revive the spirit of the humble, and to revive the heart of the contrite ones." Isa. 57:15.

The soul of the prophet, emptied of self, was filled with the light of the divine. As he witnessed to the Saviour's glory, his words were almost a counterpart of those that Christ Himself had spoken in His interview with Nicodemus. John said, "He that cometh from above is above all: he that is of the earth is earthly, and speaketh of the earth: He that cometh from heaven is above all. . . . For He whom God hath sent speaketh the words of God: for God giveth not the Spirit by measure unto Him." Christ could say, "I seek not Mine own will, but the will of the Father which hath sent Me." John 5:30. To Him it is declared, "Thou hast loved righteousness, and hated iniquity; therefore God, even Thy God, hath anointed Thee with the oil of gladness above Thy fellows." Heb. 1:9. The Father "giveth not the Spirit by measure unto Him." [180-181]

So with the followers of Christ. We can receive of heaven's light only as we are willing to be emptied of self. We cannot discern the character of God, or accept Christ by faith, unless we consent to the bringing into captivity of every thought to the obedience of Christ. To all who do this the Holy Spirit is given without measure. In Christ "dwelleth all the fullness of the Godhead bodily, and in Him ye are made full." Col. 2:9, 10, R. V.

The disciples of John had declared that all men were coming to Christ; but with clearer insight, John said, "No man receiveth His witness;" so few were ready to accept Him as the Saviour from sin. But "he that hath received His witness hath set his seal to this, that God is true." John 3:33, R. V. "He that believeth on the Son hath everlasting life." No need of disputation as to whether Christ's baptism or John's purified from sin. It is the grace of Christ that gives life to the soul. Apart from Christ, baptism, like any other service, is a worthless form. "He that believeth not the Son shall not see life."

The success of Christ's work, which the Baptist had received with such joy, was reported also to the authorities at Jerusalem. The priests and rabbis had been jealous of John's influence as they saw the people leaving the synagogues and flocking to the wilderness; but here was One who had still greater power to attract the multitudes. Those leaders in Israel were not willing to say with John, "He must increase, but I must decrease."

this the opposite of self-promotion?_____

_____

_____. Lord, lend me John's joy: being happy at the success of others, and not jealous: _____

_____

_____

5. What must the soul be emptied of, to be filled with the light of the divine? (181). _____
____ Why? _____
_____
_____

"We cannot discern the character of God, or accept Christ by faith, unless we c_____ to the bringing into captivity of every t_____ to the obedience of Christ." Lord, I can't control every thought, but I can consent, giving You permission. Remind me: _____

_____

6. "The priests and rabbis had been jealous of John's influence...Those leaders in Israel were not willing to say with John, [about Christ] 'He must increase,

but I must d_____
_____.'" (181). Am I willing? _____ How do I know? _____
_____
_____

I want You, Lord, and You only, to be seen. Help me be empty of self; how is self manifested? _____
_____
_____

7. We "should try to avoid all that may lead to discord and misapprehension. For whenever these arise, they result in the loss of s_____." I think I understand now, Lord. But what about when I am in the middle of it? Would You help me remember the loss of souls? _____
_____
_____

Prayer Journal: _____
_____
_____
_____
_____
_____
_____

They arose with a new determination to put an end to the work that was drawing the people away from them.

Jesus knew that they would spare no effort to create a division between His own disciples and those of John. He knew that the storm was gathering which would sweep away one of the greatest prophets ever given to the world. Wishing to avoid all occasion for misunderstanding or dissension, He quietly ceased His labors, and withdrew to Galilee. We also, while loyal to truth, should try to avoid all that may lead to discord and misapprehension. For whenever these arise, they result in the loss of souls. Whenever circumstances occur that threaten to cause division, we should follow the example of Jesus and of John the Baptist.

John had been called to lead out as a reformer. Because of this, his disciples were in danger of fixing their attention upon him, feeling that the success of the work depended upon his labors, and losing sight of the fact that he was only an instrument through which God had wrought. But the work of John was not sufficient to lay the foundation of the [181-182] Christian church. When he had fulfilled his mission, another work was to be done, which his testimony could not accomplish. His disciples did not understand this. When they saw Christ coming in to take the work, they were jealous and dissatisfied.

The same dangers still exist. God calls a man to do a certain work; and when he has carried it as far as he is qualified to take it, the Lord brings in others, to carry it still farther. But, like John's disciples, many feel that the success of the work depends on the first laborer. Attention is fixed upon the human instead of the divine, jealousy comes in, and the work of God is marred. The one thus unduly honored is tempted to cherish self-confidence. He does not realize his dependence on God. The people are taught to rely on man for guidance, and thus they fall into error, and are led away from God.

The work of God is not to bear the image and superscription of man. From time to time the Lord will bring in different agencies, through whom His purpose can best be accomplished. Happy are they who are willing for self to be humbled, saying with John the Baptist, "He must increase, but I must decrease."

Chapter 19

At Jacob's Well
[This chapter is based on John 4:1-42.]

On the way to Galilee Jesus passed through Samaria. It was noon when He reached the beautiful Vale of Shechem. At the opening of this valley was Jacob's well. Wearied with His journey, He sat down here to rest while His disciples went to buy food.

The Jews and the Samaritans were bitter enemies, and as far as possible avoided all dealing with each other. To trade with the Samaritans in case of necessity was indeed counted lawful by the rabbis; but all social intercourse with them was condemned. A Jew would not borrow from a Samaritan, nor receive a kindness, not even a morsel of bread or a cup of water. The disciples, in buying food, were acting in harmony with the custom of their nation. But beyond this they did not go. To ask a favor of the Samaritans, or in any way seek to benefit them, did not enter into the thought of even Christ's disciples.

As Jesus sat by the well side, He was faint from hunger and thirst. The journey since morning had been long, and now the sun of noontide beat upon Him. His thirst was increased by the thought of the cool, refreshing water so near, yet inaccessible to Him; for He had no rope nor water jar, and the well was deep. The lot of humanity was His, and He waited for someone to come to draw.

A woman of Samaria approached, and seeming unconscious of His presence, filled her pitcher with water. As she turned to go away, Jesus asked her for a drink. Such a favor no Oriental would withhold. In the East, water was called "the gift of God." To offer a drink to the thirsty traveler was held to be a duty so sacred that the Arabs of [183-184] the desert would go out of their way in order to perform it. The hatred between Jews and Samaritans prevented the woman from offering a kindness to Jesus; but the Saviour was seeking to find the key to this heart, and with the tact born of divine love, He asked, not offered, a favor. The offer of a kindness

1. Why did Jesus ask a favor of the woman at the well, instead of offering a favor? _____

_____

_____

An offer of kindness might have been r_____; but t_____ awakens trust. (184). That's how Jesus treated the woman; that's how He treats me. How do I, how should I treat others, Lord? _____

_____

_____

2. "The woman had not comprehended the words of Christ, but she felt their solemn i_____." What should I do if I have the same experience? ____

_____

Instead of light banter, dig for deeper thoughts? Wait for further illumination? Ask questions? What is living water, Lord? I want to hear what You have to say about living water: _____

_____

_____

3. "How many thirsty souls are today c_____ by the living fountain, yet looking far away for the wellsprings of l_____!" Jesus, You are my everything! I don't need to be looking anywhere else. Where am I looking?

_____

_____

May You be the first Per-

might have been rejected; but trust awakens trust. The King of heaven came to this outcast soul, asking a service at her hands. He who made the ocean, who controls the waters of the great deep, who opened the springs and channels of the earth, rested from His weariness at Jacob's well, and was dependent upon a stranger's kindness for even the gift of a drink of water.

The woman saw that Jesus was a Jew. In her surprise she forgot to grant His request, but tried to learn the reason for it. "How is it," she said, "that Thou, being a Jew, askest drink of me, which am a woman of Samaria?"

Jesus answered, "If thou knewest the gift of God, and who it is that saith to thee, Give Me to drink; thou wouldest have asked of Him, and He would have given thee living water." You wonder that I should ask of you even so small a favor as a draught of water from the well at our feet. Had you asked of Me, I would have given you to drink of the water of everlasting life.

The woman had not comprehended the words of Christ, but she felt their solemn import. Her light, bantering manner began to change. Supposing that Jesus spoke of the well before them, she said, "Sir, Thou hast nothing to draw with, and the well is deep: from whence then hast Thou that living water? Art Thou greater than our father Jacob, which gave us the well, and drank thereof himself?" She saw before her only a thirsty traveler, wayworn and dusty. In her mind she compared Him with the honored patriarch Jacob. She cherished the feeling, which is so natural, that no other well could be equal to that provided by the fathers. She was looking backward to the fathers, forward to the Messiah's coming, while the Hope of the fathers, the Messiah Himself, was beside her, and she knew Him not. How many thirsting souls are today close by the living fountain, yet looking far away for the wellsprings of life! "Say not in thine heart, Who shall ascend into heaven? (that is, to bring Christ down from above:) or, Who shall descend into the deep? (that is, to bring up Christ again from the dead.) . . . The word is nigh thee, even in thy mouth, and in thy heart: . . . if thou shalt confess with thy mouth the Lord Jesus, and shalt believe in thine heart that God hath raised Him from the dead, thou shalt be saved." Rom. 10:6-9. [184-187]

Jesus did not immediately answer the question in regard to Himself, but with solemn earnestness He said,

"Whosoever drinketh of this water shall thirst again: but whosoever drinketh of the water that I shall give him shall never thirst; but the water that I shall give him shall be in him a well of water springing up into everlasting life."

He who seeks to quench his thirst at the fountains of this world will drink only to thirst again. Everywhere men are unsatisfied. They long for something to supply the need of the soul. Only One can meet that want. The need of the world, "The Desire of all nations," is Christ. The divine grace which He alone can impart, is as living water, purifying, refreshing, and invigorating the soul.

Jesus did not convey the idea that merely one draft of the water of life would suffice the receiver. He who tastes of the love of Christ will continually long for more; but he seeks for nothing else. The riches, honors, and pleasures of the world do not attract him. The constant cry of his heart is, More of Thee. And He who reveals to the soul its necessity is waiting to satisfy its hunger and thirst. Every human resource and dependence will fail. The cisterns will be emptied, the pools become dry; but our Redeemer is an inexhaustible fountain. We may drink, and drink again, and ever find a fresh supply. He in whom Christ dwells has within himself the fountain of blessing,--"a well of water springing up into everlasting life." From this source he may draw strength and grace sufficient for all his needs.

As Jesus spoke of the living water, the woman looked upon Him with wondering attention. He had aroused her interest, and awakened a desire for the gift of which He spoke. She perceived that it was not the water of Jacob's well to which He referred; for of this she used continually, drinking, and thirsting again. "Sir," she said, "give me this water, that I thirst not, neither come hither to draw."

Jesus now abruptly turned the conversation. Before this soul could receive the gift He longed to bestow, she must be brought to recognize her sin and her Saviour. He "saith unto her, Go, call thy husband, and come hither." She answered, "I have no husband." Thus she hoped to prevent all questioning in that direction. But the Saviour continued, "Thou hast well said, I have no husband: for thou hast had five husbands; and he whom thou now hast is not thy husband: in that saidst thou truly."

The listener trembled. A mysterious hand was turn-

son I turn to: _____
_____

4. "He who seeks to quench his thirst at the fountains of this w_____ will drink only to thirst again... The need of the world, 'The Desire of all nations,' [Desire of Ages] is C_____." (187). Where could I go but to the Lord? Only He satisfies, He always satisfies, and fulfills. He is the ultimate desire. Lord, I long to worship You. "The c_____ cry of his heart is, More of Thee."

ing the pages of her life history, bringing to view that which she had hoped to keep forever [187-188] hidden. Who was He that could read the secrets of her life? There came to her thoughts of eternity, of the future Judgment, when all that is now hidden shall be revealed. In its light, conscience was awakened.

She could deny nothing; but she tried to evade all mention of a subject so unwelcome. With deep reverence, she said, "Sir, I perceive that Thou art a prophet." Then, hoping to silence conviction, she turned to points of religious controversy. If this was a prophet, surely He could give her instruction concerning these matters that had been so long disputed.

Patiently Jesus permitted her to lead the conversation whither she would. Meanwhile He watched for the opportunity of again bringing the truth home to her heart. "Our fathers worshiped in this mountain," she said, "and ye say, that in Jerusalem is the place where men ought to worship." Just in sight was Mount Gerizim. Its temple was demolished, and only the altar remained. The place of worship had been a subject of contention between the Jews and the Samaritans. Some of the ancestors of the latter people had once belonged to Israel; but because of their sins, the Lord suffered them to be overcome by an idolatrous nation. For many generations they were intermingled with idolaters, whose religion gradually contaminated their own. It is true they held that their idols were only to remind them of the living God, the Ruler of the universe; nevertheless the people were led to reverence their graven images.

When the temple at Jerusalem was rebuilt in the days of Ezra, the Samaritans wished to join the Jews in its erection. This privilege was refused them, and a bitter animosity sprang up between the two peoples. The Samaritans built a rival temple on Mount Gerizim. Here they worshiped in accordance with the Mosaic ritual, though they did not wholly renounce idolatry. But disasters attended them, their temple was destroyed by their enemies, and they seemed to be under a curse; yet they still clung to their traditions and their forms of worship. They would not acknowledge the temple at Jerusalem as the house of God, nor admit that the religion of the Jews was superior to their own.

In answer to the woman, Jesus said, "Believe Me, the hour cometh, when ye shall neither in this mountain, nor yet at Jerusalem, worship the Father. Ye worship ye know not what: we know what we worship: for salvation is of the Jews." Jesus had shown that He was free from Jewish prejudice against the Samaritans. Now He sought to break down [188-189] the prejudice of this Samaritan against the Jews. While referring to the fact that the faith of the Samaritans was corrupted with idolatry, He declared that the great truths of redemption had been committed to the Jews, and that from among them the Messiah was to appear. In the Sacred Writings they had a clear presentation of the character of God and the principles of His government. Jesus classed Himself with the Jews as those to whom God had given a knowledge of Himself.

He desired to lift the thoughts of His hearer above matters of form and ceremony, and questions of controversy. "The hour cometh," He said, "and now is, when the true worshipers shall worship the Father in spirit and in truth: for the Father seeketh such to worship Him. God is a Spirit: and they that worship Him must worship Him in spirit and in truth."

Here is declared the same truth that Jesus had revealed to Nicodemus when He said, "Except a man be born from above, he cannot see the kingdom of God." John 3:3, margin. Not by seeking a holy mountain or a sacred temple are men brought into communion with heaven. Religion is not to be confined to external forms and ceremonies. The religion that comes from God is the only religion that will lead to God. In order to serve Him aright, we must be born of the divine Spirit. This will purify the heart and renew the mind, giving us a new capacity for knowing and loving God. It will give us a willing obedience to all His requirements. This is true worship. It is the fruit of the working of the Holy Spirit. By the Spirit every sincere prayer is indited, and such prayer is acceptable to God. Wherever a soul reaches out after God, there the Spirit's working is manifest, and God will reveal Himself to that soul. For such worshipers He is seeking. He waits to receive them, and to make them His sons and daughters.

As the woman talked with Jesus, she was impressed with His words. Never had she heard such sentiments from the priests of her own people or from the Jews. As the past of her life had been spread out before her, she had been made sensible of her great want. She realized her soul thirst, which the waters of the well of Sychar could never satisfy. Nothing that had hitherto come

5. Jesus "desired to lift the thoughts of His hearer above matters of form and ceremony, and questions of c_____ _____." Worship of the Father is done "in spirit and in t_____...The religion that comes from God is the only one that will lead to God." (189). Genuine religion brings me closer to God, giving me a "new capacity for knowing and loving God." Lord, lift my thoughts; I thirst for this new capacity for knowing and loving You: _____
_____
_____

6. "She realized her soul thirst...Nothing that had hitherto come in contact

with her had so awakened her to a h_____ need. Jesus had convinced her that He read the secrets of her life; yet she felt that He was her f_____, pitying and loving her." Lord, that's me. You know me better than I know myself. Take me, I'm yours. Thanks for being my best Friend! _____

_____

_____

When I speak to others in admonition, do they know I am a friend? _____

_____

in contact with her had so awakened her to a higher need. Jesus had convinced her that He read the secrets of her life; yet she felt that He was her friend, pitying and loving her. While the very purity of His presence condemned her sin, He had spoken no word of denunciation, but had told her of His grace, that could renew [189-190] the soul. She began to have some conviction of His character. The question arose in her mind, Might not this be the long-looked-for Messiah? She said to Him, "I know that Messias cometh, which is called Christ: when He is come, He will tell us all things." Jesus answered, "I that speak unto thee am He."

As the woman heard these words, faith sprang up in her heart. She accepted the wonderful announcement from the lips of the divine Teacher.

This woman was in an appreciative state of mind. She was ready to receive the noblest revelation; for she was interested in the Scriptures, and the Holy Spirit had been preparing her mind to receive more light. She had studied the Old Testament promise, "The Lord thy God will raise up unto thee a Prophet from the midst of thee, of thy brethren, like unto me; unto Him ye shall hearken." Deut. 18:15. She longed to understand this prophecy. Light was already flashing into her mind. The water of life, the spiritual life which Christ gives to every thirsty soul, had begun to spring up in her heart. The Spirit of the Lord was working with her.

The plain statement made by Christ to this woman could not have been made to the self-righteous Jews. Christ was far more reserved when He spoke to them. That which had been withheld from the Jews, and which the disciples were afterward enjoined to keep secret, was revealed to her. Jesus saw that she would make use of her knowledge in bringing others to share His grace.

When the disciples returned from their errand, they were surprised to find their Master speaking with the woman. He had not taken the refreshing draught that He desired, and He did not stop to eat the food His disciples had brought. When the woman had gone, the disciples entreated Him to eat. They saw Him silent, absorbed, as in rapt meditation. His face was beaming with light, and they feared to interrupt His communion with heaven. But they knew that He was faint and weary, and thought it their duty to remind Him of His physical necessities. Jesus recognized their loving interest, and He said, "I have meat to eat that ye know not of."

7. "His face was beaming with light, and they feared to interrupt His c_____ _____ with heaven...'I have meat to eat that ye know not

The disciples wondered who could have brought Him food; but He explained, "My meat is to do the will of Him that sent Me, and to accomplish His work." John 4:34, R. V. As His words to the woman had aroused her conscience, Jesus rejoiced. He saw her drinking of the water [190-191] of life, and His own hunger and thirst were satisfied. The accomplishment of the mission which He had left heaven to perform strengthened the Saviour for His labor, and lifted Him above the necessities of humanity. To minister to a soul hungering and thirsting for the truth was more grateful to Him than eating or drinking. It was a comfort, a refreshment, to Him. Benevolence was the life of His soul.

Our Redeemer thirsts for recognition. He hungers for the sympathy and love of those whom He has purchased with His own blood. He longs with inexpressible desire that they should come to Him and have life. As the mother watches for the smile of recognition from her little child, which tells of the dawning of intelligence, so does Christ watch for the expression of grateful love, which shows that spiritual life is begun in the soul.

The woman had been filled with joy as she listened to Christ's words. The wonderful revelation was almost overpowering. Leaving her waterpot, she returned to the city, to carry the message to others. Jesus knew why she had gone. Leaving her waterpot spoke unmistakably as to the effect of His words. It was the earnest desire of her soul to obtain the living water; and she forgot her errand to the well, she forgot the Saviour's thirst, which she had purposed to supply. With heart overflowing with gladness, she hastened on her way, to impart to others the precious light she had received.

"Come, see a man, which told me all things that ever I did," she said to the men of the city. "Is not this the Christ?" Her words touched their hearts. There was a new expression on her face, a change in her whole appearance. They were interested to see Jesus. "Then they went out of the city, and came unto Him."

As Jesus still sat at the well side, He looked over the fields of grain that were spread out before Him, their tender green touched by the golden sunlight. Pointing His disciples to the scene, He employed it as a symbol: "Say not ye, There are yet four months, and then cometh harvest? behold, I say unto you, Lift up your eyes, and look on the fields; for they are white already to harvest." And as He spoke, He looked on the groups

of'... To minister to a soul hungering and thirsting for the truth was more g____ _____ to Him than eating or drinking. It was a comfort, a refreshment, to Him. B_____ was the life of His soul." (190-191). Lord, I want to know of this meat, to taste it. Bring me in contact with individuals who are hungering and thirsting, and grant me spiritual sensitivity to recognize it: __
_____
_____
_____

8. "As the mother watches for the s_____ of recognition from her little child, which tells of the dawning of intelligence, so does Christ w_____ for the expression of grateful love, which s_____ that spiritual life is begun in the soul." Thank You, Lord. You mean everything to me. Forgive me for taking You for granted: _____
_____

that were coming to the well. It was four months to the time for harvesting the grain, but here was a harvest ready for the reaper.

"He that reapeth," He said, "receiveth wages, and gathereth fruit unto life eternal: that both he that soweth and he that reapeth may rejoice [191-192] together. And herein is that saying true, One soweth, and another reapeth." Here Christ points out the sacred service owed to God by those who receive the gospel. They are to be His living agencies. He requires their individual service. And whether we sow or reap, we are working for God. One scatters the seed; another gathers in the harvest; and both the sower and the reaper receive wages. They rejoice together in the reward of their labor.

Jesus said to the disciples, "I sent you to reap that whereon ye bestowed no labor: other men labored, and ye are entered into their labors." The Saviour was here looking forward to the great ingathering on the day of Pentecost. The disciples were not to regard this as the result of their own efforts. They were entering into other men's labors. Ever since the fall of Adam Christ had been committing the seed of the word to His chosen servants, to be sown in human hearts. And an unseen agency, even an omnipotent power, had worked silently but effectually to produce the harvest. The dew and rain and sunshine of God's grace had been given, to refresh and nourish the seed of truth. Christ was about to water the seed with His own blood. His disciples were privileged to be laborers together with God. They were coworkers with Christ and with the holy men of old. By the outpouring of the Holy Spirit at Pentecost, thousands were to be converted in a day. This was the result of Christ's sowing, the harvest of His work.

In the words spoken to the woman at the well, good seed had been sown, and how quickly the harvest was received. The Samaritans came and heard Jesus, and believed on Him. Crowding about Him at the well, they plied Him with questions, and eagerly received His explanations of many things that had been obscure to them. As they listened, their perplexity began to clear away. They were like a people in great darkness tracing up a sudden ray of light till they had found the day. But they were not satisfied with this short conference. They were anxious to hear more, and to have their friends also listen to this wonderful teacher. They invited Him to their city, and begged Him to remain with them. For two days He tarried in Samaria, and many more believed on Him.

The Pharisees despised the simplicity of Jesus. They ignored His miracles, and demanded a sign that He was the Son of God. But the Samaritans asked no sign, and Jesus performed no miracles among them, save in revealing the secrets of her life to the woman at the well. Yet many received Him. In their new joy they said to the woman, [192-193] "Now we believe, not because of thy saying: for we have heard Him ourselves, and know that this is indeed the Christ, the Saviour of the world."

The Samaritans believed that the Messiah was to come as the Redeemer, not only of the Jews, but of the world. The Holy Spirit through Moses had foretold Him as a prophet sent from God. Through Jacob it had been declared that unto Him should the gathering of the people be; and through Abraham, that in Him all the nations of the earth should be blessed. On these scriptures the people of Samaria based their faith in the Messiah. The fact that the Jews had misinterpreted the later prophets, attributing to the first advent the glory of Christ's second coming, had led the Samaritans to discard all the sacred writings except those given through Moses. But as the Saviour swept away these false interpretations, many accepted the later prophecies and the words of Christ Himself in regard to the kingdom of God.

Jesus had begun to break down the partition wall between Jew and Gentile, and to preach salvation to the world. Though He was a Jew, He mingled freely with the Samaritans, setting at nought the Pharisaic customs of His nation. In face of their prejudices He accepted the hospitality of this despised people. He slept under their roofs, ate with them at their tables,--partaking of the food prepared and served by their hands,--taught in their streets, and treated them with the utmost kindness and courtesy.

In the temple at Jerusalem a low wall separated the outer court from all other portions of the sacred building. Upon this wall were inscriptions in different languages, stating that none but Jews were allowed to pass this boundary. Had a Gentile presumed to enter the inner enclosure, he would have desecrated the temple, and would have paid the penalty with his life. But Jesus, the originator of the temple and its service, drew the Gentiles to Him by the tie of human sympathy, while His divine grace brought to them the salvation which the Jews rejected.

The stay of Jesus in Samaria was designed to be a blessing to His disciples, who were still under the influence of Jewish bigotry. They felt that loyalty to their own nation required them to cherish enmity toward the Samaritans. They wondered at the conduct of Jesus. They could not refuse to follow His example, and during the two days in Samaria, fidelity to Him kept their prejudices under control; yet in heart they were unreconciled. They were slow to learn that their contempt and [193-194] hatred must give place to pity and sympathy. But after the Lord's ascension, His lessons came back to them with a new meaning. After the outpouring of the Holy Spirit, they recalled the Saviour's look, His words, the respect and tenderness of His bearing toward these despised strangers. When Peter went to preach in Samaria, he brought the same spirit into his own work. When John was called to Ephesus and Smyrna, he remembered the experience at Shechem, and was filled with gratitude to the divine Teacher, who, foreseeing the difficulties they must meet, had given them help in His own example.

The Saviour is still carrying forward the same work as when He proffered the water of life to the woman of Samaria. Those who call themselves His followers may despise and shun the outcast ones; but no circumstance of birth or nationality, no condition of life, can turn away His love from the children of men. To every soul, however sinful, Jesus says, If thou hadst asked of Me, I would have given thee living water.

The gospel invitation is not to be narrowed down, and presented only to a select few, who, we suppose, will do us honor if they accept it. The message is to be given to all. Wherever hearts are open to receive the truth, Christ is ready to instruct them. He reveals to them the Father, and the worship acceptable to Him who reads the heart. For such He uses no parables. To them, as to the woman at the well, He says, "I that speak unto thee am He."

When Jesus sat down to rest at Jacob's well, He had come from Judea, where His ministry had produced little fruit. He had been rejected by the priests and rabbis, and even the people who professed to be His disciples had failed of perceiving His divine character. He was faint and weary; yet He did not neglect the opportunity of speaking to one woman, though she was a stranger, an alien from Israel, and living in open sin.

The Saviour did not wait for congregations to assemble. Often He began His lessons with only a few gathered about Him, but one by one the passers-by paused to listen, until a multitude heard with wonder and awe the words of God through the heaven-sent Teacher. The worker for Christ should not feel that he cannot speak with the same earnestness to a few hearers as to a larger company. There may be only one to hear the message; but who can tell how far-reaching will be its influence? It seemed a small matter, even to His disciples, for the Saviour to spend [194-195] His time upon a woman of Samaria. But He reasoned more earnestly and eloquently with her than with kings, councilors, or high priests. The lessons He gave to that woman have been repeated to the earth's remotest bounds.

As soon as she had found the Saviour the Samaritan woman brought others to Him. She proved herself a more effective missionary than His own disciples. The disciples saw nothing in Samaria to indicate that it was an encouraging field. Their thoughts were fixed upon a great work to be done in the future. They did not see that right around them was a harvest to be gathered. But through the woman whom they despised, a whole cityful were brought to hear the Saviour. She carried the light at once to her countrymen.

This woman represents the working of a practical faith in Christ. Every true disciple is born into the kingdom of God as a missionary. He who drinks of the living water becomes a fountain of life. The receiver becomes a giver. The grace of Christ in the soul is like a spring in the desert, welling up to refresh all, and making those who are ready to perish eager to drink of the water of life.

9. "It seemed a small matter, even to His disciples, for the Savior to spend His t_____ upon a woman of Samaria. But He reasoned more earnestly and eloquently with her than with kings, councilors, or high priests." (194, 195). What lessons should I learn from Jesus' example? _____

_____

_____

"Every true disciple is born into the kingdom of God as a m_____. He who drinks of the living water b_____ a fountain of life. The receiver becomes a g____ ____. The grace of Christ in the soul is like a spring in the desert, welling up to refresh all, and making those who are ready to perish e_____ to drink of the water of life." Lord, let me bask in Your grace. I have tasted Your living water. Let me be a fountain of Your grace, for others to taste. _____

_____

_____

Prayer Journal: _____

_____

_____

_____

_____

_____

_____

_____

Chapter 20

"Except Ye See Signs and Wonders"

[This chapter is based on John 4:43-54.]

1. Why did Jesus not visit Nazareth on His way to Cana? _____ _____. Could my lack of believing on Him, limit Christ from visiting me? _____ "A prophet has no h_____ in his own country." Why? Does familiarity render it ordinary?_____ _____ Lord, having heard the gospel story for years, have I let it become ordinary? Help my response to You not be casual, but rather to see Your value and to honor You: _____ _____ _____

2. "Men estimate character by that which they themselves are capable of a_____... They could not appreciate the p_____ of that spirit upon which was no stain of sin." Lord, I don't want my lack of spirituality to be the end point of knowing You and Your character. That would be infinitly shallow. Help me to better fathom Your purity of spirit, and my estimation of Your character to exponentially grow: _____

The Galileans who returned from the Passover brought back the report of the wonderful works of Jesus. The judgment passed upon His acts by the dignitaries at Jerusalem opened His way in Galilee. Many of the people lamented the abuse of the temple and the greed and arrogance of the priests. They hoped that this Man, who had put the rulers to flight, might be the looked-for Deliverer. Now tidings had come that seemed to confirm their brightest anticipations. It was reported that the prophet had declared Himself to be the Messiah.

But the people of Nazareth did not believe on Him. For this reason, Jesus did not visit Nazareth on His way to Cana. The Saviour declared to His disciples that a prophet has no honor in his own country. Men estimate character by that which they themselves are capable of appreciating. The narrow and worldly-minded judged of Christ by His humble birth, His lowly garb, and daily toil. They could not appreciate the purity of that spirit upon which was no stain of sin.

The news of Christ's return to Cana soon spread throughout Galilee, bringing hope to the suffering and distressed. In Capernaum the tidings attracted the attention of a Jewish nobleman who was an officer in the [196-197] king's service. A son of the officer was suffering from what seemed to be an incurable disease. Physicians had given him up to die; but when the father heard of Jesus, he determined to seek help from Him. The child was very low, and, it was feared, might not live till his return; yet the nobleman felt that he must present the case in person. He hoped that a father's prayers might awaken the sympathy of the Great Physician.

On reaching Cana he found a throng surrounding Jesus. With an anxious heart he pressed through to the Saviour's presence. His faith faltered when he saw only a plainly dressed man, dusty and worn with travel. He doubted that this Person could do what he had come to ask of Him; yet he secured an interview with Jesus, told his errand, and besought the Saviour to accompany him to his home. But already his [197-198] sorrow was known to Jesus. Before the officer had left his home, the Saviour had beheld his affliction.

But He knew also that the father had, in his own mind, made conditions concerning his belief in Jesus. Unless his petition should be granted, he would not receive Him as the Messiah. While the officer waited in an agony of suspense, Jesus said, "Except ye see signs and wonders, ye will not believe."

Notwithstanding all the evidence that Jesus was the Christ, the petitioner had determined to make his belief in Him conditional on the granting of his own request. The Saviour contrasted this questioning unbelief with the simple faith of the Samaritans, who asked for no miracle or sign. His word, the ever-present evidence of His divinity, had a convincing power that reached their hearts. Christ was pained that His own people, to whom the Sacred Oracles had been committed, should fail to hear the voice of God speaking to them in His Son.

Yet the nobleman had a degree of faith; for he had come to ask what seemed to him the most precious of all blessings. Jesus had a greater gift to bestow. He desired, not only to heal the child, but to make the officer and his household sharers in the blessings of salvation, and to kindle a light in Capernaum, which was so soon to be the field of His own labors. But the nobleman must realize his need before he would desire the grace of Christ. This courtier represented many of his nation. They were interested in Jesus from selfish motives. They hoped to receive some special benefit through His power, and they staked their faith on the granting of this temporal favor; but they were ignorant as to their spiritual disease, and saw not their need of divine grace.

Like a flash of light, the Saviour's words to the nobleman laid bare his heart. He saw that his motives in seeking Jesus were selfish. His vacillating faith appeared to him in its true character. In deep distress he realized that his doubt might cost the life of his son. He knew that he was in the presence of One who could read the thoughts, and to whom all things were possible. In an agony of supplication he cried, "Sir, come down ere my child die." His faith took hold upon Christ as did

3. A Jewish nobleman "made c_____ concerning his belief in Jesus. Unless his petition should be granted [son with an incurable disease], he would not receive Him as the M_____." (198). Is my belief, is my availability to You, Lord, conditional upon continued blessings, of things going right? _____
_____
_____

4. "The Savior contrasted this q_____ unbelief with the simple faith of the Samaritans, who asked for no miracle or sign...Christ was p_____ that His own people, to whom the Sacred Oracles had been committed, should fail to hear the voice of God speaking to them in His Son." Do I add to Your pain, Lord, in waiting for one more endtime sign, before making the radical commitment to You? _____
_____
_____
_____

5. "But the nobleman must realize his n_____ before he would desire the grace of Christ." To what degree do I see my need? _____
_____
_____
What would help me?_____

If I don't desire the grace of Christ, can I still place myself to be exposed to it? _____

6. Why did Jacob have to wrestle with the angel so long? _____

(Pleading his great need, pleading for a blessing? Who is reluctant?)_____

7. Jesus is "desirous of blessing us...The Savior longs to give us a

Jacob, when, wrestling with the Angel, he cried, "I will not let Thee go, except Thou bless me." Gen. 32:26.

Like Jacob he prevailed. The Saviour cannot withdraw from the soul that clings to Him, pleading its great need. "Go thy way," He said; "thy son liveth." The nobleman left the Saviour's presence with a peace [198-199] and joy he had never known before. Not only did he believe that his son would be restored, but with strong confidence he trusted in Christ as the Redeemer.

At the same hour the watchers beside the dying child in the home at Capernaum beheld a sudden and mysterious change. The shadow of death was lifted from the sufferer's face. The flush of fever gave place to the soft glow of returning health. The dim eyes brightened with intelligence, and strength returned to the feeble, emaciated frame. No signs of his malady lingered about the child. His burning flesh had become soft and moist, and he sank into a quiet sleep. The fever had left him in the very heat of the day. The family were amazed, and great was the rejoicing.

Cana was not so far from Capernaum but that the officer might have reached his home on the evening after his interview with Jesus; but he did not hasten on the homeward journey. It was not until the next morning that he reached Capernaum. What a homecoming was that! When he went to find Jesus, his heart was heavy with sorrow. The sunshine seemed cruel to him, the songs of the birds a mockery. How different his feelings now! All nature wears a new aspect. He sees with new eyes. As he journeys in the quiet of the early morning, all nature seems to be praising God with him. While he is still some distance from his own dwelling, servants come out to meet him, anxious to relieve the suspense they are sure he must feel. He shows no surprise at the news they bring, but with a depth of interest they cannot know he asks at what hour the child began to mend. They answer, "Yesterday at the seventh hour the fever left him." At the very moment when the father's faith grasped the assurance, "Thy son liveth," divine love touched the dying child. [199-200]

The father hurries on to greet his son. He clasps him to his heart as one restored from the dead, and thanks God again and again for this wonderful restoration.

The nobleman longed to know more of Christ. As he afterward heard His teaching, he and all his household became disciples. Their affliction was sanctified to the conversion of the entire family. Tidings of the miracle spread; and in Capernaum, where so many of His mighty works were performed, the way was prepared for Christ's personal ministry.

He who blessed the nobleman at Capernaum is just as desirous of blessing us. But like the afflicted father, we are often led to seek Jesus by the desire for some earthly good; and upon the granting of our request we rest our confidence in His love. The Saviour longs to give us a greater blessing than we ask; and He delays the answer to our request that He may show us the evil of our own hearts, and our deep need of His grace. He desires us to renounce the selfishness that leads us to seek Him. Confessing our helplessness and bitter need, we are to trust ourselves wholly to His love.

The nobleman wanted to see the fulfillment of his prayer before he should believe; but he had to accept the word of Jesus that his request was heard and the blessing granted. This lesson we also have to learn. Not because we see or feel that God hears us are we to believe. We are to trust in His promises. When we come to Him in faith, every petition enters the heart of God. When we have asked for His blessing, we should believe that we receive it, and thank Him that we have received it. Then we are to go about our duties, assured that the blessing will be realized when we need it most. When we have learned to do this, we shall know that our prayers are answered. God will do for us "exceeding abundantly," "according to the riches of His glory," and "the working of His mighty power." Eph. 3:20, 16; 1:19.

g_____ blessing than we ask." (200). Where is my vision of Your goodness, Lord? _____

_____

8. Jesus "delays the answer to our request that He may show us the e_____ of our own hearts, and our deep need of His grace. He desires us to renounce the s_____ that leads us to seek Him." Lord, have I been selfish in seeking You? You say so; but I need You to show me. I want to love You for who You are! _____

9. I have an important lesson to learn regarding prayer. "Not because we see or feel that God hears us are we to b_____. We are to trust in His p_____ ....We should believe that we receive it, and thank Him that we have received it. Then we are to go about our duties, assured that the blessing will be realized when we n_____ it most." Lord, thank You for Your promises. I trust You and Your word. Give me opportunities to help my faith grow:

_____

Prayer journal: _____

_____

_____

_____

Chapter 21

Bethesda and the Sanhedrin
[This chapter is based on John 5.]

"Now there is at Jerusalem by the sheep market a pool, which is called in the Hebrew tongue Bethesda, having five porches. In these lay a great multitude of impotent folk, of blind, halt, withered, waiting for the moving of the water."

At certain seasons the waters of this pool were agitated, and it was commonly believed that this was the result of supernatural power, and that whoever first after the troubling of the pool stepped into the waters, would be healed of whatever disease he had. Hundreds of sufferers visited the place; but so great was the crowd when the water was troubled that they rushed forward, trampling underfoot men, women, and children, weaker than themselves. Many could not get near the pool. Many who had succeeded in reaching it died upon its brink. Shelters had been erected about the place, that the sick might be protected from the heat by day and the chilliness of the night. There were some who spent the night in these porches, creeping to the edge of the pool day after day, in the vain hope of relief.

Jesus was again at Jerusalem. Walking alone, in apparent meditation and prayer, He came to the pool. He saw the wretched sufferers watching for that which they supposed to be their only chance of cure. He longed to exercise His healing power, and make every sufferer whole. But it was the Sabbath day. Multitudes were going to the temple for worship, [201-202] and He knew that such an act of healing would so excite the prejudice of the Jews as to cut short His work.

But the Saviour saw one case of supreme wretchedness. It was that of a man who had been a helpless cripple for thirty-eight years. His disease was in a great degree the result of his own sin, and was looked upon as a judgment from God. Alone and friendless, feeling that he was shut out from God's mercy, the sufferer had

1. "Walking alone, in apparent m_____ and prayer." For His spiritual walk, Jesus took a walk. Jesus was in His Father's presence wherever He went. It was a companionship of abiding together. And that is what I want, too, Lord: _____

_____

_____

2. Jesus "knew that such an act of healing [on the Sabbath day] would so excite the p_____ of the Jews as to c_____ short His work." (202). How

passed long years of misery. At the time when it was expected that the waters would be troubled, those who pitied his helplessness would bear him to the porches. But at the favored moment he had no one to help him in. He had seen the rippling of the water, but had never been able to get farther than the edge of the pool. Others stronger than he would plunge in before him. He could not contend successfully with the selfish, scrambling crowd. His persistent efforts toward the one object, and his anxiety and continual disappointment, were fast wearing away the remnant of his strength.

The sick man was lying on his mat, and occasionally lifting his head to gaze at the pool, when a tender, compassionate face bent over him, and the words, "Wilt thou be made whole?" arrested his attention. Hope came to his heart. He felt that in some way he was to have help. But the glow of encouragement soon faded. He remembered how often he had tried to reach the pool, and now he had little prospect of living till it should again be troubled. He turned away wearily, saying, "Sir, I have no man, when the water is troubled, to put me into the pool: but while I am coming, another steppeth down before me."

Jesus does not ask this sufferer to exercise faith in Him. He simply says, "Rise, take up thy bed, and walk." But the man's faith takes hold [202-203] upon that word. Every nerve and muscle thrills with new life, and healthful action comes to his crippled limbs. Without question he sets his will to obey the command of Christ, and all his muscles respond to his will. Springing to his feet, he finds himself an active man.

Jesus had given him no assurance of divine help. The man might have stopped to doubt, and lost his one chance of healing. But he believed Christ's word, and in acting upon it he received strength.

Through the same faith we may receive spiritual healing. By sin we have been severed from the life of God. Our souls are palsied. Of ourselves we are no more capable of living a holy life than was the impotent man capable of walking. There are many who realize their helplessness, and who long for that spiritual life which will bring them into harmony with God; they are vainly striving to obtain it. In despair they cry, "O wretched man that I am! who shall deliver me from this body of death?" Rom. 7:24, margin. Let these desponding, struggling ones look up. The Saviour is bending over

---

can I balance the admonitions of giving the trumpet a certain sound, giving the straight testimony, and being tactful, trying not to excite the prejudice of the person I'm trying to win?

_____

_____

3. Jesus simply says to the cripple of _____ years, 'Rise, take up thy bed, and walk.' "Without q_____, he sets his will to obey the command of Christ." (203). The faith of this man! And without knowing Christ! I am put to shame, Lord, by my lack of faith:

_____

But faith is not my savior (175). What is it?

_____

_____

4. "Do not wait to f_____ that you are made whole. B_____ His word, and it will be fulfilled. Put your w_____ on the side of Christ. Will to serve Him, and in a_____ upon His word you will receive strength." I'm on Your side, Lord. Take my will. What is a reliance on Your Word that acts? _____

_____

_____

5. The Jews had so perverted the law with m_____ requirements that it became a yoke of bondage, and a byword among other nations. (204). In what light am I known as a 'law keeper?' Restricting or joyful? _____ _____ How can I change my witness to a positive one?_____

_____

_____

_____

the purchase of His blood, saying with inexpressible tenderness and pity, "Wilt thou be made whole?" He bids you arise in health and peace. Do not wait to feel that you are made whole. Believe His word, and it will be fulfilled. Put your will on the side of Christ. Will to serve Him, and in acting upon His word you will receive strength. Whatever may be the evil practice, the master passion which through long indulgence binds both soul and body, Christ is able and longs to deliver. He will impart life to the soul that is "dead in trespasses." Eph. 2:1. He will set free the captive that is held by weakness and misfortune and the chains of sin.

The restored paralytic stooped to take up his bed, which was only a rug and a blanket, and as he straightened himself again with a sense of delight, he looked around for his Deliverer; but Jesus was lost in the crowd. The man feared that he would not know Him if he should see Him again. As he hurried on his way with firm, free step, praising God and rejoicing in his newfound strength, he met several of the Pharisees, and immediately told them of his cure. He was surprised at the coldness with which they listened to his story.

With lowering brows they interrupted him, asking why he was carrying his bed on the Sabbath day. They sternly reminded him that it was not lawful to bear burdens on the Lord's day. In his joy the man had forgotten that it was the Sabbath; yet he felt no condemnation for obeying the command of One who had such power from God. He [203-204] answered boldly, "He that made me whole, the same said unto me, Take up thy bed, and walk." They asked who it was that had done this, but he could not tell. These rulers knew well that only One had shown Himself able to perform this miracle; but they wished for direct proof that it was Jesus, that they might condemn Him as a Sabbath-breaker. In their judgment He had not only broken the law in healing the sick man on the Sabbath, but had committed sacrilege in bidding him bear away his bed.

The Jews had so perverted the law that they made it a yoke of bondage. Their meaningless requirements had become a byword among other nations. Especially was the Sabbath hedged in by all manner of senseless restrictions. It was not to them a delight, the holy of the Lord, and honorable. The scribes and Pharisees had made its observance an intolerable burden. A Jew was not allowed to kindle a fire nor even to light a candle on the Sabbath. As a consequence the people were dependent upon the Gentiles for many services which their rules forbade them to do for themselves. They did not reflect that if these acts were sinful, those who employed others to perform them were as guilty as if they had done the work themselves. They thought that salvation was restricted to the Jews, and that the condition of all others, being already hopeless, could be made no worse. But God has given no commandments which cannot be obeyed by all. His laws sanction no unreasonable or selfish restrictions.

In the temple Jesus met the man who had been healed. He had come to bring a sin offering and also a thank offering for the great mercy he had received. Finding him among the worshipers, Jesus made Himself known, with the warning words, "Behold, thou art made whole: sin no more, lest a worse thing come unto thee."

The healed man was overjoyed at meeting his Deliverer. Ignorant of the enmity toward Jesus, he told the Pharisees who had questioned him, that this was He who had performed the cure. "Therefore did the Jews persecute Jesus, and sought to slay Him, because He had done these things on the Sabbath day."

Jesus was brought before the Sanhedrin to answer the charge of Sabbathbreaking. Had the Jews at this time been an independent nation, such a charge would have served their purpose for putting Him to death. This their subjection to the Romans prevented. The Jews had not the power to inflict capital punishment, and the accusations brought against [204-205] Christ would have no weight in a Roman court. There were other objects, however, which they hoped to secure. Notwithstanding their efforts to counteract His work, Christ was gaining, even in Jerusalem, an influence over the people greater than their own. Multitudes who were not interested in the harangues of the rabbis were attracted by His teaching. They could understand His words, and their hearts were warmed and comforted. He spoke of God, not as an avenging judge, but as a tender father, and He revealed the image of God as mirrored in Himself. His words were like balm to the wounded spirit. Both by His words and by His works of mercy He was breaking the oppressive power of the old traditions and man-made commandments, and presenting the love of God in its exhaustless fullness.

6. "Multitudes who were not interested in the harangues of the rabbis were a_____ by His teaching...He spoke of God, not as an a_____ judge, but as a t_____ father." (205). What is my witness for You, Lord? Is it attractive and uplifting? _____
_____

In one of the earliest prophecies of Christ it is written, "The scepter shall not depart from Judah, nor a lawgiver from between his feet, until Shiloh come; and unto Him shall the gathering of the people be." Gen. 49:10. The people were gathering to Christ. The sympathetic hearts of the multitude accepted lessons of love and benevolence in preference to the rigid ceremonies required by the priests. If the priests and rabbis had not interposed, His teaching would have wrought such a reformation as this world has never witnessed. But in order to maintain their own power, these leaders determined to break down the influence of Jesus. His arraignment before the Sanhedrin, and an open condemnation of His teachings, would aid in effecting this; for the people still had great reverence for their religious leaders. Whoever dared to condemn the rabbinical requirements, or attempt to lighten the burdens they had brought upon the people, was regarded as guilty, not only of blasphemy, but of treason. On this ground the rabbis hoped to excite suspicion of Christ. They represented Him as trying to overthrow the established customs, thus causing division among the people, and preparing the way for complete subjugation by the Romans.

But the plans which these rabbis were working so zealously to fulfill originated in another council than that of the Sanhedrin. After Satan had failed to overcome Christ in the wilderness, he combined his forces to oppose Him in His ministry, and if possible to thwart His work. What he could not accomplish by direct, personal effort, he determined to effect by strategy. No sooner had he withdrawn from the conflict in the wilderness than in council with his confederate angels he matured his plans for still further blinding the minds of the Jewish people, that [205-206] they might not recognize their Redeemer. He planned to work through his human agencies in the religious world, by imbuing them with his own enmity against the champion of truth. He would lead them to reject Christ and to make His life as bitter as possible, hoping to discourage Him in His mission. And the leaders in Israel became instruments of Satan in warring against the Saviour.

Jesus had come to "magnify the law, and make it honorable." He was not to lessen its dignity, but to exalt it. The scripture says, "He shall not fail nor be discouraged, till He have set judgment in the earth." Isa. 42:21, 4. He had come to free the Sabbath from those burden-

7. Satan made plans for "further blinding the minds of the Jewish people, that they might not r_____ their Redeemer. He planned to work through his human agencies in the r_____ world." (205, 206). Satan's goal is for me to not recognize my Redeemer. How might he do that? _____
_____
_____

What will it take to defeat Satan's plans for me?
_____
_____

some requirements that had made it a curse instead of a blessing.

For this reason He had chosen the Sabbath upon which to perform the act of healing at Bethesda. He could have healed the sick man as well on any other day of the week; or He might simply have cured him, without bidding him bear away his bed. But this would not have given Him the opportunity He desired. A wise purpose underlay every act of Christ's life on earth. Everything He did was important in itself and in its teaching. Among the afflicted ones at the pool He selected the worst case upon whom to exercise His healing power, and bade the man carry his bed through the city in order to publish the great work that had been wrought upon him. This would raise the question of what it was lawful to do on the Sabbath, and would open the way for Him to denounce the restrictions of the Jews in regard to the Lord's day, and to declare their traditions void.

Jesus stated to them that the work of relieving the afflicted was in harmony with the Sabbath law. It was in harmony with the work of God's angels, who are ever descending and ascending between heaven and earth to minister to suffering humanity. Jesus declared, "My Father worketh hitherto, and I work." All days are God's, in which to carry out His plans for the human race. If the Jews' interpretation of the law was correct, then Jehovah was at fault, whose work has quickened and upheld every living thing since first He laid the foundations of the earth; then He who pronounced His work good, and instituted the Sabbath to commemorate its completion, must put a period to His labor, and stop the never-ending routine of the universe.

Should God forbid the sun to perform its office upon the Sabbath, cut off its genial rays from warming the earth and nourishing vegetation? Must the system of worlds stand still through that holy day? Should He [206-207] command the brooks to stay from watering the fields and forests, and bid the waves of the sea still their ceaseless ebbing and flowing? Must the wheat and corn stop growing, and the ripening cluster defer its purple bloom? Must the trees and flowers put forth no bud nor blossom on the Sabbath?

In such a case, men would miss the fruits of the earth, and the blessings that make life desirable. Nature must continue her unvarying course. God could not for a moment stay His hand, or man would faint and die.

And man also has a work to perform on this day. The necessities of life must be attended to, the sick must be cared for, the wants of the needy must be supplied. He will not be held guiltless who neglects to relieve suffering on the Sabbath. God's holy rest day was made for man, and acts of mercy are in perfect harmony with its intent. God does not desire His creatures to suffer an hour's pain that may be relieved upon the Sabbath or any other day.

The demands upon God are even greater upon the Sabbath than upon other days. His people then leave their usual employment, and spend the time in meditation and worship. They ask more favors of Him on the Sabbath than upon other days. They demand His special attention. They crave His choicest blessings. God does not wait for the Sabbath to pass before He grants these requests. Heaven's work never ceases, and men should never rest from doing good. The Sabbath is not intended to be a period of useless inactivity. The law forbids secular labor on the rest day of the Lord; the toil that gains a livelihood must cease; no labor for worldly pleasure or profit is lawful upon that day; but as God ceased His labor of creating, and rested upon the Sabbath and blessed it, so man is to leave the occupations of his daily life, and devote those sacred hours to healthful rest, to worship, and to holy deeds. The work of Christ in healing the sick was in perfect accord with the law. It honored the Sabbath.

Jesus claimed equal rights with God in doing a work equally sacred, and of the same character with that which engaged the Father in heaven. But the Pharisees were still more incensed. He had not only broken the law, according to their understanding, but in calling God "His own Father" had declared Himself equal with God. John 5:18, R. V.

The whole nation of the Jews called God their Father, therefore they would not have been so enraged if Christ had represented Himself as standing in the same relation to God. But they accused Him of [207-208] blasphemy, showing that they understood Him as making this claim in the highest sense.

These adversaries of Christ had no arguments with which to meet the truths He brought home to their consciences. They could only cite their customs and traditions, and these seemed weak and vapid when compared with the arguments Jesus had drawn from the word of

God and the unceasing round of nature. Had the rabbis felt any desire to receive light, they would have been convinced that Jesus spoke the truth. But they evaded the points He made concerning the Sabbath, and sought to stir up anger against Him because He claimed to be equal with God. The fury of the rulers knew no bounds. Had they not feared the people, the priests and rabbis would have slain Jesus on the spot. But the popular sentiment in His favor was strong. Many recognized in Jesus the friend who had healed their diseases and comforted their sorrows, and they justified His healing of the sufferer at Bethesda. So for the time the leaders were obliged to restrain their hatred.

Jesus repelled the charge of blasphemy. My authority, He said, for doing the work of which you accuse Me, is that I am the Son of God, one with Him in nature, in will, and in purpose. In all His works of creation and providence, I co-operate with God. "The Son can do nothing of Himself, but what He seeth the Father do." The priests and rabbis were taking the Son of God to task for the very work He had been sent into the world to do. By their sins they had separated themselves from God, and in their pride were moving independently of Him. They felt sufficient in themselves for all things, and realized no need of a higher wisdom to direct their acts. But the Son of God was surrendered to the Father's will, and dependent upon His power. So utterly was Christ emptied of self that He made no plans for Himself. He accepted God's plans for Him, and day by day the Father unfolded His plans. So should we depend upon God, that our lives may be the simple outworking of His will.

When Moses was about to build the sanctuary as a dwelling place for God, he was directed to make all things according to the pattern shown him in the mount. Moses was full of zeal to do God's work; the most talented, skillful men were at hand to carry out his suggestions. Yet he was not to make a bell, a pomegranate, a tassel, a fringe, a curtain, or any vessel of the sanctuary, except according to the pattern shown him. God called him into the mount, and revealed to him the heavenly things. The Lord covered him with His own glory, that he might see [208-209] the pattern, and according to it all things were made. So to Israel, whom He desired to make His dwelling place, He had revealed His glorious ideal of character. The pattern was shown them in the

8. "So utterly was Christ emptied of s_____ that He made no plans for Himself. He accepted God's plans for Him, and day by day the Father unfolded His plans. So should we d_____ upon God, that our lives may be the simple outworking of His will." (208). Your agenda, Lord. Not mine. Your goals, Your vision for my life. That's what I want. May that be my daily prayer: _____
_____
_____

mount when the law was given from Sinai, and when the Lord passed by before Moses and proclaimed, "The Lord, The Lord God, merciful and gracious, long-suffering, and abundant in goodness and truth, keeping mercy for thousands, forgiving iniquity and transgression and sin." Ex. 34:6, 7.

Israel had chosen their own ways. They had not builded according to the pattern; but Christ, the true temple for God's indwelling, molded every detail of His earthly life in harmony with God's ideal. He said, "I delight to do Thy will, O My God: yea, Thy law is within My heart." Ps. 40:8. So our characters are to be builded "for an habitation of God through the Spirit." Eph. 2:22. And we are to "make all things according to the pattern," even Him who "suffered for us, leaving us an example, that ye should follow His steps." Heb. 8:5; 1 Peter 2:21.

The words of Christ teach that we should regard ourselves as inseparably bound to our Father in heaven. Whatever our position, we are dependent upon God, who holds all destinies in His hands. He has appointed us our work, and has endowed us with faculties and means for that work. So long as we surrender the will to God, and trust in His strength and wisdom, we shall be guided in safe paths, to fulfill our appointed part in His great plan. But the one who depends upon his own wisdom and power is separating himself from God. Instead of working in unison with Christ, he is fulfilling the purpose of the enemy of God and man.

The Saviour continued: "What things soever He [the Father] doeth, these also doeth the Son likewise. . . . As the Father raiseth up the dead, and quickeneth them; even so the Son quickeneth whom He will." The Sadducees held that there would be no resurrection of the body; but Jesus tells them that one of the greatest works of His Father is raising the dead, and that He Himself has power to do the same work. "The hour is coming, and now is, when the dead shall hear the voice of the Son of God: and they that hear shall live." The Pharisees believed in the resurrection of the dead. Christ declares that even now the power which gives life to the dead is among them, and they are to behold its manifestation. This same resurrection power is that which gives life to the soul "dead in trespasses and sins." Eph. 2:1. That spirit of life in Christ Jesus, "the power of His resurrection," sets men "free from [209-210] the law of sin

9. "So long as we surrender the will to God, and trust in His strength and wisdom, we shall be guided in s_____ paths, to fulfill our appointed part in His great plan. But the one who depends upon his o_____ wisdom and power is s_____ himself from God. Instead of working in unison with Christ, he is fulfilling the purpose of the e_____ of God and man." (209). Show me Lord, how I use my own strength. I certainly don't want separation. Show me, moment by moment:

and death." Phil. 3:10; Rom. 8:2. The dominion of evil is broken, and through faith the soul is kept from sin. He who opens his heart to the Spirit of Christ becomes a partaker of that mighty power which shall bring forth his body from the grave.

The humble Nazarene asserts His real nobility. He rises above humanity, throws off the guise of sin and shame, and stands revealed, the Honored of the angels, the Son of God, One with the Creator of the universe. His hearers are spellbound. No man has ever spoken words like His, or borne himself with such a kingly majesty. His utterances are clear and plain, fully declaring His mission, and the duty of the world. "For the Father judgeth no man, but hath committed all judgment unto the Son: that all men should honor the Son, even as they honor the Father. He that honoreth not the Son honoreth not the Father which hath sent Him. . . . For as the Father hath life in Himself; so hath He given to the Son to have life in Himself; and hath given Him authority to execute judgment also, because He is the Son of man."

The priests and rulers had set themselves up as judges to condemn Christ's work, but He declared Himself their judge, and the judge of all the earth. The world has been committed to Christ, and through Him has come every blessing from God to the fallen race. He was the Redeemer before as after His incarnation. As soon as there was sin, there was a Saviour. He has given light and life to all, and according to the measure of light given, each is to be judged. And He who has given the light, He who has followed the soul with tenderest entreaty, seeking to win it from sin to holiness, is in one its advocate and judge. From the opening of the great controversy in heaven, Satan has maintained his cause through deception; and Christ has been working to unveil his schemes and to break his power. It is He who has encountered the deceiver, and who through all the ages has been seeking to wrest the captives from his grasp, who will pass judgment upon every soul.

And God "hath given Him authority to execute judgment also, because He is the Son of man." Because He has tasted the very dregs of human affliction and temptation, and understands the frailties and sins of men; because in our behalf He has victoriously withstood the temptations of Satan, and will deal justly and tenderly with the souls that His own blood has been poured out to save,--because of this, the Son of man is appointed to execute the judgment.

But Christ's mission was not for judgment, but for salvation. "God sent not His Son into the world to condemn the world; but that the [210-211] world through Him might be saved." John 3:17. And before the Sanhedrin Jesus declared, "He that heareth My word, and believeth Him that sent Me, hath eternal life, and cometh not into judgment, but hath passed out of death into life." John 5:24, R. V.

Bidding His hearers marvel not, Christ opened before them, in still wider view, the mystery of the future. "The hour cometh," He said, "in which all that are in the tombs shall hear His voice, and shall come forth; they that have done good, unto the resurrection of life; and they that have done ill, unto the resurrection of judgment." John 5:28, 29, R. V.

This assurance of the future life was that for which Israel had so long waited, and which they had hoped to receive at the Messiah's advent. The only light that can lighten the gloom of the grave was shining upon them. But self-will is blind. Jesus had violated the traditions of the rabbis, and disregarded their authority, and they would not believe.

The time, the place, the occasion, the intensity of feeling that pervaded the assembly, all combined to make the words of Jesus before the Sanhedrin the more impressive. The highest religious authorities of the nation were seeking the life of Him who declared Himself the restorer of Israel. The Lord of the Sabbath was arraigned before an earthly tribunal to answer the charge of breaking the Sabbath law. When He so fearlessly declared His mission, His judges looked upon Him with astonishment and rage; but His words were unanswerable. They could not condemn Him. He denied the right of the priests and rabbis to question Him, or to interfere with His work. They were invested with no such authority. Their claims were based upon their own pride and arrogance. He refused to plead guilty of their charges, or to be catechized by them.

Instead of apologizing for the act of which they complained, or explaining His purpose in doing it, Jesus turned upon the rulers, and the accused became the accuser. He rebuked them for the hardness of their hearts, and their ignorance of the Scriptures. He declared that they had rejected the word of God, inasmuch as they had rejected Him whom God had sent. "Ye search the Scriptures, because ye think that in them ye have eternal life; and these are they which bear witness of Me." John 5:39, R. V.

In every page, whether history, or precept, or prophecy, the Old Testament Scriptures are irradiated with the glory of the Son of God. So far as it was of divine institution, the entire system of Judaism was a compacted prophecy of the gospel. To Christ "give all the prophets witness." Acts 10:43. From the promise given to Adam, down through [211-212] the patriarchal line and the legal economy, heaven's glorious light made plain the footsteps of the Redeemer. Seers beheld the Star of Bethlehem, the Shiloh to come, as future things swept before them in mysterious procession. In every sacrifice Christ's death was shown. In every cloud of incense His righteousness ascended. By every jubilee trumpet His name was sounded. In the awful mystery of the holy of holies His glory dwelt.

The Jews had the Scriptures in their possession, and supposed that in their mere outward knowledge of the word they had eternal life. But Jesus said, "Ye have not His word abiding in you." Having rejected Christ in His word, they rejected Him in person. "Ye will not come to Me," He said, "that ye might have life."

The Jewish leaders had studied the teachings of the prophets concerning the kingdom of the Messiah; but they had done this, not with a sincere desire to know the truth, but with the purpose of finding evidence to sustain their ambitious hopes. When Christ came in a manner contrary to their expectations, they would not receive Him; and in order to justify themselves, they tried to prove Him a deceiver. When once they had set their feet in this path, it was easy for Satan to strengthen their opposition to Christ. The very words that should have been received as evidence of His divinity were interpreted against Him. Thus they turned the truth of God into a lie, and the more directly the Saviour spoke to them in His works of mercy, the more determined they were in resisting the light.

Jesus said, "I receive not honor from men." It was not the influence of the Sanhedrin, it was not their sanction He desired. He could receive no honor from their approbation. He was invested with the honor and authority of Heaven. Had He desired it, angels would have come to do Him homage; the Father would again have

10. "The Jews had the Scriptures in their possession, and supposed that in their mere outward k_____ of the word they had eternal life. But Jesus said, 'Ye have not His word abiding in you.'" (212). You are the Word, Lord. I open my heart. Please abide there. Knowledge of the truth leads to a relationship with the Truth; and You are the Truth. What is my attitude towards this devotional walk: outward knowledge or aerobics for the heart? _____

testified to His divinity. But for their own sake, for the sake of the nation whose leaders they were, He desired the Jewish rulers to discern His character, and receive the blessings He came to bring them.

"I am come in My Father's name, and ye receive Me not: if another shall come in his own name, him ye will receive." Jesus came by the authority of God, bearing His image, fulfilling His word, and seeking His glory; yet He was not accepted by the leaders in Israel; but when others should come, assuming the character of Christ, but actuated by their own will and seeking their own glory, they would be received. And why? Because he who is seeking his own glory appeals to the desire for self-exaltation in others. To such appeals the Jews could respond. [212-213] They would receive the false teacher because he flattered their pride by sanctioning their cherished opinions and traditions. But the teaching of Christ did not coincide with their ideas. It was spiritual, and demanded the sacrifice of self; therefore they would not receive it. They were not acquainted with God, and to them His voice through Christ was the voice of a stranger.

Is not the same thing repeated in our day? Are there not many, even religious leaders, who are hardening their hearts against the Holy Spirit, making it impossible for them to recognize the voice of God? Are they not rejecting the word of God, that they may keep their own traditions?

"Had ye believed Moses," said Jesus, "ye would have believed Me: for he wrote of Me. But if ye believe not his writings, how shall ye believe My words?" It was Christ who had spoken to Israel through Moses. If they had listened to the divine voice that spoke through their great leader, they would have recognized it in the teachings of Christ. Had they believed Moses, they would have believed Him of whom Moses wrote.

Jesus knew that the priests and rabbis were determined to take His life; yet He clearly explained to them His unity with the Father, and His relation to the world. They saw that their opposition to Him was without excuse, yet their murderous hatred was not quenched. Fear seized them as they witnessed the convincing power that attended His ministry; but they resisted His appeals, and locked themselves in darkness.

They had signally failed to subvert the authority of Jesus or to alienate the respect and attention of the

11. "The teaching of Christ did not coincide with their ideas [of the leaders in Israel]. It was spiritual, and demanded the sacrifice of s_____; therefore they would not r_____ it. They were not acquainted with God, and to them His voice through Christ was the voice of a s_____." (213). So self gets in the way of knowing You? Then I choose 'self' to be the stranger, not You. Help me. How can I be aware and responsive to Your help?

people, many of whom were convicted by His words. The rulers themselves had felt deep condemnation as He had pressed their guilt home upon their consciences; yet this only made them the more bitter against Him. They were determined to take His life. They sent messengers all over the country to warn the people against Jesus as an impostor. Spies were sent to watch Him, and report what He said and did. The precious Saviour was now most surely standing under the shadow of the cross.

Prayer journal: _____
_____
_____
_____
_____
_____
_____
_____

Imprisonment and Death of John

[This chapter is based on Matt. 11:1-11; 14:1-11;
Mark 6:17-28; Luke 7:19-28.]

John the Baptist had been first in heralding Christ's kingdom, and he was first also in suffering. From the free air of the wilderness and the vast throngs that had hung upon his words, he was now shut in by the walls of a dungeon cell. He had become a prisoner in the fortress of Herod Antipas. In the territory east of Jordan, which was under the dominion of Antipas, much of John's ministry had been spent. Herod himself had listened to the preaching of the Baptist. The dissolute king had trembled under the call to repentance. "Herod feared John, knowing that he was a just man and an holy; . . . and when he heard him, he did many things, and heard him gladly." John dealt with him faithfully, denouncing his iniquitous alliance with Herodias, his brother's wife. For a time Herod feebly sought to break the chain of lust that bound him; but Herodias fastened him the more firmly in her toils, and found revenge upon the Baptist by inducing Herod to cast him into prison.

The life of John had been one of active labor, and the gloom and inaction of his prison life weighed heavily upon him. As week after week passed, bringing no change, despondency and doubt crept over him. His disciples did not forsake him. They were allowed access to the prison, and they brought him tidings of the works of Jesus, and told how the people were flocking to Him. But they questioned why, if this [214-215] new teacher was the Messiah, He did nothing to effect John's release. How could He permit His faithful herald to be deprived of liberty and perhaps of life?

These questions were not without effect. Doubts which otherwise would never have arisen were suggested to John. Satan rejoiced to hear the words of these disciples, and to see how they bruised the soul of the

1.   John's   disciples "questioned why, if this new teacher was the M_____, He did nothing to effect John's r_____?" (215) What effect did these questions have? _____

_____

Does Satan rejoice at what I say? Or do You, Lord? ____

_____

Lord's messenger. Oh, how often those who think them-selves the friends of a good man, and who are eager to show their fidelity to him, prove to be his most danger-ous enemies! How often, instead of strengthening his faith, their words depress and dishearten!

Like the Saviour's disciples, John the Baptist did not understand the nature of Christ's kingdom. He expected Jesus to take the throne of David; and as time passed, and the Saviour made no claim to kingly authority, John became perplexed and troubled. He had declared to the people that in order for the way to be prepared before the Lord, the prophecy of Isaiah must be fulfilled; the mountains and hills must be brought low, the crooked made straight, and the rough places plain. He had looked for the high places of human pride and power to be cast down. He had pointed to the Messiah as the One whose fan was in His hand, and who would thoroughly purge His floor, who would gather the wheat into His garner, and burn up the chaff with unquenchable fire. Like the prophet Elijah, in whose spirit and power he had come to Israel, he looked for the Lord to reveal Himself as a God that answereth by fire.

In his mission the Baptist had stood as a fearless reprover of iniquity, both in high places and in low. He had dared to face King Herod with the plain rebuke of sin. He had not counted his life dear unto himself, that he might fulfill his appointed work. And now from his dungeon he watched for the Lion of the tribe of Judah to cast down the pride of the oppressor, and to deliver the poor and him that cried. But Jesus seemed to content Himself with gathering disciples about Him, and heal-ing and teaching the people. He was eating at the tables of the publicans, while every day the Roman yoke rest-ed more heavily upon Israel, while King Herod and his vile paramour worked their will, and the cries of the poor and suffering went up to heaven. [215-216]

To the desert prophet all this seemed a mystery be-yond his fathoming. There were hours when the whis-perings of demons tortured his spirit, and the shadow of a terrible fear crept over him. Could it be that the long-hoped-for Deliverer had not yet appeared? Then what meant the message that he himself had been impelled to bear? John had been bitterly disappointed in the result of his mission. He had expected that the message from God would have the same effect as when the law was read in the days of Josiah and of Ezra (2 Chronicles 34;

2. "John the Baptist did n_____ understand the na-ture of Christ's kingdom" He watched for the pride of the o_____ to be cast down, for the poor to be delivered. "But Jesus seemed to c_____ ___ Himself with gather-ing disciples about Him, and healing and teaching the people...while ev-ery day the Roman yoke rested more h_____ ____ upon Israel." (215). How should I feel, Lord, when You don't seem to care, or You're not com-ing through like I think You should? _____
_____
_____

3. "The shadow of a ter-rible fear crept over him...John was troubled

to see that through love for him, his own disciples were cherishing u_____ __ in regard to Jesus... But the Baptist did not s_____ his faith in Christ." John remembered five evidences. "John would not d_____ his doubts and anxieties with his companions." (216). When Satan assails me with doubts, Lord, help me be like John, not to spread the negativity, but rather to remember the evidences of Your grace:

_____
_____
_____
_____

4. Why was the question, 'Art Thou He that should come, or do we look for another?' keenly bitter and disappointing? _____

_____
_____
_____ Lord, I don't want to cause You that pain. May my conversation reflect faith, and not the lack of it: _____

_____

Nehemiah 8, 9); that there would follow a deep-seated work of repentance and returning unto the Lord. For the success of this mission his whole life had been sacrificed. Had it been in vain?

John was troubled to see that through love for him, his own disciples were cherishing unbelief in regard to Jesus. Had his work for them been fruitless? Had he been unfaithful in his mission, that he was now cut off from labor? If the promised Deliverer had appeared, and John had been found true to his calling, would not Jesus now overthrow the oppressor's power, and set free His herald?

But the Baptist did not surrender his faith in Christ. The memory of the voice from heaven and the descending dove, the spotless purity of Jesus, the power of the Holy Spirit that had rested upon John as he came into the Saviour's presence, and the testimony of the prophetic scriptures,--all witnessed that Jesus of Nazareth was the Promised One.

John would not discuss his doubts and anxieties with his companions. He determined to send a message of inquiry to Jesus. This he entrusted to two of his disciples, hoping that an interview with the Saviour would confirm their faith, and bring assurance to their brethren. And he longed for some word from Christ spoken directly for himself.

The disciples came to Jesus with their message, "Art Thou He that should come, or do we look for another?"

How short the time since the Baptist had pointed to Jesus, and proclaimed, "Behold the Lamb of God, which taketh away the sin of the world." "He it is, who coming after me is preferred before me." John 1:29, 27. And now the question, "Art Thou He that should come?" It was keenly bitter and disappointing to human nature. If John, the faithful forerunner, failed to discern Christ's mission, what could be expected from the self-seeking multitude?

The Saviour did not at once answer the disciples' question. As they stood wondering at His silence, the sick and afflicted were coming to Him to be healed. The blind were groping their way through the crowd; [216-217] diseased ones of all classes, some urging their own way, some borne by their friends, were eagerly pressing into the presence of Jesus. The voice of the mighty Healer penetrated the deaf ear. A word, a touch of His hand, opened the blind eyes to behold the light of day, the scenes of nature, the faces of friends, and the face of the Deliverer. Jesus rebuked disease and banished fever. His voice reached the ears of the dying, and they arose in health and vigor. Paralyzed demoniacs obeyed His word, their madness left them, and they worshiped Him. While He healed their diseases, He taught the people. The poor peasants and laborers, who were shunned by the rabbis as unclean, gathered close about Him, and He spoke to them the words of eternal life.

Thus the day wore away, the disciples of John seeing and hearing all. At last Jesus called them to Him, and bade them go and tell John what they had witnessed, adding, "Blessed is he, whosoever shall find none occasion of stumbling in Me." Luke 7:23, R. V. The evidence of His divinity was seen in its adaptation to the needs of suffering humanity. His glory was shown in His condescension to our low estate.

The disciples bore the message, and it was enough. John recalled the prophecy concerning the Messiah, "The Lord hath anointed Me to preach good tidings unto the meek; He hath sent Me to bind up the brokenhearted, to proclaim liberty to the captives, and the opening of the prison to them that are bound; to proclaim the acceptable year of the Lord." Isa. 61:1, 2. The works of Christ not only declared Him to be the Messiah, but showed in what manner His kingdom was to be established. To John was opened the same truth that had come to Elijah in the desert, when "a great and strong wind rent the mountains, and brake in pieces the rocks before the Lord; but the Lord was not in the wind: and after the wind an earthquake; but the Lord was not in the earthquake: and after the earthquake a fire; but the Lord was not in the fire:" and after the fire, God spoke to the prophet by "a still small voice." 1 Kings 19:11, 12. So Jesus was to do His work, not with the clash of arms and the overturning of thrones and kingdoms, but through speaking to the hearts of men by a life of mercy and self-sacrifice. [217-218]

The principle of the Baptist's own life of self-abnegation was the principle of the Messiah's kingdom. John well knew how foreign all this was to the principles and hopes of the leaders in Israel. That which was to him convincing evidence of Christ's divinity would be no evidence to them. They were looking for a Messiah who had not been promised. John saw that the

5. Wondering at His silence, John's disciples stayed the day, "seeing and hearing a_____...The evidence of His divinity was seen in it's a_____ to the needs of suffering humanity." (217). How will people know that I am Your disciple, Lord? _____

_____

_____

_____

6. "He, the forerunner, was but d_____ of the cup which Christ Himself must drain to its dregs." (218). That should give me perspective: I may be experiencing what Jesus did, and my character is developing because of it. I can be a "sharer in the sufferings of Christ." (223.9). "Of all the gifts that Heaven can bestow upon men, f_____ _____ with Christ in His suffering is the most weighty t_____ and the highest honor." (225.2) Can this help my attitude in difficult times? _____

_____

_____

7. "John had spoken with equal plainness. He was no t_____ reed, swayed by the winds of human p_____ or prejudice…In his faithfulness to principle he was as firm as a r_____." (218). Can I be like John? _____ How? _____

_____

Saviour's mission could win from them only hatred and condemnation. He, the forerunner, was but drinking of the cup which Christ Himself must drain to its dregs.

The Saviour's words, "Blessed is he, whosoever shall find none occasion of stumbling in Me," were a gentle reproof to John. It was not lost upon him. Understanding more clearly now the nature of Christ's mission, he yielded himself to God for life or for death, as should best serve the interests of the cause he loved.

After the messengers had departed, Jesus spoke to the people concerning John. The Saviour's heart went out in sympathy to the faithful witness now buried in Herod's dungeon. He would not leave the people to conclude that God had forsaken John, or that his faith had failed in the day of trial. "What went ye out into the wilderness to see?" He said. "A reed shaken with the wind?"

The tall reeds that grew beside the Jordan, bending before every breeze, were fitting representatives of the rabbis who had stood as critics and judges of the Baptist's mission. They were swayed this way and that by the winds of popular opinion. They would not humble themselves to receive the heart-searching message of the Baptist, yet for fear of the people they dared not openly oppose his work. But God's messenger was of no such craven spirit. The multitudes who were gathered about Christ had been witnesses to the work of John. They had heard his fearless rebuke of sin. To the self-righteous Pharisees, the priestly Sadducees, King Herod and his court, princes and soldiers, publicans and peasants, John had spoken with equal plainness. He was no trembling reed, swayed by the winds of human praise or prejudice. In the prison he was the same in his loyalty to God and his zeal for righteousness as when he preached God's message in the wilderness. In his faithfulness to principle he was as firm as a rock.

Jesus continued, "But what went ye out for to see? A man clothed in soft raiment? Behold, they which are gorgeously appareled, and live delicately, are in kings' courts." John had been called to reprove the sins and excesses of his time, and his plain dress and self-denying life [218-219] were in harmony with the character of his mission. Rich apparel and the luxuries of this life are not the portion of God's servants, but of those who live "in kings' courts," the rulers of this world, to whom pertain its power and its riches. Jesus wished to direct attention to the contrast between the clothing of John, and that worn by the priests and rulers. These officials arrayed themselves in rich robes and costly ornaments. They loved display, and hoped to dazzle the people, and thus command greater consideration. They were more anxious to gain the admiration of men than to obtain the purity of heart which would win the approval of God. Thus they revealed that their allegiance was not given to God, but to the kingdom of this world.

"But what," said Jesus, "went ye out for to see? A prophet? yea, I say unto you, and more than a prophet. For this is he, of whom it is written,--

"Behold, I send My messenger before Thy face, which shall prepare Thy way before Thee.

"Verily I say unto you, Among them that are born of women there hath not risen a greater than John the Baptist." In the announcement to Zacharias before the birth of John, the angel had declared, "He shall be great in the sight of the Lord." Luke 1:15. In the estimation of Heaven, what is it that constitutes greatness? Not that which the world accounts greatness; not wealth, or rank, or noble descent, or intellectual gifts, in themselves considered. If intellectual greatness, apart from any higher consideration, is worthy of honor, then our homage is due to Satan, whose intellectual power no man has ever equaled. But when perverted to self-serving, the greater the gift, the greater curse it becomes. It is moral worth that God values. Love and purity are the attributes He prizes most. John was great in the sight of the Lord, when, before the messengers from the Sanhedrin, before the people, and before his own disciples, he refrained from seeking honor for himself, but pointed all to Jesus as the Promised One. His unselfish joy in the ministry of Christ presents the highest type of nobility ever revealed in man.

The witness borne of him after his death, by those who had heard his testimony to Jesus, was, "John did no miracle: but all things that John spake of this Man were true." John 10:41. It was not given to John to call down fire from heaven, or to raise the dead, as Elijah did, nor [219-220] to wield Moses' rod of power in the name of God. He was sent to herald the Saviour's advent, and to call upon the people to prepare for His coming. So faithfully did he fulfill his mission, that as the people recalled what he had taught them of Jesus, they could

8. In the estimation of heaven, what is it that constitutes greatness? "It is m_____ worth that God values. Love and purity are the attributes he prizes m_____....His [John's] unselfish joy in the ministry of Christ presents the highest type of n_____ ever revealed in man." (219). Lord, help me today to be loving and pure, and unselfish. May my ministry be inspired by joy, and not martyrdom: _____

_____

9. So faithfully did John "fulfill his mission, that as

the people recalled what he had taught them of Jesus, they could say, 'All things that John spake of this Man were t_____.' Such witness to Christ e_____ disciple of the Master is called upon to b_____." (220). Help me be that disciple, Lord, around the clock: _____

10. What did Jesus mean by stating "He that is least in the kingdom of heaven is greater than he?" _____
_____
_____
_____

say, "All things that John spake of this Man were true." Such witness to Christ every disciple of the Master is called upon to bear.

As the Messiah's herald, John was "much more than a prophet." For while prophets had seen from afar Christ's advent, to John it was given to behold Him, to hear the testimony from heaven to His Messiahship, and to present Him to Israel as the Sent of God. Yet Jesus said, "He that is least in the kingdom of heaven is greater than he."

The prophet John was the connecting link between the two dispensations. As God's representative he stood forth to show the relation of the law and the prophets to the Christian dispensation. He was the lesser light, which was to be followed by a greater. The mind of John was illuminated by the Holy Spirit, that he might shed light upon his people; but no other light ever has shone or ever will shine so clearly upon fallen man as that which emanated from the teaching and example of Jesus. Christ and His mission had been but dimly understood as typified in the shadowy sacrifices. Even John had not fully comprehended the future, immortal life through the Saviour.

Aside from the joy that John found in his mission, his life had been one of sorrow. His voice had been seldom heard except in the wilderness. His was a lonely lot. And he was not permitted to see the result of his own labors. It was not his privilege to be with Christ and witness the manifestation of divine power attending the greater light. It was not for him to see the blind restored to sight, the sick healed, and the dead raised to life. He did not behold the light that shone through every word of Christ, shedding glory upon the promises of prophecy. The least disciple who saw Christ's mighty works and heard His words was in this sense more highly privileged than John the Baptist, and therefore is said to have been greater than he.

Through the vast throngs that had listened to John's preaching, his fame had spread throughout the land. A deep interest was felt as to the result of his imprisonment. Yet his blameless life, and the strong public sentiment in his favor, led to the belief that no violent measures would be taken against him.

Herod believed John to be a prophet of God, and he fully intended [220-221] to set him at liberty. But he delayed his purpose from fear of Herodias.

Herodias knew that by direct measures she could never win Herod's consent to the death of John, and she resolved to accomplish her purpose by stratagem. On the king's birthday an entertainment was to be given to the officers of state and the nobles of the court. There would be feasting and drunkenness. Herod would thus be thrown off his guard, and might then be influenced according to her will.

When the great day arrived, and the king with his lords was feasting and drinking, Herodias sent her daughter into the banqueting hall to dance for the entertainment of the guests. Salome was in the first flush of womanhood, and her voluptuous beauty captivated the senses of the lordly revelers. It was not customary for the ladies of the court to appear at these festivities, and a flattering compliment was paid to Herod when this daughter of Israel's priests and princes danced for the amusement of his guests.

The king was dazed with wine. Passion held sway, and reason was dethroned. He saw only the hall of pleasure, with its reveling guests, the banquet table, the sparkling wine and the flashing lights, and the young girl dancing before him. In the recklessness of the moment, he desired to make some display that would exalt him before the great men of his realm. With an oath he promised to give the daughter of Herodias whatever she might ask, even to the half of his kingdom.

Salome hastened to her mother, to know what she should ask. The answer was ready,--the head of John the Baptist. Salome knew not of the thirst for revenge in her mother's heart, and she shrank from presenting the request; but the determination of Herodias prevailed. The girl returned with the terrible petition, "I will that thou forthwith give me in a charger the head of John the Baptist." Mark 6:25, R. V.

Herod was astonished and confounded. The riotous mirth ceased, and an ominous silence settled down upon the scene of revelry. The king was horror-stricken at the thought of taking the life of John. Yet his word was pledged, and he was unwilling to appear fickle or rash. The oath had been made in honor of his guests, and if one of them had offered a word against the fulfillment of his promise, he would gladly have spared the prophet. He gave them opportunity to speak in the prisoner's behalf. They had traveled long distances in order to hear the preaching of John, and they knew him to be a man without crime, and a servant of God. But though shocked at the girl's demand, they were [221-222] too besotted to interpose a remonstrance. No voice was raised to save the life of Heaven's messenger. These men occupied high positions of trust in the nation, and upon them rested grave responsibilities; yet they had given themselves up to feasting and drunkenness until the senses were benumbed. Their heads were turned with the giddy scene of music and dancing, and conscience lay dormant. By their silence they pronounced the sentence of death upon the prophet of God to satisfy the revenge of an abandoned woman.

Herod waited in vain to be released from his oath; then he reluctantly commanded the execution of the prophet. Soon the head of John was brought in before the king and his guests. Forever sealed were those lips that had faithfully warned Herod to turn from his life of sin. Never more would that voice be heard calling men to repentance. The revels of one night had cost the life of one of the greatest of the prophets.

Oh, how often has the life of the innocent been sacrificed through the intemperance of those who should have been guardians of justice! He who puts the intoxicating cup to his lips makes himself responsible for all the injustice he may commit under its besotting power. By benumbing his senses he makes it impossible for him to judge calmly or to have a clear perception of right and wrong. He opens the way for Satan to work through him in oppressing and destroying the innocent. "Wine is a mocker, strong drink is raging: and whosoever is deceived thereby is not wise." Prov. 20:1. Thus it is that "judgment is turned away backward, . . . and he that departeth from evil maketh himself a prey." Isa. 59:14, 15. Those who have jurisdiction over the lives of their fellow men should be held guilty of a crime when they yield to intemperance. All who execute the laws should be lawkeepers. They should be men of self-control. They need to have full command of their physical, mental, and moral powers, that they may possess vigor of intellect, and a high sense of justice.

The head of John the Baptist was carried to Herodias, who received it with fiendish satisfaction. She exulted in her revenge, and flattered herself that Herod's conscience would no longer be troubled. But no happiness resulted to her from her sin. Her name became notorious and abhorred, while Herod was more tormented by remorse than he had been by the warnings of the prophet. The influence of John's teachings was not silenced; it was to extend to every generation till the close of time. [222-223]

Herod's sin was ever before him. He was constantly seeking to find relief from the accusings of a guilty conscience. His confidence in John was unshaken. As he recalled his life of self-denial, his solemn, earnest appeals, his sound judgment in counsel, and then remembered how he had come to his death, Herod could find no rest. Engaged in the affairs of the state, receiving honors from men, he bore a smiling face and dignified mien, while he concealed an anxious heart, ever oppressed with the fear that a curse was upon him.

Herod had been deeply impressed by the words of John, that nothing can be hidden from God. He was convinced that God was present in every place, that He had witnessed the revelry of the banqueting room, that He had heard the command to behead John, and had seen the exultation of Herodias, and the insult she offered to the severed head of her reprover. And many things that Herod had heard from the lips of the prophet now spoke to his conscience more distinctly than had the preaching in the wilderness.

When Herod heard of the works of Christ, he was exceedingly troubled. He thought that God had raised John from the dead, and sent him forth with still greater power to condemn sin. He was in constant fear that John would avenge his death by passing condemnation upon him and his house. Herod was reaping that which God had declared to be the result of a course of sin,--"a trembling heart, and failing of eyes, and sorrow of mind: and thy life shall hang in doubt before thee; and thou shalt fear day and night, and shalt have none assurance of thy life: in the morning thou shalt say, Would God it were even! and at even thou shalt say, Would God it were morning! for the fear of thine heart wherewith thou shalt fear, and for the sight of thine eyes which thou shalt see." Deut. 28:65-67. The sinner's own thoughts are his accusers; and there can be no torture keener than the stings of a guilty conscience, which give him no rest day nor night.

To many minds a deep mystery surrounds the fate of John the Baptist. They question why he should have been left to languish and die in prison. The mystery of

11. "No h_____ resulted from her [Herodias's] sin. Her name became notorious and abhorred, while Herod was more t_____ by remorse than he had been by the warnings of the prophet." (222). "The sinner's own t_____ are his accusers; and there can be no torture k_____ than the stings of a guilty conscience, which give him no rest day nor night." (223). What a hard way to learn a lesson. Help me to learn from this story, Lord. I want to be transparent with You and conscience-free:

_____
_____
_____

this dark providence our human vision cannot penetrate; but it can never shake our confidence in God when we remember that John was but a sharer in the sufferings of Christ. All who follow Christ will wear the crown of sacrifice. They will surely be misunderstood by selfish men, and will be made a mark for the fierce assaults of Satan. It is this principle of self-sacrifice that his kingdom is established to destroy, and he will war against it wherever manifested. [223-224]

The childhood, youth, and manhood of John had been characterized by firmness and moral power. When his voice was heard in the wilderness saying, "Prepare ye the way of the Lord, make His paths straight" (Matt. 3:3), Satan feared for the safety of his kingdom. The sinfulness of sin was revealed in such a manner that men trembled. Satan's power over many who had been under his control was broken. He had been unwearied in his efforts to draw away the Baptist from a life of unreserved surrender to God; but he had failed. And he had failed to overcome Jesus. In the temptation in the wilderness, Satan had been defeated, and his rage was great. Now he determined to bring sorrow upon Christ by striking John. The One whom he could not entice to sin he would cause to suffer.

Jesus did not interpose to deliver His servant. He knew that John would bear the test. Gladly would the Saviour have come to John, to brighten the dungeon gloom with His own presence. But He was not to place Himself in the hands of enemies and imperil His own mission. Gladly would He have delivered His faithful servant. But for the sake of thousands who in after years must pass from prison to death, John was to drink the cup of martyrdom. As the followers of Jesus should languish in lonely cells, or perish by the sword, the rack, or the fagot, apparently forsaken by God and man, what a stay to their hearts would be the thought that John the Baptist, to whose faithfulness Christ Himself had borne witness, had passed through a similar experience!

Satan was permitted to cut short the earthly life of God's messenger; but that life which "is hid with Christ in God," the destroyer could not reach. Col. 3:3. He exulted that he had brought sorrow upon Christ, but he had failed of conquering John. Death itself only placed him forever beyond the power of temptation. In this warfare, Satan was revealing his own character. Before the witnessing universe he made manifest his enmity toward God and man.

Though no miraculous deliverance was granted John, he was not forsaken. He had always the companionship of heavenly angels, who opened to him the prophecies concerning Christ, and the precious promises of Scripture. These were his stay, as they were to be the stay of God's people through the coming ages. To John the Baptist, as to those that came after him, was given the assurance, "Lo, I am with you all the days, even unto the end." Matt. 28:20, R. V., margin.

God never leads His children otherwise than they would choose to be led, if they could see the end from the beginning, and discern the glory [224-225] of the purpose which they are fulfilling as co-workers with Him. Not Enoch, who was translated to heaven, not Elijah, who ascended in a chariot of fire, was greater or more honored than John the Baptist, who perished alone in the dungeon. "Unto you it is given in the behalf of Christ, not only to believe on Him, but also to suffer for His sake." Phil. 1:29. And of all the gifts that Heaven can bestow upon men, fellowship with Christ in His sufferings is the most weighty trust and the highest honor.

12. 'God never leads His children otherwise than t_____ would c_____ to be led, if they could see the end from the beginning, and discern the glory of the p_____ which they are fulfilling as co-workers with Him." (224, 225). What will be my "stay" during the upcoming times of trouble? _____

_____

_____

(precious p_____ of Scripture).

Prayer Journal: _____

_____

_____

_____

_____

_____

_____

_____

_____

Chapter 23

"The Kingdom of God Is at Hand"

"Jesus came into Galilee, preaching the gospel of the kingdom of God, and saying, The time is fulfilled, and the kingdom of God is at hand: repent ye, and believe the gospel." Mark 1:14, 15.

The Messiah's coming had been first announced in Judea. In the temple at Jerusalem the birth of the forerunner had been foretold to Zacharias as he ministered before the altar. On the hills of Bethlehem the angels had proclaimed the birth of Jesus. To Jerusalem the magi had come in search of Him. In the temple Simeon and Anna had testified to His divinity. "Jerusalem, and all Judea" had listened to the preaching of John the Baptist; and the deputation from the Sanhedrin, with the multitude, had heard his testimony concerning Jesus. In Judea, Christ had received His first disciples. Here much of His early ministry had been spent. The flashing forth of His divinity in the cleansing of the temple, His miracles of healing, and the lessons of divine truth that fell from His lips, all proclaimed that which after the healing at Bethesda He had declared before the Sanhedrin,--His Sonship to the Eternal.

If the leaders in Israel had received Christ, He would have honored them as His messengers to carry the gospel to the world. To them first was given the opportunity to become heralds of the kingdom and grace [231-232] of God. But Israel knew not the time of her visitation. The jealousy and distrust of the Jewish leaders had ripened into open hatred, and the hearts of the people were turned away from Jesus.

The Sanhedrin had rejected Christ's message and was bent upon His death; therefore Jesus departed from Jerusalem, from the priests, the temple, the religious leaders, the people who had been instructed in the law, and turned to another class to proclaim His message, and to gather out those who should carry the gospel to all nations.

As the light and life of men was rejected by the

1. Israel knew not the t_____ of her visitation...As the light and l_____ of men was rejected by the ecclesiastical authorities in the days of Christ, so it has been re-

ecclesiastical authorities in the days of Christ, so it has been rejected in every succeeding generation. Again and again the history of Christ's withdrawal from Judea has been repeated. When the Reformers preached the word of God, they had no thought of separating themselves from the established church; but the religious leaders would not tolerate the light, and those that bore it were forced to seek another class, who were longing for the truth. In our day few of the professed followers of the Reformers are actuated by their spirit. Few are listening for the voice of God, and ready to accept truth in whatever guise it may be presented. Often those who follow in the steps of the Reformers are forced to turn away from the churches they love, in order to declare the plain teaching of the word of God. And many times those who are seeking for light are by the same teaching obliged to leave the church of their fathers, that they may render obedience.

The people of Galilee were despised by the rabbis of Jerusalem as rude and unlearned, yet they presented a more favorable field for the Saviour's work. They were more earnest and sincere; less under the control of bigotry; their minds were more open for the reception of truth. In going to Galilee, Jesus was not seeking seclusion or isolation. The province was at this time the home of a crowded population, with a much larger admixture of people of other nations than was found in Judea.

As Jesus traveled through Galilee, teaching and healing, multitudes flocked to Him from the cities and villages. Many came even from Judea and the adjoining provinces. Often He was obliged to hide Himself from the people. The enthusiasm ran so high that it was necessary to take precautions lest the Roman authorities should be aroused to fear an insurrection. Never before had there been such a period as this for the world. Heaven was brought down to men. Hungering and thirsting souls that had waited long for the redemption of Israel now feasted upon the grace of a merciful Saviour. [232-233]

The burden of Christ's preaching was, "The time is fulfilled, and the kingdom of God is at hand; repent ye, and believe the gospel." Thus the gospel message, as given by the Saviour Himself, was based on the prophecies. The "time" which He declared to be fulfilled was the period made known by the angel Gabriel to Daniel.

jected in e_____ succeeding generation." (232). Lord, am I "listening for the v_____ of God, ready to accept truth in whatever guise it may be presented?" ____ _____.

What a tragedy to miss Your visit in my life! ___ _____ _____ _____

2. "The people of Galilee, despised by the rabbis of Jerusalem as rude and unlearned... were more o_____ for the reception of truth." What does it mean to be open for truth, Lord? _____ _____ _____ (willing to unlearn, and learn?)

3. "The b_____ of Christ's preaching was, 'Time is fulfilled, and the k_____ of God is at hand: repent ye, and believe the g_____.'" (233).

What did Jesus mean by 'fulfilled'? _____
_____
_____

With the Messiah's arrival, so is the kingdom of God also at hand. Is it not high time for me to repent of all that hinders my walk with You, Lord? Today is the day of salvation. Everyday is:

_____
_____
_____
_____

"Seventy weeks," said the angel, "are determined upon thy people and upon thy holy city, to finish the transgression, and to make an end of sins, and to make reconciliation for iniquity, and to bring in everlasting righteousness, and to seal up the vision and prophecy, and to anoint the most holy." Dan. 9:24. A day in prophecy stands for a year. See Num. 14:34; Ezek. 4:6. The seventy weeks, or four hundred and ninety days, represent four hundred and ninety years. A starting point for this period is given: "Know therefore and understand, that from the going forth of the commandment to restore and to build Jerusalem unto the Messiah the Prince shall be seven weeks, and threescore and two weeks," sixty-nine weeks, or four hundred and eighty-three years. Dan. 9:25. The commandment to restore and build Jerusalem, as completed by the decree of Artaxerxes Longimanus (see Ezra 6:14; 7:1, 9, margin), went into effect in the autumn of B. C. 457. From this time four hundred and eighty-three years extend to the autumn of A. D. 27. According to the prophecy, this period was to reach to the Messiah, the Anointed One. In A. D. 27, Jesus at His baptism received the anointing of the Holy Spirit, and soon afterward began His ministry. Then the message was proclaimed. "The time is fulfilled."

Then, said the angel, "He shall confirm the covenant with many for one week [seven years]." For seven years after the Saviour entered on His ministry, the gospel was to be preached especially to the Jews; for three and a half years by Christ Himself; and afterward by the apostles. "In the midst of the week He shall cause the sacrifice and the oblation to cease." Dan. 9:27. In the spring of A. D. 31, Christ the true sacrifice was offered on Calvary. Then the veil of the temple was rent in twain, showing that the sacredness and significance of the sacrificial service had departed. The time had come for the earthly sacrifice and oblation to cease.

The one week--seven years--ended in A. D. 34. Then by the stoning of Stephen the Jews finally sealed their rejection of the gospel; the disciples who were scattered abroad by persecution "went everywhere preaching the word" (Acts 8:4); and shortly after, Saul the persecutor was converted, and became Paul, the apostle to the Gentiles. [233-234]

The time of Christ's coming, His anointing by the Holy Spirit, His death, and the giving of the gospel to the Gentiles, were definitely pointed out. It was the privilege of the Jewish people to understand these prophecies, and to recognize their fulfillment in the mission of Jesus. Christ urged upon His disciples the importance of prophetic study. Referring to the prophecy given to Daniel in regard to their time, He said, "Whoso readeth, let him understand." Matt. 24:15. After His resurrection He explained to the disciples in "all the prophets" "the things concerning Himself." Luke 24:27. The Saviour had spoken through all the prophets. "The Spirit of Christ which was in them" "testified beforehand the sufferings of Christ, and the glory that should follow." 1 Peter 1:11.

It was Gabriel, the angel next in rank to the Son of God, who came with the divine message to Daniel. It was Gabriel, "His angel," whom Christ sent to open the future to the beloved John; and a blessing is pronounced on those who read and hear the words of the prophecy, and keep the things written therein. Rev. 1:3.

"The Lord God will do nothing, but He revealeth His secret unto His servants and prophets." While "the secret things belong unto the Lord our God," "those things which are revealed belong unto us and to our children forever." Amos 3:7; Deut. 29:29. God has given these things to us, and His blessing will attend the reverent, prayerful study of the prophetic scriptures.

As the message of Christ's first advent announced the kingdom of His grace, so the message of His second advent announces the kingdom of His glory. And the second message, like the first, is based on the prophecies. The words of the angel to Daniel relating to the last days were to be understood in the time of the end. At that time, "many shall run to and fro, and knowledge shall be increased." "The wicked shall do wickedly: and none of the wicked shall understand; but the wise shall understand." Dan. 12:4, 10. The Saviour Himself has given signs of His coming, and He says, "When ye see these things come to pass, know ye that the kingdom of God is nigh at hand." "And take heed to yourselves, lest at any time your hearts be overcharged with surfeiting, and drunkenness, and cares of this life, and so that day come upon you unawares." "Watch ye therefore, and pray always, that ye may be accounted worthy to escape all these things that shall come to pass, and to stand before the Son of man." Luke 21:31, 34, 36. [234-235]

We have reached the period foretold in these scrip-

4. "As the message of Christ's first advent announced the kingdom of His g_____, so the message of His second advent announces the kingdom of His g_____." (234). The experience of God's grace takes place before I will experience the kingdom of glory. The atmosphere for the experience of grace is the time spent contemplating the life of Christ. Lord, help me not to keep looking for the short cut, the fast track, but rather learn to daily relish Your presence; and that Your grace will mold my heart for the kingdom of glory: _____

_____

5. "The time of the e_____ _____ is come." (235). What does this mean to me? ___

_____

_____

_____

The nearness can't be any closer than a split-second fatal auto accident. The time to be ready is NOW. Lord, help me to detect any of Satan's tactics of delay or procrastination. And then help my motivation not to be fear of the end time, but rather to have fallen in love with You: _____

_____

_____

_____

Prayer Journal: _____

_____

_____

_____

_____

_____

_____

_____

tures. The time of the end is come, the visions of the prophets are unsealed, and their solemn warnings point us to our Lord's coming in glory as near at hand.

The Jews misinterpreted and misapplied the word of God, and they knew not the time of their visitation. The years of the ministry of Christ and His apostles,-- the precious last years of grace to the chosen people,-- they spent in plotting the destruction of the Lord's messengers. Earthly ambitions absorbed them, and the offer of the spiritual kingdom came to them in vain. So today the kingdom of this world absorbs men's thoughts, and they take no note of the rapidly fulfilling prophecies and the tokens of the swift-coming kingdom of God.

"But ye, brethren, are not in darkness, that that day should overtake you as a thief. Ye are all the children of light, and the children of the day: we are not of the night, nor of darkness." While we are not to know the hour of our Lord's return, we may know when it is near. "Therefore let us not sleep, as do others; but let us watch and be sober." 1 Thess. 5:4-6.

Chapter 24

"Is Not This the Carpenter's Son?"

[This chapter is based on Luke 4:16-30.]

Across the bright days of Christ's ministry in Galilee, one shadow lay. The people of Nazareth rejected Him. "Is not this the carpenter's son?" they said.

During His childhood and youth, Jesus had worshiped among His brethren in the synagogue at Nazareth. Since the opening of His ministry He had been absent from them, but they had not been ignorant of what had befallen Him. As He again appeared among them, their interest and expectation were excited to the highest pitch. Here were the familiar forms and faces of those whom He had known from infancy. Here were His mother, His brothers and sisters, and all eyes were turned upon Him as He entered the synagogue upon the Sabbath day, and took His place among the worshipers.

In the regular service for the day, the elder read from the prophets, and exhorted the people still to hope for the Coming One, who would bring in a glorious reign, and banish all oppression. He sought to encourage his hearers by rehearsing the evidence that the Messiah's coming was near. He described the glory of His advent, keeping prominent the thought that He would appear at the head of armies to deliver Israel.

When a rabbi was present at the synagogue, he was expected to deliver the sermon, and any Israelite might give the reading from the prophets. Upon this Sabbath Jesus was requested to take part in the service. He "stood up to read. And there was delivered unto Him a roll of the prophet Isaiah." Luke 4:16, 17, R. V., margin. The scripture which He read was one that was understood as referring to the Messiah: [236-237]

"The Spirit of the Lord is upon Me,
Because He hath anointed Me to preach the gospel
to the poor;

1. "Jesus stood before the people as a living e_____ of the prophecies concerning Himself...His words t_____ the hearers with a power they had never felt before." (237). When the Holy Spirit accompanies the reading of the Word, power speaks to the soul like nothing can. It's not just theory, or hope, but present fulfillment. Lord, may Your life and Your words find a responsive chord in me and thrill me!

_____

_____

2. But in applying the Isaiah passage to themselves, their p_____ was offended. Why? _____

_____

_____

Do I sometimes have the same response to the Holy Spirit prompting an application of Scripture to my life? _____ In what areas? _____

_____

_____ A prayer of willingness to accept God's word and will, sets for a better reception. Lord, draw me close to You, and nurture within me a willing attitude:

_____

3. "Who is this Jesus? they questioned...Although His life had been

He hath sent Me to heal the brokenhearted,
  To preach deliverance to the captives,
  And recovering of sight to the blind,
  To set at liberty them that are bruised,
To preach the acceptable year of the Lord."

"And He closed the roll, and gave it back to the attendant: . . . and the eyes of all in the synagogue were fastened on Him. . . . And all bare Him witness, and wondered at the words of grace which proceeded out of His mouth." Luke 4:20-22, R. V., margin.

Jesus stood before the people as a living expositor of the prophecies concerning Himself. Explaining the words He had read, He spoke of the Messiah as a reliever of the oppressed, a liberator of captives, a healer of the afflicted, restoring sight to the blind, and revealing to the world the light of truth. His impressive manner and the wonderful import of His words thrilled the hearers with a power they had never felt before. The tide of divine influence broke every barrier down; like Moses, they beheld the Invisible. As their hearts were moved upon by the Holy Spirit, they responded with fervent amens and praises to the Lord.

But when Jesus announced, "This day is this scripture fulfilled in your ears," they were suddenly recalled to think of themselves, and of the claims of Him who had been addressing them. They, Israelites, children of Abraham, had been represented as in bondage. They had been addressed as prisoners to be delivered from the power of evil; as in darkness, and needing the light of truth. Their pride was offended, and their fears were roused. The words of Jesus indicated that His work for them was to be altogether different from what they desired. Their deeds might be investigated too closely. Notwithstanding their exactness in outward ceremonies, they shrank from inspection by those clear, searching eyes.

Who is this Jesus? they questioned. He who had claimed for Himself the glory of the Messiah was the son of a carpenter, and had worked at His trade with His father Joseph. They had seen Him toiling up and down the hills, they were acquainted with His brothers and sisters, and knew His life and labors. They had seen Him develop from childhood to youth, and from youth to manhood. Although His life had been spotless, they would not believe that He was the Promised One. [237-238]

What a contrast between His teaching in regard to the new kingdom and that which they had heard from their elder! Jesus had said nothing of delivering them from the Romans. They had heard of His miracles, and had hoped that His power would be exercised for their advantage, but they had seen no indication of such purpose.

As they opened the door to doubt, their hearts became so much the harder for having been momentarily softened. Satan was determined that blind eyes should not that day be opened, nor souls bound in slavery be set at liberty. With intense energy he worked to fasten them in unbelief. They made no account of the sign already given, when they had been stirred by the conviction that it was their Redeemer who addressed them.

But Jesus now gave them an evidence of His divinity by revealing their secret thoughts. "He said unto them, Doubtless ye will say unto Me this parable, Physician, heal thyself: whatsoever we have heard done at Capernaum, do also here in Thine own country. And He said, Verily I say unto you, No prophet is acceptable in his own country. But of a truth I say unto you, There were many widows in Israel in the days of Elijah, when the heaven was shut up three years and six months, when there came a great famine over all the land; and unto none of them was Elijah sent, but only to Zarephath, in the land of Sidon, unto a woman that was a widow. And there were many lepers in Israel in the time of Elisha the prophet; and none of them was cleansed, but only Naaman, the Syrian." Luke 4:23-27, R. V.

By this relation of events in the lives of the prophets, Jesus met the questionings of His hearers. The servants whom God had chosen for a special work were not allowed to labor for a hardhearted and unbelieving people. But those who had hearts to feel and faith to believe were especially favored with evidences of His power through the prophets. In the days of Elijah, Israel had departed from God. They clung to their sins, and rejected the warnings of the Spirit through the Lord's messengers. Thus they cut themselves off from the channel by which God's blessing could come to them. The Lord passed by the homes of Israel, and found a refuge for His servant in a heathen land, with a woman who did not belong to the chosen people. But this woman was favored because she had followed the light she had received, and her heart was open to the greater light

spotless, they would not believe that He was the P_____
O_____."

4. "As they opened the door to doubt, their hearts became so much the h_____ for having been momentarily softened. S_____ was determined that blind eyes should not that day be opened, nor souls bound in slavery be set at liberty." (238). Lord, I don't want to make it harder for the Holy Spirit to get through to me. I know You want me to respond to every prompting of the Spirit. At that moment, please remind me of this hardening principle: ____

_____

5. What point was Jesus making by using Elijah and Elisha as illustrations? _____

_____

_____

If a youth preaches, and a point sinks home to me; if one of my own children, during family worship, makes a comment that hits home for me, how do I respond?

_____

_____

_____

6. "The Lord p_____ by the homes of Israel, and found refuge for His servant

in a heathen land…But this women was favored because she had followed the light she had received, and her heart was o_____ to the g_____ light that God sent her through His prophet." How faithful am I in following the light that I have received? _____. I don't want to miss out on greater light:

_____

7. "Naaman…felt his great n_____ of help. He was in a c_____ to receive the gifts of God's grace." (239). What is the condition? _____

_____

Lord, help me sense my great need. I am the worst of sinners. I am in awe of Your grace, love, and acceptance: _____

8. "Our standing before God depends, not upon the amount of light we have received, but upon the u_____ we make of what we have." Heathen can be better off than I am? How? (239)._____

_____

that God sent her through His prophet. [238-239]

It was for the same reason that in Elisha's time the lepers of Israel were passed by. But Naaman, a heathen nobleman, had been faithful to his convictions of right, and had felt his great need of help. He was in a condition to receive the gifts of God's grace. He was not only cleansed from his leprosy, but blessed with a knowledge of the true God.

Our standing before God depends, not upon the amount of light we have received, but upon the use we make of what we have. Thus even the heathen who choose the right as far as they can distinguish it are in a more favorable condition than are those who have had great light, and profess to serve God, but who disregard the light, and by their daily life contradict their profession.

The words of Jesus to His hearers in the synagogue struck at the root of their self-righteousness, pressing home upon them the bitter truth that they had departed from God and forfeited their claim to be His people. Every word cut like a knife as their real condition was set before them. They now scorned the faith with which Jesus had at first inspired them. They would not admit that He who had sprung from poverty and lowliness was other than a common man.

Their unbelief bred malice. Satan controlled them, and in wrath they cried out against the Saviour. They had turned from Him whose mission [239-240] it was to heal and restore; now they manifested the attributes of the destroyer.

When Jesus referred to the blessings given to the Gentiles, the fierce national pride of His hearers was aroused, and His words were drowned in a tumult of voices. These people had prided themselves on keeping the law; but now that their prejudices were offended, they were ready to commit murder. The assembly broke up, and laying hands upon Jesus, they thrust Him from the synagogue, and out of the city. All seemed eager for His destruction. They hurried Him to the brow of a precipice, intending to cast Him down headlong. Shouts and maledictions filled the air. Some were casting stones at Him, when suddenly He disappeared from among them. The heavenly messengers who had been by His side in the synagogue were with Him in the midst of that maddened throng. They shut Him in from His enemies, and conducted Him to a place of safety.

So angels protected Lot, and led him out safely from the midst of Sodom. So they protected Elisha in the little mountain city. When the encircling hills were filled with the horses and chariots of the king of Syria, and the great host of his armed men, Elisha beheld the nearer hill slopes covered with the armies of God,--horses and chariots of fire round about the servant of the Lord.

So, in all ages, angels have been near to Christ's faithful followers. The vast confederacy of evil is arrayed against all who would overcome; but Christ would have us look to the things which are not seen, to the armies of heaven encamped about all who love God, to deliver them. From what dangers, seen and unseen, we have been preserved through the interposition of the angels, we shall never know, until in the light of eternity we see the providences of God. Then we shall know that the whole family of heaven was interested in the family here below, and that messengers from the throne of God attended our steps from day to day.

When Jesus in the synagogue read from the prophecy, He stopped short of the final specification concerning the Messiah's work. Having read the words, "To proclaim the acceptable year of the Lord," He omitted the phrase, "and the day of vengeance of our God." Isa. 61:2. This was just as much truth as was the first of the prophecy, and by His silence Jesus did not deny the truth. But this last expression was that upon which His hearers delighted to dwell, and which they were desirous of fulfilling. They denounced judgments against the heathen, not discerning [240-241] that their own guilt was even greater than that of others. They themselves were in deepest need of the mercy they were so ready to deny to the heathen. That day in the synagogue, when Jesus stood among them, was their opportunity to accept the call of Heaven. He who "delighteth in mercy" (Micah 7:18) would fain have saved them from the ruin which their sins were inviting.

Not without one more call to repentance could He give them up. Toward the close of His ministry in Galilee, He again visited the home of His childhood. Since His rejection there, the fame of His preaching and His miracles had filled the land. None now could deny that He possessed more than human power. The people of Nazareth knew that He went about doing good, and healing all that were oppressed by Satan. About them were whole villages where there was not a moan of

9 . Why did Jesus omit the phrase "and the day of vengeance of our God"? (240).

_____

_____

_____

Lord, help me not to read Scripture, with an attitude of how this applies to someone else. May I never miss what the Spirit is trying to say to me, because I'm busy being self-righteous:

_____

_____

_____

_____

sickness in any house; for He had passed through them, and healed all their sick. The mercy revealed in every act of His life testified to His divine anointing.

Again as they listened to His words the Nazarenes were moved by the Divine Spirit. But even now they would not admit that this Man, who had been brought up among them, was other or greater than themselves. Still there rankled the bitter memory that while He had claimed for Himself to be the Promised One, He had really denied them a place with Israel; for He had shown them to be less worthy of God's favor than a heathen man and woman. Hence though they questioned, "Whence hath this Man this wisdom, and these mighty works?" they would not receive Him as the Christ of God. Because of their unbelief, the Saviour could not work many miracles among them. Only a few hearts were open to His blessing, and reluctantly He departed, never to return.

Unbelief, having once been cherished, continued to control the men of Nazareth. So it controlled the Sanhedrin and the nation. With priests and people, the first rejection of the demonstration of the Holy Spirit's power was the beginning of the end. In order to prove that their first resistance was right, they continued ever after to cavil at the words of Christ. Their rejection of the Spirit culminated in the cross of Calvary, in the destruction of their city, in the scattering of the nation to the winds of heaven.

Oh, how Christ longed to open to Israel the precious treasures of the truth! But such was their spiritual blindness that it was impossible to [241-242] reveal to them the truths relating to His kingdom. They clung to their creed and their useless ceremonies when the truth of Heaven awaited their acceptance. They spent their money for chaff and husks, when the bread of life was within their reach. Why did they not go to the word of God, and search diligently to know whether they were in error? The Old Testament Scriptures stated plainly every detail of Christ's ministry, and again and again He quoted from the prophets, and declared, "This day is this scripture fulfilled in your ears." If they had honestly searched the Scriptures, bringing their theories to the test of God's word, Jesus need not have wept over their impenitence. He need not have declared, "Behold, your house is left unto you desolate." Luke 13:35. They might have been acquainted with the evidence of His

10. "Because of their unbelief, the Savior could not work many m_____ among them. Only a few hearts were open to His blessing, and reluctantly He departed, never to r_____." (241). Jesus "wept over their impenitence." (242). Pass me not, oh gentle Savior. May I always be receptive, and responsive. I don't want You to ever leave. How do I express unbelief? _____
_____
_____
_____

Messiahship, and the calamity that laid their proud city in ruins might have been averted. But the minds of the Jews had become narrowed by their unreasoning bigotry. The lessons of Christ revealed their deficiencies of character, and demanded repentance. If they accepted His teachings, their practices must be changed, and their cherished hopes relinquished. In order to be honored by Heaven, they must sacrifice the honor of men. If they obeyed the words of this new rabbi, they must go contrary to the opinions of the great thinkers and teachers of the time.

Truth was unpopular in Christ's day. It is unpopular in our day. It has been unpopular ever since Satan first gave man a disrelish for it by presenting fables that lead to self-exaltation. Do we not today meet theories and doctrines that have no foundation in the word of God? Men cling as tenaciously to them as did the Jews to their traditions.

The Jewish leaders were filled with spiritual pride. Their desire for the glorification of self manifested itself even in the service of the sanctuary. They loved the highest seats in the synagogue. They loved greetings in the market places, and were gratified with the sound of their titles on the lips of men. As real piety declined, they became more jealous for their traditions and ceremonies.

Because their understanding was darkened by selfish prejudice, they could not harmonize the power of Christ's convicting words with the humility of His life. They did not appreciate the fact that real greatness can dispense with outward show. This Man's poverty seemed wholly inconsistent with His claim to be the Messiah. They questioned, If He was what He claimed to be, why was He so unpretending? If He was satisfied to be without the force of arms, what would become of their [242-243] nation? How could the power and glory so long anticipated bring the nations as subjects to the city of the Jews? Had not the priests taught that Israel was to bear rule over all the earth? and could it be possible that the great religious teachers were in error?

But it was not simply the absence of outward glory in His life that led the Jews to reject Jesus. He was the embodiment of purity, and they were impure. He dwelt among men an example of spotless integrity. His blameless life flashed light upon their hearts. His sincerity revealed their insincerity. It made manifest the

11. "T_____ was unpopular in Christ's day. It is unpopular in our day." I've got to check everything by Scripture. It doesn't matter who is saying or writing it. It doesn't matter if it's the way I've always thought. It's got to be in harmony with Scripture. Lord, keep me faithful. Show me where I am compromising for the sake of popularity:

_____
_____
_____
_____

Am I teachable? _____
_____

hollowness of their pretentious piety, and discovered iniquity to them in its odious character. Such a light was unwelcome.

If Christ had called attention to the Pharisees, and had extolled their learning and piety, they would have hailed Him with joy. But when He spoke of the kingdom of heaven as a dispensation of mercy for all mankind, He was presenting a phase of religion they would not tolerate. Their own example and teaching had never been such as to make the service of God seem desirable. When they saw Jesus giving attention to the very ones they hated and repulsed, it stirred up the worst passions of their proud hearts. Notwithstanding their boast that under the "Lion of the tribe of Judah" (Rev. 5:5), Israel should be exalted to pre-eminence over all nations, they could have borne the disappointment of their ambitious hopes better than they could bear Christ's reproof of their sins, and the reproach they felt even from the presence of His purity.

Prayer Journal: _____
_____
_____
_____
_____
_____
_____
_____
_____

Chapter 25

The Call by the Sea

[This chapter is based on Matt. 4:18-22;
Mark 1:16-20; Luke 5:1-11.]

Day was breaking over the Sea of Galilee. The disciples, weary with a night of fruitless toil, were still in their fishing boats on the lake. Jesus had come to spend a quiet hour by the waterside. In the early morning He hoped for a little season of rest from the multitude that followed Him day after day. But soon the people began to gather about Him. Their numbers rapidly increased, so that He was pressed upon all sides. Meanwhile the disciples had come to land. In order to escape the pressure of the multitude, Jesus stepped into Peter's boat, and bade him pull out a little from the shore. Here Jesus could be better seen and heard by all, and from the boat He taught the multitude on the beach.

What a scene was this for angels to contemplate; their glorious Commander, sitting in a fisherman's boat, swayed to and fro by the restless waves, and proclaiming the good news of salvation to the listening throng that were pressing down to the water's edge! He who was the Honored of heaven was declaring the great things of His kingdom in the open air, to the common people. Yet He could have had no more fitting scene for His labors. The lake, the mountains, the spreading [244-245] fields, the sunlight flooding the earth, all furnished objects to illustrate His lessons and impress them upon the mind. And no lesson of Christ's fell fruitless. Every message from His lips came to some soul as the word of eternal life.

Every moment added to the multitude upon the shore. Aged men leaning upon their staffs, hardy peasants from the hills, fishermen from their toil on the lake, merchants and rabbis, the rich and learned, old and young, bringing their sick and suffering ones, pressed to hear the words of the divine Teacher. To such scenes as this the prophets had looked forward, and they wrote:

"The land of Zebulon and the land of Naphtali,
Toward the sea, beyond Jordan,

1. "Through the H_____ S_____, that voice which was speaking from the fisherman's boat on the Sea of Galilee would be heard speaking p_____ to human hearts to the close of t_____." (245). Lord, give me the peace that only You can give. Let me have ears to hear, and a heart to embrace. Help me place myself in the atmosphere of the Holy Spirit: _____

_____

_____

2. With the miracle of the catch of fish, being in the presence of Jesus revealed to Peter his own "u_____. Love for his Master, shame for his own u_____, gratitude for the condescension of Christ, above all, the sense of his uncleanness in the presence of infinite purity, o_____ him." (246). Being in Your presence Lord, will touch me, won't it? I can't be neutral, or unresponsive. To be unresponsive is to be as if not having even been in Your presence: _____

_____

_____

3. "Humanity, with its weakness and sin, was brought in contrast with the perfection of divinity, and he felt altogeth-

Galilee of the Gentiles,
The people which sat in darkness
Saw a great light,
And to them which sat in the region and
shadow of death,
To them did light spring up." R. V.

Beside the throng on the shores of Gennesaret, Jesus in His sermon by the sea had other audiences before His mind. Looking down the ages, He saw His faithful ones in prison and judgment hall, in temptation and loneliness and affliction. Every scene of joy and conflict and perplexity was open before Him. In the words spoken to those gathered about Him, He was speaking also to these other souls the very words that would come to them as a message of hope in trial, of comfort in sorrow, and heavenly light in darkness. Through the Holy Spirit, that voice which was speaking from the fisherman's boat on the Sea of Galilee, would be heard speaking peace to human hearts to the close of time.

The discourse ended, Jesus turned to Peter, and bade him launch out into the sea, and let down his net for a draught. But Peter was disheartened. All night he had taken nothing. During the lonely hours he had thought of the fate of John the Baptist, who was languishing alone in his dungeon. He had thought of the prospect before Jesus and His followers, of the ill success of the mission to Judea, and the malice of the priests and rabbis. Even his own occupation had failed him; and as he watched by the empty nets, the future had seemed dark with discouragement. "Master," he said, "we have toiled all the night, and have taken nothing: nevertheless at Thy word I will let down the net." [245-246]

Night was the only favorable time for fishing with nets in the clear waters of the lake. After toiling all night without success, it seemed hopeless to cast the net by day; but Jesus had given the command, and love for their Master moved the disciples to obey. Simon and his brother together let down the net. As they attempted to draw it in, so great was the quantity of fish enclosed that it began to break. They were obliged to summon James and John to their aid. When the catch was secured, both the boats were so heavily laden that they were in danger of sinking.

But Peter was unmindful now of boats or lading. This miracle, above any other he had ever witnessed, was to him a manifestation of divine power. In Jesus he saw One who held all nature under His control. The presence of divinity revealed his own unholiness. Love for his Master, shame for his own unbelief, gratitude for the condescension of Christ, above all, the sense of his uncleanness in the presence of infinite purity, overwhelmed him. While his companions were securing the contents of the net, Peter fell at the Saviour's feet, exclaiming, "Depart from me; for I am a sinful man, O Lord."

It was the same presence of divine holiness that had caused the prophet Daniel to fall as one dead before the angel of God. He said, "My comeliness was turned in me into corruption, and I retained no strength." So when Isaiah beheld the glory of the Lord, he exclaimed, "Woe is me! for I am undone; because I am a man of unclean lips, and I dwell in the midst of a people of unclean lips: for mine eyes have seen the King, the Lord of hosts." Dan. 10:8; Isa. 6:5. Humanity, with its weakness and sin, was brought in contrast with the perfection of divinity, and he felt altogether deficient and unholy. Thus it has been with all who have been granted a view of God's greatness and majesty.

Peter exclaimed, "Depart from me; for I am a sinful man;" yet he clung to the feet of Jesus, feeling that he could not be parted from Him. The Saviour answered, "Fear not; from henceforth thou shalt catch men." It was after Isaiah has beheld the holiness of God and his own unworthiness that he was entrusted with the divine message. It was after Peter had been led to self-renunciation and dependence upon divine power that he received the call to his work for Christ.

Until this time none of the disciples had fully united as colaborers with Jesus. They had witnessed many of His miracles, and had listened to His teaching; but they had not entirely forsaken their former employment. [246-249] The imprisonment of John the Baptist had been to them all a bitter disappointment. If such were to be the outcome of John's mission, they could have little hope for their Master, with all the religious leaders combined against Him. Under the circumstances it was a relief to them to return for a short time to their fishing. But now Jesus called them to forsake their former life, and unite their interests with His. Peter had accepted the call. Upon reaching the shore, Jesus bade the three other disciples, "Follow Me, and I will make you fishers of men." Immediately they left all, and followed Him.

er d_____ and u_____. Thus it has been with all who have been granted a view of God's greatness and majesty." But what a privilege, to be granted this view! Peter exclaimed, "Depart from me; for I am a sinful man;" yet he clung to the feet of Jesus. Lord, if I am sensing my unholiness, You are not condemning me, but I am seeing my need, and desiring to be drawn even closer to You: _____

_____

_____

4. "It was after Isaiah had beheld the holiness of God and his own u_____, that he was e_____ with the divine message. It was after Peter had been led to self-renunciation and d_____ upon divine power that he received the c_____ to his work for Christ." It is an important and helpful step / realization. Bring me to that point, Lord: _____

_____

5. Jesus called them to forsake their former life, and unite their i_____ with His...'Follow Me...' Immediately they left all, and followed Him." (249). Have I responded to that call of uniting my interests with Yours, Lord? _____

_____

6. "During that sad night on the lake, when they were s_____ from Christ, the disciples were pressed hard by unbelief, and weary with fruitless toil. But His p_____ kindled their faith, and brought them joy and success. So it is with us; a_____ from Christ, our work is fruitless, and it is easy to distrust and m_____. But when He is near, and we labor under His direction, we rejoice in the evidence of His power. It is S_____ work to discourage the soul; it is Christ's work to i_____ with faith and hope." (249). Lord, when I am discouraged, help me to remember the separation issue, and to immediately make myself available to You again. And may my words be inspired by You, and not the enemy: _____

_____

_____

7. "The Lord Jesus seeks the co-operation of those who will become u_____ channels for the communication of His grace. The first thing to be learned by all who would become workers together with God is the lesson of s_____; then they are prepared

Before asking them to leave their nets and fishing boats, Jesus had given them the assurance that God would supply their needs. The use of Peter's boat for the work of the gospel had been richly repaid. He who is "rich unto all that call upon Him," has said, "Give, and it shall be given unto you; good measure, pressed down, and shaken together, and running over." Rom. 10:12; Luke 6:38. In this measure He had rewarded the disciple's service. And every sacrifice that is made in His ministry will be recompensed according to "the exceeding riches of His grace." Eph. 3:20; 2:7.

During that sad night on the lake, when they were separated from Christ, the disciples were pressed hard by unbelief, and weary with fruitless toil. But His presence kindled their faith, and brought them joy and success. So it is with us; apart from Christ, our work is fruitless, and it is easy to distrust and murmur. But when He is near, and we labor under His direction, we rejoice in the evidence of His power. It is Satan's work to discourage the soul; it is Christ's work to inspire with faith and hope.

The deeper lesson which the miracle conveyed for the disciples is a lesson for us also,--that He whose word could gather the fishes from the sea could also impress human hearts, and draw them by the cords of His love, so that His servants might become "fishers of men."

They were humble and unlearned men, those fishers of Galilee; but Christ, the light of the world, was abundantly able to qualify them for the position for which He had chosen them. The Saviour did not despise education; for when controlled by the love of God, and devoted to His service, intellectual culture is a blessing. But He passed by the wise men of His time, because they were so self-confident that they could not sympathize with suffering humanity, and become colaborers with the Man of Nazareth. In their bigotry they scorned to be taught by Christ. The Lord Jesus seeks the co-operation of those who will become unobstructed [249-250] channels for the communication of His grace. The first thing to be learned by all who would become workers together with God is the lesson of self-distrust; then they are prepared to have imparted to them the character of Christ. This is not to be gained through education in the most scientific schools. It is the fruit of wisdom that is obtained from the divine Teacher alone.

Jesus chose unlearned fishermen because they had

not been schooled in the traditions and erroneous customs of their time. They were men of native ability, and they were humble and teachable,--men whom He could educate for His work. In the common walks of life there is many a man patiently treading the round of daily toil, unconscious that he possesses powers which, if called into action, would raise him to an equality with the world's most honored men. The touch of a skillful hand is needed to arouse those dormant faculties. It was such men that Jesus called to be His colaborers; and He gave them the advantage of association with Himself. Never had the world's great men such a teacher. When the disciples came forth from the Saviour's training, they were no longer ignorant and uncultured. They had become like Him in mind and character, and men took knowledge of them that they had been with Jesus.

It is not the highest work of education to communicate knowledge merely, but to impart that vitalizing energy which is received through the contact of mind with mind, and soul with soul. It is only life that can beget life. What privilege, then, was theirs who for three years were in daily contact with that divine life from which has flowed every life-giving impulse that has blessed the world! Above all his companions, John the beloved disciple yielded himself to the power of that wondrous life. He says, "The life was manifested, and we have seen it, and bear witness, and show unto you that eternal life, which was with the Father, and was manifested unto us." "Of His fullness have all we received, and grace for grace." 1 John 1:2; John 1:16.

In the apostles of our Lord there was nothing to bring glory to themselves. It was evident that the success of their labors was due only to God. The lives of these men, the characters they developed, and the mighty work that God wrought through them, are a testimony to what He will do for all who are teachable and obedient.

He who loves Christ the most will do the greatest amount of good. There is no limit to the usefulness of one who, by putting self aside, [250-251] makes room for the working of the Holy Spirit upon his heart, and lives a life wholly consecrated to God. If men will endure the necessary discipline, without complaining or fainting by the way, God will teach them hour by hour, and day by day. He longs to reveal His grace. If His people will remove the obstructions, He will pour forth

to have imparted to them the c_____ ___ of Christ." (249, 250). Sounds so wonderful! Your character, channel of Your grace! Help me see the obstructions of self in my heart:_____

8. Why did Jesus choose unlearned fishermen? ___
_____
_____"When the disciples came forth from the Savior's training, they were no longer ignorant and uncultured. They had become like Him in m_____ and character, and men took knowledge of them that they had b_____ with Jesus." Lord, I pray that that is my influence, that I have been with You. Remind me to take and make time: ____
_____
_____

9. "There is no l_____ to the usefulness of one who, by putting s_____ aside, m_____ room for the working of the Holy Spirit upon his h_____, and lives a life wholly consecrated to God." (250, 251). Lord, keep giving me that vision of Yours. I give You permission to turn that vision into reality. You'll have to help

me, though, in working on putting self aside. What does it mean, Lord, to make room for the Holy Spirit to work? _____
_____
_____
_____

10. What is the highest of all schools? _____
_____
_____

Prayer journal: _____
_____
_____
_____
_____
_____
_____

the waters of salvation in abundant streams through the human channels. If men in humble life were encouraged to do all the good they could do, if restraining hands were not laid upon them to repress their zeal, there would be a hundred workers for Christ where now there is one.

God takes men as they are, and educates them for His service, if they will yield themselves to Him. The Spirit of God, received into the soul, will quicken all its faculties. Under the guidance of the Holy Spirit, the mind that is devoted unreservedly to God develops harmoniously, and is strengthened to comprehend and fulfill the requirements of God. The weak, vacillating character becomes changed to one of strength and steadfastness. Continual devotion establishes so close a relation between Jesus and His disciple that the Christian becomes like Him in mind and character. Through a connection with Christ he will have clearer and broader views. His discernment will be more penetrative, his judgment better balanced. He who longs to be of service to Christ is so quickened by the life-giving power of the Sun of Righteousness that he is enabled to bear much fruit to the glory of God.

Men of the highest education in the arts and sciences have learned precious lessons from Christians in humble life who were designated by the world as unlearned. But these obscure disciples had obtained an education in the highest of all schools. They had sat at the feet of Him who spoke as "never man spake."

Chapter 26

At Capernaum

At Capernaum Jesus dwelt in the intervals of His journeys to and fro, and it came to be known as "His own city." It was on the shores of the Sea of Galilee, and near the borders of the beautiful plain of Gennesaret, if not actually upon it.

The deep depression of the lake gives to the plain that skirts its shores the genial climate of the south. Here in the days of Christ flourished the palm tree and the olive, here were orchards and vineyards, green fields, and brightly blooming flowers in rich luxuriance, all watered by living streams bursting from the cliffs. The shores of the lake, and the hills that at a little distance encircle it, were dotted with towns and villages. The lake was covered with fishing boats. Everywhere was the stir of busy, active life.

Capernaum itself was well adapted to be the center of the Saviour's work. Being on the highway from Damascus to Jerusalem and Egypt, and to the Mediterranean Sea, it was a great thoroughfare of travel. People from many lands passed through the city, or tarried for rest in their journeyings to and fro. Here Jesus could meet all nations and all ranks, the rich and great as well as the poor and lowly, and His lessons would be carried to other countries and into many households. [252-253] Investigation of the prophecies would thus be excited, attention would be directed to the Saviour, and His mission would be brought before the world.

Notwithstanding the action of the Sanhedrin against Jesus, the people eagerly awaited the development of His mission. All heaven was astir with interest. Angels were preparing the way for His ministry, moving upon men's hearts, and drawing them to the Saviour.

In Capernaum the nobleman's son whom Christ had healed was a witness to His power. And the court official and his household joyfully testified of their faith. When it was known that the Teacher Himself was among them, the whole city was aroused. Multitudes flocked to His presence. On the Sabbath the people crowded the synagogue until great numbers had to turn away, unable

1. "All heaven was astir with interest. Angels were p_____ the way for His ministry, moving upon men's hearts, and drawing them to the Savior." (253). This is no small event. Heaven is involved in drawing me to Christ! I'd better pay attention. I want to pay attention. I don't want to miss one

tug of that drawing power:

_____

2. The crowds that heard the Savior were "astonished at His doctrine: for His word was with p_____." When the scribes and elders taught, "n_____ inspiration from God stirred their own h_____ or the hearts of their hearers." But I can't depend on the teacher or preacher. Lord, as I read the Word, as I contemplate Your life during this spiritual walk, may I sense the Spirit stirring my own heart:

_____

_____

3. "Jesus had nothing to do with the various subjects of d_____ among the Jews. It was His work to present the t_____." When I read the Word, it is easy to get caught up in applying the passage to another person, because of some deficiency they have. That gets me and them nowhere. I need to read for edification and stirring of my own heart. Lord, tell me the Truth that I (!) need to hear. Help me be receptive:

_____

_____

to find entrance.

All who heard the Saviour "were astonished at His doctrine: for His word was with power." "He taught them as one having authority, and not as the scribes." Luke 4:32; Matt. 7:29. The teaching of the scribes and elders was cold and formal, like a lesson learned by rote. To them the word of God possessed no vital power. Their own ideas and traditions were substituted for its teaching. In the accustomed round of service they professed to explain the law, but no inspiration from God stirred their own hearts or the hearts of their hearers.

Jesus had nothing to do with the various subjects of dissension among the Jews. It was His work to present the truth. His words shed a flood of light upon the teachings of patriarchs and prophets, and the Scriptures came to men as a new revelation. Never before had His hearers perceived such a depth of meaning in the word of God.

Jesus met the people on their own ground, as one who was acquainted with their perplexities. He made truth beautiful by presenting it in the most direct and simple way. His language was pure, refined, and clear as a running stream. His voice was as music to those who had listened to the monotonous tones of the rabbis. But while His teaching was simple, He spoke as one having authority. This characteristic set His teaching in contrast with that of all others. The rabbis spoke with doubt and hesitancy, as if the Scriptures might be interpreted to mean one thing or exactly the opposite. The hearers were daily involved in greater uncertainty. But Jesus taught the Scriptures as of unquestionable authority. Whatever His subject, it was presented with power, as if His words could not be controverted. [253-254]

Yet He was earnest, rather than vehement. He spoke as one who had a definite purpose to fulfill. He was bringing to view the realities of the eternal world. In every theme God was revealed. Jesus sought to break the spell of infatuation which keeps men absorbed in earthly things. He placed the things of this life in their true relation, as subordinate to those of eternal interest; but He did not ignore their importance. He taught that heaven and earth are linked together, and that a knowledge of divine truth prepares men better to perform the duties of everyday life. He spoke as one familiar with heaven, conscious of His relationship to God, yet recognizing His unity with every member of the human family.

His messages of mercy were varied to suit His audience. He knew "how to speak a word in season to him that is weary" (Isa. 50:4); for grace was poured upon His lips, that He might convey to men in the most attractive way the treasures of truth. He had tact to meet the prejudiced minds, and surprise them with illustrations that won their attention. Through the imagination He reached the heart. His illustrations were taken from the things of daily life, and although they were simple, they had in them a wonderful depth of meaning. The birds of the air, the lilies of the field, the seed, the shepherd and the sheep,--with these objects Christ illustrated immortal truth; and ever afterward, when His hearers chanced to see these things of nature, they recalled His words. Christ's illustrations constantly repeated His lessons.

Christ never flattered men. He never spoke that which would exalt their fancies and imaginations, nor did He praise them for their clever inventions; but deep, unprejudiced thinkers received His teaching, and found that it tested their wisdom. They marveled at the spiritual truth expressed in the simplest language. The most highly educated were charmed with His words, and the uneducated were always profited. He had a message for the illiterate; and He made even the heathen to understand that He had a message for them.

His tender compassion fell with a touch of healing upon weary and troubled hearts. Even amid the turbulence of angry enemies He was surrounded with an atmosphere of peace. The beauty of His countenance, the loveliness of His character, above all, the love expressed in look and tone, drew to Him all who were not hardened in unbelief. Had it not been for the sweet, sympathetic spirit that shone out in every look and word, He would not have attracted the large congregations that He did. The afflicted ones who came to Him felt that He linked His [254-255] interest with theirs as a faithful and tender friend, and they desired to know more of the truths He taught. Heaven was brought near. They longed to abide in His presence, that the comfort of His love might be with them continually.

Jesus watched with deep earnestness the changing countenances of His hearers. The faces that expressed interest and pleasure gave Him great satisfaction. As the arrows of truth pierced to the soul, breaking through the barriers of selfishness, and working contrition, and

4. "The beauty of His countenance, the loveliness of His c_____, above all, the love expressed in look and tone, drew to Him a_____ who were not hardened in unbelief. Had it not been for the sweet, sympathetic spirit that shone out in every l_____ and word, He would not have attracted the l_____ congregations that He did." (254). I can imagine the tone; yes, the character and sympathy does draw me; and thank You Jesus. How do others experience my looks and tones? _____

_____

May I be like You! _____

_____

_____

5. "The afflicted ones who came to Him felt that He linked His interest with theirs as a faithful and tender f_____, and they desired to know more of the truths He taught. Heaven was brought n_____. They longed to abide in His p_____." (254, 255). Can I be that kind of friend? Can I represent Your friendship to others? How? _____

_____

_____

finally gratitude, the Saviour was made glad. When His eye swept over the throng of listeners, and He recognized among them the faces He had before seen, His countenance lighted up with joy. He saw in them hopeful subjects for His kingdom. When the truth, plainly spoken, touched some cherished idol, He marked the change of countenance, the cold, forbidding look, which told that the light was unwelcome. When He saw men refuse the message of peace, His heart was pierced to the very depths.

6. "When He saw men refuse the message of peace, His heart was p_____ to the very depths." Jesus, forgive me, when I opt for a course other than peace. Help me to see how it pains You, me, and others: __
_____
_____

Jesus in the synagogue spoke of the kingdom He had come to establish, and of His mission to set free the captives of Satan. He was interrupted by a shriek of terror. A madman rushed forward from among the people, crying out, "Let us alone; what have we to do with Thee, Thou Jesus of Nazareth? art Thou come to destroy us? I know Thee who Thou art; the Holy One of God."

All was now confusion and alarm. The attention of the people was diverted from Christ, and His words were unheeded. This was Satan's purpose in leading his victim to the synagogue. But Jesus rebuked the demon, saying, "Hold thy peace, and come out of him. And when the devil had thrown him in the midst, he came out of him, and hurt him not."

The mind of this wretched sufferer had been darkened by Satan, but in the Saviour's presence a ray of light had pierced the gloom. He was roused to long for freedom from Satan's control; but the demon resisted the power of Christ. When the man tried to appeal to Jesus for help, the evil spirit put words into his mouth, and he cried out in an agony of fear. The demoniac partially comprehended that he was in the presence of One who could set him free; but when he tried to come within reach of that mighty hand, another's will held him, another's words found utterance through him. The conflict between the power of Satan and his own desire for freedom was terrible. [255-256]

He who had conquered Satan in the wilderness of temptation was again brought face to face with His enemy. The demon exerted all his power to retain control of his victim. To lose ground here would be to give Jesus a victory. It seemed that the tortured man must lose his life in the struggle with the foe that had been the ruin of his manhood. But the Saviour spoke with authority, and set the captive free. The man who had been possessed stood before the wondering people happy in the free-dom of self-possession. Even the demon had testified to the divine power of the Saviour.

The man praised God for his deliverance. The eye that had so lately glared with the fire of insanity, now beamed with intelligence, and overflowed with grate-ful tears. The people were dumb with amazement. As soon as they recovered speech they exclaimed, one to another, "What is this? a new teaching! with authority He commandeth even the unclean spirits, and they obey Him." Mark 1:27, R. V.

The secret cause of the affliction that had made this man a fearful spectacle to his friends and a burden to himself was in his own life. He had been fascinated by the pleasures of sin, and had thought to make life a grand carnival. He did not dream of becoming a terror to the world and the reproach of his family. He thought his time could be spent in innocent folly. But once in the downward path, his feet rapidly descended. Intemper-ance and frivolity perverted the noble attributes of his nature, and Satan took absolute control of him.

Remorse came too late. When he would have sac-rificed wealth and pleasure to regain his lost manhood, he had become helpless in the grasp of the evil one. He had placed himself on the enemy's ground, and Satan had taken possession of all his faculties. The tempter had allured him with many charming presentations; but when once the wretched man was in his power, the fiend became relentless in his cruelty, and terrible in his angry visitations. So it will be with all who yield to evil; the fascinating pleasure of their early career ends in the darkness of despair or the madness of a ruined soul.

The same evil spirit that tempted Christ in the wil-derness, and that possessed the maniac of Capernaum, controlled the unbelieving Jews. But with them he as-sumed an air of piety, seeking to deceive them as to their motives in rejecting the Saviour. Their condition was more hopeless than that of the demoniac, for they felt no need of Christ and were therefore held fast under the power of Satan. [256-257]

The period of Christ's personal ministry among men was the time of greatest activity for the forces of the kingdom of darkness. For ages Satan with his evil angels had been seeking to control the bodies and the souls of men, to bring upon them sin and suffering; then he had charged all this misery upon God. Jesus was re-

7. What was the secret cause of this man's afflic-tion? He was fascinated by the p_____ of sin. (256). "Intemperance and frivolity perverted the n_____ attributes of his nature, and Satan took absolute control of him." Lord, You enjoyed social-izing. Yet, I can see the di-rection Satan wants to take me. The transition would be subtle and gradual. Help me, Lord, to differentiate between Your pleasures, and the pleasures of the sin: _____

_____

_____

8. "Their condition [un-believing Jews] was more h_____ than that of the demoniac, for they felt no n_____ of Christ and were therefore held fast under the power of Satan." Lord, please guard me from that state of mind. I see my need of You, but not nearly as desperately as I should. How can my awareness grow? _____

_____

_____

_____

9. "Satan summoned all his forces, and at every step c__ _____ the work of Christ." (257). As my goal is a walk with You, Lord, what should I expect from Satan? _____
_____
_____
_____

10. "The only m_____ by which they could have withstood evil spirits," was by the w_____ of God. That is how Christ overcame the wicked one. What is my situation if I am not in Your word for a stretch? _____
_____
What does it mean to place myself on the enemy's ground? _____
_____
_____

vealing to men the character of God. He was breaking Satan's power, and setting his captives free. New life and love and power from heaven were moving upon the hearts of men, and the prince of evil was aroused to contend for the supremacy of his kingdom. Satan summoned all his forces, and at every step contested the work of Christ.

So it will be in the great final conflict of the controversy between righteousness and sin. While new life and light and power are descending from on high upon the disciples of Christ, a new life is springing up from beneath, and energizing the agencies of Satan. Intensity is taking possession of every earthly element. With a subtlety gained through centuries of conflict, the prince of evil works under a disguise. He appears clothed as an angel of light, and multitudes are "giving heed to seducing spirits, and doctrines of devils." 1 Tim. 4:1.

In the days of Christ the leaders and teachers of Israel were powerless to resist the work of Satan. They were neglecting the only means by which they could have withstood evil spirits. It was by the word of God that Christ overcame the wicked one. The leaders of Israel professed to be the expositors of God's word, but they had studied it only to sustain their traditions, and enforce their man-made observances. By their interpretation they made it express sentiments that God had never given. Their mystical construction made indistinct that which He had made plain. They disputed over insignificant technicalities, and practically denied the most essential truths. Thus infidelity was sown broadcast. God's word was robbed of its power, and evil spirits worked their will. [257-258]

History is repeating. With the open Bible before them, and professing to reverence its teachings, many of the religious leaders of our time are destroying faith in it as the word of God. They busy themselves with dissecting the word, and set their own opinions above its plainest statements. In their hands God's word loses its regenerating power. This is why infidelity runs riot, and iniquity is rife.

When Satan has undermined faith in the Bible, he directs men to other sources for light and power. Thus he insinuates himself. Those who turn from the plain teaching of Scripture and the convicting power of God's Holy Spirit are inviting the control of demons. Criticism and speculation concerning the Scriptures have opened the way for spiritism and theosophy--those modernized forms of ancient heathenism--to gain a foothold even in the professed churches of our Lord Jesus Christ.

Side by side with the preaching of the gospel, agencies are at work which are but the medium of lying spirits. Many a man tampers with these merely from curiosity, but seeing evidence of the working of a more than human power, he is lured on and on, until he is controlled by a will stronger than his own. He cannot escape from its mysterious power.

The defenses of the soul are broken down. He has no barrier against sin. When once the restraints of God's word and His Spirit are rejected, no man knows to what depths of degradation he may sink. Secret sin or master passion may hold him a captive as helpless as was the demoniac of Capernaum. Yet his condition is not hopeless.

The means by which we can overcome the wicked one is that by which Christ overcame,--the power of the word. God does not control our minds without our consent; but if we desire to know and to do His will, His promises are ours: "Ye shall know the truth, and the truth shall make you free." "If any man willeth to do His will, he shall know of the teaching." John 8:32; 7:17, R. V. Through faith in these promises, every man may be delivered from the snares of error and the control of sin.

Every man is free to choose what power he will have to rule over him. None have fallen so low, none are so vile, but that they can find deliverance in Christ. The demoniac, in place of prayer, could utter only the words of Satan; yet the heart's unspoken appeal was heard. No cry from a soul in need, though it fail of utterance in words, will be unheeded. Those who will consent to enter into covenant relation with the God of heaven are not left to the power of Satan or to the infirmity of their own [258-259] nature. They are invited by the Saviour, "Let him take hold of My strength, that he may make peace with Me; and he shall make peace with Me." Isa. 27:5. The spirits of darkness will battle for the soul once under their dominion, but angels of God will contend for that soul with prevailing power. The Lord says, "Shall the prey be taken from the mighty, or the lawful captive delivered? . . . Thus saith the Lord, Even the captives of the mighty shall be taken away, and the prey of the terrible shall be delivered: for I will contend

11. "None have fallen so low, none are so vile, but that they can find d_____ in Christ." (258). There is power in the Word of God and its promises. Give me confidence Lord, to rely on You and Your promises: _____

with him that contendeth with thee, and I will save thy children." Isa. 49:24, 25.

While the congregation in the synagogue were still spellbound with awe, Jesus withdrew to the home of Peter for a little rest. But here also a shadow had fallen. The mother of Peter's wife lay sick, stricken with a "great fever." Jesus rebuked the disease, and the sufferer arose, and ministered to the wants of the Master and His disciples.

Tidings of the work of Christ spread rapidly throughout Capernaum. For fear of the rabbis, the people dared not come for healing upon the Sabbath; but no sooner had the sun disappeared below the horizon than there was a great commotion. From the homes, the shops, the market places, the inhabitants of the city pressed toward the humble dwelling that sheltered Jesus. The sick were brought upon couches, they came leaning upon staffs, or, supported by friends, they tottered feebly into the Saviour's presence.

Hour after hour they came and went; for none could know whether tomorrow would find the Healer still among them. Never before had Capernaum witnessed a day like this. The air was filled with the voice of triumph and shouts of deliverance. The Saviour was joyful in the joy He had awakened. As He witnessed the sufferings of those who had come to Him, His heart was stirred with sympathy, and He rejoiced in His power to restore them to health and happiness.

Not until the last sufferer had been relieved did Jesus cease His work. It was far into the night when the multitude departed, and silence settled down upon the home of Simon. The long, exciting day was past, and Jesus sought rest. But while the city was still wrapped in slumber, the Saviour, "rising up a great while before day, . . . went out, and departed into a solitary place, and there prayed."

Thus were spent the days in the earthly life of Jesus. He often dismissed His disciples to visit their homes and rest; but He gently resisted their efforts to draw Him away from His labors. All day He toiled, [259-260] teaching the ignorant, healing the sick, giving sight to the blind, feeding the multitude; and at the eventide or in the early morning, He went away to the sanctuary of the mountains for communion with His Father. Often He passed the entire night in prayer and meditation, returning at daybreak to His work among the people.

12. After the long, exciting day of healing, "Jesus sought rest. But while the city was still wrapped in slumber, the Savior, 'rising up a great while before d_____,... went out, and departed into a solitary place, and there p_____.'" (259). "Often He passed the entire night in prayer and m_____, returning at daybreak to His work among the people." (260). It was critical to Jesus. It should be to me. Lord, be my alarm clock, so I will have that quiet, quality time with You. What more can I do to have that daily experience and walk? _____
_____
_____

Early in the morning, Peter and his companions came to Jesus, saying that already the people of Capernaum were seeking Him. The disciples had been bitterly disappointed at the reception which Christ had met hitherto. The authorities at Jerusalem were seeking to murder Him; even His own townsmen had tried to take His life; but at Capernaum He was welcomed with joyful enthusiasm, and the hopes of the disciples kindled anew. It might be that among the liberty-loving Galileans were to be found the supporters of the new kingdom. But with surprise they heard Christ's words, "I must preach the kingdom of God to other cities also: for therefore am I sent."

In the excitement which then pervaded Capernaum, there was danger that the object of His mission would be lost sight of. Jesus was not satisfied to attract attention to Himself merely as a wonder worker or a healer of physical diseases. He was seeking to draw men to Him as their Saviour. While the people were eager to believe that He had come as a king, to establish an earthly reign, He desired to turn their minds away from the earthly to the spiritual. Mere worldly success would interfere with His work.

And the wonder of the careless crowd jarred upon His spirit. In His life no self-assertion mingled. The homage which the world gives to position, or wealth, or talent, was foreign to the Son of man. None of the means that men employ to win allegiance or command homage did Jesus use. Centuries before His birth, it had been prophesied of Him, [260-261] "He shall not cry, nor lift up, nor cause His voice to be heard in the street. A bruised reed shall He not break, and the dimly burning flax shall He not quench: He shall bring forth judgment unto truth. He shall not fail nor be discouraged, till He have set judgment in the earth." Isa. 42:2-4, margin.

The Pharisees sought distinction by their scrupulous ceremonialism, and the ostentation of their worship and charities. They proved their zeal for religion by making it the theme of discussion. Disputes between opposing sects were loud and long, and it was not unusual to hear on the streets the voice of angry controversy from learned doctors of the law.

In marked contrast to all this was the life of Jesus. In that life no noisy disputation, no ostentatious worship, no act to gain applause, was ever witnessed. Christ was hid in God, and God was revealed in the character

13. In the life of Christ "no noisy disputation, no ostentatious worship, no act to gain applause, was ever w_____. Christ was hid in God, and God was revealed in the c_____ of His Son.

To this revelation Jesus desired the m_____ of the people to be directed, their homage to be given." (261). Lord, take away the desire for attention. May all I say and do, be done to Your honor and glory. May You be revealed in my character. Show me how quickly and easily self pops up: _____

_____

_____

_____

Prayer journal: _____

_____

_____

_____

_____

_____

_____

of His Son. To this revelation Jesus desired the minds of the people to be directed, and their homage to be given.

The Sun of Righteousness did not burst upon the world in splendor, to dazzle the senses with His glory. It is written of Christ, "His going forth is prepared as the morning." Hosea 6:3. Quietly and gently the daylight breaks upon the earth, dispelling the shadow of darkness, and waking the world to life. So did the Sun of Righteousness arise, "with healing in His wings." Mal. 4:2.

Chapter 27

"Thou Canst Make Me Clean"

[This chapter is based on Matt. 8:2-4; 9:1-8, 32-34;
Mark 1:40-45; 2:1-12; Luke 5:12-28.]

Of all diseases known in the East the leprosy was most dreaded. Its incurable and contagious character, and its horrible effect upon its victims, filled the bravest with fear. Among the Jews it was regarded as a judgment on account of sin, and hence was called "the stroke," "the finger of God." Deep-rooted, ineradicable, deadly, it was looked upon as a symbol of sin. By the ritual law, the leper was pronounced unclean. Like one already dead, he was shut out from the habitations of men. Whatever he touched was unclean. The air was polluted by his breath. One who was suspected of having the disease must present himself to the priests, who were to examine and decide his case. If pronounced a leper, he was isolated from his family, cut off from the congregation of Israel, and was doomed to associate with those only who were similarly afflicted. The law was inflexible in its requirement. Even kings and rulers were not exempt. A monarch who was attacked by this terrible disease must yield up the scepter, and flee from society.

Away from his friends and his kindred, the leper must bear the curse of his malady. He was obliged to publish his own calamity, to rend his garments, and sound the alarm, warning all to flee from his contaminating presence. The cry, "Unclean! unclean!" coming in mournful tones from the lonely exile, was a signal heard with fear and abhorrence.

In the region of Christ's ministry, there were many of these sufferers, and the news of His work reached them, kindling a gleam of hope. But since the days of Elisha the prophet, such a thing had never been known [262-263] as the cleansing of one upon whom this disease had fastened. They dared not expect Jesus to do for them what He had never done for any man. There was one, however, in whose heart faith began to spring up. Yet the man knew not how to reach Jesus. Debarred as he was from contact with his fellow men, how could

1. "Among the Jews, it [leprosy] was regarded as a j_____ on account of sin...Like one already dead, he was s_____ out from the habitations of men...isolated from family, cut off from the congregation... obliged to p_____ his own calamity." Am I treated as a leper? Do I treat others as a leper? What would Jesus do?

_____

_____

_____

_____

2. On hearing the news of Jesus, f_____ began to spring up in one leper. And "he questioned if Christ would heal him. Would He stoop to notice one believed to be suffering under the judgment of G__ _____?" (263). Where do these thoughts come from, Lord? May this theology not influence my response to You. You DO stoop to help the one addicted to drugs, cyber-porn, grudges, or self-centeredness!

_____

_____

3. The leper "thought of all that had been told him of Jesus." What had he heard? "Not one who had sought His help had been t_____ away." There's the picture of You that draws me. May You be my first thought in my hour of need, and in my moments of praise: _____

_____

4. The leper draws nearer to the throng gathered around Jesus. "The r_____ laid upon him, the safety of the people, and the f_____ with which all men regard him are f_____. He thinks only of the blessed hope of h_____." What hindrances do I face, in my approach to Christ for acceptance, forgiveness, and healing? _____

he present himself to the Healer? And he questioned if Christ would heal *him* . Would He stoop to notice one believed to be suffering under the judgment of God? Would He not, like the Pharisees, and even the physicians, pronounce a curse upon him, and warn him to flee from the haunts of men? He thought of all that had been told him of Jesus. Not one who had sought His help had been turned away. The wretched man determined to find the Saviour. Though shut out from the cities, it might be that he could cross His path in some byway along the mountain roads, or find Him as He was teaching outside the towns. The difficulties were great, but this was his only hope.

The leper is guided to the Saviour. Jesus is teaching beside the lake, and the people are gathered about Him. Standing afar off, the leper catches a few words from the Saviour's lips. He sees Him laying His hands upon the sick. He sees the lame, the blind, the paralytic, and those dying of various maladies rise up in health, praising God for their deliverance. Faith strengthens in his heart. He draws nearer and yet nearer to the gathered throng. The restrictions laid upon him, the safety of the people, and the fear with which all men regard him are forgotten. He thinks only of the blessed hope of healing.

He is a loathsome spectacle. The disease has made frightful inroads, and his decaying body is horrible to look upon. At sight of him the people fall back in terror. They crowd upon one another in their eagerness to escape from contact with him. Some try to prevent him from approaching Jesus, but in vain. He neither sees nor hears them. Their expressions of loathing are lost upon him. He sees only the Son of God. He hears only the voice that speaks life to the dying. Pressing to Jesus, he casts himself at His feet with the cry, "Lord, if Thou wilt, Thou canst make me clean."

Jesus replied, "I will; be thou made clean," and laid His hand upon him. Matt. 8:3, R. V.

Immediately a change passed over the leper. His flesh became healthy, the nerves sensitive, the muscles firm. The rough, scaly surface peculiar to leprosy disappeared, and a soft glow, like that upon the skin of a healthy child, took its place. [263-264]

Jesus charged the man not to make known the work that had been wrought, but straightway to present himself with an offering at the temple. Such an offering could not be accepted until the priests had made examination and pronounced the man wholly free from the disease. However unwilling they might be to perform this service, they could not evade an examination and decision of the case.

The words of Scripture show with what urgency Christ enjoined upon the man the necessity of silence and prompt action. "He straitly charged him, and forthwith sent him away; and saith unto him, See thou say nothing to any man: but go thy way, show thyself to the priest, and offer for thy cleansing those things which Moses commanded, for a testimony unto them." Had the priests known the facts concerning the healing of the leper, their hatred of Christ might have led them to render a dishonest sentence. Jesus desired the man to present himself at the temple before any rumors concerning the miracle had reached them. Thus an impartial decision could be secured, and the restored leper would be permitted to unite once more power of this Great Healer. He did not understand that every such manifestation made the priests and elders more determined to destroy Jesus. The restored man felt that the boon of health was very precious. He rejoiced in the vigor of manhood, and in his restoration to his family and society, and felt it impossible to refrain from giving glory to the Physician who had made him whole. But his act in blazing abroad the matter resulted in hindering the Saviour's work. It caused the people to flock to Him in such multitudes that He was forced for a time to cease His labors.

Every act of Christ's ministry was far-reaching in its purpose. It comprehended more than appeared in the act itself. So in the case of the leper. While Jesus ministered to all who came unto Him, He yearned to bless those who came not. While He drew the publicans, the heathen, and the Samaritans, He longed to reach the priests and teachers who were shut in by prejudice and tradition. He left untried no means by which they might be reached. In sending the healed leper to the priests, He gave them a testimony calculated to disarm their prejudices.

The Pharisees had asserted that Christ's teaching was opposed to the law which God had given through Moses; but His direction to the cleansed leper to present an offering according to the law disproved this charge. It was sufficient testimony for all who were willing to

___ (Theology? Judmental and gossiping people? etc).

5. "In sending the healed leper to the priests, He gave them a testimony calculated to d_____ their prejudices..."

be convinced.

The leaders at Jerusalem had sent out spies to find some pretext for putting Christ to death. He responded by giving them an evidence of His love for humanity, His respect for the law, and His power to deliver from sin and death. Thus He bore witness of them: "They have rewarded Me evil for good, and hatred for My love." Ps. 109:5. He who on the mount gave the precept, "Love your enemies," Himself exemplified the principle, not rendering "evil for evil, or railing for railing: but contrariwise blessing." Matt. 5:44; 1 Peter 3:9.

The same priests who condemned the leper to banishment certified his cure. This sentence, publicly pronounced and registered, was a standing testimony for Christ. And as the healed man was reinstated in the congregation of Israel, upon the priests' own assurance that there [265-266] was not a taint of the disease upon him, he himself was a living witness for his Benefactor. Joyfully he presented his offering, and magnified the name of Jesus. The priests were convinced of the divine power of the Saviour. Opportunity was granted them to know the truth and to be profited by the light. Rejected, it would pass away, never to return. By many the light was rejected; yet it was not given in vain. Many hearts were moved that for a time made no sign. During the Saviour's life, His mission seemed to call forth little response of love from the priests and teachers; but after His ascension "a great company of the priests were obedient to the faith." Acts 6:7.

The work of Christ in cleansing the leper from his terrible disease is an illustration of His work in cleansing the soul from sin. The man who came to Jesus was "full of leprosy." Its deadly poison permeated his whole body. The disciples sought to prevent their Master from touching him; for he who touched a leper became himself unclean. But in laying His hand upon the leper, Jesus received no defilement. His touch imparted life-giving power. The leprosy was cleansed. Thus it is with the leprosy of sin,--deep-rooted, deadly, and impossible to be cleansed by human power. "The whole head is sick, and the whole heart faint. From the sole of the foot even unto the head there is no soundness in it; but wounds, and bruises, and putrefying sores." Isa. 1:5, 6. But Jesus, coming to dwell in humanity, receives no pollution. His presence has healing virtue for the sinner. Whoever will fall at His feet, saying in faith, "Lord, if Thou wilt,

The priests were c_____ of the divine power of the Savior. Opportunity was granted them to know the truth and to be profited by the light. Rejected, it would pass a_____, never to return. By many the light was rejected; yet it was not given in vain." (265, 266). Lord, I want to notice the light, understand it, and respond to it. I don't want it to pass by. I need Your eye salve:

_____

_____

_____

_____

6. "The work of Christ in cleansing the leper from his terrible disease is an illustration of His work in cleansing the soul from s_____...His t_____ imparted life-giving power." (266). He touched me, and oh the joy that floods my soul. Touch me Lord, grant me the joy of harmony and purity with You:____

_____

_____

_____

Thou canst make me clean," shall hear the answer, "I will; be thou made clean." Matt. 8:2, 3, R. V.

In some instances of healing, Jesus did not at once grant the blessing sought. But in the case of leprosy, no sooner was the appeal made than it was granted. When we pray for earthly blessings, the answer to our prayer may be delayed, or God may give us something other than we ask, but not so when we ask for deliverance from sin. It is His will to cleanse us from sin, to make us His children, and to enable us to live a holy life. Christ "gave Himself for our sins, that He might deliver us from this present evil world, according to the will of God and our Father." Gal. 1:4. And "this is the confidence that we have in Him, that, if we ask anything according to His will, He heareth us: and if we know that He hear us, whatsoever we ask, we know that we have the petitions that we desired of Him." 1 John 5:14, 15. "If we confess our sins, He is faithful and just to forgive us our sins, and to cleanse us from all unrighteousness." 1 John 1:9. [266-267]

In the healing of the paralytic at Capernaum, Christ again taught the same truth. It was to manifest His power to forgive sins that the miracle was performed. And the healing of the paralytic also illustrates other precious truths. It is full of hope and encouragement, and from its connection with the caviling Pharisees it has a lesson of warning as well.

Like the leper, this paralytic had lost all hope of recovery. His disease was the result of a life of sin, and his sufferings were embittered by remorse. He had long before appealed to the Pharisees and doctors, hoping for relief from mental suffering and physical pain. But they coldly pronounced him incurable, and abandoned him to the wrath of God. The Pharisees regarded affliction as an evidence of divine displeasure, and they held themselves aloof from the sick and the needy. Yet often these very ones who exalted themselves as holy were more guilty than the sufferers they condemned.

The palsied man was entirely helpless, and, seeing no prospect of aid from any quarter, he had sunk into despair. Then he heard of the wonderful works of Jesus. He was told that others as sinful and helpless as he had been healed; even lepers had been cleansed. And the friends who reported these things encouraged him to believe that he too might be cured if he could be carried to Jesus. But his hope fell when he remembered how the

7. "But his [paralytic's] hope fell when he remembered how the disease had

been brought on him. He f_____ that the pure Physician would not t_____ him in His presence. Yet, it was not physical restoration the paralytic desired so much as relief from the b_____ of s_____." (267). Lord, may You help me silence Satan's voice, when he crushes me with the thought that You won't tolerate me in my sinner's approach to You: _____

_____

_____

8. In the house of P_____ "the power of the Lord was present to heal. The Spirit of l_____ brooded over the assembly, but Pharisees and doctors did not d_____ its presence. They felt no sense of n_____." (268). Wow, to miss the Spirit because I am so content with myself. Lord, please help me to see and value what I am missing! ____

_____

_____

9. "The sick man looked about him in unutterable a_____. When the longed-for help was so near, how could he relinquish hope?...Jesus had watched the first glimmer of faith grow into a belief

disease had been brought upon him. He feared that the pure Physician would not tolerate him in His presence.

Yet it was not physical restoration he desired so much as relief from the burden of sin. If he could see Jesus, and receive the assurance of forgiveness and peace with Heaven, he would be content to live or die, according to God's will. The cry of the dying man was, Oh that I might come into His presence! There was no time to lose; already his wasted flesh was showing signs of decay. He besought his friends to carry him on his bed to Jesus, and this they gladly undertook to do. But so dense was the crowd that had assembled in and about the house where the Saviour was, that it was impossible for the sick man and his friends to reach Him, or even to come within hearing of His voice.

Jesus was teaching in the house of Peter. According to their custom, His disciples sat close about Him, and "there were Pharisees and doctors of the law sitting by, which were come out of every town of Galilee, and Judea, and Jerusalem." These had come as spies, seeking an accusation against Jesus. Outside of these officials thronged the promiscuous multitude, the eager, the reverent, the curious, and the unbelieving. Different [267-268] nationalities and all grades of society were represented. "And the power of the Lord was present to heal." The Spirit of life brooded over the assembly, but Pharisees and doctors did not discern its presence. They felt no sense of need, and the healing was not for them. "He hath filled the hungry with good things; and the rich He hath sent empty away." Luke 1:53.

Again and again the bearers of the paralytic tried to push their way through the crowd, but in vain. The sick man looked about him in unutterable anguish. When the longed-for help was so near, how could he relinquish hope? At his suggestion his friends bore him to the top of the house and, breaking up the roof, let him down at the feet of Jesus. The discourse was interrupted. The Saviour looked upon the mournful countenance, and saw the pleading eyes fixed upon Him. He understood the case; He had drawn to Himself that perplexed and doubting spirit. While the paralytic was yet at home, the Saviour had brought conviction to his conscience. When he repented of his sins, and believed in the power of Jesus to make him whole, the life-giving mercies of the Saviour had first blessed his longing heart. Jesus had watched the first glimmer of faith grow into a belief that

He was the sinner's only helper, and had seen it grow stronger with every effort to come into His presence.

Now, in words that fell like music on the sufferer's ear, the Saviour said, "Son, be of good cheer; thy sins be forgiven thee."

The burden of despair rolls from the sick man's soul; the peace of forgiveness rests upon his spirit, and shines out upon his countenance. His physical pain is gone, and his whole being is transformed. The helpless paralytic is healed! the guilty sinner is pardoned!

In simple faith he accepted the words of Jesus as the boon of new life. He urged no further request, but lay in blissful silence, too happy for words. The light of heaven irradiated his countenance, and the people looked with awe upon the scene.

The rabbis had waited anxiously to see what disposition Christ would make of this case. They recollected how the man had appealed to them for help, and they had refused him hope or sympathy. Not satisfied with this, they had declared that he was suffering the curse of God for his sins. These things came fresh to their minds when they saw the sick man before them. They marked the interest with which all were watching the scene, and they felt a terrible fear of losing their own influence over the people. [268-269]

These dignitaries did not exchange words together, but looking into one another's faces they read the same thought in each, that something must be done to arrest the tide of feeling. Jesus had declared that the sins of the paralytic were forgiven. The Pharisees caught at these words as blasphemy, and conceived that they could present this as a sin worthy of death. They said in their hearts, "He blasphemeth: who can forgive sins but One, even God?" Mark 2:7, R. V.

Fixing His glance upon them, beneath which they cowered, and drew back, Jesus said, "Wherefore think ye evil in your hearts? For whether is easier, to say, Thy sins be forgiven thee; or to say, Arise, and walk? But that ye may know that the Son of man hath power on earth to forgive sins," He said, turning to the paralytic, "Arise, take up thy bed, and go unto thine house."

Then he who had been borne on a litter to Jesus rises to his feet with the elasticity and strength of youth. The life-giving blood bounds through his veins. Every organ of his body springs into sudden activity. The glow of health succeeds the pallor of approaching death. "And

that He was the sinner's o_____ helper, and had seen it grow stronger with every e_____ to c_____ into His presence." Do I see my need to the point of being desperate? Is there anguish, till confession and forgiveness is experienced? Do I understand that my only Helper, for my real problem, is You, Lord? __
_____
_____
_____

10. "He urged no further request, but lay in blissful silence, too happy for words…

immediately he arose, took up the bed, and went forth before them all; insomuch that they were all amazed, and glorified God, saying, We never saw it on this fashion."

Oh, wondrous love of Christ, stooping to heal the guilty and the afflicted! Divinity sorrowing over and soothing the ills of suffering humanity! Oh, marvelous power thus displayed to the children of men! Who can doubt the message of salvation? Who can slight the mercies of a compassionate Redeemer?

It required nothing less than creative power to restore health to that decaying body. The same voice that spoke life to man created from [269-270] the dust of the earth had spoken life to the dying paralytic. And the same power that gave life to the body had renewed the heart. He who at the creation "spake, and it was," who "commanded, and it stood fast," (Ps. 33:9), had spoken life to the soul dead in trespasses and sins. The healing of the body was an evidence of the power that had renewed the heart. Christ bade the paralytic arise and walk, "that ye may know," He said, "that the Son of man hath power on earth to forgive sins."

The paralytic found in Christ healing for both the soul and the body. The spiritual healing was followed by physical restoration. This lesson should not be overlooked. There are today thousands suffering from physical disease, who, like the paralytic, are longing for the message, "Thy sins are forgiven." The burden of sin, with its unrest and unsatisfied desires, is the foundation of their maladies. They can find no relief until they come to the Healer of the soul. The peace which He alone can give, would impart vigor to the mind, and health to the body.

Jesus came to "destroy the works of the devil." "In Him was life," and He says, "I am come that they might have life, and that they might have it more abundantly." He is "a quickening spirit." 1 John 3:8; John 1:4; 10:10; 1 Cor. 15:45. And He still has the same life-giving power as when on earth He healed the sick, and spoke forgiveness to the sinner. He "forgiveth all thine iniquities," He "healeth all thy diseases." Ps. 103:3.

The effect produced upon the people by the healing of the paralytic was as if heaven had opened, and revealed the glories of the better world. As the man who had been cured passed through the multitude, blessing

Oh, wondrous love of Christ...Who can doubt the message of s_____? Who can s_____ the mercies of a compassionate Redeemer?" (268, 269). This was the ultimate. What more could he ask? May I understand that truth, Lord, and experience that ultimate and complete satisfaction: _____

God at every step, and bearing his burden as if it were a feather's weight, the people fell back to give him room, and with awe-stricken faces gazed upon him, whispering softly among themselves, "We have seen strange things today."

The Pharisees were dumb with amazement and overwhelmed with defeat. They saw that here was no opportunity for their jealousy to inflame the multitude. The wonderful work wrought upon the man whom they had given over to the wrath of God had so impressed the people that the rabbis were for the time forgotten. They saw that Christ possessed a power which they had ascribed to God alone; yet the gentle dignity of His manner was in marked contrast to their own haughty bearing. They were disconcerted and abashed, recognizing, but not confessing, the presence of a superior being. The stronger the evidence that Jesus had power on earth to forgive sins, the more firmly [270-271] they entrenched themselves in unbelief. From the home of Peter, where they had seen the paralytic restored by His word, they went away to invent new schemes for silencing the Son of God.

Physical disease, however malignant and deep-seated, was healed by the power of Christ; but the disease of the soul took a firmer hold upon those who closed their eyes against the light. Leprosy and palsy were not so terrible as bigotry and unbelief.

In the home of the healed paralytic there was great rejoicing when he returned to his family, carrying with ease the couch upon which he had been slowly borne from their presence but a short time before. They gathered round with tears of joy, scarcely daring to believe their eyes. He stood before them in the full vigor of manhood. Those arms that they had seen lifeless were quick to obey his will. The flesh that had been shrunken and leaden-hued was now fresh and ruddy. He walked with a firm, free step. Joy and hope were written in every lineament of his countenance; and an expression of purity and peace had taken the place of the marks of sin and suffering. Glad thanksgiving went up from that home, and God was glorified through His Son, who had restored hope to the hopeless, and strength to the stricken one. This man and his family were ready to lay down their lives for Jesus. No doubt dimmed their faith, no unbelief marred their fealty to Him who had brought light into their darkened home.

11. The Pharisees "were disconcerted and abashed, recognizing, but not c_____, the presence of a superior being." (270). Do I recognize, but not confess? What does that mean? How would I be doing that, Lord? ____

_____

_____

_____

Prayer journal: _____

_____

_____

_____

_____

_____

_____

_____

_____

Chapter 28

Levi-Matthew

[This chapter is based on Matt. 9:9-17;
Mark 2:14-22; Luke 5:27-39.]

Of the Roman officials in Palestine, none were more hated than the publicans. The fact that the taxes were imposed by a foreign power was a continual irritation to the Jews, being a reminder that their independence had departed. And the taxgatherers were not merely the instruments of Roman oppression; they were extortioners on their own account, enriching themselves at the expense of the people. A Jew who accepted this office at the hands of the Romans was looked upon as betraying the honor of his nation. He was despised as an apostate, and was classed with the vilest of society.

To this class belonged Levi-Matthew, who, after the four disciples at Gennesaret, was the next to be called to Christ's service. The Pharisees had judged Matthew according to his employment, but Jesus saw in this man a heart open for the reception of truth. Matthew had listened to the Saviour's teaching. As the convicting Spirit of God revealed his sinfulness, he longed to seek help from Christ; but he was accustomed to the exclusiveness of the rabbis, and had no thought that this Great Teacher would notice him. [272-273]

Sitting at his toll booth one day, the publican saw Jesus approaching. Great was his astonishment to hear the words addressed to himself, "Follow Me."

Matthew "left all, rose up, and followed Him." There was no hesitation, no questioning, no thought of the lucrative business to be exchanged for poverty and hardship. It was enough for him that he was to be with Jesus, that he might listen to His words, and unite with Him in His work.

So it was with the disciples previously called. When Jesus bade Peter and his companions follow Him, immediately they left their boats and nets. Some of these disciples had friends dependent on them for support; but when they received the Saviour's invitation, they did not hesitate, and inquire, How shall I live, and sustain my family? They were obedient to the call; and when

1. A tax gatherer was hated because he was an "i_____ of Roman oppression" and an extortioner of the people. Levi - Matthew, a Jew and a tax gatherer, was "classed with the v_____ of society...Jesus saw in this man a heart o_____ for the reception of truth." Lord, do I judge others the way the Pharisees did?

_____

How can I avoid portraying the exclusiveness of the rabbis? _____

_____ (I am the chief of sinners myself).

2. Matthew was astonished to be addressed by Jesus with, "Follow Me." As the disciples were tested, so is "every soul tested, as to whether the desire for temporal good or for

afterward Jesus asked them, "When I sent you without purse, and scrip, and shoes, lacked ye anything?" they could answer, "Nothing." Luke 22:35.

To Matthew in his wealth, and to Andrew and Peter in their poverty, the same test was brought; the same consecration was made by each. At the moment of success, when the nets were filled with fish, and the impulses of the old life were strongest, Jesus asked the disciples at the sea to leave all for the work of the gospel. So every soul is tested as to whether the desire for temporal good or for fellowship with Christ is strongest.

Principle is always exacting. No man can succeed in the service of God unless his whole heart is in the work and he counts all things but loss for the excellency of the knowledge of Christ. No man who makes any reserve can be the disciple of Christ, much less can he be His colaborer. When men appreciate the great salvation, the self-sacrifice seen in Christ's life will be seen in theirs. Wherever He leads the way, they will rejoice to follow.

The calling of Matthew to be one of Christ's disciples excited great indignation. For a religious teacher to choose a publican as one of his immediate attendants was an offense against the religious, social, and national customs. By appealing to the prejudices of the people the Pharisees hoped to turn the current of popular feeling against Jesus.

Among the publicans a widespread interest was created. Their hearts were drawn toward the divine Teacher. In the joy of his new discipleship, Matthew longed to bring his former associates to Jesus. Accordingly [273-274] he made a feast at his own house, and called together his relatives and friends. Not only were publicans included, but many others who were of doubtful reputation, and were proscribed by their more scrupulous neighbors.

The entertainment was given in honor of Jesus, and He did not hesitate to accept the courtesy. He well knew that this would give offense to the Pharisaic party, and would also compromise Him in the eyes of the people. But no question of policy could influence His movements. With Him external distinctions weighed nothing. That which appealed to His heart was a soul thirsting for the water of life.

Jesus sat as an honored guest at the table of the publicans, by His sympathy and social kindliness showing

f_____ with Christ is the strongest." (273). How is it with me? Does fellowship take priority? _____

_____

In my daily affairs? ____

_____

"No man can succeed in the service of God unless his w_____ heart is in the work and he counts all things but l_____ for the excellency of the knowledge of Christ."

3. "In the j_____ of his new discipleship, Matthew longed to bring his former associates to Jesus." Do I have the same sense of joy? _____. Jesus "did not hesitate to accept the courtesy. He well knew that this would give o_____ to the Pharisaic party, and would c_____ Him in the eyes of the people." (273, 274). Lord, You are a true Friend, not just when it is politically expedient to do so. Am I that kind of friend? To others? To Jesus? _____

_____

_____

_____

4. What was it about Jesus, that men at this party "longed to become w_____ of His confidence?" _____

_____

_____

What is a "thirsty heart?"

_____

_____

_____

5. The rabbis operated differently. "They seized the opportunity of a_____ Him... This is the way in which S_____ has worked ever since the disaffection in heaven; and all who try to cause discord and a_____ are actuated by his spirit." (275). And yet I fall into this operation all too often. I am sorry, Lord. Help me see its ugliness:

_____

_____

6. Lord, what did You mean when You stated: "I will have mercy and not sacrifice: I am not come to call the righteous, but sinners to repentance?"

_____

_____

_____

_____

7. The Pharisees were in a worse condition than the publicans and the Gentiles, who were "less bigoted and self-s_____,"

that He recognized the dignity of humanity; and men longed to become worthy of His confidence. Upon their thirsty hearts His words fell with blessed, life-giving power. New impulses were awakened, and the possibility of a new life opened to these outcasts of society.

At such gatherings as this, not a few were impressed by the Saviour's teaching who did not acknowledge Him until after His ascension. When [274-275] the Holy Spirit was poured out, and three thousand were converted in a day, there were among them many who first heard the truth at the table of the publicans, and some of these became messengers of the gospel. To Matthew himself the example of Jesus at the feast was a constant lesson. The despised publican became one of the most devoted evangelists, in his own ministry following closely in his Master's steps.

When the rabbis learned of the presence of Jesus at Matthew's feast, they seized the opportunity of accusing Him. But they chose to work through the disciples. By arousing their prejudices they hoped to alienate them from their Master. It was their policy to accuse Christ to the disciples, and the disciples to Christ, aiming their arrows where they would be most likely to wound. This is the way in which Satan has worked ever since the disaffection in heaven; and all who try to cause discord and alienation are actuated by his spirit.

"Why eateth your Master with publicans and sinners?" questioned the envious rabbis.

Jesus did not wait for His disciples to answer the charge, but Himself replied: "They that be whole need not a physician, but they that are sick. But go ye and learn what that meaneth, I will have mercy, and not sacrifice: for I am not come to call the righteous, but sinners to repentance." The Pharisees claimed to be spiritually whole, and therefore in no need of a physician, while they regarded the publicans and Gentiles as perishing from diseases of the soul. Then was it not His work, as a physician, to go to the very class that needed His help?

But although the Pharisees thought so highly of themselves, they were really in a worse condition than the ones they despised. The publicans were less bigoted and self-sufficient, and thus were more open to the influence of truth. Jesus said to the rabbis, "Go ye and learn what that meaneth, I will have mercy, and not sacrifice." Thus He showed that while they claimed to expound the word of God, they were wholly ignorant of its spirit.

The Pharisees were silenced for the time, but only became more determined in their enmity. They next sought out the disciples of John the Baptist, and tried to set them against the Saviour. These Pharisees had not accepted the mission of the Baptist. They had pointed in scorn to his abstemious life, his simple habits, his coarse garments, and had declared him a fanatic. Because he denounced their hypocrisy, they had resisted his words, and had tried to stir up the people against him. The [275-276] Spirit of God had moved upon the hearts of these scorners, convicting them of sin; but they had rejected the counsel of God, and had declared that John was possessed of a devil.

Now when Jesus came mingling with the people, eating and drinking at their tables, they accused Him of being a glutton and a winebibber. The very ones who made this charge were themselves guilty. As God is misrepresented, and clothed by Satan with his own attributes, so the Lord's messengers were falsified by these wicked men.

The Pharisees would not consider that Jesus was eating with publicans and sinners in order to bring the light of heaven to those who sat in darkness. They would not see that every word dropped by the divine Teacher was a living seed that would germinate and bear fruit to the glory of God. They had determined not to accept the light; and although they had opposed the mission of the Baptist, they were now ready to court the friendship of his disciples, hoping to secure their co-operation against Jesus. They represented that Jesus was setting at nought the ancient traditions; and they contrasted the austere piety of the Baptist with the course of Jesus in feasting with publicans and sinners.

The disciples of John were at this time in great sorrow. It was before their visit to Jesus with John's message. Their beloved teacher was in prison, and they passed their days in mourning. And Jesus was making no effort to release John, and even appeared to cast discredit on his teaching. If John had been sent by God, why did Jesus and His disciples pursue a course so widely different?

The disciples of John had not a clear understanding of Christ's work; they thought there might be some foundation for the charges of the Pharisees. They observed many of the rules prescribed by the rabbis, and even hoped to be justified by the works of the law. Fast-

and thus were more open the i_____ of the truth." Lord, how can I be more open to the influence of truth? _____

_____

_____How can I unlearn self-sufficiency?

_____

_____

_____

_____

ing was practiced by the Jews as an act of merit, and the most rigid among them fasted two days in every week. The Pharisees and John's disciples were fasting when the latter came to Jesus with the inquiry, "Why do we and the Pharisees fast oft, but Thy disciples fast not?"

Very tenderly Jesus answered them. He did not try to correct their erroneous conception of fasting, but only to set them right in regard to His own mission. And He did this by employing the same figure that the Baptist himself had used in his testimony to Jesus. John had said, "He that hath the bride is the bridegroom: but the friend of the bridegroom, which standeth and heareth him, rejoiceth greatly because of [276-277] the bridegroom's voice: this my joy therefore is fulfilled." John 3:29. The disciples of John could not fail to recall these words of their teacher, as, taking up the illustration, Jesus said, "Can ye make the children of the bridechamber fast, while the bridegroom is with them?"

The Prince of heaven was among His people. The greatest gift of God had been given to the world. Joy to the poor; for Christ had come to make them heirs of His kingdom. Joy to the rich; for He would teach them how to secure eternal riches. Joy to the ignorant; He would make them wise unto salvation. Joy to the learned; He would open to them deeper mysteries than they had ever fathomed; truths that had been hidden from the foundation of the world would be opened to men by the Saviour's mission.

John the Baptist had rejoiced to behold the Saviour. What occasion for rejoicing had the disciples who were privileged to walk and talk with the Majesty of heaven! This was not a time for them to mourn and fast. They must open their hearts to receive the light of His glory, that they might shed light upon those who sat in darkness and in the shadow of death.

It was a bright picture which the words of Christ had called up, but across it lay a heavy shadow, which His eye alone discerned. "The days will come," He said, "when the bridegroom shall be taken away from them, and then shall they fast in those days." When they should see their Lord betrayed and crucified, the disciples would mourn and fast. In His last words to them in the upper chamber, He said, "A little while, and ye shall not see Me: and again, a little while, and ye shall see Me. Verily, verily, I say unto you, That ye shall weep and lament, but the world shall rejoice: and ye shall be sorrowful, but your sorrow shall be turned into joy." John 16:19, 20.

When He should come forth from the tomb, their sorrow would be turned to joy. After His ascension He was to be absent in person; but through the Comforter He would still be with them, and they were not to spend their time in mourning. This was what Satan wanted. He desired them to give the world the impression that they had been deceived and disappointed; but by faith they were to look to the sanctuary above, where Jesus was ministering for them; they were to open their hearts to the Holy Spirit, His representative, and to rejoice in the light of His presence. Yet days of temptation and trial would come, when they would be brought into conflict with the rulers of this world, and the leaders of the kingdom of darkness; when Christ was not personally [277-278] with them, and they failed to discern the Comforter, then it would be more fitting for them to fast.

The Pharisees sought to exalt themselves by their rigorous observance of forms, while their hearts were filled with envy and strife. "Behold," says the Scripture, "ye fast for strife and debate, and to smite with the fist of wickedness: ye shall not fast as ye do this day, to make your voice to be heard on high. Is it such a fast that I have chosen? a day for a man to afflict his soul? is it to bow down his head as a bulrush, and to spread sackcloth and ashes under him? wilt thou call this a fast, and an acceptable day to the Lord?" Isa. 58:4, 5.

The true fast is no mere formal service. The Scripture describes the fast that God has chosen,--"to loose the bands of wickedness, to undo the heavy burdens, and to let the oppressed go free, and that ye break every yoke;" to "draw out thy soul to the hungry, and satisfy the afflicted soul." Isa. 58:6, 10. Here is set forth the very spirit and character of the work of Christ. His whole life was a sacrifice of Himself for the saving of the world. Whether fasting in the wilderness of temptation or eating with the publicans at Matthew's feast, He was giving His life for the redemption of the lost. Not in idle mourning, in mere bodily humiliation and multitudinous sacrifices, is the true spirit of devotion manifested, but it is shown in the surrender of self in willing service to God and man.

Continuing His answer to the disciples of John, Jesus spoke a parable, saying, "No man putteth a piece

8. "After His ascension He was to be absent in person...and they were not to spend their time in m_____. This was what Satan wanted. He desired them to give the world the impression that they had been deceived and d_____." (277). How is my witness, Lord? That knowing You is a life of disappointment?

_____

_____

_____

_____

9. What is the fast that God has chosen?

a) loose the bands of
w_____

b) undo the heavy
b_____

c) let the oppressed go
f_____

d) break every y_____

e) draw out thy soul to
the h_____

f) satisfy the
a_____ soul (278).

"Here is set forth the very spirit and character of the w_____ of Christ." Lord, help me not to get caught t up in self-righteous behaviors, to be seen and noticed. May my fast be the one You have chosen:

_____

_____

of a new garment upon an old; if otherwise, then both the new maketh a rent, and the piece that was taken out of the new agreeth not with the old." The message of John the Baptist was not to be interwoven with tradition and superstition. An attempt to blend the pretense of the Pharisees with the devotion of John would only make more evident the breach between them.

Nor could the principles of Christ's teaching be united with the forms of Pharisaism. Christ was not to close up the breach that had been made by the teachings of John. He would make more distinct the separation between the old and the new. Jesus further illustrated this fact, saying, "No man putteth new wine into old bottles; else the new wine will burst the bottles, and be spilled, and the bottles shall perish." The skin bottles which were used as vessels to contain the new wine, after a time became dry and brittle, and were then worthless to serve the same purpose again. In this familiar illustration Jesus presented the condition of the Jewish leaders. Priests and scribes and rulers were [278-279] fixed in a rut of ceremonies and traditions. Their hearts had become contracted, like the dried-up wine skins to which He had compared them. While they remained satisfied with a legal religion, it was impossible for them to become the depositaries of the living truth of heaven. They thought their own righteousness all-sufficient, and did not desire that a new element should be brought into their religion. The good will of God to men they did not accept as something apart from themselves. They connected it with their own merit because of their good works. The faith that works by love and purifies the soul could find no place for union with the religion of the Pharisees, made up of ceremonies and the injunctions of men. The effort to unite the teachings of Jesus with the established religion would be vain. The vital truth of God, like fermenting wine, would burst the old, decaying bottles of the Pharisaical tradition.

The Pharisees thought themselves too wise to need instruction, too righteous to need salvation, too highly honored to need the honor that comes from Christ. The Saviour turned away from them to find others who would receive the message of heaven. In the untutored fishermen, in the publican at the market place, in the woman of Samaria, in the common people who heard Him gladly, He found His new bottles for the new wine. The instrumentalities to be used in the gospel work are those souls who gladly receive the light which God sends them. These are His agencies for imparting the knowledge of truth to the world. If through the grace of Christ His people will become new bottles, He will fill them with new wine.

The teaching of Christ, though it was represented by the new wine, was not a new doctrine, but the revelation of that which had been taught from the beginning. But to the Pharisees the truth of God had lost its original significance and beauty. To them Christ's teaching was new in almost every respect, and it was unrecognized and unacknowledged.

Jesus pointed out the power of false teaching to destroy the appreciation and desire for truth. "No man," He said, "having drunk old wine straightway desireth new: for he saith, The old is better." All the truth that has been given to the world through patriarchs and prophets shone out in new beauty in the words of Christ. But the scribes and Pharisees had no desire for the precious new wine. Until emptied of the old traditions, customs, and practices, they had no place in mind or heart for the teachings of Christ. They clung to the dead forms, and turned away from the living truth and the power of God. [279-280]

It was this that proved the ruin of the Jews, and it will prove the ruin of many souls in our own day. Thousands are making the same mistake as did the Pharisees whom Christ reproved at Matthew's feast. Rather than give up some cherished idea, or discard some idol of opinion, many refuse the truth which comes down from the Father of light. They trust in self, and depend upon their own wisdom, and do not realize their spiritual poverty. They insist on being saved in some way by which they may perform some important work. When they see that there is no way of weaving self into the work, they reject the salvation provided.

A legal religion can never lead souls to Christ; for it is a loveless, Christless religion. Fasting or prayer that is actuated by a self-justifying spirit is an abomination in the sight of God. The solemn assembly for worship, the round of religious ceremonies, the external humiliation, the imposing sacrifice, proclaim that the doer of these things regards himself as righteous, and as entitled to heaven; but it is all a deception. Our own works can never purchase salvation.

As it was in the days of Christ, so it is now; the

10. "A legal religion can never lead souls to Christ; for it is a l_____, Christless religion. Fasting or prayer that is actuated by a self-justifying spirit is an a_____ in the sight of God...The

sacrifices of God are a b_____ spirit: a broken and a c_____ heart…When s_____ is renounced, then the Lord can make man a new creature." (280). There's that self again! It is not an easy thing to conquer. Lord, thank You for being patient with me, bringing me over the same ground, nudging my spirit to be like Yours. Thank You for helping the old to be gone, and the new to come: _____

_____

_____

Prayer journal: _____

_____

_____

_____

_____

_____

_____

_____

Pharisees do not know their spiritual destitution. To them comes the message, "Because thou sayest, I am rich, and increased with goods, and have need of nothing; and knowest not that thou art wretched, and miserable, and poor, and blind, and naked: I counsel thee to buy of Me gold tried in the fire, that thou mayest be rich; and white raiment, that thou mayest be clothed, and that the shame of thy nakedness do not appear." Rev. 3:17, 18. Faith and love are the gold tried in the fire. But with many the gold has become dim, and the rich treasure has been lost. The righteousness of Christ is to them as a robe unworn, a fountain untouched. To them it is said, "I have somewhat against thee, because thou hast left thy first love. Remember therefore from whence thou art fallen, and repent, and do the first works; or else I will come unto thee quickly, and will remove thy candlestick out of his place, except thou repent." Rev. 2:4, 5.

"The sacrifices of God are a broken spirit: a broken and a contrite heart, O God, Thou wilt not despise." Ps. 51:17. Man must be emptied of self before he can be, in the fullest sense, a believer in Jesus. When self is renounced, then the Lord can make man a new creature. New bottles can contain the new wine. The love of Christ will animate the believer with new life. In him who looks unto the Author and Finisher of our faith the character of Christ will be manifest.

Chapter 29

The Sabbath

The Sabbath was hallowed at the creation. As ordained for man, it had its origin when "the morning stars sang together, and all the sons of God shouted for joy." Job 38:7. Peace brooded over the world; for earth was in harmony with heaven. "God saw everything that He had made, and, behold, it was very good;" and He rested in the joy of His completed work. Gen. 1:31.

Because He had rested upon the Sabbath, "God blessed the seventh day, and sanctified it,"--set it apart to a holy use. He gave it to Adam as a day of rest. It was a memorial of the work of creation, and thus a sign of God's power and His love. The Scripture says, "He hath made His wonderful works to be remembered." "The things that are made," declare "the invisible things of Him since the creation of the world," "even His everlasting power and divinity." Gen. 2:3; Ps. 111:4; Rom. 1:20, R. V.

All things were created by the Son of God. "In the beginning was the Word, and the Word was with God. . . . All things were made by Him; and without Him was not anything made that was made." John 1: 1-3. And since the Sabbath is a memorial of the work of creation, it is a token of the love and power of Christ.

The Sabbath calls our thoughts to nature, and brings us into communion with the Creator. In the song of the bird, the sighing of the trees, and the music of the sea, we still may hear His voice who talked [281-282] with Adam in Eden in the cool of the day. And as we behold His power in nature we find comfort, for the word that created all things is that which speaks life to the soul. He "who commanded the light to shine out of darkness, hath shined in our hearts, to give the light of the knowledge of the glory of God in the face of Jesus Christ." 2 Cor. 4:6.

It was this thought that awoke the song,--

"Thou, Lord, hast made me glad through
Thy work;

1. What does it mean that God blessed the seventh-day, and sanctified it? Set it apart to a h_____ use. God sees it as very special. And I wonder why I can't bring common, ordinary elements into it! It's holy use is to enhance a special relationship between You and me, right, Lord?

_____

_____

_____

2. "Sabbath is a memorial of God's work of creation," and thus a token of His l_____ and His p_____. Lord, how can I increase my awareness of Your love from the evidence of creation? _____

_____

_____

_____

> I will triumph in the works of Thy hands.
> O Lord, how great are Thy works!
> And Thy thoughts are very deep."
>
> Ps. 92:4,5.

And the Holy Spirit through the prophet Isaiah declares: "To whom then will ye liken God? or what likeness will ye compare unto Him? . . . Have ye not known? have ye not heard? hath it not been told you from the beginning? have ye not understood from the foundations of the earth? It is He that sitteth upon the circle of the earth, and the inhabitants thereof are as grasshoppers; that stretcheth out the heavens as a curtain, and spreadeth them out as a tent to dwell in. . . . To whom then will ye liken Me, or shall I be equal? saith the Holy One. Lift up your eyes on high, and behold who hath created these things, that bringeth out their host by number: He calleth them all by names by the greatness of His might, for that He is strong in power; not one faileth. Why sayest thou, O Jacob, and speakest, O Israel, My way is hid from the Lord, and my judgment is passed over from my God? Hast thou not known? hast thou not heard, that the everlasting God, the Lord, the Creator of the ends of the earth, fainteth not, neither is weary? . . . He giveth power to the faint; and to them that have no [282-283] might He increaseth strength." "Fear thou not; for I am with thee: be not dismayed; for I am thy God: I will strengthen thee; yea, I will help thee; yea, I will uphold thee with the right hand of My righteousness." "Look unto Me, and be ye saved, all the ends of the earth: for I am God, and there is none else." This is the message written in nature, which the Sabbath is appointed to keep in memory. When the Lord bade Israel hallow His Sabbaths, He said, "They shall be a sign between Me and you, that ye may know that I am Jehovah your God." Isa. 40:18-29; 41:10; 45:22; Ezek. 20:20, R. V.

The Sabbath was embodied in the law given from Sinai; but it was not then first made known as a day of rest. The people of Israel had a knowledge of it before they came to Sinai. On the way thither the Sabbath was kept. When some profaned it, the Lord reproved them, saying, "How long refuse ye to keep My commandments and My laws?" Ex. 16:28.

The Sabbath was not for Israel merely, but for the world. It had been made known to man in Eden, and,

---

3. The Sabbath is appointed to keep in memory what message written in nature? (283). "I am t____ God: I will s_____ thee, yea, I will help thee; yea, I will u_____ thee with the right hand of My righteousness...I am God, and there is n_____ else." Lord, lead me into Your nature, and direct my thoughts in this wonderful understanding – You are MY God!

_____

_____

_____

like the other precepts of the Decalogue, it is of imperishable obligation. Of that law of which the fourth commandment forms a part, Christ declares, "Till heaven and earth pass, one jot or one tittle shall in nowise pass from the law." So long as the heavens and the earth endure, the Sabbath will continue as a sign of the Creator's power. And when Eden shall bloom on earth again, God's holy rest day will be honored by all beneath the sun. "From one Sabbath to another" the inhabitants of the glorified new earth shall go up "to worship before Me, saith the Lord." Matt. 5:18; Isa. 66:23.

No other institution which was committed to the Jews tended so fully to distinguish them from surrounding nations as did the Sabbath. God designed that its observance should designate them as His worshipers. It was to be a token of their separation from idolatry, and their connection with the true God. But in order to keep the Sabbath holy, men must themselves be holy. Through faith they must become partakers of the righteousness of Christ. When the command was given to Israel, "Remember the Sabbath day, to keep it holy," the Lord said also to them, "Ye shall be holy men unto Me." Ex. 20:8; 22:31. Only thus could the Sabbath distinguish Israel as the worshipers of God.

As the Jews departed from God, and failed to make the righteousness of Christ their own by faith, the Sabbath lost its significance to them. Satan was seeking to exalt himself and to draw men away from Christ, and he worked to pervert the Sabbath, because it is the sign of the [283-284] power of Christ. The Jewish leaders accomplished the will of Satan by surrounding God's rest day with burdensome requirements. In the days of Christ the Sabbath had become so perverted that its observance reflected the character of selfish and arbitrary men rather than the character of the loving heavenly Father. The rabbis virtually represented God as giving laws which it was impossible for men to obey. They led the people to look upon God as a tyrant, and to think that the observance of the Sabbath, as He required it, made men hard-hearted and cruel. It was the work of Christ to clear away these misconceptions. Although the rabbis followed Him with merciless hostility, He did not even appear to conform to their requirements, but went straight forward, keeping the Sabbath according to the law of God.

Upon one Sabbath day, as the Saviour and His dis-

4. "In order to keep the Sabbath holy, men must themselves be h_____." How can this be? "Through f_____ they must become partakers of the r_____ of Christ." Lord, strengthen this faith! Show me how to make room for Your righteousness in my life! _____

_____

_____

5. How can the Sabbath lose its significance to me, as it did for the Jews? When I fail "to make the r_____ of Christ" my "o_____ by faith:" _____

_____

6. Satan sought "to draw men a_____ from Christ, and he worked to p_____ the Sabbath." Burdensome requirements led "people to look upon God as a t_____." God was represented as giving laws which were i_____ for men to obey. "It was the work of Christ to clear away these misconceptions." (283, 284). Satan knows there is something special here, and wants to counter it. I need to guard, to keep from losing that specialness, to keep Satan from having his way: _____

_____

ciples returned from the place of worship, they passed
through a field of ripening grain. Jesus had continued
His work to a late hour, and while passing through the
fields, the disciples began to gather the heads of grain,
and to eat the kernels after rubbing them in their hands.
On any other day this act would have excited no comment, for one passing through a field of grain, an orchard, or a vineyard, was at liberty to gather what he
desired to eat. See Deut. 23:24, 25. But to do this on the
Sabbath was held to be an act of desecration. Not only
was the gathering of the grain a kind of reaping, but
the rubbing of it in the hands was a kind of threshing.
Thus, in the opinion of the rabbis, there was a double
offense.

The spies at once complained to Jesus, saying, "Behold, Thy disciples do that which is not lawful to do
upon the Sabbath day."

When accused of Sabbathbreaking at Bethesda, Jesus defended Himself by affirming His Sonship to God,
and declaring that He worked in harmony with the Father. Now that the disciples are attacked, He cites [284-
285] His accusers to examples from the Old Testament,
acts performed on the Sabbath by those who were in the
service of God.

The Jewish teachers prided themselves on their
knowledge of the Scriptures, and in the Saviour's answer there was an implied rebuke for their ignorance of
the Sacred Writings. "Have ye not read so much as this,"
He said, "what David did, when himself was an hungered, and they which were with him; how he went into
the house of God, and did take and eat the shewbread, .
. . which it is not lawful to eat but for the priests alone?"
"And He said unto them, The Sabbath was made for
man, and not man for the Sabbath." "Have ye not read
in the law, how that on the Sabbath days the priests in
the temple profane the Sabbath, and are blameless? But
I say unto you, That in this place is one greater than the
temple." "The Son of man is Lord also of the Sabbath."
Luke 6:3, 4; Mark 2:27, 28; Matt. 12:5, 6.

If it was right for David to satisfy his hunger by
eating of the bread that had been set apart to a holy use,
then it was right for the disciples to supply their need by
plucking the grain upon the sacred hours of the Sabbath.
Again, the priests in the temple performed greater labor
on the Sabbath than upon other days. The same labor
in secular business would be sinful; but the work of the

priests was in the service of God. They were performing those rites that pointed to the redeeming power of
Christ, and their labor was in harmony with the object
of the Sabbath. But now Christ Himself had come. The
disciples, in doing the work of Christ, were engaged
in God's service, and that which was necessary for the
accomplishment of this work it was right to do on the
Sabbath day.

Christ would teach His disciples and His enemies
that the service of God is first of all. The object of God's
work in this world is the redemption of man; therefore
that which is necessary to be done on the Sabbath in the
accomplishment of this work is in accord with the Sabbath law. Jesus then crowned His argument by declaring Himself the "Lord of the Sabbath,"--One above all
question and above all law. This infinite Judge acquits
the disciples of blame, appealing to the very statutes
they are accused of violating.

Jesus did not let the matter pass with administer-
ing a rebuke to His enemies. He declared that in their
blindness they had mistaken the object of the Sabbath.
He said, "If ye had known what this meaneth, I will
have mercy, and not sacrifice, ye would not have condemned the guiltless." Matt. 12:7. Their many heartless
rites could not supply the [285-286] lack of that truthful
integrity and tender love which will ever characterize
the true worshiper of God.

Again Christ reiterated the truth that the sacrifices
were in themselves of no value. They were a means, and
not an end. Their object was to direct men to the Saviour, and thus to bring them into harmony with God. It
is the service of love that God values. When this is lacking, the mere round of ceremony is an offense to Him.
So with the Sabbath. It was designed to bring men into
communion with God; but when the mind was absorbed
with wearisome rites, the object of the Sabbath was
thwarted. Its mere outward observance was a mockery.

Upon another Sabbath, as Jesus entered a synagogue. He saw there a man who had a withered hand.
The Pharisees watched Him, eager to see what He
would do. The Saviour well knew that in healing on the
Sabbath He would be regarded as a transgressor, but He
did not hesitate to break down the wall of traditional requirements that barricaded the Sabbath. Jesus bade the
afflicted man stand forth, and then asked, "It is lawful to
do good on the Sabbath days, or to do evil? to save life,

7. Christ's point [rubbing heads of grain in hands, on Sabbath] was that "service of God is f_____ of all...That which is neces-sary to be done... in the ac-complishment of this work [of man's redemption] is in a_____ [and ap-propriate] with the Sabbath law." (285) Lord, show me how to keep my heart in service of You, especially on the Sabbath hours: ____
_____
_____

8. "Sacrifices were in them-selves of n_____ value. They were a means, and not an end. Their object was to direct men to the Savior, and thus to bring them into h_____ with God. It is the service of l_____ that God values." When this is lacking, the mere out-ward observance is a m_____. (286). Sabbath experi-ence without love, then, is an offense, a mockery. Lord, I have offended You. I'm sorry! Help me to see what I am missing, and to enter in the true spirit of the Sabbath: _____

9. "It was a maxim among the Jews that a failure to do good, when one had the opportunity, was to do e__ _____." Refraining from bad behavior, is that the extent of my ethics? ____

_____

Lord, help me to see the loftier vision of Your character and Your plans for my character: _____
_____
_____

10. "It is lawful to do w_____ on the Sabbath days," Jesus stated. What does this mean?
_____
_____
_____
_____

or to kill?" It was a maxim among the Jews that a failure to do good, when one had opportunity, was to do evil; to neglect to save life was to kill. Thus Jesus met the rabbis on their own ground. "But they held their peace. And when He had looked round about on them with anger, being grieved for the hardness of their hearts, He saith unto the man, Stretch forth thine hand. And he stretched it out: and his hand was restored whole as the other." Mark 3:4, 5.

When questioned, "Is it lawful to heal on the Sabbath days?" Jesus answered, "What man shall there be among you, that shall have one sheep, and if it fall into a pit on the Sabbath day, will he not lay hold on it, and lift it out? How much then is a man better than a sheep? Wherefore it is lawful to do well on the Sabbath days." Matt. 12:10-12.

The spies dared not answer Christ in the presence of the multitude, for fear of involving themselves in difficulty. They knew that He had spoken the truth. Rather than violate their traditions, they would leave a man to suffer, while they would relieve a brute because of the loss to the owner if it were neglected. Thus greater care was shown for a dumb animal than for man, who is made in the image of God. This illustrates the working of all false religions. They originate in man's desire to exalt himself above God, but they result in degrading man [286-287] below the brute. Every religion that wars against the sovereignty of God defrauds man of the glory which was his at the creation, and which is to be restored to him in Christ. Every false religion teaches its adherents to be careless of human needs, sufferings, and rights. The gospel places a high value upon humanity as the purchase of the blood of Christ, and it teaches a tender regard for the wants and woes of man. The Lord says, "I will make a man more precious than fine gold; even a man than the golden wedge of Ophir." Isa. 13:12.

When Jesus turned upon the Pharisees with the question whether it was lawful on the Sabbath day to do good or to do evil, to save life or to kill, He confronted them with their own wicked purposes. They were hunting His life with bitter hatred, while He was saving life and bringing happiness to multitudes. Was it better to slay upon the Sabbath, as they were planning to do, than to heal the afflicted, as He had done? Was it more righteous to have murder in the heart upon God's holy day than love to all men, which finds expression in deeds of mercy?

In the healing of the withered hand, Jesus condemned the custom of the Jews, and left the fourth commandment standing as God had given it. "It is lawful to do well on the Sabbath days," He declared. By sweeping away the senseless restrictions of the Jews, Christ honored the Sabbath, while those who complained of Him were dishonoring God's holy day.

Those who hold that Christ abolished the law teach that He broke the Sabbath and justified His disciples in doing the same. Thus they are really taking the same ground as did the caviling Jews. In this they contradict the testimony of Christ Himself, who declared, "I have kept My Father's commandments, and abide in His love." John 15:10. Neither the Saviour nor His followers broke the law of the Sabbath. Christ was a living representative of the law. No violation of its holy precepts was found in His life. Looking upon a nation of witnesses who were seeking occasion to condemn Him, He could say unchallenged, "Which of you convicteth Me of sin?" John 8:46, R. V.

The Saviour had not come to set aside what patriarchs and prophets had spoken; for He Himself had spoken through these representative men. All the truths of God's word came from Him. But these priceless gems had been placed in false settings. Their precious light had been made to minister to error. God desired them to be removed from their [287-288] settings of error and replaced in the framework of truth. This work only a divine hand could accomplish. By its connection with error, the truth had been serving the cause of the enemy of God and man. Christ had come to place it where it would glorify God, and work the salvation of humanity.

"The Sabbath was made for man, and not man for the Sabbath," Jesus said. The institutions that God has established are for the benefit of mankind. "All things are for your sakes." "Whether Paul, or Apollos, or Cephas, or the world, or life, or death, or things present, or things to come; all are yours; and ye are Christ's; and Christ is God's." 2 Cor. 4:15; 1 Cor. 3:22, 23. The law of Ten Commandments, of which the Sabbath forms a part, God gave to His people as a blessing. "The Lord commanded us," said Moses, "to do all these statutes, to fear the Lord our God, for our good always, that He

11. Lord, how does the Sabbath benefit me? (Made for man? 288): _____
_____
_____
_____

might preserve us alive." Deut. 6:24. And through the psalmist the message was given to Israel, "Serve the Lord with gladness: come before His presence with singing. Know ye that the Lord He is God: it is He that hath made us, and not we ourselves; we are His people, and the sheep of His pasture. Enter into His gates with thanksgiving, and into His courts with praise." Ps. 100:2-4. And of all who keep "the Sabbath from polluting it," the Lord declares, "Even them will I bring to My holy mountain, and make them joyful in My house of prayer." Isa. 56:6, 7.

12. The Sabbath points to Christ "as both the C_____ and S_____...By His power we are r_____ to God." Lord, how can I increase this awareness during the Sabbath? ___

—————————————
—————————————
—————————————
—————————————
—————————————

"Wherefore the Son of man is Lord also of the Sabbath." These words are full of instruction and comfort. Because the Sabbath was made for man, it is the Lord's day. It belongs to Christ. For "all things were made by Him; and without Him was not anything made that was made." John 1:3. Since He made all things, He made the Sabbath. By Him it was set apart as a memorial of the work of creation. It points to Him as both the Creator and the Sanctifier. It declares that He who created all things in heaven and in earth, and by whom all things hold together, is the head of the church, and that by His power we are reconciled to God. For, speaking of Israel, He said, "I gave them My Sabbaths, to be a sign between Me and them, that they might know that I am the Lord that sanctify them,"--make them holy. Ezek. 20:12. Then the Sabbath is a sign of Christ's power to make us holy. And it is given to all whom Christ makes holy. As a sign of His sanctifying power, the Sabbath is given to all who through Christ become a part of the Israel of God. [288-289]

13. "To all who receive the Sabbath as a sign of Christ's c_____ and redeeming power, it will be a d_____." (289). Lord, help me to enjoy time with You as my Creator and Redeemer, on the date You've asked to have with me: _____

—————————————
—————————————

Prayer Journal: _____
—————————————
—————————————
—————————————
—————————————
—————————————
—————————————

And the Lord says, "If thou turn away thy foot from the Sabbath, from doing thy pleasure on My holy day; and call the Sabbath a delight, the holy of the Lord, honorable; . . . then shalt thou delight thyself in the Lord." Isa. 58:13, 14. To all who receive the Sabbath as a sign of Christ's creative and redeeming power, it will be a delight. Seeing Christ in it, they delight themselves in Him. The Sabbath points them to the works of creation as an evidence of His mighty power in redemption. While it calls to mind the lost peace of Eden, it tells of peace restored through the Saviour. And every object in nature repeats His invitation, "Come unto Me, all ye that labor and are heavy-laden, and I will give you rest." Matt 11:28.

Chapter 30

"He Ordained Twelve"

[This chapter is based on Mark 3:13-19; Luke 6:12-16.]

"And He goeth up into a mountain, and calleth unto Him whom He would: and they came unto Him. And He ordained twelve, that they should be with Him, and that He might send them forth to preach."

It was beneath the sheltering trees of the mountain-side, but a little distance from the Sea of Galilee, that the twelve were called to the apostolate, and the Sermon on the Mount was given. The fields and hills were the favorite resorts of Jesus, and much of His teaching was given under the open sky, rather than in the temple or the synagogues. No synagogue could have received the throngs that followed Him; but not for this reason only did He choose to teach in the fields and groves. Jesus loved the scenes of nature. To Him each quiet retreat was a sacred temple.

It was under the trees of Eden that the first dwellers on earth had chosen their sanctuary. There Christ had communed with the father of mankind. When banished from Paradise, our first parents still worshiped in the fields and groves, and there Christ met them with the gospel of His grace. It was Christ who spoke with Abraham under the [290-291] oaks at Mamre; with Isaac as he went out to pray in the fields at the eventide; with Jacob on the hillside at Bethel; with Moses among the mountains of Midian; and with the boy David as he watched his flocks. It was at Christ's direction that for fifteen centuries the Hebrew people had left their homes for one week every year, and had dwelt in booths formed from the green branches "of goodly trees, branches of palm trees, and boughs of thick trees, and willows of the brook." Lev. 23:40.

In training His disciples, Jesus chose to withdraw from the confusion of the city to the quiet of the fields and hills, as more in harmony with the lessons of self-abnegation He desired to teach them. And during His ministry He loved to gather the people about Him under the blue heavens, on some grassy hillside, or on the beach beside the lake. Here, surrounded by the works

1. "In training His disciples, Jesus chose to withdraw from the confusion of the city to the quiet of the fields and hills, as m_____ in h_____ with the lessons of self-a_____ He desired to teach them." (291). Lord, help me to be extra careful of the trap of self-absorption; and am I providing You with enough quiet time to show me these things? _____

_____

_____

_____

2. "Surrounded by the works of His own creation, He could turn the thoughts of His hearers from the a_____ to the n_____. In the growth and development of nature were revealed the p_____ of His kingdom" As we go into the fields with Christ in our hearts, we can feel ourselves surrounded with a h_____ i_____. (291). Lord, how much artificial do I have in my life? ___

_____

_____ I'd rather chose Your holy influence: _____

3. The disciples' "office was the most i_____ to which human beings had ever been c_____, and was second only to that of C_____ Himself. They were to be workers together with God for the s_____ of the world." Lord, how much of Your disciple am I? Do I sense the importance of Your calling? (second only to Your office!) _____

_____

_____

of His own creation, He could turn the thoughts of His hearers from the artificial to the natural. In the growth and development of nature were revealed the principles of His kingdom. As men should lift up their eyes to the hills of God, and behold the wonderful works of His hands, they could learn precious lessons of divine truth. Christ's teaching would be repeated to them in the things of nature. So it is with all who go into the fields with Christ in their hearts. They will feel themselves surrounded with a holy influence. The things of nature take up the parables of our Lord, and repeat His counsels. By communion with God in nature, the mind is uplifted, and the heart finds rest.

The first step was now to be taken in the organization of the church that after Christ's departure was to be His representative on earth. No costly sanctuary was at their command, but the Saviour led His disciples to the retreat He loved, and in their minds the sacred experiences of that day were forever linked with the beauty of mountain and vale and sea.

Jesus had called His disciples that He might send them forth as His witnesses, to declare to the world what they had seen and heard of Him. Their office was the most important to which human beings had ever been called, and was second only to that of Christ Himself. They were to be workers together with God for the saving of the world. As in the Old Testament the twelve patriarchs stand as representatives of Israel, so the twelve apostles were to stand as representatives of the gospel church.

The Saviour knew the character of the men whom He had chosen; all their weaknesses and errors were open before Him; He knew the [291-292] perils through which they must pass, the responsibility that would rest upon them; and His heart yearned over these chosen ones. Alone upon a mountain near the Sea of Galilee He spent the entire night in prayer for them, while they were sleeping at the foot of the mountain. With the first light of dawn He summoned them to meet Him; for He had something of importance to communicate to them.

These disciples had been for some time associated with Jesus in active labor. John and James, Andrew and Peter, with Philip, Nathanael, and Matthew, had been more closely connected with Him than the others, and had witnessed more of His miracles. Peter, James, and John stood in still nearer relationship to Him. They were almost constantly with Him, witnessing His miracles, and hearing His words. John pressed into still closer intimacy with Jesus, so that he is distinguished as the one whom Jesus loved. The Saviour loved them all, but John's was the most receptive spirit. He was younger than the others, and with more of the child's confiding trust he opened his heart to Jesus. Thus he came more into sympathy with Christ, and through him the Saviour's deepest spiritual teaching was communicated to His people.

At the head of one of the groups into which the apostles are divided stands the name of Philip. He was the first disciple to whom Jesus addressed the distinct command, "Follow Me." Philip was of Bethsaida, the city of Andrew and Peter. He had listened to the teaching of John the Baptist, and had heard his announcement of Christ as the Lamb of God. Philip was a sincere seeker for truth, but he was slow of heart to believe. Although he had joined himself to Christ, yet his announcement of Him to Nathanael shows that he was not fully convinced of the divinity of Jesus. Though Christ had been proclaimed by the voice from heaven as the Son of God, to Philip He was "Jesus of Nazareth, the son of Joseph." John 1:45. Again, when the five thousand were [292-293] fed, Philip's lack of faith was shown. It was to test him that Jesus questioned, "Whence shall we buy bread, that these may eat?" Philip's answer was on the side of unbelief: "Two hundred pennyworth of bread is not sufficient for them, that every one of them may take a little." John 6:5, 7. Jesus was grieved. Although Philip had seen His works and felt His power, yet he had not faith. When the Greeks inquired of Philip concerning Jesus, he did not seize upon the opportunity of introducing them to the Saviour, but he went to tell Andrew. Again, in those last hours before the crucifixion, the words of Philip were such as to discourage faith. When Thomas said to Jesus, "Lord, we know not whither Thou goest; and how can we know the way?" the Saviour answered, "I am the Way, the Truth, and the Life. . . . If ye had known Me, ye should have known My Father also." From Philip came the response of unbelief: "Lord, show us the Father, and it sufficeth us." John 14:5-8. So slow of heart, so weak in faith, was that disciple who for three years had been with Jesus.

In happy contrast to Philip's unbelief was the childlike trust of Nathanael. He was a man of intensely ear-

4. Does Jesus play favorites? How is it that John is known as the one whom Jesus loved? (292).

_____

_____

_____

_____ (most receptive s_____?).
I know You love me, Lord. But I also desire a receptivity (on my part) that is intimate with You. What can I do to nurture that? _____

_____

_____

nest nature, one whose faith took hold upon unseen realities. Yet Philip was a student in the school of Christ, and the divine Teacher bore patiently with his unbelief and dullness. When the Holy Spirit was poured out upon the disciples, Philip became a teacher after the divine order. He knew whereof he spoke, and he taught with an assurance that carried conviction to the hearers.

While Jesus was preparing the disciples for their ordination, one who had not been summoned urged his presence among them. It was Judas Iscariot, a man who professed to be a follower of Christ. He now came forward, soliciting a place in this inner circle of disciples. With great earnestness and apparent sincerity he declared, "Master, I will follow Thee whithersoever Thou goest." Jesus neither repulsed nor welcomed him, but uttered only the mournful words: "The foxes have holes, and the birds of the air have nests; but the Son of man [293-294] hath not where to lay His head." Matt. 8:19, 20. Judas believed Jesus to be the Messiah; and by joining the apostles, he hoped to secure a high position in the new kingdom. This hope Jesus designed to cut off by the statement of His poverty.

The disciples were anxious that Judas should become one of their number. He was of commanding appearance, a man of keen discernment and executive ability, and they commended him to Jesus as one who would greatly assist Him in His work. They were surprised that Jesus received him so coolly.

5. "The after history of Judas would show the other disciples the danger of allowing any w_____ consideration to have w_____ in deciding the f_____ ___ of men for the work of God." (294). Lord, do I think those worldly considerations have weight? What aspects do I think make me influential?

_____

_____

_____

Lord, know my heart. That's what counts. And help my heart to be pure:

_____

_____

_____

The disciples had been much disappointed that Jesus had not tried to secure the co-operation of the leaders in Israel. They felt that it was a mistake not to strengthen His cause by securing the support of these influential men. If He had repulsed Judas, they would, in their own minds, have questioned the wisdom of their Master. The after history of Judas would show them the danger of allowing any worldly consideration to have weight in deciding the fitness of men for the work of God. The co-operation of such men as the disciples were anxious to secure would have betrayed the work into the hands of its worst enemies.

Yet when Judas joined the disciples, he was not insensible to the beauty of the character of Christ. He felt the influence of that divine power which was drawing souls to the Saviour. He who came not to break the bruised reed nor quench the smoking flax would not repulse this soul while even one desire was reaching toward the light. The Saviour read the heart of Judas; He knew the depths of iniquity to which, unless delivered by the grace of God, Judas would sink. In connecting this man with Himself, He placed him where he might, day by day, be brought in contact with the outflowing of His own unselfish love. If he would open his heart to Christ, divine grace would banish the demon of selfishness, and even Judas might become a subject of the kingdom of God.

God takes men as they are, with the human elements in their character, and trains them for His service, if they will be disciplined and learn of Him. They are not chosen because they are perfect, but notwithstanding their imperfections, that through the knowledge and practice of the truth, through the grace of Christ, they may become transformed into His image.

Judas had the same opportunities as had the other disciples. He listened to the same precious lessons. But the practice of the truth, [294-295] which Christ required, was at variance with the desires and purposes of Judas, and he would not yield his ideas in order to receive wisdom from Heaven.

How tenderly the Saviour dealt with him who was to be His betrayer! In His teaching, Jesus dwelt upon principles of benevolence that struck at the very root of covetousness. He presented before Judas the heinous character of greed, and many a time the disciple realized that his character had been portrayed, and his sin pointed out; but he would not confess and forsake his unrighteousness. He was self-sufficient, and instead of resisting temptation, he continued to follow his fraudulent practices. Christ was before him, a living example of what he must become if he reaped the benefit of the divine mediation and ministry; but lesson after lesson fell unheeded on the ears of Judas.

Jesus dealt him no sharp rebuke for his covetousness, but with divine patience bore with this erring man, even while giving him evidence that He read his heart as an open book. He presented before him the highest incentives for right doing; and in rejecting the light of Heaven, Judas would be without excuse.

6. "God takes men as they a_____, with the human elements in their character, and t_____ them for His service, if they will be disciplined and learn of Him. They are not chosen because they are p_____, but notwithstanding their imperfections, that through the k_____ and p_____ of the truth, through the g_____ of Christ, they may become transformed into His i_____." Take me, Lord, as I am, imperfect, unfit. Train me, by Your grace, into Your image. Tell me what knowledge and practice of the truth is: _____

_____

_____

7. "In His teaching, Jesus dwelt upon principles of b_____ that struck at the very root of c_____. He presented before Judas the heinous character of g_____...Christ was before him, a living example of what he must become if he reaped the benefit of the divine m_____ and ministry; but lesson after lesson fell u_____ _____ on the ears of Judas...[Jesus] presented before him the highest i_____ for right doing." (295). Lord, I pray for a soft heart, responsive

to Your patient appeals. May none go unheeded. Confront me when I do. What is that highest incentive?

_____

_____

8. "Instead of walking in the light, Judas chose to retain his defects. Evil desires, r_____ passions, dark and sullen thoughts, were c_____ _____, until Satan had full control of the man." Lord, there is too much of Judas in me! Help me not to minimize the dangers. Keep me walking in Your light, every morning, and throughout the day:

_____

_____

_____

_____

9. "All the disciples had serious f_____ when Jesus called them to His s_____...Evil temper, r_____, the spirit of criticism, were all in the beloved disciple [John]. He was proud, and ambitious to be f_____ in the kingdom of God." Lord, use me and train me like You did the twelve. Catch me in my spirit of criticism. May walking in Your grace help me to let it go: _____

_____

10. But d____ by day, John "beheld the

Instead of walking in the light, Judas chose to retain his defects. Evil desires, revengeful passions, dark and sullen thoughts, were cherished, until Satan had full control of the man. Judas became a representative of the enemy of Christ.

When he came into association with Jesus, he had some precious traits of character that might have been made a blessing to the church. If he had been willing to wear the yoke of Christ, he might have been among the chief of the apostles; but he hardened his heart when his defects were pointed out, and in pride and rebellion chose his own selfish ambitions, and thus unfitted himself for the work that God would have given him to do.

All the disciples had serious faults when Jesus called them to His service. Even John, who came into closest association with the meek and lowly One, was not himself naturally meek and yielding. He and his brother were called "the sons of thunder." While they were with Jesus, any slight shown to Him aroused their indignation and combativeness. Evil temper, revenge, the spirit of criticism, were all in the beloved disciple. He was proud, and ambitious to be first in the kingdom of God. But day by day, in contrast with his own violent spirit, he beheld the tenderness and forbearance of Jesus, and heard His lessons of humility and patience. He opened his heart to the divine influence, [295-296] and became not only a hearer but a doer of the Saviour's words. Self was hid in Christ. He learned to wear the yoke of Christ and to bear His burden.

Jesus reproved His disciples, He warned and cautioned them; but John and his brethren did not leave Him; they chose Jesus, notwithstanding the reproofs. The Saviour did not withdraw from them because of their weakness and errors. They continued to the end to share His trials and to learn the lessons of His life. By beholding Christ, they became transformed in character.

The apostles differed widely in habits and disposition. There were the publican, Levi-Matthew, and the fiery zealot Simon, the uncompromising hater of the authority of Rome; the generous, impulsive Peter, and the mean-spirited Judas; Thomas, truehearted, yet timid and fearful, Philip, slow of heart, and inclined to doubt, and the ambitious, outspoken sons of Zebedee, with their brethren. These were brought together, with their different faults, all with inherited and cultivated tendencies to evil; but in and through Christ they were to dwell in the family of God, learning to become one in faith, in doctrine, in spirit. They would have their tests, their grievances, their differences of opinion; but while Christ was abiding in the heart, there could be no dissension. His love would lead to love for one another; the lessons of the Master would lead to the harmonizing of all differences, bringing the disciples into unity, till they would be of one mind and one judgment. Christ is the great center, and they would approach one another just in proportion as they approached the center.

When Jesus had ended His instruction to the disciples, He gathered the little band close about Him, and kneeling in the midst of them, and laying His hands upon their heads, He offered a prayer dedicating them to His sacred work. Thus the Lord's disciples were ordained to the gospel ministry.

As His representatives among men, Christ does not choose angels who have never fallen, but human beings, men of like passions with those they seek to save. Christ took upon Himself humanity, that He might reach humanity. Divinity needed humanity; for it required both the divine and the human to bring salvation to the world. Divinity needed humanity, that humanity might afford a channel of communication between God and man. So with the servants and messengers of Christ. Man needs a power outside of and beyond himself, to restore him to the likeness of God, and enable him to do the work of God; but this [296-297] does not make the human agency unessential. Humanity lays hold upon divine power, Christ dwells in the heart by faith; and through co-operation with the divine, the power of man becomes efficient for good.

He who called the fisherman of Galilee is still calling men to His service. And He is just as willing to manifest His power through us as through the first disciples. However imperfect and sinful we may be, the Lord holds out to us the offer of partnership with Himself, of apprenticeship to Christ. He invites us to come under the divine instruction, that, uniting with Christ, we may work the works of God.

"We have this treasure in earthen vessels, that the exceeding greatness of the power may be of God, and not from ourselves." 2 Cor. 4:7, R. V. This is why the preaching of the gospel was committed to erring men rather than to the angels. It is manifest that the power

t_____ and forbearance of Jesus, and heard His lessons of h_____ and p_____. He opened his heart to the divine influence… By beholding Christ, they became t_____ in character." (295, 296). Yes, Lord. There is hope for me! Day by day, beholding You, contemplating Your life and Your character. Transform my character, please! _____

_____

11. "In and through Christ they were to dwell in the family of God, learning to become one in faith, in doctrine, in s_____. They would have their tests, their grievances, their differences of opinion; but while Christ was abiding in the h_____, there could be no d_____." Lord, may our relationship spill over into my other relationships. May I always operate from the point of Your grace and Spirit, from its rich fountain: _____

_____

_____

12. Why is the preaching of the gospel committed to erring men rather than to the angels? (297). _____

(be a connecting link to
fasten their trembling faith
upon Christ). Lord, I ac-
cept Your offer of partnership with Yourself. May
others see in my life, only
Your power: _____

Prayer journal: _____

_____

_____

_____

_____

which works through the weakness of humanity is the
power of God; and thus we are encouraged to believe
that the power which can help others as weak as ourselves can help us. And those who are themselves "compassed with infirmity" should be able to "have compassion on the ignorant, and on them that are out of the
way." Heb. 5:2. Having been in peril themselves, they
are acquainted with the dangers and difficulties of the
way, and for this reason are called to reach out for others in like peril. There are souls perplexed with doubt,
burdened with infirmities, weak in faith, and unable to
grasp the Unseen; but a friend whom they can see, coming to them in Christ's stead, can be a connecting link to
fasten their trembling faith upon Christ.

We are to be laborers together with the heavenly
angels in presenting Jesus to the world. With almost impatient eagerness the angels wait for our co-operation;
for man must be the channel to communicate with man.
And when we give ourselves to Christ in wholehearted
devotion, angels rejoice that they may speak through
our voices to reveal God's love.

Chapter 31

The Sermon on the Mount

[This chapter is based on Matt. 5; 6; 7.]

Christ seldom gathered His disciples alone to receive His words. He did not choose for His audience those only who knew the way of life. It was His work to reach the multitudes who were in ignorance and error. He gave His lessons of truth where they could reach the darkened understanding. He Himself was the Truth, standing with girded loins and hands ever outstretched to bless, and in words of warning, entreaty, and encouragement, seeking to uplift all who would come unto Him.

The Sermon on the Mount, though given especially to the disciples, was spoken in the hearing of the multitude. After the ordination of the apostles, Jesus went with them to the seaside. Here in the early morning the people had begun to assemble. Besides the usual crowds from the Galilean towns, there were people from Judea, and even from Jerusalem itself; from Perea, from Decapolis, from Idumea, away to the south of Judea; and from Tyre and Sidon, the Phoenician cities on the shore of the Mediterranean. "When they had heard what great things He did," they "came to hear Him, and to be healed of their diseases: . . . there went virtue out of Him, and healed them all." Mark 3:8; Luke 6:17-19.

The narrow beach did not afford even standing room within reach of His voice for all who desired to hear Him, and Jesus led the way back to the mountainside. Reaching a level space that offered a pleasant gathering place for the vast assembly, He seated Himself on the grass, and the disciples and the multitude followed His example. [298-299]

The disciples' place was always next to Jesus. The people constantly pressed upon Him, yet the disciples understood that they were not to be crowded away from His presence. They sat close beside Him, that they might not lose a word of His instruction. They were attentive listeners, eager to understand the truths they were to make known to all lands and all ages.

With a feeling that something more than usual might

1. "The disciples' place was always n_____ to Jesus...They understood that they were not to be c_____ away from His presence." (299). What things do I allow to crowd me out of Your presence?

_____

_____

_____

be expected, they now pressed about their Master. They believed that the kingdom was soon to be established, and from the events of the morning they gathered assurance that some announcement concerning it was about to be made. A feeling of expectancy pervaded the multitude also, and eager faces gave evidence of the deep interest. As the people sat upon the green hillside, awaiting the words of the divine Teacher, their hearts were filled with thoughts of future glory. There were scribes and Pharisees who looked forward to the day when they should have dominion over the hated Romans, and possess the riches and splendor of the world's great empire. The poor peasants and fishermen hoped to hear the assurance that their wretched hovels, the scanty food, the life of toil, and fear of want were to be exchanged for mansions of plenty and days of ease. In place of the one coarse garment which was their covering by day, and their blanket at night, they hoped that Christ would give them the rich and costly robes of their conquerors. All hearts thrilled with the proud hope that Israel was soon to be honored before the nations as the chosen of the Lord, and Jerusalem exalted as the head of a universal kingdom.

Christ disappointed the hope of worldly greatness. In the Sermon on the Mount He sought to undo the work that had been wrought by false education, and to give His hearers a right conception of His kingdom and of His own character. Yet He did not make a direct attack on the errors of the people. He saw the misery of the world on account of sin, yet He did not present before them a vivid delineation of their wretchedness. He taught them of something infinitely better than they had known. Without combating their ideas of the kingdom of God, He told them the conditions of entrance therein, leaving them to draw their own conclusions as to its nature. The truths He taught are no less important to us than to the multitude that followed Him. We no less than they need to learn the foundation principles of the kingdom of God.

Christ's first words to the people on the mount were words of blessing. Happy are they, He said, who recognize their spiritual poverty, and [299-300] feel their need of redemption. The gospel is to be preached to the poor. Not to the spiritually proud, those who claim to be rich and in need of nothing, is it revealed, but to those who are humble and contrite. One fountain only has

---

2. "As the people sat upon the green hillside, awaiting…their hearts were filled with the thoughts of future g_____…In the Sermon on the Mount, He sought…to give His hearers a r_____ conception of His k_____ and His own c_____ _____." Lord, I want to know You, Your character, the principles of Your kingdom. Help me to hunger and thirst for You. What are some of my misconceptions?

_____
_____
_____
_____

3. How can I be happy by recognizing my spiritual poverty? _____
_____
_____

I praise You, Lord, for being my Redeemer, meeting my n_____ of redemption: _____
_____

been opened for sin, a fountain for the poor in spirit.

The proud heart strives to earn salvation; but both our title to heaven and our fitness for it are found in the righteousness of Christ. The Lord can do nothing toward the recovery of man until, convinced of his own weakness, and stripped of all self-sufficiency, he yields himself to the control of God. Then he can receive the gift that God is waiting to bestow. From the soul that feels his need, nothing is withheld. He has unrestricted access to Him in whom all fullness dwells. "For thus saith the high and lofty One that inhabiteth eternity, whose name is Holy; I dwell in the high and holy place, with him also that is of a contrite and humble spirit, to revive the spirit of the humble, and to revive the heart of the contrite ones." Isa. 57:15.

"Blessed are they that mourn: for they shall be comforted." By these words Christ does not teach that mourning in itself has power to remove the guilt of sin. He gives no sanction to pretense or to voluntary humility. The mourning of which He speaks does not consist in melancholy and lamentation. While we sorrow on account of sin, we are to rejoice in the precious privilege of being children of God.

We often sorrow because our evil deeds bring unpleasant consequences to ourselves; but this is not repentance. Real sorrow for sin is the result of the working of the Holy Spirit. The Spirit reveals the ingratitude of the heart that has slighted and grieved the Saviour, and brings us in contrition to the foot of the cross. By every sin Jesus is wounded afresh; and as we look upon Him whom we have pierced, we mourn for the sins that have brought anguish upon Him. Such mourning will lead to the renunciation of sin.

The worldling may pronounce this sorrow a weakness; but it is the strength which binds the penitent to the Infinite One with links that cannot be broken. It shows that the angels of God are bringing back to the soul the graces that were lost through hardness of heart and transgression. The tears of the penitent are only the raindrops that precede the sunshine of holiness. This sorrow heralds a joy which will be a living fountain in the soul. "Only acknowledge thine iniquity, that thou hast transgressed against the Lord thy God;" "and I will not cause Mine anger to fall upon you: for I am merciful, saith the Lord." Jer. 3:13, 12. "Unto them that mourn in Zion," He has appointed to give [300-301] "beauty for

4. How am I to mourn?

_____

_____

_____

"By every s_____ Jesus is w_____ afesh; and as we look upon Him whom we have pierced, we mourn for the sins that have brought a_____ upon Him. Such mourning will lead to the r_____ of sin...The tears of the penitent are only the raindrops that precede the s_____ of holiness." Lord, may I mourn over the effects of my sin upon You. I don't want to hurt You. So teach me, show me:_____

_____

_____

ashes, the oil of joy for mourning, the garment of praise for the spirit of heaviness." Isa. 61:3.

And for those also who mourn in trial and sorrow there is comfort. The bitterness of grief and humiliation is better than the indulgences of sin. Through affliction God reveals to us the plague spots in our characters, that by His grace we may overcome our faults. Unknown chapters in regard to ourselves are opened to us, and the test comes, whether we will accept the reproof and the counsel of God. When brought into trial, we are not to fret and complain. We should not rebel, or worry ourselves out of the hand of Christ. We are to humble the soul before God. The ways of the Lord are obscure to him who desires to see things in a light pleasing to himself. They appear dark and joyless to our human nature. But God's ways are ways of mercy and the end is salvation. Elijah knew not what he was doing when in the desert he said that he had had enough of life, and prayed that he might die. The Lord in His mercy did not take him at his word. There was yet a great work for Elijah to do; and when his work was done, he was not to perish in discouragement and solitude in the wilderness. Not for him the descent into the dust of death, but the ascent in glory, with the convoy of celestial chariots, to the throne on high.

God's word for the sorrowing is, "I have seen his ways, and will heal him: I will lead him also, and restore comforts unto him and to his mourners." "I will turn their mourning into joy, and will comfort them, and make them rejoice from their sorrow." Isa. 57:18; Jer. 31:13.

"Blessed are the meek." The difficulties we have to encounter may be very much lessened by that meekness which hides itself in Christ. If we possess the humility of our Master, we shall rise above the slights, the rebuffs, the annoyances, to which we are daily exposed, and they will cease to cast a gloom over the spirit. The highest evidence of nobility in a Christian is self-control. He who under abuse or cruelty fails to maintain a calm and trustful spirit robs God of His right to reveal in him His own perfection of character. Lowliness of heart is the strength that gives victory to the followers of Christ; it is the token of their connection with the courts above.

"Though the Lord be high, yet hath He respect unto the lowly." Ps. 138:6. Those who reveal the meek and

---

5. "Through a_____ _____ God reveals to us the plague spots of our c_____, that by His grace we may overcome our faults. Unknown chapters in regard to ourselves are o_____ to us, and the test comes, whether we will accept the reproof and the c_____ of God." (301). Lord, instead of feeling frustrated with affliction, I ask for a teachable spirit. Thank You for being gentle and patient with me! _____
_____
_____
_____

6. "Blessed are the meek… The highest evidence of n_____ in a Christian is s_____. He who under abuse or cruelty fails to maintain a calm and trustful spirit r_____ God of His r_____ to reveal in him His own perfection of character." You mean, it's not being up front, being a leader? It's not the tithes and offerings I give? _____
_____

lowly spirit of Christ are tenderly regarded by God. They may be looked upon with scorn by the world, but they are of great value in His sight. Not only the wise, the great, the beneficent, will gain a passport to the heavenly courts; not only [301-302] the busy worker, full of zeal and restless activity. No; the poor in spirit, who crave the presence of an abiding Christ, the humble in heart, whose highest ambition is to do God's will,--these will gain an abundant entrance. They will be among that number who have washed their robes and made them white in the blood of the Lamb. "Therefore are they before the throne of God, and serve Him day and night in His temple: and He that sitteth on the throne shall dwell among them." Rev. 7:15.

"Blessed are they which do hunger and thirst after righteousness." The sense of unworthiness will lead the heart to hunger and thirst for righteousness, and this desire will not be disappointed. Those who make room in their hearts for Jesus will realize His love. All who long to bear the likeness of the character of God shall be satisfied. The Holy Spirit never leaves unassisted the soul who is looking unto Jesus. He takes of the things of Christ and shows them unto him. If the eye is kept fixed on Christ, the work of the Spirit ceases not until the soul is conformed to His image. The pure element of love will expand the soul, giving it a capacity for higher attainments, for increased knowledge of heavenly things, so that it will not rest short of the fullness. "Blessed are they which do hunger and thirst after righteousness; for they shall be filled."

The merciful shall find mercy, and the pure in heart shall see God. Every impure thought defiles the soul, impairs the moral sense, and tends to obliterate the impressions of the Holy Spirit. It dims the spiritual vision, so that men cannot behold God. The Lord may and does forgive the repenting sinner; but though forgiven, the soul is marred. All impurity of speech or of thought must be shunned by him who would have clear discernment of spiritual truth.

But the words of Christ cover more than freedom from sensual impurity, more than freedom from that ceremonial defilement which the Jews so rigorously shunned. Selfishness prevents us from beholding God. The self-seeking spirit judges of God as altogether such a one as itself. Until we have renounced this, we cannot understand Him who is love. Only the unselfish heart,

Teach me Lord, that as I lose self-control and get defensive, I am really insecure, because I'm not grounded in Your love: ___
_____
_____
_____

7. Hungering and thirsting after righteousness. "All who l_____ to bear the likeness of the character of God shall be s_____...If the e_____ is kept f_____ on Christ, the work of the Spirit ceases n_____ until the soul is conformed to His image." (302). Lord, help the longing not to wane. Throughout the day, not just at devotion time, send me the thought to keep my eyes fixed on You. Thank You for the ceaseless ministry of the Spirit:
_____
_____
_____
_____

8. What do impure thoughts do to the work of the Holy Spirit? _____
_____
_____

"S_____ prevents us from beholding God." To be pure in heart is to have an unselfish heart, a humble and trustful spirit. Lord, I don't want the Spirit's voice to get fainter, let alone obliterated. Help me to be more sensitive to Your spirit:

_____

_____

_____

_____

the humble and trustful spirit, shall see God as "merciful and gracious, long-suffering, and abundant in goodness and truth." Ex. 34:6.

"Blessed are the peacemakers." The peace of Christ is born of truth. It is harmony with God. The world is at enmity with the law of God; [302-305] sinners are at enmity with their Maker; and as a result they are at enmity with one another. But the psalmist declares, "Great peace have they which love Thy law: and nothing shall offend them." Ps. 119:165. Men cannot manufacture peace. Human plans for the purification and uplifting of individuals or of society will fail of producing peace, because they do not reach the heart. The only power that can create or perpetuate true peace is the grace of Christ. When this is implanted in the heart, it will cast out the evil passions that cause strife and dissension. "Instead of the thorn shall come up the fir tree, and instead of the brier shall come up the myrtle tree;" and life's desert "shall rejoice, and blossom as the rose." Isa. 55:13; 35:1.

The multitudes were amazed at this teaching, which was so at variance with the precepts and example of the Pharisees. The people had come to think that happiness consisted in the possession of the things of this world, and that fame and the honor of men were much to be coveted. It was very pleasing to be called "Rabbi," and to be extolled as wise and religious, having their virtues paraded before the public. This was regarded as the crown of happiness. But in the presence of that vast throng, Jesus declared that earthly gain and honor were all the reward such persons would ever receive. He spoke with certainty, and a convincing power attended His words. The people were silenced, and a feeling of fear crept over them. They looked at one another doubtfully. Who of them would be saved if this Man's teachings were true? Many were convicted that this remarkable Teacher was actuated by the Spirit of God, and that the sentiments He uttered were divine.

After explaining what constitutes true happiness, and how it may be obtained, Jesus more definitely pointed out the duty of His disciples, as teachers chosen of God to lead others into the path of righteousness and eternal life. He knew that they would often suffer from disappointment and discouragement, that they would meet with decided opposition, that they would be insulted, and their testimony rejected. Well He knew that in the fulfillment of their mission, the humble men who listened so attentively to His words were to bear calumny, torture, imprisonment, and death, and He continued:

"Blessed are they which are persecuted for righteousness' sake: for theirs is the kingdom of heaven. Blessed are ye, when men shall revile you, and persecute you, and shall say all manner of evil against you falsely, for My sake. Rejoice, and be exceeding glad: for great is your [305-306] reward in heaven: for so persecuted they the prophets which were before you."

The world loves sin, and hates righteousness, and this was the cause of its hostility to Jesus. All who refuse His infinite love will find Christianity a disturbing element. The light of Christ sweeps away the darkness that covers their sins, and the need of reform is made manifest. While those who yield to the influence of the Holy Spirit begin war with themselves, those who cling to sin war against the truth and its representatives.

Thus strife is created, and Christ's followers are accused as troublers of the people. But it is fellowship with God that brings them the world's enmity. They are bearing the reproach of Christ. They are treading the path that has been trodden by the noblest of the earth. Not with sorrow, but with rejoicing, should they meet persecution. Each fiery trial is God's agent for their refining. Each is fitting them for their work as colaborers with Him. Each conflict has its place in the great battle for righteousness, and each will add to the joy of their final triumph. Having this in view, the test of their faith and patience will be cheerfully accepted rather than dreaded and avoided. Anxious to fulfill their obligation to the world, fixing their desire upon the approval of God, His servants are to fulfill every duty, irrespective of the fear or the favor of men.

"Ye are the salt of the earth," Jesus said. Do not withdraw yourselves from the world in order to escape persecution. You are to abide among men, that the savor of the divine love may be as salt to preserve the world from corruption.

Hearts that respond to the influence of the Holy Spirit are the channels through which God's blessing flows. Were those who serve God removed from the earth, and His Spirit withdrawn from among men, this world would be left to desolation and destruction, the fruit of Satan's dominion. Though the wicked know it

9. Persecuted for righteousness' sake. "All who refuse His infinite love will find Christianity a d_____ element...Not with sorrow, but with r_____, should we meet persecution. Each fiery trial is God's agent for their r____ ____...Each conflict has its place in the great battle for r_____, and each will add to the j_____ of their final triumph." (306). That's tough, Lord! Rejoice in the opportunity for refining, to be more like You! Help me to see it that way, in the middle of the persecution: _____
_____
_____

10. "If Christians are such in name only, they are like the salt that has lost its s_____. They have no i_____ for the good in the world. Through their misrepresentation of God they are worse than u_____ _____." In name only? Without Your love, spirit, and grace? That's about as negative as I can think! That's spiritual death. Lord, help me stay clear of that attitude and experience: __
_____
_____
_____

11. We are the "light of the world." We are to radiate from w_____. "The consistent life, the holy c_____, the unswerving integrity, the active, benevolent spirit, the godly example, -- these are the mediums through which l_____ is conveyed to the world." (307). I can only be this medium if You are dwelling within. Do I think of 'light' as externals? _____
_____ May I be continually aware of Your abiding presence, throughout the day, and may You shine out: _____
_____
_____

not, they owe even the blessings of this life to the presence, in the world, of God's people whom they despise and oppress. But if Christians are such in name only, they are like the salt that has lost its savor. They have no influence for good in the world. Through their misrepresentation of God they are worse than unbelievers.

"Ye are the light of the world." The Jews thought to confine the benefits of salvation to their own nation; but Christ showed them that [306-307] salvation is like the sunshine. It belongs to the whole world. The religion of the Bible is not to be confined between the covers of a book, nor within the walls of a church. It is not to be brought out occasionally for our own benefit, and then to be carefully laid aside again. It is to sanctify the daily life, to manifest itself in every business transaction and in all our social relations.

True character is not shaped from without, and put on; it radiates from within. If we wish to direct others in the path of righteousness, the principles of righteousness must be enshrined in our own hearts. Our profession of faith may proclaim the theory of religion, but it is our practical piety that holds forth the word of truth. The consistent life, the holy conversation, the unswerving integrity, the active, benevolent spirit, the godly example,--these are the mediums through which light is conveyed to the world.

Jesus had not dwelt on the specifications of the law, but He did not leave His hearers to conclude that He had come to set aside its requirements. He knew that spies stood ready to seize upon every word that might be wrested to serve their purpose. He knew the prejudice that existed in the minds of many of His hearers, and He said nothing to unsettle their faith in the religion and institutions that had been committed to them through Moses. Christ Himself had given both the moral and the ceremonial law. He did not come to destroy confidence in His own instruction. It was because of His great reverence for the law and the prophets that He sought to break through the wall of traditional requirements which hemmed in the Jews. While He set aside their false interpretations of the law, He carefully guarded His disciples against yielding up the vital truths committed to the Hebrews.

The Pharisees prided themselves on their obedience to the law; yet they knew so little of its principles through everyday practice that to them the Saviour's words sounded like heresy. As He swept away the rubbish under which the truth had been buried, they thought He was sweeping away the truth itself. They whispered to one another that He was making light of the law. He read their thoughts, and answered them, saying,--

"Think not that I am come to destroy the law, or the prophets: I am not come to destroy, but to fulfill." Here Jesus refutes the charge of the Pharisees. His mission to the world is to vindicate the sacred claims of that law which they charge Him with breaking. If the law [307-308] of God could have been changed or abrogated, then Christ need not have suffered the consequences of our transgression. He came to explain the relation of the law to man, and to illustrate its precepts by His own life of obedience.

God has given us His holy precepts, because He loves mankind. To shield us from the results of transgression, He reveals the principles of righteousness. The law is an expression of the thought of God; when received in Christ, it becomes our thought. It lifts us above the power of natural desires and tendencies, above temptations that lead to sin. God desires us to be happy, and He gave us the precepts of the law that in obeying them we might have joy. When at Jesus' birth the angels sang,--

"Glory to God in the highest,
And on earth peace, good will
toward men" (Luke 2:14),

they were declaring the principles of the law which He had come to magnify and make honorable.

When the law was proclaimed from Sinai, God made known to men the holiness of His character, that by contrast they might see the sinfulness of their own. The law was given to convict them of sin, and reveal their need of a Saviour. It would do this as its principles were applied to the heart by the Holy Spirit. This work it is still to do. In the life of Christ the principles of the law are made plain; and as the Holy Spirit of God touches the heart, as the light of Christ reveals to men their need of His cleansing blood and His justifying righteousness, the law is still an agent in bringing us to Christ, that we may be justified by faith. "The law of the Lord is perfect, converting the soul." Ps. 19:7.

"Till heaven and earth pass," said Jesus, "one jot or one tittle shall in nowise pass from the law, till all be fulfilled." The sun shining in the heavens, the solid

12. "When the law was proclaimed from Sinai, God made known to men the holiness of His c_____ ...
The law was given to c_____ them of sin, and reveal their need of a S_____...
This work it is s_____ to do." (308). Lord, may I better understand the relation between Your law and Your character. _____

_____

_____

_____

_____

Convict me of my falling short of Your character, of wounding You afresh:

_____

_____

_____

_____

earth upon which you dwell, are God's witnesses that His law is changeless and eternal. Though they may pass away, the divine precepts shall endure. "It is easier for heaven and earth to pass, than one tittle of the law to fail." Luke 16:17. The system of types that pointed to Jesus as the Lamb of God was to be abolished at His death; but the precepts of the Decalogue are as immutable as the throne of God.

Since "the law of the Lord is perfect," every variation from it must be evil. Those who disobey the commandments of God, and teach others [308-309] to do so, are condemned by Christ. The Saviour's life of obedience maintained the claims of the law; it proved that the law could be kept in humanity, and showed the excellence of character that obedience would develop. All who obey as He did are likewise declaring that the law is "holy, and just, and good." Rom. 7:12. On the other hand, all who break God's commandments are sustaining Satan's claim that the law is unjust, and cannot be obeyed. Thus they second the deceptions of the great adversary, and cast dishonor upon God. They are the children of the wicked one, who was the first rebel against God's law. To admit them into heaven would again bring in the elements of discord and rebellion, and imperil the well-being of the universe. No man who willfully disregards one principle of the law shall enter the kingdom of heaven.

The rabbis counted their righteousness a passport to heaven; but Jesus declared it to be insufficient and unworthy. External ceremonies and a theoretical knowledge of truth constituted Pharisaical righteousness. The rabbis claimed to be holy through their own efforts in keeping the law; but their works had divorced righteousness from religion. While they were punctilious in ritual observances, their lives were immoral and debased. Their so-called righteousness could never enter the kingdom of heaven.

The greatest deception of the human mind in Christ's day was that a mere assent to the truth constitutes righteousness. In all human experience a theoretical knowledge of the truth has been proved to be insufficient for the saving of the soul. It does not bring forth the fruits of righteousness. A jealous regard for what is termed theological truth often accompanies a hatred of genuine truth as made manifest in life. The darkest chapters of history are burdened with the record of crimes commit-

---

13. "The Saviour's life of obedience maintained the claims of the law; it proved that the law could be kept in h_____, and showed the excellence of character that obedience would d_____." (309). How can I understand "obedience developing character" in a non "righteousness by works" way, Lord?

_____
_____
_____
_____

ted by bigoted religionists. The Pharisees claimed to be children of Abraham, and boasted of their possession of the oracles of God; yet these advantages did not preserve them from selfishness, malignity, greed for gain, and the basest hypocrisy. They thought themselves the greatest religionists of the world, but their so-called orthodoxy led them to crucify the Lord of glory.

The same danger still exists. Many take it for granted that they are Christians, simply because they subscribe to certain theological tenets. But they have not brought the truth into practical life. They have not believed and loved it, therefore they have not received the power and [309-310] grace that come through sanctification of the truth. Men may profess faith in the truth; but if it does not make them sincere, kind, patient, forbearing, heavenly-minded, it is a curse to its possessors, and through their influence it is a curse to the world.

The righteousness which Christ taught is conformity of heart and life to the revealed will of God. Sinful men can become righteous only as they have faith in God and maintain a vital connection with Him. Then true godliness will elevate the thoughts and ennoble the life. Then the external forms of religion accord with the Christian's internal purity. Then the ceremonies required in the service of God are not meaningless rites, like those of the hypocritical Pharisees.

Jesus takes up the commandments separately, and explains the depth and breadth of their requirement. Instead of removing one jot of their force, He shows how far-reaching their principles are, and exposes the fatal mistake of the Jews in their outward show of obedience. He declares that by the evil thought or the lustful look the law of God is transgressed. One who becomes a party to the least injustice is breaking the law and degrading his own moral nature. Murder first exists in the mind. He who gives hatred a place in his heart is setting his feet in the path of the murderer, and his offerings are abhorrent to God.

The Jews cultivated a spirit of retaliation. In their hatred of the Romans they gave utterance to hard denunciations, and pleased the wicked one by manifesting his attributes. Thus they were training themselves to do the terrible deeds to which he led them on. In the religious life of the Pharisees there was nothing to recommend piety to the Gentiles. Jesus bade them not to

14. "Many take it for granted that they are Christians, simply because they s_____ to certain theological tenets." If truth does not make me, a professed Christian, "sincere, kind, patient, forbearing, h_____-minded, it is a curse" to me and through my influence, it is a curse to the world. (309, 310). Truth be a curse? Lord, how do I sometimes forget that You are the Way, the TRUTH, and the life? _____
_____

How is doing good to those that hate me, a wellspring of life? (311) _____
_____
_____
_____
_____
_____

deceive themselves with the thought that they could in heart rise up against their oppressors, and cherish the longing to avenge their wrongs.

It is true there is an indignation that is justifiable, even in the followers of Christ. When they see that God is dishonored, and His service brought into disrepute, when they see the innocent oppressed, a righteous indignation stirs the soul. Such anger, born of sensitive morals, is not a sin. But those who at any supposed provocation feel at liberty to indulge anger or resentment are opening the heart to Satan. Bitterness and animosity must be banished from the soul if we would be in harmony with heaven.

The Saviour goes farther than this. He says, "If thou bring thy gift to the altar, and there rememberest that thy brother hath aught against thee; leave there thy gift before the altar, and go thy way; first be [310-311] reconciled to thy brother, and then come and offer thy gift." Many are zealous in religious services, while between them and their brethren are unhappy differences which they might reconcile. God requires them to do all in their power to restore harmony. Until they do this, He cannot accept their services. The Christian's duty in this matter is clearly pointed out.

God pours His blessings upon all. "He maketh His sun to rise on the evil and on the good, and sendeth rain on the just and on the unjust." He is "kind unto the unthankful and to the evil." Luke 6:35. He bids us to be like Him. "Bless them that curse you," said Jesus; "do good to them that hate you, . . . that ye may be the children of your Father which is in heaven." These are the principles of the law, and they are the wellsprings of life.

God's ideal for His children is higher than the highest human thought can reach. "Be ye therefore perfect, even as your Father which is in heaven is perfect." This command is a promise. The plan of redemption contemplates our complete recovery from the power of Satan. Christ always separates the contrite soul from sin. He came to destroy the works of the devil, and He has made provision that the Holy Spirit shall be imparted to every repentant soul, to keep him from sinning.

The tempter's agency is not to be accounted an excuse for one wrong act. Satan is jubilant when he hears the professed followers of Christ making excuses for their deformity of character. It is these excuses that lead

15. "God's ideal for His children is h_____ than the highest human thought can reach. 'Be ye therefore perfect, even as your F_____ which is in heaven is perfect.' This command is a p_____..."

to sin. There is no excuse for sinning. A holy temper, a Christlike life, is accessible to every repenting, believing child of God.

The ideal of Christian character is Christlikeness. As the Son of man was perfect in His life, so His followers are to be perfect in their life. Jesus was in all things made like unto His brethren. He became flesh, even as we are. He was hungry and thirsty and weary. He was sustained by food and refreshed by sleep. He shared the lot of man; yet He was the blameless Son of God. He was God in the flesh. His character is to be ours. The Lord says of those who believe in Him, "I will dwell in them, and walk in them; and I will be their God, and they shall be My people." 2 Cor. 6:16.

Christ is the ladder that Jacob saw, the base resting on the earth, and the topmost round reaching to the gate of heaven, to the very threshold of glory. If that ladder had failed by a single step of reaching the earth, we should have been lost. But Christ reaches us where we are. He took our nature and overcame, that we through taking His [311-312] nature might overcome. Made "in the likeness of sinful flesh" (Rom. 8:3), He lived a sinless life. Now by His divinity He lays hold upon the throne of heaven, while by His humanity He reaches us. He bids us by faith in Him attain to the glory of the character of God. Therefore are we to be perfect, even as our "Father which is in heaven is perfect."

Jesus had shown in what righteousness consists, and had pointed to God as its source. Now He turned to practical duties. In almsgiving, in prayer, in fasting, He said, let nothing be done to attract attention or win praise to self. Give in sincerity, for the benefit of the suffering poor. In prayer, let the soul commune with God. In fasting, go not with the head bowed down, and heart filled with thoughts of self. The heart of the Pharisee is a barren and profitless soil, in which no seeds of divine life can flourish. It is he who yields himself most unreservedly to God that will render Him the most acceptable service. For through fellowship with God men become workers together with Him in presenting His character in humanity.

The service rendered in sincerity of heart has great recompense. "Thy Father which seeth in secret Himself shall reward thee openly." By the life we live through the grace of Christ the character is formed. The original loveliness begins to be restored to the soul. The attri-

---

The ideal of Christian character is C_____ _____···

He bids us by f_____ in Him to attain to the g_____ of the character of God." (311, 312). If it is by faith, Lord, then help my focus to be not on obedience, but on a faith relationship. And what a promise! To be Christlike, to be like You!

_____
_____
_____
_____

butes of the character of Christ are imparted, and the image of the Divine begins to shine forth. The faces of men and women who walk and work with God express the peace of heaven. They are surrounded with the atmosphere of heaven. For these souls the kingdom of God has begun. They have Christ's joy, the joy of being a blessing to humanity. They have the honor of being accepted for the Master's use; they are trusted to do His work in His name.

"No man can serve two masters." We cannot serve God with a divided heart. Bible religion is not one influence among many others; its influence is to be supreme, pervading and controlling every other. It is not to be like a dash of color brushed here and there upon the canvas, but it is to pervade the whole life, as if the canvas were dipped into the color, until every thread of the fabric were dyed a deep, unfading hue.

"If therefore thine eye be single, thy whole body shall be full of light. But if thine eye be evil, thy whole body shall be full of darkness." Purity and steadfastness of purpose are the conditions of receiving light from God. He who desires to know the truth must be willing to accept all that it reveals. He can make no compromise with error. To be [312-313] wavering and halfhearted in allegiance to truth is to choose the darkness of error and satanic delusion.

Worldly policy and the undeviating principles of righteousness do not blend into each other imperceptibly, like the colors of the rainbow. Between the two a broad, clear line is drawn by the eternal God. The likeness of Christ stands out as distinct from that of Satan as midday in contrast with midnight. And only those who live the life of Christ are His co-workers. If one sin is cherished in the soul, or one wrong practice retained in the life, the whole being is contaminated. The man becomes an instrument of unrighteousness.

All who have chosen God's service are to rest in His care. Christ pointed to the birds flying in the heavens, to the flowers of the field, and bade His hearers consider these objects of God's creation. "Are not ye of much more value than they?" He said. Matt. 6:26, R. V. The measure of divine attention bestowed on any object is proportionate to its rank in the scale of being. The little brown sparrow is watched over by Providence. The flowers of the field, the grass that carpets the earth, share the notice and care of our heavenly Father.

The great Master Artist has taken thought for the lilies, making them so beautiful that they outshine the glory of Solomon. How much more does He care for man, who is the image and glory of God. He longs to see His children reveal a character after His similitude. As the sunbeam imparts to the flowers their varied and delicate tints, so does God impart to the soul the beauty of His own character.

All who choose Christ's kingdom of love and righteousness and peace, making its interest paramount to all other, are linked to the world above, and every blessing needed for this life is theirs. In the book of God's providence, the volume of life, we are each given a page. That page contains every particular of our history; even the hairs of the head are numbered. God's children are never absent from His mind.

"Be not therefore anxious for the morrow." Matt. 6:34, R. V. We are to follow Christ day by day. God does not bestow help for tomorrow. He does not give His children all the directions for their life journey at once, lest they should become confused. He tells them just as much as they can remember and perform. The strength and wisdom imparted are for the present emergency. "If any of you lack wisdom,"--for today,--"let him ask of God, that giveth to all men liberally, and upbraideth not; and it shall be given him." James 1:5. [313-314] "Judge not, that ye be not judged." Do not think yourself better than other men, and set yourself up as their judge. Since you cannot discern motive, you are incapable of judging another. In criticizing him, you are passing sentence upon yourself; for you show that you are a participant with Satan, the accuser of the brethren. The Lord says, "Examine yourselves, whether ye be in the faith; prove your own selves." This is our work. "If we would judge ourselves, we should not be judged." 2 Cor. 13:5; 1 Cor. 11:31.

The good tree will produce good fruit. If the fruit is unpalatable and worthless, the tree is evil. So the fruit borne in the life testifies as to the condition of the heart and the excellence of the character. Good works can never purchase salvation, but they are an evidence of the faith that acts by love and purifies the soul. And though the eternal reward is not bestowed because of our merit, yet it will be in proportion to the work that has been done through the grace of Christ.

Thus Christ set forth the principles of His kingdom,

16. Since I cannot discern motive, I am incapable of judging another. In criticizing him, I pass sentence upon myself; for I show that I am a "participant with S_____, the a_____ of the brethren." (314). I need a lot of help here, Lord. Participating with the enemy? Jar me awake, while it is happening, Lord: ___

_____

_____

_____

and showed them to be the great rule of life. To impress the lesson He adds an illustration. It is not enough, He says, for you to hear My words. By obedience you must make them the foundation of your character. Self is but shifting sand. If you build upon human theories and inventions, your house will fall. By the winds of temptation, the tempests of trial, it will be swept away. But these principles that I have given will endure. Receive Me; build on My words.

"Everyone therefore which heareth these words of Mine, and doeth them, shall be likened unto a wise man, which built his house upon the rock: and the rain descended, and the floods came, and the winds blew, and beat upon that house; and it fell not: for it was founded upon the rock." Matt. 7:24, 25, R.V.

Prayer Journal: _____
_____
_____
_____
_____
_____
_____
_____

Chapter 32

The Centurion

[This chapter is based on Matt. 8:5-13; Luke 7:1-17.]

Christ had said to the nobleman whose son He healed, "Except ye see signs and wonders, ye will not believe." John 4:48. He was grieved that His own nation should require these outward signs of His Messiahship. Again and again He had marveled at their unbelief. But He marveled at the faith of the centurion who came to Him. The centurion did not question the Saviour's power. He did not even ask Him to come in person to perform the miracle. "Speak the word only," he said, "and my servant shall be healed."

The centurion's servant had been stricken with palsy, and lay at the point of death. Among the Romans the servants were slaves, bought and sold in the market places, and treated with abuse and cruelty; but the centurion was tenderly attached to his servant, and greatly desired his recovery. He believed that Jesus could heal him. He had not seen the Saviour, but the reports he heard had inspired him with faith. Notwithstanding the formalism of the Jews, this Roman was convinced that their religion was superior to his own. Already he had broken through the barriers of national prejudice and hatred that separated the conquerors from the conquered people. He had manifested respect for the service of God, and had shown kindness to the Jews as His worshipers. In the teaching of Christ, as it had been reported to him, he found that which met the need of the soul. All that was spiritual within him responded to the Saviour's words. But he felt unworthy to come into the presence of Jesus, and he appealed to the Jewish elders to make request for the healing of his servant. They were acquainted with the [315-316] Great Teacher, and would, he thought, know how to approach Him so as to win His favor.

As Jesus entered Capernaum, He was met by a delegation of the elders, who told Him of the centurion's desire. They urged "that he was worthy for whom He should do this: for he loveth our nation, and he hath built us a synagogue."

Jesus immediately set out for the officer's home; but, pressed by the multitude, He advanced slowly. The

1. The centurion "believed that Jesus could heal him [a servant]. He had not seen the Savior, but the reports he heard had i_____ him with faith." Lord, what is my report about You? What effect does it have? Does it inspire faith, or does it discredit You?

_____

_____

_____

2. The delegation of elders sent by the centurion, urged Jesus that the centurion was worthy of his request. The centurion had a different opinion of himself. "In his self-d_____, [he] sent Him the message, 'Lord, trouble not Thyself: for I am n___worthy that Thou shouldest enter under my roof.'" (316). What is my attitude? Do I think that You owe me anything? Do I expect You to help things go a certain way for me, because of my faithfulness, stewardship, etc? The only thing that recommends me to You, God, is my need: _____

_____

_____

_____

3. "I have not found so great faith, no, not in Israel." What contrast would You make today, Lord? Not in all Christian homes? Not in my home? Not in my heart? _____

_____

_____

_____

4. The Jewish elders "did not recognize that our great need is our o_____ claim on God's mercy." The centurion's argument WAS his great need. "He did not believe in Him merely as a worker of miracles, but as the f_____ and Savior of mankind." (317).

news of His coming preceded Him, and the centurion, in his self-distrust, sent Him the message, "Lord, trouble not Thyself: for I am not worthy that Thou shouldest enter under my roof." But the Saviour kept on His way, and the centurion, venturing at last to approach Him, completed the message, saying, "Neither thought I myself worthy to come unto Thee;" "but speak the word only, and my servant shall be healed. For I am a man under authority, having soldiers under me: and I say to this man, Go, and he goeth; and to another, Come, and he cometh; and to my servant, Do this, and he doeth it." As I represent the power of Rome, and my soldiers recognize my authority as supreme, so dost Thou represent the power of the Infinite God, and all created things obey Thy word. Thou canst command the disease to depart, and it shall obey Thee. Thou canst summon Thy heavenly messengers, and they shall impart healing virtue. Speak but the word, and my servant shall be healed.

"When Jesus heard these things, He marveled at him, and turned Him about, and said unto the people that followed Him, I say unto you, I have not found so great faith, no, not in Israel." And to the centurion He said, "As thou hast believed, so be it done unto thee. And his servant was healed in the selfsame hour."

The Jewish elders who recommended the centurion to Christ had [316-317] shown how far they were from possessing the spirit of the gospel. They did not recognize that our great need is our only claim on God's mercy. In their self-righteousness they commended the centurion because of the favor he had shown to "our nation." But the centurion said of himself, "I am not worthy." His heart had been touched by the grace of Christ. He saw his own unworthiness; yet he feared not to ask help. He trusted not to his own goodness; his argument was his great need. His faith took hold upon Christ in His true character. He did not believe in Him merely as a worker of miracles, but as the friend and Saviour of mankind.

It is thus that every sinner may come to Christ. "Not by works of righteousness which we have done, but according to His mercy He saved us." Titus 3:5. When Satan tells you that you are a sinner, and cannot hope to receive blessing from God, tell him that Christ came into the world to save sinners. We have nothing to recommend us to God; but the plea that we may urge now and ever is our utterly helpless condition that makes

His redeeming power a necessity. Renouncing all self-dependence, we may look to the cross of Calvary and say,--

> "In my hand no price I bring;
> Simply to Thy cross I cling."

The Jews had been instructed from childhood concerning the work of the Messiah. The inspired utterances of patriarchs and prophets and the symbolic teaching of the sacrificial service had been theirs. But they had disregarded the light; and now they saw in Jesus nothing to be desired. But the centurion, born in heathenism, educated in the idolatry of imperial Rome, trained as a soldier, seemingly cut off from spiritual life by his education and surroundings, and still further shut out by the bigotry of the Jews, and by the contempt of his own countrymen for the people of Israel,--this man perceived the truth to which the children of Abraham were blinded. He did not wait to see whether the Jews themselves would receive the One who claimed to be their Messiah. As the "light, which lighteth every man that cometh into the world" (John 1:9) had shone upon him, he had, though afar off, discerned the glory of the Son of God.

To Jesus this was an earnest of the work which the gospel was to accomplish among the Gentiles. With joy He looked forward to the gathering of souls from all nations to His kingdom. With deep sadness He pictured to the Jews the result of their rejection of His grace: "I [317-318] say unto you, That many shall come from the east and west, and shall sit down with Abraham, and Isaac, and Jacob, in the kingdom of heaven. But the children of the kingdom shall be cast out into outer darkness: there shall be weeping and gnashing of teeth." Alas, how many are still preparing for the same fatal disappointment! While souls in heathen darkness accept His grace, how many there are in Christian lands upon whom the light shines only to be disregarded.

More than twenty miles from Capernaum, on a tableland overlooking the wide, beautiful plain of Esdraelon, lay the village of Nain, and thither Jesus next bent His steps. Many of His disciples and others were with Him, and all along the way the people came, longing for His words of love and pity, bringing their sick for His healing, and ever with the hope that He who wielded such wondrous power would make Himself known as the King of Israel. A multitude thronged His

Recognizing my need is to possess the spirit of the g_____. How is that? _____

_____

Any other attitude is to discount or negate the gospel for me. Humble me, Lord. Satan keeps me thinking that I'm a pretty decent Christian. I don't have the addictions of drugs, alcohol, adultery, gambling, or foul language. I attend church, and help others. I'm not perfect, but I am better than quite a few! What about pride, You ask? And self-righteousness? That's where I need Your help. Humble me, Lord: _____

_____

_____

steps, and it was a glad, expectant company that followed Him up the rocky path toward the gate of the mountain village.

As they draw near, a funeral train is seen coming from the gates. With slow, sad steps it is proceeding to the place of burial. On an open bier carried in front is the body of the dead, and about it are the mourners, filling the air with their wailing cries. All the people of the town seem to have gathered to show their respect for the dead and their sympathy with the bereaved.

It was a sight to awaken sympathy. The deceased was the only son of his mother, and she a widow. The lonely mourner was following to the grave her sole earthly support and comfort. "When the Lord saw her, He had compassion on her." As she moved on blindly, weeping, noting not His presence, He came close beside her, and gently said, "Weep not." Jesus was about to change her grief to joy, yet He could not forbear this expression of tender sympathy.

"He came and touched the bier;" to Him even contact with death could impart no defilement. The bearers stood still, and the lamentations of the mourners ceased. The two companies gathered about the bier, hoping against hope. One was present who had banished disease and vanquished demons; was death also subject to His power?

In clear, authoritative voice the words are spoken, "Young man, I say unto thee, Arise." That voice pierces the ears of the dead. The young man opens his eyes. Jesus takes him by the hand, and lifts him up. His gaze falls upon her who has been weeping beside him, and mother and son unite in a long, clinging, joyous embrace. The multitude [318-319] look on in silence, as if spellbound. "There came a fear on all." Hushed and reverent they stood for a little time, as if in the very presence of God. Then they "glorified God, saying, That a great prophet is risen up among us; and, That God hath visited His people." The funeral train returned to Nain as a triumphal procession. "And this rumor of Him went forth throughout all Judea, and throughout all the region round about."

He who stood beside the sorrowing mother at the gate of Nain, watches with every mourning one beside the bier. He is touched with sympathy for our grief. His heart, that loved and pitied, is a heart of unchangeable tenderness. His word, that called the dead to life, is no

5. Jesus was about to change her [widow of Nain's] grief to j_____ ...the funeral train to a t_____ procession. (318, 319). Are there transformations that You would like to make Jesus, in my life, if I gave You permission, was willing to let go of some things and some attitudes? _____

6. "He is t_____ with sympathy for our grief. His heart, that loved and pitied, is a heart of unchangeable t_____." He knows my name, my hurts; He cares; He heals. Thank You, Lord, for being my Friend: _____

less efficacious now than when spoken to the young man of Nain. He says, "All power is given unto Me in heaven and in earth." Matt. 28:18. That power is not diminished by the lapse of years, nor exhausted by the ceaseless activity of His overflowing grace. To all who believe on Him He is still a living Saviour. [319-320]

Jesus changed the mother's grief to joy when He gave back her son; yet the youth was but called forth to this earthly life, to endure its sorrows, its toils, and its perils, and to pass again under the power of death. But Jesus comforts our sorrow for the dead with a message of infinite hope: "I am He that liveth, and was dead; and, behold, I am alive forevermore, . . . and have the keys of hell and of death." "Forasmuch then as the children are partakers of flesh and blood, He also Himself likewise took part of the same; that through death He might destroy him that had the power of death, that is, the devil; and deliver them who through fear of death were all their lifetime subject to bondage." Rev. 1:18; Heb. 2:14, 15.

Satan cannot hold the dead in his grasp when the Son of God bids them live. He cannot hold in spiritual death one soul who in faith receives Christ's word of power. God is saying to all who are dead in sin, "Awake thou that sleepest, and arise from the dead." Eph. 5:14. That word is eternal life. As the word of God which bade the first man live, still gives us life; as Christ's word, "Young man, I say unto thee, Arise," gave life to the youth of Nain, so that word, "Arise from the dead," is life to the soul that receives it. God "hath delivered us from the power of darkness, and hath translated us into the kingdom of His dear Son." Col. 1:13. It is all offered us in His word. If we receive the word, we have the deliverance.

And "if the Spirit of Him that raised up Jesus from the dead dwell in you, He that raised up Christ from the dead shall also quicken your mortal bodies by His Spirit that dwelleth in you." "For the Lord Himself shall descend from heaven with a shout, with the voice of the Archangel, and with the trump of God: and the dead in Christ shall rise first: then we which are alive and remain shall be caught up together with them in the clouds, to meet the Lord in the air: and so shall we ever be with the Lord." Rom. 8:11; 1 Thess. 4:16, 17. This is the word of comfort wherewith He bids us comfort one another.

7. Satan "cannot hold in spiritual d_____ one soul who in faith r_____ Christ's word of power...It is all offered us in His w_____." (320). Lord, increase my time in Your Word, so that in faith, I may receive Your word of power. May Satan not have his way, nor hold me in spiritual death any longer:

_____
_____
_____
_____
_____

Prayer journal: _____
_____
_____
_____
_____
_____
_____
_____

Chapter 33

Who Are My Brethren?

[This chapter is based on Matt. 12:22-50; Mark 3:20-35.]

1. Jesus' brothers "felt keenly the reproach that came upon them through their r_____ to Jesus." What am I saying when I act embarrassed or timid about my relation to You, Lord? _____

_____

_____

_____

2. "In attributing the work of the Holy Spirit to S_____," I "cut myself off from the fountain of blessing." (322). I would not flagrantly do this, but how about in more subtle ways? _____

_____

(Labeling something too fanatical, new-in-the-faith, immature? How about too on-fire, too happy, too new and non-traditional?) _____

_____

Holy Spirit convict me, please:_____

___ _____

_____

The sons of Joseph were far from being in sympathy with Jesus in His work. The reports that reached them in regard to His life and labors filled them with astonishment and dismay. They heard that He devoted entire nights to prayer, that through the day He was thronged by great companies of people, and did not give Himself time so much as to eat. His friends felt that He was wearing Himself out by His incessant labor; they were unable to account for His attitude toward the Pharisees, and there were some who feared that His reason was becoming unsettled.

His brothers heard of this, and also of the charge brought by the Pharisees that He cast out devils through the power of Satan. They felt keenly the reproach that came upon them through their relation to Jesus. They knew what a tumult His words and works created, and were not only alarmed at His bold statements, but indignant at His denunciation of the scribes and Pharisees. They decided that He must be persuaded or constrained to cease this manner of labor, and they induced Mary to unite with them, thinking that through His love for her they might prevail upon Him to be more prudent.

It was just before this that Jesus had a second time performed the miracle of healing a man possessed, blind and dumb, and the Pharisees had reiterated the charge, "He casteth out devils through the prince of the devils." Matt. 9:34. Christ told them plainly that in attributing the [321-322] work of the Holy Spirit to Satan, they were cutting themselves off from the fountain of blessing. Those who had spoken against Jesus Himself, not discerning His divine character, might receive forgiveness; for through the Holy Spirit they might be brought to see their error and repent. Whatever the sin, if the soul repents and believes, the guilt is washed away in the blood of Christ; but he who rejects the work of the Holy Spirit is placing himself where repentance and faith cannot come to him. It is by the Spirit that God works upon the heart; when men willfully reject the

Spirit, and declare It to be from Satan, they cut off the channel by which God can communicate with them. When the Spirit is finally rejected, there is no more that God can do for the soul.

The Pharisees to whom Jesus spoke this warning did not themselves believe the charge they brought against Him. There was not one of those dignitaries but had felt drawn toward the Saviour. They had heard the Spirit's voice in their own hearts declaring Him to be the Anointed of Israel, and urging them to confess themselves His disciples. In the light of His presence they had realized their unholiness, and had longed for a righteousness which they could not create. But after their rejection of Him it would be too humiliating to receive Him as the Messiah. Having set their feet in the path of unbelief, they were too proud to confess their error. And in order to avoid acknowledging the truth, they tried with desperate violence to dispute the Saviour's teaching. The evidence of His power and mercy exasperated them. They could not prevent the Saviour from working miracles, they could not silence His teaching; but they did everything in their power to misrepresent Him and to falsify His words. Still the convicting Spirit of God followed them, and they had to build up many barriers in order to withstand its power. The mightiest agency that can be brought to bear upon the human heart was striving with them, but they would not yield.

It is not God that blinds the eyes of men or hardens their hearts. He sends them light to correct their errors, and to lead them in safe paths; it is by the rejection of this light that the eyes are blinded and the heart hardened. Often the process is gradual, and almost imperceptible. Light comes to the soul through God's word, through His servants, or by the direct agency of His Spirit; but when one ray of light is disregarded, there is a partial benumbing of the spiritual perceptions, and the second revealing of light is less clearly discerned. So the darkness increases, until it is night in the soul. Thus it had been with [322-323] these Jewish leaders. They were convinced that a divine power attended Christ, but in order to resist the truth, they attributed the work of the Holy Spirit to Satan. In doing this they deliberately chose deception; they yielded themselves to Satan, and henceforth they were controlled by his power.

Closely connected with Christ's warning in regard to the sin against the Holy Spirit is a warning against

3. "In the light of Jesus' presence, the Pharisees had realized their unholiness, and had l_____ for a righteousness which they could not create…Having set their feet in the path of u_____, they were too p_____ to confess their error." So close, and then to close the door? Just like Judas did at the footwashing. Are there times, Lord, that I am like that? _____
_____

4. The Pharisees "had to build up many b_____ in order to withstand its [H_____ S_____'s] power." That tells me, Lord, that I have to deliberately resist Your drawing power. Thank You for Your patience of my stubbornness. Are there barriers that I have put up in the past and forgotten about, but still withstand the power? Show me Lord:
_____
_____

5. What causes eyes to be blinded and hearts to be hardened? By gradual and imperceptible r_____ ___ of this light. "When o_____ ray of light is disregarded, there is a partial b_____ of the spiritual perceptions, and the second revealing of light is less c_____

discerned. So the d____ _____ increases, until it is night in the soul." Lord, may Your Spirit send warning alarms off at the moment of disregarding Your light. Because I do NOT want to benumb any spiritual perceptions. I want them more sensitive to the slightest whisper, nudge, glimmer: ____

_____

_____

6. "Words are more than indication of character [or of which is in the heart]; they have power to r_____ on the character. Men are i_____ by their own words…It is dangerous to utter a word of doubt, dangerous to question and criticize divine light. The habit of c_____ and irreverent criticism reacts upon the character, in fostering irreverence and unbelief." (323). Lord, to help me learn this truth; guide me to a negative example in my life, of this truth, and a positive one, so I may learn: _____

_____

_____

_____

7. "It is not only by resistance but by n_____ that the soul is destroyed…

idle and evil words. The words are an indication of that which is in the heart. "Out of the abundance of the heart the mouth speaketh." But the words are more than an indication of character; they have power to react on the character. Men are influenced by their own words. Often under a momentary impulse, prompted by Satan, they give utterance to jealousy or evil surmising, expressing that which they do not really believe; but the expression reacts on the thoughts. They are deceived by their words, and come to believe that true which was spoken at Satan's instigation. Having once expressed an opinion or decision, they are often too proud to retract it, and try to prove themselves in the right, until they come to believe that they are. It is dangerous to utter a word of doubt, dangerous to question and criticize divine light. The habit of careless and irreverent criticism reacts upon the character, in fostering irreverence and unbelief. Many a man indulging this habit has gone on unconscious of danger, until he was ready to criticize and reject the work of the Holy Spirit. Jesus said, "Every idle word that men shall speak, they shall give account thereof in the day of judgment. For by thy words thou shalt be justified, and by thy words thou shalt be condemned."

Then He added a warning to those who had been impressed by His words, who had heard Him gladly, but who had not surrendered themselves for the indwelling of the Holy Spirit. It is not only by resistance but by neglect that the soul is destroyed. "When the unclean spirit is gone out of a man," said Jesus, "he walketh through dry places, seeking rest, and findeth none. Then he saith, I will return into my house from whence I came out; and when he is come, he findeth it empty, swept, and garnished. Then goeth he, and taketh with himself seven other spirits more wicked than himself, and they enter in and dwell there."

There were many in Christ's day, as there are today, over whom the control of Satan for the time seemed broken; through the grace of God they were set free from the evil spirits that had held dominion over [323-324] the soul. They rejoiced in the love of God; but, like the stony-ground hearers of the parable, they did not abide in His love. They did not surrender themselves to God daily, that Christ might dwell in the heart; and when the evil spirit returned, with "seven other spirits more wicked than himself," they were wholly dominated by the power of evil.

When the soul surrenders itself to Christ, a new power takes possession of the new heart. A change is wrought which man can never accomplish for himself. It is a supernatural work, bringing a supernatural element into human nature. The soul that is yielded to Christ becomes His own fortress, which He holds in a revolted world, and He intends that no authority shall be known in it but His own. A soul thus kept in possession by the heavenly agencies is impregnable to the assaults of Satan. But unless we do yield ourselves to the control of Christ, we shall be dominated by the wicked one. We must inevitably be under the control of the one or the other of the two great powers that are contending for the supremacy of the world. It is not necessary for us deliberately to choose the service of the kingdom of darkness in order to come under its dominion. We have only to neglect to ally ourselves with the kingdom of light. If we do not co-operate with the heavenly agencies, Satan will take possession of the heart, and will make it his abiding place. The only defense against evil is the indwelling of Christ in the heart through faith in His righteousness. Unless we become vitally connected with God, we can never resist the unhallowed effects of self-love, self-indulgence, and temptation to sin. We may leave off many bad habits, for the time we may part company with Satan; but without a vital connection with God, through the surrender of ourselves to Him moment by moment, we shall be overcome. Without a personal acquaintance with Christ, and a continual communion, we are at the mercy of the enemy, and shall do his bidding in the end.

"The last state of that man is worse than the first. Even so," said Jesus, "shall it be also unto this wicked generation." There are none so hardened as those who have slighted the invitation of mercy, and done despite to the Spirit of grace. The most common manifestation of the sin against the Holy Spirit is in persistently slighting Heaven's invitation to repent. Every step in the rejection of Christ is a step toward the rejection of salvation, and toward the sin against the Holy Spirit.

In rejecting Christ the Jewish people committed the unpardonable sin; and by refusing the invitation of mercy, we may commit the same [324-325] error. We offer insult to the Prince of life, and put Him to shame before the synagogue of Satan and before the heavenly

It is not necessary for us deliberately to c_____ _____ the service of the kingdom of darkness in order to come under its domain. We have only to neglect to a_____ ourselves with the kingdom of light." (323, 324). What happens on the days that I don't intentionally ally myself in the morning?

_____
_____

8. "Without a v_____ connection with God, through the surrender of ourselves to Him m_____ by moment, we shall be o_____ ___." Does 'vital' mean a life-support kind of connection? _____ How do I accomplish that moment by moment? I can't be a monk all day. _____

_____
_____
_____ (Can I be like Enoch, educating my heart and mind to ever be in the presence of God?)
_____
_____
_____

universe when we refuse to listen to His delegated messengers, and instead listen to the agents of Satan, who would draw the soul away from Christ. So long as one does this, he can find no hope or pardon, and he will finally lose all desire to be reconciled to God.

While Jesus was still teaching the people, His disciples brought the message that His mother and His brothers were without, and desired to see Him. He knew what was in their hearts, and "He answered and said unto him that told Him, Who is My mother? and who are My brethren? And He stretched forth His hand toward His disciples, and said, Behold My mother and My brethren! For whosoever shall do the will of My Father which is in heaven, the same is My brother, and sister, and mother."

All who would receive Christ by faith were united to Him by a tie closer than that of human kinship. They would become one with Him, as He was one with the Father. As a believer and doer of His words, His mother was more nearly and savingly related to Him than through her natural relationship. His brothers would receive no benefit from their connection with Him unless they accepted Him as their personal Saviour.

What a support Christ would have found in His earthly relatives if they had believed in Him as one from heaven, and had co-operated with Him in doing the work of God! Their unbelief cast a shadow over the earthly life of Jesus. It was a part of the bitterness of that cup of woe which He drained for us. [325-326]

The enmity kindled in the human heart against the gospel was keenly felt by the Son of God, and it was most painful to Him in His home; for His own heart was full of kindness and love, and He appreciated tender regard in the family relation. His brothers desired that He should concede to their ideas, when such a course would have been utterly out of harmony with His divine mission. They looked upon Him as in need of their counsel. They judged Him from their human point of view, and thought that if He would speak only such things as would be acceptable to the scribes and Pharisees, He would avoid the disagreeable controversy that His words aroused. They thought that He was beside Himself in claiming divine authority, and in placing Himself before the rabbis as a reprover of their sins. They knew that the Pharisees were seeking occasion to accuse Him, and they felt that He had given them suf-

9. "All who would receive Christ by faith were united to Him, by a tie c_____ than that of human k___ _____. They would become one with Him, as He was one with the F_____." (325). Thank You, Jesus, for that wonderful privilege. What would help to make this more real? Every day? Moment by moment? _____

10. "The enmity kindled in the human heart against the gospel was k_____ felt by the Son of God, and it was most p_____ to Him in His home..."

ficient occasion.

With their short measuring line they could not fathom the mission which He came to fulfill, and therefore could not sympathize with Him in His trials. Their coarse, unappreciative words showed that they had no true perception of His character, and did not discern that the divine blended with the human. They often saw Him full of grief; but instead of comforting Him, their spirit and words only wounded His heart. His sensitive nature was tortured, His motives were misunderstood, His work was uncomprehended.

His brothers often brought forward the philosophy of the Pharisees, which was threadbare and hoary with age, and presumed to think that they could teach Him who understood all truth, and comprehended all mysteries. They freely condemned that which they could not understand. Their reproaches probed Him to the quick, and His soul was wearied and distressed. They avowed faith in God, and thought they were vindicating God, when God was with them in the flesh, and they knew Him not.

These things made His path a thorny one to travel. So pained was Christ by the misapprehension in His own home that it was a relief to Him to go where it did not exist. There was one home that He loved to visit,-- the home of Lazarus, and Mary, and Martha; for in the atmosphere of faith and love His spirit had rest. Yet there were none on earth who could comprehend His divine mission, or know the burden which He bore in behalf of humanity. Often He could find relief only in being alone, and communing with His heavenly Father. [326-327] Those who are called to suffer for Christ's sake, who have to endure misapprehension and distrust, even in their own home, may find comfort in the thought that Jesus has endured the same. He is moved with compassion for them. He bids them find companionship in Him, and relief where He found it, in communion with the Father.

Those who accept Christ as their personal Saviour are not left as orphans, to bear the trials of life alone. He receives them as members of the heavenly family; He bids them call His Father their Father. They are His "little ones," dear to the heart of God, bound to Him by the most tender and abiding ties. He has toward them an exceeding tenderness, as far surpassing what our father or mother has felt toward us in our helplessness as the

His sensitive nature was t_____, His motives were misunderstood, His work was uncomprehended...[In] the home of Lazarus, Mary and Martha... in this atmosphere of faith and l_____ His spirit had r_____." (326). What is the relationship between this 'torture' and that of the demon in proximity to Your purity, Lord? (Lu 8:28). And the cry of those begging the rocks to fall on them? (Rev 6:16). Lord, may You find rest, not torture, in my heart, in my home: _____

_____

_____

_____

11. Jesus bids me to find relief where He found it, "in c_____ with the F_____." Jesus bids me to call His Father my Father. I am "d_____ __ to the heart of God, bound to Him by the most t_____ and abiding ties." (327). Fantastic! Dear to the heart of God! Yes, Lord, I want that communion. Thank You for

that picture of You. May I claim the promise, even when I don't feel it: ____

_____

_____

_____

12. "If we do hold the relation of k_____ to Him, with what t____ _____ should we regard those who are brethren and s_____ of our Lord?" The kinship is vertical and horizontal. Others around me are also dear to God's heart. Lord, what are the claims of divine relationship?

_____

_____

_____

Prayer journal: _____

_____

_____

_____

_____

divine is above the human.

Of Christ's relation to His people, there is a beautiful illustration in the laws given to Israel. When through poverty a Hebrew had been forced to part with his patrimony, and to sell himself as a bondservant, the duty of redeeming him and his inheritance fell to the one who was nearest of kin. See Lev. 25:25, 47-49; Ruth 2:20. So the work of redeeming us and our inheritance, lost through sin, fell upon Him who is "near of kin" unto us. It was to redeem us that He became our kinsman. Closer than father, mother, brother, friend, or lover is the Lord our Saviour. "Fear not," He says, "for I have redeemed thee, I have called thee by thy name; thou art Mine." "Since thou wast precious in My sight, thou hast been honorable, and I have loved thee: therefore will I give men for thee, and people for thy life." Isa. 43:1, 4.

Christ loves the heavenly beings that surround His throne; but what shall account for the great love wherewith He has loved us? We cannot understand it, but we can know it true in our own experience. And if we do hold the relation of kinship to Him, with what tenderness should we regard those who are brethren and sisters of our Lord! Should we not be quick to recognize the claims of our divine relationship? Adopted into the family of God, should we not honor our Father and our kindred?

Chapter 34

The Invitation
[This chapter is based on Matt. 11:28-30.]

"Come unto Me, all ye that labor and are heavy-laden, and I will give you rest."

These words of comfort were spoken to the multitude that followed Jesus. The Saviour had said that only through Himself could men receive a knowledge of God. He had spoken of His disciples as the ones to whom a knowledge of heavenly things had been given. But He left none to feel themselves shut out from His care and love. All who labor and are heavy-laden may come unto Him.

Scribes and rabbis, with their punctilious attention to religious forms, had a sense of want that rites of penance could never satisfy. Publicans and sinners might pretend to be content with the sensual and earthly, but in their hearts were distrust and fear. Jesus looked upon the distressed and heart burdened, those whose hopes were blighted, and who with earthly joys were seeking to quiet the longing of the soul, and He invited all to find rest in Him.

Tenderly He bade the toiling people, "Take My yoke upon you, and learn of Me; for I am meek and lowly in heart: and ye shall find rest unto your souls."

In these words Christ is speaking to every human being. Whether they know it or not, all are weary and heavy-laden. All are weighed down with burdens that only Christ can remove. The heaviest burden that we bear is the burden of sin. If we were left to bear this burden, it [328-329] would crush us. But the Sinless One has taken our place. "The Lord hath laid on Him the iniquity of us all." Isa. 53:6. He has borne the burden of our guilt. He will take the load from our weary shoulders. He will give us rest. The burden of care and sorrow also He will bear. He invites us to cast all our care upon Him; for He carries us upon His heart.

The Elder Brother of our race is by the eternal throne. He looks upon every soul who is turning his face toward Him as the Saviour. He knows by experience what are the weaknesses of humanity, what are

1. "[Even the] Scribes and rabbis, with their punctilious attention to religious forms, had a sense of w_____ that rites of penance could never s_____...Jesus looked upon the distressed and heart burdened, those whose hopes were blighted, and who with e_____ joys were seeking to quiet the l_____ of the soul, and He invited all to find rest i_____ Him." In what ways Lord, do I seek to quiet the longing of the soul with earthly joys? _____

_____

_____

_____

2. Whether I know it or not, a_____ are weary and heavy-laden. "The heaviest burden that we bear is the burden of s_____. If we were left to bear this burden, it would c_____ us." Is this literal? _____

_____. What did Jesus feel as He was made my sin in the garden and on the cross? _____

_____

_____ How can I have a better comprehension of the strength sin has in my life? _____

_____

_____

3. "Are you wounded? He will h_____...."Come unto M_____," is His i_____." (329). I come as I am, bruised, broken, wounded. Thank You, Lord, that I have You to come to: _____

_____

_____

4. "The weaker and more helpless you know y_____ to be, the stronger will you become in H_____ strength. The heavier your burdens, the more b_____ the r_____ in casting them upon the Burden Bearer." Lord, help me realize how dependent I am on You, that I am nothing without You, that only IN You am I safe, satisfied, and strong. Let me taste of this blessed rest, in some small area, helping me to know what to do with the heavier burdens: _____

_____

_____

_____

5. "The yoke is an instrument of s_____ ...The yoke that binds to service is the l_____ of God. The great law of l_____ revealed in Eden, proclaimed upon Sinai, and in the new covenant written in the h_____, is that which binds the human worker to the will of G_____." Do I really

our wants, and where lies the strength of our temptations; for He was in all points tempted like as we are, yet without sin. He is watching over you, trembling child of God. Are you tempted? He will deliver. Are you weak? He will strengthen. Are you ignorant? He will enlighten. Are you wounded? He will heal. The Lord "telleth the number of the stars;" and yet "He healeth the broken in heart, and bindeth up their wounds." Ps. 147:4, 3. "Come unto Me," is His invitation. Whatever your anxieties and trials, spread out your case before the Lord. Your spirit will be braced for endurance. The way will be opened for you to disentangle yourself from embarrassment and difficulty. The weaker and more helpless you know yourself to be, the stronger will you become in His strength. The heavier your burdens, the more blessed the rest in casting them upon the Burden Bearer. The rest that Christ offers depends upon conditions, but these conditions are plainly specified. They are those with which all can comply. He tells us just how His rest is to be found.

"Take My yoke upon you," Jesus says. The yoke is an instrument of service. Cattle are yoked for labor, and the yoke is essential that they may labor effectually. By this illustration Christ teaches us that we are called to service as long as life shall last. We are to take upon us His yoke, that we may be co-workers with Him.

The yoke that binds to service is the law of God. The great law of love revealed in Eden, proclaimed upon Sinai, and in the new covenant written in the heart, is that which binds the human worker to the will of God. If we were left to follow our own inclinations, to go just where our will would lead us, we should fall into Satan's ranks and become possessors of his attributes. Therefore God confines us to His will, which is high, and noble, and elevating. He desires that we shall patiently and wisely take up the duties of service. The yoke of service Christ Himself has borne in humanity. He said, "I delight to do Thy will, O My God: yea, Thy law is within My heart."

Ps. 40:8. "I came down [329-330] from heaven, not to do Mine own will, but the will of Him that sent Me." John 6:38. Love for God, zeal for His glory, and love for fallen humanity, brought Jesus to earth to suffer and to die. This was the controlling power of His life. This principle He bids us adopt.

There are many whose hearts are aching under a load of care because they seek to reach the world's standard. They have chosen its service, accepted its perplexities, adopted its customs. Thus their character is marred, and their life made a weariness. In order to gratify ambition and worldly desires, they wound the conscience, and bring upon themselves an additional burden of remorse. The continual worry is wearing out the life forces. Our Lord desires them to lay aside this yoke of bondage. He invites them to accept His yoke; He says, "My yoke is easy, and My burden is light." He bids them seek first the kingdom of God and His righteousness, and His promise is that all things needful to them for this life shall be added. Worry is blind, and cannot discern the future; but Jesus sees the end from the beginning. In every difficulty He has His way prepared to bring relief. Our heavenly Father has a thousand ways to provide for us, of which we know nothing. Those who accept the one principle of making the service and honor of God supreme will find perplexities vanish, and a plain path before their feet.

want to be bound to the will of God? _____
_____How can I have this experience?
_____
_____

_____ May Your law of love, Lord, be in my heart, and stir me in service of others, a guiding yoke that helps me, in helping others. _____
_____
_____

6. "L_____ for God, zeal for His glory, and love for fallen h_____, brought Jesus to earth to suffer and to die. This was the c_____ power of His life. This principle He bids us to a_____." (330). What does 'controlling power' mean, Lord?
_____
_____
_____

7. "Worry is b_____, and cannot discern the future…Those who accept the one principle of making the s_____ and honor of God supreme will find perplexities v_____, and a plain path before their feet." All perplexities? By making God supreme? Including finances, marriage, pride, selfishness? _____. Why does that seem like a stretch?
_____

8. "Redemption is that process by which the soul is t_____ for heaven." What does this mean?

_____

_____

"Learn of Me," is a knowledge of Christ. So it's more than just coming to You, Lord? _____

_____

_____ Deliver me from that which hinders this training, Lord. Show me how to let them go: _____

_____

_____

9. "It is the love of s_____ that brings unrest...The yoke is placed upon the oxen to aid them in drawing the load, to l_____ __ the burden...When our will is s_____ up in the will of God, and we use His gifts to bless others, we shall find life's burden light." (330, 331). Lord, I want Your yoke, not the burden of self-love. I surrender my will. Sit on the throne of my will, my heart. Alert me when I am taking it back: _____

_____

"Learn of Me," says Jesus; "for I am meek and lowly in heart: and ye shall find rest." We are to enter the school of Christ, to learn from Him meekness and lowliness. Redemption is that process by which the soul is trained for heaven. This training means a knowledge of Christ. It means emancipation from ideas, habits, and practices that have been gained in the school of the prince of darkness. The soul must be delivered from all that is opposed to loyalty to God.

In the heart of Christ, where reigned perfect harmony with God, there was perfect peace. He was never elated by applause, nor dejected by censure or disappointment. Amid the greatest opposition and the most cruel treatment, He was still of good courage. But many who profess to be His followers have an anxious, troubled heart, because they are afraid to trust themselves with God. They do not make a complete surrender to Him; for they shrink from the consequences that such a surrender may involve. Unless they do make this surrender, they cannot find peace.

It is the love of self that brings unrest. When we are born from above, the same mind will be in us that was in Jesus, the mind that led [330-331] Him to humble Himself that we might be saved. Then we shall not be seeking the highest place. We shall desire to sit at the feet of Jesus, and learn of Him. We shall understand that the value of our work does not consist in making a show and noise in the world, and in being active and zealous in our own strength. The value of our work is in proportion to the impartation of the Holy Spirit. Trust in God brings holier qualities of mind, so that in patience we may possess our souls.

The yoke is placed upon the oxen to aid them in drawing the load, to lighten the burden. So with the yoke of Christ. When our will is swallowed up in the will of God, and we use His gifts to bless others, we shall find life's burden light. He who walks in the way of God's commandments is walking in company with Christ, and in His love the heart is at rest. When Moses prayed, "Show me now Thy way, that I may know Thee," the Lord answered him, "My presence shall go with thee, and I will give thee rest." And through the prophets the message was given, "Thus saith the Lord, Stand ye in the ways, and see, and ask for the old paths, where is the good way, and walk therein, and ye shall find rest for your souls." Ex. 33:13, 14; Jer. 6:16. And He says, "O that thou hadst hearkened to My commandments! then had thy peace been as a river, and thy righteousness as the waves of the sea." Isa. 48:18.

Those who take Christ at His word, and surrender their souls to His keeping, their lives to His ordering, will find peace and quietude. Nothing of the world can make them sad when Jesus makes them glad by His presence. In perfect acquiescence there is perfect rest. The Lord says, "Thou wilt keep him in perfect peace, whose mind is stayed on Thee: because he trusteth in Thee." Isa. 26:3. Our lives may seem a tangle; but as we commit ourselves to the wise Master Worker, He will bring out the pattern of life and character that will be to His own glory. And that character which expresses the glory--character--of Christ will be received into the Paradise of God. A renovated race shall walk with Him in white, for they are worthy.

As through Jesus we enter into rest, heaven begins here. We respond to His invitation, Come, learn of Me, and in thus coming we begin the life eternal. Heaven is a ceaseless approaching to God through Christ. The longer we are in the heaven of bliss, the more and still more of glory will be opened to us; and the more we know of God, the more intense will be our happiness. As we walk with Jesus in this life, we may be filled with His love, satisfied with His presence. All that human [331-332] nature can bear, we may receive here. But what is this compared with the hereafter? There "are they before the throne of God, and serve Him day and night in His temple: and He that sitteth on the throne shall dwell among them. They shall hunger no more, neither thirst any more; neither shall the sun light on them, nor any heat. For the Lamb which is in the midst of the throne shall feed them, and shall lead them unto living fountains of waters: and God shall wipe away all tears from their eyes." Rev. 7:15-17.

10. "Nothing of the world can make them s_____ when Jesus makes them g_____ by His p_____. In perfect acquiescence there is perfect r_____." Teach me how to be in Your presence all day, in all circumstances. Teach me the gladness and value of Your presence. Teach me perfect acquiescence. I never want to be separated from Your presence: _____

_____
_____
_____
_____

11. "As through Jesus we enter into rest, h_____ begins h_____. We respond to His invitation, Come, learn of Me, and in thus coming we begin the life e_____. Heaven is a c_____ approaching to God through Christ." Lord, I want that heaven of bliss now, and every day. May I never cease in my desire of approaching You:

_____
_____

Prayer journal: _____

_____
_____
_____
_____
_____

Chapter 35

"Peace, Be Still"

[This chapter is based on Matt. 8:23-34;
Mark 4:35-41; 5:1-20; Luke 8:22-39.]

It had been an eventful day in the life of Jesus. Beside the Sea of Galilee He had spoken His first parables, by familiar illustrations again explaining to the people the nature of His kingdom and the manner in which it was to be established. He had likened His own work to that of the sower; the development of His kingdom to the growth of the mustard seed and the effect of leaven in the measure of meal. The great final separation of the righteous and the wicked He had pictured in the parables of the wheat and tares and the fishing net. The exceeding preciousness of the truths He taught had been illustrated by the hidden treasure and the pearl of great price, while in the parable of the householder He taught His disciples how they were to labor as His representatives.

All day He had been teaching and healing; and as evening came on the crowds still pressed upon Him. Day after day He had ministered to them, scarcely pausing for food or rest. The malicious criticism and misrepresentation with which the Pharisees constantly pursued Him made His labors much more severe and harassing; and now the close of the day found Him so utterly wearied that He determined to seek retirement in some solitary place across the lake.

The eastern shore of Gennesaret was not uninhabited, for there were towns here and there beside the lake; yet it was a desolate region when [333-334] compared with the western side. It contained a population more heathen than Jewish, and had little communication with Galilee. Thus it offered Jesus the seclusion He sought, and He now bade His disciples accompany Him thither.

After He had dismissed the multitude, they took Him, even "as He was," into the boat, and hastily set off. But they were not to depart alone. There were other fishing boats lying near the shore, and these were quickly crowded with people who followed Jesus, eager still

1. "Day after day, Jesus had ministered, scarcely pausing for food or r_____. The malicious criticism and m_____ with which the Pharisees constantly pursued Him made His labors much more s_____ and h_____."
Jesus was so u_____ wearied. He needed rest. Lord, may I be sensitive to how You feel, with all of the demands, expectations, and being blamed. How do I sometimes add to Your hurt? _____
_____
_____

to see and hear Him.

The Saviour was at last relieved from the pressure of the multitude, and, overcome with weariness and hunger, He lay down in the stern of the boat, and soon fell asleep. The evening had been calm and pleasant, and quiet rested upon the lake; but suddenly darkness overspread the sky, the wind swept wildly down the mountain gorges along the eastern shore, and a fierce tempest burst upon the lake.

The sun had set, and the blackness of night settled down upon the stormy sea. The waves, lashed into fury by the howling winds, dashed fiercely over the disciples' boat, and threatened to engulf it. Those hardy fishermen had spent their lives upon the lake, and had guided their craft safely through many a storm; but now their strength and skill availed nothing. They were helpless in the grasp of the tempest, and hope failed them as they saw that their boat was filling.

Absorbed in their efforts to save themselves, they had forgotten that Jesus was on board. Now, seeing their labor vain and only death before them, they remembered at whose command they had set out to cross the sea. In Jesus was their only hope. In their helplessness and despair they cried, "Master, Master!" But the dense darkness hid Him from their sight. Their voices were drowned by the roaring of the tempest, and there was no reply. Doubt and fear assailed them. Had Jesus forsaken them? Was He who had conquered disease and demons, and even death, powerless to help His disciples now? Was He unmindful of them in their distress?

Again they call, but there is no answer except the shrieking of the angry blast. Already their boat is sinking. A moment, and apparently they will be swallowed up by the hungry waters.

Suddenly a flash of lightning pierces the darkness, and they see Jesus lying asleep, undisturbed by the tumult. In amazement and despair they exclaim, "Master, carest Thou not that we perish?" How can He rest so peacefully, while they are in danger and battling with death? [334-335]

Their cry arouses Jesus. As the lightning's glare reveals Him, they see the peace of heaven in His face; they read in His glance self-forgetful, tender love, and, their hearts turning to Him, cry, "Lord, save us: we perish."

Never did a soul utter that cry unheeded. As the dis-

2. "Those h_____ fisherman had spent their lives upon the lake, and had guided their craft s_____ through many a storm; but now their s_____ and skill availed n_____. They were h_____ in the grasp of the tempest, and h____ failed them." (334). In the storms of my life, where is my reliance? _____

_____. Are there things I recognize that I cannot handle? _____

3. As the lightning's glare pierces the darkness of the storm and reveals Jesus, the disciples "see the p_____ of h_____ in His face; they read in His glance self-f_____, tender l_____, and, their hearts turning to Him, cry, "Lord, save us: we p_____." (335). What gave Jesus His serenity? _____

What is self-forgetful love and how do I get it?

4. "Never did a soul utter that cry unheeded."

What cry? _____

_____

_____ How completely /
thoroughly have I uttered
that cry? To what degree do
I understand what I am saying? _____

_____

_____

5. "'Peace be still'...A
h_____ fell upon
the disciples. Even Peter
did not attempt to express
the a_____ that filled his
heart." Do I stop ('be still')
and meditate on His power
to declare "Peace"? Have
I sat in awe, struck by His
matchless character? May-
be I'm too busy. Evidence
of God's availability is
there each day, and I'm not
recognizing it. God wants
to offer peace that is out
of this world, and I keep
rowing and bailing. Why,
Lord? _____

_____

_____

ciples grasp their oars to make a last effort, Jesus rises.
He stands in the midst of His disciples, while the tempest rages, the waves break over them, and the lightning
illuminates His countenance. He lifts His hand, so often
employed in deeds of mercy, and says to the angry sea,
"Peace, be still."

The storm ceases. The billows sink to rest. The
clouds roll away, and the stars shine forth. The boat
rests upon a quiet sea. Then turning to His disciples,
Jesus asks sorrowfully, "Why are ye fearful? have ye
not yet faith?" Mark 4:40, R.V.

A hush fell upon the disciples. Even Peter did not
attempt to express the awe that filled his heart. The
boats that had set out to accompany Jesus had been in
the same peril with that of the disciples. Terror and despair had seized their occupants; but the command of
Jesus brought quiet to the scene of tumult. The fury of
the storm had driven the boats into close proximity, and
all on board beheld the miracle. In the calm that followed, fear was forgotten. The people whispered among
themselves, "What manner of man is this, that even the
winds and the sea obey Him?" [335-336]

When Jesus was awakened to meet the storm, He
was in perfect peace. There was no trace of fear in word
or look, for no fear was in His heart. But He rested not
in the possession of almighty power. It was not as the
"Master of earth and sea and sky" that He reposed in
quiet. That power He had laid down, and He says, "I
can of Mine own self do nothing." John 5:30. He trusted
in the Father's might. It was in faith--faith in God's love
and care--that Jesus rested, and the power of that word
which stilled the storm was the power of God.

As Jesus rested by faith in the Father's care, so we
are to rest in the care of our Saviour. If the disciples had
trusted in Him, they would have been kept in peace.
Their fear in the time of danger revealed their unbelief.
In their efforts to save themselves, they forgot Jesus;
and it was only when, in despair of self-dependence,
they turned to Him that He could give them help.

How often the disciples' experience is ours! When
the tempests of temptation gather, and the fierce lightnings flash, and the waves sweep over us, we battle with
the storm alone, forgetting that there is One who can
help us. We trust to our own strength till our hope is
lost, and we are ready to perish. Then we remember Jesus, and if we call upon Him to save us, we shall not cry

in vain. Though He sorrowfully reproves our unbelief and self-confidence, He never fails to give us the help we need. Whether on the land or on the sea, if we have the Saviour in our hearts, there is no need of fear. Living faith in the Redeemer will smooth the sea of life, and will deliver us from danger in the way that He knows to be best.

There is another spiritual lesson in this miracle of the stilling of the tempest. Every man's experience testifies to the truth of the words of Scripture, "The wicked are like the troubled sea, when it cannot rest. . . . There is no peace, saith my God, to the wicked." Isa. 57:20, 21. Sin has destroyed our peace. While self is unsubdued, we can find no rest. The masterful passions of the heart no human power can control. We are as helpless here as were the disciples to quiet the raging storm. But He who spoke peace to the billows of Galilee has spoken the word of peace for every soul. However fierce the tempest, those who turn to Jesus with the cry, "Lord, save us," will find deliverance. His grace, that reconciles the soul to God, quiets the strife of human passion, and in His love the heart is at rest. "He maketh the storm a calm, so that the waves thereof are still. Then are they glad because they be quiet; [336-337] so He bringeth them unto their desired haven." Ps. 107:29, 30. "Being justified by faith, we have peace with God through our Lord Jesus Christ." "The work of righteousness shall be peace; and the effect of righteousness quietness and assurance forever." Rom. 5:1; Isa. 32:17.

In the early morning the Saviour and His companions came to shore, and the light of the rising sun touched sea and land as with the benediction of peace. But no sooner had they stepped upon the beach than their eyes were greeted by a sight more terrible than the fury of the tempest. From some hiding place among the tombs, two madmen rushed upon them as if to tear them in pieces. Hanging about these men were parts of chains which they had broken in escaping from confinement. Their flesh was torn and bleeding where they had cut themselves with sharp stones. Their eyes glared out from their long and matted hair, the very likeness of humanity seemed to have been blotted out by the demons that possessed them, and they looked more like wild beasts than like men.

The disciples and their companions fled in terror; but presently they noticed that Jesus was not with them,

6. Though Jesus "sorrowfully reproves our unbelief and self-c_____, He never fails to give us the h_____ we need." (336). Thank You, Lord, for your patient understanding. How may I presume it? _____ _____ _____

7. "He who spoke peace to the b_____ of Galilee has spoken the word of peace for every s_____. However f_____ the tempest, those who turn to Jesus with the cry, "Lord, Save us," will find d_____." It is no less a miracle; the same power is involved. This is a promise I can claim! Why don't I? _____ _____ _____ _____

8. In the early morning, they reach shore and are greeted by a sight more t_____ than the fury of the tempest. The disciples fled in terror, but presently noticed that Jesus was not with them, and they turned to look for Him.

"He was standing where they had l_____ Him." (337). Lord, what are the situations where I leave You behind? _____
_____
_____
_____

9. "A marvelous change had come over the demoniacs. Light had shone in their m_____. Their eyes beamed with i_____. The countenances, so long deformed into the image of Satan, became suddenly m_____, the blood-stained hands were q_____, and with glad voices the men p_____ _____ God for their deliverance." (338). What a transformation! Lord, the changes You're bringing into my life. do they show in my eyes? My countenance? _____
_____

10. "The two demoniacs had been the t_____ of the country…Now these men were clothed and in their r_____ mind, sitting at the f_____ of Jesus." Where is it that it all comes together for me; my priorities, values, meaning? _____
_____

and they turned to look for Him. He was standing where they had left Him. He who had stilled the tempest, who had before met Satan and conquered him, did not flee before these demons. When the men, gnashing their teeth, and foaming at the mouth, approached Him, Jesus raised that hand which had beckoned the waves to rest, and the men could come no nearer. They stood raging but helpless before Him.

With authority He bade the unclean spirits come out of them. His words penetrated the darkened minds of the unfortunate men. They [337-338] realized dimly that One was near who could save them from the tormenting demons. They fell at the Saviour's feet to worship Him; but when their lips were opened to entreat His mercy, the demons spoke through them, crying vehemently, "What have I to do with Thee, Jesus, Thou Son of God most high? I beseech Thee, torment me not."

Jesus asked, "What is thy name?" And the answer was, "My name is Legion: for we are many." Using the afflicted men as mediums of communication, they besought Jesus not to send them out of the country. Upon a mountainside not far distant a great herd of swine was feeding. Into these the demons asked to be allowed to enter, and Jesus suffered them. Immediately a panic seized the herd. They rushed madly down the cliff, and, unable to check themselves upon the shore, plunged into the lake, and perished.

Meanwhile a marvelous change had come over the demoniacs. Light had shone into their minds. Their eyes beamed with intelligence. The countenances, so long deformed into the image of Satan, became suddenly mild, the bloodstained hands were quiet, and with glad voices the men praised God for their deliverance.

From the cliff the keepers of the swine had seen all that had occurred, and they hurried away to publish the news to their employers and to all the people. In fear and amazement the whole population flocked to meet Jesus. The two demoniacs had been the terror of the country. No one had been safe to pass the place where they were; for they would rush upon every traveler with the fury of demons. Now these men were clothed and in their right mind, sitting at the feet of Jesus, listening to His words, and glorifying the name of Him who had made them whole. But the people who beheld this wonderful scene did not rejoice. The loss of the swine seemed to them of greater moment than the deliverance of these captives of Satan.

It was in mercy to the owners of the swine that this loss had been permitted to come upon them. They were absorbed in earthly things, and cared not for the great interests of spiritual life. Jesus desired to break the spell of selfish indifference, that they might accept His grace. [338-339] But regret and indignation for their temporal loss blinded their eyes to the Saviour's mercy.

The manifestation of supernatural power aroused the superstitions of the people, and excited their fears. Further calamities might follow from having this Stranger among them. They apprehended financial ruin, and determined to be freed from His presence. Those who had crossed the lake with Jesus told of all that had happened on the preceding night, of their peril in the tempest, and how the wind and the sea had been stilled. But their words were without effect. In terror the people thronged about Jesus, beseeching Him to depart from them, and He complied, taking ship at once for the opposite shore.

The people of Gergesa had before them the living evidence of Christ's power and mercy. They saw the men who had been restored to reason; but they were so fearful of endangering their earthly interests that He who had vanquished the prince of darkness before their eyes was treated as an intruder, and the Gift of heaven was turned from their doors. We have not the opportunity of turning from the person of Christ as had the Gergesenes; but still there are many who refuse to obey His word, because obedience would involve the sacrifice of some worldly interest. Lest His presence shall cause them pecuniary loss, many reject His grace, and drive His Spirit from them.

But far different was the feeling of the restored demoniacs. They desired the company of their deliverer. In His presence they felt secure from the demons that had tormented their lives and wasted their manhood. As Jesus was about to enter the boat, they kept close to His side, knelt at His feet, and begged Him to keep them near Him, where they might ever listen to His words. But Jesus bade them go home and tell what great things the Lord had done for them.

Here was a work for them to do,--to go to a heathen home, and tell of the blessing they had received from Jesus. It was hard for them to be separated from the Saviour. Great difficulties were sure to beset them in as-

11. "The manifestation of supernatural power aroused the s_____ _____ of the people, and excited their f_____. Further calamities might follow from having this Stranger a_____ them. They apprehended financial ruin, and determined to be f_____ from His p_____." (339). Sounds similar to the reaction of the wicked at the second coming. What about my reaction, now. Do I ever want to be freed from Your presence, Lord? I certainly hope not. How about when prayer time is kept at a minimum? _____ _____ _____ _____

12. "In doing this work [of telling what great things the Lord had done for them], they [the demoniacs] could receive a g_____ blessing than if, merely for benefit to them-_____, they had remained in His presence. It is in working to spread the good news of salvation that we are brought n_____ to the Savior." (339, 340). Lord, I need to be challenged in reaching out and telling others. Thank You for the understanding that though not in Your physical presence, I can be brought near to You, through spreading the good news:

_____

_____

_____

13. "As witnesses for Christ, we are to tell what we k_____, what we ourselves have s_____ and h_____ and f____ …This is the witness for which our Lord calls, and for w_____ of which the world is p_____." Like John disciples, like the two demoniacs, You want us to share what we've seen You do in our lives. Let me remember: _____

_____

_____

_____

sociation with their heathen countrymen. And their long isolation from society seemed to have disqualified them for the work He had indicated. But as soon as Jesus pointed out their duty they were ready to obey. Not only did they tell their own households and neighbors about Jesus, but they went throughout Decapolis, everywhere declaring His power to save, and describing how He had freed them from the demons. In doing this work they could receive a greater [339-340] blessing than if, merely for benefit to themselves, they had remained in His presence. It is in working to spread the good news of salvation that we are brought near to the Saviour.

The two restored demoniacs were the first missionaries whom Christ sent to preach the gospel in the region of Decapolis. For a few moments only these men had been privileged to hear the teachings of Christ. Not one sermon from His lips had ever fallen upon their ears. They could not instruct the people as the disciples who had been daily with Christ were able to do. But they bore in their own persons the evidence that Jesus was the Messiah. They could tell what they knew; what they themselves had seen, and heard, and felt of the power of Christ. This is what everyone can do whose heart has been touched by the grace of God. John, the beloved disciple, wrote: "That which was from the beginning, which we have heard, which we have seen with our eyes, which we have looked upon, and our hands have handled, of the Word of life; . . . that which we have seen and heard declare we unto you." 1 John 1:1-3. As witnesses for Christ, we are to tell what we know, what we ourselves have seen and heard and felt. If we have been following Jesus step by step, we shall have something right to the point to tell concerning the way in which He has led us. We can tell how we have tested His promise, and found the promise true. We can bear witness to what we have known of the grace of Christ. This is the witness for which our Lord calls, and for want of which the world is perishing.

Though the people of Gergesa had not received Jesus, He did not leave them to the darkness they had chosen. When they bade Him depart from them, they had not heard His words. They were ignorant of that which they were rejecting. Therefore He again sent the light to them, and by those to whom they would not refuse to listen.

In causing the destruction of the swine, it was Satan's purpose to turn the people away from the Saviour, and prevent the preaching of the gospel in that region. But this very occurrence roused the whole country as nothing else could have done, and directed attention to Christ. Though the Saviour Himself departed, the men whom He had healed remained as witnesses to His power. Those who had been mediums of the prince of darkness became channels of light, messengers of the Son of God. Men marveled as they listened to the wondrous news. A door was opened to the gospel throughout that region. When Jesus returned to Decapolis, the people flocked about Him, and for three [340-341] days, not merely the inhabitants of one town, but thousands from all the surrounding region, heard the message of salvation. Even the power of demons is under the control of our Saviour, and the working of evil is overruled for good.

The encounter with the demoniacs of Gergesa had a lesson for the disciples. It showed the depths of degradation to which Satan is seeking to drag the whole human race, and the mission of Christ to set men free from his power. Those wretched beings, dwelling in the place of graves, possessed by demons, in bondage to uncontrolled passions and loathsome lusts, represent what humanity would become if given up to satanic jurisdiction. Satan's influence is constantly exerted upon men to distract the senses, control the mind for evil, and incite to violence and crime. He weakens the body, darkens the intellect, and debases the soul. Whenever men reject the Saviour's invitation, they are yielding themselves to Satan. Multitudes in every department in life, in the home, in business, and even in the church, are doing this today. It is because of this that violence and crime have overspread the earth, and moral darkness, like the pall of death, enshrouds the habitations of men. Through his specious temptations Satan leads men to worse and worse evils, till utter depravity and ruin are the result. The only safeguard against his power is found in the presence of Jesus. Before men and angels Satan has been revealed as man's enemy and destroyer; Christ, as man's friend and deliverer. His Spirit will develop in man all that will ennoble the character and dignify the nature. It will build man up for the glory of God in body and soul and spirit. "For God hath not given us the spirit of fear; but of power, and of love, and of a sound mind." 2 Tim. 1:7. He has called us "to the

14. "Whenever men reject the Savior's invitation, they are y_____ themselves to Satan. Multitudes in every department in life, in the home, in business, and even in the c_____, are doing this today…The only s_____ against his [Satan's] power is found in the p_____ of Jesus." (341). Lord, help me not to be complacent, thinking that since I don't foam at the mouth, I'm clear of Satan's agenda. I need and I want to continually be in Your presence, like Enoch was: ____

——————————————
——————————————
——————————————

Prayer journal: _____

_____

_____

_____

_____

_____

_____

_____

obtaining of the glory"--character--"of our Lord Jesus Christ;" has called us to be "conformed to the image of His Son." 2 Thess. 2:14; Rom. 8:29.

And souls that have been degraded into instruments of Satan are still through the power of Christ transformed into messengers of righteousness, and sent forth by the Son of God to tell what "great things the Lord hath done for thee, and hath had compassion on thee."

Chapter 36

The Touch of Faith

[This chapter is based on Matt. 9:18-26;
Mark 5:21-43; Luke 8:40-56.]

Returning from Gergesa to the western shore, Jesus found a multitude gathered to receive Him, and they greeted Him with joy. He remained by the seaside for a time, teaching and healing, and then repaired to the house of Levi-Matthew to meet the publicans at the feast. Here Jairus, the ruler of the synagogue, found Him.

This elder of the Jews came to Jesus in great distress, and cast himself at His feet, exclaiming, "My little daughter lieth at the point of death: I pray Thee, come and lay Thy hands on her, that she may be healed; and she shall live."

Jesus set out at once with the ruler for his home. Though the disciples had seen so many of His works of mercy, they were surprised at His compliance with the entreaty of the haughty rabbi; yet they accompanied their Master, and the people followed, eager and expectant.

The ruler's house was not far distant, but Jesus and His companions advanced slowly, for the crowd pressed Him on every side. The anxious father was impatient of delay; but Jesus, pitying the people, stopped now and then to relieve some suffering one, or to comfort a troubled heart.

While they were still on the way, a messenger pressed through the crowd, bearing to Jairus the news that his daughter was dead, and it was useless to trouble the Master further. The word caught the ear of [342-343] Jesus. "Fear not," He said; "believe only, and she shall be made whole."

Jairus pressed closer to the Saviour, and together they hurried to the ruler's home. Already the hired mourners and flute players were there, filling the air with their clamor. The presence of the crowd, and the tumult jarred upon the spirit of Jesus. He tried to silence them, saying, "Why make ye this ado, and weep? the

1. As Jesus, Jairus, and the crowd slowly advanced, a messenger came with the news that his "daughter was dead, and it was u_____ to trouble the Master further." How might Satan use that line on me? _____

———————————————

———————————————

By putting doubts in my head about being spiritually dead; that it is useless to pray, God won't hear me anyway; why trouble God with my problems? _____

———————————————

———————————————

———————————————

2. "Fear not," Jesus said, "b_____ only,

and she shall be made whole...Why make ye this a_____, and weep? The damsel is not dead, but s_____." Hired m_____ and the flute players were indignant, and laughed Him to scorn. (343). Jesus deals in a reality behind the obvious facts. God accomplishes the impossible, the unimaginable. I have to step back, get out of the way, and marvel at God's work. There's an impossible spiritual death of mine on which God does the miraculous quite regularly. Thank You, Lord! _____

_____

_____

3. A woman, suffering for t_____ years and all her m_____ spent on physicians and remedies, tried to get to Jesus at the seaside, and again at Levi-Matthew's house, but was unable both tries, and "she had begun to d_____." Lord, are there things I do, or the church does, that makes it difficult for someone to reach You? _____

_____

_____ (too busy; too program oriented, and not people oriented; not sensitive to providing a safe atmosphere for personal needs / shortcomings).

damsel is not dead, but sleepeth." They were indignant at the words of the Stranger. They had seen the child in the embrace of death, and they laughed Him to scorn. Requiring them all to leave the house, Jesus took with Him the father and mother of the maiden, and the three disciples, Peter, James, and John, and together they entered the chamber of death.

Jesus approached the bedside, and, taking the child's hand in His own, He pronounced softly, in the familiar language of her home, the words, "Damsel, I say unto thee, arise."

Instantly a tremor passed through the unconscious form. The pulses of life beat again. The lips unclosed with a smile. The eyes opened widely as if from sleep, and the maiden gazed with wonder on the group beside her. She arose, and her parents clasped her in their arms, and wept for joy.

On the way to the ruler's house, Jesus had met, in the crowd, a poor woman who for twelve years had suffered from a disease that made her life a burden. She had spent all her means upon physicians and remedies, only to be pronounced incurable. But her hopes revived when she heard of the cures that Christ performed. She felt assured that if she could only go to Him she would be healed. In weakness and suffering she came to the seaside where He was teaching, and tried to press through the crowd, but in vain. Again she followed Him from the house of Levi-Matthew, but was still unable to reach Him. She had begun to despair, when, in making His way through the multitude, He came near where she was.

The golden opportunity had come. She was in the presence of the Great Physician! But amid the confusion she could not speak to Him, nor catch more than a passing glimpse of His figure. Fearful of losing her one chance of relief, she pressed forward, saying to herself, "If I may but touch His garment, I shall be whole." As He was passing, she reached forward, and succeeded in barely touching the border of His garment. But in that moment she knew that she was healed. In that one touch she was concentrated the faith of her life, and instantly her pain and feebleness gave place to the vigor of perfect health. [343-344] With a grateful heart she then tried to withdraw from the crowd; but suddenly Jesus stopped, and the people halted with Him. He turned, and looking about asked in a voice distinctly heard above the confusion of the multitude, "Who touched Me?" The people answered this query with a look of amazement. Jostled upon all sides, and rudely pressed hither and thither, as He was, it seemed a strange inquiry.

Peter, ever ready to speak, said, "Master, the multitude throng Thee and press Thee, and sayest Thou, Who touched Me?" Jesus answered, "Somebody hath touched Me: for I perceive that virtue is gone out of Me." The Saviour could distinguish the touch of faith from the casual contact of the careless throng. Such trust should not be passed without comment. He would speak to the humble woman words of comfort that would be to her a wellspring of joy,--words that would be a blessing to His followers to the close of time.

Looking toward the woman, Jesus insisted on knowing who had touched Him. Finding concealment vain, she came forward tremblingly, [344-347] and cast herself at His feet. With grateful tears she told the story of her suffering, and how she had found relief. Jesus gently said, "Daughter, be of good comfort: thy faith hath made thee whole; go in peace." He gave no opportunity for superstition to claim healing virtue for the mere act of touching His garments. It was not through the outward contact with Him, but through the faith which took hold on His divine power, that the cure was wrought.

The wondering crowd that pressed close about Christ realized no accession of vital power. But when the suffering woman put forth her hand to touch Him, believing that she would be made whole, she felt the healing virtue. So in spiritual things. To talk of religion in a casual way, to pray without soul hunger and living faith, avails nothing. A nominal faith in Christ, which accepts Him merely as the Saviour of the world, can never bring healing to the soul. The faith that is unto salvation is not a mere intellectual assent to the truth. He who waits for entire knowledge before he will exercise faith, cannot receive blessing from God. It is not enough to believe about Christ; we must believe in Him. The only faith that will benefit us is that which embraces Him as a personal Saviour; which appropriates His merits to ourselves. Many hold faith as an opinion. Saving faith is a transaction by which those who receive Christ join themselves in covenant relation with God. Genuine faith is life. A living faith means an increase of vigor, a confiding trust, by which the soul becomes a

4. "In making His way through the multitude He came n_____ where she was. The g_____ opportunity had come. She was in the presence of the Great P_____!" Are there opportunities I miss, Lord? You are near, Your Spirit is whispering, and I don't sense the opportunity? _____

_____

_____

Thank You for being near, and help me to be better tuned in: _____

_____

5. "The Savior could distinguish the touch of f_____ from the c_____ contact of the careless throng." (344). On reflection, Lord, is my devotion time with You a casual touch or a touch of faith? On a scale of one to ten, one being a casual "contact" and ten being a "touch of faith," where do You think my devotion time is, Lord? _____ What do I need to do to nudge it to a ten? _

_____

_____

6. "Many hold faith as an opinion [believe about Christ]. Saving faith is a t_____ by which those who receive Christ j_____ themselves in c_____ relation with God. Genuine faith

is l_____. A living faith means an increase of vigor, a c_____ trust." (347). A covenant relationship with You sounds good. In faith, I join You, trust You to always know what is best for me; I want my life (my faith) to depend on You. What do I normally depend on?: _____
_____

7. "Our confession of His f_____ is heaven's c_____ agency for r_____ Christ to the world…These precious acknowledgments to the praise of the glory of His grace, when supported by a Christ-like l_____, have an i_____ power that works for the salvation of souls." Lord, help my paths to cross someone else's, so I may confess Your grace to them. May I have been in Your grace that day, and every day, so I have a testimony of Your new and fresh (daily) compassions: _____
_____
_____
_____

8. "It is for our own benefit to keep every gift of God f_____ in our memory. Thus faith is s_____ to claim and to receive more and more. There is great-

conquering power.

After healing the woman, Jesus desired her to acknowledge the blessing she had received. The gifts which the gospel offers are not to be secured by stealth or enjoyed in secret. So the Lord calls upon us for confession of His goodness. "Ye are My witnesses, saith the Lord, that I am God." Isa. 43:12.

Our confession of His faithfulness is Heaven's chosen agency for revealing Christ to the world. We are to acknowledge His grace as made known through the holy men of old; but that which will be most effectual is the testimony of our own experience. We are witnesses for God as we reveal in ourselves the working of a power that is divine. Every individual has a life distinct from all others, and an experience differing essentially from theirs. God desires that our praise shall ascend to Him, marked by our own individuality. These precious acknowledgments to the praise of the glory of His grace, when supported by a Christ-like life, have an irresistible power that works for the salvation of souls. [347-348]

When the ten lepers came to Jesus for healing, He bade them go and show themselves to the priest. On the way they were cleansed, but only one of them returned to give Him glory. The others went their way, forgetting Him who had made them whole. How many are still doing the same thing! The Lord works continually to benefit mankind. He is ever imparting His bounties. He raises up the sick from beds of languishing, He delivers men from peril which they do not see, He commissions heavenly angels to save them from calamity, to guard them from "the pestilence that walketh in darkness" and "the destruction that wasteth at noonday" (Ps. 91:6); but their hearts are unimpressed. He has given all the riches of heaven to redeem them, and yet they are unmindful of His great love. By their ingratitude they close their hearts against the grace of God. Like the heath in the desert they know not when good cometh, and their souls inhabit the parched places of the wilderness.

It is for our own benefit to keep every gift of God fresh in our memory. Thus faith is strengthened to claim and to receive more and more. There is greater encouragement for us in the least blessing we ourselves receive from God than in all the accounts we can read of the faith and experience of others. The soul that responds to the grace of God shall be like a watered garden. His health shall spring forth speedily; his light shall rise in obscurity, and the glory of the Lord shall be seen upon him. Let us then remember the loving-kindness of the Lord, and the multitude of His tender mercies. Like the people of Israel, let us set up our stones of witness, and inscribe upon them the precious story of what God has wrought for us. And as we review His dealings with us in our pilgrimage, let us, out of hearts melted with gratitude, declare, "What shall I render unto the Lord for all His benefits toward me? I will take the cup of salvation, and call upon the name of the Lord. I will pay my vows unto the Lord now in the presence of all His people." Ps. 116:12-14.

er encouragement for us in the least blessing we o_____ receive from God than in a_____ the accounts we can read of the faith and experience of o_____." (348). Forgive me Lord, of taking all Your many blessings for me, for granted. Help me recognize even the smallest blessing: _____

_____

_____

Prayer journal: _____

_____

_____

_____

_____

_____

_____

_____

Chapter 37

The First Evangelists

[This chapter is based on Matt. 10; Mark 6:7-11; Luke 9:1-6.]

1. "As Jesus ministered to the vast multitudes that gathered about Him, His disciples assisted, eager to do His bidding and to l_____ His labor...They watched for i_____ hearers, and explained the Scriptures to them." What can I do, Lord, to lighten Your load and participate in Your ministry? _____

_____

_____

The apostles were members of the family of Jesus, and they had accompanied Him as He traveled on foot through Galilee. They had shared with Him the toils and hardships that overtook them. They had listened to His discourses, they had walked and talked with the Son of God, and from His daily instruction they had learned how to work for the elevation of humanity. As Jesus ministered to the vast multitudes that gathered about Him, His disciples were in attendance, eager to do His bidding and to lighten His labor. They assisted in arranging the people, bringing the afflicted ones to the Saviour, and promoting the comfort of all. They watched for interested hearers, explained the Scriptures to them, and in various ways worked for their spiritual benefit. They taught what they had learned of Jesus, and were every day obtaining a rich experience. But they needed also an experience in laboring alone. They were still in need of much instruction, great patience and tenderness. Now, while He was personally with them, to point out their errors, and counsel and correct them, the Saviour sent them forth as His representatives.

While they had been with Him, the disciples had often been perplexed by the teaching of the priests and Pharisees, but they had brought their perplexities to Jesus. He had set before them the truths of Scripture in contrast with tradition. Thus He had strengthened their confidence in God's word, and in a great measure had set them free from their fear of the rabbis and their bondage to tradition. In the [349-350] training of the disciples the example of the Saviour's life was far more effective than any mere doctrinal instruction. When they were separated from Him, every look and tone and word came back to them. Often when in conflict with the enemies of the gospel, they repeated His words, and as they saw their effect upon the people, they rejoiced greatly.

2. "In the training of the disciples the e_____ of the Savior's l_____ was far more effective than any mere doctrinal instruction." (350). How should this inform my hermeneutics (Bible interpretation.)? How should this inform my sharing the fundamental beliefs with others?

Calling the twelve about Him, Jesus bade them go out two and two through the towns and villages. None were sent forth alone, but brother was associated with brother, friend with friend. Thus they could help and encourage each other, counseling and praying together, each one's strength supplementing the other's weakness. In the same manner He afterward sent forth the seventy. It was the Saviour's purpose that the messengers of the gospel should be associated in this way. In our own time evangelistic work would be far more successful if this example were more closely followed.

The disciples' message was the same as that of John the Baptist and of Christ Himself: "The kingdom of heaven is at hand." They were to enter into no controversy with the people as to whether Jesus of Nazareth was the Messiah; but in His name they were to do the same works of mercy as He had done. He bade them, "Heal the sick, cleanse the lepers, raise the dead, cast out devils: freely ye have received, freely give."

During His ministry Jesus devoted more time to healing the sick than to preaching. His miracles testified to the truth of His words, that He came not to destroy but to save. His righteousness went before Him, and the glory of the Lord was His rearward. Wherever He went, the tidings of His mercy preceded Him. Where He had passed, the objects of His compassion were rejoicing in health, and making trial of their new-found powers. Crowds were collecting around them to hear from their lips the works that the Lord had wrought. His voice was the first sound that many had ever heard, His name the first word they had ever spoken, His face the first they had ever looked upon. Why should they not love Jesus, and sound His praise? As He passed through the towns and cities He was like a vital current, diffusing life and joy wherever He went.

The followers of Christ are to labor as He did. We are to feed the hungry, clothe the naked, and comfort the suffering and afflicted. We are to minister to the despairing, and inspire hope in the hopeless. And to us also the promise will be fulfilled, "Thy righteousness shall go before thee; the glory of the Lord shall be thy rearward." Isa. 58:8. The love of Christ, manifested in unselfish ministry, will be more effective in reforming the evildoer than will the sword or the court of [350-351] justice. These are necessary to strike terror to the lawbreaker, but the loving missionary can do more than this. Often the heart will harden under reproof; but it will melt under the love of Christ. The missionary can-

Lord, in my training to be Your disciple, to walk like Enoch did, may Your life teach me the walk, and inspire me: _____

_____

_____

_____

3. Why did Jesus bade His evangelists to go two by two? _____

_____

_____

_____. How can my walk with You, Lord, be assisted also, in partnering with someone?

_____

_____

_____

4. "During His ministry Jesus devoted more time to h_____...than to preaching...The followers of Christ are to l_____ as He did. We are to f_____ the hungry, clothe the naked, and c_____ the suffering and afflicted. We are to minister to the despairing, and inspire h_____ in the hopeless." (350). Lord, give me your heart of compassion; and give me those opportunities to labor as You did, and to recognize them. What might a possible sample be? _____

_____

_____

5. "Often the heart will harden under r_____; but it will m_____ under the love of Christ." Lord, how do I balance this statement with calling sin by its right name? (350)

_____

_____

_____

_____

"He was never rude, never needlessly spoke a s_____ word, never gave needless pain to a sensitive soul. He did not censure human w_____. He fearlessly denounced hypocrisy, unbelief, and iniquity, but t_____ were in His voice as He uttered His scathing rebukes." (353). Lord, whenever I try to help straighten someone out, it comes across as self-righteous. Am I comparing myself to them, rather than to You? Help me to melt hearts with Your love:

_____

_____

_____

not only relieve physical maladies, but he can lead the sinner to the Great Physician, who can cleanse the soul from the leprosy of sin. Through His servants, God designs that the sick, the unfortunate, those possessed of evil spirits, shall hear His voice. Through His human agencies He desires to be a Comforter such as the world knows not.

The disciples on their first missionary tour were to go only to "the lost sheep of the house of Israel." If they had now preached the gospel to the Gentiles or the Samaritans, they would have lost their influence with the Jews. By exciting the prejudice of the Pharisees they would have involved themselves in controversy which would have discouraged them at the outset of their labors. Even the apostles were slow to understand that the gospel was to be carried to all nations. Until they themselves could grasp this truth they were not prepared to labor for the Gentiles. If the Jews would receive the gospel, God purposed to make them His messengers to the Gentiles. Therefore they were first to hear the message.

All over the field of Christ's labor there were souls awakened to their need, and hungering and thirsting for the truth. The time had come to send the tidings of His love to these longing hearts. To all these the disciples were to go as His representatives. The believers would thus be led to look upon them as divinely appointed teachers, and when the Saviour should be taken from them they would not be left without instructors.

On this first tour the disciples were to go only where Jesus had been before them, and had made friends. Their preparation for the journey was to be of the simplest kind. Nothing must be allowed to divert their minds from their great work, or in any way excite opposition and close the door for further labor. They were not to adopt the dress of the religious teachers, nor use any guise in apparel to distinguish them from the humble peasants. They were not to enter into the synagogues and call the people together for public service; their efforts were to be put forth in house-to-house labor. They were not to waste time in needless salutations, or in going from house to house for entertainment. But in every place they were to accept the hospitality of those who were worthy, those who would welcome them heartily as if entertaining Christ Himself. They were to enter the dwelling with the beautiful salutation, "Peace be to this house." Luke 10:5. That home would be blessed by their prayers, their [351-352] songs of praise, and the opening of the Scriptures in the family circle.

These disciples were to be heralds of the truth, to prepare the way for the coming of their Master. The message they had to bear was the word of eternal life, and the destiny of men depended upon their reception or rejection of it. To impress the people with its solemnity, Jesus bade His disciples, "Whosoever shall not receive you, nor hear your words, when ye depart out of that house or city, shake off the dust of your feet. Verily I say unto you, It shall be more tolerable for the land of Sodom and Gomorrah in the day of judgment, than for that city."

Now the Saviour's eye penetrates the future; He beholds the broader fields in which, after His death, the disciples are to be witnesses for Him. His prophetic glance takes in the experience of His servants through all the ages till He shall come the second time. He shows His followers the conflicts they must meet; He reveals the character and plan of the battle. He lays open before them the perils they must encounter, the self-denial that will be required. He desires them to count the cost, that they may not be taken unawares by the enemy. Their warfare is not to be waged against flesh and blood, but "against the principalities, against the powers, against the world rulers of this darkness, against the spiritual hosts of wickedness in the heavenly places." Eph. 6:12, R. V. They are to contend with supernatural forces, but they are assured of supernatural help. All the intelligences of heaven are in this army. And more than angels are in the ranks. The Holy Spirit, the representative of the Captain of the Lord's host, comes down to direct the battle. Our infirmities may be many, our sins and mistakes grievous; but the grace of God is for all who seek it with contrition. The power of Omnipotence is enlisted in behalf of those who trust in God. [352-353]

"Behold," said Jesus, "I send you forth as sheep in the midst of wolves: be ye therefore wise as serpents, and harmless as doves." Christ Himself did not suppress one word of truth, but He spoke it always in love. He exercised the greatest tact, and thoughtful, kind attention in His intercourse with the people. He was never rude, never needlessly spoke a severe word, never gave needless pain to a sensitive soul. He did not censure human weakness. He fearlessly denounced hypocrisy,

6. God's evangelist's will have to contend, down through the ages, with "supernatural f_____, but they are assured of supernatural h_____. All the intelligences of heaven are in this a_____." Angels are in the ranks. The Holy Spirit comes down to d___ _____ the battle. (352). Lord, if You are before me, who can stand against me? Allow experiences now, Lord, that will strengthen my faith and confidence in You for the upcoming battles: _____

_____

unbelief, and iniquity, but tears were in His voice as He uttered His scathing rebukes. He wept over Jerusalem, the city He loved, that refused to receive Him, the Way, the Truth, and the Life. They rejected Him, the Saviour, but He regarded them with pitying tenderness, and sorrow so deep that it broke His heart. Every soul was precious in His eyes. While He always bore Himself with divine dignity, He bowed with tenderest regard to every member of the family of God. In all men He saw fallen souls whom it was His mission to save.

The servants of Christ are not to act out the dictates of the natural heart. They need to have close communion with God, lest, under provocation, self rise up, and they pour forth a torrent of words that are unbefitting, that are not as dew or the still showers that refresh the withering plants. This is what Satan wants them to do; for these are his methods. It is the dragon that is wroth; it is the spirit of Satan that is revealed in anger and accusing. But God's servants are to be representatives of Him. He desires them to deal only in the currency of heaven, the truth that bears His own image and superscription. The power by which they are to overcome evil is the power of Christ. The glory of Christ is their strength. They are to fix their eyes upon His loveliness. Then they can present the gospel with divine tact and gentleness. And the spirit that is kept gentle under provocation will speak more effectively in favor of the truth than will any argument, however forcible.

Those who are brought in controversy with the enemies of truth have to meet, not only men, but Satan and his agents. Let them remember the Saviour's words, "Behold, I send you forth as lambs among wolves." Luke 10:3. Let them rest in the love of God, and the spirit will be kept calm, even under personal abuse. The Lord will clothe them with a divine panoply. His Holy Spirit will influence the mind and heart, so that their voices shall not catch the notes of the baying of the wolves. [353-354]

Continuing His instruction to His disciples, Jesus said, "Beware of men." They were not to put implicit confidence in those who knew not God, and open to them their counsels; for this would give Satan's agents an advantage. Man's inventions often counterwork God's plans. Those who build the temple of the Lord are to build according to the pattern shown in the mount,-- the divine similitude. God is dishonored and the gospel

---

7 "The power by which they are to overcome evil is the power of C_____. The glory of Christ is their strength. They are to f_____ their eyes upon His loveliness. Then they can present the gospel with divine tact and gentleness. And the spirit that is kept gentle under provocation will speak m_____ effectively in favor of the truth than will any argument, however forcible." (353). An argument won does not mean a heart is won. God, may I keep my eyes fixed on You and Your loveliness. May I resist the devil by drawing nigh unto You: _____
_____
_____

is betrayed when His servants depend on the counsel of men who are not under the guidance of the Holy Spirit. Worldly wisdom is foolishness with God. Those who rely upon it will surely err.

"They will deliver you up to councils, . . . yea and before governors and kings shall ye be brought for My sake, for a testimony to them and to the Gentiles." Matt. 10:17, 18, R. V. Persecution will spread the light. The servants of Christ will be brought before the great men of the world, who, but for this, might never hear the gospel. The truth has been misrepresented to these men. They have listened to false charges concerning the faith of Christ's disciples. Often their only means of learning its real character is the testimony of those who are brought to trial for their faith. Under examination these are required to answer, and their judges to listen to the testimony borne. God's grace will be dispensed to His servants to meet the emergency. "It shall be given you," says Jesus, "in that same hour what ye shall speak. For it is not ye that speak, but the Spirit of your Father which speaketh in you." As the Spirit of God illuminates the minds of His servants, the truth will be presented in its divine power and preciousness. Those who reject the truth will stand to accuse and oppress the disciples. But under loss and suffering, even unto death, the Lord's children are to reveal the meekness of their divine Example. Thus will be seen the contrast between Satan's agents and the representatives of Christ. The Saviour will be lifted up before the rulers and the people.

The disciples were not endowed with the courage and fortitude of the martyrs until such grace was needed. Then the Saviour's promise was fulfilled. When Peter and John testified before the Sanhedrin council, men "marveled; and they took knowledge of them, that they had been with Jesus." Acts 4:13. Of Stephen it is written that "all that sat in the council, looking steadfastly on him, saw his face as it had been the face of an angel." Men "were not able to resist the wisdom and the spirit by which he spake." Acts 6:15, 10. And Paul, writing of his own trial at the court of the Caesars, says, "At my first defense no one took my [354-355] part, but all forsook me. . . . But the Lord stood by me, and strengthened me; that through me the message might be fully proclaimed, and that all the Gentiles might hear: and I was delivered out of the mouth of the lion." 2 Tim. 4:16, 17, R. V.

8. The evangelist's preparation was to be "made d_____ by day in treasuring up the precious truths of God's w_____, and through prayer strengthening their faith. When they were brought into trial, the Holy Spirit would bring to their r_____ the very truths that would be needed." (355). Treasuring up is not done over night, so I can't wait till the last sign of the end, to start. Today is the day of salvation. Lord, through my daily walk with You, may Your scripture become a natural response to every day events in my life: _____

_____

_____

_____

The servants of Christ were to prepare no set speech to present when brought to trial. Their preparation was to be made day by day in treasuring up the precious truths of God's word, and through prayer strengthening their faith. When they were brought into trial, the Holy Spirit would bring to their remembrance the very truths that would be needed.

A daily, earnest striving to know God, and Jesus Christ whom He has sent, would bring power and efficiency to the soul. The knowledge obtained by diligent searching of the Scriptures would be flashed into the memory at the right time. But if any had neglected to acquaint themselves with the words of Christ, if they had never tested the power of His grace in trial, they could not expect that the Holy Spirit would bring His words to their remembrance. They were to serve God daily with undivided affection, and then trust Him.

So bitter would be the enmity to the gospel that even the tenderest earthly ties would be disregarded. The disciples of Christ would be betrayed to death by the members of their own households. "Ye shall be hated of all men for My name's sake," He added; "but he that shall endure unto the end, the same shall be saved." Mark 13:13. But He bade them not to expose themselves unnecessarily to persecution. He Himself often left one field of labor for another, in order to escape from those who were seeking His life. When He was rejected at Nazareth, and His own townsmen tried to kill Him, He went down to Capernaum, and there the people were astonished at His teaching; "for His word was with power." Luke 4:32. So His servants were not to be discouraged by persecution, but to seek a place where they could still labor for the salvation of souls.

The servant is not above his master. The Prince of heaven was called Beelzebub, and His disciples will be misrepresented in like manner. But whatever the danger, Christ's followers must avow their principles. They should scorn concealment. They cannot remain uncommitted until assured of safety in confessing the truth. They are set as watchmen, to warn men of their peril. The truth received from Christ must be imparted to all, freely and openly. Jesus said, "What I tell you in darkness, that speak ye in light: and what ye hear in the ear, that preach ye upon the housetops." [355-356]

Jesus Himself never purchased peace by compromise. His heart overflowed with love for the whole human race, but He was never indulgent to their sins. He was too much their friend to remain silent while they were pursuing a course that would ruin their souls,--the souls He had purchased with His own blood. He labored that man should be true to himself, true to his higher and eternal interest. The servants of Christ are called to the same work, and they should beware lest, in seeking to prevent discord, they surrender the truth. They are to "follow after the things which make for peace" (Rom. 14:19); but real peace can never be secured by compromising principle. And no man can be true to principle without exciting opposition. A Christianity that is spiritual will be opposed by the children of disobedience. But Jesus bade His disciples, "Fear not them which kill the body, but are not able to kill the soul." Those who are true to God need not fear the power of men nor the enmity of Satan. In Christ their eternal life is secure. Their only fear should be lest they surrender the truth, and thus betray the trust with which God has honored them.

It is Satan's work to fill men's hearts with doubt. He leads them to look upon God as a stern judge. He tempts them to sin, and then to regard themselves as too vile to approach their heavenly Father or to excite His pity. The Lord understands all this. Jesus assures His disciples of God's sympathy for them in their needs and weaknesses. Not a sigh is breathed, not a pain felt, not a grief pierces the soul, but the throb vibrates to the Father's heart.

The Bible shows us God in His high and holy place, not in a state of inactivity, not in silence and solitude, but surrounded by ten thousand times ten thousand and thousands of thousands of holy intelligences, all waiting to do His will. Through channels which we cannot discern He is in active communication with every part of His dominion. But it is in this speck of a world, in the souls that He gave His only-begotten Son to save, that His interest and the interest of all heaven is centered. God is bending from His throne to hear the cry of the oppressed. To every sincere prayer He answers, "Here am I." He uplifts the distressed and downtrodden. In all our afflictions He is afflicted. In every temptation and every trial the angel of His presence is near to deliver.

Not even a sparrow falls to the ground without the Father's notice. Satan's hatred against God leads him to hate every object of the Saviour's care. He seeks to mar

9. "No man can be true to p_____ without exciting o_____."
(356) What does this mean?

_____
_____
_____
_____

If I am not experiencing opposition, am I too accommodating, or compromising, or selling out?

_____
_____
_____

10. "It is Satan's work to fill men's hearts with d_____. He leads them to look upon God as a s_____ judge. He tempts them to sin, and then to regard themselves as too vile to a_____ their heavenly Father or to excite His pity. The Lord understands all this. Jesus assures His disciples of God's s_____ for them in their needs and weaknesses. Not a sigh is breathed, not a pain felt, not a g_____ pierces the soul, but the throb vibrates to the Father's h_____." (356). I'm glad that I am not left with just Satan's portrayal. Thank You, Jesus, for showing me the love of the Father. How can I, as Your evangelist, show that same love to others? _____

_____
_____
_____

the handiwork of God, and he delights in destroying [356-357] even the dumb creatures. It is only through God's protecting care that the birds are preserved to gladden us with their songs of joy. But He does not forget even the sparrows. "Fear ye not therefore, ye are of more value than many sparrows."

Jesus continues: As you confess Me before men, so I will confess you before God and the holy angels. You are to be My witnesses upon earth, channels through which My grace can flow for the healing of the world. So I will be your representative in heaven. The Father beholds not your faulty character, but He sees you as clothed in My perfection. I am the medium through which Heaven's blessings shall come to you. And everyone who confesses Me by sharing My sacrifice for the lost shall be confessed as a sharer in the glory and joy of the redeemed.

He who would confess Christ must have Christ abiding in him. He cannot communicate that which he has not received. The disciples might speak fluently on doctrines, they might repeat the words of Christ Himself; but unless they possessed Christlike meekness and love, they were not confessing Him. A spirit contrary to the spirit of Christ would deny Him, whatever the profession. Men may deny Christ by evilspeaking, by foolish talking, by words that are untruthful or unkind. They may deny Him by shunning life's burdens, by the pursuit of sinful pleasure. They may deny Him by conforming to the world, by uncourteous behavior, by the love of their own opinions, by justifying self, by cherishing doubt, borrowing trouble, and dwelling in darkness. In all these ways they declare that Christ is not in them. And "whosoever shall deny Me before men," He says, "him will I also deny before My Father which is in heaven."

The Saviour bade His disciples not to hope that the world's enmity to the gospel would be overcome, and that after a time its opposition would cease. He said, "I came not to send peace, but a sword." This creating of strife is not the effect of the gospel, but the result of opposition to it. Of all persecution the hardest to bear is variance in the home, the estrangement of dearest earthly friends. But Jesus declares, "He that loveth father or mother more than Me is not worthy of Me: and he that loveth son or daughter more than Me is not worthy of Me. And he that taketh not his cross, and followeth after

11. "A spirit contrary to the spirit of Christ would deny Him, whatever the profession. Men may deny Christ by evil speaking, by f_____ talking, by words that are untruthful or u_____... They may deny Him by conforming to the world, by u_____ behavior, by the love of their own o_____, by justifying s_____, by cherishing doubt, borrowing trouble, and dwelling in darkness." (357). This is denying like Peter did, causing You similar pain? Lord, I am too familiar with this list. I need Your help. How can I be more available to Your help, in thinking before I speak or act? _____
_____
_____
_____

Me, is not worthy of Me."

The mission of Christ's servants is a high honor, and a sacred trust. "He that receiveth you," He says, "receiveth Me, and he that receiveth [357-358] Me receiveth Him that sent Me." No act of kindness shown to them in His name will fail to be recognized and rewarded. And in the same tender recognition He includes the feeblest and lowliest of the family of God: "Whosoever shall give to drink unto one of these little ones"--those who are as children in their faith and their knowledge of Christ--"a cup of cold water only in the name of a disciple, verily I say unto you, he shall in nowise lose his reward."

Thus the Saviour ended His instruction. In the name of Christ the chosen twelve went out, as He had gone, "to preach the gospel to the poor, . . . to heal the brokenhearted, to preach deliverance to the captives, and recovering of sight to the blind, to set at liberty them that are bruised, to preach the acceptable year of the Lord." Luke 4:18, 19.

Prayerjournal:_____

Chapter 38

Come Rest Awhile

[This chapter is based on Matt. 14:1, 2, 12, 13;
Mark 6:30-32; Luke 9:7-10.]

On returning from their missionary tour, "the apostles gathered themselves together unto Jesus, and told Him all things, both what they had done, and what they had taught. And He said unto them, Come ye yourselves apart into a desert place, and rest awhile: for there were many coming and going, and they had no leisure so much as to eat."

The disciples came to Jesus and told Him all things. Their intimate relationship with Him encouraged them to lay before Him their favorable and unfavorable experiences, their joy at seeing results from their labors, and their sorrow at their failures, their faults, and their weaknesses. They had committed errors in their first work as evangelists, and as they frankly told Christ of their experiences, He saw that they needed much instruction. He saw, too, that they had become weary in their labors, and that they needed to rest.

But where they then were they could not obtain the needed privacy; "for there were many coming and going, and they had no leisure so much as to eat." The people were thronging after Christ, anxious to be healed, and eager to listen to His words. Many felt drawn to Him; for He seemed to them to be the fountain of all blessings. Many of those who then thronged about Christ to receive the precious boon of health accepted Him as their Saviour. Many others, afraid then to confess Him, because of the Pharisees, were converted at the descent [359-360] of the Holy Spirit, and, before the angry priests and rulers, acknowledged Him as the Son of God.

But now Christ longed for retirement, that He might be with His disciples; for He had much to say to them. In their work they had passed through the test of conflict, and had encountered opposition in various forms. Hitherto they had consulted Christ in everything; but for some time they had been alone, and at times they had been much troubled to know what to do. They had found much encouragement in their work; for Christ did not send them away without His Spirit, and by faith

1. "The disciples came to Jesus and told Him all things. Their i_____ relationship with Him encouraged them to lay before Him their favorable and unfavorable experiences, their joy at seeing results from their labors, and their sorrow at their f_____, their faults, and their weaknesses." Lord, isn't my walk with You suppose to be intimate, open, transparent, and trusting? Help me to be the kind of friend that confides: _____

_____
_____
_____

in Him they worked many miracles; but they needed now to feed on the Bread of Life. They needed to go to a place of retirement, where they could hold communion with Jesus and receive instruction for future work.

"And He said unto them, Come ye yourselves apart into a desert place, and rest awhile." Christ is full of tenderness and compassion for all in His service. He would show His disciples that God does not require sacrifice, but mercy. They had been putting their whole souls into labor for the people, and this was exhausting their physical and mental strength. It was their duty to rest.

As the disciples had seen the success of their labors, they were in danger of taking credit to themselves, in danger of cherishing spiritual pride, and thus falling under Satan's temptations. A great work was before them, and first of all they must learn that their strength was not in self, but in God. Like Moses in the wilderness of Sinai, like David among the hills of Judea, or Elijah by the brook Cherith, the disciples needed to come apart from the scenes of their busy activity, to commune with Christ, with nature, and with their own hearts.

While the disciples had been absent on their missionary tour, Jesus had visited other towns and villages, preaching the gospel of the kingdom. It was about this time that He received tidings of the Baptist's death. This event brought vividly before Him the end to which His own steps were tending. The shadows were gathering thickly about His path. Priests and rabbis were watching to compass His death, spies hung upon His steps, and on every hand plots for His ruin were multiplying. News of the preaching of the apostles throughout Galilee reached Herod, calling his attention to Jesus and His work. "This is John the Baptist," he said; "he is risen from the dead;" and he expressed a desire to see Jesus. Herod was in constant fear lest a revolution might be secretly carried forward, with the object of unseating him from the throne, and breaking the Roman yoke from the Jewish nation. Among the people the spirit [360-361] of discontent and insurrection was rife. It was evident that Christ's public labors in Galilee could not be long continued. The scenes of His suffering were drawing near, and He longed to be apart for a season from the confusion of the multitude.

With saddened hearts the disciples of John had borne his mutilated body to its burial. Then they "went and told Jesus." These disciples had been envious of

2. What two dangers often accompany success? (360). _____ _____ _____ _____ _____

_____ Lord, forgive my attitude. Help me to remember that my strength is not is self, but in You: _____ _____ _____ _____

3. "The disciples needed to come apart from the scenes of their b_____ activity, to commune with
[a] C_____, with
[b] n_____, and with
[c] their own h_____."
Why my heart, Lord? I need to learn from You! Oh, You mean there are still corners of my heart that need surrendering and softening? Gently show me: _____ _____ _____ _____ _____ _____

Christ when He seemed to be drawing the people away from John. They had sided with the Pharisees in accusing Him when He sat with the publicans at Matthew's feast. They had doubted His divine mission because He did not set the Baptist at liberty. But now that their teacher was dead, and they longed for consolation in their great sorrow, and for guidance as to their future work, they came to Jesus, and united their interest with His. They too needed a season of quiet for communion with the Saviour.

Near Bethsaida, at the northern end of the lake, was a lonely region, now beautiful with the fresh green of spring, that offered a welcome retreat to Jesus and His disciples. For this place they set out, going in their boat across the water. Here they would be away from the thoroughfares of travel, and the bustle and agitation of the city. The scenes of nature were in themselves a rest, a change grateful to the senses. Here they could listen to the words of Christ without hearing the angry interruptions, the retorts and accusations of the scribes and Pharisees. Here they could enjoy a short season of precious fellowship in the society of their Lord.

The rest which Christ and His disciples took was not self-indulgent rest. The time they spent in retirement was not devoted to pleasure seeking. They talked together regarding the work of God, and the possibility of bringing greater efficiency to the work. The disciples had been with Christ, and could understand Him; to them He need not talk in parables. He corrected their errors, and made plain to them the right way of approaching the people. He opened more fully to them the precious treasures of divine truth. They were vitalized by divine power, and inspired with hope and courage.

Though Jesus could work miracles, and had empowered His disciples to work miracles, He directed His worn servants to go apart into the country and rest. When He said that the harvest was great, and the laborers were few, He did not urge upon His disciples the necessity of ceaseless toil, but said, "Pray ye therefore the Lord of the harvest, that He will send forth laborers into His harvest." Matt. 9:38. God has [361-362] appointed to every man his work, according to his ability (Eph. 4:11-13), and He would not have a few weighted with responsibilities while others have no burden, no travail of soul.

Christ's words of compassion are spoken to His

4. Resting in nature at the north end of the lake, "they talked together regarding the work of God, and the possibility of bringing greater e_____ to the work...They were v_____ by divine power, and inspired with hope and c_____." (361). Lord, I need to be vitalized, inspired with courage. The walk with You sure helps! Power and inspiration come from You, not my own thinking. Help me to take time, to hear You: _____

_____

_____

_____

_____

workers today just as surely as they were spoken to His disciples. "Come ye yourselves apart, . . . and rest awhile," He says to those who are worn and weary. It is not wise to be always under the strain of work and excitement, even in ministering to men's spiritual needs; for in this way personal piety is neglected, and the powers of mind and soul and body are overtaxed. Self-denial is required of the disciples of Christ, and sacrifices must be made; but care must also be exercised lest through their overzeal Satan take advantage of the weakness of humanity, and the work of God be marred.

In the estimation of the rabbis it was the sum of religion to be always in a bustle of activity. They depended upon some outward performance to show their superior piety. Thus they separated their souls from God, and built themselves up in self-sufficiency. The same dangers still exist. As activity increases and men become successful in doing any work for God, there is danger of trusting to human plans and methods. There is a tendency to pray less, and to have less faith. Like the disciples, we are in danger of losing sight of our dependence on God, and seeking to make a savior of our activity. We need to look constantly to Jesus, realizing that it is His power which does the work. While we are to labor earnestly for the salvation of the lost, we must also take time for meditation, for prayer, and for the study of the word of God. Only the work accomplished with much prayer, and sanctified by the merit of Christ, will in the end prove to have been efficient for good.

No other life was ever so crowded with labor and responsibility as was that of Jesus; yet how often He was found in prayer! How constant was His communion with God! Again and again in the history of His earthly life are found records such as these: "Rising up a great while before day, He went out, and departed into a solitary place, and there prayed." "Great multitudes came together to hear, and to be healed by Him of their infirmities. And He withdrew Himself into the wilderness, and prayed." "And it came to pass in those days, that He went out into a mountain to pray, and continued all night in prayer to God." Mark 1:35; Luke 5:15, 16; 6:12.

In a life wholly devoted to the good of others, the Saviour found [362-363] it necessary to withdraw from the thoroughfares of travel and from the throng that followed Him day after day. He must turn aside from a

5. "S_____ is required of the disciples of Christ, and sacrifices must be made; but care must also be exercised lest through their overzeal Satan take advantage of the w_____ ____ of humanity, and the work of God be m_____." (362). Rest is a spiritual duty, a spiritual safeguard; something like the Sabbath? _____
Where am I overzealous?
_____
_____
_____
Where do I need to deny self?
_____
_____
_____
_____

6. "No other life was ever so crowded with labor and responsibility as was that of J_____; yet how often He was found in p_____! How c_____ was His communion with God." Weren't You, Jesus, ever (always) in Your Father's presence? And my walk with You can be the same! How do I let things crowd You out? _____
_____
_____

What's important?

_____
_____
_____

7. "We need more s_____, more trust and c_____ in our Savior." (363). What does this mean, and how can I nurture that attitude? _____
_____
_____

8. "We must individually h_____ Him speaking to the h_____ _____. When every other voice is hushed, and in q_____ we wait before Him, the silence of the soul makes more d_____ the voice of God." Waiting in silence, that's a point to work on. I'm usually in a bit of a hurry, Lord, compressing things into the shortest time possible. But that doesn't work, here. Waiting in silence, helps Your voice to be more distinct. That's what I want! Teach me patience. Teach me how to listen, my heart how to listen to You:

_____
_____

Prayer journal: _____
_____
_____
_____
_____
_____

life of ceaseless activity and contact with human needs, to seek retirement and unbroken communion with His Father. As one with us, a sharer in our needs and weaknesses, He was wholly dependent upon God, and in the secret place of prayer He sought divine strength, that He might go forth braced for duty and trial. In a world of sin Jesus endured struggles and torture of soul. In communion with God He could unburden the sorrows that were crushing Him. Here He found comfort and joy.

In Christ the cry of humanity reached the Father of infinite pity. As a man He supplicated the throne of God till His humanity was charged with a heavenly current that should connect humanity with divinity. Through continual communion He received life from God, that He might impart life to the world. His experience is to be ours.

"Come ye yourselves apart," He bids us. If we would give heed to His word, we should be stronger and more useful. The disciples sought Jesus, and told Him all things; and He encouraged and instructed them. If today we would take time to go to Jesus and tell Him our needs, we should not be disappointed; He would be at our right hand to help us. We need more simplicity, more trust and confidence in our Saviour. He whose name is called "The mighty God, The everlasting Father, The Prince of Peace;" He of whom it is written, "The government shall be upon His shoulder," is the Wonderful Counselor. We are invited to ask wisdom of Him. He "giveth to all men liberally, and upbraideth not." Isa. 9:6; James 1:5.

In all who are under the training of God is to be revealed a life that is not in harmony with the world, its customs, or its practices; and everyone needs to have a personal experience in obtaining a knowledge of the will of God. We must individually hear Him speaking to the heart. When every other voice is hushed, and in quietness we wait before Him, the silence of the soul makes more distinct the voice of God. He bids us, "Be still, and know that I am God." Ps. 46:10. Here alone can true rest be found. And this is the effectual preparation for all who labor for God. Amid the hurrying throng, and the strain of life's intense activities, the soul that is thus refreshed will be surrounded with an atmosphere of light and peace. The life will breathe out fragrance, and will reveal a divine power that will reach men's hearts.

Chapter 39

"Give Ye Them to Eat"

[This chapter is based on Matt. 14:13-21;
Mark 6:32-44; Luke 9:10-17; John 6:1-13.]

Christ had retired to a secluded place with His disciples, but this rare season of peaceful quietude was soon broken. The disciples thought they had retired where they would not be disturbed; but as soon as the multitude missed the divine Teacher, they inquired, "Where is He?" Some among them had noticed the direction in which Christ and His disciples had gone. Many went by land to meet them, while others followed in their boats across the water. The Passover was at hand, and, from far and near, bands of pilgrims on their way to Jerusalem gathered to see Jesus. Additions were made to their number, until there were assembled five thousand men besides women and children. Before Christ reached the shore, a multitude were waiting for Him. But He landed unobserved by them, and spent a little time apart with the disciples.

From the hillside He looked upon the moving multitude, and His heart was stirred with sympathy. Interrupted as He was, and robbed of His rest, He was not impatient. He saw a greater necessity demanding His attention as He watched the people coming and still coming. He "was moved with compassion toward them, because they were as sheep not having a shepherd." Leaving His retreat, He found a convenient place where He could minister to them. They received no help from [364-365] the priests and rulers; but the healing waters of life flowed from Christ as He taught the multitude the way of salvation.

The people listened to the words of mercy flowing so freely from the lips of the Son of God. They heard the gracious words, so simple and so plain that they were as the balm of Gilead to their souls. The healing of His divine hand brought gladness and life to the dying, and ease and health to those suffering with disease. The day seemed to them like heaven upon earth, and they were utterly unconscious of how long it had been since they had eaten anything.

At length the day was far spent. The sun was sinking in the west, and yet the people lingered. Jesus had

1. "From the hillside Jesus looked upon the approaching multitude, and His heart was s_____ with sympathy...The people listened...they heard the gracious words, so simple and so plain that they were as the b_____ of Gilead to their souls.... The day seemed to them like h_____ upon earth, and they were utterly unconscious of how l_____ it had been since they had eaten anything." (364, 365). You, Lord, are like that balm, a healing; time with You is, not wanting it to end; it is heaven on earth. How do I let go of the hurts, and let You heal? _____

_____

_____

_____

labored all day without food or rest. He was pale from weariness and hunger, and the disciples besought Him to cease from His toil. But He could not withdraw Himself from the multitude that pressed upon Him.

The disciples finally came to Him, urging that for their own sake the people should be sent away. Many had come from far, and had eaten nothing since morning. In the surrounding towns and villages they might be able to buy food. But Jesus said, "Give ye them to eat," and then, turning to Philip, questioned, "Whence shall we buy bread, that these may eat?" This He said to test the faith of the disciple. Philip looked over the sea of heads, and thought how impossible it would be to provide food to satisfy the wants of such a crowd. He answered that two hundred pennyworth of bread would not be nearly enough to divide among them, so that each might have a little. Jesus inquired how much food could be found among the company. "There is a lad here," said Andrew, "which hath five barley loaves, and two small fishes; but what are they among so many?" Jesus directed that these be brought to Him. Then He bade the disciples seat the people on the grass in parties of fifty or a hundred, to preserve order, and that all might witness what He was about to do. When this was accomplished, Jesus took the food, "and looking up to heaven, He blessed, and brake, and gave the loaves to His disciples, and the disciples to the multitude." "And they did all eat, and were filled. And they took up twelve baskets full of the fragments, and of the fishes."

He who taught the people the way to secure peace and happiness was just as thoughtful of their temporal necessities as of their spiritual need. The people were weary and faint. There were mothers with babes in their arms, and little children clinging to their skirts. Many had been standing for hours. They had been so intensely interested [365-366] in Christ's words that they had not once thought of sitting down, and the crowd was so great that there was danger of their trampling on one another. Jesus would give them a chance to rest, and He bade them sit down. There was much grass in the place, and all could rest in comfort.

Christ never worked a miracle except to supply a genuine necessity, and every miracle was of a character to lead the people to the tree of life, whose leaves are for the healing of the nations. The simple food [366-367] passed round by the hands of the disciples contained a whole treasure of lessons. It was humble fare that had been provided; the fishes and barley loaves were the daily food of the fisher folk about the Sea of Galilee. Christ could have spread before the people a rich repast, but food prepared merely for the gratification of appetite would have conveyed no lesson for their good. Christ taught them in this lesson that the natural provisions of God for man had been perverted. And never did people enjoy the luxurious feasts prepared for the gratification of perverted taste as this people enjoyed the rest and the simple food which Christ provided so far from human habitations.

If men today were simple in their habits, living in harmony with nature's laws, as did Adam and Eve in the beginning, there would be an abundant supply for the needs of the human family. There would be fewer imaginary wants, and more opportunities to work in God's ways. But selfishness and the indulgence of unnatural taste have brought sin and misery into the world, from excess on the one hand, and from want on the other.

Jesus did not seek to attract the people to Him by gratifying the desire for luxury. To that great throng, weary and hungry after the long, exciting day, the simple fare was an assurance not only of His power, but of His tender care for them in the common needs of life. The Saviour has not promised His followers the luxuries of the world; their fare may be plain, and even scanty; their lot may be shut in by poverty; but His word is pledged that their need shall be supplied, and He has promised that which is far better than worldly good,-- the abiding comfort of His own presence.

In feeding the five thousand, Jesus lifts the veil from the world of nature, and reveals the power that is constantly exercised for our good. In the production of earth's harvests God is working a miracle every day. Through natural agencies the same work is accomplished that was wrought in the feeding of the multitude. Men prepare the soil and sow the seed, but it is the life from God that causes the seed to germinate. It is God's rain and air and sunshine that cause it to put forth, "first the blade, then the ear, after that the full corn in the ear." Mark 4:28. It is God who is every day feeding millions from earth's harvest fields. Men are called upon to co-operate with God in the care of the grain and the preparation of the loaf, and because of this they lose sight of the divine agency. They do not give

2. "Jesus did not seek to attract the people to Him by gratifying the desire for l_____...His word is pledged that their n_____ shall be supplied, and He has promised that which is far better than worldly good –the abiding comfort of His own p_____." (367). There are benefits Lord, to our relationship. I am in it, though, not so much for those benefits, or miracles, or the city of gold; but for being Your friend: _____

_____

_____

3. Jesus "desires us to recognize Him i_____ His gifts, that they may be, as He intended, a blessing to us. It was to accomplish this purpose that the m___ _____ of Christ were performed." (368). "Every miracle was of a character to lead the people to the t_____ of life." (366). It is You, Lord, in Your gifts. The gift of salvation, friendship, life, health, jobs, homes, children, nourishment, love, beauty, etc. It is You! Let me glory in You, and not the gift:

_____

_____

_____

4. "Nothing is to be wasted...And there should be the same carefulness in spiritual things. When the baskets of fragments were collected, the people thought of their f_____ at home. They wanted them to share in the bread that Christ had blessed...Not one word that concerned their eternal salvation was to fall u_____ to the ground." Lord, You know how easy it is for me to procrastinate spiritually; there is always tomorrow; what's

God the glory due unto [367-368] His holy name. The working of His power is ascribed to natural causes or to human instrumentality. Man is glorified in place of God, and His gracious gifts are perverted to selfish uses, and made a curse instead of a blessing. God is seeking to change all this. He desires that our dull senses shall be quickened to discern His merciful kindness and to glorify Him for the working of His power. He desires us to recognize Him in His gifts, that they may be, as He intended, a blessing to us. It was to accomplish this purpose that the miracles of Christ were performed.

After the multitude had been fed, there was an abundance of food left. But He who had all the resources of infinite power at His command said, "Gather up the fragments that remain, that nothing be lost." These words meant more than putting the bread into the baskets. The lesson was twofold. Nothing is to be wasted. We are to let slip no temporal advantage. We should neglect nothing that will tend to benefit a human being. Let everything be gathered up that will relieve the necessity of earth's hungry ones. And there should be the same carefulness in spiritual things. When the baskets of fragments were collected, the people thought of their friends at home. They wanted them to share in the bread that Christ had blessed. The contents of the baskets were distributed among the eager throng, and were carried away into all the region round about. So those who were at the feast were to give to others the bread that comes down from heaven, to satisfy the hunger of the soul. They were to repeat what they had learned of the wonderful things of God. Nothing was to be lost. Not one word that concerned their eternal salvation was to fall useless to the ground.

The miracle of the loaves teaches a lesson of dependence upon God. When Christ fed the five thousand, the food was not nigh at hand. Apparently He had no means at His command. Here He was, with five thousand men, besides women and children, in the wilderness. He had not invited the large multitude to follow Him; they came without invitation or command; but He knew that after they had listened so long to His instruction, they would feel hungry and faint; for He was one with them in their need of food. They were far from home, and the night was close at hand. Many of them were without means to purchase food. He who for their sake had fasted forty days in the wilderness would not suffer them to return fasting to their homes. The providence of God had placed Jesus where He was; and He depended on His heavenly Father for the means to relieve the necessity. [368-369]

And when we are brought into strait places, we are to depend on God. We are to exercise wisdom and judgment in every action of life, that we may not, by reckless movements, place ourselves in trial. We are not to plunge into difficulties, neglecting the means God has provided, and misusing the faculties He has given us. Christ's workers are to obey His instructions implicitly. The work is God's, and if we would bless others His plans must be followed. Self cannot be made a center; self can receive no honor. If we plan according to our own ideas, the Lord will leave us to our own mistakes. But when, after following His directions, we are brought into strait places, He will deliver us. We are not to give up in discouragement, but in every emergency we are to seek help from Him who has infinite resources at His command. Often we shall be surrounded with trying circumstances, and then, in the fullest confidence, we must depend upon God. He will keep every soul that is brought into perplexity through trying to keep the way of the Lord.

Christ has bidden us, through the prophet, "Deal thy bread to the hungry," and "satisfy the afflicted soul;" "when thou seest the naked, that thou cover him," and "bring the poor that are cast out to thy house." Isa. 58:7-10. He has bidden us, "Go ye into all the world, and preach the gospel to every creature." Mark 16:15. But how often our hearts sink, and faith fails us, as we see how great is the need, and how small the means in our hands. Like Andrew looking upon the five barley loaves and the two little fishes, we exclaim, "What are they among so many?" Often we hesitate, unwilling to give all that we have, fearing to spend and to be spent for others. But Jesus has bidden us, "Give ye them to eat." His command is a promise; and behind it is the same power that fed the multitude beside the sea.

In Christ's act of supplying the temporal necessities of a hungry multitude is wrapped up a deep spiritual lesson for all His workers. Christ received from the Father; He imparted to the disciples; they imparted to the multitude; and the people to one another. So all who are united to Christ will receive from Him the bread of life, the heavenly food, and impart it to others.

the harm in one day's delay? (Like in starting that diet.) But You're saying not to let one spiritual opportunity fall useless to the ground. So help me, Lord. Help my sensitivity to You, to treasure every blessing. Bring them to mind, so I'll learn to catch them next time: _____ _____ _____

5. "How often our hearts sink, and faith fails us, as we see how g_____ is the need, and how s_____ the means in our hands...But Jesus has bidden us, 'Give ye them to eat.' His command is a p _____." (369). Lord, there is power in all of Your directives, isn't there? Like 'Follow Me,' and 'Abide in Me,' and 'Glorify Your Father.' Help me to let Your power have room to operate in my life: ____ _____ _____ _____

6. "Christ received from the Father; He imparted to the disciples; they imparted to the m_____;

and the people to one another." It is such good news, how can I keep it to myself? Give me a divine appointment today, Lord, to witness for You. Let it be part of my spiritual walk with You: _____

_____

_____

7. "We can impart only that which we r_____ from Christ; and we can receive o_____ as we impart to others." (370). The experience consists of ever abiding and learning on the one hand, and ever sharing on the other. Why will a decrease in sharing be matched in abiding? _____

_____

_____

_____. I know that You'll help me, Lord, to be open and available for both experiences, on a regular basis. _____

_____

_____

8. "Successful work for Christ depends not so much on numbers or talent as upon pureness of p_____, the true simplicity of earnest, dependent f_____. Personal responsibilities must be borne, personal duties must be taken up, personal e_____ must be made for those who do not

In full reliance upon God, Jesus took the small store of loaves; and although there was but a small portion for His own family of disciples, He did not invite them to eat, but began to distribute to them, bidding them serve the people. The food multiplied in His hands; and the hands of the disciples, reaching out to Christ Himself the Bread of [369-370] Life, were never empty. The little store was sufficient for all. After the wants of the people had been supplied, the fragments were gathered up, and Christ and His disciples ate together of the precious, Heaven-supplied food.

The disciples were the channel of communication between Christ and the people. This should be a great encouragement to His disciples today. Christ is the great center, the source of all strength. His disciples are to receive their supplies from Him. The most intelligent, the most spiritually minded, can bestow only as they receive. Of themselves they can supply nothing for the needs of the soul. We can impart only that which we receive from Christ; and we can receive only as we impart to others. As we continue imparting, we continue to receive; and the more we impart, the more we shall receive. Thus we may be constantly believing, trusting, receiving, and imparting.

The work of building up the kingdom of Christ will go forward, though to all appearance it moves slowly and impossibilities seem to testify against advance. The work is of God, and He will furnish means, and will send helpers, true, earnest disciples, whose hands also will be filled with food for the starving multitude. God is not unmindful of those who labor in love to give the word of life to perishing souls, who in their turn reach forth their hands for food for other hungry souls.

In our work for God there is danger of relying too largely upon what man with his talents and ability can do. Thus we lose sight of the one Master Worker. Too often the worker for Christ fails to realize his personal responsibility. He is in danger of shifting his burden upon organizations, instead of relying upon Him who is the source of all strength. It is a great mistake to trust in human wisdom or numbers in the work of God. Successful work for Christ depends not so much on numbers or talent as upon pureness of purpose, the true simplicity of earnest, dependent faith. Personal responsibilities must be borne, personal duties must be taken up, personal efforts must be made for those who do not know Christ. In the place of shifting your responsibility upon someone whom you think more richly endowed than you are, work according to your ability.

When the question comes home to your heart, "Whence shall we buy bread, that these may eat?" let not your answer be the response of unbelief. When the disciples heard the Saviour's direction, "Give ye them to eat," all the difficulties arose in their minds. They questioned, [370-371] Shall we go away into the villages to buy food? So now, when the people are destitute of the bread of life, the Lord's children question, Shall we send for someone from afar, to come and feed them? But what said Christ? "Make the men sit down," and He fed them there. So when you are surrounded by souls in need, know that Christ is there. Commune with Him. Bring your barley loaves to Jesus.

The means in our possession may not seem to be sufficient for the work; but if we will move forward in faith, believing in the all-sufficient power of God, abundant resources will open before us. If the work be of God, He Himself will provide the means for its accomplishment. He will reward honest, simple reliance upon Him. The little that is wisely and economically used in the service of the Lord of heaven will increase in the very act of imparting. In the hand of Christ the small supply of food remained undiminished until the famished multitude were satisfied. If we go to the Source of all strength, with our hands of faith outstretched to receive, we shall be sustained in our work, even under the most forbidding circumstances, and shall be enabled to give to others the bread of life.

The Lord says, "Give, and it shall be given unto you." "He that soweth sparingly shall reap also sparingly; and he that soweth with blessings shall reap also with blessings. . . . And God is able to make all grace abound unto you; that ye, having always all sufficiency in everything, may abound unto every good work; as it is written,--

"He hath scattered abroad, he hath given to the poor: His righteousness abideth forever.

"And He that supplieth seed to the sower and bread for food, shall supply and multiply your seed for sowing, and increase the fruits of your righteousness: ye being enriched in everything unto all liberality, which worketh through us thanksgiving to God." Luke 6:38; 2 Cor. 9:6-11, R. V., margin.

k_____ Christ." Lord, help me to better realize that the numbers and talent thing is really self-reliance. Teach me a purity of purpose and motive: _____
_____
_____
_____
_____
_____

9. "The little that is wisely and economically used in the service of the Lord of heaven will increase in the very a_____ of imparting." (371). Like sticking my foot in the Jordan river before it parts, I need to trust You to supply, as I am giving. Lord, give me that faith and strengthen it! _____
_____
_____
_____

Prayer journal: _____
_____
_____
_____
_____
_____
_____
_____

Chapter 40

A Night on the Lake

[This chapter is based on Matt. 14:22-33;
Mark 6:45-52; John 6:14-21.]

Seated upon the grassy plain, in the twilight of the spring evening, the people ate of the food that Christ had provided. The words they had heard that day had come to them as the voice of God. The works of healing they had witnessed were such as only divine power could perform. But the miracle of the loaves appealed to everyone in that vast multitude. All were sharers in its benefit. In the days of Moses, God had fed Israel with manna in the desert; and who was this that had fed them that day but He whom Moses had foretold? No human power could create from five barley loaves and two small fishes food sufficient to feed thousands of hungry people. And they said one to another, "This is of a truth that Prophet that should come into the world."

All day the conviction has strengthened. That crowning act is assurance that the long-looked-for Deliverer is among them. The hopes of the people rise higher and higher. This is He who will make Judea an earthly paradise, a land flowing with milk and honey. He can satisfy every desire. He can break the power of the hated Romans. He can deliver Judah and Jerusalem. He can heal the soldiers who are wounded in battle. He can supply whole armies with food. He can conquer the nations, and give to Israel the long-sought dominion. [377-378]

1. "In their enthusiasm the people are ready at once to crown Him king. They see that He makes no effort to attract a_____ or secure h_____ to Himself." (378). What would a comparison say to the priests and rulers? Or to me?

_____

_____

_____

_____

In their enthusiasm the people are ready at once to crown Him king. They see that He makes no effort to attract attention or secure honor to Himself. In this He is essentially different from the priests and rulers, and they fear that He will never urge His claim to David's throne. Consulting together, they agree to take Him by force, and proclaim Him the king of Israel. The disciples unite with the multitude in declaring the throne of David the rightful inheritance of their Master. It is the modesty of Christ, they say, that causes Him to refuse such honor. Let the people exalt their Deliverer. Let the arrogant priests and rulers be forced to honor Him who comes clothed with the authority of God.

They eagerly arrange to carry out their purpose; but Jesus sees what is on foot, and understands, as they cannot, what would be the result of such a movement. Even now the priests and rulers are hunting His life. They accuse Him of drawing the people away from them. Violence and insurrection would follow an effort to place Him on the throne, and the work of the spiritual kingdom would be hindered. Without delay the movement must be checked. Calling His disciples, Jesus bids them take the boat and return at once to Capernaum, leaving Him to dismiss the people.

Never before had a command from Christ seemed so impossible of fulfillment. The disciples had long hoped for a popular movement to place Jesus on the throne; they could not endure the thought that all this enthusiasm should come to nothing. The multitudes that were assembling to keep the Passover were anxious to see the new prophet. To His followers this seemed the golden opportunity to establish their beloved Master on the throne of Israel. In the glow of this new ambition it was hard for them to go away by themselves, and leave Jesus alone upon that desolate shore. They protested against the arrangement; but Jesus now spoke with an authority He had never before assumed toward them. They knew that further opposition on their part would be useless, and in silence they turned toward the sea.

Jesus now commands the multitude to disperse; and His manner is so decisive that they dare not disobey. The words of praise and exaltation die on their lips. In the very act of advancing to seize Him their steps are stayed, and the glad, eager look fades from their countenances. In that throng are men of strong mind and firm determination; but the kingly bearing of Jesus, and His few quiet words of command, quell the tumult, and frustrate their designs. They recognize [378-379] in Him a power above all earthly authority, and without a question they submit.

When left alone, Jesus "went up into a mountain apart to pray." For hours He continued pleading with God. Not for Himself but for men were those prayers. He prayed for power to reveal to men the divine character of His mission, that Satan might not blind their understanding and pervert their judgment. The Saviour knew that His days of personal ministry on earth were nearly ended, and that few would receive Him as their

2. "Never before had a command from Christ seemed so i_____ of fulfillment. The disciples had long hoped for a popular movement to place Jesus on the throne; they could not endure the thought that all this e_____ should come to n_____." All the popular enthusiasm, all the logical points in favor, do not mean it is the expedient thing to do. Trusting You, Lord, to know the right course, often defies my human reasoning. But the course I want to take is trusting You. Even if it is the unpopular thing to do: _____
_____
_____
_____

3. For hours Jesus prayed. "He prayed for power to reveal to men the divine character of His mission, that Satan might not b_____ their understanding and p_____ their

judgment…In t_____ and conflict of soul He prayed for His disciples." (379). Lord, I need to be a prayer warrior for myself, my family. Impress upon me the urgency of it all. Hours of agonizing prayer? Why don't I? _____

_____

_____

_____

4. "In the place of His exaltation to the throne of David they were to witness His c_____. This was to be indeed His true c_____. But they did not discern this…Without the Holy Spirit to enlighten the mind and e_____ the comprehension the faith of the disciples would f_____." Could it be that what I would consider a significant milestone in my life, a satisfying accomplishment, is not what You, Lord, have in mind for me. Instead, a faith-testing, a crucifixion of pride? Show me how:

_____

_____

_____

_____

Oh Lord, I need Your prayers! I know that You are praying for me: _____

_____

5. The disciples "left Jesus with d_____ hearts, more i_____ _____ with Him than ever

Redeemer. In travail and conflict of soul He prayed for His disciples. They were to be grievously tried. Their long-cherished hopes, based on a popular delusion, were to be disappointed in a most painful and humiliating manner. In the place of His exaltation to the throne of David they were to witness His crucifixion. This was to be indeed His true coronation. But they did not discern this, and in consequence strong temptations would come to them, which it would be difficult for them to recognize as temptations. Without the Holy Spirit to enlighten the mind and enlarge the comprehension the faith of the disciples would fail. It was painful to Jesus that their conceptions of His kingdom were, to so great a degree, limited to worldly aggrandizement and honor. For them the burden was heavy upon His heart, and He poured out His supplications with bitter agony and tears.

The disciples had not put off immediately from the land, as Jesus directed them. They waited for a time, hoping that He would come to [379-380] them. But as they saw that darkness was fast gathering, they "entered into a ship, and went over the sea toward Capernaum." They had left Jesus with dissatisfied hearts, more impatient with Him than ever before since acknowledging Him as their Lord. They murmured because they had not been permitted to proclaim Him king. They blamed themselves for yielding so readily to His command. They reasoned that if they had been more persistent they might have accomplished their purpose.

Unbelief was taking possession of their minds and hearts. Love of honor had blinded them. They knew that Jesus was hated by the Pharisees, and they were eager to see Him exalted as they thought He should be. To be united with a teacher who could work mighty miracles, and yet to be reviled as deceivers, was a trial they could ill endure. Were they always to be accounted followers of a false prophet? Would Christ never assert His authority as king? Why did not He who possessed such power reveal Himself in His true character, and make their way less painful? Why had He not saved John the Baptist from a violent death? Thus the disciples reasoned until they brought upon themselves great spiritual darkness. They questioned, Could Jesus be an impostor, as the Pharisees asserted?

The disciples had that day witnessed the wonderful works of Christ. It had seemed that heaven had come down to the earth. The memory of that precious, glorious day should have filled them with faith and hope. Had they, out of the abundance of their hearts, been conversing together in regard to these things, they would not have entered into temptation. But their disappointment had absorbed their thoughts. The words of Christ, "Gather up the fragments, . . . that nothing be lost," were unheeded. Those were hours of large blessing to the disciples, but they had forgotten it all. They were in the midst of troubled waters. Their thoughts were stormy and unreasonable, and the Lord gave them something else to afflict their souls and occupy their minds. God often does this when men create burdens and troubles for themselves. The disciples had no need to make trouble. Already danger was fast approaching.

A violent tempest had been stealing upon them, and they were unprepared for it. It was a sudden contrast, for the day had been perfect; and when the gale struck them, they were afraid. They forgot their disaffection, their unbelief, their impatience. Everyone worked to keep the boat from sinking. It was but a short distance by sea from Bethsaida to the point where they expected to meet Jesus, and in ordinary weather the journey required but a few hours; but now they were driven farther [380-381] and farther from the point they sought. Until the fourth watch of the night they toiled at the oars. Then the weary men gave themselves up for lost. In storm and darkness the sea had taught them their own helplessness, and they longed for the presence of their Master.

Jesus had not forgotten them. The Watcher on the shore saw those fear-stricken men battling with the tempest. Not for a moment did He lose sight of His disciples. With deepest solicitude His eyes followed the storm-tossed boat with its precious burden; for these men were to be the light of the world. As a mother in tender love watches her child, so the compassionate

before since acknowledging Him as their Lord. They m_____ …Thus the disciples reasoned until they brought upon themselves great spiritual d_____. They questioned, Could Jesus be an i_____, as the Pharisees asserted?" (380).

Why these Mt. Carmel experiences, from triumph to travail? Lord, I identify with Elijah and with the disciples. But why does it happen again and again? _____

_____

_____

_____ Could it be that love of h_____ blinds me, so that I temporarily forget the wonderful evidences of Your love and power? _____ __

_____

_____. Had the disciples been conversing about the memory of that precious, glorious day, they would have been filled with faith and hope, and "would not have entered into t_____." What's the lesson here?

_____

_____

_____

6. The disciples' "thoughts were stormy and u_____ _____, and the Lord gave them something else to afflict their souls and o_____ their

minds. God often does this when men c_____ burdens and troubles for themselves...Until the fourth watch of the night they toiled at the oars. Then the weary men gave themselves u__ for lost. In storm and darkness the sea had taught them their own h_____, and they longed for the presence of their Master." (380, 381). Thank You, Lord, for patiently working with me, when I'm self-centered and complaining. Thank You for occupying me with something else for a while. Thanks for guiding me till I see my need: __

_____

_____

7. "As a mother in tender love watches her child, so the c_____ Master watched His disciples. When their hearts were s_____, their unholy ambitions quelled, and in h_____ they prayed for help, it was given them." Thank You, Lord, for bringing my heart to a proper attitude. What are my unholy ambitions? _____

_____

_____

8. "At the m_____ when they believe themselves l_____, a gleam of light reveals a mysterious figure approaching them upon the waters." Is

Master watched His disciples. When their hearts were subdued, their unholy ambition quelled, and in humility they prayed for help, it was given them.

At the moment when they believe themselves lost, a gleam of light reveals a mysterious figure approaching them upon the water. But they know not that it is Jesus. The One who has come for their help they count as an enemy. Terror overpowers them. The hands that have grasped the oars with muscles like iron let go their hold. The boat rocks at the will of the waves; all eyes are riveted on this vision of a man walking upon the white-capped billows of the foaming sea.

They think it a phantom that omens their destruction, and they cry out for fear. Jesus advances as if He would pass them; but they recognize Him, and cry out, entreating His help. Their beloved Master turns, His voice silences their fear, "Be of good cheer: it is I; be not afraid."

As soon as they could credit the wondrous fact, Peter was almost beside himself with joy. As if he could scarcely yet believe, he cried out, "Lord, if it be Thou, bid me come unto Thee on the water. And He said, Come."

Looking unto Jesus, Peter walks securely; but as in self-satisfaction he glances back toward his companions in the boat, his eyes are turned from the Saviour. The wind is boisterous. The waves roll high, and come directly between him and the Master; and he is afraid. For a moment Christ is hidden from his view, and his faith gives way. He begins to sink. But while the billows talk with death, Peter lifts his eyes from the angry waters, and fixing them upon Jesus, cries, "Lord, save me." Immediately Jesus grasps the outstretched hand, saying, "O thou of little faith, wherefore didst thou doubt?"

Walking side by side, Peter's hand in that of his Master, they stepped into the boat together. But Peter was now subdued and silent. He had no reason to boast over his fellows, for through unbelief and self-exaltation [381-382] he had very nearly lost his life. When he turned his eyes from Jesus, his footing was lost, and he sank amid the waves.

When trouble comes upon us, how often we are like Peter! We look upon the waves, instead of keeping our eyes fixed upon the Saviour. Our footsteps slide, and the proud waters go over our souls. Jesus did not bid Peter come to Him that he should perish; He does not call us to follow Him, and then forsake us. "Fear not," He says; "for I have redeemed thee, I have called thee by thy name; thou art Mine. When thou passest through the waters, I will be with thee; and through the rivers, they shall not overflow thee: when thou walkest through the fire, thou shalt not be burned; neither shall the flame kindle upon thee. For I am the Lord thy God, the Holy One of Israel, thy Saviour." Isa. 43:1-3.

Jesus read the character of His disciples. He knew how sorely their faith was to be tried. In this incident on the sea He desired to reveal to Peter his own weakness,--to show that his safety was in constant dependence upon divine power. Amid the storms of temptation he could walk safely only as in utter self-distrust he should rely upon the Saviour. It was on the point where he thought himself strong that Peter was weak; and not until he discerned his weakness could he realize his need of dependence upon Christ. Had he learned the lesson that Jesus sought to teach him in that experience on the sea, he would not have failed when the great test came upon him.

Day by day God instructs His children. By the circumstances of the daily life He is preparing them to act their part upon that wider stage to which His providence has appointed them. It is the issue of the daily test that determines their victory or defeat in life's great crisis.

Those who fail to realize their constant dependence upon God will be overcome by temptation. We may now suppose that our feet stand secure, and that we shall never be moved. We may say with confidence, "I know in whom I have believed; nothing can shake my faith in God and in His word." But Satan is planning to take advantage of our hereditary and cultivated traits of character, and to blind our eyes to our own necessities and defects. Only through realizing our own weakness and looking steadfastly unto Jesus can we walk securely.

No sooner had Jesus taken His place in the boat than the wind ceased, "and immediately the ship was at the land whither they went." The night of horror was succeeded by the light of dawn. The disciples, and others who also were on board, bowed at the feet of Jesus with thankful hearts, saying, "Of a truth Thou art the Son of God!"

there a lesson for me here?
_____
_____

9. "Looking unto Jesus, Peter walks securely, but as in s_____ he glances back towards his companions in the boat, his eyes turned f_____ the Savior…For a moment Christ is hidden from his view, and his faith gives way." Why is my focus diverted? _____
_____
_____
(Recognition?   Waves?)

10. "In this incident on the sea Jesus desired to reveal to Peter his own weakness,--   to show that his safety was in c_____ dependence upon divine power…It is the issue of the d_____ test that determines their victory or defeat in life's great crisis… Only through realizing our own w_____ and looking s_____ unto Jesus can we walk securely." (382). Lord, as You helped Peter and Enoch walk with You, help me to 'constantly' be aware of You and not self: _____
_____
_____

Prayer journal: _____
_____
_____

Chapter 41

The Crisis in Galilee

[This chapter is based on John 6:22-71.]

When Christ forbade the people to declare Him king, He knew that a turning point in His history was reached. Multitudes who desired to exalt Him to the throne today would turn from Him tomorrow. The disappointment of their selfish ambition would turn their love to hatred, and their praise to curses. Yet knowing this, He took no measures to avert the crisis. From the first He had held out to His followers no hope of earthly rewards. To one who came desiring to become His disciple He had said, "The foxes have holes, and the birds of the air have nests; but the Son of man hath not where to lay His head." Matt. 8:20. If men could have had the world with Christ, multitudes would have proffered Him their allegiance; but such service He could not accept. Of those now connected with Him there were many who had been attracted by the hope of a worldly kingdom. These must be undeceived. The deep spiritual teaching in the miracle of the loaves had not been comprehended. This was to be made plain. And this new revelation would bring with it a closer test.

The miracle of the loaves was reported far and near, and very early next morning the people flocked to Bethsaida to see Jesus. They came in great numbers, by land and sea. Those who had left Him the preceding night returned, expecting to find Him still there; for there had been no boat by which He could pass to the other side. But their search was fruitless, and many repaired to Capernaum, still seeking Him. [383-384]

Meanwhile He had arrived at Gennesaret, after an absence of but one day. As soon as it was known that He had landed, the people "ran through that whole region round about, and began to carry about in beds those that were sick, where they heard He was." Mark 6:55.

After a time He went to the synagogue, and there those who had come from Bethsaida found Him. They learned from His disciples how He had crossed the sea. The fury of the storm, and the many hours of fruitless rowing against adverse winds, the appearance of Christ

1. From the first He had held out "no hope of earthly r_____...Of those now connected with Jesus there were many who had been attracted by the hope of a worldly k_____. These must be u_____."

Who has done the deceiving? _____

_____

Have I been deceived as to the true nature of God's kingdom being of service and humility and not recognition? _____

_____

How does the enemy keep getting me? _____

_____

_____

_____

walking upon the water, the fears thus aroused, His re-assuring words, the adventure of Peter and its result, with the sudden stilling of the tempest and landing of the boat, were all faithfully recounted to the wondering crowd. Not content with this, however, many gathered about Jesus, questioning, "Rabbi, when camest Thou hither?" They hoped to receive from His own lips a further account of the miracle.

Jesus did not gratify their curiosity. He sadly said, "Ye seek Me, not because ye saw the miracles, but because ye did eat of the loaves, and were filled." They did not seek Him from any worthy motive; but as they had been fed with the loaves, they hoped still to receive temporal benefit by attaching themselves to Him. The Saviour bade them, "Labor not for the meat which perisheth, but for that meat which endureth unto [384-385] everlasting life." Seek not merely for material benefit. Let it not be the chief effort to provide for the life that now is, but seek for spiritual food, even that wisdom which will endure unto everlasting life. This the Son of God alone can give; "for Him hath God the Father sealed."

For the moment the interest of the hearers was awakened. They exclaimed, "What shall we do, that we might work the works of God?" They had been performing many and burdensome works in order to recommend themselves to God; and they were ready to hear of any new observance by which they could secure greater merit. Their question meant, What shall we do that we may deserve heaven? What is the price we are required to pay in order to obtain the life to come?

"Jesus answered and said unto them, This is the work of God, that ye believe on Him whom He hath sent." The price of heaven is Jesus. The way to heaven is through faith in "the Lamb of God, which taketh away the sin of the world." John 1:29.

But the people did not choose to receive this statement of divine truth. Jesus had done the very work which prophecy had foretold that the Messiah would do; but they had not witnessed what their selfish hopes had pictured as His work. Christ had indeed once fed the multitude with barley loaves; but in the days of Moses Israel had been fed with manna forty years, and far greater blessings were expected from the Messiah. Their dissatisfied hearts queried why, if Jesus could perform so many wondrous works as they had witnessed,

2. Many did not seek Jesus "from any worthy motive; but as they had been fed with the loaves, they hoped still to receive temporal benefit by a___ _____ themselves to Him." (384). How do I react when I feel used?

_____

_____

_____

Do I in any way use You, Lord? To fit in, to look good, to enhance my standing, to have things go my way?

_____

_____

_____

_____

324 Can We Walk, Together?

3. "The fact the He claimed to be the S_____ of God, and yet refused to be Israel's king, was a m_____ which they could not fathom. His refusal was misinterpreted. Many concluded that He dare not assert His claims because He Himself d_____ as to the d_____ character of His mission." (385). What does it mean to have a heart open to unbelief? Do I have one, Lord? ____

_____
_____
_____
_____
_____

4. Manna was a t_____ of the real bread from heaven. "The life-giving Spirit, flowing from the infinite fullness of God, is the t_____ manna." (386). A spirit-filled life is not merely an optional, fringe-benefit that I can do okay without. It is essential, for it is "l_____-giving." What is a Christian that is not Spirit filled? Is it possible?

_____
_____
_____
_____

could He not give health, strength, and riches to all His people, free them from their oppressors, and exalt them to power and honor? The fact that He claimed to be the Sent of God, and yet refused to be Israel's king, was a mystery which they could not fathom. His refusal was misinterpreted. Many concluded that He dared not assert His claims because He Himself doubted as to the divine character of His mission. Thus they opened their hearts to unbelief, and the seed which Satan had sown bore fruit of its kind, in misunderstanding and defection.

Now, half mockingly, a rabbi questioned, "What sign showest Thou then, that we may see, and believe Thee? what dost Thou work? Our fathers did eat manna in the desert; as it is written, He gave them bread from heaven to eat."

The Jews honored Moses as the giver of the manna, ascribing praise to the instrument, and losing sight of Him by whom the work had been accomplished. Their fathers had murmured against Moses, and had doubted and denied his divine mission. Now in the same spirit the [385-386] children rejected the One who bore the message of God to themselves. "Then said Jesus unto them, Verily, verily, I say unto you, Moses gave you not that bread from heaven." The giver of the manna was standing among them. It was Christ Himself who had led the Hebrews through the wilderness, and had daily fed them with the bread from heaven. That food was a type of the real bread from heaven. The life-giving Spirit, flowing from the infinite fullness of God, is the true manna. Jesus said, "The bread of God is that which cometh down out of heaven, and giveth life unto the world." John 6:33, R. V.

Still thinking that it was temporal food to which Jesus referred, some of His hearers exclaimed, "Lord, evermore give us this bread." Jesus then spoke plainly: "I am the bread of life."

The figure which Christ used was a familiar one to the Jews. Moses, by the inspiration of the Holy Spirit, had said, "Man doth not live by bread only, but by every word that proceedeth out of the mouth of the Lord." And the prophet Jeremiah had written, "Thy words were found, and I did eat them; and Thy word was unto me the joy and rejoicing of mine heart." Deut. 8:3; Jer. 15:16. The rabbis themselves had a saying, that the eating of bread, in its spiritual significance, was the study of the law and the practice of good works; and it was often said that at the Messiah's coming all Israel would be fed. The teaching of the prophets made plain the deep spiritual lesson in the miracle of the loaves. This lesson Christ was seeking to open to His hearers in the synagogue. Had they understood the Scriptures, they would have understood His words when He said, "I am the bread of life." Only the day before, the great multitude, when faint and weary, had been fed by the bread which He had given. As from that bread they had received physical strength and refreshment, so from Christ they might receive spiritual strength unto eternal life. "He that cometh to Me," He said, "shall never hunger; and he that believeth on Me shall never thirst." But He added, "Ye also have seen Me, and believe not."

They had seen Christ by the witness of the Holy Spirit, by the revelation of God to their souls. The living evidences of His power had been before them day after day, yet they asked for still another sign. Had this been given, they would have remained as unbelieving as before. If they were not convinced by what they had seen and heard, it was useless to show them more marvelous works. Unbelief will ever find excuse for doubt, and will reason away the most positive proof.

Again Christ appealed to those stubborn hearts. "Him that cometh [386-387] to Me I will in nowise cast out." All who received Him in faith, He said, should have eternal life. Not one could be lost. No need for Pharisees and Sadducees to dispute concerning the future life. No longer need men mourn in hopeless grief over their dead. "This is the will of Him that sent Me, that everyone which seeth the Son, and believeth on Him, may have everlasting life: and I will raise him up at the last day."

But the leaders of the people were offended, "and they said, Is not this Jesus, the son of Joseph, whose father and mother we know? how is it then that He saith, I came down from heaven?" They tried to arouse prejudice by referring scornfully to the lowly origin of Jesus. They contemptuously alluded to His life as a Galilean laborer, and to His family as being poor and lowly. The claims of this uneducated carpenter, they said, were unworthy of their attention. And on account of His mysterious birth they insinuated that He was of doubtful parentage, thus representing the human circumstances of His birth as a blot upon His history.

5. "Yet they asked for still another sign...Unbelief will ever find e_____ for doubt, and will r_____ away the most positive proof." How do I let Satan reason away evidences of God's care and love to me? _____
_____
_____
_____

Jesus did not attempt to explain the mystery of His birth. He made no answer to the questionings in regard to His having come down from heaven, as He had made none to the questions concerning His crossing the sea. He did not call attention to the miracles that marked His life. Voluntarily He had made Himself of no reputation, and taken upon Him the form of a servant. But His words and works revealed His character. All whose hearts were open to divine illumination would recognize in Him "the Only-begotten of the Father, full of grace and truth." John 1:14.

The prejudice of the Pharisees lay deeper than their questions would indicate; it had its root in the perversity of their hearts. Every word and act of Jesus aroused antagonism in them; for the spirit which they cherished could find in Him no answering chord.

"No man can come to Me, except the Father which hath sent Me draw him: and I will raise him up at the last day. It is written in the prophets, And they shall be all taught of God. Every man therefore that hath heard, and hath learned of the Father, cometh unto Me." None will ever come to Christ, save those who respond to the drawing of the Father's love. But God is drawing all hearts unto Him, and only those who resist His drawing will refuse to come to Christ.

In the words, "They shall be all taught of God," Jesus referred to the prophecy of Isaiah: "All thy children shall be taught of the Lord; and great shall be the peace of thy children." Isa. 54:13. This scripture [387-388] the Jews appropriated to themselves. It was their boast that God was their teacher. But Jesus showed how vain is this claim; for He said, "Every man therefore that hath heard, and hath learned of the Father, cometh unto Me." Only through Christ could they receive a knowledge of the Father. Humanity could not endure the vision of His glory. Those who had learned of God had been listening to the voice of His Son, and in Jesus of Nazareth they would recognize Him who through nature and revelation has declared the Father.

"Verily, verily, I say unto you, He that believeth on Me hath everlasting life." Through the beloved John, who listened to these words, the Holy Spirit declared to the churches, "This is the record, that God hath given to us eternal life, and this life is in His Son. He that hath the Son hath life." 1 John 5:11, 12. And Jesus said, "I will raise him up at the last day." Christ became one

6. "The prejudice of the Pharisees lay deeper than their questions would indicate; it had its root in the p_____ of their hearts. Every word and act of Jesus aroused a_____ in them; for the spirit which they cherished could find in Him no answering c_____." (387). What spirit do I cherish? _____ Does self-promotion or revenge match Your spirit, Lord? How can my spirit and Your spirit experience harmony?

_____
_____
_____

7. "God is drawing a_____ hearts unto Him, and only those who r_____ His drawing will refuse to come to Christ." Show me ways, that I might be resisting, Lord: _____

_____

_____ And help me recognize ways that You are drawing me so that I may be open and responsive as it is happening: _____

_____

flesh with us, in order that we might become one spirit with Him. It is by virtue of this union that we are to come forth from the grave,--not merely as a manifestation of the power of Christ, but because, through faith, His life has become ours. Those who see Christ in His true character, and receive Him into the heart, have everlasting life. It is through the Spirit that Christ dwells in us; and the Spirit of God, received into the heart by faith, is the beginning of the life eternal.

The people had referred Christ to the manna which their fathers ate in the wilderness, as if the furnishing of that food was a greater miracle than Jesus had performed; but He shows how meager was that gift when compared with the blessings He had come to bestow. The manna could sustain only this earthly existence; it did not prevent the approach of death, nor insure immortality; but the bread of heaven would nourish the soul unto everlasting life. The Saviour said, "I am that bread of life. Your fathers did eat manna in the wilderness, and are dead. This is the bread which cometh down from heaven, that a man may eat thereof, and not die. I am the living bread which came down from heaven: if any man eat of this bread, he shall live forever." To this figure Christ now adds another. Only through dying could He impart life to men, and in the words that follow He points to His death as the means of salvation. He says, "The bread that I will give is My flesh, which I will give for the life of the world."

The Jews were about to celebrate the Passover at Jerusalem, in commemoration of the night of Israel's deliverance, when the destroying angel smote the homes of Egypt. In the paschal lamb God desired them [388-389] to behold the Lamb of God, and through the symbol receive Him who gave Himself for the life of the world. But the Jews had come to make the symbol all-important, while its significance was unnoticed. They discerned not the Lord's body. The same truth that was symbolized in the paschal service was taught in the words of Christ. But it was still undiscerned.

Now the rabbis exclaimed angrily, "How can this Man give us His flesh to eat?" They affected to understand His words in the same literal sense as did Nicodemus when he asked, "How can a man be born when he is old?" John 3:4. To some extent they comprehended the meaning of Jesus, but they were not willing to acknowledge it. By misconstruing His words, they hoped

8. "Those who s_____ Christ in His true character, and r_____ Him into the heart, have everlasting life." (388). As I contemplate Your life, Lord, as I walk with You, may it be more than Your story that I become familiar with; may it be Your true character that I see and receive into my heart. What will help me value this, as much as entering the city gates? _____

_____

_____

_____

9. "In the paschal lamb God desired them to b_____ the Lamb of God, and through the symbol receive Him who gave Himself for the l_____ of the world. But the Jews had come to make the symbol all-important, while its significance was u_____." (388, 389). Reality is in receiving You, and not letting You get lost in the symbol of the paschal lamb, the elements of communion and footwashing, the mechanics of tithing, Sabbathkeeping, and devotions. May I take the time to recognize You and receive You in these opportunities:

_____

_____

_____

_____

to prejudice the people against Him.

Christ did not soften down His symbolical representation. He reiterated the truth in yet stronger language: "Verily, verily, I say unto you, Except ye eat the flesh of the Son of man, and drink His blood, ye have no life in you. Whoso eateth My flesh, and drinketh My blood, hath eternal life; and I will raise him up at the last day. For My flesh is meat indeed, and My blood is drink indeed. He that eateth My flesh, and drinketh My blood, dwelleth in Me, and I in him."

To eat the flesh and drink the blood of Christ is to receive Him as a personal Saviour, believing that He forgives our sins, and that we are complete in Him. It is by beholding His love, by dwelling upon it, by drinking it in, that we are to become partakers of His nature. What food is to the body, Christ must be to the soul. Food cannot benefit us unless we eat it, unless it becomes a part of our being. So Christ is of no value to us if we do not know Him as a personal Saviour. A theoretical knowledge will do us no good. We must feed upon Him, receive Him into the heart, so that His life becomes our life. His love, His grace, must be assimilated.

But even these figures fail to present the privilege of the believer's relation to Christ. Jesus said, "As the living Father hath sent Me, and I live by the Father: so he that eateth Me, even he shall live by Me." As the Son of God lived by faith in the Father, so are we to live by faith in Christ. So fully was Jesus surrendered to the will of God that the Father alone appeared in His life. Although tempted in all points like as we are, He stood before the world untainted by the evil that surrounded Him. Thus we also are to overcome as Christ overcame.

Are you a follower of Christ? Then all that is written concerning the spiritual life is written for you, and may be attained through uniting yourself [389-390] to Jesus. Is your zeal languishing? has your first love grown cold? Accept again of the proffered love of Christ. Eat of His flesh, drink of His blood, and you will become one with the Father and with the Son.

The unbelieving Jews refused to see any except the most literal meaning in the Saviour's words. By the ritual law they were forbidden to taste blood, and they now construed Christ's language into a sacrilegious speech, and disputed over it among themselves. Many even of the disciples said, "This is an hard saying; who

10. "To eat the flesh and drink the blood of Christ is to r_____ Him as personal Savior, believing that He forgives my sins, and that I am complete in Him. It is by beholding His love, by d_____ upon it, by drinking it in, that we are to become partakers of His nature." Is that the walk, Lord? Beholding, dwelling (contemplating), and drinking it in? _____ _____ How much time is involved in 'dwelling' upon Your love? _____ _____ Help me to make time for this walk. _____ _____ _____

can hear it?"

The Saviour answered them: "Doth this offend you? What and if ye shall see the Son of man ascend up where He was before? It is the spirit that quickeneth; the flesh profiteth nothing: the words that I speak unto you, they are spirit, and they are life."

The life of Christ that gives life to the world is in His word. It was by His word that Jesus healed disease and cast out demons; by His word He stilled the sea, and raised the dead; and the people bore witness that His word was with power. He spoke the word of God, as He had spoken through all the prophets and teachers of the Old Testament. The whole Bible is a manifestation of Christ, and the Saviour desired to fix the faith of His followers on the word. When His visible presence should be withdrawn, the word must be their source of power. Like their Master, they were to live "by every word that proceedeth out of the mouth of God." Matt. 4:4.

As our physical life is sustained by food, so our spiritual life is sustained by the word of God. And every soul is to receive life from God's word for himself. As we must eat for ourselves in order to receive nourishment, so we must receive the word for ourselves. We are not to obtain it merely through the medium of another's mind. We should carefully study the Bible, asking God for the aid of the Holy Spirit, that we may understand His word. We should take one verse, and concentrate the mind on the task of ascertaining the thought which God has put in that verse for us. We should dwell upon the thought until it becomes our own, and we know "what saith the Lord."

In His promises and warnings, Jesus means me. God so loved the world, that He gave His only-begotten Son, that I by believing in Him, might not perish, but have everlasting life. The experiences related in God's word are to be my experiences. Prayer and promise, precept and warning, are mine. "I am crucified with Christ: nevertheless I live; yet not I, but Christ liveth in me: and the life which I now live in the flesh I live by the faith of the Son of God, who loved me , and gave Himself [390-391] for me." Gal. 2:20. As faith thus receives and assimilates the principles of truth, they become a part of the being and the motive power of the life. The word of God, received into the soul, molds the thoughts, and enters into the development of character.

11. "The life of Christ that gives life to the world is in His w_____...When His visible presence should be withdrawn, the word must be their source of p_____ ...We should c_____ study the Bible, asking God for the a_____ of the Holy Spirit...We should take o_____ verse, and c_____ the mind on the task of a_____ the thought which God has put in that verse for u___. We should dwell upon the thought until it becomes our own, and we know 'what saith the Lord.'" (390). What a privilege and adventure: to read, knowing that You are talking to me, sharing in a beautiful friendship. Give me a hunger for You and Your Word, so I am providing more than five minutes for Bible reading, for this Is life, this is where it is at, what it's all about! _____

_____

_____

By looking constantly to Jesus with the eye of faith, we shall be strengthened. God will make the most precious revelations to His hungering, thirsting people. They will find that Christ is a personal Saviour. As they feed upon His word, they find that it is spirit and life. The word destroys the natural, earthly nature, and imparts a new life in Christ Jesus. The Holy Spirit comes to the soul as a Comforter. By the transforming agency of His grace, the image of God is reproduced in the disciple; he becomes a new creature. Love takes the place of hatred, and the heart receives the divine similitude. This is what it means to live "by every word that proceedeth out of the mouth of God." This is eating the Bread that comes down from heaven.

Christ had spoken a sacred, eternal truth regarding the relation between Himself and His followers. He knew the character of those who claimed to be His disciples, and His words tested their faith. He declared that they were to believe and act upon His teaching. All who received Him would partake of His nature, and be conformed to His character. This involved the relinquishment of their cherished ambitions. It required the complete surrender of themselves to Jesus. They were called to become self-sacrificing, meek and lowly in heart. They must walk in the narrow path traveled by the Man of Calvary, if they would share in the gift of life and the glory of heaven.

The test was too great. The enthusiasm of those who had sought to take Him by force and make Him king grew cold. This discourse in the synagogue, they declared, had opened their eyes. Now they were undeceived. In their minds His words were a direct confession that He was not the Messiah, and that no earthly rewards were to be realized from connection with Him. They had welcomed His miracle-working power; they were eager to be freed from disease and suffering; but they would not come into sympathy with His self-sacrificing life. They cared not for the mysterious spiritual kingdom of which He spoke. The insincere, the selfish, who had sought Him, no longer desired Him. If He would not devote His power and influence to obtaining their freedom from the Romans, they would have nothing to do with Him.

Jesus told them plainly, "There are some of you that believe not;" adding, "Therefore said I unto you, that no man can come unto Me, [391-392] except it

12. "The Word d_____ _____ the natural, earthly nature, and imparts a new l_____ in Christ Jesus." (391). In what area of my life has this happened, or the Holy Spirit has convicted me to let it happen? _____

_____

_____

_____

(holding a grudge, withholding forgiveness; being self-centered?). "If they were not drawn to Him it was because their hearts were not o_____ to the Holy Spirit." (392).

were given unto him of My Father." He wished them to understand that if they were not drawn to Him it was because their hearts were not open to the Holy Spirit. "The natural man receiveth not the things of the Spirit of God: for they are foolishness unto him: neither can he know them, because they are spiritually discerned." 1 Cor. 2:14. It is by faith that the soul beholds the glory of Jesus. This glory is hidden, until, through the Holy Spirit, faith is kindled in the soul.

By the public rebuke of their unbelief these disciples were still further alienated from Jesus. They were greatly displeased, and wishing to wound the Saviour and gratify the malice of the Pharisees, they turned their backs upon Him, and left Him with disdain. They had made their choice,--had taken the form without the spirit, the husk without the kernel. Their decision was never afterward reversed; for they walked no more with Jesus.

"Whose fan is in His hand, and He will throughly purge His floor, and gather His wheat into the garner." Matt. 3:12. This was one of the times of purging. By the words of truth, the chaff was being separated from the wheat. Because they were too vain and self-righteous to receive reproof, too world-loving to accept a life of humility, many turned away from Jesus. Many are still doing the same thing. Souls are tested today as were those disciples in the synagogue at Capernaum. When truth is brought home to the heart, they see that their lives are not in accordance with the will of God. They see the need of an entire change in themselves; but they are not willing to take up the self-denying work. Therefore they are angry when their sins are discovered. They go away offended, even as the disciples left Jesus, murmuring, "This is an hard saying; who can hear it?"

Praise and flattery would be pleasing to their ears; but the truth is unwelcome; they cannot hear it. When the crowds follow, and the multitudes are fed, and the shouts of triumph are heard, their voices are loud in praise; but when the searching of God's Spirit reveals their sin, and bids them leave it, they turn their backs upon the truth, and walk no more with Jesus.

As those disaffected disciples turned away from Christ, a different spirit took control of them. They could see nothing attractive in Him whom they had once found so interesting. They sought out His enemies, for they were in harmony with their spirit and work. They misinterpreted His words, falsified His statements, and impugned His motives. They sustained their course by gathering up every item that could be [392-393] turned against Him; and such indignation was stirred up by these false reports that His life was in danger.

The news spread swiftly that by His own confession Jesus of Nazareth was not the Messiah. And thus in Galilee the current of popular feeling was turned against Him, as, the year before, it had been in Judea. Alas for Israel! They rejected their Saviour, because they longed for a conqueror who would give them temporal power. They wanted the meat which perishes, and not that which endures unto everlasting life.

With a yearning heart, Jesus saw those who had been His disciples departing from Him, the Life and the Light of men. The consciousness that His compassion was unappreciated, His love unrequited, His mercy slighted, His salvation rejected, filled Him with sorrow that was inexpressible. It was such developments as these that made Him a man of sorrows, and acquainted with grief.

Without attempting to hinder those who were leaving Him, Jesus turned to the twelve and said, "Will ye also go away?"

Peter replied by asking, "Lord, to whom shall we go?" "Thou hast the words of eternal life," he added. "And we believe and are sure that Thou art that Christ, the Son of the living God."

"To whom shall we go?" The teachers of Israel were slaves to formalism. The Pharisees and Sadducees were in constant contention. To leave Jesus was to fall among sticklers for rites and ceremonies, and ambitious men who sought their own glory. The disciples had found more peace and joy since they had accepted Christ than in all their previous lives. How could they go back to those who had scorned and persecuted the Friend of sinners? They had long been looking for the Messiah; now He had come, and they could not turn from His presence to those who were hunting His life, and had persecuted them for becoming His followers.

"To whom shall we go?" Not from the teaching of Christ, His lessons of love and mercy, to the darkness of unbelief, the wickedness of the world. While the Saviour was forsaken by many who had witnessed His wonderful works, Peter expressed the faith of the

13. "The consciousness that His compassion was u_____, His love unrequited, His mercy s_____, His salvation rejected, filled Him with sorrow that was i_____." (393). Jesus, do I add to Your sorrow? Do I lack appreciation for Your salvation and friendship? I am so sorry! I do not want to add to Your heart ache: _____ _____ _____ _____

disciples,--"Thou art that Christ." The very thought of losing this anchor of their souls filled them with fear and pain. To be destitute of a Saviour was to be adrift on a dark and stormy sea.

Many of the words and acts of Jesus appear mysterious to finite minds, but every word and act had its definite purpose in the work for our redemption; each was calculated to produce its own result. If we [393-394] were capable of understanding His purposes, all would appear important, complete, and in harmony with His mission.

While we cannot now comprehend the works and ways of God, we can discern His great love, which underlies all His dealings with men. He who lives near to Jesus will understand much of the mystery of godliness. He will recognize the mercy that administers reproof, that tests the character, and brings to light the purpose of the heart.

When Jesus presented the testing truth that caused so many of His disciples to turn back, He knew what would be the result of His words; but He had a purpose of mercy to fulfill. He foresaw that in the hour of temptation every one of His beloved disciples would be severely tested. His agony in Gethsemane, His betrayal and crucifixion, would be to them a most trying ordeal. Had no previous test been given, many who were actuated by merely selfish motives would have been connected with them. When their Lord was condemned in the judgment hall; when the multitude who had hailed Him as their king hissed at Him and reviled Him; when the jeering crowd cried, "Crucify Him!"--when their worldly ambitions were disappointed, these self-seeking ones would, by renouncing their allegiance to Jesus, have brought upon the disciples a bitter, heart-burdening sorrow, in addition to their grief and disappointment in the ruin of their fondest hopes. In that hour of darkness, the example of those who turned from Him might have carried others with them. But Jesus brought about this crisis while by His personal presence He could still strengthen the faith of His true followers.

Compassionate Redeemer, who in the full knowledge of the doom that awaited Him, tenderly smoothed the way for the disciples, prepared them for their crowning trial, and strengthened them for the final test!

14. "He who lives near to Jesus will understand much of the mystery of g_____. He will recognize the m_____ that administers reproof, that tests the c_____, and brings to light the p_____ of the heart...Jesus brought about this crisis while by His personal presence He could still s_____ the faith of His true followers." (394). In a crisis, Lord, help me to view things from Your perspective, what You're wanting to get accomplished in me, in my heart. What is the purpose of my heart?

_____

_____

_____

_____

_____

Prayer journal: _____

_____

_____

_____

_____

_____

_____

_____

Chapter 42

Tradition

[This chapter is based on Matt. 15:1-20; Mark 7:1-23.]

1. Traditional precepts were "professedly designed to guard the o_____ of the law, but they were regarded as more s_____ than the law itself." Lord, how do I let concern for the adherence to traditional guidelines for Sabbath observance, get in the way of the purpose of the Sabbath (of setting aside time for increasing my awareness of You, and for my relationship with You)?

_____

_____

_____

2. "While the people were occupied with t_____ distinctions and observances which God had not required, their attention was turned away from the great p_____ of His law." (396). And that is Satan's goal, isn't it? My attention turned away from You, Lord. Am I caught up in trifling distinctions? _____

_____

_____

The scribes and Pharisees, expecting to see Jesus at the Passover, had laid a trap for Him. But Jesus, knowing their purpose, had absented Himself from this gathering. "Then came together unto Him the Pharisees, and certain of the scribes." As He did not go to them, they came to Him. For a time it had seemed that the people of Galilee would receive Jesus as the Messiah, and that the power of the hierarchy in that region would be broken. The mission of the twelve, indicating the extension of Christ's work, and bringing the disciples more directly into conflict with the rabbis, had excited anew the jealousy of the leaders at Jerusalem. The spies they sent to Capernaum in the early part of His ministry, who had tried to fix on Him the charge of Sabbathbreaking, had been put to confusion; but the rabbis were bent on carrying out their purpose. Now another deputation was sent to watch His movements, and find some accusation against Him.

As before, the ground of complaint was His disregard of the traditional precepts that encumbered the law of God. These were professedly designed to guard the observance of the law, but they were regarded as more sacred than the law itself. When they came in collision with the commandments given from Sinai, preference was given to the rabbinical precepts.

Among the observances most strenuously enforced was that of ceremonial purification. A neglect of the forms to be observed before eating [395-396] was accounted a heinous sin, to be punished both in this world and in the next; and it was regarded as a virtue to destroy the transgressor.

The rules in regard to purification were numberless. The period of a lifetime was scarcely sufficient for one to learn them all. The life of those who tried to observe the rabbinical requirements was one long struggle against ceremonial defilement, an endless round of washings and purifications. While the people were occupied with trifling distinctions, and observances which God had not required, their attention was turned away from the great principles of His law.

Christ and His disciples did not observe these ceremonial washings, and the spies made this neglect the ground of their accusation. They did not, however, make a direct attack on Christ, but came to Him with criticism of His disciples. In the presence of the multitude they said, "Why do Thy disciples transgress the tradition of the elders? for they wash not their hands when they eat bread."

Whenever the message of truth comes home to souls with special power, Satan stirs up his agents to start a dispute over some minor question. Thus he seeks to attract attention from the real issue. Whenever a good work is begun, there are cavilers ready to enter into dispute over forms or technicalities, to draw minds away from the living realities. When it appears that God is about to work in a special manner for His people, let them not be enticed into a controversy that will work only ruin of souls. The questions that most concern us are, Do I believe with saving faith on the Son of God? Is my life in harmony with the divine law? "He that believeth on the Son hath everlasting life: and he that believeth not the Son shall not see life." "And hereby we do know that we know Him, if we keep His commandments." John 3:36; 1 John 2:3.

Jesus made no attempt to defend Himself or His disciples. He made no reference to the charges against Him, but proceeded to show the spirit that actuated these sticklers for human rites. He gave them an example of what they were repeatedly doing, and had done just before coming in search of Him. "Full well ye reject the commandment of God," He said, "that ye may keep your own tradition. For Moses said, Honor thy father and thy mother; and, Whoso curseth father or mother, let him die the death: but ye say, If a man shall say to his father or mother, It is Corban, that is to say, a gift, by whatsoever thou mightest be profited by me; he shall be free. And ye suffer him no more to do aught for his father or his mother." They set aside the fifth commandment as of [396-397] no consequence, but were very exact in carrying out the traditions of the elders. They taught the people that the devotion of their property to the temple was a duty more sacred than even the support of their parents; and that, however great the necessity, it was sacrilege to impart to father or mother any part of what had been thus consecrated. An undutiful child had only to pronounce the word "Corban" over his

3. When it appears that God is about to work in a special manner for His people, "Satan stirs up his agents to start a d_____ over some minor question. Thus he seeks to attract attention f_____ the real issue... from the living realities." What questions should most concern me? _____
_____
_____
_____

4. The Scribes and Pharisees "taught the people that the devotion of their property to the temple was a duty more s_____ than even the support of their p_____...[A per-

son] was at liberty, both at life and in death, to d_____ and defraud his parents, under the cover of a pretended d_____ to God…The apparent zeal for God on the part of the priests and rabbis was a p_____ to cover their desire for s_____." (397). Satan will employ religious language and rationale, to disarm my radar guarding against his schemes, which is to draw me away from Christ. Lord, I need to know You, Your Spirit, and Your truth, to not be taken in by Satan:

_____

_____

_____

5. "The people draweth nigh unto Me with their mouth, and honoreth Me with their l____; but their h_____ is far f____ me." Lord, help me to see how half-hearted, or even disengaged I am, AS I am spending time with You! What would help to change this? _____

_____

_____

_____

6. "Jesus explained that defilement comes not from w_____, but from w_____." It is the heart that is desperately wicked, that is the source of

property, thus devoting it to God, and he could retain it for his own use during his lifetime, and after his death it was to be appropriated to the temple service. Thus he was at liberty, both in life and in death, to dishonor and defraud his parents, under cover of a pretended devotion to God.

Never, by word or deed, did Jesus lessen man's obligation to present gifts and offerings to God. It was Christ who gave all the directions of the law in regard to tithes and offerings. When on earth He commended the poor woman who gave her all to the temple treasury. But the apparent zeal for God on the part of the priests and rabbis was a pretense to cover their desire for self-aggrandizement. The people were deceived by them. They were bearing heavy burdens which God had not imposed. Even the disciples of Christ were not wholly free from the yoke that had been bound upon them by inherited prejudice and rabbinical authority. Now, by revealing the true spirit of the rabbis, Jesus sought to free from the bondage of tradition all who were really desirous of serving God.

"Ye hypocrites," He said, addressing the wily spies, "well did Esaias prophesy of you, saying, This people draweth nigh unto Me with their mouth, and honoreth Me with their lips; but their heart is far from Me. But in vain they do worship Me, teaching for doctrines the commandments of men." The words of Christ were an arraignment of the whole system of Pharisaism. He declared that by placing their requirements above the divine precepts the rabbis were setting themselves above God.

The deputies from Jerusalem were filled with rage. They could not accuse Christ as a violator of the law given from Sinai, for He spoke as its defender against their traditions. The great precepts of the law, which He had presented, appeared in striking contrast to the petty rules that men had devised.

To the multitude, and afterward more fully to His disciples, Jesus explained that defilement comes not from without, but from within. Purity and impurity pertain to the soul. It is the evil deed, the evil word, the evil thought, the transgression of the law of God, not the neglect of external, man-made ceremonies, that defiles a man. [397-398]

The disciples noted the rage of the spies as their false teaching was exposed. They saw the angry looks, and heard the half-muttered words of dissatisfaction and revenge. Forgetting how often Christ had given evidence that He read the heart as an open book, they told Him of the effect of His words. Hoping that He might conciliate the enraged officials, they said to Jesus, "Knowest Thou that the Pharisees were offended, after they heard this saying?"

He answered, "Every plant, which My heavenly Father hath not planted, shall be rooted up." The customs and traditions so highly valued by the rabbis were of this world, not from heaven. However great their authority with the people, they could not endure the testing of God. Every human invention that has been substituted for the commandments of God will be found worthless in that day when "God shall bring every work into judgment, with every secret thing, whether it be good, or whether it be evil." Eccl. 12:14.

The substitution of the precepts of men for the commandments of God has not ceased. Even among Christians are found institutions and usages that have no better foundation than the traditions of the fathers. Such institutions, resting upon mere human authority, have supplanted those of divine appointment. Men cling to their traditions, and revere their customs, and cherish hatred against those who seek to show them their error. In this day, when we are bidden to call attention to the commandments of God and the faith of Jesus, we see the same enmity as was manifested in the days of Christ. Of the remnant people of God it is written, "The dragon was wroth with the woman, and went to make war with the remnant of her seed, which keep the commandments of God, and have the testimony of Jesus Christ." Rev. 12:17.

But "every plant, which My heavenly Father hath not planted, shall be rooted up." In place of the authority of the so-called fathers of the church, God bids us accept the word of the eternal Father, the Lord of heaven and earth. Here alone is truth unmixed with error. David said, "I have more understanding than all my teachers: for Thy testimonies are my meditation. I understand more than the ancients, because I keep Thy precepts." Ps. 119:99, 100. Let all who accept human authority, the customs of the church, or the traditions of the fathers, take heed to the warning conveyed in the words of Christ, "In vain they do worship Me, teaching for doctrines the commandments of men."

evil behavior. Lord, take out the heart of stone, and give me a new heart. Renew my mind, by reminding me throughout the day to ever be in Your presence, like Enoch did:

_____

_____

7. "Men cling to their traditions, and revere their customs, and c_____ ____ hatred against those who seek to show them their error. In this day, when we are bidden to call a_____ to the commandments of God and the faith of Jesus, we see the same e_____ as was manifested the days of Christ." (398). How do I react when an opinion I hold is shown to be non-biblical? Am I willing to let go of cherished traditions? _____

_____

_____

_____

Prayer journal: _____

_____

_____

_____

_____

_____

_____

_____

Chapter 43

Barriers Broken Down

[This chapter is based on Matt. 15:21-28; Mark 7:24-30.]

After the encounter with the Pharisees, Jesus withdrew from Capernaum, and crossing Galilee, repaired to the hill country on the borders of Phoenicia. Looking westward, He could see, spread out upon the plain below, the ancient cities of Tyre and Sidon, with their heathen temples, their magnificent palaces and marts of trade, and the harbors filled with shipping. Beyond was the blue expanse of the Mediterranean, over which the messengers of the gospel were to bear its glad tidings to the centers of the world's great empire. But the time was not yet. The work before Him now was to prepare His disciples for their mission. In coming to this region He hoped to find the retirement He had failed to secure at Bethsaida. Yet this was not His only purpose in taking this journey.

"Behold, a Canaanitish woman came out from those borders, and cried, saying, Have mercy on me, O Lord, Thou Son of David; my daughter is grievously vexed with a devil." Matt. 15:22, R. V. The people of this district were of the old Canaanite race. They were idolaters, and were despised and hated by the Jews. To this class belonged the woman who now came to Jesus. She was a heathen, and was therefore excluded from the advantages which the Jews daily enjoyed. There [399-400] were many Jews living among the Phoenicians, and the tidings of Christ's work had penetrated to this region. Some of the people had listened to His words and had witnessed His wonderful works. This woman had heard of the prophet, who, it was reported, healed all manner of diseases. As she heard of His power, hope sprang up in her heart. Inspired by a mother's love, she determined to present her daughter's case to Him. It was her resolute purpose to bring her affliction to Jesus. He must heal her child. She had sought help from the heathen gods, but had obtained no relief. And at times she was tempted to think, What can this Jewish teacher do for me? But the word had come, He heals all manner of diseases, whether those who come to Him for help are

1. "The work before Him n_____ was to p_____ His disciples for their mission." Lord, am I self-centered in my walk with You? Do I bask in Your grace, with hardly a thought of others sharing in the same experience? _____
_____
_____

2. A Canaanitish woman's daughter was grievously vexed with a d_____. As a heathen idolater, she was despised and hated by the Jews, "e_____ __ from the advantages which the Jews daily enjoyed...she determined to present her daughter's case to Him. In was her r_____ purpose to bring her affliction to Je-

rich or poor. She determined not to lose her only hope.

Christ knew this woman's situation. He knew that she was longing to see Him, and He placed Himself in her path. By ministering to her sorrow, He could give a living representation of the lesson He designed to teach. For this He had brought His disciples into this region. He desired them to see the ignorance existing in cities and villages close to the land of Israel. The people who had been given every opportunity to understand the truth were without a knowledge of the needs of those around them. No effort was made to help souls in darkness. The partition wall which Jewish pride had erected, shut even the disciples from sympathy with the heathen world. But these barriers were to be broken down.

Christ did not immediately reply to the woman's request. He received this representative of a despised race as the Jews would have done. In this He designed that His disciples should be impressed with the cold and heartless manner in which the Jews would treat such a case, as evinced by His reception of the woman, and the compassionate manner in which He would have them deal with such distress, as manifested by His subsequent granting of her petition.

But although Jesus did not reply, the woman did not lose faith. As He passed on, as if not hearing her, she followed Him, continuing her supplications. Annoyed by her importunities, the disciples asked Jesus to send her away. They saw that their Master treated her with indifference, and they therefore supposed that the prejudice of the Jews against the Canaanites was pleasing to Him. But it was a pitying Saviour to whom the woman made her plea, and in answer to the request of the disciples, Jesus said, "I am not sent but unto the lost sheep of the house [400-401] of Israel." Although this answer appeared to be in accordance with the prejudice of the Jews, it was an implied rebuke to the disciples, which they afterward understood as reminding them of what He had often told them,--that He came to the world to save all who would accept Him.

The woman urged her case with increased earnestness, bowing at Christ's feet, and crying, "Lord, help me." Jesus, still apparently rejecting her entreaties, according to the unfeeling prejudice of the Jews, answered, "It is not meet to take the children's bread, and to cast it to dogs." This was virtually asserting that it was not just to lavish the blessings brought to the fa-

sus…She d_____ not to lose her only hope." (399, 400). Am I as determined to connect with You, Lord? Do I not sense the urgency? _____ _____ _____

3. "Christ knew this woman's situation. He knew that she was l_____ to see Him, and He placed Himself in her p_____." Lord, You know my longing and my need. How will I encounter You in my path today? _____ _____

You've done this for me before, haven't You, Lord? When was that again? _____ _____ _____ _____

Help me not to miss it!

4. Jesus came to these borders of Phoencia to teach a lesson. The Jewish "people who had been given every opportunity to understand the truth were w_____ _____ a knowledge of the n_____ of those around them." Even the disciples were without sympathy. How about me? Do I know the needs of those around me? My neighbors, coworkers? _____ _____ _____ Give me sensitivity and discernment,

Lord: _____

_____

5. "Although Jesus did not reply, the woman did not l_____ faith…This answer would have utterly discouraged a less e_____ seeker. But the woman saw that her o_____ had come. Beneath the apparent refusal of Jesus, she saw a compassion that He could not h_____." (400, 401). True character always shines out. Lord, I am a hypocrite, I fake compassion. You could not fake a lack of compassion. I want to be like You, genuine and true: _____

_____

6. "She who has been regarded as an o_____ from Israel is no longer an alien, but a child in God's h_____ …

vored people of God upon strangers and aliens from Israel. This answer would have utterly discouraged a less earnest seeker. But the woman saw that her opportunity had come. Beneath the apparent refusal of Jesus, she saw a compassion that He could not hide. "Truth, Lord," she answered, "yet the dogs eat of the crumbs which fall from their masters' table." While the children of the household eat at the father's table, even the dogs are not left unfed. They have a right to the crumbs that fall from the table abundantly supplied. So while there were many blessings given to Israel, was there not also a blessing for her? She was looked upon as a dog, and had she not then a dog's claim to a crumb from His bounty?

Jesus had just departed from His field of labor because the scribes and Pharisees were seeking to take His life. They murmured and complained. They manifested unbelief and bitterness, and refused the salvation so freely offered them. Here Christ meets one of an unfortunate and despised race, that has not been favored with the light of God's word; yet she yields at once to the divine influence of Christ, and has implicit faith in His ability to grant the favor she asks. She begs for the crumbs that fall from the Master's table. If she may have the privilege of a dog, she is willing to be regarded as a dog. She has no national or religious prejudice or pride to influence her course, and she immediately acknowledges Jesus as the Redeemer, and as being able to do all that she asks of Him.

The Saviour is satisfied. He has tested her faith in Him. By His dealings with her, He has shown that she who has been regarded as an outcast from Israel is no longer an alien, but a child in God's household. As a child it is her privilege to share in the Father's gifts. Christ now grants her request, and finishes the lesson to the disciples. Turning to her with a look of pity and love, He says, "O woman, great is thy faith: [401-402] be it unto thee even as thou wilt." From that hour her daughter became whole. The demon troubled her no more. The woman departed, acknowledging her Saviour, and happy in the granting of her prayer.

This was the only miracle that Jesus wrought while on this journey. It was for the performance of this act that He went to the borders of Tyre and Sidon. He wished to relieve the afflicted woman, and at the same time to leave an example in His work of mercy toward one of a despised people for the benefit of His disciples when He should no longer be with them. He wished to lead them from their Jewish exclusiveness to be interested in working for others besides their own people.

Jesus longed to unfold the deep mysteries of the truth which had been hid for ages, that the Gentiles should be fellow heirs with the Jews, and "partakers of His promise in Christ by the gospel." Eph. 3:6. This truth the disciples were slow to learn, and the divine Teacher gave them lesson upon lesson. In rewarding the faith of the centurion at Capernaum, and preaching the gospel to the inhabitants of Sychar, He had already given evidence that He did not share the intolerance of the Jews. But the Samaritans had some knowledge of God; and the centurion had shown kindness to Israel. Now Jesus brought the disciples in contact with a heathen, whom they regarded as having no reason above any of her people, to expect favor from Him. He would give an example of how such a one should be treated. The disciples had thought that He dispensed too freely the gifts of His grace. He would show that His love was not to be circumscribed to race or nation.

When He said, "I am not sent but unto the lost sheep of the house of Israel," He stated the truth, and in His work for the Canaanite woman He was fulfilling His commission. This woman was one of the lost sheep that Israel should have rescued. It was their appointed work, the work which they had neglected, that Christ was doing.

This act opened the minds of the disciples more fully to the labor that lay before them among the Gentiles. They saw a wide field of usefulness outside of Judea. They saw souls bearing sorrows unknown to those more highly favored. Among those whom they had been taught to despise were souls longing for help from the mighty Healer, hungering for the light of truth, which had been so abundantly given to the Jews.

Afterward, when the Jews turned still more persistently from the disciples, because they declared Jesus to be the Saviour of the world, [402-403] and when the partition wall between Jew and Gentile was broken down by the death of Christ, this lesson, and similar ones which pointed to the gospel work unrestricted by custom or nationality, had a powerful influence upon the representatives of Christ, in directing their labors.

The Saviour's visit to Phoenicia and the miracle

...[Jesus] wished to lead them [His disciples] from their Jewish exclusiveness" to His work of mercy. (401, 402). Lord, the cardboard city people deserve Your mercy. Ex-convicts deserve Your mercy. Help my attitude, Lord: _____

_____

_____

_____

7. "The disciples had thought that He dispensed too f_____ the gifts of His grace." (402). Do I have the same attitude towards those freely forgiven?

_____

____ Does that mean I was more deserving of forgiveness than others? _____

_____ Lord, what is in my heart? Show me:

_____

_____

there performed had a yet wider purpose. Not alone for the afflicted woman, nor even for His disciples and those who received their labors, was the work accomplished; but also "that ye might believe that Jesus is the Christ, the Son of God; and that believing ye might have life through His name." John 20:31. The same agencies that barred men away from Christ eighteen hundred years ago are at work today. The spirit which built up the partition wall between Jew and Gentile is still active. Pride and prejudice have built strong walls of separation between different classes of men. Christ and His mission have been misrepresented, and multitudes feel that they are virtually shut away from the ministry of the gospel. But let them not feel that they are shut away from Christ. There are no barriers which man or Satan can erect but that faith can penetrate.

In faith the woman of Phoenicia flung herself against the barriers that had been piled up between Jew and Gentile. Against discouragement, regardless of appearances that might have led her to doubt, she trusted the Saviour's love. It is thus that Christ desires us to trust in Him. The blessings of salvation are for every soul. Nothing but his own choice can prevent any man from becoming a partaker of the promise in Christ by the gospel.

Caste is hateful to God. He ignores everything of this character. In His sight the souls of all men are of equal value. He "hath made of one blood all nations of men for to dwell on all the face of the earth, and hath determined the times before appointed, and the bounds of their habitation; that they should seek the Lord, if haply they might feel after Him, and find Him, though He be not far from every one of us." Without distinction of age, or rank, or nationality, or religious privilege, all are invited to come unto Him and live. "Whosoever believeth on Him shall not be ashamed. For there is no difference." "There is neither Jew nor Greek, there is neither bond nor free." "The rich and poor meet together: the Lord is the Maker of them all." "The same Lord over all is rich unto all that call upon Him. For whosoever shall call upon the name of the Lord shall be saved." Acts 17:26, 27; Gal. 3:28; Prov. 22:2; Rom. 10:11-13.

8. "The spirit which built up the partition wall between Jews and Gentiles is still a_____. Pride and prejudice have built strong walls of s_____ between different classes of men." (403). How does this apply to me? _____

_____ (in the neighborhood, in the work place). "There are no barriers which man or Satan can erect but that faith can p_____."

9. "For w_____ _____ shall call upon the name of the Lord shall be s_____." A beautiful promise for everyone, Lord. Help my walk with You spill over into my attitude to others, and may my attitude be equally inclusive: _____

Prayer journal: _____

Chapter 44

The True Sign

[This chapter is based on Matt. 15:29-39; 16:1-12;
Mark 7:31-37; 8:1-21.]

"Again He went out from the borders of Tyre, and came through Sidon unto the Sea of Galilee, through the midst of the borders of Decapolis." Mark 7:31, R. V.

It was in the region of Decapolis that the demoniacs of Gergesa had been healed. Here the people, alarmed at the destruction of the swine, had constrained Jesus to depart from among them. But they had listened to the messengers He left behind, and a desire was aroused to see Him. As He came again into that region, a crowd gathered about Him, and a deaf, stammering man was brought to Him. Jesus did not, according to His custom, restore the man by a word only. Taking him apart from the multitude, He put His fingers in his ears, and touched his tongue; looking up to heaven, He sighed at thought of the ears that would not be open to the truth, the tongues that refused to acknowledge the Redeemer. At the word, "Be opened," the man's speech was restored, and, disregarding the command to tell no man, he published abroad the story of his cure.

Jesus went up into a mountain, and there the multitude flocked to Him, bringing their sick and lame, and laying them at His feet. He healed them all; and the people, heathen as they were, glorified the God of Israel. For three days they continued to throng about the Saviour, sleeping at night in the open air, and through the day pressing eagerly to hear the words of Christ, and to see His works. At the end of three [404-405] days their food was spent. Jesus would not send them away hungry, and He called upon His disciples to give them food. Again the disciples revealed their unbelief. At Bethsaida they had seen how, with Christ's blessing, their little store availed for the feeding of the multitude; yet they did not now bring forward their all, trusting His power to multiply it for the hungry crowds. Moreover, those whom He fed at Bethsaida were Jews; these were Gentiles and heathen. Jewish prejudice was still strong in the hearts of the disciples, and they answered Jesus, "Whence can

1. Jesus returned to Decapolis where the d_____ of Gergesa had been healed. The people "had constrained Jesus to depart from among them. But they had listened to the messengers He left behind, and a d_____ was roused to see Him." What a turn around, through a simple testimony of what Jesus had done for them, and the help of the Holy Spirit. Lord, please use me in the same way. Give me an opportunity to tell others what You do for me, what You mean to me (which is):

_____
_____
_____
_____
_____
_____

2. How did the disciples reveal their unbelief? (405): _____

_____

Lord, help me not to reveal unbelief by forgetting Your providences; which are: _____

a man satisfy these men with bread here in the wilderness?" But obedient to His word they brought Him what they had,--seven loaves and two fishes. The multitude were fed, seven large baskets of fragments remaining. Four thousand men, besides women and children, were thus refreshed, and Jesus sent them away with glad and grateful hearts.

Then taking a boat with His disciples, He crossed the lake to Magdala, at the southern end of the plain of Gennesaret. In the border of Tyre and Sidon His spirit had been refreshed by the confiding trust of the Syrophoenician woman. The heathen people of Decapolis had received Him with gladness. Now as He landed once more in Galilee, where His power had been most strikingly manifested, where most of His works of mercy had been performed, and His teaching given, He was met with contemptuous unbelief.

A deputation of Pharisees had been joined by representatives from the rich and lordly Sadducees, the party of the priests, the skeptics and aristocracy of the nation. The two sects had been at bitter enmity. The Sadducees courted the favor of the ruling power in order to maintain their own position and authority. The Pharisees, on the other hand, fostered the popular hatred against the Romans, longing for the time when they could throw off the yoke of the conqueror. But Pharisee and Sadducee now united against Christ. Like seeks like; and evil, wherever it exists, leagues with evil for the destruction of the good. [405-406]

Now the Pharisees and Sadducees came to Christ, asking for a sign from heaven. When in the days of Joshua Israel went out to battle with the Canaanites at Bethhoron, the sun had stood still at the leader's command until victory was gained; and many similar wonders had been manifest in their history. Some such sign was demanded of Jesus. But these signs were not what the Jews needed. No mere external evidence could benefit them. What they needed was not intellectual enlightenment, but spiritual renovation.

"O ye hypocrites," said Jesus, "ye can discern the face of the sky,"--by studying the sky they could foretell the weather,--"but can ye not discern the signs of the times?" Christ's own words, spoken with the power of the Holy Spirit that convicted them of sin, were the sign that God had given for their salvation. And signs direct from heaven had been given to attest the mission of

3. After being so warmly received by the heathen, when Jesus landed in Galilee, "He was met with c_____ unbelief." Two sects, the Pharisees and the Sadducees, had been at bitter enmity. But "now u_____ against Christ. Like seeks like; and evil, wherever it exists, l_____ with evil for the destruction of the g_____." Teach me, Lord. I may not normally listen to gossip, but since this person has recently hurt me, out of disguised revenge, I go ahead and listen to it. Is that me, in league with evil? _____

4. "The Pharisees and Sadducees came to Christ asking for a s_____ from heaven…[But] no mere e_____ evidence could benefit them. What they needed was not intellectual enlightenment, but s_____ renova-

Christ. The song of the angels to the shepherds, the star that guided the wise men, the dove and the voice from heaven at His baptism, were witnesses for Him.

"And He sighed deeply in His spirit, and saith, Why doth this generation seek after a sign?" "There shall no sign be given unto it, but the sign of the prophet Jonas." As Jonah was three days and three nights in the belly of the whale, Christ was to be the same time "in the heart of the earth." And as the preaching of Jonah was a sign to the Ninevites, so Christ's preaching was a sign to His generation. But what a contrast in the reception of the word! The people of the great heathen city trembled as they heard the warning from God. Kings and nobles humbled themselves; the high and the lowly together cried to the God of heaven, and His mercy was granted unto them. "The men of Nineveh shall rise in judgment with this generation," Christ had said, "and shall condemn it: because they repented at the preaching of Jonas; and, behold, a greater than Jonas is here." Matt. 12:40, 41.

Every miracle that Christ performed was a sign of His divinity. He was doing the very work that had been foretold of the Messiah; but to the Pharisees these works of mercy were a positive offense. The Jewish leaders looked with heartless indifference on human suffering. In many cases their selfishness and oppression had caused the affliction that Christ relieved. Thus His miracles were to them a reproach.

That which led the Jews to reject the Saviour's work was the highest evidence of His divine character. The greatest significance of His miracles is seen in the fact that they were for the blessing of humanity. [406-407] The highest evidence that He came from God is that His life revealed the character of God. He did the works and spoke the words of God. Such a life is the greatest of all miracles.

When the message of truth is presented in our day, there are many who, like the Jews, cry, Show us a sign. Work us a miracle. Christ wrought no miracle at the demand of the Pharisees. He wrought no miracle in the wilderness in answer to Satan's insinuations. He does not impart to us power to vindicate ourselves or to satisfy the demands of unbelief and pride. But the gospel is not without a sign of its divine origin. Is it not a miracle that we can break from the bondage of Satan? Enmity against Satan is not natural to the human heart; it is im-

tion." (406). Why am I more impressed with an external sign, than an internal one? Do I favor having a safety net of distancing myself from any personal application? _____

_____

_____

_____

5. "Christ's own w_____, spoken with the power of the Holy Spirit that convicted them of sin, were the s_____ that God had given for their salvation…There shall no sign be given it, but the sign of the prophet J_____…As the preaching of Jonah was a sign to the Ninevites, so Christ's p_____ was a sign to His generation." Lord, help me to comprehend the significance of Your preaching, of Your Word, in my life, a sign for my salvation!

_____

_____

_____

6. Why were Jesus' miracles of mercy a positive offense to the Pharisees?

_____

_____

_____

(heartless indifference to human suffering; often being the cause of suffering that Jesus relieved). _____

_____

_____

7. "The highest evidence that He came from God is that His life revealed the c_____ of God. He did the works and spoke the words of God. Such a l_____ is the greatest of all miracles." (407). Lord, may I reflect Your character; and sense the wondrous opportunity to be part of Your miracle!

_____

_____

_____

"A consistent life i_____
Christ is a great miracle."

planted by the grace of God. When one who has been controlled by a stubborn, wayward will is set free, and yields himself wholeheartedly to the drawing of God's heavenly agencies, a miracle is wrought; so also when a man who has been under strong delusion comes to understand moral truth. Every time a soul is converted, and learns to love God and keep His commandments, the promise of God is fulfilled, "A new heart also will I give you, and a new spirit will I put within you." Ezek. 36:26. The change in human hearts, the transformation of human characters, is a miracle that reveals an ever-living Saviour, working to rescue souls. A consistent life in Christ is a great miracle. In the preaching of the word of God, the sign that should be manifest now and always is the presence of the Holy Spirit, to make the word a regenerating power to those that hear. This is God's witness before the world to the divine mission of His Son.

Those who desired a sign from Jesus had so hardened their hearts in unbelief that they did not discern in His character the likeness of God. They would not see that His mission was in fulfillment of the Scriptures. In the parable of the rich man and Lazarus, Jesus said to the Pharisees, "If they hear not Moses and the prophets, neither will they be persuaded, though one rose from the dead." Luke 16:31. No sign that could be given in heaven or earth would benefit them.

Jesus "sighed deeply in His spirit," and, turning from the group of cavilers, re-entered the boat with His disciples. In sorrowful silence they again crossed the lake. They did not, however, return to the place they had left, but directed their course toward Bethsaida, near where the five thousand had been fed. Upon reaching the farther side, Jesus said, "Take heed and beware of the leaven of the Pharisees and of the [407-408] Sadducees." The Jews had been accustomed since the days of Moses to put away leaven from their houses at the Passover season, and they had thus been taught to regard it as a type of sin. Yet the disciples failed to understand Jesus. In their sudden departure from Magdala they had forgotten to take bread, and they had with them only one loaf. To this circumstance they understood Christ to refer, warning them not to buy bread of a Pharisee or a Sadducee. Their lack of faith and spiritual insight had often led them to similar misconception of His words. Now Jesus reproved them for thinking that He who had fed thousands with a few fishes and barley loaves could in that solemn warning have referred merely to temporal food. There was danger that the crafty reasoning of the Pharisees and the Sadducees would leaven His disciples with unbelief, causing them to think lightly of the works of Christ.

The disciples were inclined to think that their Master should have granted the demand for a sign in the heavens. They believed that He was fully able to do this, and that such a sign would put His enemies to silence. They did not discern the hypocrisy of these cavilers.

Months afterward, "when there were gathered together an innumerable multitude of people, insomuch that they trode one upon another," Jesus repeated the same teaching. "He began to say unto His disciples first of all, Beware ye of the leaven of the Pharisees, which is hypocrisy." Luke 12:1.

The leaven placed in the meal works imperceptibly, changing the whole mass to its own nature. So if hypocrisy is allowed to exist in the heart, it permeates the character and the life. A striking example of the hypocrisy of the Pharisees, Christ had already rebuked in denouncing the practice of "Corban," by which a neglect of filial duty was concealed under a pretense of liberality to the temple. The scribes and Pharisees were insinuating deceptive principles. They concealed the real tendency of their doctrines, and improved every occasion to instill them artfully into the minds of their hearers. These false principles, when once accepted, worked like leaven in the meal, permeating and transforming the character. It was this deceptive teaching that made it so hard for the people to receive the words of Christ.

The same influences are working today through those who try to explain the law of God in such a way as to make it conform to their practices. This class do not attack the law openly, but put forward [408-409] speculative theories that undermine its principles. They explain it so as to destroy its force.

The hypocrisy of the Pharisees was the product of self-seeking. The glorification of themselves was the object of their lives. It was this that led them to pervert and misapply the Scriptures, and blinded them to the purpose of Christ's mission. This subtle evil even the disciples of Christ were in danger of cherishing. Those who classed themselves with the followers of Jesus, but who had not left all in order to become His disciples,

8. There was danger that Christ's disciples would be leavened "with u_____, causing them to think l_____ of the works of Christ." (408). Is this a danger with me, Lord? How?
_____
_____
_____

were influenced in a great degree by the reasoning of the Pharisees. They were often vacillating between faith and unbelief, and they did not discern the treasures of wisdom hidden in Christ. Even the disciples, though outwardly they had left all for Jesus' sake, had not in heart ceased to seek great things for themselves. It was this spirit that prompted the strife as to who should be greatest. It was this that came between them and Christ, making them so little in sympathy with His mission of self-sacrifice, so slow to comprehend the mystery of redemption. As leaven, if left to complete its work, will cause corruption and decay, so does the self-seeking spirit, cherished, work the defilement and ruin of the soul.

Among the followers of our Lord today, as of old, how widespread is this subtle, deceptive sin! How often our service to Christ, our communion with one another, is marred by the secret desire to exalt self! How ready the thought of self-gratulation, and the longing for human approval! It is the love of self, the desire for an easier way than God has appointed that leads to the substitution of human theories and traditions for the divine precepts. To His own disciples the warning words of Christ are spoken, "Take heed and beware of the leaven of the Pharisees."

The religion of Christ is sincerity itself. Zeal for God's glory is the motive implanted by the Holy Spirit; and only the effectual working of the Spirit can implant this motive. Only the power of God can banish self-seeking and hypocrisy. This change is the sign of His working. When the faith we accept destroys selfishness and pretense, when it leads us to seek God's glory and not our own, we may know that it is of the right order. "Father, glorify Thy name" (John 12:28), was the keynote of Christ's life, and if we follow Him, this will be the keynote of our life. He commands us to "walk, even as He walked;" and "hereby we do know that we know Him, if we keep His commandments."1 John 2:6, 3.

9. As leaven, a cherished self-seeking spirit works within. "It was this that came between the disciples and C_____, making them so little in s_____ _____ with His mission of self-sacrifice, so slow to c_____ the mystery of redemption." (409). Lord, show me how I manifest the same spirit. I do not want anything to come between us. May my spirit be molded into Your Spirit: _____

Prayer journal: _____

Chapter 45

The Foreshadowing of the Cross

[This chapter is based on Matt. 16:13-28;
Mark 8:27-38; Luke 9:18-27.]

The work of Christ on earth was hastening to a close. Before Him, in vivid outline, lay the scenes whither His feet were tending. Even before He took humanity upon Him, He saw the whole length of the path He must travel in order to save that which was lost. Every pang that rent His heart, every insult that was heaped upon His head, every privation that He was called to endure, was open to His view before He laid aside His crown and royal robe, and stepped down from the throne, to clothe His divinity with humanity. The path from the manger to Calvary was all before His eyes. He knew the anguish that would come upon Him. He knew it all, and yet He said, "Lo, I come: in the volume of the Book it is written of Me, I delight to do Thy will, O My God: yea, Thy law is within My heart." Ps. 40:7, 8.

Ever before Him He saw the result of His mission. His earthly life, so full of toil and self-sacrifice, was cheered by the prospect that He would not have all this travail for nought. By giving His life for the life of men, He would win back the world to its loyalty to God. Although the baptism of blood must first be received; although the sins of the world were to weigh upon His innocent soul; although the shadow of an unspeakable woe was upon Him; yet for the joy that was set before Him, He chose to endure the cross, and despised the shame.

From the chosen companions of His ministry the scenes that lay before Him were as yet hidden; but the time was near when they must [410-411] behold His agony. They must see Him whom they had loved and trusted, delivered into the hands of His enemies, and hung upon the cross of Calvary. Soon He must leave them to face the world without the comfort of His visible presence. He knew how bitter hate and unbelief would persecute them, and he desired to prepare them for their trials.

Jesus and His disciples had now come into one

1. "Even before He took h_____ upon Him, He saw the whole length of the path He must travel in order to s____ ____ that which was lost. Every pang that rent His heart, every i_____ that was heaped upon His head, every privation that He was called to endure, was open to His view b_____ He laid aside His crown and royal robe, and stepped down from the throne...and yet He said, 'Lo, I come.'" Lord, I can't imagine how difficult of a choice that was. Knowing of my denials, my rejections, my insults to You, You STILL came! Tell me why? ____

_____

_____

_____

_____

2. "Yet for the j_____ that was set before Him, He chose to endure the cross, and despised the shame." You mean, I am Your joy, that helped You endure humanity, Gethsemane, sin, Calvary? _____

_____

_____ (How does this statement fit with the one on page 753, paragraph 2 (chapter 78, "Calvary"):

"The Savior could not see t_____ the portals of the tomb. Hope did not present to Him His coming forth from the grave a c_____?".) My thoughts: _____

_____

_____

3. "Time was near when Jesus' disciples must behold His a_____ ...But first He went away alone, and p_____ that their hearts might be p_____ to receive His words." (410, 411). Is there a point here about my approach to meeting You, be it church, reading Your Word, or any devotion time? _____

_____

_____

_____

of the towns about Caesarea Philippi. They were beyond the limits of Galilee, in a region where idolatry prevailed. Here the disciples were withdrawn from the controlling influence of Judaism, and brought into closer contact with the heathen worship. Around them were represented forms of superstition that existed in all parts of the world. Jesus desired that a view of these things might lead them to feel their responsibility to the heathen. During His stay in this region, He endeavored to withdraw from teaching the people, and to devote Himself more fully to His disciples.

He was about to tell them of the suffering that awaited Him. But first He went away alone, and prayed that their hearts might be prepared to receive His words. Upon joining them, He did not at once communicate that which He desired to impart. Before doing this, He gave them an opportunity of confessing their faith in Him that they might be strengthened for the coming trial. He asked, "Whom do men say that I the Son of man am?"

Sadly the disciples were forced to acknowledge that Israel had failed to recognize their Messiah. Some indeed, when they saw His miracles, had declared Him to be the Son of David. The multitudes that had been fed at Bethsaida had desired to proclaim Him king of Israel. Many were ready to accept Him as a prophet; but they did not believe Him to be the Messiah.

Jesus now put a second question, relating to the disciples themselves: "But whom say ye that I am?" Peter answered, "Thou art the Christ, the Son of the living God."

From the first, Peter had believed Jesus to be the Messiah. Many others who had been convicted by the preaching of John the Baptist, and had accepted Christ, began to doubt as to John's mission when he was imprisoned and put to death; and they now doubted that Jesus was the Messiah, for whom they had looked so long. Many of the disciples who had ardently expected Jesus to take His place on David's throne left Him when they perceived that He had no such intention. But Peter and his [411-412] companions turned not from their allegiance. The vacillating course of those who praised yesterday and condemned today did not destroy the faith of the true follower of the Saviour. Peter declared, "Thou art the Christ, the Son of the living God." He waited not for kingly honors to crown his Lord, but accepted Him in His humiliation.

Peter had expressed the faith of the twelve. Yet the disciples were still far from understanding Christ's mission. The opposition and misrepresentation of the priests and rulers, while it could not turn them away from Christ, still caused them great perplexity. They did not see their way clearly. The influence of their early training, the teaching of the rabbis, the power of tradition, still intercepted their view of truth. From time to time precious rays of light from Jesus shone upon them, yet often they were like men groping among shadows. But on this day, before they were brought face to face with the great trial of their faith, the Holy Spirit rested upon them in power. For a little time their eyes were turned away from "the things which are seen," to behold "the things which are not seen." 2 Cor. 4:18. Beneath the guise of humanity they discerned the glory of the Son of God.

Jesus answered Peter, saying, "Blessed art thou, Simon Bar-jona: for flesh and blood hath not revealed it unto thee, but My Father which is in heaven."

The truth which Peter had confessed is the foundation of the believer's faith. It is that which Christ Himself has declared to be eternal life. But the possession of this knowledge was no ground for self-glorification. Through no wisdom or goodness of his own had it been revealed to Peter. Never can humanity, of itself, attain to a knowledge of the divine. "It is as high as heaven; what canst thou do? deeper than hell; what canst thou know?" Job 11:8. Only the spirit of adoption can reveal to us the deep things of God, which "eye hath not seen, nor ear heard, neither have entered into the heart of man." "God hath revealed them unto us by His Spirit: for the Spirit searcheth all things, yea, the deep things of God." 1 Cor. 2:9, 10. "The secret of the Lord is with them that fear Him;" and the fact that Peter discerned the glory of Christ was an evidence that he had been "taught of God." Ps. 25:14; John 6:45. Ah, indeed, "blessed art thou, Simon Bar-jona: for flesh and blood hath not revealed it unto thee."

Jesus continued: "I say also unto thee, That thou art Peter, and upon this rock I will build My church; and the gates of hell shall not prevail [412-413] against it." The word Peter signifies a stone,--a rolling stone. Peter was not the rock upon which the church was founded. The gates of hell did prevail against him when he denied his

4. "Flesh and blood hath not r_____ it unto thee, but My Father which is in heaven...Never can humanity, of itself, attain to the knowledge of the d_____...The fact that Peter discerned the glory of Christ was an evidence that he had been, " 't_____ of God.'" (412). Lord, even these spiritual thoughts, from this work out on my walk with You, is revealed by You, the Father, and the Spirit, to me. How exciting that You know of my personal quest and are gently guiding me with each thought, each and every day: _____

_____

Lord with cursing and swearing. The church was built upon One against whom the gates of hell could not prevail.

Centuries before the Saviour's advent Moses had pointed to the Rock of Israel's salvation. The psalmist had sung of "the Rock of my strength." Isaiah had written, "Thus saith the Lord God, Behold, I lay in Zion for a foundation a stone, a tried stone, a precious cornerstone, a sure foundation." Deut. 32:4; Ps. 62:7; Isa. 28:16. Peter himself, writing by inspiration, applies this prophecy to Jesus. He says, "If ye have tasted that the Lord is gracious: unto whom coming, a living stone, rejected indeed of men, but with God elect, precious, ye also, as living stones, are built up a spiritual house." 1 Peter 2:3-5, R. V.

"Other foundation can no man lay than that is laid, which is Jesus Christ." 1 Cor. 3:11. "Upon this rock," said Jesus, "I will build My church." In the presence of God, and all the heavenly intelligences, in the presence of the unseen army of hell, Christ founded His church upon the living Rock. That Rock is Himself,--His own body, for us broken and bruised. Against the church built upon this foundation, the gates of hell shall not prevail.

How feeble the church appeared when Christ spoke these words! There was only a handful of believers, against whom all the power of demons and evil men would be directed; yet the followers of Christ were not to fear. Built upon the Rock of their strength, they could not be overthrown.

For six thousand years, faith has builded upon Christ. For six thousand years the floods and tempests of satanic wrath have beaten upon the Rock of our salvation; but it stands unmoved.

Peter had expressed the truth which is the foundation of the church's faith, and Jesus now honored him as the representative of the whole body of believers. He said, "I will give unto thee the keys of the kingdom of heaven: and whatsoever thou shalt bind on earth shall be bound in heaven: and whatsoever thou shalt loose on earth shall be loosed in heaven."

"The keys of the kingdom of heaven" are the words of Christ. All the words of Holy Scripture are His, and are here included. These words have power to open and to shut heaven. They declare the conditions [413-414] upon which men are received or rejected. Thus the work

5. Peter, as the representative of the whole body of b_____, was given the k_____ of the kingdom of heaven, which includes all of the Holy S_____ ...Those

of those who preach God's word is a savor of life unto life or of death unto death. Theirs is a mission weighted with eternal results.

The Saviour did not commit the work of the gospel to Peter individually. At a later time, repeating the words that were spoken to Peter, He applied them directly to the church. And the same in substance was spoken also to the twelve as representatives of the body of believers. If Jesus had delegated any special authority to one of the disciples above the others, we should not find them so often contending as to who should be the greatest. They would have submitted to the wish of their Master, and honored the one whom He had chosen.

Instead of appointing one to be their head, Christ said to the disciples, "Be not ye called Rabbi;" "neither be ye called masters: for one is your Master, even Christ." Matt. 23:8, 10.

"The head of every man is Christ." God, who put all things under the Saviour's feet, "gave Him to be the head over all things to the church, which is His body, the fullness of Him that filleth all in all." 1 Cor. 11:3; Eph. 1:22, 23. The church is built upon Christ as its foundation; it is to obey Christ as its head. It is not to depend upon man, or be controlled by man. Many claim that a position of trust in the church gives them authority to dictate what other men shall believe and what they shall do. This claim God does not sanction. The Saviour declares, "All ye are brethren." All are exposed to temptation, and are liable to error. Upon no finite being can we depend for guidance. The Rock of faith is the living presence of Christ in the church. Upon this the weakest may depend, and those who think themselves the strongest will prove to be the weakest, unless they make Christ their efficiency. "Cursed be the man that trusteth in man, and maketh flesh his arm." The Lord "is the Rock, His work is perfect." "Blessed are all they that put their trust in Him." Jer. 17:5; Deut. 32:4; Ps. 2:12.

After Peter's confession, Jesus charged the disciples to tell no man that He was the Christ. This charge was given because of the determined opposition of the scribes and Pharisees. More than this, the people, and even the disciples, had so false a conception of the Messiah that a public announcement of Him would give them no true idea of His character or His work. But day by day He was revealing Himself to them as the Saviour, and thus He desired to give them a true conception

who preach God's word... [have] a mission weighted with e_____ results." (413, 414). What a responsibility and privilege, to be Your ambassador, urging others to accept Your abundant life, for life or death hang in the balance. What would it take, Lord, for me to have a passion for the lost as you do?

_____

_____

_____

_____

of Him as the Messiah. [414-415]

The disciples still expected Christ to reign as a temporal prince. Although He had so long concealed His design, they believed that He would not always remain in poverty and obscurity; the time was near when He would establish His kingdom. That the hatred of the priests and rabbis would never be overcome, that Christ would be rejected by His own nation, condemned as a deceiver, and crucified as a malefactor,--such a thought the disciples had never entertained. But the hour of the power of darkness was drawing on, and Jesus must open to His disciples the conflict before them. He was sad as He anticipated the trial.

Hitherto He had refrained from making known to them anything relative to His sufferings and death. In His conversation with Nicodemus He had said, "As Moses lifted up the serpent in the wilderness, even so must the Son of man be lifted up: that whosoever believeth in Him should not perish, but have eternal life." John 3:14, 15. But the disciples did not hear this, and had they heard, would not have understood. But now they have been with Jesus, listening to His words, beholding His works, until, notwithstanding the humility of His surroundings, and the opposition of priests and people, they can join in the testimony of Peter, "Thou art the Christ, the Son of the living God." Now the time has come for the veil that hides the future to be withdrawn. "From that time forth began Jesus to show unto His disciples, how that He must go unto Jerusalem, and suffer many things of the elders and chief priests and scribes, and be killed, and be raised again the third day."

Speechless with grief and amazement, the disciples listened. Christ had accepted Peter's acknowledgment of Him as the Son of God; and now His words pointing to His suffering and death seemed incomprehensible. Peter could not keep silent. He laid hold upon his Master, as if to draw Him back from His impending doom, exclaiming, "Be it far from Thee, Lord: this shall not be unto Thee."

Peter loved his Lord; but Jesus did not commend him for thus manifesting the desire to shield Him from suffering. Peter's words were not such as would be a help and solace to Jesus in the great trial before Him. They were not in harmony with God's purpose of grace toward a lost world, nor with the lesson of self-sacrifice that Jesus had come to teach by His own example. Peter

6. "Now the time has come for the veil that hides the future to be withdrawn... Speechless with grief and a_____, the disciples listened...His words...seemed i_____." (415). Lord, I don't want to cheapen or undervalue Your sacrificial love, Your amazing love! May my heart be moved, melted, and molded, as I contemplate Your suffering, Your passion: _____

did not desire to see the cross in the work of Christ. The impression which his words would make was directly opposed to that which Christ desired to make on the minds of His followers, and the Saviour was moved to utter one of the sternest rebukes [415-416] that ever fell from His lips: "Get thee behind Me, Satan: thou art an offense unto Me: for thou savorest not the things that be of God, but those that be of men."

Satan was trying to discourage Jesus, and turn Him from His mission; and Peter, in his blind love, was giving voice to the temptation. The prince of evil was the author of the thought. His instigation was behind that impulsive appeal. In the wilderness, Satan had offered Christ the dominion of the world on condition of forsaking the path of humiliation and sacrifice. Now he was presenting the same temptation to the disciple of Christ. He was seeking to fix Peter's gaze upon the earthly glory, that he might not behold the cross to which Jesus desired to turn his eyes. And through Peter, Satan was again pressing the temptation upon Jesus. But the Saviour heeded it not; His thought was for His disciple. Satan had interposed between Peter and his Master, that the heart of the disciple might not be touched at the vision of Christ's humiliation for him. The words of Christ were spoken, not to Peter, but to the one who was trying to separate him from his Redeemer. "Get thee behind Me, Satan." No longer interpose between Me and My erring servant. Let Me come face to face with Peter, that I may reveal to him the mystery of My love.

It was to Peter a bitter lesson, and one which he learned but slowly, that the path of Christ on earth lay through agony and humiliation. The disciple shrank from fellowship with his Lord in suffering. But in the heat of the furnace fire he was to learn its blessing. Long afterward, when his active form was bowed with the burden of years and labors, he wrote, "Beloved, think it not strange concerning the fiery trial which is to try you, as though some strange thing happened unto you: but rejoice, inasmuch as ye are partakers of Christ's sufferings; that, when His glory shall be revealed, ye may be glad also with exceeding joy." 1 Peter 4:12, 13.

Jesus now explained to His disciples that His own life of self-abnegation was an example of what theirs should be. Calling about Him, with the disciples, the people who had been lingering near, He said, "If any man will come after Me, let him deny himself, and take

7. "Satan was trying to d_____ Jesus, and turn Him from His mission; and Peter, in his blind l_____, was giving voice to the temptation." (416). Lord, I sure don't want to hear one of the sternest rebukes that ever fell from Your lips, "Get thee behind Me, Satan." How do I discourage You from Your mission?

_____
_____
_____
_____

8. "It was to Peter a bitter lesson, and one which he learned but s_____, that the path of Christ on earth lay through a_____ and h_____..." Jesus now explained to His disciples that His own life of self-a_____ was an example of what theirs should be." Your example is for me too, right Lord? I learn slowly, too: instead of self-centeredness (which I am blind to), give me opportunities for self-abnegation:

_____
_____
_____

356

Can We Walk, Together?

9. "If any man will come after Me, let him d_____ himself, and take up his c_____ daily, and follow Me...

up his cross daily, and follow Me." The cross was associated with the power of Rome. It was the instrument of the most cruel and humiliating form of death. The lowest criminals were required to bear the cross to the place of execution; and often as it was about to be laid upon their shoulders, they resisted with desperate violence, until they were overpowered, and [416-417] the instrument of torture was bound upon them. But Jesus bade His followers take up the cross and bear it after Him. To the disciples His words, though dimly comprehended, pointed to their submission to the most bitter humiliation,--submission even unto death for the sake of Christ. No more complete self-surrender could the Saviour's words have pictured. But all this He had accepted for them. Jesus did not count heaven a place to be desired while we were lost. He left the heavenly courts for a life of reproach and insult, and a death of shame. He who was rich in heaven's priceless treasure, became poor, that through His poverty we might be rich. We are to follow in the path He trod.

Love for souls for whom Christ died means crucifixion of self. He who is a child of God should henceforth look upon himself as a link in the chain let down to save the world, one with Christ in His plan of mercy, going forth with Him to seek and save the lost. The Christian is ever to realize that he has consecrated himself to God, and that in character he is to reveal Christ to the world. The self-sacrifice, the sympathy, the love, manifested in the life of Christ are to reappear in the life of the worker for God.

The self-sacrifice, the sympathy, the l_____, manifested in the life of Christ are to reappear in the l____ of the worker of God." (416, 417). Lord, help me to meditate on Your life more, to learn of Your humility, and to melt away my self-seeking. Whatever it takes, Lord, I am willing. Teach me to be more willing:

_____
_____
_____

"Whosoever will save his life shall lose it; but whosoever shall lose his life for My sake and the gospel's, the same shall save it." Selfishness is death. No organ of the body could live should it confine its service to itself. The heart, failing to send its lifeblood to the hand and the head, would quickly lose its power. As our lifeblood, so is the love of Christ diffused through every part of His mystical body. We are members one of another, and the soul that refuses to impart will perish. And "what is a man profited," said Jesus, "if he shall gain the whole world, and lose his own soul? or what shall a man give in exchange for his soul?"

Beyond the poverty and humiliation of the present, He pointed the disciples to His coming in glory, not in the splendor of an earthly throne, but with the glory of God and the hosts of heaven. And then, He said, "He shall reward every man according to his works." Then for their encouragement He gave the promise, "Verily I say unto you, There be some standing here, which shall not taste of death, till they see the Son of man coming in His kingdom." But the disciples did not comprehend His words. The glory seemed far away. Their eyes were fixed upon the nearer view, the earthly life of poverty, humiliation, and suffering. Must their glowing expectations of the Messiah's kingdom be relinquished? Were they not to see their Lord exalted to the throne of [417-418] David? Could it be that Christ was to live a humble, homeless wanderer, to be despised, rejected, and put to death? Sadness oppressed their hearts, for they loved their Master. Doubt also harassed their minds, for it seemed incomprehensible that the Son of God should be subjected to such cruel humiliation. They questioned why He should voluntarily go to Jerusalem to meet the treatment which He had told them He was there to receive. How could He resign Himself to such a fate, and leave them in greater darkness than that in which they were groping before He revealed Himself to them?

In the region of Caesarea Philippi, Christ was out of the reach of Herod and Caiaphas, the disciples reasoned. He had nothing to fear from the hatred of the Jews or from the power of the Romans. Why not work there, at a distance from the Pharisees? Why need He give Himself up to death? If He was to die, how was it that His kingdom was to be established so firmly that the gates of hell should not prevail against it? To the disciples this was indeed a mystery.

They were even now journeying along the shores of the Sea of Galilee toward the city where all their hopes were to be crushed. They dared not remonstrate with Christ, but they talked together in low, sorrowful tones in regard to what the future would be. Even amid their questionings they clung to the thought that some unforeseen circumstance might avert the doom which seemed to await their Lord. Thus they sorrowed and doubted, hoped and feared, for six long, gloomy days.

Prayer journal: _____

Chapter 46

He Was Transfigured

[This chapter is based on Matt. 17:1-8 ;
Mark 9:2-8; Luke 9:28-36.]

1. Jesus "has often spent entire nights in the mountains in p_____.··· The Man of Sorrows pours out His supplications with strong crying and t_____.··· He must Himself gain a fresh hold on omnipotence, for only thus can He c_____ the future." (419, 420). Lord, You knew the challenges and trials ahead of Yourself; You knew Your need of the Father's presence. I don't know those things like You did. Satan has the pattern of my thought process focused on self. Keep bringing me to new thought patterns, Lord, so that my mind is stayed on You, each day, each moment of each day. I want to pray like You did, feeling an urgent need. But I can't generate that sense. You can keep bringing the realization to me. Nag me if You have to, Lord. Thank You.

Evening is drawing on as Jesus calls to His side three of His disciples, Peter, James, and John, and leads them across the fields, and far up a rugged path, to a lonely mountainside. The Saviour and His disciples have spent the day in traveling and teaching, and the mountain climb adds to their weariness. Christ has lifted burdens from mind and body of many sufferers; He has sent the thrill of life through their enfeebled frames; but He also is compassed with humanity, and with His disciples He is wearied with the ascent.

The light of the setting sun still lingers on the mountain top, and gilds with its fading glory the path they are traveling. But soon the light dies out from hill as well as valley, the sun disappears behind the western horizon, and the solitary travelers are wrapped in the darkness of night. The gloom of their surroundings seems in harmony with their sorrowful lives, around which the clouds are gathering and thickening.

The disciples do not venture to ask Christ whither He is going, or for what purpose. He has often spent entire nights in the mountains in prayer. He whose hand formed mountain and valley is at home with nature, and enjoys its quietude. The disciples follow where Christ leads the way; yet they wonder why their Master should lead them up this toilsome ascent when they are weary, and when He too is in need of rest.

Presently Christ tells them that they are now to go no farther. Stepping a little aside from them, the Man of Sorrows pours out His [419-420] supplications with strong crying and tears. He prays for strength to endure the test in behalf of humanity. He must Himself gain a fresh hold on Omnipotence, for only thus can He contemplate the future. And He pours out His heart longings for His disciples, that in the hour of the power of darkness their faith may not fail. The dew is heavy upon His bowed form, but He heeds it not. The shadows of night gather thickly about Him, but He regards not their gloom. So the hours pass slowly by. At first the disciples unite their prayers with His in sincere devotion; but after a time they are overcome with weariness, and, even while trying to retain their interest in the scene, they fall asleep. Jesus has told them of His sufferings; He has taken them with Him that they might unite with Him in prayer; even now He is praying for them. The Saviour has seen the gloom of His disciples, and has longed to lighten their grief by an assurance that their faith has not been in vain. Not all, even of the twelve, can receive the revelation He desires to give. Only the three who are to witness His anguish in Gethsemane have been chosen to be with Him on the mount. Now the burden of His prayer is that they may be given a manifestation [420-421] of the glory He had with the Father before the world was, that His kingdom may be revealed to human eyes, and that His disciples may be strengthened to behold it. He pleads that they may witness a manifestation of His divinity that will comfort them in the hour of His supreme agony with the knowledge that He is of a surety the Son of God and that His shameful death is a part of the plan of redemption.

His prayer is heard. While He is bowed in lowliness upon the stony ground, suddenly the heavens open, the golden gates of the city of God are thrown wide, and holy radiance descends upon the mount, enshrouding the Saviour's form. Divinity from within flashes through humanity, and meets the glory coming from above. Arising from His prostrate position, Christ stands in godlike majesty. The soul agony is gone. His countenance now shines "as the sun," and His garments are "white as the light."

The disciples, awaking, behold the flood of glory that illuminates the mount. In fear and amazement they gaze upon the radiant form of their Master. As they become able to endure the wondrous light, they see that Jesus is not alone. Beside Him are two heavenly beings, in close converse with Him. They are Moses, who upon Sinai had talked with God; and Elijah, to whom the high privilege was given--granted to but one other of the sons of Adam--never to come under the power of death.

Upon Mount Pisgah fifteen centuries before, Moses had stood gazing upon the Land of Promise. But because of his sin at Meribah, it was not for him to enter there. Not for him was the joy of leading the host of Israel into the inheritance of their fathers. His agonized

2. Now the burden of His prayer is that Peter, James, John may 1) be given a manifestation of the g_____ He had with the Father before the world was, 2) that His kingdom may be r_____ to human eyes, 3) be comforted with the knowledge that He is of a s_____ the Son of God, that 4) His shameful d_____ ____ is a part of the plan of redemption. (421). Through the testimony of these three, Lord, aren't all disciples to be encouraged? _____ I want to join my prayer with Yours, that I might be privileged with a vision of Your glory and Your kingdom, even in the cross. What can I do to prepare for this vision, to place myself where I am more likely to experience this vision? _____ _____ _____ _____

3. "His prayer is heard... D_____ from within flashes through humanity, and meets the glory coming from above..."

entreaty, "I pray Thee, let me go over, and see the good land that is beyond Jordan, that goodly mountain, and Lebanon" (Deut. 3:25), was refused. The hope that for forty years had lighted up the darkness of the desert wanderings must be denied. A wilderness grave was the goal of those years of toil and heart-burdening care. But He who is "able to do exceeding abundantly above all that we ask or think" (Eph. 3:20), had in this measure answered His servant's prayer. Moses passed under the dominion of death, but he was not to remain in the tomb. Christ Himself called him forth to life. Satan the tempter had claimed the body of Moses because of his sin; but Christ the Saviour brought him forth from the grave. Jude 9.

Moses upon the mount of transfiguration was a witness to Christ's victory over sin and death. He represented those who shall come forth [421-422] from the grave at the resurrection of the just. Elijah, who had been translated to heaven without seeing death, represented those who will be living upon the earth at Christ's second coming, and who will be "changed, in a moment, in the twinkling of an eye, at the last trump;" when "this mortal must put on immortality," and "this corruptible must put on incorruption." 1 Cor. 15:51-53. Jesus was clothed with the light of heaven, as He will appear when He shall come "the second time without sin unto salvation." For He will come "in the glory of His Father with the holy angels." Heb. 9:28; Mark 8:38. The Saviour's promise to the disciples was now fulfilled. Upon the mount the future kingdom of glory was represented in miniature,--Christ the King, Moses a representative of the risen saints, and Elijah of the translated ones.

The disciples do not yet comprehend the scene; but they rejoice that the patient Teacher, the meek and lowly One, who has wandered to and fro a helpless stranger, is honored by the favored ones of heaven. They believe that Elijah has come to announce the Messiah's reign, and that the kingdom of Christ is about to be set up on the earth. The memory of their fear and disappointment they would banish forever. Here, where the glory of God is revealed, they long to tarry. Peter exclaims, "Master, it is good for us to be here: and let us make three tabernacles; one for Thee, and one for Moses, and one for Elias." The disciples are confident that Moses and Elijah have been sent to protect their Master, and to establish His authority as king.

Moses upon the mount of transfiguration was a witness to Christ's victory over s_____ and d_____...Elijah, who had been t_____ to heaven without seeing death, represented those who will be living on the earth at Christ's s_____ coming...Upon the mount the future kingdom of g_____ was represented in miniature, -- Christ the King, Moses a representative of the r_____ saints, and Elijah of the t_____ ones." (421, 422). Yes, Christ's prayer was heard. All sincere prayer is heard. This prayer was spectacularly answered. You are worthy, Lord! Worthy of this glory and honor! I want You to be glorified in my prayers, and in my life: _____
_____
_____

But before the crown must come the cross. Not the inauguration of Christ as king, but the decease to be accomplished at Jerusalem, is the subject of their conference with Jesus. Bearing the weakness of humanity, and burdened with its sorrow and sin, Jesus walked alone in the midst of men. As the darkness of the coming trial pressed upon Him, He was in loneliness of spirit, in a world that knew Him not. Even His loved disciples, absorbed in their own doubt and sorrow and ambitious hopes, had not comprehended the mystery of His mission. He had dwelt amid the love and fellowship of heaven; but in the world that He had created, He was in solitude. Now heaven had sent its messengers to Jesus; not angels, but men who had endured suffering and sorrow, and who could sympathize with the Saviour in the trial of His earthly life. Moses and Elijah had been colaborers with Christ. They had shared His longing for the salvation of men. Moses had pleaded for Israel: "Yet now, if Thou wilt forgive their sin--; and if not, blot me, I pray Thee, out of Thy book which Thou hast written." Ex. 32:32. Elijah [422-425] had known loneliness of spirit, as for three years and a half of famine he had borne the burden of the nation's hatred and its woe. Alone he had stood for God upon Mount Carmel. Alone he had fled to the desert in anguish and despair. These men, chosen above every angel around the throne, had come to commune with Jesus concerning the scenes of His suffering, and to comfort Him with the assurance of the sympathy of heaven. The hope of the world, the salvation of every human being, was the burden of their interview.

Through being overcome with sleep, the disciples heard little of what passed between Christ and the heavenly messengers. Failing to watch and pray, they had not received that which God desired to give them,--a knowledge of the sufferings of Christ, and the glory that should follow. They lost the blessing that might have been theirs through sharing His self-sacrifice. Slow of heart to believe were these disciples, little appreciative of the treasure with which Heaven sought to enrich them.

Yet they received great light. They were assured that all heaven knew of the sin of the Jewish nation in rejecting Christ. They were given a clearer insight into the work of the Redeemer. They saw with their eyes and heard with their ears things that were beyond the

4. "Before the c_____ must come the c_____. Not the inauguration of Christ as k_____, but the d_____ [death] to be accomplished at Jerusalem, is the subject of their conference with Jesus." Lord, what cross experience in my life is needed, before the crown? _____

_____

_____

_____

5. "He [Jesus] had dwelt amid the l_____ and fellowship of h_____ __; but in the world that He created, He was in s_____." Lord, may I better appreciate Your sacrifice. My heart goes out to comfort Your solitude: _____

_____

6. Moses and Elijah, "chosen above every a_____ around the throne, had come to c_____ with Jesus concerning the scenes of His s_____ ____, and to comfort Him with the assurance of the s_____ of heaven. The h_____ of the world, the salvation of every human being, was the b_____ of this interview." (425). So like You, Lord! The weight of suffering and humanity's salvation burdened You, yet You prayed for Your dis-

ciples. May I think of You more, what You were feeling, isolated from heaven. May I think less of how I benefit from salvation, and more on Your experience. May my love and deep appreciation for You grow:

_____

_____

7. "Failing to watch and p_____, the disciples had not received that which God desired to give them...Slow of heart to b_____ were these disciples, little a_____ ____ of the t_____ with which heaven sought to enrich them." While they received great light, there was more that they missed out on. Little appreciation of the treasure--is that me, Lord? Is my walk with You, increasing the sense of value of Your treasure?

_____

_____

Prayer journal: _____

_____

_____

_____

_____

_____

_____

_____

comprehension of man. They were "eyewitnesses of His majesty" (2 Peter 1:16), and they realized that Jesus was indeed the Messiah, to whom patriarchs and prophets had witnessed, and that He was recognized as such by the heavenly universe.

While they were still gazing on the scene upon the mount, "a bright cloud overshadowed them: and behold a voice out of the cloud, which said, This is My beloved Son, in whom I am well pleased; hear ye Him." As they beheld the cloud of glory, brighter than that which went before the tribes of Israel in the wilderness; as they heard the voice of God speak in awful majesty that caused the mountain to tremble, the disciples fell smitten to the earth. They remained prostrate, their faces hidden, till Jesus came near, and touched them, dispelling their fears with His well-known voice, "Arise, and be not afraid." Venturing to lift up their eyes, they saw that the heavenly glory had passed away, the forms of Moses and Elijah had disappeared. They were upon the mount, alone with Jesus.

Chapter 47

Ministry

[This chapter is based on Matt. 17:9-21 ;
Mark 9:9-29; Luke 9:37-45.]

The entire night had been passed in the mountain; and as the sun arose, Jesus and His disciples descended to the plain. Absorbed in thought, the disciples were awed and silent. Even Peter had not a word to say. Gladly would they have lingered in that holy place which had been touched with the light of heaven, and where the Son of God had manifested His glory; but there was work to be done for the people, who were already searching far and near for Jesus.

At the foot of the mountain a large company had gathered, led hither by the disciples who had remained behind, but who knew whither Jesus had resorted. As the Saviour drew near, He charged His three companions to keep silence concerning what they had witnessed, saying, "Tell the vision to no man, until the Son of man be risen again from the dead." The revelation made to the disciples was to be pondered in their own hearts, not to be published abroad. To relate it to the multitudes would excite only ridicule or idle wonder. And even the nine apostles would not understand the scene until after Christ had risen from the dead. How slow of comprehension even the three favored disciples were, is seen in the fact that notwithstanding all that Christ had said of what was before Him, they queried among themselves what the rising from the dead [426-427] should mean. Yet they asked no explanation from Jesus. His words in regard to the future had filled them with sorrow; they sought no further revelation concerning that which they were fain to believe might never come to pass.

As the people on the plain caught sight of Jesus, they ran to meet Him, greeting Him with expressions of reverence and joy. Yet His quick eye discerned that they were in great perplexity. The disciples appeared troubled. A circumstance had just occurred that had caused them bitter disappointment and humiliation.

1. Jesus charged the three disciples that accompanied Him to the mount of transfiguration, "to keep s_____ concerning what they had witnessed...To relate it to the multitude would excite only r_____ or i_____ wonder." Those are extremes to avoid, aren't they, Lord? Contempt or indifference. I want to be impressionable, in awe of Your character; my heart inspired and molded. What will move me beyond idle wonder? _____
_____
_____
_____

364 Can We Walk, Together?

2. "Authority over unclean spirits…had been conferred on the disciples when Jesus sent out the twelve…[But in this circumstance] the demon only m_____ them with a fresh display of his power." The rabbis were quick to try and prove that the disciples and "their Master were d_____... A feeling of c_____ and scorn pervaded the crowd." (427). Lord, to be mocked by the forces of evil, is to realize that they know I am not genuine. Instead, I desire You to take me through whatever experience necessary, that my character is molded into the genuine article:

_____

_____

3. Jesus inquired of the scribes, "What question ye with them?" "But the voices so bold and d____ _____ before were now s_____." Why?

_____

_____

_____

Is the boldness ill founded, with no credibility?

_____

_____

_____

4. "Jesus looked about Him upon the awe-stricken multitude, the caviling scribes , the perplexed disciples. He read the

While they were waiting at the foot of the mountain, a father had brought to them his son, to be delivered from a dumb spirit that tormented him. Authority over unclean spirits, to cast them out, had been conferred on the disciples when Jesus sent out the twelve to preach through Galilee. As they went forth strong in faith, the evil spirits had obeyed their word. Now in the name of Christ they commanded the torturing spirit to leave his victim; but the demon only mocked them by a fresh display of his power. The disciples, unable to account for their defeat, felt that they were bringing dishonor upon themselves and their Master. And in the crowd there were scribes who made the most of this opportunity to humiliate them. Pressing around the disciples, they plied them with questions, seeking to prove that they and their Master were deceivers. Here, the rabbis triumphantly declared, was an evil spirit that neither the disciples nor Christ Himself could conquer. The people were inclined to side with the scribes, and a feeling of contempt and scorn pervaded the crowd.

But suddenly the accusations ceased. Jesus and the three disciples were seen approaching, and with a quick revulsion of feeling the people turned to meet them. The night of communion with the heavenly glory had left its trace upon the Saviour and His companions. Upon their countenances was a light that awed the beholders. The scribes drew back in fear, while the people welcomed Jesus.

As if He had been a witness of all that had occurred, the Saviour came to the scene of conflict, and fixing His gaze upon the scribes inquired, "What question ye with them?"

But the voices so bold and defiant before were now silent. A hush had fallen upon the entire company. Now the afflicted father made his way through the crowd, and falling at the feet of Jesus, poured out the story of his trouble and disappointment. [427-428]

"Master," he said, "I have brought unto Thee my son, which hath a dumb spirit; and wheresoever he taketh him, he teareth him: . . . and I spake to Thy disciples that they should cast him out; and they could not."

Jesus looked about Him upon the awe-stricken multitude, the caviling scribes, the perplexed disciples. He read the unbelief in every heart; and in a voice filled with sorrow He exclaimed, "O faithless generation, how long shall I be with you? how long shall I suffer you?" Then He bade the distressed father, "Bring thy son hither."

The boy was brought, and as the Saviour's eyes fell upon him, the evil spirit cast him to the ground in convulsions of agony. He lay wallowing and foaming, rending the air with unearthly shrieks.

Again the Prince of life and the prince of the powers of darkness had met on the field of battle,--Christ in fulfillment of His mission to "preach deliverance to the captives, . . . to set at liberty them that are bruised" (Luke 4:18), Satan seeking to hold his victim under his control. Angels of light and the hosts of evil angels, unseen, were pressing near to behold the conflict. For a moment, Jesus permitted the evil spirit to display his power, that the beholders might comprehend the deliverance about to be wrought.

The multitude looked on with bated breath, the father in an agony of hope and fear. Jesus asked, "How long is it ago since this came unto him?" The father told the story of long years of suffering, and then, as if he could endure no more, exclaimed, "If Thou canst do anything, have compassion on us, and help us." "If Thou canst!" Even now the father questioned the power of Christ.

Jesus answers, "If thou canst believe, all things are possible to him that believeth." There is no lack of power on the part of Christ; the healing of the son depends upon the father's faith. With a burst of tears, realizing his own weakness, the father casts himself upon Christ's mercy, with the cry, "Lord, I believe; help Thou mine unbelief."

Jesus turns to the suffering one, and says, "Thou dumb and deaf spirit, I charge thee, come out of him, and enter no more into him." There is a cry, an agonized struggle. The demon, in passing, seems about to rend the life from his victim. Then the boy lies motionless, and apparently lifeless. The multitude whisper, "He is dead." But Jesus takes him by the hand, and lifting him up, presents him, in perfect soundness of mind and body, to his father. Father and son praise the name of [428-429] their Deliverer. The multitude are "amazed at the mighty power of God," while the scribes, defeated and crestfallen, turn sullenly away.

"If Thou canst do anything, have compassion on us, and help us." How many a sin-burdened soul has echoed that prayer. And to all, the pitying Saviour's an-

u_____ in e_____ heart." (428). God, You know my heart, don't You? How do You minister to my unbelief?

_____
_____
_____
_____
_____

5. "For a moment, Jesus permitted the evil spirit to d_____ his power, that the beholders might c_____ the deliverance about to be wrought." Lord, any delay in Your help might prolong my suffering in temptation, but since I need to have my eyes opened to Satan's power, and Your power, and since You won't let any temptation come along that is beyond my cope level (with Your help), I will trust You to do what is best: _____
_____
_____

6. "With a burst of tears, realizing his o_____ weakness, the father cast himself upon Christ's mercy, with the cry, "Lord, I believe; help Thou mine u_____." Lord, I pray the same prayer. I'm opening my heart to You the best way I know how. Keep showing me

more, and I will my heart to respond: _____

_____

_____

7. "It is faith that connects us with h_____, and brings us strength for coping with the powers of darkness...Faith comes by the w_____ of God. Then grasp His p_____, 'Him that cometh to Me I will in no wise cast out'...You can n_____ perish while you do this – never." (429). Lord, help me to never forget this prayer. What a wonderful promise! To be used every day! _____

_____

_____

8. "It was an object lesson of r_____, -- the Divine One from the Father's glory stooping to save the lost. It represented also the disciples' m_____. Not alone upon the mountain top with Jesus, in hours of s_____ illumination, is the life of Christ's servants to be spent." How then? _____

_____

_____

_____

(working the plain; sharing words of faith and prayer) _____

_____

Is there balance in the way I use my time? _____

_____

swer is, "If thou canst believe, all things are possible to him that believeth." It is faith that connects us with heaven, and brings us strength for coping with the powers of darkness. In Christ, God has provided means for subduing every sinful trait, and resisting every temptation, however strong. But many feel that they lack faith, and therefore they remain away from Christ. Let these souls, in their helpless unworthiness, cast themselves upon the mercy of their compassionate Saviour. Look not to self, but to Christ. He who healed the sick and cast out demons when He walked among men is the same mighty Redeemer today. Faith comes by the word of God. Then grasp His promise, "Him that cometh to Me I will in no wise cast out." John 6:37. Cast yourself at His feet with the cry, "Lord, I believe; help Thou mine unbelief." You can never perish while you do this--never.

In a brief space of time the favored disciples have beheld the extreme of glory and of humiliation. They have seen humanity as transfigured into the image of God, and as debased into the likeness of Satan. From the mountain where He has talked with the heavenly messengers, and has been proclaimed the Son of God by the voice from the radiant glory, they have seen Jesus descend to meet that most distressing and revolting spectacle, the maniac boy, with distorted countenance, gnashing his teeth in spasms of agony that no human power could relieve. And this mighty Redeemer, who but a few hours before stood glorified before His wondering disciples, stoops to lift the victim of Satan from the earth where he is wallowing, and in health of mind and body restores him to his father and his home.

It was an object lesson of redemption,--the Divine One from the Father's glory stooping to save the lost. It represented also the disciples' mission. Not alone upon the mountaintop with Jesus, in hours of spiritual illumination, is the life of Christ's servants to be spent. There is work for them down in the plain. Souls whom Satan has enslaved are waiting for the word of faith and prayer to set them free.

The nine disciples were yet pondering upon the bitter fact of their own failure; and when Jesus was once more alone with them, they questioned, "Why could not we cast him out?" Jesus answered them, [429-430] "Because of your unbelief: for verily I say unto you, If ye have faith as a grain of mustard seed, ye shall say unto this mountain, Remove hence to yonder place; and it shall remove; and nothing shall be impossible unto you. Howbeit this kind goeth not out but by prayer and fasting." Their unbelief, that shut them out from deeper sympathy with [430-431] Christ, and the carelessness with which they regarded the sacred work committed to them, had caused their failure in the conflict with the powers of darkness.

The words of Christ pointing to His death had brought sadness and doubt. And the selection of the three disciples to accompany Jesus to the mountain had excited the jealousy of the nine. Instead of strengthening their faith by prayer and meditation on the words of Christ, they had been dwelling on their discouragements and personal grievances. In this state of darkness they had undertaken the conflict with Satan.

In order to succeed in such a conflict they must come to the work in a different spirit. Their faith must be strengthened by fervent prayer and fasting, and humiliation of heart. They must be emptied of self, and be filled with the Spirit and power of God. Earnest, persevering supplication to God in faith--faith that leads to entire dependence upon God, and unreserved consecration to His work--can alone avail to bring men the Holy Spirit's aid in the battle against principalities and powers, the rulers of the darkness of this world, and wicked spirits in high places.

"If ye have faith as a grain of mustard seed," said Jesus, "ye shall say unto this mountain, Remove hence to yonder place; and it shall remove." Though the grain of mustard seed is so small, it contains that same mysterious life principle which produces growth in the loftiest tree. When the mustard seed is cast into the ground, the tiny germ lays hold of every element that God has provided for its nutriment, and it speedily develops a sturdy growth. If you have faith like this, you will lay hold upon God's word, and upon all the helpful agencies He has appointed. Thus your faith will strengthen, and will bring to your aid the power of heaven. The obstacles that are piled by Satan across your path, though apparently as insurmountable as the eternal hills, shall disappear before the demand of faith. "Nothing shall be impossible unto you."

9. The disciples unbelief, that shut them out from d_____ sympathy with Christ, and the c_____ with which they regarded the s_____ work committed to them, had caused their f_____ in the conflict with the powers of darkness." (430-1). Do I have a careless attitude towards what You have asked me to do? _____
_____. Help my attitude, Lord: _____
_____

10. What alone, can avail to bring men the Holy Spirit's aid in the battle against rulers of darkness? f_____
___ prayer, fasting, h____
_____ of heart, emptied of s_____; earnest, persevering supplications to God in f_____; unreserved c_____ to His work. (431). Teach me, Lord, of that emptiness of self, and the filling of the Spirit: _____
_____

11. "If you have faith like this [what? m_____
_____], you will lay hold upon God's w_____, and upon all the helpful a_____ He has appointed. Thus your faith will be s_____, and will bring to your aid the p_____ of heaven." Satan's obstacles, hills, will "disappear before the

d_____ of faith."
Lord, I believe, help my unbelief. Help me to lay hold
of Your word, Your prom-
ises, to test Your reliability
to fulfill, and help in time
of need: _____

_____

_____

_____

Prayer journal: _____

_____

_____

_____

_____

1. While Jesus again
tried to prepare His dis-
ciples for the scenes of
His death, "a spirit of
r_____ found a place
in their hearts. They disputed among themselves
which should be accounted
g_____ in the king-
dom...This strife they
thought to c_____
from Jesus, and they
did not, as usual, press
c_____ to His side."

Who Is the Greatest?

[This chapter is based on Matt. 17:22-27; 18:1-20;
Mark 9:30-50; Luke 9:46-48.]

On returning to Capernaum, Jesus did not repair to
the well-known resorts where He had taught the people,
but with His disciples quietly sought the house that was
to be His temporary home. During the remainder of His
stay in Galilee it was His object to instruct the disciples
rather than to labor for the multitudes.

On the journey through Galilee, Christ had again
tried to prepare the minds of His disciples for the scenes
before Him. He told them that He was to go up to Jerusalem to be put to death and to rise again. And He added
the strange and solemn announcement that He was to be
betrayed into the hands of His enemies. The disciples
did not even now comprehend His words. Although
the shadow of a great sorrow fell upon them, a spirit
of rivalry found a place in their hearts. They disputed
among themselves which should be accounted greatest
in the kingdom. This strife they thought to conceal from
Jesus, and they did not, as usual, press close to His side,
but loitered behind, so that He was in advance of them
as they entered Capernaum. Jesus read their thoughts,
and He longed to counsel and instruct them. But for this
He awaited a quiet hour, when their hearts should be
open to receive His words.

Soon after they reached the town, the collector of
the temple revenue came to Peter with the question,

"Doth not your Master pay tribute?" [432-433] This tribute was not a civil tax, but a religious contribution, which every Jew was required to pay annually for the support of the temple. A refusal to pay the tribute would be regarded as disloyalty to the temple,--in the estimation of the rabbis a most grievous sin. The Saviour's attitude toward the rabbinical laws, and His plain reproofs to the defenders of tradition, afforded a pretext for the charge that He was seeking to overthrow the temple service. Now His enemies saw an opportunity of casting discredit upon Him. In the collector of the tribute they found a ready ally.

Peter saw in the collector's question an insinuation touching Christ's loyalty to the temple. Zealous for his Master's honor, he hastily answered, without consulting Him, that Jesus would pay the tribute.

But Peter only partially comprehended the purpose of his questioner. There were some classes who were held to be exempt from the payment of the tribute. In the time of Moses, when the Levites were set apart for the service of the sanctuary, they were given no inheritance among the people. The Lord said, "Levi hath no part nor inheritance with his brethren; the Lord is his inheritance." Deut. 10:9. In the days of Christ the priests and Levites were still regarded as especially devoted to the temple, and were not required to make the annual contribution for its support. Prophets also were exempted from this payment. In requiring the tribute from Jesus, the rabbis were setting aside His claim as a prophet or teacher, and were dealing with Him as with any commonplace person. A refusal on His part to pay the tribute would be represented as disloyalty to the temple; while, on the other hand, the payment of it would be taken as justifying their rejection of Him as a prophet.

Only a little before, Peter had acknowledged Jesus as the Son of God; but he now missed an opportunity of setting forth the character of his Master. By his answer to the collector, that Jesus would pay the tribute, he had virtually sanctioned the false conception of Him to which the priests and rulers were trying to give currency.

When Peter entered the house, the Saviour made no reference to what had taken place, but inquired, "What thinkest thou, Simon? of whom do the kings of the earth take custom or tribute? of their own children, or of strangers?" Peter answered, "Of strangers." And Jesus

What does this say about the nature of sin? _____
_____
_____

Lord, whenever I am avoiding You, keeping at a distance, focus my thought process to know why: ____
_____
_____
_____

2. Jesus "longed to counsel and instruct them. But for this He waited a q_____ hour, when their hearts should be o_____ to receive His words." Lord, thanks for knowing me, and being gentle with me; when I am open vs defensive:
_____
_____
_____
_____

3. "A refusal on Jesus' part to pay the temple tribute would be represented as d_____ to the temple; while, on the other hand, the payment of it would be taken as justifying their r_____ __ of Him as a prophet." (433). Why? _____
_____
_____.

A cleaver trap? Either answer is wrong for Jesus. They had Him in a lose-lose situation. Satan manipulates me like that. But Lord, I thank You that You don't corner me, but gently knock at the door, winning me over with Your matchless love! _____

_____

_____

4. "Lest He [Jesus] give offense by withholding the tribute, He did that which He could not justly be r_____ to do. This lesson would be of great v_____ to His disciples...While Christians are not to sacrifice one p_____ of truth, they should avoid c_____ whenever it is possible to do so." (434). Lord, sometimes when I really believe that I am right, I get a little argumentative. You're telling me that having all the truth on my side, does not justify speaking outside of love (1 Cor 13)? I should avoid controversy, without compromising truth. Alright, but I'll need Your spirit: _____

_____

said, "Then are the children free." While the people of a country are taxed for the maintenance of their king, the monarch's own children are exempt. So Israel, the professed people of God, were required to [433-434] maintain His service; but Jesus, the Son of God, was under no such obligation. If priests and Levites were exempt because of their connection with the temple, how much more He to whom the temple was His Father's house.

If Jesus had paid the tribute without a protest, He would virtually have acknowledged the justice of the claim, and would thus have denied His divinity. But while He saw good to meet the demand, He denied the claim upon which it was based. In providing for the payment of the tribute He gave evidence of His divine character. It was made manifest that He was one with God, and therefore was not under tribute as a mere subject of the kingdom.

"Go thou to the sea," He directed Peter, "and cast an hook, and take up the fish that first cometh up; and when thou hast opened his mouth, thou shalt find a piece of money: that take, and give unto them for Me and thee."

Though He had clothed His divinity with humanity, in this miracle He revealed His glory. It was evident that this was He who through David had declared, "Every beast of the forest is Mine, and the cattle upon a thousand hills. I know all the fowls of the mountains; and the wild beasts of the field are Mine. If I were hungry, I would not tell thee: for the world is Mine, and the fullness thereof." Ps. 50:10-12.

While Jesus made it plain that He was under no obligation to pay the tribute, He entered into no controversy with the Jews in regard to the matter; for they would have misinterpreted His words, and turned them against Him. Lest He should give offense by withholding the tribute, He did that which He could not justly be required to do. This lesson would be of great value to His disciples. Marked changes were soon to take place in their relation to the temple service, and Christ taught them not to place themselves needlessly in antagonism to established order. So far as possible, they were to avoid giving occasion for misinterpretation of their faith. While Christians are not to sacrifice one principle of truth, they should avoid controversy whenever it is possible to do so.

When Christ and the disciples were alone in the

house, while Peter was gone to the sea, Jesus called the others to Him, and asked, "What was it that ye disputed among yourselves by the way?" The presence of Jesus, and His question, put the matter in an entirely different light from that in which it had appeared to them while they were contending [434-435] by the way. Shame and self-condemnation kept them silent. Jesus had told them that He was to die for their sake, and their selfish ambition was in painful contrast to His unselfish love.

When Jesus told them that He was to be put to death and to rise again, He was trying to draw them into conversation in regard to the great test of their faith. Had they been ready to receive what He desired to make known to them, they would have been saved bitter anguish and despair. His words would have brought consolation in the hour of bereavement and disappointment. But although He had spoken so plainly of what awaited Him, His mention of the fact that He was soon to go to Jerusalem again kindled their hope that the kingdom was about to be set up. This had led to questioning as to who should fill the highest offices. On Peter's return from the sea, the disciples told him of the Saviour's question, and at last one ventured to ask Jesus, "Who is the greatest in the kingdom of heaven?"

The Saviour gathered His disciples about Him, and said to them, "If any man desire to be first, the same shall be last of all, and servant of all." There was in these words a solemnity and impressiveness which the disciples were far from comprehending. That which Christ discerned they could not see. They did not understand the nature of Christ's kingdom, and this ignorance was the apparent cause of their contention. But the real cause lay deeper. By explaining the nature of the kingdom, Christ might for the time have quelled their strife; but this would not have touched the underlying cause. Even after they had received the fullest knowledge, any question of precedence might have renewed the trouble. Thus disaster would have been brought to the church after Christ's departure. The strife for the highest place was the outworking of that same spirit which was the beginning of the great controversy in the worlds above, and which had brought Christ from heaven to die. There rose up before Him a vision of Lucifer, the "son of the morning," in glory surpassing all the angels that surround the throne, and united in closest ties to the Son of God. Lucifer had said, "I will be like the Most High"

5. "The presence of Jesus, and His question, put the matter [who's greatest] in an entirely d_____ light." Why the difference, or what changed? _____

_____

Help me not to stray from Your presence, Lord. Be my companion throughout the day. May Your unselfish love quiet my selfish ambitions: _____

_____

6. At last, a disciple "ventured to ask Jesus, 'Who is the g_____ in the kingdom of heaven?' The Savior… [answered], 'If any man desire to be f_____, the same shall be last of all, and s_____ ____ of all.'" (435). Why were the disciples far from c_____ it's solemnity and impresssiveness? _____

_____

_____ What about me?

_____
_____
_____

7. The disciples "did not u_____ the nature of Christ's k_____… But the real cause lay d_____ …The strife for the highest place was the outworking of that same spirit which

was the beginning of the great c_____ in the worlds above, and which had brought Christ from heaven to d____." (435). The spirit of Lucifer has done a lot of damage. If that is what the disciples were toying with, and what I indulge in, then Lord, please help me to stay clear of it altogether! ___

_____

_____

_____

8. "L_____ said, 'I will be like the Most High.'" He "desired God's p_____, but not His c_____." Is that for me, also? Impressed with God's position, power and influence, and less with His character? Do I enjoy positions of power and influence in my associations?

_____

_____

(Isa. 14:12, 14); and the desire for self-exaltation had brought strife into the heavenly courts, and had banished a multitude of the hosts of God. Had Lucifer really desired to be like the Most High, he would never have deserted his appointed place in heaven; for the spirit of the Most High is manifested in unselfish ministry. Lucifer desired God's power, but not His character. He sought for himself the highest [435-436] place, and every being who is actuated by his spirit will do the same. Thus alienation, discord, and strife will be inevitable. Dominion becomes the prize of the strongest. The kingdom of Satan is a kingdom of force; every individual regards every other as an obstacle in the way of his own advancement, or a steppingstone on which he himself may climb to a higher place.

While Lucifer counted it a thing to be grasped to be equal with God, Christ, the Exalted One, "made Himself of no reputation, and took upon Him the form of a servant, and was made in the likeness of men: and being found in fashion as a man, He humbled Himself, and became obedient unto death, even the death of the cross." Phil. 2:7, 8. Now the cross was just before Him; and His own disciples were so filled with self-seeking--the very principle of Satan's kingdom--that they could not enter into sympathy with their Lord, or even understand Him as He spoke of His humiliation for them.

Very tenderly, yet with solemn emphasis, Jesus tried to correct the evil. He showed what is the principle that bears sway in the kingdom of heaven, and in what true greatness consists, as estimated by the standard of the courts above. Those who were actuated by pride and love of distinction were thinking of themselves, and of the rewards they were to have, rather than how they were to render back to God the gifts they had received. They would have no place in the kingdom of heaven, for they were identified with the ranks of Satan.

Before honor is humility. To fill a high place before men, Heaven chooses the worker who, like John the Baptist, takes a lowly place before God. The most childlike disciple is the most efficient in labor for God. The heavenly intelligences can co-operate with him who is seeking, not to exalt self, but to save souls. He who feels most deeply his need of divine aid will plead for it; and the Holy Spirit will give unto him glimpses of Jesus that will strengthen and uplift the soul. From communion with Christ he will go forth to work for those who are perishing in their sins. He is anointed for his mission; and he succeeds where many of the learned and intellectually wise would fail.

But when men exalt themselves, feeling that they are a necessity for the success of God's great plan, the Lord causes them to be set aside. It is made evident that the Lord is not dependent upon them. The work does not stop because of their removal from it, but goes forward with greater power. [436-437]

It was not enough for the disciples of Jesus to be instructed as to the nature of His kingdom. What they needed was a change of heart that would bring them into harmony with its principles. Calling a little child to Him, Jesus set him in the midst of them; then tenderly folding the little one in His arms He said, "Except ye be converted, and become as little children, ye shall not enter into the kingdom of heaven." The simplicity, the self-forgetfulness, and the confiding love of a little child are the attributes that Heaven values. These are the characteristics of real greatness.

Again Jesus explained to the disciples that His kingdom is not characterized by earthly dignity and display. At the feet of Jesus all these distinctions are forgotten. The rich and the poor, the learned and the ignorant, meet together, with no thought of caste or worldly preeminence. All meet as blood-bought souls, alike dependent upon One who has redeemed them to God.

The sincere, contrite soul is precious in the sight of God. He places His own signet upon men, not by their rank, not by their wealth, not by their intellectual greatness, but by their oneness with Christ. The Lord of glory is satisfied with those who are meek and lowly in heart. "Thou hast also given me," said David, "the shield of Thy salvation: . . . and Thy gentleness"--as an element in the human character--"hath made me great." Ps. 18:35.

"Whosoever shall receive one of such children in My name," said Jesus, "receiveth Me: and whosoever shall receive Me, receiveth not Me, but Him that sent Me." "Thus saith the Lord, The heaven is My throne, and the earth is My footstool: . . . but to this man will I look, even to him that is poor and of a contrite spirit, and trembleth at My word." Isa. 66:1, 2.

The Saviour's words awakened in the disciples a feeling of self-distrust. No one had been specially pointed out in the reply; but John was led to question whether

9. "It was not enough for the disciples of Jesus to be instructed as to the n_____ of His kingdom. What they needed was a change of h_____ ___ that would bring them into h_____ with i_____ principles." (437). Only by Your promise of a new heart and a new spirit, Lord. And You can't do it unless I give You permission every day, and seek to be in Your influence every day. Help me to be willing: _____
_____
_____

10. To enter the kingdom of heaven, I need to become as a little c_____. These characteristics of real greatness are: s_____, self-f_____, c_____ love. What is self-forgetfulness, Lord? Not holding onto a grudge? _____
_____
_____
And confiding love, is that like trust? Children do that real well. And I should be that way. OK, Lord. Help me out: _____
_____

11. "The sincere, contrite soul is p_____ ___ in the sight of God. He places His own signet upon men, not by their rank, not by their w_____

__, not by their intellectual greatness, but by their o_____ with Christ." How am I to be one with You, Lord? _____

_____ By daily abiding in You, and You in me. I invite You and that experience into my life. I want to walk together: _____

_____

_____

12. "Every soul whom God has made willing is a c_____ through which Christ will reveal His p_____ love. How careful we should be lest we discourage one of God's l_____ bearers, and thus intercept the rays that He would have s_____ to the world!" (438). Lord, help me to not indulge in a narrow, exclusive spirit; but when someone's approach to worship is different from mine, may I encourage them to continue being a channel of light, rather than criticize them, and discouraging them: _____

_____

_____

_____

in one case his action had been right. With the spirit of a child he laid the matter before Jesus. "Master," he said, "we saw one casting out devils in Thy name, and he followeth not us: and we forbade him, because he followeth not us."

James and John had thought that in checking this man they had had in view their Lord's honor; they began to see that they were jealous for their own. They acknowledged their error, and accepted the reproof of Jesus, "Forbid him not: for there is no man which shall do a miracle in My name, that can lightly speak evil of Me." None who showed [437-438] themselves in any way friendly to Christ were to be repulsed. There were many who had been deeply moved by the character and the work of Christ, and whose hearts were opening to Him in faith; and the disciples, who could not read motives, must be careful not to discourage these souls. When Jesus was no longer personally among them, and the work was left in their hands, they must not indulge a narrow, exclusive spirit, but manifest the same far-reaching sympathy which they had seen in their Master.

The fact that one does not in all things conform to our personal ideas or opinions will not justify us in forbidding him to labor for God. Christ is the Great Teacher; we are not to judge or to command, but in humility each is to sit at the feet of Jesus, and learn of Him. Every soul whom God has made willing is a channel through which Christ will reveal His pardoning love. How careful we should be lest we discourage one of God's light bearers, and thus intercept the rays that He would have shine to the world!

Harshness or coldness shown by a disciple toward one whom Christ was drawing--such an act as that of John in forbidding one to work miracles in Christ's name--might result in turning the feet into the path of the enemy, and causing the loss of a soul. Rather than for one to do this, said Jesus, "it is better for him that a millstone were hanged about his neck, and he were cast into the sea." And He added, "If thy hand cause thee to stumble, cut it off: it is good for thee to enter into life maimed, rather than having thy two hands to go into hell, into the unquenchable fire. And if thy foot cause thee to stumble, cut it off: it is good for thee to enter into life halt, rather than having thy two feet to be cast into hell." Mark 9:43-45, R. V.

Why this earnest language, than which none can be stronger? Because "the Son of man is come to save that which was lost." Shall His disciples show less regard for the souls of their fellow men than the Majesty of heaven has shown? Every soul has cost an infinite price, and how terrible is the sin of turning one soul away from Christ, so that for him the Saviour's love and humiliation and agony shall have been in vain.

"Woe unto the world because of occasions of stumbling! for it must needs be that the occasions come." Matt. 18:7, R. V. The world, inspired by Satan, will surely oppose the followers of Christ, and seek to destroy their faith; but woe to him who has taken Christ's name, and yet is found [438-439] doing this work. Our Lord is put to shame by those who claim to serve Him, but who misrepresent His character; and multitudes are deceived, and led into false paths.

Any habit or practice that would lead into sin, and bring dishonor upon Christ, would better be put away, whatever the sacrifice. That which dishonors God cannot benefit the soul. The blessing of heaven cannot attend any man in violating the eternal principles of right. And one sin cherished is sufficient to work the degradation of the character, and to mislead others. If the foot or the hand would be cut off, or even the eye would be plucked out, to save the body from death, how much more earnest should we be to put away sin, that brings death to the soul!

In the ritual service, salt was added to every sacrifice. This, like the offering of incense, signified that only the righteousness of Christ could make the service acceptable to God. Referring to this practice, Jesus said, "Every sacrifice shall be salted with salt." "Have salt in yourselves, and have peace one with another." All who would present themselves "a living sacrifice, holy, acceptable unto God" (Rom. 12:1), must receive the saving salt, the righteousness of our Saviour. Then they become "the salt of the earth," restraining evil among men, as salt preserves from corruption. Matt. 5:13. But if the salt has lost its savor; if there is only a profession of godliness, without the love of Christ, there is no power for good. The life can exert no saving influence upon the world. Your energy and efficiency in the upbuilding of My kingdom, Jesus says, depend upon your receiving of My Spirit. You must be partakers of My grace, in order to be a savor of life unto life. Then

13. "Every soul has cost an i_____ price...Our Lord is put to shame by those who claim to serve Him, but who m_____ His character." (438, 439). Lord, may my walk with You, help me reflect Your character to others: _____

there will be no rivalry, no self-seeking, no desire for the highest place. You will have that love which seeks not her own, but another's wealth.

Let the repenting sinner fix his eyes upon "the Lamb of God, which taketh away the sin of the world" (John 1:29); and by beholding, he becomes changed. His fear is turned to joy, his doubts to hope. Gratitude springs up. The stony heart is broken. A tide of love sweeps into the soul. Christ is in him a well of water springing up unto everlasting life. When we see Jesus, a Man of Sorrows and acquainted with grief, working to save the lost, slighted, scorned, derided, driven from city to city till His mission was accomplished; when we behold Him in Gethsemane, sweating great drops of blood, and on the cross dying in agony,--when we see this, self will no longer clamor to be recognized. Looking unto Jesus, we shall be ashamed of our coldness, our lethargy, our self-seeking. [440-441] We shall be willing to be anything or nothing, so that we may do heart service for the Master. We shall rejoice to bear the cross after Jesus, to endure trial, shame, or persecution for His dear sake.

"We then that are strong ought to bear the infirmities of the weak, and not to please ourselves." Rom. 15:1. No soul who believes in Christ, though his faith may be weak, and his steps wavering as those of a little child, is to be lightly esteemed. By all that has given us advantage over another,--be it education and refinement, nobility of character, Christian training, religious experience,--we are in debt to those less favored; and, so far as lies in our power, we are to minister unto them. If we are strong, we are to stay up the hands of the weak. Angels of glory, that do always behold the face of the Father in heaven, joy in ministering to His little ones. Trembling souls, who have many objectionable traits of character, are their special charge. Angels are ever present where they are most needed, with those who have the hardest battle with self to fight, and whose surroundings are the most discouraging. And in this ministry Christ's true followers will co-operate.

If one of these little ones shall be overcome, and commit a wrong against you, then it is your work to seek his restoration. Do not wait for him to make the first effort for reconciliation. "How think ye?" said Jesus; "if a man have an hundred sheep, and one of them be gone astray, doth he not leave the ninety and nine, and goeth into the mountains, and seeketh that which is

14. "Do not wait for him to make the first effort for   r_____

gone astray? And if so be that he find it, verily I say unto you, he rejoiceth more of that sheep, than of the ninety and nine which went not astray. Even so it is not the will of your Father which is in heaven, that one of these little ones should perish."

In the spirit of meekness, "considering thyself, lest thou also be tempted," (Gal. 6:1), go to the erring one, and "tell him his fault between thee and him alone." Do not put him to shame by exposing his fault to others, nor bring dishonor upon Christ by making public the sin or error of one who bears His name. Often the truth must be plainly spoken to the erring; he must be led to see his error, that he may reform. But you are not to judge or to condemn. Make no attempt at self-justification. Let all your effort be for his recovery. In treating the wounds of the soul, there is need of the most delicate touch, the finest sensibility. Only the love that flows from the Suffering One of Calvary can avail here. With pitying tenderness, let brother deal with brother, knowing that if you succeed, you will "save a soul from death," and "hide a multitude of sins." James 5:20. [440-441]

But even this effort may be unavailing. Then, said Jesus, "take with thee one or two more." It may be that their united influence will prevail where that of the first was unsuccessful. Not being parties to the trouble, they will be more likely to act impartially, and this fact will give their counsel greater weight with the erring one.

If he will not hear them, then, and not till then, the matter is to be brought before the whole body of believers. Let the members of the church, as the representatives of Christ, unite in prayer and loving entreaty that the offender may be restored. The Holy Spirit will speak through His servants, pleading with the wanderer to return to God. Paul the apostle, speaking by inspiration, says, "As though God did beseech you by us: we pray you in Christ's stead, be ye reconciled to God." 2 Cor. 5:20. He who rejects this united overture has broken the tie that binds him to Christ, and thus has severed himself from the fellowship of the church. Henceforth, said Jesus, "let him be unto thee as an heathen man and a publican." But he is not to be regarded as cut off from the mercy of God. Let him not be despised or neglected by his former brethren, but be treated with tenderness and compassion, as one of the lost sheep that Christ is still seeking to bring to His fold.

Christ's instruction as to the treatment of the err-

...Often the truth must be plainly spoken to the erring; he must be led to s_____ his error, that he may r_____." But I am not to j_____ or to c_____. "Only the love that flows from the Suffering One of Calvary can a_____ here."

ing repeats in more specific form the teaching given to Israel through Moses: "Thou shalt not hate thy brother in thine heart: thou shalt in anywise rebuke thy neighbor, that thou bear not sin for him." Lev. 19:17, margin. That is, if one neglects the duty Christ has enjoined, of trying to restore those who are in error and sin, he becomes a partaker in the sin. For evils that we might have checked, we are just as responsible as if we were guilty of the acts ourselves.

But it is to the wrongdoer himself that we are to present the wrong. We are not to make it a matter of comment and criticism among ourselves; nor even after it is told to the church, are we at liberty to repeat it to others. A knowledge of the faults of Christians will be only a cause of stumbling to the unbelieving world; and by dwelling upon these things, we ourselves can receive only harm; for it is by beholding that we become changed. While we seek to correct the errors of a brother, the Spirit of Christ will lead us to shield him, as far as possible, from the criticism of even his own brethren, and how much more from the censure of the unbelieving world. We ourselves are erring, and need Christ's pity and forgiveness, and just as we wish Him to deal with us, He bids us deal with one another. [441-442]

"Whatsoever ye shall bind on earth shall be bound in heaven: and whatsoever ye shall loose on earth shall be loosed in heaven." You are acting as the ambassadors of heaven, and the issues of your work are for eternity.

But we are not to bear this great responsibility alone. Wherever His word is obeyed with a sincere heart, there Christ abides. Not only is He present in the assemblies of the church, but wherever disciples, however few, meet in His name, there also He will be. And He says, "If two of you shall agree on earth as touching anything that they shall ask, it shall be done for them of My Father which is in heaven."

Jesus says, " My Father which is in heaven," as reminding His disciples that while by His humanity He is linked with them, a sharer in their trials, and sympathizing with them in their sufferings, by His divinity He is connected with the throne of the Infinite. Wonderful assurance! The heavenly intelligences unite with men in sympathy and labor for the saving of that which was lost. And all the power of heaven is brought to combine with human ability in drawing souls to Christ.

I am "not to make it a matter of comment and c_____... By dwelling upon these things, we ourselves can receive o____ harm, for it is by b____ that we become changed. (440, 441). Lord, may my walk help me to see only Your character in others: ____

Prayer journal: ____

At the Feast of Tabernacles
[This chapter is based on John 7:1-15, 37-39.]

Three times a year the Jews were required to assemble at Jerusalem for religious purposes. Enshrouded in the pillar of cloud, Israel's invisible Leader had given the directions in regard to these gatherings. During the captivity of the Jews, they could not be observed; but when the people were restored to their own land, the observance of these memorials was once more begun. It was God's design that these anniversaries should call Him to the minds of the people. But with few exceptions, the priests and leaders of the nation had lost sight of this purpose. He who had ordained these national assemblies and understood their significance witnessed their perversion.

The Feast of Tabernacles was the closing gathering of the year. It was God's design that at this time the people should reflect on His goodness and mercy. The whole land had been under His guidance, receiving His blessing. Day and night His watchcare had continued. The sun and rain had caused the earth to produce her fruits. From the valleys and plains of Palestine the harvest had been gathered. The olive berries had been picked, and the precious oil stored in bottles. The palm had yielded her store. The purple clusters of the vine had been trodden in the wine press. [447-448]

The feast continued for seven days, and for its celebration the inhabitants of Palestine, with many from other lands, left their homes, and came to Jerusalem. From far and near the people came, bringing in their hands a token of rejoicing. Old and young, rich and poor, all brought some gift as a tribute of thanksgiving to Him who had crowned the year with His goodness, and made His paths drop fatness. Everything that could please the eye, and give expression to the universal joy, was brought from the woods; the city bore the appearance of a beautiful forest.

This feast was not only the harvest thanksgiving, but the memorial of God's protecting care over Israel in the wilderness. In commemoration of their tent life, the

1. "The Feast of Tabernacles was the closing gathering of the year. It was God's design that at this time the people should reflect on His g_____ and m_____ ... This feast was not only the h_____ thanksgiving, but the memorial of God's protecting c_____ over Israel in the wilderness." (447, 448). Lord, when was the last time I thanked You? I have taken Your protection and blessings for granted. I am sorry; sorry for slighting You. Please help me through out the day, to recognize these blessings and acknowledge them in gratitude. You are so good to me. How may my walk with You each day, be aware of Your care? _____

_____

2. "A little before the feast was the Day of A_____ _____, when, after confession of their sins, the people were declared to be at p _____ with heaven. Thus the way was prepared for the r_____ of the feast." Why should I experience rejoicing after confessing? Shouldn't I be sorrowful, self-condemning, contrite? Lord, is confession something I should look forward to and be happy about? Why is saying 'sorry' so difficult, then? _____

_____

_____ Is true rejoicing possible without preparing for it with confession? ____

_____

_____

Israelites during the feast dwelt in booths or tabernacles of green boughs. These were erected in the streets, in the courts of the temple, or on the housetops. The hills and valleys surrounding Jerusalem were also dotted with these leafy dwellings, and seemed to be alive with people.

With sacred song and thanksgiving the worshipers celebrated this occasion. A little before the feast was the Day of Atonement, when, after confession of their sins, the people were declared to be at peace with Heaven. Thus the way was prepared for the rejoicing of the feast. "O give thanks unto the Lord; for He is good: for His mercy endureth forever" (Ps. 106:1) rose triumphantly, while all kinds of music, mingled with shouts of hosanna, accompanied the united singing. The temple was the center of the universal joy. Here was the pomp of the sacrificial ceremonies. Here, ranged on either side of the white marble steps of the sacred building, the choir of Levites led the service of song. The multitude of worshipers, waving their branches of palm and myrtle, took up the strain, and echoed the chorus; and again the melody was caught up by voices near and afar off, till the encircling hills were vocal with praise.

At night the temple and its court blazed with artificial light. The music, the waving of palm branches, the glad hosannas, the great concourse of people, over whom the light streamed from the hanging lamps, the array of the priests, and the majesty of the ceremonies, combined to make a scene that deeply impressed the beholders. But the most impressive ceremony of the feast, one that called forth greatest rejoicing, was one commemorating an event in the wilderness sojourn.

At the first dawn of day, the priests sounded a long, shrill blast upon their silver trumpets, and the answering trumpets, and the glad shouts of the people from their booths, echoing over hill and valley, welcomed [448-449] the festal day. Then the priest dipped from the flowing waters of the Kedron a flagon of water, and, lifting it on high, while the trumpets were sounding, he ascended the broad steps of the temple, keeping time with the music with slow and measured tread, chanting meanwhile, "Our feet shall stand within thy gates, O Jerusalem." Ps. 122:2.

He bore the flagon to the altar, which occupied a central position in the court of the priests. Here were two silver basins, with a priest standing at each one.

The flagon of water was poured into one, and a flagon of wine into the other; and the contents of both flowed into a pipe which communicated with the Kedron, and was conducted to the Dead Sea. This display of the consecrated water represented the fountain that at the command of God had gushed from the rock to quench the thirst of the children of Israel. Then the jubilant strains rang forth, "The Lord Jehovah is my strength and my song;" "therefore with joy shall ye draw water out of the wells of salvation." Isa. 12:2, 3. [449-450]

As the sons of Joseph made preparation to attend the Feast of Tabernacles, they saw that Christ made no movement signifying His intention of attending. They watched Him with anxiety. Since the healing at Bethesda He had not attended the national gatherings. To avoid useless conflict with the leaders at Jerusalem, He had restricted His labors to Galilee. His apparent neglect of the great religious assemblies, and the enmity manifested toward Him by the priests and rabbis, were a cause of perplexity to the people about Him, and even to His own disciples and His kindred. In His teachings He had dwelt upon the blessings of obedience to the law of God, and yet He Himself seemed to be indifferent to the service which had been divinely established. His mingling with publicans and others of ill repute, His disregard of the rabbinical observances, and the freedom with which He set aside the traditional requirements concerning the Sabbath, all seeming to place Him in antagonism to the religious authorities, excited much questioning. His brothers thought it a mistake for Him to alienate the great and learned men of the nation. They felt that these men must be in the right, and that Jesus was at fault in placing Himself in antagonism to them. But they had witnessed His blameless life, and though they did not rank themselves with His disciples, they had been deeply impressed by His works. His popularity in Galilee was gratifying to their ambition; they still hoped that He would give an evidence of His power which would lead the Pharisees to see that He was what He claimed to be. What if He were the Messiah, the Prince of Israel! They cherished this thought with proud satisfaction.

So anxious were they about this that they urged Christ to go to Jerusalem. "Depart hence," they said, "and go into Judea, that Thy disciples also may see the works that Thou doest. For there is no man that doeth

3. Jesus' brothers thought, "If He knew that He was the Messiah, why this strange r_____ and i_____?...Present yourself at the capitol, w_____ the support of the priests and rulers and u_____ the nation in establishing the new kingdom." (450). The 'if' expressed doubt and unbelief. Do I use that word or that thought in my prayers to You, Lord? _____

_____

"If it be according to Thy will" is a phrase I use a lot. But do I want to be expressing doubt with it? Help me to be confident of Your will, and Who You are: _____

_____

4. "They were o_____ _____ because, instead of seeking a temporal throne, Christ had declared Himself to be the b_____ of life." (451). Lord, am I offended by Your spiritual nature and humility? Am I that out of harmony with You?

_____

_____

Please, as I walk with You, may I understand Your nature and value it: _____

_____

_____

5. "I go not up yet unto this feast; for My time is not yet f_____ come...The world cannot hate you,...

anything in secret, and he himself seeketh to be known openly. If Thou do these things, show Thyself to the world." The "if" expressed doubt and unbelief. They attributed cowardice and weakness to Him. If He knew that He was the Messiah, why this strange reserve and inaction? If He really possessed such power, why not go boldly to Jerusalem, and assert His claims? Why not perform in Jerusalem the wonderful works reported of Him in Galilee? Do not hide in secluded provinces, they said, and perform your mighty works for the benefit of ignorant peasants and fishermen. Present yourself at the capital, win the support of the priests and rulers, and unite the nation in establishing the new kingdom. [450-451]

These brothers of Jesus reasoned from the self-ish motive so often found in the hearts of those ambitious for display. This spirit was the ruling spirit of the world. They were offended because, instead of seeking a temporal throne, Christ had declared Himself to be the bread of life. They were greatly disappointed when so many of His disciples forsook Him. They themselves turned from Him to escape the cross of acknowledging what His works revealed--that He was the Sent of God.

"Then Jesus said unto them, My time is not yet come: but your time is alway ready. The world cannot hate you; but Me it hateth, because I testify of it, that the works thereof are evil. Go ye up unto this feast: I go not up yet unto this feast; for My time is not yet full come. When He had said these words unto them, He abode still in Galilee." His brothers had spoken to Him in a tone of authority, prescribing the course He should pursue. He cast their rebuke back to them, classing them not with His self-denying disciples, but with the world. "The world cannot hate you," He said, "but Me it hateth, because I testify of it, that the works thereof are evil." The world does not hate those who are like it in spirit; it loves them as its own.

The world for Christ was not a place of ease and self-aggrandizement. He was not watching for an opportunity to seize its power and its glory. It held out no such prize for Him. It was the place into which His Father had sent Him. He had been given for the life of the world, to work out the great plan of redemption. He was accomplishing His work for the fallen race. But He was not to be presumptuous, not to rush into danger, not to hasten a crisis. Each event in His work had its appointed hour. He must wait patiently. He knew that He was to receive the world's hatred; He knew that His work would result in His death; but to prematurely expose Himself would not be the will of His Father.

From Jerusalem the report of Christ's miracles had spread wherever the Jews were dispersed; and although for many months He had been absent from the feasts, the interest in Him had not abated. Many from all parts of the world had come up to the Feast of Tabernacles in the hope of seeing Him. At the beginning of the feast many inquiries were made for Him. The Pharisees and rulers looked for Him to come, hoping for an opportunity to condemn Him. They anxiously inquired, "Where is He?" but no one knew. The thought of Him was uppermost in all minds. Through fear of the priests and rulers, none dared acknowledge [451-452] Him as the Messiah, but everywhere there was quiet yet earnest discussion concerning Him. Many defended Him as one sent from God, while others denounced Him as a deceiver of the people.

Meanwhile Jesus had quietly arrived at Jerusalem. He had chosen an unfrequented route by which to go, in order to avoid the travelers who were making their way to the city from all quarters. Had He joined any of the caravans that went up to the feast, public attention would have been attracted to Him on His entrance into the city, and a popular demonstration in His favor would have aroused the authorities against Him. It was to avoid this that He chose to make the journey alone.

In the midst of the feast, when the excitement concerning Him was at its height, He entered the court of the temple in the presence of the multitude. Because of His absence from the feast, it had been urged that He dared not place Himself in the power of the priests and rulers. All were surprised at His presence. Every voice was hushed. All wondered at the dignity and courage of His bearing in the midst of powerful enemies who were thirsting for His life.

Standing thus, the center of attraction to that vast throng, Jesus addressed them as no man had ever done. His words showed a knowledge [452-453] of the laws and institutions of Israel, of the sacrificial service and the teachings of the prophets, far exceeding that of the priests and rabbis. He broke through the barriers of formalism and tradition. The scenes of the future life seemed outspread before Him. As one who beheld

but M___ it hateth…The world does not hate those who are l_____ it in spirit; it loves them as its own." Where is my heart, Lord? Is my spirit like the world's, or Your's? _____

_____
_____

6. "Many from all parts of the world had come to the Feat of Tabernacles in hope of s_____ Him… The thought of Him was uppermost in a_____ minds." Not all had good motives. But in a positive way, is it my hope to see You at church, and as a companion throughout each day?

_____
_____ Is the thought of You uppermost in my mind? _____

_____
_____ Like Enoch, I want to ever be in Your presence:
_____
_____
_____

7. Jesus chose an u_____ ____ route. "Had He joined any of the caravans that went up to the feast, public attention would have been a_____ to Him on His entrance into the city, and a popular d_____ in His favor would have a_____ the authorities against Him." (452). How can the reception to my sharing

of the gospel be enhanced rather than hindered? _____

_____

_____

Lord, I need Your timing and sensitivity: _____

_____

8. "Jesus addressed them as no man had e_____ done...He had given them every possible proof that He came forth from G___, and made every possible effort to bring them to repentance. He would not be rejected and m_____ _____ by His o_____ nation if He c_____ save them from the guilt of such a deed." (452, 453). You were slain from the foundation of the world, yet here You are trying to save Your people from the guilt of murder. What unconditional love! Keep revealing and teaching me about Your love. You are worthy of praise! Who can I share that love with, today? _____

_____

_____

9. "There had been nothing in all this round of ceremonies to meet the wants of the s_____, nothing to satisfy the t_____ of the soul." Lord, do I seek to satisfy my restless

the Unseen, He spoke of the earthly and the heavenly, the human and the divine, with positive authority. His words were most clear and convincing; and again, as at Capernaum, the people were astonished at His teaching; "for His word was with power." Luke 4:32. Under a variety of representations He warned His hearers of the calamity that would follow all who rejected the blessings He came to bring them. He had given them every possible proof that He came forth from God, and made every possible effort to bring them to repentance. He would not be rejected and murdered by His own nation if He could save them from the guilt of such a deed.

All wondered at His knowledge of the law and the prophecies; and the question passed from one to another, "How knoweth this Man letters, having never learned?" No one was regarded as qualified to be a religious teacher unless he had studied in the rabbinical schools, and both Jesus and John the Baptist had been represented as ignorant because they had not received this training. Those who heard them were astonished at their knowledge of the Scriptures, "having never learned." Of men they had not, truly; but the God of heaven was their teacher, and from Him they had received the highest kind of wisdom.

As Jesus spoke in the temple court, the people were held spellbound. The very men who were the most violent against Him felt themselves powerless to do Him harm. For the time, all other interests were forgotten.

Day after day He taught the people, until the last, "that great day of the feast." The morning of this day found the people wearied from the long season of festivity. Suddenly Jesus lifted up His voice, in tones that rang through the courts of the temple:

"If any man thirst, let him come unto Me, and drink. He that believeth on Me, as the scripture hath said, out of his belly shall flow rivers of living water." The condition of the people made this appeal very forcible. They had been engaged in a continued scene of pomp and festivity, their eyes had been dazzled with light and color, and their ears regaled with the richest music; but there had been nothing in all this round of ceremonies to meet the wants of the spirit, nothing to [453-454] satisfy the thirst of the soul for that which perishes not. Jesus invited them to come and drink of the fountain of life, of that which would be in them a well of water, springing up unto everlasting life.

The priest had that morning performed the ceremony which commemorated the smiting of the rock in the wilderness. That rock was a symbol of Him who by His death would cause living streams of salvation to flow to all who are athirst. Christ's words were the water of life. There in the presence of the assembled multitude He set Himself apart to be smitten, that the water of life might flow to the world. In smiting Christ, Satan thought to destroy the Prince of life; but from the smitten rock there flowed living water. As Jesus thus spoke to the people, their hearts thrilled with a strange awe, and many were ready to exclaim, with the woman of Samaria, "Give me this water, that I thirst not." John 4:15.

Jesus knew the wants of the soul. Pomp, riches, and honor cannot satisfy the heart. "If any man thirst, let him come unto Me." The rich, the poor, the high, the low, are alike welcome. He promises to relieve the burdened mind, to comfort the sorrowing, and to give hope to the despondent. Many of those who heard Jesus were mourners over disappointed hopes, many were nourishing a secret grief, many were seeking to satisfy their restless longing with the things of the world and the praise of men; but when all was gained, they found that they had toiled only to reach a broken cistern, from which they could not quench their thirst. Amid the glitter of the joyous scene they stood, dissatisfied and sad. That sudden cry, "If any man thirst," startled them from their sorrowful meditation, and as they listened to the words that followed, their minds kindled with a new hope. The Holy Spirit presented the symbol before them until they saw in it the offer of the priceless gift of salvation.

The cry of Christ to the thirsty soul is still going forth, and it appeals to us with even greater power than to those who heard it in the temple on that last day of the feast. The fountain is open for all. The weary and exhausted ones are offered the refreshing draught of eternal life. Jesus is still crying, "If any man thirst, let him come unto Me, and drink." "Let him that is athirst come. And whosoever will, let him take the water of life freely." "Whosoever drinketh of the water that I shall give him shall never thirst; but the water that I shall give him shall be in him a well of water springing up into everlasting life." Rev. 22:17; John 4:14.

longing with the things of the world and the praise of men? May I hear Your hopeful invitation, If you thirst, come to Me: _____

_____

_____

10. "Christ's w_____ were the water of life... The Holy Spirit presented the symbol before them until they saw in it the offer of the priceless gift of s_____." (454). Lord, may I drink from Your word and know true satisfaction. May I sense the difference when I don't partake (as in drought):

_____

_____

Prayer journal: _____

_____

_____

_____

_____

_____

_____

Chapter 50

Among Snares

[This chapter is based on John 7:16-36, 40-53; 8:1-11.]

1. The priests and rulers "wanted to h_____ his Galilean rabbi b_____ the people." Lord, how should I compare this treatment, this lack of security, with treatment stemming from a grounding in Your love? (Eph. 3:17)? _____

_____

_____

_____

2. "The perception and a_____ of truth, He said, depends less upon the mind than upon the heart. Truth must be received into the s_____; it claims the homage of the will…its reception depends upon the r_____ of every sin that the Spirit of God reveals." Lord, may I always approach dedicated time with You, with an open mind, but also an open heart. Convict me of sin, Lord. I want nothing to be in the way of the Spirit, nothing in the way of truth, nothing in the way of our walk together: _____

_____

_____

All the while Jesus was at Jerusalem during the feast He was shadowed by spies. Day after day new schemes to silence Him were tried. The priests and rulers were watching to entrap Him. They were planning to stop Him by violence. But this was not all. They wanted to humble this Galilean rabbi before the people.

On the first day of His presence at the feast, the rulers had come to Him, demanding by what authority He taught. They wished to divert attention from Him to the question of His right to teach, and thus to their own importance and authority.

"My teaching is not Mine," said Jesus, "but His that sent Me. If any man willeth to do His will, he shall know of the teaching, whether it be of God, or whether I speak from Myself." John 7:16, 17, R. V. The question of these cavilers Jesus met, not by answering the cavil, but by opening up truth vital to the salvation of the soul. The perception and appreciation of truth, He said, depends less upon the mind than upon the heart. Truth must be received into the soul; it claims the homage of the will. If truth could be submitted to the reason alone, pride would be no hindrance in the way of its reception. But it is to be received through the work of grace in the heart; and its reception depends upon the renunciation of every sin that the Spirit of God reveals. Man's advantages for obtaining a knowledge of the truth, however great these may be, will prove of no benefit to him unless the heart is open to receive [455-456] the truth, and there is a conscientious surrender of every habit and practice that is opposed to its principles. To those who thus yield themselves to God, having an honest desire to know and to do His will, the truth is revealed as the power of God for their salvation. These will be able to distinguish between him who speaks for God, and him who speaks merely from himself. The Pharisees had not put their will on the side of God's will. They were not seeking to know the truth, but to find some excuse for evading it; Christ showed that this was why they did not understand His teaching.

He now gave a test by which the true teacher might be distinguished from the deceiver: "He that speaketh from himself seeketh his own glory: but he that seeketh the glory of Him that sent him, the same is true, and no unrighteousness is in him." John 7:18, R. V. He that seeketh his own glory is speaking only from himself. The spirit of self-seeking betrays its origin. But Christ was seeking the glory of God. He spoke the words of God. This was the evidence of His authority as a teacher of the truth.

Jesus gave the rabbis an evidence of His divinity by showing that He read their hearts. Ever since the healing at Bethesda they had been plotting His death. Thus they were themselves breaking the law which they professed to be defending. "Did not Moses give you the law," He said, "and yet none of you keepeth the law? Why go ye about to kill Me?"

Like a swift flash of light these words revealed to the rabbis the pit of ruin into which they were about to plunge. For an instant they were filled with terror. They saw that they were in conflict with Infinite Power. But they would not be warned. In order to maintain their influence with the people, their murderous designs must be concealed. Evading the question of Jesus, they exclaimed, "Thou hast a devil: who goeth about to kill Thee?" They insinuated that the wonderful works of Jesus were instigated by an evil spirit.

To this insinuation Christ gave no heed. He went on to show that His work of healing at Bethesda was in harmony with the Sabbath law, and that it was justified by the interpretation which the Jews themselves put upon the law. He said, "Moses therefore gave unto you circumcision; . . . and ye on the Sabbath day circumcise a man." According to the law, every child must be circumcised on the eighth day. Should the appointed time fall upon the Sabbath, the rite must then be performed. How much more must it be in harmony with the [456-457] spirit of the law to make a man "every whit whole on the Sabbath day." And He warned them to "judge not according to the appearance, but judge righteous judgment."

The rulers were silenced; and many of the people exclaimed, "Is not this He, whom they seek to kill? But, lo, He speaketh boldly, and they say nothing unto Him. Do the rulers know indeed that this is the very Christ?"

3. "Like a swift flash of light these words revealed to the rabbis the pit of r_____ into which they were about to plunge. For an instant they were filled with terror. They saw that they were in conflict with Infinite power." (456). Lord, let me see the fullness of sin (Rom 1:18), the pit of ruin. The ultimate pit of sin being how You were made sin on the cross and experienced separation from the Father. May Your conflict with sin help me steer clear of it: _____

_____

_____

_____

Many among Christ's hearers who were dwellers at Jerusalem, and who were not ignorant of the plots of the rulers against Him, felt themselves drawn to Him by an irresistible power. The conviction pressed upon them that He was the Son of God. But Satan was ready to suggest doubt; and for this the way was prepared by their own erroneous ideas of the Messiah and His coming. It was generally believed that Christ would be born at Bethlehem, but that after a time He would disappear, and at His second appearance none would know whence He came. There were not a few who held that the Messiah would have no natural relationship to humanity. And because the popular conception of the glory of the Messiah was not met by Jesus of Nazareth, many gave heed to the suggestion, "Howbeit we know this Man whence He is: but when Christ cometh, no man knoweth whence He is."

While they were thus wavering between doubt and faith, Jesus took up their thoughts and answered them: "Ye both know Me, and ye know whence I am: and I am not come of Myself, but He that sent Me is true, whom ye know not." They claimed a knowledge of what the origin of Christ should be, but they were in utter ignorance of it. If they had lived in accordance with the will of God, they would have known His Son when He was manifested to them.

The hearers could not but understand Christ's words. Clearly they were a repetition of the claim He had made in the presence of the Sanhedrin many months before, when He declared Himself the Son of God. As the rulers then tried to compass His death, so now they sought to take Him; but they were prevented by an unseen power, which put a limit to their rage, saying to them, Thus far shalt thou go, and no farther.

Among the people many believed on Him, and they said, "When Christ cometh, will He do more miracles than these which this Man hath done?" The leaders of the Pharisees, who were anxiously watching the course of events, caught the expressions of sympathy among the throng. Hurrying away to the chief priests, they laid their plans to arrest Him. [457-458] They arranged, however, to take Him when He was alone; for they dared not seize Him in the presence of the people. Again Jesus made it manifest that He read their purpose. "Yet a little while am I with you," He said, "and then I go unto Him that sent Me. Ye shall seek Me, and shall not find Me: and where I am, thither ye cannot come." Soon He would find a refuge beyond the reach of their scorn and hate. He would ascend to the Father, to be again the Adored of the angels; and thither His murderers could never come.

Sneeringly the rabbis said, "Whither will He go, that we shall not find Him? will He go unto the dispersed among the Gentiles, and teach the Gentiles?" Little did these cavilers dream that in their mocking words they were picturing the mission of the Christ! All day long He had stretched forth His hands unto a disobedient and gainsaying people; yet He would be found of them that sought Him not; among a people that had not called upon His name He would be manifest. Rom. 10:20, 21.

Many who were convinced that Jesus was the Son of God were misled by the false reasoning of the priests and rabbis. These teachers had repeated with great effect the prophecies concerning the Messiah, that He would "reign in Mount Zion, and in Jerusalem, and before His ancients gloriously;" that He would "have dominion also from sea to sea, and from the river unto the ends of the earth." Isa. 24:23; Ps. 72:8. Then they made contemptuous comparisons between the glory here pictured and the humble appearance of Jesus. The very words of prophecy were so perverted as to sanction error. Had the people in sincerity studied the word for themselves, they would not have been misled. The sixty-first chapter of Isaiah testifies that Christ was to do the very work He did. Chapter fifty-three sets forth His rejection and sufferings in the world, and chapter fifty-nine describes the character of the priests and rabbis.

God does not compel men to give up their unbelief. Before them are light and darkness, truth and error. It is for them to decide which they will accept. The human mind is endowed with power to discriminate between right and wrong. God designs that men shall not decide from impulse, but from weight of evidence, carefully comparing scripture with scripture. Had the Jews laid by their prejudice and compared written prophecy with the facts characterizing the life of Jesus, they would have perceived a beautiful harmony between the prophecies and their fulfillment in the life and ministry of the lowly Galilean. [458-459]

Many are deceived today in the same way as were the Jews. Religious teachers read the Bible in the light

4. "God does not c_____ _____ men to give up their u_____. Before them are light and darkness, truth and error. It is for them to d_____ which they will accept...God designs that men shall not decide from i_____, but from weight of e_____ _____, carefully comparing scripture with scripture." (458). Thank You, Lord, for inviting me to a belief relationship, asking me to believe in You based on evidence of Your love. May I ever keep learning the height, depth, width, and length of Your love. How do I pass on values to my children: compel or weight of evidence? _____

_____

_____

_____

of their own understanding and traditions; and the people do not search the Scriptures for themselves, and judge for themselves as to what is truth; but they yield up their judgment, and commit their souls to their leaders. The preaching and teaching of His word is one of the means that God has ordained for diffusing light; but we must bring every man's teaching to the test of Scripture. Whoever will prayerfully study the Bible, desiring to know the truth, that he may obey it, will receive divine enlightenment. He will understand the Scriptures. "If any man willeth to do His will, he shall know of the teaching." John 7:17, R. V.

On the last day of the feast, the officers sent out by the priests and rulers to arrest Jesus, returned without Him. They were angrily questioned, "Why have ye not brought Him?" With solemn countenance they answered, "Never man spake like this Man."

Hardened as were their hearts, they were melted by His words. While He was speaking in the temple court, they had lingered near, to catch something that might be turned against Him. But as they listened, the purpose for which they had been sent was forgotten. They stood as men entranced. Christ revealed Himself to their souls. They saw that which priests and rulers would not see,--humanity flooded with the glory of divinity. They returned, so filled with this thought, so impressed by His words, that to the inquiry, "Why have ye not brought Him?" they could only reply, "Never man spake like this Man."

The priests and rulers, on first coming into the presence of Christ, had felt the same conviction. Their hearts were deeply moved, and the thought was forced upon them, "Never man spake like this Man." But they had stifled the conviction of the Holy Spirit. Now, enraged that even the instruments of the law should be influenced by the hated Galilean, they cried, "Are ye also deceived? Have any of the rulers or of the Pharisees believed on Him? But this people who knoweth not the law are cursed."

Those to whom the message of truth is spoken seldom ask, "Is it true?" but, "By whom is it advocated?" Multitudes estimate it by the numbers who accept it; and the question is still asked, "Have any of the learned men or religious leaders believed?" Men are no more favorable to real godliness now than in the days of Christ. They are just as intently seeking earthly good, to the

5. Failing to arrest Jesus, their answer was, "'N_____ man spake like this Man.' Hardened as were their hearts, they were m_____ by His words." (459). Lord, I know You don't compel, but I am sure glad that there is a wonderful power to Your words, to melt a hardened heart like mine. How did my heart get hardened, Lord? ____
_____
_____
_____
_____

neglect of eternal riches; and it is not an [459-460] argument against the truth, that large numbers are not ready to accept it, or that it is not received by the world's great men, or even by the religious leaders.

Again the priests and rulers proceeded to lay plans for arresting Jesus. It was urged that if He were longer left at liberty, He would draw the people away from the established leaders, and the only safe course was to silence Him without delay. In the full tide of their discussion, they were suddenly checked. Nicodemus questioned, "Doth our law judge any man, before it hear him, and know what he doeth?" Silence fell on the assembly. The words of Nicodemus came home to their consciences. They could not condemn a man unheard. But it was not for this reason alone that the haughty rulers remained silent, gazing at him who had dared to speak in favor of justice. They were startled and chagrined that one of their own number had been so far impressed by the character of Jesus as to speak a word in His defense. Recovering from their astonishment, they addressed Nicodemus with cutting sarcasm, "Art thou also of Galilee? Search and look: for out of Galilee ariseth no prophet."

Yet the protest resulted in staying the proceedings of the council. The rulers were unable to carry out their purpose and condemn Jesus without a hearing. Defeated for the time, "every man went unto his own house. Jesus went unto the Mount of Olives."

From the excitement and confusion of the city, from the eager crowds and the treacherous rabbis, Jesus turned away to the quiet of the olive groves, where He could be alone with God. But in the early morning He returned to the temple, and as the people gathered about Him, He sat down and taught them.

He was soon interrupted. A group of Pharisees and scribes approached Him, dragging with them a terror-stricken woman, whom with hard, eager voices they accused of having violated the seventh commandment. Having pushed her into the presence of Jesus, they said to Him, with a hypocritical show of respect, "Moses in the law commanded us, that such should be stoned: but what sayest Thou?"

Their pretended reverence veiled a deep-laid plot for His ruin. They had seized upon this opportunity to secure His condemnation, thinking that whatever decision He might make, they would find occasion to ac-

6. The Pharisees' "p____ ____ reverence veiled a deep-laid plot for His ruin. They had seized upon this opportunity to secure His c_____." (460). Could I have a pretended reverence, Lord? A hypocritical show of respect? Is my zealousness for one theological point, my way of compensating, for a different theological blind spot? Help me, Lord, to not be like the Pharisees:

_____
_____
_____

cuse Him. Should He acquit the woman, He might be charged with despising the law of Moses. Should He declare her worthy of death, [460-461] He could be accused to the Romans as one who was assuming authority that belonged only to them.

Jesus looked for a moment upon the scene,--the trembling victim in her shame, the hard-faced dignitaries, devoid of even human pity. His spirit of stainless purity shrank from the spectacle. Well He knew for what purpose this case had been brought to Him. He read the heart, and knew the character and life history of everyone in His presence. These would-be guardians of justice had themselves led their victim into sin, that they might lay a snare for Jesus. Giving no sign that He had heard their question, He stooped, and fixing His eyes upon the ground, began to write in the dust.

Impatient at His delay and apparent indifference, the accusers drew nearer, urging the matter upon His attention. But as their eyes, following those of Jesus, fell upon the pavement at His feet, their countenances changed. There, traced before them, were the guilty secrets of their own lives. The people, looking on, saw the sudden change of expression, and pressed forward to discover what it was that they were regarding with such astonishment and shame.

With all their professions of reverence for the law, these rabbis, in bringing the charge against the woman, were disregarding its provisions. It was the husband's duty to take action against her, and the guilty parties were to be punished equally. The action of the accusers was wholly unauthorized. Jesus, however, met them on their own ground. The law specified that in punishment by stoning, the witnesses in the case should be the first to cast a stone. Now rising, and fixing His eyes upon the plotting elders, Jesus said, "He that is without sin among you, let him first cast a stone at her." And stooping down, He continued writing on the ground.

He had not set aside the law given through Moses, nor infringed upon the authority of Rome. The accusers had been defeated. Now, their robe of pretended holiness torn from them, they stood, guilty and condemned, in the presence of Infinite Purity. They trembled lest the hidden iniquity of their lives should be laid open to the multitude; and one by one, with bowed heads and downcast eyes, they stole away, leaving their victim with the pitying Saviour.

7. "Jesus read the heart, and knew the c_____ _____ and life history of everyone in His presence." (461). Lord, everything is transparent before You. Why do I try to pretend, put up a good front? You know me better than I know myself. What is it that I am trying to hide? _____ _____ _____ _____ _____ _____

8. "Their robe of pretended h_____ torn from them, they stood, g____ _____ and condemned, in the presence of Infinite P_____. They trembled lest the h_____ iniquity of their lives should be laid o_____ to the multitude." Lord, I want to be transparent with You. I am a sinner. I can't pretend otherwise. So the help I need, is not for me to live, but You to live in me. What is the reason that on some days, I don't invite You? _____ _____ _____

Jesus arose, and looking at the woman said, "Woman, where are those thine accusers? hath no man condemned thee? She said, No man, Lord. And Jesus said unto her, Neither do I condemn thee: go, and sin no more." [461-462]

The woman had stood before Jesus, cowering with fear. His words, "He that is without sin among you, let him first cast a stone," had come to her as a death sentence. She dared not lift her eyes to the Saviour's face, but silently awaited her doom. In astonishment she saw her accusers depart speechless and confounded; then those words of hope fell upon her ear, "Neither do I condemn thee: go, and sin no more." Her heart was melted, and she cast herself at the feet of Jesus, sobbing out her grateful love, and with bitter tears confessing her sins.

This was to her the beginning of a new life, a life of purity and peace, devoted to the service of God. In the uplifting of this fallen soul, Jesus performed a greater miracle than in healing the most grievous physical disease; He cured the spiritual malady which is unto death everlasting. This penitent woman became one of His most steadfast followers. With self-sacrificing love and devotion she repaid His forgiving mercy.

In His act of pardoning this woman and encouraging her to live a better life, the character of Jesus shines forth in the beauty of perfect righteousness. While He does not palliate sin, nor lessen the sense of guilt, He seeks not to condemn, but to save. The world had for this erring woman only contempt and scorn; but Jesus speaks words of comfort and hope. The Sinless One pities the weakness of the sinner, and reaches to her a helping hand. While the hypocritical Pharisees denounce, Jesus bids her, "Go, and sin no more."

It is not Christ's follower that, with averted eyes, turns from the erring, leaving them unhindered to pursue their downward course. Those who are forward in accusing others, and zealous in bringing them to justice, are often in their own lives more guilty than they. Men hate the sinner, while they love the sin. Christ hates the sin, but loves the sinner. This will be the spirit of all who follow Him. Christian love is slow to censure, quick to discern penitence, ready to forgive, to encourage, to set the wanderer in the path of holiness, and to stay his feet therein.

9. "In the act of pardoning this woman and encouraging her to live a better life, the c_____ of Jesus shines forth in the beauty of p_____ righteousness." (462). Not mercy at the expense of justice. This is perfect justice, perfect righteousness. And it is who You are! O Lord, may my character reflect Your character: _____
_____

10. "Those who are forward in accusing others, and zealous in bringing them to j_____, are often in their own lives more g_____ than they. Men hate the sinner, while they love the sin. Christ hates the sin, but loves the sinner… Christian love is slow to c_____, quick to discern p_____ _____, ready to forgive, to e_____, to set the wanderer in the path of holiness, and to s_____ his feet therein." Lord, show me how this goes further than church business meeting votes for disfellowshipping. Lord, show me my self-righteousness, my hypocrisy. May I be pure and true like You:
_____
_____

Prayer journal: _____
_____
_____
_____

Chapter 51

"The Light of Life"

[This chapter is based on John 8:12-59; 9.]

Then spake Jesus again unto them, saying, I am the light of the world: he that followeth Me shall not walk in darkness, but shall have the light of life."

When He spoke these words, Jesus was in the court of the temple specially connected with the services of the Feast of Tabernacles. In the center of this court rose two lofty standards, supporting lampstands of great size. After the evening sacrifice, all the lamps were kindled, shedding their light over Jerusalem. This ceremony was in commemoration of the pillar of light that guided Israel in the desert, and was also regarded as pointing to the coming of the Messiah. At evening when the lamps were lighted, the court was a scene of great rejoicing. Gray-haired men, the priests of the temple and the rulers of the people, united in the festive dances to the sound of instrumental music and the chants of the Levites.

In the illumination of Jerusalem, the people expressed their hope of the Messiah's coming to shed His light upon Israel. But to Jesus the scene had a wider meaning. As the radiant lamps of the temple lighted up all about them, so Christ, the source of spiritual light, illumines the darkness of the world. Yet the symbol was imperfect. That great light which His own hand had set in the heavens was a truer representation of the glory of His mission.

It was morning; the sun had just risen above the Mount of Olives, and its rays fell with dazzling brightness on the marble palaces, and [463-464] lighted up the gold of the temple walls, when Jesus, pointing to it, said, "I am the light of the world."

By one who listened to these words, they were long afterward re-echoed in that sublime passage, "In Him was life; and the life was the light of men. And the light shineth in the darkness; and the darkness apprehended it not." "That was the true light, which lighteth every

---

1. After the evening sacrifice at the Feast of Tabernacles, "all the l_____ were kindled, shedding their light over Jerusalem. This ceremony was in commemoration of the p_____ of light that guided Israel in the desert, and was also regarded as pointing to the coming of the M_____." Lord, Thank You that You came. In what ways do You let me know that Your coming again, even knocking at the door of my heart?

_____

_____

_____

man that cometh into the world." John 1:4, 5, R. V., 9. And long after Jesus had ascended to heaven, Peter also, writing under the illumination of the divine Spirit, recalled the symbol Christ had used: "We have also a more sure word of prophecy; whereunto ye do well that ye take heed, as unto a light that shineth in a dark place, until the day dawn, and the daystar arise in your hearts." 2 Peter 1:19.

In the manifestation of God to His people, light had ever been a symbol of His presence. At the creative word in the beginning, light had shone out of darkness. Light had been enshrouded in the pillar of cloud by day and the pillar of fire by night, leading the vast armies of Israel. Light blazed with awful grandeur about the Lord on Mount Sinai. Light rested over the mercy seat in the tabernacle. Light filled the temple of Solomon at its dedication. Light shone on the hills of Bethlehem when the angels brought the message of redemption to the watching shepherds.

God is light; and in the words, "I am the light of the world," Christ declared His oneness with God, and His relation to the whole human family. It was He who at the beginning had caused "the light to shine out of darkness." 2 Cor. 4:6. He is the light of sun and moon and star. He was the spiritual light that in symbol and type and prophecy had shone upon Israel. But not to the Jewish nation alone was the light given. As the sunbeams penetrate to the remotest corners of the earth, so does the light of the Sun of Righteousness shine upon every soul.

"That was the true light, which lighteth every man that cometh into the world." The world has had its great teachers, men of giant intellect and wonderful research, men whose utterances have stimulated thought, and opened to view vast fields of knowledge; and these men have been honored as guides and benefactors of their race. But there is One who stands higher than they. "As many as received Him, to them gave He power to become the sons of God." "No man hath seen God at any time; the only-begotten Son, which is in the bosom of the Father, He hath declared Him." John 1:12, 18. We can trace the line of the world's great teachers as far back as human records extend; but the [464-465] Light was before them. As the moon and the stars of the solar system shine by the reflected light of the sun, so, as far as their teaching is true, do the world's great think-

2. "In the manifestation of God to His people, light had ever been a symbol of His p_____." (464). In the words, "I am the light of the world," how did Jesus "declare Himself the M_____?" (465):

ers reflect the rays of the Sun of Righteousness. Every gem of thought, every flash of the intellect, is from the Light of the world. In these days we hear much about "higher education." The true "higher education" is that imparted by Him "in whom are hid all the treasures of wisdom and knowledge." "In Him was life; and the life was the light of men." Col. 2:3; John 1:4. "He that followeth Me," said Jesus, "shall not walk in darkness, but shall have the light of life."

In the words, "I am the light of the world," Jesus declared Himself the Messiah. The aged Simeon, in the temple where Christ was now teaching, had spoken of Him as "a light to lighten the Gentiles, and the glory of Thy people Israel." Luke 2:32. In these words he was applying to Him a prophecy familiar to all Israel. By the prophet Isaiah, the Holy Spirit had declared, "It is too light a thing that Thou shouldest be My servant to raise up the tribes of Jacob, and to restore the preserved of Israel: I will also give Thee for a light to the Gentiles, that Thou mayest be My salvation unto the end of the earth." Isa. 49:6, R. V. This prophecy was generally understood as spoken of the Messiah, and when Jesus said, "I am the light of the world," the people could not fail to recognize His claim to be the Promised One.

3. The Pharisees and rulers were "bent on forcing Jesus to directly declare Himself the Christ. His appearance and His work were so at v_____ with the expectations of the people, that, as His wily enemies believed, a direct announcement of Himself as the Messiah would cause Him to be r_____ as an imposter." Are my expectations of Christ and His Spirit at variance of how they truly operate, so I end up rejecting spiritual light as an imposter?

_____
_____
_____
_____

To the Pharisees and rulers this claim seemed an arrogant assumption. That a man like themselves should make such pretensions they could not tolerate. Seeming to ignore His words, they demanded, "Who art Thou?" They were bent upon forcing Him to declare Himself the Christ. His appearance and His work were so at variance with the expectations of the people, that, as His wily enemies believed, a direct announcement of Himself as the Messiah would cause Him to be rejected as an impostor.

But to their question, "Who art Thou?" Jesus replied, "Even that which I have also spoken unto you from the beginning." John 8:25, R.V. That which had been revealed in His words was revealed also in His character. He was the embodiment of the truths He taught. "I do nothing of Myself," He continued; "but as My Father hath taught Me, I speak these things. And He that sent Me is with Me: the Father hath not left Me alone; for I do always those things that please Him." He did not attempt to prove His Messianic claim, but showed His unity with God. If their minds had been open to God's love, they would have received Jesus.

[465-466]

Among His hearers many were drawn to Him in faith, and to them He said, "if ye continue in My word, then are ye My disciples indeed; and ye shall know the truth, and the truth shall make you free."

These words offended the Pharisees. The nation's long subjection to a foreign yoke, they disregarded, and angrily exclaimed, "We be Abraham's seed, and were never in bondage to any man: how sayest Thou, Ye shall be made free?" Jesus looked upon these men, the slaves of malice, whose thoughts were bent upon revenge, and sadly answered, "Verily, verily, I say unto you, Whosoever committeth sin is the servant of sin." They were in the worst kind of bondage,--ruled by the spirit of evil.

Every soul that refuses to give himself to God is under the control of another power. He is not his own. He may talk of freedom, but he is in the most abject slavery. He is not allowed to see the beauty of truth, for his mind is under the control of Satan. While he flatters himself that he is following the dictates of his own judgment, he obeys the will of the prince of darkness. Christ came to break the shackles of sin-slavery from the soul. "If the Son therefore shall make you free, ye shall be free indeed." "The law of the Spirit of life in Christ Jesus" sets us "free from the law of sin and death." Rom. 8:2.

In the work of redemption there is no compulsion. No external force is employed. Under the influence of the Spirit of God, man is left free to choose whom he will serve. In the change that takes place when the soul surrenders to Christ, there is the highest sense of freedom. The expulsion of sin is the act of the soul itself. True, we have no power to free ourselves from Satan's control; but when we desire to be set free from sin, and in our great need cry out for a power out of and above ourselves, the powers of the soul are imbued with the divine energy of the Holy Spirit, and they obey the dictates of the will in fulfilling the will of God.

The only condition upon which the freedom of man is possible is that of becoming one with Christ. "The truth shall make you free;" and Christ is the truth. Sin can triumph only by enfeebling the mind, and destroying the liberty of the soul. Subjection to God is restoration to one's self,--to the true glory and dignity of man. The divine law, to which we are brought into subjection, is "the law of liberty." James 2:12.

The Pharisees had declared themselves the children

4. "Every soul that refuses to give himself to God is under the c_____ of another power. He is not his o_____." (466). When Satan talks about freedom, he means:

_____

_____

_____

(not allowed to see the beauty of truth). When Christ talks about freedom He means: _____

_____

_____

_____

____ (oneness with Christ).

of Abraham. Jesus told them that this claim could be established only by doing the works of Abraham. The true children of Abraham would live, as he did, a life of obedience to God. They would not try to kill One who was speaking the truth that was given Him from God. In plotting [466-467] against Christ, the rabbis were not doing the works of Abraham. A mere lineal descent from Abraham was of no value. Without a spiritual connection with him, which would be manifested in possessing the same spirit, and doing the same works, they were not his children.

This principle bears with equal weight upon a question that has long agitated the Christian world,-- the question of apostolic succession. Descent from Abraham was proved, not by name and lineage, but by likeness of character. So the apostolic succession rests not upon the transmission of ecclesiastical authority, but upon spiritual relationship. A life actuated by the apostles' spirit, the belief and teaching of the truth they taught, this is the true evidence of apostolic succession. This is what constitutes men the successors of the first teachers of the gospel.

Jesus denied that the Jews were children of Abraham. He said, "Ye do the deeds of your father." In mockery they answered, "We be not born of fornication; we have one Father, even God." These words, in allusion to the circumstances of His birth, were intended as a thrust against Christ in the presence of those who were beginning to believe on Him. Jesus gave no heed to the base insinuation, but said, "If God were your Father, ye would love Me: for I proceeded forth and came from God."

Their works testified of their relationship to him who was a liar and a murderer. "Ye are of your father the devil," said Jesus, "and the lusts of your father it is your will to do. He was a murderer from the beginning, and stood not in the truth, because there is no truth in him. . . . Because I say the truth, ye believe Me not." John 8:44, 45, R. V. The fact that Jesus spoke the truth, and that with certainty, was why He was not received by the Jewish leaders. It was the truth that offended these self-righteous men. The truth exposed the fallacy of error; it condemned their teaching and practice, and it was unwelcome. They would rather close their eyes to the truth than humble themselves to confess that they had been in error. They did not love the truth. They did not

---

5. "Descent from Abraham was proved, not by name and l_____, but by likeness of c____ _____." (467). Is there parallel truth to being a "Christian"? Being one, or being a disciple is not in name only, but in likeness of character. Does my character mean my behavior? _____

_____

Lord, let me focus on whose I am, and what I do will follow naturally:

_____
_____
_____
_____

desire it, even though it was truth.

"Which of you convicteth [Revised Version] Me of sin? And if I say the truth, why do ye not believe Me?" Day by day for three years His enemies had been following Christ, trying to find some stain in His character. Satan and all the confederacy of evil had been seeking to overcome Him; but they had found nothing in Him by which to gain an advantage. Even the devils were forced to confess, "Thou art the Holy One of God." Mark 1:24. Jesus lived the law in the sight of heaven, in the [467-468] sight of unfallen worlds, and in the sight of sinful men. Before angels, men, and demons, He had spoken, unchallenged, words that from any other lips would have been blasphemy: "I do always those things that please Him."

The fact that although they could find no sin in Christ the Jews would not receive Him proved that they themselves had no connection with God. They did not recognize His voice in the message of His Son. They thought themselves passing judgment on Christ; but in rejecting Him they were pronouncing sentence upon themselves. "He that is of God," said Jesus, "heareth God's words: ye therefore hear them not, because ye are not of God."

The lesson is true for all time. Many a man who delights to quibble, to criticize, seeking for something to question in the word of God, thinks that he is thereby giving evidence of independence of thought, and mental acuteness. He supposes that he is sitting in judgment on the Bible, when in truth he is judging himself. He makes it manifest that he is incapable of appreciating truths that originate in heaven, and that compass eternity. In presence of the great mountain of God's righteousness, his spirit is not awed. He busies himself with hunting for sticks and straws, and in this betrays a narrow and earthly nature, a heart that is fast losing its capacity to appreciate God. He whose heart has responded to the divine touch will be seeking for that which will increase his knowledge of God, and will refine and elevate the character. As a flower turns to the sun, that the bright rays may touch it with tints of beauty, so will the soul turn to the Sun of Righteousness, that heaven's light may beautify the character with the graces of the character of Christ.

Jesus continued, drawing a sharp contrast between the position of the Jews and that of Abraham: "Your

6. How can I reverse the trend of a heart that is fast losing its capacity to appreciate God? (468). Instead of trying to give evidence of independence of thought and sitting in judgment on the Bible, turn towards the sun of righteousness, that heaven's light may b____

_____ the character with the graces of the character of Christ. Lord, do I appreciate You? _____

_____

_____

_____

father Abraham rejoiced to see My day: and he saw it, and was glad."

Abraham had greatly desired to see the promised Saviour. He offered up the most earnest prayer that before his death he might behold the Messiah. And he saw Christ. A supernatural light was given him, and he acknowledged Christ's divine character. He saw His day, and was glad. He was given a view of the divine sacrifice for sin. Of this sacrifice he had an illustration in his own experience. The command came to him, "Take now thy son, thine only son Isaac, whom thou lovest, . . . and offer him . . . for a burnt offering." Gen. 22:2. [468-469] Upon the altar of sacrifice he laid the son of promise, the son in whom his hopes were centered. Then as he waited beside the altar with knife upraised to obey God, he heard a voice from heaven saying, "Lay not thine hand upon the lad, neither do thou anything unto him: for now I know that thou fearest God, seeing thou hast not withheld thy son, thine only son from Me." Gen. 22:12. This terrible ordeal was imposed upon Abraham that he might see the day of Christ, and realize the great love of God for the world, so great that to raise it from its degradation, He gave His only-begotten Son to a most shameful death.

7. In Abraham's willingness to sacrifice Isaac, he "learned of God the greatest l_____ ever given to a mortal. His prayer that he might see C_____ before he should die was answered." (469). What are you telling me, Lord? _____

_____ Understanding that "God was making a greater and more wonderful s_____ than ever man could make." How can I learn this lesson? _____

Abraham learned of God the greatest lesson ever given to mortal. His prayer that he might see Christ before he should die was answered. He saw Christ; he saw all that mortal can see, and live. By making an entire surrender, he was able to understand the vision of Christ, which had been given him. He was shown that in giving His only-begotten Son to save sinners from eternal ruin, God was making a greater and more wonderful sacrifice than ever man could make.

Abraham's experience answered the question: "Wherewith shall I come before the Lord, and bow myself before the high God? Shall I come before Him with burnt offerings, with calves of a year old? Will the Lord be pleased with thousands of rams, or with ten thousands of rivers of oil? shall I give my first-born for my transgression, the fruit of my body for the sin of my soul?" Micah 6:6, 7. In the words of Abraham, "My son, God will provide Himself a lamb for a burnt offering," (Gen. 22:8), and in God's provision of a sacrifice instead of Isaac, it was declared that no man could make expiation for himself. The pagan system of sacrifice was wholly unacceptable to God. No father was to offer up his son or his daughter for a sin offering. The Son of God alone can bear the guilt of the world.

Through his own suffering, Abraham was enabled to behold the Saviour's mission of sacrifice. But Israel would not understand that which was so unwelcome to their proud hearts. Christ's words concerning Abraham conveyed to His hearers no deep significance. The Pharisees saw in them only fresh ground for caviling. They retorted with a sneer, as if they would prove Jesus to be a madman, "Thou art not yet fifty years old, and hast Thou seen Abraham?"

With solemn dignity Jesus answered, "Verily, verily, I say unto you, Before Abraham was, I Am."

Silence fell upon the vast assembly. The name of God, given to Moses to express the idea of the eternal presence, had been claimed as [469-470] His own by this Galilean Rabbi. He had announced Himself to be the self-existent One, He who had been promised to Israel, "whose goings forth have been from of old, from the days of eternity." Micah 5:2, margin.

Again the priests and rabbis cried out against Jesus as a blasphemer. His claim to be one with God had before stirred them to take His life, and a few months later they plainly declared, "For a good work we stone Thee not; but for blasphemy; and because that Thou, being a man, makest Thyself God." John 10:33. Because He was, and avowed Himself to be, the Son of God, they were bent on destroying Him. Now many of the people, siding with the priests and rabbis, took up stones to cast at Him. "But Jesus hid Himself, and went out of the temple, going through the midst of them, and so passed by."

The Light was shining in darkness; but "the darkness apprehended it not." John 1:5, R. V.

"As Jesus passed by, He saw a man which was blind from his birth. And His disciples asked Him, saying, Master, who did sin, this man, or his parents, that he was born blind? Jesus answered, Neither hath this man sinned, nor his parents: but that the works of God should be made manifest in him. . . . When He had thus spoken, He spat on the ground, and made clay of the spittle, and He anointed the eyes of the blind man with the clay, and said unto him, Go, wash in the pool of Siloam, (which is by interpretation, Sent). He went his way therefore, and washed, and came seeing." [470-471]

It was generally believed by the Jews that sin is

punished in this life. Every affliction was regarded as the penalty of some wrongdoing, either of the sufferer himself or of his parents. It is true that all suffering results from the transgression of God's law, but this truth had become perverted. Satan, the author of sin and all its results, had led men to look upon disease and death as proceeding from God,--as punishment arbitrarily inflicted on account of sin. Hence one upon whom some great affliction or calamity had fallen had the additional burden of being regarded as a great sinner.

Thus the way was prepared for the Jews to reject Jesus. He who "hath borne our griefs, and carried our sorrows" was looked upon by the Jews as "stricken, smitten of God, and afflicted;" and they hid their faces from Him. Isa. 53:4, 3.

God had given a lesson designed to prevent this. The history of Job had shown that suffering is inflicted by Satan, and is overruled by God for purposes of mercy. But Israel did not understand the lesson. The same error for which God had reproved the friends of Job was repeated by the Jews in their rejection of Christ.

The belief of the Jews in regard to the relation of sin and suffering was held by Christ's disciples. While Jesus corrected their error, He did not explain the cause of the man's affliction, but told them what would be the result. Because of it the works of God would be made manifest. "As long as I am in the world," He said, "I am the light of the world." Then having anointed the eyes of the blind man, He sent him to wash in the pool of Siloam, and the man's sight was restored. Thus Jesus answered the question of the disciples in a practical way, as He usually answered questions put to Him from curiosity. The disciples were not called upon to discuss the question as to who had sinned or had not sinned, but to understand the power and mercy of God in giving sight to the blind. It was evident that there was no healing virtue in the clay, or in the pool wherein the blind man was sent to wash, but that the virtue was in Christ.

The Pharisees could not but be astonished at the cure. Yet they were more than ever filled with hatred; for the miracle had been performed on the Sabbath day.

The neighbors of the young man, and those who knew him before in his blindness, said, "Is not this he that sat and begged?" They looked upon him with doubt; for when his eyes were opened, his countenance was changed and brightened, and he appeared like an-

---

8. "Satan, the author of sin and all its results, had led men to look upon disease and death as proceeding from G_____,-- as punishment a_____ inflicted on account of sin." (471). The truth is, suffering is inflicted by S_____. So why is it, that when circumstances sour, I immediately think, because I did something wicked or evil? _____

_____

_____

_____

_____

_____

other man. From [471-472] one to another the question passed. Some said, "This is he;" others, "He is like him." But he who had received the great blessing settled the question by saying, "I am he." He then told them of Jesus, and by what means he had been healed, and they inquired, "Where is He? He said, I know not."

Then they brought him before a council of the Pharisees. Again the man was asked how he had received his sight. "He said unto them, He put clay upon mine eyes, and I washed, and do see. Therefore said some of the Pharisees, This man is not of God, because He keepeth not the Sabbath day." The Pharisees hoped to make Jesus out to be a sinner, and therefore not the Messiah. They knew not that it was He who had made the Sabbath and knew all its obligation, who had healed the blind man. They appeared wonderfully zealous for the observance of the Sabbath, yet were planning murder on that very day. But many were greatly moved at hearing of this miracle, and were convicted that He who had opened the eyes of the blind was more than a common man. In answer to the charge that Jesus was a sinner because He kept not the Sabbath day, they said, "How can a man that is a sinner do such miracles?"

Again the rabbis appealed to the blind man, "What sayest thou of Him, that He hath opened thine eyes? He said, He is a prophet." The Pharisees then asserted that he had not been born blind and received his sight. They called for his parents, and asked them, saying, "Is this your son, who ye say was born blind?"

There was the man himself, declaring that he had been blind, and had had his sight restored; but the Pharisees would rather deny the evidence of their own senses than admit that they were in error. So powerful is prejudice, so distorting is Pharisaical righteousness.

The Pharisees had one hope left, and that was to intimidate the man's parents. With apparent sincerity they asked, "How then doth he now see?" The parents feared to compromise themselves; for it had been declared that whoever should acknowledge Jesus as the Christ should be "put out of the synagogue;" that is, should be excluded from the synagogue for thirty days. During this time no child could be circumcised nor dead be lamented in the offender's home. The sentence was regarded as a great calamity; and if it failed to produce repentance, a far heavier penalty followed. The great work wrought for their son had brought conviction to the parents, yet they answered, "We know that this is our son, and that he was born blind: but by what means he now [472-473] seeth, we know not; or who hath opened his eyes, we know not: he is of age; ask him: he shall speak for himself." Thus they shifted all responsibility from themselves to their son; for they dared not confess Christ.

The dilemma in which the Pharisees were placed, their questioning and prejudice, their unbelief in the facts of the case, were opening the eyes of the multitude, especially of the common people. Jesus had frequently wrought His miracles in the open street, and His work was always of a character to relieve suffering. The question in many minds was, Would God do such mighty works through an impostor, as the Pharisees insisted that Jesus was? The controversy was becoming very earnest on both sides.

The Pharisees saw that they were giving publicity to the work done by Jesus. They could not deny the miracle. The blind man was filled with joy and gratitude; he beheld the wondrous things of nature, and was filled with delight at the beauty of earth and sky. He freely related his experience, and again they tried to silence him, saying, "Give God the praise: we know that this Man is a sinner." That is, Do not say again that this Man gave you sight; it is God who has done this.

The blind man answered, "Whether He be a sinner or no, I know not: one thing I know, that, whereas I was blind, now I see."

Then they questioned again, "What did He to thee? how opened He thine eyes?" With many words they tried to confuse him, so that he might think himself deluded. Satan and his evil angels were on the side of the Pharisees, and united their energies and subtlety with man's reasoning in order to counteract the influence of Christ. They blunted the convictions that were deepening in many minds. Angels of God were also on the ground to strengthen the man who had had his sight restored. [473-474]

The Pharisees did not realize that they had to deal with any other than the uneducated man who had been born blind; they knew not Him with whom they were in controversy. Divine light shone into the chambers of the blind man's soul. As these hypocrites tried to make him disbelieve, God helped him to show, by the vigor

---

9. "'He is of age; ask him: he shall speak for himself.' Thus they shifted all r_____ from themselves to their son; for they dared not c____ _____ Christ." (473). Lord, I guess that there are times that I am not confessing You very well. May my walk with You help me be more alert to what my confession and witness of You really is:

_____
_____
_____

"I have told you already, and ye did not hear: wherefore would ye hear it again? Will ye also be His disciples?" (474). I love the humor, Lord. You must chuckle at my attempts to be blind to what is spiritually obvious. Open my eyes, Lord: ___

_____
_____

and pointedness of his replies, that he was not to be en-snared. He answered, "I have told you already, and ye did not hear: wherefore would ye hear it again? will ye also be His disciples? Then they reviled him, and said, Thou art His disciple; but we are Moses' disciples. We know that God spake unto Moses: as for this fellow, we know not from whence He is."

The Lord Jesus knew the ordeal through which the man was passing, and He gave him grace and utterance, so that he became a witness for Christ. He answered the Pharisees in words that were a cutting rebuke to his questioners. They claimed to be the expositors of Scrip-ture, the religious guides of the nation; and yet here was One performing miracles, and they were confessedly ig-norant as to the source of His power, and as to His char-acter and claims. "Why herein is a marvelous thing," said the man, "that ye know not from whence He is, and yet He hath opened mine eyes. Now we know that God heareth not sinners: but if any man be a worshiper of God, and doeth His will, him He heareth. Since the world began was it not heard that any man opened the eyes of one that was born blind. If this Man were not of God, He could do nothing."

The man had met his inquisitors on their own ground. His reasoning was unanswerable. The Phari-sees were astonished, and they held their peace,--spell-bound before his pointed, determined words. For a few moments there was silence. Then the frowning priests and rabbis gathered about them their robes, as though they feared contamination from contact with him; they shook off the dust from their feet, and hurled denuncia-tions against him,--"Thou wast altogether born in sins, and dost thou teach us?" And they excommunicated him.

Jesus heard what had been done; and finding him soon after, He said, "Dost thou believe on the Son of God?"

For the first time the blind man looked upon the face of his Restorer. Before the council he had seen his parents troubled and perplexed; he had looked upon the frowning faces of the rabbis; now his eyes rested upon the loving, peaceful countenance of Jesus. Already, at great cost to himself, he had acknowledged Him as a delegate of divine power; now a higher revelation was granted him. [474-475]

To the Saviour's question, "Dost thou believe on the

Son of God?" the blind man replied by asking, "Who is He, Lord, that I might believe on Him?" And Jesus said, "Thou hast both seen Him, and it is He that talketh with thee." The man cast himself at the Saviour's feet in worship. Not only had his natural sight been restored, but the eyes of his understanding had been opened. Christ had been revealed to his soul, and he received Him as the Sent of God.

A group of Pharisees had gathered near, and the sight of them brought to the mind of Jesus the contrast ever manifest in the effect of His words and works. He said, "For judgment I am come into this world, that they which see not might see; and that they which see might be made blind." Christ had come to open the blind eyes, to give light to them that sit in darkness. He had declared Himself to be the light of the world, and the miracle just performed was in attestation of His mission. The people who beheld the Saviour at His advent were favored with a fuller manifestation of the divine presence than the world had ever enjoyed before. The knowledge of God was revealed more perfectly. But in this very revelation, judgment was passing upon men. Their character was tested, their destiny determined.

The manifestation of divine power that had given to the blind man both natural and spiritual sight had left the Pharisees in yet deeper darkness. Some of His hearers, feeling that Christ's words applied to them, inquired, "Are we blind also?" Jesus answered, "If ye were blind, ye should have no sin." If God had made it impossible for you to see the truth, your ignorance would involve no guilt. "But now ye say, We see." You believe yourselves able to see, and reject the means through which alone you could receive sight. To all who realized their need, Christ came with infinite help. But the Pharisees would confess no need; they refused to come to Christ, and hence they were left in blindness,--a blindness for which they were themselves guilty. Jesus said, "Your sin remaineth."

10. "The manifestation of divine power that had given the blind man both natural and s_____ _____ sight, had left the Pharisees in yet deeper d_____." (475). Am I also blind? Do I value the Light of the world and the healing miracle of being called out of darkness?

_____
_____
_____
_____

Prayer journal: _____
_____
_____
_____
_____
_____
_____
_____
_____

Chapter 52

The Divine Shepherd

[This chapter is based on John 10:1-30.]

"I am the Good Shepherd: the good shepherd giveth his life for the sheep." "I am the Good Shepherd, and know My sheep, and am known of Mine. As the Father knoweth Me, even so know I the Father: and I lay down My life for the sheep."

Again Jesus found access to the minds of His hearers by the pathway of their familiar associations. He had likened the Spirit's influence to the cool, refreshing water. He had represented Himself as the light, the source of life and gladness to nature and to man. Now in a beautiful pastoral picture He represents His relation to those that believe on Him. No picture was more familiar to His hearers than this, and Christ's words linked it forever with Himself. Never could the disciples look on the shepherds tending their flocks without recalling the Saviour's lesson. They would see Christ in each faithful shepherd. They would see themselves in each helpless and dependent flock.

This figure the prophet Isaiah had applied to the Messiah's mission, in the comforting words, "O Zion, that bringest good tidings, get thee up into the high mountain; O Jerusalem, that bringest good tidings, lift up thy voice with strength; lift it up, be not afraid; say unto the cities of Judah, Behold your God! . . . He shall feed His flock like a shepherd: He shall gather the lambs with His arm, and carry them in His bosom." Isa. 40:9-11. David had sung, "The Lord is my shepherd; [476-477] I shall not want." Ps. 23:1. And the Holy Spirit through Ezekiel had declared: "I will set up one Shepherd over them, and He shall feed them." "I will seek that which was lost, and bring again that which was driven away, and will bind up that which was broken, and will strengthen that which was sick." "And I will make with them a covenant of peace." "And they shall no more be a prey to the heathen; . . . but they shall dwell safely, and none shall make them afraid." Ezek. 34:23, 16, 25, 28.

Christ applied these prophecies to Himself, and He showed the contrast between His own character and that of the leaders in Israel. The Pharisees had just driven one from the fold, because he dared to bear witness to the power of Christ. They had cut off a soul whom the True Shepherd was drawing to Himself. In this they had shown themselves ignorant of the work committed to them, and unworthy of their trust as shepherds of the flock. Jesus now set before them the contrast between them and the Good Shepherd, and He pointed to Himself as the real keeper of the Lord's flock. Before doing this, however, He speaks of Himself under another figure.

He said, "He that entereth not by the door into the sheepfold, but climbeth up some other way, the same is a thief and a robber. But he that entereth in by the door is the shepherd of the sheep." The Pharisees did not discern that these words were spoken against them. When they reasoned in their hearts as to the meaning, Jesus told them plainly, "I am the door: by Me if any man enter in, he shall be saved, and shall go in and out, and find pasture. The thief cometh not, but for to steal, and to kill, and to destroy: I am come that they might have life, and that they might have it more abundantly."

Christ is the door to the fold of God. Through this door all His children, from the earliest times, have found entrance. In Jesus, as shown in types, as shadowed in symbols, as manifested in the revelation of the prophets, as unveiled in the lessons given to His disciples, and in the miracles wrought for the sons of men, they have beheld "the Lamb of God, which taketh away the sin of the world" (John 1:29), and through Him they are brought within the fold of His grace. Many have come presenting other objects for the faith of the world; ceremonies and systems have been devised by which men hope to receive justification and peace with God, and thus find entrance to His fold. But the only door is Christ, and all who have interposed something to take the place [477-478] of Christ, all who have tried to enter the fold in some other way, are thieves and robbers.

The Pharisees had not entered by the door. They had climbed into the fold by another way than Christ, and

---

1. "Jesus told them plainly, I am the door…The t_____ cometh not, but for to steal, and to kill, and to destroy: I am come that they might have life, and that they might have it more a_____." (477). Satan has switched it around, hasn't he, Lord? He suggests that if I follow You, I'll have all the fun taken out of my life. The reality is, Satan is the thief. He robs me of lasting satisfaction. What are some ways that he still gets me on this point? __

_____

_____

_____

2. "The only door is C___ _____" for those who "hope to receive justification and p_____ with God." Do I try other entrances, like busy missionary work, church positions, extra stewardship, or comparing myself with others and relying on self-righteousness? _____

_____

_____

_____

they were not fulfilling the work of the true shepherd. The priests and rulers, the scribes and Pharisees, destroyed the living pastures, and defiled the wellsprings of the water of life. Faithfully do the words of inspiration describe those false shepherds: "The diseased have ye not strengthened, neither have ye healed that which was sick, neither have ye bound up that which was broken, neither have ye brought again that which was driven away; . . . but with force and with cruelty have ye ruled them." Ezek. 34:4.

In all ages, philosophers and teachers have been presenting to the world theories by which to satisfy the soul's need. Every heathen nation has had its great teachers and religious systems offering some other means of redemption than Christ, turning the eyes of men away from the Father's face, and filling their hearts with fear of Him who has given them only blessing. The trend of their work is to rob God of that which is His own, both by creation and by redemption. And these false teachers rob man as well. Millions of human beings are bound down under false religions, in the bondage of slavish fear, of stolid indifference, toiling like beasts of burden, bereft of hope or joy or aspiration here, and with only a dull fear of the hereafter. It is the gospel of the grace of God alone that can uplift the soul. The contemplation of the love of God manifested in His Son will stir the heart and arouse the powers of the soul as nothing else can. Christ came that He might re-create the image of God in man; and whoever turns men away from Christ is turning them away from the source of true development; he is defrauding them of the hope and purpose and glory of life. He is a thief and a robber.

"He that entereth in by the door is the shepherd of the sheep." Christ is both the door and the shepherd. He enters in by Himself. It is through His own sacrifice that He becomes the shepherd of the sheep. "To Him the porter openeth; and the sheep hear His voice: and He calleth His own sheep by name, and leadeth them out. And when He putteth forth His own sheep, He goeth before them, and the sheep follow Him: for they know His voice."

Of all creatures the sheep is one of the most timid and helpless, and in the East the shepherd's care for his flock is untiring and incessant. [478-479] Anciently as now there was little security outside of the walled towns. Marauders from the roving border tribes, or beasts of

3. Millions have been robbed by false religions, which turn their eyes "away from the Father's f_____, and filling their hearts with f_____ of Him who has given them only blessing." (478). I want to do just the opposite, then. Help me to reject as false, any thoughts of avoiding You or distancing myself from You: _____

_____

_____

4. "It is the gospel of the grace of God alone that can uplift the soul. The contemplation of the l_____ of God manifested in His S_____ will s_____ the heart and will arouse the powers of the soul as nothing else can." Lord, as I walk with You, and contemplate Your love, stir my heart; inspire a devotion and commitment to You that is unfaltering: _____

_____

_____

_____

5. "Of all the creatures the s_____ is one of the most timid and h_____ _____, and in the East the shepherd's care for his flock is u_____ and incessant." Lord, You

are both my door and my shepherd. Your care for me is untiring and incessant. That means You are available for our walk together, 24-7. You're always there, waiting for me to join you. I don't want to ever slight You and Your love by neglecting to take that morning walk with You: __

_____

_____

6. "Caring tenderly for the sickly and feeble, his [the shepherd's] life comes to be o____ with theirs. A strong and tender a_____ unites him to the objects of his care. However large the flock, the shepherd k_____ every sheep. Every one has its name, and r_____ to the name at the shepherd's call." (479). Thank You , Lord, for Your love for me and wanting to be one with me. Whenever I am tempted to question whether my walk is real, if there is any point to it, any benefit from it, remind me how much of a Shepherd You are: _____

_____

_____

_____

7. "Every souls is as fully k_____ to Jesus as if he were the o_____ one for whom the Savior died...He cares for e_____ one as if there were not another on the face of the

prey from their hiding places in the rocks, lay in wait to plunder the flocks. The shepherd watched his charge, knowing that it was at the peril of his own life. Jacob, who kept the flocks of Laban in the pasture grounds of Haran, describing his own unwearied labor, said, "In the day the drought consumed me, and the frost by night; and my sleep departed from mine eyes." Gen. 31:40. And it was while guarding his father's sheep that the boy David, single-handed, encountered the lion and the bear, and rescued from their teeth the stolen lamb.

As the shepherd leads his flock over the rocky hills, through forest and wild ravines, to grassy nooks by the riverside; as he watches them on the mountains through the lonely night, shielding from robbers, caring tenderly for the sickly and feeble, his life comes to be one with theirs. A strong and tender attachment unites him to the objects of his care. However large the flock, the shepherd knows every sheep. Every one has its name, and responds to the name at the shepherd's call.

As an earthly shepherd knows his sheep, so does the divine Shepherd know His flock that are scattered throughout the world. "Ye My flock, the flock of My pasture, are men, and I am your God, saith the Lord God." Jesus says, "I have called thee by thy name; thou art Mine." "I have graven thee upon the palms of My hands." Ezek. 34:31; Isa. 43:1; 49:16.

Jesus knows us individually, and is touched with the feeling of our infirmities. He knows us all by name. He knows the very house in which we live, the name of each occupant. He has at times given directions to His servants to go to a certain street in a certain city, to such a house, to find one of His sheep. [479-480]

Every soul is as fully known to Jesus as if he were the only one for whom the Saviour died. The distress of every one touches His heart. The cry for aid reaches His ear. He came to draw all men unto Himself. He bids them, "Follow Me," and His Spirit moves upon their hearts to draw them to come to Him. Many refuse to be drawn. Jesus knows who they are. He also knows who gladly hear His call, and are ready to come under His pastoral care. He says, "My sheep hear My voice, and I know them, and they follow Me." He cares for each one as if there were not another on the face of the earth.

"He calleth His own sheep by name, and leadeth them out. . . . And the sheep follow Him: for they know His voice." The Eastern shepherd does not drive his sheep. He depends not upon force or fear; but going before, he calls them. They know his voice, and obey the call. So does the Saviour-Shepherd with His sheep. The Scripture says, "Thou leddest Thy people like a flock by the hand of Moses and Aaron." Through the prophet, Jesus declares, "I have loved thee with an everlasting love: therefore with loving-kindness have I drawn thee." He compels none to follow Him. "I drew them," He says, "with cords of a man, with bands of love." Ps. 77:20; Jer. 31:3; Hosea 11:4.

It is not the fear of punishment, or the hope of everlasting reward, that leads the disciples of Christ to follow Him. They behold the Saviour's matchless love, revealed throughout His pilgrimage on earth, from the manger of Bethlehem to Calvary's cross, and the sight of Him attracts, it softens and subdues the soul. Love awakens in the heart of the beholders. They hear His voice, and they follow Him.

As the shepherd goes before his sheep, himself first encountering the perils of the way, so does Jesus with His people. "When He putteth forth His own sheep, He goeth before them." The way to heaven is consecrated by the Saviour's footprints. The path may be steep and rugged, but Jesus has traveled that way; His feet have pressed down the cruel thorns, to make the pathway easier for us. Every burden that we are called to bear He Himself has borne.

Though now He has ascended to the presence of God, and shares the throne of the universe, Jesus has lost none of His compassionate nature. Today the same tender, sympathizing heart is open to all the woes of humanity. Today the hand that was pierced is reached forth to bless more abundantly His people that are in the world. "And they shall never perish, neither shall any man pluck them out of My hand." [480-483] The soul that has given himself to Christ is more precious in His sight than the whole world. The Saviour would have passed through the agony of Calvary that one might be saved in His kingdom. He will never abandon one for whom He has died. Unless His followers choose to leave Him, He will hold them fast.

Through all our trials we have a never-failing Helper. He does not leave us alone to struggle with temp-

earth." (480). How can I turn that down? You died for me! You were willing to die for just me! Unbelievable! Help mine unbelief! May I respond to You, as though I am the only one to thank You:

_____

_____

"The Savior would have passed through the a_____ of Calvary that one might be saved in His kingdom." (483).

8. A "shepherd does not drive his sheep, he depends not upon force or f_____; but going b_____, he calls them... I have loved thee with an e_____ _____ love: therefore with loving-kindness I have d_____ thee." What leads me, calls me, to follow Christ? _____

_____

I behold the Savior's matchless love, and the "sight of Him attracts, it s_____ and subdues the soul. Love awakens in the heart of the beholders." May that be the experience of my walk with You, Lord: _____

_____

_____

tation, to battle with evil, and be finally crushed with burdens and sorrow. Though now He is hidden from mortal sight, the ear of faith can hear His voice saying, Fear not; I am with you. "I am He that liveth, and was dead; and, behold, I am alive forevermore." Rev. 1:18. I have endured your sorrows, experienced your struggles, encountered your temptations. I know your tears; I also have wept. The griefs that lie too deep to be breathed into any human ear, I know. Think not that you are desolate and forsaken. Though your pain touch no responsive chord in any heart on earth, look unto Me, and live. "The mountains shall depart, and the hills be removed; but My kindness shall not depart from thee, neither shall the covenant of My peace be removed, saith the Lord that hath mercy on thee." Isa. 54:10.

However much a shepherd may love his sheep, he loves his sons and daughters more. Jesus is not only our shepherd; He is our "everlasting Father." And He says, "I know Mine own, and Mine own know Me, even as the Father knoweth Me, and I know the Father." John 10:14, 15, R. V. What a statement is this!--the only-begotten Son, He who is in the bosom of the Father, He whom God has declared to be "the Man that is My fellow" (Zech. 13:7),--the communion between Him and the eternal God is taken to represent the communion between Christ and His children on the earth!

Because we are the gift of His Father, and the reward of His work, Jesus loves us. He loves us as His children. Reader, He loves you. Heaven itself can bestow nothing greater, nothing better. Therefore trust.

Jesus thought upon the souls all over the earth who were misled by false shepherds. Those whom He longed to gather as the sheep of His pasture were scattered among wolves, and He said, "Other sheep I have, which are not of this fold: them also I must bring, and they shall hear My voice; and they shall become one flock, one shepherd." John 10:16, R. V.

"Therefore doth My Father love Me, because I lay down My life, that I might take it again." That is, My Father has so loved you, that [483-484] He even loves Me more for giving My life to redeem you. In becoming your substitute and surety, by surrendering My life, by taking your liabilities, your transgressions, I am endeared to My Father.

"I lay down My life, that I might take it again. No man taketh it from Me, but I lay it down of Myself. I

9. "I know mine own, and mine own know Me, even as the F_____ knoweth Me, and I know the Father...The communion between Him and the eternal God is taken to r_____ the communion between Christ and His c_____ on the earth!" (483). What a treasured friendship, Lord! Help me to be less sporadic, and more driven for the honor of communion with You! _____
_____
_____

10. "Heaven itself can bestow nothing greater, nothing better." What can I compare it to? _____
_____
_____ "Therefore trust." What inspires trust? _____
_____
_____
_____
_____

11. "I lay it down of Myself...He could have with-

have power to lay it down, and I have power to take it again." While as a member of the human family He was mortal, as God He was the fountain of life for the world. He could have withstood the advances of death, and refused to come under its dominion; but voluntarily He laid down His life, that He might bring life and immortality to light. He bore the sin of the world, endured its curse, yielded up His life as a sacrifice, that men might not eternally die. "Surely He hath borne our griefs, and carried our sorrows. . . . He was wounded for our transgressions, He was bruised for our iniquities: the chastisement of our peace was upon Him; and with His stripes we are healed. All we like sheep have gone astray; we have turned every one to his own way; and the Lord hath laid on Him the iniquity of us all." Isa. 53:4-6.

stood the advances of d_____, and refused to come under its dominion; but v_____ He laid down His life, that He might bring life and immortality to l_____" [He] "yielded up His life as a s_____, that men might not eternally die." (484). Lord, I am trying to better understand the science of salvation. Your death is a sacrifice; and it brings life to light; meaning, You are showing me, wanting me to understand life. Help me to grasp how Your death goes deeper than simply the wages or punishment of my sins. You're bringing me to a point of light, of comprehension, of belief, of trust, of healing what causes me to sin in the first place: _____

_____
_____
_____
_____
_____

Prayer journal: _____
_____
_____
_____
_____
_____
_____

Chapter 53

The Last Journey From Galilee

[This chapter is based on Luke 9:51-56; 10:1-24.]

1. "Heretofore, Jesus had sought to shun excitement and p_____. He had r_____ the homage of the people...But He now set out to return [to Jerusalem], traveling in the most p_____ manner." Why?

_____

_____

_____ The great sacrifice was not to merely be accomplished, on some planet in some far corner of the universe. But the sacrifice was to demonstrate and share God's love. It was to be a witness, to be noticed. Otherwise, what is gained? _____

_____

Lord, do I devalue the great sacrifice, by treating it merely as a story too often repeated? Draw my attention, Lord, and draw my heart anew. _____

_____

_____

As the close of His ministry drew near, there was a change in Christ's manner of labor. Heretofore He had sought to shun excitement and publicity. He had refused the homage of the people, and had passed quickly from place to place when the popular enthusiasm in His favor seemed kindling beyond control. Again and again He had commanded that none should declare Him to be the Christ.

At the time of the Feast of Tabernacles His journey to Jerusalem was made swiftly and secretly. When urged by His brothers to present Himself publicly as the Messiah, His answer was, "My time is not yet come." John 7:6. He made His way to Jerusalem unobserved, and entered the city unannounced, and unhonored by the multitude. But not so with His last journey. He had left Jerusalem for a season because of the malice of the priests and rabbis. But He now set out to return, traveling in the most public manner, by a circuitous route, and preceded by such an announcement of His coming as He had never made before. He was going forward to the scene of His great sacrifice, and to this the attention of the people must be directed.

"As Moses lifted up the serpent in the wilderness, even so must the Son of man be lifted up." John 3:14. As the eyes of all Israel had been directed to the uplifted serpent, the symbol appointed for their healing, so all eyes must be drawn to Christ, the sacrifice that brought salvation to the lost world.

It was a false conception of the Messiah's work, and a lack of faith [485-486] in the divine character of Jesus, that had led His brothers to urge Him to present Himself publicly to the people at the Feast of Tabernacles. Now, in a spirit akin to this, the disciples would have prevented Him from making the journey to Jerusalem. They remembered His words concerning what was to befall Him there, they knew the deadly hostility of the religious leaders, and they would fain have dissuaded their Master from going thither.

To the heart of Christ it was a bitter task to press His way against the fears, disappointment, and unbelief of His beloved disciples. It was hard to lead them forward to the anguish and despair that awaited them at Jerusalem. And Satan was at hand to press his temptations upon the Son of man. Why should He now go to Jerusalem, to certain death? All around Him were souls hungering for the bread of life. On every hand were suffering ones waiting for His word of healing. The work to be wrought by the gospel of His grace was but just begun. And He was full of the vigor of manhood's prime. Why not go forward to the vast fields of the world with the words of His grace, the touch of His healing power? Why not take to Himself the joy of giving light and gladness to those darkened and sorrowing millions? Why leave the harvest gathering to His disciples, so weak in faith, so dull of understanding, so slow to act? Why face death now, and leave the work in its infancy? The foe who in the wilderness had confronted Christ assailed Him now with fierce and subtle temptations. Had Jesus yielded for a moment, had He changed His course in the least particular to save Himself, Satan's agencies would have triumphed, and the world would have been lost.

But Jesus had "steadfastly set His face to go to Jerusalem." The one law of His life was the Father's will. In the visit to the temple in His boyhood, He had said to Mary, "Wist ye not that I must be about My Father's business?" Luke 2:49. At Cana, when Mary desired Him to reveal His miraculous power, His answer was, "Mine hour is not yet come." John 2:4. With the same words He replied to His brothers when they urged Him to go to the feast. But in God's great plan the hour had been appointed for the offering of Himself for the sins of men, and that hour was soon to strike. He would not fail nor falter. His steps are turned toward Jerusalem, where His foes have long plotted to take His life; now He will lay it down. He set His face steadfastly to go to persecution, denial, rejection, condemnation, and death.

And He "sent messengers before His face: and they went, and entered into a village of the Samaritans, to make ready for Him." But [486-487] the people refused to receive Him, because He was on His way to Jerusalem. This they interpreted as meaning that Christ

2. "To the heart of Christ it was a b_____ task to press His way against the fears, d_____ ___, and unbelief of His beloved disciples. It was hard to lead them forward to the anguish and despair that awaited them at Jerusalem." (486). How does my attitude affect You, Lord? Forgive me for not understanding You and Your mission better. How can I be more supportive:

_____

_____

showed a preference for the Jews, whom they hated with intense bitterness. Had He come to restore the temple and worship upon Mount Gerizim, they would gladly have received Him; but He was going to Jerusalem, and they would show Him no hospitality. Little did they realize that they were turning from their doors the best gift of heaven. Jesus invited men to receive Him, He asked favors at their hands, that He might come near to them, to bestow the richest blessings. For every favor manifested toward Him, He requited a more precious grace. But all was lost to the Samaritans because of their prejudice and bigotry.

James and John, Christ's messengers, were greatly annoyed at the insult shown to their Lord. They were filled with indignation because He had been so rudely treated by the Samaritans whom He was honoring by His presence. They had recently been with Him on the mount of transfiguration, and had seen Him glorified by God, and honored by Moses and Elijah. This manifest dishonor on the part of the Samaritans, should not, they thought, be passed over without marked punishment.

Coming to Christ, they reported to Him the words of the people, telling Him that they had even refused to give Him a night's lodging. They thought that a grievous wrong had been done Him, and seeing Mount Carmel in the distance, where Elijah had slain the false prophets, they said, "Wilt Thou that we command fire to come down from heaven, and consume them, even as Elias did?" They were surprised to see that Jesus was pained by their words, and still more surprised as His rebuke fell upon their ears, "Ye know not what manner of spirit ye are of. For the Son of man is not come to destroy men's lives, but to save them." And He went to another village.

It is no part of Christ's mission to compel men to receive Him. It is Satan, and men actuated by his spirit, that seek to compel the conscience. Under a pretense of zeal for righteousness, men who are confederate with evil angels bring suffering upon their fellow men, in order to convert them to their ideas of religion; but Christ is ever showing mercy, ever seeking to win by the revealing of His love. He can admit no rival in the soul, nor accept of partial service; but He desires only voluntary service, the willing surrender of the heart under the constraint of love. There can be no more conclusive evidence that we possess the spirit of Satan than the dis-

3. James and John were "surprised to see that Jesus was p_____ by their words, and still more surprised as His rebuke fell upon their ears, "Ye know not what manner of s_____ ye are of...There can be no more conclusive evidence that we possess the spirit of Satan than the

position to hurt and destroy those who do not appreciate our work, or who act contrary to our ideas. [487-488]

Every human being, in body, soul, and spirit, is the property of God. Christ died to redeem all. Nothing can be more offensive to God than for men, through religious bigotry, to bring suffering upon those who are the purchase of the Saviour's blood.

"And He arose from thence, and cometh into the coasts of Judea by the farther side of Jordan: and the people resort unto Him again; and, as He was wont, He taught them again." Mark 10:1.

A considerable part of the closing months of Christ's ministry was spent in Perea, the province on "the farther side of Jordan" from Judea. Here the multitude thronged His steps, as in His early ministry in Galilee, and much of His former teaching was repeated.

As He had sent out the twelve, so He "appointed seventy others, and sent them two and two before His face into every city and place, whither He Himself was about to come." Luke 10:1, R. V. These disciples had been for some time with Him, in training for their work. When the twelve were sent out on their first separate mission, other disciples accompanied Jesus in His journey through Galilee. Thus they had the privilege of intimate association with Him, and direct personal instruction. Now this larger number also were to go forth on a separate mission.

The directions to the seventy were similar to those that had been given to the twelve; but the command to the twelve, not to enter into any city of the Gentiles or of the Samaritans, was not given to the seventy. Though Christ had just been repulsed by the Samaritans, His love toward them was unchanged. When the seventy went forth in His name, they visited, first of all, the cities of Samaria.

The Saviour's own visit to Samaria, and later, the commendation of the good Samaritan, and the grateful joy of that leper, a Samaritan, who alone of the ten returned to give thanks to Christ, were full of significance to the disciples. The lesson sank deep into their hearts. In His commission to them, just before His ascension, Jesus mentioned Samaria with Jerusalem and Judea as the places where they were first to preach the gospel. This commission His teaching had prepared them to fulfill. When in their Master's name they went to Samaria, they found the people ready to receive them. The Sa-

disposition to h_____ and destroy those who do not a_____ our work, or who act contrary to our ideas." (487). But Lord, when I see You slighted, or mocked, it is hard to think kind thoughts about them. Maybe I get defensive for myself, but thinking that I am defending You. In either case, Lord, I obviously need help, to see myself and my need. I don't want to cause You pain. What situations might You be sending me to help me practice Your spirit, and not Satan's?

_____

_____

_____

_____

4. "Though Christ had just been repulsed by the Samaritans, His love toward them was u_____." He sent the seventy disciples to their cities. The

Samaritans had heard of Christ's words of c_____ _____ [the good Samaritan] and His works of mercy for men of their nation…and their hearts were w_____." (488). Lord, my love is so self-centered. I know that I have repulsed You many times. You have an amazing, compassionate heart. I praise You for it. Thank You for not stopping to love me. I wish I could reciprocate, but I am still learning and growing in the area of spiritual love:

_____

_____

_____

5. "How g_____ a thing it is to refuse the Lord's message…Every

maritans had heard of Christ's words of commendation and His works of mercy for men of their nation. They saw that, notwithstanding their rude treatment of Him, He had only thoughts of love toward them, and their hearts were won. After His ascension they welcomed the Saviour's messengers, and the disciples gathered a precious harvest from among those who had once been their bitterest enemies. [488-489] "A bruised reed shall He not break, and the dimly burning flax shall He not quench: He shall bring forth judgment unto truth." "And in His name shall the Gentiles trust." Isa. 42:3, margin; Matt. 12:21.

In sending out the seventy, Jesus bade them, as He had bidden the twelve, not to urge their presence where they were unwelcome. "Into whatsoever city ye enter, and they receive you not," He said, "go your ways out into the streets of the same, and say, Even the very dust of your city, which cleaveth on us, we do wipe off against you: notwithstanding be ye sure of this, that the kingdom of God is come nigh unto you." They were not to do this from motives of resentment or through wounded dignity, but to show how grievous a thing it is to refuse the Lord's message or His messengers. To reject the Lord's servants is to reject Christ Himself.

"I say unto you," Jesus added, "that it shall be more tolerable in that day for Sodom, than for that city." Then His mind reverted to the Galilean towns where so much of His ministry had been spent. In deeply sorrowful accents He exclaimed, "Woe unto thee, Chorazin! woe unto thee, Bethsaida! for if the mighty works had been done in Tyre and Sidon, which have been done in you, they had a great while ago repented, sitting in sackcloth and ashes. But it shall be more tolerable for Tyre and Sidon at the judgment, than for you. And thou, Capernaum, which art exalted to heaven, shalt be thrust down to hell."

To those busy towns about the Sea of Galilee, heaven's richest blessings had been freely offered. Day after day the Prince of life had gone in and out among them. The glory of God, which prophets and kings had longed to see, had shone upon the multitudes that thronged the Saviour's steps. Yet they had refused the heavenly Gift.

With a great show of prudence the rabbis had warned the people against receiving the new doctrines taught by this new teacher; for His theories and practices were contrary to the teachings of the fathers. The people gave credence to what the priests and Pharisees taught, in place of seeking to understand the word of God for themselves. They honored the priests and rulers instead of honoring God, and rejected the truth that they might keep their own traditions. Many had been impressed and almost persuaded; but they did not act upon their convictions, and were not reckoned on the side of Christ. Satan presented his temptations, until the light appeared as darkness. Thus many rejected the truth that would have proved the saving of the soul.

The True Witness says, "Behold, I stand at the door, and knock." Rev. 3:20. Every warning, reproof, and entreaty in the word of God or [489-490] through His messengers is a knock at the door of the heart. It is the voice of Jesus asking for entrance. With every knock unheeded, the disposition to open becomes weaker. The impressions of the Holy Spirit if disregarded today, will not be as strong tomorrow. The heart becomes less impressible, and lapses into a perilous unconsciousness of the shortness of life, and of the great eternity beyond. Our condemnation in the judgment will not result from the fact that we have been in error, but from the fact that we have neglected heaven-sent opportunities for learning what is truth.

Like the apostles, the seventy had received supernatural endowments as a seal of their mission. When their work was completed, they returned with joy, saying, "Lord, even the devils are subject unto us through Thy name." Jesus answered, "I beheld Satan as lightning fall from heaven."

The scenes of the past and the future were presented to the mind of Jesus. He beheld Lucifer as he was first cast out from the heavenly places. He looked forward to the scenes of His own agony, when before all the worlds the character of the deceiver should be unveiled. He heard the cry, "It is finished" (John 19:30), announcing that the redemption of the lost race was forever made certain, that heaven was made eternally secure against the accusations, the deceptions, the pretensions, that Satan would instigate.

Beyond the cross of Calvary, with its agony and shame, Jesus looked forward to the great final day, when the prince of the power of the air will meet his destruction in the earth so long marred by his rebellion. Jesus beheld the work of evil forever ended, and the peace of

warning, reproof, and entreaty in the word of God or through His m_____ _____ is a knock at the door of the heart. It is the voice of Jesus asking for entrance. With every knock u_____, the disposition to open becomes weaker." (489, 490). Is this serious, Lord? "The heart becomes less i_____, and lapses into a perilous unconsciousness of the shortness of life, and of the great eternity beyond." Help me, Lord, to hear and be responsive to every whisper of the Holy Spirit:

_____

_____

_____

God filling heaven and earth.

Henceforward Christ's followers were to look upon Satan as a conquered foe. Upon the cross, Jesus was to gain the victory for them; that victory He desired them to accept as their own. "Behold," He said, "I give unto you power to tread on serpents and scorpions, and over all the power of the enemy: and nothing shall by any means hurt you."

The omnipotent power of the Holy Spirit is the defense of every contrite soul. Not one that in penitence and faith has claimed His protection will Christ permit to pass under the enemy's power. The Saviour is by the side of His tempted and tried ones. With Him there can be no such thing as failure, loss, impossibility, or defeat; we can do all things through Him who strengthens us. When temptations and trials [490-493] come, do not wait to adjust all the difficulties, but look to Jesus, your helper.

There are Christians who think and speak altogether too much about the power of Satan. They think of their adversary, they pray about him, they talk about him, and he looms up greater and greater in their imagination. It is true that Satan is a powerful being; but, thank God, we have a mighty Saviour, who cast out the evil one from heaven. Satan is pleased when we magnify his power. Why not talk of Jesus? Why not magnify His power and His love?

The rainbow of promise encircling the throne on high is an everlasting testimony that "God so loved the world, that He gave His only-begotten Son, that whosoever believeth in Him should not perish, but have everlasting life." John 3:16. It testifies to the universe that God will never forsake His people in their struggle with evil. It is an assurance to us of strength and protection as long as the throne itself shall endure.

Jesus added, "Notwithstanding in this rejoice not, that the spirits are subject unto you; but rather rejoice, because your names are written in heaven." Rejoice not in the possession of power, lest you lose sight of your dependence upon God. Be careful lest self-sufficiency come in, and you work in your own strength, rather than in the spirit and strength of your Master. Self is ever ready to take the credit if any measure of success attends the work. Self is flattered and exalted, and the impression is not made upon other minds that God is all and in all. The apostle Paul says, "When I am weak, then

---

6. "Not one that in penitence and faith has claimed His protection will Christ permit to pass under the enemy's p_____ ...With Him there can be no such thing as failure, loss, i_____, or defeat; we can do a_____ things through H_____ who strengthens us... Satan is pleased when we magnify his power. Why not talk of Jesus? Why not m___ _____ His power and His love?" (490, 493). Thank You, Lord for Your protection, Your strong arm. Help me not to minimize Satan's subtle strategies (a roaring lion that devours), nor to be intimidated by them. You are my strength! _____
_____
_____

7. "Be careful lest self-s_____ come in, and you work in your own strength, rather than in the spirit and strength of your M_____ ...

am I strong." 2 Cor. 12:10. When we have a realization of our weakness, we learn to depend upon a power not inherent. Nothing can take so strong a hold on the heart as the abiding sense of our responsibility to God. Nothing reaches so fully down to the deepest motives of conduct as a sense of the pardoning love of Christ. We are to come in touch with God, then we shall be imbued with His Holy Spirit, that enables us to come in touch with our fellow men. Then rejoice that through Christ you have become connected with God, members of the heavenly family. While you look higher than yourself, you will have a continual sense of the weakness of humanity. The less you cherish self, the more distinct and full will be your comprehension of the excellence of your Saviour. The more closely you connect yourself with the source of light and power, the greater light will be shed upon you, and the greater power will be yours to work for God. Rejoice that you are one with God, one with Christ, and with the whole family of heaven. [493-494]

As the seventy listened to the words of Christ, the Holy Spirit was impressing their minds with living realities, and writing truth upon the tablets of the soul. Though multitudes surrounded them, they were as though shut in with God.

Knowing that they had caught the inspiration of the hour, Jesus "rejoiced in spirit, and said, I thank Thee, O Father, Lord of heaven and earth, that Thou hast hid these things from the wise and prudent, and hast revealed them unto babes: even so, Father; for so it seemed good in Thy sight. All things are delivered to Me of My Father: and no man knoweth who the Son is, but the Father, and who the Father is, but the Son, and he to whom the Son will reveal Him."

The honored men of the world, the so-called great and wise men, with all their boasted wisdom, could not comprehend the character of Christ. They judged Him from outward appearance, from the humiliation that came upon Him as a human being. But to fishermen and publicans it had been given to see the Invisible. Even the disciples failed of understanding all that Jesus desired to reveal to them; but from time to time, as they surrendered themselves to the Holy Spirit's power, their minds were illuminated. They realized that the mighty God, clad in the garb of humanity, was among them. Jesus rejoiced that though this knowledge was not pos-

The less you cherish s_____, the more distinct and full will be your comprehension of the e_____ of your Savior." That is a much more uplifting focus, Your excellence instead of myself. I want my daily walk with You to focus on Your excellence. What can I do to help? _____
_____
_____

Can We Walk, Together?

sessed by the wise and prudent, it had been revealed to these humble men. Often as He had presented the Old Testament Scriptures, and showed their application to Himself and His work of atonement, they had been awakened by His Spirit, and lifted into a heavenly atmosphere. Of the spiritual truths spoken by the prophets they had a clearer understanding than had the original writers themselves. Hereafter they would read the Old Testament Scriptures, not as the doctrines of the scribes and Pharisees, not as the utterances of wise men who were dead, but as a new revelation from God. They beheld Him "whom the world cannot receive, because it seeth Him not, neither knoweth Him: but ye know Him; for He dwelleth with you, and shall be in you." John 14:17.

8. The only way in which we can gain a more perfect apprehension of truth is by keeping the heart t_____ and subdued by the Spirit of Christ. The soul must be cleansed from vanity and p_____, and vacated of all that has held it in possession, and Christ must be e_____ ___ within." (494). What holds possession of my soul, Lord? Show me, for I want You sitting on the throne: _____
_____
_____
_____

The only way in which we can gain a more perfect apprehension of truth is by keeping the heart tender and subdued by the Spirit of Christ. The soul must be cleansed from vanity and pride, and vacated of all that has held it in possession, and Christ must be enthroned within. Human science is too limited to comprehend the atonement. The plan of redemption is so far-reaching that philosophy cannot explain it. It will [494-495] ever remain a mystery that the most profound reasoning cannot fathom. The science of salvation cannot be explained; but it can be known by experience. Only he who sees his own sinfulness can discern the preciousness of the Saviour.

Full of instruction were the lessons which Christ taught as He slowly made His way from Galilee toward Jerusalem. Eagerly the people listened to His words. In Perea as in Galilee the people were less under the control of Jewish bigotry than in Judea, and His teaching found a response in their hearts.

During these last months of His ministry, many of Christ's parables were spoken. The priests and rabbis pursued Him with ever-increasing bitterness, and His warnings to them He veiled in symbols. They could not mistake His meaning, yet they could find in His words nothing on which to ground an accusation against Him. In the parable of the Pharisee and the publican, the self-sufficient prayer, "God, I thank Thee that I am not as the rest of men," stood out in sharp contrast to the penitent's plea, "Be merciful to me the sinner." Luke 18:11, 13, R. V., margin. Thus Christ rebuked the hypocrisy of the Jews. And under the figures of the barren fig tree and the great supper He foretold the doom about to fall upon the impenitent nation. Those who had scornfully rejected the invitation to the gospel feast heard His warning words: "I say unto you, That none of those men which were bidden shall taste of My supper." Luke 14:24.

Very precious was the instruction given to the disciples. The parable of the importunate widow and the friend asking for bread at midnight gave new force to His words, "Ask, and it shall be given you; seek, and ye shall find; knock, and it shall be opened unto you." Luke 11:9. And often their wavering faith was strengthened by the memory that Christ had said, "Shall not God do justice for His elect, which cry to Him day and night, and He is long-suffering over them? I say unto you, that He will do them justice speedily." Luke 18:7, 8, R. V., margin.

The beautiful parable of the lost sheep Christ repeated. And He carried its lesson still farther, as He told of the lost piece of silver and the prodigal son. The force of these lessons the disciples could not then fully appreciate; but after the outpouring of the Holy Spirit, as they saw the ingathering of the Gentiles and the envious anger of the Jews, they better understood the lesson of the prodigal son, and could enter into the joy of Christ's words, "It was meet that we should make merry, [495-496] and be glad;" "for this my son was dead, and is alive again; he was lost, and is found." Luke 15:32, 24. And as they went out in their Master's name, facing reproach and poverty and persecution, they often strengthened their hearts by repeating His injunction, spoken on this last journey, "Fear not, little flock; for it is your Father's good pleasure to give you the kingdom. Sell that ye have, and give alms; provide yourselves bags which wax not old, a treasure in the heavens that faileth not, where no thief approacheth, neither moth corrupteth. For where your treasure is, there will your heart be also." Luke 12:32-34.

9. "Very precious was the instruction given to the disciples...The force of these lessons [the lost sheep, the lost piece of silver, and the prodigal son] the disciples could not then fully a___ _____; but after the outpouring of the Holy Spirit, as they saw the ingathering of the Gentiles and the envious anger of the Jews, they better understood the lesson of the prodigal son, and could enter into the j_____ of Christ's words" [make merry, lost is found]. (495). Thank You for Your Word, Your parables. I learn wonderful truths of Your character and the Father's. Thank You also for the Spirit's help in applying Your instruction. I don't always get it from one reading. Your love is new with every reading! New every morning! How can I see the precious value of this treasure? _____

_____

_____

_____

Prayer journal: _____

_____

_____

_____

_____

_____

_____

_____

_____

1. The story of the Good Samaritan illustrates that true religion consists in the "performance of l_____ _____ deeds, in bringing the greatest g_____ to others, in genuine goodness." Should I also understand, Lord, that true religion does not solely consist of my intimate walk with You? My quiet, private time with You? But from my time in Your grace, I share Your grace to others. What are some examples of how I can be a theater of Your grace: _____ _____ _____ _____

2. What shall I do to inherit e_____ life? The lawyer answered his own question, love God and love n_____. Isn't this too simplistic, Lord? Might people misunderstand and think that all that is required is say 'I do?' _____

_____

But I am sensing that something deeper is being stressed from this story; that a paradigm shift is encouraged here. To love God and neighbor includes the total, summarizes the total, is the essence of the total, AND is to be the motive behind keeping and living the total Help me comprehend, Lord, the depth, the height, of that love: _____

_____

Chapter 54

The Good Samaritan

[This chapter is based on Luke 10:25-37.]

In the story of the good Samaritan, Christ illustrates the nature of true religion. He shows that it consists not in systems, creeds, or rites, but in the performance of loving deeds, in bringing the greatest good to others, in genuine goodness.

As Christ was teaching the people, "a certain lawyer stood up, and tempted Him, saying, Master, what shall I do to inherit eternal life?" With breathless attention the large congregation awaited the answer. The priests and rabbis had thought to entangle Christ by having the lawyer ask this question. But the Saviour entered into no controversy. He required the answer from the questioner himself. "What is written in the law?" He said; "how readest thou?" The Jews still accused Jesus of lightly regarding the law given from Sinai; but He turned the question of salvation upon the keeping of God's commandments.

The lawyer said, "Thou shalt love the Lord thy God with all thy heart, and with all thy soul, and with all thy strength, and with all thy mind; and thy neighbor as thyself." Jesus said, "Thou hast answered right: this do, and thou shalt live."

The lawyer was not satisfied with the position and works of the Pharisees. He had been studying the Scriptures with a desire to learn their real meaning. He had a vital interest in the matter, and had asked in sincerity, "What shall I do?" In his answer as to the requirements [497-498] of the law, he passed by all the mass of ceremonial and ritualistic precepts. For these he claimed no value, but presented the two great principles on which hang all the law and the prophets. This answer, being commended by Christ, placed the Saviour on vantage ground with the rabbis. They could not condemn Him for sanctioning that which had been advanced by an expositor of the law.

"This do, and thou shalt live," Jesus said. He presented the law as a divine unity, and in this lesson taught that it is not possible to keep one precept, and break another; for the same principle runs through them all. Man's destiny will be determined by his obedience to the whole law. Supreme love to God and impartial love to man are the principles to be wrought out in the life.

The lawyer found himself a lawbreaker. He was convicted under Christ's searching words. The righteousness of the law, which he claimed to understand, he had not practiced. He had not manifested love toward his fellow man. Repentance was demanded; but instead of repenting, he tried to justify himself. Rather than acknowledge the truth, he sought to show how difficult of fulfillment the commandment is. Thus he hoped both to parry conviction and to vindicate himself in the eyes of the people. The Saviour's words had shown that his question was needless, since he had been able to answer it himself. Yet he put another question, saying, "Who is my neighbor?"

Among the Jews this question caused endless dispute. They had no doubt as to the heathen and the Samaritans; these were strangers and enemies. But where should the distinction be made among the people of their own nation, and among the different classes of society? Whom should the priest, the rabbi, the elder, regard as neighbor? They spent their lives in a round of ceremonies to make themselves pure. Contact with the ignorant and careless multitude, they taught, would cause defilement that would require wearisome effort to remove. Were they to regard the "unclean" as neighbors?

Again Jesus refused to be drawn into controversy. He did not denounce the bigotry of those who were watching to condemn Him. But by a simple story He held up before His hearers such a picture of the outflowing of heaven-born love as touched all hearts, and drew from the lawyer a confession of the truth.

The way to dispel darkness is to admit light. The best way to deal with error is to present truth. It is the revelation of God's love that makes manifest the deformity and sin of the heart centered in self. [498-499]

"A certain man," said Jesus, "was going down from Jerusalem to Jericho; and he fell among robbers, which both stripped him and beat him, and departed, leaving him half dead. And by chance a certain priest was going down that way: and when he saw him, he passed by on the other side. And in like manner a Levite also, when he came to the place, and saw him, passed by on the other side." Luke 10:30-32, R. V. This was no imagi-

3. "The lawyer was convicted under Christ's s_____ words... Repentance was demanded, but instead of repenting, he tried to j_____ himself." (498). What is the lesson here, Lord? When you search me and convict me, self-justification, rationalization, or defensiveness are not the best responses. How do I justify myself? _____

_____

_____ I ask for the gift of repentance.

4. "The way to dispel darkness is to admit l_____
_____. The best way to deal with e_____ is to present t_____. It is the revelation of God's love that makes manifest the deformity and sin of the heart centered in s_____." Lord, may I treat others, the way You treat me. Show me ways that I may allow Your love to dispel the darkness of sin and self in me: _____

_____

_____

5. "The priest and the L_____ who passed by on the other side [of the wounded traveler] were in the c_____ that listened to Christ's words." (499)...

nary scene, but an actual occurrence, which was known to be exactly as represented. The priest and the Levite who had passed by on the other side were in the company that listened to Christ's words.

In journeying from Jerusalem to Jericho, the traveler had to pass through a portion of the wilderness of Judea. The road led down a wild, rocky ravine, which was infested by robbers, and was often the scene of violence. It was here that the traveler was attacked, stripped of all that was valuable, wounded and bruised, and left half dead by the wayside. As he lay thus, the priest came that way; but he merely glanced toward the wounded man. Then the Levite appeared. Curious to know what had happened, he stopped and looked at the sufferer. He was convicted of what he ought to do; but it was not an agreeable duty. He wished that he had not come that way, so that he need not have seen the wounded man. He persuaded himself that the case was no concern of his.

Both these men were in sacred office, and professed to expound the Scriptures. They were of the class specially chosen to be representatives of God to the people. They were to "have compassion on the ignorant, and on them that are out of the way" (Heb. 5:2), that they might lead [499-500] men to understand God's great love toward humanity. The work they were called to do was the same that Jesus had described as His own when He said, "The Spirit of the Lord is upon Me, because He hath anointed Me to preach the gospel to the poor; He hath sent Me to heal the brokenhearted, to preach deliverance to the captives, and recovering of sight to the blind, to set at liberty them that are bruised." Luke 4:18.

The angels of heaven look upon the distress of God's family upon the earth, and they are prepared to co-operate with men in relieving oppression and suffering. God in His providence had brought the priest and the Levite along the road where the wounded sufferer lay, that they might see his need of mercy and help. All heaven watched to see if the hearts of these men would be touched with pity for human woe. The Saviour was the One who had instructed the Hebrews in the wilderness; from the pillar of cloud and of fire He had taught a very different lesson from that which the people were now receiving from their priests and teachers. The merciful provisions of the law extended even to the lower animals, which cannot express in words their want and suffering. Directions had been given to Moses for the children of Israel to this effect: "If thou meet thine enemy's ox or his ass going astray, thou shalt surely bring it back to him again. If thou see the ass of him that hateth thee lying under his burden, and wouldest forbear to help him, thou shalt surely help with him." Ex. 23:4, 5. But in the man wounded by robbers, Jesus presented the case of a brother in suffering. How much more should their hearts have been moved with pity for him than for a beast of burden! The message had been given them through Moses that the Lord their God, "a great God, a mighty, and a terrible," "doth execute the judgment of the fatherless and widow, and loveth the stranger." Wherefore He commanded, "Love ye therefore the stranger." "Thou shalt love him as thyself." Deut. 10:17-19; Lev. 19:34.

Job had said, "The stranger did not lodge in the street: but I opened my doors to the traveler." And when the two angels in the guise of men came to Sodom, Lot bowed himself with his face toward the ground, and said, "Behold now, my lords, turn in, I pray you, into your servant's house, and tarry all night." Job 31:32; Gen. 19:2. With all these lessons the priest and the Levite were familiar, but they had not brought them into practical life. Trained in the school of national bigotry, they had become selfish, narrow, and exclusive. When they looked upon the wounded man, they could not tell whether he was of their nation or not. They thought he might be of the Samaritans, and they turned away. [500-503]

In their action, as Christ had described it, the lawyer saw nothing contrary to what he had been taught concerning the requirements of the law. But now another scene was presented:

A certain Samaritan, in his journey, came where the sufferer was, and when he saw him, he had compassion on him. He did not question whether the stranger was a Jew or a Gentile. If a Jew, the Samaritan well knew that, were their condition reversed, the man would spit in his face, and pass him by with contempt. But he did not hesitate on account of this. He did not consider that he himself might be in danger of violence by tarrying in the place. It was enough that there was before him a human being in need and suffering. He took off his own garment with which to cover him. The oil and wine pro-

"With all these lessons the priest and the Levite were familiar, but they had not brought them into p_____ _____ life. Trained in the school of national bigotry, they had become selfish, narrow, and e_____." (500). Lord, send me on the Jericho roads of life, that I may have opportunities to put spiritual lessons into practical life. Reveal to me where I have failed to see You, in the least:

_____

_____

_____

_____

6. "In their action, as Christ had described it, the lawyer saw nothing c_____ to what he had been t_____ __ concerning the requirements of the law." (503). What does this say about the teaching of the time?

_____

_____

_____

Or of the views of my time? _____

_____

_____

_____

vided for his own journey he used to heal and refresh the wounded man. He lifted him on his own beast, and moved slowly along with even pace, so that the stranger might not be jarred, and made to suffer increased pain. He brought him to an inn, and cared for him through the night, watching him tenderly. In the morning, as the sick man had improved, the Samaritan ventured to go on his way. But before doing this, he placed him in the care of the innkeeper, paid the charges, and left a deposit for his benefit; and not satisfied even with this, he made provision for any further need, saying to the host, "Take care of him; and whatsoever thou spendest more, when I come again, I will repay thee."

The story ended, Jesus fixed His eyes upon the lawyer, in a glance that seemed to read his soul, and said, "Which of these three, thinkest thou, proved neighbor unto him that fell among the robbers?" Luke 10:36, R. V.

The lawyer would not, even now, take the name Samaritan upon his lips, and he made answer, "He that showed mercy on him." Jesus said, "Go, and do thou likewise."

Thus the question, "Who is my neighbor?" is forever answered. Christ has shown that our neighbor does not mean merely one of the church or faith to which we belong. It has no reference to race, color, or class distinction. Our neighbor is every person who needs our help. Our neighbor is every soul who is wounded and bruised by the adversary. Our neighbor is everyone who is the property of God.

In the story of the good Samaritan, Jesus gave a picture of Himself and His mission. Man had been deceived, bruised, robbed, and ruined by Satan, and left to perish; but the Saviour had compassion on our [503-504] helpless condition. He left His glory, to come to our rescue. He found us ready to die, and He undertook our case. He healed our wounds. He covered us with His robe of righteousness. He opened to us a refuge of safety, and made complete provision for us at His own charges. He died to redeem us. Pointing to His own example, He says to His followers, "These things I command you, that ye love one another." "As I have loved you, that ye also love one another." John 15:17; 13:34.

The lawyer's question to Jesus had been, "What shall I do?" And Jesus, recognizing love to God and man as the sum of righteousness, had said, "This do,

7. "Our neighbor is every person who n_____ our h_____. Our neighbor is every soul who is wounded and b_____ by the adversary. Our neighbor is everyone who is the p_____ of God." Lord, I need Your compassion. Open my eyes to recognize opportunities to share Your love with my 'neighbor.' _____
__ _____
_____
_____

and thou shalt live." The Samaritan had obeyed the dictates of a kind and loving heart, and in this had proved himself a doer of the law. Christ bade the lawyer, "Go, and do thou likewise." Doing, and not saying merely, is expected of the children of God. "He that saith he abideth in Him ought himself also so to walk, even as He walked." 1 John 2:6.

The lesson is no less needed in the world today than when it fell from the lips of Jesus. Selfishness and cold formality have well-nigh extinguished the fire of love, and dispelled the graces that should make fragrant the character. Many who profess His name have lost sight of the fact that Christians are to represent Christ. Unless there is practical self-sacrifice for the good of others, in the family circle, in the neighborhood, in the church, and wherever we may be, then whatever our profession, we are not Christians.

Christ has linked His interest with that of humanity, and He asks us to become one with Him for the saving of humanity. "Freely ye have received," He says, "freely give." Matt. 10:8. Sin is the greatest of all evils, and it is ours to pity and help the sinner. There are many who err, and who feel their shame and their folly. They are hungry for words of encouragement. They look upon their mistakes and errors, until they are driven almost to desperation. These souls we are not to neglect. If we are Christians, we shall not pass by on the other side, keeping as far as possible from the very ones who most need our help. When we see human beings in distress, whether through affliction or through sin, we shall never say, This does not concern me.

"Ye which are spiritual, restore such an one in the spirit of meekness." Gal. 6:1. By faith and prayer press back the power of the enemy. Speak words of faith and courage that will be as a healing balsam to the bruised and wounded one. Many, many, have fainted and become discouraged [504-505] in the great struggle of life, when one word of kindly cheer would have strengthened them to overcome. Never should we pass by one suffering soul without seeking to impart to him of the comfort wherewith we are comforted of God.

All this is but a fulfillment of the principle of the law,--the principle that is illustrated in the story of the good Samaritan, and made manifest in the life of Jesus. His character reveals the true significance of the law, and shows what is meant by loving our neighbor

8. "Doing, and not s_____ merely, is expected of the children of God. He that saith he abideth in Him ought himself also so to w_____, even as He walked." (504). Lord, may the Holy Spirit reach me, telling me when I'm only giving lip service to compassion and inclusiveness:

_____
_____
_____

9. "Unless there is practical self-s_____ for the good of o_____, in the family circle, in the neighborhood, in the church, and w_____ we may be, then whatever our profession, we are n_____ Christians." Wow, Lord! What do You mean by practical self-sacrifice? __

_____
_____
_____

(If it is not practical not convenient, don't do it?)

Can We Walk, Together?

10. "The spirit we manifest toward our brethren, d_____ what i____ our spirit toward God. The love of God in the heart is the o_____ spring of love toward our neighbor." (505). Lord, show me more of Your love. May it be my contemplation more and more, throughout the day. And You deserve my love. May it be manifested in my spirit towards my neighbor:

_____

_____

_____

Prayer journal: _____

_____

_____

_____

_____

_____

_____

as ourselves. And when the children of God manifest mercy, kindness, and love toward all men, they also are witnessing to the character of the statutes of heaven. They are bearing testimony to the fact that "the law of the Lord is perfect, converting the soul." Ps. 19:7. And whoever fails to manifest this love is breaking the law which he professes to revere. For the spirit we manifest toward our brethren declares what is our spirit toward God. The love of God in the heart is the only spring of love toward our neighbor. "If a man say, I love God, and hateth his brother, he is a liar: for he that loveth not his brother whom he hath seen, how can he love God whom he hath not seen?" Beloved, "if we love one another, God dwelleth in us, and His love is perfected in us." 1 John 4:20, 12.

Chapter 55

Not With Outward Show

[This chapter is based on Luke 17:20-22.]

Some of the Pharisees had come to Jesus demanding "when the kingdom of God should come." More than three years had passed since John the Baptist gave the message that like a trumpet call had sounded through the land, "The kingdom of heaven is at hand." Matt. 3:2. And as yet these Pharisees saw no indication of the establishment of the kingdom. Many of those who rejected John, and at every step had opposed Jesus, were insinuating that His mission had failed.

Jesus answered, "The kingdom of God cometh not with outward show; [margin]: neither shall they say, Lo here! or, lo there! for, behold, the kingdom of God is within you." The kingdom of God begins in the heart. Look not here or there for manifestations of earthly power to mark its coming.

"The days will come," He said, turning to His disciples, "when ye shall desire to see one of the days of the Son of man, and ye shall not see it." Because it is not attended by worldly pomp, you are in danger of failing to discern the glory of My mission. You do not realize how great is your present privilege in having among you, though veiled in humanity, Him who is the life and the light of men. The days will come when you will look back with longing upon the opportunities you now enjoy to walk and talk with the Son of God.

Because of their selfishness and earthliness, even the disciples of Jesus [506-507] could not comprehend the spiritual glory which He sought to reveal unto them. It was not until after Christ's ascension to His Father, and the outpouring of the Holy Spirit upon the believers, that the disciples fully appreciated the Saviour's character and mission. After they had received the baptism of the Spirit, they began to realize that they had been

1. "The kingdom of God cometh not with o_____ show: neither shall they say, Lo here! or, lo there! for, behold, the kingdom of God is w_____ you. The kingdom of God begins in the h_____." Lord, I invite You to the throne of my heart. May You reign supreme. You are the most important entity in my life. How can I nurture Your Kingdom's values to find resonance in my heart? _____

_____

_____

_____

2. "Because it is not attended by worldly pomp, you are in danger of failing to d_____ the glory of My mission...The days will come when you will look back with longing upon the opportunities you now enjoy to w_____ and talk with the Son of God." What is the difference between glory and worldly pomp?

_____

_____

Lord, I do long to walk and talk with You! May I notice in Your kingdom, Your mission, a richness, a deep thrill of oneness with You. How may I take full advantage of the opportunities to walk and talk?

_____

_____

_____

3. "It was not until after Christ's ascension to His Father, and the o_____ _____ of the Holy Spirit upon the believers, that the disciples f_____ appreciated the Savior's c___ _____ and mission." (507). Lord, may I sense my need of the Spirit, to help me know You more fully. Remind me to pray for the help of the Spirit and to be available to It: _____

_____

_____

4. "'I have yet many things to say unto you, but ye cannot bear them now.' How eager they were to know it all! They grieved that their f_____ had been so feeble, that their ideas had been so wide of the mark, that they had so failed of c_____ the reality... How dull were our

in the very presence of the Lord of glory. As the sayings of Christ were brought to their remembrance, their minds were opened to comprehend the prophecies, and to understand the miracles which He had wrought. The wonders of His life passed before them, and they were as men awakened from a dream. They realized that "the Word was made flesh, and dwelt among us, (and we beheld His glory, the glory as of the Only-begotten of the Father,) full of grace and truth." John 1:14. Christ had actually come from God to a sinful world to save the fallen sons and daughters of Adam. The disciples now seemed, to themselves, of much less importance than before they realized this. They never wearied of rehearsing His words and works. His lessons, which they had but dimly understood, now came to them as a fresh revelation. The Scriptures became to them a new book.

As the disciples searched the prophecies that testified of Christ, they were brought into fellowship with the Deity, and learned of Him who had ascended to heaven to complete the work He had begun on earth. They recognized the fact that in Him dwelt knowledge which no human being, unaided by divine agency, could comprehend. They needed the help of Him whom kings, prophets, and righteous men had foretold. With amazement they read and reread the prophetic delineations of His character and work. How dimly had they comprehended the prophetic scriptures! how slow they had been in taking in the great truths which testified of Christ! Looking upon Him in His humiliation, as He walked a man among men, they had not understood the mystery of His incarnation, the dual character of His nature. Their eyes were holden, so that they did not fully recognize divinity in humanity. But after they were illuminated by the Holy Spirit, how they longed to see Him again, and to place themselves at His feet! How they wished that they might come to Him, and have Him explain the scriptures which they could not comprehend! How attentively would they listen to His words! What had Christ meant when He said, "I have yet many things to say unto you, but ye cannot bear them now"? John 16:12. How eager they were to know it all! They grieved that their faith had been so [507-508] feeble, that their ideas had been so wide of the mark, that they had so failed of comprehending the reality.

A herald had been sent from God to proclaim the coming of Christ, and to call the attention of the Jewish nation and of the world to His mission, that men might prepare for His reception. The wonderful personage whom John had announced had been among them for more than thirty years, and they had not really known Him as the One sent from God. Remorse took hold of the disciples because they had allowed the prevailing unbelief to leaven their opinions and becloud their understanding. The Light of this dark world had been shining amid its gloom, and they had failed to comprehend whence were its beams. They asked themselves why they had pursued a course that made it necessary for Christ to reprove them. They often repeated His conversations, and said, Why did we allow earthly considerations and the opposition of priests and rabbis to confuse our senses, so that we did not comprehend that a greater than Moses was among us, that One wiser than Solomon was instructing us? How dull were our ears! how feeble was our understanding!

Thomas would not believe until he had thrust his finger into the wound made by the Roman soldiers. Peter had denied Him in His humiliation and rejection. These painful remembrances came before them in distinct lines. They had been with Him, but they had not known or appreciated Him. But how these things now stirred their hearts as they recognized their unbelief!

As priests and rulers combined against them, and they were brought before councils and thrust into prison, the followers of Christ rejoiced "that they were counted worthy to suffer shame for His name." Acts 5:41. They rejoiced to prove, before men and angels, that they recognized the glory of Christ, and chose to follow Him at the loss of all things.

It is as true now as in apostolic days, that without the illumination of the divine Spirit, humanity cannot discern the glory of Christ. The truth and the work of God are unappreciated by a world-loving and compromising Christianity. Not in the ways of ease, of earthly honor or worldly conformity, are the followers of the Master found. They are far in advance, in the paths of toil, and humiliation, and reproach, in the front of the battle "against the principalities, against the powers, against the world rulers of this darkness, against the spiritual hosts of wickedness in the heavenly places." Eph. 6:12, R. V. And now, as in [508-509] Christ's day, they are misunderstood and reproached and oppressed by the priests and Pharisees of their time.

ears! How feeble was our understanding! (507, 508). Lord, I don't want to have the regrets, what might have been if I had listened more intently. Help me to, like Samuel, daily say, Speak Lord, for Thy servant heareth: _____

_____

_____

5. The disciples "had been w_____ Him, but they had not k_____ or a_____ Him. But how these things n_____ ____ stirred their hearts as they recognized their unbelief." Like being with my spouse, and not appreciating him/her, am I with You, Lord, and yet not appreciating You? _____

_____

_____

6. "It is as true n_____ as in apostolic days, that without the illumination of the divine Spirit, humanity c_____ discern the g_____ of Christ." So

to more fully comprehend Christ's glory, I should place myself in the atmosphere where God's Spirit can illumine me. Where might that atmosphere be? What are some sites that are more likely and less likely to invite the Spirit's presence? _____ _____ _____ _____

7. "The gospel of the grace of God, with its spirit of self-abnegation, can n_____ be in harmony with the spirit of the w_____. The two principles are a_____." (509). Lord, show me how I have compromised Your grace, Your spirit of self-abnegation, with the spirit of the world: _____ _____ _____ _____ _____

8. "Not by the decision of c_____ or councils or legislative assemblies, not by the patronage of worldly great men, is the kingdom of Christ established, but by the i___ _____ of Christ's n_____ in humanity through the work of the Holy Spirit." Lord,

The kingdom of God comes not with outward show. The gospel of the grace of God, with its spirit of self-abnegation, can never be in harmony with the spirit of the world. The two principles are antagonistic. "The natural man receiveth not the things of the Spirit of God: for they are foolishness unto him: neither can he know them, because they are spiritually discerned." 1 Cor. 2:14.

But today in the religious world there are multitudes who, as they believe, are working for the establishment of the kingdom of Christ as an earthly and temporal dominion. They desire to make our Lord the ruler of the kingdoms of this world, the ruler in its courts and camps, its legislative halls, its palaces and market places. They expect Him to rule through legal enactments, enforced by human authority. Since Christ is not now here in person, they themselves will undertake to act in His stead, to execute the laws of His kingdom. The establishment of such a kingdom is what the Jews desired in the days of Christ. They would have received Jesus, had He been willing to establish a temporal dominion, to enforce what they regarded as the laws of God, and to make them the expositors of His will and the agents of His authority. But He said, "My kingdom is not of this world." John 18:36. He would not accept the earthly throne.

The government under which Jesus lived was corrupt and oppressive; on every hand were crying abuses,--extortion, intolerance, and grinding cruelty. Yet the Saviour attempted no civil reforms. He attacked no national abuses, nor condemned the national enemies. He did not interfere with the authority or administration of those in power. He who was our example kept aloof from earthly governments. Not because He was indifferent to the woes of men, but because the remedy did not lie in merely human and external measures. To be efficient, the cure must reach men individually, and must regenerate the heart.

Not by the decisions of courts or councils or legislative assemblies, not by the patronage of worldly great men, is the kingdom of Christ established, but by the implanting of Christ's nature in humanity through the work of the Holy Spirit. "As many as received Him, to them gave He power to become the sons of God, even to them that believe on His name: which were born, not of blood, nor of the will of the flesh, nor of the will of man, but of God." John 1:12, 13. Here is the only power that [509-510] can work the uplifting of mankind. And the human agency for the accomplishment of this work is the teaching and practicing of the word of God.

When the apostle Paul began his ministry in Corinth, that populous, wealthy, and wicked city, polluted by the nameless vices of heathenism, he said, "I determined not to know anything among you, save Jesus Christ, and Him crucified." 1 Cor. 2:2. Writing afterward to some of those who had been corrupted by the foulest sins, he could say, "But ye are washed, but ye are sanctified, but ye are justified in the name of the Lord Jesus, and by the Spirit of our God." "I thank my God always on your behalf, for the grace of God which is given you by Jesus Christ." 1 Cor. 6:11; 1:4.

Now, as in Christ's day, the work of God's kingdom lies not with those who are clamoring for recognition and support by earthly rulers and human laws, but with those who are declaring to the people in His name those spiritual truths that will work in the receivers the experience of Paul: "I am crucified with Christ: nevertheless I live; yet not I, but Christ liveth in me." Gal. 2:20. Then they will labor as did Paul for the benefit of men. He said, "Now then we are ambassadors for Christ, as though God did beseech you by us: we pray you in Christ's stead, be ye reconciled to God." 2 Cor. 5:20.

help my church board to understand the role of the Holy Spirit in establishing Your kingdom. Sometimes we take actions that seem to try and legislate morality. Help me, Lord, in my home, in the rules that we set up, to make room for the role of the Holy Spirit in implementing Your nature. In my heart, Lord, help me not to rely on behavioral rules, but on Your Spirit, to implement Your nature: __

_____

9. "The human agency for the accomplishment of this work [of uplifting mankind], is the t_____ and p_____ of the word of God." (510). Lord, I can't generate Your nature in my life. I rely on You, for that. My part, is to make myself available to Your Spirit, and placing myself where the atmosphere of the Spirit is likely to be. That includes the teaching and preaching of the word of God. Help me avail myself of all those opportunities: ____

_____
_____

Prayer journal: _____
_____
_____
_____
_____

Chapter 56

Blessing the Children

[This chapter is based on Matt. 19:13-15;
Mark 10:13-16; Luke 18:15-17.]

Jesus was ever a lover of children. He accepted their childish sympathy and their open, unaffected love. The grateful praise from their pure lips was music in His ears, and refreshed His spirit when oppressed by contact with crafty and hypocritical men. Wherever the Saviour went, the benignity of His countenance, and His gentle, kindly manner won the love and confidence of children.

Among the Jews it was customary for children to be brought to some rabbi, that he might lay his hands upon them in blessing; but the Saviour's disciples thought His work too important to be interrupted in this way. When the mothers came to Him with their little ones, the disciples looked on them with disfavor. They thought these children too young to be benefited by a visit to Jesus, and concluded that He would be displeased at their presence. But it was the disciples with whom He was displeased. The Saviour understood the care and burden of the mothers who were seeking to train their children according to the word of God. He had heard their prayers. He Himself had drawn them into His presence.

One mother with her child had left her home to find Jesus. On the way she told a neighbor her errand, and the neighbor wanted to have Jesus bless her children. Thus several mothers came together, with their little ones. Some of the children had passed beyond the years of [511-512] infancy to childhood and youth. When the mothers made known their desire, Jesus heard with sympathy the timid, tearful request. But He waited to see how the disciples would treat them. When He saw them send the mothers away, thinking to do Him a favor, He showed them their error, saying, "Suffer the little children to come unto Me, and forbid them not: for of such is the kingdom of God." He took the children in His arms, He laid His hands upon them, and gave them the blessing for which they came.

1. "Wherever the Savior went, the benignity of His countenance, and His g_____, kindly manner won the love and c_____ of children." Lord, may my walk with You increase my awareness and value of Your gentleness. Win my love and confidence, Lord. Thank You for being so warm and caring to me. But why is it, Lord, that as adults, we tend to be more skeptical? _____

_____

_____

_____

2. "The disciples thought His work too i_____ _____ to be interrupted" to lay His hands upon children in b_____. "They thought these children too y_____ to be benefited by a visit to Jesus." Do I communicate the same attitude to my children, Lord? or the children at church? _____

_____

_____ Too young to benefit? They are the most responsive! _____

The mothers were comforted. They returned to their homes strengthened and blessed by the words of Christ. They were encouraged to take up their burden with new cheerfulness, and to work hopefully for their children. The mothers of today are to receive His words with the same faith. Christ is as verily a personal Saviour today as when He lived a man among men. He is as verily the helper of mothers today as when He gathered the little ones to His arms in Judea. The children of our hearths are as much the purchase of His blood as were the children of long ago.

Jesus knows the burden of every mother's heart. He who had a mother that struggled with poverty and privation sympathizes with every mother in her labors. He who made a long journey in order to relieve the anxious heart of a Canaanite woman will do as much for the mothers of today. He who gave back to the widow of Nain her only son, and who in His agony upon the cross remembered His own mother, is touched today by the mother's sorrow. In every grief and every need He will give comfort and help.

Let mothers come to Jesus with their perplexities. They will find grace sufficient to aid them in the management of their children. The gates are open for every mother who would lay her burdens at the Saviour's feet. He who said, "Suffer the little children to come unto Me, and forbid them not," still invites the mothers to lead up their little ones to be blessed by Him. Even the babe in its mother's arms may dwell as under the shadow of the Almighty through the faith of the praying mother. John the Baptist was filled with the Holy Spirit from his birth. If we will live in communion with God, we too may expect the divine Spirit to mold our little ones, even from their earliest moments.

In the children who were brought in contact with Him, Jesus saw the men and women who should be heirs of His grace and subjects of His kingdom, and some of whom would become martyrs for His sake. [512-515] He knew that these children would listen to Him and accept Him as their Redeemer far more readily than would grown-up people, many of whom were the worldly-wise and hardhearted. In His teaching He came down to their level. He, the Majesty of heaven, did not disdain to answer their questions, and simplify His important lessons to meet their childish understanding. He planted in their minds the seeds of truth, which in after

3. The disciples thought Jesus would be d_____ _____ at the children's presence. (511). Thinking to do Him a f_____, they sent the mothers and children away. (512). What are the occasions where I think I am helping You, Lord, only through misunderstanding Your character, I hurt You and others? Like Saul was before He became Paul?

_____
_____
_____

4. "Let mothers come to Jesus with their p____ _____. They will find g_____ sufficient to aid them in the management of their children... John the Baptist was filled with the Holy Spirit from his b_____. If we will live in c_____ with God, we too may expect the divine Spirit to mold our little ones, even from their e_____ moments." (512). Thank You Lord, for Your interest and help in our young ones. And it continues throughout our life. I do want to live in communion with You, throughout the day: _____
_____

5. "He knew that these children would l_____ to Him and accept Him as their Redeemer far more r_____ than would

grown-up people, many of whom were the worldly-wise and hardhearted...It is still true that children are the most s_____ to the teachings of the gospel; their hearts are o____ ____ to divine influences, and strong to r_____ ___ the lessons received... They need to be educated in spiritual things, and parents should give them every a_____, that they may form characters after the s_____ of the character of C_____." (515). Lord, help me to be like a child, again. To listen, to be susceptible, to be open to Your Spirit: _____ _____ _____

6. "The little ones who trust and obey their m___ _____ are learning to trust and obey the S_____ __." What a responsibility for mothers and fathers. Lord, what are the behaviors and tones of voice of mine, that don't represent You? _____ _____ _____

years would spring up, and bear fruit unto eternal life.

It is still true that children are the most susceptible to the teachings of the gospel; their hearts are open to divine influences, and strong to retain the lessons received. The little children may be Christians, having an experience in accordance with their years. They need to be educated in spiritual things, and parents should give them every advantage, that they may form characters after the similitude of the character of Christ.

Fathers and mothers should look upon their children as younger members of the Lord's family, committed to them to educate for heaven. The lessons that we ourselves learn from Christ we should give to our children, as the young minds can receive them, little by little opening to them the beauty of the principles of heaven. Thus the Christian home becomes a school, where the parents serve as underteachers, while Christ Himself is the chief instructor.

In working for the conversion of our children, we should not look for violent emotion as the essential evidence of conviction of sin. Nor is it necessary to know the exact time when they are converted. We should teach them to bring their sins to Jesus, asking His forgiveness, and believing that He pardons and receives them as He received the children when He was personally on earth.

As the mother teaches her children to obey her because they love her, she is teaching them the first lessons in the Christian life. The mother's love represents to the child the love of Christ, and the little ones who trust and obey their mother are learning to trust and obey the Saviour.

Jesus was the pattern for children, and He was also the father's example. He spoke as one having authority, and His word was with power; yet in all His intercourse with rude and violent men He did not use one unkind or discourteous expression. The grace of Christ in the heart will impart a heaven-born dignity and sense of propriety. It will soften whatever is harsh, and subdue all that is coarse and unkind. It will lead fathers and mothers to treat their children as intelligent beings, as they themselves would like to be treated. [515-516]

Parents, in the training of your children, study the lessons that God has given in nature. If you would train a pink, or rose, or lily, how would you do it? Ask the gardener by what process he makes every branch and leaf to flourish so beautifully, and to develop in symmetry and loveliness. He will tell you that it was by no rude touch, no violent effort; for this would only break the delicate stems. It was by little attentions, often repeated. He moistened the soil, and protected the growing plants from the fierce blasts and from the scorching sun, and God caused them to flourish and to blossom into loveliness. In dealing with your children, follow the method of the gardener. By gentle touches, by loving ministrations, seek to fashion their characters after the pattern of the character of Christ.

Encourage the expression of love toward God and toward one another. The reason why there are so many hardhearted men and women in the world is that true affection has been regarded as weakness, and has been discouraged and repressed. The better nature of these persons was stifled in childhood; and unless the light of divine love shall melt away their cold selfishness, their happiness will be forever ruined. If we wish our children to possess the tender spirit of Jesus, and the sympathy that angels manifest for us, we must encourage the generous, loving impulses of childhood.

Teach the children to see Christ in nature. Take them out into the open air, under the noble trees, into the garden; and in all the wonderful works of creation teach them to see an expression of His love. Teach them that He made the laws which govern all living things, that He has made laws for us, and that these laws are for our happiness and joy. Do [516-517] not weary them with long prayers and tedious exhortations, but through nature's object lessons teach them obedience to the law of God.

As you win their confidence in you as followers of Christ, it will be easy to teach them of the great love wherewith He has loved us. As you try to make plain the truths of salvation, and point the children to Christ as a personal Saviour, angels will be by your side. The Lord will give to fathers and mothers grace to interest their little ones in the precious story of the Babe of Bethlehem, who is indeed the hope of the world.

When Jesus told the disciples not to forbid the children to come to Him, He was speaking to His followers in all ages,--to officers of the church, to ministers, helpers, and all Christians. Jesus is drawing the children, and He bids us, Suffer them to come; as if He would say, They will come if you do not hinder them.

7. "In dealing with your children, follow the method of the g_____.
[It was by little a_____ _____ often repeated.] By gentle t_____, by loving ministrations, seek to fashion their characters after the pattern of the character of C_____."
(516). Lord, help to be like the gardener, little attentions and touches, often repeated, and may characters be fashioned after Yours. "The reason why there are so many h_____ men and women in the world is that true affection has been regarded as weakness, and has been discouraged and r_____."

8. "If we wish our children to possess the t_____ spirit of Jesus, and the sympathy that angels manifest for us, we must encourage the g_____, loving impulses of childhood." And keep doing so on into adulthood. I mean, I want Your tender spirit. What can I do today, to encourage generous loving impulses? _____
_____
_____

9. "The Lord will give to fathers and mothers grace to i_____ their little ones in the precious story of the Babe of Bethlehem, who is indeed the h____ of the world." (517). What

a promise, Lord! In today's fast-paced, television generation, it is hard to interest them in spiritual matters. Thank You for Your help, the extra grace to interest my young ones in You. What do I do, Lord, that makes it all seem boring or irrelevant to them?_____

_____

_____

_____

10. "The Savior regards with i_____ tenderness the souls whom He has purchased with His own blood. He looks upon them with unutterable l_____
___." Thank You Lord, for Your tenderness and passion for me. May I be secure and confident in Your love. Please be encouraged, that I long to be close to You. How can I demonstrate my love for You?

_____

_____

_____

Prayer journal:_____

_____

_____

_____

_____

_____

_____

_____

Let not your un-Christlike character misrepresent Jesus. Do not keep the little ones away from Him by your coldness and harshness. Never give them cause to feel that heaven will not be a pleasant place to them if you are there. Do not speak of religion as something that children cannot understand, or act as if they were not expected to accept Christ in their childhood. Do not give them the false impression that the religion of Christ is a religion of gloom, and that in coming to the Saviour they must give up all that makes life joyful.

As the Holy Spirit moves upon the hearts of the children, co-operate with His work. Teach them that the Saviour is calling them, that nothing can give Him greater joy than for them to give themselves to Him in the bloom and freshness of their years.

The Saviour regards with infinite tenderness the souls whom He has purchased with His own blood. They are the claim of His love. He looks upon them with unutterable longing. His heart is drawn out, not only to the best-behaved children, but to those who have by inheritance objectionable traits of character. Many parents do not understand how much they are responsible for these traits in their children. They have not the tenderness and wisdom to deal with the erring ones whom they have made what they are. But Jesus looks upon these children with pity. He traces from cause to effect.

The Christian worker may be Christ's agent in drawing these children to the Saviour. By wisdom and tact he may bind them to his heart, he may give them courage and hope, and through the grace of Christ may see them transformed in character, so that of them it may be said, "Of such is the kingdom of God."

Chapter 57

"One Thing Thou Lackest"

[This chapter is based on Matt. 19:16-22;
Mark 10:17-22; Luke 18:18-23.]

And when He was gone forth into the way, there came one running, and kneeled to Him, and asked Him, Good Master, what shall I do that I may inherit eternal life?"

The young man who asked this question was a ruler. He had great possessions, and occupied a position of responsibility. He saw the love that Christ manifested toward the children brought to Him; he saw how tenderly He received them, and took them up in His arms, and his heart kindled with love for the Saviour. He felt a desire to be His disciple. He was so deeply moved that as Christ was going on His way, he ran after Him, and kneeling at His feet, asked with sincerity and earnestness the question so important to his soul and to the soul of every human being, "Good Master, what shall I do that I may inherit eternal life?"

"Why callest thou Me good?" said Christ, "there is none good but One, that is, God." Jesus desired to test the ruler's sincerity, and to draw from him the way in which he regarded Him as good. Did he realize that the One to whom he was speaking was the Son of God? What was the true sentiment of his heart?

This ruler had a high estimate of his own righteousness. He did not really suppose that he was defective in anything, yet he was not altogether satisfied. He felt the want of something that he did not possess. Could not Jesus bless him as He blessed the little children, and satisfy his soul want?

In reply to this question Jesus told him that obedience to the commandments of God was necessary if he would obtain eternal life; and He quoted several of the commandments which show man's duty to his [518-519] fellow men. The ruler's answer was positive: "All these things have I kept from my youth up: what lack I yet?"

Christ looked into the face of the young man, as if reading his life and searching his character. He loved

1. The young man who had great possessions and responsibility, saw the l_____ that Christ manifested...and was so deeply m_____ that...he ran after Him." I too, can be deeply inspired by beholding and contemplating Your love. Where can I behold it? _____

_____ Have I taken time to allow that special drawing experience to happen?

_____

2. "This ruler had a high estimate of his own r_____...Yet he was not altogether s_____." Why is it that I will never be satisfied by focusing on my own righteousness?

_____

(compared to Christ's, mine is f_____ rags).

3. "Christ looked into the face of the young man, as if reading his life and s_____ his character. He loved him, and

He h_____ to give him that peace and grace and joy." (519). When I let God search my heart, should I be nervous about His attitude towards me? What will He see? _____

_____

_____ How does peace, grace, and joy "m_____ change my character?" ___

_____

_____

_____

(Not a new label, or folder name change, but deleting files of self-centeredness, etc).

4. Jesus "longed to see… [a] heart, conscious of the supreme l_____ to be given to God, and hiding its lack in the p_ _____ of Christ."

5. "If the ruler had then given himself to Christ, he would have g_____ in the a_____ of His presence." How can I grow, Lord? _____

_____

_____

_____ (Placing my self and my heart where the atmosphere of Your presence is, and _____

_____

_____) What does 'giving myself to You' mean? _____

_____

_____ (Abandoning

him, and He hungered to give him that peace and grace and joy which would materially change his character. "One thing thou lackest," He said; "go thy way, sell whatsoever thou hast, and give to the poor, and thou shalt have treasure in heaven: and come, take up the cross, and follow Me."

Christ was drawn to this young man. He knew him to be sincere in his assertion, "All these things have I kept from my youth." The Redeemer longed to create in him that discernment which would enable him to see the necessity of heart devotion and Christian goodness. He longed to see in him a humble and contrite heart, conscious of the supreme love to be given to God, and hiding its lack in the perfection of Christ.

Jesus saw in this ruler just the help He needed if the young man would become a colaborer with Him in the work of salvation. If he would place himself under Christ's guidance, he would be a power for good. In a marked degree the ruler could have represented Christ; for he possessed qualifications, which, if he were united with the Saviour, would enable him to become a divine force among men. Christ, seeing into his character, loved him. Love for Christ was awakening in the ruler's heart; for love begets love. Jesus longed to see him a co-worker with Him. He longed to make him like Himself, a mirror in which the likeness of God would be reflected. He longed to develop the excellence of his character, and sanctify it to the Master's use. If the ruler had then given himself to Christ, he would have grown in the atmosphere of His presence. If he had made this choice, how different would have been his future!

myself, abandoning my
all, trusting in only You).

"One thing thou lackest," Jesus said. "If thou wilt be perfect, go and sell that thou hast, and give to the poor, and thou shalt have treasure in heaven: and come and follow Me." Christ read the ruler's heart. Only one thing he lacked, but that was a vital principle. He needed the love of God in the soul. This lack, unless supplied, would prove fatal to him; his whole nature would become corrupted. By indulgence, selfishness would strengthen. That he might receive the love of God, his supreme love of self must be surrendered.

6. "One thing thou lackest...if thou wilt be p____ _____... Only one thing he lacked, but that was a v_____ principle. He needed the l_____ of God in his soul." Lord, to be perfect is to have Your love in my soul? __ _____. I want to love You completely and thoroughly. But I don't always. Can I hide my lack of supreme love for You, in Your perfection? (see item #4): _____

7. "By indulgence, selfishness would s_____ _____." (519). Denial of selfishness then, Lord, instead of being penance or works, should help me 'weaken' selfishness, and further my awareness of Your love. Please give me the grace to deny self. Where in my life and heart can I attempt that?

Christ gave this man a test. He called upon him to choose between the heavenly treasure and worldly greatness. The heavenly treasure was assured him if he would follow Christ. But self must yield; his will must be given into Christ's control. The very holiness of God was [519-520] offered to the young ruler. He had the privilege of becoming a son of God, and a coheir with Christ to the heavenly treasure. But he must take up the cross, and follow the Saviour in the path of self-denial.

Christ's words were verily to the ruler the invitation, "Choose you this day whom ye will serve." Joshua 24:15. The choice was left with him. Jesus was yearning for his conversion. He had shown him the plague spot in his character, and with what deep interest He watched the issue as the young man weighed the question! If he decided to follow Christ, he must obey His words in everything. He must turn from his ambitious projects.

8. "The very h_____ ____ of God was offered to the young ruler. He had the privilege of becoming a s_____ of God, and a c_____ with Christ to the heavenly treasure." (519, 520). What a treasure, Lord! Have I

walked away from You, not even sad, because I haven't seen the value of what You are offering?

---

9. "With what earnest, anxious l_____, what soul hunger, did the Savior look at the young man, hoping that he would yield to the i_____ of the Spirit of God." (520). Lord, I make spiritual decisions, face temptations, so casually; so flippantly; and there You are: earnest, longing, anxious for me. Thank You for being on my side. May I be bolstered by that picture of You cheering me on. _____

---

10. "His exalted position and his p_____ were exerting a subtle influence for evil upon his character. If c_____, they would supplant God in his a_____." Lord, do equity, bank accounts, vehicles, household goods, have my affections? Do I trust them for security? Search my heart, Lord, and show me what to do: _____

With what earnest, anxious longing, what soul hunger, did the Saviour look at the young man, hoping that he would yield to the invitation of the Spirit of God!

Christ made the only terms which could place the ruler where he would perfect a Christian character. His words were words of wisdom, though they appeared severe and exacting. In accepting and obeying them was the ruler's only hope of salvation. His exalted position and his possessions were exerting a subtle influence for evil upon his character. If cherished, they would supplant God in his affections. To keep back little or much from God was to retain that which would lessen his moral strength and efficiency; for if the things of this world are cherished, however uncertain and unworthy they may be, they will become all-absorbing.

The ruler was quick to discern all that Christ's words involved, and he became sad. If he had realized the value of the offered gift, quickly would he have enrolled himself as one of Christ's followers. He was a member of the honored council of the Jews, and Satan was tempting him with flattering prospects of the future. He wanted the heavenly treasure, but he wanted also the temporal advantages his riches would bring him. He was sorry that such conditions existed; he desired eternal life, but he was not willing to make the sacrifice. The cost of eternal life seemed too great, and he went away sorrowful; "for he had great possessions."

His claim that he had kept the law of God was a deception. He showed that riches were his idol. He could not keep the commandments of God while the world was first in his affections. He loved the gifts of God more than he loved the Giver. Christ had offered the young man fellowship with Himself. "Follow Me," He said. But the Saviour was not so much to him as his own name among men or his possessions. To give up his earthly treasure, that was seen, for the heavenly treasure, that was unseen, was too great a risk. He refused the offer of eternal life, and went away, and ever after the world was to receive his worship. [520-523] Thousands are passing through this ordeal, weighing Christ against the world; and many choose the world. Like the young ruler, they turn from the Saviour, saying in their hearts, I will not have this Man as my leader.

Christ's dealing with the young man is presented

as an object lesson. God has given us the rule of conduct which every one of His servants must follow. It is
obedience to His law, not merely a legal obedience, but
an obedience which enters into the life, and is exemplified in the character. God has set His own standard
of character for all who would become subjects of His
kingdom. Only those who will become co-workers with
Christ, only those who will say, Lord, all I have and
all I am is Thine, will be acknowledged as sons and
daughters of God. All should consider what it means to
desire heaven, and yet to turn away because of the conditions laid down. Think of what it means to say "No"
to Christ. The ruler said, No, I cannot give You all. Do
we say the same? The Saviour offers to share with us
the work God has given us to do. He offers to use the
means God has given us, to carry forward His work in
the world. Only in this way can He save us.

The ruler's possessions were entrusted to him that
he might prove himself a faithful steward; he was to
dispense these goods for the blessing of those in need.
So God now entrusts men with means, with talents and
opportunities, that they may be His agents in helping the
poor and the suffering. He who uses his entrusted gifts
as God designs becomes a co-worker with the Saviour.
He wins souls to Christ, because he is a representative
of His character.

To those who, like the young ruler, are in high positions of trust and have great possessions, it may seem
too great a sacrifice to give up all in order to follow
Christ. But this is the rule of conduct for all who would
become His disciples. Nothing short of obedience can
be accepted. Self-surrender is the substance of the
teachings of Christ. Often it is presented and enjoined
in language that seems authoritative, because there is
no other way to save man than to cut away those things
which, if entertained, will demoralize the whole being.

When Christ's followers give back to the Lord His
own, they are accumulating treasure which will be giv-
en to them when they shall hear the words, "Well done,
good and faithful servant; . . . enter thou into the joy of
thy Lord." "Who for the joy that was set before Him endured the cross, despising the shame, and is set down at
the right hand of the throne of God." Matt. 25:23; Heb.
12:2. The joy of seeing souls redeemed, souls eternally
saved, is the reward of all that put their feet in the footprints of Him who said, "Follow Me."

11. God entrusts me, as a steward, with means, with talent, and with o_____ _____, which are to be used for blessing those in need. (523). Lord, I am to be a steward of even op-portunities? How often to I squander them, not even recognizing the opportu-nity, or recognizing You as one of the least? _____

_____
_____

12. "Self-surrender is the s_____ of the teaching of Christ." Should that be a doctrine, or fundamental belief? Lord, teach me again, and again, over and over. Self is so much a part of me, my lifestyle. I need major help, eye salve to see it: _____

_____
_____

Prayer journal: _____
_____
_____
_____
_____
_____
_____
_____

Chapter 58

"Lazarus, Come Forth"

[This chapter is based on Luke 10:38-42; John 11:1-44.]

1. Jesus "loves a_____ the human family, but to some He is bound by peculiarly t_____ associations." What kind of relationship do I have had with You, Lord? Do You want to come to my house? _____

_____

Is there a comfort level for us both? _____

_____

2. Here Jesus "found a s_____ welcome, and pure, h_____ friendship. Here He could speak with simplicity and perfect freedom, knowing that His words would be u_____ and treasured." Lord, I know how frustrating it is to have everything I say be scrutinized and picked apart; and the relief to be among friends who accept me and my miss statements. I so appreciate Your friendship, being able to verbalize my ups and downs. How can I reciprocate that friendship to You? _____

_____

_____

What is a 'holy' friendship? _____

_____

Among the most steadfast of Christ's disciples was Lazarus of Bethany. From their first meeting his faith in Christ had been strong; his love for Him was deep, and he was greatly beloved by the Saviour. It was for Lazarus that the greatest of Christ's miracles was performed. The Saviour blessed all who sought His help; He loves all the human family, but to some He is bound by peculiarly tender associations. His heart was knit by a strong bond of affection to the family at Bethany, and for one of them His most wonderful work was wrought.

At the home of Lazarus, Jesus had often found rest. The Saviour had no home of His own; He was dependent on the hospitality of His friends and disciples, and often, when weary, thirsting for human fellowship, He had been glad to escape to this peaceful household, away from the suspicion and jealousy of the angry Pharisees. Here He found a sincere welcome, and pure, holy friendship. Here He could speak with simplicity and perfect freedom, knowing that His words would be understood and treasured.

Our Saviour appreciated a quiet home and interested listeners. He longed for human tenderness, courtesy, and affection. Those who received the heavenly instruction He was always ready to impart were greatly blessed. As the multitudes followed Christ through the open [524-525] fields, He unfolded to them the beauties of the natural world. He sought to open the eyes of their understanding, that they might see how the hand of God upholds the world. In order to call out an appreciation of God's goodness and benevolence, He called the attention of His hearers to the gently falling dew, to the soft showers of rain and the bright sunshine, given alike to good and evil. He desired men to realize more fully the regard that God bestows on the human instrumentalities He has created. But the multitudes were slow of hearing, and in the home at Bethany Christ found rest from the weary conflict of public life. Here He opened to an appreciative audience the volume of Providence.

In these private interviews He unfolded to His hearers that which He did not attempt to tell to the mixed multitude. He needed not to speak to His friends in parables.

As Christ gave His wonderful lessons, Mary sat at His feet, a reverent and devoted listener. On one occasion, Martha, perplexed with the care of preparing the meal, went to Christ, saying, "Lord, dost Thou not care that my sister hath left me to serve alone? bid her therefore that she help me." This was the time of Christ's first visit to Bethany. The Saviour and His disciples had just made the toilsome journey on foot from Jericho. Martha was anxious to provide for their comfort, and in her anxiety she forgot the courtesy due to her Guest. Jesus answered her with mild and patient words, "Martha, Martha, thou art careful and troubled about many things: but one thing is needful: and Mary hath chosen that good part, which shall not be taken away from her." Mary was storing her mind with the precious words falling from the Saviour's lips, words that were more precious to her than earth's most costly jewels.

The "one thing" that Martha needed was a calm, devotional spirit, a deeper anxiety for knowledge concerning the future, immortal life, and the graces necessary for spiritual advancement. She needed less anxiety for the things which pass away, and more for those things which endure forever. Jesus would teach His children to seize every opportunity of gaining that knowledge which will make them wise unto salvation. The cause of Christ needs careful, energetic workers. There is a wide field for the Marthas, with their zeal in active religious work. But let them first sit with Mary at the feet of Jesus. Let diligence, promptness, and energy be sanctified by the grace of Christ; then the life will be an unconquerable power for good.

Sorrow entered the peaceful home where Jesus had rested. Lazarus was stricken with sudden illness, and his sisters sent to the Saviour, [525-526] saying, "Lord, behold, he whom Thou lovest is sick." They saw the violence of the disease that had seized their brother, but they knew that Christ had shown Himself able to heal all manner of diseases. They believed that He would sympathize with them in their distress; therefore they made no urgent demand for His immediate presence, but sent only the confiding message, "He whom Thou lovest is sick." They thought that He would immediately respond to their message, and be with them as soon

3. "The 'one thing' Martha needed was a calm, d_____ spirit, a deeper anxiety for knowledge concerning the future, immortal life, and the g_____ necessary for spiritual advancement." (525). What are those 'graces?' Something I have to attain? _____ _____ Or is it a gift of God, of His attitude of love towards me? _____ _____ _____

4. "S_____ every opportunity" to "first sit with Mary at the feet of J_____." What are those opportunities? _____ _____ _____ _____

Do I take those opportunities merely when they are convenient? What does it mean to 'seize?' _____ _____ _____ _____

as He could reach Bethany.

Anxiously they waited for a word from Jesus. As long as the spark of life was yet alive in their brother, they prayed and watched for Jesus to come. But the messenger returned without Him. Yet he brought the message, "This sickness is not unto death," and they clung to the hope that Lazarus would live. Tenderly they tried to speak words of hope and encouragement to the almost unconscious sufferer. When Lazarus died, they were bitterly disappointed; but they felt the sustaining grace of Christ, and this kept them from reflecting any blame on the Saviour.

When Christ heard the message, the disciples thought He received it coldly. He did not manifest the sorrow they expected Him to show. Looking up to them, He said, "This sickness is not unto death, but for the glory of God, that the Son of God might be glorified thereby." For two days He remained in the place where He was. This delay was a mystery to the disciples. What a comfort His presence would be to the afflicted household! they thought. His strong affection for the family at Bethany was well known to the disciples, and they were surprised that He did not respond to the sad message, "He whom Thou lovest is sick."

During the two days Christ seemed to have dismissed the message from His mind; for He did not speak of Lazarus. The disciples thought of John the Baptist, the forerunner of Jesus. They had wondered why Jesus, with the power to perform wonderful miracles, had permitted John to languish in prison, and to die a violent death. Possessing such power, why did not Christ save John's life? This question had often been asked by the Pharisees, who presented it as an unanswerable argument against Christ's claim to be the Son of God. The Saviour had warned His disciples of trials, losses, and persecution. Would He forsake them in trial? Some questioned if they had mistaken His mission. All were deeply troubled.

After waiting for two days, Jesus said to the disciples, "Let us go into Judea again." The disciples questioned why, if Jesus were going to Judea, He had waited two days. But anxiety for Christ and for themselves [526-527] was now uppermost in their minds. They could see nothing but danger in the course He was about to pursue. "Master," they said, "the Jews of late sought to stone Thee; and goest Thou thither again? Je-

5. Regarding the two day delay: "The Savior had warned His disciples of trials, losses, and persecution. Would He f_____ them in trial? Some questioned if they had mistaken His mission. All were deeply troubled." (526). How is my faith in You, Lord, when I question a delay, or don't understand Your answers to my prayers? _____
_____
_____
_____

How do You feel, Lord, when I wonder if You are for real? _____
_____
_____

sus answered, Are there not twelve hours in the day?" I am under the guidance of My Father; as long as I do His will, My life is safe. My twelve hours of day are not yet ended. I have entered upon the last remnant of My day; but while any of this remains, I am safe.

"If any man walk in the day," He continued, "he stumbleth not, because he seeth the light of this world." He who does the will of God, who walks in the path that God has marked out, cannot stumble and fall. The light of God's guiding Spirit gives him a clear perception of his duty, and leads him aright till the close of his work. "But if a man walk in the night, he stumbleth, because there is no light in him." He who walks in a path of his own choosing, where God has not called him, will stumble. For him day is turned into night, and wherever he may be, he is not secure.

"These things said He: and after that He saith unto them, Our friend Lazarus sleepeth; but I go that I may awake him out of sleep." "Our friend Lazarus sleepeth." How touching the words! how full of sympathy! In the thought of the peril their Master was about to incur by going to Jerusalem, the disciples had almost forgotten the bereaved family at Bethany. But not so Christ. The disciples felt rebuked. They had been disappointed because Christ did not respond more promptly to the message. They had been tempted to think that He had not the tender love for Lazarus and his sisters that they had thought He had, or He would have hastened back with the messenger. But the words, "Our friend Lazarus sleepeth," awakened right feelings in their minds. They were convinced that Christ had not forgotten His suffering friends.

"Then said His disciples, Lord, if he sleep, he shall do well. Howbeit Jesus spake of his death: but they thought that He had spoken of taking of rest in sleep." Christ represents death as a sleep to His believing children. Their life is hid with Christ in God, and until the last trump shall sound those who die will sleep in Him.

"Then said Jesus unto them plainly, Lazarus is dead. And I am glad for your sakes that I was not there, to the intent ye may believe; nevertheless let us go unto him." Thomas could see nothing but death in store for his Master if he went to Judea; but he girded up his spirit, and said to the other disciples, "Let us also go, that we may die with Him." He knew the hatred of the Jews toward Christ. It was their [527-528] purpose to

6. "Christ represents death as a s_____ to his believing children. Their life is h_____ with Christ in God, and until the last t_____ shall sound those who die will sleep i____ Him." (527). Lord, I don't benefit from communication with loved relatives who have died the sleep in You. I DO benefit from hope that the sleep in You is NOT final:

_____

_____

_____

compass His death, but this purpose had not succeeded, because some of His allotted time still remained. During this time Jesus had the guardianship of heavenly angels; and even in the regions of Judea, where the rabbis were plotting how they might take Him and put Him to death, no harm could come to Him.

The disciples marveled at Christ's words when He said, "Lazarus is dead. And I am glad . . . that I was not there." Did the Saviour by His own choice avoid the home of His suffering friends? Apparently Mary and Martha and the dying Lazarus were left alone. But they were not alone. Christ beheld the whole scene, and after the death of Lazarus the bereaved sisters were upheld by His grace. Jesus witnessed the sorrow of their rent hearts, as their brother wrestled with his strong foe, death. He felt every pang of anguish, as He said to His disciples, "Lazarus is dead." But Christ had not only the loved ones at Bethany to think of; He had the training of His disciples to consider. They were to be His representatives to the world, that the Father's blessing might embrace all. For their sake He permitted Lazarus to die. Had He restored him from illness to health, the miracle that is the most positive evidence of His divine character, would not have been performed.

Had Christ been in the sickroom, Lazarus would not have died; for Satan would have had no power over him. Death could not have aimed his dart at Lazarus in the presence of the Life-giver. Therefore Christ remained away. He suffered the enemy to exercise his power, that He might drive him back, a conquered foe. He permitted Lazarus to pass under the dominion of death; and the suffering sisters saw their brother laid in the grave. Christ knew that as they looked on the dead face of their brother their faith in their Redeemer would be severely tried. But He knew that because of the struggle through which they were now passing their faith would shine forth with far greater power. He suffered every pang of sorrow that they endured. He loved them no less because He tarried; but He knew that for them, for Lazarus, for Himself, and for His disciples, a victory was to be gained.

"For your sakes," "to the intent ye may believe." To all who are reaching out to feel the guiding hand of God, the moment of greatest discouragement is the time when divine help is nearest. They will look back with thankfulness upon the darkest part of their way.

7. "To all who are reaching out to feel the guiding hand of God, the moment of greatest d_____ _____ is the time when divine help is n_____. They will look back with thankfulness upon the d_____ part of their

"The Lord knoweth how to deliver the godly," 2 Peter 2:9. From every temptation and every trial He will bring them forth with firmer faith and a richer experience. [528-529]

In delaying to come to Lazarus, Christ had a purpose of mercy toward those who had not received Him. He tarried, that by raising Lazarus from the dead He might give to His stubborn, unbelieving people another evidence that He was indeed "the resurrection, and the life." He was loath to give up all hope of the people, the poor, wandering sheep of the house of Israel. His heart was breaking because of their impenitence. In His mercy He purposed to give them one more evidence that He was the Restorer, the One who alone could bring life and immortality to light. This was to be an evidence that the priests could not misinterpret. This was the reason of His delay in going to Bethany. This crowning miracle, the raising of Lazarus, was to set the seal of God on His work and on His claim to divinity.

On His journey to Bethany, Jesus, according to His custom, ministered to the sick and the needy. Upon reaching the town He sent a messenger to the sisters with the tidings of His arrival. Christ did not at once enter the house, but remained in a quiet place by the wayside. The great outward display observed by the Jews at the death of friends or relatives was not in harmony with the spirit of Christ. He heard the sound of wailing from the hired mourners, and He did not wish to meet the sisters in the scene of confusion. Among the mourning friends were relatives of the family, some of whom held high positions of responsibility in Jerusalem. Among these were some of Christ's bitterest enemies. Christ knew their purposes, and therefore He did not at once make Himself known.

The message was given to Martha so quietly that others in the room did not hear. Absorbed in her grief, Mary did not hear the words. Rising at once, Martha went out to meet her Lord, but thinking that she had gone to the place where Lazarus was buried, Mary sat still in her sorrow, making no outcry.

Martha hastened to meet Jesus, her heart agitated by conflicting emotions. In His expressive face she read the same tenderness and love that had always been there. Her confidence in Him was unbroken, but she thought of her dearly loved brother, whom Jesus also had loved. With grief surging in her heart because Christ had not

way." (528). I have to take that promise by faith, Lord. Because it sure doesn't feel that way. I suppose Your help is nearest, not that You adjust Your distance, but that I adjust my search and openness to You: _____
_____
_____
_____

Remind me of times of darkness, opportunities I had to appreciate Your nearness:
_____
_____
_____
_____

8. "This was the reason of His d_____, in going to Bethany. This crowning miracle, the raising of Lazarus, was to set the seal of God on His work and on His claim to d_____." (529). Could a delay for me, also be a significant message from You, Lord? _____
_____
_____
_____

452 Can We Walk, Together?

come before, yet with hope that even now He would do something to comfort them, she said, "Lord, if Thou hadst been here, my brother had not died." Over and over again, amid the tumult made by the mourners, the sisters had repeated these words.

With human and divine pity Jesus looked into her sorrowful, careworn [529-530] face. Martha had no inclination to recount the past; all was expressed by the pathetic words, "Lord, if Thou hadst been here, my brother had not died." But looking into that face of love, she added, "I know, that even now, whatsoever Thou wilt ask of God, God will give it Thee."

Jesus encouraged her faith, saying, "Thy brother shall rise again." His answer was not intended to inspire hope of an immediate change. He carried Martha's thoughts beyond the present restoration of her brother, and fixed them upon the resurrection of the just. This He did that she might see in the resurrection of Lazarus a pledge of the resurrection of all the righteous dead, and an assurance that it would be accomplished by the Saviour's power.

Martha answered, "I know that he shall rise again in the resurrection at the last day."

Still seeking to give a true direction to her faith, Jesus declared, "I am the resurrection, and the life." In Christ is life, original, unborrowed, underived. "He that hath the Son hath life." 1 John 5:12. The divinity of Christ is the believer's assurance of eternal life. "He that believeth in Me," said Jesus, "though he were dead, yet shall he live: and whosoever liveth and believeth in Me shall never die. Believest thou this?" Christ here looks forward to the time of His second coming. Then the righteous dead shall be raised incorruptible, and the living righteous shall be translated to heaven without seeing death. The miracle which Christ was about to perform, in raising Lazarus from the dead, would represent the resurrection of all the righteous dead. By His word and His works He declared Himself the Author of the resurrection. He who Himself was soon to die upon the cross stood with the keys of death, a conqueror of the grave, and asserted His right and power to give eternal life.

To the Saviour's words, "Believest thou?" Martha responded, "Yea, Lord: I believe that Thou art the Christ, the Son of God, which should come into the world." She did not comprehend in all their significance

9. "This He did that she might see in the resurrection of Lazarus a p_____ of the resurrection of all the righteous dead, and an a_____ _____ that it would be accomplished by the Savior's power...In Christ is life, original, unborrowed, underived...By His word and His works Jesus declared Himself the A_____ of the resurrection." (530). Thank You, Lord, for these blessed promises. I don't think I could cope with the loss of loved ones, without these wonderful words from You: _____ _____ _____

the words spoken by Christ, but she confessed her faith in His divinity, and her confidence that He was able to perform whatever it pleased Him to do.

"And when she had so said, she went her way, and called Mary her sister secretly, saying, The Master is come, and calleth for thee." She delivered her message as quietly as possible; for the priests and rulers were prepared to arrest Jesus when opportunity offered. The cries of the mourners prevented her words from being heard. [530-533]

On hearing the message, Mary rose hastily, and with an eager look on her face left the room. Thinking that she had gone to the grave to weep, the mourners followed her. When she reached the place where Jesus was waiting, she knelt at His feet, and said with quivering lips, "Lord, if Thou hadst been here, my brother had not died." The cries of the mourners were painful to her; for she longed for a few quiet words alone with Jesus. But she knew of the envy and jealousy cherished in the hearts of some present against Christ, and she was restrained from fully expressing her grief.

"When Jesus therefore saw her weeping, and the Jews also weeping which came with her, He groaned in the spirit, and was troubled." He read the hearts of all assembled. He saw that with many, what passed as a demonstration of grief was only pretense. He knew that some in the company, now manifesting hypocritical sorrow, would erelong be planning the death, not only of the mighty miracle worker, but of the one to be raised from the dead. Christ could have stripped from them their robe of pretended sorrow. But He restrained His righteous indignation. The words He could in all truth have spoken, He did not speak, because of the loved one kneeling at His feet in sorrow, who truly believed in Him.

"Where have ye laid him?" He asked, "They said unto Him, Lord, come and see." Together they proceeded to the grave. It was a mournful scene. Lazarus had been much beloved, and his sisters wept for him with breaking hearts, while those who had been his friends mingled their tears with those of the bereaved sisters. In view of this human distress, and of the fact that the afflicted friends could mourn over the dead while the Saviour of the world stood by,--"Jesus wept." Though He was the Son of God, yet He had taken human nature upon Him, and He was moved by human sorrow. His

10. "Jesus wept." "He was moved by human s_____ _____. His tender, pitying

heart is ever awakened to sympathy by s_____ _____. He weeps w_____ ____ those that weep, and rejoices w_____ those that rejoice." (533). Thank You, Lord, for feeling my pain. For being there with me. May I be there for You:

_____

_____

11. "He wept because many of those now mourning for Lazarus would soon plan the d_____ of Him who was the r_____ _____ and the life." (533). Jesus wept also on account of the weight of the g_____ of ages was upon Him. (534). Lord, how can I see sin as a weight of grief, like You do? _____

_____

_____

12. Jesus' attitude towards the sinful race, transgressors of God's law, is a "fountain of tears" "broken

tender, pitying heart is ever awakened to sympathy by suffering. He weeps with those that weep, and rejoices with those that rejoice.

But it was not only because of His human sympathy with Mary and Martha that Jesus wept. In His tears there was a sorrow as high above human sorrow as the heavens are higher than the earth. Christ did not weep for Lazarus; for He was about to call him from the grave. He wept because many of those now mourning for Lazarus would soon plan the death of Him who was the resurrection and the life. But how unable were the unbelieving Jews rightly to interpret His tears! Some, who [533-534] could see nothing more than the outward circumstances of the scene before Him as a cause for His grief, said softly, "Behold how He loved him!" Others, seeking to drop the seed of unbelief into the hearts of those present, said derisively, "Could not this Man, which opened the eyes of the blind, have caused that even this man should not have died?" If it were in Christ's power to save Lazarus, why then did He suffer him to die?

With prophetic eye Christ saw the enmity of the Pharisees and the Sadducees. He knew that they were premeditating His death. He knew that some of those now apparently so sympathetic would soon close against themselves the door of hope and the gates of the city of God. A scene was about to take place, in His humiliation and crucifixion, that would result in the destruction of Jerusalem, and at that time none would make lamentation for the dead. The retribution that was coming upon Jerusalem was plainly portrayed before Him. He saw Jerusalem compassed by the Roman legions. He knew that many now weeping for Lazarus would die in the siege of the city, and in their death there would be no hope.

It was not only because of the scene before Him that Christ wept. The weight of the grief of ages was upon Him. He saw the terrible effects of the transgression of God's law. He saw that in the history of the world, beginning with the death of Abel, the conflict between good and evil had been unceasing. Looking down the years to come, He saw the suffering and sorrow, tears and death, that were to be the lot of men. His heart was pierced with the pain of the human family of all ages and in all lands. The woes of the sinful race were heavy upon His soul, and the fountain of His tears was broken up as He longed to relieve all their distress.

"Jesus therefore again groaning in Himself cometh to the grave." Lazarus had been laid in a cave in a rock, and a massive stone had been placed before the entrance. "Take ye away the stone," Christ said. Thinking that He only wished to look upon the dead, Martha objected, saying that the body had been buried four days, and corruption had already begun its work. This statement, made before the raising of Lazarus, left no room for Christ's enemies to say that a deception had been practiced. In the past the Pharisees had circulated false statements regarding the most wonderful manifestations of the power of God. When Christ raised to life the daughter of Jairus, He had said, "The damsel is not dead, but sleepeth." Mark 5:39. As she had been sick only [534-535] a short time, and was raised immediately after death, the Pharisees declared that the child had not been dead; that Christ Himself had said she was only asleep. They had tried to make it appear that Christ could not cure disease, that there was foul play about His miracles. But in this case, none could deny that Lazarus was dead.

When the Lord is about to do a work, Satan moves upon someone to object. "Take ye away the stone," Christ said. As far as possible, prepare the way for My work. But Martha's positive and ambitious nature asserted itself. She was unwilling that the decomposing body should be brought to view. The human heart is slow to understand Christ's words, and Martha's faith had not grasped the true meaning of His promise.

Christ reproved Martha, but His words were spoken with the utmost gentleness. "Said I not unto thee, that, if thou wouldest believe, thou shouldest see the glory of God?" Why should you doubt in regard to My power? Why reason in opposition to My requirements? You have My word. If you will believe, you shall see the glory of God. Natural impossibilities cannot prevent the work of the Omnipotent One. Skepticism and unbelief are not humility. Implicit belief in Christ's word is true humility, true self-surrender.

"Take ye away the stone." Christ could have commanded the stone to remove, and it would have obeyed His voice. He could have bidden the angels who were close by His side to do this. At His bidding, invisible hands would have removed the stone. But it was to be taken away by human hands. Thus Christ would show

up as He l_____ to r_____ all their distress." I don't deserve any of Your compassion, Lord. Thank You for Your tears, Your longing to heal. May I give You room to do so: ___

_____

_____

that humanity is to co-operate with divinity. What human power can do divine power is not summoned to do. God does not dispense with man's aid. He strengthens him, co-operating with him as he uses the powers and capabilities given him.

The command is obeyed. The stone is rolled away. Everything is done openly and deliberately. All are given a chance to see that no deception is practiced. There lies the body of Lazarus in its rocky grave, cold and silent in death. The cries of the mourners are hushed. Surprised and expectant, the company stand around the sepulcher, waiting to see what is to follow.

Calmly Christ stands before the tomb. A sacred solemnity rests upon all present. Christ steps closer to the sepulcher. Lifting His eyes to heaven, He says, "Father, I thank Thee that Thou hast heard Me." Not long before this, Christ's enemies had accused Him of blasphemy, and had taken up stones to cast at Him because He claimed to be the Son of [535-536] God. They accused Him of performing miracles by the power of Satan. But here Christ claims God as His Father, and with perfect confidence declares that He is the Son of God.

In all that He did, Christ was co-operating with His Father. Ever He had been careful to make it evident that He did not work independently; it was by faith and prayer that He wrought His miracles. Christ desired all to know His relationship with His Father. "Father," He said, "I thank Thee that Thou hast heard Me. And I knew that Thou hearest Me always: but because of the people which stand by I said it, that they may believe that Thou hast sent Me." Here the disciples and the people were to be given the most convincing evidence in regard to the relationship existing between Christ and God. They were to be shown that Christ's claim was not a deception.

"And when He thus had spoken, He cried with a loud voice, Lazarus, come forth." His voice, clear and penetrating, pierces the ear of the dead. As He speaks, divinity flashes through humanity. In His face, which is lighted up by the glory of God, the people see the assurance of His power. Every eye is fastened on the entrance to the cave. Every ear is bent to catch the slightest sound. With intense and painful interest all wait for the test of Christ's divinity, the evidence that is to substantiate His claim to be the Son of God, or to extinguish the hope forever.

13. "Every eye is fastened on the entrance to the cave. Every e_____ is bent to catch the slightest sound. With intense and painful i_____ all wait for the test of Christ's d____ _____, the evidence that is to substantiate His claim to be the S_____ of God, or to extinguish the hope forever...Inexpressible scene of rejoic-

There is a stir in the silent tomb, and he who was dead stands at the door of the sepulcher. His movements are impeded by the graveclothes in which he was laid away, and Christ says to the astonished spectators, "Loose him, and let him go." Again they are shown that the human worker is to co-operate with God. Humanity is to work for humanity. Lazarus is set free, and stands before the company, not as one emaciated from disease, and with feeble, tottering limbs, but as a man in the prime of life, and in the vigor of a noble manhood. His eyes beam with intelligence and with love for his Saviour. He casts himself in adoration at the feet of Jesus.

The beholders are at first speechless with amazement. Then there follows an inexpressible scene of rejoicing and thanksgiving. The sisters receive their brother back to life as the gift of God, and with joyful tears they brokenly express their thanks to the Saviour. But while brother, sisters, and friends are rejoicing in this reunion, Jesus withdraws from the scene. When they look for the Life-giver, He is not to be found.

ing and t_____"
follows. (536). How can I better appreciate the magnitude of the miracle of my resurrection from spiritual death and darkness?
_____
_____. I need that miracle every day. Remind me to pray and be open for that miracle every day! Did I thank You? _____
_____
_____

Prayer journal: _____
_____
_____
_____
_____
_____

Chapter 59

Priestly Plottings

[This chapter is based on John 11:47-54.]

1. The raising-of-Lazarus miracle was the "crowning e_____ offered by God to men that He had sent His Son into the world for their s_____." Did Jesus have power over death, even before the Calvary experience? _____.

Could Calvary's meaning be other than that of power? _____ What is Calvary all about, then, Lord? Keep showing me:

_____

_____

_____

_____

2. The Sadducees, not believing in the possibility of a resurrection, were "shown to be ignorant both of the Scriptures and the p_____ of God." (538). What is the difference between a knowledge of Scriptures, and of God's power? _____

_____

_____

What knowledge do I have? _____

_____

_____

Bethany was so near Jerusalem that the news of the raising of Lazarus was soon carried to the city. Through spies who had witnessed the miracle the Jewish rulers were speedily in possession of the facts. A meeting of the Sanhedrin was at once called to decide as to what should be done. Christ had now fully made manifest His control of death and the grave. That mighty miracle was the crowning evidence offered by God to men that He had sent His Son into the world for their salvation. It was a demonstration of divine power sufficient to convince every mind that was under the control of reason and enlightened conscience. Many who witnessed the resurrection of Lazarus were led to believe on Jesus. But the hatred of the priests against Him was intensified. They had rejected all lesser evidence of His divinity, and they were only enraged at this new miracle. The dead had been raised in the full light of day, and before a crowd of witnesses. No artifice could explain away such evidence. For this very reason the enmity of the priests grew deadlier. They were more than ever determined to put a stop to Christ's work.

The Sadducees, though not favorable to Christ, had not been so full of malignity toward Him as were the Pharisees. Their hatred had not been so bitter. But they were now thoroughly alarmed. They did not [537-538] believe in a resurrection of the dead. Producing so-called science, they had reasoned that it would be an impossibility for a dead body to be brought to life. But by a few words from Christ their theory had been overthrown. They were shown to be ignorant both of the Scriptures and of the power of God. They could see no possibility of removing the impression made on the people by the miracle. How could men be turned away from Him who had prevailed to rob the grave of its dead? Lying reports were put in circulation, but the miracle could not be denied, and how to counteract its effect they knew not. Thus far the Sadducees had not encouraged the plan of putting Christ to death. But after the resurrection of Lazarus they decided that only by His death could His fearless denunciations against them be stopped.

The Pharisees believed in the resurrection, and they could not but see that this miracle was an evidence that the Messiah was among them. But they had ever opposed Christ's work. From the first they had hated Him because He had exposed their hypocritical pretensions. He had torn aside the cloak of rigorous rites under which their moral deformity was hidden. The pure religion that He taught had condemned their hollow professions of piety. They thirsted to be revenged upon Him for His pointed rebukes. They had tried to provoke Him to say or do something that would give them occasion to condemn Him. Several times they had attempted to stone Him, but He had quietly withdrawn, and they had lost sight of Him.

The miracles He performed on the Sabbath were all for the relief of the afflicted, but the Pharisees had sought to condemn Him as a Sabbathbreaker. They had tried to arouse the Herodians against Him. They represented that He was seeking to set up a rival kingdom, and consulted with them how to destroy Him. To excite the Romans against Him, they had represented Him as trying to subvert their authority. They had tried every pretext to cut Him off from influencing the people. But so far their attempts had been foiled. The multitudes who witnessed His works of mercy and heard His pure and holy teachings knew that these were not the deeds and words of a Sabbathbreaker or blasphemer. Even the officers sent by the Pharisees had been so influenced by His words that they could not lay hands on Him. In desperation the Jews had finally passed an edict that any man who professed faith in Jesus should be cast out of the synagogue.

So, as the priests, the rulers, and the elders gathered for consultation, it was their fixed determination to silence Him who did such marvelous [538-539] works that all men wondered. Pharisees and Sadducees were more nearly united than ever before. Divided hitherto, they became one in their opposition to Christ. Nicode-

3. "In desperation the Jews had finally passed an edict that any man who professed f_____ in Jesus should be cast o_____ of the synagogue." Worship in the synagogue was to be directed to Jesus. But now professing faith IN Jesus meant being cast out? ___
_____.

Lord, in what ways do I cast out? Or am unavailable, avoiding, or unfriendly? Show me my behaviors that give that message:
_____
_____
_____
_____

mus and Joseph had, in former councils, prevented the condemnation of Jesus, and for this reason they were not now summoned. There were present at the council other influential men who believed on Jesus, but their influence prevailed nothing against that of the malignant Pharisees.

Yet the members of the council were not all agreed. The Sanhedrin was not at this time a legal assembly. It existed only by tolerance. Some of its number questioned the wisdom of putting Christ to death. They feared that this would excite an insurrection among the people, causing the Romans to withhold further favors from the priesthood, and to take from them the power they still held. The Sadducees were united in their hatred of Christ, yet they were inclined to be cautious in their movements, fearing that the Romans would deprive them of their high standing.

In this council, assembled to plan the death of Christ, the Witness was present who heard the boastful words of Nebuchadnezzar, who witnessed the idolatrous feast of Belshazzar, who was present when Christ in Nazareth announced Himself the Anointed One. This Witness was now impressing the rulers with the work they were doing. Events in the life of Christ rose up before them with a distinctness that alarmed them. They remembered the scene in the temple, when Jesus, then a child of twelve, stood before the learned doctors of the law, asking them questions at which they wondered. The miracle just performed bore witness that Jesus was none other than the Son of God. In their true significance, the Old Testament Scriptures regarding Christ flashed before their minds. Perplexed and troubled, the rulers asked, "What do we?" There was a division in the council. Under the impression of the Holy Spirit, the priests and rulers could not banish the conviction that they were fighting against God.

While the council was at the height of its perplexity, Caiaphas the high priest arose. Caiaphas was a proud and cruel man, overbearing and intolerant. Among his family connections were Sadducees, proud, bold, reckless, full of ambition and cruelty, which they hid under a cloak of pretended righteousness. Caiaphas had studied the prophecies, and although ignorant of their true meaning, he spoke with great authority and assurance: "Ye know nothing at all, nor consider that it is expedient for us, that one man should die for the people, and that

4. A council was convened, to silence Jesus and plan His death. But "under the impression of the H_____ S_____, the priests and rulers could not banish the conviction that they were f_____ against God." (539). Have I ever been "impressed" by the Holy Spirit that I'm fighting God? When?

_____
_____
_____
_____

It's a wonder that the Holy Spirit came to this gathering, this council? _____

_____

But it shows how far God is willing to go to reach me: _____

_____
_____
_____

the whole nation [539-540] perish not." Even if Jesus were innocent, urged the high priest, He must be put out of the way. He was troublesome, drawing the people to Himself, and lessening the authority of the rulers. He was only one; it was better that He should die than that the authority of the rulers should be weakened. If the people were to lose confidence in their rulers, the national power would be destroyed. Caiaphas urged that after this miracle the followers of Jesus would likely rise in revolt. The Romans will then come, he said, and will close our temple, and abolish our laws, destroying us as a nation. What is the life of this Galilean worth in comparison with the life of the nation? If He stands in the way of Israel's well-being, is it not doing God a service to remove Him? Better that one man perish than that the whole nation be destroyed.

In declaring that one man should die for the nation, Caiaphas indicated that he had some knowledge of the prophecies, although it was very limited. But John, in his account of this scene, takes up the prophecy, and shows its broad and deep significance. He says, "And not for that nation only, but that also He should gather together in one the children of God that were scattered abroad." How blindly did the haughty Caiaphas acknowledge the Saviour's mission!

On the lips of Caiaphas this most precious truth was turned into a lie. The policy he advocated was based on a principle borrowed from heathenism. Among the heathen, the dim consciousness that one was to die for the human race had led to the offering of human sacrifices. So Caiaphas proposed by the sacrifice of Jesus to save the guilty nation, not from transgression, but in transgression, that they might continue in sin. And by his reasoning he thought to silence the remonstrances of those who might dare to say that as yet nothing worthy of death had been found in Jesus.

At this council Christ's enemies had been deeply convicted. The Holy Spirit had impressed their minds. But Satan strove to gain control of them. He urged upon their notice the grievances they had suffered on account of Christ. How little He had honored their righteousness. He presented a righteousness far greater, which all who would be children of God must possess. Taking no notice of their forms and ceremonies, He had encouraged sinners to go directly to God as a merciful Father, and make known their wants. Thus, in their opinion,

5. "Caiaphas urged the council that after this miracle the followers of Jesus would likely rise in r_____...If He stands in the way of Israel's well-being, is it not doing G_____ a service to remove Him? Better that o____ man perish than that the whole n___ _____ be destroyed." (540). Lord, help me not to manipulate Scripture to make a point that I want:

_____

_____

6. "Among the heathen, the dim consciousness that one was to die for the human race had led to the offering of h_____ sacrifices." Lord, help me not to drag the cross down to a heathenistic meaning. Why did You die for me? _

_____

_____

_____

_____

7. "At this council Christ's enemies had been deeply c_____. The Holy Spirit had impressed their minds. But Satan strove to gain control of them...Satan told them that in order to maintain their a_____ _____, they must put Jesus to d_____." (540, 541). It is amazing, Lord, at the battle going on behind the scenes, of my conviction and de-

ception. Please sharpen my sensitivity to Your Spirit: _____

_____

_____

8. "Such was their deception, that they were well p_____ with themselves. They regarded themselves as p_____ __, who were seeking the nations' salvation." Lord, there must be a difference between the impression Satan gives me, even suggesting that it is a spiritual impression, and genuine impressions of the Holy Spirit's. What is the difference? _____

_____

Please give me discernment: _____

_____

_____

9. A "short period of three years was as l_____ as the world could endure the p_____ of its Redeemer." What are the times that my walk with You tends towards "enduring" Your presence instead of enjoying it?_____

_____

_____

_____

He had set aside the priesthood. He had refused to acknowledge the theology of the rabbinical schools. He had exposed the evil practices of the priests, [540-541] and had irreparably hurt their influence. He had injured the effect of their maxims and traditions, declaring that though they strictly enforced the ritual law, they made void the law of God. All this Satan now brought to their minds.

Satan told them that in order to maintain their authority, they must put Jesus to death. This counsel they followed. The fact that they might lose the power they then exercised, was, they thought, sufficient reason for coming to some decision. With the exception of a few who dared not speak their minds, the Sanhedrin received the words of Caiaphas as the words of God. Relief came to the council; the discord ceased. They resolved to put Christ to death at the first favorable opportunity. In rejecting the proof of the divinity of Jesus, these priests and rulers had locked themselves in impenetrable darkness. They had come wholly under the sway of Satan, to be hurried by him over the brink of eternal ruin. Yet such was their deception that they were well pleased with themselves. They regarded themselves as patriots, who were seeking the nation's salvation.

The Sanhedrin feared, however, to take rash measures against Jesus, lest the people should become incensed, and the violence meditated toward Him should fall upon themselves. On this account the council delayed to execute the sentence they had pronounced. The Saviour understood the plotting of the priests. He knew that they longed to remove Him, and that their purpose would soon be accomplished. But it was not His place to hasten the crisis, and He withdrew from that region, taking the disciples with Him. Thus by His own example Jesus again enforced the instruction He had given to the disciples, "When they persecute you in this city, flee ye into another." Matt. 10:23. There was a wide field in which to work for the salvation of souls; and unless loyalty to Him required it, the Lord's servants were not to imperil their lives.

Jesus had now given three years of public labor to the world. His example of self-denial and disinterested benevolence was before them. His life of purity, of suffering and devotion, was known to all. Yet this short period of three years was as long as the world could endure the presence of its Redeemer.

His life had been one of persecution and insult. Driven from Bethlehem by a jealous king, rejected by His own people at Nazareth, condemned to death without a cause at Jerusalem, Jesus, with His few faithful followers, found a temporary asylum in a strange city. He who [541-542] was ever touched by human woe, who healed the sick, restored sight to the blind, hearing to the deaf, and speech to the dumb, who fed the hungry and comforted the sorrowful, was driven from the people He had labored to save. He who walked upon the heaving billows, and by a word silenced their angry roaring, who cast out devils that in departing acknowledged Him to be the Son of God, who broke the slumbers of the dead, who held thousands entranced by His words of wisdom, was unable to reach the hearts of those who were blinded by prejudice and hatred, and who stubbornly rejected the light.

Prayer journal: _____
_____
_____
_____
_____
_____
_____
_____

Chapter 60

The Law of the New Kingdom

[This chapter is based on Matt. 20:20-28; Mark 10:32-45; Luke 18:31-34.]

The time of the Passover was drawing near, and again Jesus turned toward Jerusalem. In His heart was the peace of perfect oneness with the Father's will, and with eager steps He pressed on toward the place of sacrifice. But a sense of mystery, of doubt and fear, fell upon the disciples. The Saviour "went before them: and they were amazed; and as they followed, they were afraid."

Again Christ called the twelve about Him, and with greater definiteness than ever before, He opened to them His betrayal and sufferings. "Behold," He said, "we go up to Jerusalem, and all things that are written by the prophets concerning the Son of man shall be accomplished. For He shall be delivered unto the Gentiles, and shall be mocked, and spitefully entreated, and spitted on: and they shall scourge Him, and put Him to death: and the third day He shall rise again. And they understood none of these things: and this saying was hid from them, neither knew they the things which were spoken."

Had they not just before proclaimed everywhere, "The kingdom of heaven is at hand"? Had not Christ Himself promised that many should sit down with Abraham and Isaac and Jacob in the kingdom of God? Had He not promised to all who had left aught for His sake a hundredfold in this life, and a part in His kingdom? And had He not given to the twelve the special promise of positions of high honor in His kingdom,--to sit on thrones judging the twelve tribes of Israel? Even [547-548] now He had said that all things written in the prophets concerning Him should be fulfilled. And had not the prophets foretold the glory of the Messiah's reign? In the light of these thoughts, His words in regard to betrayal, persecution, and death seemed vague and shadowy. Whatever difficulties might intervene, they believed that the kingdom was soon to be established.

John, the son of Zebedee, had been one of the first

---

1. Jesus, with greater d_____ than ever before, opened to His disciples His betrayal and sufferings... "They shall scourge Him, and put Him to death: and the third day He shall rise again. And they understood n_____ of these things." It seems so plain to me, Lord. What was wrong? Is it the power of pre-conceived ideas? _____ Do pre-conceived ideas get in the way of my knowing You, Lord? Are my expectations of our walk together different from Yours? Do You have something different in mind? _____

_____

_____

_____

2. "Had not the prophets foretold the g_____ of the Messiah's reign? In light of these thoughts, His words in regard to betrayal, persecution and death seemed v_____ and shadowy." (548). In

two disciples who had followed Jesus. He and his brother James had been among the first group who had left all for His service. Gladly they had forsaken home and friends that they might be with Him; they had walked and talked with Him; they had been with Him in the privacy of the home, and in the public assemblies. He had quieted their fears, delivered them from danger, relieved their sufferings, comforted their grief, and with patience and tenderness had taught them, till their hearts seemed linked with His, and in the ardor of their love they longed to be nearest to Him in His kingdom. At every possible opportunity, John took his place next the Saviour, and James longed to be honored with as close connection with Him.

Their mother was a follower of Christ, and had ministered to Him freely of her substance. With a mother's love and ambition for her sons, she coveted for them the most honored place in the new kingdom. For this she encouraged them to make request.

Together the mother and her sons came to Jesus, asking that He would grant a petition on which their hearts were set.

"What would ye that I should do for you?" He questioned.

The mother answered, "Grant that these my two sons may sit, the one on Thy right hand, and the other on the left, in Thy kingdom."

Jesus bears tenderly with them, not rebuking their selfishness in seeking preference above their brethren. He reads their hearts, He knows the depth of their attachment to Him. Their love is not a mere human affection; though defiled by the earthliness of its human channel, it is an outflowing from the fountain of His own redeeming love. He will not rebuke, but deepen and purify. He said, "Are ye able to drink of the cup that I shall drink of, and to be baptized with the baptism that I am baptized with?" They recall His mysterious words, pointing to trial and suffering, yet answer confidently, "We are able." They would count it highest honor to prove their loyalty by sharing all that is to befall their Lord.

"Ye shall drink indeed of My cup, and be baptized with the baptism that I am baptized with," He said; before Him a cross instead of a [548-549] throne, two malefactors His companions at His right hand and His left. John and James were to share with their Master in

reading the Bible, Lord, I guess I should be purposeful in taking all the scriptures, considering all the evidence, and not just selecting what I want to hear. Am I really open to hearing what the Spirit has for me? _____

_____

3. "At e_____ opportunity, John took his place next the Savior." John, James and their mother made a petition of Jesus. "He knows the depth of their a_____ to Him. Their love...is an outflowing from the fountain of His own redeeming love. He will not rebuke, but d_____ and p_____." Do I have this depth of attachment for Jesus? _____

_____

Why not? _____

_____

_____

What can I do? _____

_____

_____

Seek every opportunity to sit next to You, the fountain of Your love will be the source of my love for You: _____

_____

_____

suffering; the one, first of the brethren to perish with the sword; the other, longest of all to endure toil, and reproach, and persecution.

"But to sit on My right hand, and on My left," He continued, "is not Mine to give, but it shall be given to them for whom it is prepared of My Father." In the kingdom of God, position is not gained through favoritism. It is not earned, nor is it received through an arbitrary bestowal. It is the result of character. The crown and the throne are the tokens of a condition attained; they are the tokens of self-conquest through our Lord Jesus Christ.

Long afterward, when the disciple had been brought into sympathy with Christ through the fellowship of His sufferings, the Lord revealed to John what is the condition of nearness in His kingdom. "To him that overcometh," Christ said, "will I grant to sit with Me in My throne, even as I also overcame, and am set down with My Father in His throne." "Him that overcometh will I make a pillar in the temple of My God, and he shall go no more out: and I will write upon him the name of My God, . . . and I will write upon him My new name." Rev. 3:21, 12. So Paul the apostle wrote, "I am now ready to be offered, and the time of my departure is at hand. I have fought a good fight, I have finished my course, I have kept the faith: henceforth there is laid up for me a crown of righteousness, which the Lord, the righteous Judge, shall give me at that day." 2 Tim. 4:6-8.

The one who stands nearest to Christ will be he who on earth has drunk most deeply of the spirit of His self-sacrificing love,--love that "vaunteth not itself, is not puffed up, . . . seeketh not her own, is not easily provoked, thinketh no evil" (1 Cor. 13:4, 5),--love that moves the disciple, as it moved our Lord, to give all, to live and labor and sacrifice, even unto death, for the saving of humanity. This spirit was made manifest in the life of Paul. He said, "For to me to live is Christ;" for his life revealed Christ to men; "and to die is gain,"--gain to Christ; death itself would make manifest the power of His grace, and gather souls to Him. "Christ shall be magnified in my body," he said, "whether it be by life or by death." Phil. 1:21, 20.

4. "In the kingdom of God, position is not gained through f_____. It is not e_____ …It is the result of c_____." (549). Crowns and thrones are related not to position, but to self-conquest. Ok, Lord, what do You want me to do? Character comes from where? _____

_____ Sitting next to You? So Your character will inspire my character in the conquest of self: _____

5. "The one who stands n_____ to Christ will be he who on earth has drunk most deeply of the spirit of His self-s_____ love." What love is this? It moves me "to give a_____, to live and labor and s__ _____, even unto death, for the saving of humanity." Lord, help me to drink more deeply of Your self-sacrificing love! What can I do today?

When the ten heard of the request of James and John, they were much displeased. The highest place in the kingdom was just what every one of them was seeking for himself, and they were angry that the two disciples had gained a seeming advantage over them. [549-550]

Again the strife as to which should be greatest seemed about to be renewed, when Jesus, calling them to Him, said to the indignant disciples, "Ye know that they which are accounted to rule over the Gentiles exercise lordship over them; and their great ones exercise authority upon them. But so shall it not be among you."

In the kingdoms of the world, position meant self-aggrandizement. The people were supposed to exist for the benefit of the ruling classes. Influence, wealth, education, were so many means of gaining control of the masses for the use of the leaders. The higher classes were to think, decide, enjoy, and rule; the lower were to obey and serve. Religion, like all things else, was a matter of authority. The people were expected to believe and practice as their superiors directed. The right of man as man, to think and act for himself, was wholly unrecognized.

Christ was establishing a kingdom on different principles. He called men, not to authority, but to service, the strong to bear the infirmities of the weak. Power, position, talent, education, placed their possessor under the greater obligation to serve his fellows. To even the lowliest of Christ's disciples it is said, "All things are for your sakes." 2 Cor. 4:15.

"The Son of man came not to be ministered unto, but to minister, and to give His life a ransom for many." Among His disciples Christ was in every sense a caretaker, a burden bearer. He shared their poverty, He practiced self-denial on their account, He went before them to smooth the more difficult places, and soon He would consummate His work on earth by laying down His life. The principle on which Christ acted is to actu-

When I am in heaven, will I be jealous of someone sitting next to You? _____

6. "When the ten heard of the request of James and John, they were much d_____." They were angry at the two for such an unholy display of character? No; they didn't see the gross and ugly self-centeredness. Instead, they saw the advantage lost to James and John. Lord, thank You for gently showing me what my heart is like:

7. "In the kingdoms of the world, p_____ meant self-aggrandizement." Religion was a matter of a_____. Christ's kingdom has different principles. "He called men, not to authority, but to s_____." (550). Lord, I want to be like You. Give me opportunity to put into practice the grace of having been with You, grace to serve: _____

8. "Power, p_____ _____, talent, education, placed their possessor under the greater o_____

to s_____ his fel-
lows." Show me, Lord,
the ways that I mis-
understand this point:

_____
_____
_____

9. "The plan and g_____
____ of salvation is love."
Lord, what does this mean?
Show me: _____
_____
_____

From Your motivation, to
the basis, to the benefits,
to the by-product. It is all
love: _____
_____

Prayer journal: _____
_____
_____
_____
_____
_____
_____
_____

ate the members of the church which is His body. The plan and ground of salvation is love. In the kingdom of Christ those are greatest who follow the example He has given, and act as shepherds of His flock.

The words of Paul reveal the true dignity and honor of the Christian life: "Though I be free from all men, yet have I made myself servant unto all," "not seeking mine own profit, but the profit of many, that they may be saved." 1 Cor. 9:19; 10:33.

In matters of conscience the soul must be left untrammeled. No one is to control another's mind, to judge for another, or to prescribe his duty. God gives to every soul freedom to think, and to follow his own convictions. "Every one of us shall give account of himself to God." No one has a right to merge his own individuality in that of another. In all matters where principle is involved, "let every man be fully persuaded in his own mind." Rom. 14:12, 5. In Christ's kingdom there is no lordly [550-551] oppression, no compulsion of manner. The angels of heaven do not come to the earth to rule, and to exact homage, but as messengers of mercy, to co-operate with men in uplifting humanity.

The principles and the very words of the Saviour's teaching, in their divine beauty, dwelt in the memory of the beloved disciple. To his latest days the burden of John's testimony to the churches was, "This is the message that ye heard from the beginning, that we should love one another." "Hereby perceive we the love of God, because He laid down His life for us: and we ought to lay down our lives for the brethren." 1 John 3:11, 16.

This was the spirit that pervaded the early church. After the outpouring of the Holy Spirit, "the multitude of them that believed were of one heart and of one soul: neither said any of them that aught of the things which he possessed was his own." "Neither was there any among them that lacked." "And with great power gave the apostles witness of the resurrection of the Lord Jesus: and great grace was upon them all." Acts 4:32, 34, 33.

Chapter 61

Zacchaeus

[This chapter is based on Luke 19:1-10.]

On the way to Jerusalem "Jesus entered and passed through Jericho." A few miles from the Jordan, on the western edge of the valley that here spread out into a plain, the city lay in the midst of tropic verdure and luxuriance of beauty. With its palm trees and rich gardens watered by living springs, it gleamed like an emerald in the setting of limestone hills and desolate ravines that interposed between Jerusalem and the city of the plain.

Many caravans on their way to the feast passed through Jericho. Their arrival was always a festive season, but now a deeper interest stirred the people. It was known that the Galilean Rabbi who had so lately brought Lazarus to life was in the throng; and though whispers were rife as to the plottings of the priests, the multitudes were eager to do Him homage.

Jericho was one of the cities anciently set apart for the priests, and at this time large numbers of priests had their residence there. But the city had also a population of a widely different character. It was a great center of traffic, and Roman officials and soldiers, with strangers from different quarters, were found there, while the collection of customs made it the home of many publicans.

"The chief among the publicans," Zacchaeus, was a Jew, and detested by his countrymen. His rank and wealth were the reward of a calling [552-553] they abhorred, and which was regarded as another name for injustice and extortion. Yet the wealthy customs officer was not altogether the hardened man of the world that he seemed. Beneath the appearance of worldliness and pride was a heart susceptible to divine influences. Zacchaeus had heard of Jesus. The report of One who had borne Himself with kindness and courtesy toward the proscribed classes had spread far and wide. In this chief of the publicans was awakened a longing for a better life. Only a few miles from Jericho, John the Baptist had preached at the Jordan, and Zacchaeus had heard of the call to repentance. The instruction to the publicans,

1. Though a publican, which is another name for i_____ and e_____, Zacchaeus had a "heart susceptible to divine i_____." (553). Am I born with a certain susceptibility?_____ _____ Can it be increased?_____ How? _____ _____ _____ _____

2. "Zaccheaus had heard the call to repentance" of John the Baptist and he "began at o_____ to follow the conviction that had taken hold upon him." What happens if I wait? _____
_____
_____
_____

Why do I wait, Lord?
_____
_____
_____

3. Zacchaeus was "beginning to realize how b_____ are the fruits of sin, and how d_____ the path of him who tries to return from the course of wrong." What are the fruits of sin? _____
_____
_____
_____

The strength of a habit is known only as I try to quit. But Lord, You promised sufficient strength in 1 Cor 10:13: _____
_____
_____
_____

4. Zacchaeus was misunderstood, met with s____ _____ and distrust in his efforts to correct his errors. Lord, do I make it difficult through distrust, for someone trying to return? How do I treat someone who caused me pain or difficulties? ____
_____

"Exact no more than that which is appointed you" (Luke 3:13), though outwardly disregarded, had impressed his mind. He knew the Scriptures, and was convicted that his practice was wrong. Now, hearing the words reported to have come from the Great Teacher, he felt that he was a sinner in the sight of God. Yet what he had heard of Jesus kindled hope in his heart. Repentance, reformation of life, was possible, even to him; was not one of the new Teacher's most trusted disciples a publican? Zacchaeus began at once to follow the conviction that had taken hold upon him, and to make restitution to those whom he had wronged.

Already he had begun thus to retrace his steps, when the news sounded through Jericho that Jesus was entering the town. Zacchaeus determined to see Him. He was beginning to realize how bitter are the fruits of sin, and how difficult the path of him who tries to return from a course of wrong. To be misunderstood, to be met with suspicion and distrust in the effort to correct his errors, was hard to bear. The chief publican longed to look upon the face of Him whose words had brought hope to his heart.

The streets were crowded, and Zacchaeus, who was small of stature, could see nothing over the heads of the people. None would give way for him; so, running a little in advance of the multitude, to where a wide-branching fig tree hung over the way, the rich tax collector climbed to a seat among the boughs, whence he could survey the procession as it passed below. The crowd comes near, it is going by, and Zacchaeus scans with eager eyes to discern the one figure he longs to see.

Above the clamor of priests and rabbis and the shouts of welcome from the multitude, that unuttered desire of the chief publican spoke to the heart of Jesus. Suddenly, just beneath the fig tree, a group halts, the company before and behind come to a standstill, and One looks upward whose glance seems to read the soul. Almost doubting his senses, [553-554] the man in the tree hears the words, "Zacchaeus, make haste, and come down; for today I must abide at thy house."

The multitude give way, and Zacchaeus, walking as in a dream, leads the way toward his own home. But the rabbis look on with scowling faces, and murmur in discontent and scorn, "that He was gone to be guest with a man that is a sinner."

Zacchaeus had been overwhelmed, amazed, and silenced at the love and condescension of Christ in stooping to him, so unworthy. Now love and loyalty to his new-found Master unseal his lips. He will make public his confession and his repentance. [554-555]

In the presence of the multitude, "Zacchaeus stood, and said unto the Lord; Behold, Lord, the half of my goods I give to the poor; and if I have taken anything from any man by false accusation, I restore him fourfold.

"And Jesus said unto him, This day is salvation come to this house, forsomuch as he also is a son of Abraham."

When the rich young ruler had turned away from Jesus, the disciples had marveled at their Master's saying, "How hard is it for them that trust in riches to enter into the kingdom of God!" They had exclaimed one to another, "Who then can be saved?" Now they had a demonstration of the truth of Christ's words, "The things which are impossible with men are possible with God." Mark 10:24, 26; Luke 18:27. They say how, through the grace of God, a rich man could enter into the kingdom.

5. "Above the clamor of priests and rabbis and the shouts of welcome from the multitude, that u_____ _____ desire of the chief publican spoke to the h_____ of Jesus." Thank You for hearing my unspoken and quiet moods of the heart, Lord, and for being so responsive. You are there before I need You: _____

6. "Today I must abide in thy house...[Zacchaeus] walking as in a d_____ _____...rabbis look on with scowling faces, and murmur in discontent and scorn." (554). Why the different responses to Your statement, Lord?

How do I feel about inviting You Lord, to my home right now?

7. About the rich young ruler, Jesus commented, "How hard it is for them that t_____in riches to e_____ into the kingdom of God." (555). Is the issue "riches" or "trust"? _____

What does 'entering the kingdom' mean? _____
_____
_____
_____

Zacchaeus demonstrates for us, that "through the grace of God, a rich man could enter into the kingdom." What does this grace do for a rich person? _____
_____
_____

8. "Before being accused by man, he had confessed his sin. He had y_____ _____ to the conviction of the Holy Spirit." Confession after accusation is not the same is it? Your Spirit is always working on me, Lord. May I be attentive to its voice, and act upon its prompting:
_____
_____

9. "The very first r_____ _____ of Zacchaeus to the l_____ of Christ was in manifesting c____ _____ toward the poor and suffering." Has it happened the same way for me? _____
_____ Lord, I guess I need a new look at Your love. Thank You for helping my walk with You to be meaningful. May Your love stir a response within me: _____

Before Zacchaeus had looked upon the face of Christ, he had begun the work that made him manifest as a true penitent. Before being accused by man, he had confessed his sin. He had yielded to the conviction of the Holy Spirit, and had begun to carry out the teaching of the words written for ancient Israel as well as for ourselves. The Lord had said long before, "If thy brother be waxen poor, and fallen in decay with thee; then thou shalt relieve him: yea, though he be a stranger, or a sojourner; that he may live with thee. Take thou no usury of him, or increase: but fear thy God; that thy brother may live with thee. Thou shalt not give him thy money upon usury, nor lend him thy victuals for increase." "Ye shall not therefore oppress one another; but thou shalt fear thy God." Lev. 25:35-37, 17. These words had been spoken by Christ Himself when He was enshrouded in the pillar of cloud, and the very first response of Zacchaeus to the love of Christ was in manifesting compassion toward the poor and suffering.

Among the publicans there was a confederacy, so that they could oppress the people, and sustain one another in their fraudulent practices. In their extortion they were but carrying out what had become an almost universal custom. Even the priests and rabbis who despised them were guilty of enriching themselves by dishonest practices under cover of their sacred calling. But no sooner did Zacchaeus yield to the influence of the Holy Spirit than he cast aside every practice contrary to integrity.

No repentance is genuine that does not work reformation. The righteousness of Christ is not a cloak to cover unconfessed and unforsaken [555-556] sin; it is a principle of life that transforms the character and controls the conduct. Holiness is wholeness for God; it is the entire surrender of heart and life to the indwelling of the principles of heaven.

The Christian in his business life is to represent to the world the manner in which our Lord would conduct business enterprises. In every transaction he is to make it manifest that God is his teacher. "Holiness unto the Lord" is to be written upon daybooks and ledgers, on deeds, receipts, and bills of exchange. Those who profess to be followers of Christ, and who deal in an unrighteous manner, are bearing false witness against the character of a holy, just, and merciful God. Every converted soul will, like Zacchaeus, signalize the entrance of Christ into his heart by an abandonment of the unrighteous practices that have marked his life. Like the chief publican, he will give proof of his sincerity by making restitution. The Lord says, "If the wicked restore the pledge, give again that he had robbed, walk in the statutes of life, without committing iniquity; . . . none of his sins that he hath committed shall be mentioned unto him: . . . He shall surely live." Ezek. 33:15, 16.

If we have injured others through any unjust business transaction, if we have overreached in trade, or defrauded any man, even though it be within the pale of the law, we should confess our wrong, and make restitution as far as lies in our power. It is right for us to restore not only that which we have taken, but all that it would have accumulated if put to a right and wise use during the time it has been in our possession.

To Zacchaeus the Saviour said, "This day is salvation come to this house." Not only was Zacchaeus himself blessed, but all his household with him. Christ went to his home to give him lessons of truth, and to instruct his household in the things of the kingdom. They had been shut out from the synagogues by the contempt of rabbis and worshipers; but now, the most favored household in all Jericho, they gathered in their own home about the divine Teacher, and heard for themselves the words of life.

It is when Christ is received as a personal Saviour that salvation comes to the soul. Zacchaeus had received

10. "No repentance is genuine that does not work r_____."
If our character is being transformed our conduct will be controlled. Lord, may my reformation not be mere airs to prove my 'repentance.' Rather, may it be a natural outflow:

_____

11. "Those who profess to be f_____ of Christ, and who deal in an u_____ manner, are bearing false witness against the character of a h_____, just, and merciful God." (556). Lord, You are holy, the ruler of the universe. May I properly understand my witness for You. I bear false witness against You quite a bit. Show me ways that I do: _____

_____

You have to live in my heart and help my witness. Please abide there: _____

_____

12. "It is when Christ is received as a p_____ Savior that s_____ _____ comes to the soul." Has salvation come to my home, does Christ abide in my soul t_____?

_____

Prayer journal: _____
_____
_____
_____
_____
_____
_____
_____
_____

Jesus, not merely as a passing guest in his home, but as One to abide in the soul temple. The scribes and Pharisees accused him as a sinner, they murmured against Christ for becoming his guest, but the Lord recognized him as a son of Abraham. For "they which are of faith, the same are the children of Abraham." Gal. 3:7.

Chapter 62

The Feast at Simon's House

[This chapter is based on Matt. 26:6-13;
Mark 14:3-11; Luke 7:36-50; John 11:55-57; 12:1-11.]

Simon of Bethany was accounted a disciple of Jesus. He was one of the few Pharisees who had openly joined Christ's followers. He acknowledged Jesus as a teacher, and hoped that He might be the Messiah, but he had not accepted Him as a Saviour. His character was not transformed; his principles were unchanged.

Simon had been healed of the leprosy, and it was this that had drawn him to Jesus. He desired to show his gratitude, and at Christ's last visit to Bethany he made a feast for the Saviour and His disciples. This feast brought together many of the Jews. There was at this time much excitement at Jerusalem. Christ and His mission were attracting greater attention than ever before. Those who had come to the feast closely watched His movements, and some of them with unfriendly eyes.

The Saviour had reached Bethany only six days before the Passover, and according to His custom had sought rest at the home of Lazarus. The crowds of travelers who passed on to the city spread the tidings that He was on His way to Jerusalem, and that He would rest over the Sabbath at Bethany. Among the people there was great enthusiasm. Many flocked to Bethany, some out of sympathy with Jesus, and others from curiosity to see one who had been raised from the dead.

Many expected to hear from Lazarus a wonderful account of scenes witnessed after death. They were surprised that he told them nothing. [557-558] He had nothing of this kind to tell. Inspiration declares, "The dead know not anything. . . . Their love, and their hatred, and their envy, is now perished." Eccl. 9:5, 6. But Lazarus did have a wonderful testimony to bear in regard to the work of Christ. He had been raised from the dead for this purpose. With assurance and power he declared that

1. Simon, a Pharisee, "o_____ joined Christ's followers...[He] hoped that He might be the M_____, but had not accepted Him as a S_____." What is the difference? _____

_____

_____

_____

_____

_____

What is my response to You, Lord? _____

_____

_____

_____

Can We Walk, Together?

Jesus was the Son of God.

2. "The people were eager to see and hear Jesus... Would [He] be crowned k_____ at the Passover? The priests and rulers...and their r_____ against Jesus grew more bitter...They were fearful that Jesus had now r_____ _____ their purposes against Him, and would remain away." (558). Are there plans and agendas in my life that I don't want exposed?

_____

_____

It is liberating to come clean and be transparent before You, Lord; You read me like a book. _____

_____

_____

_____

The reports carried back to Jerusalem by the visitors to Bethany increased the excitement. The people were eager to see and hear Jesus. There was a general inquiry as to whether Lazarus would accompany Him to Jerusalem, and if the prophet would be crowned king at the Passover. The priests and rulers saw that their hold upon the people was still weakening, and their rage against Jesus grew more bitter. They could hardly wait for the opportunity of removing Him forever from their way. As time passed, they began to fear that after all He might not come to Jerusalem. They remembered how often He had baffled their murderous designs, and they were fearful that He had now read their purposes against Him, and would remain away. They could ill conceal their anxiety, and questioned among themselves, "What think ye, that He will not come to the feast?"

A council of the priests and Pharisees was called. Since the raising of Lazarus the sympathies of the people were so fully with Christ that it would be dangerous to seize upon Him openly. So the authorities determined to take Him secretly, and carry on the trial as quietly as possible. They hoped that when His condemnation became known, the fickle tide of public opinion would set in their favor.

Thus they proposed to destroy Jesus. But so long as Lazarus lived, the priests and rabbis knew that they were not secure. The very existence of a man who had been four days in the grave, and who had been restored by a word from Jesus, would sooner or later cause a reaction. The people would be avenged on their leaders for taking the life of One who could perform such a miracle. The Sanhedrin therefore decided that Lazarus also must die. To such lengths do envy and prejudice lead their slaves. The hatred and unbelief of the Jewish leaders had increased until they would even take the life of one whom infinite power had rescued from the grave.

While this plotting was going on at Jerusalem, Jesus and His friends were invited to Simon's feast. At the table the Saviour sat with Simon, whom He had cured of a loathsome disease, on one side, and Lazarus, whom He had raised from the dead, on the other. Martha served at the table, but Mary was earnestly listening to every word from the lips of [558-559] Jesus. In His mercy, Jesus had pardoned her sins, He had called forth her beloved brother from the grave, and Mary's heart was filled with gratitude. She had heard Jesus speak of His approaching death, and in her deep love and sorrow she had longed to show Him honor. At great personal sacrifice she had purchased an alabaster box of "ointment of spikenard, very costly," with which to anoint His body. But now many were declaring that He was about to be crowned king. Her grief was turned to joy, and she was eager to be first in honoring her Lord. Breaking her box of ointment, she poured its contents upon the head and feet of Jesus; then, as she knelt weeping, moistening them with her tears, she wiped His feet with her long, flowing hair.

She had sought to avoid observation, and her movements might have passed unnoticed, but the ointment filled the room with its fragrance, and published her act to all present. Judas looked upon this act with great displeasure. Instead of waiting to hear what Christ would say of the matter, he began to whisper his complaints to those near him, throwing reproach upon Christ for suffering such waste. Craftily he made suggestions that would be likely to cause disaffection.

Judas was treasurer for the disciples, and from their little store he had secretly drawn for his own use, thus narrowing down their resources to a meager pittance. He was eager to put into the bag all that he could obtain. The treasure in the bag was often drawn upon to relieve the poor; and when something that Judas did not think essential was bought, he would say, Why is this waste? why was not the cost of this put into the bag that I carry for the poor? Now the act of Mary was in such marked contrast to his selfishness that he was put to shame; and according to his custom, he sought to assign a worthy motive for his objection to her gift. Turning to the disciples, he asked, "Why was not this ointment sold for three hundred pence, and given to the poor? This he said, not that he cared for the poor; but because he was a thief, and had the bag, and bare what was put therein." Judas had no heart for the poor. Had Mary's ointment been sold, and the proceeds fallen into his possession, the poor would have received no benefit.

Judas had a high opinion of his own executive ability. As a financier he thought himself greatly superior to his fellow disciples, and he had led them to regard him in the same light. He had gained their confidence, and had a strong influence over them. His professed sympa-

3. Judas, noticed the fragrance and Mary. "Craftily he made suggestions that would be likely to cause d_____." (559). Sounds like Lucifer in heaven. Lord, what should I do if I hear similar sentiments? _____

_____

_____

_____

_____

4. "The act of Mary was of such marked c_____ _____ to his selfishness that Judas was put to s_____; and according to his custom, he sought to assign a worthy m_____ _____ for his objection to her gift." Lord, how do I play similar games?

_____

_____

_____ When I do, who is being fooled? _____

_____

_____

_____

thy for the poor deceived them, and his artful insinuation caused them to look [559-560] distrustfully upon Mary's devotion. The murmur passed round the table, "To what purpose is this waste? For this ointment might have been sold for much, and given to the poor."

5. "Mary heard the words of c_____. Her heart trembled within her...[Jesus] saw that she was embarrassed and distressed...Lifting His voice above the m_____ of criticism..." (560). When no one understands me, Lord, You do. Thank You for being my best friend:
_____
_____

The gift "gladdened His heart with the assurance of her faith and love." Lord, may I gladden Your heart with my love and faith: ____
_____
_____

Mary heard the words of criticism. Her heart trembled within her. She feared that her sister would reproach her for extravagance. The Master, too, might think her improvident. Without apology or excuse she was about to shrink away, when the voice of her Lord was heard, "Let her alone; why trouble ye her?" He saw that she was embarrassed and distressed. He knew that in this act of service she had expressed her gratitude for the forgiveness of her sins, and He brought relief to her mind. Lifting His voice above the murmur of criticism, He said, "She hath wrought a good work on Me. For ye have the poor with you always, and whensoever ye will ye may do them good: but Me ye have not always. She hath done what she could: she is come aforehand to anoint My body to the burying."

The fragrant gift which Mary had thought to lavish upon the dead body of the Saviour she poured upon His living form. At the burial its sweetness could only have pervaded the tomb; now it gladdened His heart with the assurance of her faith and love. Joseph of Arimathaea and Nicodemus offered not their gift of love to Jesus in His life. With bitter tears they brought their costly spices for His cold, unconscious form. The women who bore spices to the tomb found their errand in vain, for He had risen. But Mary, pouring out her love upon the Saviour while He was conscious of her devotion, was anointing Him for the burial. And as He went down into the darkness of His great trial, He carried with Him the memory of that deed, an earnest of the love that would be His from His redeemed ones forever.

"And as He went down into the darkness of His great trial, He c_____ with Him the memory of the deed, an e_____ ___ of the love that would be His from His redeemed ones forever." Wow! That made the gift doubly valuable! Lord, You are worthy of my best, my all! How do I give You my best?
_____
_____
_____

Many there are who bring their precious gifts for the dead. As they stand about the cold, silent form, words of love are freely spoken. Tenderness, appreciation, devotion, all are lavished upon one who sees not nor hears. Had these words been spoken when the weary spirit needed them so much, when the ear could hear and the heart could feel, how precious would have been their fragrance!

Mary knew not the full significance of her deed of love. She could not answer her accusers. She could not explain why she had chosen that occasion for anointing

Jesus. The Holy Spirit had planned for her, and she had obeyed His promptings. Inspiration stoops to give no reason. An unseen presence, it speaks to mind and soul, and moves the heart to action. It is its own justification.

Christ told Mary the meaning of her act, and in this He gave her [560-563] more than He had received. "In that she hath poured this ointment on My body," He said, "she did it for My burial." As the alabaster box was broken, and filled the whole house with its fragrance, so Christ was to die, His body was to be broken; but He was to rise from the tomb, and the fragrance of His life was to fill the earth. Christ "hath loved us, and hath given Himself for us an offering and a sacrifice to God for a sweet-smelling savor." Eph. 5:2.

"Verily I say unto you," Christ declared, "Wheresoever this gospel shall be preached throughout the whole world, this also that she hath done shall be spoken of for a memorial of her." Looking into the future, the Saviour spoke with certainty concerning His gospel. It was to be preached throughout the world. And as far as the gospel extended, Mary's gift would shed its fragrance, and hearts would be blessed through her unstudied act. Kingdoms would rise and fall; the names of monarchs and conquerors would be forgotten; but this woman's deed would be immortalized upon the pages of sacred history. Until time should be no more, that broken alabaster box would tell the story of the abundant love of God for a fallen race.

Mary's act was in marked contrast with that which Judas was about to do. What a sharp lesson Christ might have given him who had dropped the seed of criticism and evil thinking into the minds of the disciples! How justly the accuser might have been accused! He who reads the motives of every heart, and understands every action, might have opened before those at the feast dark chapters in the experience of Judas. The hollow pretense on which the traitor based his words might have been laid bare; for, instead of sympathizing with the poor, he was robbing them of the money intended for their relief. Indignation might have been excited against him for his oppression of the widow, the orphan, and the hireling. But had Christ unmasked Judas, this would have been urged as a reason for the betrayal. And though charged with being a thief, Judas would have gained sympathy, even among the disciples. The Saviour reproached

6. "As far as the gospel extended, Mary's gift would shed its f_____ ... that broken alabaster box would tell the story of the a_____ love of God for a fallen race." (563). Lord, how might my life be a fragrance to those around me, of Your amazing love? _____
_____
_____

7. "Had Christ u_____ ___ Judas, this would have been urged as a reason for the betrayal...The Savior r_____ him not, and

thus avoided giving him an e_____ for his treachery." Lord, when Mary was embarrassed, You gave her dignity. You did not unmask Judas publicly. You wrote in the sand. Thank You for Your thoughtfulness. As I encounter others today, show me how I can treat others the way You treat me: _____

_____

_____

_____

8. From the look of Jesus, Judas knew that Jesus knew, had penetrated his hypocrisy. "In commending Mary's action… Christ had rebuked Judas… Now the reproof r_____ in his heart. He determined to be revenged." (563) What "should" happen when You read my heart?

_____

_____

_____

"Judas had indulged a_____ _____ until it overpowered every good trait of his character." (564). That can't be good for my walk with You, Lord! How do I indulge?   _____

_____

_____

9. "Acts of love and reverence for Jesus are an evidence of f_____ in Him as the Son of God." How can I give You

him not, and thus avoided giving him an excuse for his treachery.

But the look which Jesus cast upon Judas convinced him that the Saviour penetrated his hypocrisy, and read his base, contemptible character. And in commending Mary's action, which had been so severely condemned, Christ had rebuked Judas. Prior to this, the Saviour had never given him a direct rebuke. Now the reproof rankled in his heart. He determined to be revenged. From the supper he went directly to [563-564] the palace of the high priest, where he found the council assembled, and he offered to betray Jesus into their hands.

The priests were greatly rejoiced. These leaders of Israel had been given the privilege of receiving Christ as their Saviour, without money and without price. But they refused the precious gift offered them in the most tender spirit of constraining love. They refused to accept that salvation which is of more value than gold, and bought their Lord for thirty pieces of silver.

Judas had indulged avarice until it overpowered every good trait of his character. He grudged the offering made to Jesus. His heart burned with envy that the Saviour should be the recipient of a gift suitable for the monarchs of the earth. For a sum far less than the box of ointment cost, he betrayed his Lord.

The disciples were not like Judas. They loved the Saviour. But they did not rightly appreciate His exalted character. Had they realized what He had done for them, they would have felt that nothing bestowed upon Him was wasted. The wise men from the East, who knew so little of Jesus, had shown a truer appreciation of the honor due Him. They brought precious gifts to the Saviour, and bowed in homage before Him when He was but a babe, and cradled in a manger.

Christ values acts of heartfelt courtesy. When anyone did Him a favor, with heavenly politeness He blessed the actor. He did not refuse the simplest flower plucked by the hand of a child, and offered to Him in love. He accepted the offerings of children, and blessed the givers, inscribing their names in the book of life. In the Scriptures, Mary's anointing of Jesus is mentioned as distinguishing her from the other Marys. Acts of love and reverence for Jesus are an evidence of faith in Him as the Son of God. And the Holy Spirit mentions, as evidences of woman's loyalty to Christ: "If she have washed the saints' feet, if she have relieved the afflicted, if she have diligently followed every good work." 1 Tim. 5:10.

Christ delighted in the earnest desire of Mary to do the will of her Lord. He accepted the wealth of pure affection which His disciples did not, would not, understand. The desire that Mary had to do this service for her Lord was of more value to Christ than all the precious ointment in the world, because it expressed her appreciation of the world's Redeemer. It was the love of Christ that constrained her. The matchless excellence of the character of Christ filled her soul. That ointment was a symbol of the heart of the giver. It was the outward demonstration of a love fed by heavenly streams until it overflowed. [564-565]

The work of Mary was just the lesson the disciples needed to show them that the expression of their love for Him would be pleasing to Christ. He had been everything to them, and they did not realize that soon they would be deprived of His presence, that soon they could offer Him no token of their gratitude for His great love. The loneliness of Christ, separated from the heavenly courts, living the life of humanity, was never understood or appreciated by the disciples as it should have been. He was often grieved because His disciples did not give Him that which He should have received from them. He knew that if they were under the influence of the heavenly angels that accompanied Him, they too would think no offering of sufficient value to declare the heart's spiritual affection.

Their afterknowledge gave them a true sense of the many things they might have done for Jesus expressive of the love and gratitude of their hearts, while they were near Him. When Jesus was no longer with them, and they felt indeed as sheep without a shepherd, they began to see how they might have shown Him attentions that would have brought gladness to His heart. They no longer cast blame upon Mary, but upon themselves. Oh, if they could have taken back their censuring, their presenting the poor as more worthy of the gift than was Christ! They felt the reproof keenly as they took from the cross the bruised body of their Lord.

The same want is evident in our world today. But few appreciate all that Christ is to them. If they did, the great love of Mary would be expressed, the anointing would be freely bestowed. The expensive ointment would not be called a waste. Nothing would be thought

acts of love and reverence? _____
_____
_____
_____

Why wouldn't the disciples understand pure affection? _____
_____ Do I?
_____

"The matchless e_____ _____ of the character of Christ filled her soul…

"When Jesus was n__ longer with them [disciples]… they began to see how they might have shown Him a_____ that would have brought gladness to His heart…They felt the r_____ keenly as they took from the cross the bruised body of their Lord….Few a___ _____all that Christ is to them." (564, 565). Lord, how can I be more aware, and bring gladness to Your heart? _____
_____
_____
_____

Nothing is too costly. No self-denial, no self-sacrifice too great: _____
_____
_____

too costly to give for Christ, no self-denial or self-sacrifice too great to be endured for His sake.

10. "In the gift of Jesus, God gave a_____ heaven." Was it a waste?

_____

Was all of heaven at risk?

_____

_____

The words spoken in indignation, "To what purpose is this waste?" brought vividly before Christ the greatest sacrifice ever made,--the gift of Himself as the propitiation for a lost world. The Lord would be so bountiful to His human family that it could not be said of Him that He could do more. In the gift of Jesus, God gave all heaven. From a human point of view, such a sacrifice was a wanton waste. To human reasoning the whole plan of salvation is a waste of mercies and resources. Self-denial and wholehearted sacrifice meet us everywhere. Well may the heavenly host look with amazement upon the human family who refuse to be uplifted and enriched with the boundless love expressed in Christ. Well may they exclaim, Why this great waste?

But the atonement for a lost world was to be full, abundant, and [565-566] complete. Christ's offering was exceedingly abundant to reach every soul that God had created. It could not be restricted so as not to exceed the number who would accept the great Gift. All men are not saved; yet the plan of redemption is not a waste because it does not accomplish all that its liberality has provided for. There must be enough and to spare.

Simon the host had been influenced by the criticism of Judas upon Mary's gift, and he was surprised at the conduct of Jesus. His Pharisaic pride was offended. He knew that many of his guests were looking upon Christ with distrust and displeasure. Simon said in his heart, "This Man, if He were a prophet, would have known who and what manner of woman this is that toucheth Him: for she is a sinner."

By curing Simon of leprosy, Christ had saved him from a living death. But now Simon questioned whether the Saviour were a prophet. Because Christ allowed this woman to approach Him, because He did not indignantly spurn her as one whose sins were too great to be forgiven, because He did not show that He realized she had fallen, Simon was tempted to think that He was not a prophet. Jesus knows nothing of this woman who is so free in her demonstrations, he thought, or He would not allow her to touch Him.

But it was Simon's ignorance of God and of Christ that led him to think as he did. He did not realize that God's Son must act in God's way, with compassion, tenderness, and mercy. Simon's way was to take no notice of Mary's penitent service. Her act of kissing Christ's feet and anointing them with ointment was exasperating to his hardheartedness. He thought that if Christ were a prophet, He would recognize sinners and rebuke them.

To this unspoken thought the Saviour answered: "Simon, I have somewhat to say unto thee. . . . There was a certain creditor which had two debtors: the one owed five hundred pence, and the other fifty. And when they had nothing to pay, he frankly forgave them both. Tell Me therefore, which of them will love him most? Simon answered and said, I suppose that he, to whom he forgave most. And He said unto him, Thou hast rightly judged."

As did Nathan with David, Christ concealed His home thrust under the veil of a parable. He threw upon His host the burden of pronouncing sentence upon himself. Simon had led into sin the woman he now despised. She had been deeply wronged by him. By the two debtors of the parable, Simon and the woman were represented. Jesus did not design to teach that different degrees of obligation should be felt by the [566-567] two persons, for each owed a debt of gratitude that never could be repaid. But Simon felt himself more righteous than Mary, and Jesus desired him to see how great his guilt really was. He would show him that his sin was greater than hers, as much greater as a debt of five hundred pence exceeds a debt of fifty pence.

Simon now began to see himself in a new light. He saw how Mary was regarded by One who was more than a prophet. He saw that with keen prophetic eye Christ read her heart of love and devotion. Shame seized upon him, and he realized that he was in the presence of One superior to himself.

"I entered into thine house," Christ continued, "thou gavest Me no water for My feet;" but with tears of repentance, prompted by love, Mary hath washed My feet, and wiped them with the hair of her head. "Thou gavest Me no kiss: but this woman," whom you despise, "since the time I came in hath not ceased to kiss My feet." Christ recounted the opportunities Simon had had to show his love for his Lord, and his appreciation of what had been done for him. Plainly, yet with delicate politeness, the Saviour assured His disciples that His heart is grieved when His children neglect to show their gratitude to Him by words and deeds of love.

The Heart Searcher read the motive that led to

11. Jesus was not ignorant of the kind of woman Mary was. But Simon was ignorant of God, His compassion, tenderness, and mercy. Mary's gift was "e_____" to Simon's hardheartedness. What about my heart, Lord? Is it hard towards Your compassion?

_____

_____

Simon was ignorant of his "debt of gratitude that never could be r_____...

Mary's action, and He saw also the spirit that prompted Simon's words. "Seest thou this woman?" He said to him. She is a sinner. "I say unto thee, Her sins, which are many, are forgiven; for she loved much: but to whom little is forgiven, the same loveth little."

Simon's coldness and neglect toward the Saviour showed how little he appreciated the mercy he had received. He had thought he honored Jesus by inviting Him to his house. But he now saw himself as he really was. While he thought himself reading his Guest, his Guest had been reading him. He saw how true Christ's judgment of him was. His religion had been a robe of Pharisaism. He had despised the compassion of Jesus. He had not recognized Him as the representative of God. While Mary was a sinner pardoned, he was a sinner unpardoned. The rigid rule of justice he had desired to enforce against her condemned him.

Simon was touched by the kindness of Jesus in not openly rebuking him before the guests. He had not been treated as he desired Mary to be treated. He saw that Jesus did not wish to expose his guilt to others, but sought by a true statement of the case to convince his mind, and by pitying kindness to subdue his heart. Stern denunciation would have hardened Simon against repentance, but patient admonition convinced [567-568] him of his error. He saw the magnitude of the debt which he owed his Lord. His pride was humbled, he repented, and the proud Pharisee became a lowly, self-sacrificing disciple.

Mary had been looked upon as a great sinner, but Christ knew the circumstances that had shaped her life. He might have extinguished every spark of hope in her soul, but He did not. It was He who had lifted her from despair and ruin. Seven times she had heard His rebuke of the demons that controlled her heart and mind. She had heard His strong cries to the Father in her behalf. She knew how offensive is sin to His unsullied purity, and in His strength she had overcome.

When to human eyes her case appeared hopeless, Christ saw in Mary capabilities for good. He saw the better traits of her character. The plan of redemption has invested humanity with great possibilities, and in Mary these possibilities were to be realized. Through His grace she became a partaker of the divine nature. The one who had fallen, and whose mind had been a habitation of demons, was brought very near to the Saviour

---

While he thought himself r_____ his Guest, his Guest had been reading him...He had d_____ ___ the compassion of Jesus." (566, 567). Lord, am I so out of harmony with Your character, that I find Your character exasperating, that I despise Your compassion to others?

_____

_____

_____ Help me Lord, to better understand the depths from which I have been delivered and forgiven, to better appreciate and value Your character: _____

_____

_____

12. "Simon was t_____ _____ by the kindness of Jesus in not openly rebuking him before the guests. He had not been treated as he d_____ __ Mary to be treated...

Through His grace, she became a p_____ of the divine nature...Jesus in fellowship and ministry. It was Mary who sat at His feet and learned of Him. It was Mary who poured upon His head the precious anointing oil, and bathed His feet with her tears. Mary stood beside the cross, and followed Him to the sepulcher. Mary was first at the tomb after His resurrection. It was Mary who first proclaimed a risen Saviour.

Jesus knows the circumstances of every soul. You may say, I am sinful, very sinful. You may be; but the worse you are, the more you need Jesus. He turns no weeping, contrite one away. He does not tell to any all that He might reveal, but He bids every trembling soul take courage. Freely will He pardon all who come to Him for forgiveness and restoration.

Christ might commission the angels of heaven to pour out the vials of His wrath on our world, to destroy those who are filled with hatred of God. He might wipe this dark spot from His universe. But He does not do this. He is today standing at the altar of incense, presenting before God the prayers of those who desire His help.

The souls that turn to Him for refuge, Jesus lifts above the accusing and the strife of tongues. No man or evil angel can impeach these souls. Christ unites them to His own divine-human nature. They stand beside the great Sin Bearer, in the light proceeding from the throne of God. "Who shall lay anything to the charge of God's elect? It is God that justifieth. Who is he that condemneth? It is Christ that died, yea rather, that is risen again, who is even at the right hand of God, who also maketh intercession for us." Rom. 8:33, 34.

knows the circumstances of e_____ soul." (567, 568). Lord, I am like the Pharisaical Simon. I want to be like the pardoned Simon. By Your grace, by beholding Your grace during this walk with You, may I become a partaker of Your character, to treat others as kindly as You do me, Simon, and Mary:

_____

_____

_____

_____

Prayer journal: _____

_____

_____

_____

_____

_____

_____

Chapter 63

"Thy King Cometh"

[This chapter is based on Matt. 21:1-11;
Mark 11:1-10; Luke 19:29-44; John 12:12-19.]

"Rejoice greatly, O daughter of Zion; shout, O daughter of Jerusalem: behold, thy King cometh unto thee: He is just, and having salvation; lowly, and riding upon an ass, and upon a colt the foal of an ass." Zech. 9:9.

Five hundred years before the birth of Christ, the prophet Zechariah thus foretold the coming of the King to Israel. This prophecy is now to be fulfilled. He who has so long refused royal honors now comes to Jerusalem as the promised heir to David's throne.

It was on the first day of the week that Christ made His triumphal entry into Jerusalem. Multitudes who had flocked to see Him at Bethany now accompanied Him, eager to witness His reception. Many people were on their way to the city to keep the Passover, and these joined the multitude attending Jesus. All nature seemed to rejoice. The trees were clothed with verdure, and their blossoms shed a delicate fragrance on the air. A new life and joy animated the people. The hope of the new kingdom was again springing up.

Purposing to ride into Jerusalem, Jesus had sent two of His disciples to bring to Him an ass and its colt. At His birth the Saviour was dependent upon the hospitality of strangers. The manger in which He lay was a borrowed resting place. Now, although the cattle on a thousand hills are His, He is dependent on a stranger's kindness for an animal on [569-570] which to enter Jerusalem as its King. But again His divinity is revealed, even in the minute directions given His disciples for this errand. As He foretold, the plea, "The Lord hath need of them," was readily granted. Jesus chose for His use the colt on which never man had sat. The disciples, with glad enthusiasm, spread their garments on the beast, and seated their Master upon it. Heretofore Jesus had always traveled on foot, and the disciples had at first wondered that He should now choose to ride. But hope brightened in their hearts with the joyous thought that He was about to enter the capital, proclaim Himself King, and assert His royal power. While on their errand they communicated their glowing expectations to the friends of Jesus, and the excitement spread far and near, raising the expectations of the people to the highest pitch.

Christ was following the Jewish custom for a royal entry. The animal on which He rode was that ridden by the kings of Israel, and prophecy had foretold that thus the Messiah should come to His kingdom. No sooner was He seated upon the colt than a loud shout of triumph rent the air. The multitude hailed Him as Messiah, their King. Jesus now accepted the homage which He had never before permitted, and the disciples received this as proof that their glad hopes were to be realized by seeing Him established on the throne. The multitude were convinced that the hour of their emancipation was at hand. In imagination they saw the Roman armies driven from Jerusalem, and Israel once more an independent nation. All were happy and excited; the people vied with one another in paying Him homage. They could not display outward pomp and splendor, but they gave Him the worship of happy hearts. They were unable to present Him with costly gifts, but they spread their outer garments as a carpet in His path, and they also strewed the leafy branches of the olive and the palm in the way. They could lead the triumphal procession with no royal standards, but they cut down the spreading palm boughs, Nature's emblem of victory, and waved them aloft with loud acclamations and hosannas.

As they proceeded, the multitude was continually increased by those who had heard of the coming of Jesus and hastened to join the procession. Spectators were constantly mingling with the throng, and asking, Who is this? What does all this commotion signify? They had all heard of Jesus, and expected Him to go to Jerusalem; but they knew that He had heretofore discouraged all effort to place Him on the throne, and they were greatly astonished to learn that this was He. They wondered what could have wrought this change in Him who had declared that His kingdom was not of this world. [570-571]

Their questionings are silenced by a shout of triumph. Again and again it is repeated by the eager throng;

1. Riding on a colt "Jesus now accepted the h_____ _____ which he had never before permitted, and the disciples received this as p_____ that their glad hopes were to be realized by seeing Him established on the throne… [The multitude] wondered what could have wrought this c_____ __ in him who had declared that his kingdom was not of t_____ world …

it is taken up by the people afar off, and echoed from the surrounding hills and valleys. And now the procession is joined by crowds from Jerusalem. From the multitudes gathered to attend the Passover, thousands go forth to welcome Jesus. They greet Him with the waving of palm branches and a burst of sacred song. The priests at the temple sound the trumpet for evening service, but there are few to respond, and the rulers say to one another in alarm. "The world is gone after Him."

Never before in His earthly life had Jesus permitted such a demonstration. He clearly foresaw the result. It would bring Him to the cross. But it was His purpose thus publicly to present Himself as the Redeemer. He desired to call attention to the sacrifice that was to crown His mission to a fallen world. While the people were assembling at Jerusalem to celebrate the Passover, He, the antitypical Lamb, by a voluntary act set Himself apart as an oblation. It would be needful for His church in all succeeding ages to make His death for the sins of the world a subject of deep thought and study. Every fact connected with it should be verified beyond a doubt. It was necessary, then, that the eyes of all people should now be directed to Him; the events which preceded His great sacrifice must be such as to call attention to the sacrifice itself. After such a demonstration as that attending His entry into Jerusalem, all eyes would follow His rapid progress to the final scene.

The events connected with this triumphal ride would be the talk of every tongue, and would bring Jesus before every mind. After His crucifixion, many would recall these events in their connection with His trial and death. They would be led to search the prophecies, and would be convinced that Jesus was the Messiah; and in all lands converts to the faith would be multiplied.

In this one triumphant scene of His earthly life, the Saviour might have appeared escorted by heavenly angels, and heralded by the trump of God; but such a demonstration would have been contrary to the purpose of His mission, contrary to the law which had governed His life. He remained true to the humble lot He had accepted. The burden of humanity He must bear until His life was given for the life of the world.

This day, which seemed to the disciples the crowning day of their lives, would have been shadowed with gloomy clouds had they known that this scene of rejoicing was but a prelude to the suffering and death of their

It was necessary, then, that the eyes of all people should now be d_____ ___ to Him." It was His purpose thus publicly to present Himself as the R_____. (570, 571). Lord, have I made Your death for my sins and the sins of the world a subject of deep thought and study? _____ Draw my attention and heart, Lord, to You, as my Redeemer:

_____
_____
_____
_____

Master. Although He had repeatedly told them of His certain [571-572] sacrifice, yet in the glad triumph of the present they forgot His sorrowful words, and looked forward to His prosperous reign on David's throne.

New accessions were made continually to the procession, and, with few exceptions, all who joined it caught the inspiration of the hour, and helped to swell the hosannas that echoed and re-echoed from hill to hill and from valley to valley. The shouts went up continually, "Hosanna to the Son of David: Blessed is He that cometh in the name of the Lord! Hosanna in the highest."

Never before had the world seen such a triumphal procession. It was not like that of the earth's famous conquerors. No train of mourning captives, as trophies of kingly valor, made a feature of that scene. But about the Saviour were the glorious trophies of His labors of love for sinful man. There were the captives whom He had rescued from Satan's power, praising God for their deliverance. The blind whom He had restored to sight were leading the way. The dumb whose tongues He had loosed shouted the loudest hosannas. The cripples whom He had healed bounded with joy, and were the most active in breaking the palm branches and waving them before the Saviour. Widows and orphans were exalting the name of Jesus for His works of mercy to them. The lepers whom He had cleansed spread their untainted garments in His path, and hailed Him as the King of glory. Those whom His voice had awakened from the sleep of death were in that throng. Lazarus, whose body had seen corruption in the grave, but who now rejoiced in the strength of glorious manhood, led the beast on which the Saviour rode.

Many Pharisees witnessed the scene, and, burning with envy and malice, sought to turn the current of popular feeling. With all their authority they tried to silence the people; but their appeals and threats only increased the enthusiasm. They feared that this multitude, in the strength of their numbers, would make Jesus king. As a last resort they pressed through the crowd to where the Saviour was, and accosted Him with reproving and threatening words: "Master, rebuke Thy disciples." They declared that such noisy demonstrations were unlawful, and would not be permitted by the authorities. But they were silenced by the reply of Jesus, "I tell you that, if these should hold their peace, the stones would imme-

2. Never before had the world seen such a t_____ _____ procession... About the Savior were the glorious t_____ of His labors of love for sinful man. There were the captives whom He had rescued from Satan's p_____." The blind, dumb, cripples, widows, orphans, lepers, and Lazarus were praising God. (572). Lord, am I Your trophy of love? _____

_____

_____

3. "Man was powerless to turn aside God's purpose. Had men failed to carry out His plan, He would have given voice to the inanimate s_____, and they would have hailed His Son with acclamation of praise." If I fail to proclaim the gospel message, the remnant message, and Your praises, will I be by-passed and an inanimate object be put to use? _____. What can I do today, to proclaim Your praise?

_____
_____
_____

4. "Jesus gazes upon the scene of the temple, and the vast multitude hush their shouts, s_____ ____ by the sudden vision of beauty." Jesus was in an a_____ of tears.

diately cry out." That scene of triumph was of God's own appointing. It had been foretold by the prophet, and man was powerless to turn aside God's purpose. Had men failed to carry out His plan, He would have given a voice to the inanimate stones, and they would have hailed His Son with acclamations of praise. As the silenced Pharisees [572-575] drew back, the words of Zechariah were taken up by hundreds of voices: "Rejoice greatly, O daughter of Zion; shout, O daughter of Jerusalem: behold, thy King cometh unto thee: He is just, and having salvation; lowly, and riding upon an ass, and upon a colt the foal of an ass."

When the procession reached the brow of the hill, and was about to descend into the city, Jesus halted, and all the multitude with Him. Before them lay Jerusalem in its glory, now bathed in the light of the declining sun. The temple attracted all eyes. In stately grandeur it towered above all else, seeming to point toward heaven as if directing the people to the only true and living God. The temple had long been the pride and glory of the Jewish nation. The Romans also prided themselves in its magnificence. A king appointed by the Romans had united with the Jews to rebuild and embellish it, and the emperor of Rome had enriched it with his gifts. Its strength, richness, and magnificence had made it one of the wonders of the world.

While the westering sun was tinting and gilding the heavens, its resplendent glory lighted up the pure white marble of the temple walls, and sparkled on its gold-capped pillars. From the crest of the hill where Jesus and His followers stood, it had the appearance of a massive structure of snow, set with golden pinnacles. At the entrance to the temple was a vine of gold and silver, with green leaves and massive clusters of grapes executed by the most skillful artists. This design represented Israel as a prosperous vine. The gold, silver, and living green were combined with rare taste and exquisite workmanship; as it twined gracefully about the white and glistening pillars, clinging with shining tendrils to their golden ornaments, it caught the splendor of the setting sun, shining as if with a glory borrowed from heaven.

Jesus gazes upon the scene, and the vast multitude hush their shouts, spellbound by the sudden vision of beauty. All eyes turn upon the Saviour, expecting to see in His countenance the admiration they themselves feel.

But instead of this they behold a cloud of sorrow. They are surprised and disappointed to see His eyes fill with tears, and His body rock to and fro like a tree before the tempest, while a wail of anguish bursts from His quivering lips, as if from the depths of a broken heart. What a sight was this for angels to behold! their loved Commander in an agony of tears! What a sight was this for the glad throng that with shouts of triumph and the waving of palm branches were escorting Him to the glorious city, where they fondly hoped He was about to reign! Jesus had wept at the grave of Lazarus, but it was in a [575-576] godlike grief in sympathy with human woe. But this sudden sorrow was like a note of wailing in a grand triumphal chorus. In the midst of a scene of rejoicing, where all were paying Him homage, Israel's King was in tears; not silent tears of gladness, but tears and groans of insuppressible agony. The multitude were struck with a sudden gloom. Their acclamations were silenced. Many wept in sympathy with a grief they could not comprehend.

The tears of Jesus were not in anticipation of His own suffering. Just before Him was Gethsemane, where soon the horror of a great darkness would overshadow Him. The sheepgate also was in sight, through which for centuries the beasts for sacrificial offerings had been led. This gate was soon to open for Him, the great Anti-type, toward whose sacrifice for the sins of the world all these offerings had pointed. Near by was Calvary, the scene of His approaching agony. Yet it was not because of these reminders of His cruel death that the Redeemer wept and groaned in anguish of spirit. His was no self-ish sorrow. The thought of His own agony did not in-timidate that noble, self-sacrificing soul. It was the sight of Jerusalem that pierced the heart of Jesus--Jerusalem that had rejected the Son of God and scorned His love, that refused to be convinced by His mighty miracles, and was about to take His life. He saw what she was in her guilt of rejecting her Redeemer, and what she might have been had she accepted Him who alone could heal her wound. He had come to save her; how could He give her up?

Israel had been a favored people; God had made their temple His habitation; it was "beautiful for situa-tion, the joy of the whole earth." Ps. 48:2. The record of more than a thousand years of Christ's guardian care and tender love, such as a father bears his only child,

"It was the sight of J_____ that pierced the heart of Jesus—Jerusalem that had rejected the Son of God and s_____ His love." (575, 576). How do I scorn Your love, Lord? _____

_____

_____

5. What might have been had Jerusalem accepted Him who alone could heal her wound? _____

_____What might it be for me, Lord, as I daily walk with You, accept You alone as my healer? _____

_____

_____

was there. In that temple the prophets had uttered their solemn warnings. There had the burning censers waved, while incense, mingled with the prayers of the worshipers, had ascended to God. There the blood of beasts had flowed, typical of the blood of Christ. There Jehovah had manifested His glory above the mercy seat. There the priests had officiated, and the pomp of symbol and ceremony had gone on for ages. But all this must have an end.

Jesus raised His hand,--that had so often blessed the sick and suffering,--and waving it toward the doomed city, in broken utterances of grief exclaimed: "If thou hadst known, even thou, at least in this thy day, the things which belong unto thy peace!--" Here the Saviour paused, and left unsaid what might have been the condition of Jerusalem [576-577] had she accepted the help that God desired to give her,--the gift of His beloved Son. If Jerusalem had known what it was her privilege to know, and had heeded the light which Heaven had sent her, she might have stood forth in the pride of prosperity, the queen of kingdoms, free in the strength of her God-given power. There would have been no armed soldiers standing at her gates, no Roman banners waving from her walls. The glorious destiny that might have blessed Jerusalem had she accepted her Redeemer rose before the Son of God. He saw that she might through Him have been healed of her grievous malady, liberated from bondage, and established as the mighty metropolis of the earth. From her walls the dove of peace would have gone forth to all nations. She would have been the world's diadem of glory.

But the bright picture of what Jerusalem might have been fades from the Saviour's sight. He realizes what she now is under the Roman yoke, bearing the frown of God, doomed to His retributive judgment. He takes up the broken thread of His lamentation: "But now they are hid from thine eyes. For the days shall come upon thee, that thine enemies shall cast a trench about thee, and compass thee round, and keep thee in on every side, and shall lay thee even with the ground, and thy children within thee; and they shall not leave in thee one stone upon another; because thou knewest not the time of thy visitation."

Christ came to save Jerusalem with her children; but Pharisaical pride, hypocrisy, jealousy, and malice had prevented Him from accomplishing His purpose.

Jesus knew the terrible retribution which would be visited upon the doomed city. He saw Jerusalem encompassed with armies, the besieged inhabitants driven to starvation and death, mothers feeding upon the dead bodies of their own children, and both parents and children snatching the last morsel of food from one another, natural affection being destroyed by the gnawing pangs of hunger. He saw that the stubbornness of the Jews, as evinced in their rejection of His salvation, would also lead them to refuse submission to the invading armies. He beheld Calvary, on which He was to be lifted up, set with crosses as thickly as forest trees. He saw the wretched inhabitants suffering torture on the rack and by crucifixion, the beautiful palaces destroyed, the temple in ruins, and of its massive walls not one stone left upon another, while the city was plowed like a field. Well might the Saviour weep in agony in view of that fearful scene.

Jerusalem had been the child of His care, and as a tender father mourns over a wayward son, so Jesus wept over the beloved city. How [577-578] can I give thee up? How can I see thee devoted to destruction? Must I let thee go to fill up the cup of thine iniquity? One soul is of such value that, in comparison with it, worlds sink into insignificance; but here was a whole nation to be lost. When the fast westering sun should pass from sight in the heavens, Jerusalem's day of grace would be ended. While the procession was halting on the brow of Olivet, it was not yet too late for Jerusalem to repent. The angel of mercy was then folding her wings to step down from the golden throne to give place to justice and swift-coming judgment. But Christ's great heart of love still pleaded for Jerusalem, that had scorned His mercies, despised His warnings, and was about to imbrue her hands in His blood. If Jerusalem would but repent, it was not yet too late. While the last rays of the setting sun were lingering on temple, tower, and pinnacle, would not some good angel lead her to the Saviour's love, and avert her doom? Beautiful and unholy city, that had stoned the prophets, that had rejected the Son of God, that was locking herself by her impenitence in fetters of bondage,--her day of mercy was almost spent!

Yet again the Spirit of God speaks to Jerusalem. Before the day is done, another testimony is borne to Christ. The voice of witness is lifted up, responding to

6. "As a tender f_____ ____ mourns over a wayward son, so Jesus wept over the beloved city." (577). Lord, how have I made You mourn and weep? _____ _____ _____

_____ Thank You for understanding and comforting parents who mourn and weep: _____

7. "How can I see thee devoted to destruction? Must I let thee go to fill up the cup of thine iniquity?... Jerusalem's day of grace would be ended...If Jerusalem would but repent, it was not yet too late...she may yet be saved." (578). Thank You, Lord, for such a wonderful picture and testimony of Your passion that You are not willing that one should perish. Lord, am I devoted to destruction, rather than to You? Show me ways that I am being like Jerusalem: _____ _____ _____ _____

8. The rulers of Jerusalem have no w_____ for the Son of God. "Who is this?" Who do I say that You are? What is my testimony of what You've done for me today? _____
_____
_____
_____

Prayer journal: _____
_____
_____
_____
_____
_____
_____
_____
_____

the call from a prophetic past. If Jerusalem will hear the call, if she will receive the Saviour who is entering her gates, she may yet be saved.

Reports have reached the rulers in Jerusalem that Jesus is approaching the city with a great concourse of people. But they have no welcome for the Son of God. In fear they go out to meet Him, hoping to disperse the throng. As the procession is about to descend the Mount of Olives, it is intercepted by the rulers. They inquire the cause of the tumultuous rejoicing. As they question, "Who is this?" the disciples, filled with the spirit of inspiration, answer this question. In eloquent strains they repeat the prophecies concerning Christ:

Adam will tell you, It is the seed of the woman that shall bruise the serpent's head.

Ask Abraham, he will tell you, It is "Melchizedek King of Salem," King of Peace. Gen. 14:18.

Jacob will tell you, He is Shiloh of the tribe of Judah.

Isaiah will tell you, "Immanuel," "Wonderful, Counselor, The mighty God, The everlasting Father, The Prince of Peace." Isa. 7:14; 9:6.

Jeremiah will tell you, The Branch of David, "the Lord our Righteousness." Jer. 23:6. [578-579]

Daniel will tell you, He is the Messiah.

Hosea will tell you, He is "the Lord God of hosts; the Lord is His memorial." Hosea 12:5.

John the Baptist will tell you, He is "the Lamb of God, which taketh away the sin of the world." John 1:29.

The great Jehovah has proclaimed from His throne, "This is My beloved Son." Matt. 3:17.

We, His disciples, declare, This is Jesus, the Messiah, the Prince of life, the Redeemer of the world.

And the prince of the powers of darkness acknowledges Him, saying, "I know Thee who Thou art, the Holy One of God." Mark 1:24.

Chapter 64

A Doomed People

[This chapter is based on Mark 11:11-14, 20, 21; Matt. 21:17-19.]

The triumphal ride of Christ into Jerusalem was the dim foreshadowing of His coming in the clouds of heaven with power and glory, amid the triumph of angels and the rejoicing of the saints. Then will be fulfilled the words of Christ to the priests and Pharisees: "Ye shall not see Me henceforth, till ye shall say, Blessed is He that cometh in the name of the Lord." Matt. 23:39. In prophetic vision Zechariah was shown that day of final triumph; and he beheld also the doom of those who at the first advent had rejected Christ: "They shall look upon Me whom they have pierced, and they shall mourn for Him, as one mourneth for his only son, and shall be in bitterness for Him, as one that is in bitterness for his first-born." Zech. 12:10. This scene Christ foresaw when He beheld the city and wept over it. In the temporal ruin of Jerusalem He saw the final destruction of that people who were guilty of the blood of the Son of God.

The disciples saw the hatred of the Jews to Christ, but they did not yet see to what it would lead. They did not yet understand the true condition of Israel, nor comprehend the retribution that was to fall upon Jerusalem. This Christ opened to them by a significant object lesson.

The last appeal to Jerusalem had been in vain. The priests and rulers had heard the prophetic voice of the past echoed by the multitude, in answer to the question, "Who is this?" but they did not accept it as [580-581] the voice of Inspiration. In anger and amazement they tried to silence the people. There were Roman officers in the throng, and to them His enemies denounced Jesus as the leader of a rebellion. They represented that He was about to take possession of the temple, and reign as king in Jerusalem.

But the calm voice of Jesus hushed for a moment the clamorous throng as He again declared that He had not come to establish a temporal rule; He should soon ascend to His Father, and His accusers would see Him

1. "Too late for their salvation they would acknowledge Him." The Roman officers, "though strangers to divine influence, were m_____ as they had never been moved before. In the calm, solemn face of Jesus they read l_____, benevolence, and quiet dignity." (581). Even those not searching, experienced something powerful. If I am sincerely searching, how much more should I be stirred, Lord?

_____

_____

_____

_____

2. "The e_____ night Jesus spent in prayer." Is my need of prayer less than Yours, Lord? _____ _____ What is lacking in my life, that I am not driven to prayer like You are? _____

_____

_____

3. "This tree in full leaf gave promise of well-developed fruit. But its appearance was d_____ _____." Cursing the fig tree seemed so unlike Jesus' ways and works. "The disciples had known Him only as the Restorer, the H_____." (581, 582). How can I be protective of Your reputation, Lord? _____

no more until He should come again in glory. Then, too late for their salvation, they would acknowledge Him. These words Jesus spoke with sadness and with singular power. The Roman officers were silenced and subdued. Their hearts, though strangers to divine influence, were moved as they had never been moved before. In the calm, solemn face of Jesus they read love, benevolence, and quiet dignity. They were stirred by a sympathy they could not understand. Instead of arresting Jesus, they were more inclined to pay Him homage. Turning upon the priests and rulers, they charged them with creating the disturbance. These leaders, chagrined and defeated, turned to the people with their complaints, and disputed angrily among themselves.

Meanwhile Jesus passed unnoticed to the temple. All was quiet there, for the scene upon Olivet had called away the people. For a short time Jesus remained at the temple, looking upon it with sorrowful eyes. Then He withdrew with His disciples, and returned to Bethany. When the people sought for Him to place Him on the throne, He was not to be found.

The entire night Jesus spent in prayer, and in the morning He came again to the temple. On the way He passed a fig orchard. He was hungry, "and seeing a fig tree afar off having leaves, He came, if haply He might find anything thereon: and when He came to it, He found nothing but leaves; for the time of figs was not yet."

It was not the season for ripe figs, except in certain localities; and on the highlands about Jerusalem it might truly be said, "The time of figs was not yet." But in the orchard to which Jesus came, one tree appeared to be in advance of all the others. It was already covered with leaves. It is the nature of the fig tree that before the leaves open, the growing fruit appears. Therefore this tree in full leaf gave promise of well-developed fruit. But its appearance was deceptive. Upon searching its branches, from the lowest bough to the topmost twig, Jesus found "nothing but leaves." It was a mass of pretentious foliage, nothing more. [581-582]

Christ uttered against it a withering curse. "No man eat fruit of thee hereafter forever," He said. The next morning, as the Saviour and His disciples were again on their way to the city, the blasted branches and drooping leaves attracted their attention. "Master," said Peter, "behold, the fig tree which Thou cursedst is withered away."

Christ's act in cursing the fig tree had astonished the disciples. It seemed to them unlike His ways and works. Often they had heard Him declare that He came not to condemn the world, but that the world through Him might be saved. They remembered His words, "The Son of man is not come to destroy men's lives, but to save them." Luke 9:56. His wonderful works had been done to restore, never to destroy. The disciples had known Him only as the Restorer, the Healer. This act stood alone. What was its purpose? they questioned.

God "delighteth in mercy." "As I live, saith the Lord God, I have no pleasure in the death of the wicked." Micah 7:18; Ezek. 33:11. To Him the work of destruction and the denunciation of judgment is a "strange work." Isa. 28:21. But it is in mercy and love that He lifts the veil from the future, and reveals to men the results of a course of sin.

The cursing of the fig tree was an acted parable. That barren tree, flaunting its pretentious foliage in the very face of Christ, was a symbol of the Jewish nation. The Saviour desired to make plain to His disciples the cause and the certainty of Israel's doom. For this purpose He invested the tree with moral qualities, and made it the expositor of divine truth. The Jews stood forth distinct from all other nations, professing [582-583] allegiance to God. They had been specially favored by Him, and they laid claim to righteousness above every other people. But they were corrupted by the love of the world and the greed of gain. They boasted of their knowledge, but they were ignorant of the requirements of God, and were full of hypocrisy. Like the barren tree, they spread their pretentious branches aloft, luxuriant in appearance, and beautiful to the eye, but they yielded "nothing but leaves." The Jewish religion, with its magnificent temple, its sacred altars, its mitered priests and impressive ceremonies, was indeed fair in outward appearance, but humility, love, and benevolence were lacking.

All the trees in the fig orchard were destitute of fruit; but the leafless trees raised no expectation, and caused no disappointment. By these trees the Gentiles were represented. They were as destitute as were the Jews of godliness; but they had not professed to serve God. They made no boastful pretensions to goodness. They were blind to the works and ways of God. With them the time of figs was not yet. They were still waiting for a

4. "The cursing of the fig tree was an a_____ parable... [The Jews] boasted of their knowledge...but...were full of hypocrisy." "Humility, l_____, and benevolence were lacking." (582, 583). If I have knowledge and understanding, Lord, but lack humility, love, and benevolence, am I not better than this tree? _____ How can I foster the right fruit?

day which would bring them light and hope. The Jews, who had received greater blessings from God, were held accountable for their abuse of these gifts. The privileges of which they boasted only increased their guilt.

Jesus had come to the fig tree hungry, to find food. So He had come to Israel, hungering to find in them the fruits of righteousness. He had lavished on them His gifts, that they might bear fruit for the blessing of the world. Every opportunity and privilege had been granted them, and in return He sought their sympathy and co-operation in His work of grace. He longed to see in them self-sacrifice and compassion, zeal for God, and a deep yearning of soul for the salvation of their fellow men. Had they kept the law of God, they would have done the same unselfish work that Christ did. But love to God and man was eclipsed by pride and self-sufficiency. They brought ruin upon themselves by refusing to minister to others. The treasures of truth which God had committed to them, they did not give to the world. In the barren tree they might read both their sin and its punishment. Withered beneath the Saviour's curse, standing forth sere and blasted, dried up by the roots, the fig tree showed what the Jewish people would be when the grace of God was removed from them. Refusing to impart blessing, they would no longer receive it. "O Israel," the Lord says, "thou hast destroyed thyself." Hosea 13:9. [583-584]

The warning is for all time. Christ's act in cursing the tree which His own power had created stands as a warning to all churches and to all Christians. No one can live the law of God without ministering to others. But there are many who do not live out Christ's merciful, unselfish life. Some who think themselves excellent Christians do not understand what constitutes service for God. They plan and study to please themselves. They act only in reference to self. Time is of value to them only as they can gather for themselves. In all the affairs of life this is their object. Not for others but for themselves do they minister. God created them to live in a world where unselfish service must be performed. He designed them to help their fellow men in every possible way. But self is so large that they cannot see anything else. They are not in touch with humanity. Those who thus live for self are like the fig tree, which made every pretension but was fruitless. They observe the forms of worship, but without repentance or faith. In profession

---

5. "They brought ruin upon t_____ by refusing to minister to others... Refusing to impart blessing, they would no longer r_____ it." How can I give Jesus "sympathy and cooperation in His work of g_____?"

_____

_____

_____ (You've given me fruit to be a blessing.)

6. "No one can live the law of God without m_____ _____ to others...In the sentence pronounced on the fig tree Christ demonstrates how h_____ in His eyes is this vain p_____. He declares that the open sinner is less guilty than is he who professes to serve God, but who bears n____ fruit to His glory." (584). What is fruit to Your glory, Lord?

_____

Do I think I live Your law, but do not? _____

_____

_____

_____

they honor the law of God, but obedience is lacking. They say, but do not. In the sentence pronounced on the fig tree Christ demonstrates how hateful in His eyes is this vain pretense. He declares that the open sinner is less guilty than is he who professes to serve God, but who bears no fruit to His glory.

The parable of the fig tree, spoken before Christ's visit to Jerusalem, had a direct connection with the lesson He taught in cursing the fruitless tree. For the barren tree of the parable the gardener pleaded, Let it alone this year, until I shall dig about it and dress it; and if it bear fruit, well; but if not, then after that thou shalt cut it down. Increased care was to be given the unfruitful tree. It was to have every advantage. But if it remained fruitless, nothing could save it from destruction. In the parable the result of the gardener's work was not foretold. It depended upon that people to whom Christ's words were spoken. They were represented by the fruitless tree, and it rested with them to decide their own destiny. Every advantage that Heaven could bestow was given them, but they did not profit by their increased blessings. By Christ's act in cursing the barren fig tree, the result was shown. They had determined their own destruction.

For more than a thousand years the Jewish nation had abused God's mercy and invited His judgments. They had rejected His warnings and slain His prophets. For these sins the people of Christ's day made themselves responsible by following the same course. In the rejection [584-587] of their present mercies and warnings lay the guilt of that generation. The fetters which the nation had for centuries been forging, the people of Christ's day were fastening upon themselves.

In every age there is given to men their day of light and privilege, a probationary time in which they may become reconciled to God. But there is a limit to this grace. Mercy may plead for years and be slighted and rejected; but there comes a time when mercy makes her last plea. The heart becomes so hardened that it ceases to respond to the Spirit of God. Then the sweet, winning voice entreats the sinner no longer, and reproofs and warnings cease.

That day had come to Jerusalem. Jesus wept in anguish over the doomed city, but He could not deliver her. He had exhausted every resource. In rejecting the warnings of God's Spirit, Israel had rejected the only

7. "There is a l_____ __ to this grace." (587). Does God lose patience?
_____
_____

"Mercy may plead for years and be slighted and r_____; but there comes a time when mercy makes her last p_____. The heart becomes so h_____ that it ceases to r_____ to the Spirit of God." Do I slight the Spirit? _____ How many layers of hardness is there on my heart? _____ Lord, You can take out my hard heart of stone, and give me a new heart of flesh. I give You permission to carry out this heart surgery. I want to hear every plea of mercy, Lord. _____
_____
_____

means of help. There was no other power by which they could be delivered.

The Jewish nation was a symbol of the people of all ages who scorn the pleadings of Infinite Love. The tears of Christ when He wept over Jerusalem were for the sins of all time. In the judgments pronounced upon Israel, those who reject the reproofs and warnings of God's Holy Spirit, may read their own condemnation.

In this generation there are many who are treading on the same ground as were the unbelieving Jews. They have witnessed the manifestation of the power of God; the Holy Spirit has spoken to their hearts; but they cling to their unbelief and resistance. God sends them warnings and reproof, but they are not willing to confess their errors, and they reject His message and His messenger. The very means He uses for their recovery becomes to them a stone of stumbling.

The prophets of God were hated by apostate Israel because through them their hidden sins were brought to light. Ahab regarded Elijah as his enemy because the prophet was faithful to rebuke the king's secret iniquities. So today the servant of Christ, the reprover of sin, meets with scorn and rebuffs. Bible truth, the religion of Christ, struggles against a strong current of moral impurity. Prejudice is even stronger in the hearts of men now than in Christ's day. Christ did not fulfill men's expectations; His life was a rebuke to their sins, and they rejected Him. So now the truth of God's word does not harmonize with men's practices and their natural inclination, and thousands reject its light. Men prompted by Satan cast doubt upon God's word, and choose to exercise [587-588] their independent judgment. They choose darkness rather than light, but they do it at the peril of their souls. Those who caviled at the words of Christ, found ever-increased cause for cavil, until they turned from the Truth and the Life. So it is now. God does not propose to remove every objection which the carnal heart may bring against His truth. To those who refuse the precious rays of light which would illuminate the darkness, the mysteries of God's word remain such forever. From them the truth is hidden. They walk blindly, and know not the ruin before them.

Christ overlooked the world and all ages from the height of Olivet; and His words are applicable to every soul who slights the pleadings of divine mercy. Scorner of His love, He addresses you today. It is "thou, even

8. "The very means He uses for their recovery becomes to them a stone of s_____ _____ … [Christ's] life was a r_____ to their sins, and they rejected Him." Does reading about Christ's life in the Bible and the Desire of Ages rebuke my sins, so I stumble in wanting to read further?

_____

How should I respond, Lord? _____

thou," who shouldest know the things that belong to thy peace. Christ is shedding bitter tears for you, who have no tears to shed for yourself. Already that fatal hardness of heart which destroyed the Pharisees is manifest in you. And every evidence of the grace of God, every ray of divine light, is either melting and subduing the soul, or confirming it in hopeless impenitence.

Christ foresaw that Jerusalem would remain obdurate and impenitent; yet all the guilt, all the consequences of rejected mercy, lay at her own door. Thus it will be with every soul who is following the same course. The Lord declares, "O Israel, thou hast destroyed thyself." "Hear, O earth: behold, I will bring evil upon this people, even the fruit of their thoughts, because they have not hearkened unto My words, nor to My law, but rejected it." Hosea 13:9; Jer. 6:19.

9. "Christ is shedding bitter tears for you...Every evidence of the grace of God, every ray of divine l_____, is either m_____ and subduing the soul, or c_____ _____ it in hopeless impenitence." (588). Lord, give me eye salve to sense every ray of light, and allow it to melt my heart and soul. May my walk with You, nearness to Your heart, peel away my heart's calloused layers, render it pliable and impressionable. Thank You for Your patient love, evidenced by Your tears. Show me what those calloused layers are:

_____

_____

Prayerjournal:_____

_____

_____

_____

_____

_____

_____

Chapter 65

The Temple Cleansed Again

[This chapter is based on Matt. 21:12-16, 23-46;
Mark 11:15-19, 27-33; 12:1-12; Luke 19:45-48; 20:1-19.]

1. "Dignitaries of the temple...so completely were they c_____ by their greed of gain that in the sight of God they were no better than t_____." Lord, You know that I have an issue with greed also, not manifested in the same way as these temple dignitaries. Still, when self is so prominent in me, greed is an extension of that. I need help to see it, and its ugly nature: _____

_____

2. "The Jews had become familiar with the offering of blood, and had almost l____ sight of the fact that it was s_____ which made n_____ all this shedding of the blood of beasts." Why was it necessary for You to die, Lord?

_____

_____

_____. You experienced my full measure of sin's consequences, that I might understand the true nature of my sin, Satan's true character, and Your character, and that I might see my deplorable situation, my need of rescue and a Savior: _____

_____

_____

At the beginning of His ministry, Christ had driven from the temple those who defiled it by their unholy traffic; and His stern and godlike demeanor had struck terror to the hearts of the scheming traders. At the close of His mission He came again to the temple, and found it still desecrated as before. The condition of things was even worse than before. The outer court of the temple was like a vast cattle yard. With the cries of the animals and the sharp chinking of coin was mingled the sound of angry altercation between traffickers, and among them were heard the voices of men in sacred office. The dignitaries of the temple were themselves engaged in buying and selling and the exchange of money. So completely were they controlled by their greed of gain that in the sight of God they were no better than thieves.

Little did the priests and rulers realize the solemnity of the work which it was theirs to perform. At every Passover and Feast of Tabernacles, thousands of animals were slain, and their blood was caught by the priests and poured upon the altar. The Jews had become familiar with the offering of blood, and had almost lost sight of the fact that it was sin which made necessary all this shedding of the blood of beasts. They did not discern that it prefigured the blood of God's dear Son, [589-590] which was to be shed for the life of the world, and that by the offering of sacrifices men were to be directed to a crucified Redeemer.

Jesus looked upon the innocent victims of sacrifice, and saw how the Jews had made these great convocations scenes of bloodshed and cruelty. In place of humble repentance of sin, they had multiplied the sacrifice of beasts, as if God could be honored by a heartless service. The priests and rulers had hardened their hearts through selfishness and avarice. The very symbols pointing to the Lamb of God they had made a means of getting gain. Thus in the eyes of the people the sacredness of the sacrificial service had been in a great measure destroyed. The indignation of Jesus was stirred; He knew that His blood, so soon to be shed for the sins of the world, would be as little appreciated by the priests and elders as was the blood of beasts which they kept incessantly flowing.

Against these practices Christ had spoken through the prophets. Samuel had said, "Hath the Lord as great delight in burnt offerings and sacrifices, as in obeying the voice of the Lord? Behold, to obey is better than sacrifice, and to hearken than the fat of rams." And Isaiah, seeing in prophetic vision the apostasy of the Jews, addressed them as rulers of Sodom and Gomorrah: "Hear the word of the Lord, ye rulers of Sodom; give ear unto the law of our God, ye people of Gomorrah. To what purpose is the multitude of your sacrifices unto Me? saith the Lord: I am full of the burnt offerings of rams, and the fat of fed beasts; and I delight not in the blood of bullocks, or of lambs, or of he-goats. When ye come to appear before Me, who hath required this at your hand, to tread My courts?" "Wash you, make you clean; put away the evil of your doings from before Mine eyes; cease to do evil; learn to do well; seek judgment, relieve the oppressed, judge the fatherless, plead for the widow." 1 Sam. 15:22; Isa. 1:10-12, 16,17.

He who had Himself given these prophecies now for the last time repeated the warning. In fulfillment of prophecy the people had proclaimed Jesus king of Israel. He had received their homage, and accepted the office of king. In this character He must act. He knew that His efforts to reform a corrupt priesthood would be in vain; nevertheless His work must be done; to an unbelieving people the evidence of His divine mission must be given.

Again the piercing look of Jesus swept over the desecrated court of the temple. All eyes were turned toward Him. Priest and ruler, Pharisee [590-591] and Gentile, looked with astonishment and awe upon Him who stood before them with the majesty of heaven's King. Divinity flashed through humanity, investing Christ with a dignity and glory He had never manifested before. Those standing nearest Him drew as far away as the crowd would permit. Except for a few of His disciples, the Saviour stood alone. Every sound was hushed. The deep silence seemed unbearable. Christ spoke with a power that swayed the people like a mighty tempest: "It is written, My house shall be called the house of prayer;

3. "The i_____ ___ of Jesus was stirred; He new that His blood, so soon to be shed for the sins of the world, would be as l_____ appreciated by the priests and the elders as was the blood of the beasts which they kept i_____ _____ flowing." (590). How much have I appreciated Your sacrificial death, Lord? How much thought have I given to it, and what impact does it have on me?

_____
_____
_____
_____

4. "Divinity flashed through humanity, investing Christ with a dignity and g_____ __ He had never manifested before. Those standing nearest Him stood as f_____ away as the crowd would permit...

The displeasure of His countenance seemed like a c_____ fire." (591). How is this scene similar to the cleansing fire at the end? _____

_____

_____

Those who don't know Your glory, are out of harmony with it, will ask the rocks to hide them from You. O Lord, help me to know Your holy character, to be comfortable in Your presence now, and not itching to get as far away as possible: _____

_____

_____

_____

but ye have made it a den of thieves." His voice sounded like a trumpet through the temple. The displeasure of His countenance seemed like consuming fire. With authority He commanded, "Take these things hence." John 2:16.

Three years before, the rulers of the temple had been ashamed of their flight before the command of Jesus. They had since wondered at their own fears, and their unquestioning obedience to a single humble [591-592] Man. They had felt that it was impossible for their undignified surrender to be repeated. Yet they were now more terrified than before, and in greater haste to obey His command. There were none who dared question His authority. Priests and traders fled from His presence, driving their cattle before them.

On the way from the temple they were met by a throng who came with their sick inquiring for the Great Healer. The report given by the fleeing people caused some of these to turn back. They feared to meet One so powerful, whose very look had driven the priests and rulers from His presence. But a large number pressed through the hurrying crowd, eager to reach Him who was their only hope. When the multitude fled from the temple, many had remained behind. These were now joined by the newcomers. Again the temple court was filled by the sick and the dying, and once more Jesus ministered to them.

After a season the priests and rulers ventured back to the temple. When the panic had abated, they were seized with anxiety to know what would be the next movement of Jesus. They expected Him to take the throne of David. Quietly returning to the temple, they heard the voices of men, women, and children praising God. Upon entering, they stood transfixed before the wonderful scene. They saw the sick healed, the blind restored to sight, and deaf receive their hearing, and the crippled leap for joy. The children were foremost in the rejoicing. Jesus had healed their maladies; He had clasped them in His arms, received their kisses of grateful affection, and some of them had fallen asleep upon His breast as He was teaching the people. Now with glad voices the children sounded His praise. They repeated the hosannas of the day before, and waved palm branches triumphantly before the Saviour. The temple echoed and re-echoed with their acclamations, "Blessed be He that cometh in the name of the Lord!" "Behold, thy King cometh unto thee; He is just, and having salvation!" Ps. 118:26; Zech. 9:9. "Hosanna to the Son of David!"

The sound of these happy, unrestrained voices was an offense to the rulers of the temple. They set about putting a stop to such demonstrations. They represented to the people that the house of God was desecrated by the feet of the children and the shouts of rejoicing. Finding that their words made no impression on the people, the rulers appealed to Christ: "Hearest Thou what these say? And Jesus saith unto them, Yea; have ye never read, Out of the mouth of babes and sucklings [592-593] Thou hast perfected praise?" Prophecy had foretold that Christ should be proclaimed as king, and that word must be fulfilled. The priests and rulers of Israel refused to herald His glory, and God moved upon the children to be His witnesses. Had the voices of the children been silent, the very pillars of the temple would have sounded the Saviour's praise.

The Pharisees were utterly perplexed and disconcerted. One whom they could not intimidate was in command. Jesus had taken His position as guardian of the temple. Never before had He assumed such kingly authority. Never before had His words and works possessed so great power. He had done marvelous works throughout Jerusalem, but never before in a manner so solemn and impressive. In presence of the people who had witnessed His wonderful works, the priests and rulers dared not show Him open hostility. Though enraged and confounded by His answer, they were unable to accomplish anything further that day.

The next morning the Sanhedrin again considered what course to pursue toward Jesus. Three years before, they had demanded a sign of His Messiahship. Since that time He had wrought mighty works throughout the land. He had healed the sick, miraculously fed thousands of people, walked upon the waves, and spoken peace to the troubled sea. He had repeatedly read the hearts of men as an open book; He had cast out demons, and raised the dead. The rulers had before them the evidences of His Messiahship. They now decided to demand no sign of His authority, but to draw out some admission or declaration by which He might be condemned.

Repairing to the temple where He was teaching, they proceeded to question Him: "By what authority

5. "The sound of these happy, unrestrained voices was an o_____ to the rulers of the temple." (592). Why, Lord? Why are some praising You, and others are offended by the praise?

_____

_____

_____

doest Thou these things? and who gave Thee this authority?" They expected Him to claim that His authority was from God. Such an assertion they intended to deny. But Jesus met them with a question apparently pertaining to another subject, and He made His reply to them conditional on their answering this question. "The baptism of John," He said, "whence was it? from heaven, or of men?"

The priests saw that they were in a dilemma from which no sophistry could extricate them. If they said that John's baptism was from heaven, their inconsistency would be made apparent. Christ would say, Why have ye not then believed on him? John had testified of Christ, "Behold [593-594] the Lamb of God, which taketh away the sin of the world." John 1:29. If the priests believed John's testimony, how could they deny the Messiahship of Christ? If they declared their real belief, that John's ministry was of men, they would bring upon themselves a storm of indignation; for the people believed John to be a prophet.

With intense interest the multitude awaited the decision. They knew that the priests had professed to accept the ministry of John, and they expected them to acknowledge without a question that he was sent from God. But after conferring secretly together, the priests decided not to commit themselves. Hypocritically professing ignorance, they said, "We cannot tell." "Neither tell I you," said Christ, "by what authority I do these things."

Scribes, priests, and rulers were all silenced. Baffled and disappointed, they stood with lowering brows, not daring to press further questions upon Christ. By their cowardice and indecision they had in a great measure forfeited the respect of the people, who now stood by, amused to see these proud, self-righteous men defeated.

All these sayings and doings of Christ were important, and their influence was to be felt in an ever-increasing degree after His crucifixion and ascension. Many of those who had anxiously awaited the result of the questioning of Jesus were finally to become His disciples, first drawn toward Him by His words on that eventful day. The scene in the temple court was never to fade from their minds. The contrast between Jesus and the high priest as they talked together was marked. The proud dignitary of the temple was clothed in rich and

6. "Many of those who had anxiously awaited the result of the questioning of Jesus were finally to become His disciples, first d_____ toward Him by His words on that eventful day...The c_____ between Jesus and the high priest as they talked together was marked." (594). What was the difference? ____

_____
_____
_____What impresses me, about You, Lord? What draws me?
_____
_____
_____

costly garments. Upon his head was a glittering tiara. His bearing was majestic, his hair and his long flowing beard were silvered by age. His appearance awed the beholders. Before this august personage stood the Majesty of heaven, without adornment or display. His garments were travel stained; His face was pale, and expressed a patient sadness; yet written there were dignity and benevolence that contrasted strangely with the proud, self-confident, and angry air of the high priest. Many of those who witnessed the words and deeds of Jesus in the temple from that time enshrined Him in their hearts as a prophet of God. But as the popular feeling turned in His favor, the hatred of the priests toward Jesus increased. The wisdom by which He escaped the snares set for His feet, being a new evidence of His divinity, added fuel to their wrath.

In His contest with the rabbis, it was not Christ's purpose to humiliate His opponents. He was not glad to see them in a hard place. He had [594-595] an important lesson to teach. He had mortified His enemies by allowing them to be entangled in the net they had spread for Him. Their acknowledged ignorance in regard to the character of John's baptism gave Him an opportunity to speak, and He improved the opportunity by presenting before them their real position, adding another warning to the many already given.

"What think ye?" He said. "A certain man had two sons; and he came to the first, and said, Son, go work today in my vineyard. He answered and said, I will not: but afterward he repented, and went. And he came to the second, and said likewise. And he answered and said, I go, sir: and went not. Whether of them twain did the will of his father?"

This abrupt question threw His hearers off their guard. They had followed the parable closely, and now immediately answered, "The first." Fixing His steady eye upon them, Jesus responded in stern and solemn tones: "Verily I say unto you, That the publicans and the harlots go into the kingdom of God before you. For John came unto you in the way of righteousness, and ye believed him not: but the publicans and the harlots believed him: and ye, when ye had seen it, repented not afterward, that ye might believe him."

The priests and rulers could not but give a correct answer to Christ's question, and thus He obtained their opinion in favor of the first son. This son represented the publicans, those who were despised and hated by the Pharisees. The publicans had been grossly immoral. They had indeed been transgressors of the law of God, showing in their lives an absolute resistance to His requirements. They had been unthankful and unholy; when told to go and work in the Lord's vineyard, they had given a contemptuous refusal. But when John came, preaching repentance and baptism, the publicans received his message and were baptized.

The second son represented the leading men of the Jewish nation. Some of the Pharisees had repented and received the baptism of John; but the leaders would not acknowledge that he came from God. His warnings and denunciations did not lead them to reformation. They "rejected the counsel of God against themselves, being not baptized of him." Luke 7:30. They treated his message with disdain. Like the second son, who, when called, said, "I go, sir," but went not, the priests and rulers professed obedience, but acted disobedience. They made great professions of piety, they claimed to be obeying the law of God, but they rendered only a false obedience. The publicans were denounced and cursed by the Pharisees as infidels; but they showed by their faith and works that [595-596] they were going into the kingdom of heaven before those self-righteous men who had been given great light, but whose works did not correspond to their profession of godliness.

The priests and rulers were unwilling to bear these searching truths; they remained silent, however, hoping that Jesus would say something which they could turn against Him; but they had still more to bear.

"Hear another parable," Christ said: "There was a certain householder, which planted a vineyard, and hedged it round about, and digged a wine press in it, and built a tower, and let it out to husbandmen, and went into a far country: and when the time of the fruit drew near, he sent his servants to the husbandmen, that they might receive the fruits of it. And the husbandmen took his servants, and beat one, and killed another, and stoned another. Again, he sent other servants more than the first: and they did unto them likewise. But last of all he sent unto them his son, saying, They will reverence my son. But when the husbandmen saw the son, they said among themselves, This is the heir; come, let us kill him, and let us seize on his inheritance. And they caught him, and cast him out of the vineyard, and slew

7. "Like the second son, who said, "I go, sir," but went not, the priests and rulers... made great profession of p_____, they claimed to be obeying the law of God, but they rendered only a false obedience." (595). Lord, what is false obedience? Is that what I offer You? _____

_____

_____

him. When the lord therefore of the vineyard cometh, what will he do unto those husbandmen?"

Jesus addressed all the people present; but the priests and rulers answered. "He will miserably destroy those wicked men," they said, "and will let out his vineyard unto other husbandmen, which shall render him the fruits in their seasons." The speakers had not at first perceived the application of the parable, but they now saw that they had pronounced their own condemnation. In the parable the householder represented God, the vineyard the Jewish nation, and the hedge the divine law which was their protection. The tower was a symbol of the temple. The lord of the vineyard had done everything needful for its prosperity. "What could have been done more to my vineyard," he says, "that I have not done in it." Isa. 5:4. Thus was represented God's unwearied care for Israel. And as the husbandmen were to return to the lord a due proportion of the fruits of the vineyard, so God's people were to honor Him by a life corresponding to their sacred privileges. But as the husbandmen had killed the servants whom the master sent to them for fruit, so the Jews had put to death the prophets whom God sent to call them to repentance. Messenger after messenger had been slain. Thus far the application of the parable could not be questioned, and in what followed it was not less evident. In the beloved son whom the lord of the vineyard finally sent to his disobedient servants, and whom they [596-597] seized and slew, the priests and rulers saw a distinct picture of Jesus and His impending fate. Already they were planning to slay Him whom the Father had sent to them as a last appeal. In the retribution inflicted upon the ungrateful husbandmen was portrayed the doom of those who should put Christ to death.

Looking with pity upon them, the Saviour continued, "Did ye never read in the Scriptures, The stone which the builders rejected, the same is become the head of the corner: this is the Lord's doing, and it is marvelous in our eyes? Therefore say I unto you, The kingdom of God shall be taken from you, and given to a nation bringing forth the fruits thereof. And whosoever shall fall on this stone shall be broken: but on whomsoever it shall fall, it will grind him to powder."

This prophecy the Jews had often repeated in the synagogues, applying it to the coming Messiah. Christ was the cornerstone of the Jewish economy, and of

8. The priests and rulers "had not at first p_____ _____ the application of the parable [of the husbandman], but they now saw that they had pronounced their o_____ condemnation...Already they were planning to s_____ Him." (596, 597). Lord, You had Nathan use a story to have king David render his own verdict. I guess I am the same way. Why don't I see it before the story? How does Satan blind me to my faults, my true character? _____
_____
_____
_____

the whole plan of salvation. This foundation stone the Jewish builders, the priests and rulers of Israel, were now rejecting. The Saviour called their attention to the prophecies that would show them their danger. By every means in His power He sought to make plain to them the nature of the deed they were about to do.

And His words had another purpose. In asking the question, "When the lord therefore of the vineyard cometh, what will he do unto those husbandmen?" Christ designed that the Pharisees should answer as they did. He designed that they should condemn themselves. His warnings, failing to arouse them to repentance, would seal their doom, and He wished them to see that they had brought ruin on themselves. He designed to show them the justice of God in the withdrawal of their national privileges, which had already begun, and which would end, not only in the destruction of their temple and their city, but in the dispersion of the nation.

The hearers recognized the warning. But notwithstanding the sentence they themselves had pronounced, the priests and rulers were ready to fill out the picture by saying, "This is the heir; come, let us kill him." "But when they sought to lay hands on Him, they feared the multitude," for the public sentiment was in Christ's favor.

In quoting the prophecy of the rejected stone, Christ referred to an actual occurrence in the history of Israel. The incident was connected with the building of the first temple. While it had a special application at the time of Christ's first advent, and should have appealed with special force to the Jews, it has also a lesson for us. When the temple of Solomon [597-598] was erected, the immense stones for the walls and the foundation were entirely prepared at the quarry; after they were brought to the place of building, not an instrument was to be used upon them; the workmen had only to place them in position. For use in the foundation, one stone of unusual size and peculiar shape had been brought; but the workmen could find no place for it, and would not accept it. It was an annoyance to them as it lay unused in their way. Long it remained a rejected stone. But when the builders came to the laying of the corner, they searched for a long time to find a stone of sufficient size and strength, and of the proper shape, to take that particular place, and bear the great weight which would rest upon it. Should they make an unwise choice

9. Jesus "designed that they [the Pharisees] should condemn t_____. His warnings, failing to arouse them to repentance, would seal their doom, and He wished them to see that they had b_____ ruin on t_____."

for this important place, the safety of the entire building would be endangered. They must find a stone capable of resisting the influence of the sun, of frost, and of tempest. Several stones had at different times been chosen, but under the pressure of immense weights they had crumbled to pieces. Others could not bear the test of the sudden atmospheric changes. But at last attention was called to the stone so long rejected. It had been exposed to the air, to sun and storm, without revealing the slightest crack. The builders examined this stone. It had borne every test but one. If it could bear the test of severe pressure, they decided to accept it for the cornerstone. The trial was made. The stone was accepted, brought to its assigned position, and found to be an exact fit. In prophetic vision, Isaiah was shown that this stone was a symbol of Christ. He says:

"Sanctify the Lord of hosts Himself; and let Him be your fear, and let Him be your dread. And He shall be for a sanctuary; but for a stone of stumbling and for a rock of offense to both the houses of Israel, for a gin and for a snare to the inhabitants of Jerusalem. And many among them shall stumble, and fall, and be broken, and be snared, and be taken." Carried down in prophetic vision to the first advent, the prophet is shown that Christ is to bear trials and tests of which the treatment of the chief cornerstone in the temple of Solomon was symbolic. "Therefore thus saith the Lord God, Behold, I lay in Zion for a foundation a stone, a tried stone, a precious cornerstone, a sure foundation: he that believeth shall not make haste." Isa. 8:13-15; 28:16.

In infinite wisdom, God chose the foundation stone, and laid it Himself. He called it "a sure foundation." The entire world may lay upon it their burdens and griefs; it can endure them all. With perfect safety they may build upon it. Christ is a "tried stone." Those who trust in Him, He never disappoints. He has borne every test. He has endured the pressure [598-599] of Adam's guilt, and the guilt of his posterity, and has come off more than conqueror of the powers of evil. He has borne the burdens cast upon Him by every repenting sinner. In Christ the guilty heart has found relief. He is the sure foundation. All who make Him their dependence rest in perfect security.

In Isaiah's prophecy, Christ is declared to be both a sure foundation and a stone of stumbling. The apostle Peter, writing by inspiration of the Holy Spirit, clearly

10. "Christ is a 'tried stone.' Those who trust in Him, He n_____ disappoints." (598).

shows to whom Christ is a foundation stone, and to whom a rock of offense:

"If so be ye have tasted that the Lord is gracious. To whom coming, as unto a living stone, disallowed indeed of men, but chosen of God, and precious, ye also, as lively stones, are built up a spiritual house, an holy priesthood, to offer up spiritual sacrifices, acceptable to God by Jesus Christ. Wherefore also it is contained in the Scripture, Behold, I lay in Sion a chief cornerstone, elect, precious: and he that believeth on Him shall not be confounded. Unto you therefore which believe He is precious: but unto them which be disobedient, the stone which the builders disallowed, the same is made the head of the corner, and a stone of stumbling, and a rock of offense, even to them which stumble at the word, being disobedient." 1 Peter 2:3-8.

To those who believe, Christ is the sure foundation. These are they who fall upon the Rock and are broken. Submission to Christ and faith in Him are here represented. To fall upon the Rock and be broken is to give up our self-righteousness and to go to Christ with the humility of a child, repenting of our transgressions, and believing in His forgiving love. And so also it is by faith and obedience that we build on Christ as our foundation.

Upon this living stone, Jews and Gentiles alike may build. This is the only foundation upon which we may securely build. It is broad enough for all, and strong enough to sustain the weight and burden of the whole world. And by connection with Christ, the living stone, all who build upon this foundation become living stones. Many persons are by their own endeavors hewn, polished, and beautified; but they cannot become "living stones," because they are not connected with Christ. Without this connection, no man can be saved. Without the life of Christ in us, we cannot withstand the storms of temptation. Our eternal safety depends upon our building upon the sure foundation. Multitudes are today building upon foundations that have not been tested. When the rain falls, and the tempest rages, and the floods come, [599-600] their house will fall, because it is not founded upon the eternal Rock, the chief cornerstone Christ Jesus.

"To them which stumble at the word, being disobedient," Christ is a rock of offense. But "the stone which the builders disallowed, the same is made the

"To fall upon the Rock and be broken is to give u__ our self-righteousness...believing in His forgiving love." (599). Lord, what does it take to learn the lesson of my own unreliability, and Your absolute reliability? I want to be broken. Give me the experiences that will break me: _____
_____
_____
_____

head of the corner." Like the rejected stone, Christ in His earthly mission had borne neglect and abuse. He was "despised and rejected of men; a man of sorrows, and acquainted with grief: . . . He was despised, and we esteemed Him not." Isa. 53:3. But the time was near when He would be glorified. By the resurrection from the dead He would be declared "the Son of God with power." Rom. 1:4. At His second coming He would be revealed as Lord of heaven and earth. Those who were now about to crucify Him would recognize His greatness. Before the universe the rejected stone would become the head of the corner.

And on "whomsoever it shall fall, it will grind him to powder." The people who rejected Christ were soon to see their city and their nation destroyed. Their glory would be broken, and scattered as the dust before the wind. And what was it that destroyed the Jews? It was the rock which, had they built upon it, would have been their security. It was the goodness of God despised, the righteousness spurned, the mercy slighted. Men set themselves in opposition to God, and all that would have been their salvation was turned to their destruction. All that God ordained unto life they found to be unto death. In the Jews' crucifixion of Christ was involved the destruction of Jerusalem. The blood shed upon Calvary was the weight that sank them to ruin for this world and for the world to come. So it will be in the great final day, when judgment shall fall upon the rejecters of God's grace. Christ, their rock of offense, will then appear to them as an avenging mountain. The glory of His countenance, which to the righteous is life, will be to the wicked a consuming fire. Because of love rejected, grace despised, the sinner will be destroyed.

By many illustrations and repeated warnings, Jesus showed what would be the result to the Jews of rejecting the Son of God. In these words He was addressing all in every age who refuse to receive Him as their Redeemer. Every warning is for them. The desecrated temple, the disobedient son, the false husbandmen, the contemptuous builders, have their counterpart in the experience of every sinner. Unless he repent, the doom which they foreshadowed will be his.

11. Rock of offense or stumbling stone: "all that would have been their s_____ was turned to their destruction. All that God ordained unto l_____ they found to be unto death...The glory of His countenance, which to the righteous is l_____ ___, will be to the wicked a consuming f_____." (600). Stumbling Stone - Rock of Offense, or Sure Foundation? Every appeal, every warning is for me. How do I respond?

_____

_____

_____

___ "It was the goodness of God d_____, the righteousness spurned, the mercy slighted... Because of love r_____ __, grace despised." How much do I appreciate You, Lord, Your presence and Your character? _____

_____

_____

Prayer journal: _____

_____

_____

_____

_____

_____

_____

Chapter 66

Controversy

[This chapter is based on Matt. 22:15-46;
Mark 12:13-40; Luke 20:20-47.]

1. The priests and rulers sent to Jesus spies, "which should f_____ them-selves just men," that they might entrap Him. Lord, help me to be real and authentic: in a group prayer, do I put on airs, feigning myself a just person?

Do I act shocked at some gossip, feigning myself a just person, more righteous than the subject of the gossip? How about when correcting or counseling my children? _____

2. "Those who put the question to Jesus [lawful to give tribute to Caesar?] thought that they had sufficiently d_____ their purpose." (602). Is

The priests and rulers had listened in silence to Christ's pointed rebukes. They could not refute His charges. But they were only the more determined to entrap Him, and with this object they sent to Him spies, "which should feign themselves just men, that they might take hold of His words, that so they might deliver Him unto the power and authority of the governor." They did not send the old Pharisees whom Jesus had often met, but young men, who were ardent and zealous, and whom, they thought, Christ did not know. These were accompanied by certain of the Herodians, who were to hear Christ's words, that they might testify against Him at His trial. The Pharisees and Herodians had been bitter enemies, but they were now one in enmity to Christ.

The Pharisees had ever chafed under the exaction of tribute by the Romans. The payment of tribute they held to be contrary to the law of God. Now they saw opportunity to lay a snare for Jesus. The spies came to Him, and with apparent sincerity, as though desiring to know their duty, said, "Master, we know that Thou sayest and teachest rightly, neither acceptest Thou the person of any, but teachest the way of God truly: is it lawful for us to give tribute unto Caesar, or no?" [601-602]

The words, "We know that Thou sayest and teachest rightly," had they been sincere, would have been a wonderful admission. But they were spoken to deceive; nevertheless their testimony was true. The Pharisees did know that Christ said and taught rightly, and by their own testimony will they be judged.

Those who put the question to Jesus thought that they had sufficiently disguised their purpose; but Jesus read their hearts as an open book, and sounded their hypocrisy. "Why tempt ye Me?" He said; thus giving them a sign they had not asked, by showing that He read their hidden purpose. They were still more confused when He added, "Show Me a penny." They brought it, and He asked them, "Whose image and superscription hath it? They answered and said, Caesar's." Pointing to the inscription on the coin, Jesus said, "Render therefore unto Caesar the things which are Caesar's; and unto God the things that are God's."

The spies had expected Jesus to answer their question directly, in one way or the other. If He should say, It is unlawful to give tribute to Caesar, He would be reported to the Roman authorities and arrested for inciting rebellion. But in case He should pronounce it lawful to pay the tribute, they designed to accuse Him to the people as opposing the law of God. Now they felt themselves baffled and defeated. Their plans were disarranged. The summary manner in which their question had been settled left them nothing further to say.

Christ's reply was no evasion, but a candid answer to the question. Holding in His hand the Roman coin, upon which were stamped the name and image of Caesar, He declared that since they were living under the protection of the Roman power, they should render to that power the support it claimed, so long as this did not conflict with a higher duty. But while peaceably subject to the laws of the land, they should at all times give their first allegiance to God.

The Saviour's words, "Render . . . unto God the things that are God's," were a severe rebuke to the intriguing Jews. Had they faithfully fulfilled their obligations to God, they would not have become a broken nation, subject to a foreign power. No Roman ensign would have waved over Jerusalem, no Roman sentinel would have stood at her gates, no Roman governor would have ruled within her walls. The Jewish nation was then paying the penalty of its apostasy from God.

When the Pharisees heard Christ's answer, "they marveled, and left Him, and went their way." He had rebuked their hypocrisy and presumption, [602-603] and in doing this He had stated a great principle, a principle that clearly defines the limits of man's duty to the civil government and his duty to God. In many minds a vexed question had been settled. Ever after they held to the right principle. And although many went away dissatisfied, they saw that the principle underlying the question had been clearly set forth, and they marveled at Christ's far-seeing discernment.

No sooner were the Pharisees silenced than the Sadducees came forward with their artful questions. The

"sufficient" even possible with You Lord? _____

_____ There is no hiding anything from You. You know my thoughts, my heart, my moods better than I do. Why do I even try pretending? _____

_____

_____

3. Jesus "stated a great principle, a principle that clearly defines the limits of man's d_____ to the civil government, and his duty to G_____." (603) The principle being: render to that power the s_____ it claimed, so long as this did not c_____ with a higher duty. (602). Lord, in showing support to a neighbor, how do I sometimes compromise my integrity with You? _____

_____

two parties stood in bitter opposition to each other. The Pharisees were rigid adherents to tradition. They were exact in outward ceremonies, diligent in washings, fastings, and long prayers, and ostentatious in almsgiving. But Christ declared that they made void the law of God by teaching for doctrines the commandments of men. As a class they were bigoted and hypocritical; yet among them were persons of genuine piety, who accepted Christ's teachings and became His disciples. The Sadducees rejected the traditions of the Pharisees. They professed to believe the greater portion of the Scriptures, and to regard them as the rule of action; but practically they were skeptics and materialists.

The Sadducees denied the existence of angels, the resurrection of the dead, and the doctrine of a future life, with its rewards and punishments. On all these points they differed with the Pharisees. Between the two parties the resurrection was especially a subject of controversy. The Pharisees had been firm believers in the resurrection, but in these discussions [603-604] their views in regard to the future state became confused. Death became to them an inexplicable mystery. Their inability to meet the arguments of the Sadducees gave rise to continual irritation. The discussions between the two parties usually resulted in angry disputes, leaving them farther apart than before.

In numbers the Sadducees fell far below their opponents, and they had not so strong a hold upon the common people; but many of them were wealthy, and they had the influence which wealth imparts. In their ranks were included most of the priests, and from among them the high priest was usually chosen. This was, however, with the express stipulation that their skeptical opinions should not be made prominent. On account of the numbers and popularity of the Pharisees, it was necessary for the Sadducees to concede outwardly to their doctrines when holding any priestly office; but the very fact that they were eligible to such office gave influence to their errors.

The Sadducees rejected the teaching of Jesus; He was animated by a spirit which they would not acknowledge as manifesting itself thus; and His teaching in regard to God and the future life contradicted their theories. They believed in God as the only being superior to man; but they argued that an overruling providence and a divine foresight would deprive man of free moral

4. The Sadducees did not believe in the resurrection. "The Pharisees had been firm believers in the resurrection, but in these discussions their views in regard to the future state became c_____...[The Sadducees believed] that, having created man, God had l_____ him to himself, independent of a h_____ influence...Their ideas of God m_____ their own character." (603, 604). Lord, I am grateful for Your higher influence, through Your Spirit and the angels. This doesn't make me a slave, depriving me of free moral agency. Lord, may I not be confused; help my beliefs and values to be clearly based on Scriptures, that they lead to a belief in You. And may I help others to have the same

agency, and degrade him to the position of a slave. It was their belief, that, having created man, God had left him to himself, independent of a higher influence. They held that man was free to control his own life and to shape the events of the world; that his destiny was in his own hands. They denied that the Spirit of God works through human efforts or natural means. Yet they still held that, through the proper employment of his natural powers, man could become elevated and enlightened; that by rigorous and austere exactions his life could be purified.

Their ideas of God molded their own character. As in their view He had no interest in man, so they had little regard for one another; there was little union among them. Refusing to acknowledge the influence of the Holy Spirit upon human action, they lacked His power in their lives. Like the rest of the Jews, they boasted much of their birthright as children of Abraham, and of their strict adherence to the requirements of the law; but of the true spirit of the law and the faith and benevolence of Abraham, they were destitute. Their natural sympathies were brought within a narrow compass. They believed it possible for all men to secure [604-605] the comforts and blessings of life; and their hearts were not touched by the wants and sufferings of others. They lived for themselves.

By His words and His works, Christ testified to a divine power that produces supernatural results, to a future life beyond the present, to God as a Father of the children of men, ever watchful of their true interests. He revealed the working of divine power in benevolence and compassion that rebuked the selfish exclusiveness of the Sadducees. He taught that both for man's temporal and for his eternal good, God moves upon the heart by the Holy Spirit. He showed the error of trusting to human power for that transformation of character which can be wrought only by the Spirit of God.

This teaching the Sadducees were determined to discredit. In seeking a controversy with Jesus, they felt confident of bringing Him into disrepute, even if they could not secure His condemnation. The resurrection was the subject on which they chose to question Him. Should He agree with them, He would give still further offense to the Pharisees. Should He differ with them, they designed to hold His teaching up to ridicule.

The Sadducees reasoned that if the body is to be

belief in You. _____
_____

____Lord, if my character is unforgiving, is that my idea of You? If I am exacting with my children, is that my idea of You?
_____
_____
_____

Change my ideas and my character, Lord: _____
_____
_____
_____

5. "By His words and His works, Christ testified…to God as a F_____ of the children of men, ever w_____ of their true interests. He revealed the working of divine power in benevolence and c_____ that rebuked the selfish exclusiveness of the Sadducees…He showed the error of trusting to h_____ power for that transformation of character which can be wrought only by the Spirit of God." (605). Lord, as I walk with You, contemplating Your words and works, may Your Spirit transform my character: _____
_____

composed of the same particles of matter in its immortal as in its mortal state, then when raised from the dead it must have flesh and blood, and must resume in the eternal world the life interrupted on earth. In that case they concluded that earthly relationships would be resumed, husband and wife would be reunited, marriages consummated, and all things go on the same as before death, the frailties and passions of this life being perpetuated in the life beyond.

In answer to their questions, Jesus lifted the veil from the future life. "In the resurrection," He said, "they neither marry, nor are given in marriage, but are as the angels of God in heaven." He showed that the Sadducees were wrong in their belief. Their premises were false. "Ye do err," He added, "not knowing the Scriptures, nor the power of God." He did not charge them, as He had charged the Pharisees, with hypocrisy, but with error of belief.

The Sadducees had flattered themselves that they of all men adhered most strictly to the Scriptures. But Jesus showed that they had not known their true meaning. That knowledge must be brought home to the heart by the enlightenment of the Holy Spirit. Their ignorance of the Scriptures and the power of God He declared to be the cause of their [605-606] confusion of faith and darkness of mind. They were seeking to bring the mysteries of God within the compass of their finite reasoning. Christ called upon them to open their minds to those sacred truths that would broaden and strengthen the understanding. Thousands become infidels because their finite minds cannot comprehend the mysteries of God. They cannot explain the wonderful exhibition of divine power in His providences, therefore they reject the evidences of such power, attributing them to natural agencies which they can comprehend still less. The only key to the mysteries that surround us is to acknowledge in them all the presence and power of God. Men need to recognize God as the Creator of the universe, One who commands and executes all things. They need a broader view of His character, and of the mystery of His agencies.

Christ declared to His hearers that if there were no resurrection of the dead, the Scriptures which they professed to believe would be of no avail. He said, "But as touching the resurrection of the dead, have ye not read that which was spoken unto you by God, saying, I am

6. "That knowledge must be brought h_____ to the h_____ by the enlightenment of the Holy Spirit. Their [the Sadducees'] ignorance of the Scriptures and the p_____ of God, He declared to be the cause of their confusion of faith and d_____ ___ of mind." (605, 606). Lord, do I have knowledge, but not the power? Why haven't I allowed it to be brought home to my heart? Is there something I am not willing to let go of, so there's no room?

_____
_____
_____
_____
_____

the God of Abraham, and the God of Isaac, and the God of Jacob? God is not the God of the dead, but of the living." God counts the things that are not as though they were. He sees the end from the beginning, and beholds the result of His work as though it were now accomplished. The precious dead, from Adam down to the last saint who dies, will hear the voice of the Son of God, and will come forth from the grave to immortal life. God will be their God, and they shall be His people. There will be a close and tender relationship between God and the risen saints. This condition, which is anticipated in His purpose, He beholds as if it were already existing. The dead live unto Him.

By the words of Christ the Sadducees were put to silence. They could not answer Him. Not a word had been spoken of which the least advantage could be taken for His condemnation. His adversaries had gained nothing but the contempt of the people.

The Pharisees, however, did not yet despair of driving Him to speak that which they could use against Him. They prevailed upon a certain learned scribe to question Jesus as to which of the ten precepts of the law was of the greatest importance.

The Pharisees had exalted the first four commandments, which point out the duty of man to his Maker, as of far greater consequence than the other six, which define man's duty to his fellow man. As the result, [606-607] they greatly failed of practical godliness. Jesus had shown the people their great deficiency, and had taught the necessity of good works, declaring that the tree is known by its fruits. For this reason He had been charged with exalting the last six commandments above the first four.

The lawyer approached Jesus with a direct question, "Which is the first commandment of all?" The answer of Christ is direct and forcible: "The first of all the commandments is, Hear, O Israel; The Lord our God is one Lord: and thou shalt love the Lord thy God with all thy heart, and with all thy soul, and with all thy mind, and with all thy strength: this is the first commandment." The second is like the first, said Christ; for it flows out of it, "Thou shalt love thy neighbor as thyself. There is none other commandment greater than these." "On these two commandments hang all the law and the prophets."

The first four of the Ten Commandments are

7. "The Pharisees had exalted the first four commandments...as of far greater consequence than the other six.. As the result, they greatly failed of practical g_____." (606, 607). Lord, do I have this experience? _____
_____ What is practical godliness? _____
_____
_____

What application of loving my neighbor am I missing?
_____
_____
_____
_____

summed up in the one great precept, "Thou shalt love the Lord thy God with all thy heart." The last six are included in the other, "Thou shalt love thy neighbor as thyself." Both these commandments are an expression of the principle of love. The first cannot be kept and the second broken, nor can the second be kept while the first is broken. When God has His rightful place on the throne of the heart, the right place will be given to our neighbor. We shall love him as ourselves. And only as we love God supremely is it possible to love our neighbor impartially.

And since all the commandments are summed up in love to God and man, it follows that not one precept can be broken without violating this principle. Thus Christ taught His hearers that the law of God is not so many separate precepts, some of which are of great importance, while others are of small importance and may with impunity be ignored. Our Lord presents the first four and the last six commandments as a divine whole, and teaches that love to God will be shown by obedience to all His commandments.

The scribe who had questioned Jesus was well read in the law, and he was astonished at His words. He did not expect Him to manifest so deep and thorough a knowledge of the Scriptures. He had gained a broader view of the principles underlying the sacred precepts. Before the assembled priests and rulers he honestly acknowledged that Christ had given the right interpretation to the law, saying:

"Well, Master, Thou hast said the truth: for there is one God; and there is none other but He: and to love Him with all the heart, and [607-608] with all the understanding, and with all the soul, and with all the strength, and to love his neighbor as himself, is more than all whole burnt offerings and sacrifices."

The wisdom of Christ's answer had convicted the scribe. He knew that the Jewish religion consisted in outward ceremonies rather than inward piety. He had some sense of the worthlessness of mere ceremonial offerings, and the faithless shedding of blood for expiation of sin. Love and obedience to God, and unselfish regard for man, appeared to him of more value than all these rites. The readiness of this man to acknowledge the correctness of Christ's reasoning, and his decided and prompt response before the people, manifested a spirit entirely different from that of the priests and rul-

---

8. "Both these commandments are an expression of the p_____ of love. The first c_____ be kept and the second broken, nor can the second be k_____ while the first is broken." Lord, how can I be better guided by this principle?_____
_____
_____
_____ (beholding Your love more and more?)

9. "He had some sense of the w_____ of mere ceremonial offerings, and the f_____ _____ shedding of blood for expiation of sin." (608). Lord, is Your shed blood wasted on me, because my attitude is faithless, understanding Calvary as merely electronic transfer of balance between accounts? Help me see the cost, the price, the sacrifice, the love, and have it move me: _____
_____

ers. The heart of Jesus went out in pity to the honest scribe who had dared to face the frowns of the priests and the threats of the rulers to speak the convictions of his heart. "And when Jesus saw that he answered discreetly, He said unto him, Thou art not far from the kingdom of God."

The scribe was near to the kingdom of God, in that he recognized deeds of righteousness as more acceptable to God than burnt offerings and sacrifices. But he needed to recognize the divine character of Christ, and through faith in Him receive power to do the works of righteousness. The ritual service was of no value, unless connected with Christ by living faith. Even the moral law fails of its purpose, unless it is understood in its relation to the Saviour. Christ had repeatedly shown that His Father's law contained something deeper than mere authoritative commands. In the law is embodied the same principle that is revealed in the gospel. The law points out man's duty and shows him his guilt. To Christ he must look for pardon and for power to do what the law enjoins.

The Pharisees had gathered close about Jesus as He answered the question of the scribe. Now turning He put a question to them: "What think ye of Christ? whose son is He?" This question was designed to test their belief concerning the Messiah,--to show whether they regarded Him simply as a man or as the Son of God. A chorus of voices answered, "The Son of David." This was the title which prophecy had given to the Messiah. When Jesus revealed His divinity by His mighty miracles, when He healed the sick and raised the dead, the people had inquired among themselves, "Is not this the Son of David?" The Syrophoenician woman, blind Bartimaeus, and many others had cried to Him for help, "Have mercy on me, O Lord, Thou Son of David." Matt. 15:22. While riding into Jerusalem He had been hailed with the [608-609] joyful shout, "Hosanna to the Son of David: Blessed is He that cometh in the name of the Lord." Matt. 21:9. And the little children in the temple had that day echoed the glad ascription. But many who called Jesus the Son of David did not recognize His divinity. They did not understand that the Son of David was also the Son of God.

In reply to the statement that Christ was the Son of David, Jesus said, "How then doth David in Spirit [the Spirit of Inspiration from God] call Him Lord, say-

10. "Thou art not f____ from the kingdom of God...In the law is embodied the same principle that is revealed in the g_____ ____...To Christ he must look for pardon and for p__ _____ to do what the law enjoins." Lord, may the law be for me good news, leading me to You, for pardon and power, for acceptance and harmony with You:

_____
_____
_____
_____

ing, The Lord said unto my Lord, Sit Thou on My right hand, till I make Thine enemies Thy footstool? If David then call Him Lord, how is He his son? And no man was able to answer Him a word, neither durst any man from that day forth ask Him any more questions."

Chapter 67

Woes on the Pharisees

[This chapter is based on Matt. 23; Mark 12:41-44;
Luke 20:45-47; 21:1-4.]

It was the last day of Christ's teaching in the temple. Of the vast throngs that were gathered at Jerusalem, the attention of all had been attracted to Him; the people had crowded the temple courts, watching the contest that had been in progress, and they eagerly caught every word that fell from His lips. Never before had such a scene been witnessed. There stood the young Galilean, bearing no earthly honor or royal badge. Surrounding Him were priests in their rich apparel, rulers with robes and badges significant of their exalted station, and scribes with scrolls in their hands, to which they made frequent reference. Jesus stood calmly before them, with the dignity of a king. As one invested with the authority of heaven, He looked unflinchingly upon His adversaries, who had rejected and despised His teachings, and who thirsted for His life. They had assailed Him in great numbers, but their schemes to ensnare and condemn Him had been in vain. Challenge after challenge He had met, presenting the pure, bright truth in contrast to the darkness and errors of the priests and Pharisees. He had set before these leaders their real condition, and the retribution sure to follow persistence in their evil deeds. The warning had been faithfully given. Yet another [610-611] work remained for Christ to do. Another purpose was still to be accomplished.

The interest of the people in Christ and His work had steadily increased. They were charmed with His teaching, but they were also greatly perplexed. They had respected the priests and rabbis for their intelligence and apparent piety. In all religious matters they had ever yielded implicit obedience to their authority. Yet they now saw these men trying to cast discredit upon Jesus, a teacher whose virtue and knowledge shone forth the brighter from every assault. They looked upon the lowering countenances of the priests and elders, and there saw discomfiture and confusion. They marveled that the rulers would not believe on Jesus, when His teachings

1. Jesus "had set before these leaders their r_____ condition, and the retribution sure to follow p_____ in their evil deeds...Another purpose was still to be acomplished...

were so plain and simple. They themselves knew not what course to take. With eager anxiety they watched the movements of those whose counsel they had always followed.

In the parables which Christ had spoken, it was His purpose both to warn the rulers and to instruct the people who were willing to be taught. But there was need to speak yet more plainly. Through their reverence for tradition and their blind faith in a corrupt priesthood, the people were [611-612] enslaved. These chains Christ must break. The character of the priests, rulers, and Pharisees must be more fully exposed.

"The scribes and the Pharisees," He said, "sit in Moses' seat: all therefore whatsoever they bid you observe, that observe and do; but do not ye after their works: for they say, and do not." The scribes and Pharisees claimed to be invested with divine authority similar to that of Moses. They assumed to take his place as expounders of the law and judges of the people. As such they claimed from the people the utmost deference and obedience. Jesus bade His hearers do that which the rabbis taught according to the law, but not to follow their example. They themselves did not practice their own teaching.

And they taught much that was contrary to the Scriptures. Jesus said, "They bind heavy burdens and grievous to be borne, and lay them on men's shoulders; but they themselves will not move them with one of their fingers." The Pharisees enjoined a multitude of regulations, having their foundation in tradition, and unreasonably restricting personal liberty. And certain portions of the law they so explained as to impose upon the people observances which they themselves secretly ignored, and from which, when it served their purpose, they actually claimed exemption.

To make a show of their piety was their constant aim. Nothing was held too sacred to serve this end. To Moses God had said concerning His commandments, "Thou shalt bind them for a sign upon thine hand, and they shall be as frontlets between thine eyes." Deut. 6:8. These words have a deep meaning. As the word of God is meditated upon and practiced, the whole man will be ennobled. In righteous and merciful dealing, the hands will reveal, as a signet, the principles of God's law. They will be kept clean from bribes, and from all that is corrupt and deceptive. They will be active in works of

---

In the parables which Christ had spoken, it was His purpose both to w_____ the rulers and to i_____ the people who were willing to be taught. But there was need to speak yet more p_____. Through their reverence for t_____ _____ and their blind faith in a corrupt priesthood, the people were e_____ _____. These chains Christ must break. The c_____ _____ of the priests, rulers, and Pharisees must be more fully e_____ _____." (610-612). Lord, do You need to speak more plainly to me? _____ _____ Is there something in my character that You need to expose to me? _____ _____ _____ _____ Something I don't know the hold it has on me? _____ _____ _____ Some trait I don't recognize? _____ _____ __ _____

love and compassion. The eyes, directed toward a noble purpose, will be clear and true. The expressive countenance, the speaking eye, will testify to the blameless character of him who loves and honors the word of God. But by the Jews of Christ's day all this was undiscerned. The command given to Moses was construed into a direction that the precepts of Scripture should be worn upon the person. They were accordingly written upon strips of parchment, and bound in a conspicuous manner about the head and wrists. But this did not cause the law of God to take a firmer hold of the mind and heart. These parchments were worn merely as badges, [612-613] to attract attention. They were thought to give the wearers an air of devotion which would command the reverence of the people. Jesus struck a blow at this vain pretense:

"But all their works they do for to be seen of men: they make broad their phylacteries, and enlarge the borders of their garments, and love the uppermost rooms at feasts, and the chief seats in the synagogues, and greetings in the markets, and to be called of men, Rabbi, Rabbi. But be not ye called Rabbi: for one is your Master, even Christ; and all ye are brethren. And call no man your father upon the earth: for One is your Father, which is in heaven. Neither be ye called master: for One is your Master, even Christ." In such plain words the Saviour revealed the selfish ambition that was ever reaching for place and power, displaying a mock humility, while the heart was filled with avarice and envy. When persons were invited to a feast, the guests were seated according to their rank, and those who were given the most honorable place received the first attention and special favors. The Pharisees were ever scheming to secure these honors. This practice Jesus rebuked.

He also reproved the vanity shown in coveting the title of rabbi, or master. Such a title, He declared, belonged not to men, but to Christ. Priests, scribes, and rulers, expounders and administrators of the law, were all brethren, children of one Father. Jesus impressed upon the people that they were to give no man a title of honor indicating his control of their conscience or their faith.

If Christ were on earth today, surrounded by those who bear the title of "Reverend" or "Right Reverend," would He not repeat His saying, "Neither be ye called masters: for One is your Master, even Christ"? The

2. "The command given to Moses was c_____ into a direction that the precepts of Scripture should be w_____ upon the person." (612). Would this help the law of God to take a f_____ hold of the mind and h_____? _____ Do I ever carry the Bible around for show? _____ _____ Or recite Scripture to impress? _____ _____

3. "In such p_____ words the Savior revealed the s_____ ambition that was ever reaching for p_____ and power, displaying a mock h_____ _____, while the heart was filled with avarice and e_____." (613). Lord, sometimes when I deliberately practice humility, I wonder if I am helping. Is it mock humility? _____ Help me recognize if I am practicing, to be recognized. _____ _____ _____

4. "Priests, scribes, and rulers, e_____ and administrators of the law, were all b_____, children of one Father. Jesus impressed upon the people that they were to give no man a t_____ of honor indicating his c__ _____ of their conscience

or their faith." Do the titles "Pastor" or "Elder" carry this meaning? _____

_____

_____

5. "Again and again Christ had taught that t_____ greatness is measured by m_____ worth. In the estimation of heaven, greatness of character consists in living for the w_____ of our fellow men, in doing works of l_____ and m_____." (613, 614). Lord, reveal to me the way that I may be striving for title, position, or power. Rather, may I find of value living Your character of love and mercy: _____

_____

_____

Scripture declares of God, "Holy and reverend is His name." Ps. 111:9. To what human being is such a title befitting? How little does man reveal of the wisdom and righteousness it indicates! How many of those who assume this title are misrepresenting the name and character of God! Alas, how often have worldly ambition, despotism, and the basest sins been hidden under the broidered garments of a high and holy office! The Saviour continued:

"But he that is greatest among you shall be your servant. And whosoever shall exalt himself shall be abased; and he that shall humble himself shall be exalted." Again and again Christ had taught that true greatness is measured by moral worth. In the estimation of heaven, greatness of character consists in living for the welfare of our fellow men, in [613-614] doing works of love and mercy. Christ the King of glory was a servant to fallen man.

"Woe unto you, scribes and Pharisees, hypocrites," said Jesus; "for ye shut up the kingdom of heaven against men: for ye neither go in yourselves, neither suffer ye them that are entering to go in." By perverting the Scriptures, the priests and lawyers blinded the minds of those who would otherwise have received a knowledge of Christ's kingdom, and that inward, divine life which is essential to true holiness.

"Woe unto you, scribes and Pharisees, hypocrites! for ye devour widows' houses, and for a pretense make long prayer: therefore ye shall receive the greater damnation." The Pharisees had great influence with the people, and of this they took advantage to serve their own interests. They gained the confidence of pious widows, and then represented it as a duty for them to devote their property to religious purposes. Having secured control of their money, the wily schemers used it for their own benefit. To cover their dishonesty, they offered long prayers in public, and made a great show of piety. This hypocrisy Christ declared would bring them the greater damnation. The same rebuke falls upon many in our day who make a high profession of piety. Their lives are stained by selfishness and avarice, yet they throw over it all a garment of seeming purity, and thus for a time deceive their fellow men. But they cannot deceive God. He reads every purpose of the heart, and will judge every man according to his deeds.

Christ unsparingly condemned abuses, but He was

careful not to lessen obligation. He rebuked the selfishness that extorted and misapplied the widow's gifts. At the same time He commended the widow who brought her offering for God's treasury. Man's abuse of the gift could not turn God's blessing from the giver.

Jesus was in the court where were the treasure chests, and He watched those who came to deposit their gifts. Many of the rich brought large sums, which they presented with great ostentation. Jesus looked upon them sadly, but made no comment on their liberal offerings. Presently His countenance lighted as He saw a poor widow approach hesitatingly, as though fearful of being observed. As the rich and haughty swept by, to deposit their offerings, she shrank back as if hardly daring to venture farther. And yet she longed to do something, little though it might be, for the cause she loved. She looked at the gift in her hand. It was very small in comparison with the gifts of those around her, yet it was her all. [614-615] Watching her opportunity, she hurriedly threw in her two mites, and turned to hasten away. But in doing this she caught the eye of Jesus, which was fastened earnestly upon her.

The Saviour called His disciples to Him, and bade them mark the widow's poverty. Then His words of commendation fell upon her ear: "Of a truth I say unto you, that this poor widow hath cast in more than they all." Tears of joy filled her eyes as she felt that her act was understood and appreciated. Many would have advised her to keep her pittance for her own use; given into the hands of the well-fed priests, it would be lost sight of among the many costly gifts brought to the treasury. But Jesus understood her motive. She believed the service of the temple to be of God's appointment, and she was anxious to do her utmost to sustain it. She did what she could, and her act was to be a monument to her memory through all time, and her joy in eternity. Her heart went with her gift; its value was estimated, not by the worth of the coin, but by the love to God and the interest in His work that had prompted the deed.

Jesus said of the poor widow, She "hath cast in more than they all." The rich had bestowed from their abundance, many of them to be seen and honored by men. Their large donations had deprived them of no comfort, or even luxury; they had required no sacrifice, and could not be compared in value with the widow's mite.

It is the motive that gives character to our acts,

6. Jesus "saw a poor widow approaching h____ _____, as though fearful of being o_____ __...Yet she l_____ to do something...Watching her opportunity, she hurriedly threw in her t_____ mites, and turned to hasten away...Tears of j____ filled her eyes as she felt her act was understood and a_____." (614, 615). What was her attitude? _____ _____ "Her h_____ ___ went with her gift; its value was estimated, not by the worth of the c_____, but by the l_____ to God and the interest in His work that had prompted the deed." What are my offerings worth? _____ _____ _____

stamping them with ignominy or with high moral worth. Not the great things which every eye sees and every tongue praises does God account most precious. The little duties cheerfully done, the little gifts which make no show, and which to human eyes may appear worthless, often stand highest in His sight. A heart of faith and love is dearer to God than the most costly gift. The poor widow gave her living to do the little that she did. She deprived herself of food in order to give those two mites to the cause she loved. And she did it in faith, believing that her heavenly Father would not overlook her great need. It was this unselfish spirit and childlike faith that won the Saviour's commendation.

Among the poor there are many who long to show their gratitude to God for His grace and truth. They greatly desire to share with their more prosperous brethren in sustaining His service. These souls should not be repulsed. Let them lay up their mites in the bank of heaven. If given from a heart filled with love for God, these seeming trifles become consecrated gifts, priceless offerings, which God smiles upon and blesses. [615-616]

When Jesus said of the widow, She "hath cast in more than they all," His words were true, not only of the motive, but of the results of her gift. The "two mites which make a farthing" have brought to God's treasury an amount of money far greater than the contributions of those rich Jews. The influence of that little gift has been like a stream, small in its beginning, but widening and deepening as it flowed down through the ages. In a thousand ways it has contributed to the relief of the poor and the spread of the gospel. Her example of self-sacrifice has acted and reacted upon thousands of hearts in every land and in every age. It has appealed to both the rich and the poor, and their offerings have swelled the value of her gift. God's blessing upon the widow's mite has made it the source of great results. So with every gift bestowed and every act performed with a sincere desire for God's glory. It is linked with the purposes of Omnipotence. Its results for good no man can measure.

The Saviour continued His denunciations of the scribes and Pharisees: "Woe unto you, ye blind guides, which say, Whosoever shall swear by the temple, it is nothing; but whosoever shall swear by the gold of the temple, he is a debtor! Ye fools and blind: for whether is

---

7. "The little duties c__ _____ done, the little gifts which make no s__ _____, and which to human eyes may appear worthless, often stand h_____ in His sight." Lord, may I give from my heart, cheerfully. Reveal to me the self that pops up so easily: _____

_____

_____

8. "So with every gift bestowed and every act performed with a sincere desire for God's g_____ ____. It is linked with the purposes of Omnipotence. Its results for good no man can m_____." (616). Lord, may I share in that thrill, of being linked with Your purposes:

_____

_____

greater, the gold, or the temple that sanctifieth the gold? and, Whosoever shall swear by the altar, it is nothing; but whosoever sweareth by the gift that is upon it, he is guilty. Ye fools and blind: for whether is greater, the gift, or the altar that sanctifieth the gift?" The priests interpreted God's requirements according to their own false and narrow standard. They presumed to make nice distinctions as to the comparative guilt of various sins, passing over some lightly, and treating others of perhaps less consequence as unpardonable. For a money consideration they excused persons from their vows. And for large sums of money they sometimes passed over aggravated crimes. At the same time these priests and rulers would in other cases pronounce severe judgment for trivial offenses.

"Woe unto you, scribes and Pharisees, hypocrites! for ye pay tithe of mint and anise and cummin, and have omitted the weightier matters of the law, judgment, mercy, and faith: these ought ye to have done, and not to leave the other undone." In these words Christ again condemns the abuse of sacred obligation. The obligation itself He does not set aside. The tithing system was ordained by God, and it had been observed from the earliest times. Abraham, the father of the faithful, paid tithes of all that he possessed. The Jewish rulers recognized the obligation of tithing, and this was right; but they did not leave the people to carry [616-617] out their own convictions of duty. Arbitrary rules were laid down for every case. The requirements had become so complicated that it was impossible for them to be fulfilled. None knew when their obligations were met. As God gave it, the system was just and reasonable; but the priests and rabbis had made it a wearisome burden.

All that God commands is of consequence. Christ recognized the payment of tithes as a duty; but He showed that this could not excuse the neglect of other duties. The Pharisees were very exact in tithing garden herbs, such as mint, anise, and rue; this cost them little, and it gave them a reputation for exactness and sanctity. At the same time their useless restrictions oppressed the people and destroyed respect for the sacred system of God's own appointing. They occupied men's minds with trifling distinctions, and turned their attention from essential truths. The weightier matters of the law, justice, mercy, and truth, were neglected. "These," Christ said, "ought ye to have done, and not to leave the other

9. The Pharisees "occupied men's minds with t_____ distinctions, and turned their attention from e_____ truths. The weightier matters of the law, justice, mercy, and truth, were n_____." (617). Lord, is my tithing exact, but the weightier matters vague? _____
_____
_____Convict me:
_____
_____

undone."

Other laws had been perverted by the rabbis in like manner. In the directions given through Moses it was forbidden to eat any unclean thing. The use of swine's flesh, and the flesh of certain other animals, was prohibited, as likely to fill the blood with impurities, and to shorten life. But the Pharisees did not leave these restrictions as God had given them. They went to unwarranted extremes. Among other things the people were required to strain all the water used, lest it should contain the smallest insect, which might be classed with the unclean animals. Jesus, contrasting these trivial exactions with the magnitude of their actual sins, said to the Pharisees, "Ye blind guides, which strain at a gnat, and swallow a camel."

"Woe unto you, scribes and Pharisees, hypocrites! for ye are like unto whited sepulchers, which indeed appear beautiful outward, but are within full of dead men's bones, and of all uncleanness." As the whited and beautifully decorated tomb concealed the putrefying remains within, so the outward holiness of the priests and rulers concealed iniquity. Jesus continued:

"Woe unto you, scribes and Pharisees, hypocrites! because ye build the tombs of the prophets, and garnish the sepulchers of the righteous, and say, If we had been in the days of our fathers, we would not have been partakers with them in the blood of the prophets. Wherefore ye be witnesses unto yourselves, that ye are the children of them which [617-618] killed the prophets." To show their esteem for the dead prophets, the Jews were very zealous in beautifying their tombs; but they did not profit by their teachings, nor give heed to their reproofs.

In the days of Christ a superstitious regard was cherished for the resting places of the dead, and vast sums of money were lavished upon their decoration. In the sight of God this was idolatry. In their undue regard for the dead, men showed that they did not love God supremely, nor their neighbor as themselves. The same idolatry is carried to great lengths today. Many are guilty of neglecting the widow and the fatherless, the sick and the poor, in order to build expensive monuments for the dead. Time, money, and labor are freely spent for this purpose, while duties to the living--duties which Christ has plainly enjoined--are left undone.

The Pharisees built the tombs of the prophets, and

adorned their sepulchers, and said one to another, If we had lived in the days of our fathers, we would not have united with them in shedding the blood of God's servants. At the same time they were planning to take the life of His Son. This should be a lesson to us. It should open our eyes to the power of Satan to deceive the mind that turns from the light of truth. Many follow in the track of the Pharisees. They revere those who have died for their faith. They wonder at the blindness of the Jews in rejecting Christ. Had we lived in His day, they declare, we would gladly have received His teaching; we would never have been partakers in the guilt of those who rejected the Saviour. But when obedience to God requires self-denial and humiliation, these very persons stifle their convictions, and refuse obedience. Thus they manifest the same spirit as did the Pharisees whom Christ condemned.

Little did the Jews realize the terrible responsibility involved in rejecting Christ. From the time when the first innocent blood was shed, when righteous Abel fell by the hand of Cain, the same history had been repeated, with increasing guilt. In every age prophets had lifted up their voices against the sins of kings, rulers, and people, speaking the words which God gave them, and obeying His will at the peril of their lives. From generation to generation there had been heaping up a terrible punishment for the rejecters of light and truth. This the enemies of Christ were now drawing down upon their own heads. The sin of the priests and rulers was greater than that of any preceding generation. By their rejection of the Saviour, they were making themselves responsible [618-619] for the blood of all the righteous men slain from Abel to Christ. They were about to fill to overflowing their cup of iniquity. And soon it was to be poured upon their heads in retributive justice. Of this, Jesus warned them:

"That upon you may come all the righteous blood shed upon the earth, from the blood of righteous Abel unto the blood of Zacharias son of Barachias, whom ye slew between the temple and the altar. Verily I say unto you, All these things shall come upon this generation."

The scribes and Pharisees who listened to Jesus knew that His words were true. They knew how the prophet Zacharias had been slain. While the words of warning from God were upon his lips, a satanic fury seized the apostate king, and at his command the proph-

10. "They wonder at the blindness of the Jews in r_____ Christ...But when obedience to God requires self-d_____ and humiliation, these very persons stifle their convictions, and refuse obedience." (618). Lord, am I rejecting You as I stifle convictions? _____

_____
_____ Do I realize the responsibility involved in rejecting You? _____
_____
_____

Can We Walk, Together?

et was put to death. His blood had imprinted itself upon the very stones of the temple court, and could not be erased; it remained to bear testimony against apostate Israel. As long as the temple should stand, there would be the stain of that righteous blood, crying to God to be avenged. As Jesus referred to these fearful sins, a thrill of horror ran through the multitude.

Looking forward, Jesus declared that the impenitence of the Jews and their intolerance of God's servants would be the same in the future as it had been in the past:

"Wherefore, behold, I send unto you prophets, and wise men, and scribes: and some of them ye shall kill and crucify; and some of them shall ye scourge in your synagogues, and persecute them from city to city." Prophets and wise men, full of faith and the Holy Ghost,--Stephen, James, and many others,--would be condemned and slain. With hand uplifted to heaven, and a divine light enshrouding His person, Christ spoke as a judge to those before Him. His voice, that had so often been heard in gentleness and entreaty, was now heard in rebuke and condemnation. The listeners shuddered. Never was the impression made by His words and His look to be effaced.

Christ's indignation was directed against the hypocrisy, the gross sins, by which men were destroying their own souls, deceiving the people and dishonoring God. In the specious deceptive reasoning of the priests and rulers He discerned the working of satanic agencies. Keen and searching had been His denunciation of sin; but He spoke no words of retaliation. He had a holy wrath against the prince of darkness; but He manifested no irritated temper. So the Christian who lives in harmony with God, possessing the sweet attributes of love and mercy, will feel a righteous [619-620] indignation against sin; but he will not be roused by passion to revile those who revile him. Even in meeting those who are moved by a power from beneath to maintain falsehood, in Christ he will still preserve calmness and self-possession.

Divine pity marked the countenance of the Son of God as He cast one lingering look upon the temple and then upon His hearers. In a voice choked by deep anguish of heart and bitter tears He exclaimed, "O Jerusalem, Jerusalem, thou that killest the prophets, and stonest them which are sent unto thee, how often would

I have gathered thy children together, even as a hen gathereth her chickens under her wings, and ye would not!" This is the separation struggle. In the lamentation of Christ the very heart of God is pouring itself forth. It is the mysterious farewell of the long-suffering love of the Deity.

Pharisees and Sadducees were alike silenced. Jesus summoned His disciples, and prepared to leave the temple, not as one defeated and forced from the presence of his adversaries, but as one whose work was accomplished. He retired a victor from the contest.

The gems of truth that fell from Christ's lips on that eventful day were treasured in many hearts. For them new thoughts started into life, new aspirations were awakened, and a new history began. After the crucifixion and resurrection of Christ, these persons came to the front, and fulfilled their divine commission with a wisdom and zeal corresponding to the greatness of the work. They bore a message that appealed to the hearts of men, weakening the old superstitions that had long dwarfed the lives of thousands. Before their testimony human theories and philosophies became as idle fables. Mighty were the results flowing from the words of the Saviour to that wondering, awestruck crowd in the temple at Jerusalem.

But Israel as a nation had divorced herself from God. The natural branches of the olive tree were broken off. Looking for the last time upon the interior of the temple, Jesus said with mournful pathos, "Behold, your house is left unto you desolate. For I say unto you, Ye shall not see Me henceforth, till ye shall say, Blessed is He that cometh in the name of the Lord." Hitherto He had called the temple His Father's house; but now, as the Son of God should pass out from those walls, God's presence would be withdrawn forever from the temple built to His glory. Henceforth its ceremonies would be meaningless, its services a mockery.

11. "How often would I have g_____ thy children together, even as a hen gathered her chickens under her w_____, and ye would not...It is the mysterious f_____ of the long-suffering l_____ ____ of the Deity...God's p_____ would be withdrawn forever from the temple built for His glory. Henceforth its cere-monies would be m_____, its service a mockery." (620). Do I hear the lamentations from Your heart, Lord? Have I slighted Your love and protection? Please don't withdraw Your presence form me. I lift You up, as I walk with You and contemplate Your life. You promised that I would be drawn to You if I did:

_____
_____
_____

Prayer journal: _____
_____
_____
_____
_____
_____
_____
_____

Chapter 68

In the Outer Court

[This chapter is based on John 12:20-43.]

1. "Sir, we w_____ ____ see Jesus." How did this request make Jesus feel? _____

_____ "In the request of the Greeks He saw an e_____ of the results of His great sacrifice." Lord, increase my hunger and thirst to see You. May it be my highest desire: _____

"And there were certain Greeks among them that came up to worship at the feast: the same came therefore to Philip, which was of Bethsaida of Galilee, and desired him, saying, Sir, we would see Jesus. Philip cometh and telleth Andrew: and again Andrew and Philip tell Jesus."

At this time Christ's work bore the appearance of cruel defeat. He had been victor in the controversy with the priests and Pharisees, but it was evident that He would never be received by them as the Messiah. The final separation had come. To His disciples the case seemed hopeless. But Christ was approaching the consummation of His work. The great event which concerned not only the Jewish nation, but the whole world, was about to take place. When Christ heard the eager request, "We would see Jesus," echoing the hungering cry of the world, His countenance lighted up, and He said, "The hour is come, that the Son of man should be glorified." In the request of the Greeks He saw an earnest of the results of His great sacrifice.

These men came from the West to find the Saviour at the close of His life, as the wise men had come from the East at the beginning. At the time of Christ's birth the Jewish people were so engrossed with their own ambitious plans that they knew not of His advent. The magi [621-622] from a heathen land came to the manger with their gifts, to worship the Saviour. So these Greeks, representing the nations, tribes, and peoples of the world, came to see Jesus. So the people of all lands and all ages would be drawn by the Saviour's cross. So shall many "come from the east and west, and shall sit down with Abraham, and Isaac, and Jacob, in the kingdom of heaven." Matt. 8:11.

The Greeks had heard of Christ's triumphal entry into Jerusalem. Some supposed, and had circulated the report, that He had driven the priests and rulers from the temple, and that He was to take possession of David's throne, and reign as king of Israel. The Greeks longed to know the truth in regard to His mission. "We would see Jesus," they said. Their desire was granted. When the request was brought to Jesus, He was in that part of the temple from which all except Jews were excluded, but He went out to the Greeks in the outer court, and had a personal interview with them.

The hour of Christ's glorification had come. He was standing in the shadow of the cross, and the inquiry of the Greeks showed Him that the sacrifice He was about to make would bring many sons and daughters to God. He knew that the Greeks would soon see Him in a position they did not then dream of. They would see Him placed beside Barabbas, a robber and murderer, who would be chosen for release before the Son of God. They would hear the people, inspired by the priests and rulers, making their choice. And to the question, "What shall I do then with Jesus which is called Christ?" the answer would be given, "Let Him be crucified." Matt. 27:22. By making this propitiation for the sins of men, Christ knew that His kingdom would be perfected, and would extend throughout the world. He would work as the Restorer, and His Spirit would prevail. For a moment He looked into futurity, and heard the voices proclaiming in all parts of the earth, "Behold the Lamb of God, which taketh away the sin of the world." John 1:29. In these strangers He saw the pledge of a great harvest, when the partition wall between Jew and Gentile should be broken down, and all nations, tongues, and peoples should hear the message of salvation. The anticipation of this, the consummation of His hopes, is expressed in the words, "The hour is come, that the Son of man should be glorified." But the way in which this glorification must take place was never absent from Christ's mind. The gathering in of the Gentiles was to follow His approaching death. Only by His death could the world be saved. Like a grain of wheat, the [622-623] Son of man must be cast into the ground and die, and be buried out of sight; but He was to live again.

Christ presented His future, illustrating it by the things of nature, that the disciples might understand. The true result of His mission was to be reached by His death. "Verily, verily, I say unto you," He said, "Except a corn of wheat fall into the ground and die, it abideth alone: but if it die, it bringeth forth much fruit." When the grain of wheat falls into the ground and dies, it springs up, and bears fruit. So the death of Christ would

2. "All except Jews were e_____, but He went out to the Greeks in the outer court, and had a personal interview with them." (622). Lord, may I never limit the sense of welcome You have for others; or my voice sound disapproving and suggesting that You are unapproachable: _____

_____

_____

3. "The anticipation of this, the consummation of His h_____, is expressed in the words, 'The hour is come, that the Son of man should be g_____.'" (622). Lord, are You glorified as people comprehend and appreciate the reconciliation You offer? _____ May I not lessen Your glory, by taking Your offer for granted. Show me the depths of Your love, Lord, that I may respond from the depths of my heart: __

_____

_____

_____

result in fruit for the kingdom of God. In accordance with the law of the vegetable kingdom, life was to be the result of His death.

Those who till the soil have the illustration ever before them. Year by year man preserves his supply of grain by apparently throwing away the choicest part. For a time it must be hidden under the furrow, to be watched over by the Lord. Then appears the blade, then the ear, and then the corn in the ear. But this development cannot take place unless the grain is buried out of sight, hidden, and to all appearance, lost.

The seed buried in the ground produces fruit, and in turn this is planted. Thus the harvest is multiplied. So the death of Christ on the cross of Calvary will bear fruit unto eternal life. The contemplation of this sacrifice will be the glory of those who, as the fruit of it, will live through the eternal ages.

The grain of wheat that preserves its own life can produce no fruit. It abides alone. Christ could, if He chose, save Himself from death. But should He do this, He must abide alone. He could bring no sons and daughters to God. Only by yielding up His life could He impart life to humanity. Only by falling into the ground to die could He become the seed of that vast harvest,--the great multitude that out of every nation, and kindred, and tongue, and people, are redeemed to God.

With this truth Christ connects the lesson of self-sacrifice that all should learn: "He that loveth his life shall lose it; and he that hateth his life in this world shall keep it unto life eternal." All who would bring forth fruit as workers together with Christ must first fall into the ground and die. The life must be cast into the furrow of the world's need. Self-love, self-interest, must perish. And the law of self-sacrifice is the law of self-preservation. The husbandman preserves his grain by casting it away. So in human life. To give is to live. The life that will be preserved is the life that is freely given in service to God and man. Those who for [623-624] Christ's sake sacrifice their life in this world will keep it unto life eternal.

The life spent on self is like the grain that is eaten. It disappears, but there is no increase. A man may gather all he can for self; he may live and think and plan for self; but his life passes away, and he has nothing. The law of self-serving is the law of self-destruction.

"If any man serve Me," said Jesus, "let him follow

---

4. "Life was to be the r__ _____ of His death...Only by yielding up His life could He i_____ life to humanity." (623). Lord, bring my mind to the 'contemplation of this sacrifice' again and again. What does it mean? _____

_____

_____

5. "All who would bring forth f_____ as workers together with Christ must first fall into the ground and die...Self-l_____, self-i_____ _____ must perish. And the law of self-sacrifice is the law of self-p_____ _____...The law of self-serving is the law of self-destruction." (623-624). Lord, You were so selfless in Your sacrifice. I want to be like You. As I contemplate Your life and character, may Satan's package of self-centeredness grow strangely dim: _____

_____

_____

_____

_____

Me; and where I am, there shall also My servant be: if any man serve Me, him will My Father honor." All who have borne with Jesus the cross of sacrifice will be sharers with Him of His glory. It was the joy of Christ in His humiliation and pain that His disciples should be glorified with Him. They are the fruit of His self-sacrifice. The outworking in them of His own character and spirit is His reward, and will be His joy throughout eternity. This joy they share with Him as the fruit of their labor and sacrifice is seen in other hearts and lives. They are workers together with Christ, and the Father will honor them as He honors His Son.

The message of the Greeks, foreshadowing as it did the gathering in of the Gentiles, brought to the mind of Jesus His entire mission. The work of redemption passed before Him, from the time when in heaven the plan was laid, to the death that was now so near at hand. A mysterious cloud seemed to enshroud the Son of God. Its gloom was felt by those near Him. He sat rapt in thought. At last the silence was broken by His mournful voice, "Now is My soul troubled; and what shall I say? Father, save Me from this hour?" In anticipation Christ was already drinking the cup of bitterness. His humanity shrank from the hour of abandonment, when to all appearance He would be deserted even by God, when all would see Him stricken, smitten of God, and afflicted. He shrank from public exposure, from being treated as the worst of criminals, from a shameful and dishonored death. A foreboding of His conflict with the powers of darkness, a sense of the awful burden of human transgression, and the Father's wrath because of sin caused the spirit of Jesus to faint, and the pallor of death to overspread His countenance.

Then came divine submission to His Father's will. "For this cause," He said, "came I unto this hour. Father, glorify Thy name." Only through the death of Christ could Satan's kingdom be overthrown. Only thus could man be redeemed, and God be glorified. Jesus consented to the agony, He accepted the sacrifice. The Majesty of heaven consented to suffer as the Sin Bearer. "Father, glorify Thy name," He said. As [624-625] Christ spoke these words, a response came from the cloud which hovered above His head: "I have both glorified it, and will glorify it again." Christ's whole life, from the manger to the time when these words were spoken, had glorified God; and in the coming trial His divine-human suffer-

6. "The outworking in them of His own character and spirit is His reward, and will be His j_____ throughout eternity." That's how I can make You happy? By letting You work Your character in me? By all means! Tell me what I am doing that limits You: _____

_____

_____

_____

_____

7. "His humanity shrank from the hour of a_____

_____, when all would see Him stricken, smitten of God and afflicted...As the voice was heard, a light darted from the cloud, and encircled Christ, as if the arms of Infinite Power were thrown about Him like a w____ of fire." (624-625). Lord, help me see that sin is separation from You, and Your presence is like a wall of fire. I want to treasure Your presence more and more:

_____

_____

_____

_____

ings would indeed glorify His Father's name.

As the voice was heard, a light darted from the cloud, and encircled Christ, as if the arms of Infinite Power were thrown about Him like a wall of fire. The people beheld this scene with terror and amazement. No one dared to speak. With silent lips and bated breath all stood with eyes fixed upon Jesus. The testimony of the Father having been given, the cloud lifted, and scattered in the heavens. For the time the visible communion between the Father and the Son was ended.

"The people therefore, that stood by, and heard it, said that it thundered: others said, An angel spake to Him." But the inquiring Greeks saw the cloud, heard the voice, comprehended its meaning, and discerned Christ indeed; to them He was revealed as the Sent of God.

The voice of God had been heard at the baptism of Jesus at the beginning of His ministry, and again at His transfiguration on the mount. Now at the close of His ministry it was heard for the third time, by a larger number of persons, and under peculiar circumstances. Jesus had just spoken the most solemn truth regarding the condition of the Jews. He had made His last appeal, and pronounced their doom. Now God again set His seal to the mission of His Son. He recognized the One whom Israel had rejected. "This voice came not because of Me," said Jesus, "but for your sakes." It was the crowning evidence of His Messiahship, the signal from the Father that Jesus had spoken the truth, and was the Son of God.

"Now is the judgment of this world," Christ continued; "now shall the prince of this world be cast out. And I, if I be lifted up from the earth, will draw all unto Me. This He said, signifying what death He should die." This is the crisis of the world. If I become the propitiation for the sins of men, the world will be lighted up. Satan's hold upon the souls of men will be broken. The defaced image of God will be restored in humanity, and a family of believing saints will finally inherit the heavenly home. This is the result of Christ's death. The Saviour is lost in contemplation of the scene of triumph called up before Him. He sees the cross, the cruel, ignominious cross, with all its attending horrors, blazing with glory. [625-626]

8. "But the work of h___ ___ redemption is not all that is accomplished by the cross. The love of God is m_____

But the work of human redemption is not all that is accomplished by the cross. The love of God is manifested to the universe. The prince of this world is cast out. The accusations which Satan has brought against God are refuted. The reproach which he has cast upon heaven is forever removed. Angels as well as men are drawn to the Redeemer. "I, if I be lifted up from the earth," He said, "will draw all unto Me."

Many people were round about Christ as He spoke these words, and one said, "We have heard out of the law that Christ abideth forever: and how sayest Thou, The Son of man must be lifted up? who is this Son of man? Then Jesus said unto them, Yet a little while is the light with you. Walk while ye have the light, lest darkness come upon you: for he that walketh in darkness knoweth not whither he goeth. While ye have light, believe in the light, that ye may be the children of light."

"But though He had done so many miracles before them, yet they believed not on Him." They had once asked the Saviour, "What sign showest Thou then, that we may see, and believe Thee?" John 6:30. Innumerable signs had been given; but they had closed their eyes and hardened their hearts. Now that the Father Himself had spoken, and they could ask for no further sign, they still refused to believe.

"Nevertheless among the chief rulers also many believed on Him; but because of the Pharisees they did not confess Him, lest they should be put out of the synagogue." They loved the praise of men rather than the approval of God. To save themselves from reproach and shame, they denied Christ, and rejected the offer of eternal life. And how many through all the centuries since have been doing the same thing! To them all the Saviour's warning words apply: "He that loveth his life shall lose it." "He that rejecteth Me," said Jesus, "and receiveth not My words, hath one that judgeth him: the word that I have spoken, the same shall judge him in the last day." John 12:48.

Alas for those who knew not the time of their visitation! Slowly and regretfully Christ left forever the precincts of the temple.

to the universe...The accusation which Satan has brought against God are r_____...A_____ as well as men are drawn to the Redeemer." (626). Lord, teach me a deeper appreciation of the risks You took, and what atonement means: _____
_____
_____
_____

9. "To save themselves from reproach and shame, they denied Christ and r_____ the offer of eternal life...Alas for those who knew not the time of their visitation! Slowly and r_____ Christ left forever the precincts of the temple." Oh Lord, I don't want to deny You or reject You. I don't want to turn my back on You and make You leave. Draw me close to You, Lord! _____
_____
_____
_____

Prayer journal: _____
_____
_____
_____
_____
_____
_____
_____

Chapter 69

On the Mount of Olives

[This chapter is based on Matt. 24; Mark 13; Luke 21:5-38.]

Christ's words to the priests and rulers, "Behold, your house is left unto you desolate" (Matt. 23:38), had struck terror to their hearts. They affected indifference, but the question kept rising in their minds as to the import of these words. An unseen danger seemed to threaten them. Could it be that the magnificent temple, which was the nation's glory, was soon to be a heap of ruins? The foreboding of evil was shared by the disciples, and they anxiously waited for some more definite statement from Jesus. As they passed with Him out of the temple, they called His attention to its strength and beauty. The stones of the temple were of the purest marble, of perfect whiteness, and some of them of almost fabulous size. A portion of the wall had withstood the siege by Nebuchadnezzar's army. In its perfect masonry it appeared like one solid stone dug entire from the quarry. How those mighty walls could be overthrown the disciples could not comprehend.

As Christ's attention was attracted to the magnificence of the temple, what must have been the unuttered thoughts of that Rejected One! The view before Him was indeed beautiful, but He said with sadness, I see it all. The buildings are indeed wonderful. You point to these walls as apparently indestructible; but listen to My words: The day will come when "there shall not be left one stone upon another, that shall not be thrown down." [627-628]

Christ's words had been spoken in the hearing of a large number of people; but when He was alone, Peter, John, James, and Andrew came to Him as He sat upon the Mount of Olives. "Tell us," they said, "when shall these things be? and what shall be the sign of Thy coming, and of the end of the world?" Jesus did not answer His disciples by taking up separately the destruction of Jerusalem and the great day of His coming. He mingled the description of these two events. Had He opened to His disciples future events as He beheld them, they would have been unable to endure the sight. In mercy to

1. "They would have been unable to e_____ the sight. In m_____

them He blended the description of the two great crises, leaving the disciples to study out the meaning for themselves. When He referred to the destruction of Jerusalem, His prophetic words reached beyond that event to the final conflagration in that day when the Lord shall rise out of His place to punish the world for their iniquity, when the earth shall disclose her blood, and shall no more cover her slain. This entire discourse was given, not for the disciples only, but for those who should live in the last scenes of this earth's history.

Turning to the disciples, Christ said, "Take heed that no man deceive you. For many shall come in My name, saying, I am Christ; and shall deceive many." Many false messiahs will appear, claiming to work miracles, and declaring that the time of the deliverance of the Jewish nation has come. These will mislead many. Christ's words were fulfilled. Between His death and the siege of Jerusalem many false messiahs appeared. But this warning was given also to those who live in this age of the world. The same deceptions practiced prior to the destruction of Jerusalem have been practiced through the ages, and will be practiced again.

"And ye shall hear of wars and rumors of wars: see that ye be not troubled: for all these things must come to pass, but the end is not yet." Prior to the destruction of Jerusalem, men wrestled for the supremacy. Emperors were murdered. Those supposed to be standing next the throne were slain. There were wars and rumors of wars. "All these things must come to pass," said Christ, "but the end [of the Jewish nation as a nation] is not yet. For nation shall rise against nation, and kingdom against kingdom: and there shall be famines, and pestilences, and earthquakes, in divers places. All these are the beginning of sorrows." Christ said, As the rabbis see these signs, they will declare them to be God's judgments upon the nations for holding in bondage His chosen people. They will declare that these signs are the token of the advent of [628-629] the Messiah. Be not deceived; they are the beginning of His judgments. The people have looked to themselves. They have not repented and been converted that I should heal them. The signs that they represent as tokens of their release from bondage are signs of their destruction.

"Then shall they deliver you up to be afflicted, and shall kill you: and ye shall be hated of all nations for My name's sake. And then shall many be offended, and

___ to them He blended the destruction of these two crises." (628). Lord, thank You for only giving or allowing me what I can handle with Your help. If it seems overwhelming, remind me of 1 Cor 10:13:

_____

_____

_____

_____

2. "Many f_____ messiahs will appear, claiming to work miracles." Lord, I'm not sure how Satan will succeed on me with this one. It doesn't seem possible. Could he lull me into complacency, that I am caught off guard? _____

_____

I had better know You, the true Messiah, Your character, Your spirit, so the look-a-like messiah won't get me: _____

_____

_____

_____

3. "They will declare that these signs are the token of the advent of the Messiah...The signs that they represent as tokens of their r_____ from bondage are signs of their d_____." (628, 629). When God sends admonition, do I try to reinterpret it as approval, blessing, or acceptance?

_____

4. "Ye shall be h_____
_____ of all nations for
My name's s_____."
Lord, are there things I do
for the sake of peculiarity,
rather than for Your name's
sake? _____

_____
What's the difference?
_____
_____
_____

5. "The authorities will
make laws to r_____
religious liberty…They
will think they can f___
_____ the conscience,
which God alone should
control. Even n_____
they are making a b___
_____." (630). Desire
of Ages was copyrighted
in 1898. Where do things
stand now? Will Home-
land Security be the basis
of loss of freedoms? ____

_____
_____
_____

shall betray one another, and shall hate one another."
All this the Christians suffered. Fathers and mothers
betrayed their children. Children betrayed their parents.
Friends delivered their friends up to the Sanhedrin. The
persecutors wrought out their purpose by killing Stephen, James, and other Christians. [629-630]

Through His servants, God gave the Jewish people
a last opportunity to repent. He manifested Himself
through His witnesses in their arrest, in their trial, and
in their imprisonment. Yet their judges pronounced on
them the death sentence. They were men of whom the
world was not worthy, and by killing them the Jews crucified afresh the Son of God. So it will be again. The
authorities will make laws to restrict religious liberty.
They will assume the right that is God's alone. They
will think they can force the conscience, which God
alone should control. Even now they are making a beginning; this work they will continue to carry forward
till they reach a boundary over which they cannot step.
God will interpose in behalf of His loyal, command-
ment-keeping people.

On every occasion when persecution takes place,
those who witness it make decisions either for Christ
or against Him. Those who manifest sympathy for the
ones wrongly condemned show their attachment for
Christ. Others are offended because the principles of
truth cut directly across their practice. Many stumble
and fall, apostatizing from the faith they once advocated. Those who apostatize in time of trial will, to secure
their own safety, bear false witness, and betray their
brethren. Christ has warned us of this, that we may not
be surprised at the unnatural, cruel course of those who
reject the light.

Christ gave His disciples a sign of the ruin to come
on Jerusalem, and He told them how to escape: "When
ye shall see Jerusalem compassed with armies, then
know that the desolation thereof is nigh. Then let them
which are in Judea flee to the mountains; and let them
which are in the midst of it depart out; and let not them
that are in the countries enter thereinto. For these be
the days of vengeance, that all things which are written
may be fulfilled." This warning was given to be heeded
forty years after, at the destruction of Jerusalem. The
Christians obeyed the warning, and not a Christian perished in the fall of the city.

"Pray ye that your flight be not in the winter; neither on the Sabbath day," Christ said. He who made the Sabbath did not abolish it, nailing it to His cross. The Sabbath was not rendered null and void by His death. Forty years after His crucifixion it was still to be held sacred. For forty years the disciples were to pray that their flight might not be on the Sabbath day.

From the destruction of Jerusalem, Christ passed on rapidly to the greater event, the last link in the chain of this earth's history,--the coming of the Son of God in majesty and glory. Between these two events, there lay open to Christ's view long centuries of darkness, centuries for His [630-631] church marked with blood and tears and agony. Upon these scenes His disciples could not then endure to look, and Jesus passed them by with a brief mention. "Then shall be great tribulation," He said, "such as was not since the beginning of the world to this time, no, nor ever shall be. And except those days should be shortened, there should no flesh be saved: but for the elect's sake those days shall be shortened." For more than a thousand years such persecution as the world had never before known was to come upon Christ's followers. Millions upon millions of His faithful witnesses were to be slain. Had not God's hand been stretched out to preserve His people, all would have perished. "But for the elect's sake," He said, "those days shall be shortened."

Now, in unmistakable language, our Lord speaks of His second coming, and He gives warning of dangers to precede His advent to the world. "If any man shall say unto you, Lo, here is Christ, or there; believe it not. For there shall arise false christs, and false prophets, and shall show great signs and wonders; insomuch that, if it were possible, they shall deceive the very elect. Behold, I have told you before. Wherefore if they shall say unto you, Behold, He is in the desert; go not forth: behold, He is in the secret chambers; believe it not. For as the lightning cometh out of the east, and shineth even unto the west; so shall also the coming of the Son of man be." As one of the signs of Jerusalem's destruction, Christ had said, "Many false prophets shall rise, and shall deceive many." False prophets did rise, deceiving the people, and leading great numbers into the desert. Magicians and sorcerers, claiming miraculous power, drew the people after them into the mountain solitudes. But this prophecy was spoken also for the last days. This sign is given as a sign of the second advent. Even now false christs and false prophets are showing signs and wonders to seduce His disciples. Do we not hear the cry, "Behold, He is in the desert"? Have not thousands gone forth into the desert, hoping to find Christ? And from thousands of gatherings where men profess to hold communion with departed spirits is not the call now heard, "Behold, He is in the secret chambers"? This is the very claim that spiritism puts forth. But what says Christ? "Believe it not. For as the lightning cometh out of the east, and shineth even unto the west; so shall also the coming of the Son of man be."

6. "T_____ generation shall not pass, till all these things be fulfilled." (632). What does this mean?

_____

_____

_____

(The generation that sees the signs?) _____

_____

_____

_____

The Saviour gives signs of His coming, and more than this, He fixes the time when the first of these signs shall appear: "Immediately after the tribulation of those days shall the sun be darkened, and the moon [631-632] shall not give her light, and the stars shall fall from heaven, and the powers of the heavens shall be shaken: and then shall appear the sign of the Son of man in heaven: and then shall all the tribes of the earth mourn, and they shall see the Son of man coming in the clouds of heaven with power and great glory. And He shall send His angels with a great sound of a trumpet, and they shall gather together His elect from the four winds, from one end of heaven to the other."

At the close of the great papal persecution, Christ declared, the sun should be darkened, and the moon should not give her light. Next, the stars should fall from heaven. And He says, "Learn a parable of the fig tree; When his branch is yet tender, and putteth forth leaves, ye know that summer is nigh: so likewise ye, when ye shall see all these things, know that He is near, even at the doors." Matt. 24:32, 33, margin.

Christ has given signs of His coming. He declares that we may know when He is near, even at the doors. He says of those who see these signs, "This generation shall not pass, till all these things be fulfilled." These signs have appeared. Now we know of a surety that the Lord's coming is at hand. "Heaven and earth shall pass away," He says, "but My words shall not pass away."

7. "He will come to honor those who have loved Him, and kept His commandments, and to take them to H_____. He has not forgotten t_____ nor His promise. There will be a r_____

Christ is coming with clouds and with great glory. A multitude of shining angels will attend Him. He will come to raise the dead, and to change the living saints from glory to glory. He will come to honor those who have loved Him, and kept His commandments, and to take them to Himself. He has not forgotten them nor His promise. There will be a relinking of the family chain. When we look upon our dead, we may think of the morning when the trump of God shall sound, when "the dead shall be raised incorruptible, and we shall be changed." 1 Cor. 15:52. A little longer, and we shall see the King in His beauty. A little longer, and He will wipe all tears from our eyes. A little longer, and He will present us "faultless before the presence of His glory with exceeding joy." Jude 24. Wherefore, when He gave the signs of His coming He said, "When these things begin to come to pass, then look up, and lift up your heads; for your redemption draweth nigh."

But the day and the hour of His coming Christ has not revealed. He stated plainly to His disciples that He Himself could not make known the day or the hour of His second appearing. Had He been at liberty to reveal this, why need He have exhorted them to maintain an attitude of constant expectancy? There are those who claim to know the very day and hour of our Lord's appearing. Very earnest are they in mapping out [632-633] the future. But the Lord has warned them off the ground they occupy. The exact time of the second coming of the Son of man is God's mystery.

Christ continues, pointing out the condition of the world at His coming: "As the days of Noah were, so shall also the coming of the Son of man be. For as in the days that were before the Flood they were eating and drinking, marrying and giving in marriage, until the day that Noah entered into the ark, and knew not until the Flood came, and took them all away; so shall also the coming of the Son of man be." Christ does not here bring to view a temporal millennium, a thousand years in which all are to prepare for eternity. He tells us that as it was in Noah's day, so will it be when the Son of man comes again.

How was it in Noah's day? "God saw that the wickedness of man was great in the earth, and that every imagination of the thoughts of his heart was only evil continually." Gen. 6:5. The inhabitants of the antediluvian world turned from Jehovah, refusing to do His holy will. They followed their own unholy imagination and perverted ideas. It was because of their wickedness that they were destroyed; and today the world is following the same way. It presents no flattering signs of millennial glory. The transgressors of God's law are filling the earth with wickedness. Their betting, their horse racing, their gambling, their dissipation, their lustful practices,

of the family chain." Lord, thank You for the promise that You will return and take me to Yourself. I know You will. You keep Your word. May I be found living my love for You: _

_____

_____

8. "Had He been at liberty to reveal this, why need He have exhorted them to maintain an attitude of c_____
expectancy?...The exact time of the second coming of the Son of Man is G_____ mystery." (632, 633). Lord, how do I keep this attitude fresh?

_____

_____

_____

their untamable passions, are fast filling the world with violence.

In the prophecy of Jerusalem's destruction Christ said, "Because iniquity shall abound, the love of many shall wax cold. But he that shall endure unto the end, the same shall be saved. And this gospel of the kingdom shall be preached in all the world for a witness unto all nations; and then shall the end come." This prophecy will again be fulfilled. The abounding iniquity of that day finds its counterpart in this generation. So with the prediction in regard to the preaching of the gospel. Before the fall of Jerusalem, Paul, writing by the Holy Spirit, declared that the gospel was preached to "every creature which is under heaven." Col. 1:23. So now, before the coming of the Son of man, the everlasting gospel is to be preached "to every nation, and kindred, and tongue, and people." Rev. 14:6, 14. God "hath appointed a day, in the which He will judge the world." Acts 17:31. Christ tells us when that day shall be ushered in. He does not say that all the world will be converted, but that "this gospel of the kingdom shall be preached in all the world for a witness unto all nations; and then shall the end come." By giving the gospel to the world it is in our power to hasten our Lord's return. We are not only to look for but to hasten the coming of the day of God. 2 Peter 3:12, margin. Had [633-634] the church of Christ done her appointed work as the Lord ordained, the whole world would before this have been warned, and the Lord Jesus would have come to our earth in power and great glory.

After He had given the signs of His coming, Christ said, "When ye see these things come to pass, know ye that the kingdom of God is nigh at hand." "Take ye heed, watch and pray." God has always given men warning of coming judgments. Those who had faith in His message for their time, and who acted out their faith, in obedience to His commandments, escaped the judgments that fell upon the disobedient and unbelieving. The word came to Noah, "Come thou and all thy house into the ark; for thee have I seen righteous before Me." Noah obeyed and was saved. The message came to Lot, "Up, get you out of this place; for the Lord will destroy this city." Gen. 7:1; 19:14. Lot placed himself under the guardianship of the heavenly messengers, and was saved. So Christ's disciples were given warning of the destruction of Jerusalem. Those who watched for

9. "By giving the gospel to the world it is in our power to h_____ our Lord's return. We are not only to l_____ for but to hasten the coming of the day of God. Had the church of Christ done her appointed work as the Lord ordained, the whole world would b_____ this have been warned." (633, 634). What can I do, Lord? Just watching satellite evangelism isn't enough. I have been so blessed by the good news and Your friendship, give me opportunities, divine appointments, to share, to help fulfill the gospel commission, and so hasten Your coming: _____

_____

_____

the sign of the coming ruin, and fled from the city, escaped the destruction. So now we are given warning of Christ's second coming and of the destruction to fall upon the world. Those who heed the warning will be saved.

Because we know not the exact time of His coming, we are commanded to watch. "Blessed are those servants, whom the Lord when He cometh shall find watching." Luke 12:37. Those who watch for the Lord's coming are not waiting in idle expectancy. The expectation of Christ's coming is to make men fear the Lord, and fear His judgments upon transgression. It is to awaken them to the great sin of rejecting His offers of mercy. Those who are watching for the Lord are purifying their souls by obedience to the truth. With vigilant watching they combine earnest working. Because they know that the Lord is at the door, their zeal is quickened to co-operate with the divine intelligences in working for the salvation of souls. These are the faithful and wise servants who give to the Lord's household "their portion of meat in due season." Luke 12:42. They are declaring the truth that is now specially applicable. As Enoch, Noah, Abraham, and Moses each declared the truth for his time, so will Christ's servants now give the special warning for their generation.

But Christ brings to view another class: "If that evil servant shall say in his heart, My lord delayeth his coming; and shall begin to smite his fellow servants, and to eat and drink with the drunken; the lord of that servant shall come in a day when he looketh not for him." [634-635] The evil servant says in his heart, "My lord delayeth his coming." He does not say that Christ will not come. He does not scoff at the idea of His second coming. But in his heart and by his actions and words he declares that the Lord's coming is delayed. He banishes from the minds of others the conviction that the Lord is coming quickly. His influence leads men to presumptuous, careless delay. They are confirmed in their worldliness and stupor. Earthly passions, corrupt thoughts, take possession of the mind. The evil servant eats and drinks with the drunken, unites with the world in pleasure seeking. He smites his fellow servants, accusing and condemning those who are faithful to their Master. He mingles with the world. Like grows with like in transgression. It is a fearful assimilation. With the world he is taken in the snare. "The lord of that servant shall come . . . in an

10. "Those who watch for the Lord's coming are not waiting in i_____ expectancy. The expectation of Christ's coming is…to awaken them to the great sin of r_____ His offers of mercy…to purifying their souls…to cooperate with the divine intelligence in w_____ for the salvation of souls." Lord, wake me up. It's not just a waiting game. May I grow in Your mercy and Your pure character. And I am available to divine appointments for sharing the good news: _____
_____
_____
_____

11. "In his h_____ and by his a_____ and words, he [the evil servant] declares that the Lord's coming is d_____ _____." (635). What's in my heart, Lord?_____
_____
_____
_____

hour that he is not aware of, and shall cut him asunder, and appoint him his portion with the hypocrites."

"If therefore thou shalt not watch, I will come on thee as a thief, and thou shalt not know what hour I will come upon thee." Rev. 3:3. The advent of Christ will surprise the false teachers. They are saying, "Peace and safety." Like the priests and teachers before the fall of Jerusalem, they look for the church to enjoy earthly prosperity and glory. The signs of the times they interpret as foreshadowing this. But what saith the word of Inspiration? "Sudden destruction cometh upon them." 1 Thess. 5:3. Upon all who dwell on the face of the whole earth, upon all who make this world their home, the day of God will come as a snare. It comes to them as a prowling thief.

The world, full of rioting, full of godless pleasure, is asleep, asleep in carnal security. Men are putting afar off the coming of the Lord. They laugh at warnings. The proud boast is made, "All things continue as they were from the beginning." "Tomorrow shall be as this day, and much more abundant." 2 Peter 3:4; Isa. 56:12. We will go deeper into pleasure loving. But Christ says, "Behold, I come as a thief." Rev. 16:15. At the very time when the world is asking in scorn, "Where is the promise of His coming?" the signs are fulfilling. While they cry, "Peace and safety," sudden destruction is coming. When the scorner, the rejecter of truth, has become presumptuous; when the routine of work in the various money-making lines is carried on without regard to principle; when the student is eagerly seeking knowledge of everything but his Bible, Christ comes as a thief. [635-636]

Everything in the world is in agitation. The signs of the times are ominous. Coming events cast their shadows before. The Spirit of God is withdrawing from the earth, and calamity follows calamity by sea and by land. There are tempests, earthquakes, fires, floods, murders of every grade. Who can read the future? Where is security? There is assurance in nothing that is human or earthly. Rapidly are men ranging themselves under the banner they have chosen. Restlessly are they waiting and watching the movements of their leaders. There are those who are waiting and watching and working for our Lord's appearing. Another class are falling into line under the generalship of the first great apostate. Few believe with heart and soul that we have a hell to shun

12. "There are those who are waiting and watch-ing and w_____ for our Lord's appearing... Few believe with heart and soul that we have a hell to s_____ and a heaven

and a heaven to win.

The crisis is stealing gradually upon us. The sun shines in the heavens, passing over its usual round, and the heavens still declare the glory of God. Men are still eating and drinking, planting and building, marrying, and giving in marriage. Merchants are still buying and selling. Men are jostling one against another, contending for the highest place. Pleasure lovers are still crowding to theaters, horse races, gambling hells. The highest excitement prevails, yet probation's hour is fast closing, and every case is about to be eternally decided. Satan sees that his time is short. He has set all his agencies at work that men may be deceived, deluded, occupied and entranced, until the day of probation shall be ended, and the door of mercy be forever shut.

Solemnly there come to us down through the centuries the warning words of our Lord from the Mount of Olives: "Take heed to yourselves, lest at any time your hearts be overcharged with surfeiting, and drunkenness, and cares of this life, and so that day come upon you unawares." "Watch ye therefore, and pray always, that ye may be accounted worthy to escape all these things that shall come to pass, and to stand before the Son of man."

to w_____…Satan sees that his time is short. He has set all his agencies at work that men may be deceived, deluded, o____ _____ and entranced…so that the day come upon you unawares." (636). Lord, there is so much of this world I am tired of. I want Your coming now! How can I let Satan occupy me into delaying Your coming? _____

_____. Keep me awake, watching, working, winning heaven. _____

_____

_____

_____

Prayer journal: _____

_____

_____

_____

_____

_____

_____

Chapter 70

"The Least of These My Brethren"

[This chapter is based on Matt. 25:31-46.]

1. "Christ on the Mount of Olives pictured to His disciples the scene of the great j_____ day. And He represented its decision turning upon o_____ point...Eternal destiny will be determined by what we have done or have n_____ to do for Him in the person of the p_____ and the suffering." Lord, I should not minister to the poor to get credit for heaven. How do I get the heart that ministers genuinely?

_____

_____

_____

2. "I____ all who suffer for My name, said Jesus, you are to recognize M__ ____. As you would minister to Me, s_____ you are to minister to them. This is the evidence that you are My d_____." (638). Lord, help me to remember that it is the evidence, not the basis of discipleship. So I start by responding to the call to follow You. And out of that relationship, out of the

When the Son of man shall come in His glory, and all the holy angels with Him, then shall He sit upon the throne of His glory: and before Him shall be gathered all nations: and He shall separate them one from another." Thus Christ on the Mount of Olives pictured to His disciples the scene of the great judgment day. And He represented its decision as turning upon one point. When the nations are gathered before Him, there will be but two classes, and their eternal destiny will be determined by what they have done or have neglected to do for Him in the person of the poor and the suffering.

In that day Christ does not present before men the great work He has done for them in giving His life for their redemption. He presents the faithful work they have done for Him. To those whom He sets upon His right hand He will say, "Come, ye blessed of My Father, inherit the kingdom prepared for you from the foundation of the world: for I was an hungered, and ye gave Me meat: I was thirsty, and ye gave Me drink: I was a stranger, and ye took Me in: naked, and ye clothed Me: I was sick, and ye visited Me: I was in prison, and ye came unto Me." But those whom Christ commends know not that they have been ministering unto Him. To their perplexed inquiries He answers, "Inasmuch as ye have done it unto one of the least of these My brethren, ye have done it unto Me."

Jesus had told His disciples that they were to be hated of all men, to be persecuted and afflicted. Many would be driven from their homes, and brought to poverty. Many would be in distress through disease and [637-638] privation. Many would be cast into prison. To all who forsook friends or home for His sake He had promised in this life a hundredfold. Now He assured a special blessing to all who should minister to their brethren. In all who suffer for My name, said Jesus, you are to recognize Me. As you would minister to Me, so you are to minister to them. This is the evidence that you are My disciples.

All who have been born into the heavenly family are in a special sense the brethren of our Lord. The love of Christ binds together the members of His family, and wherever that love is made manifest there the divine relationship is revealed. "Everyone that loveth is born of God, and knoweth God." 1 John 4:7.

Those whom Christ commends in the judgment may have known little of theology, but they have cherished His principles. Through the influence of the divine Spirit they have been a blessing to those about them. Even among the heathen are those who have cherished the spirit of kindness; before the words of life had fallen upon their ears, they have befriended the missionaries, even ministering to them at the peril of their own lives. Among the heathen are those who worship God ignorantly, those to whom the light is never brought by human instrumentality, yet they will not perish. Though ignorant of the written law of God, they have heard His voice speaking to them in nature, and have done the things that the law required. Their works are evidence that the Holy Spirit has touched their hearts, and they are recognized as the children of God.

How surprised and gladdened will be the lowly among the nations, and among the heathen, to hear from the lips of the Saviour, "Inasmuch as ye have done it unto one of the least of these My brethren, ye have done it unto Me"! How glad will be the heart of Infinite Love as His followers look up with surprise and joy at His words of approval!

But not to any class is Christ's love restricted. He identifies Himself with every child of humanity. That we might become members of the heavenly family, He became a member of the earthly family. He is the Son of man, and thus a brother to every son and daughter of Adam. His followers are not to feel themselves detached from the perishing world around them. They are a part of the great web of humanity; and Heaven looks upon them as brothers to sinners as well as to saints. The fallen, the erring, and the sinful, Christ's love embraces; and every deed of kindness done to uplift a fallen soul, every act of mercy, is accepted as done to Him. [638-639]

The angels of heaven are sent forth to minister to those who shall be heirs of salvation. We know not now who they are; it is not yet made manifest who shall overcome, and share the inheritance of the saints in

heart of that relationship, comes this ministry: ____

____

____

"Wherever that love is made m_____ there the d_____ relationship is revealed."

____

____

3. What does it mean to worship God ignorantly?

____

____

"Though ignorant of theology and the written l_____ of God, they have heard God's voice speaking to them in n_____...The Holy Spirit has t_____ ____ their hearts." Lord, I have the added blessing of Scripture. What's the response of my heart? Have I allowed the Holy Spirit to touch my heart?

____

____

____

4. "How glad will be the h_____ of Infinite Love as His followers look up with surprise and joy at His words of approval!" Lord, I want Your heart to experience this gladness. In the least of these, may I recognize You and the opportunity to share love. ____

____

____

5. "Angels of heaven are passing throughout the length and breadth of the earth, seeking to comfort the sorrowing, to protect the imperiled, to w_____ the hearts of men to Christ. Not one is neglected or p_____ by." (639). How is it that with the ministry to the needy, there is a "sacred atmosphere of joy and peace?" _____

_____
_____
_____

6. "The Father from His throne numbers the u_____ _____ workers among His most p_____ treasures." Where are my values? _____

How can they be like Yours? _____
_____
_____
_____

7. Those "who had neglected Him in the person of the poor and the suffering, were u_____ _____ of their guilt." Lord, how do I keep from feeling "superior" to my poor brethren, and mercy dying out of my heart? Do I "shut" myself away from the poor in my costly dwelling and splendid church?_____

_____

light; but angels of heaven are passing throughout the length and breadth of the earth, seeking to comfort the sorrowing, to protect the imperiled, to win the hearts of men to Christ. Not one is neglected or passed by. God is no respecter of persons, and He has an equal care for all the souls He has created.

As you open your door to Christ's needy and suffering ones, you are welcoming unseen angels. You invite the companionship of heavenly beings. They bring a sacred atmosphere of joy and peace. They come with praises upon their lips, and an answering strain is heard in heaven. Every deed of mercy makes music there. The Father from His throne numbers the unselfish workers among His most precious treasures.

Those on the left hand of Christ, those who had neglected Him in the person of the poor and the suffering, were unconscious of their guilt. Satan had blinded them; they had not perceived what they owed to their brethren. They had been self-absorbed, and cared not for others' needs.

To the rich, God has given wealth that they may relieve and comfort His suffering children; but too often they are indifferent to the wants of others. They feel themselves superior to their poor brethren. They do not put themselves in the poor man's place. They do not understand the temptations and struggles of the poor, and mercy dies out of their hearts. In costly dwellings and splendid churches, the rich shut themselves away from the poor; the means that God has given to bless the needy is spent in pampering pride and selfishness. The poor are robbed daily of the education they should have concerning the tender mercies of God; for He has made ample provision that they should be comforted with the necessities of life. They are compelled to feel the poverty that narrows life, and are often tempted to become envious, jealous, and full of evil surmisings. Those who themselves have not endured the pressure of want too often treat the poor in a contemptuous way, and make them feel that they are looked upon as paupers.

But Christ beholds it all, and He says, It was I who was hungry and thirsty. It was I who was a stranger. It was I who was sick. It was I who was in prison. While you were feasting at your bountifully spread table, I was famishing in the hovel or the empty street. While you were at ease in your luxurious home, I had not where to lay My head. While [639-640] you crowded your wardrobe with rich apparel, I was destitute. While you pursued your pleasures, I languished in prison.

When you doled out the pittance of bread to the starving poor, when you gave those flimsy garments to shield them from the biting frost, did you remember that you were giving to the Lord of glory? All the days of your life I was near you in the person of these afflicted ones, but you did not seek Me. You would not enter into fellowship with Me. I know you not.

Many feel that it would be a great privilege to visit the scenes of Christ's life on earth, to walk where He trod, to look upon the lake beside which He loved to teach, and the hills and valleys on which His eyes so often rested. But we need not go to Nazareth, to Capernaum, or to Bethany, in order to walk in the steps of Jesus. We shall find His footprints beside the sickbed, in the hovels of poverty, in the crowded alleys of the great city, and in every place where there are human hearts in need of consolation. In doing as Jesus did when on earth, we shall walk in His steps.

All may find something to do. "The poor always ye have with you," (John 12:8), Jesus said, and none need feel that there is no place where they can labor for Him. Millions upon millions of human souls ready to perish, bound in chains of ignorance and sin, have never so much as heard of Christ's love for them. Were our condition and theirs to be reversed, what would we desire them to do for us? All this, so far as lies in our power, we are under the most solemn obligation to do for them. Christ's rule of life, by which every one of us must stand or fall in the judgment, is, "Whatsoever ye would that men should do to you, do ye even so to them." Matt. 7:12.

The Saviour has given His precious life in order to establish a church capable of caring for sorrowful, tempted souls. A company of believers may be poor, uneducated, and unknown; yet in Christ they may do a work in the home, the neighborhood, the church, and even in "the regions beyond," whose results shall be as far-reaching as eternity.

It is because this work is neglected that so many young disciples never advance beyond the mere alphabet of Christian experience. The light which was glowing in their own hearts when Jesus spoke to them, "Thy sins be forgiven thee," they might have kept alive by helping those in need. The restless energy that is so of-

"All the days of your life I was n_____ you in the person of these afflicted one, but you did not seek Me. You would not enter in f_____ with Me. I know you not." (639, 640). I don't ever want to hear those words, Lord. Help me to have Your character of compassion:

_____
_____
_____
_____

8. "Millions upon millions of human souls ready to p_____, bound in chains of ignorance and sin, have never so much as h_____ of Christ's l_____ for them. Were our condition and theirs to be reversed, what would we desire them to do for us?" _____
_____
_____

ten a source of danger to the young might be directed into channels through which it would [640-641] flow out in streams of blessing. Self would be forgotten in earnest work to do others good.

Those who minister to others will be ministered unto by the Chief Shepherd. They themselves will drink of the living water, and will be satisfied. They will not be longing for exciting amusements, or for some change in their lives. The great topic of interest will be, how to save the souls that are ready to perish. Social intercourse will be profitable. The love of the Redeemer will draw hearts together in unity.

When we realize that we are workers together with God, His promises will not be spoken with indifference. They will burn in our hearts, and kindle upon our lips. To Moses, when called to minister to an ignorant, undisciplined, and rebellious people, God gave the promise, "My presence shall go with thee, and I will give thee rest." And He said, "Certainly I will be with thee." Ex. 33:14; 3:12. This promise is to all who labor in Christ's stead for His afflicted and suffering ones.

Love to man is the earthward manifestation of the love of God. It was to implant this love, to make us children of one family, that the King of glory became one with us. And when His parting words are fulfilled, "Love one another, as I have loved you" (John 15:12); when we love the world as He has loved it, then for us His mission is accomplished. We are fitted for heaven; for we have heaven in our hearts.

But "if thou forbear to deliver them that are drawn unto death, and those that are ready to be slain; if thou sayest, Behold, we knew it not; doth not He that pondereth the heart consider it? and He that keepeth thy soul, doth not He know it? and shall not He render to every man according to his works?" Prov. 24:11, 12. In the great Judgment day, those who have not worked for Christ, who have drifted along thinking of themselves, caring for themselves, will be placed by the Judge of the whole earth with those who did evil. They receive the same condemnation.

To every soul a trust is given. Of everyone the Chief Shepherd will demand, "Where is the flock that was given thee, thy beautiful flock?" And "what wilt thou say when He shall punish thee?" Jer. 13:20, 21.

---

9. "Self would be f_____ _____ in earnest work to do others good…They themselves will drink of the living water, and will be s_____. They will not be l_____ for exciting amusements… The great topic of i____ _____ will be, how to s_____ the souls that are ready to perish." (641). These are wonderful results, Lord. I just got to get out and do it. Don't let up on me till I do, Lord:

_____
_____
_____

10. "When we love the world as He loved it, then for us His m_____ is accomplished." What did I think His mission was? __
_____

What do I understand it to be now? _____
_____

"We are f_____ for heaven; for we have heaven in our hearts."

Prayer journal: _____
_____
_____
_____
_____
_____
_____

Chapter 71

A Servant of Servants

[This chapter is based on Luke 22:7-18, 24; John 13:1-17.]

In the upper chamber of a dwelling at Jerusalem, Christ was sitting at table with His disciples. They had gathered to celebrate the Passover. The Saviour desired to keep this feast alone with the twelve. He knew that His hour was come; He Himself was the true paschal lamb, and on the day the Passover was eaten He was to be sacrificed. He was about to drink the cup of wrath; He must soon receive the final baptism of suffering. But a few quiet hours yet remained to Him, and these were to be spent for the benefit of His beloved disciples.

The whole life of Christ had been a life of unselfish service. "Not to be ministered unto, but to minister," (Matt. 20:28), had been the lesson of His every act. But not yet had the disciples learned the lesson. At this last Passover supper, Jesus repeated His teaching by an illustration that impressed it forever on their minds and hearts.

The interviews between Jesus and His disciples were usually seasons of calm joy, highly prized by them all. The Passover suppers had been scenes of special interest; but upon this occasion Jesus was troubled. His heart was burdened, and a shadow rested upon His countenance. [642-643] As He met the disciples in the upper chamber, they perceived that something weighed heavily upon His mind, and although they knew not its cause, they sympathized with His grief.

As they were gathered about the table, He said in tones of touching sadness, "With desire I have desired to eat this Passover with you before I suffer: for I say unto you, I will not any more eat thereof, until it be fulfilled in the kingdom of God. And He took the cup, and gave thanks, and said, Take this, and divide it among yourselves: for I say unto you, I will not drink of the fruit of the vine, until the kingdom of God shall come."

Christ knew that the time had come for Him to depart out of the world, and go to His Father. And having loved His own that were in the world, He loved them unto the end. He was now in the shadow of the

1. "He was about to drink the cup of wrath...But a few quiet hours yet remained to Him, and these were to be spent for the b_____ _____ of His beloved disciples...With desire I have desired to eat this passover w_____ you... He was now in the shadow of the cross, and the pain was t_____His heart...

His thoughts of what He Himself must suffer were ever c_____ with His disciples. He did not think of H_____. His c_____ for them was uppermost in His mind." (642, 643). Lord, You were facing the most trying experience ever, being made sin, and You think of Your disciples? _____ _____. What is Your vision of my relationship with You? _____
_____
_____
_____

2. "Moments passed in silence. Jesus appeared to be waiting." Why?
_____
_____
_____
_____

"His sorrowful words, pointing to His own suffering, had made l_____ _____ impression. The glances they cast upon each other, told of jealousy and c_____." Lord, I am sure there are times You have something to share with me, but You can see in my heart, that I am not able to hear it. But Lord, I don't want to miss out on anything You have to say to me: _____
_____
_____

cross, and the pain was torturing His heart. He knew that He would be deserted in the hour of His betrayal. He knew that by the most humiliating process to which criminals were subjected He would be put to death. He knew the ingratitude and cruelty of those He had come to save. He knew how great the sacrifice that He must make, and for how many it would be in vain. Knowing all that was before Him, He might naturally have been overwhelmed with the thought of His own humiliation and suffering. But He looked upon the twelve, who had been with Him as His own, and who, after His shame and sorrow and painful usage were over, would be left to struggle in the world. His thoughts of what He Himself must suffer were ever connected with His disciples. He did not think of Himself. His care for them was uppermost in His mind.

On this last evening with His disciples, Jesus had much to tell them. If they had been prepared to receive what He longed to impart, they would have been saved from heartbreaking anguish, from disappointment and unbelief. But Jesus saw that they could not bear what He had to say. As He looked into their faces, the words of warning and comfort were stayed upon His lips. Moments passed in silence. Jesus appeared to be waiting. The disciples were ill at ease. The sympathy and tenderness awakened by Christ's grief seemed to have passed away. His sorrowful words, pointing to His own suffering, had made little impression. The glances they cast upon each other told of jealousy and contention.

There was "a strife among them, which of them should be accounted the greatest." This contention, carried on in the presence of Christ, grieved and wounded Him. The disciples clung to their favorite idea that Christ would assert His power, and take His position on the throne of David. And in heart each still longed for the highest place in the [643-644] kingdom. They had placed their own estimate upon themselves and upon one another, and, instead of regarding their brethren as more worthy, they had placed themselves first. The request of James and John to sit on the right and left of Christ's throne had excited the indignation of the others. That the two brothers should presume to ask for the highest position so stirred the ten that alienation threatened. They felt that they were misjudged, that their fidelity and talents were not appreciated. Judas was the most severe upon James and John.

When the disciples entered the supper room, their hearts were full of resentful feelings. Judas pressed next to Christ on the left side; John was on the right. If there was a highest place, Judas was determined to have it, and that place was thought to be next to Christ. And Judas was a traitor.

Another cause of dissension had arisen. At a feast it was customary for a servant to wash the feet of the guests, and on this occasion preparation had been made for the service. The pitcher, the basin, and the towel were there, in readiness for the feet washing; but no servant was present, and it was the disciples' part to perform it. But each of the disciples, yielding to wounded pride, determined not to act the part of a servant. All manifested a stoical unconcern, seeming unconscious that there was anything for them to do. By their silence they refused to humble themselves.

How was Christ to bring these poor souls where Satan would not gain over them a decided victory? How could He show that a mere profession of discipleship did not make them disciples, or insure them a place in His kingdom? How could He show that it is loving service, true humility, which constitutes real greatness? How was He to kindle love in their hearts, and enable them to comprehend what He longed to tell them?

The disciples made no move toward serving one another. Jesus waited for a time to see what they would do. Then He, the divine Teacher, rose from the table. Laying aside the outer garment that would have impeded

3. "This c_____ _____, carried on in the presence of Christ, grieved and w_____ Him..."

Each of the disciples, yielding to wounded p__ _____, determined n_____ to act the part of a servant. All manifested a stoical unconcern, seeming u_____ that there was anything for them to do. By their s_____ they refused to humble themselves." (643, 644). Do I ever use that tactic, pretending to be unaware that any apology is needed? Why do I let my pride grieve and wound You, Lord? I am so embarrassed:

_____
_____

4. "How could He show that it is loving service, true h_____, which constitutes real g_____

…[Jesus'] action opened the e_____ of the disciples. Bitter shame and h_____ filled their hearts. They understood the unspoken rebuke, and s_____ themselves in altogether a new light" What did they see?

_____

_____

_____Putting myself in their shoes, what would I see about myself, Lord?

_____

_____

_____ Not that I want greatness, Lord, but how will You help me to have real greatness?

_____

_____

5. Jesus "knew that the Father had given a_____ things into His hands, and that He came from God, and went to God. He had a full consciousness of His d_____; but He laid a_____ His royal crown and kingly robes, and had taken the form of a s_____." (645). If I get just a little authority, power, or position, Lord, how do I use it? _____

_____

_____

6. "When the Savior's hand were bathing those soiled feet, and wiping them with the towel, the h_____ of Judas t_____ through and t_____ with

His movements, He took a towel, and girded Himself. With surprised interest the disciples looked on, and in silence waited to see what was to follow. "After that He poureth water into a basin, and began to wash the disciples' feet, and to wipe them with the towel wherewith He was girded." This action opened the eyes of the disciples. Bitter shame and humiliation filled their hearts. They understood the unspoken rebuke, and saw themselves in altogether a new light.

So Christ expressed His love for His disciples. Their selfish spirit filled Him with sorrow, but He entered into no controversy with them [644-645] regarding their difficulty. Instead He gave them an example they would never forget. His love for them was not easily disturbed or quenched. He knew that the Father had given all things into His hands, and that He came from God, and went to God. He had a full consciousness of His divinity; but He had laid aside His royal crown and kingly robes, and had taken the form of a servant. One of the last acts of His life on earth was to gird Himself as a servant, and perform a servant's part.

Before the Passover Judas had met a second time with the priests and scribes, and had closed the contract to deliver Jesus into their hands. Yet he afterward mingled with the disciples as though innocent of any wrong, and interested in the work of preparing for the feast. The disciples knew nothing of the purpose of Judas. Jesus alone could read his secret. Yet He did not expose him. Jesus hungered for his soul. He felt for him such a burden as for Jerusalem when He wept over the doomed city. His heart was crying, How can I give thee up? The constraining power of that love was felt by Judas. When the Saviour's hands were bathing those soiled feet, and wiping them with the towel, the heart of Judas thrilled through and through with the impulse then and there to confess his sin. But he would not humble himself. He hardened his heart against repentance; and the old impulses, for the moment put aside, again controlled him. Judas was now offended at Christ's act in washing the feet of His disciples. If Jesus could so humble Himself, he thought, He could not be Israel's king. All hope of worldly honor in a temporal kingdom was destroyed. Judas was satisfied that there was nothing to be gained by following Christ. After seeing Him degrade Himself, as he thought, he was confirmed in his purpose to disown Him, and confess himself deceived. He was possessed by a demon, and he resolved to complete the work he had agreed to do in betraying his Lord.

Judas, in choosing his position at table, had tried to place himself first, and Christ as a servant served him first. John, toward whom Judas had felt so much bitterness, was left till the last. But John did not take this as a rebuke or slight. As the disciples watched Christ's action, they were greatly moved. When Peter's turn came, he exclaimed with astonishment, "Lord, dost Thou wash my feet?" Christ's condescension broke his heart. He was filled with shame to think that one of the disciples was not performing this service. "What I do," Christ said, "thou knowest not now; but thou shalt know hereafter." Peter could not bear to see his Lord, whom he believed to be the Son of God, acting the part of a servant. His whole soul rose up against this humiliation. [645-646] He did not realize that for this Christ came into the world. With great emphasis he exclaimed, "Thou shalt never wash my feet."

Solemnly Christ said to Peter, "If I wash thee not, thou hast no part with Me." The service which Peter refused was the type of a higher cleansing. Christ had come to wash the heart from the stain of sin. In refusing to allow Christ to wash his feet, Peter was refusing the higher cleansing included in the lower. He was really rejecting his Lord. It is not humiliating to the Master to allow Him to work for our purification. The truest humility is to receive with thankful heart any provision made in our behalf, and with earnestness do service for Christ.

At the words, "If I wash thee not, thou hast no part with Me," Peter surrendered his pride and self-will. He could not endure the thought of separation from Christ; that would have been death to him. "Not my feet only," he said, "but also my hands and my head. Jesus saith to him, He that is washed needeth not save to wash his feet, but is clean every whit."

These words mean more than bodily cleanliness. Christ is still speaking of the higher cleansing as illustrated by the lower. He who came from the bath was clean, but the sandaled feet soon became dusty, and again needed to be washed. So Peter and his brethren had been washed in the great fountain opened for sin and uncleanness. Christ acknowledged them as His. But temptation had led them into evil, and they still needed His cleansing grace. When Jesus girded Himself with a

the impulse then and there to confess his sin." Lord, Can I have this exciting experience of confession?

_____

_____

Why do I think confession is such a downer?

_____

_____

_____

7. "Judas h_____ _____ his heart against repentance…Judas was now o_____ at Christ's act in washing the feet of His disciples." Lord, why do I harden my heart against repentance, against Your constraining power of love? ___

_____

_____

_____

_____

8. What is the higher cleansing of which the footwashing is a type? (646). _____

_____

____ (h_____, from the stain of sin). "Truest humility is to r_____ ____ with thankful heart any provision made in our behalf, and with earnestness do service for Christ."

9. Peter "could not endure the thought of s_____ _____ from Christ; that would have been d_____ ____ to him." Lord, may I have tasted of the blessed

abiding fellowship and friendship with You, so that the thought of separation is a major dread: ___

_____

_____

10. "He desired by that very act to wash the alienation, jealousy, and p_____ from their hearts...With the spirit the disciples then had, not one of them was prepared for c_____ with Christ." Show me my heart, Lord. What is in the way of communion with You? _____

_____

_____

_____

towel to wash the dust from their feet, He desired by that very act to wash the alienation, jealousy, and pride from their hearts. This was of far more consequence than the washing of their dusty feet. With the spirit they then had, not one of them was prepared for communion with Christ. Until brought into a state of humility and love, they were not prepared to partake of the paschal supper, or to share in the memorial service which Christ was about to institute. Their hearts must be cleansed. Pride and self-seeking create dissension and hatred, but all this Jesus washed away in washing their feet. A change of feeling was brought about. Looking upon them, Jesus could say, "Ye are clean." Now there was union of heart, love for one another. They had become humble and teachable. Except Judas, each was ready to concede to another the highest place. Now with subdued and grateful hearts hey could receive Christ's words.

Like Peter and his brethren, we too have been washed in the blood of Christ, yet often through contact with evil the heart's purity is soiled. We must come to Christ for His cleansing grace. Peter shrank from bringing his soiled feet in contact with the hands of his Lord and Master; [646-649] but how often we bring our sinful, polluted hearts in contact with the heart of Christ! How grievous to Him is our evil temper, our vanity and pride! Yet all our infirmity and defilement we must bring to Him. He alone can wash us clean. We are not prepared for communion with Him unless cleansed by His efficacy.

Jesus said to the disciples, "Ye are clean, but not all." He had washed the feet of Judas, but the heart had not been yielded to Him. It was not purified. Judas had not submitted himself to Christ.

After Christ had washed the disciples' feet, and had taken His garments and sat down again, He said to them, "Know ye what I have done to you? Ye call Me Master and Lord: and ye say well; for so I am. If I then, your Lord and Master, have washed your feet; ye also ought to wash one another's feet. For I have given you an example, that ye should do as I have done to you. Verily, verily, I say unto you, The servant is not greater than his lord; neither he that is sent greater than he that sent him."

Christ would have His disciples understand that although He had washed their feet, this did not in the least detract from His dignity. "Ye call Me Master and

Lord: and ye say well; for so I am." And being so infinitely superior, He imparted grace and significance to the service. No one was so exalted as Christ, and yet He stooped to the humblest duty. That His people might not be misled by the selfishness which dwells in the natural heart, and which strengthens by self-serving, Christ Himself set the example of humility. He would not leave this great subject in man's charge. Of so much consequence did He regard it, that He Himself, One equal with God, acted as servant to His disciples. While they were contending for the highest place, He to whom every knee shall bow, He whom the angels of glory count it honor to serve, bowed down to wash the feet of those who called Him Lord. He washed the feet of His betrayer.

In His life and lessons, Christ has given a perfect exemplification of the unselfish ministry which has its origin in God. God does not live for Himself. By creating the world, and by upholding all things, He is constantly ministering for others. "He maketh His sun to rise on the evil and on the good, and sendeth rain on the just and on the unjust." Matt. 5:45. This ideal of ministry God has committed to His Son. Jesus was given to stand at the head of humanity, that by His example He might teach what it means to minister. His whole life was under a law of service. He served all, ministered to all. Thus He lived the law of God, and by His example showed how we are to obey it. [649-650]

Again and again Jesus had tried to establish this principle among His disciples. When James and John made their request for pre-eminence, He had said, "Whosoever will be great among you, let him be your minister." Matt. 20:26. In My kingdom the principle of preference and supremacy has no place. The only greatness is the greatness of humility. The only distinction is found in devotion to the service of others.

Now, having washed the disciples' feet, He said, "I have given you an example, that ye should do as I have done to you." In these words Christ was not merely enjoining the practice of hospitality. More was meant than the washing of the feet of guests to remove the dust of travel. Christ was here instituting a religious service. By the act of our Lord this humiliating ceremony was made a consecrated ordinance. It was to be observed by the disciples, that they might ever keep in mind His lessons of humility and service.

11. Jesus "would not leave this great subject in man's charge. Of so much

c_____

did He regard it, that He Himself, one equal to God, acted as servant to His disciples." (649).

This ordinance is Christ's appointed preparation for the sacramental service. While pride, variance, and strife for supremacy are cherished, the heart cannot enter into fellowship with Christ. We are not prepared to receive the communion of His body and His blood. Therefore it was that Jesus appointed the memorial of His humiliation to be first observed.

As they come to this ordinance, the children of God should bring to remembrance the words of the Lord of life and glory: "Know ye what I have done to you? Ye call Me Master and Lord: and ye say well; for so I am. If I then, your Lord and Master, have washed your feet; ye also ought to wash one another's feet. For I have given you an example, that ye should do as I have done to you. Verily, verily, I say unto you, The servant is not greater than his lord; neither he that is sent greater than he that sent him. If ye know these things, happy are ye if ye do them." There is in man a disposition to esteem himself more highly than his brother, to work for self, to seek the highest place; and often this results in evil surmisings and bitterness of spirit. The ordinance preceding the Lord's Supper is to clear away these misunderstandings, to bring man out of his selfishness, down from his stilts of self-exaltation, to the humility of heart that will lead him to serve his brother.

The holy Watcher from heaven is present at this season to make it one of soul searching, of conviction of sin, and of the blessed assurance of sins forgiven. Christ in the fullness of His grace is there to change the current of the thoughts that have been running in selfish channels. The Holy Spirit quickens the sensibilities of those who follow the example of their Lord. As the Saviour's humiliation for us is remembered, thought [650-651] links with thought; a chain of memories is called up, memories of God's great goodness and of the favor and tenderness of earthly friends. Blessings forgotten, mercies abused, kindnesses slighted, are called to mind. Roots of bitterness that have crowded out the precious plant of love are made manifest. Defects of character, neglect of duties, ingratitude to God, coldness toward our brethren, are called to remembrance. Sin is seen in the light in which God views it. Our thoughts are not thoughts of self-complacency, but of severe self-censure and humiliation. The mind is energized to break down every barrier that has caused alienation. Evil thinking and evilspeaking are put away. Sins are confessed, they

12. "The holy Watcher from heaven is p_____ _____ at this season to make it one of soul s____ _____, of conviction of sin, and of the blessed a_____ of sins forgiven...The Holy Spirit quickens the s_____ _____ of those who follow the example of their Lord...Roots of bitterness that have c_____ out of the precious plant of love are made manifest... The desire is kindled for a h_____ spiritual life." (650, 651). Lord, quicken my sensibilities; I don't want anything to crowd You or Your love out. May the footwashing experience provide this quickening: _____ _____

are forgiven. The subduing grace of Christ comes into the soul, and the love of Christ draws hearts together in a blessed unity.

As the lesson of the preparatory service is thus learned, the desire is kindled for a higher spiritual life. To this desire the divine Witness will respond. The soul will be uplifted. We can partake of the Communion with a consciousness of sins forgiven. The sunshine of Christ's righteousness will fill the chambers of the mind and the soul temple. We "behold the Lamb of God, which taketh away the sin of the world." John 1:29.

To those who receive the spirit of this service, it can never become a mere ceremonial. Its constant lesson will be, "By love serve one another." Gal. 5:13. In washing the feet of His disciples, Christ gave evidence that He would do any service, however humble, that would make them heirs with Him of the eternal wealth of heaven's treasure. His disciples, in performing the same rite, pledge themselves in like manner to serve their brethren. Whenever this ordinance is rightly celebrated, the children of God are brought into a holy relationship, to help and bless each other. They covenant that the life shall be given to unselfish ministry. And this, not only for one another. Their field of labor is as wide as their Master's was. The world is full of those who need our ministry. The poor, the helpless, the ignorant, are on every hand. Those who have communed with Christ in the upper chamber will go forth to minister as He did.

Prayerjournal:_____

Jesus, the served of all, came to be the servant of all. And because He ministered to all, He will again be served and honored by all. And those who would partake of His divine attributes, and share with Him the joy of seeing souls redeemed, must follow His example of unselfish ministry.

All this was comprehended in the words of Jesus, "I have given you an example, that ye should do as I have done to you." This was the intent of the service He established. And He says, "If ye know these things," if you know the purpose of His lessons, "happy are ye if ye do them."

Chapter 72

"In Remembrance of Me"

[This chapter is based on Matt. 26:20-29;
Mark 14:17-25; Luke 22:14-23; John 13:18-30.]

"The Lord Jesus the same night in which He was betrayed took bread: and when He had given thanks, He brake it, and said, Take, eat: this is My body, which is broken for you: this do in remembrance of Me. After the same manner also He took the cup, when He had supped, saying, This cup is the new testament in My blood: this do ye, as oft as ye drink it, in remembrance of Me. For as often as ye eat this bread, and drink this cup, ye do show the Lord's death till He come." 1 Cor. 11:23-26.

Christ was standing at the point of transition between two economies and their two great festivals. He, the spotless Lamb of God, was about to present Himself as a sin offering, that He would thus bring to an end the system of types and ceremonies that for four thousand years had pointed to His death. As He ate the Passover with His disciples, He instituted in its place the service that was to be the memorial of His great sacrifice. The national festival of the Jews was to pass away forever. The service which Christ established was to be observed by His followers in all lands and through all ages.

The Passover was ordained as a commemoration of the deliverance of Israel from Egyptian bondage. God had directed that, year by year, as the children should ask the meaning of this ordinance, the history should be repeated. Thus the wonderful deliverance was to be kept fresh in the minds of all. The ordinance of the Lord's Supper was given [652-653] to commemorate the great deliverance wrought out as the result of the death of Christ. Till He shall come the second time in power and glory, this ordinance is to be celebrated. It is the means by which His great work for us is to be kept fresh in our minds.

At the time of their deliverance from Egypt, the children of Israel ate the Passover supper standing, with their loins girded, and with their staves in their hands, ready for their journey. The manner in which they cel-

1. "The Passover was ordained as a commemoration of the deliverance of Israel from Egyptian b_____ ...The ordinance of the Lord's Supper was given to commemorate the great d____ _____ wrought out as the result of the death of Christ." (652, 653). How is my slavery as real as that of the pyramid builders, Lord? _____ _____ _____

ebrated this ordinance harmonized with their condition; for they were about to be thrust out of the land of Egypt, and were to begin a painful and difficult journey through the wilderness. But in Christ's time the condition of things had changed. They were not now about to be thrust out of a strange country, but were dwellers in their own land. In harmony with the rest that had been given them, the people then partook of the Passover supper in a reclining position. Couches were placed about the table, and the guests lay upon them, resting upon the left arm, and having the right hand free for use in eating. In this position a guest could lay his head upon the breast of the one who sat next above him. And the feet, being at the outer edge of the couch, could be washed by one passing around the outside of the circle.

Christ is still at the table on which the paschal supper has been spread. The unleavened cakes used at the Passover season are before Him. The Passover wine, untouched by fermentation, is on the table. These emblems Christ employs to represent His own unblemished sacrifice. Nothing corrupted by fermentation, the symbol of sin and death, could represent the "Lamb without blemish and without spot." 1 Peter 1:19.

"And as they were eating, Jesus took bread, and blessed it, and brake it, and gave it to the disciples, and said, Take, eat; this is My body. And He took the cup, and gave thanks, and gave it to them, saying, Drink ye all of it; for this is My blood of the new testament, which is shed for many for the remission of sins. But I say unto you, I will not drink henceforth of this fruit of the vine, until that day when I drink it new with you in My Father's kingdom."

Judas the betrayer was present at the sacramental service. He received from Jesus the emblems of His broken body and His spilled blood. He heard the words, "This do in remembrance of Me." And sitting there in the very presence of the Lamb of God, the betrayer brooded upon his own dark purposes, and cherished his sullen, revengeful thoughts.

At the feet washing, Christ had given convincing proof that He understood the character of Judas. "Ye are not all clean" (John 13:11), [653-654] He said. These words convinced the false disciple that Christ read his secret purpose. Now Christ spoke out more plainly. As they were seated at the table He said, looking upon His disciples, "I speak not of you all: I know whom I have

2. "Sitting there in the very p_____ of the Lamb of God, the betrayer brooded upon his own dark purposes, and c_____ his sullen, revengeful thoughts." Lord, even as I am in the ritual of worship or devotion, I give the enemy ac-

cess to my mind? It is just too exhausting, constantly guarding against this guy! I am helpless. But You are so helpful. May my availability to You and only You continually increase: _____

_____

_____

3. "At these words amazement and c_____ _____ seized them. They could not comprehend how any one of them could deal t_____ with their divine Teacher... Whose heart could give birth to such a design?...Surely not one of the favored twelve...for whom He had shown such a great regard by bringing them into close c_____ with Himself!" (654). Lord, help me to see how even the slightest betrayal or denial of my relationship with You is treacherous to You, and for me: _____

_____

_____

_____

Open my eyes, to ways that I have unknowingly done so: _____

_____

_____

_____

_____

The disciples "remembered how true His sayings were, [and] fear and self-d_____ seized them. They began to s_____ their

chosen: but that the scripture may be fulfilled, He that eateth bread with Me hath lifted up his heel against Me."

Even now the disciples did not suspect Judas. But they saw that Christ appeared greatly troubled. A cloud settled over them all, a premonition of some dreadful calamity, the nature of which they did not understand. As they ate in silence, Jesus said, "Verily I say unto you, that one of you shall betray Me." At these words amazement and consternation seized them. They could not comprehend how any one of them could deal treacherously with their divine Teacher. For what cause could they betray Him? and to whom? Whose heart could give birth to such a design? Surely not one of the favored twelve, who had been privileged above all others to hear His teachings, who had shared His wonderful love, and for whom He had shown such great regard by bringing them into close communion with Himself!

As they realized the import of His words, and remembered how true His sayings were, fear and self-distrust seized them. They began to search their own hearts to see if one thought against their Master were harbored there. With the most painful emotion, one after another inquired, "Lord, is it I?" But Judas sat silent. John in deep distress at last inquired, "Lord, who is it?" And Jesus answered, "He that dippeth his hand with Me in the dish, the same shall betray Me. The Son of man goeth as it is written of Him: but woe unto that man by whom the Son of man is betrayed! it had been good for that man if he had not been born." The disciples had searched one another's faces closely as they asked, "Lord, is it I?" And now the silence of Judas drew all eyes to him. Amid the confusion of questions and expressions of astonishment, Judas had not heard the words of Jesus in answer to John's question. But now, to escape the scrutiny of the disciples, he asked as they had done, "Master, is it I?" Jesus solemnly replied, "Thou hast said."

In surprise and confusion at the exposure of his purpose, Judas rose hastily to leave the room. "Then said Jesus unto him, That thou doest, do quickly. . . . He then having received the sop went immediately out: and it was night." Night it was to the traitor as he turned away from Christ into the outer darkness.

Until this step was taken, Judas had not passed beyond the possibility of repentance. But when he left the presence of his Lord and his [654-655] fellow disciples, the final decision had been made. He had passed the boundary line.

Wonderful had been the long-suffering of Jesus in His dealing with this tempted soul. Nothing that could be done to save Judas had been left undone. After he had twice covenanted to betray his Lord, Jesus still gave him opportunity for repentance. By reading the secret purpose of the traitor's heart, Christ gave to Judas the final, convincing evidence of His divinity. This was to the false disciple the last call to repentance. No appeal that the divine-human heart of Christ could make had been spared. The waves of mercy, beaten back by stubborn pride, returned in a stronger tide of subduing love. But although surprised and alarmed at the discovery of his guilt, Judas became only the more determined. From the sacramental supper he went out to complete the work of betrayal.

In pronouncing the woe upon Judas, Christ also had a purpose of mercy toward His disciples. He thus gave them the crowning evidence of His Messiahship. "I tell you before it come," He said, "that, when it is come to pass, ye may believe that I AM." Had Jesus remained silent, in apparent ignorance of what was to come upon Him, the disciples might have thought that their Master had not divine foresight, and had been surprised and betrayed into the hands of the murderous mob. A year

own hearts to see if one thought against their Master were harbored there."

4. "When he [Judas] left the p_____ of his Lord and his fellow disciples, the final decision had been made. He had passed the b_____ ___ line." (654, 655). What line? _____

_____

_____ Lord, I don't want to leave Your presence; but like Enoch, to ever BE IN Your presence. _____

When You convict me, do I sulk and become unavailable? _____

_____

_____

5. "By reading the secret purpose of the traitor's heart, Christ gave to Judas the final, convincing e___ _____ of His divinity…No appeal that the divine-human heart of Christ could make had been s__ _____. The waves of mercy, b_____-back by stubborn pride, returned in a stronger tide of subduing l_____."
Lord, I guess to resist You, I have to purposefully beat back Your love. Show me how I am a bit like Judas:

_____

_____

Thank You for not giving up by my slightest sign of

resistance, for Your "patience and mercy...toward the most g_____ erring." That's me, alright! _____

before, Jesus had told the disciples that He had chosen twelve, and that one was a devil. Now His words to Judas, showing that his treachery was fully known to his Master, would strengthen the faith of Christ's true followers during His humiliation. And when Judas should have come to his dreadful end, they would remember the woe that Jesus had pronounced upon the betrayer.

And the Saviour had still another purpose. He had not withheld His ministry from him whom He knew to be a traitor. The disciples did not understand His words when He said at the feet washing, "Ye are not all clean," nor yet when at the table He declared, "He that eateth bread with Me hath lifted up his heel against Me." John 13:11, 18. But afterward, when His meaning was made plain, they had something to consider as to the patience and mercy of God toward the most grievously erring.

Though Jesus knew Judas from the beginning, He washed his feet. And the betrayer was privileged to unite with Christ in partaking of the sacrament. A long-suffering Saviour held out every inducement for the sinner to receive Him, to repent, and to be cleansed from the defilement of sin. This example is for us. When we suppose one to be in error and sin, we are not to divorce ourselves from him. By no careless [655-656] separation are we to leave him a prey to temptation, or drive him upon Satan's battleground. This is not Christ's method. It was because the disciples were erring and faulty that He washed their feet, and all but one of the twelve were thus brought to repentance.

Christ's example forbids exclusiveness at the Lord's Supper. It is true that open sin excludes the guilty. This the Holy Spirit plainly teaches. 1 Cor. 5:11. But beyond this none are to pass judgment. God has not left it with men to say who shall present themselves on these occasions. For who can read the heart? Who can distinguish the tares from the wheat? "Let a man examine himself, and so let him eat of that bread, and drink of that cup." For "whosoever shall eat this bread, and drink this cup of the Lord, unworthily, shall be guilty of the body and blood of the Lord." "He that eateth and drinketh unworthily, eateth and drinketh damnation to himself, not discerning the Lord's body." 1 Cor. 11:28, 27, 29.

When believers assemble to celebrate the ordinances, there are present messengers unseen by human eyes. There may be a Judas in the company, and if so, messengers from the prince of darkness are there, for they attend all who refuse to be controlled by the Holy Spirit. Heavenly angels also are present. These unseen visitants are present on every such occasion. There may come into the company persons who are not in heart servants of truth and holiness, but who may wish to take part in the service. They should not be forbidden. There are witnesses present who were present when Jesus washed the feet of the disciples and of Judas. More than human eyes beheld the scene.

Christ by the Holy Spirit is there to set the seal to His own ordinance. He is there to convict and soften the heart. Not a look, not a thought of contrition, escapes His notice. For the repentant, brokenhearted one He is waiting. All things are ready for that soul's reception. He who washed the feet of Judas longs to wash every heart from the stain of sin.

None should exclude themselves from the Communion because some who are unworthy may be present. Every disciple is called upon to participate publicly, and thus bear witness that he accepts Christ as a personal Saviour. It is at these, His own appointments, that Christ meets His people, and energizes them by His presence. Hearts and hands that are unworthy may even administer the ordinance, yet Christ is there to minister to His children. All who come with their faith fixed upon Him will be greatly blessed. All who neglect these seasons of divine privilege will suffer loss. Of them it may appropriately be said, "Ye are not all clean."

In partaking with His disciples of the bread and wine, Christ pledged [656-659] Himself to them as their Redeemer. He committed to them the new covenant, by which all who receive Him become children of God, and joint heirs with Christ. By this covenant every blessing that heaven could bestow for this life and the life to come was theirs. This covenant deed was to be ratified with the blood of Christ. And the administration of the Sacrament was to keep before the disciples the infinite sacrifice made for each of them individually as a part of the great whole of fallen humanity.

But the Communion service was not to be a season of sorrow. This was not its purpose. As the Lord's disciples gather about His table, they are not to remember and lament their shortcomings. They are not to dwell upon their past religious experience, whether that experience has been elevating or depressing. They are not to recall the differences between them and their

6. "He is there to convict and s_____ the heart...For the repentant, b_____ one He is waiting...He who washed the feet of Judas l_____ to wash every heart from the stain of sin." (656). Let that be me! How can this longing to be washed be mine? _____
_____
_____

7. "Every disciple is called upon to participate p_____ ___, and thus bear witness that he accepts Christ as a p_____ Savior. It is at these, His own a_____ _____, that Christ meets His people, and energizes them by His presence." Lord, I don't want to miss any appointment that You have set up for me. How do I shift seeing the Sabbath and Lord's Supper as an obligation, over to a thrill that You want time with me?
_____
_____
_____

8. "In partaking w_____ His disciples of the bread and wine, Christ pledged Himself to them as their Redeemer. He committed to them the new covenant...By this covenant every b_____ that heaven could bestow for this life and the life to come was theirs." (656, 659). Every blessing of heaven

is mine? Thank You Lord; I enter the covenant, with You! Well, what should 'entering a covenant' look like to me? _____
_____
_____

9. "The preparatory service has embraced all this. The self-examination, the c__ _____ of sin, the rec-onciling of differences, has all been done. Now they come to meet with C_____ _____." Lord, help me not to lessen the fullness of the communion service by ne-glecting the thoroughness of the preparatory service. Bring to mind confessions and reconciliation I need:
_____
_____

10. "Christ has instituted this service that it may speak to our senses of the love of God." It is to be kept fresh in my memory. (660). Lord, how can I avoid ritualizing this ser-vice? _____
_____
_____

11. "Nothing less than the d_____ of Christ could make His love efficacious for us." Is it the magnitude

brethren. The preparatory service has embraced all this. The self-examination, the confession of sin, the recon-ciling of differences, has all been done. Now they come to meet with Christ. They are not to stand in the shadow of the cross, but in its saving light. They are to open the soul to the bright beams of the Sun of Righteousness. With hearts cleansed by Christ's most precious blood, in full consciousness of His presence, although unseen, they are to hear His words, "Peace I leave with you, My peace I give unto you: not as the world giveth, give I unto you." John 14:27.

Our Lord says, Under conviction of sin, remember that I died for you. When oppressed and persecuted and afflicted for My sake and the gospel's, remember My love, so great that for you I gave My life. When your duties appear stern and severe, and your burdens too heavy to bear, remember that for your sake I endured the cross, despising the shame. When your heart shrinks from the trying ordeal, remember that your Redeemer liveth to make intercession for you.

The Communion service points to Christ's second coming. It was designed to keep this hope vivid in the minds of the disciples. Whenever they met together to commemorate His death, they recounted how "He took the cup, and gave thanks, and gave it to them, saying, Drink ye all of it; for this is My blood of the new testa-ment, which is shed for many for the remission of sins. But I say unto you, I will not drink henceforth of this fruit of the vine, until that day when I drink it new with you in My Father's kingdom." In their tribulation they found comfort in the hope of their Lord's return. Un-speakably precious to them was the thought, "As often as ye eat this bread, and drink this cup, ye do show the Lord's death till He come." 1 Cor. 11:26. [659-660]

These are the things we are never to forget. The love of Jesus, with its constraining power, is to be kept fresh in our memory. Christ has instituted this service that it may speak to our senses of the love of God that has been expressed in our behalf. There can be no union between our souls and God except through Christ. The union and love between brother and brother must be ce-mented and rendered eternal by the love of Jesus. And nothing less than the death of Christ could make His love efficacious for us. It is only because of His death that we can look with joy to His second coming. His sacrifice is the center of our hope. Upon this we must fix our faith.

The ordinances that point to our Lord's humiliation and suffering are regarded too much as a form. They were instituted for a purpose. Our senses need to be quickened to lay hold of the mystery of godliness. It is the privilege of all to comprehend, far more than we do, the expiatory sufferings of Christ. "As Moses lifted up the serpent in the wilderness," even so has the Son of man been lifted up, "that whosoever believeth in Him should not perish, but have eternal life." John 3:14, 15. To the cross of Calvary, bearing a dying Saviour, we must look. Our eternal interests demand that we show faith in Christ.

Our Lord has said, "Except ye eat the flesh of the Son of man, and drink His blood, ye have no life in you. . . . For My flesh is meat indeed, and My blood is drink indeed." John 6:53-55. This is true of our physical nature. To the death of Christ we owe even this earthly life. The bread we eat is the purchase of His broken body. The water we drink is bought by His spilled blood. Never one, saint or sinner, eats his daily food, but he is nourished by the body and the blood of Christ. The cross of Calvary is stamped on every loaf. It is reflected in every water spring. All this Christ has taught in appointing the emblems of His great sacrifice. The light shining from that Communion service in the upper chamber makes sacred the provisions for our daily life. The family board becomes as the table of the Lord, and every meal a sacrament.

And how much more are Christ's words true of our spiritual nature. He declares, "Whoso eateth My flesh, and drinketh My blood, hath eternal life." It is by receiving the life for us poured out on Calvary's cross, that we can live the life of holiness. And this life we receive by receiving His word, by doing those things which He has commanded. Thus we become one with Him. "He that eateth My flesh," He says, "and drinketh My blood, dwelleth in Me, and I in him. As the living [660-661] Father hath sent Me, and I live by the Father: so he that eateth Me, even he shall live by Me." John 6:54, 56, 57. To the holy Communion this scripture in a special sense applies. As faith contemplates our Lord's great sacrifice, the soul assimilates the spiritual life of Christ. That soul will receive spiritual strength from every Communion. The service forms a living connection by which the believer is bound up with Christ, and thus

of the sacrifice, the cost, that awakens my heart's response, and anything less would not have reached that depth of response: ___

_____

_____May Your costly gift, its efficacy, not be wasted by any lack of a full response from me. What would a full response be?

_____

_____

_____

12. "Whoso eateth My flesh, and drinketh My blood, hath eternal life. It is by receiving the life for us poured out on Calvary's cross, that we can l_____ ___ the life of holiness." How? "This life we receive by receiving His word, by doing those things which He has commanded. Thus we become o_____ with Him...forms a living c_____." (660, 661). Lord, help me realize ever more fully, what receiving Your life means:

_____

_____

_____

_____

bound up with the Father. In a special sense it forms a connection between dependent human beings and God.

As we receive the bread and wine symbolizing Christ's broken body and spilled blood, we in imagination join in the scene of Communion in the upper chamber. We seem to be passing through the garden consecrated by the agony of Him who bore the sins of the world. We witness the struggle by which our reconciliation with God was obtained. Christ is set forth crucified among us.

Looking upon the crucified Redeemer, we more fully comprehend the magnitude and meaning of the sacrifice made by the Majesty of heaven. The plan of salvation is glorified before us, and the thought of Calvary awakens living and sacred emotions in our hearts. Praise to God and the Lamb will be in our hearts and on our lips; for pride and self-worship cannot flourish in the soul that keeps fresh in memory the scenes of Calvary.

He who beholds the Saviour's matchless love will be elevated in thought, purified in heart, transformed in character. He will go forth to be a light to the world, to reflect in some degree this mysterious love. The more we contemplate the cross of Christ, the more fully shall we adopt the language of the apostle when he said, "God forbid that I should glory, save in the cross of our Lord Jesus Christ, by whom the world is crucified unto me, and I unto the world." Gal. 6:14.

13. "He who beholds the Savior's matchless love will be elevated in t____ _____, purified in h_____, transformed in c_____. He will go forth to be a light to the world, to reflect in some degree this mysterious love." So by beholding, I will reflect? Lord, may my walk consist of beholding Your matchless love. Give me some examples of reflecting Your love: _____

_____

_____

_____

Prayer journal: _____

_____

_____

_____

_____

_____

_____

Chapter 73

"Let Not Your Heart Be Troubled"

[This chapter is based on John 13:31-38; 14-17.]

Looking upon His disciples with divine love and with the tenderest sympathy, Christ said, "Now is the Son of man glorified, and God is glorified in Him." Judas had left the upper chamber, and Christ was alone with the eleven. He was about to speak of His approaching separation from them; but before doing this He pointed to the great object of His mission. It was this that He kept ever before Him. It was His joy that all His humiliation and suffering would glorify the Father's name. To this He first directs the thoughts of His disciples.

Then addressing them by the endearing term, "Little children," He said, "Yet a little while I am with you. Ye shall seek Me: and as I said unto the Jews, Whither I go, ye cannot come; so now I say to you."

The disciples could not rejoice when they heard this. Fear fell upon them. They pressed close about the Saviour. Their Master and Lord, their beloved Teacher and Friend, He was dearer to them than life. To Him they had looked for help in all their difficulties, for comfort in their sorrows and disappointments. Now He was to leave them, a lonely, dependent company. Dark were the forebodings that filled their hearts.

But the Saviour's words to them were full of hope. He knew that they were to be assailed by the enemy, and that Satan's craft is most successful against those who are depressed by difficulties. Therefore He pointed them away from "the things which are seen," to "the things which are not seen." 2 Cor. 4:18. From earthly exile He turned their thoughts to the heavenly home. [662-663]

"Let not your heart be troubled," He said; "ye believe in God, believe also in Me. In My Father's house are many mansions: if it were not so, I would have told you. I go to prepare a place for you. And if I go and prepare a place for you, I will come again, and receive you unto Myself; that were I am, there ye may be also. And whither I go ye know, and the way ye know." For your sake I came into the world. I am working in your

1. "It was His j_____ that all His humiliation and suffering would g_____ the Father's name." Lord, what makes the difference between a self-pitying martyr and being joyful in suffering?

_____

_____

_____

2. "Their Master and Lord, their beloved Teacher and F_____, He was dearer to them than life. To Him they had looked for help in all their difficulties, for c_____ in their sorrows and disappointments." Lord, I desire that kind of friendship with You. If my relationship now boils down to a mere hour or two a week at church, that's probably for credit and not friendship, isn't it? _____ Help my walk to grow deeper: ____

_____

behalf. When I go away, I shall still work earnestly for you. I came into the world to reveal Myself to you, that you might believe. I go to the Father to co-operate with Him in your behalf. The object of Christ's departure was the opposite of what the disciples feared. It did not mean a final separation. He was going to prepare a place for them, that He might come again, and receive them unto Himself. While He was building mansions for them, they were to build characters after the divine similitude.

Still the disciples were perplexed. Thomas, always troubled by doubts, said, "Lord, we know not whither Thou goest; and how can we know the way? Jesus saith unto him, I am the way, the truth, and the life; no man cometh unto the Father, but by Me. If ye had known Me, ye should have known My Father also: and from henceforth ye know Him, and have seen Him."

There are not many ways to heaven. Each one may not choose his own way. Christ says, "I am the way: . . . no man cometh unto the Father, but by Me." Since the first gospel sermon was preached, when in Eden it was declared that the seed of the woman should bruise the serpent's head, Christ had been uplifted as the way, the truth, and the life. He was the way when Adam lived, when Abel presented to God the blood of the slain lamb, representing the blood of the Redeemer. Christ was the way by which patriarchs and prophets were saved. He is the way by which alone we can have access to God.

"If ye had known Me," Christ said, "ye should have known My Father also: and from henceforth ye know Him, and have seen Him." But not yet did the disciples understand. "Lord, show us the Father," exclaimed Philip, "and it sufficeth us."

Amazed at his dullness of comprehension, Christ asked with pained surprise, "Have I been so long time with you, and yet hast thou not known Me, Philip?" Is it possible that you do not see the Father in the works He does through Me? Do you not believe that I came to testify of the Father? "How sayest thou then, Show us the Father?" "He that hath seen Me hath seen the Father." Christ had not ceased to be [663-664] God when He became man. Though He had humbled Himself to humanity, the Godhead was still His own. Christ alone could represent the Father to humanity, and this representation the disciples had been privileged to behold for over three years.

3. "Christ alone could represent the Father to humanity…

"Believe Me that I am in the Father, and the Father in Me: or else believe Me for the very works' sake." Their faith might safely rest on the evidence given in Christ's works, works that no man, of himself, ever had done, or ever could do. Christ's work testified to His divinity. Through Him the Father had been revealed.

If the disciples believed this vital connection between the Father and the Son, their faith would not forsake them when they saw Christ's suffering and death to save a perishing world. Christ was seeking to lead them from their low condition of faith to the experience they might receive if they truly realized what He was,--God in human flesh. He desired them to see that their faith must lead up to God, and be anchored there. How earnestly and perseveringly our compassionate Saviour sought to prepare His disciples for the storm of temptation that was soon to beat upon them. He would have them hid with Him in God.

As Christ was speaking these words, the glory of God was shining from His countenance, and all present felt a sacred awe as they listened with rapt attention to His words. Their hearts were more decidedly drawn to Him; and as they were drawn to Christ in greater love, they were drawn to one another. They felt that heaven was very near, and that the words to which they listened were a message to them from their heavenly Father.

"Verily, verily, I say unto you," Christ continued, "He that believeth on Me, the works that I do shall he do also." The Saviour was deeply anxious for His disciples to understand for what purpose His divinity was united to humanity. He came to the world to display the glory of God, that man might be uplifted by its restoring power. God was manifested in Him that He might be manifested in them. Jesus revealed no qualities, and exercised no powers, that men may not have through faith in Him. His perfect humanity is that which all His followers may possess, if they will be in subjection to God as He was.

"And greater works than these shall he do; because I go unto My Father." By this Christ did not mean that the disciples' work would be of a more exalted character than His, but that it would have greater extent. He did not refer merely to miracle working, but to all that would take place under the working of the Holy Spirit. [664-667]

After the Lord's ascension, the disciples realized

They felt that h_____ was very near, and that the words to which they listened were a message to them from their heavenly F_____...[Jesus came] to display the g__ _____ of God, that man might be uplifted by its restoring power. God was manifest in Him that He might be manifest i____ them. Jesus revealed no qualities, and exercised no powers, that men may not h_____ through faith in Him." (664). How is the Father to be manifest in me? _____

_____

_____ By my walk of contemplating Your display of the Father's glory.

the fulfillment of His promise. The scenes of the crucifixion, resurrection, and ascension of Christ were a living reality to them. They saw that the prophecies had been literally fulfilled. They searched the Scriptures, and accepted their teaching with a faith and assurance unknown before. They knew that the divine Teacher was all that He had claimed to be. As they told their experience, and exalted the love of God, men's hearts were melted and subdued, and multitudes believed on Jesus.

The Saviour's promise to His disciples is a promise to His church to the end of time. God did not design that His wonderful plan to redeem men should achieve only insignificant results. All who will go to work, trusting not in what they themselves can do, but in what God can do for and through them, will certainly realize the fulfillment of His promise. "Greater works than these shall ye do," He declares; "because I go unto My Father."

4. "As yet the disciples were u_____ ____ with the Savior's u_____ resources and power...He explained that the secret of their success would be in a_____ for strength and grace in His name... E_____ _____ sincere prayer is heard in heaven." (667). You mean, my walk can be successful, based not on my determination and persistence, but in daily asking for Your unlimited power (grace)? _____

_____

_____

As yet the disciples were unacquainted with the Saviour's unlimited resources and power. He said to them, "Hitherto have ye asked nothing in My name." John 16:24. He explained that the secret of their success would be in asking for strength and grace in His name. He would be present before the Father to make request for them. The prayer of the humble suppliant He presents as His own desire in that soul's behalf. Every sincere prayer is heard in heaven. It may not be fluently expressed; but if the heart is in it, it will ascend to the sanctuary where Jesus ministers, and He will present it to the Father without one awkward, stammering word, beautiful and fragrant with the incense of His own perfection.

The path of sincerity and integrity is not a path free from obstruction, but in every difficulty we are to see a call to prayer. There is no one living who has any power that he has not received from God, and the source whence it comes is open to the weakest human being. "Whatsoever ye shall ask in My name," said Jesus, "that will I do, that the Father may be glorified in the Son. If ye shall ask anything in My name, I will do it."

"In My name," Christ bade His disciples pray. In Christ's name His followers are to stand before God. Through the value of the sacrifice made for them, they are of value in the Lord's sight. Because of the imputed righteousness of Christ they are accounted precious.

For Christ's sake the Lord pardons those that fear Him. He does not see in them the vileness of the sinner. He recognizes in them the likeness of His Son, in whom they believe. [667-668]

The Lord is disappointed when His people place a low estimate upon themselves. He desires His chosen heritage to value themselves according to the price He has placed upon them. God wanted them, else He would not have sent His Son on such an expensive errand to redeem them. He has a use for them, and He is well pleased when they make the very highest demands upon Him, that they may glorify His name. They may expect large things if they have faith in His promises.

But to pray in Christ's name means much. It means that we are to accept His character, manifest His spirit, and work His works. The Saviour's promise is given on condition. "If ye love Me," He says, "keep My commandments." He saves men, not in sin, but from sin; and those who love Him will show their love by obedience.

All true obedience comes from the heart. It was heart work with Christ. And if we consent, He will so identify Himself with our thoughts and aims, so blend our hearts and minds into conformity to His will, that when obeying Him we shall be but carrying out our own impulses. The will, refined and sanctified, will find its highest delight in doing His service.

When we know God as it is our privilege to know Him, our life will be a life of continual obedience. Through an appreciation of the character of Christ,

5. "The Lord is disappointed when His people place a l_____ estimate upon themselves. He desires His c_____ heritage to value themselves according to the p_____ He has placed upon them...He is well pleased when they make the very h_____ ___ demands upon Him, that they may glorify His name." (668). Lord, help me to turn a deaf ear to the enemy's whispers of my total depreciation. The price that You and the Father paid, for me, powerfully draws me and commits my heart to You: _____

_____

_____

6. To pray in Christ's name "means that we are to accept His c_____, manifest His s_____, and work His works...If we c_____, He will so identify Himself with our thoughts and aims, so b_____ our hearts and minds into conformity with His will, that when obeying Him we shall be but carrying out our own impulses." Lord, what a beautiful picture of oneness. I consent. I consent. Blend and conform my heart with Yours: _____

_____

_____

7. "When we know God as it is our p_____

to know Him, our life will be a life of continual obedience. Through an appreciation of the character of Christ, through c_____ _____ with God, sin will become h_____ to us." My privilege; not my duty? Lord, change my concepts to joyful anticipation. And how am I to appreciate Your character when there are times, like Simon and Judas, it is offensive to me? (566, 645). _____

_____. Lord, help me. Help our walk together, the communion, to continue to change my taste buds, from loving sin to hating sin, from offensiveness to Your character to appreciation of Your character. Help me to taste and see that You are good, to daily walk and contemplate Your goodness:

_____
_____
_____

through communion with God, sin will become hateful to us.

As Christ lived the law in humanity, so we may do if we will take hold of the Strong for strength. But we are not to place the responsibility of our duty upon others, and wait for them to tell us what to do. We cannot depend for counsel upon humanity. The Lord will teach us our duty just as willingly as He will teach somebody else. If we come to Him in faith, He will speak His mysteries to us personally. Our hearts will often burn within us as One draws nigh to commune with us as He did with Enoch. Those who decide to do nothing in any line that will displease God, will know, after presenting their case before Him, just what course to pursue. And they will receive not only wisdom, but strength. Power for obedience, for service, will be imparted to them, as Christ has promised. Whatever was given to Christ--the "all things" to supply the need of fallen men--was given to Him as the head and representative of humanity. And "whatsoever we ask, we receive of Him, because we keep His commandments, and do those things that are pleasing in His sight." 1 John 3:22.

Before offering Himself as the sacrificial victim, Christ sought for the most essential and complete gift to bestow upon His followers, a gift that [668-669] would bring within their reach the boundless resources of grace. "I will pray the Father," He said, "and He shall give you another Comforter, that He may abide with you forever; even the Spirit of truth; whom the world cannot receive, because it seeth Him not, neither knoweth Him: but ye know Him; for He dwelleth with you, and shall be in you. I will not leave you orphans: I will come to you." John 14:16-18, margin.

Before this the Spirit had been in the world; from the very beginning of the work of redemption He had been moving upon men's hearts. But while Christ was on earth, the disciples had desired no other helper. Not until they were deprived of His presence would they feel their need of the Spirit, and then He would come.

The Holy Spirit is Christ's representative, but divested of the personality of humanity, and independent thereof. Cumbered with humanity, Christ could not be in every place personally. Therefore it was for their interest that He should go to the Father, and send the Spirit to be His successor on earth. No one could then have any advantage because of his location or his personal contact with Christ. By the Spirit the Saviour would be accessible to all. In this sense He would be nearer to them than if He had not ascended on high.

"He that loveth Me shall be loved of My Father, and I will love him, and will manifest Myself to him." Jesus read the future of His disciples. He saw one brought to the scaffold, one to the cross, one to exile among the lonely rocks of the sea, others to persecution and death. He encouraged them with the promise that in every trial He would be with them. That promise has lost none of its force. The Lord knows all about His faithful servants who for His sake are lying in prison or who are banished to lonely islands. He comforts them with His own presence. When for the truth's sake the believer stands at the bar of unrighteous tribunals, Christ stands by his side. All the reproaches that fall upon him, fall upon Christ. Christ is condemned over again in the person of His disciple. When one is incarcerated in prison walls, Christ ravishes the heart with His love. When one suffers death for His sake, Christ says, "I am He that liveth, and was dead; and, behold, I am alive forevermore, . . . and have the keys of hell and of death." Rev. 1:18. The life that is sacrificed for Me is preserved unto eternal glory.

At all times and in all places, in all sorrows and in all afflictions, when the outlook seems dark and the future perplexing, and we feel helpless and alone, the Comforter will be sent in answer to the prayer of [669-670] faith. Circumstances may separate us from every earthly friend; but no circumstance, no distance, can separate us from the heavenly Comforter. Wherever we are, wherever we may go, He is always at our right hand to support, sustain, uphold, and cheer.

The disciples still failed to understand Christ's words in their spiritual sense, and again He explained His meaning. By the Spirit, He said, He would manifest Himself to them. "The Comforter, which is the Holy Ghost, whom the Father will send in My name, He shall teach you all things." No more will you say, I cannot comprehend. No longer will you see through a glass, darkly. You shall "be able to comprehend with all saints what is the breadth, and length, and depth, and height; and to know the love of Christ, which passeth knowledge." Eph. 3:18, 19.

The disciples were to bear witness to the life and work of Christ. Through their word He was to speak to

8. "In this sense He would be n_____ to them than if He had not ascended on high...No circumstance, no distance, can s_____ _____ us from the heavenly Comforter. Wherever we are where ever we may go, He is always at the right hand to s_____ ___, sustain, uphold, and c_____." (669, 670). Lord, I never want to be separated from You. What are the atmospheres that I put myself in, that the Holy Spirit feels unwelcome?

_____
_____
_____
_____
_____

all the people on the face of the earth. But in the humiliation and death of Christ they were to suffer great trial and disappointment. That after this experience their word might be accurate, Jesus promised that the Comforter should "bring all things to your remembrance, whatsoever I have said unto you."

"I have yet many things to say unto you," He continued, "but ye cannot bear them now. Howbeit when He, the Spirit of truth, is come, He will guide you into all truth: for He shall not speak of Himself; but whatsoever He shall hear, that shall He speak: and He will show you things to come. He shall glorify Me: for He shall receive of Mine, and shall show it unto you." Jesus had opened before His disciples a vast tract of truth. But it was most difficult for them to keep His lessons distinct from the traditions and maxims of the scribes and Pharisees. They had been educated to accept the teaching of the rabbis as the voice of God, and it still held a power over their minds, and molded their sentiments. Earthly ideas, temporal things, still had a large place in their thoughts. They did not understand the spiritual nature of Christ's kingdom, though He had so often explained it to them. Their minds had become confused. They did not comprehend the value of the scriptures Christ presented. Many of His lessons seemed almost lost upon them. Jesus saw that they did not lay hold of the real meaning of His words. He compassionately promised that the Holy Spirit should recall these sayings to their minds. And He had left unsaid many things that could not be comprehended by the disciples. These also would be opened to them by the Spirit. The Spirit was to quicken their [670-671] understanding, that they might have an appreciation of heavenly things. "When He, the Spirit of truth, is come," said Jesus, "He will guide you into all truth."

9. "The Spirit was to quicken their understanding, that they might have an a_____ of heavenly things...The Holy

The Comforter is called "the Spirit of truth." His work is to define and maintain the truth. He first dwells in the heart as the Spirit of truth, and thus He becomes the Comforter. There is comfort and peace in the truth, but no real peace or comfort can be found in falsehood. It is through false theories and traditions that Satan gains his power over the mind. By directing men to false standards, he misshapes the character. Through the Scriptures the Holy Spirit speaks to the mind, and impresses truth upon the heart. Thus He exposes error, and expels it from the soul. It is by the Spirit of truth, working through the word of God, that Christ subdues His chosen people to Himself.

In describing to His disciples the office work of the Holy Spirit, Jesus sought to inspire them with the joy and hope that inspired His own heart. He rejoiced because of the abundant help He had provided for His church. The Holy Spirit was the highest of all gifts that He could solicit from His Father for the exaltation of His people. The Spirit was to be given as a regenerating agent, and without this the sacrifice of Christ would have been of no avail. The power of evil had been strengthening for centuries, and the submission of men to this satanic captivity was amazing. Sin could be resisted and overcome only through the mighty agency of the Third Person of the Godhead, who would come with no modified energy, but in the fullness of divine power. It is the Spirit that makes effectual what has been wrought out by the world's Redeemer. It is by the Spirit that the heart is made pure. Through the Spirit the believer becomes a partaker of the divine nature. Christ has given His Spirit as a divine power to overcome all hereditary and cultivated tendencies to evil, and to impress His own character upon His church.

Of the Spirit Jesus said, "He shall glorify Me." The Saviour came to glorify the Father by the demonstration of His love; so the Spirit was to glorify Christ by revealing His grace to the world. The very image of God is to be reproduced in humanity. The honor of God, the honor of Christ, is involved in the perfection of the character of His people.

"When He [the Spirit of truth] is come, He will reprove the world of sin, and of righteousness, and of judgment." The preaching of the word will be of no avail without the continual presence and aid of the Holy Spirit. This is the only effectual teacher of divine truth. Only [671-672] when the truth is accompanied to the heart by the Spirit will it quicken the conscience or transform the life. One might be able to present the letter of the word of God, he might be familiar with all its commands and promises; but unless the Holy Spirit sets home the truth, no souls will fall on the Rock and be broken. No amount of education, no advantages, however great, can make one a channel of light without the co-operation of the Spirit of God. The sowing of the gospel seed will not be a success unless the seed is quickened into life by the dew of heaven. Before one book of the New Testa-

---

Spirit was the highest of all g_____...[It] was to be given as a r_____ _____ agent, and without this the sacrifice of Christ would be to no avail...

Through the Spirit the believer becomes a p_____ ___ of the divine nature." (670, 671). Lord, may Your Spirit regenerate my appreciation for Your character, and regenerate my character. Give me a thirst for Your Spirit; I don't want Your sacrifice to be to no avail:

_____

_____

_____

10. "Only when the truth is accompanied to the h_____ by the Spirit will it q_____ the conscience or transform the life." (672) Lord, how do I sometimes read Your Word, and hear the preaching of Your Word, and not let the Spirit apply it to my heart? _____

_____

_____

_____

ment was written, before one gospel sermon had been preached after Christ's ascension, the Holy Spirit came upon the praying apostles. Then the testimony of their enemies was, "Ye have filled Jerusalem with your doctrine." Acts 5:28.

Christ has promised the gift of the Holy Spirit to His church, and the promise belongs to us as much as to the first disciples. But like every other promise, it is given on conditions. There are many who believe and profess to claim the Lord's promise; they talk *about* Christ and *about* the Holy Spirit, yet receive no benefit. They do not surrender the soul to be guided and controlled by the divine agencies. We cannot use the Holy Spirit. The Spirit is to use us. Through the Spirit God works in His people "to will and to do of His good pleasure." Phil. 2:13. But many will not submit to this. They want to manage themselves. This is why they do not receive the heavenly gift. Only to those who wait humbly upon God, who watch for His guidance and grace, is the Spirit given. The power of God awaits their demand and reception. This promised blessing, claimed by faith, brings all other blessings in its train. It is given according to the riches of the grace of Christ, and He is ready to supply every soul according to the capacity to receive.

In His discourse to the disciples, Jesus made no mournful allusion to His own sufferings and death. His last legacy to them was a legacy of peace. He said, "Peace I leave with you, My peace I give unto you: not as the world giveth, give I unto you. Let not your heart be troubled, neither let it be afraid."

Before leaving the upper chamber, the Saviour led His disciples in a song of praise. His voice was heard, not in the strains of some mournful lament, but in the joyful notes of the Passover hallel:

"O praise the Lord, all ye nations:
Praise Him, all ye people.
For His merciful kindness is great toward us:
And the truth of the Lord endureth forever.
Praise ye the Lord." Psalm 117. [672-673]

After the hymn, they went out. Through the crowded streets they made their way, passing out of the city gate toward the Mount of Olives. Slowly they proceeded, each busy with his own thoughts. As they began to descend toward the mount, Jesus said, in a tone of deep-

1. "They talk about Christ and about the Holy Spirit, yet receive no benefit." Why? "They do not surrender the soul to be g____ ___ and c_____ by the divine agencies." Lord, am I willing to let the Spirit control me? What does that mean? _____
_____
_____
_____

est sadness, "All ye shall be offended because of Me this night: for it is written, I will smite the shepherd, and the sheep of the flock shall be scattered abroad." Matt. 26:31. The disciples listened in sorrow and amazement. They remembered how in the synagogue at Capernaum, when Christ spoke of Himself as the bread of life, many had been offended, and had turned away from Him. But the twelve had not shown themselves unfaithful. Peter, speaking for his brethren, had then declared his loyalty to Christ. Then the Saviour had said, "Have not I chosen you twelve, and one of you is a devil?" John 6:70. In the upper chamber Jesus said that one of the twelve would betray Him, and that Peter would deny Him. But now His words include them all.

Now Peter's voice is heard vehemently protesting, "Although all shall be offended, yet will not I." In the upper chamber he had declared, "I will lay down my life for Thy sake." Jesus had warned him that he would that very night deny his Saviour. Now Christ repeats the warning: "Verily I say unto thee, That this day, even in this night, before the cock crow twice, thou shalt deny Me thrice." But Peter only "spake the more vehemently, If I should die with Thee, I will not deny Thee in anywise. Likewise also said they all." Mark 14:29, 30, 31. In their self-confidence they denied the repeated statement of Him who knew. They were unprepared for the test; when temptation should overtake them, they would understand their own weakness.

When Peter said he would follow his Lord to prison and to death, he meant it, every word of it; but he did not know himself. Hidden in his heart were elements of evil that circumstances would fan into life. Unless he was made conscious of his danger, these would prove his eternal ruin. The Saviour saw in him a self-love and assurance that would overbear even his love for Christ. Much of infirmity, of unmortified sin, carelessness of spirit, unsanctified temper, heedlessness in entering into temptation, had been revealed in his experience. Christ's solemn warning was a call to heart searching. Peter needed to distrust himself, and to have a deeper faith in Christ. Had he in humility received the warning, he would have appealed to the Shepherd of the flock to keep His sheep. When on the Sea of Galilee he was about to sink, he cried, "Lord, save me." Matt. 14:30. Then the hand of Christ was outstretched [673-674] to grasp his hand. So now if he had cried to Jesus, Save me

2. Peter vehemently protested, "Although all shall be o_____, yet will not I." This was stated in s_____ - confidence. Later, "they would understand their o_____ weakness." (673). Lord, what does it mean to be offended? _____

_____

_____

(Embarrassed by? Want to disown or disassociate? Values clash?) _____

_____

_____

_____

3. Peter "meant it, every word of it; but he did not k_____ himself." He needed to be "made c_____ _____ of his danger... Christ's solemn warning was a call to h_____ searching. Peter needed to d_____ himself, and to have a d_____ _____ faith in Christ." I know I don't know myself, and not as well as I need to. Not forgetting the value You have of me, I need to learn to distrust myself, and to depend totally on You. _____

_____

_____

from myself, he would have been kept. But Peter felt that he was distrusted, and he thought it cruel. He was already offended, and he became more persistent in his self-confidence.

Jesus looks with compassion on His disciples. He cannot save them from the trial, but He does not leave them comfortless. He assures them that He is to break the fetters of the tomb, and that His love for them will not fail. "After I am risen again," He says, "I will go before you into Galilee." Matt. 26:32. Before the denial, they have the assurance of forgiveness. After His death and resurrection, they knew that they were forgiven, and were dear to the heart of Christ.

Jesus and the disciples were on the way to Gethsemane, at the foot of Mount Olivet, a retired spot which He had often visited for meditation and prayer. The Saviour had been explaining to His disciples His mission to the world, and the spiritual relation to Him which they were to sustain. Now He illustrates the lesson. The moon is shining bright, and reveals to Him a flourishing grapevine. Drawing the attention of the disciples to it, He employs it as a symbol.

"I am the true Vine," He says. Instead of choosing the graceful palm, the lofty cedar, or the strong oak, Jesus takes the vine with its clinging tendrils to represent Himself. The palm tree, the cedar, and the oak stand alone. They require no support. But the vine entwines about the trellis, and thus climbs heavenward. So Christ in His humanity was [674-675] dependent upon divine power. "I can of Mine own self do nothing," He declared. John 5:30.

"I am the true Vine." The Jews had always regarded the vine as the most noble of plants, and a type of all that was powerful, excellent, and fruitful. Israel had been represented as a vine which God had planted in the Promised Land. The Jews based their hope of salvation on the fact of their connection with Israel. But Jesus says, I am the real Vine. Think not that through a connection with Israel you may become partakers of the life of God, and inheritors of His promise. Through Me alone is spiritual life received.

"I am the true Vine, and My Father is the husbandman." On the hills of Palestine our heavenly Father had planted this goodly Vine, and He Himself was the husbandman. Many were attracted by the beauty of this Vine, and declared its heavenly origin. But to the leaders in Israel it appeared as a root out of a dry ground. They took the plant, and bruised it, and trampled it under their unholy feet. Their thought was to destroy it forever. But the heavenly Husbandman never lost sight of His plant. After men thought they had killed it, He took it, and replanted it on the other side of the wall. The vine stock was to be no longer visible. It was hidden from the rude assaults of men. But the branches of the Vine hung over the wall. They were to represent the Vine. Through them grafts might still be united to the Vine. From them fruit has been obtained. There has been a harvest which the passers-by have plucked.

"I am the Vine, ye are the branches," Christ said to His disciples. Though He was about to be removed from them, their spiritual union with Him was to be unchanged. The connection of the branch with the vine, He said, represents the relation you are to sustain to Me. The scion is engrafted into the living vine, and fiber by fiber, vein by vein, it grows into the vine stock. The life of the vine becomes the life of the branch. So the soul dead in trespasses and sins receives life through connection with Christ. By faith in Him as a personal Saviour the union is formed. The sinner unites his weakness to Christ's strength, his emptiness to Christ's fullness, his frailty to Christ's enduring might. Then he has the mind of Christ. The humanity of Christ has touched our humanity, and our humanity has touched divinity. Thus through the agency of the Holy Spirit man becomes a partaker of the divine nature. He is accepted in the Beloved. [675-676]

This union with Christ, once formed, must be maintained. Christ said, "Abide in Me, and I in you. As the branch cannot bear fruit of itself, except it abide in the vine; no more can ye, except ye abide in Me." This is no casual touch, no off-and-on connection. The branch becomes a part of the living vine. The communication of life, strength, and fruitfulness from the root to the branches is unobstructed and constant. Separated from the vine, the branch cannot live. No more, said Jesus, can you live apart from Me. The life you have received from Me can be preserved only by continual communion. Without Me you cannot overcome one sin, or resist one temptation.

"Abide in Me, and I in you." Abiding in Christ means a constant receiving of His Spirit, a life of unreserved surrender to His service. The channel of com-

4. "By f_____ in Him as a personal Savior the u_____ is formed [branch to the vine]. The sinner unites his w_____ _ to Christ's strength, his emptiness to Christ's fullness…Then he has the m__ _____ of Christ…Thus through the agency of the Holy Spirit man becomes a p_____ of the divine nature." (675). Are there three steps here, Lord: faith, union, partaker? _____ Increase my desire for this union, Lord. How do unite my will to Your strength?

_____

_____

5. "Abide in Me, and I in you…This is no casual touch, no o____-and-on connection… Without Me you cannot overcome one sin, or resist one t_____ …Abiding in Christ means a c_____ receiving of His Spirit, a life of unreserved surrender to His service…We are to cling

to Jesus, and receive from Him by f_____ the strength and p_____ _____ of His own character." (676). Remind me Lord, to continually receive Your Spirit, 24-7, throughout the day, to ever be in Your presence, no matter where I am, what I am doing, who I am talking with. I am with You: _____

_____

_____

6. "The pruning will cause pain, but it is the F_____ ____ who applies the knife. He works with no wanton hand or i_____ heart... The husbandman

munication must be open continually between man and his God. As the vine branch constantly draws the sap from the living vine, so are we to cling to Jesus, and receive from Him by faith the strength and perfection of His own character.

The root sends its nourishment through the branch to the outermost twig. So Christ communicates the current of spiritual strength to every believer. So long as the soul is united to Christ, there is no danger that it will wither or decay.

The life of the vine will be manifest in fragrant fruit on the branches. "He that abideth in Me," said Jesus, "and I in him, the same bringeth forth much fruit: for without Me ye can do nothing." When we live by faith on the Son of God, the fruits of the Spirit will be seen in our lives; not one will be missing.

"My Father is the husbandman. Every branch in Me that beareth not fruit He taketh away." While the graft is outwardly united with the vine, there may be no vital connection. Then there will be no growth or fruitfulness. So there may be an apparent connection with Christ without a real union with Him by faith. A profession of religion places men in the church, but the character and conduct show whether they are in connection with Christ. If they bear no fruit, they are false branches. Their separation from Christ involves a ruin as complete as that represented by the dead branch. "If a man abide not in Me," said Christ, "he is cast forth as a branch, and is withered; and men gather them, and cast them into the fire, and they are burned."

"And every branch that beareth fruit, He purgeth [pruneth] it, that it may bring forth more fruit." From the chosen twelve who had followed [676-677] Jesus, one as a withered branch was about to be taken away; the rest were to pass under the pruning knife of bitter trial. Jesus with solemn tenderness explained the purpose of the husbandman. The pruning will cause pain, but it is the Father who applies the knife. He works with no wanton hand or indifferent heart. There are branches trailing upon the ground; these must be cut loose from the earthly supports to which their tendrils are fastening. They are to reach heavenward, and find their support in God. The excessive foliage that draws away the life current from the fruit must be pruned off. The overgrowth must be cut out, to give room for the healing beams of the Sun of Righteousness. The husbandman prunes away the harmful growth, that the fruit may be richer and more abundant.

"Herein is My Father glorified," said Jesus, "that ye bear much fruit." God desires to manifest through you the holiness, the benevolence, the compassion, of His own character. Yet the Saviour does not bid the disciples labor to bear fruit. He tells them to abide in Him. "If ye abide in Me," He says, "and My words abide in you, ye shall ask what ye will, and it shall be done unto you." It is through the word that Christ abides in His followers. This is the same vital union that is represented by eating His flesh and drinking His blood. The words of Christ are spirit and life. Receiving them, you receive the life of the Vine. You live "by every word that proceedeth out of the mouth of God." Matt. 4:4. The life of Christ in you produces the same fruits as in Him. Living in Christ, adhering to Christ, supported by Christ, drawing nourishment from Christ, you bear fruit after the similitude of Christ.

In this last meeting with His disciples, the great desire which Christ expressed for them was that they might love one another as He had loved them. Again and again He spoke of this. "These things I command you," He said repeatedly, "that ye love one another." His very first injunction when alone with them in the upper chamber was, "A new commandment I give unto you, That ye love one another; as I have loved you, that ye also love one another." To the disciples this commandment was new; for they had not loved one another as Christ had loved them. He saw that new ideas and impulses must control them; that new principles must be practiced by them; through His life and death they were to receive a new conception of love. The command to love one another had a new meaning in the light of His self-sacrifice. The whole [677-678] work of grace is one continual service of love, of self-denying, self-sacrificing effort. During every hour of Christ's sojourn upon the earth, the love of God was flowing from Him in irrepressible streams. All who are imbued with His Spirit will love as He loved. The very principle that actuated Christ will actuate them in all their dealing one with another.

This love is the evidence of their discipleship. "By this shall all men know that ye are My disciples," said Jesus, "if ye have love one to another." When men are bound together, not by force or self-interest, but

prunes away the harmful growth, that the fruit may be r_____ and more abundant." (677). I can get discouraged at the pain of the pruning, or I can anticipate the richer fruit in store, a closer harmony with You: _____
_____

7. "The Savior does not bid the disciples l_____ ____ to bear fruit. He tells them to a_____ in Him." How do I abide? __
_____
_____

"It is through the w__ _____ that Christ abides in His followers." _____ Lord, may my focus be on abiding in You through Your word. This walk of contemplating Your character will bear fruit naturally; Your character will be manifested. Thank You for being a Friend that abides. _____
_____

8. "During every hour of Christ's sojourn upon earth, the love of God was f_____ from Him in i_____ streams. All who are imbued with His Spirit will love a_____ He loved." It's not a feeling, but a p_____ __. (678). But Lord, as a principle, does that mean it is a forced behavior? If it is going to flow, it

has to flow naturally, and not be a struggle, doesn't it? _____

_____

_____

by love, they show the working of an influence that is above every human influence. Where this oneness exists, it is evidence that the image of God is being restored in humanity, that a new principle of life has been implanted. It shows that there is power in the divine nature to withstand the supernatural agencies of evil, and that the grace of God subdues the selfishness inherent in the natural heart.

This love, manifested in the church, will surely stir the wrath of Satan. Christ did not mark out for His disciples an easy path. "If the world hate you," He said, "ye know that it hated Me before it hated you. If ye were of the world, the world would love his own: but because ye are not of the world, but I have chosen you out of the world, therefore the world hateth you. Remember the word that I said unto you, The servant is not greater than his lord. If they have persecuted Me, they will also persecute you; if they have kept My saying, they will keep yours also. But all these things will they do unto you for My name's sake, because they know not Him that sent Me." The gospel is to be carried forward by aggressive warfare, in the midst of opposition, peril, loss, and suffering. But those who do this work are only following in their Master's steps.

As the world's Redeemer, Christ was constantly confronted with apparent failure. He, the messenger of mercy to our world, seemed to do little of the work He longed to do in uplifting and saving. Satanic influences were constantly working to oppose His way. But He would not be discouraged. Through the prophecy of Isaiah He declares, "I have labored in vain, I have spent My strength for nought, and in vain: yet surely My judgment is with the Lord, and My work with My God. . . . Though Israel be not gathered, yet shall I be glorious in the eyes of the Lord, and My God shall be My strength." It is to Christ that the promise is given, "Thus saith the Lord, the Redeemer of Israel, and His Holy One, to Him whom man despiseth, to Him whom the nation [678-679] abhorreth; . . . thus saith the Lord: . . . I will preserve Thee, and give Thee for a covenant of the people, to establish the earth, to cause to inherit the desolate heritages; that Thou mayest say to the prisoners, Go forth; to them that are in darkness, Show yourselves. . . . They shall not hunger nor thirst; neither shall the heat nor sun smite them: for He that hath mercy on them shall lead them, even by the springs of water shall

He guide them." Isa. 49:4, 5, 7-10.

Upon this word Jesus rested, and He gave Satan no advantage. When the last steps of Christ's humiliation were to be taken, when the deepest sorrow was closing about His soul, He said to His disciples, "The prince of this world cometh, and hath nothing in Me." "The prince of this world is judged." Now shall he be cast out. John 14:30; 16:11; 12:31. With prophetic eye Christ traced the scenes to take place in His last great conflict. He knew that when He should exclaim, "It is finished," all heaven would triumph. His ear caught the distant music and the shouts of victory in the heavenly courts. He knew that the knell of Satan's empire would then be sounded, and the name of Christ would be heralded from world to world throughout the universe.

Christ rejoiced that He could do more for His followers than they could ask or think. He spoke with assurance, knowing that an almighty decree had been given before the world was made. He knew that truth, armed with the omnipotence of the Holy Spirit, would conquer in the contest with evil; and that the bloodstained banner would wave triumphantly over His followers. He knew that the life of His trusting disciples would be like His, a series of uninterrupted victories, not seen to be such here, but recognized as such in the great hereafter.

"These things I have spoken unto you," He said, "that in Me ye might have peace. In the world ye shall have tribulation: but be of good cheer; I have overcome the world." Christ did not fail, neither was He discouraged, and His followers are to manifest a faith of the same enduring nature. They are to live as He lived, and work as He worked, because they depend on Him as the great Master Worker. Courage, energy, and perseverance they must possess. Though apparent impossibilities obstruct their way, by His grace they are to go forward. Instead of deploring difficulties, they are called upon to surmount them. They are to despair of nothing, and to hope for everything. With the golden chain of His matchless love Christ has bound them to the throne of God. It is His purpose that the highest influence in the universe, emanating from the source of all power, shall be theirs. They are to have power [679-680] to resist evil, power that neither earth, nor death, nor hell can master, power that will enable them to overcome as Christ overcame.

9. Christ's followers are to "despair of nothing, and to h_____ for everything. With the golden chain of His matchless love Christ has b_____ them to the t_____ of God. It is His purpose that the highest i_____ ___ in the universe, emanating from the source of all power, shall be theirs." (679). Lord, may I be influenced, and be an influence. Thank You for this wonderful gift: _____
_____
_____
_____

Christ designs that heaven's order, heaven's plan of government, heaven's divine harmony, shall be represented in His church on earth. Thus in His people He is glorified. Through them the Sun of Righteousness will shine in undimmed luster to the world. Christ has given to His church ample facilities, that He may receive a large revenue of glory from His redeemed, purchased possession. He has bestowed upon His people capabilities and blessings that they may represent His own sufficiency. The church, endowed with the righteousness of Christ, is His depositary, in which the riches of His mercy, His grace, and His love, are to appear in full and final display. Christ looks upon His people in their purity and perfection, as the reward of His humiliation, and the supplement of His glory,--Christ, the great Center, from whom radiates all glory.

10. "The church, endowed with the righteousness of Christ, is His depositary, in which the riches of His mercy, His g_____, and His love, are to appear in full and final d_____." (680). Lord, is my bank open for business? How can I increase my capacity for deposits? ———

Prayer journal: ———

With strong, hopeful words the Saviour ended His instruction. Then He poured out the burden of His soul in prayer for His disciples. Lifting His eyes to heaven, He said, "Father, the hour is come; glorify Thy Son, that Thy Son also may glorify Thee: as Thou hast given Him power over all flesh, that He should give eternal life to as many as Thou hast given Him. And this is life eternal, that they might know Thee the only true God, and Jesus Christ, whom Thou hast sent."

Christ had finished the work that was given Him to do. He had glorified God on the earth. He had manifested the Father's name. He had gathered out those who were to continue His work among men. And He said, "I am glorified in them. And now I am no more in the world, but these are in the world, and I come to Thee. Holy Father, keep through Thine own name those whom Thou hast given Me, that they may be one, as We are." "Neither pray I for these alone, but for them also which shall believe on Me through their word; that they all may be one; . . . I in them, and Thou in Me, that they may be made perfect in one; and that the world may know that Thou hast sent Me, and hast loved them, as Thou hast loved Me."

Thus in the language of one who has divine authority, Christ gives His elect church into the Father's arms. As a consecrated high priest He intercedes for His people. As a faithful shepherd He gathers His flock under the shadow of the Almighty, in the strong and sure refuge. For Him there waits the last battle with Satan, and He goes forth to meet it.

Chapter 74

Gethsemane

[This chapter is based on Matt. 26:36-56; Mark 14:32-50; Luke 22:39-53; John 18:1-12.]

In company with His disciples, the Saviour slowly made His way to the garden of Gethsemane. The Passover moon, broad and full, shone from a cloudless sky. The city of pilgrims' tents was hushed into silence.

Jesus had been earnestly conversing with His disciples and instructing them; but as He neared Gethsemane, He became strangely silent. He had often visited this spot for meditation and prayer; but never with a heart so full of sorrow as upon this night of His last agony. Throughout His life on earth He had walked in the light of God's presence. When in conflict with men who were inspired by the very spirit of Satan, He could say, "He that sent Me is with Me: the Father hath not left Me alone; for I do always those things that please Him." John 8:29. But now He seemed to be shut out from the light of God's sustaining presence. Now He was numbered with the transgressors. The guilt of fallen humanity He must bear. Upon Him who knew no sin must be laid the iniquity of us all. So dreadful does sin appear to Him, so great is the weight of guilt which He must bear, that He is tempted to fear it will shut Him out forever from His Father's love. Feeling how terrible is the wrath of God against transgression, He exclaims, "My soul is exceeding sorrowful, even unto death."

As they approached the garden, the disciples had marked the change that came over their Master. Never before had they seen Him so utterly [685-686] sad and silent. As He proceeded, this strange sadness deepened; yet they dared not question Him as to the cause. His form swayed as if He were about to fall. Upon reaching the garden, the disciples looked anxiously for His usual place of retirement, that their Master might rest. Every step that He now took was with labored effort. He groaned aloud, as if suffering under the pressure of a terrible burden. Twice His companions supported Him, or He would have fallen to the earth.

Near the entrance to the garden, Jesus left all but

1. "As He neared Gethsemane, He became strangely s_____... Through out His life on earth He had w_____ in the light of God's presence...But now He seemed to be shut out from the light of God's sustaining p_____. Now He is numbered with the transgressors...So dreadful does it appear to Him... that He is tempted to f_____ it will shut Him out f_____ from His Father's love." Lord, may I walk as You did, in the light of Your presence. And may the thought of any separation be uncomfortable: _____

_____

_____

2. "With Peter, James, and John He entered the garden's secluded recesses... [He] desired their presence n_____ Him...He desired them to spend the night with Him in p_____ _____." (686). Most of the time, Lord, I pray to You for support. Help me to be less self-centered, and think more often of what You are going through, to pray for You, and support You: _____

_____

3. "He felt that by sin He was being s_____ _____ from His Father. The gulf was so broad, so b_____, so deep, that His spirit shuddered before it. As man He must suffer the c_____ of man's sin. As man He must endure the w_____ of God against transgression." Lord, I am noticing the association of God's wrath, or a definition. It seems that it is the awful consequence of sin, which is separation. Instead of anger, it is dissonance between purity and evil. How You experienced being made sin, is opening my eyes to what sin is. And I contrast this with the enemy's portrayal of what sin is (and I guess how I often view it myself): _____

_____

_____

_____

three of the disciples, bidding them pray for themselves and for Him. With Peter, James, and John, He entered its secluded recesses. These three disciples were Christ's closest companions. They had beheld His glory on the mount of transfiguration; they had seen Moses and Elijah talking with Him; they had heard the voice from heaven; now in His great struggle, Christ desired their presence near Him. Often they had passed the night with Him in this retreat. On these occasions, after a season of watching and prayer, they would sleep undisturbed at a little distance from their Master, until He awoke them in the morning to go forth anew to labor. But now He desired them to spend the night with Him in prayer. Yet He could not bear that even they should witness the agony He was to endure.

"Tarry ye here," He said, "and watch with Me."

He went a little distance from them--not so far but that they could both see and hear Him--and fell prostrate upon the ground. He felt that by sin He was being separated from His Father. The gulf was so broad, so black, so deep, that His spirit shuddered before it. This agony He must not exert His divine power to escape. As man He must suffer the consequences of man's sin. As man He must endure the wrath of God against transgression.

Christ was now standing in a different attitude from that in which He had ever stood before. His suffering can best be described in the words of the prophet, "Awake, O sword, against My shepherd, and against the man that is My fellow, saith the Lord of hosts." Zech. 13:7. As the substitute and surety for sinful man, Christ was suffering under divine justice. He saw what justice meant. Hitherto He had been as an intercessor for others; now He longed to have an intercessor for Himself.

As Christ felt His unity with the Father broken up, He feared that in His human nature He would be unable to endure the coming conflict with the powers of darkness. In the wilderness of temptation the destiny of the human race had been at stake. Christ was then conqueror. Now [686-687] the tempter had come for the last fearful struggle. For this he had been preparing during the three years of Christ's ministry. Everything was at stake with him. If he failed here, his hope of mastery was lost; the kingdoms of the world would finally become Christ's; he himself would be overthrown and cast out. But if Christ could be overcome, the earth would become Satan's kingdom, and the human race would be forever in his power. With the issues of the conflict before Him, Christ's soul was filled with dread of separation from God. Satan told Him that if He became the surety for a sinful world, the separation would be eternal. He would be identified with Satan's kingdom, and would nevermore be one with God.

And what was to be gained by this sacrifice? How hopeless appeared the guilt and ingratitude of men! In its hardest features Satan pressed the situation upon the Redeemer: The people who claim to be above all others in temporal and spiritual advantages have rejected You. They are seeking to destroy You, the foundation, the center and seal of the promises made to them as a peculiar people. One of Your own disciples, who has listened to Your instruction, and has been among the foremost in church activities, will betray You. One of Your most zealous followers will deny You. All will forsake You. Christ's whole being abhorred the thought. That those whom He had undertaken to save, those whom He loved so much, should unite in the plots of Satan, this pierced His soul. The conflict was terrible. Its measure was the guilt of His nation, of His accusers and betrayer, the guilt of a world lying in wickedness. The sins of men weighed heavily upon Christ, and the sense of God's wrath against sin was crushing out His life.

Behold Him contemplating the price to be paid for the human soul. In His agony He clings to the cold ground, as if to prevent Himself from being drawn farther from God. The chilling dew of night falls upon His prostrate form, but He heeds it not. From His pale lips comes the bitter cry, "O My Father, if it be possible, let this cup pass from Me." Yet even now He adds, "Nevertheless not as I will, but as Thou wilt."

The human heart longs for sympathy in suffering. This longing Christ felt to the very depths of His being. In the supreme agony of His soul He came to His disciples with a yearning desire to hear some words of comfort from those whom He had so often blessed and comforted, and shielded in sorrow and distress. The One who had always had words of sympathy for them was now suffering superhuman agony, and He longed to know that they were praying for Him and for themselves. [687-688] How dark seemed the malignity of sin! Terrible was the temptation to let the human race bear the consequences of its own guilt, while He stood

(Innocent, fun and exciting, no harm done, I'm immune, etc). Through this contemplation of Your life, especially the closing scenes, may my perspective of sin change from the enemy's to Yours: _____

_____

_____

4. "Christ's soul was filled with d_____ of separation from God. Satan told Him that if He became the s_____ for a sinful world, the separation would be e_____... How hopeless appeared the guilt and i_____ of men! In its hardest features Satan pressed the situation upon the Redeemer." (687). Which included:

_____

_____

Lord, show me how I unite in the plots of Satan; and how this pierces Your soul:

_____

_____

_____

5. "The human heart longs for s_____ in suffering. This longing Christ felt to the very d_____ of His being..."

If He could only know that His disciples understood and a_____ this, He would be s_____ _____." Lord, help me to understand and appreciate what You went through, and You go through: _____

_____

_____

6. The disciples "gave Him the strongest assurance that they would" not be offended because of Him. Yet "when the Savior was m_____ in need of their sympathy and prayers, they were found asleep." (688, 689). Lord, how can I realize the necessity of watchfulness and earnest prayer in order to withstand temptation? _____

_____

_____

innocent before God. If He could only know that His disciples understood and appreciated this, He would be strengthened.

Rising with painful effort, He staggered to the place where He had left His companions. But He "findeth them asleep." Had He found them praying, He would have been relieved. Had they been seeking refuge in God, that satanic agencies might not prevail over them, He would have been comforted by their steadfast faith. But they had not heeded the repeated warning, "Watch and pray." At first they had been much troubled to see their Master, usually so calm and dignified, wrestling with a sorrow that was beyond comprehension. They had prayed as they heard the strong cries of the sufferer. They did not intend to forsake their Lord, but they seemed paralyzed by a stupor which they might have shaken off if they had continued pleading with God. They did not realize the necessity of watchfulness and earnest prayer in order to withstand temptation.

Just before He bent His footsteps to the garden, Jesus had said to the disciples, "All ye shall be offended because of Me this night." They had given Him the strongest assurance that they would go with Him to prison and to death. And poor, self-sufficient Peter had added, "Although all shall be offended, yet will not I." Mark 14:27, 29. But the [688-689] disciples trusted to themselves. They did not look to the mighty Helper as Christ had counseled them to do. Thus when the Saviour was most in need of their sympathy and prayers, they were found asleep. Even Peter was sleeping.

And John, the loving disciple who had leaned upon the breast of Jesus, was asleep. Surely, the love of John for his Master should have kept him awake. His earnest prayers should have mingled with those of his loved Saviour in the time of His supreme sorrow. The Redeemer had spent entire nights praying for His disciples, that their faith might not fail. Should Jesus now put to James and John the question He had once asked them, "Are ye able to drink of the cup that I shall drink of, and to be baptized with the baptism that I am baptized with?" they would not have ventured to answer, "We are able." Matt. 20:22.

The disciples awakened at the voice of Jesus, but they hardly knew Him, His face was so changed by anguish. Addressing Peter, Jesus said, "Simon, sleepest thou? couldest not thou watch one hour? Watch ye and pray, lest ye enter into temptation. The spirit truly is ready, but the flesh is weak." The weakness of His disciples awakened the sympathy of Jesus. He feared that they would not be able to endure the test which would come upon them in His betrayal and death. He did not reprove them, but said, "Watch ye and pray, lest ye enter into temptation." Even in His great agony, He was seeking to excuse their weakness. "The spirit truly is ready," He said, "but the flesh is weak."

Again the Son of God was seized with superhuman agony, and fainting and exhausted, He staggered back to the place of His former struggle. His suffering was even greater than before. As the agony of soul came upon Him, "His sweat was as it were great drops of blood falling down to the ground." The cypress and palm trees were the silent witnesses of His anguish. From their leafy branches dropped heavy dew upon His stricken form, as if nature wept over its Author wrestling alone with the powers of darkness.

A short time before, Jesus had stood like a mighty cedar, withstanding the storm of opposition that spent its fury upon Him. Stubborn wills, and hearts filled with malice and subtlety, had striven in vain to confuse and overpower Him. He stood forth in divine majesty as the Son of God. Now He was like a reed beaten and bent by the angry storm. He had approached the consummation of His work a conqueror, having at each step gained the victory over the powers of darkness. As [689-690] one already glorified, He had claimed oneness with God. In unfaltering accents He had poured out His songs of praise. He had spoken to His disciples in words of courage and tenderness. Now had come the hour of the power of darkness. Now His voice was heard on the still evening air, not in tones of triumph, but full of human anguish. The words of the Saviour were borne to the ears of the drowsy disciples, "O My Father, if this cup may not pass away from Me, except I drink it, Thy will be done."

The first impulse of the disciples was to go to Him; but He had bidden them tarry there, watching unto prayer. When Jesus came to them, He found them still sleeping. Again He had felt a longing for companionship, for some words from His disciples which would bring relief, and break the spell of darkness that well-nigh overpowered Him. But their eyes were heavy; "neither wist they what to answer Him." His presence aroused them. They saw His face marked with the bloody sweat of agony, and they were filled with fear. His anguish of mind they could not understand. "His visage was so marred more than any man, and His form more than the sons of men." Isa. 52:14.

Turning away, Jesus sought again His retreat, and fell prostrate, overcome by the horror of a great darkness. The humanity of the Son of God trembled in that trying hour. He prayed not now for His disciples that their faith might not fail, but for His own tempted, agonized soul. The awful moment had come--that moment which was to decide the destiny of the world. The fate of humanity trembled in the balance. Christ might even now refuse to drink the cup apportioned to guilty man. It was not yet too late. He might wipe the bloody sweat from His brow, and leave man to perish in his iniquity. He might say, Let the transgressor receive the penalty of his sin, and I will go back to My Father. Will the Son of God drink the bitter cup of humiliation and agony? Will the innocent suffer the consequences of the curse of sin, to save the guilty? The words fall tremblingly from the pale lips of Jesus, "O My Father, if this cup may not pass away from Me, except I drink it, Thy will be done."

Three times has He uttered that prayer. Three times has humanity shrunk from the last, crowning sacrifice. But now the history of the human race comes up before the world's Redeemer. He sees that the transgressors of the law, if left to themselves, must perish. He sees the helplessness of man. He sees the power of sin. The woes and lamentations of a doomed world rise before Him. He beholds its impending [690-693] fate, and His decision is made. He will save man at any cost to Himself. He accepts His baptism of blood, that through Him perishing millions may gain everlasting life. He has left the courts of heaven, where all is purity, happiness, and glory, to save the one lost sheep, the one world that has fallen by transgression. And He will not turn from His mission. He will become the propitiation of a race that has willed to sin. His prayer now breathes only submission: "If this cup may not pass away from Me, except I drink it, Thy will be done."

Having made the decision, He fell dying to the ground from which He had partially risen. Where now were His disciples, to place their hands tenderly beneath the head of their fainting Master, and bathe that brow,

7. Jesus "fell prostrate, overcome by the h____ _____ of a great darkness...The awful moment had come – that moment which was to decide the d_____ of the world... He sees the h_____ ____ of man. He sees the p_____ of sin...His decision is made. He will save man at a____ cost to Himself." (690, 693). Lord, I am overwhelmed with love for You. May I be more thoughtful, of what You experienced, before yielding so casually to temptation. Help my decision, to trust Your strength, and be faithful, no matter what the cost, or what I think I have to give up:

_____

_____

marred indeed more than the sons of men? The Saviour trod the wine press alone, and of the people there was none with Him.

But God suffered with His Son. Angels beheld the Saviour's agony. They saw their Lord enclosed by legions of satanic forces, His nature weighed down with a shuddering, mysterious dread. There was silence in heaven. No harp was touched. Could mortals have viewed the amazement of the angelic host as in silent grief they watched the Father separating His beams of light, love, and glory from His beloved Son, they would better understand how offensive in His sight is sin.

The worlds unfallen and the heavenly angels had watched with intense interest as the conflict drew to its close. Satan and his confederacy of evil, the legions of apostasy, watched intently this great crisis in the work of redemption. The powers of good and evil waited to see what answer would come to Christ's thrice-repeated prayer. Angels had longed to bring relief to the divine sufferer, but this might not be. No way of escape was found for the Son of God. In this awful crisis, when everything was at stake, when the mysterious cup trembled in the hand of the sufferer, the heavens opened, a light shone forth amid the stormy darkness of the crisis hour, and the mighty angel who stands in God's presence, occupying the position from which Satan fell, came to the side of Christ. The angel came not to take the cup from Christ's hand, but to strengthen Him to drink it, with the assurance of the Father's love. He came to give power to the divine-human suppliant. He pointed Him to the open heavens, telling Him of the souls that would be saved as the result of His sufferings. He assured Him that His Father is greater and more powerful than Satan, that His death would result in the utter discomfiture of Satan, and that the kingdom of this world would be given to the saints of the Most High. He told Him that He [693-694] would see of the travail of His soul, and be satisfied, for He would see a multitude of the human race saved, eternally saved.

Christ's agony did not cease, but His depression and discouragement left Him. The storm had in nowise abated, but He who was its object was strengthened to meet its fury. He came forth calm and serene. A heavenly peace rested upon His bloodstained face. He had borne that which no human being could ever bear; for He had tasted the sufferings of death for every man.

8. "God s_____ with His Son...Could mortals have viewed the a_____ _____ of the angelic host as in s_____ grief they watched the Father s_____ His beams of light, love, and glory from His beloved Son, they would better understand how o_____ ____ in His sight is sin." As I turn my eyes upon You, Lord, things of earth will grow strangely dim. As I taste and see that You are good, may sin become distasteful and offensive to me: _____
_____
_____

9. Jesus "had borne that which no human being could ever bear; for He had t_____ the sufferings of d_____ for every man." Lord, this took place in the garden of Gethsemane, not on Calvary; what does this mean, that You tasted the sufferings of death? _____
_____
_____

The sleeping disciples had been suddenly awakened by the light surrounding the Saviour. They saw the angel bending over their prostrate Master. They saw him lift the Saviour's head upon his bosom, and point toward heaven. They heard his voice, like sweetest music, speaking words of comfort and hope. The disciples recalled the scene upon the mount of transfiguration. They remembered the glory that in the temple had encircled Jesus, and the voice of God that spoke from the cloud. Now that same glory was again revealed, and they had no further fear for their Master. He was under the care of God; a mighty angel had been sent to protect Him. Again the disciples in their weariness yield to the strange stupor that overpowers them. Again Jesus finds them sleeping.

Looking sorrowfully upon them He says, "Sleep on now, and take your rest: behold, the hour is at hand, and the Son of man is betrayed into the hands of sinners."

Even as He spoke these words, He heard the footsteps of the mob in search of Him, and said, "Rise, let us be going: behold, he is at hand that doth betray Me."

No traces of His recent agony were visible as Jesus stepped forth to meet His betrayer. Standing in advance of His disciples He said, "Whom seek ye?" They answered, "Jesus of Nazareth." Jesus replied, "I am He." As these words were spoken, the angel who had lately ministered to Jesus moved between Him and the mob. A divine light illuminated the Saviour's face, and a dove-like form overshadowed Him. In the presence of this divine glory, the murderous throng could not stand for a moment. They staggered back. Priests, elders, soldiers, and even Judas, fell as dead men to the ground.

The angel withdrew, and the light faded away. Jesus had opportunity to escape, but He remained, calm and self-possessed. As one glorified He stood in the midst of that hardened band, now prostrate and helpless at His feet. The disciples looked on, silent with wonder and awe. [694-695]

But quickly the scene changed. The mob started up. The Roman soldiers, the priests and Judas, gathered about Christ. They seemed ashamed of their weakness, and fearful that He would yet escape. Again the question was asked by the Redeemer, "Whom seek ye?" They had had evidence that He who stood before them was the Son of God, but they would not be convinced. To the question, "Whom seek ye?" again they answered,

"Jesus of Nazareth." The Saviour then said, "I have told you that I am He: if therefore ye seek Me, let these go their way"--pointing to the disciples. He knew how weak was their faith, and He sought to shield them from temptation and trial. For them He was ready to sacrifice Himself.

Judas the betrayer did not forget the part he was to act. When the mob entered the garden, he had led the way, closely followed by the high priest. To the pursuers of Jesus he had given a sign, saying, "Whomsoever I shall kiss, that same is He: hold Him fast." Matt. 26:48. Now he pretends to have no part with them. Coming close to [695-696] Jesus, he takes His hand as a familiar friend. With the words, "Hail, Master," he kisses Him repeatedly, and appears to weep as if in sympathy with Him in His peril.

Jesus said to him, "Friend, wherefore art thou come?" His voice trembled with sorrow as He added, "Judas, betrayest thou the Son of man with a kiss?" This appeal should have aroused the conscience of the betrayer, and touched his stubborn heart; but honor, fidelity, and human tenderness had forsaken him. He stood bold and defiant, showing no disposition to relent. He had given himself up to Satan, and he had no power to resist him. Jesus did not refuse the traitor's kiss.

The mob grew bold as they saw Judas touch the person of Him who had so recently been glorified before their eyes. They now laid hold of Jesus, and proceeded to bind those precious hands that had ever been employed in doing good.

The disciples had thought that their Master would not suffer Himself to be taken. For the same power that had caused the mob to fall as dead men could keep them helpless, until Jesus and His companions should escape. They were disappointed and indignant as they saw the cords brought forward to bind the hands of Him whom they loved. Peter in his anger rashly drew his sword and tried to defend his Master, but he only cut off an ear of the high priest's servant. When Jesus saw what was done, He released His hands, though held firmly by the Roman soldiers, and saying, "Suffer ye thus far," He touched the wounded ear, and it was instantly made whole. He then said to Peter, "Put up again thy sword into his place: for all they that take the sword shall perish with the sword. Thinkest thou that I cannot now pray to My Father, and He shall presently give Me more than

10. "B_____ thou the Son of man with a kiss?' This appeal should have aroused the conscience of the betrayer, and t_____ his stubborn heart." (696). Lord, do I betray You with a kiss? Expose to me my self-righteousness, how my witness and testimony is self-promoting: _____

_____

_____

11. "The disciples had thought their Master would not s_____ Himself to be taken. For the same p_____ that had caused the mob to fall as dead men could keep them helpless, until Jesus and His companions should es-

cape... Oh, w_____, the disciples thought, does He not save Himself and us?...They were o_____ _____ that He should suffer this humiliation to Himself and t_____ ...They blamed Him for submitting to the mob... They all f_____ Him and fled." (696, 697). Lord, am I that kind of disciple, offended, self-centered, denying, betraying, forsaking? _____

_____ How can I be a more true friend?

_____

_____

_____

_____

Prayer journal: _____

_____

_____

_____

_____

_____

_____

twelve legions of angels?"--a legion in place of each one of the disciples. Oh, why, the disciples thought, does He not save Himself and us? Answering their unspoken thought, He added, "But how then shall the scriptures be fulfilled, that thus it must be?" "The cup which My Father hath given Me, shall I not drink it?"

The official dignity of the Jewish leaders had not prevented them from joining in the pursuit of Jesus. His arrest was too important a matter to be trusted to subordinates; the wily priests and elders had joined the temple police and the rabble in following Judas to Gethsemane. What a company for those dignitaries to unite with--a mob that was eager for excitement, and armed with all kinds of implements, as if in pursuit of a wild beast! [696-697]

Turning to the priests and elders, Christ fixed upon them His searching glance. The words He spoke they would never forget as long as life should last. They were as the sharp arrows of the Almighty. With dignity He said: You come out against Me with swords and staves as you would against a thief or a robber. Day by day I sat teaching in the temple. You had every opportunity of laying hands upon Me, and you did nothing. The night is better suited to your work. "This is your hour, and the power of darkness."

The disciples were terrified as they saw Jesus permit Himself to be taken and bound. They were offended that He should suffer this humiliation to Himself and them. They could not understand His conduct, and they blamed Him for submitting to the mob. In their indignation and fear, Peter proposed that they save themselves. Following this suggestion, "they all forsook Him, and fled." But Christ had foretold this desertion, "Behold," He had said, "the hour cometh, yea, is now come, that ye shall be scattered, every man to his own, and shall leave Me alone: and yet I am not alone, because the Father is with Me." John 16:32.

Chapter 75

Before Annas
and the Court of Caiaphas

[This chapter is based on Matt. 26:57-75; 27:1;
Mark 14:53-72; 15:1; Luke 22:54-71; John 18:13-27.]

Over the brook Kedron, past gardens and olive groves, and through the hushed streets of the sleeping city, they hurried Jesus. It was past midnight, and the cries of the hooting mob that followed Him broke sharply upon the still air. The Saviour was bound and closely guarded, and He moved painfully. But in eager haste His captors made their way with Him to the palace of Annas, the ex-high priest.

Annas was the head of the officiating priestly family, and in deference to his age he was recognized by the people as high priest. His counsel was sought and carried out as the voice of God. He must first see Jesus a captive to priestly power. He must be present at the examination of the prisoner, for fear that the less-experienced Caiaphas might fail of securing the object for which they were working. His artifice, cunning, and subtlety must be used on this occasion; for, at all events, Christ's condemnation must be secured.

Christ was to be tried formally before the Sanhedrin; but before Annas He was subjected to a preliminary trial. Under the Roman rule the Sanhedrin could not execute the sentence of death. They could only examine a prisoner, and pass judgment, to be ratified by the Roman authorities. It was therefore necessary to bring against Christ charges [698-699] that would be regarded as criminal by the Romans. An accusation must also be found which would condemn Him in the eyes of the Jews. Not a few among the priests and rulers had been convicted by Christ's teaching, and only fear of excommunication prevented them from confessing Him. The priests well remembered the question of Nicodemus, "Doth our law judge any man, before it hear him, and know what he doeth?" John 7:51. This question had for the time broken up the council, and thwarted their plans. Joseph of Arimathaea and Nicodemus were not now to be summoned, but there were others who

1. "Not a f_____ among the priests and rulers had been c_____ by Christ's teaching, and only fear of excommunication prevented them from c_____

Him…The trial must be so conducted as to u_____ _____ the members of the Sanhedrin a_____ Christ." (699). Lord, are there certain associations I have, that I would refrain from confessing You, for fear of excommunication or reprisals? _____
_____.
Why am I shy about it?
_____
_____
_____
_____

might dare to speak in favor of justice. The trial must be so conducted as to unite the members of the Sanhedrin against Christ. There were two charges which the priests desired to maintain. If Jesus could be proved a blasphemer, He would be condemned by the Jews. If convicted of sedition, it would secure His condemnation by the Romans. The second charge Annas tried first to establish. He questioned Jesus concerning His disciples and His doctrines, hoping the prisoner would say something that would give him material upon which to work. He thought to draw out some statement to prove that He was seeking to establish a secret society, with the purpose of setting up a new kingdom. Then the priests could deliver Him to the Romans as a disturber of the peace and a creator of insurrection.

Christ read the priest's purpose as an open book. As if reading the inmost soul of His questioner, He denied that there was between Him and His followers any secret bond of union, or that He gathered them secretly and in the darkness to conceal His designs. He had no secrets in regard to His purposes or doctrines. "I spake openly to the world," He answered; "I ever taught in the synagogue, and in the temple, whither the Jews always resort; and in secret have I said nothing."

The Saviour contrasted His own manner of work with the methods of His accusers. For months they had hunted Him, striving to entrap Him and bring Him before a secret tribunal, where they might obtain by perjury what it was impossible to gain by fair means. Now they were carrying out their purpose. The midnight seizure by a mob, the mockery and abuse before He was condemned, or even accused, was their manner of work, not His. Their action was in violation of the law. Their own rules declared that every man should be treated as innocent until proved guilty. By their own rules the priests stood condemned.

Turning upon His questioner, Jesus said, "Why askest thou Me?" Had not the priests and rulers sent spies to watch His movements, and report His every word? Had not these been present at every gathering [699-700] of the people, and carried to the priests information of all His sayings and doings? "Ask them which heard Me, what I have said unto them," replied Jesus; "behold, they know what I said."

Annas was silenced by the decision of the answer. Fearing that Christ would say something regarding his course of action that he would prefer to keep covered up, he said nothing more to Him at this time. One of his officers, filled with wrath as he saw Annas silenced, struck Jesus on the face, saying, "Answerest Thou the high priest so?"

Christ calmly replied, "If I have spoken evil, bear witness of the evil: but if well, why smitest thou Me?" He spoke no burning words of retaliation. His calm answer came from a heart sinless, patient, and gentle, that would not be provoked.

Christ suffered keenly under abuse and insult. At the hands of the beings whom He had created, and for whom He was making an infinite sacrifice, He received every indignity. And He suffered in proportion to the perfection of His holiness and His hatred of sin. His trial by men who acted as fiends was to Him a perpetual sacrifice. To be surrounded by human beings under the control of Satan was revolting to Him. And He knew that in a moment, by the flashing forth of His divine power, He could lay His cruel tormentors in the dust. This made the trial the harder to bear.

The Jews were looking for a Messiah to be revealed in outward show. They expected Him, by one flash of overmastering will, to change the current of men's thoughts, and force from them an acknowledgment of His supremacy. Thus, they believed, He was to secure His own exaltation, and gratify their ambitious hopes. Thus when Christ was treated with contempt, there came to Him a strong temptation to manifest His divine character. By a word, by a look, He could compel His persecutors to confess that He was Lord above kings and rulers, priests and temple. But it was His difficult task to keep to the position He had chosen as one with humanity.

The angels of heaven witnessed every movement made against their loved Commander. They longed to deliver Christ. Under God the angels are all-powerful. On one occasion, in obedience to the command of Christ, they slew of the Assyrian army in one night one hundred and eighty-five thousand men. How easily could the angels, beholding the shameful scene of the trial of Christ, have testified their indignation by consuming the adversaries of God! But they were not commanded to do this. He who could have doomed His enemies to death bore with [700-703] their cruelty. His love for His Father, and His pledge, made from the

2. Jesus "spoke no burning words of r_____ _____. His calm answer came from a heart sinless, patient, and gentle, that would not be p_____ _____." (700). Lord, what does it take to be like that?

_____

_____

_____

If I am cherishing sin in my heart, the enemy has an easier time provoking me? _____ Show me, Lord, what I can let go of:

_____

_____

3. Jesus "suffered in proportion to the perfection of His h_____ and His hatred of s_____." Lord, as our walk together becomes more meaningful, and my character molded more like Yours, how will I treat those chosing not to walk with You? Will I abandon them, isolate myself in self-righteousness, and be intolerant towards them?

_____

_____ What should I do? What did You do? _____

_____

_____

_____ Didn't You eat and socialize with sinners?

4. "By a word, by a l___ _____, Jesus could c___ _____ His persecutors to confess that He was Lord." What would

be wrong with that? How would it be out of harmony with Your goals? _____

_____

_____

_____

5. "It was part of His m_____ to bear, in His humanity, all the taunts and a_____ that men could heap upon Him...

foundation of the world, to become the Sin Bearer, led Him to endure uncomplainingly the coarse treatment of those He came to save. It was a part of His mission to bear, in His humanity, all the taunts and abuse that men could heap upon Him. The only hope of humanity was in this submission of Christ to all that He could endure from the hands and hearts of men.

Christ had said nothing that could give His accusers an advantage; yet He was bound, to signify that He was condemned. There must, however, be a pretense of justice. It was necessary that there should be the form of a legal trial. This the authorities were determined to hasten. They knew the regard in which Jesus was held by the people, and feared that if the arrest were noised abroad, a rescue would be attempted. Again, if the trial and execution were not brought about at once, there would be a week's delay on account of the celebration of the Passover. This might defeat their plans. In securing the condemnation of Jesus they depended largely upon the clamor of the mob, many of them the rabble of Jerusalem. Should there be a week's delay, the excitement would abate, and a reaction would be likely to set in. The better part of the people would be aroused in Christ's favor; many would come forward with testimony in His vindication, bringing to light the mighty works He had done. This would excite popular indignation against the Sanhedrin. Their proceedings would be condemned, and Jesus would be set free, to receive new homage from the multitudes. The priests and rulers therefore determined that before their purpose could become known, Jesus should be delivered into the hands of the Romans.

But first of all, an accusation was to be found. They had gained nothing as yet. Annas ordered Jesus to be taken to Caiaphas. Caiaphas belonged to the Sadducees, some of whom were now the most desperate enemies of Jesus. He himself, though wanting in force of character, was fully as severe, heartless, and unscrupulous as was Annas. He would leave no means untried to destroy Jesus. It was now early morning, and very dark; by the light of torches and lanterns the armed band with their prisoner proceeded to the high priest's palace. Here, while the members of the Sanhedrin were coming together, Annas and Caiaphas again questioned Jesus, but without success.

When the council had assembled in the judgment

hall, Caiaphas took his seat as presiding officer. On either side were the judges, and those specially interested in the trial. The Roman soldiers were stationed on [703-704] the platform below the throne. At the foot of the throne stood Jesus. Upon Him the gaze of the whole multitude was fixed. The excitement was intense. Of all the throng He alone was calm and serene. The very atmosphere surrounding Him seemed pervaded by a holy influence.

Caiaphas had regarded Jesus as his rival. The eagerness of the people to hear the Saviour, and their apparent readiness to accept His teachings, had aroused the bitter jealousy of the high priest. But as Caiaphas now looked upon the prisoner, he was struck with admiration for His noble and dignified bearing. A conviction came over him that this Man was akin to God. The next instant he scornfully banished the thought. Immediately [704-705] his voice was heard in sneering, haughty tones demanding that Jesus work one of His mighty miracles before them. But his words fell upon the Saviour's ears as though He heard them not. The people compared the excited and malignant deportment of Annas and Caiaphas with the calm, majestic bearing of Jesus. Even in the minds of that hardened multitude arose the question, Is this man of godlike presence to be condemned as a criminal?

Caiaphas, perceiving the influence that was obtaining, hastened the trial. The enemies of Jesus were in great perplexity. They were bent on securing His condemnation, but how to accomplish this they knew not. The members of the council were divided between the Pharisees and the Sadducees. There was bitter animosity and controversy between them; certain disputed points they dared not approach for fear of a quarrel. With a few words Jesus could have excited their prejudices against each other, and thus have averted their wrath from Himself. Caiaphas knew this, and he wished to avoid stirring up a contention. There were plenty of witnesses to prove that Christ had denounced the priests and scribes, that He had called them hypocrites and murderers; but this testimony it was not expedient to bring forward. The Sadducees in their sharp contentions with the Pharisees had used to them similar language. And such testimony would have no weight with the Romans, who were themselves disgusted with the pretensions of the Pharisees. There was abundant evidence that Je-

Of all the throng, He alone was c_____ and serene. The very a_____ _____ surrounding Him seemed pervaded by a holy influence...

The people compared the e_____ and malignant deportment of Annas and Caiaphas with the calm, m_____ bearing of Jesus. Even in the minds of that h_____ _____ multitude arose the question, Is this man of godlike p_____ _____ to be condemned as a criminal?" (703-705). Lord, what is my bearing under stress? _____ _____ _____ _____ Is it my mission also, to bear taunts and abuse? _____ _____ How can I have an atmosphere of holy influence? _____ _____ _____

sus had disregarded the traditions of the Jews, and had spoken irreverently of many of their ordinances; but in regard to tradition the Pharisees and Sadducees were at swords' points; and this evidence also would have no weight with the Romans. Christ's enemies dared not accuse Him of Sabbathbreaking, lest an examination should reveal the character of His work. If His miracles of healing were brought to light, the very object of the priests would be defeated.

False witnesses had been bribed to accuse Jesus of inciting rebellion and seeking to establish a separate government. But their testimony proved to be vague and contradictory. Under examination they falsified their own statements.

Early in His ministry Christ had said, "Destroy this temple, and in three days I will raise it up." In the figurative language of prophecy, He had thus foretold His own death and resurrection. "He spake of the temple of His body." John 2:19, 21. These words the Jews had understood in a literal sense, as referring to the temple at Jerusalem. Of all that Christ had said, the priests could find nothing to use against Him [705-706] save this. By misstating these words they hoped to gain an advantage. The Romans had engaged in rebuilding and embellishing the temple, and they took great pride in it; any contempt shown to it would be sure to excite their indignation. Here Romans and Jews, Pharisees and Sadducees, could meet; for all held the temple in great veneration. On this point two witnesses were found whose testimony was not so contradictory as that of the others had been. One of them, who had been bribed to accuse Jesus, declared, "This fellow said, I am able to destroy the temple of God, and to build it in three days." Thus Christ's words were misstated. If they had been reported exactly as He spoke them, they would not have secured His condemnation even by the Sanhedrin. Had Jesus been a mere man, as the Jews claimed, His declaration would only have indicated an unreasonable, boastful spirit, but could not have been construed into blasphemy. Even as misrepresented by the false witnesses, His words contained nothing which would be regarded by the Romans as a crime worthy of death.

Patiently Jesus listened to the conflicting testimonies. No word did He utter in self-defense. At last His accusers were entangled, confused, and maddened. The trial was making no headway; it seemed that their plottings were to fail. Caiaphas was desperate. One last resort remained; Christ must be forced to condemn Himself. The high priest started from the judgment seat, his face contorted with passion, his voice and demeanor plainly indicating that were it in his power he would strike down the prisoner before him. "Answerest Thou nothing?" he exclaimed; "what is it which these witness against Thee?"

Jesus held His peace. "He was oppressed, and He was afflicted, yet He opened not His mouth: He is brought as a lamb to the slaughter, and as a sheep before her shearers is dumb, so He openeth not His mouth." Isaiah 53:7.

At last, Caiaphas, raising his right hand toward heaven, addressed Jesus in the form of a solemn oath: "I adjure Thee by the living God, that Thou tell us whether Thou be the Christ, the Son of God."

To this appeal Christ could not remain silent. There was a time to be silent, and a time to speak. He had not spoken until directly questioned. He knew that to answer now would make His death certain. But the appeal was made by the highest acknowledged authority of the nation, and in the name of the Most High. Christ would not fail to show proper respect for the law. More than this, His own relation to the Father was called in question. He must plainly declare His character and mission. [706-707] Jesus had said to His disciples, "Whosoever therefore shall confess Me before men, him will I confess also before My Father which is in heaven." Matt. 10:32. Now by His own example He repeated the lesson.

Every ear was bent to listen, and every eye was fixed on His face as He answered, "Thou hast said." A heavenly light seemed to illuminate His pale countenance as He added, "Nevertheless I say unto you, Hereafter shall ye see the Son of man sitting on the right hand of power, and coming in the clouds of heaven."

For a moment the divinity of Christ flashed through His guise of humanity. The high priest quailed before the penetrating eyes of the Saviour. That look seemed to read his hidden thoughts, and burn into his heart. Never in afterlife did he forget that searching glance of the persecuted Son of God.

"Hereafter," said Jesus, "shall ye see the Son of man sitting on the [707-708] right hand of power, and coming in the clouds of heaven." In these words Christ

6. Caiaphas asked Jesus whether He was the Christ, the Son of God. "To this appeal Christ could not remain s_____...
His own r_____
to the Father was called in question." (706). Lord, under very little pressure, my testimony as to my relation to the Father has been one of denial. You are my Friend. I am privileged and honored! Why can't I faithfully speak well of our relationship?
_____
_____
_____

7. "The high priest quailed before the p_____
_____ eyes of the Savior. That look seemed to read his h_____ thoughts, and burn into his heart. Never in afterlife did he forget that s_____
_____ glance of the persecuted Son of God." (707). I don't want to quail, Lord, but to invite Your search of my heart: _____
_____
_____
_____

presented the reverse of the scene then taking place. He, the Lord of life and glory, would be seated at God's right hand. He would be the judge of all the earth, and from His decision there could be no appeal. Then every secret thing would be set in the light of God's countenance, and judgment be passed upon every man according to his deeds.

The words of Christ startled the high priest. The thought that there was to be a resurrection of the dead, when all would stand at the bar of God, to be rewarded according to their works, was a thought of terror to Caiaphas. He did not wish to believe that in future he would receive sentence according to his works. There rushed before his mind as a panorama the scenes of the final judgment. For a moment he saw the fearful spectacle of the graves giving up their dead, with the secrets he had hoped were forever hidden. For a moment he felt as if standing before the eternal Judge, whose eye, which sees all things, was reading his soul, bringing to light mysteries supposed to be hidden with the dead.

The scene passed from the priest's vision. Christ's words cut him, the Sadducee, to the quick. Caiaphas had denied the doctrine of the resurrection, the judgment, and a future life. Now he was maddened by satanic fury. Was this man, a prisoner before him, to assail his most cherished theories? Rending his robe, that the people might see his pretended horror, he demanded that without further preliminaries the prisoner be condemned for blasphemy. "What further need have we of witnesses?" he said; "behold, now ye have heard His blasphemy. What think ye?" And they all condemned Him.

Conviction mingled with passion led Caiaphas to do as he did. He was furious with himself for believing Christ's words, and instead of rending his heart under a deep sense of truth, and confessing that Jesus was the Messiah, he rent his priestly robes in determined resistance. This act was deeply significant. Little did Caiaphas realize its meaning. In this act, done to influence the judges and secure Christ's condemnation, the high priest had condemned himself. By the law of God he was disqualified for the priesthood. He had pronounced upon himself the death sentence.

A high priest was not to rend his garments. By the Levitical law, this was prohibited under sentence of death. Under no circumstances, on no occasion, was the priest to rend his robe. It was the custom among the

---

8. "The thought...when all would stand at the bar of God, to be rewarded according to their works, was a thought of t_____ to Caiaphas...furious with himself for b_____ Christ's words...he rent his priestly robes in determined resistance," in p_____ horror. (708). Lord, I don't want terror to be my response; but rather, like Judas, to thrill to confess, to be read like a book, to come clean and be transparent with You. How can I lessen my resistence to Your drawing me into greater openness with You? _____

_____

Jews for the garments to be rent at the death of friends, but this [708-709] custom the priests were not to observe. Express command had been given by Christ to Moses concerning this. Lev. 10:6.

Everything worn by the priest was to be whole and without blemish. By those beautiful official garments was represented the character of the great antitype, Jesus Christ. Nothing but perfection, in dress and attitude, in word and spirit, could be acceptable to God. He is holy, and His glory and perfection must be represented by the earthly service. Nothing but perfection could properly represent the sacredness of the heavenly service. Finite man might rend his own heart by showing a contrite and humble spirit. This God would discern. But no rent must be made in the priestly robes, for this would mar the representation of heavenly things. The high priest who dared to appear in holy office, and engage in the service of the sanctuary, with a rent robe, was looked upon as having severed himself from God. By rending his garment he cut himself off from being a representative character. He was no longer accepted by God as an officiating priest. This course of action, as exhibited by Caiaphas, showed human passion, human imperfection.

By rending his garments, Caiaphas made of no effect the law of God, to follow the tradition of men. A man-made law provided that in case of blasphemy a priest might rend his garments in horror at the sin, and be guiltless. Thus the law of God was made void by the laws of men.

Each action of the high priest was watched with interest by the people; and Caiaphas thought for effect to display his piety. But in this act, designed as an accusation against Christ, he was reviling the One of whom God had said, "My name is in Him." Ex. 23:21. He himself was committing blasphemy. Standing under the condemnation of God, he pronounced sentence upon Christ as a blasphemer.

When Caiaphas rent his garment, his act was significant of the place that the Jewish nation as a nation would thereafter occupy toward God. The once favored people of God were separating themselves from Him, and were fast becoming a people disowned by Jehovah. When Christ upon the cross cried out, "It is finished" (John 19:30), and the veil of the temple was rent in twain, the Holy Watcher declared that the Jewish people had rejected Him who was the antitype of all their types, the substance of all their shadows. Israel was divorced from God. Well might Caiaphas then rend his official robes, which signified that he claimed to be a representative of the great High Priest; for no longer had they any meaning for him or for the people. Well might the high priest rend his robes in horror for himself and for the nation. [709-710]

The Sanhedrin had pronounced Jesus worthy of death; but it was contrary to the Jewish law to try a prisoner by night. In legal condemnation nothing could be done except in the light of day and before a full session of the council. Notwithstanding this, the Saviour was now treated as a condemned criminal, and given up to be abused by the lowest and vilest of humankind. The palace of the high priest surrounded an open court in which the soldiers and the multitude had gathered. Through this court, Jesus was taken to the guardroom, on every side meeting with mockery of His claim to be the Son of God. His own words, "sitting on the right hand of power," and, "coming in the clouds of heaven," were jeeringly repeated. While in the guardroom, awaiting His legal trial, He was not protected. The ignorant rabble had seen the cruelty with which He was treated before the council, and from this they took license to manifest all the satanic elements of their nature. Christ's very nobility and godlike bearing goaded them to madness. His meekness, His innocence, His majestic patience, filled them with hatred born of Satan. Mercy and justice were trampled upon. Never was criminal treated in so inhuman a manner as was the Son of God.

But a keener anguish rent the heart of Jesus; the blow that inflicted the deepest pain no enemy's hand could have dealt. While He was undergoing the mockery of an examination before Caiaphas, Christ had been denied by one of His own disciples.

After deserting their Master in the garden, two of the disciples had ventured to follow, at a distance, the mob that had Jesus in charge. These disciples were Peter and John. The priests recognized John as a well-known disciple of Jesus, and admitted him to the hall, hoping that as he witnessed the humiliation of his Leader, he would scorn the idea of such a one being the Son of God. John spoke in favor of Peter, and gained an entrance for him also.

In the court a fire had been kindled; for it was the

1. "They took license to manifest all the satanic elements of their nature. Christ's very nobility and godlike bearing goaded them to m_____. His meekness, His innocence, His majestic patience, filled them with hatred born of S_____." (710). Lord, how do I respond to someone's response of kindness to my meanness?_____

2. "A keener a_____ rent the heart of Jesus; the blow that inflicted the d_____ pain" was being denied by one of His o_____ disciples.

coldest hour of the night, being just before the dawn. A company drew about the fire, and Peter presumptuously took his place with them. He did not wish to be recognized as a disciple of Jesus. By mingling carelessly with the crowd, he hoped to be taken for one of those who had brought Jesus to the hall.

But as the light flashed upon Peter's face, the woman who kept the door cast a searching glance upon him. She had noticed that he came in with John, she marked the look of dejection on his face, and thought [710-711] that he might be a disciple of Jesus. She was one of the servants of Caiaphas' household, and was curious to know. She said to Peter, "Art not thou also one of this Man's disciples?" Peter was startled and confused; the eyes of the company instantly fastened upon him. He pretended not to understand her; but she was persistent, and said to those around her that this man was with Jesus. Peter felt compelled to answer, and said angrily, "Woman, I know Him not." This was the first denial, and immediately the cock crew. O Peter, so soon ashamed of thy Master! so soon to deny thy Lord!

The disciple John, upon entering the judgment hall, did not try to conceal the fact that he was a follower of Jesus. He did not mingle with the rough company who were reviling his Master. He was not questioned, for he did not assume a false character, and thus lay himself liable to suspicion. He sought a retired corner secure from the notice [711-712] of the mob, but as near Jesus as it was possible for him to be. Here he could see and hear all that took place at the trial of his Lord.

Peter had not designed that his real character should be known. In assuming an air of indifference he had placed himself on the enemy's ground, and he became an easy prey to temptation. If he had been called to fight for his Master, he would have been a courageous soldier; but when the finger of scorn was pointed at him, he proved himself a coward. Many who do not shrink from active warfare for their Lord are driven by ridicule to deny their faith. By associating with those whom they should avoid, they place themselves in the way of temptation. They invite the enemy to tempt them, and are led to say and do that of which under other circumstances they would never have been guilty. The disciple of Christ who in our day disguises his faith through dread of suffering or reproach denies his Lord as really as did Peter in the judgment hall.

"By mingling carelessly with the crowd, he hoped to be taken for one of those who had b_____ _____ Jesus to the hall...

Peter had not designed that his real c_____ should be known. In assuming an air of i_____ __ he had placed himself on the enemy's ground...If he had been called to fight for his Master, he would have been a c_____ ____ soldier; but when the finger of s_____ was pointed at him, he proved himself a c_____." (710-712). Lord, I know I have given You pain, by denying You. Sometimes I don't even know that I am doing it. Show me when I am being indifferent. I don't want to give You any more pain: _____ _____ _____ _____

3. "The disciple of Christ who in our day d_____ _____ his faith through dread of suffering or reproach d_____ his Lord

as really as did Peter in the judgment hall." Lord, forgive Me for disguising my faith, my relationship with You. I am honored to be Your disciple. Please help me to recognize when I am disguising my faith: (for example)

_____

_____

_____

4. "The Savior turned from the frowning judges, and looked full upon His p____ ____ disciple. At the same time Peter's eyes were drawn to his Master." (713). What did Peter see in the gaze? _____

_____

5. "Peter had just declared that he k_____ not Jesus, but he now realized with bitter g_____ how well his Lord knew him, and how accurately He had read his heart, the falseness of which was u_____ _____ even to himself...It

Peter tried to show no interest in the trial of his Master, but his heart was wrung with sorrow as he heard the cruel taunts, and saw the abuse He was suffering. More than this, he was surprised and angry that Jesus should humiliate Himself and His followers by submitting to such treatment. In order to conceal his true feelings, he endeavored to join with the persecutors of Jesus in their untimely jests. But his appearance was unnatural. He was acting a lie, and while seeking to talk unconcernedly he could not restrain expressions of indignation at the abuse heaped upon his Master.

Attention was called to him the second time, and he was again charged with being a follower of Jesus. He now declared with an oath, "I do not know the Man." Still another opportunity was given him. An hour had passed, when one of the servants of the high priest, being a near kinsman of the man whose ear Peter had cut off, asked him, "Did not I see thee in the garden with Him?" "Surely thou art one of them: for thou art a Galilean, and thy speech agreeth thereto." At this Peter flew into a rage. The disciples of Jesus were noted for the purity of their language, and in order fully to deceive his questioners, and justify his assumed character, Peter now denied his Master with cursing and swearing. Again the cock crew. Peter heard it then, and he remembered the words of Jesus, "Before the cock crow twice, thou shalt deny Me thrice." Mark 14:30.

While the degrading oaths were fresh upon Peter's lips, and the shrill [712-713] crowing of the cock was still ringing in his ears, the Saviour turned from the frowning judges, and looked full upon His poor disciple. At the same time Peter's eyes were drawn to his Master. In that gentle countenance he read deep pity and sorrow, but there was no anger there.

The sight of that pale, suffering face, those quivering lips, that look of compassion and forgiveness, pierced his heart like an arrow. Conscience was aroused. Memory was active. Peter called to mind his promise of a few short hours before that he would go with his Lord to prison and to death. He remembered his grief when the Saviour told him in the upper chamber that he would deny his Lord thrice that same night. Peter had just declared that he knew not Jesus, but he now realized with bitter grief how well his Lord knew him, and how accurately He had read his heart, the falseness of which was unknown even to himself.

A tide of memories rushed over him. The Saviour's tender mercy, His kindness and long-suffering, His gentleness and patience toward His erring disciples,--all was remembered. He recalled the caution, "Simon, behold, Satan hath desired to have you, that he may sift you as wheat: but I have prayed for thee, that thy faith fail not." Luke 22:31, 32. He reflected with horror upon his own ingratitude, his falsehood, his perjury. Once more he looked at his Master, and saw a sacrilegious hand raised to smite Him in the face. Unable longer to endure the scene, he rushed, heartbroken, from the hall.

He pressed on in solitude and darkness, he knew not and cared not whither. At last he found himself in Gethsemane. The scene of a few hours before came vividly to his mind. The suffering face of his Lord, stained with bloody sweat and convulsed with anguish, rose before him. He remembered with bitter remorse that Jesus had wept and agonized in prayer alone, while those who should have united with Him in that trying hour were sleeping. He remembered His solemn charge, "Watch and pray, that ye enter not into temptation." Matt. 26:41. He witnessed again the scene in the judgment hall. It was torture to his bleeding heart to know that he had added the heaviest burden to the Saviour's humiliation and grief. On the very spot where Jesus had poured out His soul in agony to His Father, Peter fell upon his face, and wished that he might die.

It was in sleeping when Jesus bade him watch and pray that Peter had prepared the way for his great sin. All the disciples, by sleeping [713-714] in that critical hour, sustained a great loss. Christ knew the fiery ordeal through which they were to pass. He knew how Satan would work to paralyze their senses that they might be unready for the trial. Therefore it was that He gave them warning. Had those hours in the garden been spent in watching and prayer, Peter would not have been left to depend upon his own feeble strength. He would not have denied his Lord. Had the disciples watched with Christ in His agony, they would have been prepared to behold His suffering upon the cross. They would have understood in some degree the nature of His overpowering anguish. They would have been able to recall His words that foretold His sufferings, His death, and His resurrection. Amid the gloom of the most trying hour, some rays of hope would have lighted up the darkness

was torture to his bleeding heart to know that he had added the h_____ burden to the Savior's humiliation and grief." (713). How might this torture be similar or different, from the torture experienced by the wicked in the end?

_____

_____

Lord, I don't to be a burden to Your heart. But I don't know my own falseness. Help me; forgive me, for "every i_____ _____ look, word, and act against" You. (715).

6. "It was in sleeping when Jesus bade him watch and pray that Peter had p_____ the way for his great sin. All the disciples, by sleeping in that critical hour, sustained a great loss." Help me,

Lord, to know when I am 'sleeping.' What are those attitudes? _____

_____

_____

7. "A satanic fury took possession of the people. The roar of voices was like that of wild beasts." How does Satan disguise his possessing people today? _____

_____

_____

and sustained their faith.

As soon as it was day, the Sanhedrin again assembled, and again Jesus was brought into the council room. He had declared Himself the Son of God, and they had construed His words into a charge against Him. But they could not condemn Him on this, for many of them had not been present at the night session, and they had not heard His words. And they knew that the Roman tribunal would find in them nothing worthy of death. But if from His own lips they could all hear those words repeated, their object might be gained. His claim to the Messiahship they might construe into a seditious political claim.

"Art Thou the Christ?" they said, "tell us." But Christ remained silent. They continued to ply Him with questions. At last in tones of mournful pathos He answered, "If I tell you, ye will not believe; and if I also ask you, ye will not answer Me, nor let Me go." But that they might be left without excuse He added the solemn warning, "Hereafter shall the Son of man sit on the right hand of the power of God."

"Art Thou then the Son of God?" they asked with one voice. He said unto them, "Ye say that I am." They cried out, "What need we any further witness? for we ourselves have heard of His own mouth."

And so by the third condemnation of the Jewish authorities, Jesus was to die. All that was now necessary, they thought, was for the Romans to ratify this condemnation, and deliver Him into their hands.

Then came the third scene of abuse and mockery, worse even than that received from the ignorant rabble. In the very presence of the priests and rulers, and with their sanction, this took place. Every feeling of sympathy or humanity had gone out of their hearts. If their arguments [714-715] were weak, and failed to silence His voice, they had other weapons, such as in all ages have been used to silence heretics,--suffering, and violence, and death.

When the condemnation of Jesus was pronounced by the judges, a satanic fury took possession of the people. The roar of voices was like that of wild beasts. The crowd made a rush toward Jesus, crying, He is guilty, put Him to death! Had it not been for the Roman soldiers, Jesus would not have lived to be nailed to the cross of Calvary. He would have been torn in pieces before His judges, had not Roman authority interfered, and by force of arms restrained the violence of the mob.

Heathen men were angry at the brutal treatment of one against whom nothing had been proved. The Roman officers declared that the Jews in pronouncing condemnation upon Jesus were infringing upon the Roman power, and that it was even against the Jewish law to condemn a man to death upon his own testimony. This intervention brought a momentary lull in the proceedings; but the Jewish leaders were dead alike to pity and to shame.

Priests and rulers forgot the dignity of their office, and abused the Son of God with foul epithets. They taunted Him with His parentage. They declared that His presumption in proclaiming Himself the Messiah made Him deserving of the most ignominious death. The most dissolute men engaged in infamous abuse of the Saviour. An old garment was thrown over His head, and His persecutors struck Him in the face, saying, "Prophesy unto us, Thou Christ, Who is he that smote Thee?" When the garment was removed, one poor wretch spat in His face.

Prayer journal: _____

The angels of God faithfully recorded every insulting look, word, and act against their beloved Commander. One day the base men who scorned and spat upon the calm, pale face of Christ will look upon it in its glory, shining brighter than the sun.

Chapter 76

Judas

The history of Judas presents the sad ending of a life that might have been honored of God. Had Judas died before his last journey to Jerusalem he would have been regarded as a man worthy of a place among the twelve, and one who would be greatly missed. The abhorrence which has followed him through the centuries would not have existed but for the attributes revealed at the close of his history. But it was for a purpose that his character was laid open to the world. It was to be a warning to all who, like him, should betray sacred trusts.

A little before the Passover, Judas had renewed his contract with the priests to deliver Jesus into their hands. Then it was arranged that the Saviour should be taken at one of His resorts for meditation and prayer. Since the feast at the house of Simon, Judas had had opportunity to reflect upon the deed which he had covenanted to perform, but his purpose was unchanged. For thirty pieces of silver--the price of a slave--he sold the Lord of glory to ignominy and death.

Judas had naturally a strong love for money; but he had not always been corrupt enough to do such a deed as this. He had fostered the evil spirit of avarice until it had become the ruling motive of his life. The love of mammon overbalanced his love for Christ. Through becoming the slave of one vice he gave himself to Satan, to be driven to any lengths in sin.

Judas had joined the disciples when multitudes were following Christ. The Saviour's teaching moved their hearts as they hung entranced upon His words, spoken in the synagogue, by the seaside, upon the mount. [716-717] Judas saw the sick, the lame, the blind, flock to Jesus from the towns and cities. He saw the dying laid at His feet. He witnessed the Saviour's mighty works in healing the sick, casting out devils, and raising the dead. He felt in his own person the evidence of Christ's power. He recognized the teaching of Christ as superior to all that he had ever heard. He loved the Great Teacher, and desired to be with Him. He felt a desire

1. The story of Judas was laid open to the world as a warning to those who would "b_____ sacred trusts." Could this be a warning to me? How? ___

2. "Through becoming the slave of o_____ vice he [Judas] gave himself to Satan, to be driven to any lengths in sin." How does a small cherished sin lead to such serious results?

3. Judas "felt in his own person the evidence of Christ's p_____ ...He loved the Great Teacher, and desired to be w_____ Him. He felt

to be changed in character and life, and he hoped to experience this through connecting himself with Jesus. The Saviour did not repulse Judas. He gave him a place among the twelve. He trusted him to do the work of an evangelist. He endowed him with power to heal the sick and to cast out devils. But Judas did not come to the point of surrendering himself fully to Christ. He did not give up his worldly ambition or his love of money. While he accepted the position of a minister of Christ, he did not bring himself under the divine molding. He felt that he could retain his own judgment and opinions, and he cultivated a disposition to criticize and accuse.

Judas was highly regarded by the disciples, and had great influence over them. He himself had a high opinion of his own qualifications, and looked upon his brethren as greatly inferior to him in judgment and ability. They did not see their opportunities, he thought, and take advantage of circumstances. The church would never prosper with such shortsighted men as leaders. Peter was impetuous; he would move without consideration. John, who was treasuring up the truths that fell from Christ's lips, was looked upon by Judas as a poor financier. Matthew, whose training had taught him accuracy in all things, was very particular in regard to honesty, and he was ever contemplating the words of Christ, and became so absorbed in them that, as Judas thought, he could not be trusted to do sharp, far-seeing business. Thus Judas summed up all the disciples, and flattered himself that the church would often be brought into perplexity and embarrassment if it were not for his ability as a manager. Judas regarded himself as the capable one, who could not be overreached. In his own estimation he was an honor to the cause, and as such he always represented himself.

Judas was blinded to his own weakness of character, and Christ placed him where he would have an opportunity to see and correct this. As treasurer for the disciples, he was called upon to provide for the needs of the little company, and to relieve the necessities of the poor. When in the Passover chamber Jesus said to him, "That thou doest, do quickly" (John 13:27), the disciples thought He had bidden him [717-718] buy what was needed for the feast, or give something to the poor. In ministering to others, Judas might have developed an unselfish spirit. But while listening daily to the lessons of Christ and witnessing His unselfish life, Judas

a desire to be c_____ ____ in character and life, and he hoped to experience this through connecting himself with Jesus...But Judas did not come to the point of s_____ himself fully to Christ. He did not g_____ up his worldly ambition or his love of money." (717). Lord, am I that much different from Judas? He had some very spiritual and holy feelings. Lord, help me to recognize the two masters I try to serve, the level to which I do, and the danger of doing so. _____

_____
_____
_____
_____
_____

Is one of the two masters my "own opinion?"
_____
_____ Do I "cultivate a disposition to criticize and accuse?"
_____
_____
_____

4. "In his own estimation he was an h_____ to the cause, and as such he always represented himself. Judas was b____ _____ to his own weakness of character, and Christ p_____ him where he would have an opportunity to see and

618   Can We Walk, Together?

indulged his covetous disposition. The small sums that came into his hands were a continual temptation. Often when he did a little service for Christ, or devoted time to religious purposes, he paid himself out of this meager fund. In his own eyes these pretexts served to excuse his action; but in God's sight he was a thief.

Christ's oft-repeated statement that His kingdom was not of this world offended Judas. He had marked out a line upon which he expected Christ to work. He had planned that John the Baptist should be delivered from prison. But lo, John was left to be beheaded. And Jesus, instead of asserting His royal right and avenging the death of John, retired with His disciples into a country place. Judas wanted more aggressive warfare. He thought that if Jesus would not prevent the disciples from carrying out their schemes, the work would be more successful. He marked the increasing enmity of the Jewish leaders, and saw their challenge unheeded when they demanded from Christ a sign from heaven. His heart was open to unbelief, and the enemy supplied thoughts of questioning and rebellion. Why did Jesus dwell so much upon that which was discouraging? Why did He predict trial and persecution for Himself and for His disciples? The prospect of having a high place in the new kingdom had led Judas to espouse the cause of Christ. Were his hopes to be disappointed? Judas had not decided that Jesus was not the Son of God; but he was questioning, and seeking to find some explanation of His mighty works.

Notwithstanding the Saviour's own teaching, Judas was continually advancing the idea that Christ would reign as king in Jerusalem. At the feeding of the five thousand he tried to bring this about. On this occasion Judas assisted in distributing the food to the hungry multitude. He had an opportunity to see the benefit which it was in his power to impart to others. He felt the satisfaction that always comes in service to God. He helped to bring the sick and suffering from among the multitude to Christ. He saw what relief, what joy and gladness, come to human hearts through the healing power of the Restorer. He might have comprehended the methods of Christ. But he was blinded by his own selfish desires. Judas was first to take advantage of the enthusiasm excited by the miracle of the loaves. It was he who set on foot the [718-719] project to take Christ by force and make Him king. His hopes were high. His

correct this....Christ's oft repeated statement that His kingdom was not of this world o_____ Judas." Why? _____

_____
_____

disappointment was bitter.

Christ's discourse in the synagogue concerning the bread of life was the turning point in the history of Judas. He heard the words, "Except ye eat the flesh of the Son of man, and drink His blood, ye have no life in you." John 6:53. He saw that Christ was offering spiritual rather than worldly good. He regarded himself as farsighted, and thought he could see that Jesus would have no honor, and that He could bestow no high position upon His followers. He determined not to unite himself so closely to Christ but that he could draw away. He would watch. And he did watch.

From that time he expressed doubts that confused the disciples. He introduced controversies and misleading sentiments, repeating the arguments urged by the scribes and Pharisees against the claims of Christ. All the little and large troubles and crosses, the difficulties and the apparent hindrances to the advancement of the gospel, Judas interpreted as evidences against its truthfulness. He would introduce texts of Scripture that had no connection with the truths Christ was presenting. These texts, separated from their connection, perplexed the disciples, and increased the discouragement that was constantly pressing upon them. Yet all this was done by Judas in such a way as to make it appear that he was conscientious. And while the disciples were searching for evidence to confirm the words of the Great Teacher, Judas would lead them almost imperceptibly on another track. Thus in a very religious, and apparently wise, way he was presenting matters in a different light from that in which Jesus had given them, and attaching to His words a meaning that He had not conveyed. His suggestions were constantly exciting an ambitious desire for temporal preferment, and thus turning the disciples from the important things they should have considered. The dissension as to which of them should be greatest was generally excited by Judas.

When Jesus presented to the rich young ruler the condition of discipleship, Judas was displeased. He thought that a mistake had been made. If such men as this ruler could be connected with the believers, they would help sustain Christ's cause. If Judas were only received as a counselor, he thought, he could suggest many plans for the advantage of the little church. His principles and methods would differ somewhat from Christ's, but in these things he thought himself wiser

The t_____ point was when Judas "saw that Christ was offering s___ _____ rather than worldly good...From that time he expressed d_____ ____ that confused the disciples...This was done by Judas in such a way as to make it appear that he was c_____." (719). Am I in it with You Lord, only for the material benefits and blessings? Am I Your friend for what I get out of it? _____

_____

_____

Please place me where I will have an opportunity to see, and to grow:

_____

than Christ. [719-720]

In all that Christ said to His disciples, there was something with which, in heart, Judas disagreed. Under his influence the leaven of disaffection was fast doing its work. The disciples did not see the real agency in all this; but Jesus saw that Satan was communicating his attributes to Judas, and thus opening up a channel through which to influence the other disciples. This, a year before the betrayal, Christ declared. "Have not I chosen you twelve," He said, "and one of you is a devil?" John 6:70.

Yet Judas made no open opposition, nor seemed to question the Saviour's lessons. He made no outward murmur until the time of the feast in Simon's house. When Mary anointed the Saviour's feet, Judas manifested his covetous disposition. At the reproof from Jesus his very spirit seemed turned to gall. Wounded pride and desire for revenge broke down the barriers, and the greed so long indulged held him in control. This will be the experience of everyone who persists in tampering with sin. The elements of depravity that are not resisted and overcome, respond to Satan's temptation, and the soul is led captive at his will.

But Judas was not yet wholly hardened. Even after he had twice pledged himself to betray the Saviour, there was opportunity for repentance. At the Passover supper Jesus proved His divinity by revealing the traitor's purpose. He tenderly included Judas in the ministry to the disciples. But the last appeal of love was unheeded. Then the case of Judas was decided, and the feet that Jesus had washed went forth to the betrayer's work.

Judas reasoned that if Jesus was to be crucified, the event must come to pass. His own act in betraying the Saviour would not change the result. If Jesus was not to die, it would only force Him to deliver Himself. At all events, Judas would gain something by his treachery. He counted that he had made a sharp bargain in betraying his Lord.

Judas did not, however, believe that Christ would permit Himself to be arrested. In betraying Him, it was his purpose to teach Him a lesson. He intended to play a part that would make the Saviour careful thenceforth to treat him with due respect. But Judas knew not that he was giving Christ up to death. How often, as the Saviour taught in parables, the scribes and Pharisees had been carried away with His striking illustrations! How

5. "At the reproof from Jesus [at Simon's house] his [Judas'] very spirit seemed turned to gall. Wounded p_____ and desire for revenge broke down the barriers, and the greed so long indulged held him in control. This will be the experience of everyone who persists in t_____ with sin." (720). Something indulged and cherished, so seemingly small, ends up controlling? Lord, please help me not to be blind to:

_____
_____
_____

6. "In betraying the Savior...it would only force Him to d_____ Him-

often they had pronounced judgment against themselves! Often when the truth was brought home to their hearts, they had been filled with rage, and had taken up stones to cast at Him; [720-721] but again and again He had made His escape. Since He had escaped so many snares, thought Judas, He certainly would not now allow Himself to be taken.

Judas decided to put the matter to the test. If Jesus really was the Messiah, the people, for whom He had done so much, would rally about Him, and would proclaim Him king. This would forever settle many minds that were now in uncertainty. Judas would have the credit of having placed the king on David's throne. And this act would secure to him the first position, next to Christ, in the new kingdom.

The false disciple acted his part in betraying Jesus. In the garden, when he said to the leaders of the mob, "Whomsoever I shall kiss, that same is He: hold Him fast" (Matt. 26:48), he fully believed that Christ would escape out of their hands. Then if they should blame him, he could say, Did I not tell you to hold Him fast?

Judas beheld the captors of Christ, acting upon his words, bind Him firmly. In amazement he saw that the Saviour suffered Himself to be led away. Anxiously he followed Him from the garden to the trial before the Jewish rulers. At every movement he looked for Him to surprise His enemies, by appearing before them as the Son of God, and setting at nought all their plots and power. But as hour after hour went by, and Jesus submitted to all the abuse heaped upon Him, a terrible fear came to the traitor that he had sold his Master to His death.

As the trial drew to a close, Judas could endure the torture of his guilty conscience no longer. Suddenly a hoarse voice rang through the hall, sending a thrill of terror to all hearts: He is innocent; spare Him, O Caiaphas!

The tall form of Judas was now seen pressing through the startled throng. His face was pale and haggard, and great drops of sweat stood on his forehead. Rushing to the throne of judgment, he threw down [721-722] before the high priest the pieces of silver that had been the price of his Lord's betrayal. Eagerly grasping the robe of Caiaphas, he implored him to release Jesus, declaring that He had done nothing worthy of death. Caiaphas angrily shook him off, but was confused, and

self… People for whom He had done so much, would r_____ about Him, and p_____ Him king…Judas would have the c_____ of having placed the king on David's throne." (720, 721). Lord, do I want credit, or recognition from others?

_____

Why? _____

_____

Do I think that I am an honor to the cause? _____

_____

_____

_____

7. "But as hour after hour went by, and Jesus submitted to all the abuse heaped upon Him, a terrible f____ _____ came to the traitor that he had sold his Master to His death." Lord, by failing to claim Your victory over the power of sin for me, am I also a traitor that has sold You to Your death?

_____

_____

_____

Help me not to be motivated to avoid fear only, but to be moved by Your great sacrifice and love, and to render back the purest love and devotion that Your abiding presence can inspire: _____

_____

_____

_____

8. By Judas' appeal to Caiaphas, the "p_____ of the priest was revealed. It was evident that they had b_____ the disciple to betray his Master." (722). Lord, how might I be encouraging others to betray You? _____ _____ _____ _____

9. Jesus "knew that Judas did n_____ repent; his confession was f_____ _____ from his guilty soul by an awful sense of c_____ and a looking for of judgment, but he felt no deep, h_____ grief that he had betrayed the spotless Son of God, and d_____ the Holy One of Israel." (722). Lord, is my "repenting," merely a formality to clear my record in heaven, or is there a recognition of the hurt and sorrow caused, and heartbreaking grief over the damage done to relationships? _____ _____ _____ _____

Prayerjournal:_____ _____ _____ _____ _____ _____ _____

knew not what to say. The perfidy of the priests was revealed. It was evident that they had bribed the disciple to betray his Master.

"I have sinned," again cried Judas, "in that I have betrayed the innocent blood." But the high priest, regaining his self-possession, answered with scorn, "What is that to us? see thou to that." Matt. 27:4. The priests had been willing to make Judas their tool; but they despised his baseness. When he turned to them with confession, they spurned him.

Judas now cast himself at the feet of Jesus, acknowledging Him to be the Son of God, and entreating Him to deliver Himself. The Saviour did not reproach His betrayer. He knew that Judas did not repent; his confession was forced from his guilty soul by an awful sense of condemnation and a looking for of judgment, but he felt no deep, heartbreaking grief that he had betrayed the spotless Son of God, and denied the Holy One of Israel. Yet Jesus spoke no word of condemnation. He looked pityingly upon Judas, and said, For this hour came I into the world.

A murmur of surprise ran through the assembly. With amazement they beheld the forbearance of Christ toward His betrayer. Again there swept over them the conviction that this Man was more than mortal. But if He was the Son of God, they questioned, why did He not free Himself from His bonds and triumph over His accusers?

Judas saw that his entreaties were in vain, and he rushed from the hall exclaiming, It is too late! It is too late! He felt that he could not live to see Jesus crucified, and in despair went out and hanged himself.

Later that same day, on the road from Pilate's hall to Calvary, there came an interruption to the shouts and jeers of the wicked throng who were leading Jesus to the place of crucifixion. As they passed a retired spot, they saw at the foot of a lifeless tree, the body of Judas. It was a most revolting sight. His weight had broken the cord by which he had hanged himself to the tree. In falling, his body had been horribly mangled, and dogs were now devouring it. His remains were immediately buried out of sight; but there was less mockery among the throng, and many a pale face revealed the thoughts within. Retribution seemed already visiting those who were guilty of the blood of Jesus.

Chapter 77

In Pilate's Judgment Hall

[This chapter is based on Matt. 27:2 , 11-31;
Mark 15:1-20; Luke 23:1-25; John 18:28-40; 19:1-16.]

In the judgment hall of Pilate, the Roman governor, Christ stands bound as a prisoner. About Him are the guard of soldiers, and the hall is fast filling with spectators. Just outside the entrance are the judges of the Sanhedrin, priests, rulers, elders, and the mob.

After condemning Jesus, the council of the Sanhedrin had come to Pilate to have the sentence confirmed and executed. But these Jewish officials would not enter the Roman judgment hall. According to their ceremonial law they would be defiled thereby, and thus prevented from taking part in the feast of the Passover. In their blindness they did not see that murderous hatred had defiled their hearts. They did not see that Christ was the real Passover lamb, and that, since they had rejected Him, the great feast had for them lost its significance.

When the Saviour was brought into the judgment hall, Pilate looked upon Him with no friendly eyes. The Roman governor had been called from his bedchamber in haste, and he determined to do his work as quickly as possible. He was prepared to deal with the prisoner with [723-724] magisterial severity. Assuming his severest expression, he turned to see what kind of man he had to examine, that he had been called from his repose at so early an hour. He knew that it must be someone whom the Jewish authorities were anxious to have tried and punished with haste.

Pilate looked at the men who had Jesus in charge, and then his gaze rested searchingly on Jesus. He had had to deal with all kinds of criminals; but never before had a man bearing marks of such goodness and nobility been brought before him. On His face he saw no sign of guilt, no expression of fear, no boldness or defiance. He saw a man of calm and dignified bearing, whose countenance bore not the marks of a criminal, but the signature of heaven.

Christ's appearance made a favorable impression upon Pilate. His better nature was roused. He had heard

1. "These Jewish officials would not enter the Roman judgment hall...they would be d_____ thereby...In their blindness they did not see that murderous hatred had defiled their h_____...Since they had rejected Him, the great feast had for them l_____ ___ its significance." Lord, in keeping and guarding the letter (of the law), does the spirit (of the law) get lost? _____

_____

If church attendance and devotions is an encounter with the letter but not the spirit, should I throw out the letter? _____

_____

_____

2. The countenance of Jesus that Pilate saw, "bore not the mark of a c_____ _____, but the signature of h_____." (724). What is that countenance Lord, and how can I have it? _____

_____

_____

of Jesus and His works. His wife had told him something of the wonderful deeds performed by the Galilean prophet, who cured the sick and raised the dead. Now this revived as a dream in Pilate's mind. He recalled rumors that he had heard from several sources. He resolved to demand of the Jews their charges against the prisoner.

Who is this Man, and wherefore have ye brought Him? he said. What accusation bring ye against Him? The Jews were disconcerted. Knowing that they could not substantiate their charges against Christ, they did not desire a public examination. They answered that He was a deceiver called Jesus of Nazareth.

Again Pilate asked, "What accusation bring ye against this Man?" The priests did not answer his question, but in words that showed their irritation, they said, "If He were not a malefactor, we would not have delivered Him up unto thee." When those composing the Sanhedrin, the first men of the nation, bring to you a man they deem worthy of death, is there need to ask for an accusation against him? They hoped to impress Pilate with a sense of their importance, and thus lead him to accede to their request without going through many preliminaries. They were eager to have their sentence ratified; for they knew that the people who had witnessed Christ's marvelous works could tell a story very different from the fabrication they themselves were now rehearsing.

3. The Sanhedrin "hoped to impress Pilate with a sense of their i_____ _____, and thus lead him to accede to their request...This they besought as a f_____ on the occasion of their great national festival...

The priests thought that with the weak and vacillating Pilate they could carry through their plans without trouble. Before this he had signed the death warrant hastily, condemning to death men they knew were not worthy of death. In his estimation the life of a prisoner was [724-725] of little account; whether he were innocent or guilty was of no special consequence. The priests hoped that Pilate would now inflict the death penalty on Jesus without giving Him a hearing. This they besought as a favor on the occasion of their great national festival.

But there was something in the prisoner that held Pilate back from this. He dared not do it. He read the purposes of the priests. He remembered how, not long before, Jesus had raised Lazarus, a man that had been dead four days; and he determined to know, before signing the sentence of condemnation, what were the charges against Him, and whether they could be proved.

If your judgment is sufficient, he said, why bring the prisoner to me? "Take ye Him, and judge Him according to your law." Thus pressed, the priests said that they had already passed sentence upon Him, but that they must have Pilate's sentence to render their condemnation valid. What is your sentence? Pilate asked. The death sentence, they answered; but it is not lawful for us to put any man to death. They asked Pilate to take their word as to Christ's guilt, and enforce their sentence. They would take the responsibility of the result.

Pilate was not a just or a conscientious judge; but weak though he was in moral power, he refused to grant this request. He would not condemn Jesus until a charge had been brought against Him.

The priests were in a dilemma. They saw that they must cloak their hypocrisy under the thickest concealment. They must not allow it to appear that Christ had been arrested on religious grounds. Were this put forward as a reason, their proceedings would have no weight with Pilate. They must make it appear that Jesus was working against the common law; then He could be punished as a political offender. Tumults and insurrection against the Roman government were constantly arising among the Jews. With these revolts the Romans had dealt very rigorously, and they were constantly on the watch to repress everything that could lead to an outbreak.

Only a few days before this the Pharisees had tried to entrap Christ with the question, "Is it lawful for us to give tribute unto Caesar?" But Christ had unveiled their hypocrisy. The Romans who were present had seen the utter failure of the plotters, and their discomfiture at His answer, "Render therefore unto Caesar the things which be Caesar's." Luke 20:22-25.

Now the priests thought to make it appear that on this occasion Christ [725-726] had taught what they hoped He would teach. In their extremity they called false witnesses to their aid, "and they began to accuse Him, saying, We found this fellow perverting the nation, and forbidding to give tribute to Caesar, saying that He Himself is Christ a King." Three charges, each without foundation. The priests knew this, but they were willing to commit perjury could they but secure their end.

Pilate saw through their purpose. He did not believe that the prisoner had plotted against the government. His meek and humble appearance was altogether out of

They saw that they must cloak their hypocrisy under the thickest c_____ _____." (724, 725). Lord, I don't want to conceal anything. Expose to me any attempt on my part, to conceal, to disguise, or to impress others with my importance. It is Your character I wish to manifest and You I want to glorify:

_____
_____
_____

4. "His meek and humble appearance was altogether

out of h_____
___ with the charge...

He stood s_____, but
His silence was eloquence.
It was as a light shining
from the inner to the o__
_____ man." (726).
Lord, how come my silence
comes across as sulking, or
martyrdom, or self-righ-
teousness?_____
_____
_____
_____

5. Jesus "knew that the
Holy Spirit was s_____
_____ with Pilate, and He
gave him opportunity to
acknowledge his convic-
tion...Pilate u_____
Christ's meaning, but p__
____ arose in his heart. He
would not acknowledge
the conviction that pressed

harmony with the charge. Pilate was convinced that a deep plot had been laid to destroy an innocent man who stood in the way of the Jewish dignitaries. Turning to Jesus he asked, "Art Thou the King of the Jews?" The Saviour answered, "Thou sayest it." And as He spoke, His countenance lighted up as if a sunbeam were shining upon it.

When they heard His answer, Caiaphas and those that were with him called Pilate to witness that Jesus had admitted the crime with which He was charged. With noisy cries, priests, scribes, and rulers demanded that He be sentenced to death. The cries were taken up by the mob, and the uproar was deafening. Pilate was confused. Seeing that Jesus made no answer to His accusers, Pilate said to Him, "Answerest Thou nothing? behold how many things they witness against Thee. But Jesus yet answered nothing."

Standing behind Pilate, in view of all in the court, Christ heard the abuse; but to all the false charges against Him He answered not a word. His whole bearing gave evidence of conscious innocence. He stood unmoved by the fury of the waves that beat about Him. It was as if the heavy surges of wrath, rising higher and higher, like the waves of the boisterous ocean, broke about Him, but did not touch Him. He stood silent, but His silence was eloquence. It was as a light shining from the inner to the outer man.

Pilate was astonished at His bearing. Does this Man disregard the proceedings because He does not care to save His life? he asked himself. As he looked at Jesus, bearing insult and mockery without retaliation, he felt that He could not be as unrighteous and unjust as were the clamoring priests. Hoping to gain the truth from Him and to escape the tumult of the crowd, Pilate took Jesus aside with him, and again questioned, "Art Thou the King of the Jews?"

Jesus did not directly answer this question. He knew that the Holy [726-727] Spirit was striving with Pilate, and He gave him opportunity to acknowledge his conviction. "Sayest thou this thing of thyself," He asked, "or did others tell it thee of Me?" That is, was it the accusations of the priests, or a desire to receive light from Christ, that prompted Pilate's question? Pilate understood Christ's meaning; but pride arose in his heart. He would not acknowledge the conviction that pressed upon him. "Am I a Jew?" he said. "Thine own nation and the chief priests have delivered Thee unto me: what hast Thou done?"

Pilate's golden opportunity had passed. Yet Jesus did not leave him without further light. While He did not directly answer Pilate's question, He plainly stated His own mission. He gave Pilate to understand that He was not seeking an earthly throne.

"My kingdom is not of this world," He said; "if My kingdom were of this world, then would My servants fight, that I should not be delivered to the Jews: but now is My kingdom not from hence. Pilate therefore said unto Him, Art Thou a king then? Jesus answered, Thou sayest that I am a king. To this end was I born, and for this cause came I into the world, that I should bear witness unto the truth. Everyone that is of the truth heareth My voice."

Christ affirmed that His word was in itself a key which would unlock the mystery to those who were prepared to receive it. It had a self-commending power, and this was the secret of the spread of His kingdom of truth. He desired Pilate to understand that only by receiving and appropriating truth could his ruined nature be reconstructed.

Pilate had a desire to know the truth. His mind was confused. He eagerly grasped the words of the Saviour, and his heart was stirred with a great longing to know what it really was, and how he could obtain it. "What is truth?" he inquired. But he did not wait for an answer. The tumult outside recalled him to the interests of the hour; for the priests were clamorous for immediate action. Going out to the Jews, he declared emphatically, "I find in Him no fault at all."

These words from a heathen judge were a scathing rebuke to the perfidy and falsehood of the rulers of Israel who were accusing the Saviour. As the priests and elders heard this from Pilate, their disappointment and rage knew no bounds. They had long plotted and waited for this opportunity. As they saw the prospect of the release of Jesus, they seemed ready to tear Him in pieces. They loudly denounced Pilate, and threatened him with the censure of the Roman government. They [727-728] accused him of refusing to condemn Jesus, who, they affirmed, had set Himself up against Caesar.

Angry voices were now heard, declaring that the seditious influence of Jesus was well known throughout the country. The priests said, "He stirreth up the people,

upon him…Pilate's golden o_____ had passed." (726, 727). Lord, may I not miss opportunities of Your working on my heart. May my pride not be a stumbling block to growth. _____
_____
_____
_____

6. Jesus made the statement, "My k_____ _____ is not of this world…If my kingdom were of this world, then would my servants f____ _____, that I should not be delivered to the Jews." Lord, if I'm fighting for a viewpoint, am I of the kingdom? _____
_____ Show me what my spirit is: _____
_____

7. "For this cause came I into the world, that I should bear w_____ _____ unto the truth…Pilate had a desire to know the truth…He eagerly grasped the words of the Savior, and his heart was s_____ with a great longing to know what it really was, and how he could obtain it. 'What is truth?' he inquired. But he did not w_____ for an answer." Lord, what is the tumult outside that distracts me from waiting for an answer?
_____
_____

teaching throughout all Jewry, beginning from Galilee to this place."

Pilate at this time had no thought of condemning Jesus. He knew that the Jews had accused Him through hatred and prejudice. He knew what his duty was. Justice demanded that Christ should be immediately released. But Pilate dreaded the ill will of the people. Should he refuse to give Jesus into their hands, a tumult would be raised, and this he feared to meet. When he heard that Christ was from Galilee, he decided to send Him to Herod, the ruler of that province, who was then in Jerusalem. By this course, Pilate thought to shift the responsibility of the trial from himself to Herod. He also thought this a good opportunity to heal an old quarrel between himself and Herod. And so it proved. The two magistrates made friends over the trial of the Saviour.

Pilate delivered Jesus again to the soldiers, and amid the jeers and insults of the mob He was hurried to the judgment hall of Herod. "When Herod saw Jesus, he was exceeding glad." He had never before met the Saviour, but "he was desirous to see Him of a long season, because he had heard many things of Him; and he hoped to have seen some miracle done by Him." This Herod was he whose hands were stained with the blood of John the Baptist. When Herod first heard of Jesus, he was terror-stricken, and said, "It is John, whom I beheaded: [728-729] he is risen from the dead;" "therefore mighty works do show forth themselves in him." Mark 6:16; Matt. 14:2. Yet Herod desired to see Jesus. Now there was opportunity to save the life of this prophet, and the king hoped to banish forever from his mind the memory of that bloody head brought to him in a charger. He also desired to have his curiosity gratified, and thought that if Christ were given any prospect of release, He would do anything that was asked of Him.

A large company of the priests and elders had accompanied Christ to Herod. And when the Saviour was brought in, these dignitaries, all speaking excitedly, urged their accusations against Him. But Herod paid little regard to their charges. He commanded silence, desiring an opportunity to question Christ. He ordered that the fetters of Christ should be unloosed, at the same time charging His enemies with roughly treating Him. Looking with compassion into the serene face of the world's Redeemer, he read in it only wisdom and purity. He as well as Pilate was satisfied that Christ had been accused through malice and envy.

Herod questioned Christ in many words, but throughout the Saviour maintained a profound silence. At the command of the king, the decrepit and maimed were then called in, and Christ was ordered to prove His claims by working a miracle. Men say that Thou canst heal the sick, said Herod. I am anxious to see that Thy widespread fame has not been belied. Jesus did not respond, and Herod still continued to urge: If Thou canst work miracles for others, work them now for Thine own good, and it will serve Thee a good purpose. Again he commanded, Show us a sign that Thou hast the power with which rumor hath accredited Thee. But Christ was as one who heard and saw not. The Son of God had taken upon Himself man's nature. He must do as man must do in like circumstances. Therefore He would not work a miracle to save Himself the pain and humiliation that man must endure when placed in a similar position.

Herod promised that if Christ would perform some miracle in his presence, He should be released. Christ's accusers had seen with their own eyes the mighty works wrought by His power. They had heard Him command the grave to give up its dead. They had seen the dead come forth obedient to His voice. Fear seized them lest He should now work a miracle. Of all things they most dreaded an exhibition of His power. Such a manifestation would prove a deathblow to their [729-730] plans, and would perhaps cost them their lives. Again the priests and rulers, in great anxiety, urged their accusations against Him. Raising their voices, they declared, He is a traitor, a blasphemer. He works His miracles through the power given Him by Beelzebub, the prince of the devils. The hall became a scene of confusion, some crying one thing and some another.

Herod's conscience was now far less sensitive than when he had trembled with horror at the request of Herodias for the head of John the Baptist. For a time he had felt the keen stings of remorse for his terrible act; but his moral perceptions had become more and more degraded by his licentious life. Now his heart had become so hardened that he could even boast of the punishment he had inflicted upon John for daring to reprove him. And he now threatened Jesus, declaring repeatedly that he had power to release or to condemn Him. But no sign from Jesus gave evidence that He heard a word.

Herod was irritated by this silence. It seemed to in-

8. Herod asked Jesus for a sign, a miracle for the decrepit and maimed. Fear seized Christ's accusers, "lest He should now work a miracle. Of all things they most d_____ an exhibition of His power." (729). Lord, would an exhibition of Your power and glory expose something negative in my heart? _____

_____

Is this why I don't give myself in abandon to You?

_____

_____

_____

9. "Herod's conscience was now far less s_____ _____ than when he had trembled with horror at the request of Herodias…Now his heart had become so h_____…" (730). What happened? "His moral perceptions had become more and more degraded by his l_____ ____ life." Lord, am I hardening my heart through the cares of this world? _____

_____

What are those cares?

_____

_____

_____

_____

dicate utter indifference to his authority. To the vain and pompous king, open rebuke would have been less offensive than to be thus ignored. Again he angrily threatened Jesus, who still remained unmoved and silent.

The mission of Christ in this world was not to gratify idle curiosity. He came to heal the brokenhearted. Could He have spoken any word to heal the bruises of sin-sick souls, He would not have kept silent. But He had no words for those who would but trample the truth under their unholy feet.

Christ might have spoken words to Herod that would have pierced the ears of the hardened king. He might have stricken him with fear and trembling by laying before him the full iniquity of his life, and the horror of his approaching doom. But Christ's silence was the severest rebuke that He could have given. Herod had rejected the truth spoken to him by the greatest of the prophets, and no other message was he to receive. Not a word had the Majesty of heaven for him. That ear that had ever been open to human woe, had no room for Herod's commands. Those eyes that had ever rested upon the penitent sinner in pitying, forgiving love had no look to bestow upon Herod. Those lips that had uttered the most impressive truth, that in tones of tenderest entreaty had pleaded with the most sinful and the most degraded, were closed to the haughty king who felt no need of a Saviour.

Herod's face grew dark with passion. Turning to the multitude, he [730-731] angrily denounced Jesus as an impostor. Then to Christ he said, If You will give no evidence of Your claim, I will deliver You up to the soldiers and the people. They may succeed in making You speak. If You are an impostor, death at their hands is only what You merit; if You are the Son of God, save Yourself by working a miracle.

No sooner were these words spoken than a rush was made for Christ. Like wild beasts, the crowd darted upon their prey. Jesus was dragged this way and that, Herod joining the mob in seeking to humiliate the Son of God. Had not the Roman soldiers interposed, and forced back the maddened throng, the Saviour would have been torn in pieces.

"Herod with his men of war set Him at nought, and mocked Him, and arrayed Him in a gorgeous robe." The Roman soldiers joined in this abuse. All that these wicked, corrupt soldiers, helped on by Herod and the

10. "Christ's s_____ _____ was the severest rebuke...The haughty king who felt no need of a Savior." Lord, may I not harden my heart, that there is nothing You can say or do to reach me: _____ _____ _____ _____

Jewish dignitaries, could instigate was heaped upon the Saviour. Yet His divine patience failed not.

Christ's persecutors had tried to measure His character by their own; they had represented Him as vile as themselves. But back of all the present appearance another scene intruded itself,--a scene which they will one day see in all its glory. There were some who trembled in Christ's presence. While the rude throng were bowing in mockery before Him, some who came forward for that purpose turned back, afraid and silenced. Herod was convicted. The last rays of merciful light were shining upon his sin-hardened heart. He felt that this was no common man; for divinity had flashed through humanity. At the very time when Christ was encompassed by mockers, adulterers, and murderers, Herod felt that he was beholding a God upon His throne.

Hardened as he was, Herod dared not ratify the condemnation of Christ. He wished to relieve himself of the terrible responsibility, and he sent Jesus back to the Roman judgment hall.

Pilate was disappointed and much displeased. When the Jews returned with their prisoner, he asked impatiently what they would have him do. He reminded them that he had already examined Jesus, and found no fault in Him; he told them that they had brought complaints against Him, but they had not been able to prove a single charge. He had sent Jesus to Herod, the tetrarch of Galilee, and one of their own nation, but he also had found in Him nothing worthy of death. "I will therefore chastise Him," Pilate said, "and release Him."

Here Pilate showed his weakness. He had declared that Jesus was [731-732] innocent, yet he was willing for Him to be scourged to pacify His accusers. He would sacrifice justice and principle in order to compromise with the mob. This placed him at a disadvantage. The crowd presumed upon his indecision, and clamored the more for the life of the prisoner. If at the first Pilate had stood firm, refusing to condemn a man whom he found guiltless, he would have broken the fatal chain that was to bind him in remorse and guilt as long as he lived. Had he carried out his convictions of right, the Jews would not have presumed to dictate to him. Christ would have been put to death, but the guilt would not have rested upon Pilate. But Pilate had taken step after step in the violation of his conscience. He had excused himself from judging with justice and equity, and he now found

1. "While the rude throng were bowing in mockery before Him, some who came forward for that purpose t_____ back, afraid and silenced. Herod was convicted. The last rays of m_____ light were shining upon his sin-hardened heart. He felt that this was no common man; for d_____ had flashed through humanity. At the very time when Christ was encompassed by m_____, adulterers, and murderers, Herod felt that he was beholding a God upon His t_____." (731). Lord, this was not Your throne, yet Herod felt that way. In the midst of such evil, You are extending rays of mercy from Your throne. Thank You for Your persistent optimism, for not giving up on me: _____
_____
_____
_____

2. Pilate "had declared that Jesus was i_____ _____, yet he was willing for Him to be scourged to p_____ His accusers. He would sacrifice j____ _____ and principle in order to c_____ with the mob. This placed him at a d_____..."

His wavering and i_____ _____ proved his ruin." (731, 732). Lord, are You convicting me of compromising? _____ _____.

Do I at one point agree that You're right, and then not live by that truth? _____ _____ _____

_____ How do I stall with indecision and non-responsiveness? _____ _____ _____

3. Pilate's wife "had n___ ___ doubt of Christ's character or mission. She knew Him to be the P_____ of God." She sent a letter to Pilate, "Have thou nothing to do with this j_____ Man." Lord, help me to be as responsive to conviction as she was. So much of the time I am second-guessing, evaluating, wavering, slighting. May I act, instead of delay: _____ _____ _____

himself almost helpless in the hands of the priests and rulers. His wavering and indecision proved his ruin.

Even now Pilate was not left to act blindly. A message from God warned him from the deed he was about to commit. In answer to Christ's prayer, the wife of Pilate had been visited by an angel from heaven, and in a dream she had beheld the Saviour and conversed with Him. Pilate's wife was not a Jew, but as she looked upon Jesus in her dream, she had no doubt of His character or mission. She knew Him to be the Prince of God. She saw Him on trial in the judgment hall. She saw the hands tightly bound as the hands of a criminal. She saw Herod and his soldiers doing their dreadful work. She heard the priests and rulers, filled with envy and malice, madly accusing. She heard the words, "We have a law, and by our law He ought to die." She saw Pilate give Jesus to the scourging, after he had declared, "I find no fault in Him." She heard the condemnation pronounced by Pilate, and saw him give Christ up to His murderers. She saw the cross uplifted on Calvary. She saw the earth wrapped in darkness, and heard the mysterious cry, "It is finished." Still another scene met her gaze. She saw Christ seated upon the great white cloud, while the earth reeled in space, and His murderers fled from the presence of His glory. With a cry of horror she awoke, and at once wrote to Pilate words of warning.

While Pilate was hesitating as to what he should do, a messenger pressed through the crowd, and handed him the letter from his wife, which read:

"Have thou nothing to do with that just Man: for I have suffered many things this day in a dream because of Him." [732-733]

Pilate's face grew pale. He was confused by his own conflicting emotions. But while he had been delaying to act, the priests and rulers were still further inflaming the minds of the people. Pilate was forced to action. He now bethought himself of a custom which might serve to secure Christ's release. It was customary at this feast to release some one prisoner whom the people might choose. This custom was of pagan invention; there was not a shadow of justice in it, but it was greatly prized by the Jews. The Roman authorities at this time held a prisoner named Barabbas, who was under sentence of death. This man had claimed to be the Messiah. He claimed authority to establish a different order of things, to set the world right. Under satanic delusion he claimed that whatever he could obtain by theft and robbery was his own. He had done wonderful things through satanic agencies, he had gained a following among the people, and had excited sedition against the Roman government. Under cover of religious enthusiasm he was a hardened and desperate villain, bent on rebellion and cruelty. By giving the people a choice between this man and the innocent Saviour, Pilate thought to arouse them to a sense of justice. He hoped to gain their sympathy for Jesus in opposition to the priests and rulers. So, turning to the crowd, he said with great earnestness, "Whom will ye that I release unto you? Barabbas, or Jesus which is called Christ?"

Like the bellowing of wild beasts came the answer of the mob, "Release unto us Barabbas!" Louder and louder swelled the cry, Barabbas! Barabbas! Thinking that the people had not understood his question, Pilate asked, "Will ye that I release unto you the King of the Jews?" But they cried out again, "Away with this Man, and release unto us Barabbas"! "What shall I do then with Jesus which is called Christ?" Pilate asked. Again the surging multitude roared like demons. Demons themselves, in human form, were in the crowd, and what could be expected but the answer, "Let Him be crucified"?

Pilate was troubled. He had not thought it would come to that. He shrank from delivering an innocent man to the most ignominious and cruel death that could be inflicted. After the roar of voices had ceased, he turned to the people, saying, "Why, what evil hath He done?" But the case had gone too far for argument. It was not evidence of Christ's innocence that they wanted, but His condemnation.

Still Pilate endeavored to save Him. "He said unto them the third time, Why, what evil hath He done? I have found no cause of death [733-734] in Him: I will therefore chastise Him, and let Him go." But the very mention of His release stirred the people to a tenfold frenzy. "Crucify Him, crucify Him," they cried. Louder and louder swelled the storm that Pilate's indecision had called forth.

Jesus was taken, faint with weariness and covered with wounds, and scourged in the sight of the multitude. "And the soldiers led Him away into the hall, called Praetorium, and they call together the whole band. And they clothed Him with purple, and platted a crown of

4. "By giving the people a c_____ between this Barabbas and the innocent Savior, Pilate thought to arouse them to a sense of j_____. He hoped to gain their s_____ for Jesus... Like the bellowing of wild b_____ came the answer of the mob, 'Release unto us Barabbas!'...The surging multitude roared like d_____. Demons themselves, in h_____ form, were in the crowd." Lord, could this happen to me? _____
_____ Not that I would recognize the demons in me: _____
_____
When I yield to temptation, am I crying out 'Release to me self-gratification?' and 'Crucify Jesus?' _____
_____
_____
_____

thorns, and put it about His head, and began to salute Him, Hail, King of the Jews! And they . . . did spit upon Him, and bowing their knees worshiped Him." Occasionally some wicked hand snatched the reed that had been placed in His hand, and struck the crown upon His brow, forcing the thorns into His temples, and sending the blood trickling down His face and beard.

Wonder, O heavens! and be astonished, O earth! Behold the oppressor and the oppressed. A maddened throng enclose the Saviour of the world. Mocking and jeering are mingled with the coarse oaths of blasphemy. His lowly birth and humble life are commented upon by the unfeeling mob. His claim to be the Son of God is ridiculed, and the vulgar jest and insulting sneer are passed from lip to lip.

Satan led the cruel mob in its abuse of the Saviour. It was his purpose to provoke Him to retaliation if possible, or to drive Him to perform a miracle to release Himself, and thus break up the plan of salvation. One stain upon His human life, one failure of His humanity to endure the terrible test, and the Lamb of God would have been an imperfect offering, and the redemption of man a failure. But He who by a command could bring the heavenly host to His aid--He who could have driven that mob in terror from His sight by the flashing forth of His divine majesty--submitted with perfect calmness to the coarsest insult and outrage.

Christ's enemies had demanded a miracle as evidence of His divinity. They had evidence far greater than any they had sought. As their cruelty degraded His torturers below humanity into the likeness of Satan, so did His meekness and patience exalt Jesus above humanity, and prove His kinship to God. His abasement was the pledge of His exaltation. The blood drops of agony that from His wounded temples flowed down His face and beard were the pledge of His anointing with "the oil of gladness" (Heb. 1:9.) as our great high priest. [734-735]

Satan's rage was great as he saw that all the abuse inflicted upon the Saviour had not forced the least murmur from His lips. Although He had taken upon Him the nature of man, He was sustained by a godlike fortitude, and departed in no particular from the will of His Father.

When Pilate gave Jesus up to be scourged and mocked, he thought to excite the pity of the multitude.

5. "Satan led the cruel mob in its abuse of the Savior. It was his purpose to provoke Him to r_____ if possible, or to drive Him to perform a miracle to r_____ Himself, and thus break up the plan of salvation." (734). If the enemy wanted to break up the plan of salvation, to not have Jesus die, why were demons in the mob yelling "Crucify Him?"

_____
_____
_____

6. "As their cruelty degraded His torturers below humanity into the likeness of S_____, so did His meekness and p_____ exalt Jesus above humanity, and prove His k_____ to God." Lord, what do my characteristics convey regarding my relationship to You? __
_____
_____
_____

He hoped they would decide that this was sufficient punishment. Even the malice of the priests, he thought, would now be satisfied. But with keen perception the Jews saw the weakness of thus punishing a man who had been declared innocent. They knew that Pilate was trying to save the life of the prisoner, and they were determined that Jesus should not be released. To please and satisfy us, Pilate has scourged Him, they thought, and if we press the matter to a decided issue, we shall surely gain our end.

Pilate now sent for Barabbas to be brought into the court. He then presented the two prisoners side by side, and pointing to the Saviour he said in a voice of solemn entreaty, "Behold the Man!" "I bring Him forth to you, that ye may know that I find no fault in Him."

There stood the Son of God, wearing the robe of mockery and the crown of thorns. Stripped to the waist, His back showed the long, cruel stripes, from which the blood flowed freely. His face was stained with blood, and bore the marks of exhaustion and pain; but never had it appeared more beautiful than now. The Saviour's visage was not marred before His enemies. Every feature expressed gentleness and resignation and the tenderest pity for His cruel foes. In His manner there was no cowardly weakness, but the strength and dignity of long-suffering. In striking contrast was the prisoner at His side. Every line of the countenance of Barabbas proclaimed him the hardened ruffian that he was. The contrast spoke to every beholder. Some of the spectators were weeping. As they looked upon Jesus, their hearts were full of sympathy. Even the priests and rulers were convicted that He was all that He claimed to be.

The Roman soldiers that surrounded Christ were not all hardened; some were looking earnestly into His face for one evidence that He was a criminal or dangerous character. From time to time they would turn and cast a look of contempt upon Barabbas. It needed no deep insight to read him through and through. Again they would turn to the One upon trial. They looked at the divine sufferer with feelings of deep pity. The silent submission of Christ stamped upon their minds [735-736] the scene, never to be effaced until they either acknowledged Him as the Christ, or by rejecting Him decided their own destiny.

Pilate was filled with amazement at the uncomplaining patience of the Saviour. He did not doubt that

7. "Behold the Man...The Savior's visage was not marred before His enemies. Every feature expressed g_____ and resignation and the tenderest p_____ for His cruel foes. In His manner there was no cowardly weakness, but the strength and d_____ of long-suffering...The contrast [of Barabbas and Jesus] spoke to every beholder... Even the priests and rulers were c_____ that He was all that He claimed to be." (735). Lord, with so much cruel ill-treatment, how could You be gentle and have pity? Does that dignity come only with suffering long? _____ _____ Is there a contrast between me and someone who doesn't know You? _____ What should the contrast be? _____ _____ _____ Does the contrast speak to the viewer? _____ _____ _____ _____

the sight of this Man, in contrast with Barabbas, would move the Jews to sympathy. But he did not understand the fanatical hatred of the priests for Him, who, as the Light of the world, had made manifest their darkness and error. They had moved the mob to a mad fury, and again priests, rulers, and people raised that awful cry, "Crucify Him, crucify Him." At last, losing all patience with their unreasoning cruelty, Pilate cried out despairingly, "Take ye Him, and crucify Him: for I find no fault in Him."

The Roman governor, though familiar with cruel scenes, was moved with sympathy for the suffering prisoner, who, condemned and scourged, with bleeding brow and lacerated back, still had the bearing of a king upon his throne. But the priests declared, "We have a law, and by our law He ought to die, because He made Himself the Son of God."

Pilate was startled. He had no correct idea of Christ and His mission; but he had an indistinct faith in God and in beings superior to humanity. A thought that had once before passed through his mind now took more definite shape. He questioned whether it might not be a divine being that stood before him, clad in the purple robe of mockery, and crowned with thorns.

Again he went into the judgment hall, and said to Jesus, "Whence art Thou?" But Jesus gave him no answer. The Saviour had spoken freely to Pilate, explaining His own mission as a witness to the truth. Pilate had disregarded the light. He had abused the high office of judge by yielding his principles and authority to the demands of the mob. Jesus had no further light for him. Vexed at His silence, Pilate said haughtily:

"Speakest Thou not unto me? knowest Thou not that I have power to crucify Thee, and have power to release Thee?"

Jesus answered, "Thou couldest have no power at all against Me, except it were given thee from above: therefore he that delivered Me unto thee hath the greater sin."

Thus the pitying Saviour, in the midst of His intense suffering and grief, excused as far as possible the act of the Roman governor who gave Him up to be crucified. What a scene was this to hand down to the world for all time! What a light it sheds upon the character of Him who is the Judge of all the earth! [736-737]

"He that delivered Me unto thee," said Jesus, "hath

8. "Thus the pitying Savior, in the midst of His intense s_____ and grief, e_____ as far as possible the act of the Roman governor who gave Him up to be crucified...What a light it sheds upon the c_____ of Him who is the Judge of all the earth!" (736). Lord, what does this say about You, and how You treat me? _____ _____ _____

the greater sin." By this Christ meant Caiaphas, who, as high priest, represented the Jewish nation. They knew the principles that controlled the Roman authorities. They had had light in the prophecies that testified of Christ, and in His own teachings and miracles. The Jewish judges had received unmistakable evidence of the divinity of Him whom they condemned to death. And according to their light would they be judged.

The greatest guilt and heaviest responsibility belonged to those who stood in the highest places in the nation, the depositaries of sacred trusts that they were basely betraying. Pilate, Herod, and the Roman soldiers were comparatively ignorant of Jesus. They thought to please the priests and rulers by abusing Him. They had not the light which the Jewish nation had so abundantly received. Had the light been given to the soldiers, they would not have treated Christ as cruelly as they did.

Again Pilate proposed to release the Saviour. "But the Jews cried out, saying, If thou let this man go, thou art not Caesar's friend." Thus these hypocrites pretended to be jealous for the authority of Caesar. Of all the opponents of the Roman rule, the Jews were most bitter. When it was safe for them to do so, they were most tyrannical in enforcing their own national and religious requirements; but when they desired to bring about some purpose of cruelty, they exalted the power of Caesar. To accomplish the destruction of Christ, they would profess loyalty to the foreign rule which they hated.

"Whosoever maketh himself a king," they continued, "speaketh against Caesar." This was touching Pilate in a weak point. He was under suspicion by the Roman government, and he knew that such a report would be ruin to him. He knew that if the Jews were thwarted, their rage would be turned against him. They would leave nothing undone to accomplish their revenge. He had before him an example of the persistence with which they sought the life of One whom they hated without reason.

Pilate then took his place on the judgment seat, and again presented Jesus to the people, saying, "Behold your King!" Again the mad cry was heard, "Away with Him, crucify Him." In a voice that was heard far and near, Pilate asked, "Shall I crucify your King?" But from profane, blasphemous lips went forth the words, "We have no king but Caesar."

Thus by choosing a heathen ruler, the Jewish na-

9. "To accomplish the destruction of Christ, they would profess l_____ to the foreign rule which they hated...We have no king but Caesar...Thus by choosing a heathen ruler, the Jewish nation had

w_____ from the t_____. They had re-jected God as their k____. Hence-forth they had no d_____." (737, 738). Lord, how do I unknowing-ly declare, I have no king but self? _____

_____

_____

_____

10. "Rather than lose his worldly power, he chose to sacrifice an innocent life. How many, to escape l_____ or suffering, in like manner, sacrifice p_____. Con-science and duty point one way, and self-interest points another. The current sets strongly in the w_____ _____ direction." Lord, I guess going with the flow is not the way to go. I think the enemy blinds me as to when I am sacrificing prin-ciple. Lord, I need Your eye salve. Help me to al-ways choose You, and be faithful to You: _____

_____

_____

_____

tion had withdrawn [737-738] from the theocracy. They had rejected God as their king. Henceforth they had no deliverer. They had no king but Caesar. To this the priests and teachers had led the people. For this, with the fearful results that followed, they were responsible. A nation's sin and a nation's ruin were due to the religious leaders.

"When Pilate saw that he could prevail nothing, but that rather a tumult was made, he took water, and washed his hands before the multitude, saying, I am innocent of the blood of this just Person: see ye to it." In fear and self-condemnation Pilate looked upon the Saviour. In the vast sea of upturned faces, His alone was peaceful. About His head a soft light seemed to shine. Pilate said in his heart, He is a God. Turning to the multitude he declared, I am clear of His blood. Take ye Him, and crucify Him. But mark ye, priests and rulers, I pronounce Him a just man. May He whom He claims as His Father judge you and not me for this day's work. Then to Jesus he said, Forgive me for this act; I cannot save You. And when he had again scourged Jesus, he delivered Him to be crucified.

Pilate longed to deliver Jesus. But he saw that he could not do this, and yet retain his own position and honor. Rather than lose his worldly power, he chose to sacrifice an innocent life. How many, to escape loss or suffering, in like manner sacrifice principle. Conscience and duty point one way, and self-interest points another. The current sets strongly in the wrong direction, and he who compromises with evil is swept away into the thick darkness of guilt.

Pilate yielded to the demands of the mob. Rather than risk losing his position, he delivered Jesus up to be crucified. But in spite of his precautions, the very thing he dreaded afterward came upon him. His honors were stripped from him, he was cast down from his high office, and, stung by remorse and wounded pride, not long after the crucifixion he ended his own life. So all who compromise with sin will gain only sorrow and ruin. "There is a way which seemeth right unto a man, but the end thereof are the ways of death." Prov. 14:12.

When Pilate declared himself innocent of the blood of Christ, Caiaphas answered defiantly, "His blood be on us, and on our children." The awful words were taken up by the priests and rulers, and echoed by the crowd in an inhuman roar of voices. The whole multitude answered and said, "His blood be on us, and on our children."

The people of Israel had made their choice. Pointing to Jesus they [738-739] had said, "Not this man, but Barabbas." Barabbas, the robber and murderer, was the representative of Satan. Christ was the representative of God. Christ had been rejected; Barabbas had been chosen. Barabbas they were to have. In making this choice they accepted him who from the beginning was a liar and a murderer. Satan was their leader. As a nation they would act out his dictation. His works they would do. His rule they must endure. That people who chose Barabbas in the place of Christ were to feel the cruelty of Barabbas as long as time should last.

Looking upon the smitten Lamb of God, the Jews had cried, "His blood be on us, and on our children." That awful cry ascended to the throne of God. That sentence, pronounced upon themselves, was written in heaven. That prayer was heard. The blood of the Son of God was upon their children and their children's children, a perpetual curse.

Terribly was it realized in the destruction of Jerusalem. Terribly has it been manifested in the condition of the Jewish nation for eighteen hundred years,--a branch severed from the vine, a dead, fruitless branch, to be gathered up and burned. From land to land throughout the world, from century to century, dead, dead in trespasses and sins!

Terribly will that prayer be fulfilled in the great judgment day. When Christ shall come to the earth again, not as a prisoner surrounded by a rabble will men see Him. They will see Him then as heaven's King. Christ will come in His own glory, in the glory of His Father, and the glory of the holy angels. Ten thousand times ten thousand, and thousands of thousands of angels, the beautiful and triumphant sons of God, possessing surpassing loveliness and glory, will escort Him on His way. Then shall He sit upon the throne of His glory, and before Him shall be gathered all nations. Then every eye shall see Him, and they also that pierced Him. In the place of a crown of thorns, He will wear a crown of glory,--a crown within a crown. In place of that old purple kingly robe, He will be clothed in raiment of whitest white, "so as no fuller on earth can white them." Mark 9:3. And on His vesture and on His thigh a name will be written, "King of kings, and Lord of lords." Rev. 19:16.

Those who mocked and smote Him will be there. The priests and rulers will behold again the scene in the judgment hall. Every circumstance will appear before them, as if written in letters of fire. Then those who prayed, "His blood be on us, and on our children," will receive the answer to their prayer. Then the whole world will know [739-740] and understand. They will realize who and what they, poor, feeble, finite beings, have been warring against. In awful agony and horror they will cry to the mountains and rocks, "Fall on us, and hide us from the face of Him that sitteth on the throne, and from the wrath of the Lamb: for the great day of His wrath is come; and who shall be able to stand?" Rev. 6:16, 17.

Chapter 78

Calvary

[This chapter is based on Matt. 27:31-53; Mark 15:20-38; Luke 23:26-46; John 19:16-30.]

"And when they were come to the place, which is called Calvary, there they crucified Him."

"That He might sanctify the people with His own blood," Christ "suffered without the gate." Heb. 13:12. For transgression of the law of God, Adam and Eve were banished from Eden. Christ, our substitute, was to suffer without the boundaries of Jerusalem. He died outside the gate, where felons and murderers were executed. Full of significance are the words, "Christ hath redeemed us from the curse of the law, being made a curse for us." Gal. 3:13.

A vast multitude followed Jesus from the judgment hall to Calvary. The news of His condemnation had spread throughout Jerusalem, and people of all classes and all ranks flocked toward the place of crucifixion. The priests and rulers had been bound by a promise not to molest Christ's followers if He Himself were delivered to them, and the disciples and believers from the city and the surrounding region joined the throng that followed the Saviour.

As Jesus passed the gate of Pilate's court, the cross which had been prepared for Barabbas was laid upon His bruised and bleeding shoulders. Two companions of Barabbas were to suffer death at the same time with Jesus, and upon them also crosses were placed. The Saviour's burden [741-742] was too heavy for Him in His weak and suffering condition. Since the Passover supper with His disciples, He had taken neither food nor drink. He had agonized in the garden of Gethsemane in conflict with satanic agencies. He had endured the anguish of the betrayal, and had seen His disciples forsake Him and flee. He had been taken to Annas, then to Caiaphas, and then to Pilate. From Pilate He had been sent to Herod, then sent again to Pilate. From insult to renewed insult, from mockery to mockery, twice tortured by the scourge,--all that night there had been scene after scene of a character to try the soul of man to the uttermost.

1. "The Savior's burden [the cross] was too heavy for Him in His weak and s_____ condition...He had a_____ in the garden of Gethsemane in conflict with s_____ agencies. He had endured the a_____ of the betrayal, and had seen His disciples f_____ Him and flee." (741-742). Certainly not to the same

degree, Lord, but shouldn't I be agonizing in conflict with satanic agencies also?

_____

Lord, help me. How can I avoid being complacent, or self-sufficient, and instead, to see my need, and to lean on You? _____

_____

_____

_____

2. "The bearing of the cross of Calvary was a b_____ _____ to Simon, and he was ever after g_____ ____ for this providence." Thank You, Lord, for the providences that lead me to the point of making a choice. What challenges have I had recently, and how can I see them as opportunities and blessings?

_____

_____

_____

_____

Christ had not failed. He had spoken no word but that tended to glorify God. All through the disgraceful farce of a trial He had borne Himself with firmness and dignity. But when after the second scourging the cross was laid upon Him, human nature could bear no more. He fell fainting beneath the burden.

The crowd that followed the Saviour saw His weak and staggering steps, but they manifested no compassion. They taunted and reviled Him because He could not carry the heavy cross. Again the burden was laid upon Him, and again He fell fainting to the ground. His persecutors saw that it was impossible for Him to carry His burden farther. They were puzzled to find anyone who would bear the humiliating load. The Jews themselves could not do this, because the defilement would prevent them from keeping the Passover. None even of the mob that followed Him would stoop to bear the cross.

At this time a stranger, Simon a Cyrenian, coming in from the country, meets the throng. He hears the taunts and ribaldry of the crowd; he hears the words contemptuously repeated, Make way for the King of the Jews! He stops in astonishment at the scene; and as he expresses his compassion, they seize him and place the cross upon his shoulders.

Simon had heard of Jesus. His sons were believers in the Saviour, but he himself was not a disciple. The bearing of the cross to Calvary was a blessing to Simon, and he was ever after grateful for this providence. It led him to take upon himself the cross of Christ from choice, and ever cheerfully stand beneath its burden.

Not a few women are in the crowd that follow the Uncondemned to His cruel death. Their attention is fixed upon Jesus. Some of them have seen Him before. Some have carried to Him their sick and suffering ones. Some have themselves been healed. The story of the scenes that have taken place is related. They wonder at the hatred of the crowd toward Him for whom their own hearts are melting and ready to break. [742-743] And notwithstanding the action of the maddened throng, and the angry words of the priests and rulers, these women give expression to their sympathy. As Jesus falls fainting beneath the cross, they break forth into mournful wailing.

This was the only thing that attracted Christ's attention. Although full of suffering, while bearing the sins of the world, He was not indifferent to the expression of grief. He looked upon these women with tender compassion. They were not believers in Him; He knew that they were not lamenting Him as one sent from God, but were moved by feelings of human pity. He did not despise their sympathy, but it awakened in His heart a deeper sympathy for them. "Daughters of Jerusalem," He said, "weep not for Me, but weep for yourselves, and for your children." From the scene before Him, Christ looked forward to the time of Jerusalem's destruction. In that terrible scene, many of those who were now weeping for Him were to perish with their children.

From the fall of Jerusalem the thoughts of Jesus passed to a wider judgment. In the destruction of the impenitent city He saw a symbol of the final destruction to come upon the world. He said, "Then shall they begin to say to the mountains, Fall on us; and to the hills, Cover us. For if they do these things in a green tree, what shall be done in the dry?" By the green tree, Jesus represented Himself, the innocent Redeemer. God suffered His wrath against transgression to fall on His beloved Son. Jesus was to be crucified for the sins of men. What suffering, then, would the sinner bear who continued in sin? All the impenitent and unbelieving would know a sorrow and misery that language would fail to express.

Of the multitude that followed the Saviour to Calvary, many had attended Him with joyful hosannas and the waving of palm branches as He rode triumphantly into Jerusalem. But not a few who had then shouted His praise, because it was popular to do so, now swelled the cry of "Crucify Him, crucify Him." When Christ rode into Jerusalem, the hopes of the disciples had been raised to the highest pitch. They had pressed close about their Master, feeling that it was a high honor to be connected with Him. Now in His humiliation they followed Him at a distance. They were filled with grief, and bowed down with disappointed hopes. How were the words of Jesus verified: "All ye shall be offended because of Me this night: for it is written, I will smite the shepherd, and the sheep of the flock shall be scattered abroad." Matt. 26:31. [743-744]

Arriving at the place of execution, the prisoners were bound to the instruments of torture. The two thieves wrestled in the hands of those who placed them on the cross; but Jesus made no resistance. The mother

3. "Of the multitude that followed the Savior to Calvary, many had attended Him with j_____ hosannas and the waving of palm branches as He rode t_____ into Jerusalem. But not a few who had then shouted His praise, because it was p_____ to do so, now swelled the cry of 'c_____ Him, c_____ Him.'" (743). Lord, how is my praise and worship? Is it merely popular, going along with the crowd? Is it focused and heartfelt? ____

————————————————

————————————————

————————————————

4. The disciples "had pressed c_____ about their Master, feeling that it was a high honor to be connected with Him. Now in His humiliation they followed Him at a d_____ _____." Lord, am I Your friend for what I get out of it? The benefits, or recognition? _____

————————————————

____ I want to be a friend to You! Thank You for gently showing me my motives:

————————————————

————————————————

————————————————

of Jesus, supported by John the beloved disciple, had followed the steps of her Son to Calvary. She had seen Him fainting under the burden of the cross, and had longed to place a supporting hand beneath His wounded head, and to bathe that brow which had once been pillowed upon her bosom. But she was not permitted this mournful privilege. With the disciples she still cherished the hope that Jesus would manifest His power, and deliver Himself from His enemies. Again her heart would sink as she recalled the words in which He had foretold the very scenes that were then taking place. As the thieves were bound to the cross, she looked on with agonizing suspense. Would He who had given life to the dead suffer Himself to be crucified? Would the Son of God suffer Himself to be thus cruelly slain? Must she give up her faith that Jesus was the Messiah? Must she witness His shame and sorrow, without even the privilege of ministering to Him in His distress? She saw His hands stretched upon the cross; the hammer and the nails were brought, and as the spikes were driven through the tender flesh, the heart-stricken disciples bore away from the cruel scene the fainting form of the mother of Jesus.

The Saviour made no murmur of complaint. His face remained calm and serene, but great drops of sweat stood upon His brow. There was no pitying hand to wipe the death dew from His face, nor words of sympathy and unchanging fidelity to stay His human heart. While the soldiers were doing their fearful work, Jesus prayed for His enemies, "Father, forgive them; for they know not what they do." His mind passed from His own suffering to the sin of His persecutors, and the terrible retribution that would be theirs. No curses were called down upon the soldiers who were handling Him so roughly. No vengeance was invoked upon the priests and rulers, who were gloating over the accomplishment of their purpose. Christ pitied them in their ignorance and guilt. He breathed only a plea for their forgiveness,--"for they know not what they do."

Had they known that they were putting to torture One who had come to save the sinful race from eternal ruin, they would have been seized with remorse and horror. But their ignorance did not remove their guilt; for it was their privilege to know and accept Jesus as their [744-745] Saviour. Some of them would yet see their sin, and repent, and be converted. Some by their

---

5. "While the soldiers were doing their fearful work, Jesus p_____ for His enemies." (744). While I was a rebellious sinner, Lord, You died for me. Why do You have this overwhelming love?

_____

_____

_____

_____

6. But their i_____ did not remove their guilt; for it was their p_____ _____ to know and accept Jesus as their Savior." Lord,

impenitence would make it an impossibility for the prayer of Christ to be answered for them. Yet, just the same, God's purpose was reaching its fulfillment. Jesus was earning the right to become the advocate of men in the Father's presence.

That prayer of Christ for His enemies embraced the world. It took in every sinner that had lived or should live, from the beginning of the world to the end of time. Upon all rests the guilt of crucifying the Son of God. To all, forgiveness is freely offered. "Whosoever will" may have peace with God, and inherit eternal life.

As soon as Jesus was nailed to the cross, it was lifted by strong men, and with great violence thrust into the place prepared for it. This caused the most intense agony to the Son of God. Pilate then wrote an inscription in Hebrew, Greek, and Latin, and placed it upon the cross, above the head of Jesus. It read, "Jesus of Nazareth the King of the Jews." This inscription irritated the Jews. In Pilate's court they had cried, "Crucify Him." "We have no king but Caesar." John 19:15. They had declared that whoever should acknowledge any other king was a traitor. Pilate wrote out the sentiment they had expressed. No offense was mentioned, except that Jesus was the King of the Jews. The inscription was a virtual acknowledgment of the allegiance of the Jews to the Roman power. It declared that whoever might claim to be the King of Israel would be judged by them worthy of death. The priests had overreached themselves. When they were plotting the death of Christ, Caiaphas had declared it expedient that one man should die to save the nation. Now their hypocrisy was revealed. In order to destroy Christ, they had been ready to sacrifice even their national existence.

The priests saw what they had done, and asked Pilate to change the inscription. They said, "Write not, The King of the Jews; but that He said, I am King of the Jews." But Pilate was angry with himself because of his former weakness, and he thoroughly despised the jealous and artful priests and rulers. He replied coldly, "What I have written I have written."

A higher power than Pilate or the Jews had directed the placing of that inscription above the head of Jesus. In the providence of God it was to awaken thought, and investigation of the Scriptures. The place where Christ was crucified was near to the city. Thousands of people from all lands were then at Jerusalem, and the inscrip-

help me not to limit my availability to Your light, thinking that I won't be responsible for it then. But rather, to seek every ray of light, every opportunity, every privilege to know You: _____
_____
_____

7. "Jesus was earning the right to become the advocate of men in the Father's presence." (745). What does this mean?
_____
_____
_____

Does Jesus' advocacy, change the Father's attitude, or the opinion of the on-looking universe?
_____
_____
_____
_____

Lord, have I given You the right to represent me?
_____

tion declaring Jesus of [745-746] Nazareth the Messiah would come to their notice. It was a living truth, transcribed by a hand that God had guided.

In the sufferings of Christ upon the cross prophecy was fulfilled. Centuries before the crucifixion, the Saviour had foretold the treatment He was to receive. He said, "Dogs have compassed Me: the assembly of the wicked have enclosed Me: they pierced My hands and My feet. I may tell all My bones: they look and stare upon Me. They part My garments among them, and cast lots upon My vesture." Ps. 22:16-18. The prophecy concerning His garments was carried out without counsel or interference from the friends or the enemies of the Crucified One. To the soldiers who had placed Him upon the cross, His clothing was given. Christ heard the men's contention as they parted the garments among them. His tunic was woven throughout without seam, and they said, "Let us not rend it, but cast lots for it, whose it shall be."

In another prophecy the Saviour declared, "Reproach hath broken My heart; and I am full of heaviness: and I looked for some to take pity, but there was none; and for comforters, but I found none. They gave Me also gall for My meat; and in My thirst they gave Me vinegar to drink." Ps. 69:20, 21. To those who suffered death by the cross, it was permitted to give a stupefying potion, to deaden the sense of pain. This was offered to Jesus; but when He had tasted it, He refused it. He would receive nothing that could becloud His mind. His faith must keep fast hold upon God. This was His only strength. To becloud His senses would give Satan an advantage.

The enemies of Jesus vented their rage upon Him as He hung upon the cross. Priests, rulers, and scribes joined with the mob in mocking the dying Saviour. At the baptism and at the transfiguration the voice of God had been heard proclaiming Christ as His Son. Again, just before Christ's betrayal, the Father had spoken, witnessing to His divinity. But now the voice from heaven was silent. No testimony in Christ's favor was heard. Alone He suffered abuse and mockery from wicked men.

"If Thou be the Son of God," they said, "come down from the cross." "Let Him save Himself, if He be Christ, the chosen of God." In the wilderness of temptation Satan had declared, "If Thou be the Son of God,

8. "He would receive nothing that could becloud His mind. His faith must keep fast h_____ upon God. This was His only strength. To becloud His senses would give Satan an a_____."
(746). Lord, what beclouds my mind? What interferes my faith from having a fast hold upon You? _____

_____

May I not give the enemy any advantage: _____

command that these stones be made bread." "If Thou be the Son of God, cast Thyself down" from the pinnacle of the temple. Matt. 4:3, 6. And Satan with his angels, in human form, was present at the [746-749] cross. The archfiend and his hosts were co-operating with the priests and rulers. The teachers of the people had stimulated the ignorant mob to pronounce judgment against One upon whom many of them had never looked, until urged to bear testimony against Him. Priests, rulers, Pharisees, and the hardened rabble were confederated together in a satanic frenzy. Religious rulers united with Satan and his angels. They were doing his bidding.

Jesus, suffering and dying, heard every word as the priests declared, "He saved others; Himself He cannot save. Let Christ the King of Israel descend now from the cross, that we may see and believe." Christ could have come down from the cross. But it is because He would not save Himself that the sinner has hope of pardon and favor with God.

In their mockery of the Saviour, the men who professed to be the expounders of prophecy were repeating the very words which Inspiration had foretold they would utter upon this occasion. Yet in their blindness they did not see that they were fulfilling the prophecy. Those who in derision uttered the words, "He trusted in God; let Him deliver Him now, if He will have Him: for He said, I am the Son of God," little thought that their testimony would sound down the ages. But although spoken in mockery, these words led men to search the Scriptures as they had never done before. Wise men heard, searched, pondered, and prayed. There were those who never rested until, by comparing scripture with scripture, they saw the meaning of Christ's mission. Never before was there such a general knowledge of Jesus as when He hung upon the cross. Into the hearts of many who beheld the crucifixion scene, and who heard Christ's words, the light of truth was shining.

To Jesus in His agony on the cross there came one gleam of comfort. It was the prayer of the penitent thief. Both the men who were crucified with Jesus had at first railed upon Him; and one under his suffering only became more desperate and defiant. But not so with his companion. This man was not a hardened criminal; he had been led astray by evil associations, but he was less guilty than many of those who stood beside the cross reviling the Saviour. He had seen and heard Jesus, and

9. "Priests, ruler, Pharisees, and the hardened rabble were c_____ _____ together in a satanic frenzy. Religious rulers u_____ with Satan and his angels. They were doing his bidding." (749). Lord, awaken me, to realize that just because I don't foam at the mouth doesn't mean the enemy has left me alone. Show me how I confederate with the enemy: _____
_____
_____
_____

10. "Although spoken in mockery, these words led men to s_____ the scriptures as they had never done before...There were those who never r_____ _____ until, by comparing scripture with scripture, they saw the m_____ of Christ's mission. Never before was there such a general knowledge of Jesus as when He hung upon the cross." Lord, as I contemplate Your life, especially the closing scenes, may I experience the same flood of knowledge:
_____
_____
_____

had been convicted by His teaching, but he had been turned away from Him by the priests and rulers. Seeking to stifle conviction, he had plunged deeper and deeper into sin, until he was arrested, tried as a criminal, and condemned to die on the cross. In the judgment hall and on the way to Calvary he had been in company with Jesus. He had heard Pilate declare, "I find no fault in Him." John 19:4. He had marked His [749-750] godlike bearing, and His pitying forgiveness of His tormentors. On the cross he sees the many great religionists shoot out the tongue with scorn, and ridicule the Lord Jesus. He sees the wagging heads. He hears the upbraiding speeches taken up by his companion in guilt: "If Thou be Christ, save Thyself and us." Among the passers-by he hears many defending Jesus. He hears them repeat His words, and tell of His works. The conviction comes back to him that this is the Christ. Turning to his fellow criminal he says, "Dost not thou fear God, seeing thou art in the same condemnation?" The dying thieves have no longer anything to fear from man. But upon one of them presses the conviction that there is a God to fear, a future to cause him to tremble. And now, all sin-polluted as it is, his life history is about to close. "And we indeed justly," he moans; "for we receive the due reward of our deeds: but this Man hath done nothing amiss."

There is no question now. There are no doubts, no reproaches. When condemned for his crime, the thief had become hopeless and despairing; but strange, tender thoughts now spring up. He calls to mind all he has heard of Jesus, how He has healed the sick and pardoned sin. He has heard the words of those who believed in Jesus and followed Him weeping. He has seen and read the title above the Saviour's head. He has heard the passers-by repeat it, some with grieved, quivering lips, others with jesting and mockery. The Holy Spirit illuminates his mind, and little by little the chain of evidence is joined together. In Jesus, bruised, mocked, and hanging upon the cross, he sees the Lamb of God, that taketh away the sin of the world. Hope is mingled with anguish in his voice as the helpless, dying soul casts himself upon a dying Saviour. "Lord, remember me," he cries, "when Thou comest into Thy kingdom."

Quickly the answer came. Soft and melodious the tone, full of love, compassion, and power the words: Verily I say unto thee today, Thou shalt be with Me in paradise.

For long hours of agony, reviling and mockery have fallen upon the ears of Jesus. As He hangs upon the cross, there floats up to Him still the sound of jeers and curses. With longing heart He has listened for some expression of faith from His disciples. He has heard only the mournful words, "We trusted that it had been He which should have redeemed Israel." How grateful then to the Saviour was the utterance of faith and love from the dying thief! While the leading Jews deny Him, and even the disciples doubt His divinity, the poor thief, upon the [750-751] brink of eternity, calls Jesus Lord. Many were ready to call Him Lord when He wrought miracles, and after He had risen from the grave; but none acknowledged Him as He hung dying upon the cross save the penitent thief who was saved at the eleventh hour.

The bystanders caught the words as the thief called Jesus Lord. The tone of the repentant man arrested their attention. Those who at the foot of the cross had been quarreling over Christ's garments, and casting lots upon His vesture, stopped to listen. Their angry tones were hushed. With bated breath they looked upon Christ, and waited for the response from those dying lips.

As He spoke the words of promise, the dark cloud that seemed to enshroud the cross was pierced by a bright and living light. To the penitent thief came the perfect peace of acceptance with God. Christ in His humiliation was glorified. He who in all other eyes appeared to be conquered was a Conqueror. He was acknowledged as the Sin Bearer. Men may exercise power over His human body. They may pierce the holy temples with the crown of thorns. They may strip from Him His raiment, and quarrel over its division. But they cannot rob Him of His power to forgive sins. In dying He bears testimony to His own divinity and to the glory of the Father. His ear is not heavy that it cannot hear, neither His arm shortened that it cannot save. It is His royal right to save unto the uttermost all who come unto God by Him.

I say unto thee today, Thou shalt be with Me in Paradise. Christ did not promise that the thief should be with Him in Paradise that day. He Himself did not go that day to Paradise. He slept in the tomb, and on the morning of the resurrection He said, "I am not yet ascended to My Father." John 20:17. But on the day of the crucifixion, the day of apparent defeat and darkness, the promise was given. "Today" while dying upon

1. "With longing heart Jesus had listened for some expression of f_____ from His disciples. He has heard only the m_____ _____ words, 'We trusted that it had been He which s_____ have redeemed Israel.' How g_____ ___ then to the Savior was the utterance of faith and l_____ from the dying thief... none a_____ _____ Him as He hung dying upon the cross save the penitent thief." (750-751). Lord, instead of self-centered perspective, help my contemplation to be about You, and how I might comfort You: _____ _____ _____

the cross as a malefactor, Christ assures the poor sinner, Thou shalt be with Me in Paradise.

The thieves crucified with Jesus were placed "on either side one, and Jesus in the midst." This was done by the direction of the priests and rulers. Christ's position between the thieves was to indicate that He was the greatest criminal of the three. Thus was fulfilled the scripture, "He was numbered with the transgressors." Isa. 53:12. But the full meaning of their act the priests did not see. As Jesus, crucified with the thieves, was placed "in the midst," so His cross was placed in the midst of a world lying in sin. And the words of pardon spoken to the penitent thief kindled a light that will shine to the earth's remotest bounds. [751-752]

With amazement the angels beheld the infinite love of Jesus, who, suffering the most intense agony of mind and body, thought only of others, and encouraged the penitent soul to believe. In His humiliation He as a prophet had addressed the daughters of Jerusalem; as priest and advocate He had pleaded with the Father to forgive His murderers; as a loving Saviour He had forgiven the sins of the penitent thief.

As the eyes of Jesus wandered over the multitude about Him, one figure arrested His attention. At the foot of the cross stood His mother, supported by the disciple John. She could not endure to remain away from her Son; and John, knowing that the end was near, had brought her again to the cross. In His dying hour, Christ remembered His mother. Looking into her grief-stricken face and then upon John, He said to her, "Woman, behold thy son!" then to John, "Behold thy mother!" John understood Christ's words, and accepted the trust. He at once took Mary to his home, and from that hour cared for her tenderly. O pitiful, loving Saviour; amid all His physical pain and mental anguish, He had a thoughtful care for His mother! He had no money with which to provide for her comfort; but He was enshrined in the heart of John, and He gave His mother to him as a precious legacy. Thus He provided for her that which she most needed,--the tender sympathy of one who loved her because she loved Jesus. And in receiving her as a sacred trust, John was receiving a great blessing. She was a constant reminder of his beloved Master.

The perfect example of Christ's filial love shines forth with undimmed luster from the mist of ages. For nearly thirty years Jesus by His daily toil had helped bear the burdens of the home. And now, even in His last agony, He remembers to provide for His sorrowing, widowed mother. The same spirit will be seen in every disciple of our Lord. Those who follow Christ will feel that it is a part of their religion to respect and provide for their parents. From the heart where His love is cherished, father and mother will never fail of receiving thoughtful care and tender sympathy.

And now the Lord of glory was dying, a ransom for the race. In yielding up His precious life, Christ was not upheld by triumphant joy. All was oppressive gloom. It was not the dread of death that weighed upon Him. It was not the pain and ignominy of the cross that caused His inexpressible agony. Christ was the prince of sufferers; but His suffering was from a sense of the malignity of sin, a knowledge that [752-753] through familiarity with evil, man had become blinded to its enormity. Christ saw how deep is the hold of sin upon the human heart, how few would be willing to break from its power. He knew that without help from God, humanity must perish, and He saw multitudes perishing within reach of abundant help.

Upon Christ as our substitute and surety was laid the iniquity of us all. He was counted a transgressor, that He might redeem us from the condemnation of the law. The guilt of every descendant of Adam was pressing upon His heart. The wrath of God against sin, the terrible manifestation of His displeasure because of iniquity, filled the soul of His Son with consternation. All His life Christ had been publishing to a fallen world the good news of the Father's mercy and pardoning love. Salvation for the chief of sinners was His theme. But now with the terrible weight of guilt He bears, He cannot see the Father's reconciling face. The withdrawal of the divine countenance from the Saviour in this hour of supreme anguish pierced His heart with a sorrow that can never be fully understood by man. So great was this agony that His physical pain was hardly felt.

Satan with his fierce temptations wrung the heart of Jesus. The Saviour could not see through the portals of the tomb. Hope did not present to Him His coming forth from the grave a conqueror, or tell Him of the Father's acceptance of the sacrifice. He feared that sin was so offensive to God that Their separation was to be eternal. Christ felt the anguish which the sinner will feel when mercy shall no longer plead for the guilty race. It was

2. "His suffering was from a sense of the m_____ _____ of sin…With the terrible weight of g____ _____ He bears, He cannot s_____ the Father's reconciling face… The Savior could not s____ ____ through the portals of the tomb. H_____ did not present to Him His coming forth from the grave a conqueror…He feared that sin was so offensive to God that Their s_____ ___ was to be eternal…It

was the sense of s_____ __, bringing the Father's wrath upon Him as man's substitute, that made the cup He drank so bitter, and b_____ the heart of the Son of God." (752-753). Lord, what a contrast to how the enemy makes sin appear, so exciting and of no consequence. May this contemplation of Your life, strengthen me against temptation:

_____
_____
_____

_____ Lord, I am sorry for my sin, for breaking Your heart: _____

_____

Lord, Your death illustrates Your love for sinners. So what is this wrath? If it is to be consistent with Your love, might it be Your reaction toward sin (vs sinner)? _____

_____

the sense of sin, bringing the Father's wrath upon Him as man's substitute, that made the cup He drank so bitter, and broke the heart of the Son of God.

With amazement angels witnessed the Saviour's despairing agony. The hosts of heaven veiled their faces from the fearful sight. Inanimate nature expressed sympathy with its insulted and dying Author. The sun refused to look upon the awful scene. Its full, bright rays were illuminating the earth at midday, when suddenly it seemed to be blotted out. Complete darkness, like a funeral pall, enveloped the cross. "There was darkness over all the land unto the ninth hour." There was no eclipse or other natural cause for this darkness, which was as deep as midnight without moon or stars. It was a miraculous testimony given by God that the faith of after generations might be confirmed.

In that thick darkness God's presence was hidden. He makes darkness His pavilion, and conceals His glory from human eyes. God and [753-754] His holy angels were beside the cross. The Father was with His Son. Yet His presence was not revealed. Had His glory flashed forth from the cloud, every human beholder would have been destroyed. And in that dreadful hour Christ was not to be comforted with the Father's presence. He trod the wine press alone, and of the people there was none with Him.

In the thick darkness, God veiled the last human agony of His Son. All who had seen Christ in His suffering had been convicted of His divinity. That face, once beheld by humanity, was never forgotten. As the face of Cain expressed his guilt as a murderer, so the face of Christ revealed innocence, serenity, benevolence,--the image of God. But His accusers would not give heed to the signet of heaven. Through long hours of agony Christ had been gazed upon by the jeering multitude. Now He was mercifully hidden by the mantle of God.

The silence of the grave seemed to have fallen upon Calvary. A nameless terror held the throng that was gathered about the cross. The cursing and reviling ceased in the midst of half-uttered sentences. Men, women, and children fell prostrate upon the earth. Vivid lightnings occasionally flashed forth from the cloud, and revealed the cross and the crucified Redeemer. Priests, rulers, scribes, executioners, and the mob, all thought that their time of retribution had come. After a while some whispered that Jesus would now come down from the

cross. Some attempted to grope their way back to the
city, beating their breasts and wailing in fear.

At the ninth hour the darkness lifted from the people, but still enveloped the Saviour. It was a symbol of
the agony and horror that weighed upon His heart. No
eye could pierce the gloom that surrounded the cross,
and none could penetrate the deeper gloom that enshrouded the suffering soul of Christ. The angry lightnings seemed to be hurled at Him as He hung upon the
cross. Then "Jesus cried with a loud voice, saying, Eloi,
Eloi, lama sabachthani?" "My God, My God, why hast
Thou forsaken Me?" As the outer gloom settled about
the Saviour, many voices exclaimed: The vengeance
of heaven is upon Him. The bolts of God's wrath are
hurled at Him, because He claimed to be the Son of
God. Many who believed on Him heard His despairing
cry. Hope left them. If God had forsaken Jesus, in what
could His followers trust?

When the darkness lifted from the oppressed spirit
of Christ, He revived to a sense of physical suffering,
and said, "I thirst." One of the [754-755] Roman soldiers, touched with pity as he looked at the parched lips,
took a sponge on a stalk of hyssop, and dipping it in
a vessel of vinegar, offered it to Jesus. But the priests
mocked at His agony. When darkness covered the earth,
they had been filled with fear; as their terror abated, the
dread returned that Jesus would yet escape them. His
words, "Eloi, Eloi, lama sabachthani?" they had misinterpreted. With bitter contempt and scorn they said,
"This man calleth for Elias." The last opportunity to relieve His sufferings they refused. "Let be," they said,
"let us see whether Elias will come to save Him."

The spotless Son of God hung upon the cross, His
flesh lacerated with stripes; those hands so often reached
out in blessing, nailed to the wooden bars; those feet
so tireless on ministries of love, spiked to the tree; that
royal head pierced by the crown of thorns; those quivering lips shaped to the cry of woe. And all that He en-
dured--the blood drops that flowed from His head, His
hands, His feet, the agony that racked His frame, and
the unutterable anguish that filled His soul at the hiding
of His Father's face--speaks to each child of humanity,
declaring, It is for thee that the Son of God consents to
bear this burden of guilt; for thee He spoils the domain
of death, and opens the gates of Paradise. He who stilled
the angry waves and walked the foam-capped billows,

who made devils tremble and disease flee, who opened blind eyes and called forth the dead to life,--offers Himself upon the cross as a sacrifice, and this from love to thee. [755-756] He, the Sin Bearer, endures the wrath of divine justice, and for thy sake becomes sin itself.

In silence the beholders watched for the end of the fearful scene. The sun shone forth; but the cross was still enveloped in darkness. Priests and rulers looked toward Jerusalem; and lo, the dense cloud had settled over the city and the plains of Judea. The Sun of Righteousness, the Light of the world, was withdrawing His beams from the once favored city of Jerusalem. The fierce lightnings of God's wrath were directed against the fated city.

Suddenly the gloom lifted from the cross, and in clear, trumpetlike tones, that seemed to resound throughout creation, Jesus cried, "It is finished." "Father, into Thy hands I commend My spirit." A light encircled the cross, and the face of the Saviour shone with a glory like the sun. He then bowed His head upon His breast, and died.

Amid the awful darkness, apparently forsaken of God, Christ had drained the last dregs in the cup of human woe. In those dreadful hours He had relied upon the evidence of His Father's acceptance heretofore given Him. He was acquainted with the character of His Father; He understood His justice, His mercy, and His great love. By faith He rested in Him whom it had ever been His joy to obey. And as in submission He committed Himself to God, the sense of the loss of His Father's favor was withdrawn. By faith, Christ was victor.

Never before had the earth witnessed such a scene. The multitude stood paralyzed, and with bated breath gazed upon the Saviour. Again darkness settled upon the earth, and a hoarse rumbling, like heavy thunder, was heard. There was a violent earthquake. The people were shaken together in heaps. The wildest confusion and consternation ensued. In the surrounding mountains, rocks were rent asunder, and went crashing down into the plains. Sepulchers were broken open, and the dead were cast out of their tombs. Creation seemed to be shivering to atoms. Priests, rulers, soldiers, executioners, and people, mute with terror, lay prostrate upon the ground.

When the loud cry, "It is finished," came from the lips of Christ, the priests were officiating in the temple.

---

3. "In those dreadful hours Jesus had r_____ upon the evidence of His Father's a_____ heretofore given Him...By f_____, Christ was victor." (756). Lord, while You experienced the consequence of my sin, separation from the Father, You leaned on the memory of Your relationship with Him. Lord, do I have a history with You to lean on? Bring to mind evidences of Your love and acceptance:

_____

_____

_____

_____

It was the hour of the evening sacrifice. The lamb representing Christ had been brought to be slain. Clothed in his significant and beautiful dress, the priest stood with lifted knife, as did Abraham when he was about to slay his son. With intense interest the people were looking on. But the earth trembles and quakes; [756-757] for the Lord Himself draws near. With a rending noise the inner veil of the temple is torn from top to bottom by an unseen hand, throwing open to the gaze of the multitude a place once filled with the presence of God. In this place the Shekinah had dwelt. Here God had manifested His glory above the mercy seat. No one but the high priest ever lifted the veil separating this apartment from the rest of the temple. He entered in once a year to make an atonement for the sins of the people. But lo, this veil is rent in twain. The most holy place of the earthly sanctuary is no longer sacred.

All is terror and confusion. The priest is about to slay the victim; but the knife drops from his nerveless hand, and the lamb escapes. Type has met antitype in the death of God's Son. The great sacrifice has been made. The way into the holiest is laid open. A new and living way is prepared for all. No longer need sinful, sorrowing humanity await the coming of the high priest. Henceforth the Saviour was to officiate as priest and advocate in the heaven of heavens. It was as if a living voice had spoken to the worshipers: There is now an end to all sacrifices and offerings for sin. The Son of God is come according to His word, "Lo, I come (in the volume of the Book it is written of Me,) to do Thy will, O God." "By His own blood" He entereth "in once into the holy place, having obtained eternal redemption for us." Heb. 10:7; 9:12.

4. In the temple "all is t_____ and confusion. The priest is about to slay the victim; but the knife drops from his nerveless hand, and the l_____ _____ escapes. Type has met a_____ in the death of God's Son. The great sacrifice has been m_____." (757). Lord, may an equally pivotal reality occur in my life; that the power of sin is broken: _____

_____
_____
_____

Prayer Journal: _____

_____
_____
_____
_____

Chapter 79

"It is Finished"

1. "It was for them [the a_
_____ and unfallen
worlds] as well as for us
that the great work of redemption had been accom-
plished. They share in the
fruits of Christ's v_____
__." Had they sinned? ____
_____

Why or how did redemp-
tion help them? _____
_____

_____ "Not until
the death of Christ was the
c_____ of
Satan clearly r_____
___ to the angels or to the
unfallen worlds...They
had not c_____ seen the
nature of his r_____
_____." Lord, if the
cross taught the angels
something, then the cross
is more than a payment
of my penalty. It should
reveal to me the nature of
Satan's and my rebellion.
I am slow, Lord. Help me
see how they are similar:
_____
_____
_____
_____

2. "Rebellion was not to
be overcome by f_____
_____... [God's] authority
rests upon g_____
___, mercy, and l_____
___; and the presentation
of these principles are the
means to be used." For the

Christ did not yield up His life till He had accomplished the work which He came to do, and with His
parting breath He exclaimed, "It is finished." John
19:30. The battle had been won. His right hand and His
holy arm had gotten Him the victory. As a Conqueror
He planted His banner on the eternal heights. Was there
not joy among the angels? All heaven triumphed in the
Saviour's victory. Satan was defeated, and knew that
his kingdom was lost.

To the angels and the unfallen worlds the cry, "It
is finished," had a deep significance. It was for them
as well as for us that the great work of redemption had
been accomplished. They with us share the fruits of
Christ's victory.

Not until the death of Christ was the character of
Satan clearly revealed to the angels or to the unfallen
worlds. The archapostate had so clothed himself with
deception that even holy beings had not understood his
principles. They had not clearly seen the nature of his
rebellion.

It was a being of wonderful power and glory that
had set himself against God. Of Lucifer the Lord says,
"Thou sealest up the sum, full of wisdom, and perfect
in beauty." Ezek. 28:12. Lucifer had been the covering
cherub. He had stood in the light of God's presence.
He had been the highest of all created beings, and had
been foremost in revealing God's purposes to the universe. After he had sinned, his power to deceive [758-
759] was the more deceptive, and the unveiling of his
character was the more difficult, because of the exalted
position he had held with the Father.

God could have destroyed Satan and his sympathiz-
ers as easily as one can cast a pebble to the earth; but
He did not do this. Rebellion was not to be overcome
by force. Compelling power is found only under Satan's
government. The Lord's principles are not of this order.
His authority rests upon goodness, mercy, and love; and
the presentation of these principles is the means to be
used. God's government is moral, and truth and love are

to be the prevailing power.

It was God's purpose to place things on an eternal basis of security, and in the councils of heaven it was decided that time must be given for Satan to develop the principles which were the foundation of his system of government. He had claimed that these were superior to God's principles. Time was given for the working of Satan's principles, that they might be seen by the heavenly universe.

Satan led men into sin, and the plan of redemption was put in operation. For four thousand years, Christ was working for man's uplifting, and Satan for his ruin and degradation. And the heavenly universe beheld it all.

When Jesus came into the world, Satan's power was turned against Him. From the time when He appeared as a babe in Bethlehem, the usurper worked to bring about His destruction. In every possible way he sought to prevent Jesus from developing a perfect childhood, a faultless manhood, a holy ministry, and an unblemished sacrifice. But he was defeated. He could not lead Jesus into sin. He could not discourage Him, or drive Him from a work He had come on earth to do. From the desert to Calvary, the storm of Satan's wrath beat upon Him, but the more mercilessly it fell, the more firmly did the Son of God cling to the hand of His Father, and

universe to be eternally secure, "t_____ must be given for Satan to develop the p_____ which were the foundation of his system of government...Time was given for the w_____ of Satan's principles, that they might be seen by the heavenly u_____." (759). Not by might nor by _____, but by My _____. Lord, help me to see the difference in the two sets of principles, and Who employs them. Satan is cleaver in attributing his own character onto Yours. And Lord, I need help in seeing which principles I live by; and through this walk of contemplating Your life, may I adopt Your principles: _____

_____

_____

"But the plan of redemption had a yet broader and deeper purpose than the salvation of man. It was not for this alone that Christ came to the earth; it was not merely that the inhabitants of this little world might regard the law of God as it should be regarded; but it was to vindicate the character of God before the universe. To this result of His great sacrifice--its influence upon the intelligences of other worlds, as well as upon man--the Saviour looked forward when just before His crucifixion He said: `Now is the judgment of this world:

now shall the prince of this world be cast out. And I, if I be lifted up from the earth, will draw all men unto Me.' John 12:31, 32. The act of Christ in dying for the salvation of man would not only make heaven accessible to men, but before all the universe it would justify God and His Son in their dealing with the rebellion of Satan. It would establish the perpetuity of the law of God and would reveal the nature and the results of sin."
Patriarchs and Prophets 68, 69.

3. "All the efforts of Satan to oppress and overcome Him only brought out in a p_____ light His spotless character. All heaven and the unfallen worlds had been w_____ _____ to the controversy. With what i_____ interest did they follow the closing scenes of the conflict." Lord, when Satan oppresses me, what is revealed of my character? Is it pure? _____
_____

Help the intensity of my interest to increase, in how this controversy affected You, and how the behind-the-scenes controversy involves me: _____
_____
_____
_____
_____
_____
_____

press on in the bloodstained path. All the efforts of Satan to oppress and overcome Him only brought out in a purer light His spotless character.

All heaven and the unfallen worlds had been witnesses to the controversy. With what intense interest did they follow the closing scenes of the conflict. They beheld the Saviour enter the garden of Gethsemane, His soul bowed down with the horror of a great darkness. They heard His bitter cry, "Father, if it be possible, let this cup pass from Me." Matt. 26:39. As the Father's presence was withdrawn, they saw Him sorrowful with a bitterness of sorrow exceeding that of the last great struggle with death. The bloody sweat was forced from His pores, and [759-760] fell in drops upon the ground. Thrice the prayer for deliverance was wrung from His lips. Heaven could no longer endure the sight, and a messenger of comfort was sent to the Son of God.

Heaven beheld the Victim betrayed into the hands of the murderous mob, and with mockery and violence hurried from one tribunal to another. It heard the sneers of His persecutors because of His lowly birth. It heard the denial with cursing and swearing by one of His best-loved disciples. It saw the frenzied work of Satan, and his power over the hearts of men. Oh, fearful scene! the Saviour seized at midnight in Gethsemane, dragged to and fro from palace to judgment hall, arraigned twice before the priests, twice before the Sanhedrin, twice before Pilate, and once before Herod, mocked, scourged, condemned, and led out to be crucified, bearing the heavy burden of the cross, amid the wailing of the daughters of Jerusalem and the jeering of the rabble.

Heaven viewed with grief and amazement Christ hanging upon the cross, blood flowing from His wounded temples, and sweat tinged with blood standing upon His brow. From His hands and feet the blood fell, drop by drop, upon the rock drilled for the foot of the cross. The wounds made by the nails gaped as the weight of His body dragged upon His hands. His labored breath grew quick and deep, as His soul panted under the burden of the sins of the world. All heaven was filled with wonder when the prayer of Christ was offered in the midst of His terrible suffering,--"Father, forgive them; for they know not what they do." Luke 23:34. Yet there stood men, formed in the image of God, joining to crush out the life of His only-begotten Son. What a sight for the heavenly universe!

The principalities and powers of darkness were assembled around the cross, casting the hellish shadow of unbelief into the hearts of men. When the Lord created these beings to stand before His throne, they were beautiful and glorious. Their loveliness and holiness were in accordance with their exalted station. They were enriched with the wisdom of God, and girded with the panoply of heaven. They were Jehovah's ministers. But who could recognize in the fallen angels the glorious seraphim that once ministered in the heavenly courts?

Satanic agencies confederated with evil men in leading the people to believe Christ the chief of sinners, and to make Him the object of detestation. Those who mocked Christ as He hung upon the cross were imbued with the spirit of the first great rebel. He filled them with vile [760-761] and loathsome speeches. He inspired their taunts. But by all this he gained nothing.

Could one sin have been found in Christ, had He in one particular yielded to Satan to escape the terrible torture, the enemy of God and man would have triumphed. Christ bowed His head and died, but He held fast His faith and His submission to God. "And I heard a loud voice saying in heaven, Now is come salvation, and strength, and the kingdom of our God, and the power of His Christ: for the accuser of our brethren is cast down, which accused them before our God day and night." Rev. 12:10.

Satan saw that his disguise was torn away. His administration was laid open before the unfallen angels and before the heavenly universe. He had revealed himself as a murderer. By shedding the blood of the Son of God, he had uprooted himself from the sympathies of the heavenly beings. Henceforth his work was restricted. Whatever attitude he might assume, he could no longer await the angels as they came from the heavenly courts, and before them accuse Christ's brethren of being clothed with the garments of blackness and the defilement of sin. The last link of sympathy between Satan and the heavenly world was broken.

Yet Satan was not then destroyed. The angels did not even then understand all that was involved in the great controversy. The principles at stake were to be more fully revealed. And for the sake of man, Satan's existence must be continued. Man as well as angels

4. "Could o_____ sin have been found in Christ, had He in one particular y_____ to Satan to escape the terrible torture, the enemy of God and man would have triumphed." (761). Lord, I know that I don't save myself, You do. But is it a big deal if I yield?

_____

_____

_____

5. Satan's "administration was laid o_____ before the unfallen angels and before the heavenly universe...The last link of s_____ between Satan and the heavenly world was broken...For the sake of man, Satan's existence must be continued." Lord, how does his existence help me? _____

_____

_____

6. "In the opening of the great controversy, Satan had declared that [a] the law of God could not be o_____, that [b] justice was i_____ _____ with mercy, and that, [c] should the law be broken, it would be i____ _____ for the sinner to be pardoned. [d] Every sin must meet its p_____ _____, urged Satan; and if God should r_____ ___ the punishment of sin, He would not be a God of truth and j_____ ___." Lord, the enemy has used those points of logic on me. Show me the times that I bought into his logic:

_____

_____

_____

_____

I am Sorry. Teach me Your values and principles, Lord, and keep me from the enemy's: _____

_____

_____

_____

7. "But man was deceived; his mind was darkened by Satan's sophistry...For him there was a hope in the k_____ of God's love. By b_____ His character he might be d_____ back to God." (762). Lord, is this how You plan to save me, to reconcile me? This is beyond paying the penalty! Help me to take time,

must see the contrast between the Prince of light and the prince of darkness. He must choose whom he will serve.

In the opening of the great controversy, Satan had declared that the law of God could not be obeyed, that justice was inconsistent with mercy, and that, should the law be broken, it would be impossible for the sinner to be pardoned. Every sin must meet its punishment, urged Satan; and if God should remit the punishment of sin, He would not be a God of truth and justice. When men broke the law of God, and defied His will, Satan exulted. It was proved, he declared, that the law could not be obeyed; man could not be forgiven. Because he, after his rebellion, had been banished from heaven, Satan claimed that the human race must be forever shut out from God's favor. God could not be just, he urged, and yet show mercy to the sinner.

But even as a sinner, man was in a different position from that of Satan. Lucifer in heaven had sinned in the light of God's glory. To him as to no other created being was given a revelation of God's love. [761-762] Understanding the character of God, knowing His goodness, Satan chose to follow his own selfish, independent will. This choice was final. There was no more that God could do to save him. But man was deceived; his mind was darkened by Satan's sophistry. The height and depth of the love of God he did not know. For him there was hope in a knowledge of God's love. By beholding His character he might be drawn back to God.

Through Jesus, God's mercy was manifested to men; but mercy does not set aside justice. The law reveals the attributes of God's character, and not a jot or tittle of it could be changed to meet man in his fallen condition. God did not change His law, but He sacrificed Himself, in Christ, for man's redemption. "God was in Christ, reconciling the world unto Himself." 2 Cor. 5:19.

The law requires righteousness,--a righteous life, a perfect character; and this man has not to give. He cannot meet the claims of God's holy law. But Christ, coming to the earth as man, lived a holy life, and developed a perfect character. These He offers as a free gift to all who will receive them. His life stands for the life of men. Thus they have remission of sins that are past, through the forbearance of God. More than this, Christ imbues men with the attributes of God. He builds up the human character after the similitude of the divine character, a goodly fabric of spiritual strength and beauty. Thus the very righteousness of the law is fulfilled in the believer in Christ. God can "be just, and the justifier of him which believeth in Jesus." Rom. 3:26.

God's love has been expressed in His justice no less than in His mercy. Justice is the foundation of His throne, and the fruit of His love. It had been Satan's purpose to divorce mercy from truth and justice. He sought to prove that the righteousness of God's law is an enemy to peace. But Christ shows that in God's plan they are indissolubly joined together; the one cannot exist without the other. "Mercy and truth are met together; righteousness and peace have kissed each other." Ps. 85:10.

By His life and His death, Christ proved that God's justice did not destroy His mercy, but that sin could be forgiven, and that the law is righteous, and can be perfectly obeyed. Satan's charges were refuted. God had given man unmistakable evidence of His love.

Another deception was now to be brought forward. Satan declared that mercy destroyed justice, that the death of Christ abrogated the Father's law. Had it been possible for the law to be changed or abrogated, then Christ need not have died. But to abrogate the law would [762-763] be to immortalize transgression, and place the world under Satan's control. It was because the law was changeless, because man could be saved only through obedience to its precepts, that Jesus was lifted up on the cross. Yet the very means by which Christ established the law Satan represented as destroying it. Here will come the last conflict of the great controversy between Christ and Satan.

That the law which was spoken by God's own voice is faulty, that some specification has been set aside, is the claim which Satan now puts forward. It is the last great deception that he will bring upon the world. He needs not to assail the whole law; if he can lead men to disregard one precept, his purpose is gained. For "whosoever shall keep the whole law, and yet offend in one point, he is guilty of all." James 2:10. By consenting to break one precept, men are brought under Satan's power. By substituting human law for God's law, Satan will seek to control the world. This work is foretold

to make room in my life to behold Your character of love, and to be further drawn to You. May this spiritual walk with You provide opportunity to behold and be drawn: ___

_____

_____

_____

8. "The law requires righteousness,--a righteous life, a perfect c_____
____; and this man has not to give…These He [Christ] offers as a f_____ gift to all who will receive them. His life stands for the life of men…Christ i_____ men with the attributes of God. He builds up the human character after the similitude of the d_____ character." Lord, I don't have a perfect character. I could never produce one. Thank You for the free gift of one, and for the work You are doing in me. Remind me to daily be available and receive this gift:

_____

_____

_____

_____

9. "Satan declared that m_____ destroys justice, that the death of Christ abrogated the Father's law. Had it been possible for the law to be changed or abrogated, then Christ need not have d_____…The very means by which Christ e_____ the law Satan represented as de-

stroying it. Here will come the last conflict of the great controversy between C___ ____ and Satan...It is the last great d_____ ____ that Satan will bring upon the world." (762-763). Lord, is the enemy deceiving me? _____ ____. Do I presume Your forgiveness and mercy? _____. Help me to better understand Your character, of love and purity, Your holy reaction to sin. How does the enemy lessen my awareness of Your holy character, by urging my carelessness towards sin? _____

_____

_____

10. "Every character will be fully developed...Satan and all who have joined him in rebellion will be cut off...reap [ing] that which they have sown. God is the fountain of life; when one chooses the service of sin, he s_____ from God, and thus cuts himself o_____ from life...God gives them existence for a time that they may develop their character...

in prophecy. Of the great apostate power which is the representative of Satan, it is declared, "He shall speak great words against the Most High, and shall wear out the saints of the Most High, and think to change times and laws: and they shall be given into his hand." Dan. 7:25.

Men will surely set up their laws to counterwork the laws of God. They will seek to compel the consciences of others, and in their zeal to enforce these laws they will oppress their fellow men.

The warfare against God's law, which was begun in heaven, will be continued until the end of time. Every man will be tested. Obedience or disobedience is the question to be decided by the whole world. All will be called to choose between the law of God and the laws of men. Here the dividing line will be drawn. There will be but two classes. Every character will be fully developed; and all will show whether they have chosen the side of loyalty or that of rebellion.

Then the end will come. God will vindicate His law and deliver His people. Satan and all who have joined him in rebellion will be cut off. Sin and sinners will perish, root and branch, (Mal. 4:1),--Satan the root, and his followers the branches. The word will be fulfilled to the prince of evil, "Because thou hast set thine heart as the heart of God; . . . I will destroy thee, O covering cherub, from the midst of the stones of fire. . . . Thou shalt be a terror, and never shalt thou be any more." Then "the wicked shall not be: yea, thou shalt diligently consider his place, and it shall not be;" "they shall be as though they had not been." Ezek. 28:6-19; Ps. 37:10; Obadiah 16. [763-764]

This is not an act of arbitrary power on the part of God. The rejecters of His mercy reap that which they have sown. God is the fountain of life; and when one chooses the service of sin, he separates from God, and thus cuts himself off from life. He is "alienated from the life of God." Christ says, "All they that hate Me love death." Eph. 4:18; Prov. 8:36. God gives them existence for a time that they may develop their character and reveal their principles. This accomplished, they receive the results of their own choice. By a life of rebellion, Satan and all who unite with him place themselves so out of harmony with God that His very presence is to them a consuming fire. The glory of Him who is love will destroy them.

At the beginning of the great controversy, the angels did not understand this. Had Satan and his host then been left to reap the full result of their sin, they would have perished; but it would not have been apparent to heavenly beings that this was the inevitable result of sin. A doubt of God's goodness would have remained in their minds as evil seed, to produce its deadly fruit of sin and woe.

But not so when the great controversy shall be ended. Then, the plan of redemption having been completed, the character of God is revealed to all created intelligences. The precepts of His law are seen to be perfect and immutable. Then sin has made manifest its nature, Satan his character. Then the extermination of sin will vindicate God's love and establish His honor before a universe of beings who delight to do His will, and in whose heart is His law.

Well, then, might the angels rejoice as they looked upon the Saviour's cross; for though they did not then understand all, they knew that the destruction of sin and Satan was forever made certain, that the redemption of man was assured, and that the universe was made eternally secure. Christ Himself fully comprehended the results of the sacrifice made upon Calvary. To all these He looked forward when upon the cross He cried out, "It is finished."

By a life of rebellion, Satan and all who unite with him place themselves so out of h_____ with God that His very p_____ is to t_____ a consuming fire. The g_____ of Him who is love will destroy them." (763, 764). Lord, what is the difference between "an act of arbitrary power on the part of God," and "the inevitable result of sin?"

_____

_____

_____

_____

Lord, show me: am I out of harmony with Your presence, or am I comfortable in Your presence? _____

_____

_____

Prayer journal: _____

_____

_____

_____

_____

_____

_____

_____

_____

Chapter 80

In Joseph's Tomb

At last Jesus was at rest. The long day of shame and torture was ended. As the last rays of the setting sun ushered in the Sabbath, the Son of God lay in quietude in Joseph's tomb. His work completed, His hands folded in peace, He rested through the sacred hours of the Sabbath day.

In the beginning the Father and the Son had rested upon the Sabbath after Their work of creation. When "the heavens and the earth were finished, and all the host of them" (Gen. 2:1), the Creator and all heavenly beings rejoiced in contemplation of the glorious scene. "The morning stars sang together, and all the sons of God shouted for joy." Job 38:7. Now Jesus rested from the work of redemption; and though there was grief among those who loved Him on earth, yet there was joy in heaven. Glorious to the eyes of heavenly beings was the promise of the future. A restored creation, a redeemed race, that having conquered sin could never fall,--this, the result to flow from Christ's completed work, God and angels saw. With this scene the day upon which Jesus rested is forever linked. For "His work is perfect;" and "whatsoever God doeth, it shall be forever." Deut. 32:4; Eccl. 3:14. When there shall be a "restitution of all things, which God hath spoken by the mouth of all His holy prophets since the world began" (Acts 3:21), the creation Sabbath, the [769-770] day on which Jesus lay at rest in Joseph's tomb, will still be a day of rest and rejoicing. Heaven and earth will unite in praise, as "from one Sabbath to another" (Isa. 66:23) the nations of the saved shall bow in joyful worship to God and the Lamb.

In the closing events of the crucifixion day, fresh evidence was given of the fulfillment of prophecy, and new witness borne to Christ's divinity. When the darkness had lifted from the cross, and the Saviour's dying cry had been uttered, immediately another voice was heard, saying, "Truly this was the Son of God." Matt. 27:54.

These words were said in no whispered tones. All eyes were turned to see whence they came. Who had spoken? It was the centurion, the Roman soldier. The divine patience of the Saviour, and His sudden death, with the cry of victory upon His lips, had impressed this heathen. In the bruised, broken body hanging upon the cross, the centurion recognized the form of the Son of God. He could not refrain from confessing his faith. Thus again evidence was given that our Redeemer was to see of the travail of His soul. Upon the very day of His death, three men, differing widely from one another, had declared their faith,--he who commanded the Roman guard, he who bore the cross of the Saviour, and he who died upon the cross at His side.

As evening drew on, an unearthly stillness hung over Calvary. The crowd dispersed, and many returned to Jerusalem greatly changed in spirit from what they had been in the morning. Many had flocked to the crucifixion from curiosity, and not from hatred toward Christ. Still they believed the accusations of the priests, and looked upon Christ as a malefactor. Under an unnatural excitement they had united with the mob in railing against Him. But when the earth was wrapped in blackness, and they stood accused by their own consciences, they felt guilty of a great wrong. No jest or mocking laughter was heard in the midst of that fearful gloom; and when it was lifted, they made their way to their homes in solemn silence. They were convinced that the charges of the priests were false, that Jesus was no pretender; and a few weeks later, when Peter preached upon the day of Pentecost, they were among the thousands who became converts to Christ.

But the Jewish leaders were unchanged by the events they had witnessed. Their hatred of Jesus had not abated. The darkness that had mantled the earth at the crucifixion was not more dense than that which still enveloped the minds of the priests and rulers. At His birth the star [770-771] had known Christ, and had guided the wise men to the manger where He lay. The heavenly hosts had known Him, and had sung His praise over the plains of Bethlehem. The sea had known His voice, and had obeyed His command. Disease and death had recognized His authority, and had yielded to Him their

1. "'Truly this was the Son of God'...The divine p_____ of the Savior, and His sudden death, with the cry of victory upon His lips, had impressed this heathen. In the bruised, broken body hanging upon the cross, the centurion recognized the form of the Son of God. He could not r_____ from confessing his faith." (770). Lord, when I face another spiritual failure, may I hear Your cry of victory. May I not give up, feeling defeated, but believe Your victory, be uplifted and hopeful. How do I confess my faith? _____

_____

_____

2. "Many returned to Jerusalem greatly changed in s_____ from what they had been in the morning...they stood accused by their own c_____ ... They were c_____ _____ that the charges of the high priests were false, that Jesus was no p____ _____." Lord, I am trying to imagine how I would feel if I had just united with the mob in railing against You, and participated in the cause of Your death: _____

_____. And the tragedy is, I keep doing it! __

_____

_____

_____

3. "Inanimate nature had k_____ Christ, and had born witness to His divinity. But the priests and ruler of Israel knew n_____ the Son of God." (771). Is my appreciation of You, Lord, any greater than what the inanimate objects have?

———————————
———————————
———————————

4. "They d_____ the dead Christ more, far more, than they had ever f_____ the living Christ." The aftermath of sin is never pleasant, is it Lord? Would You please bring that thought to my mind, as I am being tempted? ——————

———————————
———————————

5. "The S_____ was now drawing on, and it would be a violation of its s_____ for the bodies to hang upon the cross." What's the dichotomy?

———————————

_____ Lord, show me how I can be zealous towards keeping one commandment (4th), and yet be blind to my falling way short in another (sixth):

———————————
———————————
———————————

How do I avoid that trap?
———————————

prey. The sun had known Him, and at the sight of His dying anguish, had hidden its face of light. The rocks had known Him, and had shivered into fragments at His cry. Inanimate nature had known Christ, and had borne witness to His divinity. But the priests and rulers of Israel knew not the Son of God.

Yet the priests and rulers were not at rest. They had carried out their purpose in putting Christ to death; but they did not feel the sense of victory they had expected. Even in the hour of their apparent triumph, they were harassed with doubts as to what would next take place. They had heard the cry, "It is finished." "Father, into Thy hands I commend My spirit." John 19:30; Luke 23:46. They had seen the rocks rent, and had felt the mighty earthquake, and they were restless and uneasy.

They had been jealous of Christ's influence with the people when living; they were jealous of Him even in death. They dreaded the dead Christ more, far more, than they had ever feared the living Christ. They dreaded to have the attention of the people directed any further to the events attending His crucifixion. They feared the results of that day's work. Not on any account would they have had His body remain on the cross during the Sabbath. The Sabbath was now drawing on, and it would be a violation of its sanctity for the bodies to hang upon the cross. So, using this as a pretext, the leading Jews requested Pilate that the death of the victims might be hastened, and their bodies be removed before the setting of the sun.

Pilate was as unwilling as they for the body of Jesus to remain upon the cross. His consent having been obtained, the legs of the two thieves were broken to hasten their death; but Jesus was found to be already dead. The rude soldiers had been softened by what they had heard and seen of Christ, and they were restrained from breaking His limbs. Thus in the offering of the Lamb of God was fulfilled the law of the Passover, "They shall leave none of it unto the morning, nor break any bone of it: according to all the ordinances of the Passover they shall keep it." Num. 9:12

The priests and rulers were amazed to find that Christ was dead. Death by the cross was a lingering process; it was difficult to determine [771-772] when life had ceased. It was an unheard-of thing for one to die within six hours of crucifixion. The priests wished to make sure of the death of Jesus, and at their suggestion a soldier thrust a spear into the Saviour's side. From the wound thus made, there flowed two copious and distinct streams, one of blood, the other of water. This was noted by all the beholders, and John states the occurrence very definitely. He says, "One of the soldiers with a spear pierced His side, and forthwith came there out blood and water. And he that saw it bare record, and his record is true: and he knoweth that he saith true, that ye might believe. For these things were done, that the scripture should be fulfilled, A bone of Him shall not be broken. And again another scripture saith, They shall look on Him whom they pierced." John 19:34-37.

After the resurrection the priests and rulers circulated the report that Christ did not die upon the cross, that He merely fainted, and was afterward revived. Another report affirmed that it was not a real body of flesh and bone, but the likeness of a body, that was laid in the tomb. The action of the Roman soldiers disproves these falsehoods. They broke not His legs, because He was already dead. To satisfy the priests, they pierced His side. Had not life been already extinct, this wound would have caused instant death.

But it was not the spear thrust, it was not the pain of the cross, that caused the death of Jesus. That cry, uttered "with a loud voice" (Matt. 27:50; Luke 23:46), at the moment of death, the stream of blood and water that flowed from His side, declared that He died of a broken heart. His heart was broken by mental anguish. He was slain by the sin of the world.

With the death of Christ the hopes of His disciples perished. They looked upon His closed eyelids and drooping head, His hair matted with blood, His pierced hands and feet, and their anguish was indescribable. Until the last they had not believed that He would die; they could hardly believe that He was really dead. Overwhelmed with sorrow, they did not recall His words foretelling this very scene. Nothing that He had said now gave them comfort. They saw only the cross and its bleeding Victim. The future seemed dark with despair. Their faith in Jesus had perished; but never had they loved their Lord as now. Never before had they so felt His worth, and their need of His presence.

Even in death, Christ's body was very precious to His disciples. They longed to give Him an honored

_____ May I so value our relationship, that my focus is not on keeping the commandments, but on keeping the relationship, our abiding together; that the desire to be in harmony with Your will and law will naturally follow: _____

6. "He died of a broken heart. His heart was broken by mental a_____." (772). Lord, I need this sensitivity to the heinous nature of sin. Will this walk of beholding Your life of love and purity increase my response to Your love and purity, including recoiling from sin? _____

Change my heart, O Lord!

7. "The hopes of the disciples perished...Their f_____ in Jesus had perished; but never had they l_____ their Lord as now. Never before had they so felt His w_____, and their need of His presence."

Lord, why do I wait till the loss of a loved one, to realize their worth and the value of a loving relationship? I guess that is why I am walking daily, to share that love now, and not have regrets, when it is too late:

_____

_____

_____

burial, but knew not how to accomplish [772-773] this. Treason against the Roman government was the crime for which Jesus was condemned, and persons put to death for this offense were consigned to a burial ground especially provided for such criminals. The disciple John with the women from Galilee had remained at the cross. They could not leave the body of their Lord to be handled by the unfeeling soldiers, and buried in a dishonored grave. Yet they could not prevent it. They could obtain no favors from the Jewish authorities, and they had no influence with Pilate.

In this emergency, Joseph of Arimathaea and Nicodemus came to the help of the disciples. Both these men were members of the Sanhedrin, and were acquainted with Pilate. Both were men of wealth and influence. They were determined that the body of Jesus should have an honorable burial.

Joseph went boldly to Pilate, and begged from him the body of Jesus. For the first time, Pilate learned that Jesus was really dead. Conflicting reports had reached him in regard to the events attending the crucifixion, but the knowledge of Christ's death had been purposely kept from him. Pilate had been warned by the priests and rulers against deception by Christ's disciples in regard to His body. Upon hearing Joseph's request, he therefore sent for the centurion who had charge at the cross, and learned for a certainty of the death of Jesus. He also drew from him an account of the scenes of Calvary, confirming the testimony of Joseph.

The request of Joseph was granted. While John was troubled about the burial of his Master, Joseph returned with Pilate's order for the body of Christ; and Nicodemus came bringing a costly mixture of myrrh and aloes, of about a hundred pounds' weight, for His embalming. The most honored in all Jerusalem could not have been shown more respect in death. The disciples were astonished to see these wealthy rulers as much interested as they themselves in the burial of their Lord.

Neither Joseph nor Nicodemus had openly accepted the Saviour while He was living. They knew that such a step would exclude them from the Sanhedrin, and they hoped to protect Him by their influence in its councils. For a time they had seemed to succeed; but the wily priests, seeing their favor to Christ, had thwarted their plans. In their absence Jesus had been condemned and delivered to be crucified. Now that He was dead, they no longer concealed their attachment to Him. While the disciples feared to show themselves openly as His followers, [773-774] Joseph and Nicodemus came boldly to their aid. The help of these rich and honored men was greatly needed at this time. They could do for their dead Master what it was impossible for the poor disciples to do; and their wealth and influence protected them, in a great measure, from the malice of the priests and rulers.

Gently and reverently they removed with their own hands the body of Jesus from the cross. Their tears of sympathy fell fast as they looked upon His bruised and lacerated form. Joseph owned a new tomb, hewn in a rock. This he was reserving for himself; but it was near Calvary, and he now prepared it for Jesus. The body, together with the spices brought by Nicodemus, was carefully wrapped in a linen sheet, and the Redeemer was borne to the tomb. There the three disciples straightened the mangled limbs, and folded the bruised hands upon the pulseless breast. The Galilean women came to see that all had been done that could be done for the lifeless form of their beloved Teacher. Then they saw the heavy stone rolled against the entrance of the tomb, and the Saviour was left at rest. The women were last at the cross, and last at the tomb of Christ. While the evening shades were gathering, Mary Magdalene and the other Marys lingered about the resting place of their Lord, shedding tears of sorrow over the fate of Him whom they loved. "And they returned, . . . and rested the Sabbath day according to the commandment." Luke 23:56.

That was a never-to-be-forgotten Sabbath to the sorrowing disciples, and also to the priests, rulers, scribes, and people. At the setting of the sun on the evening of the preparation day the trumpets sounded, signifying that the Sabbath had begun. The Passover was observed as it had been for centuries, while He to whom it pointed had been slain by wicked hands, and lay in Joseph's tomb. On the Sabbath the courts of the temple were filled with worshipers. The high priest from Golgotha was there, splendidly robed in his sacerdotal garments. White-turbaned priests, full of activity, performed their duties. But some present were not at rest as the blood of bulls and goats was offered for sin. They were not conscious that type had met antitype, that an infinite

8. "That was a never-to-be-f_____ Sabbath to the sorrowing disciples, and also to the priests, rulers, scribes, and people...The P_____ was observed as it had been for centuries, while He to whom it pointed had been s_____ by wicked hands, and l_____ in Joseph's tomb...Never

before had that service been witnessed with such c_____ feelings...A sense of strangeness pervaded everything." (774). Lord, may my devotions to You engage my heart and mind, be relevant to me and to You, true to Your vision for me: ____

_____

_____

_____

_____

sacrifice had been made for the sins of the world. They knew not that there was no further value in the performance of the ritual service. But never before had that service been witnessed with such conflicting feelings. The trumpets and musical instruments and the voices of the singers were as loud and clear as usual. But a sense of strangeness pervaded everything. [774-775] One after another inquired about a strange event that had taken place. Hitherto the most holy place had been sacredly guarded from intrusion. But now it was open to all eyes. The heavy veil of tapestry, made of pure linen, and beautifully wrought with gold, scarlet, and purple, was rent from top to bottom. The place where Jehovah had met with the high priest, to communicate His glory, the place that had been God's sacred audience chamber, lay open to every eye,--a place no longer recognized by the Lord. With gloomy presentiments the priests ministered before the altar. The uncovering of the sacred mystery of the most holy place filled them with dread of coming calamity.

Many minds were busy with thoughts started by the scenes of Calvary. From the crucifixion to the resurrection many sleepless eyes were constantly searching the prophecies, some to learn the full meaning of the feast they were then celebrating, some to find evidence that Jesus was not what He claimed to be; and others with sorrowful hearts were searching for proofs that He was the true Messiah. Though searching with different objects in view, all were convicted of the same truth,--that prophecy had been fulfilled in the events of the past few days, and that the Crucified One was the world's Redeemer. Many who at that time united in the service never again took part in the paschal rites. Many even of the priests were convicted of the true character of Jesus. Their searching of the prophecies had not been in vain, and after His resurrection they acknowledged Him as the Son of God.

Nicodemus, when he saw Jesus lifted up on the cross, remembered His words spoken by night in the Mount of Olives: "As Moses lifted up the serpent in the wilderness, even so must the Son of man be lifted up: that whosoever believeth in Him should not perish, but have eternal life." John 3:14, 15. On that Sabbath, when Christ lay in the grave, Nicodemus had opportunity for reflection. A clearer light now illuminated his mind, and the words which Jesus had spoken to him were no longer mysterious. He felt that he had lost much by not connecting himself with the Saviour during His life. Now he recalled the events of Calvary. The prayer of Christ for His murderers and His answer to the petition of the dying thief spoke to the heart of the learned councilor. Again he looked upon the Saviour in His agony; again he heard that last cry, "It is finished," spoken like the words of a conqueror. Again he beheld the reeling earth, the darkened heavens, the rent veil, the shivered rocks, and his faith was forever established. The very event that destroyed [775-776] the hopes of the disciples convinced Joseph and Nicodemus of the divinity of Jesus. Their fears were overcome by the courage of a firm and unwavering faith.

Never had Christ attracted the attention of the multitude as now that He was laid in the tomb. According to their practice, the people brought their sick and suffering ones to the temple courts, inquiring, Who can tell us of Jesus of Nazareth? Many had come from far to find Him who had healed the sick and raised the dead. On every side was heard the cry, We want Christ the Healer! Upon this occasion those who were thought to show indications of the leprosy were examined by the priests. Many were forced to hear their husbands, wives, or children pronounced leprous, and doomed to go forth from the shelter of their homes and the care of their friends, to warn off the stranger with the mournful cry, "Unclean, unclean!" The friendly hands of Jesus of Nazareth, that never refused to touch with healing the loathsome leper, were folded on His breast. The lips that had answered his petition with the comforting words, "I will; be thou clean" (Matt. 8:3), were now silent. Many appealed to the chief priests and rulers for sympathy and relief, but in vain. Apparently they were determined to have the living Christ among them again. With persistent earnestness they asked for Him. They would not be turned away. But they were driven from the temple courts, and soldiers were stationed at the gates to keep back the multitude that came with their sick and dying, demanding entrance.

The sufferers who had come to be healed by the Saviour sank under their disappointment. The streets were filled with mourning. The sick were dying for want of the healing touch of Jesus. Physicians were consulted

9. Nicodemus "felt that he had l_____ much by not c_____ himself to the Savior during His life." (775). Lord, help me to see the emptiness of my day when I don't connect with You that morning. How do overcome the comfortableness with that loss? _____

_____
_____
_____
_____
_____

10. Nicodemus "recalled the events of Calvary... again he heard that _____ _____ cry, 'It is finished,' spoken like the words of a c_____... The very event that destroyed the hopes of the disciples c_____ Joseph and Nicodemus of the divinity of Jesus." (775, 776). What's the difference?

_____
_____
_____
_____

in vain; there was no skill like that of Him who lay in Joseph's tomb.

The mourning cries of the suffering ones brought home to thousands of minds the conviction that a great light had gone out of the world. Without Christ, the earth was blackness and darkness. Many whose voices had swelled the cry of "Crucify Him, crucify Him," now realized the calamity that had fallen upon them, and would as eagerly have cried, Give us Jesus! had He still been alive.

When the people learned that Jesus had been put to death by the priests, inquiries were made regarding His death. The particulars of His trial were kept as private as possible; but during the time when He was in the grave, His name was on thousands of lips, and reports of [776-777] His mock trial, and of the inhumanity of the priests and rulers, were circulated everywhere. By men of intellect these priests and rulers were called upon to explain the prophecies of the Old Testament concerning the Messiah, and while trying to frame some falsehood in reply, they became like men insane. The prophecies that pointed to Christ's sufferings and death they could not explain, and many inquirers were convinced that the Scriptures had been fulfilled.

The revenge which the priests had thought would be so sweet was already bitterness to them. They knew that they were meeting the severe censure of the people; they knew that the very ones whom they had influenced against Jesus were now horrified by their own shameful work. These priests had tried to believe Jesus a deceiver; but it was in vain. Some of them had stood by the grave of Lazarus, and had seen the dead brought back to life. They trembled for fear that Christ would Himself rise from the dead, and again appear before them. They had heard Him declare that He had power to lay down His life and to take it again. They remembered that He had said, "Destroy this temple, and in three days I will raise it up." John 2:19. Judas had told them the words spoken by Jesus to the disciples while on the last journey to Jerusalem: "Behold, we go up to Jerusalem; and the Son of man shall be betrayed unto the chief priests and unto the scribes, and they shall condemn Him to death, and shall deliver Him to the Gentiles to mock, and to scourge, and to crucify Him: and the third day He shall rise again." Matt. 20:18, 19. When they heard

11. "The revenge which the priests had thought would be so s_____ was already b_____ to them." (777). Lord, how is the enemy able to continue enticing me with this sweetness, when the reality is bitterness? When will I learn? _____

_____

It is Your character that is truly sweet and satisfying:
_____
_____
_____

these words, they had mocked and ridiculed. But now they remembered that Christ's predictions had so far been fulfilled. He had said that He would rise again the third day, and who could say that this also would not come to pass? They longed to shut out these thoughts, but they could not. Like their father, the devil, they believed and trembled.

Now that the frenzy of excitement was past, the image of Christ would intrude upon their minds. They beheld Him as He stood serene and uncomplaining before His enemies, suffering without a murmur their taunts and abuse. All the events of His trial and crucifixion came back to them with an overpowering conviction that He was the Son of God. They felt that He might at any time stand before them, the accused to become the accuser, the condemned to condemn, the slain to demand justice in the death of His murderers.

They could rest little upon the Sabbath. Though they would not step [777-778] over a Gentile's threshold for fear of defilement, yet they held a council concerning the body of Christ. Death and the grave must hold Him whom they had crucified. "The chief priests and Pharisees came together unto Pilate, saying, Sir, we remember that that deceiver said, while He was yet alive, After three days I will rise again. Command therefore that the sepulcher be made sure until the third day, lest His disciples come by night, and steal Him away, and say unto the people, He is risen from the dead: so the last error shall be worse than the first. Pilate said unto them, Ye have a watch: go your way, make it as sure as ye can." Matt. 27:62-65.

The priests gave directions for securing the sepulcher. A great stone had been placed before the opening. Across this stone they placed cords, securing the ends to the solid rock, and sealing them with the Roman seal. The stone could not be moved without breaking the seal. A guard of one hundred soldiers was then stationed around the sepulcher to prevent it from being tampered with. The priests did all they could to keep Christ's body where it had been laid. He was sealed as securely in His tomb as if He were to remain there through all time.

So weak men counseled and planned. Little did these murderers realize the uselessness of their efforts. But by their action God was glorified. The very efforts made to prevent Christ's resurrection are the most con-

12. "The very efforts made to p_____ Christ's resurrection are the most c_____

__ arguments in its proof."
(778). Lord, when Satan
throws darkness and doubt
my way, may I experience
a greater reliance on You, a
greater conviction of Your
nearness: _____
_____

Prayer journal: _____
_____
_____
_____
_____
_____
_____
_____

vincing arguments in its proof. The greater the number
of soldiers placed around the tomb, the stronger would
be the testimony that He had risen. Hundreds of years
before the death of Christ, the Holy Spirit had declared
through the psalmist, "Why do the heathen rage, and the
people imagine a vain thing? The kings of the earth set
themselves, and the rulers take counsel together, against
the Lord, and against His anointed. . . . He that sitteth
in the heavens shall laugh: the Lord shall have them in
derision." Ps. 2:1-4. Roman guards and Roman arms
were powerless to confine the Lord of life within the
tomb. The hour of His release was near.

Chapter 81

"The Lord Is Risen"

[This chapter is based on Matt. 28:2-4, 11-15.]

The night of the first day of the week had worn slowly away. The darkest hour, just before daybreak, had come. Christ was still a prisoner in His narrow tomb. The great stone was in its place; the Roman seal was unbroken; the Roman guards were keeping their watch. And there were unseen watchers. Hosts of evil angels were gathered about the place. Had it been possible, the prince of darkness with his apostate army would have kept forever sealed the tomb that held the Son of God. But a heavenly host surrounded the sepulcher. Angels that excel in strength were guarding the tomb, and waiting to welcome the Prince of life.

"And, behold, there was a great earthquake: for the angel of the Lord descended from heaven." Clothed with the panoply of God, this angel left the heavenly courts. The bright beams of God's glory went before him, and illuminated his pathway. "His countenance was like lightning, and his raiment white as snow: and for fear of him the keepers did shake, and became as dead men."

Now, priests and rulers, where is the power of your guard? Brave soldiers that have never been afraid of human power are now as captives taken without sword or spear. The face they look upon is not the face [779-780] of mortal warrior; it is the face of the mightiest of the Lord's host. This messenger is he who fills the position from which Satan fell. It is he who on the hills of Bethlehem proclaimed Christ's birth. The earth trembles at his approach, the hosts of darkness flee, and as he rolls away the stone, heaven seems to come down to the earth. The soldiers see him removing the stone as he would a pebble, and hear him cry, Son of God, come forth; Thy Father calls Thee. They see Jesus come forth from the grave, and hear Him proclaim over the rent sepulcher, "I am the resurrection, and the life." As He comes forth in majesty and glory, the angel host bow low in adoration before the Redeemer, and welcome

1. "Hosts of evil a_____ ____ were gathered about the place...A heavenly h_____ surrounded the sepulcher." What was the atmosphere, Lord, between these two groups?

_____

_____

_____

May I recognize the significance in my life, of the conflict between these two forces, as they vie for my loyalty:

_____

_____

_____

_____

Him with songs of praise.

An earthquake marked the hour when Christ laid down His life, and another earthquake witnessed the moment when He took it up in triumph. He who had vanquished death and the grave came forth from the tomb with the tread of a conqueror, amid the reeling of the earth, the flashing of lightning, and the roaring of thunder. When He shall come to the earth again, He will shake "not the earth only, but also heaven." "The earth shall reel to and fro like a drunkard, and shall be removed like a cottage." "The heavens shall be rolled together as a scroll;" "the elements shall melt with fervent heat, the earth also and the works that are therein shall be burned up." But "the Lord will be the hope of His people, and the strength of the children of Israel." Heb. 12:26; Isa. 24:20; 34:4; 2 Peter 3:10; Joel 3:16.

At the death of Jesus the soldiers had beheld the earth wrapped in darkness at midday; but at the resurrection they saw the brightness of the angels illuminate the night, and heard the inhabitants of heaven singing with great joy and triumph: Thou hast vanquished Satan and the powers of darkness; Thou hast swallowed up death in victory!

Christ came forth from the tomb glorified, and the Roman guard beheld Him. Their eyes were riveted upon the face of Him whom they had so recently mocked and derided. In this glorified Being they beheld the prisoner whom they had seen in the judgment hall, the one for whom they had plaited a crown of thorns. This was the One who had stood unresisting before Pilate and Herod, His form lacerated by the cruel scourge. This was He who had been nailed to the cross, at whom the priests and rulers, full of self-satisfaction, had wagged their heads, saying, "He saved others; Himself He cannot save." Matt. 27:42. This was He who had been laid in Joseph's new tomb. The decree of heaven had [780-781] loosed the captive. Mountains piled upon mountains over His sepulcher could not have prevented Him from coming forth.

At sight of the angels and the glorified Saviour the Roman guard had fainted and become as dead men. When the heavenly train was hidden from their view, they arose to their feet, and as quickly as their trembling limbs could carry them, made their way to the gate of the garden. Staggering like drunken men, they

2. "At the death of Jesus the soldiers had beheld the earth wrapped in d_____ _____ at midday; but at the resurrection they saw the b_____ of the angels illuminate the night...The Roman guard beheld Him. Their eyes were riveted upon the face of Him whom they had so recently mocked and derided." (780). What a contrast Lord! I want to see Your glorified face. And may this vision keep me from mocking You, from denying You, from betraying You: _____
_____
_____
_____

hurried on to the city, telling those whom they met the wonderful news. They were making their way to Pilate, but their report had been carried to the Jewish authorities, and the chief priests and rulers sent for them to be brought first into their presence. A strange appearance those soldiers presented. Trembling with fear, their faces colorless, they bore testimony to the resurrection of Christ. The soldiers told all, just as they had seen it; they had not had time to think or speak anything but the truth. With painful utterance they said, It was the Son of God who was crucified; we have heard an angel proclaiming Him as the Majesty of heaven, the King of glory.

The faces of the priests were as those of the dead. Caiaphas tried to speak. His lips moved, but they uttered no sound. The soldiers were about to leave the council room, when a voice stayed them. Caiaphas had at last found speech. Wait, wait, he said. Tell no one the things you have seen.

A lying report was then given to the soldiers. "Say ye," said the priests, "His disciples came by night, and stole Him away while we [781-782] slept." Here the priests overreached themselves. How could the soldiers say that the disciples had stolen the body while they slept? If they were asleep, how could they know? And if the disciples had been proved guilty of stealing Christ's body, would not the priests have been first to condemn them? Or if the sentinels had slept at the tomb, would not the priests have been foremost in accusing them to Pilate?

The soldiers were horrified at the thought of bringing upon themselves the charge of sleeping at their post. This was an offense punishable with death. Should they bear false witness, deceiving the people, and placing their own lives in peril? Had they not kept their weary watch with sleepless vigilance? How could they stand the trial, even for the sake of money, if they perjured themselves?

In order to silence the testimony they feared, the priests promised to secure the safety of the guard, saying that Pilate would not desire to have such a report circulated any more than they did. The Roman soldiers sold their integrity to the Jews for money. They came in before the priests burdened with a most startling message of truth; they went out with a burden of money, and

3. "A strange appearance those soldiers presented. Trembling with fear, their faces c_____, they bore testimony to the resurrection of Christ... They had not had t_____ ____ to think or speak anything but the truth." (781). Lord, help me to follow those first instincts, not to calculate on how to cover myself, to shift the blame, but to be transparent. Show me instances that reveal my heart, Lord: _____
_____
_____
_____

4. Pilate "himself privately questioned the guard. They, fearing for their own safety, dared not c_____ anything, and Pilate drew from them an account of all that had taken place… from that time there was no p_____ for him." (782). Lord, thank You for Your Spirit, that gently persists. When I hear a spiritual truth, and then hesitate to be open to it, to apply it, may there be no peace for me, only an unsettled feeling, till I embrace the truth and experience closer harmony with You:

_____
_____
_____
_____

5. "When Jesus was laid in the grave, Satan triumphed. He dared to hope that the Savior would not t_____ up His life again…When He saw Christ come forth in triumph, he k_____ that his kingdom would have an e_____, and that he must finally die." What is it about the resurrection that secures this?

_____
_____
_____
_____

All of Lucifer's supposed improvements to running the universe prove false. And having chosen a pathway independent of the only source of life, that life

on their tongues a lying report which had been framed for them by the priests.

Meanwhile the report of Christ's resurrection had been carried to Pilate. Though Pilate was responsible for having given Christ up to die, he had been comparatively unconcerned. While he had condemned the Saviour unwillingly, and with a feeling of pity, he had felt no real compunction until now. In terror he now shut himself within his house, determined to see no one. But the priests made their way into his presence, told the story which they had invented, and urged him to overlook the sentinels' neglect of duty. Before consenting to this, he himself privately questioned the guard. They, fearing for their own safety, dared not conceal anything, and Pilate drew from them an account of all that had taken place. He did not prosecute the matter further, but from that time there was no peace for him.

When Jesus was laid in the grave, Satan triumphed. He dared to hope that the Saviour would not take up His life again. He claimed the Lord's body, and set his guard about the tomb, seeking to hold Christ a prisoner. He was bitterly angry when his angels fled at the approach of the heavenly messenger. When he saw Christ come forth in triumph, he knew that his kingdom would have an end, and that he must finally die. [782-785]

The priests, in putting Christ to death, had made themselves the tools of Satan. Now they were entirely in his power. They were entangled in a snare from which they saw no escape but in continuing their warfare against Christ. When they heard the report of His resurrection, they feared the wrath of the people. They felt that their own lives were in danger. The only hope for them was to prove Christ an impostor by denying that He had risen. They bribed the soldiers, and secured Pilate's silence. They spread their lying reports far and near. But there were witnesses whom they could not silence. Many had heard of the soldiers' testimony to Christ's resurrection. And certain of the dead who came forth with Christ appeared to many, and declared that He had risen. Reports were brought to the priests of persons who had seen these risen ones, and heard their testimony. The priests and rulers were in continual dread, lest in walking the streets, or within the privacy of their own homes, they should come face to face with Christ. They felt that there was no safety for them. Bolts and bars were but poor protection against the Son of God. By day and by night that awful scene in the judgment hall, when they had cried, "His blood be on us, and on our children," was before them. Matt. 27:25. Nevermore would the memory of that scene fade from their minds. Nevermore would peaceful sleep come to their pillows.

will be lost. Lord, may I recognize in every temptation, the enemy's goal of eternally separating me from You, and by Your abiding presence and power, resist him and the temptation:

_____
_____
_____
_____

6. The priests "felt that their own lives were in d_____ __... They b_____ the soldiers, and secured Pilate's s_____. They spread their lying reports far and near...They were in c_____ dread, lest in walking the streets, or in the privacy of their own homes, they should come f_____ to f _____ with Christ." (785). Lord, I long for just the opposite, and that is the joy of seeing You face to face. May I not cherish anything, or hang on to anything, that causes me to avoid you, or extending less than a warm and genuine welcome to You: _____

_____
_____
_____

When the voice of the mighty angel was heard at Christ's tomb, saying, Thy Father calls Thee, the Saviour came forth from the grave by the life that was in Himself. Now was proved the truth of His words, "I lay down My life, that I might take it again. . . . I have power to lay it down, and I have power to take it again." Now was fulfilled the prophecy He had spoken to the priests and rulers, "Destroy this temple, and in three days I will raise it up." John 10:17, 18; 2:19.

Over the rent sepulcher of Joseph, Christ had proclaimed in triumph, "I am the resurrection, and the life." These words could be spoken only by the Deity.

7. "The Savior came forth from the grave by the life that was in H_____ _____. Now was proved the truth of His words, 'I lay d_____ My life, that I might take it again...I have power to lay it down, and I have power to take it again.'"

What caused His death?

_____
_____
_____
_____

(His willingness to be made my sin, experiencing the fullness of heinous sin, which is separation from the Father, which is a broken heart). Lord, only by Your power, can I be resurrected from the captivity and death of sin. I invite Your abiding presence and resurrection power into my life: _____
_____
_____
_____

8. "So Christ the first f___ _____ represented the great spiritual harvest to be gathered for the kingdom of God...Those who came forth from the grave at Christ's resurrection were raised to e_____ ____ life." (786). Lord, I pray for and long for, no longer being the captive of Satan. I am Yours, Your child, a fruit of Your great sacrifice: _____
_____
_____
_____

All created beings live by the will and power of God. They are dependent recipients of the life of God. From the highest seraph to the humblest animate being, all are replenished from the Source of life. Only He who is one with God could say, I have power to lay down My life, and I have power to take it again. In His divinity, Christ possessed the power to break the bonds of death.

Christ arose from the dead as the first fruits of those that slept. He was the antitype of the wave sheaf, and His resurrection took place on [785-786] the very day when the wave sheaf was to be presented before the Lord. For more than a thousand years this symbolic ceremony had been performed. From the harvest fields the first heads of ripened grain were gathered, and when the people went up to Jerusalem to the Passover, the sheaf of first fruits was waved as a thank offering before the Lord. Not until this was presented could the sickle be put to the grain, and it be gathered into sheaves. The sheaf dedicated to God represented the harvest. So Christ the first fruits represented the great spiritual harvest to be gathered for the kingdom of God. His resurrection is the type and pledge of the resurrection of all the righteous dead. "For if we believe that Jesus died and rose again, even so them also which sleep in Jesus will God bring with Him." 1 Thess. 4:14.

As Christ arose, He brought from the grave a multitude of captives. The earthquake at His death had rent open their graves, and when He arose, they came forth with Him. They were those who had been co-laborers with God, and who at the cost of their lives had borne testimony to the truth. Now they were to be witnesses for Him who had raised them from the dead.

During His ministry, Jesus had raised the dead to life. He had raised the son of the widow of Nain, and the ruler's daughter and Lazarus. But these were not clothed with immortality. After they were raised, they were still subject to death. But those who came forth from the grave at Christ's resurrection were raised to everlasting life. They ascended with Him as trophies of His victory over death and the grave. These, said Christ, are no longer the captives of Satan; I have redeemed them. I have brought them from the grave as the first fruits of My power, to be with Me where I am, nevermore to see death or experience sorrow.

These went into the city, and appeared unto many,

declaring, Christ has risen from the dead, and we be risen with Him. Thus was immortalized the sacred truth of the resurrection. The risen saints bore witness to the truth of the words, "Thy dead men shall live, together with My dead body shall they arise." Their resurrection was an illustration of the fulfillment of the prophecy, "Awake and sing, ye that dwell in dust: for thy dew is as the dew of herbs, and the earth shall cast out the dead." Isa. 26:19.

To the believer, Christ is the resurrection and the life. In our Saviour the life that was lost through sin is restored; for He has life in Himself [786-787] to quicken whom He will. He is invested with the right to give immortality. The life that He laid down in humanity, He takes up again, and gives to humanity. "I am come," He said, "that they might have life, and that they might have it more abundantly." "Whosoever drinketh of the water that I shall give him shall never thirst; but the water that I shall give him shall be in him a well of water springing up into everlasting life." "Whoso eateth My flesh, and drinketh My blood, hath eternal life; and I will raise him up at the last day." John 10:10; 4:14; 6:54.

To the believer, death is but a small matter. Christ speaks of it as if it were of little moment. "If a man keep My saying, he shall never see death," "he shall never taste of death." To the Christian, death is but a sleep, a moment of silence and darkness. The life is hid with Christ in God, and "when Christ, who is our life, shall appear, then shall ye also appear with Him in glory." John 8:51, 52; Col. 3:4.

The voice that cried from the cross, "It is finished," was heard among the dead. It pierced the walls of sepulchers, and summoned the sleepers to arise. Thus will it be when the voice of Christ shall be heard from heaven. That voice will penetrate the graves and unbar the tombs, and the dead in Christ shall arise. At the Saviour's resurrection a few graves were opened, but at His second coming all the precious dead shall hear His voice, and shall come forth to glorious, immortal life. The same power that raised Christ from the dead will raise His church, and glorify it with Him, above all principalities, above all powers, above every name that is named, not only in this world, but also in the world to come.

9. "To the believer, Christ is the resurrection and the l_____. In our Savior the life that was lost through sin is r_____...He is invested with the r_____ ____ to give immortality." (786, 787). Lord, You will win the hearts, devotion and loyalty of the believing universe. Satan is silenced; his charges against You regarding Your use of power and fairness are groundless and forever refuted. Lord, may you today help me realize the utter bankruptcy of Satan's logic and enticements. You alone are the way, the truth, and the life. How does Satan get me?

_____
_____
_____
_____

Prayer journal: _____
_____
_____
_____
_____
_____
_____

Chapter 82

"Why Weepest Thou?"

[This chapter is based on Matt. 28:1, 5-8; Mark 16:1-8; Luke 24:1-12; John 20:1-18.]

1. "The sun of their h___ _____ had set, and night had settled down on their h_____." Do I have such a relationship with You, Lord, that a day without You is as night?

_____

_____

_____

_____

2. "Who shall roll us away the s_____?... The heavens were s_____ _____ alight with the glory that came not from the rising sun. The earth t_____. They saw the great stone was rolled away. The grave was e__ _____." This glory and trembling must not be the actual resurrection, but possibly an additional testimony just for them. And, after nearly two thousand years, the event still has power for me. Thank You Lord, for this encouragement; and may I claim the power of Your victory: __

_____

_____

_____

The women who had stood by the cross of Christ waited and watched for the hours of the Sabbath to pass. On the first day of the week, very early, they made their way to the tomb, taking with them precious spices to anoint the Saviour's body. They did not think about His rising from the dead. The sun of their hope had set, and night had settled down on their hearts. As they walked, they recounted Christ's works of mercy and His words of comfort. But they remembered not His words, "I will see you again." John 16:22.

Ignorant of what was even then taking place, they drew near the garden, saying as they went, "Who shall roll us away the stone from the door of the sepulcher?" They knew that they could not remove the stone, yet they kept on their way. And lo, the heavens were suddenly alight with glory that came not from the rising sun. The earth trembled. They saw that the great stone was rolled away. The grave was empty.

The women had not all come to the tomb from the same direction. Mary Magdalene was the first to reach the place; and upon seeing that the stone was removed, she hurried away to tell the disciples. Meanwhile the other women came up. A light was shining about the tomb, but the body of Jesus was not there. As they lingered about the place, suddenly they saw that they were not alone. A young man clothed in shining garments was sitting by the tomb. It was the angel who had rolled away the stone. He had taken the guise of humanity that he [788-789] might not alarm these friends of Jesus. Yet about him the light of the heavenly glory was still shining, and the women were afraid. They turned to flee, but the angel's words stayed their steps. "Fear not ye," he said; "for I know that ye seek Jesus, which was crucified. He is not here: for He is risen, as He said. Come, see the place where the Lord lay. And go quickly, and tell His disciples that He is risen from the dead." Again they look into the tomb, and again they hear the wonderful news. Another angel in human form is there, and he says, "Why seek ye the living among the dead? He is not here, but is risen: remember how He spake unto you when He was yet in Galilee, saying, The Son of man must be delivered into the hands of sinful men, and be crucified, and the third day rise again."

He is risen, He is risen! The women repeat the words again and again. No need now for the anointing spices. The Saviour is living, and not dead. They remember now that when speaking of His death He said that He would rise again. What a day is this to the world! Quickly the women departed from the sepulcher "with fear and great joy; and did run to bring His disciples word."

Mary had not heard the good news. She went to Peter and John with the sorrowful message, "They have taken away the Lord out of the sepulcher, and we know not where they have laid Him." The disciples hurried to the tomb, and found it as Mary had said. They saw the shroud and the napkin, but they did not find their Lord. Yet even here was testimony that He had risen. The graveclothes were not thrown heedlessly aside, but carefully folded, each in a place by itself. John "saw, and believed." He did not yet understand the scripture that Christ must rise from the dead; but he now remembered the Saviour's words foretelling His resurrection.

It was Christ Himself who had placed those graveclothes with such care. When the mighty angel came down to the tomb, he was joined by another, who with his company had been keeping guard over the Lord's body. As the angel from heaven rolled away the stone, the other entered the tomb, and unbound the wrappings from the body of Jesus. But it was the Saviour's hand that folded each, and laid it in its place. In His sight who guides alike the star and the atom, there is nothing unimportant. Order and perfection are seen in all His work.

Mary had followed John and Peter to the tomb; when they returned to Jerusalem, she remained. As she looked into the empty tomb, grief filled her heart. Looking in, she saw the two angels, one at the head and [789-790] the other at the foot where Jesus had lain. "Woman, why weepest thou?" they asked her. "Because they have taken away my Lord," she answered, "and I

3. "Why seek ye the l___ _____ among the dead?" The women "remember n_____ that when speaking of His death He said that he would rise again. What a d_____ is this to the world!" (789). Why had they not understood earlier? _____ _____ Do I use selective listening with You, Lord? _____ _____

_____ Putting myself in the women's shoes, how do I feel with this news? _____ _____ _____ _____ What does it mean to share the news "with fear and great joy?" _____ _____ _____ _____

4. "It was the S_____ ___ hand that folded each [shroud and napkin], and laid it in its place...nothing is u_____." Lord, may I recognize how You guide my life, how You use events and circumstances to nurture my character. Help me not to be casual or indifferent about my walk with You., but rather to be deliberate and joining up with You in the appointments You give me: _____ _____ _____ _____

know not where they have laid Him."

Then she turned away, even from the angels, thinking that she must find someone who could tell her what had been done with the body of Jesus. Another voice addressed her, "Woman, why weepest thou? whom seekest thou?" Through her tear-dimmed eyes, Mary saw the form of a man, and thinking that it was the gardener, she said, "Sir, if thou have borne Him hence, tell me where thou hast laid Him, and I will take Him away." If this rich man's tomb was thought too honorable a burial place for Jesus, she herself would provide a place for Him. There was a grave that Christ's own voice had made vacant, the grave where Lazarus had lain. Might she not there find a burial place for her Lord? She felt that to care for His precious crucified body would be a great consolation to her in her grief.

But now in His own familiar voice Jesus said to her, "Mary." Now she knew that it was not a stranger who was addressing her, and turning she saw before her the living Christ. In her joy she forgot that He had been crucified. Springing toward Him, as if to embrace His feet, she said, "Rabboni." But Christ raised His hand, saying, Detain Me not; "for I am not yet ascended to My Father: but go to My brethren, and say unto them, I ascend unto My Father, and your Father; and to My God, and your God." And Mary went her way to the disciples with the joyful message.

Jesus refused to receive the homage of His people until He had the assurance that His sacrifice was accepted by the Father. He ascended to the heavenly courts, and from God Himself heard the assurance that His atonement for the sins of men had been ample, that through His blood all might gain eternal life. The Father ratified the covenant made with Christ, that He would receive repentant and obedient men, and would love them even as He loves His Son. Christ was to complete His work, and fulfill His pledge to "make a man more precious than fine gold; even a man than the golden wedge of Ophir." Isa. 13:12. All power in heaven and on earth was given to the Prince of Life, and He returned to His followers in a world of sin, that He might impart to them of His power and glory.

While the Saviour was in God's presence, receiving gifts for His church, the disciples thought upon His empty tomb, and mourned and wept. The day that was

5. "Jesus refused to receive the h_____ of His people until He had the a_____ that His sacrifice was accepted by the Father...The Father r_____ the covenant made with Christ, that He would receive repentant and obedient men, and would l_____ them even as he loves His Son." (790). Lord, You didn't change the Father's heart, did You? Your Word clarifies that while I was yet a sinner, God loved me, and You came to die for me (Romans 5:8, John 3:16). Is this covenant ratified, the Father's love ratified, as a demonstration for the accuser and the onlooking universe, of this great controversy, this war between You and the dragon? _____
_____
_____

a day of rejoicing to all heaven was to the disciples a day of uncertainty, confusion, and perplexity. Their unbelief [790-793] in the testimony of the women gives evidence of how low their faith had sunk. The news of Christ's resurrection was so different from what they had anticipated that they could not believe it. It was too good to be true, they thought. They had heard so much of the doctrines and the so-called scientific theories of the Sadducees that the impression made on their minds in regard to the resurrection was vague. They scarcely knew what the resurrection from the dead could mean. They were unable to take in the great subject.

"Go your way," the angels had said to the women, "tell His disciples and Peter that He goeth before you into Galilee: there shall ye see Him, as He said unto you." These angels had been with Christ as guardian angels throughout His life on earth. They had witnessed His trial and crucifixion. They had heard His words to His disciples. This was shown by their message to the disciples, and should have convinced them of its truth. Such words could have come only from the messengers of their risen Lord.

"Tell His disciples and Peter," the angels said. Since the death of Christ, Peter had been bowed down with remorse. His shameful denial of the Lord, and the Saviour's look of love and anguish, were ever before him. Of all the disciples he had suffered most bitterly. To him the assurance is given that his repentance is accepted and his sin forgiven. He is mentioned by name.

"Tell His disciples and Peter that He goeth before you into Galilee: there shall ye see Him." All the disciples had forsaken Jesus, and the call to meet Him again includes them all. He has not cast them off. When Mary Magdalene told them she had seen the Lord, she repeated the call to the meeting in Galilee. And a third time the message was sent to them. After He had ascended to the Father, Jesus appeared to the other women, saying, "All hail. And they came and held Him by the feet, and worshiped Him. Then said Jesus unto them, Be not afraid: go tell My brethren that they go into Galilee, and there shall they see Me."

Christ's first work on earth after His resurrection was to convince His disciples of His undiminished love and tender regard for them. To give them proof that He was their living Saviour, that He had broken the fetters

6. "The day that was a day of rejoicing to all h_____ _____ was to the disciples a day of u_____, confusion, and perplexity. Their unbelief in the testimony of the women gives evidence of how low their f_____ had sunk." (790, 793). Lord, when my faith is weak, direct my thoughts to Your perspective, to better understand how the current challenge is actually an opportunity: __
_____
_____
_____

7. "Since the death of Christ, Peter had been bowed down with r_____ ____. His s_____ denial of the Lord, and the Savior's look of love and a_____, were ever before him...He had suffered most bitterly. To him the a_____ is given that his repentance is accepted and his sin forgiven." What should I do, Lord, with the painful memories of how I let you down? _____
_____
_____
_____
_____

8. "Christ's f_____ work on earth after His resurrection was to convince His disciples of His u_____ love and tender regard for

them...He would draw the b_____ of love still closer around them." Lord, I want to be available to new visions of Your love and compassions every morning. Draw Your bonds of love close and tight! Remind me to take this walk with You every day!

_____
_____
_____
_____

9. "We t_____ that it had been He which should have redeemed Israel... How many are still doing what these disciples did...He is close beside them, but their tear-blinded eyes do not discern Him...

of the tomb, and could no longer be held by the enemy death; to reveal that He had the same heart of love as when He was with them as their beloved Teacher, He appeared to them again and again. He would draw the bonds of love still closer around them. Go tell My brethren, He said, that they meet Me in Galilee. [793-794]

As they heard this appointment, so definitely given, the disciples began to think of Christ's words to them foretelling His resurrection. But even now they did not rejoice. They could not cast off their doubt and perplexity. Even when the women declared that they had seen the Lord, the disciples would not believe. They thought them under an illusion.

Trouble seemed crowding upon trouble. On the sixth day of the week they had seen their Master die; on the first day of the next week they found themselves deprived of His body, and they were accused of having stolen it away for the sake of deceiving the people. They despaired of ever correcting the false impressions that were gaining ground against them. They feared the enmity of the priests and the wrath of the people. They longed for the presence of Jesus, who had helped them in every perplexity.

Often they repeated the words, "We trusted that it had been He which should have redeemed Israel." Lonely and sick at heart they remembered His words, "If they do these things in a green tree, what shall be done in the dry?" Luke 24:21; 23:31. They met together in the upper chamber, and closed and fastened the doors, knowing that the fate of their beloved Teacher might at any time be theirs.

And all the time they might have been rejoicing in the knowledge of a risen Saviour. In the garden, Mary had stood weeping, when Jesus was close beside her. Her eyes were so blinded by tears that she did not discern Him. And the hearts of the disciples were so full of grief that they did not believe the angels' message or the words of Christ Himself.

How many are still doing what these disciples did! How many echo Mary's despairing cry, "They have taken away the Lord, . . . and we know not where they have laid Him"! To how many might the Saviour's words be spoken, "Why weepest thou? whom seekest thou?" He is close beside them, but their tear-blinded eyes do not discern Him. He speaks to them, but they do not understand.

Oh that the bowed head might be lifted, that the eyes might be opened to behold Him, that the ears might listen to His voice! "Go quickly, and tell His disciples that He is risen." Bid them look not to Joseph's new tomb, that was closed with a great stone, and sealed with the Roman seal. Christ is not there. Look not to the empty sepulcher. Mourn not as those who are hopeless and helpless. Jesus lives, and because He lives, we shall live also. From grateful hearts, from lips touched with holy fire, let the glad song ring out, Christ is risen! He lives to make intercession for us. Grasp this hope, and it will hold the soul like a sure, tried anchor. Believe, and thou shalt see the glory of God.

Oh that the bowed head might be l_____, that the eyes might be opened to b_____ Him, that ears might l_____ to His voice... M_____ not as those who are hopeless and helpless...Christ is r_____!" (794). Lord, if I am not shouting and singing, if my lips aren't touched by holy fire, if I don't have a grateful heart, then my head must be bowed, and my eyes and ears closed. How might my awareness of the magnitude of my deliverance from the power of sin that Your resurrection affords, be increased?

_____
_____
_____
_____

Prayer journal: _____

_____
_____
_____
_____
_____
_____

Chapter 83

The Walk to Emmaus
[This chapter is based on Luke 24:13-33.]

Late in the afternoon of the day of the resurrection, two of the disciples were on their way to Emmaus, a little town eight miles from Jerusalem. These disciples had had no prominent place in Christ's work, but they were earnest believers in Him. They had come to the city to keep the Passover, and were greatly perplexed by the events that had recently taken place. They had heard the news of the morning in regard to the removal of Christ's body from the tomb, and also the report of the women who had seen the angels and had met Jesus. They were now returning to their homes to meditate and pray. Sadly they pursued their evening walk, talking over the scenes of the trial and the crucifixion. Never before had they been so utterly disheartened. Hopeless and faithless, they were walking in the shadow of the cross.

They had not advanced far on their journey when they were joined by a stranger, but they were so absorbed in their gloom and disappointment that they did not observe him closely. They continued their conversation, expressing the thoughts of their hearts. They were reasoning in regard to the lessons that Christ had given, which they seemed unable to comprehend. As they talked of the events that had taken place, Jesus longed to comfort them. He had seen their grief; He understood the conflicting, perplexing ideas that brought to their minds the thought, [795-796] Can this Man, who suffered Himself to be so humiliated, be the Christ? Their grief could not be restrained, and they wept. Jesus knew that their hearts were bound up with Him in love, and He longed to wipe away their tears, and fill them with joy and gladness. But He must first give them lessons they would never forget.

"He said unto them, What manner of communications are these that ye have one to another, as ye walk, and are sad? And the one of them, whose name was Cleopas, answering said unto Him, Art Thou only a

---

1. Two travelers were "greatly p_____ by the events that had recently taken place...Never before had they been so utterly d_____. Hopeless and f_____ _____, they were walking in the shadow of the cross...Jesus l_____ to comfort them...He understood the c_____, perplexing ideas that brought to their minds the thought, can this Man, who suffered Himself to be so h_____, be the Christ?" Lord, You are so understanding, even of my doubts about You. You are very comforting to me. Why don't I come to You more quickly? _____ _____ _____

stranger in Jerusalem, and hast not known the things which are come to pass there in these days?" They told Him of their disappointment in regard to their Master, "which was a prophet mighty in deed and word before God and all the people;" but "the chief priests and our rulers," they said, "delivered Him to be condemned to death, and have crucified Him." With hearts sore with disappointment, and with quivering lips, they added, "We trusted that it had been He which should have redeemed Israel: and beside all this, today is the third day since these things were done."

Strange that the disciples did not remember Christ's words, and realize that He had foretold the events which had come to pass! They did not realize that the last part of His disclosure would be just as verily fulfilled as the first part, that the third day He would rise again. This was the part they should have remembered. The priests and rulers did not forget this. On the day "that followed the day of the preparation, the chief priests and Pharisees came together unto Pilate, saying, Sir, we remember that that deceiver said, while He was yet alive, After three days I will rise again." Matt. 27:62, 63. But the disciples did not remember these words.

"Then He said unto them, O fools, and slow of heart to believe all that the prophets have spoken: ought not Christ to have suffered these things, and to enter into His glory?" The disciples wondered who this stranger could be, that He should penetrate to their very souls, and speak with such earnestness, tenderness, and sympathy, and with such hopefulness. For the first time since Christ's betrayal, they began to feel hopeful. Often they looked earnestly at their companion, and thought that His words were just the words that Christ would have spoken. They were filled with amazement, and their hearts began to throb with joyful expectation.

Beginning at Moses, the very Alpha of Bible history, Christ expounded in all the Scriptures the things concerning Himself. Had He [796-799] first made Himself known to them, their hearts would have been satis-

2. "We t_____ that it had been He which should have redeemed Israel… Strange that the disciples did not r_____ Christ's words…that the third day He would rise again…The priests and rulers did not f_____ __ this." (796). Lord, like the disciples, do I trust in certain expectations about You, instead of trusting in You? And if those expectations aren't realized, what happens to my trust and confidence in You?

_____
_____
_____ What happens when I forget Your promises, but the enemy doesn't, and he seeks to prevent their fulfillment?_____
_____
_____ Which ones?
_____

3. "The disciples wondered who this stranger could be, that He should p___ _____ to their very souls…They were filled with amazement, and their hearts began to throb with joyful e_____ ____." Thank You, Lord, that even in my darkened moments, of doubt and perplexity, You have just the words that get through, and turn me around: ____
_____
_____
_____

4. Upon what must the faith of these two travelers be established? _____

_____ "They had looked upon His death as the d_____ of all their hopes. Now He showed from the prophets that this was the very strongest e_____ for their faith...The miracles of Christ are a proof of His divinity; but a s_____ _____ proof that He is the world's R_____ _____ is found in comparing the prophecies of the Old Testament with the history of the New." (799). Lord, what about feelings of love I have for You, and friendship? How do feelings, faith, and scriptural truth interrelate and effect my walk with You? _____

5. "The cup of suffering...the awful conflict... was the fulfillment of the c_____ made before the foundation of the world was laid. Christ must die...All this was to b_____, but it was not to end in defeat, but in glorious, eternal victory." Lord,

fied. In the fullness of their joy they would have hungered for nothing more. But it was necessary for them to understand the witness borne to Him by the types and prophecies of the Old Testament. Upon these their faith must be established. Christ performed no miracle to convince them, but it was His first work to explain the Scriptures. They had looked upon His death as the destruction of all their hopes. Now He showed from the prophets that this was the very strongest evidence for their faith.

In teaching these disciples, Jesus showed the importance of the Old Testament as a witness to His mission. Many professed Christians now discard the Old Testament, claiming that it is no longer of any use. But such is not Christ's teaching. So highly did He value it that at one time He said, "If they hear not Moses and the prophets, neither will they be persuaded, though one rose from the dead." Luke 16:31.

It is the voice of Christ that speaks through patriarchs and prophets, from the days of Adam even to the closing scenes of time. The Saviour is revealed in the Old Testament as clearly as in the New. It is the light from the prophetic past that brings out the life of Christ and the teachings of the New Testament with clearness and beauty. The miracles of Christ are a proof of His divinity; but a stronger proof that He is the world's Redeemer is found in comparing the prophecies of the Old Testament with the history of the New.

Reasoning from prophecy, Christ gave His disciples a correct idea of what He was to be in humanity. Their expectation of a Messiah who was to take His throne and kingly power in accordance with the desires of men had been misleading. It would interfere with a correct apprehension of His descent from the highest to the lowest position that could be occupied. Christ desired that the ideas of His disciples might be pure and true in every specification. They must understand as far as possible in regard to the cup of suffering that had been apportioned to Him. He showed them that the awful conflict which they could not yet comprehend was the fulfillment of the covenant made before the foundation of the world was laid. Christ must die, as every transgressor of the law must die if he continues in sin. All this was to be, but it was not to end in defeat, but in glorious, eternal victory. Jesus told them that every effort must be made to save the world from sin. His followers must live as He lived, and work as He worked, with intense, persevering effort. [799-800]

Thus Christ discoursed to His disciples, opening their minds that they might understand the Scriptures. The disciples were weary, but the conversation did not flag. Words of life and assurance fell from the Saviour's lips. But still their eyes were holden. As He told them of the overthrow of Jerusalem, they looked upon the doomed city with weeping. But little did they yet suspect who their traveling companion was. They did not think that the subject of their conversation was walking by their side; for Christ referred to Himself as though He were another person. They thought that He was one of those who had been in attendance at the great feast, and who was now returning to his home. He walked as carefully as they over the rough stones, now and then halting with them for a little rest. Thus they proceeded along the mountainous road, while the One who was soon to take His position at God's right hand, and who could say, "All power is given unto Me in heaven and in earth," walked beside them. Matt. 28:18.

During the journey the sun had gone down, and before the travelers reached their place of rest, the laborers in the fields had left their work. As the disciples were about to enter their home, the stranger appeared as though He would continue His journey. But the disciples felt drawn to Him. Their souls hungered to hear more from Him. "Abide with us," they said. He did not seem to accept the invitation, but they pressed it upon Him, urging, "It is toward evening, and the day is far spent." Christ yielded to this entreaty and "went in to tarry with them."

Had the disciples failed to press their invitation, they would not have known that their traveling companion was the risen Lord. Christ never forces His company upon anyone. He interests Himself in those who need Him. Gladly will He enter the humblest home, and cheer the lowliest heart. But if men are too indifferent to think of the heavenly Guest, or ask Him to abide with them, He passes on. Thus many meet with great loss. They do not know Christ any more than did the disciples as He walked with them by the way.

The simple evening meal of bread is soon prepared. It is placed before the guest, who has taken His seat at

Is my dying to sin, thought of as defeat, a loss, a sacrifice? _____

_____

_____ What about a victory? _____

_____

_____

6. "Christ never f_____ _____ His company on anyone. He interests Himself in those who n_____ Him...But if men are too i_____ to think of the heavenly Guest, or ask Him to abide with them, He passes on. Thus many meet with great l_____. They do not know Christ." (800). Lord, my indifference is great. My loss is great. Help me to recognize how great is my need, to open the door to Your knock: _____

_____

_____

_____

7. "Did not our heart b__ _____ within us, while He talked with us by the way, and while He o____ _____ to us the scripture?" (801). Lord, does my heart burn? How can I help experience that burn?

_____
_____

I want to be open as You open the scriptures to me.

_____
_____
_____

8. "With this great news to communicate, they c____ _____ sit and talk...Their hearts l_____ for joy. They seem to be in a new world. Christ is a l____ _____ Savior...They carry the g_____ message ever given to the world, a message of glad tidings upon which the hopes of the human family for time and for eternity d_____." Lord, set my heart on fire! Fill this land with Your glory! Who can I carry this message to? _____

_____
_____
_____

Prayer journal: _____

_____
_____
_____
_____
_____
_____
_____
_____
_____

the head of the table. Now He puts forth His hands to bless the food. The disciples start back in astonishment. Their companion spreads forth His hands in exactly the same way as their Master used to do. They look again, and lo, they see in His hands the print of nails. Both exclaim at once, It is the Lord Jesus! He has risen from the dead! [800-801]

They rise to cast themselves at His feet and worship Him, but He has vanished out of their sight. They look at the place which had been occupied by One whose body had lately lain in the grave, and say to each other, "Did not our heart burn within us, while He talked with us by the way, and while He opened to us the Scriptures?"

But with this great news to communicate they cannot sit and talk. Their weariness and hunger are gone. They leave their meal untasted, and full of joy immediately set out again on the same path by which they came, hurrying to tell the tidings to the disciples in the city. In some parts the road is not safe, but they climb over the steep places, slipping on the smooth rocks. They do not see, they do not know, that they have the protection of Him who has traveled the road with them. With their pilgrim staff in hand, they press on, desiring to go faster than they dare. They lose their track, but find it again. Sometimes running, sometimes stumbling, they press forward, their unseen Companion close beside them all the way.

The night is dark, but the Sun of Righteousness is shining upon them. Their hearts leap for joy. They seem to be in a new world. Christ is a living Saviour. They no longer mourn over Him as dead. Christ is risen--over and over again they repeat it. This is the message they are carrying to the sorrowing ones. They must tell them the wonderful story of the walk to Emmaus. They must tell who joined them by the way. They carry the greatest message ever given to the world, a message of glad tidings upon which the hopes of the human family for time and for eternity depend.

Chapter 84

"Peace Be Unto You"

[This chapter is based on Luke 24:33-48; John 20:19-29.]

On reaching Jerusalem the two disciples enter at the eastern gate, which is open at night on festal occasions. The houses are dark and silent, but the travelers make their way through the narrow streets by the light of the rising moon. They go to the upper chamber where Jesus spent the hours of the last evening before His death. Here they know that their brethren are to be found. Late as it is, they know that the disciples will not sleep till they learn for a certainty what has become of the body of their Lord. They find the door of the chamber securely barred. They knock for admission, but no answer comes. All is still. Then they give their names. The door is carefully unbarred, they enter, and Another, unseen, enters with them. Then the door is again fastened, to keep out spies.

The travelers find all in surprised excitement. The voices of those in the room break out into thanksgiving and praise, saying, "The Lord is risen indeed, and hath appeared to Simon." Then the two travelers, panting with the haste with which they have made their journey, tell the wondrous story of how Jesus has appeared to them. They have just ended, and some are saying that they cannot believe it, for it is too good to be true, when behold, another Person stands before them. Every eye is fastened upon the stranger. No one has knocked for entrance. No [802-803] footstep has been heard. The disciples are startled, and wonder what it means. Then they hear a voice which is no other than the voice of their Master. Clear and distinct the words fall from His lips, "Peace be unto you."

"But they were terrified and affrighted, and supposed that they had seen a spirit. And He said unto them, Why are ye troubled? and why do thoughts arise in your hearts? Behold My hands and My feet, that it is I Myself: handle Me, and see; for a spirit hath not flesh and bones, as ye see Me have. And when He had thus spoken, He showed them His hands and His feet."

They beheld the hands and feet marred by the cruel nails. They recognized His voice, like no other they had ever heard. "And while they yet believed not for joy, and wondered, He said unto them, Have ye here any meat? And they gave Him a piece of a broiled fish, and of an honeycomb. And He took it, and did eat before them." "Then were the disciples glad, when they saw the Lord." Faith and joy took the place of unbelief, and with feelings which no words could express they acknowledged their risen Saviour.

At the birth of Jesus the angel announced, Peace on earth, and good will to men. And now at His first appearance to the disciples after His resurrection, the Saviour addressed them with the blessed words, "Peace [803-804] be unto you." Jesus is ever ready to speak peace to souls that are burdened with doubts and fears. He waits for us to open the door of the heart to Him, and say, Abide with us. He says, "Behold, I stand at the door, and knock: if any man hear My voice, and open the door, I will come in to him, and will sup with him, and he with Me." Rev. 3:20.

The resurrection of Jesus was a type of the final resurrection of all who sleep in Him. The countenance of the risen Saviour, His manner, His speech, were all familiar to His disciples. As Jesus arose from the dead, so those who sleep in Him are to rise again. We shall know our friends, even as the disciples knew Jesus. They may have been deformed, diseased, or disfigured, in this mortal life, and they rise in perfect health and symmetry; yet in the glorified body their identity will be perfectly preserved. Then shall we know even as also we are known. 1 Cor. 13:12. In the face radiant with the light shining from the face of Jesus, we shall recognize the lineaments of those we love.

When Jesus met with His disciples, He reminded them of the words He had spoken to them before His death, that all things must be fulfilled which were written in the law of Moses, and in the prophets, and in the Psalms concerning Him. "Then opened He their understanding, that they might understand the Scriptures, and said unto them, Thus it is [804-805] written, and thus it behooved Christ to suffer, and to rise from the dead the third day: and that repentance and remission of sins should be preached in His name among all nations, beginning at Jerusalem. And ye are witnesses of these

1. "At the birth of Jesus the angel announced, P_____ on earth, and good will to men. And now at His first appearance to the disciples after His resurrection, the Savior addressed them with the words, "Peace be u_____ you." (803, 804). Lord, You know me, what my real needs are. You see my burdens, doubts and fears. So what keeps me from trusting Your word and experiencing tranquility? _____
_____
_____

2. "The resurrection of Jesus was a t_____ of the final resurrection of all who sleep in Him... We shall k_____ our friends, even as the disciples knew Jesus...In the face radiant with the light shining f_____ the face of Jesus, we shall recognize the lineaments of those we love." Lord, may my face reflect Your glory, which means I want to be exposed to Your presence as much as possible, my walk with You to continue throughout the day. When I interact with people today, may what I say and my tone of voice reflect that I have been with You, that I am with You: _____
_____

things."

The disciples began to realize the nature and extent of their work. They were to proclaim to the world the wonderful truths which Christ had entrusted to them. The events of His life, His death and resurrection, the prophecies that pointed to these events, the sacredness of the law of God, the mysteries of the plan of salvation, the power of Jesus for the remission of sins,--to all these things they were witnesses, and they were to make them known to the world. They were to proclaim the gospel of peace and salvation through repentance and the power of the Saviour.

3. What wonderful truths did Christ entrust with us? a) events of His l_____, death, and resurrection, b) the p_____ that pointed to these events, c) the s_____ of the law of God, d) the mysteries of the plan of s_____, e) the power of Jesus for the r__ _____ of sins. (805). Lord, I am blessed with these truths. May I not take them for granted, but rather more fully study and explore the experience they offer. If You entrusted them to me, they must be very special and sacred to You. How can I better understand these trusts, to better appreciate and to share this treasure? _____

_____

_____

_____

"And when He had said this, He breathed on them, and saith unto them, Receive ye the Holy Ghost: Whosesoever sins ye remit, they are remitted unto them; and whosesoever sins ye retain, they are retained." The Holy Spirit was not yet fully manifested; for Christ had not yet been glorified. The more abundant impartation of the Spirit did not take place till after Christ's ascension. Not until this was received could the disciples fulfill the commission to preach the gospel to the world. But the Spirit was now given for a special purpose. Before the disciples could fulfill their official duties in connection with the church, Christ breathed His Spirit upon them. He was committing to them a most sacred trust, and He desired to impress them with the fact that without the Holy Spirit this work could not be accomplished.

The Holy Spirit is the breath of spiritual life in the soul. The impartation of the Spirit is the impartation of the life of Christ. It imbues the receiver with the attributes of Christ. Only those who are thus taught of God, those who possess the inward working of the Spirit, and in whose life the Christ-life is manifested, are to stand as representative men, to minister in behalf of the

4. "He b_____ on them, and said unto them, Receive ye the Holy G__ _____... He was committing to them a most s_____ trust, and He desired to impress them with the fact that w_____ the Holy Spirit this work could not be accomplished." What happens if I try to honor this trust with out the Holy Spirit? _____

_____

1 Cor 2:14 _____

_____

_____

5. "The Holy Spirit is the breath of spiritual l_____ _____ in the soul...It imbues the receiver with the attributes of Christ." Without breath, there is no life; does my spiritual life have breath? _____
_____
_____
_____

What can I do to increase it? _____
_____
_____
_____

6. "The church has a duty, to warn, to instruct, and if possible to r____ _____ ...Call sin by its r_____ name...In choosing to sin, they d__ _____ Christ...But there is a b_____ side to the picture...Let this thought be kept uppermost." What is it? "In labor for the erring, let every eye be directed to C_____...speak...of the forgiving m_____ of the Savior." (805, 806). Lord, help me to remember the extent of your compassion, mercy, and forgiveness towards me, the chief of sinners. And may I be a channel of similar thoughts to others: _____
_____
_____
_____

church.

"Whosesoever sins ye remit," said Christ, "they are remitted; . . . and whosoever sins ye retain, they are retained." Christ here gives no liberty for any man to pass judgment upon others. In the Sermon on the Mount He forbade this. It is the prerogative of God. But on the church in its organized capacity He places a responsibility for the individual members. Toward those who fall into sin, the church has a duty, to warn, to instruct, and if possible to restore. "Reprove, rebuke, exhort," the Lord says, "with all long-suffering and doctrine." 2 Tim. 4:2. Deal [805-806] faithfully with wrongdoing. Warn every soul that is in danger. Leave none to deceive themselves. Call sin by its right name. Declare what God has said in regard to lying, Sabbathbreaking, stealing, idolatry, and every other evil. "They which do such things shall not inherit the kingdom of God." Gal. 5:21. If they persist in sin, the judgment you have declared from God's word is pronounced upon them in heaven. In choosing to sin, they disown Christ; the church must show that she does not sanction their deeds, or she herself dishonors her Lord. She must say about sin what God says about it. She must deal with it as God directs, and her action is ratified in heaven. He who despises the authority of the church despises the authority of Christ Himself.

But there is a brighter side to the picture. "Whosesoever sins ye remit, they are remitted." Let this thought be kept uppermost. In labor for the erring, let every eye be directed to Christ. Let the shepherds have a tender care for the flock of the Lord's pasture. Let them speak to the erring of the forgiving mercy of the Saviour. Let them encourage the sinner to repent, and believe in Him who can pardon. Let them declare, on the authority of God's word, "If we confess our sins, He is faithful and just to forgive us our sins, and to cleanse us from all unrighteousness." 1 John 1:9. All who repent have the assurance, "He will have compassion upon us; He will subdue our iniquities; and Thou wilt cast all their sins into the depths of the sea." Micah 7:19.

Let the repentance of the sinner be accepted by the church with grateful hearts. Let the repenting one be led out from the darkness of unbelief into the light of faith and righteousness. Let his trembling hand be placed in the loving hand of Jesus. Such a remission is ratified in heaven.

Only in this sense has the church power to absolve the sinner. Remission of sins can be obtained only through the merits of Christ. To no man, to no body of men, is given power to free the soul from guilt. Christ charged His disciples to preach the remission of sins in His name among all nations; but they themselves were not empowered to remove one stain of sin. The name of Jesus is the only "name under heaven given among men, whereby we must be saved." Acts 4:12.

When Jesus first met the disciples in the upper chamber, Thomas was not with them. He heard the reports of the others, and received abundant proof that Jesus had risen; but gloom and unbelief filled his heart. As he heard the disciples tell of the wonderful manifestations of the risen Saviour, it only plunged him in deeper despair. If Jesus had [806-807] really risen from the dead, there could be no further hope of a literal earthly kingdom. And it wounded his vanity to think that his Master should reveal Himself to all the disciples except him. He was determined not to believe, and for a whole week he brooded over his wretchedness, which seemed all the darker in contrast with the hope and faith of his brethren.

During this time he repeatedly declared, "Except I shall see in His hands the print of the nails, and put my finger into the print of the nails, and thrust my hand into His side, I will not believe." He would not see through the eyes of his brethren, or exercise faith which was dependent upon their testimony. He ardently loved his Lord, but he had allowed jealousy and unbelief to take possession of his mind and heart.

A number of the disciples now made the familiar upper chamber their temporary home, and at evening all except Thomas gathered here. One evening Thomas determined to meet with the others. Notwithstanding his unbelief, he had a faint hope that the good news was true. While the disciples were taking their evening meal, they talked of the evidences which Christ had given them in the prophecies. "Then came Jesus, the doors being shut, and stood in the midst, and said, Peace be unto you."

Turning to Thomas He said, "Reach hither thy finger, and behold My hands; and reach hither thy hand, and thrust it into My side: and be not faithless, but be-

7. Thomas was in deep despair. "If Jesus had really risen from the dead, there could be n_____ further hope of a literal earthly kingdom...He was d___ _____ not be believe...

He had a_____ jealousy and unbelief to take possession of his mind and heart." (806, 807). Enoch, on his walk with You Lord, educated his heart and mind to ever be in Your presence. Thomas made room in his heart and mind for something else. What are the ways that I make room in my heart and mind, for one or the other? _____

_____

_____

_____

8. "Notwithstanding his unbelief, he had a f_____ _____ hope that the good news was true." What does this say about God's persistent knocking? _____

_____

_____

_____

_____

lieving." These words showed that He was acquainted with the thoughts and words of Thomas. The doubting disciple knew that none of his companions had seen Jesus for a week. They could not have told the Master of his unbelief. He recognized the One before him as his Lord. He had no desire for further proof. His heart leaped for joy, and he cast himself at the feet of Jesus crying, "My Lord and my God."

Jesus accepted his acknowledgment, but gently reproved his unbelief: "Thomas, because thou hast seen Me, thou hast believed: blessed are they that have not seen, and yet have believed." The faith of Thomas would have been more pleasing to Christ if he had been willing to believe upon the testimony of his brethren. Should the world now follow the example of Thomas, no one would believe unto salvation; for all who receive Christ must do so through the testimony of others.

Many who are given to doubt excuse themselves by saying that if they had the evidence which Thomas had from his companions, they would believe. They do not realize that they have not only that evidence, but [807-808] much more. Many who, like Thomas, wait for all cause of doubt to be removed, will never realize their desire. They gradually become confirmed in unbelief. Those who educate themselves to look on the dark side, and murmur and complain, know not what they do. They are sowing the seeds of doubt, and they will have a harvest of doubt to reap. At a time when faith and confidence are most essential, many will thus find themselves powerless to hope and believe.

In His treatment of Thomas, Jesus gave a lesson for His followers. His example shows how we should treat those whose faith is weak, and who make their doubts prominent. Jesus did not overwhelm Thomas with reproach, nor did He enter into controversy with him. He revealed Himself to the doubting one. Thomas had been most unreasonable in dictating the conditions of his faith, but Jesus, by His generous love and consideration, broke down all the barriers. Unbelief is seldom overcome by controversy. It is rather put upon self-defense, and finds new support and excuse. But let Jesus, in His love and mercy, be revealed as the crucified Saviour, and from many once unwilling lips will be heard the acknowledgment of Thomas, "My Lord and my God."

9. "Many who, like Thomas, wait for a_____ cause of doubt to be removed, will never realize their desire...Those who educate themselves to look on the dark side, and murmur and c_____, know not what they do. They are sowing the seeds of doubt, and they will have a h_____ of doubt to reap." (808). Lord, show me how I might be educating myself to doubt:
_____
_____
_____
_____
_____

10. "Thomas had been most unreasonable in dictating the c_____ _____ of his faith... Unbelief is seldom overcome by controversy. It is rather put upon self-defense, and finds new support and e__ _____." Lord, do I have conditions to my faith? __
_____
_____
_____

Prayer journal: _____
_____
_____
_____
_____

Chapter 85

By the Sea Once More
[This chapter is based on John 21:1-22.]

Jesus had appointed to meet His disciples in Galilee; and soon after the Passover week was ended, they bent their steps thither. Their absence from Jerusalem during the feast would have been interpreted as disaffection and heresy, therefore they remained till its close; but this over, they gladly turned homeward to meet the Saviour as He had directed.

Seven of the disciples were in company. They were clad in the humble garb of fishermen; they were poor in worldly goods, but rich in the knowledge and practice of the truth, which in the sight of Heaven gave them the highest rank as teachers. They had not been students in the schools of the prophets, but for three years they had been taught by the greatest Educator the world has ever known. Under His instruction they had become elevated, intelligent, and refined, agents through whom men might be led to a knowledge of the truth.

Much of the time of Christ's ministry had been passed near the Sea of Galilee. As the disciples gathered in a place where they were not likely to be disturbed, they found themselves surrounded by reminders of Jesus and His mighty works. On this sea, when their hearts were filled with terror, and the fierce storm was hurrying them to destruction, Jesus had walked upon the billows to their rescue. Here the tempest had been hushed by His word. Within sight was the beach where above ten thousand persons had been fed from a few small loaves and fishes. Not far distant was Capernaum, the scene of so many miracles. As the disciples [809-810] looked upon the scene, their minds were full of the words and deeds of their Saviour.

The evening was pleasant, and Peter, who still had much of his old love for boats and fishing, proposed that they should go out upon the sea and cast their nets. In this plan all were ready to join; they were in need of food and clothing, which the proceeds of a successful night's fishing would supply. So they went out in their

1. Though "clad in the humble garb of fishermen…[the disciples were] r_____ in the knowledge and practice of the t_____, which in the sight of Heaven gave them the h_____ rank as teachers." Lord, show me the difference between knowledge and practice: _____ _____ _____ _____ How can I be rich in the knowledge and practice of truth? _____ _____ _____ _____ _____

boat, but they caught nothing. All night they toiled, without success. Through the weary hours they talked of their absent Lord, and recalled the wonderful events they had witnessed in His ministry beside the sea. They questioned as to their own future, and grew sad at the prospect before them.

All the while a lone watcher upon the shore followed them with His eye, while He Himself was unseen. At length the morning dawned. The boat was but a little way from the shore, and the disciples saw a stranger standing upon the beach, who accosted them with the question, "Children, have ye any meat?" When they answered, "No," "He said unto them, Cast the net on the right side of the ship, and ye shall find. They cast therefore, and now they were not able to draw it for the multitude of fishes."

John recognized the stranger, and exclaimed to Peter, "It is the Lord." Peter was so elated and so glad that in his eagerness he cast himself into the water and was soon standing by the side of his Master. The other disciples came in their boat, dragging the net with fishes. "As soon then as they were come to land, they saw a fire of coals there, and fish laid thereon, and bread."

They were too much amazed to question whence came the fire and the food. "Jesus saith unto them, Bring of the fish which ye have now caught." Peter rushed for the net, which he had dropped, and helped his brethren drag it to the shore. After the work was done, and the preparation made, Jesus bade the disciples come and dine. He broke the food, and divided it among them, and was known and acknowledged by all the seven. The miracle of feeding the five thousand on the mountainside was now brought to their minds; but a mysterious awe was upon them, and in silence they gazed upon the risen Saviour.

Vividly they recalled the scene beside the sea when Jesus had bidden them follow Him. They remembered how, at His command, they had launched out into the deep, and had let down their net, and the catch had been so abundant as to fill the net, even to breaking. Then Jesus had called them to leave their fishing boats, and had promised to make them [810-811] fishers of men. It was to bring this scene to their minds, and to deepen its impression, that He had again performed the miracle. His act was a renewal of the commission to the dis-

2. "Jesus had called them to leave their fishing boats, and had p_____ to make them fishers of m_____. It was to bring this scene to their minds and to deepen its i_____, that He had again performed the miracle. His act was a renewal of the c_____ to

ciples. It showed them that the death of their Master had not lessened their obligation to do the work He had assigned them. Though they were to be deprived of His personal companionship, and of the means of support by their former employment, the risen Saviour would still have a care for them. While they were doing His work, He would provide for their needs. And Jesus had a purpose in bidding them cast their net on the right side of the ship. On that side He stood upon the shore. That was the side of faith. If they labored in connection with Him,--His divine power combining with their human effort,--they could not fail of success.

Another lesson Christ had to give, relating especially to Peter. Peter's denial of his Lord had been in shameful contrast to his former professions of loyalty. He had dishonored Christ, and had incurred the distrust of his brethren. They thought he would not be allowed to take his former position among them, and he himself felt that he had forfeited his trust. Before being called to take up again his apostolic work, he must before them all give evidence of his repentance. Without this, his sin, though repented of, might have destroyed his influence as a minister of Christ. The Saviour gave him opportunity to regain the confidence of his brethren, and, so far as possible, to remove the reproach he had brought upon the gospel.

Here is given a lesson for all Christ's followers. The gospel makes no compromise with evil. It cannot excuse sin. Secret sins are to be confessed in secret to God; but, for open sin, open confession is required. The reproach of the disciple's sin is cast upon Christ. It causes Satan to triumph, and wavering souls to stumble. By giving proof of repentance, the disciple, so far as lies in his power, is to remove this reproach.

While Christ and the disciples were eating together by the seaside, the Saviour said to Peter, "Simon, son of Jonas, lovest thou Me more than these?" referring to his brethren. Peter had once declared, "Though all men shall be offended because of Thee, yet will I never be offended." Matt. 26:33. But he now put a truer estimate upon himself. "Yea, Lord," he said, "Thou knowest that I love Thee." There is no vehement assurance that his love is greater than that of his brethren. He does not express his own opinion of his devotion. To Him who can read all the motives of the heart he appeals to judge as

the disciples...He would provide for their needs." (810, 811). Lord, help me to recognize when I work on the wrong side of the boat. Success comes only as I labor in connection with You. May my ministry not be self-reliant, but totally dependent on You: _

_____

_____

3. "Peter's denial of his Lord had been in shameful contrast to his former professions of l_____ _____...He must...give e_____ of his repentance. Without this, his sin, though repented of, might have destroyed his i____ _____ as a minister of Christ." Lord, show me my forms of denying You that contradict my professions of loyalty: _____

_____

_____

_____ Help me recognize and deal with, a lack of my repentance and loss of influence? _____

_____

_____

4. "Peter had once declared...'I will never be o_____.' But now he put a t_____ estimate upon himself...There is no vehement a_____ ____ that his love is greater than that of his brethren. He does not express his own o_____ of his

devotion. To Him who can read all the m_____ of the heart he appeals to judge as to his sincerity." Lord, I am like Peter, not knowing myself. Help me to have a truer estimate. And thank You for being so gentle, not overwhelming me with too many of my faults all at once. I really do want my expressions of love and devotion to You to be genuine, and only You can help me, nurturing that purity. ____

_____
_____
_____

5. "Before the assembled disciples Jesus revealed the depth of Peter's repentance, and showed how t_____ humbled was the once boasting disciple...The close, testing questions of the Lord had not called out one forward, self-s_____

to his sincerity,--"Thou knowest that I love Thee." And Jesus bids him, "Feed My lambs." [811-812]

Again Jesus applied the test to Peter, repeating His former words: "Simon, son of Jonas, lovest thou Me?" This time He did not ask Peter whether he loved Him better than did his brethren. The second response was like the first, free from extravagant assurance: "Yea, Lord; Thou knowest that I love Thee." Jesus said to him, "Feed My sheep." Once more the Saviour put the trying question: "Simon, son of Jonas, lovest thou Me?" Peter was grieved; he thought that Jesus doubted his love. He knew that his Lord had cause to distrust him, and with an aching heart he answered, "Lord, Thou knowest all things; Thou knowest that I love Thee." Again Jesus said to him, "Feed My sheep."

Three times Peter had openly denied his Lord, and three times Jesus drew from him the assurance of his love and loyalty, pressing home that pointed question, like a barbed arrow to his wounded heart. Before the assembled disciples Jesus revealed the depth of Peter's repentance, and showed how thoroughly humbled was the once boasting disciple.

Peter was naturally forward and impulsive, and Satan had taken advantage of these characteristics to overthrow him. Just before the fall of Peter, Jesus had said to him, "Satan hath desired to have you, that he may sift you as wheat: but I have prayed for thee, that thy faith fail not: and when thou art converted, strengthen thy brethren." Luke 22:31, 32. That time had now come, and the transformation in Peter was evident. The close, testing questions of the Lord had not called out one forward, self-sufficient reply; and because of his humiliation and repentance, Peter was better prepared than ever before to act as shepherd to the flock.

The first work that Christ entrusted to Peter on restoring him to the ministry was to feed the lambs. This was a work in which Peter had little experience. It would require great care and tenderness, much patience and perseverance. It called him to minister to those who were young in the faith, to teach the ignorant, to open the Scriptures to them, and to educate them for usefulness in Christ's service. Heretofore Peter had not been fitted to do this, or even to understand its importance. But this was the work which Jesus now called upon him to do. For this work his own experience of suffering and repentance had prepared him.

Before his fall, Peter was always speaking unadvisedly, from the impulse of the moment. He was always ready to correct others, and to express his mind, before he had a clear comprehension of himself or of what he had to say. But the converted Peter was very different. He retained his former fervor, but the grace of Christ regulated his zeal. He was no longer impetuous, self-confident, and self-exalted, but calm, [812-815] self-possessed, and teachable. He could then feed the lambs as well as the sheep of Christ's flock.

The Saviour's manner of dealing with Peter had a lesson for him and for his brethren. It taught them to meet the transgressor with patience, sympathy, and forgiving love. Although Peter had denied his Lord, the love which Jesus bore him never faltered. Just such love should the undershepherd feel for the sheep and lambs committed to his care. Remembering his own weakness and failure, Peter was to deal with his flock as tenderly as Christ had dealt with him.

The question that Christ had put to Peter was significant. He mentioned only one condition of discipleship and service. "Lovest thou Me?" He said. This is the essential qualification. Though Peter might possess every other, yet without the love of Christ he could not be a faithful shepherd over the Lord's flock. Knowledge, benevolence, eloquence, gratitude, and zeal are all aids in the good work; but without the love of Jesus in the heart, the work of the Christian minister is a failure.

Jesus walked alone with Peter, for there was something which He wished to communicate to him only. Before His death, Jesus had said to him, "Whither I go, thou canst not follow Me now; but thou shalt follow Me afterwards." To this Peter had replied, "Lord, why cannot I follow Thee now? I will lay down my life for Thy sake." John 13:36, 37. When he said this, he little knew to what heights and depths Christ's feet would lead the way. Peter had failed when the test came, but again he was to have opportunity to prove his love for Christ. That he might be strengthened for the final test of his faith, the Saviour opened to him his future. He told him that after living a life of usefulness, when age was telling upon his strength, he would indeed follow his Lord. Jesus said, "When thou wast young, thou girdedst thyself, and walkedst whither thou wouldest: but when

reply...The converted Peter...was no longer impetuous, self-confident, and self-e_____, but calm, self-possessed, and teachable." (812, 815). Whatever it takes, Lord, for You to get through to me, I am willing. I want to be teachable. I want my love for You to grow:

_____
_____
_____
_____

6. Christ "mentioned only o____ condition of discipleship and service. 'L_____ thou Me?' He said. This is the e____ _____ qualification." Lord, search my heart. Help my priority be, to love You more completely. Delete from my mind any thoughts of my being an asset to Your cause. The only thing that commends me is my need. The only thing that qualifies me is a love relationship with You:

_____
_____
_____

thou shalt be old, thou shalt stretch forth thy hands, and another shall gird thee, and carry thee whither thou wouldest not. This spake He, signifying by what death he should glorify God."

Jesus thus made known to Peter the very manner of his death; He even foretold the stretching forth of his hands upon the cross. Again He bade His disciple, "Follow Me." Peter was not disheartened by the revelation. He felt willing to suffer any death for his Lord.

Heretofore Peter had known Christ after the flesh, as many know Him now; but he was no more to be thus limited. He knew Him no more as he had known Him in his association with Him in humanity. [815-816] He had loved Him as a man, as a heaven-sent teacher; he now loved Him as God. He had been learning the lesson that to him Christ was all in all. Now he was prepared to share in his Lord's mission of sacrifice. When at last brought to the cross, he was, at his own request, crucified with his head downward. He thought it too great an honor to suffer in the same way as his Master did.

To Peter the words "Follow Me" were full of instruction. Not only for his death, but for every step of his life, was the lesson given. Hitherto Peter had been inclined to act independently. He had tried to plan for the work of God, instead of waiting to follow out God's plan. But he could gain nothing by rushing on before the Lord. Jesus bids him, "Follow Me." Do not run ahead of Me. Then you will not have the hosts of Satan to meet alone. Let Me go before you, and you will not be overcome by the enemy.

As Peter walked beside Jesus, he saw that John was following. A desire came over him to know his future, and he "saith to Jesus, Lord, and what shall this man do? Jesus saith unto him, If I will that he tarry till I come, what is that to thee? follow thou Me." Peter should have considered that his Lord would reveal to him all that it was best for him to know. It is the duty of everyone to follow Christ, without undue anxiety as to the work assigned to others. In saying of John, "If I will that he tarry till I come," Jesus gave no assurance that this disciple should live until the Lord's second coming. He merely asserted His own supreme power, and that even if He should will this to be so, it would in no way affect Peter's work. The future of both John and Peter was in the hands of their Lord. Obedience in following

7. "For e_____ step of his life, was the lesson given...Jesus bids him, 'Follow Me.' Do not run a_____ of Me. Then you will not have the hosts of Satan to meet a_____ __." (816). Lord, show me how I run ahead of You: _____ _____

_____ Am I less than wholeheartedly submitting my plans, activities and desires for each day to You? Like Enoch, I want to follow You, each step of my life: _____ _____ _____ _____

Him was the duty required of each.

How many today are like Peter! They are interested in the affairs of others, and anxious to know their duty, while they are in danger of neglecting their own. It is our work to look to Christ and follow Him. We shall see mistakes in the lives of others, and defects in their character. Humanity is encompassed with infirmity. But in Christ we shall find perfection. Beholding Him, we shall become transformed.

John lived to be very aged. He witnessed the destruction of Jerusalem, and the ruin of the stately temple,--a symbol of the final ruin of the world. To his latest days John closely followed his Lord. The burden of his testimony to the churches was, "Beloved, let us love one another;" "he that dwelleth in love, dwelleth in God, and God in him." 1 John 4:7, 16. [816-817]

Peter had been restored to his apostleship, but the honor and authority he received from Christ had not given him supremacy over his brethren. This Christ had made plain when in answer to Peter's question, "What shall this man do?" He had said, "What is that to thee? follow thou Me." Peter was not honored as the head of the church. The favor which Christ had shown him in forgiving his apostasy, and entrusting him with the feeding of the flock, and Peter's own faithfulness in following Christ, won for him the confidence of his brethren. He had much influence in the church. But the lesson which Christ had taught him by the Sea of Galilee Peter carried with him throughout his life. Writing by the Holy Spirit to the churches, he said:

"The elders which are among you I exhort, who am also an elder, and a witness of the sufferings of Christ, and also a partaker of the glory that shall be revealed: Feed the flock of God which is among you, taking the oversight thereof, not by constraint, but willingly; not for filthy lucre, but of a ready mind; neither as being lords over God's heritage, but being ensamples to the flock. And when the Chief Shepherd shall appear, ye shall receive a crown of glory that fadeth not away." 1 Peter 5:1-4.

8. "It is our work to l____ ____ to Christ and follow Him. We shall see mistakes in the lives of others, and d_____ in their character...But in Christ we shall find p_____ ____. Beholding Him, we shall become t_____ _____." Lord, when I compare myself to others, I either inflate my value, or I become discouraged. May Your love be a protective blinder, helping me to focus on only You: _____

_____

_____

_____

9. Peter wrote: "Feed the flock of God...[not] as being l_____ over God's heritage, but being e____ _____ to the flock." (817). Lord, what is my example? I am revealing a friendship with You? Am I reflecting Your light and character? _____

_____

_____

_____

Prayer journal: _____

_____

_____

_____

_____

_____

_____

Chapter 86

Go Teach All Nations
[This chapter is based on Matt. 28:16-20.]

Standing but a step from His heavenly throne, Christ gave the commission to His disciples. "All power is given unto Me in heaven and in earth," He said. "Go ye therefore, and teach all nations." "Go ye into all the world, and preach the gospel to every creature." Mark 16:15. Again and again the words were repeated, that the disciples might grasp their significance. Upon all the inhabitants of the earth, high and low, rich and poor, was the light of heaven to shine in clear, strong rays. The disciples were to be colaborers with their Redeemer in the work of saving the world.

The commission had been given to the twelve when Christ met with them in the upper chamber; but it was now to be given to a larger number. At the meeting on a mountain in Galilee, all the believers who could be called together were assembled. Of this meeting Christ Himself, before His death, had designated the time and place. The angel at the tomb reminded the disciples of His promise to meet them in Galilee. The promise was repeated to the believers who were gathered at Jerusalem during the Passover week, and through them it reached many lonely ones who were mourning the death of their Lord. With intense interest all looked forward to the interview. They made their way to the place of meeting by circuitous routes, coming in from every direction, to avoid exciting the suspicion of the jealous Jews. With wondering hearts they came, talking earnestly together of the news that had reached them concerning Christ.

At the time appointed, about five hundred believers were collected in little knots on the mountainside, eager to learn all that could be learned [818-819] from those who had seen Christ since His resurrection. From group to group the disciples passed, telling all they had seen and heard of Jesus, and reasoning from the Scriptures as He had done with them. Thomas recounted the story of his unbelief, and told how his doubts had been swept away. Suddenly Jesus stood among them. No one could

1. "The disciples were to be c_____ with their Redeemer in the work of saving the world." What a honor, is Your invitation to partner with You in spreading the good news! Have there been divine appointments to speak on Your behalf, that I have missed? What were those?

_____

_____

_____

Open my eyes Your appointments, to be Your ambassador.

tell whence or how He came. Many who were present had never before seen Him; but in His hands and feet they beheld the marks of the crucifixion; His countenance was as the face of God, and when they saw Him, they worshiped Him.

But some doubted. So it will always be. There are those who find it hard to exercise faith, and they place themselves on the doubting side. These lose much because of their unbelief.

This was the only interview that Jesus had with many of the believers after His resurrection. He came and spoke to them saying, "All power is given unto Me in heaven and in earth." The disciples had worshiped Him before He spoke, but His words, falling from lips that had been closed in death, thrilled them with peculiar power. He was now the risen Saviour. Many of them had seen Him exercise His power in healing the sick and controlling satanic agencies. They believed that He possessed power to set up His kingdom at Jerusalem, power to quell all opposition, power over the elements of nature. He had stilled the angry waters; He had walked upon the white-crested billows; He had raised the dead to life. Now He declared that "all power" was given to Him. His words carried the minds of His hearers above earthly and temporal things to the heavenly and eternal. They were lifted to the highest conception of His dignity and glory.

Christ's words on the mountainside were the announcement that His sacrifice in behalf of man was full and complete. The conditions of the atonement had been fulfilled; the work for which He came to this world had been accomplished. He was on His way to the throne of God, to be honored by angels, principalities, and powers. He had entered upon His mediatorial work. Clothed with boundless authority, He gave His commission to the disciples: "Go ye therefore, and teach all nations," "baptizing them into the name of the Father and of the Son and of the Holy Spirit: teaching them to observe all things whatsoever I commanded you: and lo, I am with you always, even unto the end of the world." Matt. 28:19, 20, R. V.

The Jewish people had been made the depositaries of sacred truth; but Pharisaism had made them the most exclusive, the most bigoted, of [819-820] all the human race. Everything about the priests and rulers--their

2. "All power is given unto Me in heaven and in earth...His words, falling from lips that had been closed in death, t_____ _____ them with peculiar power...His words carried the minds of His hearers a_____ earthly and temporal things to the heavenly and eternal. They were lifted to the highest conception of His dignity and g_____." (819). Lord, open my eyes to the thrill of Your words, to the highest conception of Your dignity and glory. How do I short-change myself, in not taking time in Your Word, to hear and see You? _____

_____
_____
_____

dress, customs, ceremonies, traditions--made them unfit to be the light of the world. They looked upon themselves, the Jewish nation, as the world. But Christ commissioned His disciples to proclaim a faith and worship that would have in it nothing of caste or country, a faith that would be adapted to all peoples, all nations, all classes of men.

Before leaving His disciples, Christ plainly stated the nature of His kingdom. He called to their minds what He had previously told them concerning it. He declared that it was not His purpose to establish in this world a temporal, but a spiritual kingdom. He was not to reign as an earthly king on David's throne. Again He opened to them the Scriptures, showing that all He had passed through had been ordained in heaven, in the councils between the Father and Himself. All had been foretold by men inspired by the Holy Spirit. He said, You see that all I have revealed to you concerning My rejection as the Messiah has come to pass. All I have said in regard to the humiliation I should endure and the death I should die, has been verified. On the third day I rose again. Search the Scriptures more diligently, and you will see that in all these things the specifications of prophecy concerning Me have been fulfilled.

Christ commissioned His disciples to do the work He had left in their hands, beginning at Jerusalem. Jerusalem had been the scene of His amazing condescension for the human race. There He had suffered, been rejected and condemned. The land of Judea was His birthplace. There, clad in the garb of humanity, He had walked with men, and few had discerned how near heaven came to the earth when Jesus was among them. At Jerusalem the work of the disciples must begin.

In view of all that Christ had suffered there, and the unappreciated labor He had put forth, the disciples might have pleaded for a more promising field; but they made no such plea. The very ground where He had scattered the seed of truth was to be cultivated by the disciples, and the seed would spring up and yield an abundant harvest. In their work the disciples would have to meet persecution through the jealousy and hatred of the Jews; but this had been endured by their Master, and they were not to flee from it. The first offers of mercy must be made to the murderers of the Saviour.

And there were in Jerusalem many who had secret-

3. "The first offers of mercy must be made to the m_____ of the Sav-

ly believed on Jesus, and many who had been deceived by the priests and rulers. To these also the gospel was to be presented. They were to be called to [820-821] repentance. The wonderful truth that through Christ alone could remission of sins be obtained was to be made plain. While all Jerusalem was stirred by the thrilling events of the past few weeks, the preaching of the gospel would make the deepest impression.

But the work was not to stop here. It was to be extended to the earth's remotest bounds. To His disciples Christ said, You have been witnesses of My life of self-sacrifice in behalf of the world. You have witnessed My labors for Israel. Although they would not come unto Me that they might have life, although priests and rulers have done to Me as they listed, although they have rejected Me as the Scriptures foretold, they shall have still another opportunity of accepting the Son of God. You have seen that all who come to Me, confessing their sins, I freely receive. Him that cometh to Me I will in nowise cast out. All who will, may be reconciled to God, and receive everlasting life. To you, My disciples, I commit this message of mercy. It is to be given to Israel first, and then to all nations, tongues, and peoples. It is to be given to Jews and Gentiles. All who believe are to be gathered into one church.

Through the gift of the Holy Spirit the disciples were to receive a marvelous power. Their testimony was to be confirmed by signs and wonders. Miracles would be wrought, not only by the apostles, but by those who received their message. Jesus said, "In My name shall they cast out devils; they shall speak with new tongues; they shall take up serpents; and if they drink any deadly thing, it shall not hurt them; they shall lay hands on the sick, and they shall recover." Mark 16:17, 18.

At that time poisoning was often practiced. Unscrupulous men did not hesitate to remove by this means those who stood in the way of their ambition. Jesus knew that the life of His disciples would thus be imperiled. Many would think it doing God service to put His witnesses to death. He therefore promised them protection from this danger.

The disciples were to have the same power which Jesus had to heal "all manner of sickness and all manner of disease among the people." By healing in His name the diseases of the body, they would testify to His

ior...All who will, may be r_____ to God and receive everlasting life. To you, My disciples, I c_____ this message of mercy." (820, 821). Lord, I am the chief of sinners; and You're saying that I can be reconciled! I can be one with You! You want me to be Your friend! It is hard to believe, but I'll take it! AND You've entrusted me to share this message of mercy. Use me today: _____

_____

_____

_____

power for the healing of the soul. Matt. 4:23; 9:6. And a new endowment was now promised. The disciples were to preach among other nations, and they would receive power to speak other tongues. The apostles and their associates were unlettered men, yet through the outpouring of the Spirit on the day of Pentecost, their speech, whether in their own or a foreign language, became pure, simple, and accurate, both in word and in accent. [821-822]

4. "Christ gave His disciples their commission. He made f_____ provision for the prosecution of the work, and took upon Himself r_____ for its success...Everyone who hears is to r_____ the invitation. Whatever one's calling in life, his f_____ _____ interest should be to be to w_____ souls for Christ." (822). Lord, train my mind and my heart, to have that interest for sin-sick souls. You've been so good to me! So why don't I share it more? _____
_____
_____
_____

Thus Christ gave His disciples their commission. He made full provision for the prosecution of the work, and took upon Himself the responsibility for its success. So long as they obeyed His word, and worked in connection with Him, they could not fail. Go to all nations, He bade them. Go to the farthest part of the habitable globe, but know that My presence will be there. Labor in faith and confidence, for the time will never come when I will forsake you.

The Saviour's commission to the disciples included all the believers. It includes all believers in Christ to the end of time. It is a fatal mistake to suppose that the work of saving souls depends alone on the ordained minister. All to whom the heavenly inspiration has come are put in trust with the gospel. All who receive the life of Christ are ordained to work for the salvation of their fellow men. For this work the church was established, and all who take upon themselves its sacred vows are thereby pledged to be co-workers with Christ.

"The Spirit and the bride say, Come. And let him that heareth say, Come." Rev. 22:17. Everyone who hears is to repeat the invitation. Whatever one's calling in life, his first interest should be to win souls for Christ. He may not be able to speak to congregations, but he can work for individuals. To them he can communicate the instruction received from his Lord. Ministry does not consist alone in preaching. Those minister who relieve the sick and suffering, helping the needy, speaking words of comfort to the desponding and those of little faith. Nigh and afar off are souls weighed down by a sense of guilt. It is not hardship, toil, or poverty that degrades humanity. It is guilt, wrongdoing. This brings unrest and dissatisfaction. Christ would have His servants minister to sin-sick souls.

The disciples were to begin their work where they were. The hardest and most unpromising field was not to be passed by. So every one of Christ's workers is to begin where he is. In our own families may be souls hungry for sympathy, starving for the bread of life. There may be children to be trained for Christ. There are heathen at our very doors. Let us do faithfully the work that is nearest. Then let our efforts be extended as far as God's hand may lead the way. The work of many may appear to be restricted by circumstances; but, wherever it is, if performed with faith and diligence it will be felt to the uttermost parts of the earth. Christ's work when upon earth appeared to be confined to a narrow field, but multitudes from all lands heard His message. God often uses the simplest means to accomplish the greatest results. It is [822-823] His plan that every part of His work shall depend on every other part, as a wheel within a wheel, all acting in harmony. The humblest worker, moved by the Holy Spirit, will touch invisible chords, whose vibrations will ring to the ends of the earth, and make melody through eternal ages.

But the command, "Go ye into all the world," is not to be lost sight of. We are called upon to lift our eyes to the "regions beyond." Christ tears away the wall of partition, the dividing prejudice of nationality, and teaches a love for all the human family. He lifts men from the narrow circle which their selfishness prescribes; He abolishes all territorial lines and artificial distinctions of society. He makes no difference between neighbors and strangers, friends and enemies. He teaches us to look upon every needy soul as our brother, and the world as our field.

When the Saviour said, "Go, . . . teach all nations," He said also, "These signs shall follow them that believe; In My name shall they cast out devils; they shall speak with new tongues; they shall take up serpents; and if they drink any deadly thing, it shall not hurt them; they shall lay hands on the sick, and they shall recover." The promise is as far-reaching as the commission. Not that all the gifts are imparted to each believer. The Spirit divides "to every man severally as He will." 1 Cor. 12:11. But the gifts of the Spirit are promised to every believer according to his need for the Lord's work. The promise is just as strong and trustworthy now as in the days of the apostles. "These signs shall follow them that believe." This is the privilege of God's children, and faith should lay hold on all that it is possible to have as

5. "The gifts of the Spirit are p_____ to every believer according to his n_____ for the Lord's work...

an indorsement of faith.

"They shall lay hands on the sick, and they shall recover." This world is a vast lazar house, but Christ came to heal the sick, to proclaim deliverance to the captives of Satan. He was in Himself health and strength. He imparted His life to the sick, the afflicted, those possessed of demons. He turned away none who came to receive His healing power. He knew that those who petitioned Him for help had brought disease upon themselves; yet He did not refuse to heal them. And when virtue from Christ entered into these poor souls, they were convicted of sin, and many were healed of their spiritual disease, as well as of their physical maladies. The gospel still possesses the same power, and why should we not today witness the same results?

Christ feels the woes of every sufferer. When evil spirits rend a human frame, Christ feels the curse. When fever is burning up the life current, He feels the agony. And He is just as willing to heal the sick now as when He was personally on earth. Christ's servants are His [823-824] representatives, the channels for His working. He desires through them to exercise His healing power.

In the Saviour's manner of healing there were lessons for His disciples. On one occasion He anointed the eyes of a blind man with clay, and bade him, "Go, wash in the pool of Siloam. . . . He went his way therefore, and washed, and came seeing." John 9:7. The cure could be wrought only by the power of the Great Healer, yet Christ made use of the simple agencies of nature. While He did not give countenance to drug medication, He sanctioned the use of simple and natural remedies.

To many of the afflicted ones who received healing, Christ said, "Sin no more, lest a worse thing come unto thee." John 5:14. Thus He taught that disease is the result of violating God's laws, both natural and spiritual. The great misery in the world would not exist did men but live in harmony with the Creator's plan.

Christ had been the guide and teacher of ancient Israel, and He taught them that health is the reward of obedience to the laws of God. The Great Physician who healed the sick in Palestine had spoken to His people from the pillar of cloud, telling them what they must do, and what God would do for them. "If thou wilt diligently hearken to the voice of the Lord thy God," He

---

When virtue from Christ entered into these poor souls, they were c_____ of sin, and many were h_____ of their spiritual disease, as well as their physical maladies. The gospel still possesses the same p_____, and why should we today not witness the same r_____?" (823). Lord, I need healing, of many spiritual diseases: pride, self-centeredness. Do I cling to these, limiting Your virtue in entering me, and drawing me into closer harmony with You? _____

_____

6. "To many of the afflicted ones who received healing, Christ said, 'Sin no more...' Disease is the result of v_____ God's laws, both natural and spiritual. The great misery in the world would not exist did men but live in h_____ with the Creator's plan." (824). Lord, does the enemy not bring some disease, as in Job's case? _____. Yet, don't let me use that as a cover for an unhealthy lifestyle. Help me to not knowingly

said, "and wilt do that which is right in His sight, and wilt give ear to His commandments, and keep all His statutes, I will put none of these diseases upon thee, which I have brought upon the Egyptians: for I am the Lord that healeth thee." Ex. 15:26. Christ gave to Israel definite instruction in regard to their habits of life, and He assured them, "The Lord will take away from thee all sickness." Deut. 7:15. When they fulfilled the conditions, the promise was verified to them. "There was not one feeble person among their tribes." Ps. 105:37.

These lessons are for us. There are conditions to be observed by all who would preserve health. All should learn what these conditions are. The Lord is not pleased with ignorance in regard to His laws, either natural or spiritual. We are to be workers together with God for the restoration of health to the body as well as to the soul.

And we should teach others how to preserve and to recover health. For the sick we should use the remedies which God has provided in nature, and we should point them to Him who alone can restore. It is our work to present the sick and suffering to Christ in the arms of our faith. We should teach them to believe in the Great Healer. We should lay hold on His promise, and pray for the manifestation of His power. The very essence of the gospel is restoration, and the Saviour would have us bid [824-825] the sick, the hopeless, and the afflicted take hold upon His strength.

The power of love was in all Christ's healing, and only by partaking of that love, through faith, can we be instruments for His work. If we neglect to link ourselves in divine connection with Christ, the current of life-giving energy cannot flow in rich streams from us to the people. There were places where the Saviour Himself could not do many mighty works because of their unbelief. So now unbelief separates the church from her divine Helper. Her hold upon eternal realities is weak. By her lack of faith, God is disappointed, and robbed of His glory.

It is in doing Christ's work that the church has the promise of His presence. Go teach all nations, He said; "and, lo, I am with you alway, even unto the end of the world." To take His yoke is one of the first conditions of receiving His power. The very life of the church depends upon her faithfulness in fulfilling the Lord's com-

and deliberately be out of harmony with any of Your guidelines for natural and spiritual health. Show me where I am: _____
_____
_____
_____

7. "The very essence of the gospel is r_____ _____...The power of love was in all Christ's healing, and only by partaking of that love, through faith, can we be i_____ of His work...Unbelief s_____ the church from her divine Helper. Her hold upon eternal realities is weak. By her lack of faith, God is disappointed, and r_____ of His glory." (824, 825). Lord, on each and every day of my walk with You, help me not to "neglect to link" myself in "divine connection" with You. May I partake of Your love, Your new compasssions every morning:
_____
_____
_____

8. "It is in doing Christ's work, that the church has the promise of His p____ _____... To take His yoke is one of the first conditions of receiving His p_____. The very l_____ of the church depends upon her faithful-

ness in fulfilling the Lord's commission…Where there is no active labor for others, love wanes, and faith grows dim." Spiritual feebleness and decay is not my goal, Lord. That is why I am trying this daily spiritual exercise program, my walk with You. I want to claim the promise of Your presence:_____

_____

_____

_____

mission. To neglect this work is surely to invite spiritual feebleness and decay. Where there is no active labor for others, love wanes, and faith grows dim.

Christ intends that His ministers shall be educators of the church in gospel work. They are to teach the people how to seek and save the lost. But is this the work they are doing? Alas, how many are toiling to fan the spark of life in a church that is ready to die! How many churches are tended like sick lambs by those who ought to be seeking for the lost sheep! And all the time millions upon millions without Christ are perishing.

Divine love has been stirred to its unfathomable depths for the sake of men, and angels marvel to behold in the recipients of so great love a mere surface gratitude. Angels marvel at man's shallow appreciation of the love of God. Heaven stands indignant at the neglect shown to the souls of men. Would we know how Christ regards it? How would a father and mother feel, did they know that their child, lost in the cold and the snow, had been passed by, and left to perish, by those who might have saved it? Would they not be terribly grieved, wildly indignant? Would they not denounce those murderers with wrath hot as their tears, intense as their love? The sufferings of every man are the sufferings of God's child, and those who reach out no helping hand to their perishing fellow beings provoke His righteous anger. This is the wrath of the Lamb. To those who claim fellowship with Christ, yet have been indifferent to the needs of their fellow men, He will declare in the great Judgment day, "I know you not whence ye are; depart from Me, all ye workers of iniquity." Luke 13:27. [825-826]

In the commission to His disciples, Christ not only outlined their work, but gave them their message. Teach the people, He said, "to observe all things whatsoever I have commanded you." The disciples were to teach what Christ had taught. That which He had spoken, not only in person, but through all the prophets and teachers of the Old Testament, is here included. Human teaching is shut out. There is no place for tradition, for man's theories and conclusions, or for church legislation. No laws ordained by ecclesiastical authority are included in the commission. None of these are Christ's servants to teach. "The law and the prophets," with the record of His own words and deeds, are the treasure committed to the disciples to be given to the world. Christ's name is their watchword, their badge of distinction, their bond of union, the authority for their course of action, and the source of their success. Nothing that does not bear His superscription is to be recognized in His kingdom.

The gospel is to be presented, not as a lifeless theory, but as a living force to change the life. God desires that the receivers of His grace shall be witnesses to its power. Those whose course has been most offensive to Him He freely accepts; when they repent, He imparts to them His divine Spirit, places them in the highest positions of trust, and sends them forth into the camp of the disloyal to proclaim His boundless mercy. He would have His servants bear testimony to the fact that through His grace men may possess Christlikeness of character, and may rejoice in the assurance of His great love. He would have us bear testimony to the fact that He cannot be satisfied until the human race are reclaimed and reinstated in their holy privileges as His sons and daughters.

In Christ is the tenderness of the shepherd, the affection of the parent, and the matchless grace of the compassionate Saviour. His blessings He presents in the most alluring terms. He is not content merely to announce these blessings; He presents them in the most attractive way, to excite a desire to possess them. So His servants are to present the riches of the glory of the unspeakable Gift. The wonderful love of Christ will melt and subdue hearts, when the mere reiteration of doctrines would accomplish nothing. "Comfort ye, comfort ye My people, saith your God." "O Zion, that bringest good tidings, get thee up into the high mountain; O Jerusalem, that bringest good tidings, lift up thy voice with strength; lift it up, be not afraid; say unto the cities of Judah, Behold your God! . . . He shall feed His flock like a shepherd: He shall gather the lambs with His arm, and carry them in His bosom." Isa. 40:1, 9-11. [826-827] Tell the people of Him who is "the Chiefest among ten thousand," and the One "altogether lovely." The Song of Solomon 5:10, 16. Words alone cannot tell it. Let it be reflected in the character and manifested in the life. Christ is sitting for His portrait in every disciple. Every one God has predestinated to be "conformed to the image of His Son." Rom. 8:29. In every one Christ's long-suffering love, His holiness, meekness, mercy, and

9. "The gospel is to be presented, not as a l_____ ___ theory, but as a living force to c_____ the life…Bear testimony to the fact that through His grace men may possess C_____ of character, and may rejoice in the a_____ of His great love…The wonderful love of Christ will m_____ and subdue hearts, when the mere reiteration of doctrine would accomplish n_____." (826). Lord, may my contemplation of Your life and character melt my heart, and mold my character to be like Yours. What is in my heart that needs melting? _____ _____

10. "Words alone cannot tell it. Let it be r_____ _____ in the character, and manifested in the life. Christ is sitting for His p_____ in every disciple…Let Chris-

truth are to be manifested to the world.

The first disciples went forth preaching the word. They revealed Christ in their lives. And the Lord worked with them, "confirming the word with signs following." Mark 16:20. These disciples prepared themselves for their work. Before the day of Pentecost they met together, and put away all differences. They were of one accord. They believed Christ's promise that the blessing would be given, and they prayed in faith. They did not ask for a blessing for themselves merely; they were weighted with the burden for the salvation of souls. The gospel was to be carried to the uttermost parts of the earth, and they claimed the endowment of power that Christ had promised. Then it was that the Holy Spirit was poured out, and thousands were converted in a day.

So it may be now. Instead of man's speculations, let the word of God be preached. Let Christians put away their dissensions, and give themselves to God for the saving of the lost. Let them in faith ask for the blessing, and it will come. The outpouring of the Spirit in apostolic days was the "former rain," and glorious was the result. But the "latter rain" will be more abundant. Joel 2:23.

All who consecrate soul, body, and spirit to God will be constantly receiving a new endowment of physical and mental power. The inexhaustible supplies of heaven are at their command. Christ gives them the breath of His own spirit, the life of His own life. The Holy Spirit puts forth its highest energies to work in heart and mind. The grace of God enlarges and multiplies their faculties, and every perfection of the divine nature comes to their assistance in the work of saving souls. Through co-operation with Christ they are complete in Him, and in their human weakness they are enabled to do the deeds of Omnipotence.

The Saviour longs to manifest His grace and stamp His character on the whole world. It is His purchased possession, and He desires to make men free, and pure, and holy. Though Satan works to hinder this purpose, yet through the blood shed for the world there are triumphs to be achieved that will bring glory to God and the Lamb. Christ will not be satisfied till the victory is complete, and "He shall see of the travail [826-827] of His soul, and shall be satisfied." Isa. 53:11. All the na-

tians put away their d___ _____, and give themselves to God for the saving of the lost." (827). Lord, let me be a nail, from which hangs Your picture. May Your character be reflected in my life, as I behold You:. Is what I testify out of harmony with my life? How? _____
_____
_____
_____

tions of the earth shall hear the gospel of His grace. Not all will receive His grace; but "a seed shall serve Him; it shall be accounted to the Lord for a generation." Ps. 22:30. "The kingdom and dominion, and the greatness of the kingdom under the whole heaven, shall be given to the people of the saints of the Most High," and "the earth shall be full of the knowledge of the Lord, as the waters cover the sea." "So shall they fear the name of the Lord from the west, and His glory from the rising of the sun." Dan. 7:27; Isa. 11:9; 59:19.

"How beautiful upon the mountains are the feet of him that bringeth good tidings, that publisheth peace; that bringeth good tidings of good, that publisheth salvation; that saith unto Zion, Thy God reigneth! . . . Break forth into joy, sing together, ye waste places: . . . for the Lord hath comforted His people. . . . The Lord hath made bare His holy arm in the eyes of all the nations; and all the ends of the earth shall see the salvation of our God." Isa. 52:7-10.

Prayer journal: _____
_____
_____
_____
_____
_____
_____

Chapter 87

"To My Father, and Your Father"

[This chapter is based on Luke 24:50-53; Acts 1:9-12.]

1. "Not Mount Moriah... was to be thus honored... There the waves of mercy, still returning in a stronger tide of l_____, had been beaten back by hearts as hard as rock." Lord, how do I reject Your mercy and love? How does my hard heart beat back Your compassion? _____

_____

_____

May this spiritual walk, meditating on Your life, soften my heart, melt my heart, put a new heart within me. I don't want to miss any gestures of Your love. How do I beat back Your love?

_____

_____

_____

2. "In the garden of Gethsemane at the foot [of the Mount of Olives] He had prayed and a_____ alone. From this mountain He was to a_____ to heaven. Upon its summit His feet will rest when He shall come a_____ _____. Not as a man of sorrows, but as a glorious and t_____ king He will stand upon Olivet." (830). Lord, this

The time had come for Christ to ascend to His Father's throne. As a divine conqueror He was about to return with the trophies of victory to the heavenly courts. Before His death He had declared to His Father, "I have finished the work which Thou gavest Me to do." John 17:4. After His resurrection He tarried on earth for a season, that His disciples might become familiar with Him in His risen and glorified body. Now He was ready for the leave-taking. He had authenticated the fact that He was a living Saviour. His disciples need no longer associate Him with the tomb. They could think of Him as glorified before the heavenly universe.

As the place of His ascension, Jesus chose the spot so often hallowed by His presence while He dwelt among men. Not Mount Zion, the place of David's city, not Mount Moriah, the temple site, was to be thus honored. There Christ had been mocked and rejected. There the waves of mercy, still returning in a stronger tide of love, had been beaten back by hearts as hard as rock. Thence Jesus, weary and heart-burdened, had gone forth to find rest in the Mount of Olives. The holy Shekinah, in departing from the first temple, had stood upon the eastern mountain, as if loath to forsake the chosen city; so Christ stood upon Olivet, with yearning heart overlooking Jerusalem. The groves and glens of the [829-830] mountain had been consecrated by His prayers and tears. Its steeps had echoed the triumphant shouts of the multitude that proclaimed Him king. On its sloping descent He had found a home with Lazarus at Bethany. In the garden of Gethsemane at its foot He had prayed and agonized alone. From this mountain He was to ascend to heaven. Upon its summit His feet will rest when He shall come again. Not as a man of sorrows, but as a glorious and triumphant king He will stand upon Olivet, while Hebrew hallelujahs mingle with Gentile hosannas, and the voices of the redeemed as a mighty host shall swell the acclamation, "Crown

Him Lord of all!

Now with the eleven disciples Jesus made His way toward the mountain. As they passed through the gate of Jerusalem, many wondering eyes looked upon the little company, led by One whom a few weeks before the rulers had condemned and crucified. The disciples knew not that this was to be their last interview with their Master. Jesus spent the time in conversation with them, repeating His former instruction. As they approached Gethsemane, He paused, that they might call to mind the lessons He had given them on the night of His great agony. Again He looked upon the vine by which He had then represented the union of His church with Himself and His Father; again He repeated the truths He had then unfolded. All around Him were reminders of His unrequited love. Even the disciples who were so dear to His heart, had, in the hour of His humiliation, reproached and forsaken Him.

Christ had sojourned in the world for thirty-three years; He had endured its scorn, insult, and mockery; He had been rejected and crucified. Now, when about to ascend to His throne of glory,--as He reviews the ingratitude of the people He came to save,--will He not withdraw from them His sympathy and love? Will not His affections be centered upon that realm where He is appreciated, and where sinless angels wait to do His bidding? No; His promise to those loved ones whom He leaves on earth is, "I am with you alway, even unto the end of the world." Matt. 28:20.

Upon reaching the Mount of Olives, Jesus led the way across the summit, to the vicinity of Bethany. Here He paused, and the disciples gathered about Him. Beams of light seemed to radiate from His countenance as He looked lovingly upon them. He upbraided them not for their faults and failures; words of the deepest tenderness were the last that fell upon their ears from the lips of their Lord. With hands outstretched [830-831] in blessing, and as if in assurance of His protecting care, He slowly ascended from among them, drawn heavenward by a power stronger than any earthly attraction. As He passed upward, the awe-stricken disciples looked with straining eyes for the last glimpse of their ascending Lord. A cloud of glory hid Him from their sight; and the words came back to them as the cloudy chariot of angels received Him, "Lo, I am with you alway, even unto

sounds like the third coming, but I want to be there for both. You have done so much for me. I long to worship and honor You!

_____
_____
_____

3. "As He reviews the i_____ of the people He came to save, will He not w_____ ___ from them His sympathy and love? Will not His affections be centered upon that realm where He is a_____, and where sinless angels wait to do His bidding? N___." Lord, to withdraw love is what I would do. I do it a lot. How do I let Your love flow through me?

_____
_____
_____
_____

4. "He upbraided them [the disciples] not for their f___ _____ and failures; words of the deepest tenderness were the l_____ that fell upon their ears from the lips of their Lord."

What percentage of my words are encouraging?

_____

_____ How can the percentage change?

_____
_____
_____
_____

5. "With e_____ desire all heaven had waited for the end of His tarrying in a world marred by the curse of sin. The time had now come for the heavenly universe to r_____ their King." (832). Lord, will the anticipation be similar when You return to heaven the second time (with the saints)? _____

I don't want to detract from that moment, by my absence. May mediating on Your great sacrifice, increase my appreciation, and my desire to affirm You, that Your sacrifice was worth it:_____
_____
_____
_____

the end of the world." At the same time there floated down to them the sweetest and most joyous music from the angel choir.

While the disciples were still gazing upward, voices addressed them which sounded like richest music. They turned, and saw two angels in the form of men, who spoke to them, saying, "Ye men of Galilee, why stand ye gazing up into heaven? this same Jesus, which is taken up from [831-832] you into heaven, shall so come in like manner as ye have seen Him go into heaven."

These angels were of the company that had been waiting in a shining cloud to escort Jesus to His heavenly home. The most exalted of the angel throng, they were the two who had come to the tomb at Christ's resurrection, and they had been with Him throughout His life on earth. With eager desire all heaven had waited for the end of His tarrying in a world marred by the curse of sin. The time had now come for the heavenly universe to receive their King. Did not the two angels long to join the throng that welcomed Jesus? But in sympathy and love for those whom He had left, they waited to give them comfort. "Are they not all ministering spirits, sent forth to minister for them who shall be heirs of salvation?" Heb. 1:14.

Christ had ascended to heaven in the form of humanity. The disciples had beheld the cloud receive Him. The same Jesus who had walked and talked and prayed with them; who had broken bread with them; who had been with them in their boats on the lake; and who had that very day toiled with them up the ascent of Olivet,--the same Jesus had now gone to share His Father's throne. And the angels had assured them that the very One whom they had seen go up into heaven, would come again even as He had ascended. He will come "with clouds; and every eye shall see Him." "The Lord Himself shall descend from heaven with a shout, with the voice of the Archangel, and with the trump of God: and the dead in Christ shall rise." "The Son of man shall come in His glory, and all the holy angels with Him, then shall He sit upon the throne of His glory." Rev. 1:7; 1 Thess. 4:16; Matt. 25:31. Thus will be fulfilled the Lord's own promise to His disciples: "If I go and prepare a place for you, I will come again, and receive you unto Myself; that where I am, there ye may be also." John 14:3. Well might the disciples rejoice in the hope of their Lord's return.

When the disciples went back to Jerusalem, the people looked upon them with amazement. After the trial and crucifixion of Christ, it had been thought that they would appear downcast and ashamed. Their enemies expected to see upon their faces an expression of sorrow and defeat. Instead of this there was only gladness and triumph. Their faces were aglow with a happiness not born of earth. They did not mourn over disappointed hopes, but were full of praise and thanksgiving to God. With rejoicing they told the wonderful story of Christ's resurrection and His ascension to heaven, and their testimony was received by many. [832-833]

The disciples no longer had any distrust of the future. They knew that Jesus was in heaven, and that His sympathies were with them still. They knew that they had a friend at the throne of God, and they were eager to present their requests to the Father in the name of Jesus. In solemn awe they bowed in prayer, repeating the assurance, "Whatsoever ye shall ask the Father in My name, He will give it you. Hitherto have ye asked nothing in My name: ask, and ye shall receive, that your joy may be full." John 16:23, 24. They extended the hand of faith higher and higher, with the mighty argument, "It is Christ that died, yea rather, that is risen again, who is even at the right hand of God, who also maketh intercession for us." Rom. 8:34. And Pentecost brought them fullness of joy in the presence of the Comforter, even as Christ had promised.

All heaven was waiting to welcome the Saviour to the celestial courts. As He ascended, He led the way, and the multitude of captives set free at His resurrection followed. The heavenly host, with shouts and acclamations of praise and celestial song, attended the joyous train.

As they drew near to the city of God, the challenge is given by the escorting angels,--

> "Lift up your heads, O ye gates;
> And be ye lift up, ye everlasting doors;
> And the King of glory shall come in."

Joyfully the waiting sentinels respond,--

> "Who is this King of glory?"

6. The disciples were not down cast and ashamed. "They did not m_____ over disappointed hopes, but were full of p_____ ____ and thanksgiving to God...[They] no longer had any d_____ of the future. They knew that Jesus was in heaven, and that His s_____ were with them still. They knew that they had a f___ _____ at the throne of God." (832, 833). Lord, do people look upon me and my witness with amazement? _____ Why am I not, "with rejoicing," telling the "wonderful story" of Your resurrection and ascension?

_____

_____

_____

This they say, not because they know not who He is, but because they would hear the answer of exalted praise,--

> "The Lord strong and mighty,
> The Lord mighty in battle!
> Lift up your heads, O ye gates;
> Even lift them up, ye everlasting doors;
> And the King of glory shall come in."

Again is heard the challenge, "Who is this King of glory?" for the angels never weary of hearing His name exalted. The escorting angels make reply,--

> "The Lord of hosts;
> He is the King of glory." Ps. 24:7-10.

7. "Then the portals of the city of God are opened w_____, and the angelic throng sweep through the gates amid a burst of r_____ ____ music." Lord, how can I give You such a welcome to my heart? ____
_____
_____
_____
_____
_____

Then the portals of the city of God are opened wide, and the angelic throng sweep through the gates amid a burst of rapturous music. [833-834]

There is the throne, and around it the rainbow of promise. There are cherubim and seraphim. The commanders of the angel hosts, the sons of God, the representatives of the unfallen worlds, are assembled. The heavenly council before which Lucifer had accused God and His Son, the representatives of those sinless realms over which Satan had thought to establish his dominion,--all are there to welcome the Redeemer. They are eager to celebrate His triumph and to glorify their King.

But He waves them back. Not yet; He cannot now receive the coronet of glory and the royal robe. He enters into the presence of His Father. He points to His wounded head, the pierced side, the marred feet; He lifts His hands, bearing the print of nails. He points to the tokens of His triumph; He presents to God the wave sheaf, those raised with Him as representatives of that great multitude who shall come forth from the grave at His second coming. He approaches the Father, with whom there is joy over one sinner that repents; who rejoices over one with singing. Before the foundations of the earth were laid, the Father and the Son had united in a covenant to redeem man if he should be overcome by Satan. They had clasped Their hands in a solemn pledge that Christ should become the surety for the human race. This pledge Christ has fulfilled. When upon

8. Jesus "approaches the Father, with whom there is j____ over one sinner that repents; who rejoices over one with s_____." (834). Is the Father in any way reluctant to accept us?
_____
"The Father and Son had u_____ in a covenant to redeem man." For God so loved the world!
_____
_____

the cross He cried out, "It is finished," He addressed the Father. The compact had been fully carried out. Now He declares: Father, it is finished. I have done Thy will, O My God. I have completed the work of redemption. If Thy justice is satisfied, "I will that they also, whom Thou hast given Me, be with Me where I am." John 19:30; 17:24.

The voice of God is heard proclaiming that justice is satisfied. Satan is vanquished. Christ's toiling, struggling ones on earth are "accepted in the Beloved." Eph. 1:6. Before the heavenly angels and the representatives of unfallen worlds, they are declared justified. Where He is, there His church shall be. "Mercy and truth are met together; righteousness and peace have kissed each other." Ps. 85:10. The Father's arms encircle His Son, and the word is given, "Let all the angels of God worship Him." Heb. 1:6.

With joy unutterable, rulers and principalities and powers acknowledge the supremacy of the Prince of life. The angel host prostrate themselves before Him, while the glad shout fills all the courts of heaven, "Worthy is the Lamb that was slain to receive power, and riches, and wisdom, and strength, and honor, and glory, and blessing." Rev. 5:12. [834-835]

Songs of triumph mingle with the music from angel harps, till heaven seems to overflow with joy and praise. Love has conquered. The lost is found. Heaven rings with voices in lofty strains proclaiming, "Blessing, and honor, and glory, and power, be unto Him that sitteth upon the throne, and unto the Lamb forever and ever." Rev. 5:13. ----------

From that scene of heavenly joy, there comes back to us on earth the echo of Christ's own wonderful words, "I ascend unto My Father, and your Father; and to My God, and your God." John 20:17. The family of heaven and the family of earth are one. For us our Lord ascended, and for us He lives. "Wherefore He is able also to save them to the uttermost that come unto God by Him, seeing He ever liveth to make intercession for them." Heb. 7:25.

9. "The voice of God is heard proclaiming that justice is s_____. Satan is vanquished. Christ's toiling, struggling ones on earth are 'a___ _____ in the Beloved.'" Hallelujah! Lord, help keep that vision ever before me, so that I need not get defensive towards others or insecure: _____ _____

10. "L_____ has conquered." (835). Lord, may this principle govern and guide my life. In my daily life, of preparing for eternity, may I see the true value of Your love, and live it: _____ _____ _____

11. "The family of heaven and the family of earth are o_____." Lord, what does and should this mean to me? _____ _____ _____

Prayer journal: _____ _____ _____ _____ _____

1-God's Love for Man

Nature and revelation alike testify of God's love. Our Father in heaven is the source of life, of wisdom, and of joy. Look at the wonderful and beautiful things of nature. Think of their marvelous adaptation to the needs and happiness, not only of man, but of all living creatures. The sunshine and the rain, that gladden and refresh the earth, the hills and seas and plains, all speak to us of the Creator's love. It is God who supplies the daily needs of all His creatures. In the beautiful words of the psalmist--

"The eyes of all wait upon Thee;
And Thou givest them their meat in due season.
Thou openest Thine hand,
And satisfiest the desire of every living thing."
Psalm 145:15, 16.

God made man perfectly holy and happy; and the fair earth, as it came from the Creator's hand, bore no blight of decay or shadow of the curse. It is transgression of God's law--the law of love--that has brought woe and death. Yet even amid the suffering that results from sin, God's love is revealed. It is written that God cursed the ground for man's sake. Genesis 3:17. The thorn and the thistle--the difficulties and trials that make his life one of toil and care--were appointed for his good as a part of the training needful in God's plan for his uplifting from the ruin and degradation that sin has wrought. The [10] world, though fallen, is not all sorrow and misery. In nature itself are messages of hope and comfort. There are flowers upon the thistles, and the thorns are covered with roses.

"God is love" is written upon every opening bud, upon every spire of springing grass. The lovely birds making the air vocal with their happy songs, the delicately tinted flowers in their perfection perfuming the air, the lofty trees of the forest with their rich foliage

1. "It is God who supplies the d_____ needs of all His creatures... 'Thou... satisfiest the d_____ of every living thing.'" (9) Lord, as I go through the day, why am I so unaware of You? What am I preoccupied about? Sports? Meeting the expectations of the boss, the bank? Help me recognize the daily, everyday satisfactions from You, and appreciate Your expressions of love:

_____

_____

_____

2. "Even amid the s_____ that results from sin, God's love is revealed." Lord, I don't always see the flowers because of the thistles. I am sorry that I questioned Your goodness, Your love, when it was there all the time. What is the eye salve that helps me see?

_____

_____

_____

of living green--all testify to the tender, fatherly care of our God and to His desire to make His children happy.

The word of God reveals His character. He Himself has declared His infinite love and pity. When Moses prayed, "Show me Thy glory," the Lord answered, "I will make all My goodness pass before thee." Exodus 33:18, 19. This is His glory. The Lord passed before Moses, and proclaimed, "The Lord, The Lord God, merciful and gracious, long-suffering, and abundant in goodness and truth, keeping mercy for thousands, forgiving iniquity and transgression and sin." Exodus 34:6, 7. He is "slow to anger, and of great kindness," "because He delighteth in mercy." Jonah 4:2; Micah 7:18.

God has bound our hearts to Him by unnumbered tokens in heaven and in earth. Through the things of nature, and the deepest and tenderest earthly ties that human hearts can know, He has sought to reveal Himself to us. Yet these but imperfectly represent His love. Though all these evidences have been given, the enemy of good blinded the minds of men, so that they looked upon God with fear; they thought of [11] Him as severe and unforgiving. Satan led men to conceive of God as a being whose chief attribute is stern justice,--one who is a severe judge, a harsh, exacting creditor. He pictured the Creator as a being who is watching with jealous eye to discern the errors and mistakes of men, that He may visit judgments upon them. It was to remove this dark shadow, by revealing to the world the infinite love of God, that Jesus came to live among men.

The Son of God came from heaven to make manifest the Father. "No man hath seen God at any time; the only begotten Son, which is in the bosom of the Father, He hath declared Him." John 1:18. "Neither knoweth any man the Father, save the Son, and he to whomsoever the Son will reveal Him." Matthew 11:27. When one of the disciples made the request, "Show us the Father," Jesus answered, "Have I been so long time with you, and yet hast thou not known Me, Philip? He that hath seen Me hath seen the Father; and how sayest thou then, Show us the Father?" John 14:8, 9.

In describing His earthly mission, Jesus said, The Lord "hath anointed Me to preach the gospel to the poor; He hath sent Me to heal the brokenhearted, to preach deliverance to the captives, and recovering of sight to the blind, to set at liberty them that are bruised."

3. "The word of God reveals His c_____ _____ [His glory] [of] infinite love and pity...

The enemy of good b_____ _____ the minds of men, so that they looked upon God with fear; they thought of Him as severe and u_____ _____...a severe judge, a harsh, exacting creditor." (10, 11). Lord, how has Satan had success blinding my eyes, at times not seeing the evidences of Your character of love?

_____
_____
_____

4. "It was to remove this dark shadow, by revealing to the world the i_____ _____ love of God, that Jesus came to live among man...to make manifest the Father...Love, mercy,

Luke 4:18. This was His work. He went about doing good and healing all that were oppressed by Satan. There were whole villages where there was not a moan of sickness in any house, for He had passed through them and healed all their sick. His work gave evidence of His divine anointing. Love, mercy, and compassion were revealed in every act of [12] His life; His heart went out in tender sympathy to the children of men. He took man's nature, that He might reach man's wants. The poorest and humblest were not afraid to approach Him. Even little children were attracted to Him. They loved to climb upon His knees and gaze into the pensive face, benignant with love.

and compassion were revealed in every a_____ of His life." (12). Lord, I desire to draw close to You. Guide my 'Steps to Christ' as I read of Your life, of Your character and the Father's character of love. May Your love draw me close to You, and guide my walk to be instep with You. How can I let Your love be revealed in every act of my life? _____

Jesus did not suppress one word of truth, but He uttered it always in love. He exercised the greatest tact and thoughtful, kind attention in His intercourse with the people. He was never rude, never needlessly spoke a severe word, never gave needless pain to a sensitive soul. He did not censure human weakness. He spoke the truth, but always in love. He denounced hypocrisy, unbelief, and iniquity; but tears were in His voice as He uttered His scathing rebukes. He wept over Jerusalem, the city He loved, which refused to receive Him, the way, the truth, and the life. They had rejected Him, the Saviour, but He regarded them with pitying tenderness. His life was one of self-denial and thoughtful care for others. Every soul was precious in His eyes. While He ever bore Himself with divine dignity, He bowed with the tenderest regard to every member of the family of God. In all men He saw fallen souls whom it was His mission to save.

5. "Such is the character of Christ as revealed in His l_____." (12) Lord, what lessons are there for me? _____
_____

Such is the character of Christ as revealed in His life. This is the character of God. It is from the Father's heart that the streams of divine compassion, manifest in Christ, flow out to the children of men. Jesus, the tender, pitying Saviour, was God "manifest in the flesh." 1 Timothy 3:16. [13]

It was to redeem us that Jesus lived and suffered and died. He became "a Man of Sorrows," that we might be made partakers of everlasting joy. God permitted His beloved Son, full of grace and truth, to come from a world of indescribable glory, to a world marred and blighted with sin, darkened with the shadow of death and the curse. He permitted Him to leave the bosom of His love, the adoration of the angels, to suffer shame, insult, humiliation, hatred, and death. "The chastisement of our peace was upon Him; and with His stripes we are healed." Isaiah 53:5. Behold Him in the wilderness, in Gethsemane, upon the cross! The spotless Son of God took upon Himself the burden of sin. He who had been one with God, felt in His soul the awful separation that sin makes between God and man. This wrung from His lips the anguished cry, "My God, My God, why hast Thou forsaken Me?" Matthew 27:46. It was the burden of sin, the sense of its terrible enormity, of its separation of the soul from God--it was this that broke the heart of the Son of God.

But this great sacrifice was not made in order to create in the Father's heart a love for man, not to make Him willing to save. No, no! "God so loved the world, that He gave His only-begotten Son." John 3:16. The Father loves us, not because of the great propitiation, but He provided the propitiation because He loves us. Christ was the medium through which He could pour out His infinite love upon a fallen world. "God was in Christ, reconciling the world unto Himself." 2 Corinthians 5:19. God suffered with His Son. In the agony of Gethsemane, the death of [14] Calvary, the heart of Infinite Love paid the price of our redemption.

Jesus said, "Therefore doth My Father love Me, because I lay down My life, that I might take it again." John 10:17. That is, "My Father has so loved you that He even loves Me more for giving My life to redeem you. In becoming your Substitute and Surety, by surrendering My life, by taking your liabilities, your transgressions, I am endeared to My Father; for by My sacrifice, God can be just, and yet the Justifier of him who believeth in Jesus."

None but the Son of God could accomplish our redemption; for only He who was in the bosom of the Father could declare Him. Only He who knew the height and depth of the love of God could make it manifest. Nothing less than the infinite sacrifice made by Christ in behalf of fallen man could express the Father's love to lost humanity.

6. "The Father loves us, not because of the great propitiation, but He p___ _____ the propitiation because He loves us." (13). Lord, You were willing to have Your heart broken; Father, You were willing for Your Son to be made sin, to be so out of harmony as to be in a deadly clash with Your holy character, to be separated from Yourself, ALL because You both love me! Why? It is so hard to fathom:

_____
_____
_____
_____

7. "By My sacrifice, God can be j_____, and yet the Justifier of him who believeth in Jesus." (14). Lord, what do I need to learn from the truths of "Substitute," "Surety," "just," and "Justifier," on how they relate to a chapter entitled "God's Love for Man?" _____

_____
_____
_____
_____

8. "None but the Son of God could accomplish our redemption. [Why?] ... Nothing less than the infinite sacrifice made by Christ...could e_____ _____ the Father's love to lost humanity." Lord, You and the Father are one. You know love the best. Both of You are love. This sacrifice is deeper than a pay-

ment of a penalty. Thank You for this expression of Your awesome love! I want to be one with You and Your love: _____

_____

9. "He who was one with God has linked Himself with the children of men by ties that are n____ _____ to be broken." Lord, help me to understand and embrace that my walk with You is based on Your commitment and love and not my performance:

_____

_____

10. "That we should be called the sons of God... What a v_____ this places upon man!...The matchless love of God for a world that did not love Him! The thought has a subduing power upon the soul and brings the mind into   c_____ of the will of God." (15). Lord, I want that harmony and oneness with You. May I contemplate Your new compassions every morning, and study the divine character in the light of the cross: _____

_____

_____

Prayer journal: _____

_____

_____

_____

_____

_____

_____

"God so loved the world, that He gave His only-begotten Son." He gave Him not only to live among men, to bear their sins, and die their sacrifice. He gave Him to the fallen race. Christ was to identify Himself with the interests and needs of humanity. He who was one with God has linked Himself with the children of men by ties that are never to be broken. Jesus is "not ashamed to call them brethren" (Hebrews 2:11); He is our Sacrifice, our Advocate, our Brother, bearing our human form before the Father's throne, and through eternal ages one with the race He has redeemed--the Son of man. And all this that man might be uplifted from the ruin and degradation of sin that he might reflect the love of God and share the joy of holiness. [15]

The price paid for our redemption, the infinite sacrifice of our heavenly Father in giving His Son to die for us, should give us exalted conceptions of what we may become through Christ. As the inspired apostle John beheld the height, the depth, the breadth of the Father's love toward the perishing race, he was filled with adoration and reverence; and, failing to find suitable language in which to express the greatness and tenderness of this love, he called upon the world to behold it. "Behold, what manner of love the Father hath bestowed upon us, that we should be called the sons of God." 1 John 3:1. What a value this places upon man! Through transgression the sons of man become subjects of Satan. Through faith in the atoning sacrifice of Christ the sons of Adam may become the sons of God. By assuming human nature, Christ elevates humanity. Fallen men are placed where, through connection with Christ, they may indeed become worthy of the name "sons of God."

Such love is without a parallel. Children of the heavenly King! Precious promise! Theme for the most profound meditation! The matchless love of God for a world that did not love Him! The thought has a subduing power upon the soul and brings the mind into captivity to the will of God. The more we study the divine character in the light of the cross, the more we see mercy, tenderness, and forgiveness blended with equity and justice, and the more clearly we discern innumerable evidences of a love that is infinite and a tender pity surpassing a mother's yearning sympathy for her wayward child.

2-The Sinner's Need of Christ

Man was originally endowed with noble powers and a well-balanced mind. He was perfect in his being, and in harmony with God. His thoughts were pure, his aims holy. But through disobedience, his powers were perverted, and selfishness took the place of love. His nature became so weakened through transgression that it was impossible for him, in his own strength, to resist the power of evil. He was made captive by Satan, and would have remained so forever had not God specially interposed. It was the tempter's purpose to thwart the divine plan in man's creation, and fill the earth with woe and desolation. And he would point to all this evil as the result of God's work in creating man.

In his sinless state, man held joyful communion with Him "in whom are hid all the treasures of wisdom and knowledge." Colossians 2:3. But after his sin, he could no longer find joy in holiness, and he sought to hide from the presence of God. Such is still the condition of the unrenewed heart. It is not in harmony with God, and finds no joy in communion with Him. The sinner could not be happy in God's presence; he would shrink from the companionship of holy beings. Could he be permitted to enter heaven, it would have no joy for him. The spirit of unselfish love that reigns there--every heart responding to the heart of Infinite Love--would touch no answering chord in his soul. His thoughts, his interests, his motives, would be alien to [18] those that actuate the sinless dwellers there. He would be a discordant note in the melody of heaven. Heaven would be to him a place of torture; he would long to be hidden from Him who is its light, and the center of its joy. It is no arbitrary decree on the part of God that excludes the wicked from heaven; they are shut out by their own unfitness for its companionship. The glory of God would be to them a consuming fire. They would welcome destruction, that they might be hidden from the face of Him who died to redeem them.

1. "Through disobedience, his powers were perverted, and s_____ took the place of l_____." (17) Lord, why is one response easier for me, than the other? _____

_____

_____

_____

2. But after his sin, [man] could no longer find j___ _____ in holiness, and he sought to hide from the presence of God. Such is still the condition of the u_____ heart. It is not in harmony with God, and finds no joy in c_____ with Him... Heaven would be to him a place of torture...would welcome destruction." (17, 18). Lord, I give You permission to renew my heart. How might my experience in Your presence, in holiness, be one of joy instead of discomfort? _____

_____

_____

_____

It is impossible for us, of ourselves, to escape from the pit of sin in which we are sunken. Our hearts are evil, and we cannot change them. "Who can bring a clean thing out of an unclean? not one." "The carnal mind is enmity against God: for it is not subject to the law of God, neither indeed can be." Job 14:4; Romans 8:7. Education, culture, the exercise of the will, human effort, all have their proper sphere, but here they are powerless. They may produce an outward correctness of behavior, but they cannot change the heart; they cannot purify the springs of life. There must be a power working from within, a new life from above, before men can be changed from sin to holiness. That power is Christ. His grace alone can quicken the lifeless faculties of the soul, and attract it to God, to holiness.

3. "His g _____ alone can quicken the lifeless faculties of the soul, and a_____ it to God, to holiness." Lord, how can I be more available to Your grace?

_____

_____

_____

The Saviour said, "Except a man be born from above," unless he shall receive a new heart, new desires, purposes, and motives, leading to a new life, "he cannot see the kingdom of God." John 3:3, margin. The idea that it is necessary only to develop the good that [19] exists in man by nature, is a fatal deception. "The natural man receiveth not the things of the Spirit of God: for they are foolishness unto him: neither can he know them, because they are spiritually discerned." "Marvel not that I said unto thee, Ye must be born again." 1 Corinthians 2:14; John 3:7. Of Christ it is written, "In Him was life; and the life was the light of men"--the only "name under heaven given among men, whereby we must be saved." John 1:4; Acts 4:12.

4. "The natural man receiveth n_____ the things of the Spirit of God: for they are f_____ __ unto him." (19). Lord, what impact do the things of this world have, on my spiritual life? _____

_____

_____

It is not enough to perceive the loving-kindness of God, to see the benevolence, the fatherly tenderness, of His character. It is not enough to discern the wisdom and justice of His law, to see that it is founded upon the eternal principle of love. Paul the apostle saw all this when he exclaimed, "I consent unto the law that it is good." "The law is holy, and the commandment holy, and just, and good." But he added, in the bitterness of his soul-anguish and despair, "I am carnal, sold under sin." Romans 7:16, 12, 14. He longed for the purity, the righteousness, to which in himself he was powerless to attain, and cried out, "O wretched man that I am! who shall deliver me from this body of death?" Romans 7:24, margin. Such is the cry that has gone up from burdened hearts in all lands and in all ages. To all, there is but one answer, "Behold the Lamb of God, which taketh away

5. "'O wretched man that I am! Who shall deliver me?'... To all, there is but o_____ answer, 'B_____ the Lamb of God.'" Lord, help me see the depths of my self-complacency, and my desperate need to behold and connect with You:

_____

_____

_____

_____

the sin of the world." John 1:29.

Many are the figures by which the Spirit of God has sought to illustrate this truth, and make it plain to souls that long to be freed from the burden of guilt. When, after his sin in deceiving Esau, Jacob fled from his father's home, he was weighed down with a sense [20] of guilt. Lonely and outcast as he was, separated from all that had made life dear, the one thought that above all others pressed upon his soul, was the fear that his sin had cut him off from God, that he was forsaken of Heaven. In sadness he lay down to rest on the bare earth, around him only the lonely hills, and above, the heavens bright with stars. As he slept, a strange light broke upon his vision; and lo, from the plain on which he lay, vast shadowy stairs seemed to lead upward to the very gates of heaven, and upon them angels of God were passing up and down; while from the glory above, the divine voice was heard in a message of comfort and hope. Thus was made known to Jacob that which met the need and longing of his soul--a Saviour. With joy and gratitude he saw revealed a way by which he, a sinner, could be restored to communion with God. The mystic ladder of his dream represented Jesus, the only medium of communication between God and man.

This is the same figure to which Christ referred in His conversation with Nathanael, when He said, "Ye shall see heaven open, and the angels of God ascending and descending upon the Son of man." John 1:51. In the apostasy, man alienated himself from God; earth was cut off from heaven. Across the gulf that lay between, there could be no communion. But through Christ, earth is again linked with heaven. With His own merits, Christ has bridged the gulf which sin had made, so that the ministering angels can hold communion with man. Christ connects fallen man in his weakness and helplessness with the Source of infinite power. [21]

But in vain are men's dreams of progress, in vain all efforts for the uplifting of humanity, if they neglect the one Source of hope and help for the fallen race. "Every good gift and every perfect gift" (James 1:17) is from God. There is no true excellence of character apart from Him. And the only way to God is Christ. He says, "I am the way, the truth, and the life: no man cometh unto the Father, but by Me." John 14:6.

The heart of God yearns over His earthly children

6. "The mystic ladder of his [Jacob's] dream represented J_____, the only medium of communication between God and man." Lord, may my walk be grounded in You, Your love and grace. Why don't I treasure this gift, of being restored to communion with You? Do I think I don't need "comfort and hope," a Savior?____
_____
_____

7. "There is no true excellence of character a_____ ____ from Him... No man cometh unto the Father, but by Me." (21). Lord, You are my only hope! How does beholding Your character and life, mold my character? _____
_____
_____
_____

8. "In giving up His Son, He has poured out to us a_____ heaven in one gift...Motives stronger, and agencies more powerful, could never be brought into operation...What m_____ could He do?" (21, 22). Lord, help me to recognize my great need of You as my Savior. And help me to recognize Your great passion for the restoration of our fellowship. You have given everything! Your all! Do I value our fellowship a fraction as much? ____

_____

_____

I love You! _____

_____

9. "Let us avail ourselves of the means provided for us that we may be t_____ _____ into His likeness, and be restored to fellowship." Lord, I give you my schedule, my time, my self, my all; for I want to be available to all of heaven's means:

_____

_____

_____

Prayer journal: _____

_____

_____

_____

_____

with a love stronger than death. In giving up His Son, He has poured out to us all heaven in one gift. The Saviour's life and death and intercession, the ministry of angels, the pleading of the Spirit, the Father working above and through all, the unceasing interest of heavenly beings,--all are enlisted in behalf of man's redemption.

Oh, let us contemplate the amazing sacrifice that has been made for us! Let us try to appreciate the labor and energy that Heaven is expending to reclaim the lost, and bring them back to the Father's house. Motives stronger, and agencies more powerful, could never be brought into operation; the exceeding rewards for right-doing, the enjoyment of heaven, the society of the angels, the communion and love of God and His Son, the elevation and extension of all our powers throughout eternal ages--are these not mighty incentives and encouragements to urge us to give the heart's loving service to our Creator and Redeemer?

And, on the other hand, the judgments of God pronounced against sin, the inevitable retribution, the [22] degradation of our character, and the final destruction, are presented in God's word to warn us against the service of Satan.

Shall we not regard the mercy of God? What more could He do? Let us place ourselves in right relation to Him who has loved us with amazing love. Let us avail ourselves of the means provided for us that we may be transformed into His likeness, and be restored to fellowship with the ministering angels, to harmony and communion with the Father and the Son.

3-Repentance

How shall a man be just with God? How shall the sinner be made righteous? It is only through Christ that we can be brought into harmony with God, with holiness; but how are we to come to Christ? Many are asking the same question as did the multitude on the Day of Pentecost, when, convicted of sin, they cried out, "What shall we do?" The first word of Peter's answer was, "Repent." Acts 2:37, 38. At another time, shortly after, he said, "Repent, . . . and be converted, that your sins may be blotted out." Acts 3:19.

Repentance includes sorrow for sin and a turning away from it. We shall not renounce sin unless we see its sinfulness; until we turn away from it in heart, there will be no real change in the life.

There are many who fail to understand the true nature of repentance. Multitudes sorrow that they have sinned and even make an outward reformation because they fear that their wrongdoing will bring suffering upon themselves. But this is not repentance in the Bible sense. They lament the suffering rather than the sin. Such was the grief of Esau when he saw that the birthright was lost to him forever. Balaam, terrified by the angel standing in his pathway with drawn sword, acknowledged his guilt lest he should lose his life; but there was no genuine repentance for sin, no conversion of purpose, no abhorrence of evil. Judas Iscariot, after betraying his [24] Lord, exclaimed, "I have sinned in that I have betrayed the innocent blood." Matthew 27:4.

The confession was forced from his guilty soul by an awful sense of condemnation and a fearful looking for of judgment. The consequences that were to result to him filled him with terror, but there was no deep, heartbreaking grief in his soul, that he had betrayed the spotless Son of God and denied the Holy One of Israel. Pharaoh, when suffering under the judgments of God, acknowledged his sin in order to escape further punishment, but returned to his defiance of Heaven as soon as the plagues were stayed. These all lamented the results

1. "It is only through Christ that we can be brought into h_____ with God, with holiness." (23). Lord, it has nothing to do with my performance? It is only through You. The phrase "harmony with God, with holiness" tells me that all discussion of holiness is to be seen in terms of relationship, not performance: _____

_____

_____

2. "Repentance includes a s_____ for sin and a turning away from it… Lament[ing] the s_____ ____ rather than the sin" [is not repentance in the Bible sense]. Esau, Balaam, and Judas had "no genuine repentance of sin, no conversion of p_____, no a_____ of evil." Do I, Lord? Where does abhorrence come from? _____

_____

_____

Help me better understand sorrow for sin not as my suffering, but Your suffering, how I have betrayed and denied You:

_____

_____

_____

3. "When the heart yields to the influence of the Spirit of God, the conscience will be q_____...conviction takes hold upon the m_____ and heart...he sees the love of God, the beauty of holiness, the joy of p_____." (24) Lord, is the terror of appearing in my own uncleanness, is it my response to You, or to being out of harmony with You? _____

_____

I think I see the joy of purity and long to be cleansed. So why do I hesitate to yield? Do I also still long to indulge in self? Show me how: _____

_____

_____

_____

4. David's prayer: "It was not for pardon only that he prayed, but for p_____ __ of heart. He longed for the j____ of holiness—to be restored to harmony and c_____ with God...'Purge me...wash me...clean heart...restore unto me the joy of Thy salvation.'" (25) Lord, I pray David's prayer, and ask Your Spirit to guide the yielding of my heart, to be genuine and thorough. What am I hanging on to, unwilling to let go? ____

_____

_____

_____

of sin, but did not sorrow for the sin itself.

But when the heart yields to the influence of the Spirit of God, the conscience will be quickened, and the sinner will discern something of the depth and sacredness of God's holy law, the foundation of His government in heaven and on earth. The "Light, which lighteth every man that cometh into the world," illumines the secret chambers of the soul, and the hidden things of darkness are made manifest. John 1:9. Conviction takes hold upon the mind and heart. The sinner has a sense of the righteousness of Jehovah and feels the terror of appearing, in his own guilt and uncleanness, before the Searcher of hearts. He sees the love of God, the beauty of holiness, the joy of purity; he longs to be cleansed and to be restored to communion with Heaven.

The prayer of David after his fall, illustrates the nature of true sorrow for sin. His repentance was sincere and deep. There was no effort to palliate [25] his guilt; no desire to escape the judgment threatened, inspired his prayer. David saw the enormity of his transgression; he saw the defilement of his soul; he loathed his sin. It was not for pardon only that he prayed, but for purity of heart. He longed for the joy of holiness--to be restored to harmony and communion with God. This was the language of his soul:

"Blessed is he whose transgression is forgiven,
whose sin is covered.
Blessed is the man unto whom the Lord
imputeth not iniquity,
And in whose spirit there is no guile."
Psalm 32:1, 2.
"Have mercy upon me, O God, according to
Thy loving-kindness:
According unto the multitude of Thy tender
mercies blot out my transgressions. . . .
For I acknowledge my transgressions: and my
sin is ever before me. . . .
Purge me with hyssop, and I shall be clean:
wash me, and I shall be whiter than snow. . . .
Create in me a clean heart, O God;
And renew a right spirit within me.
Cast me not away from Thy presence;
And take not Thy Holy Spirit from me.
Restore unto me the joy of Thy salvation;

And uphold me with Thy free spirit. . . .
Deliver me from bloodguiltiness, O God, Thou
God of my salvation:
And my tongue shall sing aloud of Thy
righteousness." Psalm 51:1-14.

A repentance such as this, is beyond the reach of our own power to accomplish; it is obtained only from Christ, who ascended up on high and has given gifts unto men. [26]

Just here is a point on which many may err, and hence they fail of receiving the help that Christ desires to give them. They think that they cannot come to Christ unless they first repent, and that repentance prepares for the forgiveness of their sins. It is true that repentance does precede the forgiveness of sins; for it is only the broken and contrite heart that will feel the need of a Saviour. But must the sinner wait till he has repented before he can come to Jesus? Is repentance to be made an obstacle between the sinner and the Saviour?

The Bible does not teach that the sinner must repent before he can heed the invitation of Christ, "Come unto Me, all ye that labor and are heavy-laden, and I will give you rest." Matthew 11:28. It is the virtue that goes forth from Christ, that leads to genuine repentance. Peter made the matter clear in his statement to the Israelites when he said, "Him hath God exalted with His right hand to be a Prince and a Saviour, for to give repentance to Israel, and forgiveness of sins." Acts 5:31. We can no more repent without the Spirit of Christ to awaken the conscience than we can be pardoned without Christ.

Christ is the source of every right impulse. He is the only one that can implant in the heart enmity against sin. Every desire for truth and purity, every conviction of our own sinfulness, is an evidence that His Spirit is moving upon our hearts.

Jesus has said, "I, if I be lifted up from the earth, will draw all men unto Me." John 12:32. Christ must be revealed to the sinner as the Saviour dying for the sins of the world; and as we behold the Lamb of [27] God upon the cross of Calvary, the mystery of redemption begins to unfold to our minds and the goodness of God leads us to repentance. In dying for sinners, Christ manifested a love that is incomprehensible; and as the sinner beholds this love, it softens the heart, impresses

5. How does Acts 5:31 answer the question, must I first repent before I come to Christ? _____

_____

_____ "We can no more r_____ without the Spirit of Christ to waken the conscience than we can be pardoned w_____ Christ." (26) Lord, that doesn't mean that I wait, does it? _____ How can I be more available to Your Spirit to awaken my conscience?

_____

_____

_____

————————————————

6. "The g_____ of God leads us to repentance. In dying for sinners, Christ manifested a l_____ that is incomprehensible; and as the sinner beholds this love, it s_____ the heart, impresses the mind,

and inspires c_____
____ in the soul." (27) So
Lord, Your death is more
than taking my place. I am
to experience Your love
and having my heart soft-
ened: _____
_____
_____

7. "To look upon His cross,
to behold Him…What is
sin, that it should r_____
_____ such a sacrifice for
the redemption of its victim?" Draw me, Lord. Why
is Your sacrifice required?
_____
_____

May Your power draw me
to a much deeper appreciation of my need, my sin, and
Your love: _____
_____

Is Your death the only way
I would comprehend the
enmity I have, the alien-
ation I have towards You
(Col 1:20)? Is Your death
the only way for me to be
drawn and reconciled? __
_____
_____
_____

8. "If he does not r_____
____ [this love] he will be
drawn to Jesus." Lord, what
are the ways that I might
unknowingly resist Your
love? _____
_____
_____

the mind, and inspires contrition in the soul.

It is true that men sometimes become ashamed of their sinful ways, and give up some of their evil habits, before they are conscious that they are being drawn to Christ. But whenever they make an effort to reform, from a sincere desire to do right, it is the power of Christ that is drawing them. An influence of which they are unconscious works upon the soul, and the conscience is quickened, and the outward life is amended. And as Christ draws them to look upon His cross, to behold Him whom their sins have pierced, the commandment comes home to the conscience. The wickedness of their life, the deep-seated sin of the soul, is revealed to them. They begin to comprehend something of the righteousness of Christ, and exclaim, "What is sin, that it should require such a sacrifice for the redemption of its victim? Was all this love, all this suffering, all this humiliation, demanded, that we might not perish, but have everlasting life?"

The sinner may resist this love, may refuse to be drawn to Christ; but if he does not resist he will be drawn to Jesus; a knowledge of the plan of salvation will lead him to the foot of the cross in repentance for his sins, which have caused the sufferings of God's dear Son. [28]

The same divine mind that is working upon the things of nature is speaking to the hearts of men and creating an inexpressible craving for something they have not. The things of the world cannot satisfy their longing. The Spirit of God is pleading with them to seek for those things that alone can give peace and rest--the grace of Christ, the joy of holiness. Through influences seen and unseen, our Saviour is constantly at work to attract the minds of men from the unsatisfying pleasures of sin to the infinite blessings that may be theirs in Him. To all these souls, who are vainly seeking to drink from the broken cisterns of this world, the divine message is addressed, "Let him that is athirst come. And whosoever will, let him take the water of life freely." Revelation 22:17.

You who in heart long for something better than this world can give, recognize this longing as the voice of God to your soul. Ask Him to give you repentance, to reveal Christ to you in His infinite love, in His perfect purity. In the Saviour's life the principles of God's law--love to God and man--were perfectly exemplified. Benevolence, unselfish love, was the life of His soul. It is as we behold Him, as the light from our Saviour falls upon us, that we see the sinfulness of our own hearts.

We may have flattered ourselves, as did Nicodemus, that our life has been upright, that our moral character is correct, and think that we need not humble the heart before God, like the common sinner: but when the light from Christ shines into our souls, we shall see how impure we are; we shall discern the selfishness of motive, the enmity against God, that [29] has defiled every act of life. Then we shall know that our own righteousness is indeed as filthy rags, and that the blood of Christ alone can cleanse us from the defilement of sin, and renew our hearts in His own likeness.

One ray of the glory of God, one gleam of the purity of Christ, penetrating the soul, makes every spot of defilement painfully distinct, and lays bare the deformity and defects of the human character. It makes apparent the unhallowed desires, the infidelity of the heart, the impurity of the lips. The sinner's acts of disloyalty in making void the law of God, are exposed to his sight, and his spirit is stricken and afflicted under the searching influence of the Spirit of God. He loathes himself as he views the pure, spotless character of Christ.

When the prophet Daniel beheld the glory surrounding the heavenly messenger that was sent unto him, he was overwhelmed with a sense of his own weakness and imperfection. Describing the effect of the wonderful scene, he says, "There remained no strength in me:

9. "Through influences seen and unseen, our Savior is c_____ at work to attract the minds of men from the u_____ pleasures of sin to the i_____ blessings that may be theirs in Him." (28) Thank You, Lord. May I be more sensitive and responsive to these influences: _____

10. "When the light from Christ shines into our souls, we shall see how i_____ we are; we shall discern the selfishness of m_____, ...the unhallowed desires, the i_____ of the heart, the impurity of the lips." (28, 29) Lord, may Your light shine. Search me. What are some of these discoveries about me that I can let go of?

for my comeliness was turned in me into corruption, and I retained no strength." Daniel 10:8. The soul thus touched will hate its selfishness, abhor its self-love, and will seek, through Christ's righteousness, for the purity of heart that is in harmony with the law of God and the character of Christ.

Paul says that as "touching the righteousness which is in the law"--as far as outward acts were concerned--he was "blameless" (Philippians 3:6); but when the spiritual character of the law was discerned, he saw himself a sinner. Judged by the letter of the law as [30] men apply it to the outward life, he had abstained from sin; but when he looked into the depths of its holy precepts, and saw himself as God saw him, he bowed in humiliation and confessed his guilt. He says, "I was alive without the law once: but when the commandment came, sin revived, and I died." Romans 7:9. When he saw the spiritual nature of the law, sin appeared in its true hideousness, and his self-esteem was gone.

God does not regard all sins as of equal magnitude; there are degrees of guilt in His estimation, as well as in that of man; but however trifling this or that wrong act may seem in the eyes of men, no sin is small in the sight of God. Man's judgment is partial, imperfect; but God estimates all things as they really are. The drunkard is despised and is told that his sin will exclude him from heaven; while pride, selfishness, and covetousness too often go unrebuked. But these are sins that are especially offensive to God; for they are contrary to the benevolence of His character, to that unselfish love which is the very atmosphere of the unfallen universe. He who falls into some of the grosser sins may feel a sense of his shame and poverty and his need of the grace of Christ; but pride feels no need, and so it closes the heart against Christ and the infinite blessings He came to give.

11. What are the sins that are especially offensive to You, God, and why?

"Contrary to the benevolence of His character, to that unselfish love which is the very atmosphere of the unfallen universe."

The poor publican who prayed, "God be merciful to me a sinner" (Luke 18:13), regarded himself as a very wicked man, and others looked upon him in the same light; but he felt his need, and with his burden of [31] guilt and shame he came before God, asking for His mercy. His heart was open for the Spirit of God to do its gracious work and set him free from the power of sin. The Pharisee's boastful, self-righteous prayer showed that his heart was closed against the influence of the Holy Spirit. Because of his distance from God, he had no sense of his own defilement, in contrast with the perfection of the divine holiness. He felt no need, and he received nothing.

If you see your sinfulness, do not wait to make yourself better. How many there are who think they are not good enough to come to Christ. Do you expect to become better through your own efforts? "Can the Ethiopian change his skin, or the leopard his spots? then may ye also do good, that are accustomed to do evil." Jeremiah 13:23. There is help for us only in God. We must not wait for stronger persuasions, for better opportunities, or for holier tempers. We can do nothing of ourselves. We must come to Christ just as we are.

But let none deceive themselves with the thought that God, in His great love and mercy, will yet save even the rejecters of His grace. The exceeding sinfulness of sin can be estimated only in the light of the cross. When men urge that God is too good to cast off the sinner, let them look to Calvary. It was because there was no other way in which man could be saved, because without this sacrifice it was impossible for the human race to escape from the defiling power of sin, and be restored to communion with holy beings,--impossible for them again to become partakers [32] of spiritual life,--it was because of this that Christ took upon Himself the guilt of the disobedient and suffered in the sinner's stead. The love and suffering and death of the Son of God all testify to the terrible enormity of sin and declare that there is no escape from its power, no hope of the higher life, but through the submission of the soul to Christ.

12. "When men urge that God is too good to cast off the sinner, let them look to Calvary." (31) What does this mean, Lord? _____

_____ Show me the "terrible enormity of sin."

The impenitent sometimes excuse themselves by saying of professed Christians, "I am as good as they are. They are no more self-denying, sober, or circumspect in their conduct than I am. They love pleasure and self-indulgence as well as I do." Thus they make the faults of others an excuse for their own neglect of duty. But the sins and defects of others do not excuse anyone, for the Lord has not given us an erring human pattern. The spotless Son of God has been given as our example, and those who complain of the wrong course of professed Christians are the ones who should show better lives and nobler examples. If they have so high a conception of what a Christian should be, is not their own sin so much the greater? They know what is right, and yet refuse to do it.

13. "Beware of procrasti-
nation…delaying to y____
____ to the pleading voice
of God's Holy Spirit…Sin,
however small it may be
esteemed, can be i_____
_____ in only at the peril
of i_____ loss." (32,
33) Thank You, Lord, for
enlightening me as to Sa-
tan's tactics of procrastination. But I still need Your
help to guard my heart
against it: _____

_____

_____

14. "Every act of trans-
gression, every n_____
____ or rejection of the
grace of Christ, is reacting
upon yourself; it is h____
_____ the heart,
depraving the will, b____
_____ the understanding,
and not only making you
less inclined to yield, but
less c_____
of yielding, to the tender
pleading of God's Holy
Spirit…One sinful desire,
persistently cherished, will
eventually neutralize all
the power of the gospel."
(33, 34) Lord, I want to
hear the slightest whisper
of Your Spirit. Help me listen with openness and willingness: _____

Beware of procrastination. Do not put off the work
of forsaking your sins and seeking purity of heart
through Jesus. Here is where thousands upon thousands
have erred to their eternal loss. I will not here dwell
upon the shortness and uncertainty of life; but there is a
terrible danger--a danger not sufficiently understood--in
delaying to yield to the pleading voice of God's Holy
Spirit, in choosing to live in sin; for such this delay really is. Sin, however [33] small it may be esteemed, can
be indulged in only at the peril of infinite loss. What we
do not overcome, will overcome us and work out our
destruction.

Adam and Eve persuaded themselves that in so
small a matter as eating of the forbidden fruit there
could not result such terrible consequences as God had
declared. But this small matter was the transgression of
God's immutable and holy law, and it separated man
from God and opened the floodgates of death and un-
told woe upon our world. Age after age there has gone
up from our earth a continual cry of mourning, and the
whole creation groaneth and travaileth together in pain
as a consequence of man's disobedience. Heaven itself
has felt the effects of his rebellion against God. Calvary
stands as a memorial of the amazing sacrifice required
to atone for the transgression of the divine law. Let us
not regard sin as a trivial thing.

Every act of transgression, every neglect or rejection of the grace of Christ, is reacting upon yourself; it is
hardening the heart, depraving the will, benumbing the
understanding, and not only making you less inclined to
yield, but less capable of yielding, to the tender pleading of God's Holy Spirit.

Many are quieting a troubled conscience with the
thought that they can change a course of evil when they
choose; that they can trifle with the invitations of mercy,
and yet be again and again impressed. They think that
after doing despite to the Spirit of grace, after casting
their influence on the side of Satan, in a moment of terrible extremity they can change their course. But this is
not so easily done. The experience, [34] the education,
of a lifetime, has so thoroughly molded the character
that few then desire to receive the image of Jesus.

Even one wrong trait of character, one sinful desire,
persistently cherished, will eventually neutralize all the
power of the gospel. Every sinful indulgence strength-

ens the soul's aversion to God. The man who manifests an infidel hardihood, or a stolid indifference to divine truth, is but reaping the harvest of that which he has himself sown. In all the Bible there is not a more fearful warning against trifling with evil than the words of the wise man that the sinner "shall be holden with the cords of his sins." Proverbs 5:22.

Christ is ready to set us free from sin, but He does not force the will; and if by persistent transgression the will itself is wholly bent on evil, and we do not desire to be set free, if we will not accept His grace, what more can He do? We have destroyed ourselves by our determined rejection of His love. "Behold, now is the accepted time; behold, now is the day of salvation." "To-day if ye will hear His voice, harden not your hearts." 2 Corinthians 6:2; Hebrews 3:7, 8.

"Man looketh on the outward appearance, but the Lord looketh on the heart"--the human heart, with its conflicting emotions of joy and sorrow; the wandering, wayward heart, which is the abode of so much impurity and deceit. 1 Samuel 16:7. He knows its motives, its very intents and purposes. Go to Him with your soul all stained as it is. Like the psalmist, throw its chambers open to the all-seeing eye, exclaiming, "Search me, O God, and know my heart: try me, and know [35] my thoughts: and see if there be any wicked way in me, and lead me in the way everlasting." Psalm 139: 23, 24.

Many accept an intellectual religion, a form of godliness, when the heart is not cleansed. Let it be your prayer, "Create in me a clean heart, O God; and renew a right spirit within me." Psalm 51:10. Deal truly with your own soul. Be as earnest, as persistent, as you would be if your mortal life were at stake. This is a matter to be settled between God and your own soul, settled for eternity. A supposed hope, and nothing more, will prove your ruin.

Study God's word prayerfully. That word presents before you, in the law of God and the life of Christ, the great principles of holiness, without which "no man shall see the Lord." Hebrews 12:14. It convinces of sin; it plainly reveals the way of salvation. Give heed to it as the voice of God speaking to your soul.

As you see the enormity of sin, as you see yourself as you really are, do not give up to despair. It was sinners that Christ came to save. We have not to reconcile God

15. "He is wooing by His t_____ love the hearts of His erring children." (35) Draw me close to You, Lord. Thank You for tugging at my heart:

_____
_____
_____

16. "It is when we most fully comprehend the l_____ of God that we b_____ realize the sinfulness of sin." (36) Lord, I desire that "best" realization of Your love. Help me not to settle for less than the length, width, depth, and height of Your love. Draw me close to You. I don't any of my sin to separate me from You and Your love: ____

_____
_____
_____
_____

Prayer journal: _____

_____
_____
_____
_____

to us, but--O wondrous love!--God in Christ is "reconciling the world unto Himself." 2 Corinthians 5:19. He is wooing by His tender love the hearts of His erring children. No earthly parent could be as patient with the faults and mistakes of his children, as is God with those He seeks to save. No one could plead more tenderly with the transgressor. No human lips ever poured out more tender entreaties to the wanderer than does He. All His promises, His warnings, are but the breathing of unutterable love.

When Satan comes to tell you that you are a [36] great sinner, look up to your Redeemer and talk of His merits. That which will help you is to look to His light. Acknowledge your sin, but tell the enemy that "Christ Jesus came into the world to save sinners" and that you may be saved by His matchless love. 1 Timothy 1:15. Jesus asked Simon a question in regard to two debtors. One owed his lord a small sum, and the other owed him a very large sum; but he forgave them both, and Christ asked Simon which debtor would love his lord most. Simon answered, "He to whom he forgave most." Luke 7:43. We have been great sinners, but Christ died that we might be forgiven. The merits of His sacrifice are sufficient to present to the Father in our behalf. Those to whom He has forgiven most will love Him most, and will stand nearest to His throne to praise Him for His great love and infinite sacrifice. It is when we most fully comprehend the love of God that we best realize the sinfulness of sin. When we see the length of the chain that was let down for us, when we understand something of the infinite sacrifice that Christ has made in our behalf, the heart is melted with tenderness and contrition.

4-Confession

"He that covereth his sins shall not prosper: but whoso confesseth and forsaketh them shall have mercy." Proverbs 28:13.

The conditions of obtaining mercy of God are simple and just and reasonable. The Lord does not require us to do some grievous thing in order that we may have the forgiveness of sin. We need not make long and wearisome pilgrimages, or perform painful penances, to commend our souls to the God of heaven or to expiate our transgression; but he that confesseth and forsaketh his sin shall have mercy.

The apostle says, "Confess your faults one to another, and pray one for another, that ye may be healed." James 5:16. Confess your sins to God, who only can forgive them, and your faults to one another. If you have given offense to your friend or neighbor, you are to acknowledge your wrong, and it is his duty freely to forgive you. Then you are to seek the forgiveness of God, because the brother you have wounded is the property of God, and in injuring him you sinned against his Creator and Redeemer. The case is brought before the only true Mediator, our great High Priest, who "was in all points tempted like as we are, yet without sin," and who is "touched with the feeling of our infirmities," and is able to cleanse from every stain of iniquity. Hebrews 4:15.

Those who have not humbled their souls before God in acknowledging their guilt, have not yet [38] fulfilled the first condition of acceptance. If we have not experienced that repentance which is not to be repented of, and have not with true humiliation of soul and brokenness of spirit confessed our sins, abhorring our iniquity, we have never truly sought for the forgiveness of sin; and if we have never sought, we have never found the peace of God. The only reason why we do not have remission of sins that are past is that we are not willing to humble our hearts and comply with the conditions of the word of truth. Explicit instruction is given con-

1. "He that c_____ ___ his sins shall not prosper: but whoso c_____ _____ and forsaketh them shall have mercy." (38) Is it even possible to cover or hide my sins? _____ Lord, what game am I playing when I try? ____
_____
_____
_____
_____

2. "Confess your faults one to another, and pray one for another, that ye may be h_____." What insight does the missing word imply, as a purpose for my prayers that I should be open to?
_____
_____
_____

3. "Then you are to seek the forgiveness of God, because the brother you have w_____ is the property of God, and in injuring him you sinned a_____ his Creator and R_____ ___." Lord, I don't want to wound You or a brother. Help me to see the pain that my sin causes: _____
_____
_____

4. "If we...have not with true humiliation of soul and b_____ of spirit confessed our sins, a_____ our iniquity, we have never truly sought for the forgiveness of sin... have never found the p____ _____ of God." (38). Lord,

asking for forgiveness, out of duty, or to avoid further consequence, or to appear spiritually superior, means I haven't experienced Your peace? _____

_____ Help my motives to be pure and transparent. What does "repentance which is not to be repented of" mean? _____

_____

_____

5. "True confession is always of a s_____ character, and acknowledges p_____ sins." Lord, what is the likely outcome if my confession isn't? _____

_____

6. "Confession will not be acceptable to God without sincere repentance and r_____." What does this mean? "Everything o_____ to God must be put away. This is the result of genuine s_____ for sin." (39) Lord, I can't generate sorrow. Help me to be willing, for You to create enmity or offensiveness between me and sin. _

_____

_____

_____

_____

cerning this matter. Confession of sin, whether public or private, should be heartfelt and freely expressed. It is not to be urged from the sinner. It is not to be made in a flippant and careless way, or forced from those who have no realizing sense of the abhorrent character of sin. The confession that is the outpouring of the inmost soul finds its way to the God of infinite pity. The psalmist says, "The Lord is nigh unto them that are of a broken heart; and saveth such as be of a contrite spirit." Psalm 34:18.

True confession is always of a specific character, and acknowledges particular sins. They may be of such a nature as to be brought before God only; they may be wrongs that should be confessed to individuals who have suffered injury through them; or they may be of a public character, and should then be as publicly confessed. But all confession should be definite and to the point, acknowledging the very sins of which you are guilty.

In the days of Samuel the Israelites wandered from God. They were suffering the consequences of [39] sin; for they had lost their faith in God, lost their discernment of His power and wisdom to rule the nation, lost their confidence in His ability to defend and vindicate His cause. They turned from the great Ruler of the universe and desired to be governed as were the nations around them. Before they found peace they made this definite confession: "We have added unto all our sins this evil, to ask us a king." 1 Samuel 12:19. The very sin of which they were convicted had to be confessed. Their ingratitude oppressed their souls and severed them from God.

Confession will not be acceptable to God without sincere repentance and reformation. There must be decided changes in the life; everything offensive to God must be put away. This will be the result of genuine sorrow for sin. The work that we have to do on our part is plainly set before us: "Wash you, make you clean; put away the evil of your doings from before Mine eyes; cease to do evil; learn to do well; seek judgment, relieve the oppressed, judge the fatherless, plead for the widow." Isaiah 1:16, 17. "If the wicked restore the pledge, give again that he had robbed, walk in the statutes of life, without committing iniquity; he shall surely live, he shall not die." Ezekiel 33:15. Paul says, speaking of the work of repentance: "Ye sorrowed after a godly sort, what carefulness it wrought in you, yea, what clearing of yourselves, yea, what indignation, yea, what fear, yea, what vehement desire, yea, what zeal, yea, what revenge! In all things ye have approved yourselves to be clear in this matter." 2 Corinthians 7:11. [40]

When sin has deadened the moral perceptions, the wrongdoer does not discern the defects of his character nor realize the enormity of the evil he has committed; and unless he yields to the convicting power of the Holy Spirit he remains in partial blindness to his sin. His confessions are not sincere and in earnest. To every acknowledgment of his guilt he adds an apology in excuse of his course, declaring that if it had not been for certain circumstances he would not have done this or that for which he is reproved.

After Adam and Eve had eaten of the forbidden fruit, they were filled with a sense of shame and terror. At first their only thought was how to excuse their sin and escape the dreaded sentence of death. When the Lord inquired concerning their sin, Adam replied, laying the guilt partly upon God and partly upon his companion: "The woman whom Thou gavest to be with me, she gave me of the tree, and I did eat." The woman put the blame upon the serpent, saying, "The serpent beguiled me, and I did eat." Genesis 3: 12, 13. Why did You make the serpent? Why did You suffer him to come into Eden? These were the questions implied in her excuse for her sin, thus charging God with the responsibility of their fall. The spirit of self-justification originated in the father of lies and has been exhibited by all the sons and daughters of Adam. Confessions of this order are not inspired by the divine Spirit and will not be acceptable to God. True repentance will lead a man to bear his guilt himself and acknowledge it without deception or hypocrisy. Like the poor publican, not lifting up so much as his eyes unto heaven, he will cry, "God be [41] merciful to me a sinner," and those who do acknowledge their guilt will be justified, for Jesus will plead His blood in behalf of the repentant soul.

The examples in God's word of genuine repentance and humiliation reveal a spirit of confession in which there is no excuse for sin or attempt at self-justification. Paul did not seek to shield himself; he paints his sin in its darkest hue, not attempting to lessen his guilt. He

7. "When sin has d____ _____ the moral perceptions, the wrongdoer does not discern the defects of his c_____ _____ nor realize the enormity of the evil he has committed…he remains in partial b_____ to his sin." (40) And Lord, I would be calloused to the wound I am causing You and others. Help my sensitivity to sin be heightened. Show me now, my blind spots: _____ _____ _____

8. "The spirit of self-j____ _____ originated in the father of lies and has been exhibited by all the sons and daughters of Adam… True repentance will lead a man to bear his guilt h_____ and acknowledge it without deception or h_____ _____." Lord, it seems so automatic to shirk responsibility, to excuse myself and blame others. Expose to me my own hypopcrisy: _____ _____ _____

says, "Many of the saints did I shut up in prison, having received authority from the chief priests; and when they were put to death, I gave my voice against them. And I punished them oft in every synagogue, and compelled them to blaspheme; and being exceedingly mad against them, I persecuted them even unto strange cities." Acts 26: 10, 11. He does not hesitate to declare that "Christ Jesus came into the world to save sinners; of whom I am chief." 1 Timothy 1:15.

9. "Christ Jesus came into the world to s_____ sinners; of whom I am c_____." (41) Lord, I am in need of forgiveness, cleansing, and healing every day. Teach me humbleness. Thank You for coming into this dark world, becoming my sin, to save me: _____
_____
_____

The humble and broken heart, subdued by genuine repentance, will appreciate something of the love of God and the cost of Calvary; and as a son confesses to a loving father, so will the truly penitent bring all his sins before God. And it is written, "If we confess our sins, He is faithful and just to forgive us our sins, and to cleanse us from all unrighteousness." 1 John 1:9.

10. Do I appreciate the "l_____ of God and the c_____ of Calvary? _____
_____ Why will a humble and broken heart help me? _____
_____
_____

11. How can I put the promise 1Jn1:9 into more practical use? _____
_____
_____
_____

Prayer journal: _____
_____
_____
_____
_____
_____

5-Consecration

God's promise is, "Ye shall seek Me, and find Me, when ye shall search for Me with all your heart." Jeremiah 29:13.

The whole heart must be yielded to God, or the change can never be wrought in us by which we are to be restored to His likeness. By nature we are alienated from God. The Holy Spirit describes our condition in such words as these: "Dead in trespasses and sins;" "the whole head is sick, and the whole heart faint;" "no soundness in it." We are held fast in the snare of Satan, "taken captive by him at his will." Ephesians 2:1; Isaiah 1:5, 6; 2 Timothy 2:26. God desires to heal us, to set us free. But since this requires an entire transformation, a renewing of our whole nature, we must yield ourselves wholly to Him.

The warfare against self is the greatest battle that was ever fought. The yielding of self, surrendering all to the will of God, requires a struggle; but the soul must submit to God before it can be renewed in holiness.

The government of God is not, as Satan would make it appear, founded upon a blind submission, an unreasoning control. It appeals to the intellect and the conscience. "Come now, and let us reason together" is the Creator's invitation to the beings He has made. Isaiah 1:18. God does not force the will of His creatures. He cannot accept an homage that is not willingly and intelligently given. A mere forced submission would prevent all real development of mind [44] or character; it would make man a mere automaton. Such is not the purpose of the Creator. He desires that man, the crowning work of His creative power, shall reach the highest possible development. He sets before us the height of blessing to which He desires to bring us through His grace. He invites us to give ourselves to Him, that He may work His will in us. It remains for us to choose whether we will be set free from the bondage of sin, to share the glorious liberty of the sons of God.

In giving ourselves to God, we must necessarily

1. "'Search for Me with a_____ your heart'…Since this requires an e_____ transformation, a renewing of our w_____ nature… y_____ ourselves wholly to Him." (43) Lord, I seem unable to even comprehend this level. Thank You for Your gentleness, confronting one corner of my heart at a time: _____
_____
_____
_____

2. "The warfare against s_____ is the greatest battle that was ever fought." More significant than military, naval or galactic battles? Than athletic contests? How does it compare with the cosmic conflict, the war between Michael and the dragon? _____
_____ Help me not to be so casual about it: _____

3. God "cannot accept a homage that is not w_____ ____ and i_____ given." Lord, You desire for me the highest possible development, vs automaton. How have I cooperated or hindered Your desire for me? _____
_____
_____

4. "Whatever shall draw away the h_____ from God must be g____ __up... We are not God's children unless we are such e_____." (44) Lord, I want my heart to be close to You, not drawn away. Give me eye salve to see. Help me to let go of my need for recognition, my drive to overfill my day, my concern and focus on self, etc: _____

_____

_____

_____

5. "When Christ dwells in the heart, the soul will be so filled with His l_____ _____, with the joy of c__ _____ with Him, that it will cleave to Him; and in the contemplation of Him, s_____ will be forgotten." How is this greatest battle (against self) fought? _____

_____

Come into my heart, Lord. Come in today, come in to stay. Let self pale to nothingness compared to the grandeur of Your character: _____

_____

__ _____

_____

give up all that would separate us from Him. Hence the Saviour says, "Whosoever he be of you that forsaketh not all that he hath, he cannot be My disciple." Luke 14:33. Whatever shall draw away the heart from God must be given up. Mammon is the idol of many. The love of money, the desire for wealth, is the golden chain that binds them to Satan. Reputation and worldly honor are worshiped by another class. The life of selfish ease and freedom from responsibility is the idol of others. But these slavish bands must be broken. We cannot be half the Lord's and half the world's. We are not God's children unless we are such entirely.

There are those who profess to serve God, while they rely upon their own efforts to obey His law, to form a right character, and secure salvation. Their hearts are not moved by any deep sense of the love of Christ, but they seek to perform the duties of the Christian life as that which God requires of them in order to gain heaven. Such religion is worth nothing. When Christ dwells in the heart, the soul will be [45] be so filled with His love, with the joy of communion with Him, that it will cleave to Him; and in the contemplation of Him, self will be forgotten. Love to Christ will be the spring of action. Those who feel the constraining love of God, do not ask how little may be given to meet the requirements of God; they do not ask for the lowest standard, but aim at perfect conformity to the will of their Redeemer. With earnest desire they yield all and manifest an interest proportionate to the value of the object which they seek. A profession of Christ without this deep love is mere talk, dry formality, and heavy drudgery.

Do you feel that it is too great a sacrifice to yield all to Christ? Ask yourself the question, "What has Christ given for me?" The Son of God gave all--life and love and suffering--for our redemption. And can it be that we, the unworthy objects of so great love, will withhold our hearts from Him? Every moment of our lives we have been partakers of the blessings of His grace, and for this very reason we cannot fully realize the depths of ignorance and misery from which we have been saved. Can we look upon Him whom our sins have pierced, and yet be willing to do despite to all His love and sacrifice? In view of the infinite humiliation of the Lord of glory, shall we murmur because we can enter into life only through conflict and self-abasement?

The inquiry of many a proud heart is, "Why need I go in penitence and humiliation before I can have the assurance of my acceptance with God?" I point you to Christ. He was sinless, and, more than this, He was the Prince of heaven; but in man's [46] behalf He became sin for the race. "He was numbered with the transgressors; and He bare the sin of many, and made intercession for the transgressors." Isaiah 53:12.

But what do we give up, when we give all? A sin-polluted heart, for Jesus to purify, to cleanse by His own blood, and to save by His matchless love. And yet men think it hard to give up all! I am ashamed to hear it spoken of, ashamed to write it.

God does not require us to give up anything that it is for our best interest to retain. In all that He does, He has the well-being of His children in view. Would that all who have not chosen Christ might realize that He has something vastly better to offer them than they are seeking for themselves. Man is doing the greatest injury and injustice to his own soul when he thinks and acts contrary to the will of God. No real joy can be found in the path forbidden by Him who knows what is best and who plans for the good of His creatures. The path of transgression is the path of misery and destruction.

It is a mistake to entertain the thought that God is pleased to see His children suffer. All heaven is interested in the happiness of man. Our heavenly Father does not close the avenues of joy to any of His creatures. The divine requirements call upon us to shun those indulgences that would bring suffering and disappointment, that would close to us the door of happiness and heaven. The world's Redeemer accepts men as they are, with all their wants, imperfections, and weaknesses; and He will not only cleanse from sin and grant redemption through His blood, but [47] will satisfy the heart-longing of all who consent to wear His yoke, to bear His burden. It is His purpose to impart peace and rest to all who come to Him for the bread of life. He requires us to perform only those duties that will lead our steps to heights of bliss to which the disobedient can never attain. The true, joyous life of the soul is to have Christ formed within, the hope of glory.

Many are inquiring, "How am I to make the surrender of myself to God?" You desire to give yourself to Him, but you are weak in moral power, in slavery to

6. "But what do we give up, when we give a_____?" (46) _____

Lord, help me see the true value of things. What is the value of a sin-polluted heart? I want to consecrate my heart to you: _____

_____

_____

_____

7. "No r_____ joy can be found in the path forbidden by Him who knows what is b____ and who plans for the good of His creatures." How does Satan package his enticements with a different kind of joy, to divert my heart?

_____

_____

_____

doubt, and controlled by the habits of your life of sin. Your promises and resolutions are like ropes of sand. You cannot control your thoughts, your impulses, your affections. The knowledge of your broken promises and forfeited pledges weakens your confidence in your own sincerity, and causes you to feel that God cannot accept you; but you need not despair. What you need to understand is the true force of the will. This is the governing power in the nature of man, the power of decision, or of choice. Everything depends on the right action of the will. The power of choice God has given to men; it is theirs to exercise. You cannot change your heart, you cannot of yourself give to God its affections; but you can choose to serve Him. You can give Him your will; He will then work in you to will and to do according to His good pleasure. Thus your whole nature will be brought under the control of the Spirit of Christ; your affections will be centered upon Him, your thoughts will be in harmony with Him.

8. "How can I make the surrender of myself to God?...You cannot change your heart, you cannot of yourself give to God its a_____; but you can c_____ to serve Him." (47) Lord, I give You my w____; I want my affections centered on You, and my thoughts to be in harmony with You:

_____
_____
_____

Desires for goodness and holiness are right as [48] far as they go; but if you stop here, they will avail nothing. Many will be lost while hoping and desiring to be Christians. They do not come to the point of yielding the will to God. They do not now choose to be Christians.

9. "Through c_____ ___ surrender to God you will be enabled to live the new life, even the life of faith." (48). Lord, help me hear Your moment by moment reminders to surrender. Be a constant Companion and Friend this day and every day: _____

_____
_____

Through the right exercise of the will, an entire change may be made in your life. By yielding up your will to Christ, you ally yourself with the power that is above all principalities and powers. You will have strength from above to hold you steadfast, and thus through constant surrender to God you will be enabled to live the new life, even the life of faith.

Prayer journal: _____
_____
_____
_____
_____

6-Faith and Acceptance

As your conscience has been quickened by the Holy Spirit, you have seen something of the evil of sin, of its power, its guilt, its woe; and you look upon it with abhorrence. You feel that sin has separated you from God, that you are in bondage to the power of evil. The more you struggle to escape, the more you realize your helplessness. Your motives are impure; your heart is unclean. You see that your life has been filled with selfishness and sin. You long to be forgiven, to be cleansed, to be set free. Harmony with God, likeness to Him--what can you do to obtain it?

It is peace that you need--Heaven's forgiveness and peace and love in the soul. Money cannot buy it, intellect cannot procure it, wisdom cannot attain to it; you can never hope, by your own efforts, to secure it. But God offers it to you as a gift, "without money and without price." Isaiah 55:1. It is yours if you will but reach out your hand and grasp it. The Lord says, "Though your sins be as scarlet, they shall be as white as snow; though they be red like crimson, they shall be as wool." Isaiah 1:18. "A new heart also will I give you, and a new spirit will I put within you." Ezekiel 36:26.

You have confessed your sins, and in heart put them away. You have resolved to give yourself to God. Now go to Him, and ask that He will wash away your sins and give you a new heart. Then [50] believe that He does this because He has promised. This is the lesson which Jesus taught while He was on earth, that the gift which God promises us, we must believe we do receive, and it is ours. Jesus healed the people of their diseases when they had faith in His power; He helped them in the things which they could see, thus inspiring them with confidence in Him concerning things which they could not see--leading them to believe in His power to forgive sins. This He plainly stated in the healing of the man sick with palsy: "That ye may know that the Son of man hath power on earth to forgive sins, (then saith He to the sick of the palsy,) Arise, take up thy bed,

1. "Harmony with God, likeness to Him—what can you do to obtain it? It is peace that you need—Heaven's f_____ and peace and love in the soul...It is yours if you will but r_____ out your hand and grasp it." (49) Lord, thank You for Your gracious and generous offer. I don't deserve any of it. Harmony with You is not something I can earn or deserve. It is through receiving Your "forgiveness and peace and love." How do I make room for it in my life? _____
_____
_____

2. "Now go to Him, and a_____ that He will wash away your sins and give you a new h_____. Then b_____ that He does this because He has p_____." Lord, why don't I make this request every day?
_____
_____ Why do I need to "ask" You? _____
_____
_____

and go unto thine house." Matthew 9:6. So also John the evangelist says, speaking of the miracles of Christ, "These are written, that ye might believe that Jesus is the Christ, the Son of God; and that believing ye might have life through His name." John 20:31.

From the simple Bible account of how Jesus healed the sick, we may learn something about how to believe in Him for the forgiveness of sins. Let us turn to the story of the paralytic at Bethesda. The poor sufferer was helpless; he had not used his limbs for thirty-eight years. Yet Jesus bade him, "Rise, take up thy bed, and walk." The sick man might have said, "Lord, if Thou wilt make me whole, I will obey Thy word." But, no, he believed Christ's word, believed that he was made whole, and he made the effort at once; he willed to walk, and he did walk. He acted on the word of Christ, and God gave the power. He was made whole. [51]

In like manner you are a sinner. You cannot atone for your past sins; you cannot change your heart and make yourself holy. But God promises to do all this for you through Christ. You believe that promise. You confess your sins and give yourself to God. You will to serve Him. Just as surely as you do this, God will fulfill His word to you. If you believe the promise,--believe that you are forgiven and cleansed,--God supplies the fact; you are made whole, just as Christ gave the paralytic power to walk when the man believed that he was healed. It is so if you believe it.

Do not wait to feel that you are made whole, but say, "I believe it; it is so, not because I feel it, but because God has promised."

Jesus says, "What things soever ye desire, when ye pray, believe that ye receive them, and ye shall have them." Mark 11:24. There is a condition to this promise--that we pray according to the will of God. But it is the will of God to cleanse us from sin, to make us His children, and to enable us to live a holy life. So

3. From the story of the paralytic we "learn something about h_____ to believe in Him for the forgiveness of sins... he b_ _____ Christ's word ... He a_____ on the word of Christ, and God gave the p_____." (50) Lord, do I not act on Your word? _____

_____

How should a person that's been forgiven act? _____

_____

_____

_____

4. "If you believe the promise, --believe that you are forgiven and cleansed, -- God supplies the f_____; you a_____ made whole... It is s__ if you believe it." (51) Lord, thank You for that assurance. Why don't I believe?

_____

May I be secure and anchored in Your forgiveness and love: _____

_____

_____

5. Suppose the feeling of being whole isn't there? _____

_____

_____Lord, do I rely on feelings or moods, give them too much credence?

_____

_____

we may ask for these blessings, and believe that we receive them, and thank God that we have received them. It is our privilege to go to Jesus and be cleansed, and to stand before the law without shame or remorse. "There is therefore now no condemnation to them which are in Christ Jesus, who walk not after the flesh, but after the Spirit." Romans 8:1.

Henceforth you are not your own; you are bought with a price. "Ye were not redeemed with corruptible things, as silver and gold; . . . but with the precious blood of Christ, as of a lamb without blemish and [52] without spot." 1 Peter 1:18, 19. Through this simple act of believing God, the Holy Spirit has begotten a new life in your heart. You are as a child born into the family of God, and He loves you as He loves His Son.

Now that you have given yourself to Jesus, do not draw back, do not take yourself away from Him, but day by day say, "I am Christ's; I have given myself to Him;" and ask Him to give you His Spirit and keep you by His grace. As it is by giving yourself to God, and believing Him, that you become His child, so you are to live in Him. The apostle says, "As ye have therefore received Christ Jesus the Lord, so walk ye in Him." Colossians 2:6.

Some seem to feel that they must be on probation, and must prove to the Lord that they are reformed, before they can claim His blessing. But they may claim the blessing of God even now. They must have His grace, the Spirit of Christ, to help their infirmities, or they cannot resist evil. Jesus loves to have us come to Him just as we are, sinful, helpless, dependent. We may come with all our weakness, our folly, our sinfulness, and fall at His feet in penitence. It is His glory to encircle us in the arms of His love and to bind up our wounds, to cleanse us from all impurity.

Here is where thousands fail; they do not believe that Jesus pardons them personally, individually. They do not take God at His word. It is the privilege of all who comply with the conditions to know for themselves that pardon is freely extended for every sin. Put away the suspicion that God's promises are not meant for you. They are for every [53] repentant transgressor. Strength and grace have been provided through Christ to be brought by ministering angels to every believing soul. None are so sinful that they cannot find strength,

6. "We may ask for these blessings, and believe that we r_____ them, and t_____ God that we have received them." Lord, help me to act on Your promises, to give my faith in You some feet: _____ _____ _____

7. "Day by d_____ say, "I am Christ's; I have g____ _____ myself to Him;" How do I give myself to You, Lord? What does it mean? _____ _____ _____ _____

8. "Jesus l_____ to have us come to Him j_____as we are... to encircle us in the arms of His love and to bind up our w_____, to cleanse us from all i_____." Lord, thank You for Your agape love. Help me guard against satan's suggestion, that since there is no probation, that I should be casual about my commitment. Rather, Your love inspires greater devotion, a desire for oneness with You: _____ _____ _____

purity, and righteousness in Jesus, who died for them. He is waiting to strip them of their garments stained and polluted with sin, and to put upon them the white robes of righteousness; He bids them live and not die.

God does not deal with us as finite men deal with one another. His thoughts are thoughts of mercy, love, and tenderest compassion. He says, "Let the wicked forsake his way, and the unrighteous man his thoughts: and let him return unto the Lord, and He will have mercy upon him; and to our God, for He will abundantly pardon." "I have blotted out, as a thick cloud, thy transgressions, and, as a cloud, thy sins." Isaiah 55:7; 44:22.

"I have no pleasure in the death of him that dieth, saith the Lord God: wherefore turn yourselves, and live ye." Ezekiel 18:32. Satan is ready to steal away the blessed assurances of God. He desires to take every glimmer of hope and every ray of light from the soul; but you must not permit him to do this. Do not give ear to the tempter, but say, "Jesus has died that I might live. He loves me, and wills not that I should perish. I have a compassionate heavenly Father; and although I have abused His love, though the blessings He has given me have been squandered, I will arise, and go to my Father, and say, 'I have sinned against heaven, and before Thee, and am no more worthy to be called Thy son: make me as one of Thy hired servants.'" The parable tells you how [54] the wanderer will be received: "When he was yet a great way off, his father saw him, and had compassion, and ran, and fell on his neck, and kissed him." Luke 15:18-20.

But even this parable, tender and touching as it is, comes short of expressing the infinite compassion of the heavenly Father. The Lord declares by His prophet, "I have loved thee with an everlasting love: therefore with loving-kindness have I drawn thee." Jeremiah 31:3. While the sinner is yet far from the Father's house, wasting his substance in a strange country, the Father's heart is yearning over him; and every longing awakened in the soul to return to God is but the tender pleading of His Spirit, wooing, entreating, drawing the wanderer to his Father's heart of love.

With the rich promises of the Bible before you, can you give place to doubt? Can you believe that when the poor sinner longs to return, longs to forsake his sins, the Lord sternly withholds him from coming to His feet in

---

9. "Satan is ready to s___ _____ away the blessed a_____ of God." Lord, alert me as to when he is doing so, to recognize his tactics. How has he gotten me before? _____
_____
_____
_____

10. "Every longing a_____ ____ in the soul to return to God is but the tender pleading of His Spirit, wooing, entreating, d___ _____ the wanderer to his Father's h_____ of love." (54) Lord, I want

repentance? Away with such thoughts! Nothing can hurt your own soul more than to entertain such a conception of our heavenly Father. He hates sin, but He loves the sinner, and He gave Himself in the person of Christ, that all who would might be saved and have eternal blessedness in the kingdom of glory. What stronger or more tender language could have been employed than He has chosen in which to express His love toward us? He declares, "Can a woman forget her sucking child, that she should not have compassion on the son of her womb? yea, they may forget, yet will I not forget thee." Isaiah 49:15.

Look up, you that are doubting and trembling; [55] for Jesus lives to make intercession for us. Thank God for the gift of His dear Son and pray that He may not have died for you in vain. The Spirit invites you today. Come with your whole heart to Jesus, and you may claim His blessing.

As you read the promises, remember they are the expression of unutterable love and pity. The great heart of Infinite Love is drawn toward the sinner with boundless compassion. "We have redemption through His blood, the forgiveness of sins." Ephesians 1:7. Yes, only believe that God is your helper. He wants to restore His moral image in man. As you draw near to Him with confession and repentance, He will draw near to you with mercy and forgiveness.

to be more sensitive to that drawing, to being awakened. Keep that thought in my mind, help me recognize the moments of drawing, throughout this day:

_____
_____
_____

11. "Nothing can h_____ ____ your own soul more than to entertain such a conception of our heavenly Father." What conception, Lord? _____
_____

12. "As you draw near to Him with confession and repentance, He will draw n_____ to you with m_ _____ and forgiveness." Thank You, Lord, for Your boundless compassion. Thank You for Your desire to draw near to me, and to draw me to Your heart. I love You: _____
_____
_____
_____

Prayer journal: _____
_____
_____
_____
_____

7-The Test of Discipleship

"If any man be in Christ, he is a new creature: old things are passed away; behold, all things are become new." 2 Corinthians 5:17.

A person may not be able to tell the exact time or place, or trace all the chain of circumstances in the process of conversion; but this does not prove him to be unconverted. Christ said to Nicodemus, "The wind bloweth where it listeth, and thou hearest the sound thereof, but canst not tell whence it cometh, and whither it goeth: so is everyone that is born of the Spirit." John 3:8. Like the wind, which is invisible, yet the effects of which are plainly seen and felt, is the Spirit of God in its work upon the human heart. That regenerating power, which no human eye can see, begets a new life in the soul; it creates a new being in the image of God. While the work of the Spirit is silent and imperceptible, its effects are manifest. If the heart has been renewed by the Spirit of God, the life will bear witness to the fact. While we cannot do anything to change our hearts or to bring ourselves into harmony with God; while we must not trust at all to ourselves or our good works, our lives will reveal whether the grace of God is dwelling within us. A change will be seen in the character, the habits, the pursuits. The contrast will be clear and decided between what they have been and what they are. The character is revealed, not [58] by occasional good deeds and occasional misdeeds, but by the tendency of the habitual words and acts.

It is true that there may be an outward correctness of deportment without the renewing power of Christ. The love of influence and the desire for the esteem of others may produce a well-ordered life. Self-respect may lead us to avoid the appearance of evil. A selfish heart may perform generous actions. By what means, then, shall we determine whose side we are on?

Who has the heart? With whom are our thoughts? Of whom do we love to converse? Who has our warmest affections and our best energies? If we are Christ's,

1. "If the heart has been r_____ by the Spirit of God, the life will bear w_____ to the fact." What will the life witness to, Lord? _____

_____

"A change will be seen in the c_____, the habits, the pursuits."

2. "The character is revealed, not by o_____ _____ good deeds and occasional misdeeds, but by the t_____ of the habitual words and acts." Lord, help me not to yield to the temptatation of complacency, or self-confidence ("no big deal, my tendency is good"), nor to the temptation of despair and defeat because of occasional misdeeds. Keep my eyes not on my performance or lack there of, but rather on You: _____

_____

3. "A s_____ heart may perform generous actions. By what means, then, shall we determine whose s_____ we are on?"

_____

our thoughts are with Him, and our sweetest thoughts are of Him. All we have and are is consecrated to Him. We long to bear His image, breathe His spirit, do His will, and please Him in all things.

Those who become new creatures in Christ Jesus will bring forth the fruits of the Spirit, "love, joy, peace, long-suffering, gentleness, goodness, faith, meekness, temperance." Galatians 5:22, 23. They will no longer fashion themselves according to the former lusts, but by the faith of the Son of God they will follow in His steps, reflect His character, and purify themselves even as He is pure. The things they once hated they now love, and the things they once loved they hate. The proud and self-assertive become meek and lowly in heart. The vain and supercilious become serious and unobtrusive. The drunken become sober, and the profligate pure. The vain customs and fashions of the world are laid aside. Christians will seek not the "outward adorning," but "the hidden man of [59] the heart, in that which is not corruptible, even the ornament of a meek and quiet spirit." 1 Peter 3: 3, 4.

There is no evidence of genuine repentance unless it works reformation. If he restore the pledge, give again that he had robbed, confess his sins, and love God and his fellow men, the sinner may be sure that he has passed from death unto life.

When, as erring, sinful beings, we come to Christ and become partakers of His pardoning grace, love springs up in the heart. Every burden is light, for the yoke that Christ imposes is easy. Duty becomes a delight, and sacrifice a pleasure. The path that before seemed shrouded in darkness, becomes bright with beams from the Sun of Righteousness.

The loveliness of the character of Christ will be seen in His followers. It was His delight to do the will of God. Love to God, zeal for His glory, was the controlling power in our Saviour's life. Love beautified and ennobled all His actions. Love is of God. The unconsecrated heart cannot originate or produce it. It is found only in the heart where Jesus reigns. "We love, because He first loved us." 1 John 4:19, R.V. In the heart renewed by divine grace, love is the principle of action. It modifies the character, governs the impulses, controls the passions, subdues enmity, and ennobles the affections. This love, cherished in the soul, sweetens the life

4. "The l_____ of the character of Christ will be seen in His followers... It [love] modifies the character, governs the i_____ _____, controls the passions, subdues e_____, and ennobles the affections ... sheds a r_____ in-

fluence on all around." (59) Lord, how can I make room for this to happen in my life? _____

_____

_____ In beholding the loveliness of the character of Christ.

5. "If the law is written in the h_____, will it not shape the life? Obedience -- the service and allegiance of love; is the true sign of d_____."
(60) Lord, I want to be a disciple. I want to be obedient. I can't. I make myself available for You to ever keep showing me how to be motivated by Your love, to an allegiance of love:

_____

_____

_____

6. "It is faith, and faith o__ ___, that makes us partakers of the grace of Christ, which e_____ us to render obedience." Lord, I

and sheds a refining influence on all around.

There are two errors against which the children of God--particularly those who have just come to trust in His grace--especially need to guard. The first, already dwelt upon, is that of looking to their [60] own works, trusting to anything they can do, to bring themselves into harmony with God. He who is trying to become holy by his own works in keeping the law, is attempting an impossibility. All that man can do without Christ is polluted with selfishness and sin. It is the grace of Christ alone, through faith, that can make us holy.

The opposite and no less dangerous error is that belief in Christ releases men from keeping the law of God; that since by faith alone we become partakers of the grace of Christ, our works have nothing to do with our redemption.

But notice here that obedience is not a mere outward compliance, but the service of love. The law of God is an expression of His very nature; it is an embodiment of the great principle of love, and hence is the foundation of His government in heaven and earth. If our hearts are renewed in the likeness of God, if the divine love is implanted in the soul, will not the law of God be carried out in the life? When the principle of love is implanted in the heart, when man is renewed after the image of Him that created him, the new-covenant promise is fulfilled, "I will put My laws into their hearts, and in their minds will I write them." Hebrews 10:16. And if the law is written in the heart, will it not shape the life? Obedience--the service and allegiance of love--is the true sign of discipleship. Thus the Scripture says, "This is the love of God, that we keep His commandments." "He that saith, I know Him, and keepeth not His commandments, is a liar, and the truth is not in him." 1 John 5:3; 2:4. Instead of releasing man from obedience, it is faith, [61] and faith only, that makes us partakers of the grace of Christ, which enables us to render obedience.

We do not earn salvation by our obedience; for salvation is the free gift of God, to be received by faith. But obedience is the fruit of faith. "Ye know that He was manifested to take away our sins; and in Him is no sin. Whosoever abideth in Him sinneth not: whosoever sinneth hath not seen Him, neither known Him." 1 John 3:5, 6. Here is the true test. If we abide in Christ, if the love of God dwells in us, our feelings, our thoughts, our purposes, our actions, will be in harmony with the will of God as expressed in the precepts of His holy law. "Little children, let no man deceive you: he that doeth righteousness is righteous, even as He is righteous." 1 John 3:7. Righteousness is defined by the standard of God's holy law, as expressed in the ten precepts given on Sinai.

That so-called faith in Christ which professes to release men from the obligation of obedience to God, is not faith, but presumption. "By grace are ye saved through faith." But "faith, if it hath not works, is dead." Ephesians 2:8; James 2:17. Jesus said of Himself before He came to earth, "I delight to do Thy will, O My God: yea, Thy law is within My heart." Psalm 40:8. And just before He ascended again to heaven He declared, "I have kept My Father's commandments, and abide in His love." John 15:10. The Scripture says, "Hereby we do know that we know Him, if we keep His commandments. . . . He that saith he abideth in Him ought himself also so to walk even as He walked." 1 John 2:3-6. "Because Christ also [62] suffered for us, leaving us an example, that ye should follow His steps." 1 Peter 2:21.

The condition of eternal life is now just what it always has been,--just what it was in Paradise before the fall of our first parents,--perfect obedience to the law of God, perfect righteousness. If eternal life were granted on any condition short of this, then the happiness of the whole universe would be imperiled. The way would be open for sin, with all its train of woe and misery, to be immortalized.

It was possible for Adam, before the fall, to form a righteous character by obedience to God's law. But he failed to do this, and because of his sin our natures are fallen and we cannot make ourselves righteous. Since we are sinful, unholy, we cannot perfectly obey the holy law. We have no righteousness of our own with which to meet the claims of the law of God. But Christ has made a way of escape for us. He lived on earth amid trials and temptations such as we have to meet. He lived a sinless life. He died for us, and now He offers to take our sins and give us His righteousness. If you give yourself to Him, and accept Him as your Saviour, then, sinful as your life may have been, for His sake you are accounted righteous. Christ's character stands in place

invite You into my heart, and by beholding Your character, may Your abiding presence render obedience / harmony with Your will: _____

_____
_____
_____

7. "The condition of eternal life is ... perfect o_____ _____ to the law of God, perfect r_____ ...

We have n___ righteousness of our own with which to meet the claims of the law of God ... Christ's character stands in p____

___ to your character, and you are a_____ ___ before God just as if you had n___ sinned." (62) Lord, how do I let Your character stand in place of my character? _____

_____
_____
_____

8. "Our only ground of hope is in the r_____ _____ of Christ imputed to us, and in that wrought by His S_____ working i___ and through us." (63) Lord, remind me of my need of a continual surrender of my will to You, to make room for Your righteousnes in me: _____

_____
_____

9. "Where there is not only a belief in God's word, but a s_____ of the will to Him; where the heart is yielded to Him, the affections f_____ upon Him, there is faith - f_____ that works by love and purifies the soul." Lord, where are my affections? Is my heart yielded?

_____

Help me to see that faith is more than a simple decision, but a devoted love relationship with You: __

_____
_____

of your character, and you are accepted before God just as if you had not sinned.

More than this, Christ changes the heart. He abides in your heart by faith. You are to maintain this connection with Christ by faith and the continual surrender of your will to Him; and so long as you do this, He will work in you to will and to do [63] according to His good pleasure. So you may say, "The life which I now live in the flesh I live by the faith of the Son of God, who loved me, and gave Himself for me." Galatians 2:20. So Jesus said to His disciples, "It is not ye that speak, but the Spirit of your Father which speaketh in you." Matthew 10:20. Then with Christ working in you, you will manifest the same spirit and do the same good works--works of righteousness, obedience.

So we have nothing in ourselves of which to boast. We have no ground for self-exaltation. Our only ground of hope is in the righteousness of Christ imputed to us, and in that wrought by His Spirit working in and through us.

When we speak of faith, there is a distinction that should be borne in mind. There is a kind of belief that is wholly distinct from faith. The existence and power of God, the truth of His word, are facts that even Satan and his hosts cannot at heart deny. The Bible says that "the devils also believe, and tremble;" but this is not faith. James 2:19. Where there is not only a belief in God's word, but a submission of the will to Him; where the heart is yielded to Him, the affections fixed upon Him, there is faith--faith that works by love and purifies the soul. Through this faith the heart is renewed in the image of God. And the heart that in its unrenewed state is not subject to the law of God, neither indeed can be, now delights in its holy precepts, exclaiming with the psalmist, "O how love I Thy law! it is my meditation all the day." Psalm 119:97. And the righteousness of the law is fulfilled in us, "who [64] walk not after the flesh, but after the Spirit." Romans 8:1.

There are those who have known the pardoning love of Christ and who really desire to be children of God, yet they realize that their character is imperfect, their life faulty, and they are ready to doubt whether their hearts have been renewed by the Holy Spirit. To such I would say, Do not draw back in despair. We shall often have to bow down and weep at the feet of Jesus because of our shortcomings and mistakes, but we are not to be discouraged. Even if we are overcome by the enemy, we are not cast off, not forsaken and rejected of God. No; Christ is at the right hand of God, who also maketh intercession for us. Said the beloved John, "These things write I unto you, that ye sin not. And if any man sin, we have an advocate with the Father, Jesus Christ the righteous." 1 John 2:1. And do not forget the words of Christ, "The Father Himself loveth you." John 16:27. He desires to restore you to Himself, to see His own purity and holiness reflected in you. And if you will but yield yourself to Him, He that hath begun a good work in you will carry it forward to the day of Jesus Christ. Pray more fervently; believe more fully. As we come to distrust our own power, let us trust the power of our Redeemer, and we shall praise Him who is the health of our countenance.

The closer you come to Jesus, the more faulty you will appear in your own eyes; for your vision will be clearer, and your imperfections will be seen in broad and distinct contrast to His perfect nature. This is evidence that Satan's delusions have lost their [65] power; that the vivifying influence of the Spirit of God is arousing you.

No deep-seated love for Jesus can dwell in the heart that does not realize its own sinfulness. The soul that is transformed by the grace of Christ will admire His divine character; but if we do not see our own moral deformity, it is unmistakable evidence that we have not had a view of the beauty and excellence of Christ.

The less we see to esteem in ourselves, the more we shall see to esteem in the infinite purity and loveliness of our Saviour. A view of our sinfulness drives us to Him who can pardon; and when the soul, realizing its helplessness, reaches out after Christ, He will reveal Himself in power. The more our sense of need drives us to Him and to the word of God, the more exalted views we shall have of His character, and the more fully we shall reflect His image.

10. "The closer you come to Jesus, the more f_____ _____ you will appear in your own eyes; for your vision will be c_____ _____, and your imperfections will be seen in broad and distinct c_____ to His divine nature. This is e_____ that Satan's delusions have lost their power; that the vivifying i_____ of the Spirit of God is arousing you." (64) Lord, may the recognition of my need of Your forgiveness and love, drive me into Your arms, presenting a view of Your exalted character, and may my affections grow into a deep-seated love for You: _____

Prayer journal: _____

8-Growing Up Into Christ

The change of heart by which we become children of God is in the Bible spoken of as birth. Again, it is compared to the germination of the good seed sown by the husbandman. In like manner those who are just converted to Christ are, "as new-born babes," to "grow up" to the stature of men and women in Christ Jesus. 1 Peter 2:2; Ephesians 4:15. Or like the good seed sown in the field, they are to grow up and bring forth fruit. Isaiah says that they shall "be called trees of righteousness, the planting of the Lord, that He might be glorified." Isaiah 61:3. So from natural life, illustrations are drawn, to help us better to understand the mysterious truths of spiritual life.

Not all the wisdom and skill of man can produce life in the smallest object in nature. It is only through the life which God Himself has imparted, that either plant or animal can live. So it is only through the life from God that spiritual life is begotten in the hearts of men. Unless a man is "born from above," he cannot become a partaker of the life which Christ came to give. John 3:3, margin.

As with life, so it is with growth. It is God who brings the bud to bloom and the flower to fruit. It is by His power that the seed develops, "first the blade, then the ear, after that the full corn in the ear." Mark 4:28. And the prophet Hosea says of Israel, that "he shall grow as the lily." "They shall revive as the corn, and grow as the vine." Hosea 14:5, 7. And Jesus bids us "consider the lilies how [68] they grow." Luke 12:27. The plants and flowers grow not by their own care or anxiety or effort, but by receiving that which God has furnished to minister to their life. The child cannot, by any anxiety or power of its own, add to its stature. No more can you, by anxiety or effort of yourself, secure spiritual growth. The plant, the child, grows by receiving from its surroundings that which ministers to its life--air, sunshine, and food. What these gifts of nature are to animal and plant, such is Christ to those who trust in Him. He is their "everlasting light," "a sun and shield." Isaiah 60:19; Psalm 84:11. He shall be as "the dew unto

1. There are gifts of nature for animals and plants. How is Christ the same for me? (68) _____ _____ _____

Israel." "He shall come down like rain upon the mown grass." Hosea 14:5; Psalm 72:6. He is the living water, "the Bread of God . . . which cometh down from heaven, and giveth life unto the world." John 6:33.

In the matchless gift of His Son, God has encircled the whole world with an atmosphere of grace as real as the air which circulates around the globe. All who choose to breathe this life-giving atmosphere will live and grow up to the stature of men and women in Christ Jesus.

As the flower turns to the sun, that the bright beams may aid in perfecting its beauty and symmetry, so should we turn to the Sun of Righteousness, that heaven's light may shine upon us, that our character may be developed into the likeness of Christ.

2. "Turn to the Sun of Righteousness, that heaven's light may s_____ upon us, that our character may be developed into the l_____ of Christ." Lord, help me to draw my life from You. What is a day without You really like? _____
_____
_____

Jesus teaches the same thing when He says, "Abide in Me, and I in you. As the branch cannot bear fruit of itself, except it abide in the vine; no more can ye, except ye abide in Me. . . . Without Me ye [69] can do nothing." John 15:4, 5. You are just as dependent upon Christ, in order to live a holy life, as is the branch upon the parent stock for growth and fruitfulness. Apart from Him you have no life. You have no power to resist temptation or to grow in grace and holiness. Abiding in Him, you may flourish. Drawing your life from Him, you will not wither nor be fruitless. You will be like a tree planted by the rivers of water.

Many have an idea that they must do some part of the work alone. They have trusted in Christ for the forgiveness of sin, but now they seek by their own efforts to live aright. But every such effort must fail. Jesus says, "Without Me ye can do nothing." Our growth in grace, our joy, our usefulness,--all depend upon our union with Christ. It is by communion with Him, daily, hourly,--by abiding in Him,--that we are to grow in grace. He is not only the Author, but the Finisher of our faith. It is Christ first and last and always. He is to be with us, not only at the beginning and the end of our course, but at every step of the way. David says, "I have set the Lord always before me: because He is at my right hand, I shall not be moved." Psalm 16:8.

3. "It is by communion with Him, daily, h_____ ____,--by abiding in Him,-- that we grow in grace...every step of the way." (69) Lord, guide my thoughts, train my heart and mind, to ever be in Your presence, like Enoch did. I invite You to be a Companion 'every step of the way.' What can I do to train my heart and mind? _____
_____

Do you ask, "How am I to abide in Christ?" In the same way as you received Him at first. "As ye have therefore received Christ Jesus the Lord, so walk ye in Him." "The just shall live by faith." Colossians 2:6;

4. "By faith you became Christ's, and by faith you are to grow up in Him—by giving and t_____."
(70) Lord, I give myself, my heart, my will, my service, my all. I take You, opening the door for You to abide. Be my strength, my righteousness, my everlasting helper. I claim this reality in faith. What keeps me from believing this is in the bank? _____

_____

_____

_____

5. "Make this your very f_____ work...'Take me, O Lord, as w_____ Thine...' This is a daily matter. Each m_____ __ consecrate yourself to God for that day." Lord, this prayer inspires me. I give You permission to interrupt my thoughts, my routine, to remind me to express this prayer, from my heart each morning:

_____

6. "Let the mind dwell upon His love, upon the beauty, the perfection, of His character. Christ in His self-denial, Christ in His h___ _____, Christ in His purity and holiness, Christ in His matchless love—this is the subject for the soul's c_____."
Lord, nurture my thoughts to dwell on You, and may

Hebrews 10:38. You gave yourself to God, to be His wholly, to serve and obey Him, and you took Christ as your Saviour. You could not yourself atone for your sins or change your heart; but having given [70] yourself to God, you believe that He for Christ's sake did all this for you. By faith you became Christ's, and by faith you are to grow up in Him--by giving and taking. You are to give all,--your heart, your will, your service,--give yourself to Him to obey all His requirements; and you must take all,--Christ, the fullness of all blessing, to abide in your heart, to be your strength, your righteousness, your everlasting helper,--to give you power to obey.

Consecrate yourself to God in the morning; make this your very first work. Let your prayer be, "Take me, O Lord, as wholly Thine. I lay all my plans at Thy feet. Use me today in Thy service. Abide with me, and let all my work be wrought in Thee." This is a daily matter. Each morning consecrate yourself to God for that day. Surrender all your plans to Him, to be carried out or given up as His providence shall indicate. Thus day by day you may be giving your life into the hands of God, and thus your life will be molded more and more after the life of Christ.

A life in Christ is a life of restfulness. There may be no ecstasy of feeling, but there should be an abiding, peaceful trust. Your hope is not in yourself; it is in Christ. Your weakness is united to His strength, your ignorance to His wisdom, your frailty to His enduring might. So you are not to look to yourself, not to let the mind dwell upon self, but look to Christ. Let the mind dwell upon His love, upon the beauty, the perfection, of His character. Christ in His self-denial, Christ in His humiliation, Christ in [71] His purity and holiness, Christ in His matchless love--this is the subject for the soul's contemplation. It is by loving Him, copying Him, depending wholly upon Him, that you are to be transformed into His likeness.

Jesus says, "Abide in Me." These words convey the idea of rest, stability, confidence. Again He invites, "Come unto Me, . . . and I will give you rest." Matthew 11:28. The words of the psalmist express the same thought: "Rest in the Lord, and wait patiently for Him." And Isaiah gives the assurance, "In quietness and in confidence shall be your strength." Psalm 37:7; Isaiah 30:15. This rest is not found in inactivity; for in the

Saviour's invitation the promise of rest is united with the call to labor: "Take My yoke upon you: . . . and ye shall find rest." Matthew 11:29. The heart that rests most fully upon Christ will be most earnest and active in labor for Him.

When the mind dwells upon self, it is turned away from Christ, the source of strength and life. Hence it is Satan's constant effort to keep the attention diverted from the Saviour and thus prevent the union and communion of the soul with Christ. The pleasures of the world, life's cares and perplexities and sorrows, the faults of others, or your own faults and imperfections--to any or all of these he will seek to divert the mind. Do not be misled by his devices. Many who are really conscientious, and who desire to live for God, he too often leads to dwell upon their own faults and weaknesses, and thus by separating them from Christ he hopes to [72] gain the victory. We should not make self the center and indulge anxiety and fear as to whether we shall be saved. All this turns the soul away from the Source of our strength. Commit the keeping of your soul to God, and trust in Him. Talk and think of Jesus. Let self be lost in Him. Put away all doubt; dismiss your fears. Say with the apostle Paul, "I live; yet not I, but Christ liveth in me: and the life which I now live in the flesh I live by the faith of the Son of God, who loved me, and gave Himself for me." Galatians 2:20. Rest in God. He is able to keep that which you have committed to Him. If you will leave yourself in His hands, He will bring you off more than conqueror through Him that has loved you.

When Christ took human nature upon Him, He bound humanity to Himself by a tie of love that can never be broken by any power save the choice of man himself. Satan will constantly present allurements to induce us to break this tie--to choose to separate ourselves from Christ. Here is where we need to watch, to strive, to pray, that nothing may entice us to choose another master; for we are always free to do this. But let us keep our eyes fixed upon Christ, and He will preserve us. Looking unto Jesus, we are safe. Nothing can pluck us out of His hand. In constantly beholding Him, we "are changed into the same image from glory to glory, even as by the Spirit of the Lord." 2 Corinthians 3:18.

It was thus that the early disciples gained their like-

my appreciation deepen, for You and Your awesome character. What time frame is involved in letting my 'mind dwell?' _____

_____

_____

7. "It is Satan's constant effort to keep the attention d_____ from the Saviour and thus p_____ the union and communion of the soul with Christ." (71) Lord, how has he been successful in my life? ___

_____

_____ Help me guard against His diversions: _____

_____

_____ I want my mind stayed on Thee!

8. "We should not make s_____ the center and indulge anxiety and fear as to whether we shall be saved. All this turns the soul a__ _____ from the Source of our strength. Commit the keeping of your soul to God, and t_____ in Him." (72) Do I indulge in fear? Have a lack in trust? What can anchor my trust?

_____

Lord, just give me a hunger and thirst for Your communion. May the joy of divine fellowship be my focus: _____

_____

_____

9. "When Christ took human nature upon Him, He bound humanity to Him-

self by a tie of love that can n_____ be broken by any power save the choice of man himself... Nothing can pluck us out of His hand." (72) May my eyes be focused on You, Lord, and not satan's allurements. Thank You for this tie of love! May I be as committed to You as You are to me:

_____

_____

_____

10. "Day by day his heart [John's] was drawn out toward Christ, until he lost sight of s_____ in love for his Master...Christ's Spirit, His love, softens the heart, subdues the soul, and raises the thoughts and d_____ toward God and heaven." (73) Draw me nearer, nearer, blessed Lord. May self be lost in Your love. What hardens my heart, that I might let Your love soften? _____

_____

_____

_____

ness to the dear Saviour. When those disciples heard the words of Jesus, they felt their need of Him. They sought, they found, they followed Him. They [73] were with Him in the house, at the table, in the closet, in the field. They were with Him as pupils with a teacher, daily receiving from His lips lessons of holy truth. They looked to Him, as servants to their master, to learn their duty. Those disciples were men "subject to like passions as we are." James 5:17. They had the same battle with sin to fight. They needed the same grace, in order to live a holy life.

Even John, the beloved disciple, the one who most fully reflected the likeness of the Saviour, did not naturally possess that loveliness of character. He was not only self-assertive and ambitious for honor, but impetuous, and resentful under injuries. But as the character of the Divine One was manifested to him, he saw his own deficiency and was humbled by the knowledge. The strength and patience, the power and tenderness, the majesty and meekness, that he beheld in the daily life of the Son of God, filled his soul with admiration and love. Day by day his heart was drawn out toward Christ, until he lost sight of self in love for his Master. His resentful, ambitious temper was yielded to the molding power of Christ. The regenerating influence of the Holy Spirit renewed his heart. The power of the love of Christ wrought a transformation of character. This is the sure result of union with Jesus. When Christ abides in the heart, the whole nature is transformed. Christ's Spirit, His love, softens the heart, subdues the soul, and raises the thoughts and desires toward God and heaven.

When Christ ascended to heaven, the sense of His presence was still with His followers. It was a [74] personal presence, full of love and light. Jesus, the Saviour, who had walked and talked and prayed with them, who had spoken hope and comfort to their hearts, had, while the message of peace was still upon His lips, been taken up from them into heaven, and the tones of His voice had come back to them, as the cloud of angels received Him--"Lo, I am with you alway, even unto the end of the world." Matthew 28:20. He had ascended to heaven in the form of humanity. They knew that He was before the throne of God, their Friend and Saviour still; that His sympathies were unchanged; that He was still identified with suffering humanity. He was presenting before

God the merits of His own precious blood, showing His wounded hands and feet, in remembrance of the price He had paid for His redeemed. They knew that He had ascended to heaven to prepare places for them, and that He would come again and take them to Himself.

As they met together after the ascension they were eager to present their requests to the Father in the name of Jesus. In solemn awe they bowed in prayer, repeating the assurance, "Whatsoever ye shall ask the Father in My name, He will give it you. Hitherto have ye asked nothing in My name: ask, and ye shall receive, that your joy may be full." John 16:23, 24. They extended the hand of faith higher and higher with the mighty argument, "It is Christ that died, yea rather, that is risen again, who is even at the right hand of God, who also maketh intercession for us." Romans 8:34. And Pentecost brought them the presence of the Comforter, of whom [75] Christ had said, He "shall be in you." And He had further said, "It is expedient for you that I go away: for if I go not away, the Comforter will not come unto you; but if I depart, I will send Him unto you." John 14:17; 16:7. Henceforth through the Spirit, Christ was to abide continually in the hearts of His children. Their union with Him was closer than when He was personally with them. The light, and love, and power of the indwelling Christ shone out through them, so that men, beholding, "marveled; and they took knowledge of them, that they had been with Jesus." Acts 4:13.

All that Christ was to the disciples, He desires to be to His children today; for in that last prayer, with the little band of disciples gathered about Him, He said, "Neither pray I for these alone, but for them also which shall believe on Me through their word." John 17:20.

Jesus prayed for us, and He asked that we might be one with Him, even as He is one with the Father. What a union is this! The Saviour has said of Himself, "The Son can do nothing of Himself;" "the Father that dwelleth in Me, He doeth the works." John 5:19; 14:10. Then if Christ is dwelling in our hearts, He will work in us "both to will and to do of His good pleasure." Philippians 2:13. We shall work as He worked; we shall manifest the same spirit. And thus, loving Him and abiding in Him, we shall "grow up into Him in all things, which is the head, even Christ." Ephesians 4:15.

11. "Jesus prayed for us, and He asked that we might be o____ with the Father. What a union is this!" (75) Lord, growing up into You, the theme of this chapter, is believable and real, in that You are praying for me and You envision us as one. I love Your vision! And I love You!! What is contrary in my heart, to Your vision?

_____
_____
_____

Prayer journal: _____
_____
_____
_____
_____
_____
_____

9-The Work and the Life

God is the source of life and light and joy to the universe. Like rays of light from the sun, like the streams of water bursting from a living spring, blessings flow out from Him to all His creatures. And wherever the life of God is in the hearts of men, it will flow out to others in love and blessing.

Our Saviour's joy was in the uplifting and redemption of fallen men. For this He counted not His life dear unto Himself, but endured the cross, despising the shame. So angels are ever engaged in working for the happiness of others. This is their joy. That which selfish hearts would regard as humiliating service, ministering to those who are wretched and in every way inferior in character and rank, is the work of sinless angels. The spirit of Christ's self-sacrificing love is the spirit that pervades heaven and is the very essence of its bliss. This is the spirit that Christ's followers will possess, the work that they will do.

When the love of Christ is enshrined in the heart, like sweet fragrance it cannot be hidden. Its holy influence will be felt by all with whom we come in contact. The spirit of Christ in the heart is like a spring in the desert, flowing to refresh all and making those who are ready to perish, eager to drink of the water of life.

Love to Jesus will be manifested in a desire to work as He worked for the blessing and uplifting of [78] humanity. It will lead to love, tenderness, and sympathy toward all the creatures of our heavenly Father's care.

The Saviour's life on earth was not a life of ease and devotion to Himself, but He toiled with persistent, earnest, untiring effort for the salvation of lost mankind. From the manger to Calvary He followed the path of self-denial and sought not to be released from arduous tasks, painful travels and exhausting care and labor. He said, "The Son of man came not to be ministered unto, but to minister, and to give His life a ransom for many." Matthew 20:28. This was the one great object of His life. Everything else was secondary and subservient. It

1. "Our Saviour's j____ was in the uplifting and redemption of fallen men... The spirit of Christ's self-sacrificing love is the spirit that pervades heaven and is the very e_____ of its bliss. This is the spirit that Christ's followers will p_____." (77) Lord, self-sacrificing love is so foreign in our world. I love because it makes me feel good. Open my eyes and understanding, to comprehend Your love: _____
_____
_____

2. "Love to Jesus will be manifested in a desire to work as He worked for the blessing and uplifting of h_____." My love to You, Lord, is expressed by uplifting others? I am ashamed of my love; it is so self-centered. Keep working on me and molding me, Lord! How much of my attempted love for humanity is self-generated? ___
_____
_____

3. "This was the one great o_____ of His

was His meat and drink to do the will of God and to finish His work. Self and self-interest had no part in His labor.

So those who are the partakers of the grace of Christ will be ready to make any sacrifice, that others for whom He died may share the heavenly gift. They will do all they can to make the world better for their stay in it. This spirit is the sure outgrowth of a soul truly converted. No sooner does one come to Christ than there is born in his heart a desire to make known to others what a precious friend he has found in Jesus; the saving and sanctifying truth cannot be shut up in his heart. If we are clothed with the righteousness of Christ and are filled with the joy of His indwelling Spirit, we shall not be able to hold our peace. If we have tasted and seen that the Lord is good we shall have something to tell. Like Philip when he found the Saviour, we shall invite others into His presence. We shall seek to present to them [79] the attractions of Christ and the unseen realities of the world to come. There will be an intensity of desire to follow in the path that Jesus trod. There will be an earnest longing that those around us may "behold the Lamb of God, which taketh away the sin of the world." John 1:29.

And the effort to bless others will react in blessings upon ourselves. This was the purpose of God in giving us a part to act in the plan of redemption. He has granted men the privilege of becoming partakers of the divine nature and, in their turn, of diffusing blessings to their fellow men. This is the highest honor, the greatest joy, that it is possible for God to bestow upon men. Those who thus become participants in labors of love are brought nearest to their Creator.

God might have committed the message of the gospel, and all the work of loving ministry, to the heavenly angels. He might have employed other means for accomplishing His purpose. But in His infinite love He chose to make us co-workers with Himself, with Christ and the angels, that we might share the blessing, the joy, the spiritual uplifting, which results from this unselfish ministry.

We are brought into sympathy with Christ through the fellowship of His sufferings. Every act of self-sacrifice for the good of others strengthens the spirit of beneficence in the giver's heart, allying him more closely

life." (78) What was? _____

_____ What is the object of my life? _____

4. "No sooner does one come to Christ than there is born in his heart a d_____ ___ to make known to others what a precious f_____ ___ he has found in Jesus." Haven't I tasted and seen that You are good? _____

_____ Why am I hesitant to invited others into Your presence? ___

5. "This is the highest honor, the greatest joy, that it is possible for God to bestow upon men. Those who thus become participants in labors of love are brought n_____ to their Creator." (79) What is this highest, greatest, nearest experience? _____

6. "Every act of s_____-sacrifice for the good of others strengthens the spirit of beneficence in the giver's heart, allying him more c_____ to the

Redeemer…it is only as we thus fulfill the divine p_____ in our creation that life can be a b_____ to us." Lord, I want to be right in the middle of Your purpose being fulfilled. Help me recognize opportunities to be self-sacrificing, and times that I have let self control the moment: _____
_____
_____
_____

7. "You will feel the need of a deeper experience… will hunger and thirst after righteousness." (80) How? If I will go, to "w___ souls for Him." I've thought that I should wait for this hunger and thirst drive, and THEN witness. But witnessing helps me see my need, which is that hunger. Give me courage Lord, to speak for You: _____
_____
_____

8. Unselfish labor for others gives depth, stability, Christlike l_____ to the character; peace and happiness; clear spiritual perceptions, a steady, growing faith, increased power in p_____; and a working out of my own salvation. Lord, with all these benefits, it would be foolish to not seek every opportunity for unselfish labor for others. Send me those opportu-

to the Redeemer of the world, who "was rich, yet for your sakes . . . became poor, that ye through His poverty might be rich." 2 Corinthians 8:9. And it is only as we thus fulfill the divine [80] purpose in our creation that life can be a blessing to us.

If you will go to work as Christ designs that His disciples shall, and win souls for Him, you will feel the need of a deeper experience and a greater knowledge in divine things, and will hunger and thirst after righteousness. You will plead with God, and your faith will be strengthened, and your soul will drink deeper drafts at the well of salvation. Encountering opposition and trials will drive you to the Bible and prayer. You will grow in grace and the knowledge of Christ, and will develop a rich experience.

The spirit of unselfish labor for others gives depth, stability, and Christlike loveliness to the character, and brings peace and happiness to its possessor. The aspirations are elevated. There is no room for sloth or selfishness. Those who thus exercise the Christian graces will grow and will become strong to work for God. They will have clear spiritual perceptions, a steady, growing faith, and an increased power in prayer. The Spirit of God, moving upon their spirit, calls forth the sacred harmonies of the soul in answer to the divine touch. Those who thus devote themselves to unselfish effort for the good of others are most surely working out their own salvation.

The only way to grow in grace is to be disinterestedly doing the very work which Christ has enjoined upon us--to engage, to the extent of our ability, in helping and blessing those who need the help we can give them. Strength comes by exercise; activity is the very condition of life. Those who endeavor to maintain Christian life by passively accepting the blessings that come through the means of grace, and [81] doing nothing for Christ, are simply trying to live by eating without working. And in the spiritual as in the natural world, this always results in degeneration and decay. A man who would refuse to exercise his limbs would soon lose all power to use them. Thus the Christian who will not exercise his God-given powers not only fails to grow up into Christ, but he loses the strength that he already had.

The church of Christ is God's appointed agency for

the salvation of men. Its mission is to carry the gospel to the world. And the obligation rests upon all Christians. Everyone, to the extent of his talent and opportunity, is to fulfill the Saviour's commission. The love of Christ, revealed to us, makes us debtors to all who know Him not. God has given us light, not for ourselves alone, but to shed upon them.

If the followers of Christ were awake to duty, there would be thousands where there is one today proclaiming the gospel in heathen lands. And all who could not personally engage in the work, would yet sustain it with their means, their sympathy, and their prayers. And there would be far more earnest labor for souls in Christian countries.

We need not go to heathen lands, or even leave the narrow circle of the home, if it is there that our duty lies, in order to work for Christ. We can do this in the home circle, in the church, among those with whom we associate, and with whom we do business.

The greater part of our Saviour's life on earth was spent in patient toil in the carpenter's shop at Nazareth. Ministering angels attended the Lord of [82] life as He walked side by side with peasants and laborers, unrecognized and unhonored. He was as faithfully fulfilling His mission while working at His humble trade as when He healed the sick or walked upon the storm-tossed waves of Galilee. So in the humblest duties and lowliest positions of life, we may walk and work with Jesus.

The apostle says, "Let every man, wherein he is called, therein abide with God." 1 Corinthians 7:24. The businessman may conduct his business in a way that will glorify his Master because of his fidelity. If he is a true follower of Christ he will carry his religion into everything that is done and reveal to men the spirit of Christ. The mechanic may be a diligent and faithful representative of Him who toiled in the lowly walks of life among the hills of Galilee. Everyone who names the name of Christ should so work that others, by seeing his good works, may be led to glorify their Creator and Redeemer.

Many have excused themselves from rendering their gifts to the service of Christ because others were possessed of superior endowments and advantages. The opinion has prevailed that only those who are especially talented are required to consecrate their abilities to

nities, Lord! _____
_____
_____
_____

9. "If the followers of Christ were a_____ to duty, there would be thousands where there is o_____ today proclaiming the gospel in heathen lands…in the h_____ circle, in the church, among those with whom we a___ _____, and with whom we do business." (81). Lord, what does it mean to be awake to duty?_____
_____

the service of God. It has come to be understood by many that talents are given to only a certain favored class to the exclusion of others who of course are not called upon to share in the toils or the rewards. But it is not so represented in the parable. When the master of the house called his servants, he gave to every man his work.

With a loving spirit we may perform life's [83] humblest duties "as to the Lord." Colossians 3:23. If the love of God is in the heart, it will be manifested in the life. The sweet savor of Christ will surround us, and our influence will elevate and bless.

You are not to wait for great occasions or to expect extraordinary abilities before you go to work for God. You need not have a thought of what the world will think of you. If your daily life is a testimony to the purity and sincerity of your faith, and others are convinced that you desire to benefit them, your efforts will not be wholly lost.

The humblest and poorest of the disciples of Jesus can be a blessing to others. They may not realize that they are doing any special good, but by their unconscious influence they may start waves of blessing that will widen and deepen, and the blessed results they may never know until the day of final reward. They do not feel or know that they are doing anything great. They are not required to weary themselves with anxiety about success. They have only to go forward quietly, doing faithfully the work that God's providence assigns, and their life will not be in vain. Their own souls will be growing more and more into the likeness of Christ; they are workers together with God in this life and are thus fitting for the higher work and the unshadowed joy of the life to come.

10. "But by their unconscious influence they may start waves of b_____ that will widen and deepen, and the blessed results they may never know until they day of final reward." (83) Lord, may my daily life be a testimony, a sweet savor to elevate and bless others. What does 'unconscious influence' mean?

_____
_____
_____

Prayer journal: _____
_____
_____
_____
_____

10-A Knowledge of God

Many are the ways in which God is seeking to make Himself known to us and bring us into communion with Him. Nature speaks to our senses without ceasing. The open heart will be impressed with the love and glory of God as revealed through the works of His hands. The listening ear can hear and understand the communications of God through the things of nature. The green fields, the lofty trees, the buds and flowers, the passing cloud, the falling rain, the babbling brook, the glories of the heavens, speak to our hearts, and invite us to become acquainted with Him who made them all.

Our Saviour bound up His precious lessons with the things of nature. The trees, the birds, the flowers of the valleys, the hills, the lakes, and the beautiful heavens, as well as the incidents and surroundings of daily life, were all linked with the words of truth, that His lessons might thus be often recalled to mind, even amid the busy cares of man's life of toil.

God would have His children appreciate His works and delight in the simple, quiet beauty with which He has adorned our earthly home. He is a lover of the beautiful, and above all that is outwardly attractive He loves beauty of character; He would have us cultivate purity and simplicity, the quiet graces of the flowers.

If we will but listen, God's created works will teach us precious lessons of obedience and trust. [86] From the stars that in their trackless courses through space follow from age to age their appointed path, down to the minutest atom, the things of nature obey the Creator's will. And God cares for everything and sustains everything that He has created. He who upholds the unnumbered worlds throughout immensity, at the same time cares for the wants of the little brown sparrow that sings its humble song without fear. When men go forth to their daily toil, as when they engage in prayer; when they lie down at night, and when they rise in the morning; when the rich man feasts in his palace, or when the poor man

1. "The things of nature… were all linked with the words of truth, that His lessons might thus be often r_____ to mind, even amid the b_____ cares of man's life of toil." (85) Lord, how often, in a typical day, does my life encounter nature? _____ _____ What words of truth am I missing? __ _____ _____

2. "He is a lover of the beautiful, and above all that is outwardly attractive He loves beauty of c_____; He would have us cultivate p_____ __ and simplicity, the quiet g_____ of the flowers." Lord, how can I increase the time given to preparing character beauty vs time for outward beauty? _____ _____ _____

3. "No tears are shed that God does not n_____. There is no s_____ that He does not mark. If we would but fully b_____ ___ this, all undue anxiety would be d_____." (86) Lord, what keeps me from fully believing this?

_____
_____ Thank You for being an understanding Friend, throughout my day: _____
_____
_____

4. Why is it that it is "the Christian who enjoys the beauty of the earth with the highest a_____ _____?" (87) _____
_____
_____
_____ Should a creationist be less in awe than an evolutionist? ____ How might I be limiting my 'knowledge of God' by my lack of appreciation? _____
_____
_____

5. "In our c_____ and surroundings, in the changes daily taking place around us, we may find precious lessons if our hearts are but o_____ to d_____ them." Lord, help my heart to be open;

gathers his children about the scanty board, each is tenderly watched by the heavenly Father. No tears are shed that God does not notice. There is no smile that He does not mark.

If we would but fully believe this, all undue anxieties would be dismissed. Our lives would not be so filled with disappointment as now; for everything, whether great or small, would be left in the hands of God, who is not perplexed by the multiplicity of cares, or overwhelmed by their weight. We should then enjoy a rest of soul to which many have long been strangers.

As your senses delight in the attractive loveliness of the earth, think of the world that is to come, that shall never know the blight of sin and death; where the face of nature will no more wear the shadow of the curse. Let your imagination picture the home of the saved, and remember that it will be more glorious than your brightest imagination can portray. In the varied gifts of God in nature we see but the faintest [87] gleaming of His glory. It is written, "Eye hath not seen, nor ear heard, neither have entered into the heart of man, the things which God hath prepared for them that love Him." 1 Corinthians 2:9.

The poet and the naturalist have many things to say about nature, but it is the Christian who enjoys the beauty of the earth with the highest appreciation, because he recognizes his Father's handiwork and perceives His love in flower and shrub and tree. No one can fully appreciate the significance of hill and vale, river and sea, who does not look upon them as an expression of God's love to man.

God speaks to us through His providential workings and through the influence of His Spirit upon the heart. In our circumstances and surroundings, in the changes daily taking place around us, we may find precious lessons if our hearts are but open to discern them. The psalmist, tracing the work of God's providence, says, "The earth is full of the goodness of the Lord." "Whoso is wise, and will observe these things, even they shall understand the loving-kindness of the Lord." Psalm 33:5; 107:43.

God speaks to us in His word. Here we have in clearer lines the revelation of His character, of His dealings with men, and the great work of redemption. Here is open before us the history of patriarchs and prophets and other holy men of old. They were men "subject to like passions as we are." James 5:17. We see how they struggled through discouragements like our own, how they fell under temptation as we have done, and yet took heart again and conquered through the grace of God; and, beholding, we are [88] encouraged in our striving after righteousness. As we read of the precious experiences granted them, of the light and love and blessing it was theirs to enjoy, and of the work they wrought through the grace given them, the spirit that inspired them kindles a flame of holy emulation in our hearts and a desire to be like them in character--like them to walk with God.

Jesus said of the Old Testament Scriptures,--and how much more is it true of the New,--"They are they which testify of Me," the Redeemer, Him in whom our hopes of eternal life are centered. John 5:39. Yes, the whole Bible tells of Christ. From the first record of creation--for "without Him was not anything made that was made"--to the closing promise, "Behold, I come quickly," we are reading of His works and listening to His voice. John 1:3; Revelation 22:12. If you would become acquainted with the Saviour, study the Holy Scriptures.

Fill the whole heart with the words of God. They are the living water, quenching your burning thirst. They are the living bread from heaven. Jesus declares, "Except ye eat the flesh of the Son of man, and drink His blood, ye have no life in you." And He explains Himself by saying, "The words that I speak unto you, they are spirit, and they are life." John 6:53, 63. Our bodies are built up from what we eat and drink; and as in the natural economy, so in the spiritual economy: it is what we meditate upon that will give tone and strength to our spiritual nature.

The theme of redemption is one that the angels desire to look into; it will be the science and the song of the redeemed throughout the ceaseless ages of [89] eternity. Is it not worthy of careful thought and study now? The infinite mercy and love of Jesus, the sacrifice made in our behalf, call for the most serious and solemn reflection. We should dwell upon the character of our dear Redeemer and Intercessor. We should meditate upon the mission of Him who came to save His people from their sins. As we thus contemplate heavenly themes, our

grant me the eye salve to notice Your precious lessons. Bring to my mind what happened today: ____

_____
_____
_____

6. "God speaks to us in His w_____...We see how they [men of old] struggled through d_____ like our own, how they fell under temptation as we have done, and yet took heart again and conquered through the g_____ of God; and, beholding, we are e_____ _____." Lord, as I read Your word, I want to see Your character, and how You deal with men. Help me to take heart through Your graces. Show me how to live, how to apply Your grace and Your character to my situations: _____

_____
_____

7. "If you would become a_____ with the Savior, s_____ the Holy Scriptures. Fill the w_____ heart with the words of God...It is what we mediate upon that will give t_____ and s_____ _____ to our spiritual nature." (88) Lord, what do I meditate on? _____

_____

May my thoughts be filled by You. Throughout the day, may my meditation involve You: _____

_____
_____

8. "The theme of redemption...will be the science and song of the redeemed throughout the ceaseless ages of e_____ ...As we thus contemplate heavenly themes" [what will be the result?]_____
_____
_____
_____
_____
_____

9. "If God's word were studied as it should be, men would have a b_____ ____ of mind, a n_____ of character, and a stability of p_____ rarely seen in these times." (90) Lord, give me a hunger and a thirst for Your word. May it mold me and my character. I need help in organizing my time, and my priorities. I want to be in Your word more. How would You suggest I be more in Your Word? ____
_____
_____
_____
_____

faith and love will grow stronger, and our prayers will be more and more acceptable to God, because they will be more and more mixed with faith and love. They will be intelligent and fervent. There will be more constant confidence in Jesus, and a daily, living experience in His power to save to the uttermost all that come unto God by Him.

As we meditate upon the perfections of the Saviour, we shall desire to be wholly transformed and renewed in the image of His purity. There will be a hungering and thirsting of soul to become like Him whom we adore. The more our thoughts are upon Christ, the more we shall speak of Him to others and represent Him to the world.

The Bible was not written for the scholar alone; on the contrary, it was designed for the common people. The great truths necessary for salvation are made as clear as noonday; and none will mistake and lose their way except those who follow their own judgment instead of the plainly revealed will of God.

We should not take the testimony of any man as to what the Scriptures teach, but should study the words of God for ourselves. If we allow others to do our thinking, we shall have crippled energies and [90] contracted abilities. The noble powers of the mind may be so dwarfed by lack of exercise on themes worthy of their concentration as to lose their ability to grasp the deep meaning of the word of God. The mind will enlarge if it is employed in tracing out the relation of the subjects of the Bible, comparing scripture with scripture and spiritual things with spiritual.

There is nothing more calculated to strengthen the intellect than the study of the Scriptures. No other book is so potent to elevate the thoughts, to give vigor to the faculties, as the broad, ennobling truths of the Bible. If God's word were studied as it should be, men would have a breadth of mind, a nobility of character, and a stability of purpose rarely seen in these times.

But there is but little benefit derived from a hasty reading of the Scriptures. One may read the whole Bible through and yet fail to see its beauty or comprehend its deep and hidden meaning. One passage studied until its significance is clear to the mind and its relation to the plan of salvation is evident, is of more value than the perusal of many chapters with no definite purpose in view and no positive instruction gained. Keep your Bible with you. As you have opportunity, read it; fix the texts in your memory. Even while you are walking the streets you may read a passage and meditate upon it, thus fixing it in the mind.

We cannot obtain wisdom without earnest attention and prayerful study. Some portions of Scripture are indeed too plain to be misunderstood, but there are others whose meaning does not lie on the surface to be seen at a glance. Scripture must be [91] compared with scripture. There must be careful research and prayerful reflection. And such study will be richly repaid. As the miner discovers veins of precious metal concealed beneath the surface of the earth, so will he who perseveringly searches the word of God as for hid treasure find truths of the greatest value, which are concealed from the view of the careless seeker. The words of inspiration, pondered in the heart, will be as streams flowing from the fountain of life.

Never should the Bible be studied without prayer. Before opening its pages we should ask for the enlightenment of the Holy Spirit, and it will be given. When Nathanael came to Jesus, the Saviour exclaimed, "Behold an Israelite indeed, in whom is no guile!" Nathanael said, "Whence knowest Thou me?" Jesus answered, "Before that Philip called thee, when thou wast under the fig tree, I saw thee." John 1:47, 48. And Jesus will see us also in the secret places of prayer if we will seek Him for light that we may know what is truth. Angels from the world of light will be with those who in humility of heart seek for divine guidance.

The Holy Spirit exalts and glorifies the Saviour. It is His office to present Christ, the purity of His righteousness, and the great salvation that we have through Him. Jesus says, "He shall receive of Mine, and shall show it unto you." John 16:14. The Spirit of truth is the only effectual teacher of divine truth. How must God esteem the human race, since He gave His Son to die for them and appoints His Spirit to be man's teacher and continual guide!

10. "One passage studied until its s_____ ____ is clear to the mind and its r_____ to the plan of salvation is evident, is of more value." Lord, slow me down in my quiet time with You and Your Word. May I not be hasty, but rather be still and know that You are God. What's so important, that it makes me be in a hurry?
_____
_____
_____

11. "The Spirit of truth is the only effectual t_____ ____ of divine truth." (91) Lord, what is this calling for on my part? _____
_____
_____

Prayer journal: _____
_____
_____
_____
_____

11-The Privilege of Prayer

1. "Prayer is the o_____
_____ of the heart to God
as to a friend. Not that it
is necessary in order to
make k_____ to God
what we are, but in order
to enable us to r_____
_____ Him." (93) Lord,
why isn't there already,
a natural opening up to
You? How am I closed?

_____

_____

_____ Thank You
for considering me Your
friend! _____

2. Jesus "found comfort
and joy in c_____
___ with His Father. And
if the Savior of men, the
Son of God, felt the n___
_____ of prayer, how much
m_____ should feeble,
sinful mortals feel the necessity of f_____
constant prayer." (94)
Lord, how do I resist the
disease of laodicea, "I
have no major needs"?

_____

Fervent prayer brought
You comfort and joy. I
need and desire the same.
So why don't I pray more?

_____

_____

_____

Through nature and revelation, through His providence, and by the influence of His Spirit, God speaks
to us. But these are not enough; we need also to pour
out our hearts to Him. In order to have spiritual life
and energy, we must have actual intercourse with our
heavenly Father. Our minds may be drawn out toward
Him; we may meditate upon His works, His mercies,
His blessings; but this is not, in the fullest sense, communing with Him. In order to commune with God, we
must have something to say to Him concerning our actual life.

Prayer is the opening of the heart to God as to a
friend. Not that it is necessary in order to make known
to God what we are, but in order to enable us to receive
Him. Prayer does not bring God down to us, but brings
us up to Him.

When Jesus was upon the earth, He taught His disciples how to pray. He directed them to present their
daily needs before God, and to cast all their care upon
Him. And the assurance He gave them that their petitions should be heard, is assurance also to us.

Jesus Himself, while He dwelt among men, was often in prayer. Our Saviour identified Himself with our
needs and weakness, in that He became a suppliant, a
petitioner, seeking from His Father fresh supplies of
strength, that He might come forth braced for duty and
trial. He is our example in all things. He is a brother in
our infirmities, "in all points tempted like as we are;"
but as the sinless one His [94] nature recoiled from evil;
He endured struggles and torture of soul in a world of
sin. His humanity made prayer a necessity and a privilege. He found comfort and joy in communion with His
Father. And if the Saviour of men, the Son of God, felt
the need of prayer, how much more should feeble, sinful
mortals feel the necessity of fervent, constant prayer.

Our heavenly Father waits to bestow upon us the
fullness of His blessing. It is our privilege to drink largely at the fountain of boundless love. What a wonder it
is that we pray so little! God is ready and willing to
hear the sincere prayer of the humblest of His children,

and yet there is much manifest reluctance on our part to make known our wants to God. What can the angels of heaven think of poor helpless human beings, who are subject to temptation, when God's heart of infinite love yearns toward them, ready to give them more than they can ask or think, and yet they pray so little and have so little faith? The angels love to bow before God; they love to be near Him. They regard communion with God as their highest joy; and yet the children of earth, who need so much the help that God only can give, seem satisfied to walk without the light of His Spirit, the companionship of His presence.

The darkness of the evil one encloses those who neglect to pray. The whispered temptations of the enemy entice them to sin; and it is all because they do not make use of the privileges that God has given them in the divine appointment of prayer. Why should the sons and daughters of God be reluctant to pray, when prayer is the key in the hand of faith to unlock heaven's storehouse, where are treasured [95] the boundless resources of Omnipotence? Without unceasing prayer and diligent watching we are in danger of growing careless and of deviating from the right path. The adversary seeks continually to obstruct the way to the mercy seat, that we may not by earnest supplication and faith obtain grace and power to resist temptation.

There are certain conditions upon which we may expect that God will hear and answer our prayers. One of the first of these is that we feel our need of help from Him. He has promised, "I will pour water upon him that is thirsty, and floods upon the dry ground." Isaiah 44:3. Those who hunger and thirst after righteousness, who long after God, may be sure that they will be filled. The heart must be open to the Spirit's influence, or God's blessing cannot be received.

Our great need is itself an argument and pleads most eloquently in our behalf. But the Lord is to be sought unto to do these things for us. He says, "Ask, and it shall be given you." And "He that spared not His own Son, but delivered Him up for us all, how shall He not with Him also freely give us all things?" Matthew 7:7; Romans 8:32.

If we regard iniquity in our hearts, if we cling to any known sin, the Lord will not hear us; but the prayer of the penitent, contrite soul is always accepted. When

3. "God's heart of infinite love y_____ toward them, ready to give them more than they ask or t_____, and yet they pray so l_____ and have so little faith." Lord, with a shortage of prayer, I am missing so much! I am missing Your yearning heart! How can I see it as a hightest joy? _____

_____

4. "The darkness of the evil one e_____ those who n_____ to pray." Lord, do I prefer darkness to light? _____

_____ My choices are so pathetically ignorant! Forgive me and help me! _

_____
_____
_____

5. "There are certain c__ _____ upon which we may expect that God will h_____ and answer our prayers. One of the first of these is that we feel our n_____ of help from Him." (95) Lord, I am the chief of sinners. You are my all in all. You are my everything. My life is empty without You: _____

_____
_____
_____

6. "When all known wrongs are r_____, we may believe that God will answer our petitions...Another element of prevailing prayer is f_____...

When our prayers seem not to be answered, we are to cling to the p_____...

all known wrongs are righted, we may believe that God will answer our petitions. Our own merit will never commend us to the favor of God; it is the worthiness of Jesus that will save us, His blood that will cleanse us; yet we have a work to do in complying with the conditions of acceptance. [96]

Another element of prevailing prayer is faith. "He that cometh to God must believe that He is, and that He is a rewarder of them that diligently seek Him." Hebrews 11:6. Jesus said to His disciples, "What things soever ye desire, when ye pray, believe that ye receive them, and ye shall have them." Mark 11:24. Do we take Him at His word?

The assurance is broad and unlimited, and He is faithful who has promised. When we do not receive the very things we asked for, at the time we ask, we are still to believe that the Lord hears and that He will answer our prayers. We are so erring and short-sighted that we sometimes ask for things that would not be a blessing to us, and our heavenly Father in love answers our prayers by giving us that which will be for our highest good--that which we ourselves would desire if with vision divinely enlightened we could see all things as they really are. When our prayers seem not to be answered, we are to cling to the promise; for the time of answering will surely come, and we shall receive the blessing we need most. But to claim that prayer will always be answered in the very way and for the particular thing that we desire, is presumption. God is too wise to err, and too good to withhold any good thing from them that walk uprightly. Then do not fear to trust Him, even though you do not see the immediate answer to your prayers. Rely upon His sure promise, "Ask, and it shall be given you."

If we take counsel with our doubts and fears, or try to solve everything that we cannot see clearly, before we have faith, perplexities will only increase [97] and deepen. But if we come to God, feeling helpless and dependent, as we really are, and in humble, trusting faith make known our wants to Him whose knowledge is infinite, who sees everything in creation, and who governs everything by His will and word, He can and will attend to our cry, and will let light shine into our hearts. Through sincere prayer we are brought into connection with the mind of the Infinite. We may have no remarkable evidence at the time that the face of our Redeemer is bending over us in compassion and love, but this is even so. We may not feel His visible touch, but His hand is upon us in love and pitying tenderness.

When we come to ask mercy and blessing from God we should have a spirit of love and forgiveness in our own hearts. How can we pray, "Forgive us our debts, as we forgive our debtors," and yet indulge an unforgiving spirit? Matthew 6:12. If we expect our own prayers to be heard we must forgive others in the same manner and to the same extent as we hope to be forgiven.

Perseverance in prayer has been made a condition of receiving. We must pray always if we would grow in faith and experience. We are to be "instant in prayer," to "continue in prayer, and watch in the same with thanksgiving." Romans 12:12; Colossians 4:2. Peter exhorts believers to be "sober, and watch unto prayer." 1 Peter 4:7. Paul directs, "In everything by prayer and supplication with thanksgiving let your requests be made known unto God." Philippians 4:6. "But ye, beloved," says Jude, "praying in the Holy Ghost, keep yourselves in the love of God." Jude 20, 21. [98] Unceasing prayer is the unbroken union of the soul with God, so that life from God flows into our life; and from our life, purity and holiness flow back to God.

There is necessity for diligence in prayer; let nothing hinder you. Make every effort to keep open the communion between Jesus and your own soul. Seek every opportunity to go where prayer is wont to be made. Those who are really seeking for communion with God will be seen in the prayer meeting, faithful to do their duty and earnest and anxious to reap all the benefits they can gain. They will improve every opportunity of placing themselves where they can receive the rays of light from heaven.

We should pray in the family circle, and above all we must not neglect secret prayer, for this is the life of the soul. It is impossible for the soul to flourish while prayer is neglected. Family or public prayer alone is not sufficient. In solitude let the soul be laid open to the inspecting eye of God. Secret prayer is to be heard only by the prayer-hearing God. No curious ear is to receive the burden of such petitions. In secret prayer the soul is free from surrounding influences, free from excitement. Calmly, yet fervently, will it reach out after God. Sweet

We may have no remarkable evidence at the time that the face of our Redeemer is bending over us in c_____ and love, but this is even s__." (95-97) Lord, there are wrongs I need to right: ___

_____

_____ And I have faith that You answer my prayers, not because I feel something; rather, it is Your promises. Remind me of them: ____

_____

7. "P_____ in prayer has been made a condition of receiving...

Seek e_____ opportunity to go where prayer is wont to be made... They will improve every opportunity of placing themselves where they can receive the rays of l_____ from heaven." (98) Lord, increase my sensitivity to Your call to prayer. May my walk with You be one of constant, fervent prayer, constant companionship: _____

_____

8. "Secret prayer...is the l_____ of the soul." Lord, what does this mean and how can I live it?

9. "Pray in your closet, and as you go about your d___ _____ labor let your heart be often lifted up to God. It was thus that Enoch w_____ with God ...

We may keep so near to God that in every unexpected trial our thoughts will turn as n_____ as the flower turns to the sun." (98-100) Lord, help me guard my closet. I want my thoughts to turn naturally to You: _____ _____ _____

and abiding will be the influence emanating from Him who seeth in secret, whose ear is open to hear the prayer arising from the heart. By calm, simple faith the soul holds communion with God and gathers to itself rays of divine light to strengthen and sustain it in the conflict with Satan. God is our tower of strength.

Pray in your closet, and as you go about your daily labor let your heart be often uplifted to God. [99] It was thus that Enoch walked with God. These silent prayers rise like precious incense before the throne of grace. Satan cannot overcome him whose heart is thus stayed upon God.

There is no time or place in which it is inappropriate to offer up a petition to God. There is nothing that can prevent us from lifting up our hearts in the spirit of earnest prayer. In the crowds of the street, in the midst of a business engagement, we may send up a petition to God and plead for divine guidance, as did Nehemiah when he made his request before King Artaxerxes. A closet of communion may be found wherever we are. We should have the door of the heart open continually and our invitation going up that Jesus may come and abide as a heavenly guest in the soul.

Although there may be a tainted, corrupted atmosphere around us, we need not breathe its miasma, but may live in the pure air of heaven. We may close every door to impure imaginings and unholy thoughts by lifting the soul into the presence of God through sincere prayer. Those whose hearts are open to receive the support and blessing of God will walk in a holier atmosphere than that of earth and will have constant communion with heaven.

We need to have more distinct views of Jesus and a fuller comprehension of the value of eternal realities. The beauty of holiness is to fill the hearts of God's children; and that this may be accomplished, we should seek for divine disclosures of heavenly things.

Let the soul be drawn out and upward, that God may grant us a breath of the heavenly atmosphere. We may keep so near to God that in every unexpected [100] trial our thoughts will turn to Him as naturally as the flower turns to the sun.

Keep your wants, your joys, your sorrows, your cares, and your fears before God. You cannot burden Him; you cannot weary Him. He who numbers the hairs of your head is not indifferent to the wants of His children. "The Lord is very pitiful, and of tender mercy." James 5:11. His heart of love is touched by our sorrows and even by our utterances of them. Take to Him everything that perplexes the mind. Nothing is too great for Him to bear, for He holds up worlds, He rules over all the affairs of the universe. Nothing that in any way concerns our peace is too small for Him to notice. There is no chapter in our experience too dark for Him to read; there is no perplexity too difficult for Him to unravel. No calamity can befall the least of His children, no anxiety harass the soul, no joy cheer, no sincere prayer escape the lips, of which our heavenly Father is unobservant, or in which He takes no immediate interest. "He healeth the broken in heart, and bindeth up their wounds." Psalm 147:3. The relations between God and each soul are as distinct and full as though there were not another soul upon the earth to share His watchcare, not another soul for whom He gave His beloved Son.

Jesus said, "Ye shall ask in My name: and I say not unto you, that I will pray the Father for you: for the Father Himself loveth you." "I have chosen you: . . . that whatsoever ye shall ask of the Father in My name, He may give it you." John 16:26, 27; 15:16. But to pray in the name of Jesus is something more than a mere mention of that name at the beginning [101] and the ending of a prayer. It is to pray in the mind and spirit of Jesus, while we believe His promises, rely upon His grace, and work His works.

God does not mean that any of us should become hermits or monks and retire from the world in order to devote ourselves to acts of worship. The life must be like Christ's life--between the mountain and the multitude. He who does nothing but pray will soon cease to pray, or his prayers will become a formal routine. When men take themselves out of social life, away from the sphere of Christian duty and cross bearing; when they cease to work earnestly for the Master, who worked earnestly for them, they lose the subject matter of prayer and have no incentive to devotion. Their prayers become personal and selfish. They cannot pray in regard to the wants of humanity or the upbuilding of Christ's kingdom, pleading for strength wherewith to work.

We sustain a loss when we neglect the privilege of associating together to strengthen and encourage one

10. "The relations between God and e_____ soul are as distinct and full as though there were not another soul upon the earth to share His w_____ _____, not another soul for whom He g_____ His beloved Son." Lord, do I treat this as a simple child-like belief, similar to that of Santa Clause? _____ That Your watchcare and friendship is that individual and personal is fantastic! _____ _____ _____

another in the service of God. The truths of His word lose their vividness and importance in our minds. Our hearts cease to be enlightened and aroused by their sanctifying influence, and we decline in spirituality. In our association as Christians we lose much by lack of sympathy with one another. He who shuts himself up to himself is not filling the position that God designed he should. The proper cultivation of the social elements in our nature brings us into sympathy with others and is a means of development and strength to us in the service of God.

If Christians would associate together, speaking to each other of the love of God and of the precious [102] truths of redemption, their own hearts would be refreshed and they would refresh one another. We may be daily learning more of our heavenly Father, gaining a fresh experience of His grace; then we shall desire to speak of His love; and as we do this, our own hearts will be warmed and encouraged. If we thought and talked more of Jesus, and less of self, we should have far more of His presence.

If we would but think of God as often as we have evidence of His care for us we should keep Him ever in our thoughts and should delight to talk of Him and to praise Him. We talk of temporal things because we have an interest in them. We talk of our friends because we love them; our joys and our sorrows are bound up with them. Yet we have infinitely greater reason to love God than to love our earthly friends; it should be the most natural thing in the world to make Him first in all our thoughts, to talk of His goodness and tell of His power. The rich gifts He has bestowed upon us were not intended to absorb our thoughts and love so much that we should have nothing to give to God; they are constantly to remind us of Him and to bind us in bonds of love and gratitude to our heavenly Benefactor. We dwell too near the lowlands of earth. Let us raise our eyes to the open door of the sanctuary above, where the light of the glory of God shines in the face of Christ, who "is able also to save them to the uttermost that come unto God by Him." Hebrews 7:25.

We need to praise God more "for His goodness, and for His wonderful works to the children of men." Psalm 107:8. Our devotional exercises should not [103] consist wholly in asking and receiving. Let us not be

11. If we thought and talked more of J_____, and less of s_____, we should have far more of His p__ _____ ...it should be the most natural thing in the world to make Him first in a___ our thoughts, to t_____ of His goodness and tell of His p_____." (102) Lord, do I want more of Your presence?

_____ How can I train my thoughts and conversation to focus on You? _____

always thinking of our wants and never of the benefits we receive. We do not pray any too much, but we are too sparing of giving thanks. We are the constant recipients of God's mercies, and yet how little gratitude we express, how little we praise Him for what He has done for us.

Anciently the Lord bade Israel, when they met together for His service, "Ye shall eat before the Lord your God, and ye shall rejoice in all that ye put your hand unto, ye and your households, wherein the Lord thy God hath blessed thee." Deuteronomy 12:7. That which is done for the glory of God should be done with cheerfulness, with songs of praise and thanksgiving, not with sadness and gloom.

Our God is a tender, merciful Father. His service should not be looked upon as a heart-saddening, distressing exercise. It should be a pleasure to worship the Lord and to take part in His work. God would not have His children, for whom so great salvation has been provided, act as if He were a hard, exacting taskmaster. He is their best friend; and when they worship Him, He expects to be with them, to bless and comfort them, filling their hearts with joy and love. The Lord desires His children to take comfort in His service and to find more pleasure than hardship in His work. He desires that those who come to worship Him shall carry away with them precious thoughts of His care and love, that they may be cheered in all the employments of daily life, that they may have grace to deal honestly and faithfully in all things.

Prayer journal: _____
_____
_____
_____
_____
_____
_____
_____

We must gather about the cross. Christ and Him [104] crucified should be the theme of contemplation, of conversation, and of our most joyful emotion. We should keep in our thoughts every blessing we receive from God, and when we realize His great love we should be willing to trust everything to the hand that was nailed to the cross for us.

The soul may ascend nearer heaven on the wings of praise. God is worshiped with song and music in the courts above, and as we express our gratitude we are approximating to the worship of the heavenly hosts. "Whoso offereth praise glorifieth" God. Psalm 50:23. Let us with reverent joy come before our Creator, with "thanksgiving, and the voice of melody." Isaiah 51:3.

12-What to Do with Doubt

Many, especially those who are young in the Christian life, are at times troubled with the suggestions of skepticism. There are in the Bible many things which they cannot explain, or even understand, and Satan employs these to shake their faith in the Scriptures as a revelation from God. They ask, "How shall I know the right way? If the Bible is indeed the word of God, how can I be freed from these doubts and perplexities?"

God never asks us to believe, without giving sufficient evidence upon which to base our faith. His existence, His character, the truthfulness of His word, are all established by testimony that appeals to our reason; and this testimony is abundant. Yet God has never removed the possibility of doubt. Our faith must rest upon evidence, not demonstration. Those who wish to doubt will have opportunity; while those who really desire to know the truth will find plenty of evidence on which to rest their faith.

It is impossible for finite minds fully to comprehend the character or the works of the Infinite One. To the keenest intellect, the most highly educated mind, that holy Being must ever remain clothed in mystery. "Canst thou by searching find out God? canst thou find out the Almighty unto perfection? It is as high as heaven; what canst thou do? deeper than hell; what canst thou know?" Job 11:7, 8. [106] The apostle Paul exclaims, "O the depth of the riches both of the wisdom and knowledge of God! how unsearchable are His judgments, and His ways past finding out!" Romans 11:33. But though "clouds and darkness are round about Him," "righteousness and judgment are the foundation of His throne." Psalm 97:2, R.V. We can so far comprehend His dealings with us, and the motives by which He is actuated, that we may discern boundless love and mercy united to infinite power. We can understand as much of His purposes as it is for our good to know; and beyond this we must still trust the hand that is omnipotent, the heart that is full of love.

---

1. "God never asks us to believe, without giving sufficient e_____ upon which to base our faith. His existence, His c_____, the truthfulness of His word, are all e_____ by the testimony that appeals to our r_____." (105) Lord, thanks for being convincing, and not coercive, for wanting me to believe, and not just be subservient, for inviting me into a friendship relationship (John 15:15):

_____

_____

_____

2. "Our faith must rest upon evidence, not d___ _____." Lord, what does this mean? Scriptural truth vs feelings I understand. By 'demonstration' do we mean the things which we cannot explain or understand, but yet they're in front of us? These don't need to lead to skepticism; rather, be a part of a patient journey of discovery, together with You: _____

_____

_____

The word of God, like the character of its divine Author, presents mysteries that can never be fully comprehended by finite beings. The entrance of sin into the world, the incarnation of Christ, regeneration, the resurrection, and many other subjects presented in the Bible, are mysteries too deep for the human mind to explain, or even fully to comprehend. But we have no reason to doubt God's word because we cannot understand the mysteries of His providence. In the natural world we are constantly surrounded with mysteries that we cannot fathom. The very humblest forms of life present a problem that the wisest of philosophers is powerless to explain. Everywhere are wonders beyond our ken. Should we then be surprised to find that in the spiritual world also there are mysteries that we cannot fathom? The difficulty lies solely in the weakness and narrowness of the human mind. God has given us in the Scriptures sufficient evidence of their divine character, and we are not to [107] doubt His word because we cannot understand all the mysteries of His providence.

The apostle Peter says that there are in Scripture "things hard to be understood, which they that are unlearned and unstable wrest . . . unto their own destruction." 2 Peter 3:16. The difficulties of Scripture have been urged by skeptics as an argument against the Bible; but so far from this, they constitute a strong evidence of its divine inspiration. If it contained no account of God but that which we could easily comprehend; if His greatness and majesty could be grasped by finite minds, then the Bible would not bear the unmistakable credentials of divine authority. The very grandeur and mystery of the themes presented should inspire faith in it as the word of God.

The Bible unfolds truth with a simplicity and a perfect adaptation to the needs and longings of the human heart, that has astonished and charmed the most highly cultivated minds, while it enables the humblest and uncultured to discern the way of salvation. And yet these simply stated truths lay hold upon subjects so elevated, so far-reaching, so infinitely beyond the power of human comprehension, that we can accept them only because God has declared them. Thus the plan of redemption is laid open to us, so that every soul may see the steps he is to take in repentance toward God and faith toward our Lord Jesus Christ, in order to be saved in God's

3. "The entrance of sin in the world, the i_____ _____ of Christ, regeneration, the resurrection...are mysteries too d_____ for the human mind to explain, or even f_____ to comprehend." (106) Lord, are You saying, don't try? Or are You say, "the difficulty lies solely in the weakness and narrowness of the human m_____," so don't get frustrated? Keep at it: _____
_____
_____
_____

appointed way; yet beneath these truths, so easily un- derstood, lie mysteries that are the hiding of His glory- -mysteries that overpower the mind in its research, yet inspire the sincere seeker for truth with reverence and faith. The more [108] he searches the Bible, the deeper is his conviction that it is the word of the living God, and human reason bows before the majesty of divine revelation.

To acknowledge that we cannot fully comprehend the great truths of the Bible is only to admit that the finite mind is inadequate to grasp the infinite; that man, with his limited, human knowledge, cannot understand the purposes of Omniscience.

Because they cannot fathom all its mysteries, the skeptic and the infidel reject God's word; and not all who profess to believe the Bible are free from danger on this point. The apostle says, "Take heed, brethren, lest there be in any of you an evil heart of unbelief, in departing from the living God." Hebrews 3:12. It is right to study closely the teachings of the Bible and to search into "the deep things of God" so far as they are revealed in Scripture. 1 Corinthians 2:10. While "the secret things belong unto the Lord our God," "those things which are revealed belong unto us." Deuteron- omy 29:29. But it is Satan's work to pervert the inves- tigative powers of the mind. A certain pride is mingled with the consideration of Bible truth, so that men feel impatient and defeated if they cannot explain every por- tion of Scripture to their satisfaction. It is too humiliat- ing to them to acknowledge that they do not understand the inspired words. They are unwilling to wait patiently until God shall see fit to reveal the truth to them. They feel that their unaided human wisdom is sufficient to enable them to comprehend the Scripture, and failing to do this, they virtually deny its authority. It is true that many theories and doctrines popularly supposed to be derived from the Bible have no foundation in its teach- ing, and indeed are [109] contrary to the whole tenor of inspiration. These things have been a cause of doubt and perplexity to many minds. They are not, however, chargeable to God's word, but to man's perversion of it.

If it were possible for created beings to attain to a full understanding of God and His works, then, having reached this point, there would be for them no further discovery of truth, no growth in knowledge, no further development of mind or heart. God would no longer be supreme; and man, having reached the limit of knowledge and attainment, would cease to advance. Let us thank God that it is not so. God is infinite; in Him are "all the treasures of wisdom and knowledge." Colossians 2:3. And to all eternity men may be ever searching, ever learning, and yet never exhaust the treasures of His wisdom, His goodness, and His power.

God intends that even in this life the truths of His word shall be ever unfolding to His people. There is only one way in which this knowledge can be obtained. We can attain to an understanding of God's word only through the illumination of that Spirit by which the word was given. "The things of God knoweth no man, but the Spirit of God;" "for the Spirit searcheth all things, yea, the deep things of God." 1 Corinthians 2:11, 10. And the Saviour's promise to His followers was, "When He, the Spirit of truth, is come, He will guide you into all truth. . . . For He shall receive of Mine, and shall show it unto you." John 16:13, 14.

God desires man to exercise his reasoning powers; and the study of the Bible will strengthen and elevate the mind as no other study can. Yet we are to beware [110] of deifying reason, which is subject to the weakness and infirmity of humanity. If we would not have the Scriptures clouded to our understanding, so that the plainest truths shall not be comprehended, we must have the simplicity and faith of a little child, ready to learn, and beseeching the aid of the Holy Spirit. A sense of the power and wisdom of God, and of our inability to comprehend His greatness, should inspire us with humility, and we should open His word, as we would enter His presence, with holy awe. When we come to the Bible, reason must acknowledge an authority superior to itself, and heart and intellect must bow to the great I AM.

There are many things apparently difficult or obscure, which God will make plain and simple to those who thus seek an understanding of them. But without the guidance of the Holy Spirit we shall be continually liable to wrest the Scriptures or to misinterpret them. There is much reading of the Bible that is without profit and in many cases a positive injury. When the word of God is opened without reverence and without prayer; when the thoughts and affections are not fixed upon

4. "To all eternity men may be e____ searching, ever learning, and yet never e_____ the treasures of His wisdom, His goodness, and His power." (109) Lord, may each experience in Your word, be an adventure of discovery. Grant me a thirst, a quest, a desire for more. What experience in Your compassion did I have this morning? (Lam 3:23)?

_____

_____

_____

5. "If we would not have the S_____ clouded to our understanding, so that the plainest truths shall not be comprehended, we must have the simplicity and faith of a little c____ ___, ready to learn, and beseeching the aid of the H_____ S_____." (110). Lord, am I ready to learn? What does that mean? _____

_____

_____

Lord, I enter Your word with awe, with eagerness and anticipation. Don't let me be casual. May Your Spirit render my heart reverent and my mind illuminated: _____

_____

6. "There is much reading of the Bible that is without p_____ and in many cases a positive i_____." For instance: _____

_____

_____

_____

_____

_____ Lord, show me what 'affections fixed upon You' means: _____

_____

_____

_____

7. "Disguise it as they may, the real cause of doubt and skepticism, in most cases, is the l_____ of s____." (111) Lord, do I have an unwelcoming, unwilling attitude as I read? _____

_____

Help me to see where my love and affections are on sin, and not You:

_____

_____

_____

_____

8. "Evidence of e_____ ___... He bids us 'taste and see that the Lord is good'...

God, or in harmony with His will, the mind is clouded with doubts; and in the very study of the Bible, skepticism strengthens. The enemy takes control of the thoughts, and he suggests interpretations that are not correct. Whenever men are not in word and deed seeking to be in harmony with God, then, however learned they may be, they are liable to err in their understanding of Scripture, and it is not safe to trust to their explanations. Those who look to the Scriptures to find discrepancies, have not spiritual [111] insight. With distorted vision they will see many causes for doubt and unbelief in things that are really plain and simple.

Disguise it as they may, the real cause of doubt and skepticism, in most cases, is the love of sin. The teachings and restrictions of God's word are not welcome to the proud, sin-loving heart, and those who are unwilling to obey its requirements are ready to doubt its authority. In order to arrive at truth, we must have a sincere desire to know the truth and a willingness of heart to obey it. And all who come in this spirit to the study of the Bible will find abundant evidence that it is God's word, and they may gain an understanding of its truths that will make them wise unto salvation.

Christ has said, "If any man willeth to do His will, he shall know of the teaching." John 7:17, R.V. Instead of questioning and caviling concerning that which you do not understand, give heed to the light that already shines upon you, and you will receive greater light. By the grace of Christ, perform every duty that has been made plain to your understanding, and you will be enabled to understand and perform those of which you are now in doubt.

There is an evidence that is open to all,--the most highly educated, and the most illiterate,--the evidence of experience. God invites us to prove for ourselves the reality of His word, the truth of His promises. He bids us "taste and see that the Lord is good." Psalm 34:8. Instead of depending upon the word of another, we are to taste for ourselves. He declares, "Ask, and ye shall receive." John 16:24. His promises will be [112] fulfilled. They have never failed; they never can fail. And as we draw near to Jesus, and rejoice in the fullness of His love, our doubt and darkness will disappear in the light of His presence.

The apostle Paul says that God "hath delivered us

from the power of darkness, and hath translated us into the kingdom of His dear Son." Colossians 1:13. And everyone who has passed from death unto life is able to "set to his seal that God is true." John 3:33. He can testify, "I needed help, and I found it in Jesus. Every want was supplied, the hunger of my soul was satisfied; and now the Bible is to me the revelation of Jesus Christ. Do you ask why I believe in Jesus? Because He is to me a divine Saviour. Why do I believe the Bible? Because I have found it to be the voice of God to my soul." We may have the witness in ourselves that the Bible is true, that Christ is the Son of God. We know that we are not following cunningly devised fables.

Peter exhorts his brethren to "grow in grace, and in the knowledge of our Lord and Saviour Jesus Christ." 2 Peter 3:18. When the people of God are growing in grace, they will be constantly obtaining a clearer understanding of His word. They will discern new light and beauty in its sacred truths. This has been true in the history of the church in all ages, and thus it will continue to the end. "The path of the righteous is as the light of dawn, that shineth more and more unto the perfect day." Proverbs 4:18, R.V., margin.

By faith we may look to the hereafter and grasp the pledge of God for a growth of intellect, the [113] human faculties uniting with the divine, and every power of the soul being brought into direct contact with the Source of light. We may rejoice that all which has perplexed us in the providences of God will then be made plain, things hard to be understood will then find an explanation; and where our finite minds discovered only confusion and broken purposes, we shall see the most perfect and beautiful harmony. "Now we see through a glass, darkly; but then face to face: now I know in part; but then shall I know even as also I am known." 1 Corinthians 13:12.

Why do I believe the Bible? Because I have f_____ it to be the voice of God to my soul." (111-112) Lord, what would help me, to have this evidence of experience? _____
_____
_____

9. "When the people of God are g_____ in grace, they will be constantly obtaining a c_____ understanding of His word." Lord, how do I grow in grace?
_____
_____
_____ Why will my understanding get clearer?
_____
_____

10. What will happen as "every power of the soul [is] being brought into direct contact with the S_____ of light?" (113) _____
_____
_____ Lord, that is what I want, perfect and beautiful harmony with You: _____
_____
_____

Prayer Journal: _____
_____
_____
_____
_____

13-Rejoicing in the Lord

The children of God are called to be representatives of Christ, showing forth the goodness and mercy of the Lord. As Jesus has revealed to us the true character of the Father, so we are to reveal Christ to a world that does not know His tender, pitying love. "As Thou hast sent Me into the world," said Jesus, "even so have I also sent them into the world." "I in them, and Thou in Me; . . . that the world may know that Thou hast sent Me." John 17: 18, 23. The apostle Paul says to the disciples of Jesus, "Ye are manifestly declared to be the epistle of Christ," "known and read of all men." 2 Corinthians 3:3, 2. In every one of His children, Jesus sends a letter to the world. If you are Christ's follower, He sends in you a letter to the family, the village, the street, where you live. Jesus, dwelling in you, desires to speak to the hearts of those who are not acquainted with Him. Perhaps they do not read the Bible, or do not hear the voice that speaks to them in its pages; they do not see the love of God through His works. But if you are a true representative of Jesus, it may be that through you they will be led to understand something of His goodness and be won to love and serve Him.

Christians are set as light bearers on the way to heaven. They are to reflect to the world the light shining upon them from Christ. Their life and character should be such that through them others will get a right conception of Christ and of His service. [116] If we do represent Christ, we shall make His service appear attractive, as it really is. Christians who gather up gloom and sadness to their souls, and murmur and complain, are giving to others a false representation of God and the Christian life. They give the impression that God is not pleased to have His children happy, and in this they bear false witness against our heavenly Father.

Satan is exultant when he can lead the children of God into unbelief and despondency. He delights to see us mistrusting God, doubting His willingness and power to save us. He loves to have us feel that the Lord will do us harm by His providences. It is the work of

1. "As Jesus has revealed to us the true c_____ _____ of the Father, so w_____ are to reveal Christ to a world that does not know His tender, pitying l_____...In every one of His children, Jesus sends a l_____ to the world." (115) Lord, as an epistle from You, what I am saying about You? _____
_____
_____

What do I want to be saying? What do You want me to be saying? _____
_____
_____

Satan to represent the Lord as lacking in compassion and pity. He misstates the truth in regard to Him. He fills the imagination with false ideas concerning God; and instead of dwelling upon the truth in regard to our heavenly Father, we too often fix our minds upon the misrepresentations of Satan and dishonor God by distrusting Him and murmuring against Him. Satan ever seeks to make the religious life one of gloom. He desires it to appear toilsome and difficult; and when the Christian presents in his own life this view of religion, he is, through his unbelief, seconding the falsehood of Satan.

Many, walking along the path of life, dwell upon their mistakes and failures and disappointments, and their hearts are filled with grief and discouragement. While I was in Europe, a sister who had been doing this, and who was in deep distress, wrote to me, asking for some word of encouragement. The night after I had read her letter I dreamed that I was in a garden, and one who seemed to be the owner of [117] the garden was conducting me through its paths. I was gathering the flowers and enjoying their fragrance, when this sister, who had been walking by my side, called my attention to some unsightly briers that were impeding her way. There she was mourning and grieving. She was not walking in the pathway, following the guide, but was walking among the briers and thorns. "Oh," she mourned, "is it not a pity that this beautiful garden is spoiled with thorns?" Then the guide said, "Let the thorns alone, for they will only wound you. Gather the roses, the lilies, and the pinks."

Have there not been some bright spots in your experience? Have you not had some precious seasons when your heart throbbed with joy in response to the Spirit of God? When you look back into the chapters of your life experience do you not find some pleasant pages? Are not God's promises, like the fragrant flowers, growing beside your path on every hand? Will you not let their beauty and sweetness fill your heart with joy?

The briers and thorns will only wound and grieve you; and if you gather only these things, and present them to others, are you not, besides slighting the goodness of God yourself, preventing those around you from walking in the path of life?

It is not wise to gather together all the unpleasant

2. "Satan ever seeks to make the religious life one of g_____. He desires it to appear toilsome and d_____; and when the Christian presents in his own life this view of religion, he is, through his unbelief, seconding the f_____ of Satan." (116) How do I communicate a toilsome life, or rather, reflect the light shining upon me from You?

_____

_____

_____

_____

3. "A discouraged soul is filled with d_____ __, shutting out the l_____ ____ of God from his own soul and casting a shadow upon the pathway of o_____." (117) Lord, I don't want to "slight" You, or "dishonor" You; I don't want to shut out Your light. Show me how I do: _____

_____

_____

recollections of a past life,--its iniquities and disappointments,--to talk over them and mourn over them until we are overwhelmed with discouragement. A discouraged soul is filled with darkness, shutting out the light of God from his own soul and casting a shadow upon the pathway of others. [118]

Thank God for the bright pictures which He has presented to us. Let us group together the blessed assurances of His love, that we may look upon them continually: The Son of God leaving His Father's throne, clothing His divinity with humanity, that He might rescue man from the power of Satan; His triumph in our behalf, opening heaven to men, revealing to human vision the presence chamber where the Deity unveils His glory; the fallen race uplifted from the pit of ruin into which sin had plunged it, and brought again into connection with the infinite God, and having endured the divine test through faith in our Redeemer, clothed in the righteousness of Christ, and exalted to His throne--these are the pictures which God would have us contemplate.

When we seem to doubt God's love and distrust His promises we dishonor Him and grieve His Holy Spirit. How would a mother feel if her children were constantly complaining of her, just as though she did not mean them well, when her whole life's effort had been to forward their interests and to give them comfort? Suppose they should doubt her love; it would break her heart. How would any parent feel to be thus treated by his children? And how can our heavenly Father regard us when we distrust His love, which has led Him to give His only-begotten Son that we might have life? The apostle writes, "He that spared not His own Son, but delivered Him up for us all, how shall He not with Him also freely give us all things?" Romans 8:32. And yet how many, by their actions, if not in word, are saying, "The Lord does [119] not mean this for me. Perhaps He loves others, but He does not love me."

4. "Every word of doubt you utter is i_____ Satan's temptations." (119) Shut You out and invite Satan? Lord, why would I do that? Help direct my thoughts to the assurances of Your love; may that be my theme and focus each day: ____

_____

_____

All this is harming your own soul; for every word of doubt you utter is inviting Satan's temptations; it is strengthening in you the tendency to doubt, and it is grieving from you the ministering angels. When Satan tempts you, breathe not a word of doubt or darkness. If you choose to open the door to his suggestions, your mind will be filled with distrust and rebellious questioning. If you talk out your feelings, every doubt you express not only reacts upon yourself, but it is a seed that will germinate and bear fruit in the life of others, and it may be impossible to counteract the influence of your words. You yourself may be able to recover from the season of temptation and from the snare of Satan, but others who have been swayed by your influence may not be able to escape from the unbelief you have suggested. How important that we speak only those things that will give spiritual strength and life!

Angels are listening to hear what kind of report you are bearing to the world about your heavenly Master. Let your conversation be of Him who liveth to make intercession for you before the Father. When you take the hand of a friend, let praise to God be on your lips and in your heart. This will attract his thoughts to Jesus.

All have trials; griefs hard to bear, temptations hard to resist. Do not tell your troubles to your fellow mortals, but carry everything to God in prayer. Make it a rule never to utter one word of doubt or discouragement. You can do much to brighten the [120] life of others and strengthen their efforts, by words of hope and holy cheer.

There is many a brave soul sorely pressed by temptation, almost ready to faint in the conflict with self and with the powers of evil. Do not discourage such a one in his hard struggle. Cheer him with brave, hopeful words that shall urge him on his way. Thus the light of Christ may shine from you. "None of us liveth to himself." Romans 14:7. By our unconscious influence others may be encouraged and strengthened, or they may be discouraged, and repelled from Christ and the truth.

There are many who have an erroneous idea of the life and character of Christ. They think that He was devoid of warmth and sunniness, that He was stern, severe, and joyless. In many cases the whole religious experience is colored by these gloomy views.

It is often said that Jesus wept, but that He was never known to smile. Our Saviour was indeed a Man of Sorrows, and acquainted with grief, for He opened His heart to all the woes of men. But though His life was self-denying and shadowed with pain and care, His spirit was not crushed. His countenance did not wear an expression of grief and repining, but ever one of peaceful serenity. His heart was a wellspring of life, and wherever He went He carried rest and peace, joy

5. What should I do instead? "How important that we speak o_____ those things that will give spiritual s_____ and life!" Lord, how do my expressions react me, and others? _____

_____

6. "Do not tell your troubles to your fellow mortals, but carry everything to G____ __ in prayer." Lord, what about being my brother's keeper? If they are discouraged, and need someone to talk to, shouldn't I listen, and direct their thoughts to You? _____

_____
_____

7. "Our Saviour was deeply serious and intensely in e_____, but never g_____ or morose." (120) Lord, may my walk with You be filled with peace like a river, and the light of joy. Even when the enemy sends difficulties my way, there is tranquility and joy in Your presence. Please bring that thought to me right in the midst of the challenge: _____
_____
_____

and gladness.

Our Saviour was deeply serious and intensely in earnest, but never gloomy or morose. The life of those who imitate Him will be full of earnest purpose; they will have a deep sense of personal responsibility. Levity will be repressed; there will be no [121] boisterous merriment, no rude jesting; but the religion of Jesus gives peace like a river. It does not quench the light of joy; it does not restrain cheerfulness nor cloud the sunny, smiling face. Christ came not to be ministered unto but to minister; and when His love reigns in the heart, we shall follow His example.

If we keep uppermost in our minds the unkind and unjust acts of others we shall find it impossible to love them as Christ has loved us; but if our thoughts dwell upon the wondrous love and pity of Christ for us, the same spirit will flow out to others. We should love and respect one another, notwithstanding the faults and imperfections that we cannot help seeing. Humility and self-distrust should be cultivated, and a patient tenderness with the faults of others. This will kill out all narrowing selfishness and make us large-hearted and generous.

The psalmist says, "Trust in the Lord, and do good; so shalt thou dwell in the land, and verily thou shalt be fed." Psalm 37:3. "Trust in the Lord." Each day has its burdens, its cares and perplexities; and when we meet how ready we are to talk of our difficulties and trials. So many borrowed troubles intrude, so many fears are indulged, such a weight of anxiety is expressed, that one might suppose we had no pitying, loving Saviour ready to hear all our requests and to be to us a present help in every time of need.

Some are always fearing, and borrowing trouble. Every day they are surrounded with the tokens of God's love; every day they are enjoying the bounties of His providence; but they overlook these present [122] blessings. Their minds are continually dwelling upon something disagreeable which they fear may come; or some difficulty may really exist which, though small, blinds their eyes to the many things that demand gratitude. The difficulties they encounter, instead of driving them to God, the only source of their help, separate them from Him because they awaken unrest and repining.

Do we well to be thus unbelieving? Why should

we be ungrateful and distrustful? Jesus is our friend; all heaven is interested in our welfare. We should not allow the perplexities and worries of everyday life to fret the mind and cloud the brow. If we do we shall always have something to vex and annoy. We should not indulge a solicitude that only frets and wears us, but does not help us to bear trials.

You may be perplexed in business; your prospects may grow darker and darker, and you may be threatened with loss; but do not become discouraged; cast your care upon God, and remain calm and cheerful. Pray for wisdom to manage your affairs with discretion, and thus prevent loss and disaster. Do all you can on your part to bring about favorable results. Jesus has promised His aid, but not apart from our effort. When, relying upon our Helper, you have done all you can, accept the result cheerfully.

It is not the will of God that His people should be weighed down with care. But our Lord does not deceive us. He does not say to us, "Do not fear; there are no dangers in your path." He knows there are trials and dangers, and He deals with us plainly. He does not propose to take His people out of a world of sin and evil, but He points them to a never-failing [123] refuge. His prayer for His disciples was, "I pray not that Thou shouldest take them out of the world, but that Thou shouldest keep them from the evil." "In the world," He says, "ye shall have tribulation: but be of good cheer; I have overcome the world." John 17:15, 16:33.

In His Sermon on the Mount, Christ taught His disciples precious lessons in regard to the necessity of trusting in God. These lessons were designed to encourage the children of God through all ages, and they have come down to our time full of instruction and comfort. The Saviour pointed His followers to the birds of the air as they warbled their carols of praise, unencumbered with thoughts of care, for "they sow not, neither do they reap." And yet the great Father provides for their needs. The Saviour asks, "Are ye not much better than they?" Matthew 6:26. The great Provider for man and beast opens His hand and supplies all His creatures. The birds of the air are not beneath His notice. He does not drop the food into their bills, but He makes provision for their needs. They must gather the grains He has scattered for them. They must prepare the material for their little nests. They must feed their young. They go forth singing to their labor, for "your heavenly Father feedeth them." And "are ye not much better than they?" Are not you, as intelligent, spiritual worshipers, of more value than the birds of the air? Will not the Author of our being, the Preserver of our life, the One who formed us in His own divine image, provide for our necessities if we but trust in Him?

Christ pointed His disciples to the flowers of the [124] field, growing in rich profusion and glowing in the simple beauty which the heavenly Father had given them, as an expression of His love to man. He said, "Consider the lilies of the field, how they grow." The beauty and simplicity of these natural flowers far outrival the splendor of Solomon. The most gorgeous attire produced by the skill of art cannot bear comparison with the natural grace and radiant beauty of the flowers of God's creation. Jesus asks, "If God so clothe the grass of the field, which today is, and tomorrow is cast into the oven, shall He not much more clothe you, O ye of little faith?" Matthew 6: 28, 30. If God, the divine Artist, gives to the simple flowers that perish in a day their delicate and varied colors, how much greater care will He have for those who are created in His own image? This lesson of Christ's is a rebuke to the anxious thought, the perplexity and doubt, of the faithless heart.

8. What point does Jesus make that is a "rebuke to the anxious thought, the perplexity and doubt, of the faithless heart" [?] (124) _____ _____ _____ _____ _____ _____

The Lord would have all His sons and daughters happy, peaceful, and obedient. Jesus says, "My peace I give unto you: not as the world giveth, give I unto you. Let not your heart be troubled, neither let it be afraid." "These things have I spoken unto you, that My joy might remain in you, and that your joy might be full." John 14:27; 15:11.

Happiness that is sought from selfish motives, outside of the path of duty, is ill-balanced, fitful, and transitory; it passes away, and the soul is filled with loneliness and sorrow; but there is joy and satisfaction in the service of God; the Christian is not left to walk in uncertain paths; he is not left to vain regrets and disappointments. If we do not have the [125] pleasures of this life we may still be joyful in looking to the life beyond.

9. "But even here Christians may have the joy of communion w_____ Christ; they may have the light of His love, the perpetual comfort of His p_____. Every

But even here Christians may have the joy of communion with Christ; they may have the light of His love, the perpetual comfort of His presence. Every step in life may bring us closer to Jesus, may give us a deeper experience of His love, and may bring us one step nearer to the blessed home of peace. Then let us not cast away our confidence, but have firm assurance, firmer than ever before. "Hitherto hath the Lord helped us," and He will help us to the end. 1 Samuel 7:12. Let us look to the monumental pillars, reminders of what the Lord has done to comfort us and to save us from the hand of the destroyer. Let us keep fresh in our memory all the tender mercies that God has shown us,--the tears He has wiped away, the pains He has soothed, the anxieties removed, the fears dispelled, the wants supplied, the blessings bestowed,--thus strengthening ourselves for all that is before us through the remainder of our pilgrimage.

We cannot but look forward to new perplexities in the coming conflict, but we may look on what is past as well as on what is to come, and say, "Hitherto hath the Lord helped us." "As thy days, so shall thy strength be." Deuteronomy 33:25. The trial will not exceed the strength that shall be given us to bear it. Then let us take up our work just where we find it, believing that whatever may come, strength proportionate to the trial will be given.

And by and by the gates of heaven will be thrown open to admit God's children, and from the lips of the King of glory the benediction will fall on their [126] ears like richest music, "Come, ye blessed of My Father, inherit the kingdom prepared for you from the foundation of the world." Matthew 25:34.

Then the redeemed will be welcomed to the home that Jesus is preparing for them. There their companions will not be the vile of earth, liars, idolaters, the impure, and unbelieving; but they will associate with those who have overcome Satan and through divine grace have formed perfect characters. Every sinful tendency, every imperfection, that afflicts them here has been removed by the blood of Christ, and the excellence and brightness of His glory, far exceeding the brightness of the sun, is imparted to them. And the moral beauty, the perfection of His character, shines through them, in worth far exceeding this outward splendor. They are without fault before the great white throne, sharing the dignity and the privileges of the angels.

In view of the glorious inheritance that may be his,

step in life may bring us c_____ to Jesus...look to the monumental pillars." (125). What are those?

_____

_____ How do I keep these fresh in my memory?

10. "The soul redeemed and cleansed from sin, with all its noble powers dedicated to the service of God, is of surpassing w_____; and there is joy in heaven in the presence of God and the holy angels over o____ soul redeemed." (126) Lord, I am redeemed, and I love to proclaim it! Give me a sense of the great value of this worth, and may Your joy fill me. How can I let this joy spill over to others? _____
_____
_____

Prayer journal: _____
_____
_____
_____
_____

If your heart has beat more in rhythm with God's heart, through this aerobic "walk" with Him, why not repeat this exercise? It won't be going over old material, because He promises that His compassions are new every morning! Be thrilled with the privilege to be best friends with the King! --To your spiritual health!

"what shall a man give in exchange for his soul?" Matthew 16:26. He may be poor, yet he possesses in himself a wealth and dignity that the world could never bestow. The soul redeemed and cleansed from sin, with all its noble powers dedicated to the service of God, is of surpassing worth; and there is joy in heaven in the presence of God and the holy angels over one soul redeemed, a joy that is expressed in songs of holy triumph.